The Administration of Public Airports

fifth edition

Library of Congress Control Number: 2007903670

10-digit ISBN: 1-890938-10-6
13-digit ISBN: 978-1-890938-10-9

Printed in the United States of America

COAST AIRE PUBLICATIONS, LLC
290 W. Sparrow Drive
Chandler, Arizona 85286-7758
Office (480) 899-6151
Fax (480) 899-7918
E-Mail coastaire@cox.net
Web Site www.coastairepublications.com

The Administration of Public Airports

fifth edition

Laurence E. Gesell, Ph.D., A.A.E.
Arizona State University

Robin R. Sobotta, Ph.D., A.A.E.
Embry-Riddle Aeronautical University

COAST AIRE PUBLICATIONS, LLC

CONTENTS

CHAPTER 6
Environmental Management

CHAPTER 7
Aviation Noise

CHAPTER 8
Operations: Safety and Certification

CHAPTER 9
Airport and Aviation Security

CHAPTER 11
Airport Maintenance

CHAPTER 12
Airport Finance and Economics

CHAPTER 13
The Airport Marketplace: Revenues and Rates

CHAPTER 14
Public Relations, Social and Ethical Responsibilities

CHAPTER 16
Fifth Wave Infrastructure

CHAPTER 17
Airport Liability

TABLES

FIGURES

PREFACE

Air transportation has undergone revolutionary changes during the last three decades of deregulation, but especially since the tragic events of September 11, 2001. What is developing is an airline system made up of six principal market niches, leaving airports to adapt to the changing air transportation industry. It was never more true that "as the airlines go, so go the airports." Security awareness is heightened, but so are concerns about the environment. Airports are compelled to go green. Yet, in the 21st century, airports are evolving as dynamic and rapidly growing marketplaces heavily dependent upon emerging technological advancements. Concurrently, privatization in all of its forms is spreading around the globe and pressure is on public administrators to adapt to a new entrepreneurial model.

Indeed, much has happened since the last edition, let alone the first edition of this book nearly thirty years ago. Deregulatory philosophy has spread to most industries, with airports seemingly included. Yet, airport management is caught in a paradox. On the one hand there is a movement toward increased privatization. On the other hand, as changes in the economy continue to impact the airport industry, and environmental regulations challenge traditional ways of doing things, airport sponsors are being held increasingly to higher standards of responsibility and liability. One of the outcomes has been that airport sponsors have taken greater control of terminal and landside activities that were once the exclusive responsibility of private enterprise.

The enigma is that airport privatization in the deregulatory sense means that government ought to extract itself from the direct management of airports and turn the process over to the private sector either by management contract or by lease or outright sale to private investors. It has been suggested that both airports and airlines should compete freely with less government involvement and reduced subsidies—and rely more upon the natural marketplace forces. But an alternative is for public administrators to act more like private enterprise, albeit in the public interest.

The title of this book, *The Administration of Public Airports*, is an intentional play on words reflecting the fact that managers of public airports are by definition public administrators. But public administration has changed radically in the last thirty years. Airports are now big business. They are economic marketplaces and complex industrial enterprises. Since the advent of airline deregulation, airports, which were once part of an entrenched government bureaucracy, have now become dynamic and commercially oriented businesses. Privatization of public facilities, development and expansion of infrastructure through private investment, and the rise of entrepreneurship in the public sector, all suggest a "shift in paradigm" from traditional forms of public administration to the onset of a *New Public Administration.* Whereas historically, airports were expected only to break even, profit in the public sector is rapidly becoming an expectation. Profit can be converted into capital, and capital is needed to address expanding airport development needs.

Traffic volume is back up since 9/11. Many of the world's airports are again experiencing major congestion problems which could soon lead to gridlock if nothing is done to add air traffic system capacity. The problem is serious, yet all stakeholders are in a dilemma as to how to improve the system effectively. The problem with expanding the airport system to meet the demands of society is financial. With local and national budgets stretched and basic services such as education under-funded, many governments simply don't have the money to improve airports. Airport sponsors in the United States and throughout the world are looking at private investment as a way to ease the financial strain. Whether by private investment or profit generation within the new public administration paradigm, airport management is being challenged to generate the capital necessary to support the next generation of airport infrastructure development.

This fifth edition is a significant rewrite to reflect the changing nature of managing airports in the public sector today. But as it has been with all previous editions, the goal is to prepare students for airport management careers and to serve as a ready reference for those professionals already engaged in the management of public airports. This text is new, revised and expanded to meet that goal and hopefully it provides some insight. To those professionals already engaged in airport management, it is anticipated that this book might enhance individual capabilities. To the person just entering the field, it is expected this book will provide a sound foundation and a starting point from which to launch a challenging yet rewarding career.

LEG/RRS

CHAPTER 1

AIRPORT MANAGEMENT

Go through your phone book, call people and ask them to drive you to the airport. The ones who will drive you are your true friends. The rest aren't bad people; they're just acquaintances.

Jay Leno, Comedian and Television Host[1]

INTRODUCTION

Airports are an indispensable community asset, assuring unfettered freedom of movement, supporting the air transportation access needs of leisure travelers and business, and providing economic benefit to the communities they serve. In the opening quote, whether he intended two interpretations, Jay Leno illustrates both positive and negative aspects associated with airports. From his statement, it can be surmised that the existence of a nearby airport isn't just a possibility, but a reliable assumption in most communities. He would, in fact be correct in this supposition, as more than 98% of the nation's population lives within 20 miles of a federally funded public use airport.[2] His statement might also suggest, somewhat accurately, that a visit to an airport can be a confusing or distressing venture—akin to seeking a shot at the doctor's office. For these citizens, while airports may be a necessity, visiting them can be a daunting experience.

---

[1] Jay Leno, from *Laura Moncur's Motivational Questions* (date unk.), Quotations Page, http://www.quotationspage.com (visited Dec. 28, 2006).

[2] U.S. Dept. of Trans. (FAA), Report to Congress; *National Plan of Integrated Airport Systems 2005-2009* (Sep. 30, 2004), http//www.faa.gov/arp/planning/npias.

The complexities associated with the operation of larger, commercial service airports often require specialized fire, police, operations and maintenance personnel; accommodation of businesses operating at or through the airport; a host of finance, accounting and business personnel; and access to expertise in environmental, development, planning and legal matters. Airport managers must be equally equipped to respond to a host of demands from airport users, public officials, the media, and citizens located as far as 50 miles from the airport. The airport's impact far transcends its property line.

The busiest airports require a professional, capable administrator who can competently manage a multi-million dollar budget, and oversee hundreds—if not thousands—of acres of real estate and an equal number of employees. Such a director must be capable of assuring the airport's political and economic stability, and all the related economic benefits that such a facility brings to a community. In fact some of the largest commercial service airports in the United States are credited with generating more than 30,000 jobs in the surrounding communities.[3] At smaller airports, an airport manager must demonstrate immense flexibility. The manager may be solely responsible for changing the runway light bulbs, mowing the grass, dispensing fuel and collecting parking fees from transient tenants. Still, while the range of activities at all airports is vast, those who are charged with managing large and small airports share a critical commonality: they are collectively responsible for operating the facilities that comprise the backbone of the air transportation system.

This book is intended to provide insight into the complexities of airport planning, development, operations and management, and into what it means to be an airport manager in the public sector today. This work is ethnocentric in that the focus is on management of public airports in the United States, but airports the world over share common attributes and challenges. Thus, much of what is presented in this text may be just as applicable to international airports as it is to those in the U.S. Currently, the U.S. generates nearly 30% of the world's commercial aviation activity and 50% of the world's general aviation activity.[4] That means that the bulk of air transportation re-

---

[3] City of Phoenix, *Economic Impact: Sky Harbor Aviation Workers Distribution by Community* (2003), http://www.phoenix.gov/AVIATION/info_stats/econ_impact/impact_city.html.
[4] U.S. Dept. of Trans. (FAA), Report to Congress; *National Plan of Integrated Airport Systems, 2005-2009* (Sep. 30, 2004), http//www.faa.gov/arp/planning/npias.

sides outside the United States. Moreover, air transportation outside the U.S. is growing at an even faster rate.

To varying degrees, this book serves a multiplicity of audiences domestic and foreign including newly appointed airport commissioners, seasoned aviation directors, first line airport supervisors, college students exploring the field, or jack-of-all-trades airport mangers oft found at smaller airports. It is intended to provide both an overview of the complexities faced by those in airport-related professions, a quick reference handbook for exploring new industry perspectives, and some specific insight into the myriad of challenges and opportunities that airport managers face within society. A solid knowledge base is provided herein, from which one may better understand and perform the duties, responsibilities and societal outreach associated with this field.

GOVERNANCE IN THE PUBLIC SECTOR

By "public sector," it is meant that airport management is usually a job within or for the government; that is to say, the airport manager is the administrator of a public (or governmentally owned) facility. Most public-use airports are government-owned, and because the people who manage these airports are public servants, the title of this book, *The Administration of Public Airports*, is presented as intentional play on words to reflect the prevailing nature of airport management. The manager of a publicly owned airport is, by definition, a *public administrator*.

In the traditional perspective, the public administrator is a professional civil servant who carries out and provides continuity to programs authorized by elected officials.[5] As will be seen in the next chapter, the definition of public administration and the traditional role of the public administrator is rapidly changing, but suffice it to say that today's public administration is the action-oriented business side of government with an understanding of the legal and political complexities associated with civil service. To fill its ranks, the public sector draws from many professions, and airport management is but one specialty area within the broader scope of public administration.

Serving many masters, executives in public service must be many things to a broad public audience. Public administration is the accom-

---

[5] *See* Marshall E. Dimock & Gladys O. Dimock, *Public Administration* 145 (4th ed. 1969).

plishment of politically determined objectives, or in short, "the accomplishing side of government."[6] It is concerned with policy, practical problem solving and the important act of governance. "Governance is the exercise of authority by government, or more precisely, the system and method by which that authority is exercised."[7] In the case of public airports, the administrator applies his or her aviation expertise to the overriding problem-solving process and management of the airport enterprise.

Specific problems facing airport managers the world over in the 21st century include airport capacity constraints, aging infrastructure, community compatibility issues, complex environmental challenges, unique security and safety threats, the demands of new large aircraft, increasing fiscal pressures, and the imposition of unfunded regulatory requirements. In response to these and other challenges, the business of "running" airports broadly encompasses many fields of knowledge. Not only must the airport manager possess combined aviation and management skills, but must have a fair knowledge of a host of other disciplines, each of which in its own right may be a distinct career field.

The attributes of an effective public administrator are professionalism, expertise, adaptive problem-solving skills, and political sensitivity. The public administrator must produce work of sufficient quality that people will react favorably toward government. The administrator must have knowledge that stems from a close involvement in devising solutions to pressing issues of public policy. The administrator knows the subject, recommends policy, and carries out what has been decided upon, while simultaneously dealing with the competing interests of those supporting and opposing his or her programs. Ideally, the public administrator must have an awareness and deliberate avoidance of partisan politics. Above all, the public administrator must be ethical.

It is interesting to note, that when asked how airport management could more effectively confront problems facing today's airport executives, similar answers were given by nearly two dozen practicing airport managers queried, as well as experts on government and public liaison. These individuals centered their recommendations on six areas generally supported by a code of ethics. The foremost recom-

---

[6] Grover Starling, *Managing the Public Sector* 1 (6th ed. 2002).
[7] *Id.* at 2.

mendation of the airport managers surveyed was to safeguard credibility, emphasizing credibility as crucial for someone whose job is in safety-related public service. Credibility and public trust are slowly earned but quickly destroyed.

The airport managers surveyed also recommended the encouragement of teamwork and the use of computers and advanced technologies to enhance public service. They suggested that the administrator should strengthen news media contacts and should be "pro-active." Rather than attempting to hide a potentially embarrassing or damaging situation, the airport executive should be honest, disclose the problem, and clearly explain what is being done to rectify it.

The administrator should periodically take time to re-examine the community partnership, and should strive to maintain a cooperative relationship with the local community. Additionally, the administrator should reassess airport board meetings and make them meaningful, constructive sessions. The airport administrator should maintain a working relationship wherein airport board members or commissioners make policy, and airport directors shy away from making rules and forming policy. Instead, they should focus on what they do best: running airports.

And last, airport executives ought to acquaint themselves with elected representatives in Congress and in state legislatures, and should become active in the government process in order to promote airport service in the public interest.

It remains advantageous for today's airport manager to have a technical background in aviation, as did earlier predecessors. But with the advances in aviation technology made particularly since the advent of the jet aircraft in the late 1950s, the airport manager's technical aviation education, of necessity, must be much more comprehensive than that of earlier counterparts. The airport administrator is responsible for knowing an array of Federal Aviation Administration [FAA] orders, Advisory Circulars [AC], Federal Aviation Regulations [FARs], Transportation Security Regulations [TSRs] and other federal regulations and regulators. Airport managers must also be familiar with a web of interwoven state aviation laws and local ordinances.

Along with an aviation management education, the airport manager must also be competent in public relations, economics, air commerce, business management, and personnel administration. The airport administrator must be versatile in a wide range of technical areas such as finance and accounting, business and real estate law, airport planning and civil engineering, office administration, environmental and security issues, and labor relations. And the airport manager must be able to fulfill these responsibilities while at the same time walking a tightrope between politically diverging interests.

Said Charles M. "Chip" Barclay, then executive vice president of the American Association of Airport Executives [AAAE],

> *Airports have been economically deregulated and operationally over-regulated, made anti-trust eligible, sued by airlines for covering costs, prevented from suing to recover bankrupt property, and nearly defederalized, among a variety of other challenges, in just the past few years. The airport executive must be on top of each new development, as he or she follows through on the last new development, while the airport continues to run smoothly and economically as the highest public expectations can conceive . . .*[8]

The airport manager was once an aviator and an entrepreneur who peddled aviation wares such as flying lessons, aviation fuel, mechanical services, and so forth. Running the airport was just a sideline. While at smaller airports this remains the case, many airport managers have joined the ranks of public administration and become accomplished bureaucrats, skilled in the governmental process, and business management of a public institution. Now, ironically, with the introduction of privatization and entrepreneurship into the public sector, the role of the public airport administrator is seemingly coming full circle.

THE AIRPORT MARKETPLACE

An "airport" consists essentially of one or more runways for aircraft, together with associated buildings, hangars, or terminals, where passengers and air cargo (freight, mail and express) transported by the

[8] Charles M. Barclay, *Managing Airports: It's a Tough Job, and a Professional Has to Do It*, Airport Services Management (May 1984).

aircraft are processed. But airports are more than simply places where airplanes can takeoff and land or where passengers or freight are handled. They are the gateways to the modern transportation world. Airports form the terminal ends of the air transportation system, and it is the airports that provide system capacity. The capacity of a specific airport depends on its design, weather conditions, and operating limits imposed by environmental conditions.[9] But more than a component of the air traffic and airspace system, airports are a forum, or marketplace, where seemingly disparate activities are brought together to facilitate, for passengers and air cargo alike, the interchange between air and surface transport.

Airports are economic marketplaces and complex industrial enterprises. During the thirty years since the advent of airline deregulation,[10] airports, which were once part of an entrenched government bureaucracy, have now become dynamic and commercially oriented businesses. In fact, airports are big business! Since the late 1970s, what were previously operated as central or local government departments, many U.S. airports have become commercially oriented enterprises capable of generating substantial profits. European airports, historically, have also seen consistent increases in profits (i.e., surplus, as it is termed in the public sector) at their major airports.[11] The improving financial performance has been mirrored in other parts of the world as well, notably East Asia and the Pacific.[12]

Larger airports are indeed becoming more profitable, and over the last two or three decades they have begun to look more like commercial enterprises than they do government service activities. And although many airports and airport activities are becoming more privatized in one form or another, the preponderance of airports around the world are still owned and operated by central or local governments and in some cases the military. Yet, relative to the total number of airports around the world, there are few privately owned airports outside the United States. Conversely, in the U.S. there are *many* privately owned airports. But while the number of privately owned air-

---

[9] FAA, *National Airway System, Annual Report FY-1989* (Jul. 1990).
[10] *I.e.*, 1978-2008.
[11] The eighteen airports are: London Heathrow, London Gatwick, Manchester, Frankfurt, Dublin, Amsterdam, Glasgow, Nice, Rome, Copenhagen, Belfast, Milan, Birmingham, Vienna, East Midlands (UK), Marseilles, Geneva, and Basel-Mulhouse. *See* Rigas Doganis, *The Airport Business* Ch. 1 (1992).
[12] *Id.* at 3.

ports continues to rise, those airports open to the public are gradually diminishing relative to the total. Thus, uniformly around the globe, the majority of airports open to the public are owned and operated by governmental entities.

In the U.S. it is mostly local governments including cities, counties, and special districts that own the airports that are open to the public. In countries other than the United States, most airports are owned and operated by the central government and/or shared governance with one or more local city-states. In all cases and in increasing numbers, airports are becoming privatized in part or totally. Although there are numerous privately owned airfields in the United States, some of which are open to the public and others not, only a few privately owned airports are considered of major importance in terms of the air transportation system.

With the vast majority of public use airports falling under government control, public sector employees have traditionally carried out airport management and development responsibilities. Nevertheless, there is a current movement towards privatization, in any one of its many forms, by an increasing number of airport sponsors, and toward entrepreneurship in the public sector in general. But currently, the preponderance of public-use airports are owned by the public, and managed by public administrators or by their representatives. Thus, the role of the airport manager is couched within the field of public administration—*even* if the manager works for a company contracted by the airport sponsor to manage the airport.

AIRPORT EVOLUTION: PARALLELING THE INDUSTRY

Airport development has paralleled the development of the aircraft using them, and the industry built around those aircraft. The first daily scheduled international air passenger service in heavier-than-air craft began on August 25, 1919. On that day, Aircraft Transport and Travel first serviced Hounslow in London and Le Bourget in Paris using a de Havilland DH-4. It carried one passenger. Later the same day, a de Havilland DH-16 was used to transport four passengers. Still on the same day, a converted Handley-Page bomber made a proving flight to Paris carrying seven journalists as passengers.[13]

[13] Bill Gunston (ed.), *Chronicle of Aviation* (1992), at 171.

Scheduled transcontinental airmail service in the United States began in 1920. By 1926, fourteen domestic airline companies were established, from which the pedigrees of many of the United States' major airlines can be traced. Similarly, smaller lines consolidated in Europe, including Lufthansa German Airlines, the largest European airline whose pedigree reaches back to the inaugural days of flight in the first zeppelins in 1910.[14] Most European carriers were governmentally owned or subsidized, as were their airports. European air transportation focused on linking the vast reaches of its sponsors' empires. Germany developed a number of airlines in Latin America.[15] Routes from Europe to Africa and Asia were developed by Air France, the United Kingdom's Imperial Airways, the Netherlands' KLM, and Belgium's Sabena.[16]

THE EVOLUTION OF AN INDUSTRY

Aircraft technology has changed markedly since the early days of commercial aviation. The first modern passenger airliner, the Boeing 247, was built in 1933.[17] The Boeing 247 accommodated ten passengers and had a cruising speed of 155 miles per hour. The cabin was insulated to reduce engine noise; it had upholstered seats and a hot water heater to increase passenger comfort. The Douglas Aircraft Company copied and improved upon the Boeing innovations with its DC-2, which had more powerful engines and could seat two more passengers than the Boeing 247. Douglas built the DC-3, the workhorse of commercial aviation, and the first to enable airlines to actually make money by flying passengers.[18] Among its advanced features were a lighter, stress-carrying metal skin, controllable-pitch propellers, retractable landing gear, and wing flaps.[19]

More than 10,000 DC-3s were built, and many still fly today, landing at dirt strips at remote corners of the globe. The DC-3 has a range of 1,500 miles, a speed of about 200 miles per hour, and can seat twenty-four passengers. Plastic insulation quieted the cabin, and seats

---

[14] R.E.G. Davies, *Lufthansa: An Airline and Its Aircraft* 2 (1991).
[15] Peter Pletschacher, *Lufthansa Junkers Ju 52: The Story of the Old Aunty Ju*, 31-33 (1989).
[16] Newal Taneja, *Introduction to Civil Aviation*, 6, 11 (2nd ed. 1989).
[17] *Id.* at 7; *see also* R.E.G. Davies, *Airlines of the United States Since 1914*, 180 (1972).
[18] *Id.*
[19] Newal Taneja, *Introduction to Civil Aviation* 7 (2nd ed. 1989).

set in rubber reduced vibration.[20] Development of the air transportation infrastructure, including navigational aids, air traffic control systems and airport improvements followed these advancements in aircraft design.

In 1920, the U.S. Post Office Department established four aeronautical stations to maintain bonfires and assist aviators with aerial navigation at night. By the late 1920s, the bonfires had been replaced with beacon lights operated by the Department of Commerce Lighthouse Division. Navigation via electronic signals was introduced in the 1930s with the implementation of the Radio Range and its associated airway system. The Radio Range was a non-directional radio navigation system. The signal was emitted in four quadrants, two each of which were identified in Morse Code by the letters "A"(. -) and "N"(- .). Approaching the radio station, the "A" was on one side and the "N" was on the other. The area of overlap between the lettered quadrants was known as the "beam." Pilots knew they were "on the beam" when they heard the solid tone created by the overlapping of the Morse code signals. The radio range stations formed the first radio airways, each of which was identified by a color and a numerical identifier. Hence, they were known as the "colored" airways.[21]

In the chronological development of the air traffic system in the U.S., the earlier bonfire attendants were replaced by lighthouse attendants, who were later replaced by radio range attendants, who in turn provided the additional service of radio relay for en route traffic. The modern Flight Service Station [FSS], which is one of the divisions of the Federal Air Traffic Control Service, traces its origin to these early radio range attendants.[22]

Air traffic control, *per se*, traces its beginnings to the Air Commerce Act of 1926, which directed the Secretary of Commerce "to establish, operate, and maintain . . . all necessary air navigation facilities except airports." The purpose of the 1926 Act was to promote air commerce. It charged the executive branch with the operation and maintenance of an airway system, as well as providing Air Navigation Aids [NAVAIDs], and with the promotion of safety in air commerce through a system of regulation. The Department of Commerce was

---

[20] Air Transport Ass'n., *The Airline Handbook* 7-8 (1995).

[21] *See* Paul Stephen Dempsey & Laurence E. Gesell, *Air Transportation: Foundations for the 21st Century* Ch. 8 (1997).

[22] Donald D. Engen, *Air Traffic Control: The First 50 Years*, Federal Aviation news release (Jul. 3, 1986).

given jurisdiction to monitor air safety; within it was created a Bureau of Air Commerce to promulgate air safety regulation. However, the Federal government for yet another decade did not assume the actual function of controlling aircraft within an air traffic control system.

In the early 1930s, the possibility of two aircraft arriving simultaneously over the same point and at the same altitude seemed remote, and there was no single agency serving as a unified control for airborne traffic. Rather, en route locations of (airline) company planes were monitored by the individual air carriers on their own distinct radio frequencies. In the mid-1930s there were three such airline-operated centers: one in Newark, one in Cleveland, and one in Chicago. In 1936, these three centers, which constituted the skeletal beginnings of an air traffic control system, were turned over to the Bureau of Air Commerce. In 1986, the FAA celebrated the 50th anniversary of the Air Traffic Control Service based on its acquisition of the airline radio stations in 1936.

Following the further development of aircraft and the air transportation infrastructure in the 1920s and 1930s, international aviation grew robustly. United States' air traffic grew from 6,000 passengers in 1926, to 1.5 million by 1938. World War II developments brought tremendous technological advances to aviation. Larger, faster aircraft, capable of flying longer distances at higher altitudes with pressurized cabins became widely available. A British pilot, Frank Whittle, designed the first jet engine in 1930, although it was the Germans who were first to build and test a jet aircraft. Nevertheless, it would take five years to perfect the design; too late to affect the outcome of World War II. The pressurized Boeing Stratoliner, a derivation of the B-17 bomber introduced in 1940, enabled flying at 10,000 feet or more, above the weather. The Stratoliner could fly as high as 20,000 feet, and reach speeds of 200 miles per hour.[23] Improvements in navigation technology, including radar, radio communications, instrument flying, and weather forecasting also stimulated robust growth in commercial aviation.[24]

Subsequent developments in propeller-driven aircraft were also astonishing. The Douglas DC-6, and its rival, the Lockheed Constellation, powered by four engines, were both capable of carrying 50 passengers at more than 300 miles per hour. Later versions were capable

---

[23] Air Transport Ass'n., *The Airline Handbook* 8-9 (1995).
[24] Newal Taneja, *Introduction to Civil Aviation* 13 (2nd ed. 1989).

of flying across North America and across the North Atlantic nonstop. The Boeing Stratocruiser, DC-7 and Lockheed Super Constellation, each could carry a hundred passengers nonstop across the Atlantic.[25] By 1958, U.S. domestic enplanements had risen to forty-nine million. The decade of the 1960s saw a dramatic increase in aircraft development following introduction of the jet air transport. Airport development reflected those changes in aircraft design and deployment.

In 1952, British Overseas Airways Company [BOAC] (predecessor of today's British Airways) flew a thirty-six-seat British-made De Havilland jet, the Comet, from London to Johannesburg, South Africa, at a speed of 500 miles per hour. Success of the Comet offered to catapult Great Britain into the lead as a producer of air transports. Unfortunately, two years later a Comet inexplicably disintegrated after taking off from Rome, and a second disintegrated near Stromboli.[26] Following Britain's disastrous attempt to introduce the first commercial jet transport, the Boeing 707 made its maiden flight on July 15, 1954.[27] Shortly thereafter, France introduced the Caravelle, but it was only marginally successful.[28] The Comet was improved, but by then having been eclipsed by the Boeing 707, it was relegated to military service. The U.S. would thereby come to dominate jet aircraft manufacturing, and Boeing, in its introduction of the 707, would later become the world's predominant producer of jet transports.

The Boeing 707 had a range of nearly 7,500 miles, a speed 550 miles an hour, and was capable of seating 189 passengers. Its four engines had 17,000 pounds of thrust. Jet engines proved more reliable than piston engines, producing less vibration, which put less stress on the aircraft airframe and reduced maintenance costs. They also burned kerosene, which was half the cost of high-octane gasoline burned in traditional piston aircraft.[29] The jet was a huge economic success and airlines began to replace railroad passenger trains and ocean liners in the long-distance transport market. Douglas produced the DC-8 to compete with the Boeing 707, making its maiden flight in 1959. The rear-mounted three-engine Boeing 727 introduced in 1964, and two-engine DC-9 would join these aircraft. Later, the two-engine two-pilot

---

[25] *Id.*

[26] R.E.G. Davies, *Airlines of the United States Since 1914* 509 (1972).

[27] Richard Todd, *The Dream Becomes a Disaster*, in the Wings Over The World video series (1989).

[28] Newal Taneja, *Introduction to Civil Aviation* 25 (2nd ed. 1989).

[29] Air Transport Assn., *The Airline Handbook* 10 (1995).

Boeing 737, introduced in 1968, would become the dominant domestic aircraft. Traffic increase took a giant leap during the decade of the 1960s, and the nature of airport management began to change with it.

Air traffic went from 49 million passengers in 1958, to 275 million in 1978, then to 466 million by 1990.[30] The total enplaned passengers in America rose to 641.4 million by 2003, and is projected to exceed a billion by 2015.[31] The 2003 total aircraft operations figure of 62.7 million, is also expected to rise—to more than 80 million by 2015.[32]

A 65% increase in projected passengers for 2015 is forecast to be the result of a predicted 40% increase in air carrier operations. During that time, the FAA anticipates that both the average passenger trip length and average aircraft size will also increase.[33] The anticipated growth is being attributed to a variety of factors including: increased public confidence (particularly post 9/11) in flight as a safe mode of transportation, continued growth by low cost carriers (and resulting robust competition), moderate growth in the regional jet market (but not the meteoric increases seen in the 1990s), and the increased entry of *New Large Aircraft* [NLAs] at U.S. airports.

Meeting the future demand in the single-aisle class of aircraft is the Airbus A320 family (A318/A319/A320/A321 models) as well as the New Generation Boeing 737 family (the 737-600/-700/-800/-900 models). To date Boeing has won orders for more than 6,000 airplanes in the 737 family, with over 1,000 orders yet to be filled. The Next generation 737 models build on the strengths of previous models by adding advanced technology winglets and improved passenger cabins. The Boeing 737-900ER is the newest member of the New Generation series. Launched in the summer of 2006, the 737ER can carry as many as 215 passengers up to 3,200 nautical miles.[34]

The counterpart to the Boeing 737-900 is the Airbus A321, which can carry 220 passengers in single-class configuration and can fly up to 3,000 nautical miles. As of 2007, Airbus had received 4,843 total orders for A320 family aircraft, of which 2,944 had been delivered.[35]

---

[30] National Commission to Ensure a Strong, Competitive Airline Industry, *Change, Challenge and Competition* 4 (1993).

[31] U.S. Dept. of Transp. (FAA), Report to Congress; *National Plan of Integrated Airport Systems (2005-2009) – US Aviation Activity Forecast* (Sep. 30, 2004), http//www.faa.gov/arp/planning/npias.

[32] *Id.*

[33] *Id.*

[34] The Boeing Company, http://www.boeing.com (visited Dec. 28, 2006).

[35] Airbus Aircraft Families, http://www.airbus.com (visited Dec. 29, 2006).

To meet future demand Boeing will deliver the first of its 787 "Dreamliner" aircraft in the spring of 2008. The 787 is an advanced technology aircraft that, depending on the model will carry 210-330 passengers from 8,000 to 8,800 nautical miles.[36] Boeing celebrated the completion of a "virtual rollout" in December of 2006.[37] To match the Boeing 787 entry, Airbus is proposing the A350. In late 2006 Airbus gave the go-ahead to the first three of five versions covering 250-375 seat capacity and a range of roughly 8,300 to 8,500 nautical miles. The A350 family is designed to replace A340s, MD-11s and Boeing 777s as well as rival the Boeing 787. Airbus projects delivery of the first version of the A350 (the -900) around 2013.[38]

The big one of course is the Airbus A380. After two years of delay, Airbus was set to receive type certification for the A380 by the first of the year 2007. As of this writing, there were still a few certification items remaining, such as Category IIIB auto land and maximum energy brake testing. More importantly, Airbus was waiting for the U.S. Federal Aviation Administration to certify the aircraft for landing on 45 meter or roughly 150 feet-wide runways. Acceptance of the A380 at some airports may require major modifications of pavement dimensions, strengths, and revamping of terminal facilities, which some airports may decline to undertake.[39] The substantial investment to handle just a few A380 arrivals and departures is causing some airport authorities to balk. Thus, full adoption of the A380 into the air transport fleet may be limited to the few airports that will be able to accommodate it.

The big surprise in air transport development has been continuation of the Boeing 747 line. Once shut down by Boeing, 747's arc back in production with the launch of the third generation family (Boeing 747-8 International and the 747-8 Freighter models). The 747-8 Freighter was launched in November of 2005, with deliveries to begin in 2009. Lufthansa German Airlines is the launch customer for the 747-8 Intercontinental and is scheduled to take delivery of its

---

[36] The Boeing Company, http://www.boeing.com (visited Dec. 28, 2006).

[37] Michael Mecham, *Rolling Out, Virtually*, Av. Wk. & Space Tech. (Dec. 11, 2006), at 42.

[38] Robert Wall, *Miles to Go*, Av. Wk. & Space Tech. (Dec. 11, 2006), at 36.

[39] Reportedly, Clark County (Las Vegas), when approached by Airbus to discuss modifying its airports to accommodate the A-380 declined due to the attached cost relative to the value of the few passengers that may utilize the A-380 over the next decade.

first aircraft in 2010. The freighter will have a range of 4,475 nautical miles; the passenger's is 8,000 nautical miles.[40]

At the opposite end of the scale is the *Regional Jet* [RJ], a small airliner designed to fly between 35 and 100 passengers. In the early 1990s, Canadair Regional Jet [CRJ] introduced the first widely successful RJ, the CL-600. The main competitor to emerge was Embraer with its ERJ 145. Other competitors such as Dornier, de Havilland Canada, Shorts and Fokker entered the market but have since left, leaving Canadair and Embraer as the principal competitors for the RJ niche. Initially there was a clamor to obtain regional jet aircraft. However, the once booming market for regional jets suddenly collapsed. The high per-seat operation costs of the classic 50-seat RJ were exacerbated by rising fuel costs.[41] In late 2005, Canadair suspended its 50-seat CRJ-200 production line. The new trend is for larger aircraft with better economics, exemplified by Canadair's 70-seat CRJ-700 and the 70-110-seat Embraer E-Jets, which blur the line between RJs and regular single-aisle transports like the Boeing 737 and Airbus A320.[42]

POST-DEREGULATION PHASES

Clearly, much changed with airports during the last half of the 20th century. With passage of the Federal Aviation Act of 1958 came significant changes in safety oversight by the federal government. But even more profound have been the changes in the economics and finance of airports subsequent to the Airline Deregulation Act of 1978.

In reviewing the changes in the airport industry since passage of the Airline Deregulation Act, David NewMyer suggests that the U.S. experience with deregulation might offer some lessons for interna-

---

[40] Michael Mecham, *Family Addition*, Av. Wk. & Space Tech. (Dec. 11, 2006), at 39.

[41] Much of the RJ boom was attributed to the fee-per-departure structure under which they operated. Under such structures, traditional airlines contracted with a regional airline company on a per departure or per flight basis regardless of the number of passengers or the length of flight, which resulted in a form of subsidy. The traditional airline kept all the revenue from the ticket sale. In turn the regional operator was assured of consistent revenue stream and could earn a modest profit by controlling cost. However, the regional operators have been squeezed by airline bankruptcies and cost controls on the part of the traditional carriers and by increasing costs of their own operations. Marilyn Adams, *Regional Jets Appear on the Endangered Species List,* USA Today, (Nov. 2, 2005), at B.1. Regional Airline Association, *Industry Projections* http://www.raa.org/carriers_services/industryprojections.pdf (visited May 11, 2007).

[42] *Id.*

tional airport managers.[43] According to NewMyer, the impacts of deregulation on U.S. airports essentially mirror the general impacts of deregulation on the airlines. The FAA identified four distinct phases following passage of the Airline Deregulation Act;[44] these are the *expansion, consolidation, concentration, and globalization* phases. The events of 9/11 triggered a fifth phase, which is best characterized as *realignment.*

The initial period, or *expansion* phase, lasted from 1978 to 1985. The industry went from thirty large air carriers in 1978 to 105 in 1985. Expansion of the airline industry resulted in a sudden surge in demand for limited airport facilities. New airlines needed gate space, counter space, and ramp space, as did existing airlines that were expanding under the route freedom accorded them by deregulation. Increased demand put pressure on airports across the United States, especially larger airports subjected to the hub-and-spoke phenomenon. But many smaller airports were negatively impacted as well, as carriers sought more profitable routes and/or changed the size of the aircraft serving the route.

The hub-and-spoke concept, or "hubbing," is a corporate strategy where large airlines dominate traffic at select airports by forming hub-and-spoke networks. A carrier uses spoke flights, flown by its own planes or those of smaller carriers (sometimes called commuters) that major airlines control through purchase or agreement to generate passenger flow for flights to and from its hub operations. Hub-and-spoke networks have significantly altered the air transportation route structure and the airports served. The hub-and-spoke airlines may overload major airports with additional flights and transfer passengers, while leaving many airports not integrated into their hub systems without regular airline service.[45] Large airports are left with air traffic and airspace capacity constraints, while smaller airports went looking for air carrier service.[46]

The period of rapid expansion from 1978 to 1985 was followed by a *consolidation* phase, which began in 1986 and lasted just two years. During this brief period, there were eleven mergers and sixteen buy-

---

[43] David A. NewMyer, *The Impact of Deregulation on Airports: An International Perspective*, J. of Aviation/Aerospace Ed. & Research, Vol. 1 No. 1 (spring 1990).

[44] *I.e.*, 1978-1988.

[45] *See generally* Melvin A. Brenner, James O. Leet & Elihu Schott, *Airline Deregulation* (1985).

[46] Paul Stephen Dempsey & Laurence E. Gesell, *Air Transportation: Foundations for the 21st Century* 452 (1997).

outs of smaller regional and commuter airlines. Coupled with business failures, this resulted in only sixty-one carriers at the end of 1988. During consolidation, third level carriers progressively aligned themselves with major counterparts under the same or similar name and with aircraft painted the colors of the larger carrier. As competition intensified in hub-and-spoke systems, there was an increasing need to focus regional and commuter airline service on feeding the hubs. If an airport was not served by an airline with an agreement to feed the hub, the airport was subject to losing its air service.[47] Most hard hit were rural, small-community airports where service was disrupted, if not altogether lost. Small communities, fortunate enough to retain air service, found that airfares increased dramatically.[48]

In 1988, the *concentration* phase began as the four largest carriers accounted for 60.4% of the domestic traffic, as compared to 52.5% in 1978, before deregulation. The industry had become more concentrated than before deregulation! As a result of industry concentration, airports now have fewer airlines providing service to them. For the consumer this means less competition and generally higher fares. For airports, it means their bargaining position may be compromised because fewer airlines are interested in long-term leases for terminal and gate facilities.

The fourth phase, *globalization,* had its roots established in December of 1987 via United Airlines' announcement of a marketing merger with British Airways, whereby the two carriers would begin Computer Reservation System [CRS] code sharing.[49] By the mid-1990s, four major global airline systems had emerged: the United/Lufthansa alliance, the British/American alliance, the Delta/Dwarfs alliance, and the Northwest/KLM alliance.[50] Cities which have new international service as a result of global airline alli-

---

[47] David A. NewMyer, *The Impact of Deregulation on Airports: An International Perspective*, J. of Aviation/Aerospace Ed. & Research, Vol. 1 No. 1 (spring 1990), at 68.

[48] *See* Laurence E. Gesell, *Airline Re-Regulation* 60-65 (1990); *see also* Mary Kihl, *The Impacts of Deregulation on Passenger Transportation in Small Towns*, Transportation Quarterly, Vol. 42 No. 2 (1988); *see also* D.B. Vellenga & D.R. Vellenga, *An Analysis of Essential Air Service to the Southeastern U.S. Since the Airline Deregulation Act of 1978*, J. of Trans. Research Forum (Nov. 1987).

[49] *See* David A. NewMyer, *The Impact of Deregulation on Airports: An International Perspective*, J. of Aviation/Aerospace Ed. & Research, Vol. 1 No. 1 (spring 1990), at 62.

[50] Paul Stephen Dempsey & Laurence E. Gesell, *Airline Management: Strategies for the 21st Century* 451 (1997).

ances have had to adapt to the special facility and service needs of international airlines such as customs, immigration, and so forth.[51]

At the turn of the century, the fifth and current phase, *realignment*, emerged as a preeminent force. An upheaval in airline network structures was prompted by the tragic events of September 11, 2001. Networked (so-called traditional) carrier operations declined significantly, while low cost airline and regional jet operations began to change the face of the airline industry. In the 2004 edition of the *Journal of Transportation Statistics*, the MITRE Corporation reported,

> *The events of 2001 led to a massive restructuring of the airline industry that addressed weak basic business practices. The most significant changes were in capacity reductions in the number of available seat-miles and the number of flights. These necessary adjustments reflect a drop in demand, a decline in business travel, and the availability of Internet booking. In addition, a realigned fare structure narrowed the gap between premium and walkup fares and leisure fares. Finally, renegotiations of labor and other contracts, and simplification of the network structure, have also played key roles in the restructuring of the industry.* [52]

The reduced capacity adjustments ultimately "affected industry participants differently, with network carriers affected more than *Low Cost Carriers* [LCCs]." Both the LCCs and regional carriers utilizing regional jets were able to increase capacity while network carriers did not. Ultimately, the low cost and RJ carriers performed much better than their network carrier counterparts.[53]

In the MITRE report, the authors tracked airline market share (in this case, via the percentage of available seats) in each of three cate-

---

[51] David A. NewMyer, *The Impact of Deregulation on Airports: An International Perspective*, J. of Aviation/Aerospace Ed. and Research, Vol. 1 No. 1 (spring 1990), at 73.

[52] Dipasis Bhadra & Pamela Texter, *Airline Networks: An Econometric Framework to Analyze Domestic U.S. Air Travel,* Bureau of Trans. Statistics (2004), http://www.bts.gov/publications/journal_of_transportation_and_statistics/volume_07_number_01/.

[53] *Id.*

gories: network, low costs and all others (primarily regional jets, with a very small percentage of scheduled charter carriers). From 2000 to 2004, the Department of Transportation [DOT] Bureau of Transportation Statistics [BTS] reported an 11% drop in the availability of network carrier seats, while low fare seats increased by 8% and all others increased by 3%. Clearly industry realignment is occurring, although there are indications that the increasing RJ 50-seat series market trend will not continue. Currently about 1,600 RJs are in use, the majority of which are a 50-seat version.[54]

"The sleek little 50-seat regional jet that changed the industry fourteen years ago is now a falling star, the victim of changing economies," reported *USA Today* in 2005. "Small jets don't make economic sense on many routes anymore. Amid competition from low cost carriers, regional jets don't command the high fares they once did. And small jets spread high fuel costs among too many seats."[55] Some experts even predict a 100 aircraft "glut" in the 50-seat version, although the larger 70-100 seat RJs can be profitable.[56]

THE DRIVE FOR PRIVATIZATION

Perhaps the most significant impact that airline deregulation has had on airports is that its effects have fueled the drive for airport privatization. Proponents of airline deregulation suggest that airports, as well as the airlines, ought to be deregulated. More specifically, what they are suggesting is that airports should be privatized and freed of governmental oversight. An underlying belief is that management by private enterprise is generally more efficient than government management.

By executive order, President George Bush defined privatization as ". . . the disposition or transfer of an infrastructure asset, such as by sale or by long-term lease, from a state or local government to a private party."[57] In the deregulatory sense, airport privatization means that the government ought to extract itself from the direct management of airports and turn the process over to the private sector either

[54] Marilyn Adams, *Regional Jets Appear on the Endangered Species List,* USA Today (Nov. 2, 2005), at B-1.
[55] *Id.*
[56] *Id.* fact attributed to UBS analyst Peter Rozenber in the article.
[57] *Executive Order 12803* (1992).

by contractual management of the airport, by lease, or by outright sale to private investors.

Alfred Kahn, broadly recognized as the "father of airline deregulation," argued that airline deregulation, if it was to work, had to be "complete." He believed that the government needed to discontinue its economic intervention and to rely more upon natural marketplace forces to balance the economy. He also suggested that not only the airlines, but airports as well, should compete freely without government involvement and without subsidy.[58] Both the Heritage Foundation and the Reason Foundation strongly advocate the deregulation of airports as well. William Laffer of the Heritage Foundation, for example, states that the air system's problems are the result of "unfinished deregulation." The real problem (with air traffic congestion), he says, ". . . lies with the failure to deregulate the other components of America's air transportation network—the airports and the air traffic control system."[59] In like manner, Robert Poole of the Reason Foundation suggests, "Congress freed up the airlines to compete and grow, but left the essential infrastructure—the airports and Air Traffic Control [ATC] system—in their static, bureaucratic pre-deregulation condition. The result is a growing set of problems, (the) most notable (being) delays, congestion, and questions about safety levels."[60]

Indeed, airline deregulation resulted in profound changes in the air transport industry. In 1998, when he was looking back upon his career with *Airline Business* magazine, Editor Richard Whitaker marveled at how much the airline industry had changed since the magazine had been launched thirteen years earlier.[61] In 1985, Carl Icahn had just taken over Trans World Airlines; People Express was looking at acquisitions; Japan Airlines was losing its international monopoly; British Airways, Singapore Airlines and Maylasian Airlines were about to be privatized; Britain and France had signed a new air services agreement; and Dragonair was gearing up to compete against Cathay. In the first issue of the magazine, Frank Borman talked about plans to

---

[58] *See* Alfred Kahn, *Is It Time to Re-regulate the Airline Industry?* The World Economy, Vol. 5 No. 4 (1982), at 353.

[59] Tom Belden, *Privatization of Airports Gaining Favor*, The Phoenix Gazette (Thur., Mar. 28, 1991).

[60] Robert W. Poole, Jr., *Privatizing Airports*, The Reason Foundation Policy Study No. 119 (Jan. 1990).

[61] *See* Richard Whitaker, *Airline Revolution Gathers Pace*, Airline Magazine (Aug. 1998), at 7.

make Eastern Airlines a global company, and Europe's airlines were fighting the introduction of deregulation there.

Whitaker noted that many aspects of the airline industry had changed beyond recognition, as if there had been a "revolution." Eastern, Pan Am, People Express, Braniff, and British Caladonia had all vanished. Carl Icahn had sold out, Fokker Aircraft Company was out of business, McDonnell-Douglas had become part of Boeing, and Robert Crandall, the venerable CEO at American Airlines, had retired.

Although not "deregulated" in the American sense of the word, Europe's airline industry had indeed been "liberalized," as had most national markets. Nearly all government-owned airlines of any size were now in the private sector. And the industry was moving towards globalization with the emergence of the mega-alliance air carrier groups. A regional carrier before deregulation, Southwest Airlines had become an industry leader, and the package carriers (FedEx, UPS, Emery, etc.) had taken over the U.S. air cargo industry.[62]

In short, the decades of the 1980s and 1990s saw the airline industry complete its transformation from a cosseted industry that had been nurtured and subsidized by government into a profitable and mostly privatized global business. But, as Whitaker suggested, the revolution was not yet over. The remaining airline privatizations were still to take place, and "large numbers of airports" as well would enter the private sector.[63] With regard to airport privatization, Tom Gill suggests that, by the end of the 20th century there had been a "stampede to market"! Cash-strapped national and local governments worldwide were abandoning responsibility for costly airport development, and by the first decade of the 21st century Gill predicted that most international commercial airports would likely be in private hands.[64] While this prediction has not yet come to fruition, there indeed has been steady movement toward international airport privatization.

Airports, like the airlines, have evolved since deregulation. Looking at the phenomenon of airport evolution, the FAA authorized a study to examine what it considered to be the airport evolutionary process.[65] The basic objective was to identify the evolutionary life of

---

[62] *See id.*

[63] Richard Whitaker, *Airline Revolution Gathers Pace*, Airline Magazine (Aug. 1998), at 7.

[64] Tom Gill, *Stampede to Market*, Airline Business (Apr. 1998), at 50.

[65] Systems Consultants, Inc., *Airport Evolution Study*, Report No. SCI-76-4086A for the FAA (May 1977).

airports. The study's basis was that airports are like *living things*; they are initially conceived and given birth, they pass through an accelerated growth period similar to adolescence, they reach a period of maturity and stability in adulthood, and ultimately are abandoned and die. The likely scenario is that an airport, after it is born, grows for a while, then enters a period of stability, then grows more, becomes stable again, and continues the growth/stability cycle until at some point it outlives its usefulness. The number of growth stages as well as the time periods for stability varies with different airports. One airport may reach long-term maturity after a single growth period and remain operationally stable until its abandonment, while another airport, similar at birth, may proceed through numerous growth stages finally reaching maturity as a large international air carrier airport.

Applying the "living airport" scenario to airport *systems*, airports as an industry were given birth and nurtured during the 1920s, 1930s and early 1940s. In the immediate post World War II era, many airports were converted from military to civil airfields and were donated to local communities by the federal government. Others were started from scratch by aviators seeking ways to profit from their skills as flyers. Airports were a fledgling market, and the complexities of business were relatively simple compared to today. Airport management in the past had relatively more aviation-related technical requirements, but little was required of the airport operator in terms of business management and dealing with the governmental process.

ENABLING LEGISLATION

With some exceptions (particularly in Alaska), public airport administration in the United States is structured within one of three standard forms of governmental organization. Most airports are owned by a county (otherwise called a "borough" in New York or a "parish" in Louisiana), by a municipality (city, borough, town, township, or village), or by one of the sub-governmental entities known as authorities or special districts. Until 1986, there were two federally owned and operated public airports: Dulles International Airport and Washington National Airport. Both airports were transferred by lease in 1986 to a local entity, the Metropolitan Washington Airports Authority. Though still federally "owned," the two airports raise money in the private sector, and conduct their own operations and planning.

Cities, counties, authorities and special districts derive their authority to operate airports from the state within which they are located. However, before looking directly at the source of authority to administer airports given to local governments by the states, one must first question why it is that airports in a capitalist society are in the public sector at all. Why are they not a private enterprise? As mentioned in the last section, although there is a current movement to privatize certain airports, why have airports not been privatized all along? Why is it that air transportation has become a bifurcated system in the U.S., with privately owned airlines on the one hand, and publicly owned and operated airports on the other?

The foremost answer is that most airports of major importance to the nation's air transportation system are in the public domain as a function of economic expedience, if not necessity. If airports could have been profitable from the outset, they would have been privately held. But the economic reality is that airports in general are not profitable and are, therefore, unattractive as long-term ventures other than to management companies who assume only limited risk. Supporting this contention, a Congressional Budget Office study in 1984 concluded there were only 71 of the 5,000 or so airports in the then National Airport System Plan [NASP] that demonstrated economic self-sufficiency.[66] This suggests that most airports today operate at a deficit and must be subsidized. "Self-sufficiency" is defined herein as the ability to pay not only operating expenses, but also to develop sufficient revenues to finance capital spending needs. Hence, ownership and operation of public airports has been relegated to the public sector; i.e., to governments willing to subsidize airport operation in exchange for other social and economic benefits hopefully to be derived from having a community airport.

Airports have been further relegated by the federal government to the state, and especially to the local government levels as a matter of historic precedent; following a trend set early in the 19th century and carried forward into the 20th century in highway and road development. Beginning in 1832, the Jacksonian era was one of strict (constitutional) interpretation of states rights; that is to say, states would be the supreme authority in internal developments, including that of roads and highway networks. This precedent was mirrored early in the last century in the Federal Aid Road Act of 1916. Although cer-

[66] Congressional Budget Office, *Financing U.S. Airports in the 1980s* (1984).

tain highway improvements were to be funded (in part) by the federal government, states were still to retain ownership and to be responsible for construction and maintenance of (their) highways. This became the basic pattern of highway development in subsequent programs. The same pattern was adopted for early development of the air transportation system.

Air transportation in the 1920s was characterized by a fledgling industry lacking in capital, engaged in reckless competition, and highly dependent for its survival upon government subsidization. To enhance development of the new industry, Congress passed two related acts. First, contracts granted through the Air Mail Act of 1925 (and as amended in 1926) provided revenue for private capital investment. Secondly, the Air Commerce Act of 1926 provided for federal development of the (air) way. But in a seeming reflection of Jacksonian policy, development of the terminal ends (i.e., the airports) was left for the states and their local governments to accomplish. In fact, specifically prohibited was federal funding of airport development, although it might be noted that there were incidences of federal funding through Franklin Delano Roosevelt's "New Deal" work programs during the Great Depression.

Under the Federal Airport Act of 1946, and subsequent airport related legislation, the Federal government officially began participating in airport development. But, the ultimate responsibility for airport ownership and operation still remains with the state and/or local government sponsor. As exemplified in Jacksonian policy, the authority for states and local governments to own and operate airports is constitutionally grounded in the Tenth Amendment. The U.S. Constitution vests all government authority, as *specifically* stated, with the Federal government. Otherwise, authority rests with the individual states. State and local airports derive their powers through *enabling* legislation created by their individual state legislatures.

In the case of state-owned airports, enablement and authority is through legislation authorizing airport operation directly by the State. For county, city, and joint governmental operations (classified as airport authorities, port authorities, special districts, and so forth) the airport's "authority" is granted by the State through charters of incorporation or through alternative organization of these sub-governmental entities.

These public airport sponsors have the authority to acquire property for airport purposes through purchase, lease, or through exercise of their power of *eminent domain* (i.e., the inherent power of a sovereign government to take private property for public use). They may also exercise their *police powers* to regulate the operation of their airports.

LOCAL GOVERNMENT STRUCTURE

Although most airports in the United States are owned and operated by local governments, the Federal Aviation Administration is charged with the responsibility of formulating and maintaining a plan for a *national* system of airports. The National Plan of Integrated Airport Systems [NPIAS] (pronounced "nip-pee-us" throughout the industry) is comprised of airports that are open to the public. The NPIAS report, which generally encompasses a five-year projection window, "estimates the costs associated with establishing a system of airports adequate to meet the needs of civil aviation" along with the needs of the Postal Service and the Department of Defense. Airports are only included in the NPIAS if they make a significant contribution to national air transportation or provide local access to the air transportation network.[67]

There are nearly 20,000 landing sites in the U.S. However, the term "landing sites" encompasses much more than airports. Included in the larger figure are heliports, Short Take Off and Landing or "STOLports," and seaplane bases, as well as airports. Of the 19,847 U.S. landing sites in America, the NPIAS contains only 3,431 airports, and of the NPIAS airports, less than 10% are privately owned.[68] Hence, pilots and the aviation community are almost entirely dependent upon local governments to provide and maintain airport facilities. Although there are some state-owned and operated airports, none are federally operated, and, generally speaking, most NPIAS airports are owned and operated by cities, counties, or special districts.

The latitude given in the operation of the airport, and the magnitude of responsibility embodied in the airport manager, is determined by a number of factors. These factors include the size of the airport,

---

[67] U.S. DOT (FAA), Report to Congress; *National Plan of Integrated Airport Systems, 2007-2011* (Sep. 29, 2006).
[68] *Id.*

the level of service provided, the number and technical qualifications of the airport staff, the limits of the geographic area served, and by the complexities of inter-jurisdictional coordination to be accomplished.

The *county* is the governmental jurisdiction found between the state and the municipal levels. A county normally has at its head an elected body known as the Board of Supervisors or County Commissioners. Counties will also have an administrative manager who is appointed by the board. The county administrator is responsible for the overall administration of the government's operation, and is in charge of the several public service directorates such as engineering, personnel, purchasing, public utilities, and so forth. See Figure 1.1, "County Organization," for an example of a typical county organizational chart.

The manager of the airport is often at the directorate level with a direct line of communication to the county administrator. In this situation the manager of the airport will usually carry the title of airport "director" rather than airport "manager." In other cases, depending upon how large the airport is, its relative importance to the community, and the responsibility associated with the position, the airport manager may be located lower in the organizational hierarchy, subordinate to one of the directorates. For example, the airport manager may work for the director of public works or in the case of the example in Figure 1.1, for the director of general services.

With regard to smaller airports, the prevailing notion is to attempt, through consolidation, to combine airports with some other department within local government such as public works. Accordingly, the airport manager is subordinated to the director of the greater department. A precedent for this can be found at the federal level where the FAA Administrator is subordinate to the Secretary of Transportation. The same is often the case at the state level where the division of aeronautics is usually found within the state department of transportation.

At the county level, the airport manager may be answerable to one of the directors, who in turn will be responsible to the county administrator. However, when the airport manager is once or twice removed from the chief executive, communications become interrupted and other operational problems may ensue, which can negate the advantages of consolidating departments.

Figure 1.1—COUNTY ORGANIZATION

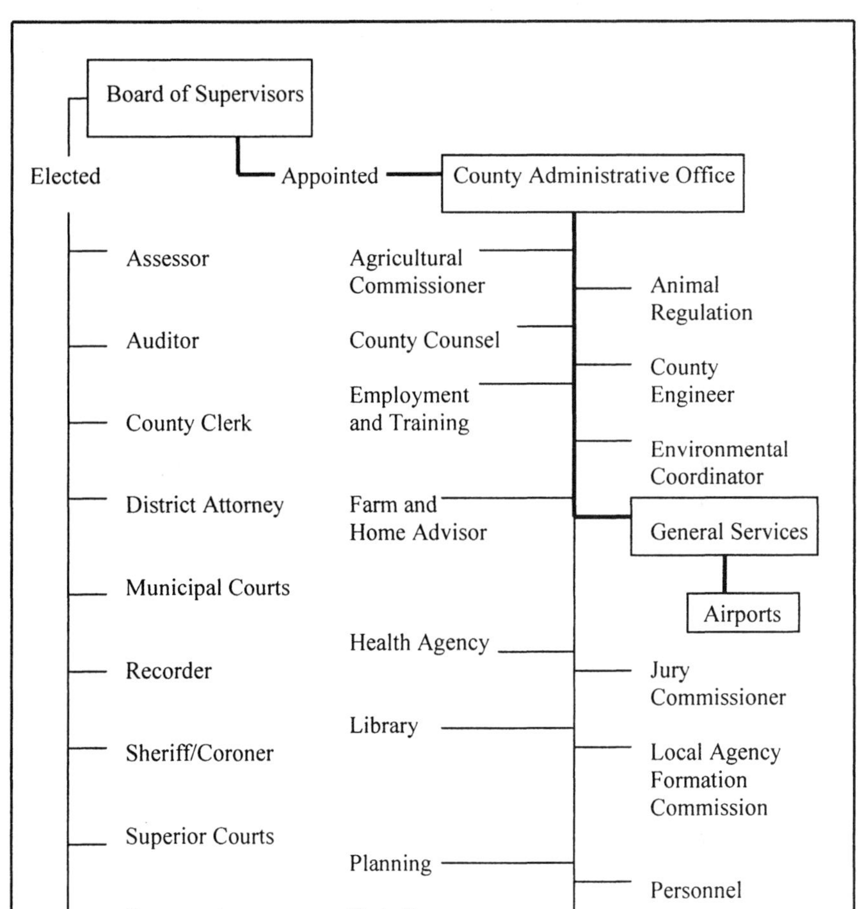

Source: County of San Luis Obispo, Calif.

Cities are the basic fundamental levels of government. They form a collective public means of solving local issues of people living in close proximity. Cities provide the same types of services as the counties but within a more specific urban locale, usually a smaller area within the county. There are some situations, however, where a city and county are combined in the same geographical area. Examples are San Francisco, California, and Arlington, Virginia, where the city and county limits are one and the same. The most common forms of city government are three: mayor-council, council-manager, and city commission:

- The *mayor-council* system includes an executive or presiding officer (the mayor), a legislative body (the council) elected at large and responsible for enacting local laws, and varying numbers of elected or appointed department heads and advisory boards (much like that found at the county level).
- The *council-manager* form of city government has at its head an elected body (the council), which makes policy decisions, enacts ordinances, approves the budget and appoints an administrative officer—the city manager. This form of city government is the one most analogous to the prevailing county organization previously discussed. As with the county administrator, the city manager oversees the activities of the various service departments and advisory boards. The city manager, through other appointees, supervises all parts of government. The manager sees that laws and ordinances are enforced, appoints and removes personnel, prepares the annual budget for approval, advises the council on financial conditions, controls purchasing, and reports and makes recommendations to the council as necessary. The council-manager organization is the most popular form of city government.
- The last major form of city organization is the *commission.* This form of government is becoming extinct, but some discussion is warranted. With the commission plan there is a constituted body of popularly elected commissioners. Together they serve as the legislative body, and singularly as heads of administrative departments. The major deficiency with this type of government is attributable to the diffusion of administrative responsibility among the several commissioners, and the lack of

> a single, unifying executive. All too often there is little coordination of activities, much duplication of effort, and a greater potential for conflict between department heads.

Airport management within the city structure is comparable to the relationship of airport management within county organizations. Figure 1.2, "City Organization," illustrates a typical city organizational chart.

The governmental organization that provides for the greatest autonomy in the operation of the airport is the *special district*, or *authority*. When the airport serves two or more governmental jurisdictions, requires special coordination in its operation, is sufficiently large and complex, and where the airport creates sufficient revenue to support its own operation,[69] the airport's interests may be best served by creating a special district, bounded by the airport property limits and administered by an airport authority.

The executive body of the special district is made up of airport board members (or a board of commissioners) who are either appointed by the city or county that established the district, or is voted into office by the public in a general election. See Figure 1.3, "Airport District," for an example of a typical airport district organizational chart. The airport manager reports directly for the airport board.

Special-purpose districts are set up by cities, towns and counties to do specific jobs. There are many kinds of special districts, of which airport districts, or authorities, are only one. Special districts are also set up to administer transportation ports, the public school system, collect garbage, supply water for domestic and irrigation purposes, build roads and bridges, move commuters, provide for sewage and garbage disposal, generate and distribute electricity, conduct air pollution control programs, and maintain fire protection facilities. Services provided by special districts and authorities can include practically the full array of local government functions.

[69] Revenue in an authority model may be "generated" via support funneled though the authority's various jurisdictions. In some cases, a greater level of funding by one member may yield additional decision-making authority for that member agency.

Figure 1.2—CITY ORGANIZATION

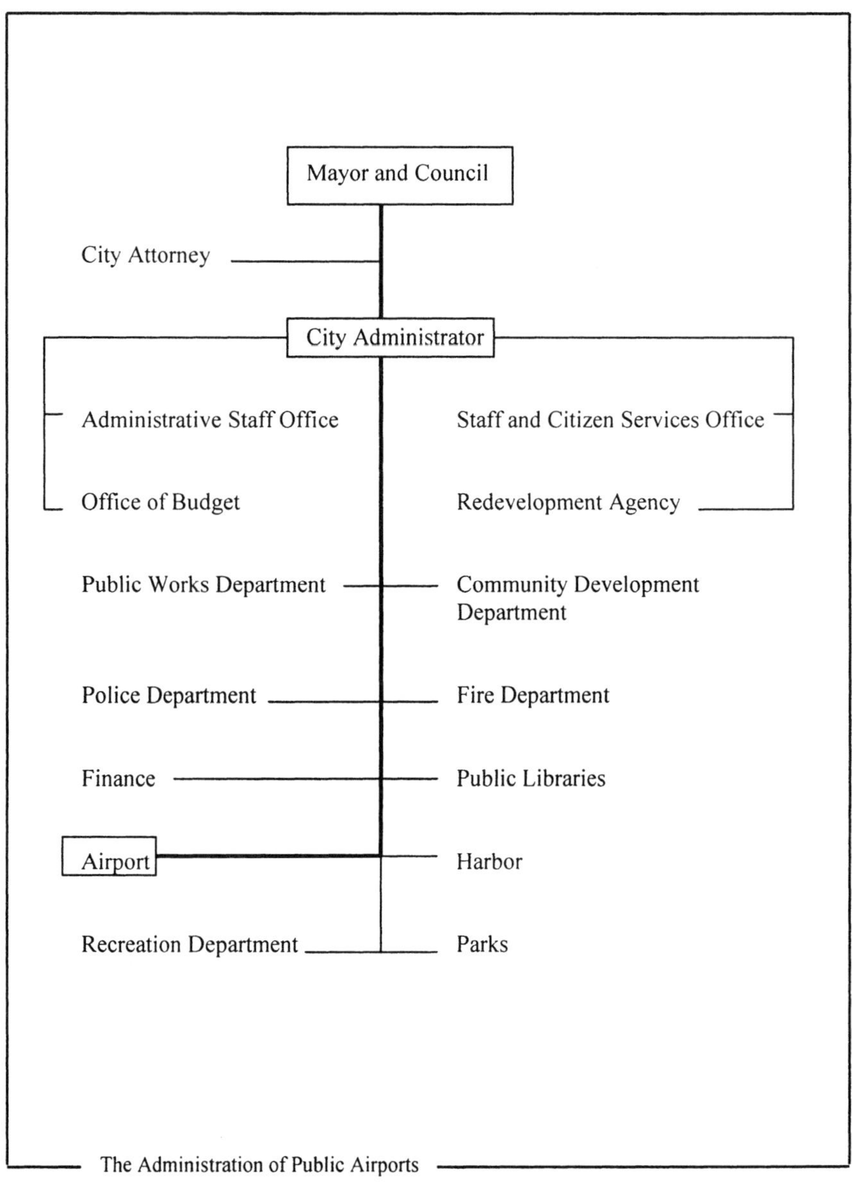

Source: City of Santa Barbara, Calif.

Figure 1.3—AIRPORT DISTRICT

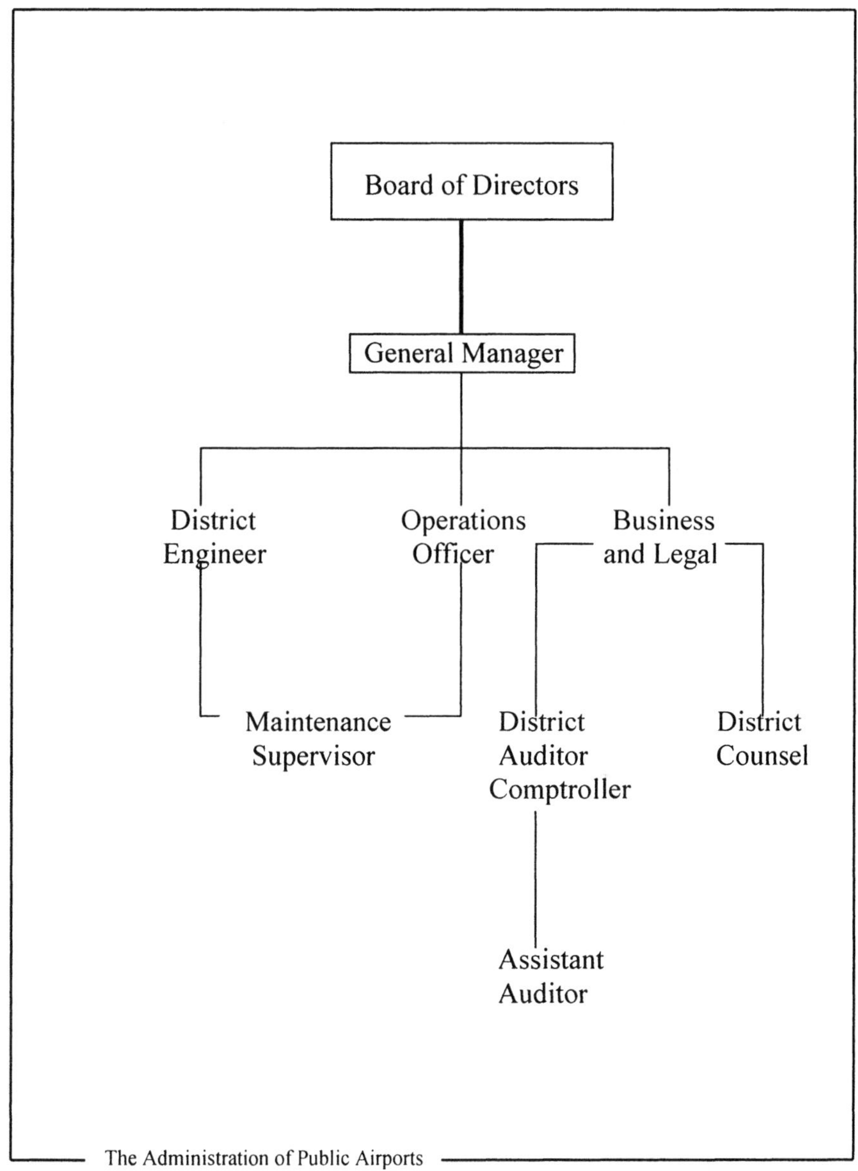

Source: Santa Maria, Calif. Airport District

Special-purpose districts now greatly outnumber traditional municipal governments. In 1990s, for example, there were 33,131 special-purpose governments, compared to 19,296 municipalities.[70] Special-purpose districts cut across municipal boundaries to embrace an entire metropolitan area or part of a state. They can range in size from such giants as the Port Authority of New York and New Jersey to the airport in Missoula, Montana. The latter was set apart by the City of Missoula as a special district, with its board members appointed by the city council. A majority of special districts are separate and distinct units of local government, and have substantial fiscal and administrative independence. Others are governed by the county board of supervisors or by the city council, such as the one in Missoula. Some are joint-powers authorities, deriving their powers from combined governmental jurisdictions, such as the New York and New Jersey Port Authority.

Since the independent special district provides airport management with the greatest autonomy amongst the various governmental forms, the interests of the airport can be served more directly, and with less interference from external political influence. The airport authority is considered self-serving, less encumbered by the sundry general welfare responsibilities of cities and counties, and is established solely for the purpose of promoting the airport and aviation service to the community.

Special districts are usually immune to the traditional political distraction associated with county and city-run airports. In situations where the county board of supervisors or the city council is responsible for the airport's operation, the elected officials are often divided in their individual support of the airport. A good illustration can be found where the politician is elected on a pro-environmental and community status quo platform. The elected official may find it difficult to promote development of the airport when it may mean increased aircraft noise and a potentially adverse impact upon the established community environment. The elected official may be in danger of losing the support of the constituency that put him or her into office. If a majority of a board or council find themselves in similar positions, airport interests may suffer accordingly. Airport promotion will ride the tide of political terms of office, waiting for a majority of

[70] The Associated Press, *Special Districts Booming*, Tribune Newspapers (Thur., Feb. 11, 1993), at A4.

the governing body to be in support of airport development. It can readily be seen how detrimental this kind of off-and-on-again support can be to the operation of an airport.

It should be noted that no matter what form of governmental organization, the airport manager is responsible to a duly constituted legislative body. As an appointed public administrator, the airport manager is an "administrative" agent for elected officials. It is the latter who are responsible directly to the public at large, and (theoretically) it is they alone who are involved in overt politics and policy-making decisions—not the airport manager. It is the airport manager's responsibility to interpret and implement the policy decisions of elected officials, to provide staff expertise on airport matters, and to provide policy feedback to them, and not to become involved in partisan politics. Certainly politics are involved, but in the classical sense the airport manager serves the public, but does so in an *administrative* capacity

THE PROFESSION

Today's airport managers must deal with complex business issues, must maneuver through a complicated local and national political maze, and must be able to balance the needs of their communities with national aviation interests. The aviation industry has become exceedingly complex in a maze of not only aviation rules and regulations but also of environmental and other contemporary social issues. Additionally, airports have become big business with operating statements in the millions of dollars. Airport managers, who in the 1940s and 1950s once thrived in the industry due to their technical skills in aviation, have since been replaced by managers with disciplined education in business management, public administration and aviation specific management or business academic preparation.

Airports link their regions with the rest of the world. They promote local economic development. They provide jobs. They generate revenue for their particular regions, often without the benefit of general tax revenues that other public enterprises enjoy. The managers of these airports must perform like major corporate executives, making decisions that affect thousands of people, generating millions of dollars in direct and indirect revenue, and making the same kinds of decisions made in successful private sector enterprises. And these managers must understand all levels of government to accomplish their policies and programs.

Airports are like cities in miniature, and their managers must provide the same types of public welfare services that other "cities" do, such as police and fire protection. They must operate their own public works, and be integrally connected to the major local emergency care centers. The task is professional in every sense of the word, yet the pay is oftentimes not what might be expected. Chip Barclay noted that,

> *. . . airport managers have some of the most responsible demanding, politically sensitive and varied jobs in the aviation industry. Airport executives are often responsible for much larger business at much lower levels of compensation than their private industry counterparts, with periodic local political examinations as a "bonus". . . .*[71]

The empirical evidence seems to demonstrate that airport executives do not enjoy the same level of compensation as their counterparts in the private sector, whether at for-profit enterprises or at nonprofit organizations. Ironically, airport executives are often responsible for high visibility organizations with significantly larger staffs, exponentially larger budgets, and with far broader economic impacts than their private sector counterparts. Yet, on average government employees are less compensated than their private sector equivalents. Airport managers' salaries seem even more suppressed by what may be called "bureaucratic rationality," although public sector employment is often considered more stable than private sector work.

The job specification for the airport manager may call for equal and sometimes even higher education, professional accreditation, and/or greater experience levels than managers further up in the hierarchy (such as say a department director, the city manager, and/or county administrator). Yet, it is reasoned that the airport manager should be paid less than superiors within whose department the airport may be situated. So why do they do it? Why are airport managers apparently willing to work for less? Charles Barclay suggests "the

---

[71] Charles M. Barclay, *Needed: Equal Pay for Equal Work*, Airport Magazine (Mar./Apr. 1991).

seduction of aviation over the economics of executive compensation presents the most plausible theory."[72] Airport managers seemingly love their jobs so much they are willing to forego higher compensation packages in exchange for doing what they like best.

AIRPORT ASSOCIATIONS AND ACCREDITATION

The two most prominent organizations representing airport interests are the American Association of Airport Executives or AAAE, and the Airports Council International [ACI]. The ACI is composed of airports and their representatives (i.e., the airport sponsors), and AAAE is made up of managers of airports (i.e., individuals).

Originally named the Airport Operators Council International [AOCI], the ACI merged with the International Civil Airports Association to form a new organization, the Airports Association Council International. The world's airports were united by this merger, in the new association named Airports Council International. More than 400 airports and authorities are members of ACI in six world regions: Africa, Europe, Asia, Latin America, North America and the Pacific. The world headquarters for ACI is in Geneva, with the ACI-North American regional office [ACI-NA] located in Washington, D.C.

The institution historically recognized for providing individual airport managers with professional certification is the AAAE, headquartered in Alexandria, Virginia. However, ACI and the International Civil Aviation Organization [ICAO] joined forces in 2007 to offer the *Airport Management Professional Accreditation Programme* [AMPAP], which can lead to award of the *International Airport Professional* [IAP] designation.[73]

The AMPAP requires the candidate to successfully complete four mandatory (five-day duration or equivalent) courses and two electives in a three-year period. Themes of the mandatory courses are: (1) Air Transportation System Overview/Airport Strategic Business Planning; (2) Airport Master Planning, Development and Environmental Management; (3) Airport Marketing, Commercial Development and Financial Administration; and (4) Airport Operations, Safety and Security. The electives are existing ICAO or ACI courses that have been

---

[72] Charles M. Barclay, *Manageing Airports: It's a Tough Job, and a Professional Has to Do It*, Airport Services Management (May 1984).
[73] ACI, *Global Training Hub Course Catalogue* (2007).

incorporated as optional AMPAP courses and other electives as they are introduced into the program. Courses are offered at a variety of locations around the world, with some courses offered on-line.

For AAAE, there are several membership options including a reduced cost academic membership for students. The AAAE confers the status of Accredited Airport Executive [AAE] upon its members who have satisfactorily demonstrated abilities in the field of airport management. The title (AAE) is awarded at the end of a multi-year process during which a candidate obtains and demonstrates a thorough knowledge of the principles of the industry.[74] In addition to the AAE certification, the AAAE also provides a Certified Member [CM] option for individuals not directly involved in the management of an airport but desiring professional certification of their airport-related knowledge.

The first step in the traditional program for an aspiring AAE candidate is to become an Affiliate member of the American Association of Airport Executives. Affiliate membership is for individuals who are "actively engaged in the management or staff functions of a public-use airport."[75] As an Affiliate with one or more year's full time experience in civil airport management, the AAE aspirant may then declare his or her intention to become an Accredited Airport Executive, upon which time the Affiliate member is reclassified as an "Executive Candidate." The successful applicant must be twenty-one years of age and must also possess a four-year college degree or eight years of civil airport management experience, or combined equivalent. Although a degree in any field is acceptable, the previous section dealing with the airport's functional areas of responsibility gives some indications as to the recommended fields, which could advantageously lead to a career in airport management.[76]

The AAE designation is earned following the AAAE's acceptance of an original management research paper relating to a topic of interest to airport managers/management, a written examination, and a final interview. The interview, designed to evaluate the candidate's knowledge and communication skills, can only be scheduled upon the candidate's completion of three year's civil airport management experience. The process is comparable to examinations in other profes-

[74] Neilson A. Bertholf, Jr., *Accreditation Adds Excellence*, Airport Magazine (Nov./Dec. 1991).
[75] AAAE, http://www.aaae.org (visited 2006).
[76] *Id.*

sional fields. Upon successful completion of these requirements, along with the signing of a code-of-ethics form, the AAE designation is awarded, and the candidate is admitted to Executive Membership. Such members are eligible to use the initials A.A.E. after their name."[77]

The preponderance of advertised openings for airport positions commonly stipulate, as a condition of employment, the desirability of some level of aviation experience. In addition, the advertised qualifications include completion of a relevant four-year college degree, and sometimes a master's degree is deemed desirable. For positions in airport management (and operations), the most commonly stipulated educational requirements are in public and/or business administration, or airport/aviation management.

For jobs in engineering (or airport planning and development), degrees in the fields of civil engineering, architecture and/or urban planning (i.e., the so called "A&E" professions) are most commonly required. Traditionally, backgrounds in architecture, engineering, or planning, normally do not lead to positions as airport managers, but rather become their own specialty field in the airport industry.

The architecture and engineering, or A&E fields, if employed directly by the airport, are normally *staff* rather than *line* assignments; in other words, they are not directly involved in airport management *per se*. More commonly, architects, engineers, and planners support airport activities as professional or staff consultants to airport management. When asked what courses of instruction airport consultants viewed as most important for entry level employment in the consulting industry, members of the Airport Consultants Council recommended three courses as most important. By order of precedence, the surveyed members recommended studies in aviation policy and planning, airport administration, and aviation law and regulation.[78]

EDUCATIONAL PREPARATION

The most common educational field leading to airport management is management itself, whether it is in business administration, public administration, or aviation management. There are approxi-

---

[77] *Id.*

[78] Michelle Fuller & Lawrence J. Truitt, *Aviation Education: Perceptions of Airport Consultants*, J. of Air Transportation World Wide, Vol. II No. 3 (Jun. 1997).

mately 200 institutions of higher learning specializing in aviation studies. However, most of these schools are two-year institutions with programs leading to an associate degree only. There are relatively few four-year programs offering a bachelor's degree in aviation management or aviation business administration, and even fewer that offer a graduate education in airport management. The recognized accrediting body for these specialized aviation management or business programs is the Aviation Accreditation Board International [AABI], formerly the Council on Aviation Accreditation [CAA].

In addition to the normal curriculum, most of these four-year schools have coordinated airport management internships or cooperative arrangements with a variety of public airports. These institutions offer excellent programs in aeronautics and aviation management, but because there are relatively few of them, and many of them are widely dispersed, the student may have to travel far from home to attend one of these schools. Moreover, many of these schools are privately owned. Attending a private school of aviation can be an expensive proposition, and for some prospective students it may be beyond their means, although the industry has scholarships available to prospective students.

Barring the availability or capability to attend an institution offering a specialized bachelor's degree, other alternatives include a junior (or community) college for two years and then transfer to a four-year institution. Recommended might be a two-year program in aviation technology to include pilot and/or aviation maintenance training. With a sound foundation in aviation, the student could then transfer to a college offering a bachelor's degree in either public or business administration. Or a student could purse a two-year program of study in management or business, and then complete the remaining two years in an aviation management or aviation business administration program at a specialized four-year institution. Either approach could provide the student with a solid undergraduate foundation for a career in airport management at a reduced cost, although the student should use care to assure the eventual transferability of credits.

Regardless of the institution or path selected, it is immeasurably advantageous for a student to seek a cooperative educational training program or an internship at a public airport. Internships are most helpful when taken in the summer before the Junior or Senior years, or immediately after graduation. Internship planning and coordination can be accomplished by going through school administration, or by directly contacting airport managers and requesting that such a program be established if one does not already exist. Coordinated education and internship programs are an excellent way to obtain experience, and in some cases, college credit. The experience can be later referenced to assist in the securing of permanent employment. Some internship positions are paid; others are not, but the experience gained is invaluable.

Sometimes it may be helpful to have some flying experience. Typical job announcements list pilot qualifications as beneficial, but rarely is it a mandatory requirement. Seemingly, a common thread running through the biographies of many airport managers is that flying is merely an extension of a more fundamental love of aviation, and that they apparently find their jobs managing airports more satisfying than flying airplanes for a career.

Growing numbers of students pursuing management careers in aviation are now seeking graduate degrees to prepare them. The most appropriate professional degree for a career in airport management is the Master of Public Administration [MPA], although a Master of Business Administration [MBA] or an aeronautical or transportation Masters degree would be appropriate as well.

Whereas there are relatively few colleges or universities offering a four-year degree in any field of aviation, there are even fewer with aviation-related masters programs, and currently, none (outside of the aeronautical or aerospace engineering fields) that offer a doctoral degree specific to airports. There are, however, Doctorates of Business Administration [DBA] and Doctorates of Public Administration [DPA] or Doctor of Philosophy [PhD] counterparts, which in some cases may be tailored for an emphasis in airport management.

In a survey, active airport managers were asked to rate the relevance of each course in the Master of Public Administration core to the management of airports. The managers reported that all MPA coursework is relevant to airport management. But not surprisingly, a course in airport management was considered most important. Next, by order of importance, were courses in public budgeting and fiscal management, public personnel management and a general course in public administration.[79]

As can be seen, the traditional master in public administration also provides a good background for a career in airport administration, but should be supplemented with airport-specific knowledge to be best prepared. The airport management aspirant may have to complete limited coursework at a school offering graduate education in aviation. And, if the student is unable, or otherwise unwilling to attend an aviation school that has a graduate curriculum, the student may be able to take at least one or two courses from such an institution. The credit could then be transferred for inclusion in the MPA or other relevant program of study at the school of choice.

SUMMARY

Airports require a specialized knowledge in their management and operation, with in many cases a combination of business administration acumen mixed with public administration skills. Airports in the United States have a rich history, strongly rooted within the public sector but with a public/private partnership in management and investment. International airports likewise have a history of government involvement, but in recent years the trend has been towards privatization of what previously was almost exclusively a public or governmental function.

From the government service perspective, the next chapter discusses what has come to be known as the "new public administration" and provides an important introduction into the field of public administration and management. In learning the basic managerial terms, tool and concepts associated with management in the public sector, one can better understand the administrative and managerial complexities associated with this complex career field. The subjects of airport finance and economics, the airport marketplace, and privatization and entrepreneurship of airports are reserved for later presentation in Chapters 12, 13, and 15, respectively.

---

[79] *See* Lawrence J. Truitt, John A. Hamman, & Klaus G. Palinkas, *Graduate Education in Airport Administration: Preparing Airport Managers for the 21st Century*, J. of Avn./Aerospace Ed. & Research (winter 1994).

CHAPTER 2

NEW PUBLIC ADMINISTRATION

Elected officials find themselves caught between explaining and defending the institutions over which they preside and the impulse to continue to criticize and change those institutions. The longer people are in office, the more likely they tend to defend the very bureaucracies and the very policies which they may once have campaigned against. The impulse to force a transformation of those institutions is gradually overwhelmed by an impulse to preside.

Newt Gingrich, Professor and Politician[1]

INTRODUCTION

In the context of management or administration in the public sector, the traditional view had been that public administration is an enterprise devoted exclusively to the objective implementation of politics decreed by popularly elected government officials.[2] The prevailing theory of government in the previous century was that political leaders set policy, and then administrators dutifully implemented it. This paralleled earlier beliefs that politics and administration were distinctly separated functions. (But, clearly, they are not.) Moreover, people often regarded public policy as something created only at the highest levels of government.[3] Examples might be something like

---

[1] Newt Gingrich, *The Conservative Movement at the Crossroads* (Apr. 18, 2005); http://www.newt.org/backpage.asp?art=1703.

[2] William L. Morrow, *Public Administration: Politics, Policy, and the Political System* 1-2 (2nd ed. 1980).

[3] *See* Grover Starling, *Managing the Public Sector* (6th ed. 2002).

"American civil rights policy," or perhaps a "balanced budget policy."

Within the "new" public administration paradigm, while elected officials generally create policy, non-elected administrators may also be responsible for assistance in shaping the policy and in creating and implementing the programs that support and implement the policy decisions. Bureaucrats are active participants in the policy-making process. Administrative actions typically modify or set policy in the process of trying to implement it. Agencies not infrequently are instructed by elected functionaries to *make* policy.[4]

Career public managers concur that policy creation is not merely a top-down exercise. Public policies are also tied to the mundane as well as the spectacular events in government. As Newt Gingrich suggested in the introductory quote (*supra*), the priorities and policies of elected officials may also change over time, creating a challenge for career public administrators who function in an important supporting role: stabilizing services and providing reliable governance. Career public administrators can serve to smooth the political leadership transitions that naturally occur in government. They can also help (or hinder) politicians efforts to implement wide-sweeping changes to public bureaucracies and implement innovative programs.

While politicians generally have notions for high-profile policies, they often rely on seasoned public managers for their years of experience. Thus, policy suggestions routinely percolate up from respected career administrators who can suggest purposeful courses of action (i.e., policies) to achieve elected officials agendas, create economic efficiencies, better manage resources, or improve the delivery of services within a community.

In program delivery, policies may be further reshaped, sometimes unwittingly, by those who interface with the public or users in the implementation of the policy. For example, when a Mayor claims a policy of "a cleaner community," programs like "more frequent garbage collection" or "24-hour graffiti removal" may be created. But, if one's garbage is neglected or wall left cluttered with "street art" after

---

[4] In an early challenge to the simplistic notion that bureaucracies as merely implementers of decisions made by elected officials, Carl Friedrich noted that public policy "is a continuous process, the formulation of which is inseparable from its execution," in Carl J. Friedrich, *Public Policy and the Nature of Administrative Responsibility*, in Carl J. Friedrich & Edward Mason (eds.), Public Policy (1940) at 6; *see also* Charles E. Lindblom & Edward J. Woodhouse, *The Policy-Making Process* 59 (3rd ed. 1993).

the program is announced, it may be perceived that those who established the policies are ineffective.

In one case example, in the 1970s the United States Congress adopted an energy savings policy. Elizabeth Dole was then Secretary of Transportation. Responsible for carrying out federal policy, she in turn created an energy-saving program. Enforcement of the 55-mile-an-hour speed limit was a Department of Transportation [DOT] policy intended to save energy resources. Likewise, an airport (city, county or special district) sponsor might adopt a "user-pays" policy. The airport manager must in turn create policy on the airport to ensure that users pay their full share of expenses incurred on the airport. Often "the latitude of those charged with carrying out policy is so substantial that . . . policy is effectively 'made' by the people who implement it."[5]

PUBLIC ADMINISTRATORS AND PUBLIC POLICY

Who are public administrators and what exactly is public policy? We begin by defining the role and then move toward the action they take. Historically public administrators were identified as those who were hired into public sector positions. But it has since been recognized that this was a short-sighted approach, as elected officials and unpaid officials in oversight positions are indeed administrators of public policy. In listing Public Administrators, one would appropriately include both governmental and non-profit administrators, mangers and officials such as: [6]

- Elected chief executives;
- Governors and Mayors;
- Administrators, commissioners, directors;
- Officials appointed to lead line agencies and their staff, if involved in running government programs; and/or
- Officials in oversight positions (legislators, boards, staff), even though they don't run agencies or manage programs.[7]

---

[5] Michael Lipsky, *Standing the Study of Public Policy Implementation on its Head*, in Walter Dean Burnham & Martha W. Weinberg (eds.), American Politics and Public Policy 397 (1978); *see also* Charles E. Lindblom & Edward J. Woodhouse, *The Policy-Making Process* 59 (3rd ed. 1993).

[6] Grover Starling, *Managing the Public Sector* (6th ed. 2002).

[7] *Id.*

What it means to be "public" has similarly expanded over the years, beyond traditional governmental structures, to include public-oriented non-profit organizations and public-benefit (private sector-run) programs.[8] Generally speaking, "public policy" is whatever governments, specifically represented by the public administrators such as those listed above, choose to do or not to do. But it takes more than a simple definition to explain what public policy is. It is an abstraction. Textbooks devoted to defining public policy traditionally give more than one definition and then make excuses for the inadequacy of each of the definitions. Then the authors go on to present their own definition, which may also be inadequate in describing what, in effect, is an abstract notion called "public policy."

In trying to define what public policy is, James Anderson, David Brady and Charles Bullock explain what public policy must incorporate. For example, a useful definition must embody the idea that public policy is a course or pattern of activity and not simply a decision to act in some particular way. In other words, it is a process and not merely a decision. Public policy is directed toward the accomplishment of some goal. It involves purposive governmental action. In sum, public policy will show a pattern of governmental activity on some topic or matter, which has a purpose or goal. It will not equate decision making with policy or confuse the stated goal of action with what is actually done.[9] In light of these parameters Anderson, Brady and Bullock offer the following by stating that public policy is,

> *. . . a goal-directed or purposive course of action followed by an actor or set of actors in an attempt to deal with a public problem.*[10]

Another definition holds that public policy, "broadly defined," is "the relationship of a governmental unit to its environment."[11] Carl Friedrich regards policy as,

---

[8] *Id.*

[9] James Anderson, David Brady & Charles Bullock III, *Public Policy and Politics in America* 4-5 (1978).

[10] *Id.* at 5.

[11] Robert Eyestone, *The Threads of Public Policy: A Study in Policy Leadership* 18 (1971), in James E. Anderson, *Public Policymaking: An Introduction* 5 (2nd ed. 1994).

> *. . . a proposed course of action of a person, group, or government within a given environment providing obstacles and opportunities which the policy was proposed to utilize and overcome in an effort to reach a goal or realize an objective or a purpose.*[12]

The process of making policy does not necessarily follow a logical sequence. In fact, award-winning author John Kingdon, suggests that policy creation is better characterized as three streams in government: (1) problem recognition, (2) formation and refining of policy proposals and (3) politics. Individually, the streams are not as powerful as they are collectively in creating and redefining policy. Kingdon states,

> *The key to understanding agenda and policy change is in the [streams'] coupling. The separate streams come together at critical times. A problem is recognized, a solution is available, the political climate makes the time right for change, and the constraints do not prohibit action.*[13]

When the seemingly meandering streams periodically intersect with one another—often as a result of trigger events (e.g., like aircraft accidents, public scandals or changes in leadership)—*policy windows* of opportunity open, allowing enterprising *policy entrepreneurs* to capitalize on the streams' convergences. Simply put, opportunity simply meets preparedness. During these convergences, policy entrepreneurs gain rather sudden support and momentum for their ideas, prompting the desired policy creation or change.[14] Clearly, the events of September 11, 2001, triggered the opening of a policy window, promoting a heretofore-unseen focus on security throughout the industry and the redirection of billions in government spending for this new effort.

While Kingdon's ideas are rather novel, generally, the policy literature presents the policy-making process as a more structured cycle

[12] Carl J. Friedrich, *Man and His Government* 79 (1963), in James E. Anderson, Public Policymaking: An Introduction 5 (2nd ed. 1994).
[13] John W. Kingson, *Agendas, Alternatives and Public Policies*, 87-88 (2nd ed. 1995).
[14] *Id.*

or set of steps. When depicting the policy-making process, the following elements in some form are generally included in models:

- *Problem identification*—wherein relief is sought from a situation that produces a human need, deprivation, or dissatisfaction. It is getting the government to perceive the problem as being one that it should handle;
- *Agenda setting*—looks at those problems, among many, which receive the government's serious attention. It is getting the government to begin to act on the problem. The problems that receive serious attention from the policy-makers compose the policy agenda;
- *Policy formulation*—is development of pertinent and acceptable courses of action for dealing with public problems. It is the government's proposed solution to the problem;
- *Policy adoption*—is development of support for a specific proposal such that the policy is legitimized or authorized. It is getting the government to accept a particular solution to the problem. Policy adoption is generally thought of as building majority support for a policy proposal;
- *Policy implementation*—is the law, rule, or order that has been adopted. It is application of the policy by the government's bureaucratic machinery to the problem. Because great authority is often delegated to agencies, which in turn make policy in the implementation process, these agencies can alter policy through implementation; and finally,
- *Policy evaluation, reformation or termination*—which is the attempt by the government to determine whether or not the policy has been effective and make necessary changes. In other words, did the policy work?[15]

Public policies in modern political systems do not just happen. Rather, they are designed to accomplish specified goals or produce definite results—even though these goals are not always met. Policy statements are formal expressions or articulations of public policy. They come in the form of legislative statutes, executive orders and

---

[15] James Anderson, David Brady & Charles Bullock III, *Public Policy and Politics in America* 7-12 (1978); *see also* James E. Anderson, *Public Policymaking: An Introduction* 37-38 (2nd ed. 1994).

decrees, administrative rules and regulations, and court opinions, as well as statements and speeches by public officials indicating the government's intentions and goals.[16] Proposed public policies may be thought of as hypotheses suggesting that specific actions should be taken in addressing problems[17] and to achieve particular results.[18]

Governmental institutions and officials through the political process (i.e., politics) develop public policies. They are distinct from other kinds of policies because they result from the actions of legitimate authorities in a political system. David Easton designates the "authorities" in a political system as the,

> *. . . elders, paramount chiefs, executives, legislators, judges, administrators, councilors, monarchs, and the like, (who) engage in the daily affairs of a political system.*[19]

Moreover, these individuals are,

> *. . . recognized by most members of the system as having responsibility for these matters, and take actions which are accepted as binding most of the time by most of the members so long as they act within the limits of their roles.*[20]

Charles Lindblom and Edward Woodhouse suggest, "presidents and prime ministers, cabinet secretaries and ministers, mayors and governors, legislators and bureaucrats are the most visible parts of the policy-making process." But there are social forces as well, which influence policy-making. Because there are so may people and social forces influencing policy outcomes, Lindblom and Woodhouse find it misleading to refer to those in positions of authority as "leaders" or "decision makers." "Unfortunately," they say, ". . . no entirely ade-

---

[16] James A. Anderson, *Public Policymaking* 7 (2nd ed. 1994).

[17] A "problem" is perceived as a situation that produces "a human need, deprivation, or dissatisfaction, self-identified or identified by others, for which relief is sought." *See* Charles O. Jones, *Introduction to the Study of Public Policy* 17 (1970).

[18] James Anderson, *Public Policymaking: An Introduction* 6 (1994).

[19] David Easton, *A Systems Analysis of Political Life* 212 (1965), in James Anderson, David Brady & Charles Bullock III, *Public Policy and Politics in America* 5 (1978).

[20] *Id.*

quate replacement for these comfortable terms is available in English" to adequately describe those who influence the creation of this abstract process called public policy.

But in general, public policy can be summarized in the following way. It,

- is purposive, goal-oriented behavior rather than random or chance behavior;
- consists of courses of action—rather than separate, discrete decisions or actions—performed by government officials;
- is what governments do—not what they say they will do or what they intend to do;
- may be either negative or positive—positive when the government takes action, negative when the government decides not to act in an area where government action is sought;
- is based on law and is authoritative; and
- it is politics.[21]

Sometimes there is disjunction "between the intensions or purposes of public administrators and the outcomes of public policy."[22] These *unintended consequences* can result from a number of factors, but must be considered when any policy decision is implemented. Reasons that these consequences may occur include:

- *Bargaining and compromise among many actors*, diluting the final policy or program to a point where it can no longer achieve the desired objective or solve the problem;
- *Public sector problems are inherently difficult*, due to the magnitude and complexity (acid rain, aviation noise, poverty) where simple solutions might not exist or haven't been tested;
- *Social science inaccuracies*, whereby the judgment used in selecting a solution or adopting an approach be incorrect and/or actually create unanticipated new problems; and
- *Effect of random events*, nullifying the assumptions and effectiveness of the original approach taken.

---

[21] James Anderson, David Brady and Charles Bullock III, *Public Policy and Politics in America* 4-5 (1978).
[22] Grover Starling, *Managing the Public Sector* (6th ed. 2002).

ADMINISTRATION

In defining "administration" in the classical sense, it refers to all those processes that contribute to the efficient implementation of a predetermined goal or policy. Administration is a mechanical and scientific enterprise. Heavy stress is placed on *how* the job is done, and with selection of the best *ways* to fulfill a predetermined objective; that is to say, to accomplish the task with "efficiency." The traditional way of promoting efficiency is within Max Weber's bureaucratic ideal. Bureaucracies are structured around a "hierarchy," where there is a clear-cut chain-of-command relationship between subordinates in organizations.[23] Secondly, bureaucracies promote the "merit" principle, meaning that selection and/or promotion of workers is based on their competency to perform well on the job.[24]

In sum, traditional public administration is grounded in classical management theory and fundamentally upon the bureaucratic ideal of Max Weber. By "ideal," Weber was not referring necessarily to the "best" way to organize, but rather to the one to which organizations most readily adapt. That is to say, organizations are most apt to conform to the bureaucratic ideal. To Weber, a disciplined bureaucracy was the only means of accomplishing social objectives "rationally." The chaos of politics was to be separated from a rational system of administration. Bureaucracies needed to be formal in structure, disciplined in behavior, and staffed by individuals chosen for their competence as specialists—their sensitivities and personalities to be sacrificed for bureaucratic rationalism. In sum, administrators would be technicians, and administration would be concerned mostly with the careful orchestration of individuals and resources toward the predetermined policy objectives of elected officials.[25]

Unfortunately, Weber's bureaucratic model has been criticized from the outset for its inflexibility and for its definition of "bureaucrats as emotionless, robot-like implementers of policy." Above all, it did not respond to the humanitarian ideals of a democratic society.[26] In this regard, Woodrow Wilson was the first American to develop a

---

[23] Max Weber, *The Theory of Social and Economic Organization* 186, 333-334 (A.M. Henderson & Talcott Parsons trans. 1947).

[24] *Id.*

[25] *Id.*

[26] William L. Morrow, *Public Administration: Politics, Policy, and the Political System* 54-58 (2nd ed. 1980).

theory of public administration that integrated Weberian doctrine with democratic values.

Wilson agreed with Weber on the universality of administrative principles, the role of careerism as a means to promote professionalism and neutrality, the legal basis of administrative authority, the goal of efficiency, and, most of all, the complete separation of politics from administration.[27] "The field of administration," said Wilson, ". . . is a field of business. It is removed from the hurry and strife of politics."[28] However, Wilson had a dilemma in confronting the contradictions inherent in the clash between democracy and efficiency. He had to find a way to make government bureaucracy more responsive to the public. A hoped-for answer to the dilemma came by way of applying Frederick Taylor's principles to the bureaucratic ideal.[29]

Traditional theories of administration were directed primarily at discovering universal principles of administration that could be applied scientifically to direct bureaucracies toward one overriding goal—the implementation of policies by the most efficient means. Reliance was placed on research and scientific principles to determine the best way to maximize efficiency.[30] Within this paradigm, Frederick Taylor originated the school of scientific management, designed to maximize productivity in the private sector. Although grounded in doctrines of private administration, scientific management would have a significant impact on public administration.

An early attempt at applying Taylor's scientific principles to public administration was made by Luther Gulick. In 1937, Gulick and Lydall Urwick wrote their classic treatise, which became the standard work on organization theory and reform in public administration.[31] In concert with Wilson and Taylor, Gulick argued that efficiency is the paramount goal of any administrative activity.[32] To this end he offered five principles of government administration:

- *Division of labor*—whereby tasks should be assigned to those technically qualified to perform them;

---

[27] *Id.*
[28] *Id.*
[29] *Id.*
[30] *Id.*
[31] Luther H. Gulick & Lydall Urwick (eds.), *Papers on the Science of Administration* (1937).
[32] Luther H. Gulick, *Notes on the Theory of Organization*, in Luther H. Gulick & Lydall Urwick (eds.), Papers on the Science of Administration (1937).

- *Coordination*—of overall objectives;
- *Span of control*—limiting the number of employees who could be supervised effectively;
- *Unity of command*—where a worker is responsible to only one supervisor; and
- *Authority commensurate with responsibility*—wherein a manager is given sufficient power to perform the tasks and responsibilities expected.

According to Gulick, management guidelines were circumscribed by *Planning*, *Organizing*, *Staffing*, *Directing*, *Coordinating*, *Reporting*, and *Budgeting* [POSDCORB].[33] Collectively, the POSDCORB guidelines and organizational formulas, as well as other principles proffered by Gulick, came to be known as the "proverbs" of public administration.[34] Nevertheless, Gulick and the entire school of scientific management eventually came under attack either for lack of scientific validation of their principles or for lack of humanitarian concern. And, although the application of Frederick Taylor's principles appeared at the time to be the answer to problems inherent in Max Weber's ideal of bureaucracy, one of the most well-publicized problems in government remains that of bureaucracy itself.

Within Woodrow Wilson's concept of public administration, a bureaucracy is to be service-oriented and responsive to public opinion. The bureaucracy is supposed to be both relevant to public needs in making policy and humanitarian in attitude toward its clients. Unfortunately, it doesn't always work out that way. Bureaucrats depend upon their agency (or bureau) for their income, security and welfare. As a result, they identify closely with their agency and its policies and practices. Their close identity with the agency nourishes what William Morrow refers to as the "institutional imperative." The institutional imperative is another expression for self-preservation, wherein institutions are, by nature, driven to endorse anything that will preserve and amplify their status, size, and importance and reject any policy or reform that will detract from those three conditions.[35]

---

[33] *See* Luther Gulick, *Notes on a Theory of Organization*, in Luther Gulick & Lyndall Urwick (eds.), Papers on the Science of Administration (1937).

[34] William L. Morrow, *Public Administration: Politics, Policy, and the Political System* 60 (2nd ed. 1980).

[35] *Id.* at 11-19.

Bureaucrats are expected to apply the rules of their agency *strictly*. They follow the rules because they take few risks in doing so. In applying the rules strictly they treat their clients—those who come to them for service—as subordinates to whom the rules and regulations must be applied. The result is often waste, duplication of service, and inefficiency. More importantly, there is a resultant detachment of bureaucrats from the needs of the very clients they are expected to serve. Bureaucrats often use the rules to justify policies that are important mostly to them and their agencies, irrespective of client needs. Hence, inherent to the bureaucratic paradigm is an "institutional imperative" for agencies to use their authority (policy-making power) in ways that help the agency grow, and to secure for its workers their self-serving interests.[36] The process is known as "bureaucratic self-perpetuation."

In the end, application of scientific management principles to the field of public administration has failed to overcome inherent weaknesses in bureaucracy. Nevertheless, theorists and political leaders have demonstrated a willingness to continue improving upon the principle. "Neo-Taylorism," as Christopher Pollitt described it, dominated government reform efforts in the United States and the United Kingdom during the 1980s. Neo-Taylorist initiatives, such as those proposed by President Ronald Reagan's Grace Commission, were concerned with efficiency and administrative control.[37] Then there was *Neo-Managerialism*, with its focus upon economic productivity, ever more sophisticated technologies, labor force discipline, and professional managers with authority and "right to manage."[38]

Scientific management in its original form was the product of engineers looking at production as if human beings could be regarded as machines, to be designed for the task, tested to improve productivity, and timed to precise measurements. Included within the classical management framework were Fayol's concerns about organizational structure.[39] In general, scientific management took a manager-centered or top-down view of how to get the right production system within an organization.[40]

---

[36] *See* William L. Morrow, *Public Administration: Politics, Policy, and the Political System* 13-17 (2nd ed. 1980).

[37] Christopher Pollitt, *Managerialism and the Public Sector: The Anglo-American Experience* (1990).

[38] Larry D. Terry, *Administrative Leadership, Neo-Managerialism, and the Public Management Movement*, Public Administration Review, Vol. 58, No. 3 (May/Jun. 1998), at 196.

[39] Henri Fayol, *General and Industrial Management* (Constance Storrs ed. 1916/1965).

[40] Susan Wright, *Anthropology of Organization* (1994).

The follow-on to scientific management was the *behavioral school*. Between 1927 and 1932, in a study of workers in the Hawthorne Plant in western Chicago and in Cicero, Illinois, industrial psychologists tested some of the principles of scientific management.[41] The so-called "Hawthorne Study" tested the impact of changing physical plant conditions (namely lighting) on worker output. The conclusion of the experiment came as some surprise, in that regardless of the change in lighting (brighter or dimmer) worker output increased. The "Hawthorne Effect," as it has come to be known, revealed that psychological factors were more important than physical conditions in achieving increased worker production.

Scientific management concentrated on the mechanics of the employee in the work environment. Through engineering and scientific selection of effective workers, Taylor and others sought efficiency believing that employees, acting as rational, economic creatures, would react favorably to incentives designed to increase their wages and overall economic security.[42] Led by Professor Elton Mayo, the Hawthorne researchers concluded that workers were influenced by informal social structures as well that encouraged them to pursue goals other than strictly economic ones. Although not replacing scientific management, the Hawthorne studies paved the way for the emergence and acceptance of the behavioral school of management.

But not only have Wilsonian notions of scientific management in public administration changed, the idea that politics and public administration can be separated has been displaced as well. As Brian Cook points out, "Public administration is as much a political institution as any legislature, court, or office of an elected executive. Administration is clearly a means to reach collective ends, but it exerts its own formative influence as well."[43]

Robert Behn argues that it is time to accept policy making as a responsibility of public administrators. According to Behn, policy making, through effective leadership, is not only a right of public managers, it is an obligation. He points out that,

> *Frederick Winslow Taylor is dead; nobody really believes that human organizations are*

---

[41] *See id.*

[42] Frederick W. Taylor, *The Principles of Scientific Management* (1947).

[43] Brian J. Cook, *Politics, Political Leadership, and Public Management*, Public Administration Review, Vol. 58, No. 3 (May/Jun. 1998), at 225.

> *like machines. Nobody really thinks that once the boxes are drawn on the organization chart and the job descriptions written, the agency will run smoothly. Nobody thinks that you could just give orders; they don't even do that in the military anymore. Everyone accepts that to get an organization to accomplish any purpose, you have to motivate people.*[44]

PARADIGM SHIFT

In practice, public administration is as old as society itself and the existence of governments needing administrators to conduct their affairs. But as a theory, public administration goes back only about a century. As an academic subject, it is now taught in most countries of the world, although in many instances only since the end of World War II.[45] It was also following WWII that students of public administration observed that, despite the views of traditionalists, the study and practice of public administration could not be separated from the study and practice of politics.[46] A basic aspect of public administration is its unavoidable involvement in politics and policy making. This stands in stark contrast to the traditional view of public administration as an enterprise devoted exclusively to implementation of politics decreed by popularly elected officials.[47]

In a democratic society, government institutions reflect the alignment of political forces that determine how policies are made within the system. And one of the major characteristics in American politics is *pluralism*. According to William Morrow, pluralism ". . . refers to the existence of a mutual balance of power among religious, ethnic, economic, and geographic groups, with overlapping membership, all of which participate in policy making through mutual adjustment of conflicting goals within political arenas."[48] As a responsive institution, public administration is pluralist in character. The fact that ad-

---

[44] Robert D. Behn, *What Right Do Public Managers Have to Lead?* Public Administration Review Vol. 58, No. 3 (May/Jun. 1998).

[45] Marshall Edward Dimock & Gladys Dimock, *Public Administation* 4 (4th ed. 1969).

[46] William L. Morrow, *Public Administration: Politics, Policy, and the Political System* 1-2 (2nd ed. 1980).

[47] *Id.*

[48] William L. Morrow, *Public Administration: Politics, Policy, and the Political System* 69 (2nd ed. 1980).

ministrative agencies reflect pluralism means that agencies are themselves representative institutions. Public administration is thereby as much a political institution as any legislature, court, or office of an elected executive.[49]

Robert Behn argues that leadership responsibility extends beyond being just internal leaders for their agencies. Leadership responsibility in the broader political scheme, and with it policy making, has been relegated to public administrators as a result of several failures in society.[50]

- First of all, there is *analytical failure*. It is intellectually impossible to design an ideal system that could contemplate all situations with a comprehensive set of rational rules with which to respond.
- There is *executive failure*, because chief executives rarely give clear instructions to their agency managers. Legislatures, too, can give directions that are ambiguous, contradictory, and often unrealistic.
- There is *political failure* as a result of "interest group" activity (or what James Madison called "factions"). If not for the public administrator, who then would check and balance these minority factions? The elected official does not have the interest, resources or the time. Neither does the legislature collectively, nor the judiciary.
- There is a *civic failure*, because the stakes for individual citizens are so small compared with the time and resources necessary to make a difference that they conclude—from a simple, implicit benefit-cost analysis—that it makes little sense to try to even figure out how to affect something in which they have anything less than a major interest.
- Finally, there is a *judicial failure*, because judges and Supreme Court justices are not infallible. As Justice Oliver Wendall Holmes, Jr., noted, ". . . great cases like hard cases make bad law."[51] What this points out is that there is nothing to guarantee

[49] Brian J. Cook, *Politics, Political Leadership, and Public Management*, Public Administration Review Vol. 58, No. 3 (May/Jun. 1998), at 225.
[50] *See* Robert D. Behn, *What Right Do Public Managers Have to Lead?*, Public Administration Review, Vol. 58, No. 3 (May/Jun. 1998), at 211-219.
[51] Oliver Wendall Holmes, Jr., *Northern Securities Co. v. United States* 192 U.S. 197 (1904).

> that the result of a single lawsuit—or even a series of lawsuits—will improve the functioning of a public agency, let alone improve the public welfare. That must be left to the agency itself.

In the final analysis, who else might exercise leadership in the public sector if not public administrators? "Still," Behn asks, "what gives public managers the right to lead?"

> *They aren't elected by anybody. Since the beginning of the republic, the legislature has been the branch of government designed to reflect the will of the people. It is the legislature, not public managers, who should set purposes, policies, and priorities. After all, the citizens elect their legislators, not their public managers. And if the citizens are unhappy with their government's purposes, policies, and priorities, they have an easy remedy: replace their legislators during the next election with people who will establish more representative purposes, policies, and priorities.*[52]

But Behn is playing the Devil's advocate. He is aware that public managers must lead and that the rhetorical premise presented above does not comport with the actual practice of American government at all levels.

Although public administration is the accomplishment of politically determined objectives, it is also concerned with policy; for bureaucracy, even with its failings, is the chief policy maker in contemporary governments.[53] Moreover, elected officials are not the only individuals authorized under the U.S. Constitution to exercise initiative. Business leaders, special interest group leaders, religious leaders, community leaders, educational leaders, intellectual leaders—even movie stars and professional athletes—all have rights to exercise initiative. Why then, asks Behn, ". . . should such an opportunity be de-

---

[52] Robert D. Behn, *What Right Do Public Managers Have to Lead?*, Public Administration Review, Vol. 58, No. 3 (May/Jun. 1998), at 215.

[53] Marshall Edward Dimock & Gladys Dimock, *Public Administation* 3 (4th ed. 1969).

nied to public managers?" Certainly, they have as much, if not more, knowledge and wisdom as other leaders when it comes to solving social issues within the purview of their departments. As a result, leadership is not just a right of public managers it is an obligation. And *leadership* is at the heart of the new public administration movement.

However, leadership within the new public administration refers to more than just the right to make public policy. It implies an ability to conduct business in a quasi-private enterprise environment, with accountability previously unknown to public administrators. Liberation management and market-driven management have emerged synergistically as dominant approaches in the field of public administration. Followers of liberation management are guided by the idea that public managers are highly skilled and committed individuals who already know how to manage. Consequently, the supposedly poor performance of public bureaucracies is not the result of managerial incompetence, malfeasance or self-serving interest, but rather, it is the result of a faulty system, which is overburdened by cumbersome, unnecessary rules and a lack of accountability.[54] As former Vice President Al Gore explained, "liberation management assumes that public managers are good people trapped in bad systems."[55]

Conversely, market-driven management is driven by two alternative concepts. One is competition, guided by the neo-classical economics belief in the economic efficiency of the marketplace. Proponents of the market-driven approach believe that public managers will increase performance levels if exposed to market forces. The second idea is tied to the general character of private sector management. Underpinning this idea is a belief that private sector management is inherently superior to that of the public sector. Entrepreneurial public management is an advanced concept that takes market-driven management well into the information age. Newt Gingrich explains, "The term 21st Century Entrepreneurial Public Management was chosen to deliberately distinguish it from Bureaucratic Public Administration, [distinguishing] between the new information age system of entrepreneurial management and the inherited agricultural age system of bu-

[54] *See* Larry D. Terry, *Administrative Leadership, Neo-Managerialism, and the Public Management Movement*, Public Administration Review, Vol. 58, No. 3 (May/Jun. 1998), at 195.
[55] Albert Gore, *From Red Tape to Results: Creating a Government that Works Better and Costs Less*, National Performance Review (1993).

reaucratic administration."[56] Gingrich suggests that this modernized form of government would yield quality services and government, along with lowering costs, but strongly cautions against the complete adoption of a private sector model:

> *The one constant is the term public. It is important to recognize that there are legitimate requirements of public activity and public responsibility which will be just as true in this new model as they were in the older model. Simply throwing the doors open to market oriented, entrepreneurial incentives with information age systems will not get the job done. The system we are developing has to meet the higher standards of accountability, prudence, and honesty which are inherent in a public activity.*[57]

The entrepreneurial public management model, as defined by a set of 23 principles, centers on a few key ideas including actively embrace information technology and looking to industry for guiding concepts like benchmarking, outsourcing and visioning. Also suggested is the revising of public manager's approaches to planning and project management, and incorporating privatization, where appropriate. With changes in recruitment, training, and education, Gingrich envisions the creation of a new generation entrepreneurial public managers who can best support a citizen-centered government that is well-linked to public resources by advanced technology.[58] He explains:

> *A customer centered, citizen centered model of governance would start with the concept that as a general rule being online is better than being in line. It would both put traditional bureaucratic functions on the internet as is*

[56] Newt Gingrich, *21st Century Entrepreneurial Public Management: Getting Government to Move at the Speed and Effectiveness of the Information Age*, http://www.newt.org/backpage.asp?art=1715.
[57] *Id.*
[58] *Id.*

> *happening in many states (paying taxes, ordering license tags, etc.) but it would also begin to rethink major functions of government in terms of the new internet based system. The information age makes possible a lot more citizen self help as defined by the citizen's needs.*[59]

Entrepreneurial public management, liberation management and market-driven management help to define the new public administration movement.[60]

Larry D. Terry argues that the new public administration is driven by more sophisticated forms of management that collectively he calls "Neo-Managerialism."[61] He says that Neo-Managerialism consists of an older tradition embodied in the work of Frederick Taylor, as well as a complex mixture of public choice theory, agency theory, and transaction-cost economics. That is to say, management in the public sector has come full circle from the scientific management of Frederick Taylor, to the organization behavior models of Henri Fayol and a whole host of writers, to more sophisticated scientific models included under the rubric of Neo-Managerialism and the new public administration.

By stating that public management theories have come full circle, the current trend toward Neo-Managerialism can be explained by looking at the past. But rather than describing a "circle," what surfaces is a synergistic, reiterative model which conceptually departs from one concept to another and then, in a reiterative process, is threaded back through the original concept to become yet another higher, more abstract form.

EVOLVING SYSTEMS

The evolution of public management follows a classical form of social development.[62] Rather than a linear model where information is added to "A", and "B" follows "A", "C" follows "B", and so forth, the model is a "synergistic loop" where "B" is pulled back through,

---

[59] *Id.*
[60] Larry D. Terry, *Administrative Leadership, Neo-Managerialism, and the Public Management Movement*, Public Administration Review, Vol. 58, No. 3 (May/Jun. 1998), at 195.
[61] *Id.* at 194.
[62] *See generally* Laurence E. Gesell, *Airline Re-Regulation* (1990).

and combined with "A" to form a "C", which is not exactly the same but still resembles "A".

This model of human development may be referred to as a "synergistic loop," and comparatively expressed as follows:

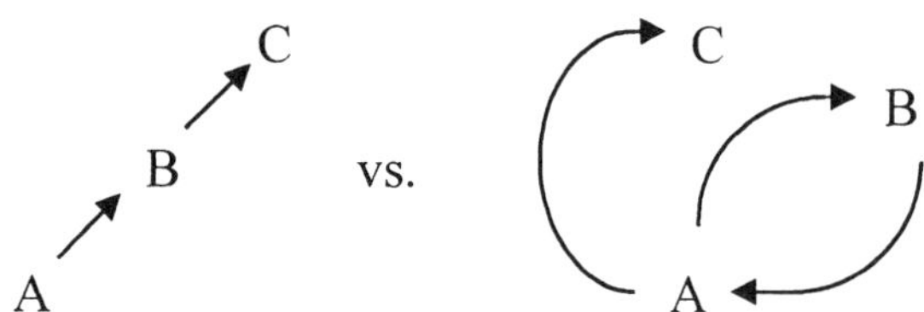

As a result, time can be thought of as curvilinear, not linear. Hence, the "pendulum" of historical development not only swings back and forth, but the whole mechanism is elevated simultaneously so that the pendulum bob never quite returns to the same place. Similarly, history doesn't "repeat itself," it only mirrors reflections of the past.

As synergistic loops are added through time—one on top of the other—they come together to form a spiral or helix. Hence, the evolution of management theory might be modeled as shown in Figure 2.1, "The Evolution of Public Management Theory."

Looking at the model of management theory development, it appears as a series of "synergistic loops," wherein the "pendulum" swings back and forth between forms of scientific and behavioral science paradigms. However, it should be realized that there is no universally accepted management theory. Rather, both ends of the spectrum coexist, often with each side borrowing heavily from the other, but from time-to-time emphasizing changes, giving favor and dominance to one over the other until the pendulum again swings. As a result, time can be thought of as curvilinear, not linear. Hence, the "pendulum" of historical development not only swings back and forth, but the whole mechanism is elevated simultaneously so that the pendulum bob never quite returns to the same place. Similarly, history doesn't "repeat itself," it only mirrors reflections of the past.

The model of modern management theory begins with the *scientific management* approach, formulated by Frederick Taylor and others between 1890 and 1930, who sought to determine the best methods for performing any task scientifically, and for selecting, training, and motivating workers. Scientific management arose in part from the

Figure 2.1—THE EVOLUTION OF PUBLIC MANAGEMENT THEORY

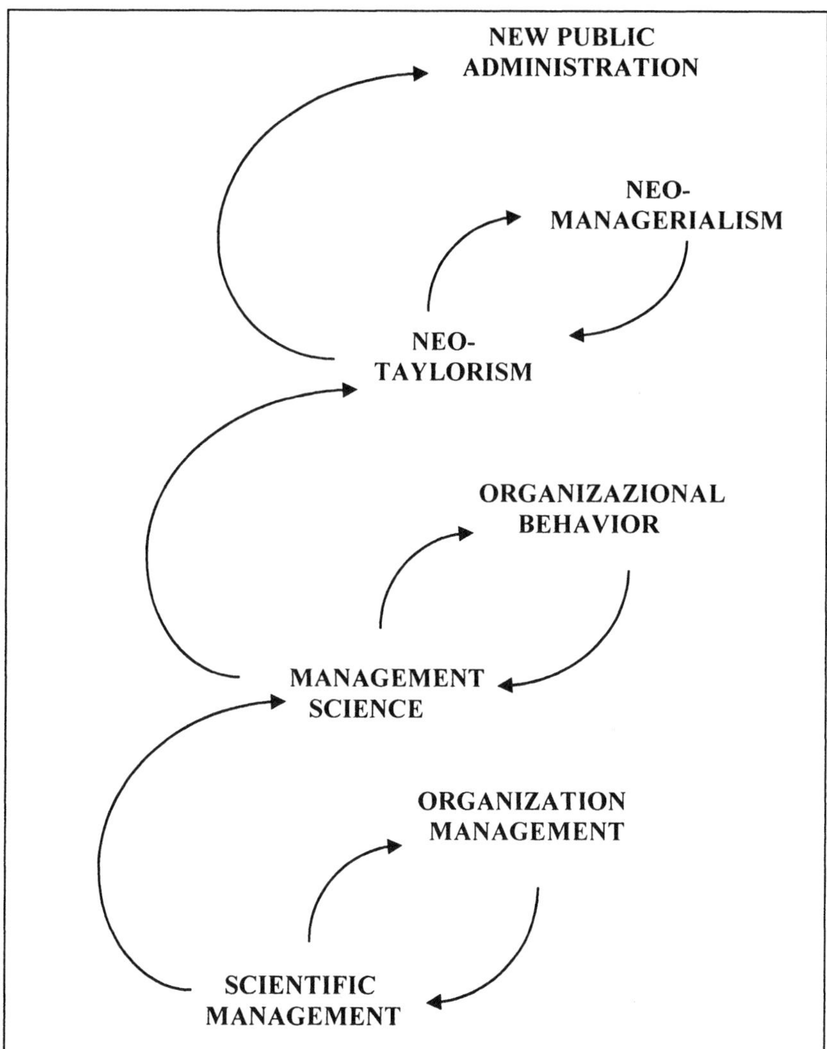

need to increase productivity. *Organization management* theory almost simultaneously grew out of the need to find guidelines for managing complex, high production organizations such as factories. It was an early attempt, pioneered by Henri Fayol, to identify principles and skills that underlie effective management.

The *management science* approach, sometimes called "operations research," evolves out of the classical school, but using more sophisticated mathematical techniques for modeling, analysis, and solution of management problems. Typical of the types of activities performed by management science teams of specialists include such activities as capital budgeting and cash flow management, production scheduling, development of product strategies, planning for human resource development programs, maintenance of optimal inventory levels, and production scheduling. Management science has not yet reached the stage where it can effectively deal with organizational behavior and human relations. Thus, seeking greater efficiency, the pendulum swings at times back to the behavioral perspective.[63]

The behavioral school emerged, in part, because managers found that the classical approach did not achieve sufficient production efficiency, nor was it conducive to harmony in the workplace. The turning point for organizational behavior was the Hawthorne experiments conducted at the Western Electric Company from 1924 to 1933. There, a group of management scholars trained in sociology, psychology, and related fields, used their diverse knowledge to understand and improve the way organizations are managed. Later researchers were more rigorously trained in the social sciences—including psychology, sociology, and anthropology—and used more sophisticated research methods. Thus, these later researchers became known as "behavioral scientists."[64]

The latest swings of the pendulum have been towards *Neo-Taylorism* in the 1980s, with its concerns with efficiency and administrative control, and *Neo-Managerialism* in the 1990's, with its focus upon economic marketplace efficiency, more sophisticated technologies, a disciplined labor force, and authoritative management. The increasing emphasis on entrepreneurship and privatization in the public sector portend an evolving new public administration.

MANAGEMENT THEORY

Privatization of public facilities, development and expansion of infrastructure through private investment, and the rise of entrepreneur-

---

[63] *See* James A.F. Stoner & R. Edward Freeman, *Management*, Ch. 2 (4th ed. 1989).
[64] *Id.*

ship in the public sector, all suggest a "shift in paradigm"[65] from traditional forms of public administration to the onset of a *New Public Administration* [NPA]. If indeed there is a "new" public administration on the horizon, in order to recognize what it is one must first understand what it is being compared against. This chapter presents an overview of the classical traditions in management theory. The semantics of "management" versus "administration" are compared to note that each of these terms connotes a different meaning. Tested is the role "leadership" plays in either management or administration in the public sector. Finally, a discussion centers on new concepts in public administration and how they might apply to public airports and the qualifications of public servants to manage them within a changing paradigm.

To begin, traditional notions of public administration are rooted in classical management theory, of which there are two schools—*scientific management* and *organizational theory*—each with its own founding pioneer. Through his experimentation and consulting experience, Frederick W. Taylor (1856-1915) laid the foundation for scientific management. Henri Fayol (1841-1925)—a contemporary of Frederick Taylor—is generally acknowledged as the founder of classical organization management, or what in contemporary terms is often referred to as "organizational behavior." While Taylor was basically concerned with organizational functions and ways to increase the efficiency of *individual* workers, Fayol was interested in the *total* organization and in identifying the principles and skills that underlie effective management.[66]

Fayol actually used the word "administration" for what has since come to be known as "management." But in the contemporary sense, is administration synonymous with management? Is there a differentiation to be made between management and leadership? Is leadership, for example, a trait to be found only in the new form of public administration, and is classical management theory just a relic of the past? Moreover, in light of privatization in the public sector, and the advent of new public administration, is entrepreneurship at odds with traditional concepts of public administration? If airport management must adapt to the NPA, are managers from the old school obsolete, or

[65] *See* Thomas Kuhn, *The Structure of Scientific Revolutions* (2nd ed. 1970).
[66] James A.F. Stoner & R. Edward Freeman, *Management* 35-42 (4th ed. 1989).

can they be "taught new tricks"? Or, conversely, is the new public management just "new wine in old bottles."[67]

A key to understanding NPA is to question whether leadership is a proper role for the *public* administrator. That is to say, should the directives issued by public administrators be limited to the policy dictates of the electorate only, or to "lead" the way? Should administrators step beyond the traditional boundaries of management in the public sector? Whether part of the old public administration or the new, John Kotter argues there is a difference between management and leadership, at least in *business*, if not in the public sector.[68] Yet both management and leadership involve three key activities:

- Deciding what needs to be done;
- Creating networks of people and relationships that can accomplish an agenda; and then
- Trying to ensure that those people actually do the job.

But Kotter maintains that managers and leaders accomplish "these three tasks in different ways." Leaders, he writes, perform these tasks by "setting direction," "aligning people," and by "motivating and inspiring." Managers, on the other hand, carry out these tasks by "planning and budgeting," "organizing and staffing," and "controlling."[69] Seemingly, Kotter is suggesting that business leaders (i.e., entrepreneurs) are *visionary strategists*, while managers are *tactically responsible* for producing the detailed plans that carry out the visions of "true" leaders.[70] Or, simply put, leaders are *strategic* while managers are *tactical*. Although presented with a slight twist, Kotter's description of what managers do is in the spirit of Henri Fayol and the classical organization theorists.[71] Again, the classical school subscribes generally to Gulick's principles of planning, organizing, commanding, coordinating, and controlling.

---

[67] *See* Linda Kaboolian, *The New Public Management: Challenging the Boundaries of the Management vs. Administration Debate*, Public Administration Review, Vol. 58, No. 3 (May/Jun. 1998), at 189.

[68] John P. Kotter, *What Leaders Really Do*, Harvard Business Review, Vol. 68 (1990), at 103-116.

[69] *Id.* at 4.

[70] *See* Robert D. Behn, *What Right Do Public Managers Have to Lead?,* Public Administration Review, Vol. 58, No. 3 (May/Jun.1998), at 212.

[71] Henri Fayol, *Industrial and General Administration*, (J.A. Courbrough trans. 1930).

Since Henri Fayol first presented his principles of management, hundreds of authors have presented takeoffs, in many cases combining certain functions (e.g., organizing and staffing can be combined into just organizing), while at the same time using different terms as if they were synonymous. For instance, "leadership" may be used in place of "commanding" and/or "directing." Hence, many texts differ in the terms used and as to the number of specific management functions involved in the management process. Most authors in the classical management school have conformed to the spirit of Fayol's frame of reference, although the terms they have used might have had slightly different connotations. Luther Gulick, for example, used his now famous acronym, POSDCORB, to frame the basic principles of management: i.e., planning, organizing, staffing, directing, coordinating, reporting, and budgeting.[72] In addition, a critical public managerial function, *linking* is discussed later in this section.

Gulick's framework, though considered somewhat dated by some scholars, provides a listing of the functions of management according to the classical school of management[73] Gulick's list or primary management functions are discussed below.

PLANNING

Planning is the key function in the management process. Planning is about devising a course of action that will enable the organization to accomplish its goals. Planning is the "who, what, where, and when" determinant of management. The purpose of planning is to determine *what* is to be done, *where* it is to be done, *who* is responsible for seeing that it is done, *when* it is to be done, and sometimes even *how* it is to be done. Planning includes all managerial activities that determine results and the appropriate means to achieve these re-

[72] *See* Luther Gulick, *Notes on a Theory of Organization*, in Luther Gulick & Lyndall Urwick (eds.), Papers on the Science of Administration (1937).

[73] The framework for discussion of the management process, as used in this section, is taken generally from the following texts: James A.F. Stoner & R. Edward Freeman, *Management* (4th ed. 1989); James H. Donnelly, Jr., James L. Gibson, & John M. Ivancevich, *Fundamentals of Management: Functions, Behavior, Models* (4th ed. 1981); Rolf E. Rogers & Robert H. McIntire, *Organization and Management Theory* (1983); and the U.S. Army Command and General Staff College, *Management Text Subcourse Manual* (Jun. 1980).

sults. It includes four interrelated phases: goal setting, forecasting, budgeting, and policy implementation.[74]

If not visionary, planning is nevertheless a creative process. Plans give the organization its objectives, and the first step in planning is the selection of goals for the organization. It is the means used to guide the organization from the present into the future in order to accomplish its goals and objectives. Planning is the key, or initiating function of management because it sets the stage for the other functions. The plan forms the basis for directives, and the directives, in turn, set the standards for the control process. And, it is against the original plan that end results are reported and compared.

ORGANIZING

Objectives are accomplished by organizations of people and resources and by the leaders who manage them. Organizing is about mobilization of material and human resources. Organizing may be defined as the process of establishing relationships between functions, resources and personnel grouped together for a common purpose. That is to say, organizations are established to accomplish specific purposes. The process of organizing typically involves three elements: determining the tasks to be completed, establishing an organizational structure, and allocating personnel and resources.

"Determining the tasks," means the dividing of the overall mission of the plan into specific tasks. At the core of the organizing function is the concept of *division of labor*. Probably more has been written on division of labor and thc organizing function than on any of the other functions of management, save perhaps planning. Hence, more is presented on this subject below.

In the second element, "establishing an organizational structure," the formal structure or hierarchy of the organization is established, the list of tasks analyzed, and the specific duties and responsibilities of individual positions are determined. At the same time, these positions are grouped into departments and sections according to types of duties involved. The end result of establishing an organizational structure is the formation of a formal *organizational chart*, which may in-

---

[74] James H. Donnelly, Jr., James L. Gibson, & John M. Ivancevich, *Fundamentals of Management: Functions, Behavior, Models*, Ch. 4 (4th ed. 1981).

clude written job descriptions containing the duties and responsibilities of each position in the organization.

After the framework for the organizational chart has been worked out, personnel are then assigned to the various tasks, they are provided with the necessary equipment, supplies, places to work, and time frames within which to accomplish assigned tasks. This is the process of staffing and allocation of resources.

STAFFING

Organizations emerge when the division of labor becomes too complex for one person to accomplish. Division of labor refers to *job specialization* at the individual level and *departmentation* and the creation of sub-units at the group or organizational level. "Division of labor" is an encompassing term for sub-dividing labor into precise skills. It is the most important single principle in classical organization design. The second principle is *bureaucracy*. Job specialization, or the specialization of labor, is the division of labor defining depth and scope of each job. A "job" is defined as the "scope of work assigned to one person."[75] The job belongs to an individual. Departmentalization, on the other hand, groups two or more people and functions. The staffing function consists of personnel management and the proper placement of individuals within the formal organizational structure both by job and by department.

Organization is a management system consisting of *vertical* and *horizontal specialization* and a hierarchy of management levels. According to Stoner and Freeman, "the systems approach to management attempts to view the organization as a unified, purposeful system composed of interrelated parts."[76]

Horizontal specialization of management is the process by which the natural sequence of a task is broken down into specialized subgroups, with each sub-group having its own manager. It is a sequence of interrelated tasks. Conversely, vertical specialization refers to a scalar chain of command and accountability that, when charted, results in a pyramidal form. The scalar chain is a hierarchy of manag-

---

[75] James H. Donnelly, Jr., James L. Gibson, & John M. Ivancevich, *Fundamentals of Management: Functions, Behavior, Models* Ch. 4 (4th ed. 1981).

[76] James A.F. Stoner & R. Edward Freeman, *Management* 56 (4th ed. 1989).

ers, often referred to as top, middle, and first-line management, below whom are situated the rank-and-file workers.

Top management is defined as having no managing supervisor above them. Top management answers to a board of directors or other policy-making agency, but has no manager, *per se*, to whom the top manager is responsible. Middle managers are defined as having managers located both above and below them. Middle managers develop operational plans and procedures, and they coordinate the work of other managers. They are closely associated with horizontal specialization, in that they coordinate the efforts of sub-unit managers. First-line or operational managers have no managers below them, only workers over whom they have direct responsibility. They coordinate operations and supervise production.

The scalar chain is otherwise known as "bureaucracy." Second to the principle of division of labor, bureaucracy is the essence of the classical school of management. Max Weber described bureaucracy as the "ideal" form of organization.[77] It has many of the characteristics of the classical organization design. That is to say, it is highly structured, with centralized control, narrow spans of control, and a rational set of rules.[78] Weber's ideal bureaucracy is characterized by:

- *Limited areas of responsibility* attached to each position within the organization, which reduces the need for subjective judgment;
- *Hierarchical authority* and a formal chain of command, with centralized control and responsibility concentrated at the top of the hierarchy;
- *Central system of file collections* summarizing the activities of the organization;
- Narrowly defined division of labor through *high job specialization and departmentation*;
- Full-time, *career employees* who are loyal to the system and rewarded with seniority;
- A *rationalized system* of rules, regulations and policy guidance;

---

[77] Max Weber, *The Theory of Social and Economic Organizations*, (Talcott Parsons, (ed.)., A.M. Henderson & Talcott Parsons, (trans.) 1947); *see also* Rolf E. Rogers & Robert H. McIntire, *Organization and Management Theory*, Ch. 1 (1983).

[78] Span of control refers to the number of people, activities or functions any one manager can reasonably and efficiently handle simultaneously.

- An *impersonal system* where employees are required to follow a set of prescribed rules;
- Promotions based on *seniority*;
- *Merit recruitment* based on skills, ability and technical knowledge; and
- A clear *separation between the private and public lives* of employees.

While today the term "bureaucracy" is oft associated with negative or even sinister implications, employing many of the basic bureaucratic components of Weber model have historically helped a vast number of organizations, particularly larger and more complex entities, to survive and thrive.

DIRECTING

To Fayol, commanding was about getting workers to do their work. What Fayol described as "commanding" is a like function to what Gulick chose to call "directing." The act might also be called "leadership." It is the function of motivating and actuating others to achieve the desired corporate goals. It is about getting the members of the organization to perform. Once plans have been drawn up, the organization has been designed, personnel assigned and equipment procured, the proper coordination effected, directives (or orders) are issued in order to implement plans and activate the organization. The process of converting plans into action is directing. A directive may be in oral or written form. Directives are the communication in which a policy is established or a specific action is ordered.

Whereas the actual issuing of directives in accordance with bureaucratic rules may be viewed as a *concrete* process, leadership takes on a more *abstract* connotation. Almost anyone can issue a directive, but not everyone can effectively motivate others to do their bidding. The latter is *leadership*.

Whereas John Kotter argues that in business, as opposed to say public administration, there is a difference between management and leadership,[79] Henry Mintzberg suggests that leadership is but one of

---

[79] John P. Kotter, *Social Choice and Individual Values* (2nd ed. 1990); *see also* Robert D. Behn, *What Right Do Public Managers Have to Lead?*, Public Administration Review (May/Jun. 1998), Vol. 58, No. 3, at 212.

the basic roles of management in virtually all managerial activities involving subordinates.[80] According to Kotter, the tasks of motivating and inspiring are key to leadership. Yet, as Robert Behn suggests, "the task of the manager is to make the human machine run smoothly and on time . . . If human organizations are machines, they don't need motivation, and they don't need inspiration, and they don't need leadership." But if getting such people within organizations to actually do their jobs requires motivation and inspiration, it requires leadership. Perhaps this suggests that Mintzberg is correct and that Kotter's differentiation between leadership and management holds little merit. Leadership is applicable to "virtually all managerial activities,"[81] public administration not excluded.

COORDINATING

Managers, or leaders if you will, also accomplish the goals and objectives of the organization by *coordinating* the efforts of individuals and facilities. Through coordination an orderly unification of group effort in pursuit of a common purpose is achieved. According to Webster, "coordination" is the process of bringing things into harmony, to bring order or relation. As a function of management, coordination is an integration of all details necessary for the accomplishment of goals and objectives. It is an integral part of planning.

There are basically two types of coordination. There is *coordination of thought*, requiring a common understanding of all parties involved. Coordination of thought is between two or more people, and it must precede *coordination of action*. The latter form of coordination involves the relationship of physical things, either with respect to time or between the items. Coordination of action involves timing and the correct order of performance for the various phases of project development.

REPORTING

Reporting is a function of accountability. It is also part of the control process. Reporting is used to measure the effectiveness of goal achievement in several ways, including profitability, marketing, pro-

---

[80] Henry Mintzberg, *The Nature of Managerial Work* (1973).
[81] *See id.*

ductivity, and by other physical and financial measures. Profitability measures might include ratios of profits to sales, to total assets, and to capital (net worth). Marketing measures relate products, markets, distribution and customer service objectives. Productivity measures are basically ratios of output to input.[82]

Physical and financial measures reflect the organization's capacity to acquire resources sufficient for its larger objectives. Some of these measures might include rate of return, liquidity, solvency, accounts receivable, working capital, and/or inventory.[83] Measuring an airport's output might include total revenue, air traffic movements, commercial air transport movements, passengers and freight handled, or "work-load units." As Rigas Doganis suggests, work-load units arose from a need by the airlines to obtain a standard measure of output combining both passengers and freight. Since the early days, the airline industry has converted passengers into a weight equivalent, namely passenger tons and/or passenger tons per mile or kilometer.[84]

Peter Drucker suggested that organizational performance could be measured by the process now famous known as Management by Objectives [MBO]. By "organizational performance," what is meant is the extent to which the goals of others are achieved. In the management of objectives process each manager (subject to higher management approval) sets goals for his or her unit.[85] Superior and subordinate managers jointly identify goals and define areas of responsibility. At designated intervals they measure results by evaluating performance achieved against the previously established goals.

BUDGETING

Budgeting is an integral part of planning. It is a plan of estimated expenditures during a given period of time.[86] There is also a close

---

[82] James H. Donnelly, Jr., James L. Gibson, & John M. Ivancevich, *Fundamentals of Management: Functions, Behavior, Models* (4th ed. 1981).

[83] *Id.*

[84] One passenger (80 kilograms) and associated baggage (20 kilograms) were assumed to be equivalent to 100 kilograms so that ten passengers made up one ton. The rationale was that an aircraft could only lift a certain payload and that a passenger and their baggage could be directly substituted by their weight in freight. Passenger and baggage weights are now assumed to be lower, wherein most airlines use a figure of 90 kilograms. Now, 11.111 passengers are equivalent to one ton. Rigas Doganis, *The Airport Business* 20 (1992).

[85] Peter Drucker, *The Practice of Management* (1954).

[86] *Id.*

relationship between the process of planning and budgeting as a control technique. There are three basic types of budgets:

- Line item;
- Program; and
- Performance.

There are also three basic approaches to budgeting:

- Fixed;
- Variable; and
- Moving.

The basic budgeting types and approaches to budgeting are discussed more thoroughly later in the book. Inasmuch as budgeting is a fiscal process, its discussion is reserved for a later chapter as well.

LINKING

For public administrators, the list above is a good start, but one function that should be separately addressed is *linking*. The linking function is also referred to as "indirect administration," "third-party government" or "government by proxy"[87] and goes beyond the more simplistic "coordinating" function as undertaken in business, where internal and external coordination heavily rely upon the established organizational structure or a written contract. This reveals a basic difference between a model that is based on the business world and one that is needed in government.

In order to effectively manage in the public sector, an administrator often needs to closely involve, engage and rely upon many individuals over whom s/he has no direct authority or control. In linking, public administrators regularly work with other representatives of government, as well as non-profit organizations and industry, to achieve their mission(s). One's linking capabilities are typically associated with strong negotiation and communication skills, as opposed to being reliant upon hierarchal structure, discipline, or financial incentives.

[87] *See* Grover Starling, *Managing the Public Sector* (6th ed. 2002).

In the case of airport managers, directors or top public administrators, having a capability to effectively link with others in positions of authority in nearby jurisdictions can mean the difference between success and failure. The impact of an airport is felt miles away, and may involve several jurisdictions. The ability to engage fellow public administrators, for example to support proper land use in the jurisdictions near the airport, is critical to the survival and future growth of the airport. Good linkages with fellow administrators and the communities they serve can help to promote a positive perception of the airport and actually help to reduce the potential for costly litigation.

AIRPORT STAFFING

Airports, the world over, are traditionally organized around three principle divisions of labor: *Administration*, *Facilities Management*, and *Operations*.[88] Into these three general areas the airport is staffed. An overview of the operational functions performed at an airport reveals the sundry positions, which might be found within an airport's staff. Naturally, at smaller airports fewer people will accomplish a wider range of the required tasks; personnel are typically less specialized. The larger the airport, the more likely it is to find each of the operational functions and/or sub-functions staffed by individual specialists, whose range of tasks is more limited, off-set by their depth of expertise in a narrowed area.

Administrative functions include the management of financial matters, chattel and real property, purchasing, personnel administration, public relations, and clerical services, to name a few of the major areas. A descriptive buzzword for administration might be "paperwork," including leases, contracts, correspondence, fiscal records, budgets, and so forth. Administration in this sense refers to management of the airport's business affairs, of keeping its paperwork in order. Also included in administration would be legal counsel, environmental services, public relations, and the services of consultants.

---

[88] Rigas Doganis divides the areas differently. He suggests that within the overall airport umbrella, the range of services include: essential operational services such as air traffic control, security and firefighting, as well as runway and building maintenance; traffic-handling services associated directly with the aircraft itself (*e.g.*, cleaning, baggage loading or unloading, and/or processing of passengers, baggage or freight); and commercial activities including restaurants, bars, and other concessionaires). *See* Rigas Doganis, *The Airport Business* 7-11 (1992).

Facilities management encompasses a broad range of activities, which include engineering, architecture and planning, and supporting functions such as building and grounds maintenance, fabrication, and custodial services. The operative word is "infrastructure," meaning buildings and other structures such as: runways, taxiways, ramps, roads and the infields. It is the proprietorship of the airport.

The area of *operations* is perhaps an even broader and more encompassing term, used herein to describe the third major airport support area. Generally, "airport operations" connotes "movement," which in turn entails the airport's functional, or line as opposed to staff, responsibilities. Airport operations includes coordination with the airlines, general aviation, air traffic control, aircraft and structural fire fighting and rescue, airport security and law enforcement, and regulatory compliance. It also encompasses automobile parking, ground transportation and vehicle circulation. And it entails the parking, movement of aircraft, and aircraft servicing activities in the terminal (or ramp) areas for which airport management, as opposed to air traffic control, is responsible.

In the classical, Weberian sense, the airport is staffed with sufficient personnel to accomplish the individual tasks associated with the three principal areas of activity identified above.[89] That is to say, at smaller airports fewer people will accomplish multiple tasks. But with increased airport size and complexity comes ever-increasing job specialization (i.e., "division of labor") and fewer tasks assigned to each individual. As the airport grows, the organizational chart develops into the traditional pyramid, or triangular shape, associated with what Max Weber described as the "bureaucratic ideal."

Common airport functions are management, personnel, finance, public relations, environmental, maintenance, engineering, and operations including security and Airport Rescue and Fire Fighting [ARFF]. Administrative assistants to the airport manager may include an assistant manager to carry out the manager's responsibilities in his or her absence, and supporting staff including a property agent, operations officer, financial accountant, public relations officer, environ-

[89] In Max Weber's perspective on capitalism (and the modern institutional order), the free market economy is dependent upon rational-legal authority, not only internal to the organization in its "bureaucracy" but also externally, upon the "rationality of economic action." *See* Max Weber, *The Theory of Social and Economic Organization*, A.M. Henderson & Talcott Parsons (trans.) 186, 333-334 (1947).

mental coordinator, airport engineer, and personnel manager. What follows are prospective titles for the various airport staff positions.

The *assistant airport manager* serves both as an assistant and a backup to the chief executive officer. This person acts as an executive officer in charge of staff functions and other administrative details. The assistant is second in command only to the airport manager in the line of authority, and will take charge of the overall operation of the airport in the manager's absence.

The *operations manager* is the supervisor in charge of the airport's functional, or movement, activities. This person is responsible for aircraft operations while aircraft are physically in the terminal area and on the parking ramps. It might be noted that it is air traffic control's responsibility to direct traffic on the air movement areas, which include the active runways and associated taxiways, but airport management is responsible for safety and movement of aircraft on the aprons and parking areas. Other operational areas for which the operations manager may be responsible are the petroleum storage and dispensing facilities, queuing and circulation of ground transportation, private and rental auto parking, airport security and law enforcement activities, airport rescue and fire fighting services, airport certification requirements, and overall airport safety conditions. Larger airports may have separate *security, ground transportation, parking, cargo, landside, airside or terminal supervisors/ managers*

The *financial manager*, *comptroller* or *Chief Financial Officer* [CFO] is responsible for airport financial services and for staff accountants and other managers who make determinations relative to the airport's economic viability. The team assists in establishing revenue rates and in making business decisions that help to maintain the airport's fiscal solvency. They may also track airport services provision, facility and resource usage, and operating costs to establish, track and revise user rates and charges. Larger airports may employ several bookkeepers or accountants.

The *business* or *property manager* is responsible for capital and real property assets, and may also be accountable for all capitalized personal (chattel) properties. The property manager researches title, arranges for land purchase or sale, becomes involved with leases and tenant agreements. Duties may also include the monitoring of insurance coverage and drafting of certain legal documents, particularly leases and other negotiated agreements. The property manager, in effect, is the airport's *real estate agent.* There might also be a separate and distinct *insurance agent* responsible for risk management. They may also authorize and oversee tenant improvements.

The *purchasing agent* is responsible for ordering supplies and inventory of operating stocks. This person maintains an inventory of all parts, equipment, and disposable goods needed to keep the airport functioning from day-to-day. The purchasing agent is also responsible for salvage and for sale or disposal of surplus equipment. The purchasing agent may also be responsible for insuring contracts for personal services (e.g., architecture, engineering and planning services).

The *personnel or human resource manager* is responsible for labor relations, for recruiting employees and for maintaining personnel and employee finance records. The actual hiring and firing is customarily done by the airport manager or by an appropriate line manager, but the personnel office will conduct the employment search, maintain records on all employees, and will advise management on labor-related legal issues, employment practices and working conditions.

Public relations and communicating with the public are perhaps the most important functions of airport management. The *public relations manager* or *Public Information Officer* [PIO] maintains compatible relations between the airport and its tenants, airport users, legislators, and the surrounding and adjacent communities. A PIO and/or *noise officer* may handle noise complaints. The PIO may respond to general complaints, to public requests for information, or act as a media spokesperson during emergencies and other issues of current and significant interest to the community. A *marketing manager* may handle both public information and promotion of the "airport as a market." The latter is discussed in greater detail in Chapter 13.

Airports must be equipped to respond to a variety of environmental concerns including those relating to air and water quality (including deicing activities), hazardous waste issues (including fuel spill clean up), aircraft noise, wildlife hazard tracking and mitigation, consumer waste disposal, etc. Depending upon the items of concern at a particular airport, a particular *environmental specialist* may be employed with specialized training to respond, record, remediate and report activities, as deemed necessary by environmental oversight agencies. Clearly, aircraft activities can be a great source of annoyance to the community. The public relations efforts of airport management might entail the designation of an *environmental coordina-*

tor, and delegating to that person the responsibility for formulating programs to improve adverse environmental impact upon the community resulting from the airport's close proximity. *Noise abatement officers or specialists* are oftentimes charged with devising noise abatement procedures and land use compatibility programs.

Facilities or *maintenance manager(s)* are responsible for the planning, construction and maintenance of the airport's physical facilities or infrastructure. This position (or several specialized positions) equate most directly with the public works director in a county or city organization. Civil engineering is the principal discipline in airport engineering and facility maintenance, but with larger airports and expanded engineering needs, other specialties such as mechanical and electrical engineering may also be employed full time. Architectural and planning services may be fully employed as well, especially where there is a need for planning and design of new facilities associated with a rapidly growing airport. Additionally, facilities management includes a wide range of maintenance (electrical, structural, mechanical, etc.) and custodial services that keep the airport clean, safe and operable. The maintenance staff will also include groundskeepers to maintain the airfield, terminal and landside area grounds.

Clerical services support the administrative staff. As with any office activity the services of secretaries, stenographers, filing clerks and other clerical assistants are required to keep the paperwork moving. Letters must be typed, records filed, and accounts posted.

Supplementing the full-time airport staff are professionals in fields that are needed from time-to-time, but for which there is usually insufficient need to fully employ their services. Typical of these specialty services are *consultants* in architecture, engineering and planning, *attorneys-at-law*, and *financial analysts*. Even though management may have the in-house capabilities, it is sometimes advantageous to have the input of an unbiased, third party opinion. Hence, it may be politically expedient or otherwise reasonable to engage the services of an outside consultant to perform specific tasks.

In addition to actual airport employees, there are other personnel who are normally found at the airport, but who do not work directly for airport management. Those unfamiliar with airport operations often misperceive that airport employees perform these services. The most glaring examples are air traffic control and security checkpoint screeners. With few exceptions, air traffic controllers do not work for the airport. They are usually employed by the Federal Aviation Administration [FAA] directly or are engaged contractually with some funding through the local government and/or the FAA's contract tower program. Technically, the FAA is a tenant on the airport, albeit at a very nominal rental rate. Since 2001, the checkpoint personnel are either employees of the Transportation Security Administration [TSA] or are privately contracted to operate under the guidance and oversight of the TSA. However, the airport sponsor provides Law Enforcement Officers [LEO], either by creation of an airport police department or by contracting for police services from a local police agency such as a city police department or the office of the county sheriff.

Other airport tenants will be airlines, Fixed Base Operators [FBO] and concessionaires. This latter group makes up the majority of the airport-related work force. The airport, in reality, is a commercial forum or marketplace. The airport owner (city, county or special district) sponsors the market "place," but the vendors (the airlines, FBOs, and concessionaires) create the "market" itself. Fixed base operators are in private business and provide such services as air taxi (i.e., on-demand passenger transportation), flight instruction, aircraft servicing, and aircraft maintenance and repair. Concessionaires include automobile rental companies, taxis or limousine services, restaurants, retail shops and other services commonly used by the traveling public. The airlines and their employees are also tenants on the airport, providing line-haul services for passengers, freight and mail.

SUMMARY

The airport is a complex system operated by public administrators who have specialized training and responsibilities, fall under legislative and community oversight, and are expected to conduct them selves in a manner that supports the best interests of its community and its users. The public administrators who run airports also provide a valuable service of *governance* that may be overlooked when compared against the provision of routine and emergency service functions. But while both are important, "governance" (i.e., responsible public oversight and proper exercise of government power, action and function) must be balanced with service provision in order for a public administrator's obligations to be fulfilled.

CHAPTER 3

THE AIRPORT

The United States has the most advanced air transportation system in the world. The backbone of the nation's air transportation system is its airports.

Arizona Department of Transportation[1]

A PHYSICAL PLACE

Airports can be many things to many people. But before they are any of those things they are places, which can be described by their physical characteristics. At the heart of the airport is the runway. It is around the runway system that airports are planned and developed. Taxiway systems, terminal buildings, aprons, parking areas, and other facilities are developed in support of the runway system

Required of early airfields was the option of taking off or landing in any direction in order to take advantage of the prevailing winds. In an attempt to retain the advantage of being able to take off in any given direction, later airports—particularly World War II vintage military airfields in the United States—were constructed with triangular shaped runway patterns. Although the triangular runway configuration did not provide for take-off operations through the full range of 360 degrees, it did provide for multiple options which if not directly into the wind, were nearly so. Many of the military airfields inherited by civilian communities had triangular runway configurations, the

---

[1] Arizona Dept. of Trans. [ADOT], *Aviation: Spreading it Wings Over Arizona*, video (1999), available from ADOT, Phoenix, Ariz.

outlines of which can still be seen underlying subsequent pavement expansions and overlays.

Commensurate with the development of larger and faster aircraft, runway length requirements became greater, and fields large enough to allow for operations in multiple directions became less and less available. It soon became necessary to develop primary runways aligned with the generally prevailing winds, and if necessary to build secondary runways which could take advantage of occasional cross-winds. Runways are currently developed in this manner; although exceptions have been made, as discussed later in this chapter. Meteorological data is analyzed to determine which runway orientation would make best use of the prevailing winds. The runway is the heart of the airport, and it is around the runway system that airports are planned and developed. Taxiway systems, terminal buildings, aprons, parking areas, and other facilities are developed in support of the runway system.

Airports really are more than just places where airplanes takeoff and land. As described in Chapter 1, they are viable marketplaces and complex industrial enterprises. Indeed, airports take on varying meanings to different people. First, however, they are places, which can be described by their physical characteristics. The paragraphs that follow describe in general the basic components that make up the airport complex.

RUNWAYS

A *runway* is a defined area on an airport prepared for the landing and taking off of aircraft. An airport may have several runways, each with a different purpose. The *primary runway*, as the name would indicate, is usually oriented in the direction of the prevailing wind, and is almost always the longest. If the airport has an instrument assisted approach, it will normally be oriented to the primary runway. *Crosswind runways* are aligned at an angle up to ninety degrees of the primary runway orientation in order to provide a usable runway when strong crosswinds make it hazardous to use the primary runway. *Parallel runways* are constructed when required for increased capacity. Small airports rarely have parallel runways, but at airports handling large volumes of traffic, both the primary and crosswind runways might have parallel counterparts.[2]

Runway length, width, and strength parameters have been determined by the Federal Aviation Administration and are presented in FAA *Advisory Circulars* [AC] in the form of graphic curves which provide adjustments for elevations, gradient, and mean average temperatures. Runway lengths vary from about 3,000 feet for utility airports, up to more than 12,000 feet for some transport airports. Runways range from 60 feet to 200 feet in width. For *utility* airports, runway lengths are determined according to the requirements of generic groups of aircraft for which the airport is designed (e.g., basic utility, general utility, etc.). Runway length determinations for *transport* category airports are determined by the requirements of the specific critical aircraft.[3]

New runway construction can be costly. The 9,000 foot runway constructed in 2006 at St. Louis Lambert Airport in St. Louis cost $1.1 billion to build, and stands as the most expensive capital improvement project ever undertaken in that city's history. The airlines are expected to pay 23% of the runway cost, amounting to a $1 surcharge for every one of Lambert's boarding passengers. "But while there were plenty of supporters for the new runway, not everyone liked Lambert's plans. Construction meant razing more than 2,000 homes, churches, schools and businesses in neighboring Bridgeton. St. Charles residents argued that the runway would bring airport noise to their living rooms."[4]

The number and orientation of the runways determine the configuration of the airport. The primary factor influencing runway orientation is wind. Ideally the runway should be aligned with the prevailing winds. Wind conditions affect all airplanes in varying degrees, but generally the smaller the airplane the more it is affected by adverse winds, especially crosswind components. The crosswind component is particularly critical to aircraft with conventional landing gear (i.e., two main wheels and a tail wheel).

---

[2] The information for this section of the chapter is largely taken from guidance provided by the FAA in AC 150/5300-13 *Airport Design*, (including all changes to that AC) and AC 150/5325-4B, *Runway Length Requirements for Airport Design*, retrieved from www.faa.gov.

[3] *See* Ch. 4 for definitions of *utility* and *transport* category aircraft.

[4] *New $1 Billion Runway Opens this Week, but It's Not Needed Anymore*, The Associated Press., (Mon., Apr. 10, 2006).

While it is commonly believed that aircraft must always operate into the wind, it is actually not uncommon for commercial airports to receive Federal Aviation Administration [FAA] waivers that permit air traffic control to ask pilots to land and depart with significant crosswinds and tailwinds. An FAA Order clarifies this point: "Under ideal conditions, aircraft takeoffs and landings should be conducted into the wind. However, other considerations such as delay and capacity problems, runway length, available approach aids, noise abatement and other factors may require aircraft operations to be conducted on runways not directly aligned into the wind." [5]

The most desirable runway orientation, based on wind, is the one that has the greatest wind coverage along its centerline axis, and with the least adverse crosswind. "Wind coverage" is the proportion of time (in percentage) for which operations are considered safe due to acceptable crosswind components. A "crosswind component" of wind direction and velocity is the resultant vector, which acts at a right angle to the runway. It is equal to the wind speed multiplied by the trigonometric sine of the angle between the wind direction and the runway direction. Normally, these wind vector triangles and computations of prevailing winds are solved graphically in FAA publications and aircraft operation manuals.

According to FAA criteria, the desirable wind coverage for an airport is 95%, based on total weather observations taken for the location. The standard for transport airports requires 95% runway wind coverage with 15 miles per hour (13 knot) crosswind component. For utility airports a 95% runway wind coverage is also required, but with a 12 miles per hour (10.5 knot) crosswind component.

Construction of more than one runway is sometimes necessary to give the desired (95%) wind coverage. If a single runway orientation is unable to attain the 95% benchmark, a crosswind runway should be added to attain at least a 95% combined wind coverage at the specified crosswind component (i.e., 12 or 15 mph respectively for utility and transport categories).

---

[5] FAA Order 8400.9, *National Safety and Operational Criteria for Runway Use Programs* (1981).

TAXIWAYS

Taxiways are constructed to facilitate aircraft movement from one part of the airport to another, primarily to and from the runway. They are considered "a defined path" as opposed to a *taixlane* which is "the portion of the aircraft parking area used for access between taxiways and aircraft parking positions." [6]

The efficiency of a runway is directly related to the capability of the taxiway system to facilitate the movement of traffic to and from the runway. Taxiways are classified into one of the following types: parallel, entrance, exit, bypass, and apron access.

A *parallel taxiway* runs parallel to its associated runway and may have several exit taxiways connecting it with the runway. At very busy airports, there may be dual parallel taxiways. The FAA recommends parallel taxiways when a runway receives more than 20,000 annual operations. The primary purpose of parallel taxiways is to improve the operational flow around the runway, thereby increasing capacity and safety.

Entrance taxiways are normally located at the ends of the runway and also serve as the last exit taxiway on a bi-directional runway. An entrance taxiway is usually at a right angle to the runway, although some operational groups advocate designs for runway entry which permit acceleration while turning onto the runway. *Apron access* taxiways connect the air movement area with other taxiways and with hangars and aprons.

Bypass taxiways serve an important purpose at busy airports, in that they allow Air Traffic Control [ATC] a limited length of parallel taxiway to maneuver aircraft around areas that may be otherwise bottlenecked. An alternative to a bypass taxiway is a *holding bay,* which provides a place for ATC to hold aircraft in a static position while awaiting gate availability or clearance to depart. *A turn-around*—which is essentially a paved area which aircraft can use to momentarily leave the runway, turn around, and reenter the runway to use it as a taxiway—is useful at less busy airfields where a full length parallel taxiway's cost could not be justified.

---

[6] The information for this section of the chapter is largely taken from guidance provided by the FAA in AC 150/5300-13 *Airport Design*, (including all changes to that AC) retrieved from www.faa.gov.

Exit taxiways should be located at frequent intervals along the runway to promote pilot acceptance of an exit, thus provide for minimum *Runway Occupancy Time* [ROT] by users. The exit taxiway should provide for free flow to the parallel taxiway, or at least to a point where the airplane is considered clear of the runway, thus enabling another operation on the runway. Exit taxiways can be constructed at right angles, or to allow for greater exit speed can be at a thirty to forty-five degree angle. Angled taxiways are commonly referred to as "acute angle," "high speed exit," or "rapid exit."

Another high-speed category is the *spiral exit* taxiway, which applies "spiral" geometry to connecting parallel runway/taxiway systems. Typically, the spiral incorporates a computer designed curving exit, connected to parallel taxiways. Spiral exits feature more strategic placement, geometric refinements, lighting and markings, which enable higher exit speeds. Spiral exit speeds range between 30 and 60 knots, as opposed to 10 to 15 knots for conventional exit speeds. The spiral can reduce the ROT from the customary 60-second range for runways with conventional high-speed exits to as low as 45 seconds.

The decision to build a high-speed (or spiral) exit taxiway is based upon analyses of existing and contemplated traffic. The idea behind it is to enhance the capacity of the runway. However, if there is insufficient demand, construction of high-speed exits is probably not necessary, and the customary perpendicular exits may suffice. The conventional 90 degree exit taxiway can be constructed at less cost, and when properly located along the runway, may achieve an acceptably efficient flow of traffic.

The widths and strengths (i.e., load-bearing capacity) of taxiways vary for each classification of airport according to the size of aircraft to be served. Taxiways typically range in width from 25 to as much as 100 feet.

APRON AND HANGAR SPACE

Aircraft parking *apron* and *hangar* space requirements are determined not only by the number of aircraft needing facilities, but also by the relationship of the number of based versus transient aircraft expected to utilize the airport. Additionally, since aircraft may be parked either in hangars or on the open ramps, the availability of one affects the need for the other.[7]

Aircraft storage space expands as a function of the volume and size of the aircraft expected to park in or on it. Apron space, for example, is sized on two factors: the number of aircraft tie-downs necessary to meet existing and forecast demand; and the aircraft mix. Logically, larger aircraft require more apron space for parking and maneuvering than do smaller aircraft. At a minimum, an individual parking space for a typical basic utility aircraft is about 1,100 to 1,200 square feet, plus the associated taxiway serving that space.

Apron areas are customarily designated by user category. *Transient ramps* are for visiting aircraft and *based aircraft ramps* are for those aircraft permanently stored at the airport. The number of *hangars* required depends upon localized demand, but as a rule, greater demand can be expected in the more severe climate areas, where protection from adverse weather conditions is more of a necessity.

Hangars and/or covered tie downs (also known as "T-Shades" or "ramadas") are developed according to the expressed demand for these facilities, usable airport space available for hangar development, and available financing to build them. Hangars may be designed for individual aircraft use or for multiple aircraft storage. Individual hangars may have conventional rectangular shapes or may be *T-hangars*; derived from the "T" shape of the walls, which conform to the outer shape of the airplane.

Multiple aircraft hangars are usually of *conventional* (rectangular) design. However, in the interest of space utilization and affordable construction, some innovative designs have evolved which do not conform to the standard conventional or T-hangar design. Some of these designs have included hangars in the shape of tents or igloos. There are also hexagonal shapes to fit on irregular shaped parcels.

Some hangars have been built like a turntable, wherein the table turns until the select airplane is located at the hangar door opening. In the obverse of the turntable design, the aircraft are parked on a fixed surface, and the hangar walls rotate around the aircraft until the hangar opening is properly positioned. One conceptual hangar design was modeled after a multi-level auto parking structure where aircraft

---

[7] The information for this section of the chapter is largely taken from guidance provided by the FAA AC 150/5300-13 *Airport Design*, (including all changes to that AC) and AC 150/5360-9 *Planning and Design of Airport Facilities at Nonhub Locations*, as retrieved from www.faa.gov.

would be raised to the appropriate hangar level by elevator. A recent and popular trend is toward moveable or *portable hangars*. Many hangars are now of portable design. They may be assigned a mobile trailer license by the State, and can be relocated on short notice.

AIRPORT LIGHTING

Airport *Navigational Aids* [NAVAIDs] are grouped into *visual* type aids, and those that emit *electronic* signals. Lighting and navigational aids extend an airport's usefulness into periods of darkness and poor visibility. A NAVAID provides point-to-point guidance information or positional data to aircraft in flight.

Airport lighting systems are made up of various lighting aids that may be installed on an airport. A quick reference list of the most common types of airport lighting are included below, followed by more in-depth discussion of these systems later in this section: [8]

- *Approach Light Systems* [ALS] provide directional guidance by which the pilot aligns the aircraft with the extended runway centerline on final approach for landing;
- *Visual Approach Slope Indicators* [VASI] provide vertical visual approach slope guidance during the approach for landing. VASIs come in a variety of variations;
- *Precision Approach Path Indicators* [PAPI] use VASI-like light units installed in single row of two or four lights;
- *Runway End Identifier Lights* [REIL] are two strobe-like, synchronized flashing lights, one on each side of the runway at the threshold end for positive identification of the approach end of the runway;
- *Runway edge lights* are used to define the lateral limits of the runway, while *Runway Centerline Light Systems* [RCLS] are used on precision instrument approach runways to increase runway visibility;

---

[8] Sources for this section include: FAA, *Federal Aviation Regulations/Aeronautical Information Manual*, published by Jeppesen (2006), and FAA AC 150/5340-30B, *Design and Installation Details for Airport Visual Aids*, (effective Aug. 1, 2006), retrieved from http://www.airweb.faa.gov/ Regulatory_and_Guidance_Library/rgAdvisoryCirculars.

- *Touchdown Zone Lights* [TDZL] are located symmetrically about the runway centerline to better define the touchdown zone;
- *Threshold lights* arranged along the runway threshold, and are bi-directional, with green showing toward approaching aircraft, while departing aircraft see red (to signify the departure end or limits of the runway);
- *Taxiway edge lights* outline the sides of taxiways in blue, while taxiway centerline lights are in-ground steady burning green lights;
- *Rotating beacons*;
- A variety of other lights are used to help keep aircraft off unwanted movement surfaces. These include *clearance bar lights, runway guard* (also called wig-wag*) lights*, and *stop bar lights*, the later of which is controlled by ATC; and
- *Obstruction lights* can be either flashing or steady burning red lights, or a bright flashing white light. Obstructions are also painted aviation orange and white for daytime marking.

In the following paragraphs, several types of lights and lighting systems, introduced above, are discussed in greater depth.[9]

The *aeronautical beacon*, or *rotating beacon*, is a visual NAVAID displaying flashes of white and green light (or green only) to indicate the location of a *land airport*. White and yellow indicates a *water airport*. The airport beacon has a vertical light distribution such as to make it most effective at angles of one to ten degrees above the horizontal from its site; however, it can be seen well above and below this peak spread. The beacon may be an omnidirectional capacitor-discharge device, or it may rotate at a constant speed, which produces the visual effect of flashes at regular intervals. Flashes are comprised of one or two colors alternately, with the total numbers of flashes as follows:[10]

---

[9] Sources for this section include: FAA, *Federal Aviation Regulations/Aeronautical Information Manual*, published by Jeppesen (2006); and FAA AC 150/5340-30B, *Design and Installation Details for Airport Visual Aids*, (effective Aug. 1, 2006), retrieved from http://www.airweb.faa.gov/ Regulatory _and_Guidance_Library/rgAdvisoryCirculars.

[10] FAA AC 150/5345-12E, *Specification for Airport and Heliport Beacons* (2006); and FAA, *Federal Aviation Regulations/Aeronautical Information Manual*, published by Jeppesen (2006).

- 24 to 30 per minute for beacons marking airports, landmarks, and points on Federal airways; and
- 30 to 45 per minute for beacons marking heliports.

The colors and color combinations of beacons are:

- White and green, or green alone—lighted land airport;
- White and yellow, or yellow alone—lighted water airport;
- White and red—landmark or navigational point (rare installation);
- White alone—unlighted land airport (rare installation); and
- Green, yellow, and white—lighted heliport.

Military airport beacons are also comprised of white and green flashes, but can be differentiated from civil beacons with their distinctive white-white-green flash sequence.

In control zones, operation of the airport beacon during the hours of daylight often indicates that the ground visibility is less than three miles and/or the ceiling is less than 1,000 feet. ATC clearance would be required for landing, takeoff and flight in the traffic pattern. At locations with control towers and if controls are provided, ATC personnel turn the beacon on. There is no regulatory requirement for daylight operation. At many airports throughout the country, the airport beacon is turned on by a photoelectric cell or time clocks and ATC personnel have no control as to when it shall be turned on.

Approach Light Systems provide the basic means for transition from instrument flight using electronic approach aids to visual flight and landing. Operational requirements dictate the sophistication and configuration of the ALS for a particular runway. Approach light systems are a configuration of signal lights starting at the landing threshold and extending into the approach area a distance of 2,400 to 3,000 feet for precision instrument runways and 1,400 to 1,500 feet for non-precision instrument runways. Some systems include sequenced flashing lights, which appear to the pilot as a ball of light traveling towards the runway at high speed twice a second. An ALS is valuable in providing assistance for landing pilots to transition from instrument flight to visual flight.[11]

---

[11] Sources for this section include: FAA, *Federal Aviation Regulations/Aeronautical Information Manual*, published by Jeppesen (2006); and FAA AC 150/5340-30B, *Design and Installa-*

The *Visual Approach Slope Indicator* is a system of lights so arranged to provide visual descent-guidance information during the approach to a runway. These lights are visible from three to five miles during the day and up to 20 miles or more at night. The visual glide path of the VASI provides safe obstruction clearance within plus or minus ten degrees of the extended runway centerline and to four nautical miles from the runway threshold. The runway or runway lights provide lateral course guidance.[12]

VASI installations may consist of two, four, six, twelve, or sixteen light units arranged in bars referred to as near, middle, and far bars. Most VASI installations consist of two bars, near and far, and may consist of two, four, or twelve light units. Some airports have VASIs consisting of three bars, near, middle, and far, which provide an additional visual glide path for use by high cockpit aircraft. This installation may consist of either six or sixteen light units. VASI installations consisting of two, four, or six light units are located on one side of the runway, usually the left (i.e., the pilot's side of the cockpit). Where the installation consists of twelve or sixteen light units, the light units are located on both sides of the runway.[13]

Two-bar VASI installations provide one visual glide path which is normally set at three degrees. Three-bar VASI installations provide two visual glide paths. The lower glide path is provided by the near and middle bars and is normally set at three degrees while the upper glide path, provided by the middle and far bars, is normally one-quarter degree higher. This higher glide path is intended for use only by high cockpit aircraft to provide a sufficient threshold crossing height. Although normal glide path angles are three degrees, angles at some locations may be as high as 4.5 degrees to give proper obstacle clearance.[14]

The basic principle of the VASI is that of color differentiation between red and white (as well as amber on the tri-color VASI discussed below). Each light unit projects a beam of light having a white segment in the upper part of the beam and red segment in the lower part of the beam. The light units are arranged so that the pilot using the VASIs—if on the desired approach path (usually set at 3 de-

---

tion Details for Airport Visual Aids, (effective Aug. 1, 2006), retrieved from http://www.airweb.faa.gov/ Regulatory_and_Guidance_Library/rgAdvisoryCirculars.

[12] *Id.*

[13] *Id.*

[14] *Id.*

grees)—sees a desired light combination. If the pilot leaves the desired approach path though, another combination of colors would be seen, signifying the aircraft is either too high or too low for the desired approach path.

Several types of non-standard visual approach slope indicators have been installed at general aviation and air carrier airports. *Tri-color VASIs* normally consist of a single light unit projecting a three-color visual approach path into the final approach area of the runway upon which the indicator is installed. The below glide path indication is red, the above-glide-path indication is amber, and the on-glide-path indication is green. These types of indicators have a useful range of approximately one-half to one mile during the day and up to five miles at night depending upon the visibility conditions.[15]

Pulsating Visual Approach Slope Indicators [PVASIs] normally consist of a single light unit projecting a two-color visual approach path into the final approach area of the runway upon which the indicator is installed. The below glide path indication is normally pulsating red and the above glide path indication is normally pulsating white. The on glide path indication for one type of system is a steady white light while for another type system the on glide path indication consists of an alternating red and white light. The useful range of these systems is about four miles during the day and up to ten miles at night.[16]

Alignment of elements systems are installed on some small general aviation airports. They are a low-cost system consisting of painted plywood panels, normally black and white or fluorescent orange. Some of these systems are lighted for night use. The useful range of these systems is approximately three-quarter miles. To use the system the pilot positions the aircraft so the elements are in alignment.[17]

The *Precision Approach Path Indicator* uses light units similar to the VASI but are installed in a single row of either two or four light units. These systems have a visual range of approximately five miles during the day and up to twenty miles at night. The row of PAPI light units is normally installed on the runway's left side.[18]

---

[15] *Id.*
[16] *Id.*
[17] *Id.*
[18] *Id.*

Runway End Identifier Lights are installed at many airfields to provide rapid and positive identification of the approach end of a particular runway. The system consists of a pair of synchronized flashing lights, one of which is located laterally on each side of the runway threshold. REILs may be either omnidirectional or unidirectional facing the approach area. They may be located longitudinally 200 feet either upwind or downwind from the runway threshold.[19]

Runway edge lights, spaced at approximate 200-foot intervals, are used to outline the edges of runways during periods of darkness and restricted visibility conditions. These light systems are classified according to the intensity or brightness they are capable of producing: they are the *High Intensity Runway Lights* [HIRL], *Medium Intensity Runway Lights* [MIRL], and the *Low Intensity Runway Lights* [LIRL]. The HIRL and MIRL systems typically have variable intensity controls.

Runway edge lights are white, except on instrument runways where yellow (or amber) lights are visible for the last 2,000 feet or half the runway length (whichever is less), to create "caution zone" for landing aircraft. The threshold lights marking the longitudinal limits of the runway emit red light toward the runway to indicate the end of runway to a departing aircraft and emit green outward from the runway end to indicate the threshold to landing aircraft.[20]

There are several types of *in-runway lighting*, including touchdown zone lighting, runway centerline lighting, runway remaining lighting, and taxiway turnoff lights. *Touchdown zone lighting* and *runway centerline lighting* are installed on some precision approach runways to facilitate landing under adverse visibility conditions. Taxiway lead-off (or turnoff) lights may be added to expedite movement of aircraft from the runway. Touchdown zone lighting consists of two rows of transverse light bars disposed symmetrically about the runway centerline in the runway touchdown zone. The system starts 100 feet from the landing threshold and extends to 3,000 feet from the threshold or the midpoint of the runway, whichever is less.[21]

Runway centerline lighting is made up of flush centerline lights spaced at fifty-foot intervals beginning 75 feet from the landing threshold and extending to within 75 feet of opposite end of the run-

[19] *Id.*
[20] *Id.*
[21] *Id.*

way. *Runway remaining lighting* is applied to centerline lighting systems in the final 3,000 feet as viewed from the takeoff or approach position. Alternate red and white lights are seen from the 3,000-foot points to the 1,000-foot points, with all red centerline lighting visible for the last 1,000 feet of the runway. From the opposite direction, these lights are seen as white lights.[22]

Runway distance remaining markers consist of signs located along the sides of a runway to indicate the remaining runway distance in increments of 1,000 feet. The signs may be located on either both sides, or only one side, of the runway. The signs have white numerals on a black background and are lighted for nighttime and low visibility operations.

Since runways rarely exist in exact multiples of 1,000 feet, the excess distance is added to the runway ends. Therefore, the last sign on each runway end may be located more, but never less, than 1,000 feet from the runway end. For this reason, the runway distance remaining markers often will not exactly coincide with distance remaining information of other runway lighting systems.[23]

Taxiway edge lights are used to outline the edges of taxiways during periods of darkness or restricted visibility conditions. These fixtures emit blue light. *Taxiway centerline lights* are used to facilitate ground traffic under low visibility conditions. They are located along the taxiway centerline in a straight line on straight portions, on the centerline of curved portions, and along designated taxiing paths in portions of runways, ramp, and apron areas. Taxiway centerline lights are steady burning and emit green light. *Taxiway lead-off lights* are flush, green (or green and yellow) lights spaced at fifty-foot intervals defining the curved path of aircraft travel from the runway centerline to a point on the adjacent taxiway.[24]

Operation of approach light systems and runway lighting is controlled by the control tower. At some locations the FSS may control the lights where there is no control tower in operation. Pilots may request that lights be turned on or off. Runway edge lights, in-pavement

---

[22] *Id.*

[23] FAA AC 150/5340-18D, *Standards for Airport Sign Systems*, (effective Dec. 6, 2004), retrieved from http://www.airweb.faa.gov/ Regulatory_and_Guidance_Library/rgAdvisoryCirculars.

[24] FAA AC 150/5340-30B, *Design and Installation Details for Airport Visual Aids*, (effective Aug. 1, 2006), retrieved from http://www.airweb.faa.gov/ Regulatory _and_Guidance_Library/rgAdvisoryCirculars.

lights and approach lights also have intensity controls, which may be varied to meet the pilot's request. For example, *Sequenced Flashing Lights* [SFL] may be turned on and off. Some sequenced flashing light systems also have intensity control. The *Medium Intensity Approach Lighting System* with *Runway Alignment Indicators* [MALSR] has been installed at many airports. The control of MALSR is activated by controllers in the *Air Traffic Control Tower* [ATCT] and/or by radio control from approaching aircraft.[25]

Pilot control of lighting by radio is available at selected airports to provide airborne or ground control of lights by keying the aircraft's microphone. Control of lighting systems is available either full-time at those locations without specified hours for lighting or with no control tower or Flight Service Station [FSS], or part-time (during unattended periods) at those locations with a part-time tower or FSS or specified hours for lighting. All lighting systems that are to be radio controlled at an airport, whether on a single runway or multiple runways, operate on the same radio frequency.[26]

With FAA approved systems, various combinations of medium intensity approach lights, runway lights, taxiway lights, VASI and/or REIL may be activated by radio control. On runways with both approach lighting and runway lighting (runway edge lights, taxiway lights, etc.) systems, the approach lighting system takes precedence for air-to-ground radio control over the runway lighting system which is set at a predetermined intensity step, based on expected visibility conditions. Runways without approach lighting may provide radio controlled intensity adjustments of runway edge lights. Other lighting systems, including VASI, REIL, and taxiway lights may be either controlled with the runway edge lights or controlled independently of the runway edge lights.[27]

The control system consists of a three-step control responsive to seven, five, and/or three microphone clicks. This three-step control will turn on lighting facilities capable of three-step, two-step or one-step operation. The three-step and two-step lighting facilities can be altered in intensity, while the one-step cannot. All lighting is illuminated for a period of 15 minutes from the most recent time of activation and may not be extinguished prior to end of the 15-minute period

---

[25] *Id.*

[26] FAA, *Federal Aviation Regulations/Aeronautical Information Manual*, published by Jeppesen (2006).

[27] *Id.*

(except for one-step and two-step REILs, which may be turned off when desired by keying the mike five or three times respectively).

AIRPORT MARKING AIDS

In the interest of safety, regularity, or efficiency of aircraft operations, the FAA has recommended the following airport marking. *Runway markings* include centerline and threshold markings, and runway designator (numbers) indicating the magnetic orientation of the runway. In this category also are taxiway markings. *Runway designators* are the runway numbers and letters, which are determined from the approach direction. The runway number is the whole number nearest to one-tenth of the magnetic azimuth of the centerline of the runway, measured clockwise from the magnetic north. The accompanying letter, or letters, differentiates between left ("L"), right ("R"), or center ("C") parallel runways, as applicable:

- For two parallel runways, "L", "R";
- For three parallel runways, "L", "C", "R".[28]

Different markings are requited, based on whether the runway is used for visual, non-precision or precision (instrument) approaches. (See Figures 3.1 and 3.2 depicting various sets of runway markings.). *Visual runway markings* are applied to runways used for operations under *Visual Flight Rules* [VFR]. Visual runway markings include:[29]

- *Designation marking* (runway numbers and letters);
- *Centerline marking* (dashed white line);
- *Threshold marking* (series of longitudinal stripes beside one another) on runways that might be used by international commercial air transport aircraft;

---

[28] On occasion, to help avoid pilot confusion, three parallel runways may be designated as: two with a common heading only with a "right" and a "left" designation, positioned next to a third runway given a slightly different numerical designation. An example of this can be found at Phoenix Sky Harbor International Airport, which when adding a third parallel runway after many years of two parallels, were convinced by air traffic officials that this would reduce confusion by users.

[29] FAA AC 150/5340-1J, *Standards for Airport Markings* (Apr. 2005).

Figure 3.1—VISUAL AND NONPRECISION RUNWAY MARKINGS

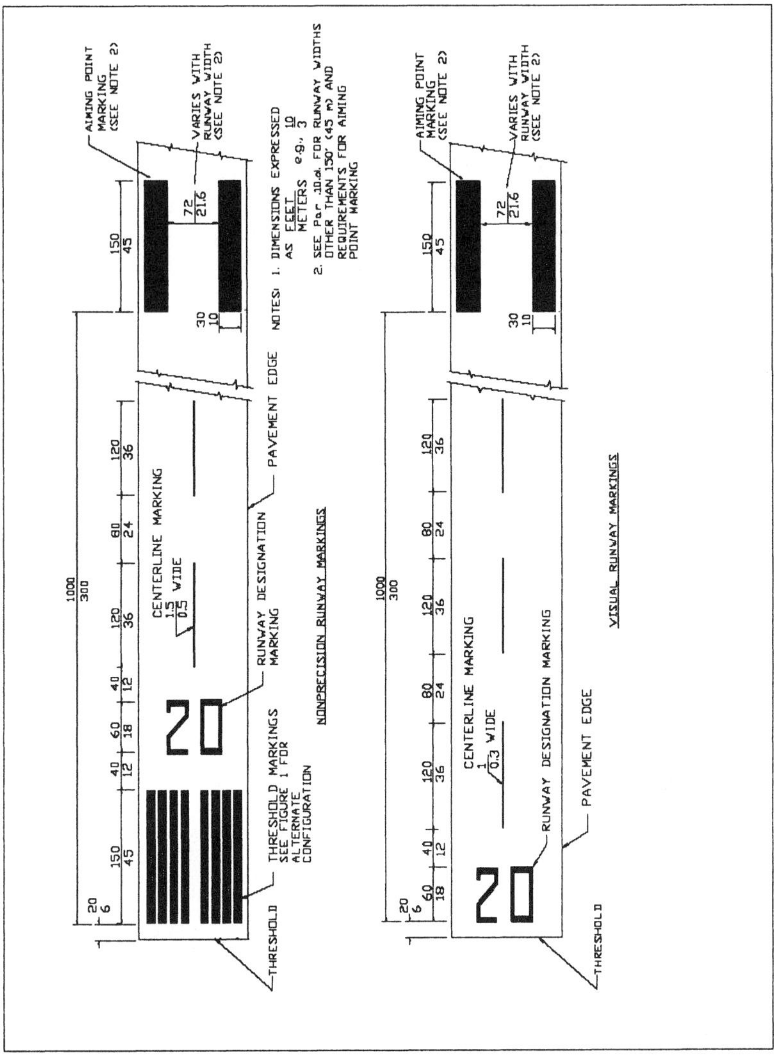

Source: FAA AC 150/5340-1J, *Standards for Airport Markings* (Apr. 2005).

Figure 3.2—PRECISION INSTRUMENT RUNWAY MARKINGS

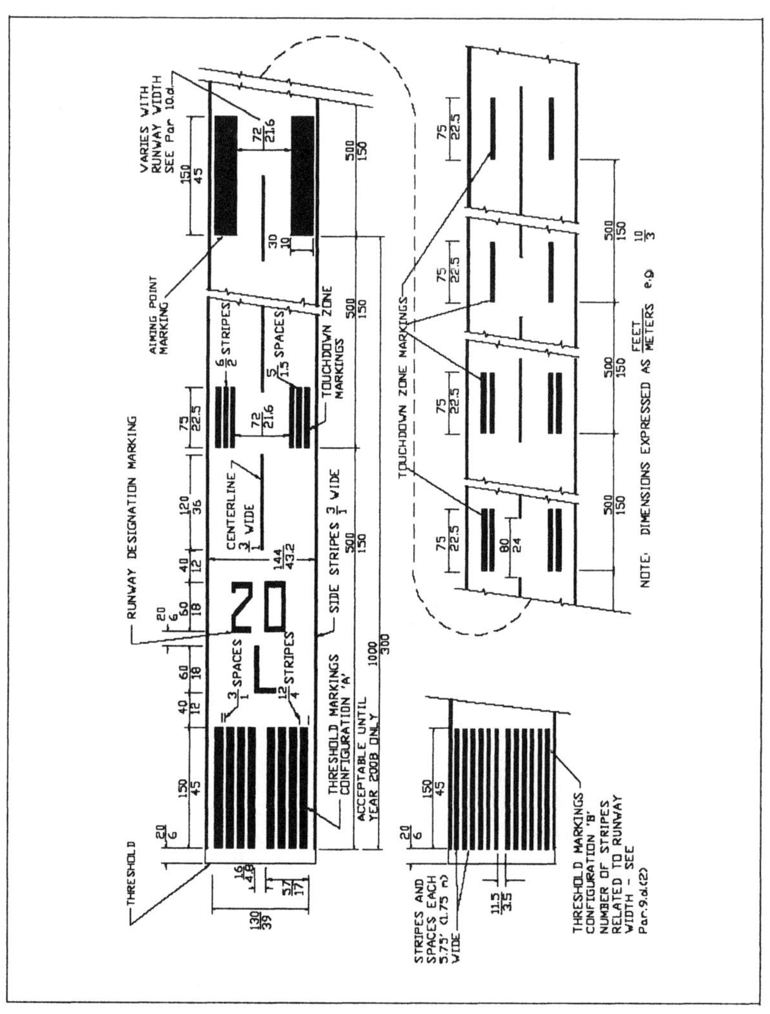

Source: FAA AC 150/5340-1J, *Standards for Airport Markings* (Apr. 2005).

- *Aiming point marking* (two rectangular markings approximately 1,000 feet from the threshold) on runways 4,000 feet or longer used by jet aircraft;
- *Side stripes* (when the full pavement width may not be available as a runway); and
- *Holding position markings* (for taxiway/runway intersections).

Non-precision instrument runway markings are used on runways served by a non-precision navigation aid and intended for landings under *Instrument Flight Rules* [IFR]. These markings are the same as required for visual runways, with the exception that threshold markings are always required (regardless of whether international commercial transport service is expected or not).

Precision instrument runway markings are placed on runways served by precision approach aids (i.e., with azimuth and glide slope information), and on runways having special operational requirements. Precision instrument runway markings include:

- Designation marking;
- Centerline marking;
- Threshold marking;
- Aiming point marking;
- Touchdown zone marking;
- Side stripes; and
- Holding position markings (for taxiway/runway intersections and ILS critical areas).

The *threshold* is the designated beginning of the runway that is available and suitable for the landing of aircraft. For operational and other safety reasons, the threshold is sometimes displaced, relocated, or marks the beginning of a special operation runway. For unusual threshold locations, special markings are applied in accordance with the current airport marking advisory circular.[30]

A *displaced threshold* (depicted in Figure 3.3) is a threshold that is not at the beginning of the full strength runway pavement. The paved area behind the displaced runway threshold is available for taxiing, the landing rollout, and the takeoff of aircraft. *Overrun and stopway*

---

[30] FAA AC 150/5340-1J, *Standards for Airport Markings* (Apr. 2005).

areas are any surface or area extending beyond the usable runway which appears usable but which, due to the nature of its structure, is unusable. A *closed runway* is a runway that is unusable and may be hazardous even though it may appear usable.

Fixed distance markers provide fixed distance information for landing of turbojet aircraft on other than a precision instrument runway. This marking is similar to the fixed distance marking on a precision instrument runway and located 1,000 feet from the threshold. A S*hort Take Off and Landing* [STOL] runway is designed for use by aircraft with special take off and landing characteristics. In addition to the normal runway number marking, the letters, "STOL," are painted on the approach end of the runway and a touchdown aim point is shown. *Helicopter landing areas* are also provided with special markings that can be found in AC 150/5340-1J, *Standards for Airport Markings*.[31]

Taxiway marking includes a taxiway centerline marked with a continuous yellow line. The taxiway edge may be marked with two continuous yellow lines six inches apart. Taxiway *holding lines* consist of two continuous and two dashed lines, spaced six inches between lines, perpendicular to the taxiway centerline; more recently, hold lines also consist of one or more signs at the edge of the taxiway, with white characters on a red sign face.

Over the last decade, several new changes have been made to the FAA's marking advisory circular. The newest changes are enhanced taxiway markings (comprised of a solid yellow centerline bordered by a dashed line on both sides and all outlined in black) at airports annually enplaning 1,500,000 or more passengers, and the extension of runway holding position markings onto the paved shoulder (at airports being served by Design Group 5 and 6 aircraft). These two forms of easier-to-see markings are considered the only acceptable means of compiling with FAR Part 139, effective June 30, 2008.

[31] *Id.*

Figure 3.3—DISPLACED THRESHOLD MARKINGS

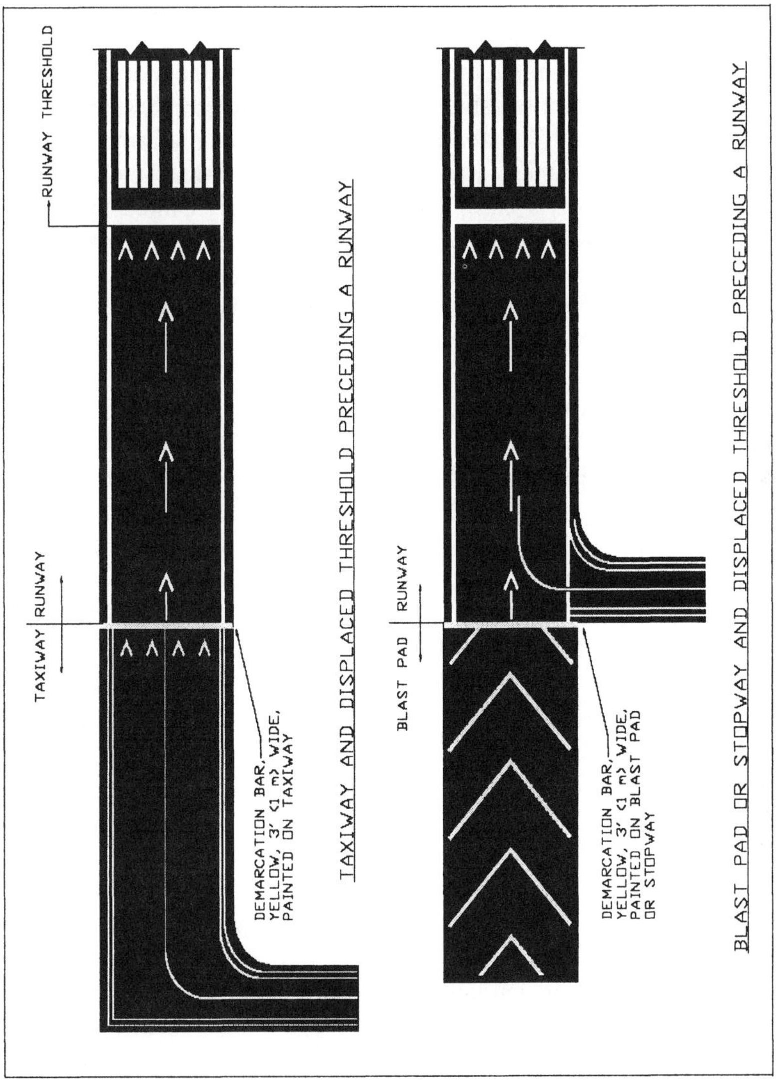

Source: FAA AC 150/5340-1J, *Standards for Airport Markings* (Apr. 2005).

Black outlining is also required in holding position markings, non-movement area boundary markings, taxiway centerlines, holding position markings, and geographic position markings. These more stringent guidelines and standards are optional at all non-specified airports, but may be adopted to help prevent runway incursions.[32]

Other surface painted signs and markings include (but are not limited to): gate identifier, apron entrance, vehicle roadway, and non-movement area boundary markings. In addition, special markings are used for the airport's compass rose and the segmented circle. The *compass rose* is a circle graduated in 360 degrees and marked on the ground at an airport. It is used as a reference to either true or magnetic direction. The *segmented circle* is a visual indicator system for traffic pattern information. The components are:

- The segmented circle itself, on the ground in a centralized location;
- The wind direction indicator;
- The landing direction indicator (a tetrahedron or wind tee);
- Landing strip indicators to show alignment of landing strips; and
- The traffic pattern indicators, used to indicate direction of turns.

Glass (reflective) beads are required to be added to many runway and taxiway markings, as they serve to highlight pavement markings. These beads are not recommended for use in black paint.

NATIONAL AIRSPACE SYSTEM

Described herein is the *National Airspace System* [NAS]; the common network of U.S. airspace, air navigation facilities, equipment and services, airports and landing areas, aeronautical charts, information and services, rules, regulations and procedures, technical information, personnel and material.[33] The FAA has responsibility of insuring the safe and expeditious flow of air traffic at and between airports and for providing terminal area facilities and equipment at qualified locations.

---

[32] FAA AC 150/5340-1J, *Standards for Airport Markings* (Apr. 2005).

[33] FAA, *National Airspace System Plan* (1985).

Other nations have similar systems that when networked together form a web of air traffic control, facilities, equipment.

Qualification for inclusion of specific facilities is determined by the FAA and normally based upon the number and types of operations. The present system and FAA's future plans are described in the *National Airspace System Plan*, which outlines the FAA's modernization program for aviation facilities, equipment and associated development. This includes over 19,000 airports, 750 ATC facilities, and approximately 45,000 pieces of equipment. Much of what follows was excerpted from the National Airspace System Plan.[34]

The air transport infrastructure in the United States is described in a National Airspace System Plan, which is an inclusive nomenclature for all, or nearly all of the components of the air transportation infrastructure. The National Airspace System is an integrated network of facilities and services, but its development has not always been well thought out or planned. Rather, the NAS evolved through a series of piecemeal adjustments and improvements. It was not until 1981 that the Federal Aviation Administration charted a comprehensive National Airspace System Plan. Thirteen years later the NAS was still being developed in general accordance with the 1981 plan. However, it has since been modified, periodically updated, and had several benchmark completion dates postponed.

By 1994, the timetable for implementation of the National Airspace System was so out of conformance that to call the NAS a "plan" had become meaningless. Delayed implementation of the National Airspace System Plan (particular the failure to promptly and efficiency modernize the air traffic control system) has subjected the FAA to harsh criticism from the airline industry and from proponents of a deregulated infrastructure who have suggested that the air traffic control system as well as the FAA's procurement system ought to be privatized.[35] The next few paragraphs will discuss both the status of the NAS "architecture" as well as a review of the General Accountability Office's review of the FAA's efforts to modernize the air traffic control system in the U.S.

The NAS architecture is a 15-year plan that includes existing and planned capital investments. In the quest for an improved ATC sys-

---

[34] U.S. DOT (FAA), Report to Congress; *National Plan of Integrated Airport Systems 2005-2009* (Sep. 30, 2004), retrieved from http//www.faa.gov/arp/planning/npias.

[35] *See* Paul Stephen Dempsey & Laurence E. Gesell, *Air Transportation: Foundations for the 21st Century* Ch. 8 (1997).

tem, the FAA and the aviation community regularly collaborate to determine which equipment still has utility and which need to be updated with new systems, capabilities and procedures via architecture updates. In 1996, NAS architecture version 2.0 focused on using the existing infrastructure while moving toward *Free Flight*. In December 1997, NAS Architecture 3.0 incorporated feedback from the aviation community. Then in January 1999, NAS Architecture 4.0 used input from the Administrator's Modernization Task Force and more realistic funding profiles. It covers 1998-2015.[36]

The most current version, NAS Architecture 5.0, differs from the prior version in that it scales back the larger investment that the FAA had previously expected to make and gives guidance to manufacturers in the form of "Operational Improvements [OI] to help users and manufacturers plan their operations and investments with confidence."[37] It is based on the FAA and industry concept of conducting flights safely and efficiently while adding greater flexibility.

Of particular interest to the U.S. Government Accountability Office [GAO] is whether the FAA is adequately and efficiently progressing toward a goal of planning for the *Next Generation Air Transportation System* [NGATS]. In its June 2006 report, the GAO reported on the progress made by two relatively new FAA organizations: the Air Traffic Organization [ATO] and the Joint Planning and Development Office [JPDO] (comprised of seven federal and non-federal partner agencies). JPDO and ATO have been given the majority of the responsibility for planning and implementing the FAA's modernization efforts, particularly the challenging NGATS. The GAO reports that the results are mixed: while the JPDO and ATO have succeeded in improving interagency coordination—and have done so in a reasonably efficient way—there are still problems in making progress toward "operating effectively as a performance-based organization, hiring and training thousands of air traffic controllers, ensuring stakeholder involvement in major system acquisitions, and keeping acquisitions on schedule and in budget." In addition, the GAO noted that the JPDO, in particular, lacks "authority

---

[36] FAA, *Blueprint for NAS Modernization* (2002), retrieved from: www.nas-architecture.faa.gov/nas5/downloads/blueprint_2002.pdf.

[37] Retrieved from www.nas-architecture.faa.gov/nas5/faq/WhatIsNAS5.cfm (visited Aug. 1, 2006).

over the key human and technological resources needed to continue developing plans and systems requirements for NGATS."[38]

NATIONAL AIRSPACE SYSTEM COMPONENTS

While air traffic control facilities and airports are both important pieces of the National Airspace System, the NAS also includes many other significant (particularly technology-based) components. Ground-to-air communications facilities allow voice radio communications between air traffic control facilities and aircraft through the use of radio. Separate facilities are provided for communication between controllers and pilots within route and terminal airspace. Other ground-to-air facilities provide communication between aircraft and flight service station specialists who advise pilots or are advised by pilots regarding their flight plans, weather, and other en route advisories. This combination of equipment, procedures and services provides users with air transportation system access during excellent visual conditions, as well as during a variety of conditions when user visibility is partially or fully obscured, referred to as *instrument conditions*.

Electronic, radio-signal emitting, facilities at airports are intended for the establishment of *instrument approach procedures,* which consist of a series of predetermined maneuvers for the orderly transition of an aircraft under instrument flight conditions from the en route airspace and beginning of the initial approach to a landing. Instrument approaches are categorized as either precision or non-precision. A *precision approach procedure* provides azimuth guidance normally aligned with the runway centerline and glide slope information. A *non-precision approach procedure* contains azimuth guidance only.

Precision instrument approach systems commonly in use are:

- The *Instrument Landing System* [ILS], which normally consists of five basic components: a localizer for azimuth information, a

[38] U.S. GAO, *Air Traffic Control Modernization: Status of the Current Program and Planning for the Next Generation Air Transportation System*, Testimony before the Subcommittee on Aviation, Committee on Transportation, Infrastructure, House of Representatives, GAO-06-653T Report (Jun., 21, 2006).

glide slope for vertical guidance, outer and middle markers for location, and an approach light system;[39]

- The *Microwave Landing System* [MLS], which is a supplementary system for the ILS facilities and operates in the microwave spectrum; and
- The *Precision Approach Radar* [PAR], wherein the air traffic controller issues guidance instructions predicated upon azimuth and glide path radar information, also known as *Ground Controlled Approach* [GCA].

Some of the nation's navigational aid equipment is obsolete, costly to maintain, and is being replaced with modern solid-state devices. The present airport electronic approach and landing system is the instrument landing system. Precision approach ILS provides both azimuth and elevation guidance to a runway from a ground facility. Marker beacons, lighting systems, *Distance Measuring Equipment* [DME], and compass locators are associated with ILS to enable equipped aircraft to fly along the approach path to the runway. There are still many vacuum tube-type ILSs in operation. Nevertheless, because of long-standing difficulties in trying to implement the MLS as a replacement, the ILS remains the standard landing system in the United States. The MLS "supplements" the ILS.[40]

Non-precision instrument approach facilities are:

- *Area Navigation* [RNAV] is a method of navigation permitting aircraft operations on any desired course within the coverage of station-referenced signals, normally derived from the Very High Frequency Omni-Directional [VOR] network;
- *Aerial Surveillance Radar* [ASR], wherein the air traffic controller issues azimuth instructions and recommended altitudes on final approach. The ASR, like the PAR, may also be called GCA;
- *Localizer* [LOC] provides azimuth guidance along a final approach course. It is used as part of an ILS, or alone in a

---

[39] The ILS has five categories: I, II, IIIa, IIIb, and IIIc. The lowest authorized ILS minimums, with all required ground and airborne system components operative range from a Decision Height [DH] of 200 feet and *Runway Visual Range* [RVR] of 2,400 for Category I; to no DH and no RVR limitations (*i.e.*, zero ceiling and zero visibility) for Category IIIc; *see Aeronautical Information Manual* [AIM] (1999).

[40] *Id.*

non-precision procedure. Known as a *Localizer Directional Aid* [LDA] when not aligned with the runway;

- *Non-Directional Beacon* [NDB] is a radio beacon transmitting non-directional signals whereby the pilot of an aircraft equipped with direction finding equipment can determine the aircraft' s bearing to or from the radio beacon and can "home" on, or track to or from the station;
- *Simplified Direction Facility* [SDF] is similar to the localizer portion of an ILS except that the SDF course may be wider than the localizer, resulting in a lower degree of accuracy;
- *Very High Frequency Omn-Directional Range* is a ground-based electronic navigation aid transmitting very high frequency navigation signals, 360 degrees in azimuth, oriented from magnetic north]; and
- *Distance Measuring Equipment* is used to measure, in nautical miles, the slant range distance of an aircraft from the DME navigational aid.

Military aircraft use the *Ultra-High Frequency* [UHF] *Tactical Air Navigation* [TACAN] system for both azimuth and distance guidance. The VOR and VOR/TACAN have been located to provide optimum guidance in heavily traveled areas. Airways are comprised of line segments between these navigational facilities.

The disadvantage of airway navigation is the lack of flexibility in routing. Aircraft equipped with RNAV can select direct routes within coverage of the ground stations. However, area navigation is limited in the present system due to limitations of the air traffic system's ability to handle aircraft flying outside the route structure. The NDB is a lower-cost, lower-capability alternative to the VOR station and is used where there is no VOR coverage. The NDBs are used for en route guidance and fixes as well as being part of landing systems.

The Department of Defense satellite-based *Global Positioning System* [GPS] is a satellite-based radio navigation aid, which provides a worldwide common grid reference system based on the earth-fixed coordinate system. The GPS provides two levels of service. *Standard Positioning Service* [SPS] provides horizontal positioning accuracy from within 100 to 300 meters. *Precise Positioning Service* [PPS] is more accurate.

LORAN is a supplementary service, which uses a network of land-based radio transmitters developed to provide an accurate system for LOng RAnge Navigation. The current system, LORAN-C, was the third version of four developed since World War II. Initially developed for maritime users, LORAN is now incorporated into the NAS for supplemental en route and non-precision approach operations. The current LORAN-C model accuracy is within 0.25 nautical miles, and with increased predictable accuracy aviation use of LORAN-C became popular, with more than 100,000 installations in aircraft by 1990. However, only about 10% of these installations are approved for IFR use during en route and terminal operations. Manufacturers of LORAN-C airborne equipment sought and were granted FAA certification of receiver models to be used for IFR non-precision instrument approach operations. However, with the advent of GPS, the use of LORAN for non-precision approaches is being cancelled.[41]

The air route procedure is used to maintain a safe and controlled airspace using existing technology. Aircraft equipped for area navigation can fly direct efficient paths, but this application is limited due to the present air traffic control system's problems with handling aircraft outside the air route structure. Low-cost, low-precision NDBs are used where the air traffic demand for an air route is not great enough to justify the more expensive VOR.

The Federal Aviation Administration is responsible for most of the Nation's en route and terminal navigation facilities. The en route system is almost wholly a function of the FAA, but state and/or local governments often elect to provide facilities in addition to the federal facilities in the terminal environment.

RADAR SYSTEMS AND DATA LINK

Two types of radar, search radar and beacon radar (sometimes known as secondary radar) currently provide surveillance of the airspace. They are generally located at the same site. *Search radar* relies only on signals reflected from aircraft. The *Air Traffic Control Radar Beacon System* [ATCRBS] receives reply signals transmitted from airborne electronic equipment called transponders. On aircraft equipped with (Mode C) altitude encoders, the transponder automatically transmits the aircraft's altitude as well. The ATCRBS is pres-

[41] FAA, *Aeronautical Information Manual* (2006).

ently the main source of surveillance information used for air traffic control.

There are, additionally, two types of search radar systems. The en route air traffic control system relies principally on *Long-Range Radar* [LRR], while the terminal air traffic control system uses shorter-range *Airport Surveillance Radar* [ASR]. Both types of radar are used extensively for flight monitoring. Some existing radar systems are tube type and obsolete, while others are solid state. Because search radar was designed for aircraft surveillance, it is presently capable of giving only limited information on weather and precipitation.

Airport Surface Detection Equipment [ASDE] is another type of radar used by tower controllers to detect aircraft and vehicles on runways and taxiways during low-visibility conditions. Although not radar, the *Direction Finder* [DF] is used to locate lost aircraft and for other emergencies. The aircraft's bearing is determined on the ground by using radio transmissions from the aircraft. The guidance information is then transmitted to the aircraft on a voice channel. The majority of the current DF systems are tube type and are located at flight service stations.

National Airspace System ground-to-air facility improvements required through the near term are proceeding forward. The main focus has been the replacement of obsolete vacuum-tube equipment with solid state. New and more capable systems such as (ATCRBS) Mode Select [Mode S] with data link, and a new generation of weather radar will also be placed into operation. Data link will enable the redirection of routine ATC-pilot communications thorough the transponder, thereby relieving radio congestion.

Replacement of maintenance-intensive equipment with solid-state systems and establishment of additional systems to provide coverage where it is required and not available today will further improve the NAS. In addition to VOR and DME equipment, which will be the primary navigational system, the Global Positioning System will gain popularity as a supplemental navigational system. This imposes rather stringent requirements upon the FAA to monitor the GPS satellites for accuracy and service availability. GPS monitors will provide the FAA the data required to certify the system and maintain the appropriate margin of safety.

The NAVAID eligibility criteria used by the FAA are based primarily on air traffic demand since volume of traffic is a tangible and measurable indication of the need for air navigation facilities and air traffic control services. They do not, however, cover all situations which may arise and are not used as a sole determination in denying a location, a terminal facility or service for which there is a demonstrated operational or air traffic control requirement. Other factors which must also be considered are the general terrain features in the vicinity of the airport, the nature of the operations, and the frequency of severe climatological phenomena such as heavy snow, ice, fog, or other local conditions that can adversely affect the safety of aircraft operations. Similarly, air traffic volume by itself does not always constitute a requirement for an air navigation facility.

Installation of visual aids may continue to be emphasized. Although lighting aids are not NAVAIDS in the strict sense, they do complement the (electronic) radio approach systems and can be instrumental in reducing the landing minima. Lighting aids not only complement the instrument approach system but they are equally beneficial to the pilot operating in visual conditions. Visual approach slope indicators are valuable in establishing a visual angle of approach when operating over water, flat terrain and other deceptive areas. They aid in keeping the aircraft on the proper glide path when transitioning from instruments in the cockpit to visual conditions on final approach, and can also aid in assuring the proper angle of descent where noise abatement procedures are necessary.

Runway End Identification Lights, mentioned earlier in this chapter, are valuable in picking out the runway from other surrounding lights and for establishing proper alignment on final approach course. The REILs may also serve as quasi-approach lighting systems where there is no ALS. The ALS is almost exclusively used to complement the ILS. The ALS is required to establish the landing minima normally expected with an ILS approach.

TERMINAL AIR TRAFFIC CONTROL

The most conspicuous area of federal influence on the airport is in air traffic control.[42] A misconception by many in the general public is that the airport authority employs air traffic controllers. However, with some exceptions (e.g., contract towers), air traffic controllers are

[42] The authors wish to thank Katherine Wallmueller for her substantive contributions to this chapter, and specifically, throughout this section.

federal employees working for the FAA. Technically, the FAA is a tenant on the airport, albeit at customarily very nominal, even token rental rates on the land to comply with minimal requirements of legal consideration under contract law. For example a rental rate of $1.00 per year may suffice. Actual facilities such as air traffic control towers, as well as other operational support facilities including navigational and approach lighting aids are usually installed, maintained and paid for by the U.S. government.

In the early 1930s, the possibility of two aircraft arriving simultaneously over the same point and at the same altitude seemed remote, and there was no single agency serving as a unified control for airborne traffic. Rather, en route locations of (airline) company planes were monitored by each of the individual air carriers, and on their own separate and distinct radio frequencies. In the mid 1930s there were three such airline-operated centers—one in Newark, one in Cleveland, and one in Chicago. In 1936, these three centers, which constituted the skeletal beginnings of an air traffic control system, were turned over to the Bureau of Air Commerce. In 1986 the FAA celebrated the 50th anniversary of the Air Traffic Control Service based on its acquisition of the airline radio stations in 1936.[43]

The *Civil Aeronautics Administration* [CAA], forerunner of the FAA, began operating air traffic control towers, *per se*, in 1941. Control towers became, and still are, necessary to assure efficient and expeditious movement of air traffic in terminal areas having substantial volumes of air traffic. As aircraft operations increase, a level is reached at which control tower services are required. The minimum level can vary depending on the type, mix, and complexity of operations.

Air traffic control towers are sometimes located atop another building, or they are free standing structures located strategically to afford unobstructed views of the "air movement areas," meaning the active runways and taxiways. Local ATC facilities control aircraft on the air movement areas and in the nearby airspace.

The *control tower cab* is a glass-enclosed structure housing the air traffic controllers and supporting equipment. The tower cab is used for visual control of aircraft. At radar terminal facilities, the radar displays are normally located in a radar room separated from the tower

---

[43] Paul Stephen Dempsey & Laurence E. Gesell, *Air Transportation, Foundations for the 21st Century* 444 (1997).

cab, as discussed below. At locations where the radar displays are in the tower cab they are referred to as a *TRACAB*.

Control towers are classified as either approach or non-approach facilities. *Non-approach towers* issue clearances for aircraft to land or take-off, relay IFR clearances, and otherwise issue advisories and clearances based on visual observations. Approach control towers may or may not be equipped with radar. These facilities issue IFR clearances directly to pilots and provide procedural and/or radar separation between IFR traffic. *Bright Radar Indicator Tower Equipment* [BRITE] is a supplemental radar display and alphanumeric system. It is designed for use in the bright-light environment of the ATCT cab.

The three major types of facilities used in terminal air traffic control are the,

- *Airport Traffic Control Tower* [ATCT];
- *Terminal Radar Approach Control* [TRACON]; and
- *Terminal Radar Approach Control in the Tower Cab* [TRACAB].

Located on airports, the ATCTs are the most common, as well as the most visible of the ATC facilities. Their purpose is to separate aircraft, sequence aircraft in the traffic pattern, expedite arrivals and departures, separate aircraft on the landing areas, and provide clearance and weather information to pilots.

The second most common facilities are the TRACONs, controlling airspace around airports having moderate-to-high-density traffic. TRACON controllers separate and sequence both arriving and departing flights. Normally, each TRACON is associated with one ATCT and located within the same building. However, a TRACON may be remotely located and may serve more than one ATCT. The third type, the TRACAB, serves a function similar to that of the TRACON. TRACABs are located within tower cabs at airports with lower-density traffic.

The current terminal ATC system consists of more than 500 Air Traffic Control Terminal Facilities [ATCTF], of which 218 are contract towers. The remaining 267 are FAA operated ATCTs which consist of 112 tower-only facilities, seven ATCT/TRACABs, 148 ATCT/TRACONs, and 19 TRACON-only facilities. In addition, as of

2005, there were 22 *Air Route Traffic Control Centers* [ARTCC] facilities (regional control facilities) in operation in the U.S.[44]

All terminal air traffic control facilities are equipped with ground-to-air radio communications; have telephone communications to air route traffic control centers and flight service stations; and have a variety of equipment for observing, detecting, receiving, and displaying weather information. Radios and telephones are major tools of the terminal controller.

At nearly all terminal ATC facilities, computers are used to relieve the controller of routine tasks and give the controller information that assists in maintaining aircraft identification. In addition, information such as altitude and aircraft speed, which must be provided by the pilot in a non-automated environment, is displayed on the controllers' screen by means of alphanumeric symbology.

The least sophisticated of the terminal automation systems is a non-programmable, numeric beacon decoder system. That is, information from an aircraft's transponder is decoded and displayed for the controller in numeric form along with normal radar data. It provides aircraft transponder code and altitude information for suitably equipped aircraft.

The *Automated Radar Terminal System II* [ARTS II] is a programmable, non-tracking data processing system. Although it does not provide tracking, the ARTS II does provide meaningful information such as aircraft identification and altitude information to the controller. ARTS II derives its information only from the aircraft's transponder. ARTS II may be interfaced with the ARTCC computer for the automatic exchange of information. ARTS II was initially installed in 70 small facilities beginning in 1974. By 1987, it was in a total of 128 sites and had been upgraded to ARTS IIA. This included a processor upgrade, ARTS IIIA-based tracking of targets, Minimum Safe Altitude Warning [MSAW], and Conflict Alert [CA]. Common ARTS IIE replaced the ARTS IIA systems by 2000.

The *Automated Radar Terminal System III* [ARTS III] is a programmable beacon tracking system. Based on information supplied by the aircraft's transponder, ARTS III detects, tracks, and predicts the position of aircraft in the terminal area. The information is displayed on the controller's radarscope by means of com-

---

[44] FAA, ATCT–TRACON Information Card,r, retrieved from http://www.faa.gov/ats/atb/Sectors/Facilities/ATCT-TRACON_InfoCard_05152003.pdf.

puter-generated symbols and alphanumeric characters, along with normal radar data. The computer screen displays aircraft identification, altitude, ground speed, and flight plan data. In addition, ARTS III is interfaced with the ARTCC computer allowing the computers to exchange information.[45]

At present, ARTS III is installed at medium-to-high activity terminal facilities. Currently, there are two unique features provided by ARTS III through software. The first is *Minimum Safe Altitude Warning*. MSAW is a function of the ARTS III computer that will alert the controller when a tracked aircraft with altitude reporting capability is below or is predicted by the computer to go below a predetermined minimum safe altitude. The second unique feature is *conflict alert.* Terminal conflict alert is a computer function, which alerts the controller to situations where aircraft are in close proximity and possibly require attention or action.[46]

The ARTS IIIA is an enhancement of the existing ARTS III designed to meet increasing traffic demands in terminal airspace. The ARTS IIIA is capable of tracking search radar targets as well as transponder-equipped aircraft. Thus, all aircraft that are within radar coverage of ARTS IIIA are candidates for computer processing. Like ARTS III, ARTS IIIA interfaces with the ARTCC's computer and contains the unique software features of MSAW and conflict alert. ARTS IIIE was developed in the early 1990s to meet the growing demands of New York TRACON. It incorporates a larger automation system utilizing a Local Area Network [LAN] for system communications. The system supports 2800 simultaneous tracks and 58 displays. ARTS IIIE has been installed at other high density facilities to replace ARTS IIIA. [47]

In the terminal area, the FAA operates several different versions of older computers, which have limited memory and processing speed. Three of these are differing versions of monochrome which are not only hard to view, but are both difficult and expensive to maintain. The *Standardized Terminal Automation Replacement System* [STARS] is a joint Department of Defense and FAA procurement program that was undertaken to replace the aging ARTS.

---

[45] FAA, *Common ARTS History* (last revised Aug. 5, 2003), retrieved from http://www.faa.gov/ats/atb/Sectors/Automation/CommonArts/history.htm.
[46] *Id.*
[47] *Id.*

STARS technology features a sizable color monitor that displays both flight information and aircraft positioning to air traffic controllers. Close-in viewing is the optimal range, which makes it ideal for controllers. The system has backup capabilities, enabling the system to continue to operate despite a component failure. In addition, in the even of a total system failure, STARS has an emergency service level through which controller can get critical information.[48]

The STARS initiative has not progressed without controversy. Controllers originally complained about the lack of user involvement in the product selection. In response, users were engaged and product requirements were increased, incurring cost overruns and causing the project to fall behind in schedule. Still, the FAA projects that more than 170 TRACONs in the U.S. will be updated with STARS technology by 2008.[49]

FLIGHT SERVICES AND WEATHER SYSTEMS

Flight Service Stations [FSS] are air traffic service facilities, which provide pilot briefing and en route communications with VFR flights, assist lost aircraft and aircraft with emergencies, relay air traffic control clearances, process *Notices to Airmen* [NOTAMs], disseminate weather information, handle flight plans, and operate the national weather typewriter system. The origin of the FSS goes back to 1920 when the Post Office Department established aeronautical stations to support the airmail routes. These original stations kept bonfires going to assist airmail pilots with navigation. They also accumulated weather information and served as radiotelegraph stations.

In the late 1920s, the aeronautical stations were incorporated into the Department of Commerce's Lighthouse Division, the forerunner of the Civil Aeronautics Administration. The flight service station of today evolved from a bonfire attendant, to a radio range attendant, to a relay station for ground-to-air communications, to its present status as the primary communications aid for VFR operations, preflight briefings, aviation weather, and search and rescue responsibilities.

---

[48] FAA, *STARS History* (revised Jan. 17, 2003), retrieved from http://www.faa.gov/ats/atb/Sectors/Automation/STARS/index.htm.

[49] GAO, *National Airspace System: Better Cost Data Could Improve FAA's Management of the Standard Terminal Automated Replacement System* (Jan. 2003), retrieved from http://www.gao.gov/new.items/d03343.pdf.

Like air traffic control towers, flight service stations are tenants of the airport owner. At some airports, and in addition to their normal duties, flight service station attendants will take weather observations, issue airport advisories, administer airman examinations, and coordinate with U.S. Customs and Immigration.

In 1981, there were more than 300 FAA flight service stations offering a broad range of pre-flight and in-flight services especially aimed at general aviation (or non-airline pilots). However, the number of operating flight service stations has been systematically reduced through automation.

The trend of modern FSS facilities is toward streamlining the operation through automation and self-service pilot briefing terminals. Automation and improvement of flight service stations and related aviation weather systems are being made to allow consolidation of facilities and reduction of operating costs.

Flight Service Stations were consolidated in the mid-1980s and implementation of automated flight service was begun. Enhancements to the flight service automation system and the central weather processor project have evolved into a modernized system of flight services and weather services. The *Integrated Terminal Weather System* [ITWS] receives data from FAA and *National Weather Service* [NWS] sensors as well as airborne aircraft flying within a few miles of airports. The ITWS uses weather products such as the *Terminal Doppler Weather Radar* [TDWR], *Next Generation Weather Radar* [NEXRAD], and upgraded Airport Surveillance Radar Model 9. Other inputs are received from the National Lightning Detection Network, NWS Rapid Update Cycle data, and the Meteorological Data Collection and Reporting System. The ITWS also uses the Low Level Wind Shear Alert System, the Automated Weather Observing System (AWOS), and the Automated Surface Observing System [ASOS].[50]

These systems provide efficient and low-cost surface observation data critical to airport operations. The AWOS and ASOS provide around-the-clock, real-time weather information at airports without adequate weather observation personnel. The basic system (AWOS I) consists of weather sensors to measure wind speed and direction, temperature, dew point, pressure, precipitation, visibility, cloud

---

[50] FAA, *Integrated Terminal Weather System*, http://www.faa.gov/ats/atb/sectors/Automation/TIPDS/ITWS (visited Apr. 25, 2007).

height and density altitude. In addition to the basic system there are two upgrades. AWOS II adds a visibility sensor, and AWOS III adds a cloud height reader. In addition to the AWOS data, ASOS provides information on the degree and type of precipitation (i.e., rain, sleet, snow, freezing rain, etc.) received in the observation area.

The instruments for AWOS/ASOS systems are located close to the touchdown zone(s), and data are processed in a computer at the observation site. Reports are updated every 60 seconds and relayed by computer-generated voice transmission over ground-to-air VOR or discrete frequency, by telephone lines, and via digital interfaces with weather communication networks. The information may be accessed from the cockpit, by telephone, or directly from the computer.

CONTROL TOWER ESTABLISHMENT

The FAA has authority to establish control towers or discontinue control tower services when activity levels and safety considerations merit such action. Criteria for establishing a control tower was initially developed and published in 1951. Prior to 1983, the establishment of new control tower facilities was a fairly straight-forward process predicated upon a sum of ratios considering the number of air carrier operations, air taxi operations, and the number of itinerant and local general aviation and military operations.

The FAA's *Airway Planning Standard Number One* (FAA Handbook 7031.2B) stated that if the sum of the computed ratio values was equal to or greater than 1.0 the airport was a candidate for a control tower. Tower candidates had to continue to meet the criteria for at least two consecutive annual counts and be projected to meet a third count for budgetary purposes. Tower candidates then competed with other qualified locations for a tower in priority order, and final approval was dependent upon congressional appropriations.

After 1983, new values were assigned based upon *cost/benefit* relationships that effectively resulted in a reduction in the towers required. About this same time, the FAA began private contracting for ATC services at the lowest activity airports as a cost-saving measure.

Current qualifications for becoming a candidate site for establishment or discontinuance of a control tower are published in FAR Part 170, "Establishment and Discontinuance Criteria for Air Traffic Control Services and Navigational Facilities."[51] The following criteria, along with general facility establishment standards, must be met:

- The airport, whether publicly or privately owned, must be open to and available for use by the public; [52]
- The airport must be part of the NPIAS;
- Airport owners/authorities must guarantee that the airport will continue in operation for a long enough period to permit the amortization of the control tower investment;
- The FAA must be furnished appropriate land without cost for construction of the control tower; and
- The airport must meet specified benefit-cost ratio criteria utilizing three consecutive FAA annual counts and projections of future traffic during the expected life of the tower facility.[53]

But even if the airport meets all the criteria listed above, it is *not* guaranteed to receive a control tower. This is where the contract tower program comes in. The FAA, responding to an airport sponsor's request for an air traffic control tower, can elect to establish a contract tower. The FAA can either elect to pay for the service in its entirety, or enter into a cost-sharing agreement with the sponsor, depending on the results of the benefit-cost analysis. Typically, the airport sponsor is responsible for 10% of the cost of construction and operations.

The FAA prescribes benefit-cost-based criteria for establishment and discontinuance of control tower facilities. Criteria and computation methods used in determining eligibility for VFR tower establishment and discontinuance are based on economic analyses of the costs and benefits of a control tower.[54] The criterion compares the

---

[51] *See* AOPA, *Criteria for Establishing Air Traffic Control Towers and the Contract Tower Program*, http://www.aopa.org/whatsnew/air_traffic/actc.html (visited Apr. 23, 2007). The criteria and computation methodology are outlined in the FAA Report FAA-APO-90-7, *Establishment and Discontinuance Criteria for Air Traffic Control Towers.*

[52] "Open to the public," as defined in the Airport and Airway Improvement Act of 1982.

[53] An FAA annual count is a fiscal year or a calendar year activity summary. Where actual traffic counts are unavailable or not recorded, adequately documented FAA estimates of the scheduled and nonscheduled activity may be used.

[54] Site-specific activity forecasts are used to estimate three categories of tower benefits: (1) benefits from prevented collisions between aircraft; (2) benefits from other prevented accidents; and (3) benefits from reduced flying time. Explicit dollar values are assigned to the prevention of fatalities and injuries and time saved. Tower establishment costs include: annual operating costs: staffing, maintenance, equipment, supplies, and leased services; and investment costs: facilities, equipment, and operational start-up.

Present Value of VFR tower Benefits [BPV] at a site with the *Present Value of VFR tower Costs* [CPV] over a 15-year time frame. A location is eligible for a control tower when the benefits derived from operating the tower exceed the installation and operation costs (i.e., the values of benefits exceed costs, or $BPV/CPV \geq 1.00$

OBSTRUCTIONS TO NAVIGABLE AIRSPACE

Navigable airspace is the airspace above minimum altitudes for safe flight, and includes the airspace needed to insure safety in take-off and landing of aircraft. Section 307 of the Federal Aviation Act of 1958 empowers the FAA to formulate policy with respect to the use of navigable airspace, and to insure the safety of aircraft and the efficient utilization of such airspace. The FAA further states,

> *All grants issued after 1946 and most surplus property deeds require that the aerial approaches to airports be free of hazards and that the sponsor prevent the creation of future hazards. Protection of the terminal airspace is not limited to merely acquiring and clearing the land in the Runway Protection Zone [RPZ] The sponsor is required to protect the terminal airspace for instrument and visual operations and procedures.*[55]

Federal Aviation Regulation [FAR] Part 77 was formulated in response to Section 307 of the 1958 Act. Part 77 establishes standards for determining obstructions in navigable airspace.

Part 77 defines the navigable airspace in the vicinity of an airport in terms of *imaginary surfaces* established with relation to the airport and to each runway. The size of each such imaginary surface is based on the category of each runway according to the type of approach available or planned for that runway. The civil airport imaginary surfaces and an associated table are shown in Figures 3.4 and 3.5, "Civil Airport Imaginary Surfaces" and "Part 77 Dimensional Standards."[56]

---

[55] FAA, Airports *Quarterly* (Mar. 30, 2004), Vol. 2, Issue 1, retrieved from http://www.faa.gov/airports_airtraffic/airports/regional_guidance/southwest/ airports_news_events/asw_newsletter/media/ASW-NEWSL-3-04.pdf.
[56] 14 CFR Part 77: *Objects Affecting Navigable Airspace*.

Figure 3.4—CIVIL AIRPORT IMAGINARY SURFACES

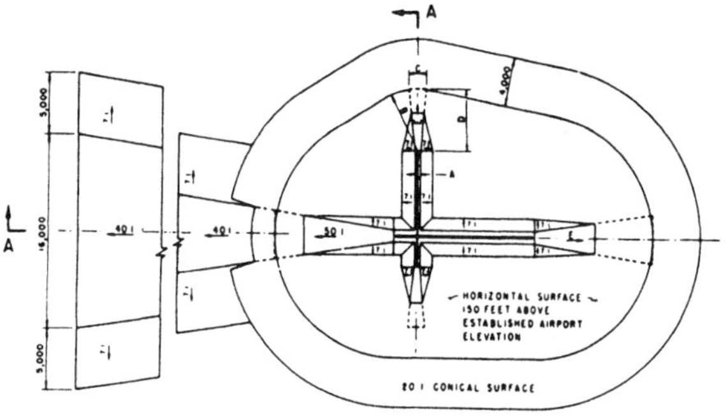

DIM	ITEM	DIMENSIONAL STANDARDS (FEET)					
		VISUAL RUNWAY		NON-PRECISION INSTRUMENT RUNWAY			PRECISION INSTRUMENT RUNWAY
		A	B	A	B		
					C	D	
A	WIDTH OF PRIMARY SURFACE AND APPROACH SURFACE WIDTH AT INNER END	250	500	500	500	1,000	1,000
B	RADIUS OF HORIZONTAL SURFACE	5,000	5,000	5,000	10,000	10,000	10,000
		VISUAL APPROACH		NON-PRECISION INSTRUMENT APPROACH			PRECISION INSTRUMENT APPROACH
		A	B	A	B		
					C	D	
C	APPROACH SURFACE WIDTH AT END	1,250	1,500	2,000	3,500	4,000	16,000
D	APPROACH SURFACE LENGTH	5,000	5,000	5,000	10,000	10,000	*
E	APPROACH SLOPE	20:1	20:1	20:1	34:1	34:1	*

A- UTILITY RUNWAYS
B- RUNWAYS LARGER THAN UTILITY
C- VISIBILITY MINIMUMS GREATER THAN 3/4 MILE
D- VISIBILITY MINIMUMS AS LOW AS 3/4 MILE
* PRECISION INSTRUMENT APPROACH SLOPE IS 50:1 FOR INNER 10,000 FEET AND 40:1 FOR AN ADDITIONAL 40,000 FEET

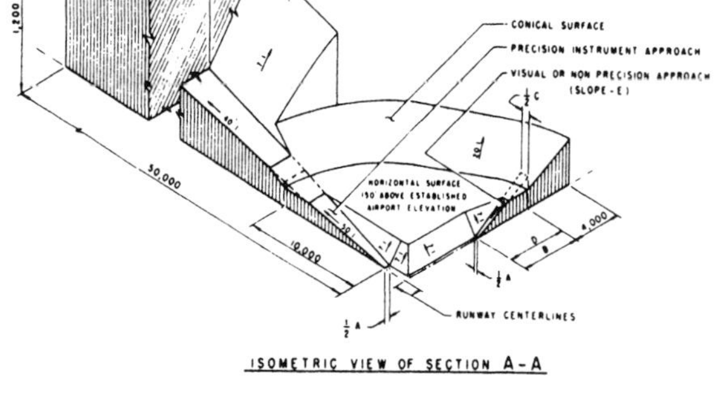

ISOMETRIC VIEW OF SECTION A-A

Source: 14 CFR Part 77: *Objects Affecting Navigable Airspace*.

Figure 3.5—PART 77 DIMENSIONAL STANDARDS

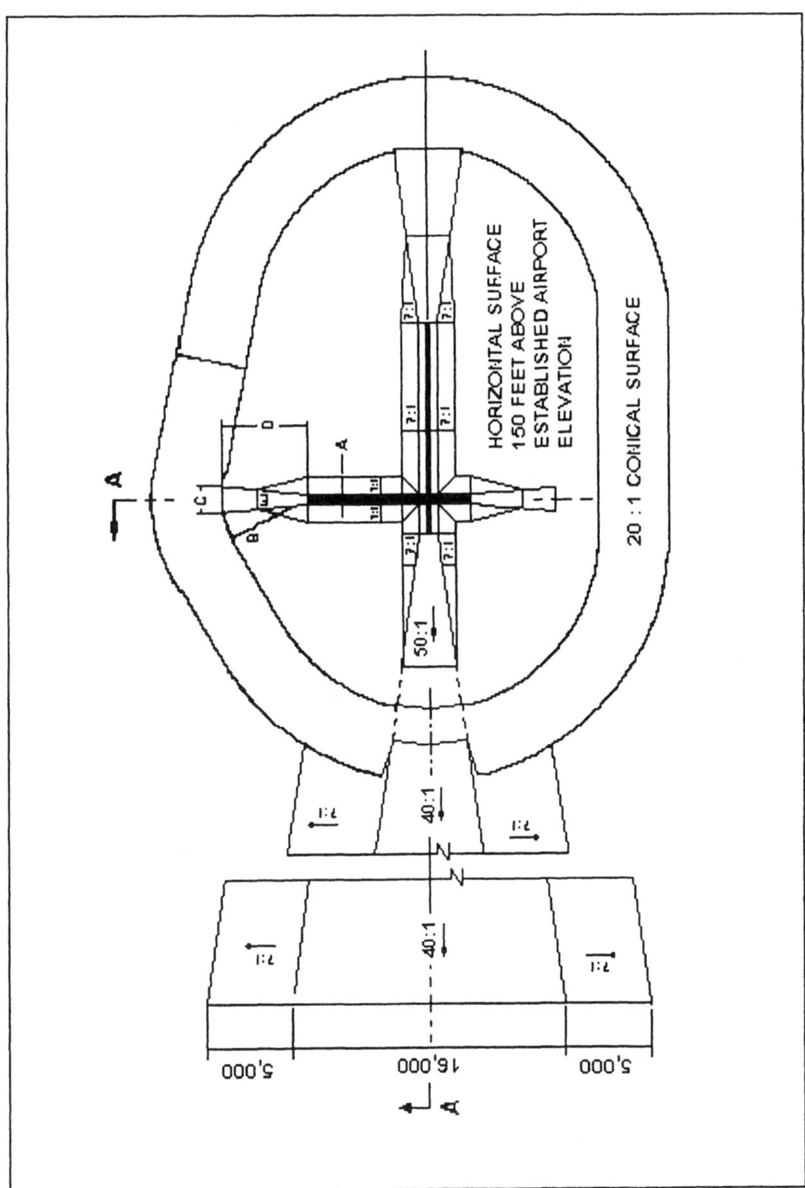

Source: 14 CFR Part 77: *Objects Affecting Navigable Airspace*.

The FAR Part 77 imaginary surfaces consist of:

- The *horizontal surface*, which is a horizontal plane 150 feet above the established airport elevations, the perimeter of which is constructed by swinging arcs of specified radii from the center of each end of the primary surface of each runway and connecting the adjacent arcs by lines tangent to those arcs. The radius of each arc is: 5,000 feet for all runways designated as utility or visual; 10,000 feet for all other runways;
- The *conical surface*, extending outward and upward from the periphery of the horizontal surface at a slope of twenty-to-one (20:1) for a horizontal distance of 4,000 feet;
- *Primary surface*, longitudinally centered on a runway, extending 200 feet beyond the ends of runway with prepared hard surfaces. The width of a primary surface varies from 250 feet for utility runways having only visual approaches to 1,000 feet for precision instrument runways;
- *Approach surface*, longitudinally centered on the extended runway centerline and extending outward and upward from each end of the primary surface. An approach surface is applied to each end of each runway based upon the type of approach available or planned for that runway end; and,
- *Transitional surfaces,* extending outward and upward at right angles to the runway centerline and extended at a slope of seven-to-one (7:1) from the sides of the primary surface and from the sides of the approach surfaces.

Although associated with the airport, the airspace delimited by the imaginary surfaces is not the property of the airport sponsor. The imaginary surfaces merely define the lower limits of airspace through which aircraft may rightfully navigate. The imaginary surfaces do not prohibit development from the ground up unless the airport operating authority owns title to the land, either in fee simple or by easement, or has some other means of controlling and prohibiting intrusion. Part 77 merely describes the standards to be used in determining whether or not structures are obstructions to air navigation. In other words, as presently written, Part 77 has no local enforcement authority. Part 77 requires "public hearings on the potentially hazardous affect on air navigation of proposed airport construction or alterations from any permanent or temporary objective from trees to construction equipment." [57]

Indirect enforcement authority for FAR Part 77 and its associated Advisory Circulars (AC 70-1 and AC 70/7460-1K) does exist,[58] though, for FAA-certificated (air carrier) airports in a "hidden" clause contained within FAR Part 139, which states, "FAA Advisory Circulars contain methods and procedures for the development of Airport Certification Manuals that are acceptable to the Administrator." Air carrier airport operators thus must comply with the established regulatory guidance and associated advisory circulars, or risk losing their certificate to operate.[59]

The FAA has sought to determine other ways in which provisions to control encroachment into the imaginary surfaces might be included. Generally, though, until such time that FAR Part 77 is re-written with enforcement authority the responsibility for controlling land use and development near airports will remain vested with local governments. The horizontal limits of the imaginary surfaces are extensive, and ownership in title or through restrictive easement of the entire area is cost prohibitive and impractical. While there are a number of controls that can be employed to restrict development near the airport,[60] how does an airport sponsor know when someone in the community is considering erecting a structure that might be a hazard to air navigation?

One tool, specifically referenced in FAR Part 77.14, enables communities to receive information on construction or other "alterations" that might create permanent or temporary obstructions: the *Notice of Proposed Construction or Alteration* Process, initiated via the completion of FAA Form 7460-1 and submittal to the FAA as well as the Manager, Air Traffic Division, FAA Regional Office in the project's jurisdiction. Communities permitting construction near an air-

---

[57] FAA, *Airports Quarterly* (Mar. 30, 2004), Vol. 2, Issue 1, retrieved from http://www.faa.gov/airports_airtraffic/airports/regional_guidance/southwest/ airports_news_events/asw_newsletter/media/ASW-NEWSL-3-04.pdf.

[58] FAA Order 7400.2F contains the FAA's Procedures for Handling Airspace Matters, (including change 1, effective date Aug. 3, 2006).

[59] *See* 14 CFR Part 139.201(d), available at http://www.gpoaccess.gov/cfr/index.html.

[60] These various controls are discussed more thoroughly in the forthcoming chapter on Environmental Management; *See also* FAA A/C 150/5190-4, *A Model Zoning Ordinance to Limit Height or Objects Around Airports.*

port can request an executed copy of the 7460-1 form prior to issuing a building permit.[61]

This disclosure form identifies a construction project sponsor, the work schedule, the location of the project, the overall height of any objects being proposed. In addition, Form 7460-1 states the work schedule, duration, and marking, painting or lighting methods to be used to mark potential obstructions. Examples of such obstructions are antenna towers, cranes, buildings, power lines and water tanks.

Obstructions are marked and lighted to warn pilots of their presence during daytime and nighttime conditions. They may be marked and/or lighted in any of the following combinations:[62]

- *Aviation red obstruction lights* that are flashing aviation red beacons and steady burning aviation red lights during nighttime operation. Aviation orange and white paint is used for daytime marking;
- *High intensity white obstruction lights* that are flashing high intensity white lights during daytime with reduced intensity for twilight and nighttime operation. When this type system is used, the marking of structures with red obstruction lights and aviation orange and white paint may be omitted; and/or
- *Dual lighting*, which is a combination of flashing aviation red beacons and steady burning aviation red lights for nighttime operation and flashing high intensity white lights for daytime operation. Aviation orange and white paint may be omitted.

High intensity flashing white lights are used to identify some supporting structures of overhead transmission lines located across rivers, chasms, gorges, and so forth. These lights flash in a (middle, top, lower light) sequence at approximately sixty flashes per minute. The top light is normally installed near the top of the supporting structure, while the lower light indicates the approximate lower portion of the wire span. The lights are beamed towards the companion structure and identify the area of the wire span.

High intensity, flashing white lights are also employed to identify tall structures, such as chimneys and towers, as obstructions to air

[61] *See* FAA AC 70/7460-2K, *Proposed Construction or Alternation of Objects that May Affect the Navigable Airspace* (effective Mar. 1, 2000).
[62] FAA AC 70/7460-1, *Obstruction Marking and Lighting*.

navigation. The lights provide 360-degree coverage about the structure at forty flashes per minute and consist of from one to seven levels of lights depending upon the height of the structure. Where more than one level is used the vertical banks flash simultaneously.

CONTROLLED AIRSPACE

Federal Aviation Regulation Part 77 is the basic document defining airport airspace predicated upon the physical runway development. Other terminal airspace limits are based upon air traffic and airspace procedures. *Controlled airspace* consists of those areas within which some or all aircraft may be subject to ATC. Safety, user needs, and volume of flight operations are some of the factors considered in the designation of controlled airspace. When so designated, the airspace is supported by ground-to-air communications, navigation aids, and air traffic services.

"Controlled airspace" is a generic term that covers the different classifications of airspace (see Figure 3.6, "Airspace Classes"):

- *Class A airspace*—is generally that airspace from 18,000 feet mean sea level up to and including flight level 600;
- *Class B airspace*—is generally that airspace from the surface to 10,000 feet surrounding the busiest airports in terms of IFR operations or passenger enplanements. The configuration of each Class B airspace area is individually tailored and consists of a surface area and two or more layers (some Class B airspace areas resemble upside-down wedding cakes), and is designed to contain all published instrument approach procedures once an aircraft enters the airspace;
- *Class C airspace*—is generally that airspace from the surface to 4,000 feet above the airport elevation surrounding those airports that have an operational control tower, are serviced by a radar approach control, and that have a certain number of IFR operations or passenger enplanements. Although the configuration of each Class C airspace area is individually tailored, the airspace usually consists of a five nautical mile radius core surface area.

Figure 3.6—AIRSPACE CLASSES

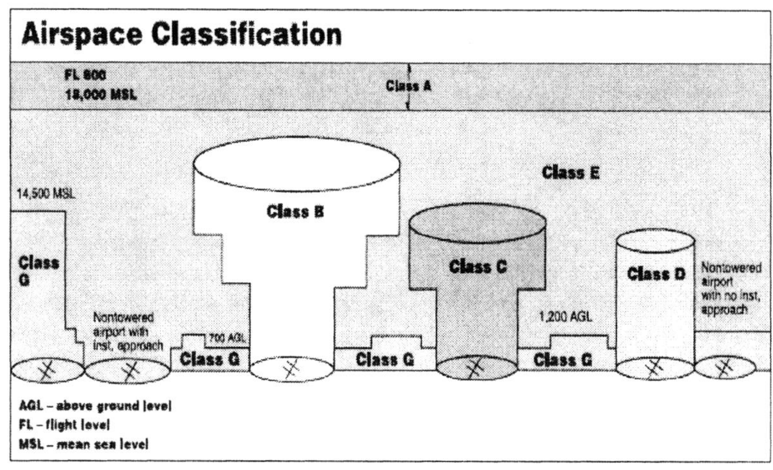

Airspace	Class A	Class B	Class C	Class D	Class E	Class G
Entry Requirements	ATC clearance	ATC clearance	Prior two-way communications	Prior two-way communications	Prior two-way communications*	Prior two-way communications*
Minimum Pilot Qualifications	Instrument Rating	Private or Student certification. Local restrictions apply	Student certificate	Student certificate	Student certificate	Student certificate
Two-Way Radio Communications	Yes	Yes	Yes	Yes	Yes, under IFR flight plan*	Yes*
Special VFR Allowed	No	Yes	Yes	Yes	Yes	N/A
VFR Visibility Minimum	N/A	3 statute miles	3 statute miles	3 statute miles	3 statute miles**	1 statute mile†
VFR Minimum Distance from Clouds	N/A	Clear of clouds	500' below, 1,000' above, 2,000' horizontal	500' below, 1,000' above, 2,000' horizontal	500' below,** 1,000' above, 2,000' horizontal	Clear of clouds†
VFR Aircraft Separation	N/A	All	IFR aircraft	Runway Operations	None	None
Traffic Advisories	Yes	Yes	Yes	Workload permitting	Workload permitting	Workload permitting
Airport Application	N/A	• Radar • Instrument Approaches • Weather • Control Tower • High Density	• Radar • Instrument Approaches • Weather • Control Tower	• Instrument Approaches • Weather • Control Tower	• Instrument Approaches • Weather	• Control Tower

*Only if a temporary tower or control tower is present is the exception.
**Only true below 10,000 feet.
†Only true during day at or below 1,200 feet AGL (see 14 CFR part 91).

Source: FAA Handbook 8083-15-1, retrieved from www. faa.gov.

Class C airspace extends from the surface up to 4,000 feet above the airport elevation, and a ten nautical mile radius shelf area that extends from 1,200 feet to 4,000 feet above airport elevation. The normal outer area radius will be twenty nautical miles, with some variations;

- *Class D airspace*—is generally that airspace from the surface to 2,500 feet above the airport elevation surrounding those airports that have an operational control tower. The configuration of each Class D airspace area is individually tailored and when instrument procedures are published, the airspace will normally be designed to contain the procedures;
- *Class E airspace*—generally, if the airspace is not Class A, Class B, Class C, or Class D, and it is controlled airspace, it is Class E airspace. Types of Class E airspace include: the surface area designated for an airport and containing all instrument procedures, an extension to a surface area, airspace used for transition to/from the terminal or en route environment; en route domestic areas, the Federal airways, and offshore airspace areas; and
- *Class G airspace*—which is uncontrolled, is that portion of the airspace that has not been designated as Class A, Class B, Class C, Class D, or Class E airspace.

Somewhat related to the controlled airspace around airports is the *Terminal Radar Service Area* [TRSA]. Airspace surrounding designated airports wherein air traffic control provides radar vectoring, sequencing, and separation on a full-time basis for all IFR and participating VFR aircraft. Service provided in a TRSA is called "Stage III Service." TRSAs were originally established at selected airports as part of the terminal radar program, then called the *Airport Radar Service Area* [ARSA],[63] which generally coincided with the airspace area now classified as Class C. It consisted of controlled airspace extending upward from the surface or higher to specified altitudes, within which all aircraft were subject to operating rules and pilot and equipment requirements specified in the federal aviation regulations.

Another airspace area associated with some airports is the *Airport Advisory Area*. The airport advisory area is the area within ten statute miles of an airport where a control tower is not operating, but where a

[63] FAA, *Aeronautical Information Manual* (1999).

flight service station is located. At such locations, the FSS provides advisory service to arriving and departing aircraft.

The operational limits of terminal instrument procedures are established using the criteria in the *United States Standard for Terminal Instrument Procedures* [TERPS]. The TERPS handbook is used to formulate, review, approve, and publish procedures for instrument approach and departure of aircraft to and from airports. Instrument approach procedures are based on navigational aids and imaginary locations ("fixes") in the air, and are oriented toward the runway system. They are established to enable aircraft to navigate using on-board radio navigation equipment in conditions of low ceilings and reduced visibility. An instrument approach procedure may have four separate segments between the en route system and landing. They are the:

- *Initial approach* segment;
- *Intermediate approach* segment;
- *Final approach* segment; and
- *Missed approach* segment.

In addition, an area for *circling* the airport under visual conditions is also considered. The approach segments begin and end at designated fixes.

In constructing the procedure, the final approach course is identified first since the landing phase is the most critical of all the segments. When the final approach has been determined, the other segments are blended with it to produce an orderly maneuvering pattern from the en route course to the final approach leg. The final approach leg is the segment in which alignment and descent for landing are accomplished. The final approach segment begins at the *Final Approach Fix* [FAF] and ends at the runway, or *Missed Approach Point* [MAP].[64]

Final approach may be made to a runway for a straight-in landing, or to a point where a circling approach to the airport can be made. A straight-in approach is aligned with the landing runway orientation. All precision approaches and most non-precision approaches are "straight-in." In a "circling" approach the final approach course is not

---

[64] *Id.*

aligned with the landing runway, but instead the aircraft must circle the airport under visual conditions to align the aircraft for landing.

A missed approach procedure is established for each instrument approach in the event the actual approach does not result in visual contact with the airport environment, or for some reason the approach must be aborted. The missed approach is a procedure by which the aircraft may return to the en route system, or to a point where another approach attempt can be made.

TERMINAL AREA

The common perception of a terminal building is that it is a place where passengers are processed for enplanements or deplanements by the airlines. In actuality a "terminal" may be any one of several buildings or facilities on the airport. As defined in the *Airport and Airway Development Act* of 1970, the terminal area is,

> *. . . that area used or intended to be used for such facilities as terminal and cargo buildings, gates, hangars, shops, and other service buildings; automobile parking, airport motels and restaurants, and garages and vehicle service-facilities used in connection with the airport; and entrance and service roads used by the public within the boundaries of the airport.*

The terminal area also includes aircraft aprons and taxiways required for the maneuvering of aircraft, and service equipment in the terminal vicinity. Additionally, all terminal facilities are not necessarily located in one area on the airport. Hangar and cargo areas may be situated at locations remote from the main terminal complex.

There are terminal buildings expressly for air carrier operations. There are terminals designed solely for general aviation. Terminals may be used jointly by air carrier and general aviation operations, or there may be separate facilities on the same airport. At some predominantly general aviation airports there are terminals established for the commuter airlines. Some airports cater to charter airline activities and will have terminals designed just for that purpose.

The air carrier terminal building is essentially the service center for the transit of passengers and cargo between surface vehicles and the air transportation system. Air carrier terminal buildings are complex structures designed primarily around volumes of passengers and relatively standard services available to those passengers. An air carrier terminal may accommodate only a few passengers a day, or may service several thousand per hour. The transfer of cargo is also a major function of the air carrier terminal. Many airports are hubs for significant amounts of air freight and will have separate facilities for the handling of scheduled freight, express and mail cargoes.

By definition, "commuter" air carrier operations are scheduled routes flown by an air taxi service. However, since deregulation of the airlines in 1978, the air transportation industry has undergone a dramatic transformation. What were once the trunk carriers have expanded into the international market, regional carriers moved into the high-density domestic (trunk) markets, and more importantly, commuters moved into the regional markets. Commuters that were once identified with small, twin-engine airplanes are now operating larger aircraft, with seating capacities up to sixty passengers. More recently, they began integrating *Regional Jets* [RJ] into their fleets.

The structure of the market has, indeed, changed, and the "commuters" of yesteryear are the "regionals" of today. They have become an integral part of the common air carrier system. Many commuter companies have formed partnerships (if not merged) with larger (Major) airlines.

With this shift from air taxi type operations to a mode more typical of larger common carriers, there is a requirement for the regional carriers to share common terminals with their larger counterparts. This has become especially so with the introduction of regional jet aircraft. No longer can the "commuters" be segregated with general aviation, away from the air carrier terminal. The commuters and their operations have been incorporated into those of the larger air carriers. Airport terminals must be planned and developed to accomplish the same end.

At some airports where there are no scheduled air carriers, but where the airport is serviced by charter airlines, there may be a passenger terminal established solely for the charter activity. Niagara Falls International Airport in New York State is an example of a charter air carrier airport. The Niagara Falls Airport terminal building contains all of the major facilities found at a scheduled service airline terminal. There are passenger check-in facilities, concessions, restaurant-snack bar, public lobby, departure cargo and passenger holding rooms, and an extensive customs and immigration processing area and baggage claim facility. The terminal provides complete passenger handling and aircraft ground servicing functions for airline charter activities.

Functional allocations of air carrier terminal building space consist of offices, airline operations, ticketing, baggage claim, public lobby, passenger waiting, Very Important Person [VIP] lounges, restrooms, security screening, concessions, restaurants and snack bars and car rental counters. Ancillary to the terminal building are auto rental and limousine parking areas, auto parking lots, airport access roads, passenger gates and the terminal aircraft parking apron. Air carrier building space requirements are usually based upon peak-hour passenger demand, or more precisely, upon the existing and forecast *Typical Peak Hour Passengers* [TPHP].

Unlike airline terminals, which can be designed around volumes of passengers and the relatively standard services made available to those passengers, a general aviation terminal area is predicated upon the level of varying types of services conducted by fixed base operators and other aviation related businesses. General aviation terminals are not restricted to pilot and passenger embarking areas, but rather, include a broad spectrum of general aviation activities including pilot and passenger lounges, briefing or flight planning areas, classrooms for flying schools, offices, restrooms, maintenance areas, salesrooms, and so forth.

Calculating areas required by general aviation business entities is highly subjective and is based upon potential development anticipated by the individual business operators, and at the same time proportionately relating it to forecasts of aircraft operations. General aviation terminal facilities are designed to accommodate airport administration and a variety of special aviation activities. The question of whether a separate general aviation terminal building is to be constructed, or space provided in part of an existing building, such as a hangar, is a local decision. Conversely, air carrier terminal buildings are required wherever there is air carrier service.

The *Air Movement Area* [AMA], consisting of the runways, taxiways, and extended safety areas, plus the aircraft parking aprons, make up the *airside* portion of the airport. That is to say, the airside portion begins at the interface between the outer wall of the terminal building and the aircraft-parking apron. The *landside* portion of the airport begins at the interface wall and extends toward the street-side access. In other words, the landside portion includes the access roads, automobile parking areas, and terminal buildings.[65]

TERMINAL APRON

Planning and development of the air carrier apron is oriented toward individual airline requirements and is designed to accommodate specific types of aircraft. The design of an apron area is a product of four primary considerations:

- Physical characteristics of the aircraft;
- The ground service equipment;
- Spatial relationship of the parked aircraft to the terminal; and
- Safety, security, and operational practices.

The primary objective of the terminal apron is to accommodate the timely interchange of airliners between the terminal and the air movement area. Involved is maximized use of the available ramp space in relationship to the terminal building configuration. The optimal operational situation allows aircraft to taxi in and out of the docking area under their own power. However, the capability to both *power-in* and *power-out* requires substantial maneuvering area, and apron space is often at a premium. The power-out maneuver requires a wide turning radius, and therefore prohibits the use of adjacent apron space for parking other aircraft.

Also of consideration is the jet-blast effect associated with the power-out maneuver. Aircraft blast is a factor in *taxi-in* and *push-out* operations as well, but it is a particular concern where aircraft taxi out under their own power. Aircraft blast has been known to lift pavement into the air, pit or blowout vehicle windshields and windows in buildings. Aircraft parking areas, vehicle parking areas and aircraft ground equipment should be staged outside areas normally affected by aircraft blast, thus increasing the need for more space to allow

[65] Some analysts divide the airport into three areas: airside, terminal, and landside.

power-out maneuvering. Normally, the maximum blast acceptable for ground equipment and personnel is thirty-five miles per hour. Higher limits may be acceptable in the case of blast impact upon buildings, depending upon their structural design. In the most extreme cases, blast fences may be installed to minimize the effects of aircraft jet blast. Slats may be installed in perimeter fencing, or fences may be otherwise constructed of concrete or special materials, to reduce blast beyond the fence line.

Apron space is often so limited that a common practice is to taxi into the docking area, but to push out when departing. In many cases the parking spaces are designed with such close tolerances that the various aircraft are segregated, and specific types of aircraft are limited to parking in predetermined docking areas only. From an airline operational standpoint, the push-out maneuver is far less desirable since it requires extra ground support equipment, and more importantly, because it requires additional personnel to operate the tow vehicles.

Fixed utilities commonly found on the terminal apron include aircraft refueling systems, electrical power, and potable water. Ancillary utilities in the form of ground support equipment are air starters, auxiliary power units, baggage conveyances, aircraft loading ramps and stairs, and passenger loading bridges.

Aircraft fuel can be supplied by either tanker or from underground or "hydrant" refueling systems, or it can be a combination of both. Potable water is normally serviced from the terminal building. And fixed electrical power can be provided through the loading bridge, or may be placed in underground cables leading to a common receptacle.

AIRPORT ACCESS

The term "airport access" has multiple meanings. In the commercial sense, it refers to the availability of terminal airline space to new entrants in the market; i.e., the "access" a new airline may have to renting or otherwise obtaining terminal building counter space, ramp space, and passenger gates. Another meaning, addressed herein, refers to physical facilities providing passenger access to the airport; i.e., roads, walkways, and so forth. "Access" can have yet another meaning. It can mean access free of impediments for the handicapped or those who are otherwise "physically challenged."

The enplaning passenger's sequence begins as the passenger begins his or her journey to the airport and is processed through the terminal building to the awaiting airplane. As the aircraft apron is designed to expeditiously shuttle aircraft in and out, so is the terminal building designed to provide for the expedient flow of passenger traffic. The terminal complex begins with a well-planned access road leading to the terminal building. Airport access is divided into three major segments:

- Access from the *Central Business District* [CBD];
- Access from the *airport perimeter* by roads (and sometimes rapid transit) to the terminal building curbs; and
- Access from *curbside* through the terminal building to awaiting aircraft.

The airport access road and terminal building capacities should be at least equal to the airport' s airside capacity. Otherwise, the landside capacity becomes a bottleneck, which then limits the overall capacity of the airport to process passengers and air traffic. Passenger driveways should be uncomplicated by any other traffic except that associated with loading and unloading of passengers.

Optimally, there should be one-way circulation in the terminal area, and parking and circulation routes should be clearly defined with roadway markings and signs. Often, at larger airports, there are separate driveways for trucks and other vehicles servicing the terminal building and its related facilities. Employee traffic may also be combined with the service access roads.

Curbsides at the front of the terminal building need to be controlled, and should have separate enplaning and deplaning areas for "arrivals" and "departures." Control of curbside space depends upon the arrangement and organization of the curb lanes, building openings, signs and curbside baggage check-in. Curb areas for limousines, taxis, and buses must be designated and separated from private vehicular areas. It is common practice to place taxis in separate queue lanes. Vehicular curb maneuvering lanes are provided for the purpose of loading and unloading passengers, and should be used only for this purpose; not as waiting, or temporary parking spaces. Control of private vehicles requires strict policing, particularly in close proximity to the terminal building. The importance of maintaining control over ground vehicular movement and parking cannot be overemphasized: first, because the smooth orderly flow of traffic depends upon it, and second, because one of the greatest sources of airport revenue is derived from charges assessed in the parking lots.

Auto parking lots are normally segregated into various user areas. Airport tenants, airport employees, and air crews should have parking areas reserved for their use. There should be short-term parking lots for those people who are temporary visitors to the airport either on business or to meet passengers. Surveys have shown that those who use airport parking lots for an average of six hours or less are mainly well-wishers, otherwise known as "meeters and greeters." Short-term parking rates are normally set higher than for long-term parking. Long-term parking lots are primarily used by passengers leaving their cars at the airport while traveling by air.

With regard to access for the physically challenged, airports must be made accessible to all! Not only is there a moral obligation to do so, there is a legal mandate as well. Several pieces of legislation have laid the regulatory foundation for accessibility including the *Architectural Barriers Act* of 1968, the *Rehabilitation Act* of 1973, the *Air Carrier Access Act* of 1986, and the *American with Disabilities* [ADA] Act of 1990.

These acts—to a varying degree and focus—each address accommodation and non-discrimination on the basis of handicap as it applies to "services, programs and activities of public entities" (ADA Title II) such as airports, and "public accommodations provide by private entities" (ADA Title III) such as the concessions that operate within airport terminals. ADA Title 1 also addresses employment discrimination issues.[66]

Airports that receive federal funding must give assurances that they will comply not only with the aforementioned Acts, but also must follow the *Uniform Federal Accessibility Standards*, implemented in 1988. The enforcement agencies monitoring compliance are the Department of Transportation [DOT] for those entities that have received federal funds, and the Department of Justice [DOJ] for

---

[66] *See* extensive historical discussion and related airport guidance in the FAA AC 150/5340-14, *Access to Airports by Individuals with Disabilities* (issued Jun. 30, 1999). For information on airline responsibilities (inside aircraft) *see* 14 CFR Part 382 (Mar. 6, 1990).

public entities, regardless of whether federal assistance was received.[67]

Airports experience three types of barriers: architectural, communication, and awareness.

- *Architectural* barriers, such as stairs, narrow doorways, or restricted toilet facility space, may not be so readily overcome. Some improvements and innovations can only be made in new construction, as it may be too costly to modify existing structures.
- *Communication* barriers present the most difficulties for those with visual or hearing impairments. As awareness problems can be rectified through training, communications problems can be readily corrected by installing telecommunication devices designed to assist the impaired.
- *Awareness*, or more appropriately, lack of problem awareness can be corrected with research and training, for which there are various disability groups who conduct such training and information exchange for airports and communities.

Major changes need to have been anticipated in the original design. Barring major renovation, oftentimes the airport sponsor's hands are tied. However, new construction affords airport operators the opportunity to incorporate provisions for the disabled. Nevertheless, there are some things that can be done short of new construction. Steps that airport operators can take to improve accessibility at their facilities include:

- Use of bigger and better signs indicating the location of handicapped parking lots;
- Enlarging "handicapped" parking spaces to standard wheel chair access size and making sure they are signed properly;
- Reducing close-in parking fees;
- Installing audible buzzer signals at traffic lights;
- Making sure there are adequate curb cuts in the passenger loading areas;

---

[67] *See* 49 CFR Part 27 for DOT enforcement information and 28 CFR Part 36 for DOJ compliance information.

- Providing a grassy area and water for guide dogs;
- Having a dedicated phone information center for the disabled;
- Centrally located *Telecommunications Devices for the Deaf* [TDD], making them readily available, and kept secure from vandalism;
- Positioning television monitors relaying flight information so that they are visible from a wheel chair;
- Installing digital readout flight information screens for the hearing impaired;
- Removing potential obstructions in hallways such as vending machines, which can impede the flow of traffic;
- Eliminating protrusions from walls, and recessing or flush mounting wall items like ashtrays, drinking fountains and telephones;
- Providing a small, secure room with a couch, a chair, and a baby-changing table;
- Providing Braille in elevators and on menus in restaurants; and
- Using large, easy to read signs.[68]

Other considerations include relocating facilities (mirrors, telephones, etc.) to wheelchair height. Color gradients in different hues can be integrated to aid the color blind. Telephones with varying volume for the hearing impaired are helpful. Consideration should be given to the needs of the elderly.[69]

TERMINAL BUILDINGS

Conceptually, there are but two basic terminal building configurations. Terminals are either centralized or decentralized, or a combination of the two. The *centralized* concept has an operating arrangement wherein passenger, ticketing, and baggage facilities of all airlines are located in the same building. The *decentralized*, or "unit" concept of terminal operation has each airline housed in a separate building, each with its own facilities for passengers, visitors, baggage, and cargo. Combined conceptual design occurs where the separate airline's facilities are segregated within the same building such as an elongated

---

[68] Recommendations of Dennis Cannon of the Architectural & Trans. Barriers Compliance Board, and Betsy Buxer of the Phoenix Transit Dept. (about 1991).

[69] Robert O'Connor, *Free Movement for All,* Airport Magazine (Sep./Oct. 1998), at 42-47.

terminal. Another example could have certain airlines such as international carriers in a central terminal, and the domestic carriers in their own separate facilities.

These two basic (centralized or decentralized) operational concepts form the basis for traditional forms of airport terminal layout. From the two basic concepts emanate terminal designs that can take any one of several forms as shown in Figure 3.7, "Terminal Concepts." The traditional airport terminal design forms include four "centralized" concepts and one decentralized concept (unit terminals), as follows:[70]

- *Simple terminals*—which consist of a single common passenger processing area containing public lobby, ticketing areas and having several exits, or gates, leading to the terminal apron. The simple terminal is adaptable to both general aviation and air carrier operations, and is normally a single level structure;
- *Linear terminals*—are an elongation of the simple terminal concept. The simple terminal is repeated in a linear extension to provide additional apron frontage, more gates, and more internal building area. The linear arrangement is also known as the "gate arrival concept." More sophisticated linear terminals often have two-level structures where enplaning passengers enter on one level, and deplaning passengers exist from the other. Both simple and linear configurations lend themselves well to close in public parking and short walking distances to aircraft;
- *Finger terminals*—or "piers," are gate concourses added to simple or linear configurations. More sophisticated forms will have passenger holding rooms along the extensions of the concourses. Normally the main central terminal building is used to process passengers and baggage. The fingers provide enclosed access from the central terminal to aircraft gates. Unless transit systems such as people movers are provided, walking distances through finger terminals are long;

---

[70] FAA AC 5360-13, *Planning and Design Guidelines for Airport Terminal Facilities.* While International Civil Aviation Organization standards generally address international perspectives on airside (runway/taxiway) development, international terminal design standards as well as some airfield standards can be found in the International Air Transport Association [IATA] *Airport Development Reference Manual* (9th ed. Jan. 2004).

Figure 3.7—TERMINAL CONCEPTS

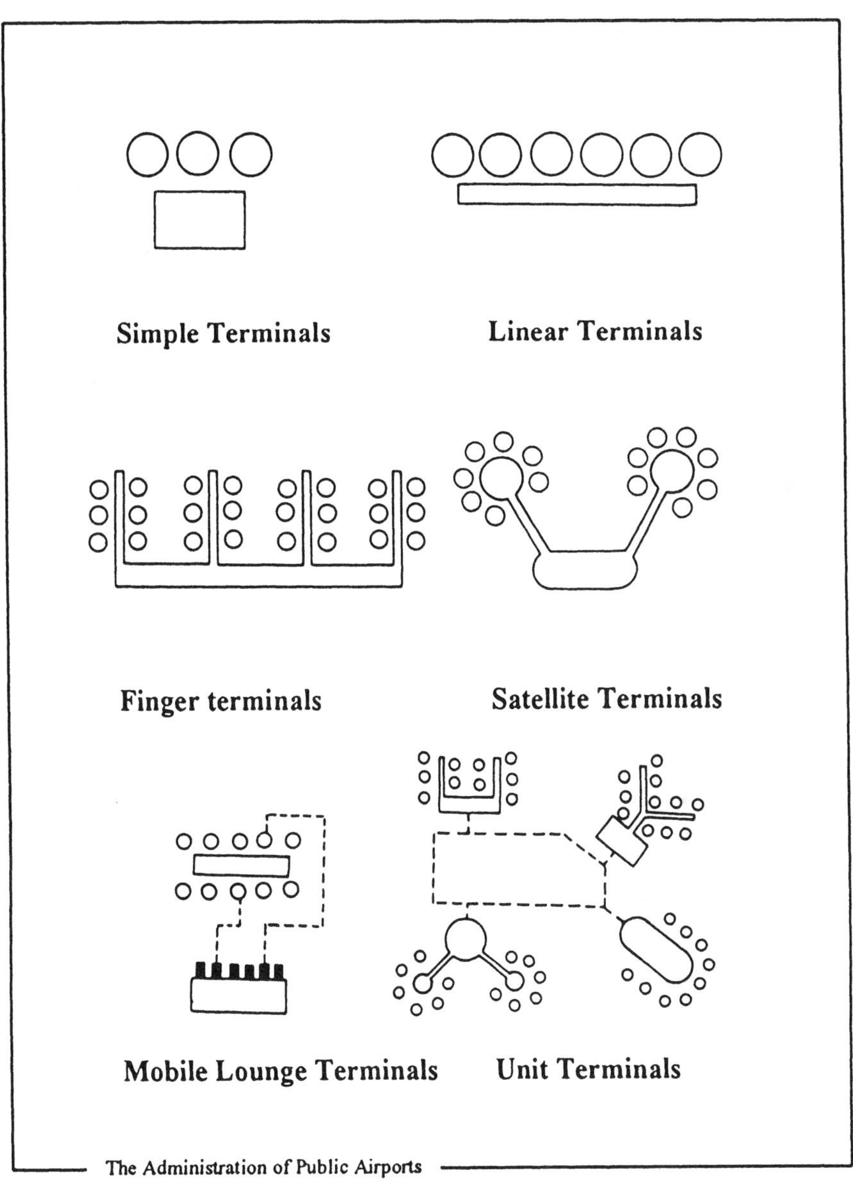

Source: FAA AC 150/5070-6.

- *Satellite terminals*—also known as the "rotunda" concept, feature a centralized terminal for ticketing, baggage handling, and other passenger services. The central terminal is connected by concourses to one or more satellite structures. Holding areas and gates are at the far extensions of the concourses in the (usually) round satellite structures. It is similar to the finger concept except the holding area is a common room at the end of the finger, as opposed to individual holding rooms along the length of the concourse.
- *Transporter or Mobile Lounge*—or "remote aircraft parking concept," has a centralized terminal, but aircraft parking aprons are remotely located. The gates at the terminal building lead to mobile passenger transporters, which carry the passengers to the awaiting aircraft. The walking distances are held to a minimum, while at the same time large volumes of passengers can be processed.
- *Unit terminals*—are a complex of individual (decentralized) airline terminals, interconnected by access and service roads and passenger transit systems. Each terminal provides complete passenger processing and aircraft parking facilities.

Paul Dempsey cites a similar list of concepts as recognized by the International Civil Aviation Organization [ICAO], with the exception that unit terminals are not mentioned. Instead a category referred to as a "hybrid" concept is included, consisting of any combination of at least two of the above concepts.[71] Richard de Neufville and Amedeo Odoni take yet another position in referring to terminals as "passenger buildings," which are generally one of five basic configurations:[72]

- *Finger Piers;*
- *Satellites (with or without finger piers;*
- *Midfield concourses*, described as "major independent passenger buildings—either linear or X-shaped;
- *Linear,* with only one side devoted to aircraft; and/or
- *Transporter*.

[71] Paul Stephen Dempsey, *Airport Planning and Development Handbook: A Global Survey* (2000).
[72] Richard de Neufville & Amedeo Odoni, *Airport Systems: Planning, Design and Management* (2003).

Increasing landside congestion at major airports has resulted in the creation of *off-airport terminals* linked to the airport by bus or rail service. For airports and airlines alike, off-airport terminals can reduce the number of automobiles using the airport access roads and curbsides. For passengers, such terminal facilities can save them parking fares, or may otherwise eliminate the need to find a ride to the airport. Off-airport terminals may also save time by allowing early check-in without having to spend the time to traverse the airport access system. Off-airport terminals are generally of three types: full-service terminals, limited service terminals and access terminals:

- *Full service terminals*—provide all the passenger services usually available at the airport such as ticketing, check-in of passengers and baggage, and baggage claim;
- *Limited service terminals*—provide only some of the above services. The simplest provides passenger ticketing only. By this definition, a travel agency could be classified as a limited service terminal; and
- *Access terminals*—which do not provide any passenger handling services, but may be limited to a sheltered waiting area. They may have amenities such as telephones, rest rooms and vending machines. More elaborate access terminals might also have a coffee shop, newsstand or a car rental agency.

ENPLANING SYSTEMS

Passageways from the terminal building to the aircraft may be as simple as a marked walkway leading from the terminal gate to steps ascending to the airplane. Access from the terminal can be provided by mobile lounges as described above. Or, more popularly, the passageway from terminal to aircraft may be any one of a variety of modern, sophisticated aircraft loading bridges. At smaller airports, and with smaller airliners, folding stairs may be built into the aircraft, which can be extended for passenger loading. Alternatively, a set of ramp stairs may be either motored or manually pushed into place against the airplane for use by enplaning passengers.

Although the mobile lounge concept is an efficient system, it has not been widely put into practice. Dulles International Airport near Washington, D.C., is perhaps the most prominent example of an airport that uses passenger transporters. Most medium-to-large air carrier airports use aircraft loading bridges extensively. The factors going into which type of loading bridge to use include the aircraft and the terminal building design (particularly the sill heights), door centerlines and fueling positions.

The various bridge configurations are predicated upon the operational flexibility required. Some are fixed while others are mobile. There are bridges affixed on pedestals and there are those that swing in a radial motion or extend linearly. More commonly, bridges are attached to terminal sills at about the same height as the aircraft entry level, but there are those that can be elevated to accommodate a mix of aircraft sizes.

UTILITIES

The adequacy of airport utilities is normally an engineering function. If the water system needs to be increased, if more electrical power is required, more telephone lines needed, etc., then the respective utility companies design and install said facilities. However, this seemingly straightforward function is often complicated by financial feasibility or by political considerations. For example, it may be economically impractical to extend city or district water systems to include the airport. A particular local government may be opposed to annexation of an airport (which may belong to a separate government entity) into its municipal services. Or, when additional telephones are needed, there may not be enough paired telephone lines available, and installation of additional lines may be prohibitively expensive. There might be any number of reasons why additional facilities are not available, and the airport may have to install its own.

The airport may drill its own water well, for example. Or, it may utilize septic systems. Larger installations may include water and sewage treatment plants. Electrical generators may be installed for back-up power, or may even be designed as the primary system. Natural gas and fuel oil can be delivered by truck and stored in tanks at individual buildings, or placed in common tanks having a pipeline distribution system within the airport boundaries. In other words, there are alternative ways of obtaining services. But in most cases it is far less expensive to obtain these services from existing utility companies. Sometimes local ordinances may even prohibit the creation of separate utility systems.

The utilities commonly considered are water, sewer, natural gas and telephone service. But also of particular concern on an airport is an adequate *storm drainage system*, an aircraft refueling system, and an auxiliary electrical power system.

STORM DRAINAGE

The nature of an airport entails large expanses of pavement. And, as the airport develops, it becomes ever harder to find ground that is not paved or otherwise covered by buildings. Even so, storm water collects and needs someplace to drain. Storm water needs open ground to percolate and to dissipate below the surface. Otherwise it requires some sort of drainage system to carry it off to other tributaries and common storm relief channels. Because of expansive pavement, and without an adequate drainage system, one of the greatest operational problems encountered by the airport manager is storm water runoff and flooding.

If water does not drain properly, it will back up and pond. Parking lots and aircraft aprons may be washed out, water running across the runway may reduce runway friction and may cause hydroplaning, and buildings may be flooded. Storm drainage may also be an environmental issue.

Common elements of drainage systems are culverts and swales, drainage inlets, cisterns and drainage pipes for the carriage of water, and retention and detention ponds to collect water until it can percolate or be carried off later. Sometimes, lift stations are required to pump the water to a higher level where it can then gravitate.

EMERGENCY POWER

Like a hospital operating room, the airport needs a reserve power system in case of emergency. An area blackout could leave airborne aircraft stranded. Most modern airports have backup generators sufficient to supply minimum electrical requirements to the basic facilities such as the runway and taxiway lighting systems, aircraft aprons, terminal buildings and other areas where passengers are serviced. Normally, the generator(s) are permanently installed, but at smaller airports the generator could be portable and either truck or trailer mounted. In the latter case, the generator would be moved to a critical location where runway and taxiway lighting systems could be plugged into it.

At a bare minimum the airport should at least have some means of illuminating the runway environment, be it with battery powered lights or even flare pots. Mass blackouts have occurred in high-density urban areas such as New York City and widespread area blackouts have happened in California, including the large metropolitan areas. But smaller airports are just as subject to needing emergency lighting capability, as demonstrated by the following story.

An Arizona pilot was in the business of supplying used cars to an auto dealer in Phoenix.[73] The pilot arranged to fly five drivers to Blythe, California, for the purpose of having them return to Phoenix driving five used cars. The pilot arrived at the fixed base operator's location at the Phoenix Sky Harbor Airport at about 6:30 p.m., and told a receptionist that he was flying to Blythe, California, and return. He then signed the FBO's lease agreement for a single-engine airplane. According to court records, he appeared in a hurry, and stated he would file a flight plan in the air. On his preflight inspection, the FBO's chief pilot and managing agent observed the pilot for five or ten minutes.

The pilot and his passengers took off at 7:01 p.m. for a night flight to Blythe. As the plane approached its destination the FAA flight service station reported that the Blythe Airport had sustained a power failure and was without runway lights. Unfortunately, the pilot only learned of the light outage when he called in over nearby Quartzite for landing instructions. In a makeshift attempt to illuminate the runway environment an automobile was placed at the end of the runway with its lights on, but with tragic consequences. Expert testimony indicated that while attempting to land, the pilot became spatially disoriented and crashed. All in the plane perished!

[73] *See Anderson Aviation v. Perez*, 508 P2d 87 (1973).

REFUELING SYSTEMS

In the sense of providing power for use by aircraft, an aviation fuel distribution system may also be considered as a utility. There was a time when the customary manner of refueling an airplane was to manually up-end a can of gasoline and pour the fuel into a funnel through a chamois-skin filter. Obviously, this would not do today. One can only imagine how long it would take to put nearly 50,000 gallons of jet fuel into a Boeing 747 aircraft. The fuel capacities of modern jumbo jets are so great that the use of the largest of tanker trucks is an exercise in inefficiency. One of the world's largest refueling trucks, for example, holds only 18,000 gallons of fuel. To fill a Boeing 747 to its capacity of more than 47,000 gallons would take more than two truckloads.

Where there is a high volume of air carrier activity, and/or where there are large, jet airplanes, refueling operations can be most efficiently accomplished through the use of *hydrants*. With hydrant systems, fuel is delivered under pressure from a common storage area through fixed piping to a hydrant valve, at either the aircraft parking space or to a common location for use in refueling more than one aircraft. At busy air carrier airports, not only are tanker trucks less efficient, but their presence can only add to the ramp congestion already caused by an array of other ground servicing equipment. This is especially true of the oversized fuel trucks. The 18,000-gallon truck referred to above, for example, is seventy feet long!

Even though hydrant systems represent the most efficient method of refueling aircraft, this efficiency is also costly and may not be warranted at other than large, very active air carrier airports. At low activity general aviation airports a small tanker of perhaps one or two thousand gallons' capacity may be the only means of refueling aircraft. The small tanker may even receive its fuel supply from a distributor located off the airport. In most cases, however, airports have at least limited, but permanent fuel storage facilities on airport property.

Fuel storage tanks can be underground or above ground. They can be made of steel, fiberglass, or in some cases rubber. At smaller general aviation fields the fuel storage has commonly been underground. However, due to environmental considerations, above ground installations (or conversions) are becoming more the norm. Typical storage capacity at small airports will consist of one or more tanks of 1,000 to 10,000 gallons' capacity each. The tanks are connected directly to fuel dispensing pumps. Fuel is then either delivered *into-truck*, or the aircraft may taxi directly to the pumps for *into-plane* delivery. Many general aviation airports use a combination of both delivery systems. Another trend seen at general aviation airports is increasing use of automated self-fueling systems operated by credit card. These systems provide the benefit of reduced costs to both buyer and seller as well as up to 24-hour fuel availability. The trade off is a loss of personal service, as well as some loss of control over the refueling operation with consequently higher risk in liability for both the purveyor and the airport.

As airports become larger and more active, their fuel storage capacities and fuel flowage rates increase proportionately to the increased demand. Although there is no established guideline for required fuel storage capacity, three days' supply has become a commonly accepted standard. As more capacity is required, more tankage is added. Tanks are then grouped together in one or more fuel farms. Tanks within the fuel farm are interconnected by pipeline, pumps and a manifold switching assembly to control the flow of petroleum products into, out of, and within the tank farm.

The size and location of fuel farms can vary depending upon the method of delivery. Fuel can be received by pipeline, transport truck, railroad tank car, ship or barge. The common elements that are found in airport fueling systems include:

- *Fuelers*—or tank trucks, which are self-propelled vehicles basically employing a tank to hold fuel and an engine-driven transfer pump;
- *Fuel servicers*—are self propelled vehicles (or towed carts) without a tank, and often without a transfer pump, used to relay fuel from a hydrant to the aircraft;
- *Pits*—or hydrants, are below-grade dispensers for delivery of fuel from a remote source into aircraft;
- *Cabinets*—which may also be called hydrants, are above grade dispensers for delivery of fuel from a remote source into aircraft;
- *Storage tanks*—can be on vehicles or in fixed installations. Above ground tanks are usually prefabricated steel plates that

are bolted together; rubber bladders may also be used above ground, particularly for temporary storage capacity. Underground containers are usually integral steel or fiberglass tanks;

- *Pumps*—are used to transfer fuel through the pipeline when there is insufficient head pressure. Type of fuel, flow rates, and pressure requirements are primary factors in designing pumps;
- *Meters*—are used to measure the volume of fuel delivered;
- *Rate-of-flow controls*—prevent exceeding the design capacity of the system and especially of the filters and meters;
- *Air eliminators*—separate air from the fuel by means of a tank and float arrangement;
- *Filters and filter/separators*—remove solid particulate matter. Filter/Separators also remove free water from the fuel;
- *Discharge hoses*—transfer fuel from dispenser to aircraft and are often stowed on hose reels; and
- *Nozzles*—which are valves attached to the dispensing hose. They may be used to dispense fuel by gravity flow such as over-the-wing refueling, or may make a tight connection for high pressure refueling such as in under-the-wing operations.

Ownership and/or oversight or aircraft or vehicular fueling systems is one of the airport's many important responsibilities. These important systems must be monitored to assure that they meet all environmental standards in fuel storage, dispensing and fuel spill cleanup. Airport can also adapt their fueling systems to be more environmentally conscientious, for example in promoting the availability and use of alternative fuels. Theses issues will be addressed in forthcoming chapters relating to environmental issues and airport operations.

SUMMARY

Described in this chapter are the elements, components and mechanical parts that when assembled form what is called an "Airport." The next chapters describe how airports are planned, designed and built and then organized into systems that collectively create a marketplace of exchange. In this chapter the airport was explored as a physical place. In the next chapter the U.S. system of airports is explored as it has evolved since the early days of flight and into the current National Plan of Integrated Airport Systems.

CHAPTER 4

AIRPORT SYSTEMS

The system as we know it right now cannot handle [the expected] growth. It is not scalable. We are going to have to transform the system and increase capacity. Without modernization, congestion will increase and the entire aviation community will suffer

Marion Blakely, FAA Administrator[1]

INTRODUCTION

In this statement, Marion Blakely of the Federal Aviation Administration [FAA] is acknowledging the sheer enormity of the challenge associated with managing the complex system of airports, airspace and related facilities that comprises the U.S. air transportation system. Over the decades, the government has continually reassessed the status of the industry, re-labeled what it then perceived, and then adjusted the formal regulatory structure, planning tools and funding mechanisms accordingly.

Airports and airlines are in a constant state of mutual flux, in an attempt to keep up with user expectations, unexpected challenges and threats, and the newest technologies needed for its modernization. As the airline industry changes, so too do airports. This cycle and synergy is not a new dance. Since the early part of last century, the government has been describing the system of airports in formal terms,

---

[1] Marion Blakey commenting on U.S. air transportation system capacity, as quoted by Randy Dufault & James Wynbrandt, *FAA Administrator Brings News on Medicals, User Fees*, EAA Air Venture Today (Jul. 27, 2006), retrieved from http://www.airventure.org/2006/thurjuly27/blakey.html.

but as the airline industry has evolved (particularly through deregulation), an informal system of airports evolved as well.

EVOLUTIONARY CONTEXT

A century has passed since the Wright Brothers' successful flight in 1903. As a mode of travel, air transportation has been evolving for almost ninety of those years. And although not necessarily in synchronization with the technical development and changes on-going within air transportation, regulation of the air transport industry by the United States Government has been evolving as well, albeit at a slightly offset pace. Regulatory oversight of air commerce began with the Air Mail Act of 1925, and as revised in 1926, in companionship with the Air Commerce Act of 1926. Regulation in earnest commenced with the Civil Aeronautics Act of 1938. But it was not until 1970 that the government took seriously its regulatory oversight of commercial airports.

In the past several decades, since passage of the *Airport and Airway Development Act* of 1970 with its companion, the *Airport and Airway Revenue Act* of 1970, airport regulation has been designed and redesigned several times to conform to changes happening in the airlines. Particularly since the advent of airline deregulation in 1978, airport regulations have been subjected to significant adaptation. In the maze of regulations surrounding the airline and airport industries, a proliferation of rules, regulations, procedures, and advisory circulars have been adopted. It has been nearly impossible for the government to produce new rules and regulations without incurring some conflict with old ones.

The history of government regulatory oversight is confusing and at times confounding. Terms and expressions have been used, often misused, and at times abused by the industry and its observers. For example, there are several definitions for "large aircraft" versus "small aircraft." "Air transport" connotes an air carrier aircraft, yet some general aviation airports have been designated as "transport" category airports. "Reliever airports" relieve air carrier airports, yet they are a category of general aviation airports. Sometimes antiquated terms such as "commuter" aircraft or airports linger in the vocabulary of those in the industry, but there no longer remain viable definitions or uses for these extinct descriptors.

Unfortunately, many obsolete terms are found in working documents, thus making it necessary for one to understand the etiology of these terms and to comprehend their meaning within the context of the current airport system picture. The purpose of this chapter is to explain these various terms and to describe the evolutionary development of airport systems, particularly in the United States.

THE CURRENT SYSTEM

Between 1992 and 2002, U.S. Passenger-Miles of Travel [PMT] increased 27 percent to a total of 5.0 trillion in 2002, or approximately 17,000 miles annually for every U.S. citizen, regardless of age.[2] Outside of transportation by private automobile—which comprises 87% of U.S. passenger miles traveled—the most popular mode of transportation is by air, comprising 10% of PMT.

Aviation is key to inter-city and international travel. In 2005, more than 745 million passengers traveled in U.S. air carriers, resulting in the completion of 788 billion Revenue Passenger Miles [RPM].[3] In addition, an estimated quarter as many more passengers use general aviation aircraft as a mode of transportation.[4] Reportedly, 25% of all trips in the United States of 100 miles or more are taken by air. Over half of the U.S. adult population has flown on a regular passenger airline, and nearly half of them traveled by air in the past year.

Air transportation is important economically, socially, and politically.[5] And, it is airports that form the terminal ends of the air transport system. Passengers begin and end their journeys at airports. In the United States, most trips begin at one of the airports in the National Plan of Integrated Airport Systems [NPIAS]. Around the globe, international passengers board aircraft at a comparable national airport within their own countries. Airports, like the air transportation system in general, are important to everyone, and not just to the direct consumers of aviation services. Airports are the gateways to commerce and to the modern transportation world.

---

[2] Bureau of Transportation Statistics [BTS], *Transportation Statistics Annual Report* (Nov. 2005), retrieved from: http://www.bts.gov/publications/transportation_statistics_annual_report/2005/html/chapter_02/passenger_miles_of_travel.html.

[3] BTS, *2005 Total Airline System Passenger Traffic Up 4.6 Percent from 2004* (Apr. 2006), retrieved from www.bts.gov.

[4] Based on a rule-of-thumb that 1 in 5 passengers boards a general aviation aircraft.

[5] *See* Robert Kane, *Air Transportation* (12th ed. 1996).

In the U.S., while there are more than 19,000 landing facilities, more than 14,000 of these civil landing areas are not open to the public. While 5,261 of these airports are open to the public, more than 1,800 are excluded from the NPIAS because they do not meet the minimum criteria.[6]

To be added to the NPIAS, an airport must meet the following minimum criteria:[7]

- Have at least 10 locally based aircraft (to be considered to have sufficient activity). Airports included in the NPIAS average 33-based aircraft each, while non-NPIAS airports average one based aircraft each.
- Be within 20 miles of the primary population served (but not closer than 20 miles to nearest NPIAS airport). Of the nearly 290 million citizens living in the US, all but 5.4 million live within 20 miles of a NPIAS airport.

The objective of federal involvement in airport development is to assure a "balanced airport system," providing reasonable access to safe and adequate air transportation and taking into account the diverse needs of different communities with respect to the various segments of aviation. NPIAS should be reasonably accessible to the community and viable to the community's interest. Historically, "reasonable access" has been defined as located within 20 miles of the community concentration, (otherwise stated as approximately 30 minutes' ground travel time). The "viability" of an airport is determined by the likelihood of it being maintained, if not further improved, by the community.[8]

The 3,444 airports included in the NPIAS are public-use airports considered necessary to provide a safe, efficient, and "integrated" system of airports to meet the needs of civil aviation, national defense, and the Postal Service.

---

[6] FAA, Report to Congress; *National Plan of Integrated Airport Systems 2007-2011* (Sep. 29, 2006).

[7] *Id.*

[8] *Id. See also* FAA Order 5090.3C, *Field Formulation of the National Plan of Integrated Airport Systems* (Dec. 4, 2000).

In order to be included in the NPIAS, a public-use airport must be either: [9]

- *Publicly owned or controlled;* or
- *Privately owned* but designated by the FAA as a "*reliever*" airport; or alternatively,
- *Privately owned* but enplane 2,500 or more passengers annually by *scheduled passenger aircraft service.*

NPIAS inclusion entitles these select airports to share an estimated $39.5 billion in total grant funding, as available from 2005 to 2009, for approved infrastructure development, and improving the condition and performance of the airport system in the following categories: safety, capacity, pavement condition, financial performance, surface accessibility, and noise.[10]

As of 2002, 510 of the NPIAS airports were commercial service airports, 278 were classified as reliever airports, while 2,556 were classified as general aviation airports (including heliports and seaplane bases). Most airports in the NPIAS are publicly owned, open for general use and have at least one paved and lighted runway. Added to this are the few significant privately owned airports that are open to the public and also included in the NPIAS.[11]

OVERVIEW OF FEDERAL INVOLVEMENT

Although there is a movement globally to privatize commercial airports, the preponderance of international airports have been sponsored by each nation's central government and/or in partnership with local governments. While U.S. airports are typically locally owned and operated, the federal governmental has played an increasingly important role in the development of American airports. A brief overview of the legislative history pertaining to airport development is presented over the next two pages to provide a preliminary foundation for discussion. Many of the pieces of legislation and associated avia-

---

[9] FAA, Report to Congress, *National Plan of Integrated Airport Systems 2005-2009* (Sep. 30, 2004), retrieved from http//www.faa.gov/arp/planning/npias.
[10] *Id.*
[11] *Id.*

tion classifications systems are discussed more in-depth later in this chapter.

The federal role in airport planning and development emanates from two principal Congressional acts: (1) the Federal Aviation Act of 1958, and (2) the Airport and Airway Development Act of 1970 (as amended or superseded). The 1958 Federal Aviation Act vests with the FAA the responsibility for the orderly development and location of landing areas reasonably necessary for use in air commerce, or in the interests of national defense.[12] In recognition of the importance of the orderly planning and development of civil airports, the Airport and Airway Development Act of 1970 directed the Secretary of Transportation to prepare, publish, and revise as necessary a *National Airport System Plan* [NASP] for the development of public airports in the United States.

To provide the necessary funding in support of the Airport and Airway Development Act of 1970, the Airport and Airway Revenue Act was passed simultaneously. It, too, has been amended to maintain its currency and compatibility with enabling legislation. The result of the Airport and Airway Revenue Act was the establishment of an *Airport and Airway Trust Fund* to be used for partially financing capital improvements at eligible airports. The "Aviation Trust Fund," or "Trust Fund," is derived from *user* taxes imposed upon the aviation community. In other words, taxes on aviation fuels, airline tickets, air cargo, the use of aircraft, and so forth, contribute to the Trust Fund. The Aviation Trust Fund is not comprised of general fund (or income tax) monies, but rather comes directly from aviation system *users*.

The Airport and Airway Development Act was amended in 1976, and was superseded by the Airport and Airway Improvement Act of 1982. The 1982 Act was re-authorized under the Airport and Airway Safety and Capacity Expansion Act of 1987, and again amended by the Aviation Safety and Capacity Expansion Act of 1990.

The Airport and Airway Improvement Act of 1982[13] has been amended many times. Examples of amendments include: the Airport and Airway Safety and Capacity Expansion Act of 1987, the Aviation Safety and Capacity Expansion Act of 1990, the Airport and Airway Safety, Capacity, Noise Improvement, and Intermodal Transportation

---

[12] In 1994 Congress consolidated and re-codified all the aviation laws and statutes into Title 49 of the United States Code.

[13] Public Law 97-248.

Act of 1992. The 1982 Act, as most recently amended by the Wendall H. Ford Aviation Investment and Reform Act for 21st Century (AIR-21), requires the biennial publication of the NPIAS. The 1982 Act also established the Airport Improvement Program [AIP] to distribute funds to NPIAS airports.[14]

The AIP, which is the current airport development grant program, provides financial support to public agencies (and to a few private entities) for the planning and development of public-use airports that are included in the NPIAS. Grant recipients are referred to as the "sponsors." Grant eligible activities, as contained in the authorizing legislation, but are limited to "capital items serving to develop and improve the airport in areas of safety, capacity, and noise compatibility."

The amount of funding varies based on the number of passengers served. Sponsors of larger airports are expected to generate more revenues than smaller airports. Thus, AIP grants typically cover 95% of small, reliever and general aviation airport costs, while they only cover 75% of large and medium "hub" costs (with up to 80% for noise program implement grants). Upon accepting the funds, airport sponsors must carry out the legal and financial obligations or *assurances* associated with the project application and grant agreement. Airport "hub" classifications and assurances are discussed in more detail later in this chapter.

THE ADVENT OF AIR TRANSPORTATION

Geography is an important factor in explaining the evolution of transportation. Landforms, for example, present alternatives to potential development. It is less expensive, say, to go around a mountain than to go over it or through it, or to go around a body of water than to bridge it. The evolution of transportation is explained by these alternatives. It was not until the advent of air transportation that topography became less of an obstacle. But even given the ability of airliners to bridge oceans and cross over high mountains, the air transport system is to some extent still limited by geography. Airport location, for example, is a critical consideration. Additionally, the availability of airspace has become a vital concern. Airport and airspace capacity

[14] FAA, *Overview: What is AIP?* (date unk.), retrieved from http://www.faa.gov/airports_airtraffic/airports/aip/overview/.

constraints threaten to limit air traffic growth in the 21st century, particularly in high-density urban areas.[15]

Technology, too, is important in describing the evolution of transportation. Rail transportation, for example, had to await development of the steel rail. Locomotives awaited the coming of the steam engine. Motor transportation needed the internal combustion engine, the pneumatic tire, and improved highway construction technology. Before there could be transport by air, the horizontal, lateral, and vertical axes of control had to be mastered. Also needed were lightweight engines. And, engines for all modes of travel awaited advances in petroleum technology, and so on.[16] As noted by the late Honorable L. Welch Pogue,

> *Our twentieth century has been filled with spectacular inventions, discoveries, and events. None have been more important to most of us than aviation. It has reduced the world to manageable proportions. It has revolutionized the world in many respects. In this global field, two events, towering above all others, were (1) the Wright Brothers' 1903 First Flight, and (2) the Frank Whittle early pioneering concept of jet power for aircraft propulsion which he later developed and made operational.*[17]

To fly had been man's vision since antiquity. That vision became a reality on December 17, 1903, when on the sands of Kitty Hawk, North Carolina, Orville Wright launched the flying machine he and his brother, Wilbur, had created. The flight covered only 120 feet from start to finish, and lasted only 12 seconds. But the Wright Brothers had done something no one else in history had been able to accomplish. They had produced a man-carrying aircraft, propelled under its own power, and capable of controlling the three axes of

---

[15] Roy J. Sampson, Martin T. Farris, & David L. Schrock, *Domestic Transportation: Practice, Theory, and Policy* 20-21 (6th ed. 1990).

[16] Paul Stephen Dempsey & Laurence E. Gesell, *Air Transportation: Foundations for the 21st Century* 1-10 (1997).

[17] L. Welch Pogue in Paul Stephen Dempsey & Laurence E. Gesell, *Air Transportation: Foundations for the 21st Century* xv (1997).

movement—vertical, horizontal and lateral. But the Wright Brothers were not alone in that quest. With better understanding of the principles of aerodynamics, numerous inventors including Joseph and Etienne Montgolfier, Sir George Cayley, Otto Lillienthal, Alberto Santos-Dumont, Ferdinand von Zeppelin, Octave Chanute, Samuel P. Langley, Glenn Curtiss, and of course the Wright Brothers, had collectively produced a variety of lighter-than-air and heavier-than-air craft before 1910. Improved through the advent of WWI, airplane technology was applied to the commercial carriage of passengers and mail.

Air transportation, as a reliable mode of travel, effectively began on August 25, 1919, with an inaugural flight from London to Paris by Aircraft Transport and Travel, a British company. It was the world's first regularly scheduled international airline flight.[18] In the United States, regularly scheduled passenger service is marked by passage of the Air Commerce Act of 1926. As a companion to the Air Mail Act of 1925 (as amended in 1926), the Air Commerce Act provided funding for development of a rudimentary airway infrastructure and a regulatory framework to support regularly scheduled passenger service by air. The Air Mail Act, on the other hand, was to provide a sufficient revenue stream to make the fledgling air transport industry economically viable through a system of subsidies provided for the carriage of mail.

EARLY AIRPORT DEVELOPMENT

Having invented the airplane, one convention necessary for the development of this new mode of transportation[19] was its infrastructure—the airports and airways. Airport facilities began as "airfields," meaning they were open, cleared fields, suitable for landing and takeoff operations of early biplanes. There were no defined "runways," and ideally aircraft could takeoff or land in any direction that would take advantage of the prevailing winds. The landing and takeoff cy-

---

[18] Arguably, the mayor of St. Petersburg, Fla., became the world's first fare paying passenger by air when, on Jan. 1, 1914, he was carried across Tampa Bay in a Benoist flying boat. However, the St. Petersburg-Tampa air service was primitive, if not experimental, and after only four months the program ended. *See* Paul Stephen Dempsey & Laurence E. Gesell, *Air Transportation: Foundations for the 21st Century* 10 (1997).

[19] The other modes of public transportation are waterway, railway, highway, and pipeline. *See* Paul Stephen Dempsey & Laurence E. Gesell, *Air Transportation: Foundations for the 21st Century* Ch. 1 (1997).

cles have always been the most hazardous of aircraft operations. In the early days of flight, landings were particularly dangerous, and often ended with a "ground loop" as the airplane lost directional control during the transition from flight to ground operations. Rather than having "conventional" landing gear with two main wheels and a steerable tail wheel, early airplanes had only a skid on the tail. Hence, the term "tail dragger" originated. Because these early airplanes could not steer while on the ground, for directional control it was important they be able to land and takeoff as nearly as possible directly into the wind. Ideally, airfields needed to be large enough to provide the option of taking off or landing into any one of 360 degrees.

There were no defined runways on the open fields. Not only were runways undefined, but typically they were not stabilized either. That is to say, they were not paved, but rather, had natural grassy surfaces. The open, unimproved sod fields worked well during fair weather, but during wet, rainy seasons they became unusable. By spreading cinders on the fields they became more useable during inclement weather, and this became an early method used to stabilize the landing/takeoff surface. As larger, more advanced aircraft were produced, extending the takeoff and landing areas beyond the limits of open fields became necessary. The elongated cinder strips were later paved and began to resemble runways as they are recognized today. The first concrete runway in the United States was constructed in Dearborn, Michigan, with others following in Glendale, California, Cheyenne, Wyoming, Louisville, Kentucky, and Cincinnati, Ohio. By the 1930s paved runways were a popular construction.

Promoted by the development of aviation during WWI, commercial air service gained general acceptance between the two world wars. Mass employment of aircraft in carrying troops and cargo during WWII acted as a catalyst to encourage development of air as the principle mode of common carriage for inter-city and international transport of passengers after the war. The introduction of gas turbine engine technology further increased speed and efficiency and solidified the position of air transport as the principal public means of moving passengers and express cargo between cities.

In the development of air transportation following World War I, the Europeans took an early lead. Air transportation advanced more rapidly in Europe as a result of government initiative and ownership. The first daily scheduled international air passenger service in heavier-than-air craft began on August 25, 1919. On that day, Aircraft Transport and Travel first serviced Hounslow in London and Le Bourget in Paris using a de Havilland DH-4. It carried one passenger. Later the same day, a de Havilland DH-16 was used to transport four passengers. Still on the same day, a converted Handley-Page bomber made a proving flight to Paris carrying seven journalists as passengers.[20]

Lufthansa German Airlines [DLH] traces its pedigree back to the inaugural days of flight in the first zeppelins in 1910.[21] Most European carriers were governmentally owned or subsidized, and focused on linking the vast reaches of their empires. Germany developed a number of airlines in Latin America.[22] Routes from Europe to Africa and Asia were developed by Air France, the U.K.'s Imperial Airways, the Netherlands' Royal Dutch Airline [KLM], and Belgium's Sabena.[23]

The fact that air transportation was being promoted faster in Europe than in the United States caused some concern among American politicians and government officials. In response to the early lead in Europe, the U.S. government likewise took initiatives to foster development of air transportation in America.

In the United States, government sponsorship would come through support from the U.S. Postal Service. The early airmail acts, especially the Air Mail Act of 1925, coupled with the Air Commerce Act of 1926, provided the needed revenue to support early airline operations. They created a rudimentary airspace infrastructure and promoted air transportation as an industry.

Operated by the government, scheduled transcontinental air mail service began in the United States in 1920, with airplanes flying mail in the day and handing off their mail to trains at night, shaving 22 hours off the coast-to-coast trip. In 1921, the Army installed rotating beacons between Columbus and Dayton, Ohio, making night flight possible.[24] This reduced the time consumed for transcontinental mail delivery to 24 hours eastbound, and 29 hours westbound (prevailing westerly winds account for the difference), two or three days less than

---

[20] Bill Gunston (ed.), *Chronicle of Aviation* (1992), at 171.
[21] R.E.G. Davies, *Lufthansa: An Airline And Its Aircraft* 2 (1991).
[22] Peter Pletschacher, *Lufthansa Junkers Ju 52: The Story of the Old Aunty Ju* 31-33 (1989).
[23] Newal Taneja, *Introduction to Civil Aviation* 6, 11 (2nd ed. 1989).
[24] R.E.G. Davies, *Airlines of the United States Since 1914* 25 (1972).

by rail.[25] Congress expanded mail subsidies with the Contract Air Mail Act (Kelly Act) of 1925.[26] The first five contracts were issued to National Air Transport (owned by the Curtiss Aeroplane Co.), Varney Air Lines, Western Air Express, Colonial Air Transport, and Robertson Aircraft Corporation[27]

Fourteen domestic airline companies were established in 1926. The pedigree of the nation's major airlines can be traced from these early airmail contract awards. National and Varney would later become important parts of the United Airlines system, which originally was a joint venture between the Boeing Airplane Company and Pratt & Whitney. Western would eventually merge with Transcontinental Air Transport (another subsidiary of Curtiss), to form Transcontinental and Western Air, which under Howard Hughes, would later become Trans World Airlines [TWA]. Robertson would become a part of the Universal Aviation Corporation, which would merge with Southern Air Transport, Colonial and others to form what became American Airlines. Juan Trippe, one of the original partners of Colonial, would form Pan American World Airways in 1927, flying mail between Key West, Florida, and Havana, Cuba. Pitcairn Aviation, another Curtiss subsidiary, would become Eastern Air Transport, predecessor of Eastern Air Lines.[28] U.S. traffic grew from 6,000 passengers in 1926, to 1.5 million in 1938.[29]

Notwithstanding government subsidies and safety regulatory intervention, the airline companies still lacked the means to develop a supporting infrastructure of their own. They had neither the money nor the capital resources needed to develop an en route system of navigation aids, nor did they have the funds necessary to develop the airports at the terminal ends of the system. Air transportation companies not only relied upon mail contracts, but they also depended on government-provided airways.[30] The Federal government actively promoted commercial air transportation through a system of airmail payments to airlines (pursuant to the Air Mail Act of 1925) and through provision of an airway system (in accordance with the Air

[25] Air Transport Association, *The Airline Handbook* 2 (1995).

[26] R.E.G. Davies, *Airlines of the United States Since 1914* 33 (1972).

[27] *Id.* at 39, 56.

[28] Air Transport Association, *The Airline Handbook* 3 (1995).

[29] *See* Paul Stephen Dempsey & Laurence E. Gesell, *Air Transportation: Foundations for the 21st Century* Ch. 2 (1997).

[30] Roy J. Sampson, Martin T. Farris & David Schrock, *Domestic Transportation: Practice, Theory, and Policy* 38 (6th ed. 1990).

Commerce Act of 1926). However, the government was less active in promoting (even prohibited from involvement with) early airport development. State and local governments have historically been more active than the federal government in promoting airports.[31] Hence, the federal government assumed responsibility for developing the airways as well as subsidizing airline operations, but as a matter of precedence, state and local governments assumed responsibility for the airport infrastructure.

The pattern of state and federal responsibility for airport development can be found in Jacksonian notions of state rights. A champion of state rights, Andrew Jackson felt strongly that the federal government ought not to be involved in road development within the sovereign states. During his administration the National Pike was abandoned as a federal project and turned over to the states. Because of Jacksonian Era policy, ownership, maintenance, and administration of roads and highways remained a state and local responsibility. But federal intervention came in 1916 with the Federal Aid Road Act. It set the basic pattern for development of a national highway system where the federal government subsidizes planning and the funding of capital improvements. But the states are responsible for ownership, the actual construction, and maintenance of their highways.[32]

The Federal Aid Road Act set the basic pattern of domestic highway development with the following fundamentals grounded in Jacksonian policy:

- State ownership, construction, and maintenance of highways;
- A formula of 50% matching federal/state funding; and
- State highway departments to coordinate, engineer, designate and contract for highway improvements.[33]

In 1926 the Air Commerce Act directed the Secretary of Commerce "to establish, operate, and maintain . . . all necessary air navigation facilities *except* airports" (emphasis added). Deferring to the states, the Air Commerce Act specifically prohibited the federal gov-

[31] *See* Stephen J. Thompson, *The Airport Improvement Program: Background, and Some Options for Using Federal Financial Resources More Effectively*, a Congressional Research Service report for Congress (Jan. 1994).
[32] Roy J. Sampson, Martin T. Farris & David Schrock, *Domestic Transportation: Practice, Theory, and Policy* 34-36 (6th ed. 1990).
[33] *See generally id.* at 24-26, 233, 674-79.

ernment from constructing or operating airports. But in spite of being prohibited by the Air Commerce Act of 1926, federal funding in airport development began as early as 1933 under several work relief programs promoted by the Roosevelt administration.[34] During the Great Depression, the Federal government participated in construction and improvement of airports as well as highways and other public works in connection with work relief programs and/or in aiding the military. Under two of these programs, the *Development of Landing Areas Program* and the *Development of Civil Landing Areas Program*, 584 airports were developed. From 1933 to 1947, the total federal funds expended under all these programs totaled approximately $912 million.[35]

The Civil Aeronautics Act of 1938 finally removed restrictions against federal involvement and prompted recommendations by the newly formed Civil Aeronautics Authority for Congress to appropriate funds for airport development. The Civil Aeronautics Act of 1938 had authorized:

- A *Civil Aeronautics Authority* to economically regulate air transportation;
- An *Administrator of Aviation* for administrative enforcement; and
- An *Air Safety Board* for aircraft accident investigation.

Under a 1939 amendment, and subsequent government reorganization in 1940, the Act collapsed the functions into two:

- A *Civil Aeronautics Board* [CAB] to economically regulate the industry and investigate accidents; and
- A *Civil Aeronautics Administration* [CAA] to promulgate and enforce safety rules.

In 1944, during Harry Truman's administration, recommendations by the Civil Aeronautics Administration led to enactment of the Federal Airport Act of 1946.

---

[34] Roy J. Sampson, Martin T. Farris & David L. Schrock, *Domestic Transportation: Practice, Theory, and Policy* 263-264 (1990).

[35] *See* FAA, *FAA Airports 50th Anniversary*, a brochure celebrating 50 years of airport development (1996).

FEDERAL AIRPORT ACT

At present, planning and development of publicly owned airports relies heavily upon financial support from the federal government. However, prior to 1946 airports were not only developed, owned and operated by local governments (e.g., cities, counties and special districts or authorities), but, with the exceptions noted above, were financed totally by local government as well. Recognizing that airports are "necessary to the social and economic structure of a community," and also acknowledging the fact that small communities needed assistance in the development of their airports, Congress passed the *Federal Airport Act* of 1946 with the overall intent of developing a *National Airport Plan* [NAP].

Congress initially authorized (general fund) appropriations in an aggregate amount of $500 million over a period of seven years to aid in the development of airports. The 1946 Act was continued through the Eisenhower, Kennedy and Johnson administrations and in 1970 was finally discontinued and replaced with new legislation. Between 1946 and 1970, Congress appropriated a total of nearly $1.2 billion (or an average of $48.5 million per year) under the *Federal Aid to Airports Program* [FAAP] of the 1946 Act.[36] A principle embodied in the Act was that the monies were to be spent only for air operations facilities. In other words, communities were to receive assistance for development of the airside, for building runways, taxiways and so forth, but would not be helped with landside development or with revenue producing facilities such as terminal buildings, hangars and other commercial development.

The airport grant program authorized a 50% federal share coupled with a 50% matching share by the local community (or airport sponsor)—the same (50/50) formula used in early highway construction under the Federal Aid Road Act of 1916. Federal funding in support of the Federal Airport Act came from general tax revenues. Rather than taxing the general public, future airport funding would be generated through a direct tax to users of the air transportation system.

Although the 1946 Act was specifically intended to help the smaller communities, its effect was just the opposite. Large cities, with already active airports, could more readily match the federal

[36] *See* FAA, *FAA Airports 50th Anniversary*, a brochure celebrating 50 years of airport development (1996).

share, either from airport generated revenues or through bonding procedures. For many small communities half of the costs for development was more than they could afford. Moreover, financial assistance for the development of airside facilities was only part of the dilemma. In many cases, the airports were transferred from the military after World War II and, by-and-large, the airside facilities were already in place. Needed most was landside and terminal development, for which no federal assistance was offered.

In 1953, President Eisenhower attempted to have the Act amended to include provisions for federal expenditure on public terminal facilities, but to no avail. The original airport development aid program was extended until 1961. In 1966, the Senate Commerce Committee approved a bill to continue federal funding of airport development until June of 1970, at which time the program expired.

The general stipulations necessary for approval of an airport project under the Federal Aid to Airports Program were as follows. The airport had to:

- Be open for *public use*, without unjust discrimination;
- Be *suitably operated*;
- Have its *aerial approaches* cleared and *protected*;
- Have *land use controls* adjacent to the airport;
- Be *open to the military*;
- Have *standardized accounting records* on all projects; and
- Make its *records available for inspection* by the FAA.

Although the airport grant program has continued through replacement legislation, the basic conditions listed above have been perpetuated in the underlying philosophies of subsequent and on-going airport aid programs. One exception is the availability of federal funding for public terminal buildings, which were eventually made an eligible item in 1976.

It is interesting to note that as one of the provisions of the 1946 Act, the airport sponsor was to implement appropriate *land use controls* to protect the airport from encroachment which might impede its continued operation. Yet, in spite of this provision, stories of severe community encroachment and inappropriate land use around the nation's airports have become classic! This particular stipulation was loosely enforced and, until more recently, had not received the attention that perhaps it should have warranted from the outset. The problem of encroachment has become one of major proportions. The mechanisms by which land uses may be corrected and controlled are discussed more thoroughly in an upcoming chapter on "Environmental Management."

AIRPORT AND AIRWAY DEVELOPMENT ACT

In 1970, Congress determined that the nation's airport and airway system was "inadequate to meet then current and projected growth in aviation," and substantial expansion and improvement of the airport and airway system was required. As a result, Congress enacted the Airport and Airway Development Act of 1970. The hallmark of the 1970 Act was the associated Airport and Airway Revenue Act of 1970, which provided for an airport and airway user tax to pay for improvements to the system. The aviation user taxes, then as now, are deposited directly into the Aviation Trust Fund. These taxes include a tax on airline tickets, on freight waybills, an international departure fee, taxes on each gallon of aviation gasoline and jet fuel, and a tax on tires and tubes. The federal share for grants under the Airport and Airway Development Act of 1970 was raised to as much as 90%, leaving only 10% for the local airport sponsor to match.

Whereas airport development historically had been an *ad hoc*, reactionary process, the Airport and Airway Development Act gave rise to proactive formalized planning and development of individual airports and systems of airports. The Secretary of Transportation was directed to prepare and publish a *National Airport System Plan* or NASP, the immediate forerunner to the current NPIAS. One part of the plan provided for airport planning, and the other part funded facility construction. The planning element was *the Planning Grant Program* [PGP], and the funding mechanism for the actual development of physical facilities was the *Airport Development Aid Program* [ADAP].

The 1970 Act gave authority to incur obligations to make grants for airport development for a period of five years, and in a total amount not to exceed $840 million. This total obligation was amended in 1971 to an aggregate of $1.46 billion for fiscal years 1971 through 1975.[37] This increased the federal dollars available for airport development to substantially more than was made available by the Federal Airport Act of 1946. The Airport and Airway Development Act of 1970, as amended in 1976, expired in 1981. However, the provisions for user taxation under the Airport and Airway Revenue Act of 1970 were continued in follow-on airport improvement legislation.

To aid in the distribution of airport planning and development funds, the federal government has categorized airports according to their perceived needs. By labeling the various categories of airports, the government also gains an element of control.

GOVERNMENT OVERSIGHT

In its regulatory oversight, the government seeks a degree of control over the agencies it regulates. For example, in air transportation the government has sought to control airline corporations as if they were individuals and by labeling the persona of each corporation. What sociologists refer to as "labeling," and the psychologists call "stereotyping," are both forms of control exercised by one person or group over another. The government labels airlines, for example, because it wants, or expects to elicit a certain kind of behavior from a given category of airline companies. It does the same thing with airports. The government categorizes airports and airlines so that it can respond to the industry in bureaucratic form; that is to say, with prepared responses to stereotyped issues. Maslow calls this process "rubricizing."[38] In the process of perceiving the world about us, he says, there is "relatively greater stress on selective, preparatory, organizing, and mobilizing actions."[39]

Stereotyping is an aid in the process of perceiving, and rubricizing is a form of stereotyping and of "recognition or discovery in the world of what we have already put there," and then labeled. Hence, by labeling airports and/or airlines, the government categorizes them into forms that can be more readily controlled through regulation. Thus, the government can dictate the characteristics of a formal organizational structure of airports. But like most formal organizations there is an informal organization as well. The airlines, for example, do not necessarily stand still while the government labels them. In

---

[38] Abraham Maslow, *Motivation and Personality* (1970).
[39] *Id.* at 205-213.

fact, they may not accept a "label" applied to them from the outside at all.

Airlines have corporate cultures that seem to be in a perpetual struggle to redefine themselves and "brand" their desired image. The government might prefer that the airlines remain static, but periodically must assess the status of the airline industry, re-label what it then perceives, and subsequently adjust the regulatory structure. Likewise, airports are in a constant state of flux. As the airline industry changes, so do airports to meet the complex demands of a variety of users while maximizing revenue generating opportunities and self-sustainability. Over the years, categories have been created for both air carriers and airports. In the following pages, several historical categories are included and discussed to illustrate the continual evolution of the industry.

AIR CARRIER CATEGORIES

The process of labeling airlines began with the Civil Aeronautics Act of 1938, out of which came 16 airlines *grandfathered* with *Certificates of Public Convenience and Necessity* [PC&N] issued to them under Section 401(e) of the 1938 Act, the "grandfather clause."[40] Air carriers, which had provided adequate and continuous airmail service from May 14, 1938, to August 22, 1938 (the effective date of the 1938 Act), would receive a permanent PC&N Certificate.[41] Subsequently, the Civil Aeronautics Board categorized the so-called "401 carriers" so that they could be regulated accordingly.

The *domestic trunk carriers* retained the medium and long stage-lengths over the highest density and therefore most profitable routes. The *international and territorial carriers*, otherwise known as "flag" carriers, operated between the United States and foreign countries and/or between the mainland and U.S. territories. Although there was service to and from the mainland, the interiors of U.S. territories like Alaska and Hawaii were not well served by either the trunk or the

[40] Robert M. Kane, *Air Transportation* (12th ed. 1996).

[41] The sixteen *grandfather carriers* originally granted PC&N Certificates under the Civil Aeronautics Act of 1938 (predecessor of the Federal Aviation Act of 1958) were: American Airlines, Braniff Airways, Chicago and Southern Airlines, Continental Airlines, Delta Air Corporation, Eastern Airlines, Inland Airlines, Mid-Continent Airlines, National Airlines, Northeast Airlines, Northwest Airlines, Pennsylvania-Central Airlines, Transcontinental and Western Air, United Airlines, Western Air Express, and Wilmington-Catalina.

international air carriers. This provided an opportunity for start-up airlines and the creation of a new category of air carrier. These airlines became the "*intra-Hawaiian*" and "*intra-Alaskan*" carriers

Pressures were exerted on the CAB for the creation of new categories of service to the mainland as well, even before World War II ended. The war effort put a significant drain on airline assets. The void was filled by issuing temporary PC&N Certificates to additional airlines and subsidizing their operations. These carriers became the *domestic local service airlines*. Because the locals were "feeding" customers to the trunks, they became known as the "feeder" airlines. With concurrence from the trunk carriers, the feeders were granted permanent Certificates of Public Convenience and Necessity in the 1950s. Two other categories emanating out of World War II were the *all cargo carriers* and the *supplemental air carriers*. Yet another category to come along during the post-war era consisted of the *helicopter carriers*. The remaining categories were the *intrastate carriers*, operating solely within the confines of one state, and the *foreign carriers*, registered in another country.[42]

Subsequent to the 1938 Civil Aeronautics Act, simultaneously developed along with economic regulation was safety regulation, promulgated first by the Civil Aeronautics Administration, and later by the Federal Aviation Agency/Administration. Evolving safety regulation was written to be compatible with the economic regulations. For example, Title 14 CFR Part 121, "Certification and operations: domestic, flag, and supplemental air carriers and commercial operators of large aircraft" (i.e., "FAR Part 121") was applicable to PC&N certificated "401 carriers," and Title 14 CFR Part 135, "Air taxi operators and commercial operators," was written around air taxi/commuter (or "Part 298") operations. The FAA maintained its ability to write safety regulations in conformance with counterpart economic regulations until the on-set of airline deregulation in the 1970s, after which time the airlines took on a new "culture" and much confusion began to reign between safety and economic regulation and as to which regulations given airline categories were subject.[43]

Even before official adoption of airline deregulatory policy, the airline companies began slipping outside of their (government-

---

[42] *See* Paul Stephen Dempsey & Laurence E. Gesell, *Air Transportation: Foundations for the 21st Century* Ch. 3 (1997).
[43] *Id.*

defined) categorical bounds. And, the government was helping them do it. The stage was set for dramatic change. The airlines took swift advantage of the opportunity to cross the categorical boundaries. By the early 1980s, all of the economic air carrier categories had been completely jumbled, and the safety regulations were grossly out of sync with their economic counterparts. It became necessary for both the FAA and the CAB to reorder or "re-label" their categorical descriptions of the air transport industry. For purposes of economic regulation subsequent to adoption of the Airline Deregulation Act of 1978, airlines were re-classified as follows, according to gross annual incomes, and whether they are Section 401 versus Part 298 carriers:

- *Majors*, with revenue of more than $1 Billion;
- *Nationals*, $100 Million to $1 Billion;
- *Large Regionals*, $20 Million to $99,999,999;
- *Medium Regionals*, $0 to $19,999,999; and
- *Small Regionals* are distinguished from the other four groups, irrespective of their incomes, by the fact they do not hold Certificates of Public Convenience and Necessity.

Small regionals are distinguished from the other four groups, irrespective of their incomes, by the fact they do not hold Certificates of Public Convenience and Necessity. That is to say, they are "Part 298" rather than "Section 401" carriers. Prior to airline deregulation in 1978, commuter category aircraft were limited to a maximum of thirty passenger seats and/or 7,500 pounds. Commuters (or what came to be known as "small regionals") have been allowed to increase the seating capacity of their aircraft up to 60 passengers. Air carriers having aircraft with more than 60 seats and/or 18,000 pounds internal capacity must apply to the Department of Transportation [DOT][44] for a "401" Certificate, and are classified according to annual revenues as a medium regional or higher.

The term "commuter" was made nearly obsolete by the reclassification of airlines in this group as small regionals. Furthermore, the term was obscured by the trend of mergers aligning smaller carriers with their major counterparts. Effectively, the airline industry has

[44] The DOT assumed all remaining responsibilities for economic regulation of air transportation when the CAB ceased operations on Dec. 31, 1984, per the "Sunset" provision of the Airline Deregulation Act of 1978.

emerged as a conglomerate of major and small regional carriers, and the other categories (i.e., medium regional, large regional, and national) have become less meaningful as industry descriptors.

Demonstrating this point, in its *Enplanement and All Cargo Activity* report in 1993, the FAA described four categories of air transportation of persons or goods for remuneration. In the process, the agency generally recognized the existence of primarily only two tiers of scheduled U.S. common air carriers, the larger "401" operators and the "298" commuter airlines. At the same time the FAA perpetuated use of the term "commuter." Categorized this way, and taking into account air taxi and foreign operators, the four groups of commercial operators are:

- *Large Certificated Route Air Carrier* [LCRAC];
- *Commuter and Small Certificated Air Carrier* [CAC];
- *Air Taxi/Commercial Operator* [ATCO]; and
- *Foreign Flag Air Carrier* [FFC].[45]

Just as the federal government has categorized airlines, it has likewise organized airports for at least two purposes. One, airports are organized to regulate them and thereby achieve a level of control over airports that are otherwise within the jurisdiction of the states. And two, airports are organized as an aid in apportioning appropriate levels of funding to various airport service levels.

AIRPORT CLASSIFICATIONS

The FAA refers to the kind of airport development that responds to the critical type of aircraft (rather than actual passenger and aircraft volumes insofar as meeting certain minimum requirements) as "fundamental airport development" However, the fundamental criteria used to describe the various categories of airports have changed, even though the FAA continues to use the same terminology. Since some of these terms have been in use for nearly thirty years, there exists the likelihood of confusing their alternate meanings. Various interpretations are presented in this text for historical background, for compari-

[45] *See* Paul Stephen Dempsey & Laurence E. Gesell, *Air Transportation: Foundations for the 21st Century* Ch. 3 (1997).

son, and to avoid confusion. Unfortunately, trying to learn the terms and there nuances is itself an exercise in confusion, if not frustration.

Because the original airport design classifications are generally associated with the National Airport System Plan era (i.e., the 1970s and early 1980s), they will be referred to herein as "NASP Airport Categories." In the NASP era, fundamental development of airports meant that airports were grouped into two generalized categories: they were either *air carrier* or *general aviation*. "General aviation" is all aviation other than military and commercial "common carriage" using "large aircraft."[46] It includes business, instructional, and personal flying, and commercial flying such as agricultural spraying and aerial photography.

General aviation airports were then sub-categorized by aircraft size. Airports designed for small aircraft were grouped into the *utility* category. A "small" airplane (for purposes of categorizing general aviation airports) is defined as having a maximum certificated takeoff weight of 12,500 pounds (5,700 kilograms) or less. Airports serving large aircraft were categorized as "transport" airports. In this case, a "large" airplane is defined as having a maximum certified takeoff weight of more than 12,500 pounds. Although "transport" has the general connotation of "air carrier transport," in the NASP era criteria, transport referred to general aviation, not air carrier, airports.

Air carrier airports were designed around *transport* (meaning "large") aircraft as well, but they were categorized as "Air Carrier," and designed around specific aircraft. Required were separate libraries of critical aircraft operating manuals to aid in their design.

---

[46] "Large aircraft" has had several meanings. Its original (1938) meaning referred to an aircraft having more than 12,500 pounds maximum gross weight. PC&N certificates were initially issued to carriers operating aircraft weighing more than 12,500 pounds. This rule still applies to type certification for pilots. 12,500 pounds is also used as a cut off in airport design. But for PC&N certification the rule was changed in the interim to aircraft with more than 30 seats and/or 7,500 pounds internal payload capacity. Thus, prior to airline deregulation in 1978 commuter category aircraft were limited to a maximum of 30 passenger seats and/or 7,500 pounds. The "30-seat" rule still applies to airport certification. Airports serving air carriers operating aircraft with more than 30 seats must be certified under FAR Part 139. The current ruling for PC&N purposes is that air carriers having aircraft with more than 60 seats and/or 18,000 pounds internal capacity must apply to the DOT for a PC&N ("401") certificate.

COMMERCIAL AIRPORT ROLES/CATEGORIES

With the advent of the Airline Deregulation Act of 1978 and subsequent shifts in market priorities, the airport categories became less clearly defined. Within the context of the old National Airport System Plan, or NASP, and the fundamental development concept, there were several ways in which air carrier airports had been grouped historically: by *operational role*, by *functional role*, and by *statistical area*. The latter method, based upon area demographics, is still used in urban planning as well as airport planning. For historical background all three methods are described below.

Regardless of the classification system that has been used, at some air carrier airports general aviation activity may far surpass the demand imposed by air carrier service. Nevertheless, the critical air carrier aircraft—because of its more demanding facility requirements—has in the past determined the design configuration of the airport.

OPERATIONAL ROLES

Operational roles helped to define airports by the critical aircraft serving the facility—as determined by aircraft size, capacity and average length of haul. Aircraft were grouped into three areas (see Table 4.1, "Airline Service Operational Roles"). The largest and fastest aircraft, and those usually used on long distance markets were in Group A. Mid-size and smaller jet transports, wide-bodied jet transports, and those aircraft normally associated with domestic trunk and regional routes were in Group B.[47]

FUNCTIONAL ROLE

The *functional role* airport classification system consisted of distinct sub-systems of airports, differentiated by level of public service (demonstrated by the number of enplaned passengers). Each sub-system was further classified into three levels of operational density (defined as aircraft operations). The functional system roles were primary, secondary, and feeder (see Table 4.2, "Airport Functional Classifications").

---

[47] It might be noted that the era wherein this system of categories was popular (*i.e.*, the 1970s) is reflected in the types of aircraft listed, many of which are no longer in common service.

Table 4.1—AIRLINE SERVICE OPERATIONAL ROLES

Aircraft Group	*Typical Aircraft*	*Length of Haul* (in miles)
A	B-747 DC-8 B-707	Code 1 - over 1,500 Code 2 - 500 to 1,500 Code 3 - 0 to 500
B	B-727/737 DC-9 L-1011	Code 1 - over 1,500 Code 2 - 500 to 1,500 Code 3 - 0 to 500
C	F-27 F-227 YS-11	Code 1 - N/A Code 2 - 500 to 1,500 Code 3 - 0 to 500

Source: *National Airport System Plan* (1972).

Table 4.2—AIRPORT FUNCTIONAL CLASSIFICATIONS

Category	*Annual Enplaned Passengers*	*Annual Aircraft Operations*
Primary	Over 1,000,000	
High Density		Over 350,000
Medium Density		250,000-350,000
Low Density		Under 250,000
Secondary	50,000-1,000,000	
High Density		Over 250,000
Medium Density		100,000-250,000
Feeder	Under 50,000	
High Density		Over 100,000
Medium Density		20,000-100,000
Low Density		Under 20,000

Source: *National Airport Classification System*, FAA AC 150/5090-2 (Jun. 1971).

The *Primary* system identified airports with the highest level of public service. Airports included in this category were in most cases, located in the largest metropolitan areas. The primary airports served high to medium flows of inter-city and international traffic. These airports were capable of handling the largest and most sophisticated aircraft in the air carrier and general aviation fleets. Airports in the primary system would have normally had parallel runways capable of independent operations in instrument meteorological conditions, would have an *Air Traffic Control* [ATC] tower, and would have a terminal building with a capacity for high-density passenger flow.

The *Secondary* system identified the next highest level of public service airports. As the name implies it consisted of those airports having a secondary, or lesser public service role than that of the primary system. Secondary airports would typically have a single, full-length runway and shorter parallel runways (excluding crosswind runways) as necessary to provide adequate capacity. The airports in this category had medium to low-density passenger flow terminal facilities. The air traffic activity levels would normally have been sufficient to justify an ATC tower.

The *Feeder* system category identified the lowest public service level of the NASP. Although the feeder airports had lower volumes of traffic, the majority of air carriers that served airports in the United States were in this category. Most of the feeder airports had as much or more general aviation traffic as they did air carrier activity. Airport configurations for this category normally had a single primary runway (excluding crosswind runways) and had low density passenger terminals. They may or may not have qualified for an ATC tower.

STATISTICAL AREA

The air carrier airport categories determined by population densities are known as the *Hub System*. The "hub system" should not be confused with the "hub-and spoke" network that is explained below. The air traffic "hub," as the term is used here, is a *Standard Metropolitan Statistical Area* [SMSA] requiring airline service. A hub represents a demographic area rather than a specific airport; therefore, within it a hub may have more than one air carrier airport. The hubs fall into four classes as determined by each community's percentage of the total annual air carrier enplaned passengers in the United States: large, medium, small, and non-hub.

The hub system remains a convenient method for ranking airports by their relative importance, rather than by any absolute measurement of activity. Hub classifications remain fairly stable. As long as a hub's passenger enplanements grow at the national average, its designation will not change. If an airport continues with above-average growth it might move from a small to a medium hub or from a medium hub to a large hub, and so forth. Conversely, continued slow growth might cause a large hub to be reclassified as a medium hub, as its share of the national enplanements decreases. Comparisons between hub categories and the current airport classifications are found in (Table 4.3, "Airport Categories").

AIRPORT AND AIRWAY DEVELOPMENT ACT AMENDMENTS

In June of 1975 the funding authorization for the 1970 Airport and Airway Development Act expired, and it was not until August 1976, that the original Act was continued, although modified slightly. Due to the lapse in amending legislation, the 1976 Amendment was received by the aviation industry as if it were a new Act. Where the original Act merely defined an airport as "any area of land or water which is used, or intended for use, for the landing and take-off of aircraft," the amended Act went on to sub-categorize airports into:

- *Air Carrier* airports were existing public airports that were regularly served or expected to be served by a CAB certificated air carrier;
- *Commuter Service* airports were air carrier airports served by one or more carriers operating under exemption from Section 401(a) of the Federal Aviation Act of 1958 (i.e., not CAB certificated);
- *General Aviation* airports were public airports which were not air carrier airports; and *Reliever* airports were general aviation airports having the primary function of relieving congestion at an air carrier airport by diverting general aviation traffic from the air carrier airport.

Table 4.3—AIRPORT CATEGORIES

<table>
<tr><th colspan="2">Airport Classifications</th><th>Hub Type: Percentage of Annual Passenger Boardings</th><th>Common Name</th></tr>
<tr><td rowspan="5">Commercial Service:
Publicly owned airports that have at least 2,500 passenger boardings each calendar year and receive scheduled passenger service
§47102(7)</td><td rowspan="4">Primary:
Have more than 10,000 passenger boardings each year
§47102(11)</td><td>Large:
1% or more</td><td>Large Hub</td></tr>
<tr><td>Medium:
At least 0.25%,
but less than 1%</td><td>Medium Hub</td></tr>
<tr><td>Small:
At least 0.05%,
but less than 0.25%</td><td>Small Hub</td></tr>
<tr><td>Nonhub:
More than 10,000.
but less than 0.05%</td><td>Nonhub Primary</td></tr>
<tr><td>Nonprimary</td><td>Nonhub:
At least 2,500
and no more than 10,000</td><td>Nonprimary Commercial Service</td></tr>
<tr><td colspan="2">Nonprimary
(Except Commercial Service)</td><td>Not Applicable</td><td>Reliever
§47102(18)</td></tr>
</table>

Source: FAA, retrieved from http://www.faa.gov/airports_airtraffic/airports/planning_capacity/passenger_allcargo_stats/categories/#table.

Commuter Service Airports, as they appeared in the NASP, were the result of the 1976 amendments to the Airport and Airway Development Act of 1970. Legislation in 1976 recognized the growing importance of the commuter service airlines and sought to provide them with some measure of improved financial assistance by creating a special funding category for commuter airports.

Though not served by carriers holding Certificates of Public Convenience and Necessity, a Commuter Service Airport was one regularly served by a commuter airline, and one that had no less than 2,500 annual enplaned passengers to be so classified. A commuter airline was CAB exempted from the Board's classification of certificated air carriers (under Part 298 of Title 14 of the Code of Federal Regulations).

The airline deregulatory movement, especially as it was implemented by then CAB Chairman Alfred Kahn, allowed many of the (former) commuter airlines to apply for, and be granted, dormant routes held by the certificated air carriers. It was a period of seeming regulatory confusion, and technically the assignment of CAB certified routes should have reclassified the commuter airlines as Local Service or, "Regional" carriers. However, the CAB and the FAA still regarded these transformed carriers as "Commuter Airlines," and airports served only by commuters were then categorized as "Commuterports."

The commuter airlines generally served smaller markets in which there was insufficient traffic to profitably support certificated local (or regional) carrier operations. While commuter airlines were identified with small communities, they also operated in and out of the largest of airports as well. As noted above, the term "commuter" seems outmoded. However, some people still refer to an airport served by small regional air carriers as a "commuter airport."

Unlike the term "commuter" the category known as "reliever" is still appropriate today within its original meaning. Then as now reliever airports are *general aviation* airports in metropolitan areas that reduce air carrier airport congestion by providing facilities and service suitable for attracting and diverting general aviation activity away from the major air carrier airports. Reliever airports are generally associated with large and medium hubs, but the term is often broadly used for any airport which relieves the congestion pressure at another (air carrier) airport. It is a misuse of the term, however, to apply it to a secondary air carrier airport as the media are oft inclined to do.

Back to the Airport and Airway Development Act amendments of 1976, there were a number of miscellaneous provisions added to the original 1970 Act. Among them were funds made available for snow removal equipment, funds for use in the purchase of noise suppression facilities and acquisition of land near airports to ensure compatible use within the noise levels of an airport, and available funding of air carrier airport terminal buildings. The Department of Transportation was authorized funding for research and development from the Aviation Trust Fund. Such funds had previously come from the general revenue fund. Additionally, in response to demands from the states, a demonstration project was initiated to allow four states to manage their own general aviation airport project funds. The latter was a pilot project to determine the feasibility of allowing the individual states more latitude in managing their own airport development projects.

The amended act directed the Secretary of Transportation to conduct a study of airports in areas where land requirements, local taxes, or a low revenue-return-per-acre may close such airports. This provision gave recognition to the fact that many publicly used, but privately owned airports were in danger of being closed, and steps would have to be taken to retain these critically needed airports for public use.

The Airport and Airway Development Act of 1970, as amended in 1976, expired September 30, 1980, extended from the original expiration date in June. As had occurred in 1975, the ADAP legislation expired without new legislation to replace it. On September 30, 1980, the Airport Development Aid Program and its attendant user tax collections expired amidst sharp disagreement between the House and Senate bills for replacement legislation. The result was termination of federally assisted airport development, and reversion to pre-ADAP user tax levels.[48] Since members of Congress could not agree, a simple one-year ADAP extension was adopted in 1981 until a more comprehensive continuation of the airport development program could be agreed upon.

---

[48] Aviation Gasoline [AVGAS] tax dropped from $.07 to $.04 per gal.; the aircraft use tax was ended; the airline passenger ticket tax was reduced from 8% to 5%; and the airfreight waybill tax was terminated.

AIRPORT AND AIRWAY IMPROVEMENT ACT

The Planning Grant Program and the Airport Development Aid Program of the original 1970 Act, as well as the Airport and Airway Development Act of 1970 itself, ultimately expired on September 30, 1981. During the active eleven-year span of the 1970 Act, 8,809 grants totaling $4.5 billion were approved for airport planning and development. The replacement program, known as the *Airport Improvement Program* [AIP], was promulgated by the *Airport and Airway Improvement Act* of 1982.[49] The declared purpose of the Airport and Airway Improvement Act is,

> *. . . the continuation of airport and airway improvement programs and more effective management and utilization of the Nation's airport and airway system are required to meet the current and projected growth of aviation and the requirements of interstate commerce, the Postal Service, and the national defense.*[50]

The Airport and Airway Improvement Act continues to provide funding for airport planning and development, but under a single, consolidated Airport Improvement Program or AIP rather than the separate PGP and ADAP programs of the previous legislation. As with the 1970 Act, funding is provided through the Aviation Trust Fund with the same (approximately) "90/10" federal/local matching share of costs, respectively.[51]

As with the 1970 Act, funding then as now is provided through the Airport and Airway Trust Fund. Taxes, or user fees, are collected from the various segments of the aviation community and placed in the trust fund. The 1982 Act allowed for the first time the use of federal funds to up-grade public-use private airports. To qualify, privately owned airports have to "relieve" air traffic congestion at commercial airports. Austin Executive Airpark, a reliever for Robert Mueller Municipal Airport in Austin, Texas, became the first private

---

[49] Title V of the *Tax Equity and Fiscal Responsibility Act* of 1982, Public Law 97-248 (Sep. 3, 1982).

[50] 49 U.S.C. App. § 2201 (1993).

[51] The federal/local share may vary depending upon federal funding levels authorized for specific projects.

airport to receive federal grant money, and was provided $1.5 million for runway improvements, lighting and acquisition of land for a clear zone. Like any airport, the money was not granted without *assurances*. In exchange for the $1.5 million grant, the airpark's owners had to make a commitment to keep the field open and available to the public for a stipulated period of time.

The 1982 Act also authorized funds for noise abatement and land-use compatibility planning pursuant to the Aviation Safety and Noise Abatement Act of 1979.[52] Noise abatement and land-use planning projects are conducted in accordance with Federal Aviation Regulation Part 150, and are commonly referred to as "FAR Part 150 (Noise) Studies."

The Airport Improvement Program—established by the Airport and Airway Improvement Act of 1982 (Public Law 97-248)—has been amended many times. More recently, the AIP was amended in passage of the Aviation Investment and Reform Act for 21st Century, commonly referred to as "AIR-21." AIP funds continue to be drawn from the Airport and Airway Trust fund which is supported by fuel taxes, user fees, and other revenue sources. The latest airport categories include: commercial service, primary, cargo service, reliever, and general aviation airports.

- *Commercial Service Airports* are publicly owned airports, which enplane 2,500 or more passengers annually and receive scheduled service;
- *Primary Airports* are commercial service airports, which enplane more than 10,000 passengers annually (non Primary Commercial Service Airports have at least 2,500 and no more than 10,000 passenger boardings annually);
- *Cargo Service Airports* are served by aircraft "providing air transportation of only cargo with a total annual landed weight of more than 100 million pounds (an airport can be both a cargo service and a commercial service airport);
- *Reliever Airports* are publicly or privately owned airports designated by the FAA as having the function of relieving congestion at a commercial service airport and providing more general aviation access to the overall community; and

[52] Public Law 96-193.

- *General Aviation Airports*, the largest grouping of airports, are all those that were not defined above. [53]

RELIEVER AIRPORTS

Although the definition has been modified through the years, essentially the purpose of a *reliever airport* is to allow greater capacity to one or more air carrier airports while simultaneously serving as a general aviation airport in a large metropolitan area.[54] The need for reliever airports was first recognized in the National Airport Plan or NAP for fiscal years 1962-1966, which stated that, "[l]arge and medium hubs need separate general aviation airports because of the very great air carrier activity and the excessive time it takes to get to an air carrier airport from many parts of a metropolitan area."[55]

Officially recognized in the National Airport System Plan, or NASP, designation as a reliever airport required conformance to a fairly strict definition like that in place in 1992, requiring a reliever airport,

- to provide substantial capacity or instrument training relief via a current or forecasted activity level of at least fifty based aircraft, or 25,000 annual itinerant operations, or 35,000 annual local operations; OR the installation or proposed installation of a precision instrument landing system, if determined to be a desirable location for instrument training activity; and/or
- be a commercial service airport that serves a Standard Metropolitan Statistical Area with a population of at least 250,000 persons or at least 250,000 annual enplaned passengers, and operates at 60% of its capacity, or operated at such a level before being a relieved airport, or is subject to restrictions that limit activity that would otherwise reach 60% of capacity.[56]

---

[53] FAA, Report to Congress; *National Plan of Integrated Airport Systems 2005-2009* (Sep. 30, 2004); retrieved from http//www.faa.gov/arp/planning/npias.

[54] For a history of the evolution of reliever airports, *see* David A. Newmyer, Stephen A. Mitchell & Jeffrey P. Smith, *Problems and Prospects of Reliever Airports*, Collegiate Aviation Review of the UAA (Sep. 1992).

[55] *See id.*

[56] *See generally* David A. Newmyer, Stephen A. Mitchell & Jeffrey P. Smith, *Problems and Prospects of Reliever Airports*, Collegiate Aviation Review of the UAA (Sep. 1992).

In the 1993 *Aviation System Capacity Plan*, the FAA proposed different types of reliever airports: traditional relievers which could reduce congestion and delay, and *supplemental airports* to *intentionally* "divert" some of the (general aviation) growth at certain air carrier airports. Supplemental airports differ from the old category of reliever airport, whose role is to "attract" general aviation activity away from busy hubs.

In the 2002 NPIAS, the FAA restated its reliever criteria, with the exception to the above former criteria being "a case-by-case review" of each reliever candidate to ascertain "whether there is a current or future significant requirement for additional general aviation capacity to relieve congestion at the commercial service airport or to enhance general aviation access to the overall community" with a requirement for at least 100 based aircraft or 25,000 annual itinerant operations.[57]

An existing or proposed public use airport "may be included in the NPIAS as a reliever airport if it relieves airport congestion at a commercial service airport and provides general aviation access to the overall community." With the revised definition, helicopters can also quality with the same numbers.

HELIPORTS

A public use heliport that doesn't meet the criteria outlined in the prior section may still be included in the NPIAS "if it makes a significant contribution to public transportation." It is also desirable to be included in a metropolitan or state airport system plan. Heliport landing areas may be included if they have:

- At least 4 based rotorcraft, or
- 800 annual itinerant operations, or
- 400 annual operations by air taxi rotorcraft.

Special or private use heliports intended "to provide community services such as police patrol, traffic surveillance, or air ambulance transportation should not be included."[58]

---

[57] FAA, Report to Congress; *National Plan of Integrated Airport Systems 2005-2009* (Sep. 30, 2004), retrieved from http//www.faa.gov/arp/planning/npias.
[58] *Id.*

Helicopters are important to communities for a variety of reasons, ranging from security to search and rescue. Emphasis placed on development and use of helicopters in the 1960s by the military carried over into the civilian sector. Corporations have increasingly turned to the helicopter for short-range air mobility. Helicopters have found widespread acceptance in commercial uses including fighting brush fires, agricultural application, traffic watch, medical evacuation, corporate transportation and offshore transportation. Public service agencies are using helicopters extensively as well. For example, it is now out of the ordinary to find a large police department that does not use the helicopter in its operations.

With this influx in helicopter traffic, especially at airports, it has become necessary to provide special air traffic procedures and landing facilities as part of the overall airport complement. Although helicopter operations and heliports are characteristically unique, they are but one extension of the overall aviation transportation system. The integration of heliports into the total airport scheme constitutes an increasingly important facet of airport operations. Heliports are particularly unique in three areas:

- *Site* selection;
- *Design* and facilities; and in
- *Airspace* and instrument procedures.

Heliports may be located on the ground or on suitable structures on land or over water. Their design can be as simple as an open area at ground level or, in comparison, may be built on a rooftop or other elevated structure. Because of the variety of locations, approach/departure paths leading to and from the heliport are a major safety consideration. There are obstruction clearance criteria designed particularly for heliports. With their unique flight capabilities, and in addition to standard instrument procedures, there are instrument approach procedures designed especially for use by helicopters, such as instrument approaches to points in space with visual transition to distant landing sites. Moreover, helicopters may operate in visual conditions far below those authorized for fixed-wing operations.

Heliports are designed around the critical (helicopter) aircraft, and rather than using approach speed and/or wingspan (which are the physical characteristics used in airport design), the characteristic that is most important in heliport design is the *main rotor diameter*. Take-off and landing areas must provide at least 1/3 rotor diameter, but not less than ten feet (three meters), horizontal clearance between the takeoff and landing area and buildings, fences, and other objects that main and/or tail rotors might strike.

For heliports serving single-rotor helicopters exclusively, the length and width, or diameter of the takeoff and landing area is designed to be at least equal to twice the rotor diameter of the critical helicopter. For heliports serving tandem-rotor helicopters, the length and width, or diameter of the takeoff and landing area is designed to be at least one rotor diameter greater than the overall length of the critical aircraft.

The important principle in the *integration* of helicopter operations at an airport is, ironically, to *segregate* their operation to the extent possible from airplane operations. This is true on the ground as well as in the air. The wind vortices produced by the helicopter's rotor blades are capable of overturning small, parked fixed-wing aircraft. Airport helipads are commonly located on remote aprons or taxiways, with hover lanes to parking areas that avoid close proximity to parked airplanes.

Planning and development of heliports and heliport systems has increased dramatically as the volume of fixed-wing aircraft traffic approaches the capacity limits of major airports and of the air traffic and airspace system. Helicopters can operate independently between heliports, thereby increasing the available capacity of major airports, and of the national airspace system.

In its campaign to establish more heliports, the *Helicopter Association International* [HAI] has pressed for more simple, *Visual Flight Rule* [VFR] heliports to serve the current generation of helicopters and the new tilt-rotor aircraft such as derivatives of the Bell/Boeing V-22 Osprey. Once established, a VFR heliport can be easily converted to *Instrument Flight Rule* [IFR] capability. Non-precision approaches, with high decision height and visibility minimums, can often satisfy heliport needs.

The HAI heliport strategy aims to establish a hub-and-spoke pattern of heliports and helistops in metropolitan areas, especially in the Northeast. A civilian model of the Osprey could carry 36-44 passengers, and it is estimated tilt-rotor transports could capture up to 10 million of the 120 million passengers traveling through the New York metropolitan area annually. Helicopter routes between Boston, New York and Washington, D.C., are also envisioned below the operating levels for conventional jet transports.

AIRPORT AND AIRWAY IMPROVEMENT ACT AMENDMENTS

The Airport and Airway Improvement Act of 1982 remains fundamentally in tact as of this writing. Nevertheless, in the promotion of safety and capacity enhancement, the Act has been significantly amended twice since 1982. The operative words in subsequent amendments to the Airport and Airway Improvement Act of 1982 were "safety" and "capacity." The 1982 Act was amended by the Airport and Airway Safety and Capacity Expansion Act of 1987 and by the Aviation Safety and Capacity Expansion Act of 1990.

The salient revisions of 1987 included a redefinition of "airports" to include heliports; to require fire fighting and rescue equipment at any airport which serves scheduled passenger operations of air carrier aircraft designed for more than 20 passenger seats; and the redefinition of "primary airport." A primary airport had been defined as one that enplaned .01 percent or more of the national air carrier passengers annually. After 1987, a primary airport is one with "more than 10,000 passengers enplaned annually."

Of particular significance, the Aviation Safety and Capacity Expansion Act of 1990 provided authority for the imposition of a *Passenger Facility Charge* [PFC]. Imposition of the PFC represents a radical departure in the way airports are financed, and represents a first step to removing the major air carrier airports from the federal funding program. Originally, the Aviation Safety and Capacity Act allowed commercial service airport authorities to impose a fee of $1.00, $2.00, or $3.00 for each paying passenger of an air carrier enplaned at such airports. In 2000, fees of $4.00 or $4.50 were deemed permissible under certain limited circumstances such as if a medium or large hub airport would use the PFCs to "make a significant contribution to air safety and security, increasing competition amongst air carriers, reducing current or anticipated congestion, or reducing the impact of aviation noise on people living near the airport."[59]

The Aviation Safety and Capacity Act was included as part of the Omnibus Budget Reconciliation Act of 1990. The Aviation Safety and Capacity Act continued the Airport Improvement Program, but renamed the "airway" portion of the program (i.e. the *Airway Improvement Program*) as the *Airway Capital Investment Plan*. The 1990 Act placed special emphasis on the conversion to civil use of appropriate former military air bases and on the identification and improvement of additional joint-use facilities. It made available 1.5% of the annual trust fund monies to sponsors of current or former military airports plus as much as $5 million a year per airport for five years after assuming responsibility for the airport.

Another part of the Omnibus Budget Reconciliation Act of 1990, known as the Airport Noise and Capacity Act of 1990, enacted a *National Aviation Noise Policy* and added provisions regarding noise associated with aircraft and airports. Yet another part of the Omnibus Budget Reconciliation Act, known as the Revenue Reconciliation Act of 1990, increased some aviation taxes and extended the authorization for the Airport and Airway Trust Fund.

The AIP authorized nearly $5.2 billion for the first five years of the program (or an average of $1.04 billion per year).[60] For the six fiscal years 1990 through 1995, AIP appropriations averaged $1.68 billion per year. Add to this the local passenger facility charges authorized by the FAA. In actual dollars, there has been a steady and substantial increase in federal airport support since the federal government first instituted the Federal Aid to Airport Program under the Federal Airport Act in 1946, initially authorizing average expenditures of only $48.5 million per year. But, as Charles ("Chip") Barclay points out, current appropriations fall way short of projected needs for airport development in the United States.[61]

The *American Association of Airport Executives* [AAAE] and the North American chapter of the *Airports Council International* [ACI]

---

[59] Code of Federal Regulations, Title 14: Aeronautics and Space, Part 158, *Passenger Facility Charges* (updated May 30, 2000).

[60] FAA, *FAA Airports 50th Anniversary*, a brochure celebrating 50 years of airport development (1996).

[61] Charles M. Barclay, *America's Future in Airport Infrastructure*, a position paper of the President of the AAAE (1996).

conduct periodic surveys to assess the capital development needs of U.S. airports. Surveys in 1990, 1992, and 1995, showed a need for $10 billion annually for airport development and capital reconstruction. In contrast, there was on average only $2.2 billion annually over the same five years for a total of $11 billion available from appropriated aviation trust funds combined with local passenger facility charge authority. This amounted to approximately one-fifth of the needed investment. Adding airport bonds and other local revenues to federal investment increased the available resources, but still to just over one-half of the airport development funds needed.[62]

The years immediately post-September 11, 2001, saw larger infusions of funds, particularly for security related expenditures at airports (through Department of Homeland Security spending measures) to fund in-line explosive detection system installations and other screening-related expenditures. In addition, at the mid-point of the first decade of this century, the AIP funding levels were at the $3.5 billion mark annually, with "significant support for airports, despite the number of competing programs. . ."[63] In 2006, the struggle for funding continued.

There is underway a seemingly perpetual search for ways to increase system capacity and for ways to pay for it. Moreover, the scope of airport development is expanding, and with that expansion there is an increasing demand upon limited resources. Some analysts suggest that perhaps limited federal airport development funds might be directed toward the highest priority airports, and that most of the funds ought to be applied to projects that will make the greatest reduction in traffic congestion and that will make the greatest improvement in operating efficiency.[64]

AIRPORT CATEGORIES

Within the national framework of airport planning, airfield development is predicated upon providing basic facilities for the specific type of aircraft expected to use the airport. Runway length and pave-

---

[62] *Id.*

[63] AAAE, Senate Panel Clears 3.52 Billion for AIP (Aug. 1, 2006), and Airport Report, *Dot Spending Bill Heads to Conference* (Nov. 1, 2005), Vol. 11, No. 15 and Vol.1, No. 21.

[64] Stephen J. Thompson, *The Airport Improvement Program: Background, and Some Options for Using Federal Financial Resources More Effectively*, a Congressional Research Service report for Congress (Jan. 31, 1994), at 23.

ment strengths are related closely to the dimensions, weight, and performance characteristics of the "critical aircraft" using the airport more or less on a daily basis.

In designing the airport elements to accommodate the critical aircraft, consideration of the physical characteristics of the critical airplane is required. The two principal physical characteristics taken into account are *approach speed* and *wingspan.*[65]

The *aircraft approach category* groups aircraft based on 1.3 times their stall speed in their landing configuration at their maximum certified landing weight. The categories are as follows:[66]

- *Category A* aircraft have approach speeds less than 91 knots;
- *Category B* aircraft have approach speeds of 91 knots or more, but less than 121 knots;
- *Category C* aircraft have approach speeds of 121 knots or more, but less than 141 knots;
- *Category D* aircraft have approach speeds of 141 knots or more, but less than 166 knots; and
- *Category E* aircraft have approach speeds of 166 knots or more.

The *airplane design group* arranges airplanes based on wingspan. The groups are as follows: [67]

- *Group I* are airplanes with wingspans up to but not including 49 feet (15 meters);
- *Group II* airplanes have wingspans of 49 feet (15 meters) up to but not including 79 feet (24 meters);
- *Group III* airplanes have wingspans of 79 feet (24 meters) up to but not including 118 feet (36 meters);
- *Group IV* airplanes have wingspans of 118 feet (36 meters) up to but not including 171 feet (52 meters);
- *Group V* airplanes have wingspans of 171 feet (52 meters) up to but not including 214 feet (65 meters); and
- *Group VI* airplanes have wingspans of 214 feet (65 meters) up to but not including 262 feet (80 meters).

---

[65] FAA A/C 150/5300-13, *Airport Design* (1989), retrieved from www.faa.gov.

[66] *Id.*

[67] *Id.*

By combining the aircraft approach categories with airplane design groups in a matrix, an *Airport Reference Code* [ARC] results (e.g., A-I, A-II, B-III, C-V, and so forth). The airport reference code identifies the groupings within which the critical aircraft is identified, and serves as a key for applying airport design criteria such as taxiway/runway lengths and widths, and navigation aids.[68]

Early airport design grouping fell within the two generalized categories of *utility* and *transport*, in response to the critical type of aircraft using the airport. Today, each term has neither a general aviation nor air carrier connotation, as was once the case. These two board categories can be roughly matched to respective ARCs.

For example, *utility airports* are designed, constructed, and maintained to serve airplanes in Aircraft Approach Category A and B. A utility airport can be expected to have the following kinds of activity:

- *Basic Utility—Stage I* airports serve 75% of the single-engine and small twin-engine airplanes used for personal and business purposes. Precision approach operations are not usually anticipated. This type of airport is designed for "small" airplanes (i.e., 12,500 pounds or less) in Airport Reference Code B-I.
- *Basic Utility—Stage II* airports serve all the airplanes of stage I, plus some small business and air taxi-type twin-engine airplanes. Precision approach operations are not usually anticipated. This airport type is also designed for small airplanes in Airport Reference Code B-I.
- *General Utility—Stage I* airports serve *all* small airplanes. Precision approach operations are not usually anticipated. This type of airport is designed for airplanes in Airport Reference Code B-II.
- *General Utility—Stage II* airports serve "large" airplanes (i.e., over 12,500 pounds) in Aircraft Approach Category A and B, and usually have the capability for precision approach operations. These airports are normally designed for Airport Reference Code B-III.

---

[68] *Id.*

All other airports fall into the *transport* category. Transport airports are designed, constructed, and maintained to serve airplanes in Aircraft Approach Category C and D. The transport category includes some of the larger business, or corporate jet-type airplanes, but the majority consists of large air carrier aircraft.

INTERNATIONAL AIRPORTS

It might be well to recognize that there is not only a national system of airports (i.e., the National Plan of Integrated Airport Systems, or NPIAS), but there is also a system of categorizing U.S. airports for customs purposes. Under Section 1109(b) of the Federal Aviation Act of 1958, the Secretary of the Treasury is authorized to ". . . designate places in the United States as ports of entry for civil aircraft arriving in the United States from any place outside thereof and for merchandise carried on such aircraft. . . ." This responsibility is assigned to the U.S. Customs Service.

Furthermore, Article 68 of the Convention on International Civil Aviation provides for the designation by the signatory Governments (referred to by the *International Civil Aviation Organization* [ICAO] as "Contracting States") of ". . . the route to be followed within its territory by an international air service and the airports which any such service may use."

The categories of *international airports* (within the United States) include:

- *Airports of Entry* are those airports, which have been designated as international airports for customs purposes. These airports are open to all international aircraft for entry and clearance purposes without the necessity of obtaining permission. However, advance notice of arrival is required in order that inspectors may be readily available. Designation as an airport of entry follows application by the airport operator and finding by the U.S. Customs Service that the airport will generate sufficient international traffic. An airport of entry must provide adequate space and facilities for Customs and Federal inspection purposes and satisfy certain other requirements established by the U.S. Customs Service.

- *Landing Rights Airports* are those airports where incoming international flights must obtain prior permission to land and must furnish advance notice of arrival to U.S. Customs. This category of airports includes most of the so-called major U.S. "International Airports" (e.g., John F. Kennedy International, Chicago-O'Hare International, Los Angeles International, et al.). Advance notice of arrival may be transmitted via flight plans at those airports where *Advise Customs* [ADCUS] service is available and such notice is treated as application for permission to land. Customs officers may, at their discretion, grant blanket "landing rights" to individuals or companies at certain airports for a specific period of time, in which case advance notices of arrival are the only requirement. This blanket permission is generally given for scheduled airline flights at busy landing rights airports.
- *International Civil Aviation Organization Designated U.S. Airports Serving International Operations* are those airports designated under Article 68 of the Convention on International Civil Aviation as airports serving international operations (for traffic or refueling purposes). U.S. airports so designated are identified in ICAO Regional Air Navigation Plans, Documents 8755 and 8733, and include those regularly served by scheduled and nonscheduled international commercial air transport, those designated as alternates, and those used regularly by international general aviation flights. U.S. airports with ICAO designations may not necessarily be airports of entry or landing rights airports as the ICAO designation is independent of any Customs requirements.

In addition to the designated international airports discussed above, there are a number of airports in the United States that are not officially so designated but which contain the word "International" within their names. These are the *Unofficially Named International Airports*. There is no prohibition against such a practice, however, without an official designation, such an airport has no international status.

AIRPORT DEREGULATION

Since airline deregulation in 1978, the *airport-as-a-market* has become more dominant than the existence of service by any one airline. Moreover, reliance upon any one airline for continued air service has become highly speculative. The overall objective of airline deregulatory policy was to return the industry to an environment of *competitive capitalism*, with many competing airlines, where none would control the market, and where price would be reduced to the marginal unit cost of production.[69] The idea was to create a more perfect economic model of competition. Deregulation radically changed the market climate of the airlines, and the air transport industry, including airports. Rather than having the government dictate where air transport markets might best be served, greater reliance was placed upon a more natural evolution of the economic marketplace.

The airlines responded to the economic freedom by attempting to *rationalize* the marketplace to their own advantage.[70] Deregulation led the carriers to want two things—market dominance and lower cost of operation.[71] A phenomenon associated with airline deregulation has been the creation of new tools of competition. After *price competition*, the principal instrument of competition coming out of deregulation has been the *hub-and-spoke* concept.[72] Thornton called it the primary "weapon of war" in the unleashed competition following deregulation.[73] Some call them "fortress hubs," where a single airline controls the lion's share of gates, takeoffs and landings, and passengers.

The hub-and-spoke has been an economic strategy designed to capture a greater share of the market. Using the hub-and-spoke system, the airline can put far more cities into its system and it can effectively capture passengers by making it difficult and expensive for them not to use the hub airline's services.[74] Airline hubs are bottleneck connections travelers have to go through when they fly to their

---

[69] The "marginal unit" is the last unit of production sold at the lowest average price commensurate with recovering all costs of production.

[70] *See generally* Paul Stephen Dempsey & Laurence E. Gesell, *Air Transportation: Foundations for the 21st Century* 121-131 (1997).

[71] Karen Walker, *Bespoke Fortunes*, Airline Business (Jan. 1997), at 35.

[72] *See id.* at 451-457.

[73] R.L. Thornton, *Airlines and Agents: Conflict and the Public Welfare*, J. of Air Law & Commerce (1986), at 52.

[74] Barbara Byer, in Karen Walker, *Bespoke Fortunes*, Airline Business (Jan. 1997), at 35.

destinations. "Hubbing" is the result of airlines offering a large number of connecting flights to other cities from a few of their "hub" airports. Hubbing came about because the airlines found the hub allowed them to take advantage of network and scale economies, while offering frequent service to a geometrically increasing array of city-pair markets.[75]

Hubbing is a corporate strategy where large airlines dominate traffic at many airports by forming hub-and-spoke networks. A carrier uses spoke flights, flown by its own planes or those of smaller commuter lines that major airlines control through purchase or agreement to generate passenger flow for flights to and from its hub operations. The introduction of regional jets is now enlarging the catchment area around strategic hubs to 500 nautical miles. The network creates sizable economies that inhibit entry into hub markets by competitors. The captive origin-and-destination passenger provides a stable base on which carriers may load fixed costs, while consumers complain of "monopoly pricing at fortress hubs."

The "hub-and-spoke" should not be confused with the DOT categorization of the airport hub system based on demographics. But in a study of forty-three airports falling under the FAA's "large-hub" classification, the U.S. Government Accountability Office [GAO] found fares to be generally "much higher" in 1995 at the ten airports that are either affected by operational constraints or where one airline accounts for the vast majority of enplanements. High fares at fortress hubs have been well documented, but the solutions are less well documented. The indisputable fact remains that the hub-and-spoke concept is now so deeply established that any fundamental change would be extremely controversial and difficult to bring about.[76]

The airlines argue that the hub-and-spoke system offers convenience and access to city-pairs that otherwise might not be viable markets.[77] This translates into convenience for the customer and higher yields to the airline.[78] The system seems to suit the traveling public, and irrespective of the higher costs noted to the consumer, the trend is

[75] Adib Kanafani & Atef Ghobrial, *Airline Hubbing—Some Implications for Airport Economics*, an unpublished seminar paper (1984).

[76] Karen Walker, *Bespoke Fortunes*, Airline Business (Jan. 1997), at 32.

[77] *Id.*

[78] "Yield" means the air transport revenue per unit of traffic carried in air transportation. It may be calculated and presented several ways (*e.g.*, passenger revenue per passenger mile, per aircraft mile, per passenger ton mile and per passenger. *See* Paul Stephen Dempsey & Laurence E. Gesell, *Air Transportation, Foundations for the 21st Century* 566 (1997).

towards even more concentration at fortress hubs. The drive is economics. The more concentrated the hub, the higher the yields to the participating airlines.

Ideally, the "hub" airport, of a hub-and-spoke network, has the following characteristics:

- It is an *interior point* geographically situated for flow from several directions, particularly a routing that incorporates most business traffic (the most lucrative share of the market);[79]
- It has a *large population base* to enhance high-yield *Origin and Destination* [O&D] traffic, preferably white collar (because business travelers typically pay more for air transportation); and,
- Preferably, there are *no nearby hubs* or competing airports dominated by another airline.[80]

Other factors affecting what makes an airport a good hub location for an airline are local market growth potential, connection potential, lack of growth constraints, market share that can be garnered, the number of gates the airline can control, and effective gate utilization.[81]

Before deregulation, while Atlanta (for Delta) and Pittsburgh (for Allegheny, now US Airways), were moderately concentrated, no airline dominated more than 45% of the capacity or market share of any major airport in the United States (as measured by gates, passengers, or takeoffs and landings). Subsequent to deregulation, airlines began consolidating their operations around hub-and-spoke networks. These networks account for 70% of the flights offered by domestic airlines.[82] Today, dominant airlines control more than half the enplanements at more than half of the nation's fifty largest airports

The infrastructure of gates and landing slots at the major airports has been consumed by the megacarriers, leaving little room for significant new entry.[83] Strategically located hubs were designed to al-

---

[79] In the U.S., the routing of most business traffic is east/west.

[80] Paul S. Dempsey, Robert Hardaway & William Thoms, 1 *Aviation Law & Regulation* § 2.12 (1993). *See also* J.P. Morgan Securities, *The U.S. Airline Industry* 17 (1993).

[81] Karen Walker, *U.S. Hubs Need to be Consolidated*, Airline Business (Feb. 1998), at 74.

[82] *American-Sponsored Study Blasts Criticism of Hubs*, Aviation Daily (Jul. 31, 1990), at 197.

[83] 88% of the gates at the nation's 66 largest airports are leased to airlines, and 85% of the leases are for exclusive use; *Intelligence*, Aviation Daily (Aug. 20, 1990), at 323. Some upstarts have focused on the remaining, smaller airports. In the early 1980s, America West focused on Phoenix and Las Vegas. In the 1990s, WesternPacific began operations at Colorado Springs, and

low the largest carriers powerful positioning from which to blanket the nation with ubiquitous service. For example, by the mid-1990s United had established hubs at Chicago, Denver, San Francisco, and Washington, D.C. (Dulles). Likewise, American Airlines had developed hubs at Chicago, Dallas/Ft. Worth, Miami, San Juan, San Jose, Nashville, and Raleigh/Durham. While Delta built hubs at Atlanta, Dallas/Ft. Worth, Salt Lake City, and Cincinnati, Northwest established hubs at Detroit, Minneapolis/St. Paul and Memphis.

Hubbing is advantageous for a number of reasons. It allows enhanced marketing opportunities via the geometric proliferation of the number of possible city-pair markets that can be served. The number of passengers enjoys a corresponding exponential growth, while labor staffing increases at a much more moderate rate.[84] Figure 4.1, "Hub-and-Spoke vs. Linear Route Model", shows the advantages of the hub-and-spoke system over linear routes by increasing the city pairs served (in this particular model) from six to thirty-six through the hub city, "H."[85]

The events of September 11, 2001 challenged the fragile stability of the nation's largest network carriers.[86] While these giants fell into bankruptcy, low-cost carriers and regional operators emerged with some impressive successes via less hub-oriented, flexible route systems. Still, it must be noted that, despite more recent economic instability issues, the creation of hub-and-spoke networks have significantly altered the nation's air transportation route structure. Just five years after 9/11, many major airports and airlines observed the return of some of the pre-9/11 delay levels. While larger airports face airfield and airspace capacity constraints, smaller airports continue to seek more and improved air carrier service.[87] This trend is both familiar and global.

American Trans Air focused operations on Indianapolis. Several major carriers (*i.e.*, TWA, Braniff and Eastern) unsuccessfully attempted to establish a hub at Kansas City. In the 1990s, upstart Vanguard Airlines also focused operations at Kansas City. *See* Aviation Daily (Jan. 30, 1996), at 150.

[84] Dan Reed, *American Eagle* 157 (1992).

[85] *See* Paul Stephen Dempsey & Laurence E. Gesell, Air *Transportation: Foundations for the 21st Century* 200-213 (1997).

[86] Dipasis Bhadra & Pamela Texter, BTS, *Airline Networks: An Econometric Framework to Analyze Domestic U.S. Air Travel* (2004), retrieved from http://www.bts.gov/publications/journal_of_transportation_and_statistics/volume_07_number_01/.

[86] *Id.*

[87] *Id.*

[87] *Id.*

Figure 4.1—HUB-AND-SPOKE vs. LINEAR ROUTE MODEL
(Hypothetical Route Structure to Serve Nine Cities)

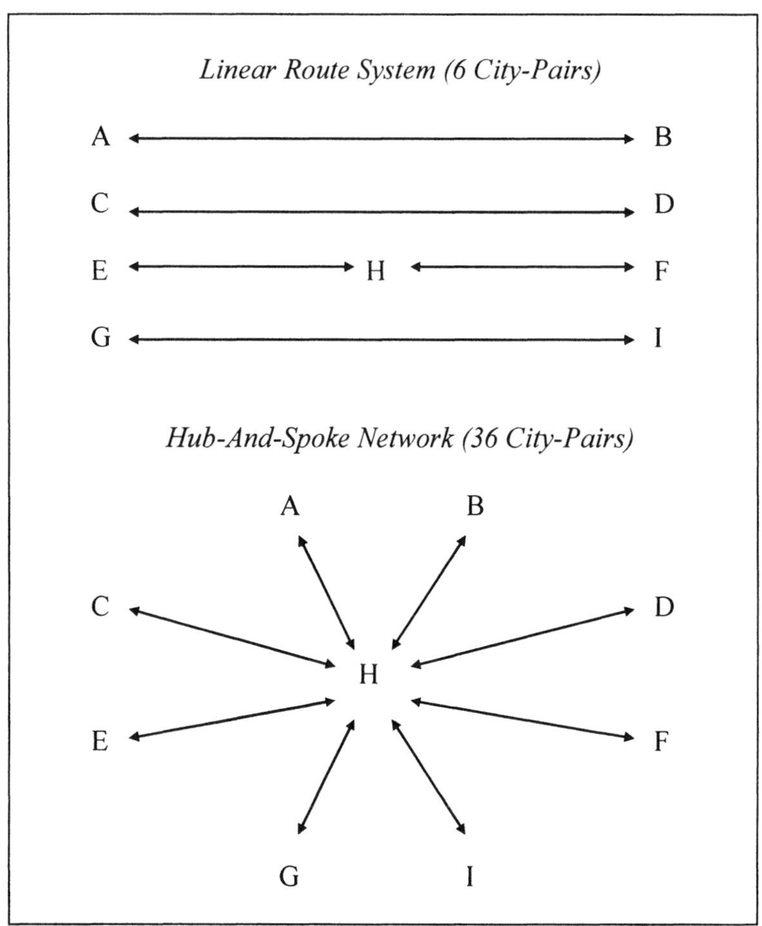

Source: Laurence E. Gesell & Paul Stephen Dempsey, *Air Transportation: Foundations for the 21st Century* (2nd ed. 2005).

One thing is clear; the aviation industry is characterized by dynamic processes and systems. The economic recessions and booms, fuel crises, and terrorism threats and responses of the 1980s, 1990s and 2000s have prompted both airlines and airports to continually reevaluate their offerings and needs, winding down many of the smaller, less efficient hubs. Over the years, hubs have been dismantled or downsized at Washington Dulles Airport (United), Denver (Continental), Dallas/Ft. Worth (Delta), Dayton (US Airways), Kansas City (TWA, Eastern and Braniff), San Jose, Nashville and Raleigh/Durham (American), and Colorado Springs (WesternPacific). Many do not have a sufficient origin and destination traffic-base on which to load fixed costs.

Downsizing a hub is a painful process, for every spoke eliminated deprives other spokes of traffic feed, causing the synergies of the hub to unravel.[88] Nevertheless, airline management must be sufficiently agile to withdraw from markets which are producing unsatisfactorily, and re-deploy resources to more lucrative markets.

Brian Harris, vice president at Wall Street's Lehman Brothers, concludes the industry remains over-hubbed and would be more economically efficient if there were fewer, larger-sized hubs. Hub economics work better (i.e., are more profitable) where there are larger (and fewer) hubs in big cities.[89]

To work, a hub must have a large number of flights ("banks," as they are called) from a large number of origins converging at an airport in close time proximity, so that passengers can readily transfer to flights departing to an equally large number of destinations. This requires a large number of gates and ground personnel. Nevertheless, significant network economies may be achieved via hubbing.

Both O&D and many connecting passengers pay a yield premium for the frequent service hubbing allows. At the concentrated "fortress hub," consumption of airport infrastructure often translates into higher yields. The most attractive hubs from a financial standpoint are congested hubs near large business communities.

The more congested the airport, the scarcer the air transportation resource becomes. And, scarce resources lead to higher prices.[90] Yields at concentrated airports are more than 20% higher per mile for passengers who begin or end their trips there than at unconcentrated airports.[91]

Hubbing also results in a yield premium for connecting traffic, particularly in the large majority of city-pair markets not served non-

---

[88] James Hirsch, *Big Airlines Scale Back Hub-Airport System To Curb Rising Costs*, Wall St. J. (Jan. 12, 1993), at A1, A6.

[89] *See* Karen Walker, *U.S. Hubs Need to be Consolidated*, Airline Business (Feb. 1998), at 74.

[90] Alexander ter Kuile, *Hub Fever*, Airline Business (Dec. 1997), at 67.

[91] GAO, *Airline Competition: Higher Fares and Reduced Competition at Concentrated Airports* (1990).

stop, for city-pairs less than 1,500 miles in distance, and for smaller cities without multiple hub connections. Some hub carriers have learned to focus on this high-yield connecting traffic, and avoid the local O&D price wars with non-union upstart airlines.[92]

Airlines with more gates, takeoff and landing slots (at capacity constrained airports), and/or "codesharing" agreements charge significantly higher prices than those without, according to the U.S. General Accounting Office. In fact, flights at airports where *majority-in-interest clauses* [93] reduce expansion opportunities result in 3% higher fares; flights at slot controlled airports result in 7% higher fares; and carriers with code sharing arrangements charge 8% higher fares.[94]

In 1988, the eight largest U.S. airlines controlled 96% of the landing and takeoff slots at the four slot-constrained airports (i.e., Chicago O'Hare, Washington National, and New York's Kennedy and LaGuardia). In 1985, before the U.S. Department of Transportation decreed these public resources could be bought and sold in the market, the eight largest airlines controlled only 70% of the slots.[95] An airline, which doubles the number of its gates, enjoys a 3.5% increase in fares.[96]

These yield advantages are achieved because of a broader economic principle, the "S-Curve," [97] which posits that the dominant car-

---

[92] Address by Maurice Myers before the Salomon Brothers Transportation Conference at New York, N.Y. (Nov. 17, 1994).

[93] *I.e.*, documents allowing airline control over some key airport decisions.

[94] Paul Dempsey, Robert Hardaway & William Thoms, *Aviation Law & Regulation* § 5.05 (1993). GAO, Testimony of Kenneth Mead before the Aviation Subcommittee of the U.S. Senate Commerce Committee 6 (Apr. 5, 1990).

[95] GAO, *Airline Competition: Industry Operating and Marketing Practices Limit Market Entry* 4 (1990).

[96] *Id.* at 6.

[97] Tretheway & Oum point to the "S-Curve" effect of flight frequency on demand and revenue, the essential premise of which is that a carrier which offers consumers a disproportionately larger number of flights in a market *vis-à-vis* its competitors will enjoy an even greater disproportionate advantage in terms of both passenger load factors and revenue. *See* Michael Tretheway & Tae Oum, *Airline Economics: Foundations for Strategy and Policy* 27 (1992); *see also* William E. O'Connor, *An Introduction to Airline Economics* 107-09 (5th ed. 1995). The S-Curve phenomenon was first identified by economist William Fruhan in 1972. Fruhan explained that travelers tend to contact the dominant carrier in the market first, due to its marketing dominance and its greater choice of scheduling options. By virtue of this advantage, carriers are incentivized to add flights to the market. But unless the market for air travel grows, excessive over-scheduling harms all competitors in the market by increasing the number of empty seats. *See* William Fruhan, *The Fight for Competitive Advantage* (1972); *see also* Paul Stephen Dempsey & Laurence E. Gesell, *Airline Management: Strategies for the 21st Century* 36 (1997).

rier in terms of frequency and capacity in any market will enjoy a disproportionate share of the traffic in terms of higher load factors and higher yields.[98]

International carriers also employ their gateways as venues for *sixth freedom* [99] connecting traffic. For example, KLM puts enough capacity on the North Atlantic to transport the entire population of the Netherlands to the United States in a single summer. Most of the traffic is funneled through its hub at Amsterdam Shiphol, from or to points beyond.

Nevertheless, hubbing sacrifices equipment and labor utilization and consumes more fuel than a linear route system in markets sufficiently dense to support nonstop service. Clearly also, the United States is overhubbed by duplicative parallel route networks connecting virtually every conceivable city-pair market. To trim costs and reduce capacity, in the 1990s, carriers began to downsize or close selected hubs. The net effect of the majors giving up their smaller hub operations was to become entrenched in the remaining larger hubs. The major airlines are now relying more than ever on their "fortress hubs."

By the mid 1990s, U.S. domestic commercial aviation had divided itself into two dominant types of service providers: (1) the *ubiquitous network hub carriers* (e.g., United, American, Delta, Northwest) emphasizing connecting traffic; and (2) the *short-haul nonstop point-to-point carriers* (e.g., Southwest) focusing on O&D traffic.[100] Internationally as well, new long-haul point-to-point carriers have emerged (e.g., Virgin Atlantic) to compete along side the established international network carriers (e.g., British Airways).

---

[98] Barbara Beyer, *The Curse and Blessing of Hubs* 3, unpublished paper delivered at the International Conference on Aviation & Airport Infrastructure in Denver, Colo. (Dec. 5-9, 1993).

[99] *Sixth freedom* is the right to carry traffic between two foreign countries via its own country of registry. Sixth freedom can also be viewed as a combination of third and fourth freedoms secured by the country of registry from two different countries. *Third freedom* is the right to carry traffic from its country of registry to another country. *Fourth freedom* is the right to carry traffic from another country to its own country of registry. *See* Paul Stephen Dempsey & Laurence E. Gesell, *Air Transportation: Foundations for the 21st Century* 304-305 (1997).

[100] The only profitable U.S. major airlines, Southwest and Jet Blue, embrace a point-to-point linear route system, which allows more productive equipment and labor utilization, and more efficient fuel consumption than does a hubbed operation. Southwest avoids congested airports, focusing instead on secondary airports in many markets, thereby allowing a quick turn around time (15 minutes is the goal).

INTERNATIONAL ALLIANCES

Airline deregulation in the United States has yielded mixed results, but for whatever reason, until the late 1990s, the airline industry had been troubled financially. To help the beleaguered airline industry, in 1993 President Bill Clinton created *The National Commission to Ensure a Strong Competitive Airline Industry* (the "Baliles Commission"), to investigate, study and make policy recommendations about the financial health and future competitiveness of the U.S. airline and aerospace industries. The airline industry, by that time, had lost $10 billion in the previous three years. Amongst its findings, the Commission determined that "The principle challenge for the country is to fashion a new, growth-oriented international aviation framework . . .," requiring ". . . a clear and decisive shift in policy by the U.S. away from the present system of bilateral regulation of air services to one based on multi-national arrangements. . . ."[101]

Formed about the same time, as the Baliles Commission to study airline conditions, was *Le Comite des Sages* (the "European Wise Men Committee") to study the causes of the on-going air transport crisis in Europe. Their report of February 1994 criticized the air carriers' slow response to the changing air transportation market.[102] Suggesting that in the *liberalization* of the European Union [EU] (formerly the European Economic Community [EEC]), "There is no way back to the previous era of nationalistic protectionism." The source of the crisis in Europe, they said, was government protection of nationalized carriers.

Despite U.S. foreign policy advocating deregulation on a global scale, few nations followed the U.S. lead in the 1970s and 1980s. But as the deregulation trend picked up speed, interest quickened in the privatization of nationalized airlines in order to remain competitive. As Europe has followed its path to liberalization under the EU, free trade advocates battle with protectionists for an open skies policy. Likewise, in Latin America a highly regulated industry of national carriers has shifted to a more competitive marketplace of largely private airlines.[103] In Asia, highly nationalized (albeit privatized) carriers like Japan Airlines [JAL] and All Nippon Airlines [ANA] are battling

---

[101] *See generally* Paul Stephen Dempsey & Laurence E. Gesell, *Airline Management: Strategies for the 21st Century* Ch. 9 (1997).
[102] James Ott & Raymond Neidl, *Airline Odyssey* 122 (1995).
[103] *Id.* at 123.

low-cost carriers such as Korean Airlines, Singapore Air, Cathay Pacific, and Thai International. Japan is among the most protective of the world's great economic powers, yet it is having to examine the prospects of liberalization as well.

Although nationalism remains an issue with most countries, global market forces, aided by U.S. policy, are moving the industry closer to an "open skies" policy worldwide. An overriding trend has been toward alliances or partnerships among the world's airlines through codesharing agreements. Codesharing allows two carriers to display a single, joint code on the computer reservations system. It differs from the old system of "interlining," where each carrier would have its own code identifier. Traditionally, passengers were handed off to the succeeding carrier for completion of a journey to a destination not served by the original carrier. Codesharing, on the other hand, allows the two carriers to act as one, thus providing what is referred to as "seamless travel." Codesharing began subsequent to deregulation, when the majors began aligning themselves with their commuter counterparts (e.g., American Eagle with American; United Express with United, Delta Connection with Delta, and so forth). The agreements allowed the smaller carriers to share the two-letter code used to identify their larger partner. Codesharing has since spread to include international partners.

By connecting multiple hubs around the world, codesharing partners can increase by several-fold the city-pairs they offer.[104] In the transatlantic market, for instance, alliance competition focuses on price and frequency. The true strength of alliances lies in their ability to connect the individual networks so that by linking the central hubs they effectively achieve maximum connectivity among stations at the highest possible frequency. According to the "S-Curve" theorem, the alliance with the highest frequency gains the largest market.

THE FUTURE SYSTEM

International marketing and equity alliances have emerged, providing by order of magnitude a wider array of city-pairs to sell to customers, and interline feed which can be significant. But concentration forces have led to only a few alliances with a global reach, each striving to achieve the lowest unit costs through increased efficiencies and

---

[104] *See* Richard Whitaker, *Hubbing Power*, Airline Business (Dec. 1966), at 32.

higher capacities. In what is referred to as a "virtuous circle," theoretically these lower airfares open new markets, resulting in extra demand for large aircraft, which in turn reduces unit costs and allows further fare reductions. What Alexander ter Kuile calls the "volume-based alliances," are carriers that operate large aircraft and provide distinct unit cost advantages over the smaller aircraft of what he refers to as "network builders."[105] The virtuous circle suggests that the alliance with the largest aircraft will have the lowest unit costs.[106] British Airways and United Airlines qualify as *volume operators*. American Airlines, KLM-Northwest, the Delta group and Lufthansa are *economy of scope operators*, which expand their networks rather than increase unit volumes.

Dominance of the (network builders versus volume-based) carriers' strategies and geographic locations will strongly influence financial results and to a great extent the future of airport system development. Generally, large congested airports provide for higher yields than do transfer hubs. Likewise, congested hubs attract volume operators with high capacity aircraft. Open hubs tend to attract frequency/network builders lacking the unit cost advantages of high capacity aircraft.[107] Nevertheless, congested airports motivate alliances to become "volume-oriented" operators through the promise of a unit cost advantage and higher yields. Thus, Alexander ter Kuile suggests that in the end, both network-builder and volume-based strategies will lead to further concentration of both airlines and airports. The significant income of volume operators will lead to predatory action by the richest players to gain new hubs, while the network builders will seek

---

[105] Alexander ter Kuile, *Hub Fever*, Airline Business (Dec. 1997), at 66-71.

[106] This explains why volume operators actively support the launch of the Airbus A380, 600-passenger plus transport, which may be crucial to their continued growth. Alexander ter Kuile, *Hub Fever*, Airline Business (Dec. 1997), at 66; *see generally* Paul Stephen Dempsey & Laurence E. Gesell, *Air Transportation: Foundations for the 21st Century* 85-88 (1997).

[107] Look, for example, at London/Heathrow Airport, which has been slot restricted for years. Conversely, Amsterdam and Munich have not as yet suffered such limitations, allowing their home carriers a relatively free choice in operating strategy. Whereas British Airways increases aircraft size per departure to accommodate growth, KLM can afford to operate smaller aircraft, focusing on frequency. British Airways had 212 seats per movement at Heathrow in 1997, while KLM had 129 seats per movement at Amsterdam. Yet, one of the strongest hub builders is KLM at Amsterdam. Congestion at Frankfurt is forcing Lufthansa to increase aircraft capacity per departure, yet the airline is building up frequency and destinations at its new Munich hub using smaller regional jets. Lufthansa averaged only 105 seats per movement at Munich in 1997. *See* Alexander ter Kuile, *Hub Fever*, Airline Business (Dec. 1997), at 66-67.

mergers and acquisitions to increase their volume in order to remain competitive.[108]

The FAA predicts the number annual domestic enplanements will be over 958.4 million by the year 2015.[109] Owing to the hub-and-spoke phenomenon, the bulk of this expansion will likely occur at the large hubs with already over-burdened facilities. Four of the largest hub airports (Atlanta Hartsfield-Jackson, Chicago O'Hare, Dallas-Ft. Worth, and Los Angeles International) reached combined enplanements of over 126 million annually in 2005.[110] Although there have been a variety of studies conducted of an impending capacity gridlock, presenting the costs and benefits of numerous alternatives, there have been few recommendations.[111]

When Donald Engen served as the FAA Administrator in the mid 1980s, he was seemingly wishing for a "magic wand" that would create four big new airports in the New York, Chicago, Atlanta and Los Angeles areas. In 1987, his successor, Alan McArtor, had a similar wish, but with a difference: He wanted "a dozen or so" new major airports. Unfortunately, according to Laurie McGinley, the chances of building any new major airports after Denver amount to a "wing and a prayer."[112]

SUMMARY

International airline alliances combined with hubbing strategies are having an impact globally. Capacity constraints and air traffic delays are not issues unique to the United States. In the U.S., the air transportation industry is showing signs of a maturing market. But airports in Europe and Asia are being taxed to their limits as well.[113]

---

[108] *Id.* at 71.
[109] DOT, *Aviation Capacity Enhancement Plan* (1994).
[110] *Id.*
[111] Stephen M. Rutner & Ray A. Mundy, *Hubs versus Hub-Nots: A Comparison of Various U.S. Airports*, Vol.1, No. 1 J. of Transp. World Wide (1996) at 82-83.
[112] Laurie McGinley, *FAA Seeks More Airports to Lessen Congestion, But Its Chances Amount to a Wing and a Prayer*, Wall St. J. (Wed., Aug. 26, 1987) at 42.
[113] In 1987 work was started on Japan's second major international airport at Osaka. Kansai International Airport has, as a prime reason for its existence, the goal of boosting the Osaka's economy, and to relieve pressure on Tokyo's Narita International Airport. Asian airports led the way in traffic growth in 1995 and 1996. Osaka (with Osaka International and Osaka Kansai) had the fastest growing airport system in the world. Lois Jones, *Asia Takes the Lead*, Airline Business (Dec. 1996), at 41; *see also* David A. Brown, *Japanese Building International Offshore Airport to Serve Osaka*, Aviation Wk. & Space Tech. (Jul. 13, 1987), at 38.

And, on the Pacific Rim and in Latin America, air transportation growth is explosive! The problem of overly taxed airports is a global issue, with the last decade of the 20th century and the first decade of the 21st century witnessing a blurring of the economic divisions among countries that once marked the industry.

Still, the path to a "new and improved" structure for not only the U.S., but for airports worldwide, is filled with numerous obstacles, pitfalls and problems.[114] It's also full of possibility, associated with new technologies that are reshaping today's air carriers and airports. This begs the question: What might a future system of airports look like? Might the airports of the future be equipped to host fleets of *Uninhabited or Unmanned Aircraft Systems* [UAS] or *New Large Aircraft* [NLA]s? Might the terminals be largely automated, reducing workload, dangers or opportunities for airport employees?

The next several chapters will investigate the myriad of challenges and endless possibilities facing the next generation of aviation managers, ranging from planning and environmental issues to security and maintenance issues, as well as many others.

---

[114] *See* Oris Dunham, *Airport Globalization*, Airport Magazine (Sep./Oct. 1990) at 5.

CHAPTER 5

AIRPORT DEVELOPMENT AND MASTER PLANNING

If and when you become a candidate for the [new large aircraft], the good news is that that you probably won't have a lot of them coming to your airport. . . . The bad news is [that most terminal building interfaces will] have to be reconstructed to accommodate the aircraft. . . . Hold rooms [must] expand [along with] support facilities. It is not necessarily the numbers. It is just that you're going to have it all happening in a very brief time period.

James E. Bennett, President and Chief Executive
Metropolitan Washington Airports Authority[1]

INTRODUCTION

Planning is indeed well underway for the next generation of aircraft—referred to as "New Large Aircraft" [NLA]. In fact, 14 U.S. airports have already indicated they will be making signification modifications for NLA by the year 2010—with the current focus on Airbus' 555-seat self-proclaimed "21st century aircraft," the A380.[2] Jim Bennett's point (supra) was that airport planners will be best prepared if they "build for the peak."[3] This would include consideration

---

[1] As cited in, *Seven Experts, One Focus: Trends in Airport Architecture, Construction and Design: Talking Trends*, Airport Magazine (Nov./Dec. 2003).
[2] Airbus S.A.S., *Airbus Aircraft Families: A380* (Sep. 2006), retrieved from http://www.airbus.com/en/aircraftfamilies/a380/; *see also* FAA, *Annual Aviation Capacity Enhancement Plan* (2003), retrieved from http://www.faa.gov/ATS/asc/ACE.html.
[3] *Id.* at 1.

of both the physical accommodations needed to allow larger aircraft to safely transit the airfield, but also the terminal and landside infrastructure and technological changes needed for the significant influxes of passenger movements that will occur with each NLA operation.[4] Clearly, landside and terminal facilities must reasonably match in their adaptation and expansion, in order to best accommodate the new large aircraft.

While new large aircraft, security challenges, environmental concerns and a host of other issues concern today's airport planners and operators, most experts agree that the major issue facing the world's air transportation industry during this century will be lack of adequate air traffic, airspace, and airport capacity. Primarily, it is the airport that provides capacity for the air transportation system. As a result, the underlying motivation behind airport master planning and development is a perpetual search for ways to increase system capacity.

THE SEARCH FOR CAPACITY

In its 2003 *Aviation Capacity Enhancement Plan* [ACE], the Federal Aviation Administration's [FAA's] Office of System Capacity states, "measuring aviation activity is a way of estimating the demand on airports and the air traffic control system. Capacity is an expression of their ability to meet that demand, so any analysis of capacity requires an analysis of current and future demand."[5]

Demand is a measure of aviation activity such as passenger enplanements, revenue ton miles, and aircraft operations. This demand is generated by one of three basic types of aviation activities: commercial passenger and cargo transportation, general aviation, and military operations. But using these measures can be somewhat limiting. The FAA explains,

> *By definition, only commercial passenger operations produce passenger enplanements and only cargo operations produce revenue ton miles, while all aviation activity produces aircraft operations (takeoffs and landings). . . .*

---

[4] *Id. at* 1.

[5] FAA, *Annual Aviation Capacity Enhancement Plan* (2003), retrieved from http://www.faa.gov/ATS/asc/ACE.html.

> *Each type uses different types of aircraft, has its own patterns of operations, and places different demands on airports and the air traffic control system.* [6]

Many airports in the United States were wartime constructions in the 1940s, post-war modifications of the 1950s, and expansions to accommodate jet travel in the 1960s. But since then *capacity* has not kept pace with *demand*. By the 1970s, analysts were beginning to note that unless something was done about it, lack of adequate capacity would become a threat to the future of air transportation. And, by the 1980s, observers were generally aware that sufficient capacity had indeed become a major concern. In the early 1980s, for example, the International Civil Aviation Organization [ICAO] recognized the increasing limitations of the air navigation systems, as well as the need for improvements, to take civil aviation into the 21st century.[7]

By the early 1990s, alarm had truly set in, and "capacity" became an operative word for the U.S. Congress in its amendments to the Airport and Airway Improvement Act of 1982.[8] Beginning in 1992, the FAA began to publish annual *Aviation Capacity Enhancement Plans,* the most current as of this writing is the 2003 plan. The FAA focused on several strategies to continue to improve airport capacity including runway "renovation, realignment, new, extension and renovations" as we ended the Centennial of Flight (1903 to 2003).[9]

Still, despite a concerted effort to increase capacity throughout the system, capacity continues to lag behind increasing demands for limited airport resources. It appears to be a dilemma for which there are no pat answers. Indeed, most experts agree that the major issue facing the world's air transportation industry in the next century, in fact, will be the lack of adequate air traffic, airspace, and airport capacity.

The development of adequate capacity is the primary motivation behind the airport planning and development process. Airport planning and development is a comprehensive subject that could easily fill

---

[6] *Id.*

[7] ICAO, *International Aviation in the 21st Century*, Avn. Safety J. (winter 1992), Vol. 2, No. 1, at 19.

[8] The Airport and Airway Development Act of 1982 Act was amended by the Airport and Airway Safety and Capacity Expansion Act of 1987 and by the Aviation Safety and Capacity Expansion Act of 1990.

[9] *Id.* at 5.

a volume of its own. And it is a significant component of airport management. As such, it deserves a comprehensive overview in this text. This chapter and the succeeding two chapters will address the subject of airport planning and development. This chapter begins with a review of the progressive clogging of the air transportation infrastructure and the impending gridlock that surely lies ahead if drastic measures are not taken to avert it. Included in this chapter is a synopsis of the alternatives available to master planners and developers for increasing airport capacity. The chapter concludes with a discussion of the responsibility for airport development, the federal grant process is outlined, and the process of selecting contract architects, engineers and planners is described.

Following the discussion of growing airport and airspace congestion and ways by which capacity can be enhanced, the actual master planning process is then addressed in the section, "Airport Master Planning." *Airport master planning* is the systematic way by which airports are developed and enhanced. But taken to the next abstraction, the underlying motivation behind airport planning and development is a perpetual search for ways to increase system capacity. As stated at the outset in this book, "it is the airport that provides capacity for the air transportation system."

Airport sponsors must follow very specific guidance, as provided by the FAA to compile their individualized airport master plans. Due to the volume of work associated with assembling a master plan, airport sponsors often employ specialized consultants to assist them with the master planning process.

Advisory Circular [AC] 150/5070-6B, *Airport Master Plans*, most recently updated in 2005, identifies an important pre-planning component, along with the following "key elements" of the airport master plan studies: [10]

- Public Involvement Program;
- Environmental Considerations;
- Existing Conditions;
- Aviation Forecasts;
- Facility Requirements;
- Alternatives Development and Evaluation;

[10] FAA, *Airport Master Plans*, AC 150/5070-6B (Jul. 29, 2005).

- Airport Layout Plans;
- Facilities Implementation Plan; and
- Financial Feasibility Analysis.

A thorough *inventory* of the subject airport's existing conditions and historic data enable production of *forecasts* of future activity demand. Analyses of *demand/capacity* relationships, in turn, provide a basis for determination of *facility requirements* and the development of alternative airside and landside concepts designed to achieve a balance in capacity among all components. Determinations are made of the physical capability of expansion, as well as its timing based on development costs versus delay-reduction benefits, operational reliability, safety considerations, and the ability of the airport sponsor to finance the improvements. The facility requirements analysis determines the need for such items as the length/strength and number of runways, terminal area requirements, number of gate positions, apron parking areas, access roads, auto parking, other modes of ground transportation, and the overall airport land area requirements. Airside capacity requirements are expressed in numbers and dimensions of runways and associated taxiways, apron areas, and so forth. Landside capacity requirements include terminal building space, auto parking and surface access.

The calculated facility requirements become the basis for feasibility site selection and *concepts* or *alternatives* in design. Should it be determined that the airport is capable of providing the required capacity, then the detailed planning steps for the *existing* site ensue. If there are serious reservations about the capacity of the existing site, there must be an investigation of alternatives such as developing new, replacement, or additional sites, modifying the role of the existing airport, or providing new aviation facilities.

Environmental issues can prevent a master plan from progressing to approval for years. The next chapter, "Environmental Management," considers the potential impact that aviation has on the environment and the steps that can be taken to mitigate that impact. In many cases, addressing environmental impact of an airport can be reduced to a two-part investigation of *land use* and *air operations* considerations. But implementation of *operational procedures* designed to reduce the adverse environmental effects of the airport upon the *surrounding community* is part of an overall strategic plan. Comprehensive environmental strategies are the result of effective master planning. Hence, the subject of the environment is grouped together with the airport planning and development process.

DEVELOPMENT RESPONSIBILITY

The responsibility for development of airports in the United States can best be described as an exercise in circular policy. It is a classic example of what has become known as "new federalism."[11] Ultimately, the responsibility belongs to the airport sponsor, but planning and development of publicly owned airports relies heavily upon financial aid from the federal government. The Federal government outlines the requirements for airports and determines where federal monies can best be spent; and once the project is complete dictates compliance with contractual assurances while at the same time absolving itself of responsibility.

The role of the Federal government is couched within airport and airway improvement legislation. Accordingly, the general policy depends upon state and local initiative, but often involves federal participation in the form of guidance and financial assistance. Federal "guidance" has increasingly dictated to the airport sponsor how the airport is to function. Perhaps, then, former FAA Administrator Allan McArtor succinctly stated the attitude, with regard to how the nation's airport resources are managed,

> *Although the initiative for airport development still resides with state and local agencies, the Federal government no longer can afford to remain in a purely reactive mode. We must and will take a more active leadership role and become the catalyst in a national campaign to expand airport capacity.*

---

[11] "Federalism" is formed by a compact between the separate states (being individual political units), which willingly subordinate their powers to the central or national government, while at the same time retaining other limited powers. It is a system unique to the U.S. "New Federalism" is a derisive term giving reference to the growing power of the central government through a civil contractual basis. For example, by accepting federal funding for airport development, the local government agrees to conform to certain assurances made part of the contract to receive the funds, and thereby relinquishes some of its independent power.

Most of the nation's airports are owned and operated by state enabled local authorities, but sometimes it is difficult to recognize that reality. The position taken by the states is similar to that of the federal government. Implied in typical state policies is that each community (or private) airport owner is responsible for its own airport, and the state's ultimate responsibilities in the development of individual airports are minimal. States recognize their responsibility to assist local communities in developing and continuing the operation of the airports in keeping with objectives within state developed airport system plans, but the onus for airport development initiative lies with the local airport sponsor.

In most cases, because they lack sufficient funds to develop their own airports, local governments must turn to the state, and principally to the federal government for financial assistance. In exchange, the local governments must develop their airports to the satisfaction of the state and federal governments—and in accordance with state and federal guidelines for airport development, and in compliance with federal laws.

The way by which local dependence upon the state and federal governments came about is classic in the evolution of financing public institutions. The Air Commerce Act of 1926 directed the Secretary of Commerce, ". . . to establish, operate, and maintain . . . all necessary air navigation facilities except airports." Thus, prior to 1933, the federal government was prohibited from participating in the development or operation of airports, a function delegated to local governments and to the private sector. However, during the Depression Era of the 1930s the Federal government did advance large sums of money for construction and improvement of airports in connection with various relief programs. The Civil Aeronautics Act of 1938 removed restrictions against federal involvement in airports and prompted recommendations by the newly formed *Civil Aeronautics Authority* [CAA] for Congress to appropriate funds for airport development. In 1944, recommendations by the CAA led to enactment of the Federal Airport Act of 1946. However, airport developments occurred *ad hoc*, and there was no systematic approach to airport planning and development.

SYSTEM CONGESTION

Congestion of airways and airports—in the United States in particular but in Europe as well—has been growing alarmingly over at least the past three decades. And by most predictions the airport and airspace system will become increasingly more congested into the foreseeable future. The necessary infrastructure is simply not being developed commensurate with growth in demand. As Lester Thurow points out, the development is "alarming" when one considers that,

> *In the United States, public infrastructure investment has been cut in half over the past twenty-five years. We (the United States) are investing less than any other G-7 nation, including the sobering statistic that we are investing at one-third the rate of the Japanese.*[12]

The cause of the capacity bind is not so much the result of a failure to anticipate growth, as it is a failure to take appropriate actions to avoid its consequences. One excuse postulated is that the growth following airline deregulation in 1978 was not anticipated. And there has been much rhetoric about the supposedly "unanticipated" growth. However, neither the records nor the data support conclusions that the growth was so unexpected. Demand for air transportation has, indeed, increased. But the growth has been generally consistent with earlier *FAA Forecasts* for 1978 to 1988 and subsequent forecasts for 1979 to 1990; in other words, forecasts that were based upon historical data and conclusions prepared before the effects of deregulation could have been realized.[13] Consequently, the growth subsequent to airline deregulation could hardly be characterized as "unexpected." The actual demand that occurred after airline deregulation in 1978 should have come as a surprise to no one. But what was clearly not anticipated was development of the *hub-and-spoke* strategy and concentration of air traffic around select hubs. The hub-and-spoke phenomenon has resulted in an unequal distribution of traffic amongst the available

---

[12] Lester Thurow, *The Future of Capitalism* (1996); *see also* Charles M. Barclay, *America's Future in Airport Infrastructure*, a position paper by the President of the American Association of Airport Executives [AAAE] (1996), at 1-1.

[13] *See* Laurence E. Gesell, *Airline Re-Regulation* (1990).

airports. The excess concentration resulted in 21 major U.S. airports experiencing more than 20,000 hours of annual delay by 1987.

Not only was the increased traffic forecast to occur, capacity constraints were "anticipated" as early as the 1960s. But the adopted solution was a determination to "fix" the problem through improved electronics; more efficient navigation aids, reduced traffic separation, and through computerization of the *Air Traffic Control* [ATC] system. Yet the "electronic" solution seemingly did little to alleviate increasing congestion. Responding to the dilemma, the late Professor Robert Horonjeff stated that the key to relieving congestion lies not in improved electronic aids, but rather by acquiring more capacity on the ground. Congestion results from the inability of the *terminal ends* to accept aircraft from the airspace system. More succinctly, Dr. Horonjeff was arguing, to relieve congestion, needed are more runways.[14]

In light of diminishing land resources, airport-planning philosophies through the 1970s and into the 1980s were predicated upon conservation and increased operational efficiency of *existing* facilities. Now in the first decade of the 21st century there are few new airports of significance actually being built. The last major airport developed in the U.S. was Denver International Airport, which after years of delayed construction and malfunctioning (principally baggage conveyor) equipment, finally opened in 1995. Before that, it was Dallas/Fort Worth, completed more than twenty years earlier in 1974.

DELAYS IN THE NATIONAL AIRSPACE SYSTEM

Understanding the term, "delay" is not a simple matter with regard to its relevance in aviation. The FAA explains,

> *Delay is the traditional measure of NAS performance, but it is not a straightforward measure to calculate for an individual flight, airport, or for the entire system. There are many delay parameters that can be (and are) tracked.*[15]

---

[14] Robert Horonjeff & Chris Orman, *The Trade-Off Between Airfield Improvements and Electronic Systems for Airport Capacity*, a paper presented at the annual meeting of the Radio Technical Commission for Aeronautics held in Arlington, Va. (Nov. 19, 1975).

[15] FAA, *Annual Aviation Capacity Enhancement Plan* (2003), retrieved from http://www.faa.gov/ATS/asc/ACE.html.

Additional measures for delay are periodically added to the metrics used by the FAA to assess problems within the *National Airspace System* [NAS]. For example, in late 2003, both the FAA and the Department of Transportation [DOT] decided to include reasons for flight delays in the FAA's monthly airline service report, as derived from its *Operational Network* [OPSNET].[16] OPSNET data is created through observation. FAA staff record any aircraft delayed in excess of fifteen minutes during any phase of that aircraft's flight. "According to OPSNET data 316,888 flights were delayed by fifteen minutes in CY 2003," which was more than a 10% increase from the prior year.[17]

In 2002, five categories were established to categorize the reason for an air carrier flight delay including: weather, NAS, security, carrier caused, and late-arriving flights.[18] These data are maintained within the *Aviation System Performance Metrics System* [ASPM] which was originally developed by nine commercial carriers (members of the Air Transport Association) in conjunction with the FAA. As of 2003, 22 air carriers were reporting flight data for flights to and from 55 airports. In addition, more than 30 of the nation's busiest airports are currently monitored for delay metrics including percent of flights on-time, airport arrival capacity and airport arrival efficiency[19].

The goal of identifying airport and air carrier delay is to determine the cause, in order to devise a remedy. But the costs associated with increasing airport capacity can be significant.

FINANCIAL CONSIDERATIONS

The principal means of increasing air transportation system capacity are: (1) to build *additional* new airports; or (2) to maximize the efficiency of *existing* airports via a variety of measures including the addition of runways, improved navigational aids, terminal expansions, and so forth.[20] But there can be many obstacles to fulfilling such objectives, not the least of which is the immense cost. A new world-class airport can cost upwards from a billion dollars (U.S.) and

---

[16] *See Airline On-time Performance and Causes of Flight Delays*, retrieved from www.bts.gov.

[17] FAA, Annual Aviation Capacity Enhancement Plan (2003), retrieved from http://www.faa.gov/ATS/asc/ACE.html.

[18] Monthly carrier filings are undertaken in accordance with 14 CFR Part 234.

[19] *Id.* at 17.

[20] *Id.*

once construction has commenced the costs can rapidly escalate out of control.

The Denver International Airport, for example, was to take an initial investment of about $1.5 billion. Before the airport opened, the cost had risen to over $5 billion! Required was a substantial commitment by the federal government for a disproportionately large portion of the aviation trust fund monies. And, although Denver was able to garner a large share of the available federal funds, other airport sponsors, such as Austin, Texas, have found out they may not be so fortunate. The aviation trust fund is insufficient to fund development of many airports like the one at Denver.

In 1988, Austin residents approved a new $698 million, four-runway airport, northeast of the existing Robert Mueller Airport. Austin officials calculated they were entitled to more than $300 million in *Airport Improvement Program* [AIP] monies, but received a letter of commitment from the FAA for only $57 million. With the letter from the FAA came an explanation that the AIP program is not "designed" to provide such large amounts of money to a single project, no matter how worthy. Nevertheless, the FAA ultimately increased its commitment level. Still, the City's share to develop the Austin-Bergstrom International Airport was $549.3 million, with approximately only one-fourth funded by the national aviation system.[21] The airport ultimately opened in 1999.

High costs are but one aspect of the obstacles to expanding the airport infrastructure. High costs in turn result from environmental restraints, including air and water pollution, automobile traffic congestion, lack of suitable land near large metropolitan areas, and perhaps most notably, objections to aircraft noise by the surrounding community.[22] Moreover, construction costs *per se* are but one aspect of airport development. The cost of land in many cases has become prohibitive. This is especially true in the dense urban areas of the East, and in the West and along the Sun Belt where there has been high in-migration from other parts of the country—the very areas where aviation growth and the need for additional airport facilities has been most pronounced. The economic and operational viability of an airport requires *complementary* location with the urban setting.

---

[21] Retrieved from www.ci.austin.tx.us/news/week1003.htm (Nov. 23, 1998).

[22] Stephen J. Thompson, *Airport Congestion: Background and Some Policy Options*, a Congressional Research Service Report to Congress (May 20, 1994), at 8.

This same complementary relationship places the airport in direct competition with other industries for the use of progressively more expensive property and increasingly limited land resources.

POLITICAL AND LEGAL CONSIDERATIONS

Besides cost and the time it takes to plan and develop an airport—typically ten to fifteen years—another significant obstacle is *competing political interests*. Airport development, particularly of a new major international airport, takes *unified* commitment! Development and/or expansion of critically needed airports will depend upon overcoming these economic, environmental, and politically sensitive hurdles. Primarily because of environmental considerations, the development of new airports has been extremely difficult, and in many cases nearly impossible. Proposed airports to be constructed in the Los Angeles and Miami areas, for example, became stalled years ago because of environmental objections.

Not only is the development of new airports difficult, but retention of already existing airport facilities in dense urban areas has become a problem as well. This is particularly true with privately owned airports, but affected have been many publicly owned facilities too. The reasons for the closings of airports are varied and complex, but the most common problem cited for the closing of privately owned airports is high cost of operation. The major problem at public airports is noise impact upon the surrounding community and development pressures to use the land for other than airport-related purposes.

It might be added that it takes local support to *retain* an airport as well as build one. The City of Santa Monica, in Southern California, for example, decided its property was too valuable to be used as an airport. The attitude of the Santa Monica City Council with regards to its airport is not uncommon in cities and counties elsewhere. Classic examples of private airport closures can be found in the fringes of New York City: Sky Acres Airport near Westchester, Deer Park on Long Island, and Red Bank, Colts Neck, and Asbury Park airports in Monmouth County, New Jersey; all closed since 1970.

Santa Monica Municipal Airport is illustrative of problems that can be encountered in trying to retain a publicly owned general aviation airport in a high-density urban area. For many years, airport operations have been the subject of controversy between the City of

Santa Monica and the residents near the airport, and two seminal lawsuits were brought against the city. In response to continuing complaints about the airport from residents, the Santa Monica City Council asked city administration to investigate the validity of the complaints and to suggest possible solutions. The result was a series of restrictive ordinances, including a ban against jet aircraft operations, imposed by city council.

Santa Monica once again got caught up in litigation, resulting in a third precedent-setting case.[23] This time though, the suit was not from local residents, but rather came from the airport users themselves (the Santa Monica Airport Association, supported by the National Business Aircraft Association and the General Aviation Manufacturers Association) in an attempt to overturn the city's ordinances. Prior to the case being settled, it was pointed out by James L. Hoyt, Member of the Santa Monica Airport Commission, that if the City could not enforce its noise abatement procedures it would surely have to rethink its commitment to maintain an airport that at best contributed $250 thousand a year to the city budget on land that was most likely worth $80 million! Since then (the late 1970s), the direct contribution to the city coffers has had only marginal increase while the value of the land particularly in California has skyrocketed.

With the exception of a ban on jets, the court upheld the city's right to prohibit certain types of operations. The FAA and the City reached an agreement that would keep the airport open until at least the year 2015, but the vice of community encroachment has increasingly tightened around it.

Recognized in the Santa Monica case is that the support of state and local officials as well as the local community can be critical to retaining airport facilities. In many cases that support may be weak or non-existent, as it was in Santa Monica. Identified is apathy particularly at the local level. Everyone seems to want adequate air transportation facilities, but not necessarily "in their backyard."[24] Not only may there not be sufficient support for development of a new airport, or for expansion of an already existing airport, but political forces may be at work to close an airport as well.

---

[23] *Santa Monica Airport Association v. City of Santa Monica*, 481 F. Supp.927 (C.D. Cal. 1979); *see also* Ch. 16.

[24] This is a situation known as the "NIMBY" ("Not In My Back Yard") syndrome. It is a term frequently used in conjunction with environmental issues.

Certain local officials and political activists may harbor resentment of the airport, and its users, and therefore may not respect the user's needs. The reason for resentment may stem from the community having other needs besides air transportation. And in the eyes of some people, these other public safety needs, social welfare considerations, and environmental concerns may take precedence over the airport. The airport is a public facility that (if it is not an air carrier airport) may be looked upon by many as serving only a small, select and well-to-do special interest group at the public taxpayer's expense.

Sometimes, however, there may be support for retention, even expansion, of an existing airport, while at the same time a locality may, for parochial reasons, be against airport development in an adjoining community. For example, during the 1960s, New York and New Jersey were considering building a fourth airport in the New York City area. When Connecticut suggested it might build an airport to compete with the New York airports, the Port Authority of New York and New Jersey organized opposition to kill the Connecticut proposal.[25]

In another instance, an airport project was proposed for the St. Louis area, but a site was selected for the new airport across the Mississippi River in Illinois. Supposedly the proposal died for at least three reasons. One, residents in the county where the new airport would be located opposed the project because of the potential noise impact. Two, the State of Missouri was in opposition because the airport would be in Illinois. And three, business interests in St. Louis did not want to lose the economic base provided by the existing airport.[26] The Mid-America Airport was built in spite of the opposition. But as of this writing it has been able to attract only limited scheduled or charter airline service.[27]

---

[25] Lyn Loyd Cresswell, *Airport Policy in the United States: The Need for Accountability, Planning and Leadership*, Trans. Law J., Vol. 19, No. 1 (1990), at 32; *see also* Stephen J. Thompson, *Airport Congestion: Background and Some Policy Options*, a Congressional Research Service Report to Congress (May 20, 1994), at 20.

[26] Lyn Loyd Cresswell, *Airport Policy in the United States: The Need for Accountability, Planning and Leadership*, Trans. Law J., Vol. 19, No. 1 (1990), at 34; *see also* Stephen J. Thompson, *Airport Congestion: Background and Some Policy Options*, a Congressional Research Service report to Congress (May 20, 1994), at 20.

[27] *See* CNN, *Headline News* (May 28, 1999).

DFW's ROCKY DEVELOPMENT

Development of the Dallas-Forth Worth Airport occurred after thirty years of bickering between the two cities involved. Both Dallas and Fort Worth fought construction of the airport. The factors keeping the cities apart were many:

- A different congressman represented each city, and each congressman supported federal funding for an airport owned by the city each represented;
- Refusal of the federal government (i.e., the Civil Aeronautics Board) to interfere in what it viewed to be a "local matter";
- Continuous squabbling between the two cities over airport location and design;
- Unsupported confidence by Fort Worth representatives in the potential for expansion of Dallas Love Field (then the air carrier airport serving the region);
- Opposition to a jointly-owned airport by Dallas business leaders and the media in Dallas; and
- Failure of the air carriers to support moving to another airport, irrespective of the city in which it might be located.

The two cities finally came together because,

- like the St. Louis example above, the threat of outside competition was introduced when Arlington, Texas, sought to sponsor an airport in their community;
- the airlines finally agreed to relocate to a new airport;
- Dallas threatened legal action against the Civil Aeronautics Board's support of a Fort Worth airport;
- the CAB and the FAA came together in unified support for locating the airport in a neutral zone between the two cities;
- the Federal government refused to fund expansion of Love Field because of its limited potential;
- homeowners attacked the City of Dallas over noise impact from Love Field;
- airline pilots declared Love Field unsafe; and

- pressure from the State of Texas for a single, jointly-owned facility.[28]

OTHER AIRPORT DEVELOPMENTAL CHALLENGES

In yet another example of political rivalry, in the mid 1990s, there was an attempt to promote development of a major regional airport midway between the urban centers of Phoenix and Tucson, Arizona. The proposed regional airport, added to the two existing city airports, would have provided the region with sufficient capacity well into the 21st century. It should be noted that Phoenix is one of the airports listed as being likely to exceed 20,000 hours of annual aircraft delay by the year 2000. But political opposition, principally from the airport sponsors in Tucson and Phoenix, and particularly from the latter, gave rise to the proposal's defeat.

In the meantime, a third runway was completed at Phoenix and a fourth is on the drawing boards. Although it was eventually completed, third runway development met stiff opposition because of environmental concerns voiced by nearby communities of Tempe and Scottsdale, although the latter was not quite as forceful as the former. And even though the project was eventually developed, dimensions of the third (and most outboard) runway were limited by available property along the Salt River. Hence, all aircraft landing and taking off from the Phoenix Sky Harbor Airport cannot utilize the new runway. As a result, limited use of the third runway detracts from the airport's full capacity potential. Another, fourth runway, has been proposed but as of this writing plans were shelved, not only because of opposition from adjacent communities, but because of opposition from, and the cost of relocating, tenants currently sitting atop the site where the fourth runway would be placed.

Chicago is another example where the airport is exceeding 20,000 hours of annual aircraft delay. Yet it, too, has been involved in jurisdictional disputes over siting and building a major new airport. Over a third major airport for the Chicago area, there were disputes between the State of Illinois and the State of Indiana, between Chicago and

[28] Lyn Loyd Cresswell, *Airport Policy in the United States: The Need for Accountability, Planning and Leadership*, Trans. Law J., Vol. 19, No. 1 (1990), at 34-35; *see also* Stephen J. Thompson, *Airport Congestion: Background and Some Policy Options*, a Congressional Research Service Report to Congress (May 20, 1994), at 21.

southern Illinois, and among other interest groups, as to where the new airport ought to go. Owing to the fact that much of the funding would come from airports owned by the City of Chicago (i.e., Midway and O'Hare Airports), the decision was deferred to the City of Chicago. However, a firm commitment to construct the third airport had, as of this writing, not been made.[29]

Resolving jurisdictional disputes often requires involvement by the federal government, as it was in the Dallas-Fort Worth Airport development. Yet the federal government has not always had a clear policy regarding airport development, nor have the respective federal agencies always been in concert. Federal policy with regard to the best use of AIP funds is far from certain. The Federal government has already stated that there are insufficient AIP funds for it to support the development of any more airports like Denver International. Still, the money will have to come from somewhere to build enough new airport capacity to eliminate congestion, and it will cost billions of dollars. In the meantime, congestion at the busiest airports is only expected to get worse. The uncertainty has prompted congressional studies to find more efficient ways to utilize available federal funds.[30] Some suggestions have included designating an airport priority list; thereby listing airports according to their propensity to relieve congestion, and then funding the select airports before any others of lesser priority receive funding support.[31]

Public policy options with regard to the most effective use of federal financial resources may help to lessen capacity constraints, but the solution to the long-standing controversy over airport congestion, as pointed out by Horonjeff years ago, remains the same—more runways are needed! Nevertheless, it is recognized that implementation of that solution may not be so easy. But *the* answer is, indeed, more runways. And it is enlightening to know that even if the Federal government does not have any firm answers as to how to magically produce needed capacity; it has finally come to realize what the root of the problem is. After years of pursuing alternative (and ultimately less

[29] Stephen J. Thompson, *Airport Congestion: Background and Some Policy Options*, a Congressional Research Service Report to Congress (May 20, 1994), at 21.
[30] *See e.g.*, Stephen J. Thompson, *The Airport Improvement Program: Background, and Some Options for Using Federal Financial Resources More Effectively*, a Congressional Research Service Report to Congress (Jan. 31, 1994); *see also* Stephen J. Thompson, *Airport Congestion: Background and Some Policy Options*, a Congressional Research Service Report to Congress (May 20, 1994).
[31] *Id.*

effective) means of improving upon existing capacity, by the mid-1980s the FAA publicly acknowledged the answer to airport congestion being the availability of more runways. In 1985, FAA Administrator Donald Engen emphasized that airport capacity is an issue transcending all other problems facing the aviation industry today. To quote,

> *. . . left untreated, the problem will grow far worse over the next ten to fifteen years. We could have as many as sixty capacity constrained air carrier airports and another forty to forty-five congested general aviation fields by the year 2000 . . . We need to begin now to improve our major air carrier airports. We need to begin now to improve our system of reliever airports . . . Washington can provide the leadership and the funding, but local support is needed to put an airport, or an airport system in place.*[32]

Admiral Engen was off in his prediction only in his assessment of time versus numbers. Thirty-three of the sixty airports became a reality by the year 2000. But the number is still growing, not only in the United States but also worldwide.

The fact the U.S. may have had so many capacity locked airports in the near future was really not news. The fact Washington was finally listening and so openly stating the problem was newsworthy! Mr. Engen was asking all segments of the industry to get behind a program to improve and build more airports. Subsequent FAA administrators have likewise called for the expansion of existing airports and the building of new ones.

But it was not so long ago that the federal government's stated policies seemed to ignore the need for more runways. In 1978, then Secretary of Transportation, Brock Adams, presented a transportation policy, which included the following on airways:

> *For the most part, the major airport and airways facilities we will need for the foreseeable*

[32] Donald Engen, in an address to the Aircraft Owners & Pilots Association [AOPA] (1985).

> *future are authorized or in place. Therefore, our policy must now change to emphasize the improved utilization and more effective management of these facilities. For the future this will involve upgrading the system to keep pace with technological improvements that offer safety or high capacity which reflect geographic changes in demand.*

Translating the policy into action, "upgrading the system," meant the expenditure of billions of dollars on the *air traffic control and airspace system*—rather than into *runways* where specifically the capacity problem could have been more adequately controlled. Not that upgrading the ATC system has been worthwhile, because certainly from a safety standpoint it has been. But it must be recognized that the air traffic and airspace system is not an area where the greatest capacity problems can be or could have been resolved.

In 1975, Professor Horonjeff and his colleague, Chris Orman, in a paper presented to the Radio Technical Commission for Aeronautics [RTCA], compared the trade-off between airfield improvements and upgraded electronic systems for improvements in airport capacity.[33] Recognized were improvements to be derived from an upgraded ATC system, but as Horonjeff stated, the *key* to relieving congestion lies not in improved electronic aids, but rather in acquiring more "landside" capacity (in this case, meaning more runways). His point was that adding a runway is the more effective measure for increasing capacity. Demonstrated was a 28% increase in capacity by adding a parallel runway, compared to only 9% by upgrading the ATC system. It should be noted that another airport could increase capacity by as much as 100%.

In those days, Horonjeff and Orman were not the only ones who were prophesying capacity doom if something were not done to correct the deficiency in capacity. From the side of the electronics advocates, Dr. Richard M. Harris of the Mitre Corporation in the early 1970s stated that unless basic improvements were made to the ATC system, most major airports would become saturated for long periods

---

[33] Robert Horonjeff, in a paper presented at the annual meeting of the RTCA held in Arlington, Va. (1975).

of time on a daily basis. Mitre Corporation was at the time under contract to assist the FAA's Office of Systems Engineering Management in the establishment of an engineering and development plan for increasing airport capacity. The FAA/Mitre study team concluded that an upgraded ATC system *would* relieve Instrument Flight Rules [IFR] and Visual Flight Rules [VFR] saturation through 1980 and beyond. Perhaps the team's expectations were greater than the actual implementation programs have produced, but clearly by the mid 1980s, capacity constraint was not averted. As well-meaning as the team may have been, and irrespective of the benefits derived from theirs (and others') work in increasing capacity through improved electronic aids, it appears evident the concerted effort spent improving the ATC system has been an unfortunate diversion from correcting the real cause of capacity constraint, that of building more runways.

As a sign of the times, during the 1970s, FAA policy was more reflective of *environmental concerns* than it was of potentially constrained capacity. Capacity problems were forecast, while aircraft noise and other environmental concerns were apparent. To quote from the same 1978 Brock Adams policy statement, "Environmental compatibility of the air commerce system, particularly in the context of aircraft noise, will weigh heavily in our future aviation policy."

The FAA's policies, and environmental concerns of the 1970s, came under critical review by the aviation industry. In a discussion paper on the allocation of limited airport capacity, the Airport Operators Council International [AOCI] stated:

> *Numerous constraints on the physical expansion of many airports are also expected to foreclose accommodation of increased user demand. At larger hubs, little or no significant physical expansion of airside facilities may be possible. Where such physical expansion is potentially possible, environmental constraint may preclude or severely limit implementation.*

Where airport capacity could have been potentially increased, conservative infrastructure development policies of the federal government may have stifled expansion. Funding limitations of Airport Development Aid Program [ADAP], the expressed philosophy of the administration that airport development could not be expected to increase at the historical rate, and the increasing recognition that few, if any, new major air carrier airports would be built in the foreseeable future, all contributed to the expectation that airport development would not keep pace with the demand for airport facilities in many large hub locations.

Times as well as policy have changed. Perhaps the change in policy was triggered by reactionary pressures built up over air traffic delays at airports like Atlanta's Hartsfield, Chicago's O'Hare, or at Denver, Kennedy, LaGuardia, and Newark in the Winter of 1984. But the cause for the reaction is not so important as the fact that Washington was finally listening, and indicating it had some motivation to address the real problem. This was a giant step in the right direction, for the first step in correcting any problem is to first *recognize the problem.* But recognizing the problem does not necessarily mean there are sufficient funds to do much about it. When signing into law the Federal Aviation Administration Authorization Act of 1994, President Clinton stated,

> *This bill . . . fulfills part of my pledge to emphasize economically valuable infrastructure investment as the way to keep our Nation competitive by committing nearly $1.7 billion to new airport development and planning grants. Overall, I believe the legislation sends the right signal—that the aviation sector continues to be a prime contributor to this country's economic health.*

The $1.7 billion committed to airport infrastructure development, referred to above in Mr. Clinton's statement, fell well short of the funds necessary to meet future airport infrastructure development needs. Nevertheless, by its actions the Federal government had assumed responsibility for development and oversight of the NPIAS. As we transition through the Bush Administration, the Federal government cannot now renege on that commitment, but unfortunately foreign events (particularly in Iraq and Afghanistan) have diverted attention away from domestic policy.

CAPACITY ENHANCEMENT

Robert Horonjeff's point that adding a runway is the more effective measure for increasing capacity may have been over simplistic in light of the realities of both fiscal and political constraints on airport system expansion. Nevertheless, acquiring more landside capacity (meaning more runways) is the simplest answer to a complex issue. But when Horonjeff referred to the "landside," what he meant was the airport versus air traffic and airspace improvements. Airport capacity enhancement is a building block process. Starting with an unimproved airfield, where the field may not be useable during inclement weather or at times when the field is wet, building an improved runway by *paving* it is the first step to adding year-round capacity.

Having built a runway, *taxiways* at each runway end, or at least *turnarounds* at each end of the runway provide a way for aircraft to clear the runway so that other aircraft may use it. To further facilitate aircraft on the ground, taxiway improvements connecting the runway and the terminal apron provide the means for aircraft to clear the air movement area. A taxiway *parallel* to the runway aids in the circular movement of traffic on the ground, further enhancing the airport's capacity.

A single runway is limited by the prevailing winds. Adding a *crosswind runway* or runways, until the desired 95% crosswind component is achieved adds more capacity. But still, only one runway can be used at a time. To allow simultaneous operations, a *parallel runway* must be added. Depending on its location a parallel runway can nearly double the capacity. Parallel runways placed at least 700 feet apart can be used simultaneously in the same direction. If the runways are 1,400 feet apart during daytime operations, or 2,800 feet for nighttime operations, they can be used independently for traffic in opposite directions. Parallel runways at least 4,300 feet apart if the thresholds are side-by-side, or between 2,500 to 4,300 feet depending on distance the thresholds are staggered from one another, can provide simultaneous IFR operations.

Parallel runways may also be used for simultaneous operations with departures from one runway and landings on the other. To take full advantage of parallel runways, each must have parallel taxiways. Two parallel taxiways for each runway would allow for two-way ground traffic, which may facilitate movement to/from the terminal area(s).

Landside improvements that are truly on the "landside" are important as well. The true landside portion of the airport begins at the interface wall and extends toward the street-side access. In other words, the landside portion includes the access roads, automobile parking areas, and terminal buildings. Landside access can help to insure the highest utilization of the airside capacity. There are also terminal improvements that can enhance capacity. The ability to taxi to and from the terminal under the aircraft's own power (i.e., "power in" and "power out") can expedite clearing terminal gates. Additionally, aprons and gates that are segregated according to aircraft size and type can facilitate aircraft movement in the terminal area. Runway and taxiway construction should be designed around the "critical" aircraft but ought to accommodate all aircraft. One final aspect of the landside perspective is the provision of adequate snow and ice removal equipment, and an efficient maintenance and repair program to expeditiously return runways and taxiways to service.

Improvements to airport capacity from the perspective of the airspace components start with basic improvements. Any *instrument approach system* is better than no instrument approach procedure at all. But instrument approach systems come in many configurations, each an enhancement over the other. For example, a *precision* approach procedure is 15% to 20% more effective in adding capacity to a single runway than is a *non-precision* approach.[34] *Lighting aids*, such as the *Visual Approach Slope Indicator* [VASI], *Omni-Directional Approach Light Systems* [ODALS], *Lead In Lights* [LDIN] and/or *Runway End Identification Lights* [REIL] can all aid in traffic movement under low visibility conditions. Most importantly, an *Approach Lighting System* [ALS], depending on the configuration, can reduce the landing minima and thereby increase capacity.

Terminal *radar systems* can improve the IFR capacity by several-fold. The capability of vectoring aircraft directly to the approach course, can reduce the time the aircraft spends to follow the complete instrument approach procedure. The air traffic and airspace capacity with and ILS approach in a radar versus non-radar environment can be three times greater.[35]

---

[34] *See* Airborne Instruments Laboratory, *Airport Capacity Handbook*, Sec. 4 (2nd ed., Jun. 1969).
[35] *Id.*

As Professor Horonjeff stated, "the key to relieving congestion lies not in improved electronic aids, but rather by acquiring more capacity on the ground" (see *supra*). When he made that statement, his comments were aimed at advocates of improving the airside capacity through reduced aircraft separation by metering and spacing techniques. Specifically, Horonjeff was being critical of the Mitre Corporation and the FAA for having spent much time and effort toward advanced design and development of the air traffic control system, rather than placing the same, or at least equal time and energy into building more runways. But from Mitre's analysis a number of basic concepts and techniques for capacity improvement were identified, and they became the basis for the FAA/Mitre plan.

Richard Harris and Frederick C. Holland, both of the Mitre Corporation, argued that airport capacity enhancement techniques fell generally into two categories: *single runway capacity* improvements and *airport system capacity* improvements. From Mitre's position, both categories incorporated metering and spacing techniques to enhance capacity, not the *addition* of more runway capacity as advocated by Horonjeff and others. And even when Mitre did address runway improvements, it did so from the perspective of "the elements of arrival spacing (control and longitudinal separation) and runway operation (exiting and departure mixing) that affect the operations of individual runways." "Airport system capacity items," Mitre said, were "those elements affecting overall capacity of the airport such as runway geometry (parallel spacing, crosswind capacity), ground traffic capability, environmental constraints on design, and improved airport economic and operational planning methods."[36]

Although not exhaustive, Mitre listed the capacity benefits of a number of ATC and runway design improvements that, in combination, it believed could increase the IFR capacity by as much as 96% within the ensuing ten to fifteen years (i.e., by the mid 1980s). A substantial portion of the effort was "directed in improving terminal air traffic control and runway design and increasing the potential IFR rate of an airport without requiring the acquisition of additional land or building a new airport." In other words, Mitre relied upon its ability to improve the capacity of the existing system rather than invest in

[36] Richard M. Harris & Frederick C. Holland, *Techniques for Increasing Airport Capacity*, a paper presented to the International Air Transport Association 19th Technical Conference in Dublin, Ireland (Oct. 23-29, 1972).

new runways. Mitre said that improvements in operations rates would come from *improved delivery* to the final approach course, *reduced lateral and longitudinal spacing* on final approach, and *improved runway design* to reduce the effects of arrival and departure runway occupancy.[37]

RUNWAY CAPACITY IMPROVEMENTS

There was a major development effort mounted to provide computer aids to the controller to improve the accuracy of delivery to the ILS "approach gate."[38] As part of the FAA's *Automated Radar Terminal Systems* [ARTS] program it developed a *Metering and Spacing* [M&S] capability. Under M&S the computer algorithm schedules the aircraft to the runway based upon the aircraft type and separation minima plus a buffer based upon the delivery precision. Basic M&S employs ARTS tracking plus the automatic computation of speed, heading and altitude commands displayed to the controller. In addition, the computer will provide separation monitoring on the final approach course.[39]

REDUCED LONGITUDINAL SPACING

Mitre recognized that reduction of the (three-mile) IFR separation standard would be a "regulatory action of great consequence," but nevertheless suggested that substantial increases in capacity could be realized if the standard were reduced. Mitre proposed that reduction in the longitudinal minimum could be achieved by overcoming three problem areas:

---

[37] *Id.* at 4.

[38] The "approach gate" is an imaginary point used within ATC as a basis for vectoring aircraft to the final approach course. The gate will be established along the final approach course 1 mile from the outer marker (or the fix used in lieu of the outer marker) on the side away from the airport for precision approaches and 1 mile from the final fix on the side away from the airport for non-precision approaches. In either case when measured along the final approach course, the gate will be no closer than 5 miles from the landing threshold. FAA Aeronautical Information Manual, *Pilot/Controller Glossary* (1999).

[39] Richard M. Harris & Frederick C. Holland, *Techniques for Increasing Airport Capacity*, a paper presented to the International Air Transport Association 19th Technical Conference in Dublin, Ireland (Oct. 23-23, 1972), at 4.

- *Controller alert* to unsafe overtaking situations, a function that Mitre claimed could be provided by the automated M&S system;
- *Wake turbulence management*; and
- *Runway design* to avoid a wave off caused by a following aircraft overtaking a preceding aircraft, and to allow interleaved departure release.

Identified as the key to reducing longitudinal separation was the reduction of the effects of *wake turbulence*. To effectively conquer the wake vortex problem there are four basic approaches under investigation:

- *Detection* of existing hazards via acoustic or pressure sensing for real-time avoidance;
- *Prediction* of hazard conditions and locations for dynamic hazard avoidance;
- *Dissipation at the source* or reduction of the vortex hazard through modification of the aerodynamic generating mechanism; and
- *Dissipation from the ground* of the vortex by ground-based means such as vacuum or blowing devices.[40]

As of this writing the above problems associated with wake vortex have not been solved sufficiently to allow significant reductions in longitudinal separation. Government and industry groups are continuing to make concerted efforts to minimize or eliminate the hazards of trailing vortices. However, the pilot must exercise the flight disciplines necessary to ensure vortex avoidance during VFR operations. In IFR operations, controllers provide separation. Other than a "heavy aircraft" (i.e., 300,000 pounds or greater) following another heavy aircraft (where the separation may be reduced to four miles), all other aircraft following a heavy aircraft on landing must be separated by at least five miles (for a small aircraft behind a heavy it is six miles).[41]

---

[40] *Id.* at 10.
[41] FAA Aeronautical Information Manual, *Wake Turbulence*, Sec. 3 (1999).

REDUCED RUNWAY OCCUPANCY

The solutions Mitre offered for reducing runway occupancy time were related to an assumed reduction in longitudinal separation. *Runway Occupancy Time* [ROT] affects capacity in two ways. First, arrivals are affected when arrival spacing time approaches runway occupancy time. Given that the longitudinal separation standard remains unchanged, this time limit does not ordinarily occur in IFR conditions because ATC allows for large inter-arrival times. But assuming reduced spacing on final approach, runway occupancy time would have to be reduced and controlled through the provision of well-spaced *high-speed exit taxiways*.

Second, departures are affected by arrival occupancy time when arrivals and departures are mixed on the same runway. One solution currently being employed is to provide *dedicated* parallel runways, one for arrivals and one for departures. As an alternative solution, Mitre proposed the *dual-lane* runway. The "dual-lane runway" is a very close-spaced IFR *dependent* runway pair with centerline spacing 700 to 2,499 feet. The dual-lane runway concept incorporates efficient spacing of high-speed exits so that the arrival runway works in concert with the departure runway. Operationally, the dual-lane runway system functions like dedicated parallel runways. The departure is released when the arrival crosses the threshold of the arrival runway, rather than having to wait while the arrival rolls out and exits the runway. The basic advantage over the common parallel runway system that the dual-lane parallel system takes up less land.[42] Additionally, in certain situations building a parallel runway might not be considered because it cannot be developed as an *independent* runway, the dual-lane runway system offers significant advantages over one runway alone.

In summary, in an era of "conservative" planning and development (see Brock Adams' statement above) what Mitre had hoped for was to provide the electronic gadgetry to avert an impending gridlock. It did not work out that way. Seemingly, the technical obstacles could not be overcome timely enough to implement Mitre's recommenda-

---

[42] Richard M. Harris & Frederick C. Holland, *Techniques for Increasing Airport Capacity*, a paper presented to the International Air Transport Association 19th Technical Conference in Dublin, Ireland (Oct. 23-28, 1972), at 10-11.

tions in a comprehensive way. The Mitre Corporation predicted that by the mid 1980s there would be:

- Reduction in *longitudinal spacing* from three to two miles, with variable spacing for wake turbulence under some meteorological conditions;
- *Improved delivery accuracy* (from ± forty seconds to ± ten seconds);
- *Reduced lateral spacing* between parallel runways from 5,000 feet to 3,500 feet with ARTS III, and 2,500 feet with the *Microwave Landing System* [MLS];
- Wide-spread *adoption of dual-lane runways*;
- *Separate facilities* for general aviation;
- *Curved approaches* via MLS; and
- *Semi-automated ground traffic control.*

Although some improvements have been realized in advanced design of the air traffic control system, billions of dollars have been expended on a system that did not measure up to its expectations. As of this writing the air traffic control system in the United States is obsolete, a growing number of major U.S. airports are experiencing more than 20,000 hours of annual delay, and the ominous threat for potential system gridlock still looms ahead.

As the Mitre team suggested more than thirty years ago, and what is perhaps one solution to solving the dilemma, will be the contribution of advanced study, modeling, and analysis of airport capacity increase. There are many *modeling techniques* for studying airports or selected aspects of airports such as single runways or runway layouts. Airports can be modeled mathematically or through computer simulation. And models can be used to study the effects of changes in air traffic, ground traffic, passengers, or all at once. This type of analysis is a vital aid both to immediate planning and to master planning for future development.[43]

---

[43] *See id.* at 16.

MASTER PLANNING STUDIES

The Airport and Airway Development Act of 1970 gave rise to a formal systemized planning and development of airports, which did not exist prior to then. After 1970, the development of airports would no longer be the random function that it had previously been.[44] The Secretary of Transportation was directed by this Act to prepare and publish a *National Airport System Plan* [NASP] for the *capital development* of public airports. But one section of the Act provided for grants of funds to planning agencies to prepare *airport master plans.* The planning element of the airport development program was called the *Planning Grant Program* [PGP], and the funding of actual development of physical facilities was entitled the "Airport Development Aid Program."

The Airport and Airway Development Act defines "airport master planning" as,

> *. . . the development for planning purposes of information and guidance to determine the extent, type, and nature of development needed at a specific airport. It may include the preparation of an airport layout plan and feasibility studies, and the conduct of such other studies, surveys, and planning actions as may be necessary to determine the short, intermediate, and long-range aeronautical demands required to be met by a particular airport as a part of a system of airports.*

The Act goes on to define "airport system planning" as,

> *. . . the development for planning purposes of information and guidance to determine the extent, type, nature, location, and timing of airport development needed in a specific area to establish a viable and balanced system of pub-*

[44] AC 150/5070-6, "Airport Master Plans," published in Feb. 1971, has guided the preparation of master plans since enactment of the Airport and Airway Development Act of 1970. The description of the airport master planning process presented herein follows the outline in, and draws heavily from an updated version of AC 150/5070-6 (Jun. 1985).

> *lic airports. It includes identification of the specific aeronautical role of each airport within the system, development of estimates of system-wide development costs, and the conduct of such studies, surveys, and other planning actions as may be necessary to determine the short, intermediate, and the long-range aeronautical demands required to be met by a particular system of airports.*

Earlier master planning was predicated upon local rather than system aviation needs. It was a form of "crisis management" where development of facilities was a spontaneous reaction to immediate needs more than it was a program of planning for future requirements. That is to say, airport planning and development in the past was "reactive" rather than "proactive."

Primarily in response to the Airport and Airway Development Act of 1970, more recent planning efforts have incorporated actual and projected demands of the air transportation system, and in a systematic way that serves future air transportation needs. Not only must the planner consider the present and future requirements of all facets of aviation, but must also compare aviation development against its associated environmental impacts, overall proposed community development, and development of other modes of transportation.

Under the current Federal guidance, there two basic types of master planning studies: *Airport Master Plans and Airport Layout Plan Updates.*[45] The planning category, "Airport Master" Plans, includes the following two choices:

- *Master Plan*—A planning process that addresses major revisions in the comprehensive study of the airport.
- *Master Plan Update*—A study that requires far less effort and only changes part of an existing Master Plan.

In order to receive federal assistance, airports are required to keep their Airport Layout Plan [ALP] current. Thus, sometimes, an airport sponsor will only undertake a master plan study to update the ALP.

---

[45] FAA, *Airport Master Plans*, AC 150/5070-6B (Jul. 29, 2005), retrieved from www.faa.gov.

Such an update of just the "drawing set" of the Master Plan is referred to as an "Airport Layout Plan Update". [46]

Master planning represents the planner's concept of the ultimate development of an airport, and synthesizes the planning research and logic into a graphic and written report—the *Airport Master Plan.* Master plans are accomplished not only for the construction of new airports, but also for modernization and expansion of existing airports. The overall objective of the airport master plan is to provide guidelines for the logical and timely development of the airport. The master plan identifies needed improvements and establishes priorities based on existing and projected aeronautical demands. The master plan is integrated into the community's transportation system, and is designed to be compatible with the generalized community development. Specific objectives of the master plan are to:

- Provide graphic representation of the ultimate airport development;
- Present land use strategies on the airport and adjacent to it;
- Establish a phased schedule for development;
- Present the back-up data which supports the master plan;
- Describe the alternative concepts for development; and
- Provide a concise, descriptive, and clearly understandable report.

A master plan facilitates approval of funds for future airport projects by federal and state agencies that participate extensively in the support of airport development. The plan also provides for the preparation of environmental assessments and impact reports where and when they are required by specific development projects. Along with the application for federal and state funds, the sponsor must also submit a plan with supporting justification for any construction. A well-conceived master plan can be used as a guide throughout the period it is intended to cover, but it has to be flexible enough to permit adjustments for technical and other changes that may occur along the way. The products of the master planning process include the following deliverables:

---

[46] *Id.*

- Technical Report—containing the results of the analysis;
- Summary Report—containing "pertinent facts, conclusions, and recommendations for public review";
- Airport Layout Plan Drawing Set;
- Web Page; and
- Public Information Kit.[47]

AIRPORT MASTER PLAN ELEMENTS

The master planning process follows a logical sequence of tasks. The process involves collecting data, forecasting demand, conducting demand/capacity analyses to determine facility requirements and developing plans and schedules. The various tasks or elements of a master planning process will vary in complexity and degree of application, depending on the size, function and problems of the individual airport. Each task is undertaken only to the extent necessary to produce a meaningful product for a specific airport, and it is not always necessary to undertake every task. Initially, the airport must organize itself and engage in the preplanning process.

As mentioned earlier in this chapter, airport master plan studies typically include a well-considered preplanning phase, followed by addressing the several key elements:

- Public Involvement Program;
- Environmental Considerations;
- Existing Conditions;
- Aviation Forecasts;
- Facility Requirements;
- Alternatives Development and Evaluation;
- Airport Layout Plans;
- Facilities Implementation Plan; and
- Financial Feasibility Analysis.[48]

---

[47] *Id.*
[48] *Id.*

PREPLANNING

In beginning the process of preparing master plan studies, thoughtful organization and preplanning efforts are important. Thorough preplanning activities can expedite a project and identify issues, decide which existing data will be used, clarify airport operator/consultant relationships, and establish schedules, financial resources and overall project scope.

The sophistication of the organization created for a master planning study will vary depending on the complexity of the project, but in all cases the airport operator should take the lead in initiating and accomplishing the project, reviewing technical reports, controlling communications regarding the project, and conducting public hearings and public information sessions that will be required throughout the process.

The preplanning process includes several components such as: initial needs determination, request for proposal and consultant selection, development of study design, negotiation of consultant contract and application for study funding.[49] For all master planning projects, a defined organizational structure is important the relationships and responsibilities of all stakeholders are understood.

After the organizational phase, but prior to awarding a contract to the consultant, the airport sponsor and the selected consultant should: (1) identify the pertinent issues involved in development of the airport; and (2) determine the type and magnitude of effort needed to address each issue individually. This step is referred to as "scoping." During this step specific aviation-related issues are reviewed and a preliminary assessment is made of what it will take to resolve them.

The length of the short, intermediate and long-term activity forecasts need to be determined. Customarily, this means five, ten, and twenty-year time frames, but there may be justification in selecting other time frames. In any event, the short-term forecast should support a *capital improvement plan*, the intermediate-term forecast should present a realistic *assessment of needs*, and the long-term forecast should present a concept-oriented *statement of needs*.

Schedules showing milestones for completion of technical products as well as coordination and review activities must be agreed upon during the scoping phase. Adhering to schedules—especially for con-

[49] *Id.*

troversial issues—can be very difficult. As a result, realistic milestones need to be agreed upon. Finally, the specific products of the master planning process should be agreed upon with regard to number, type and format of reports and drawings.

After scoping the project and selecting a consultant, the price for consulting services must be determined and contractual arrangements finalized. The consultant should be selected by an unbiased and technically qualified selection panel based upon generally accepted practices of consultants engaged in architecture, engineering and planning. The normal agreement is a *firm fixed price*, however, where the level of effort or duration of the project is uncertain, a *cost-plus-a-fixed fee* contract or *time and materials* contract may be necessary.

PUBLIC INVOLEMENT PROGRAM

An airport master plan draws widespread community and airport user interest, and the planning project must include a comprehensive public participation program of coordination and review procedures. Public support of the airport master plan is vital! A planning process that does not include an adequate public participation program may likely meet with strong citizen reaction and ultimate disapproval.

Upon the selection and contracting of a consultant, a public involvement program should be established to identify and document relevant stakeholders and their key issues. For less complex projects, the airport operator and a consultant together may constitute the organizational structure, but it is generally accepted that the FAA as well as aviation industry organizations would normally participate in the master planning process. Others that might be included in the formal organization include city, county and/or airport board representatives, citizen participation groups, and airport tenants.

The FAA identifies several tools and techniques that are valuable in increasing meaningful public involvement, including committees, public information meetings, small group meetings and a public awareness campaign.[50] Technical review committees might include air traffic and airspace experts, FAA regional and field office representatives, airline representatives, financial institutions, general aviation users, and other resource agencies. Airport management staff will

---

[50] *Id.*

likely participate in the on-going activities of the master planning process.

Generally, the earlier the public is involved, the greater the trust will be between the parties. In addition, it is much better to involve the public in constructing a plan, than to be relegated to defending a plan that was created with insufficient public involvement.

ENVIRONMENTAL CONSIDERATIONS

Existing and potential environmental impacts and appropriate mitigating measures must be considered throughout the master planning process. The master planning process is an ideal vehicle for reviewing potential environmental conflicts. Throughout the inventory process, data concerning the surrounding environment is gathered and evaluated. Particular emphasis is placed on airport generated noise, but consideration is also given to other factors such as airport drainage, erosion, light pollution, endangered species protection, and items of historic or archeological significance. This data serves as the basis for evaluation of the environmental effects of alternative development concepts, and for planning land use adjacent to the airport. It also provides the basic input for an Environmental Assessment or an Environmental Impact Statement if they are required.

The Environmental component of a master planning study is used to address environmental impacts, identify mitigating measures, and confirm compliance with the National Environmental Policy Act [NEPA] requirements, as required to obtain federal funding. Figure 5.1 presents a "Master Plan Environmental Overview" as provided by the FAA.[51]

During the environmental scoping process associated with NEPA, a determination should be made to assess the required documentation for environmental studies (i.e., *Environmental Assessment* [EA], *Environmental Impact Statement* [EIS], and so forth), and whether any categorical exclusions/inclusions might apply. A determination should be made with regard to the depth of original forecasting to be conducted. For example, other pertinent forecasts may exist, which might be used to augment and/or mitigate the forecasting effort (e.g., forecasts produced for regional or state system plans, FAA Terminal Area Forecasts, and so forth).

[51] *Id.*

Figure 5.1—MASTER PLAN ENVIRONMENTAL OVERVIEW

Air Quality Classification	Attainment Area: Non-Attainment Area: (List Pollutants) Maintenance Area: (List Pollutants)	
Aquatic Concerns	Bay: Creek: Ocean: Pond: Habitat-Endangered/ Threatened Species: Drinking Water Reservoir:	Wetlands: Floodplains: Potable Water Aquifer: Sole-Source Aquifer: Streams: Other:
Terrestrial Concerns	Contaminated Areas: Habitat-Endangered/Threatened Species: Farmland, Prime and Unique: Hazardous Material Storage Areas: Landfills:	
Cultural	Historic Properties: Archeological resources: Parks Wildlife Refuges: Residential Areas: Noise Sensitive Areas: (Churches, Schools, Hospitals, etc.) Other:	
Land Use Concerns	Traffic: Noise: Lighting: Obstructions: Environmental Justice: Zoning:	

* Note: Historic resources should be identified but the planning consultants should be wary of disclosing some information due to the sensitivity certain parties (i.e., Native Americans, Native Hawaiians) attach to these resources. A discussion should be held with these parties to decide if maps should include the identified resources.

Source: FAA, *Airport Master Plans*, AC 150/5070-6B. (Jul. 29, 2005), retrieved from www.faa.gov.

A number of permits that may be needed to remain in compliance with environmental quality regulations, including the following:

- Clean Water Act Section 404 Dredge and Fill Permit;
- Air Quality Permit (including those for site batch plans);
- Local Government Construction Permits;
- Grow Management Permits;
- Clean Water Act National Pollutant Discharge Elimination System [NPDES] Permits; and
- U.S. Fish and Wildlife, National Fisheries Services opinions, or State Wildlife and Game Commission Permits, if protected or endangered species may be impacted.

EXISTING CONDITIONS AND ISSUES

After the organization and preplanning phase, the actual airport master planning begins.[52] Existing conditions and issues are studied, and an *inventory* is made of pertinent information. As the master planning process begins, consultants literally show up at the airport study site with several empty suitcases in hand. The empty suitcases are for return to their home office filled with information about the existing airport. The inventory phase is to assemble and review all existing information pertinent to the accomplishment of subsequent planning steps. Following are three examples of the types of information gathered. Data regarding air traffic management, for example, will influence capacity determinations. Knowledge of airport rates and charges as well as historical revenues and expenses will help in determining the financial feasibility of proposed airport improvements. Or, an inventory of the condition and useful life of runways, taxiways, terminals, and so forth, is critical to determining the need for additional facilities.

There are general types of data required for most master planning projects, although the degree and emphasis of the data collection will vary substantially with the size and complexity of the project. Some of the types of data include:

[52] This section was largely drawn from FAA, *Airport Master Plans*, AC 150/5070-6B (Jul. 29, 2005), retrieved from www.faa.gov.

- Background historical information;
- The existing facilities;
- On and off-airport land uses;
- Ground access and circulation;
- Environmental information;
- Air traffic and airspace management;
- Support facilities such as Aircraft Rescue and Fire Fighting [ARFF], FAA and flight kitchens;
- Utilities such as water, power, communications and sewer systems;
- Meteorological information;
- Financial data;
- Historical aviation activity; and
- Socio-economic and demographic information.

Also included in the inventory are discussions of issues related to policy, land use and transportation planning. Some of these issues might include:

- The impacts of aviation growth on the community;
- The community's air carrier service needs;
- The potential need for new and/or expanded airport facilities;
- Capacity for expansion;
- Ground access problems;
- Issues related to relocation of persons, building or other infrastructure facilities;
- Obstructions to air navigation and objects which may affect flight; and/or
- Environmental concerns.

Data are collected on the airport and airspace infrastructure and airport-related land uses. Pertinent airport-related issues and regulatory mechanisms are defined. An inventory is taken of all existing airport facilities, area planning efforts, environmental and historical data, and socio-economic and demographic information describing the airport and its community. The inventory is a "shopping list" of information that will aid in the master planning process. Although not inclusive of all information that may be required, the following list is nevertheless comprehensive:

- Concise historical background information about how the airport evolved, its air traffic activity, military uses of the airport, airlines serving the airport, a description of facilities and dates of development, ownership record, and facts leading up to master plan decision; i.e., the results of steering committees, legislative agencies, study groups, and funding authorization;
- Data records pertinent to the study such as (IFR and VFR, and itinerant versus local) air traffic volumes, air passenger and cargo activity, based aircraft and the mix of aircraft using the airport, storage types and capacity and flowage volumes by type of fuel, itinerant versus local use of aircraft apron facilities, fixed base operator activity, and historic meteorological data;
- Airport and facility information such as a copy of the A*irport Master Record* (FAA Form 5010), information in the *Aeronautical Information Manual* [AIM] pertinent to the airport, types and conditions of hangars, runways and taxiways, and aircraft parking aprons, as well as size, condition and use of existing buildings;
- Air traffic and airspace facilities such as *Navigation Aids* [NAVAIDs], approach plates and other *Terminal Instrument Procedures* [TERPS], air traffic patterns and any airspace conflictions, associated airways, special use airspace, and known obstructions to air navigation;
- Environmental information both on and off the airport such as noise impact areas, emissions levels, historical and archeological sites that might influence development of the airport, biosystems of both vegetation and wildlife habitats, drainage and storm-water run-off, as well as types of fertilizers, herbicides, de-icing chemicals used on the airport; and proximity of the airport to water bodies and aquifers;
- Land use information both on and off airport, zoning and other height and hazard regulatory controls, land use planning commissions, state and local aeronautical commissions;

- Financial resources available from federal, state, local and private sources, historic revenues and expenses, local building costs; and
- Socio-economic and demographic information such as employment data on the airport and within the region, census trends, industrial activity, market trends, and personal income levels of the local population.

AVIATION (DEMAND) FORECASTS

Forecasting is a preliminary step in the planning process.[53] All business and public administration decisions require forecasting to some degree. The attempt in forecasting, like other rational economic actions, is to reduce uncertainty about the future. Forecasts can be used as indicators of whether or not budgetary plans and financial decisions are consistent with the future and with the goals and objectives of the airport.

Estimates of the timing of certain threshold events are the basis for effective planning and financial decisions. In airport planning, these events correspond to levels of aviation demand, which will exceed existing or planned capacities of the airport. The objective in airport forecasting is to predict when certain levels of demand will occur. The aviation demand elements to be forecast typically include types of activity, levels of activity, and peak periods of demand (see Table 5.1 "Airport Master Planning Aviation Demand Elements").

Depending upon available data and the level of assurance desired, forecasting methods can range from the very simple to the complex. Presented here are some generally accepted approaches to forecasting for management and planning of public airports. These forecasting approaches may be generally categorized as:

- Mechanical extrapolation;
- Mathematical analysis; and
- Judgmental interpolation.

[53] This section was largely drawn from FAA, *Airport Master Plans*, AC 150/5070-6B (Jul. 29, 2005), retrieved from www.faa.gov.

Table 5.1— AIRPORT MASTER PLANNING AVIATION DEMAND ELEMENTS

Required	***Included Where Appropriate***
Aircraft Operations (Annual)	
Itinerant	Domestic versus International
Air carrier	Annual Instrument Approaches
Air Taxi & Commuter (Regional)	IFR versus VFR Operations
	Air Cargo Aircraft Operations
General Aviation	Touch and Go Ops (Training)
Military	Helicopter Operations
Local	Average Load Factor
General Aviation	Fuel Use
Military	
Passengers (Annual)	
Enplanements	Passenger and Cargo Data Domestic
Air Carrier	Domestic vs. International
Commuter	General Aviation Passengers
Enplanements	Helicopter
Originating	Air Taxi
Connecting	Other
	Number of Student Pilots
	Number of Hours Flown
Aircraft	
Based	Average Seats/Aircraft
Aircraft Mix	Air Freight
Critical Aircraft	

Source: FAA, *Airport Master Plans*, AC 150/5070-6B (Jul. 29, 2005), retrieved from www.faa.gov.

No matter how complex the forecasting model might be, the results are still little more than calculated guesses tempered hopefully by sound judgment. Forecasting is an art, not a science! No one can accurately predict the future to a scientific level of acceptance. As an art form, forecasting is subjective. Hence, professional judgment (if not a gut reaction) may be appropriately used to modify seemingly firm mathematical results.

Quoting John Maynard Keynes,

> *Most major business decisions are taken as a result of animal spirits—of a spontaneous urge to action rather than inaction—and not as the outcome of a weighted average of quantitative benefits multiplied by probabilities*

Forecasting is an important tool in management and planning, but extensive mathematical analyses are not always necessary since some forecasts may already exist. As part of its comprehensive forecasting program, the FAA produces forecasts each year for the airports in the National Plan of Integrated Airport Systems. State and regional aviation activity forecasts are also important considerations, as are aviation forecasts produced by the Air Transport Association and other independent agencies.

One of the first steps in airport-related forecasting is to review already existing forecasts and to modify them according to changed local conditions. There are two noteworthy situations in which the FAA and other forecasts for a specific airport may need to be adjusted—unusual local conditions, or changed local conditions not accounted for in the existing forecasts.

For *unusual local conditions*, the forecaster needs to identify and document any ways in which the forecast factors for the area served by the specific airport differ radically from areas served by other similarly sized airports in the region. For example, the economy and population of the airport service area may be growing faster, the disposable personal income in the area may be above average, or the geographic attributes of the site may generate a higher-than-average aviation demand.

In the case of *changed local conditions*, attention should be paid to predictable changes from past trends (e.g., sharp deviations in growth trends for the local economy), disposable income, or demographic characteristics. In addition, some factors specific to the airport may be constraining demand forecasts, such as limited airport capacity or ground access or environmental constraints. To the extent plans for removal or abatement of these constraints can be documented, a basis may exist for adjusting an aviation demand forecast. For instance, if the existing forecast is based on a limited number of based aircraft, and plans to increase tie-downs or to establish a new fixed base operator can be documented there may be reason to adjust the aviation demand forecast.

If the forecaster is able to identify any unusual or changed local conditions, then adjustments should be made in the forecasts using one or more of the mechanical, mathematical, or judgmental forecasting methods. *Opinion surveying* may also be part of the judgmental process. It is perhaps the most subjective of the various forecasting techniques. Nevertheless, surveys may be used to temper existing forecasts or to collect additional data for self-generated forecasts.

Of the factors affecting demand forecasting, the following six have been found to be of particular significance and should be considered in forecasting demand for airport master plans and in updating and refining those forecasts:

- *Economic growth and changes in industrial activity*—a community's economic character affects its air traffic generating potential;
- *Demographic patterns*—the size and composition of an area's population—and its potential growth—are basic ingredients in creating demand for air transportation services;
- *Disposable personal income*—the discretionary purchasing power available to residents over any period of time is a good indicator of consumers' financial ability to travel;
- *Geographic attributes*—the geographic distribution and distances between populations and centers of commerce within the area served by the airport may have a direct bearing on the type and level of transportation services that will be demanded;
- *Other external factors*—there are a number of other factors that might affect aviation demand at all or certain types of airports or at a specific airport. Examples might be: fuel price changes,

changes in the regulatory environment, changes in levels and types of taxes, passenger fares, or currency restrictions; and

- *Local aviation actions*—there may be any number of actions that local airport authorities take that have the conscious or unintended effect of either stimulating or retarding growth in aviation demand at the airport. Examples might be changes in airport fee structures, plans for future development, an active marketing plan, or removal of political or legal constraints to growth.

Inventory data, and specifically historic activity trends, are used to develop *forecasts* of aviation demand. These forecasts are normally established for *short*, *intermediate*, and *long-range (*identified as up to 5 years, 6-10 years and beyond 10 years). Notably, these time frames are shorter than the forecast horizons associated with the larger master planning study.[54]

The five, ten and twenty-year) time periods. While twenty-year periods are usually targeted for long-range projections, a ten-year intermediate period is a more reasonable target in terms of forecast accuracy. A five-year forecast should be of sufficient accuracy to justify a short-term capital improvement program. The forecasts are of based aircraft, aircraft mix, aircraft operations, enplaned passengers, air cargo, ground transportation, and any other activities for which existing or future support facilities may be required. The various forecasts are developed for the *busy-hour* (peak-time) operations, around which airport development is determined.

Forecasts analyze the relationships between dependent variables (i.e., those factors to be predicted) and independent variables (i.e., the predicting factors). *Regression* analysis is the statistical technique for estimating the value of one variable based on knowledge of another variable and the empirical relationship between them. When only two variables are involved, the analysis is described as a simple (or "bivariate") regression. Multiple (or "multivariate") regression refers to the analysis of three or more variables. Regression has been the most commonly used of the mathematical (or econometric) forecasting methodologies, because a wide-based audience more readily interprets the results.[55] Nevertheless, since 1970 the *Autoregressive In-*

[54] *Id.*

[55] This is because correlation factors may be interpreted as a percentage of explanation.

tegrated Moving Average [ARIMA] technique has also found widespread acceptance amongst forecasters. Although ARIMA reportedly overcomes certain problems associated with regression analyses (with best fit and with definition of error terms), its sophistication is beyond the scope of this text.

The reason for including a discussion of forecasting techniques in this book is more by way of aiding the reader in understanding the process and interpreting the results, rather than as an introduction to sophisticated econometrics. Many hand-held calculators are programmed for accomplishing *bivariate* regressions. *Multivariate* programs are available on common software applications on the Personal Computer [PC] (e.g. *Excel* in Microsoft Windows), as well as highly sophisticated software packages for both PC and main frame computers (e.g., *Statistical Package for the Social Sciences* [SPSS]). Nevertheless, for readers unfamiliar with regression analyses, an introduction and description of regression is presented in Appendix A.[56]

FACILITY REQUIREMENTS (ANALYSIS AND CONCEPTS)

Having inventoried the existing airport and reviewed its condition, and then from the existing data created demand forecasts, the planning process turns to an investigation of the airport's capability to accommodate forecasted demand. Future facility requirements are based upon projected forecasts of demand, and the *demand/capacity* relationships of existing facilities. Hence, the capability of the existing airport to support forecast demand must be determined.

Although it is not always possible, ideally, an airport is planned and developed to accommodate the entire forecast demand. As a result, the *unconstrained capacity* needs to be determined. The unconstrained airside and landside capacity requirements are then imposed on the existing airport facilities and an assessment is made as to whether and/or how to expand facilities to accommodate forecast demand into the five, ten and twenty-year planning periods. Generally, the demand/capacity studies compare such things as the volume of aircraft operations against existing airfield facilities; the number of passenger enplanements against available terminal building space;

---

[56] The step by step explanation of the regression procedure is drawn heavily from the *Management Text Subcourse Manual*, U.S. Army Command and General Staff College (Jun. 1980).

airport access traffic against access road systems and other modes of ground transportation; and so forth.

In demand/capacity analyses, airside capacity is calculated and matched against aircraft demand forecasts. Landside capacity is determined for the terminal area, passenger gates, curbside and surface access, and for automobile parking. Capacities of airport facilities can be calculated by two means, either by using a demand/capacity handbook and *manually* determining capacity calculations or by *computer simulation*.

When addressing airports, "capacity" is not an absolute term, but rather implies "delays at a given movement rate." To explain, a hypothetical aircraft fuel tank in absolute terms might contain say 100 gallons, assuming the tank is in a closed and static state. But once fuel begins to flow into or from the tank, it becomes part of a fuel system. Time, vis-à-vis rate of flow, must now be considered into the "capacity" calculations. Now consider the aircraft is in flight, and has available to it aerial refueling on demand. Now what is the capacity? If the rate of flow is 10 gallons per hour, the capacity (based on movement rate) will be the original 100 gallons plus the 10 gallons. Assuming the aircraft has unlimited access to aerial refueling, and could remain in the air indefinitely, it has an "absolute" capacity of 110 gallons per hour, all things remaining equal. But to expect all things to remain unchanged may not be "practical." Suppose power from the aircraft engine is increased and the rate of flow increases to 15 gallons per hour. So long as the refueling tanker can likewise increase its fuel flow, capacity of the aircraft being refueled can increase. However, if the tanker is unable to increase the flow, the capacity of the refueled aircraft becomes "constrained." Or suppose the aircraft must experience "delay" between aerial refueling tankers, and must reduce power to conserve fuel. Then, the capacity will go below 110 gallons per hour. If the aircraft needing fuel has to wait too long for a tanker it will have to land, and the delay may become "unacceptable."

Airport capacity works in much the same way. In one definition of airport capacity, it is "that level of aircraft operations where the delays to the aircraft reach the maximum acceptable level." It is defined as a "practical" capacity that is reached when the movement rate results in an acceptable delay. In other words, airport capacity is limited by delay factors. Use of runways, taxiways, gates, and the surrounding airspace is a queuing process, wherein there is competition for use of these facilities. For example, if two aircraft wish to use the runway at the same time, one of the aircraft must wait (or queue) for the other to use the runway. The queuing time is delay, and is dependent on a number of other factors. "Movement rate" is the governing factor.[57] Other factors affecting airport capacity include:

- *Weather* (IFR versus VFR)—traffic flow is significantly reduced during instrument meteorological conditions when there are low cloud ceilings and poor visibility;
- *Runway configuration* (design) and number of runways—for example, a crosswind runway can add capacity to a single runway, but a parallel runway can nearly double capacity;
- *Training activity* (specifically the amount of touch-and-go landings)—because training aircraft occupy the runway for shorter duration, the capacity in terms of landing and takeoffs is increased;
- *Aircraft population* (mix)—a given airport system can accommodate more small than large aircraft;
- Number and location of *exit taxiways* and runway crossings—the availability of convenient taxiways of proper design can reduce *Runway Occupancy Time* [ROT];
- Location of *terminal buildings* relative to the runways and taxiways—long taxi times and/or taxiing delayed by crossing runways, or landings and takeoffs delayed by aircraft taxiing across runways reduces capacity;
- Aircraft arrival versus *departure rates*—the departure rate is higher than arrival rate, thus traffic must be balanced to increase capacity and rate of flow;
- *Airspace constraints* and proximity to other airports—airports that are too close to one another can reduce the potential capacity of each airport; and
- *Wake vortices*—causing increased separation between air traffic and consequent delays.

Airborne Instruments Laboratory [AIL] first published an airport capacity handbook in June 1963. The FAA adopted the AIL handbook, which was issued in November of 1966 as Advisory Circular

---

[57] Airborne Instruments Laboratory, *Airport Capacity Handbook* 17-3 (2nd ed., Jun. 1969).

150/5060-1, "Airport Capacity Criteria Used in Preparing the National Airport Plan."[58] This original circular presented the capacity methodology used by the FAA for determining when additional runways, taxiways, and aprons were to be recommended in the *National Airport Plan* [NAP].[59] The circular was designed as an aid to airport sponsors and engineers in developing *Airport Layout Plans* [ALP] and for determining when additional airport pavement facilities should be provided to increase airport capacity and accommodate more aircraft. The circular was updated in 1968 as AC 150/5060-1A.

At about the same time AC 150/5060-1A was published, the FAA prepared a short hand version, AC 150/5060-3, "Airport Capacity Criteria Used in Long-Range Planning," for determining the approximate practical hourly and practical annual capacities of various airport runway configurations. This latter circular was for use in "long-range" (meaning ten years or more) planning for expansion of existing airports and construction of new airports to accommodate forecast demand.

Using the AIL methodology, the FAA adopted as policy that airport facilities should be planned and developed when demand reached or was forecast to reach 60% of capacity. However, methodologies and assumptions have changed since the AIL Handbook was first published and, as will be seen in subsequent paragraphs, when this standard rule of thumb is applied, the methodology selected to calculate capacity can become critical.

To the Airborne Instruments Laboratory, "capacity" meant "an operating level, expressed as the rate of aircraft movements, which results in a given level of delay," as prescribed specifically in their definitions of *Practical Hourly Capacity* [PHOCAP] and *Practical Annual Capacity* [PANCAP]. The latter (PANCAP), AIL said, was the better measure of an airport's efficiency than hourly capacity. In either case, "practical" capacity was reached when the delay to operations reached an average of four minutes. For small aircraft the acceptable delay was an average of two minutes.

Although not adopted as an advisory circular, AIL's second edition to the *Airport Capacity Handbook* was used extensively throughout the ten-year planning period following adoption of the Airport

[58] *See* FAA, *Airport Capacity Criteria Used in Preparing the National Airport Plan*, AC 150/5060-1A (Jul. 8, 1968).
[59] The National Airport Plan was the result of the Federal Airport Act of 1946.

and Airway Development Act of 1970. Since AIL defined capacity as delay-related, it acknowledged that PHOCAP could be exceeded, but at the price of a higher delay. And in many cases there were examples of airports actually operating with air traffic levels well above what AIL determined to be their ("acceptable") capacity limits. Because airports were actually operating at higher levels, the abstractness of AIL's "practical" capacity was difficult to justify. Added to this was the problem of dealing with wide-body aircraft that had just entered production in the late 1960s.[60]

Knowing that production of wide-body aircraft was in progress, AIL allowed for capacity predictions for what it termed the "post-1975 conditions." Whereas, AIL had otherwise used techniques and calculations based on actual surveys of air traffic, for the yet to be introduced wide-body aircraft, AIL had to rely on the author's judgment of future events and upon certain assumptions. It assumed that traffic control equipment aids, particularly in the form of arrival/departure sequencing computers, would become available to air traffic controllers. In addition, and although it had no empirical evidence, AIL assumed that the wide-bodies would not behave much differently than then existing Boeing 707 and DC-8 aircraft.[61]

The lack of empirical data upon which to base their techniques for calculating actual airport capacity, the abstractness of using "practical" capacity, together with the early introduction of computerized modeling techniques for calculating capacities generally made the AIL Handbook obsolete. The changes in aircraft fleet composition, along with improvements in air traffic control practices that had subsequently occurred, outdated the AIL methodology. In the late 1970s, the FAA contracted with a project team to reexamine the procedures for determining airport capacity and to suggest im-

---

[60] In the late 1960s, the Air Force solicited bids for production of a super large transport. The principal bidders were Lockheed and Boeing. Lockheed won the bid, and subsequently introduced the C-5 Galaxy in 1968. Although Boeing lost the competition with its proposed CH-X, from the experience gained, Boeing proposed production of the 747, and in Aug. of 1966, production of the 747 commenced. The gamble paid off, and Boeing acquired a niche as the only producer of civilian jumbo-jet transports. Lockheed and Douglas, unable to match the Boeing effort, turned their attention to the so-called Jumbo Twin specification prepared by American Airlines. Subsequent discussions with American assessed a broader market, which led to a final proposal for a three-engine wide-body.[60] In response to the specified demand, Douglas produced the DC-10, and Lockheed introduced the L-1011 TriStar; Paul Stephen Dempsey & Laurence E. Gesell, *Air Transportation: Foundations for the 21st Century* 64 (1997).

[61] Airborne Instruments Laboratory, *Airport Capacity Handbook* 17-2, 17-12 (2nd ed., Jun. 1969).

provements to update them.[62] Recommendations by the project team led to cancellation of AC 150/5060-1A, *Airport Capacity Criteria Used in Preparing the National Airport Plan*, dated July 8, 1968 (i.e., the original AIL methodology handbook), and AC 150/5060-3A, *Airport Capacity Criteria Used in Long Range Planning*, dated December 24, 1969 (i.e., the shorthand AIL handbook).

Both of the outdated ACs were replaced in 1983 by AC 150/5060-5, *Airport Capacity and Delay*. It contains a chapter for "Capacity and Delay Calculations for Long Range Planning," as well as procedures for conducting more detailed calculations of capacity and delay at specific airports. Demand/capacity analyses for sample airports is presented in Appendix A.

Refined in AC 150/5060-5 are definitions of capacity and delay. It defines "capacity" as the "throughput rate," meaning the *maximum* number of operations that can take place in an hour. "Delay" is the difference in time between a constrained and an unconstrained aircraft operation. These definitions take into account that delays occur because of simultaneous demands. But rather than automatically building into the capacity calculation what an acceptable level of delay is, it leaves that decision to the airport sponsor. As a result, the acceptable level of delay will vary from airport to airport.[63]

Advisory Circular 150/5060-5 also introduced new assumptions that in many cases differed from the previously employed AIL methodology (see Table 5.2, "Methodology Assumptions"). For starters, the throughput method for calculating airport capacity and average delay per aircraft is derived from computer simulation, whereas AIL had based their calculations on empirical observations. Additionally, factors other than those used by AIL are considered for calculations, of "hourly capacity" rather than PHOCAP, and "annual service volume" rather than PANCAP, for example. Moreover, in AC 150/5060-5, "delay" is defined simply as the "difference between constrained versus unconstrained operating time." The underlying assumption is that capacity is an absolute calculation irrespective of delay, and that local airport sponsors may determine for themselves what an "acceptable" average delay is for their particular circumstances.

---

[62] The project team was headed by Douglas Aircraft Co. and included Peat, Marwick, Mitchell & Company, McDonnell Douglas Automation Co., American Airlines, Inc., & Professor Robert Horonjeff of the University of California, Berkeley as general advisor.

[63] *See* FAA, *Airport Capacity and Delay*, AC 150/5060-5 (Sep. 23, 1983).

Table 5.2—METHODOLOGY ASSUMPTIONS

Airport Capacity Handbook	*vs. Airport Capacity and Delay*
Similarities	
• Instrument Approach Weather, Visual Approach Weather, and Crosswind Conditions	Ceiling, Visibility, and Poor Visibility Conditions
• Runway Configuration	Runway Configuration
• Runway Use	Runway Use
• Aircraft Population (5 classes; A = large)	Aircraft Mix (4 classes; A = small)
• Touch-and-Go Activity	Percent Touch-and-Go
• Runway Crossing (terminal location)	Taxiway Capacity (crosswind runway)
• "Post 1975 Conditions"	Wake Vortices Effects
Unique Characteristics	
• Runway Design (length, weight, etc)	Exit Taxiway Location
• Airspace (routings)	Percent Arrivals
• Proximity of Other Airports	Gate Capacity
• Capacity (prescribes acceptable delay)	Maximum Operations (acceptable delay varies)
• Practical Hourly Capacity (PHOCAP)	Hourly Capacity
• Practical Annual Capacity (PANCAP) ("saturation" closest thing to maximum "throughput")*	Annual Service Volume (maximum throughput, but may be modified by "airfield useable time")
• Delay (calculated constraint on capacity)	Constrained versus Unconstrained Operating Time

* Note: "Saturation" was defined in FAA, *Terminal Area Forecasts 1978-1988* (Jan. 1977), as 166% of PANCAP.

ALTERNATIVES DEVELOPMENT AND EVALUATION

As alternatives are considered, a balance is expected between the needs of airport users and the airport sponsor's strategic vision. The FAA views the key components of this element to be:

- *Identification* of alternatives to address previously identified facility requirements;
- *Evaluation* of the alternatives, individual and collective, so the planners gain a thorough understanding of the strengths, weaknesses, and implications of each; and,
- *Selection* of the recommended alternative.[64]

It is important to consider a number of factors associated with each alternative including environmental, fiscal and other requirements and objectives. An "Alternatives Analysis Process" example for considering options is provided as Figure 5.2. This sample flow chart allows several airport function elements to be considered (airside, airline passenger terminal complex, cargo, general aviation, ground access, and support) as either primary or secondary elements.

Further, airport operational performance should be evaluated from a number of perspectives, including capacity, capability and efficiency. Each airport's demands, desires and future vision must be considered in fairly evaluating alternatives. In addition, a vast number of more complex considerations must be included in an airport site selection process, as discussed in detail later in this section.[65]

When evaluating alternatives, the process and considerations should be adapted to each airport's unique situation. While sophisticated analysis such as a simulation is available, it may not be appropriate, reasonable or financially feasible for all airport sponsors. Simulations are discussed in depth in the next section.

---

[64] FAA, *Airport Master Plans*, AC 150/5070-6B (Jul. 29, 2005), retrieved from www.faa.gov.
[65] *Id.* at 65.

Figure 5.2—ALTERNATIVES ANALYSIS PROCESS

1 Determine which airport functional elements (Airside, Airline Passenger Terminal Complex, Cargo, General Aviation, Ground Access, and Support) will be analyzed as Primary Elements and Secondary Elements.

PRIMARY ELEMENTS | SECONDARY ELEMENTS

2 ID Preliminary Alternatives | ID Preliminary Alternatives | ID Preliminary Alternatives

3 Preliminary Screening - By Element Mostly Subjective

4 Intermediate List | Intermediate List | Intermediate List

5 Quantitative Analysis – By Element

6 Short List | Short List | Short List

7 1 2 3 4 ... etc Merge Elements into Combined Alternatives

8 Quantitative Analysis of Combined Alternatives

9 Recommended Alternative

Secondary Analysis Needed?

10 ID Alternatives If Needed | ID Alternatives If Needed | ID Alternatives If Needed

11 Evaluate Alternatives – By Element

12 Recommended | Recommended | Recommended

13 Refined Recommended Alternative goes to ALP for development

Source: FAA, Airport *Master Plans*, AC 150/5070-6B (Jul. 29, 2005), retrieved from www.faa.gov.

SIMULATION

One area where the MITRE Corporation was right on target in 1972 was in their prediction that computer simulation and modeling would one day be vital to the master planning process.[66] A variety of simulation models have been developed for airport planning, and a careful review is needed to determine which is best for a particular application. The FAA, for example, has procured and developed a whole host of computer models for conducting airport analyses. Several of these models are used to determine the capacity and delay of airports and to study the sensitivity of capacity and delay to various airport conditions. The capacity and delay models include the *Runway Capacity Model*, the *Runway Delay Simulation Model* [RDSIM], the *Airfield Delay Simulation Model* [ADSM], and the *Airport and Airspace Delay Simulation Model* [SIMMOD]. These capacity and delay models fall into two categories, *analytic* and *simulation*, and are used to produce calculations of:

- Hourly runway, taxiway, and gate capacity;
- Hourly and daily delays, travel times, flow rates, and queuing data;
- Annual delay and annual delay costs; and annual delay savings computed from annual delay costs.[67]

Other analytic models recommended by the FAA include the *Integrated Noise Model* [INM] and *Airport Design (for Microcomputers)*. Added to FAA family of computer models is a proliferation of common software applicable to airport planning and design. To begin with there are word-processing programs like Word and Word Perfect, as well as graphics and publication packages like *Adobe* or *Pagemaker*. As already mentioned above, there are statistical packages such as Excel, SPSS, and others for conducting forecasting exercises. There is a library of programs that provide the capability to perform the usual functions of traditional transportation planning with regards to trip generation, distribution, and network assignment.

---

[66] Richard M. Harris & Frederick C. Holland, *Techniques for Increasing Airport Capacity*, a paper presented to the International Air Transport Association 19th Technical Conference in Dublin, Ireland (Oct. 23-28, 1972), at 16.
[67] FAA, retrieved from http://www.tc.faa.gov/capacity/runwayq.htm (Dec.15, 1998).

Added to the aforementioned are software programs for *Computer-Aided Design and Computer Aided Manufacturing* [CAD/CAM], as well as *Global Information Systems* [GIS] used in producing maps, plots and layout plans.

Looking specifically at the FAA programs, the *Runway Capacity Model* is an analytic model for computing airport capacity. It assumes an infinite queue of arrivals and departures, and thereby provides a theoretical maximum throughput for the runways. In computing capacity, the minimum sustainable time between successive arrivals and departures is determined, and then inverted to find the maximum number of arrivals per hour. The maximum number of departures that can be inserted between the arrivals is then calculated.

The inputs to the Runway Capacity Model are the airfield's geometry and operating strategy. Each execution consists of a geometry/strategy combination coupled with other variables such as aircraft mix, average runway occupancy time, and average separations between aircraft. The principal output of the model is the total capacity per hour for a specified arrival percentage. In addition, the output includes messages containing operating strategies for reaching given percentages of arrivals.[68]

The Runway Delay Simulation Model was primarily developed to perform runway capacity and delay analyses by simulating runway operations. By varying delay, capacity can be calculated. Graphs showing flow rates versus demand and delay versus demand can be generated and the results calculated for a single traffic hour. The model can be used to compute capacity at an acceptable level of delay and maximum throughput.

Inputs to the Runway Delay Simulation Model are similar to, but less detailed than, those used by the Airfield Delay Simulation Model. The RDSIM therefore requires far less time and effort to simulate. The inputs include runway usage, runway occupancy times, exit probabilities, aircraft demand and mix, aircraft approach speeds, aircraft separations and ATC rules and procedures. The outputs for RDSIM are similar to ADSIM. And because the RDSIM results can be produced more easily, they can be used to readily capture the main benefits of a given alternative improvement.[69]

---

[68] *Id.*
[69] *Id.*

The *Airfield Delay Simulation Model*, like RDSIM, simulates the movement of aircraft on the airport surface and in the immediate approach and departure airspace corridors. The ADSIM is one of the most detailed models available for evaluating airport operations and sources of delay. However, the advantages of using ADSIM over RDSIM must be balanced against the large investment in time and money required to set up and run the former.

The ADSIM uses a demand profile that requires more meticulous definitions than does the RDSIM, of the characteristics of the airfield surface, ATC procedures, and aircraft utilizing the airport. Inputs to the model include aircraft routings developed from a link-node diagram of the airport, runway and taxiway usage, runway occupancy times and exit probabilities, aircraft approach and taxiing speeds, aircraft operations, gate service times, aircraft demand and mix, and ATC rules and procedures.

The outputs of ADSIM are hourly arrival and departure flow rates, travel times, and arrival and departure delays for each runway. The model can also pinpoint the source of delay. Also provided are total delays for each link on the airfield, departure queue lengths, and individual aircraft delays. Additionally, the model has an animation feature that displays the movement of aircraft on the airfield and throughout the airport system.[70]

Until the Airport and Airspace Delay Simulation Model was developed, the complex airspace interactions between airports could not be adequately analyzed by a single airport model. SIMMOD is an advanced state-of-the-art, computer model that simulates both airport and airspace operations. It is an event-step simulation model, which traces the movement of individual aircraft and simulated ATC actions. It was designed to evaluate impacts of proposed operational alternatives and facility improvements including those that involve complex interactions among airports. It provides the means to quantitatively assess the impacts on capacity, delay, traffic loading, and aircraft operating costs of a wide variety of potential airport and airspace operating alternatives.[71]

Inputs to SIMMOD include traffic demand and fleet mix, route structures (both in airspace and on the airport surface), runway use configurations, separation rules and control procedures, aircraft per-

---

[70] *Id.*

[71] J.C. Bobick, ATAC Corp., *Validation of the SIMMOD Model* (Dec. 1988).

formance characteristics, airspace sectorization, interactions among multiple airports, and weather conditions. Depending on the type of aircraft, input parameters include permissible airborne speed ranges for use by ATC, runway occupancy times, safety separations, landing rollout characteristics, taxi speeds, gate utilization (by airline and aircraft type), and runway/taxiway utilization. The output consists of reports, which provide statistics describing aircraft delay, travel time, and fuel consumption. SIMMOD also has a post-processing animation presentation, which shows the movement of aircraft on the airport and in the adjoining airspace.[72]

The objective analysis of airport noise is a complex technical task involving lengthy calculations, making the use of computers essential. Mathematical models are essentially the only means of predicting noise exposure from complex operations. Many methods have been devised to compute and describe airport noise, each with one or more computer programs or models to carry out the calculations. Since Version I was released in January 1978, the *Integrated Noise Model* has been the FAA's standard tool for determining the predicted noise impact in the vicinity of airports.[73] As of this writing, the most current version of the INM was Version 7.0, released April 30, 2007.

The input of certain characteristics of the airport and its operation is a necessary step in the calculations of noise contours. The user must define runways and flight tracks and allocate the traffic of specific aircraft types. The model contains common flight profiles, noise characteristics for all common civil aircraft, and noise versus distance curves. Nevertheless, changes to the aircraft noise and performance data built into the model can be accomplished through user option commands, if necessary.

The INM was designed to offer any chosen noise metric or combination of metrics as output. Noise metrics available from the model are *Noise Exposure Forecast* [NEF], *Day-Night Average Sound Level* [DNL or Ldn], *Equivalent Sound Level* [Leq], *Community Noise Equivalent Level* [CNEL], and time of exposure above a number of user specified A-weighted sound levels in decibels [dB], decibels on the A scale [dBA], etc. All of the aforementioned metrics can be dis-

---

[72] Retrieved from http://www.tc.faa.gov/capacity/runwayq.htm. (Dec. 15, 1998).

[73] Charles R. Foster, FAA Dir. of Environmental Quality, *The Integrated Noise Model*, an environmental newsletter (about summer 1977); *see also* FAA, *Integrated Noise Model Version 3 User's Guide*, FAA-EE-81-17 (Oct. 1982).

played in the form of contours of equal noise exposure to a desired map scale.[74]

Finally, *Airport Design (For Microcomputers)* augments AC 150/5300-13, *Airport Design*, AC 150/5325-4A, *Runway Length Requirements for Airport Design*, and AC 150/5060-5, *Airport Capacity and Delay*. The Airport Design model calculates specific runway, taxiway, taxilane, and other airport item's standard width and clearance dimensions. Changing the airplane design group will change the airplane wingspan to the maximum wingspan for that group. This is the wingspan used for the standard design group method of airport design. Changing the airplane wingspan will adjust the airplane design group automatically. Input data include takeoff and landing wingspan and the undercarriage width.

In addition, the Airport Design model calculates the wind coverage for up to a six-runway configuration. Windroses are created in several computer aided design packages including *AutoCad*, *CAD2D* (formerly *Prodesign II*), and *Colorpro*. Input information consists of wind observation data in a format specified in AC 150/5313. The data can be purchased on disk from the *National Climatic Data Center*.[75] Another task that may be performed on the Airport Design model is airport capacity and delay for long range planning, in accordance with AC 150/5060-5, "Airport Capacity and Delay."

In summary, a useful tool in determining the most efficient airport configuration is the airport simulation model. Computer simulation may be warranted for a complex airport or when development of great magnitude is being considered. Simulation allows the planner to analyze the merits of alternative development proposals.

SITE SELECTION

Site selection is required in situations where there is no existing airport, or where the airport facilities cannot be adequately expanded to meet forecast demand. This may involve an entirely new airport to replace the old one, or a smaller reliever facility in addition to the principal airport.

---

[74] Charles R. Foster, FAA Dir. of Environmental Quality, *The Integrated Noise Model*, an environmental newsletter (about summer 1977).

[75] National Climatic Data Center, Federal Building, Asheville, N.C. 28801.

When the capability of the existing airport to meet forecast demand is questionable or when there has been a decision to construct a new airport, a site selection process is necessary. In the former case, the emphasis is on reviewing the need for and feasibility of a new airport. The review of potential new sites should, at least initially, be limited in scope to compiling information necessary to make that kind of a decision. In the latter case, the process will be significantly more detailed, leading to the selection of a specific site.

The site selection process is an evaluation of possible airport locations. Normally considered in the evaluation are airspace requirements, environmental factors, community growth, airport access, availability of utilities, land costs, site development costs, and political considerations.

AIRPORT PLANS

The airport *plans* and *drawings* include the airport layout plan, land use plan, terminal area plans, and the airport access plans. The Airport Layout Plan is the end result of the master planning process. It is the blueprint for future development. It is the most important product of the master planning process. Without and ALP, airport development will not be funded by the FAA.

The ALP is a detailed, scaled drawing, which depicts the existing and ultimate development of the airport (see Figure 5.3, "Sample Airport Layout Plan"). It shows prominent airport facilities such as runways, taxiways, aprons, safety areas, buildings, NAVAIDs, parking areas, roads, fencing, drainage facilities, and so forth. It often shows prominent natural and man-made features such as trees, streams, ponds, railroads, power lines, and depicts topographic elevations with contour lines. It designates areas reserved for specific uses such as general aviation fixed base operations, air carrier operations, cargo facilities, airport maintenance, and aviation fuel farms.

It will also show areas reserved for non-aviation development. Examples of such development might be motels, industrial areas, and office complexes. Airport boundaries, property lines, and easements are shown. Runway approach and clear zones are outlined in both plan and profile views and the height and location of controlling objects are indicated.

Figure 5.3—SAMPLE AIRPORT LAYOUT PLAN

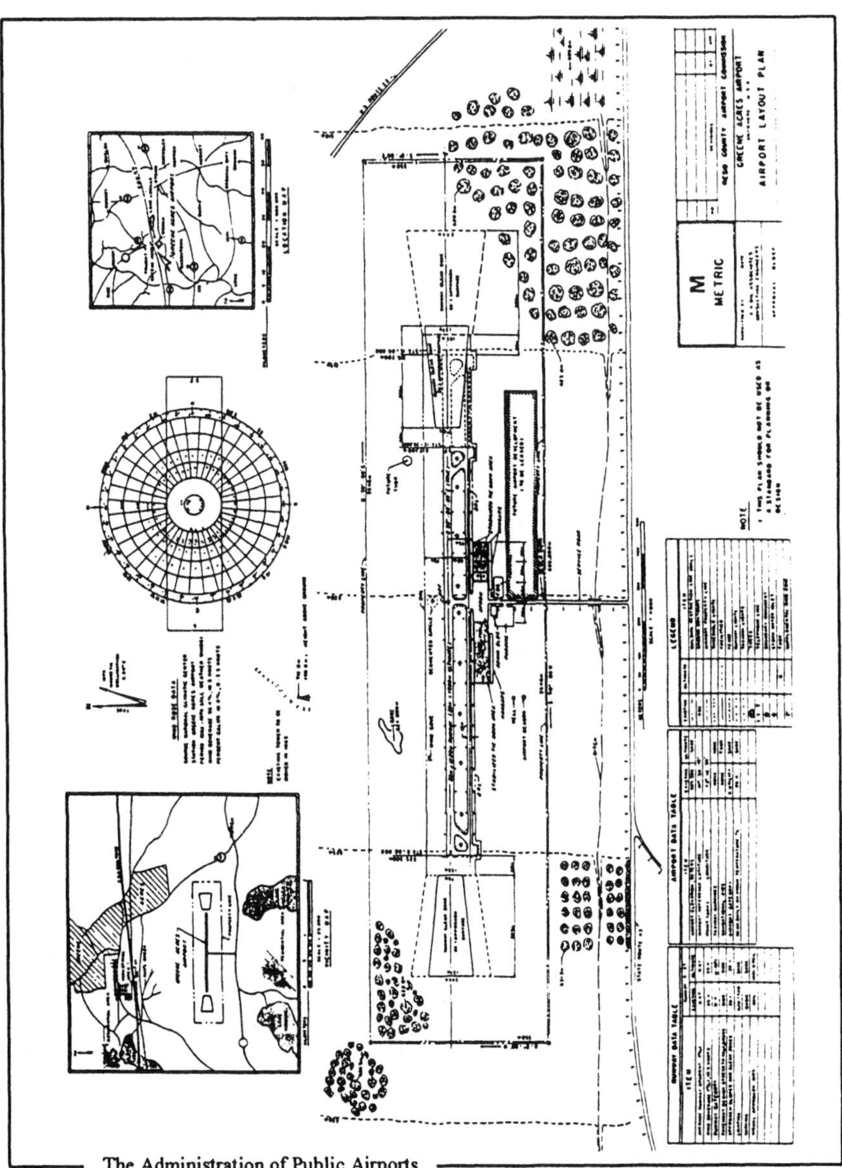

Source: FAA, AC 150/5300-4b.

Included with the airport layout plans are insets showing the geographic location of the airport and proximity to its nearest community. The location map shows the prominent cities, highways, and railroads within twenty-five to fifty miles. The vicinity map depicts the airport with its geographic relationship to the community it serves. Additionally, the ALP will have a basic data table containing such information as runway elevations, lengths, strengths, and gradients; normal or mean maximum temperature of the hottest month; and percent of wind coverage for each runway.

A wind rose is placed on the ALP with each runway orientation superimposed. Prevailing winds and wind speeds are indicated on the wind rose, and the source of the wind information is given along with dates of observation.

The *Land Use Plan* shows areas recommended for the passenger terminal complex, maintenance and cargo facilities, general aviation fixed base operator facilities, commercial and industrial areas, and other facilities within the airport boundary. Existing and recommended off-airport land uses should also be shown. The creators of the Land Use Plan should take into consideration noise levels, obstruction clearance criteria, or other activities affecting the safety of aircraft operations The *Terminal Area Plan* displays the various terminal components and their relationships. Separate large-scale drawings may be appropriate for important elements of the terminal area plan, such as terminal buildings, cargo buildings, and hangars.

Access Plans show major highway routes between the airport and the *Central Business District* [CBD], and points of connection with key arterial systems. They also show other modes of access, such as rail lines if appropriate.

FACILITIES IMPLEMENTATION PLAN

Implementation of the airport master planning process involves the preparation of development schedules and costs such that the findings and recommendations of the planning effort will come to fruition. The schedules for development must be financially feasible, and the FAA will assist the sponsor to create a Capital Improvement Plan or Program [CIP] which includes both planning and development projects planned for the airport. According to the FAA,

> *The facilities implementation plan must balance funding constraints, project sequencing limitations; environmental processing requirements; agency and tenant approvals and coordination processes; business issues, such as lease and property acquisition; and sponsor preferences. It must also be coordinate with the master plan ALP and the airport's financial plan.*[76]

The facilities implementation plan is a fluid document in the sense that it may change from year to year, depending upon changing conditions. It should be relatively simple to update after the master plan study has been completed.

A key element of the facilities implementation plan is the CIP. All projects illustrated on the ALP need to be described in detail within the CIP. Generally specific ALP projects are listed in the CIP with the following types of information:[77]

- Project identification;
- Project scope;
- Concise project purpose or objective;
- Project schedule;
- Perquisites, dependent, and interrelated projects;
- Project budget;
- Environmental processing required;
- Funding information (AIP grants, Passenger Facility Charges [PFC] or other sources);
- Special considerations (lease, property acquisition, environmental/habitat constraints, site constraints);
- Identification of responsibilities (timeframe, by activity, organization, stakeholder); and
- Benefit/cost information.

[76] FAA, *Airport Master Plans*, AC 150/5070-6B (Jul. 29, 2005), at 83, retrieved from www.faa.gov.
[77] *Id.*

In addition, project sequencing, a comprehensive master schedule, and key activities and responsibilities should be clearly established within the Facilities Implementation Plan.

FINANCIAL FEASIBLITY ANALYSIS

Financial feasibility must be considered throughout the planning process, especially during the requirements analysis and site selection activity. Financial plans are divided appropriately to mirror short, intermediate and long term (i.e., five, ten, and twenty-year) development needs.

Financial feasibility plans (or schedules) usually are included to reflect the methods in which the plan will be financed. These plans must show the sources of revenue that will cover capital improvement program costs as well as Operations and Maintenance [O&M] costs. Examples of funding sources might include federal funding, state funding, third party development, PFCs, consumer facility charge (user fees from off-airport agencies such as car agencies), bonds, and local funds.

THE GRANT PROCESS

The *Airport Improvement Program* or AIP is administered in accordance with Federal Aviation Regulations and *Office of Management and Budget* [OMB] Circular A-102, *Uniform Administrative Requirements for Grants-in-Aid to State and Local Governments*. The grant process has been subdivided into three areas: pre-grant, grant, and post-grant. The FAA has synopsized the phases of the grant process in its pamphlet entitled, "Introduction to the Airport Improvement Program." The *Pre-grant* phase is comprised of a preliminary meeting, pre-application, notice of allocation, application and the grant agreement.

In the *Preliminary Meeting*, persons interested in obtaining a grant under the AIP are invited to contact the appropriate FAA Airports office to discuss their proposed project. This meeting provides an opportunity to discuss the project scope and to familiarize the prospective applicant with grant requirements and procedures including the following:

- *Grant Procedure*—FAA personnel will be able to provide the necessary pre-application and application forms and answer any questions on completing them. Also provided may be information on deadline dates established for submission of the pre-application or application in order to be considered for inclusion in the current year's program.
- *Procurement*—OMB Circular A-102 contains the requirements for procurements under federally funded grant programs. The basic tenet is that procurements "shall be conducted in a manner that provides maximum open and free competition." Generally, this is achieved in the AIP through the use of competitive bids for construction or equipment acquisition contracts and use of competitive negotiation for professional services such as architect/engineering, legal, appraisal, etc.
- *Environment*—All proposed AIP projects must be reviewed by the FAA to determine their impact on the environment. The review can range from a determination that the proposed project is categorically excluded from further environmental analysis to a full-scale environmental impact statement. Sponsors are required to prepare the initial environmental assessment when one is necessary.
- *Airport Layout Plan*—In connection with a project for airport development, the proposed work must be shown on an airport layout plan, which has been approved by the FAA. The airport layout plan depicts the existing and future boundaries and facilities of the airport.
- *Public Hearings*—If the proposed project involves the location of an airport, an airport runway, or a major runway extension, the sponsor must offer the opportunity for a public hearing for the purpose of considering the economic, social, and environmental effects of the airport or runway and its consistency with the goals and objectives of planning carried out by the community.
- *Disadvantaged or Minority Business Enterprise* [DBE or MBE] *Program*—The purpose of such a program is to allow firms owned and controlled by traditionally underrepresented groups (such as minorities and/or women) to take part in contracts supported by Federal funds. The sponsor must be famil-

iar with the requirements of the program, which includes the setting of goals for program participation.

The formal process begins with the filing of a *pre-application.* Some projects, however, such as planning or equipment purchases, do not require a pre-application. In these instances, the formal process begins with the filing of the application.[78] Additionally, in some states, state law requires that the pre-application be submitted through a state agency.

The pre-application serves as a preliminary notice of the sponsor's interest and intent. The cost and work effort associated with submission of a pre-application is usually minimal and is eligible for reimbursement if a grant is issued for the project. The pre-application does not obligate the sponsor to undertake the proposed project, nor does acceptance by the FAA imply that the proposed project will be funded under the AIP.

The FAA reviews the pre-application for compliance with applicable requirements and considers its funding priority. If the proposed project is approved, the FAA issues a *notice of allocation.* This notice specifies the work items that have been designated for inclusion in the program and the amount of funds being reserved for these items. The notice is the first step leading to the issuance of a grant offer and provides reasonable assurance that the project will receive federal funding. It allows the sponsor to proceed with the preparation of plans and specifications and the procurement of the necessary contractor services. The allocation is contingent upon the sponsor establishing and adhering to a schedule acceptable to the FAA for submission of the application. Failure to adhere to the schedule could result in the withdrawal of the allocation.

The *application* is usually submitted after the cost of the project has been refined based upon a firm fixed price contract or unit prices received through the procurement process. The sponsor is also required to submit assurances as part of the application. These assurances address the sponsor's responsibilities during the project as well as continuing obligations, which remain in effect for the useful life of facilities developed with federal funds. The FAA reviews the application and, if satisfactory, issues a grant offer to the sponsor.

---

[78] The same FAA form is used for the pre-application and the application, only a different box is checked.

The *grant agreement* (i.e., the "grant") is based upon the amount contained in the application, which is generally about the same amount specified in the notice of allocation. The grant agreement is comprised of two parts: the offer and acceptance. The *offer* sets forth the work to be accomplished in the project, the United States share of the project, and the maximum obligation of the United States. The sponsor is responsible for paying all project costs that exceed the maximum obligation. The *acceptance* of the offer by the sponsor completes the grant agreement and becomes a legal binding contract between the sponsor and the United States.

During the *grant* or performance phase (which is that period of time when the project is actually underway), the airport sponsor is responsible for *project monitoring* to assure time schedules are being met, the approved work items are being accomplished as specified in the grant agreement, and all other terms and conditions are being complied with. The FAA periodically reviews and inspects project progress.

The FAA makes *payments* for the United States' share as the project progresses by one of the three following methods: (1) letter-of-credit, (2) advance by Treasury check, and/or (3) reimbursement by Treasury check. In the first two methods, the sponsor times the payment as close as possible to the actual disbursement of funds. Payment under the last method is made after the sponsor incurs the expense. Payment is made for the United States' share of the *allowable costs*. OMB Circular A-87, "Cost Principles for State and Local Governments," provides principles and standards for determining cost applicable under grants. A cost is allowable if it is:

- Necessary in accomplishing the project in conformity with the terms and conditions of the grant;
- Incurred after the execution of the grant agreement;[79]
- Reasonable in amount; and
- Not included in another federally assisted project.

Once the project is completed, the *post-grant* phase entails a formal audit of the records and a check on compliance by the FAA of the assurances made in the agreement. The sponsor is responsible for

[79] Note that certain project formulation and land acquisition costs may be eligible even if the costs were incurred prior to the grant agreement.

having an independent *audit* of the accounts relating to the disposition of the funds provided by the grant. The sponsor has the option of fulfilling this requirement through an organization-wide audit of its total operations or an audit confined to transactions relating directly to the project.

In accepting federal aid for other than planning, the sponsor incurs obligations which continue after the project is financially complete. The *assurances* for an airport development project include such things as:

- Keeping the airport available for public use on fair and reasonable terms;
- Not granting an exclusive right to any persons providing aeronautical services to the public;
- Suitably operating and maintaining the airport;
- Taking appropriate action, to the extent reasonable, to achieve compatible uses of lands in the vicinity of the airport;
- Submitting annual or special financial and operations reports as the Secretary of Transportation may request, as well as making any records available for the Secretary's inspection; or
- Assuring that no person is excluded from participating in any activity conducted with or benefiting from grant funds on the grounds of race, creed, color, national origin, sex, age, or handicap.

Similar assurances apply to sponsors receiving grants to implement projects contained in noise compatibility programs. Assurances for planning projects relate to the project itself and do not obligate the sponsor beyond the duration of the planning effort.

ARCHITECTURE, ENGINEERING, AND PLANNING CONTRACTS

Planning and development may sometimes be accomplished internally, either in whole or in part, through so-called "force account" procedures, where the sponsor's personnel perform some of the tasks. But in most instances these services are obtained from individuals, firms, or consultants engaged in architecture, engineering and planning, or *Architecture and Engineering* [A&E] services. The objective is to obtain qualified services at fair and reasonable costs, together with timely, complete, and acceptable performance. To this end, there are industry standards designed to insure that the highest quality architecture, engineering and planning services are obtained. In general, there are three major categories of A&E services: consultation and reports; basic (engineering) services; and special services.

Consulting services involve collecting, interpreting, and reporting information, together with drawing conclusions and making recommendations. Master planning and feasibility studies are within these services. Examples of other related services are direct personal assistance in preparation of legal proceedings or appearance in court, cost studies, management and production engineering, inspection or testing, operational services, surveying, and mapping.

The preponderance of actual engineering falls into the basic and special services categories. *Basic services* are engineering practice in which engineering design, working drawings, specifications, and other similar documents are developed, usually based upon prior study of project requirements such as the master plan or a feasibility study.

When development of projects involves studies outside the scope of basic services, it falls within the category of *special services*. These special engineering services vary greatly in scope, complexity, and timing and include such activities as soils investigation, laboratory inspections, land surveys, field surveys, photogrammetry, technical inspections, and preparation of applications for government grants, or other advances for airport projects.

The process of selecting an A&E firm normally follows a predetermined course of events. The standard procedure for selecting a consulting firm is chronologically as follows:

- Project identification;
- Advertisement;
- Pre-qualification of firms;
- Proposal submittal;
- Preliminary selection;
- Formal proposals;
- Final selection; and
- Contract agreement.

Architectural, engineering, and planning firms are duly certified professionals with standardized qualifications. They may differ, however, with specific job experience and in areas of specialization. Perhaps the most important aspect in successfully completing a project is to properly match the qualifications of the A&E firm with the task at hand. The selection process begins with an accurate and clearly defined job description. All too often the airport sponsor is uncertain as to the exact project goals and will expect the architect, engineer or planner to define the project for them. In turn, the A&E professional may not identify the same problems as envisioned by the sponsor, and may outline a program that does not respond to the sponsor's needs. When soliciting proposals from A&E firms, it greatly facilitates the selection process when the airport sponsor knows what it wants. The consultant is then in a much better position to determine if his or her company can adequately respond to the job requirements.

Depending on the nature and extent of the project, the airport sponsor may want widespread advertisement of the *Request For Proposals* [RFP], or it may choose to solicit only from a pre-selected group of firms, perhaps from companies the sponsor has used before. The idea is to consider the qualifications of an adequate number of firms capable of meeting the requirements of the project. The names of consulting firms may be obtained from professional associations such as the *American Society of Civil Engineers* [ASCE], the *American Institute of Architects* [AIA], or the *American Planning Association* [APA]; from individual state boards of registration; or from telephone directories. The FAA's Regional Airport Headquarters or local Airports Field or District Office can also be of assistance in identifying firms who have done related airport projects.

A preliminary list of consultants is compiled, and requests are sent to each of the firms asking for a statement of their interest in the project and requesting that they present their qualifications. Normally, the A&E firm's response will include a brief history of the company, a list of representative projects which are either on-going or completed, the names and addresses of past clients, and individual resumes of the personnel who would tentatively be assigned to the project. From these initial responses, the airport sponsor selects a minimum of three companies, asking each of them to submit more formal proposals and inviting them to an interview with the selection committee.

The formal proposal will include the consultant's understanding and proposed approach to the project. It will include an outlined work scope and time schedule for completion of the project, and may also have the associated costs and fee schedule if made a condition of the proposal. The interview will give both the sponsor and the potential consultant the opportunity to discuss the proposal in greater detail, and to determine the consultant's ability to competently complete the project.

The finalists are normally listed in order of their desirability. The firm considered most qualified is invited to a second interview to finalize the work scope and to negotiate the question of compensation. When all architecture, engineering and planning matters and charges have been agreed upon the contract is consummated. If all details cannot be settled, then the preferred consultant is discharged and the negotiation moves on to the next best-qualified firm until an agreement is reached. Upon the execution of a contract, all other firms who had submitted qualifications are then notified that the selection has been completed.

Terms of the contract agreement should be clearly defined between all parties to the contract, including the extent and character of work to be performed, conditions relating to time limitations, the monetary terms, and the schedule payments. Architecture, engineering and planning contracts involve highly technical services and should be prepared by someone who is thoroughly conversant with the A&E practice. A professional should assume responsibility for quality assurance in the performance of the contract as well. It may be necessary to hire a third party consultant to inspect the job and to insure compliance with the work scope specifications.

The following is a checklist of the essential provisions of an agreement for A&E services:

- *Date* of agreement;
- *Parties* to the agreement;
- Acknowledgement of the *selection process*;
- *Nature*, extent, and character of the project;
- Project *location*;
- Time *limitations*;
- *Services* rendered by the A&E firm;
- *Services* rendered by the *client*;

- Statement that data, design drawings, and specifications become the *property of the client*;
- Provisions for *termination* of services;
- Compensation and *payment schedule*;
- Provisions for *alteration of work scope*; and
- Time *schedule* for execution of professional services.

Charges for A&E services will vary with the nature and conditions of the services rendered to the client. Charges are usually computed on one of the following bases, or in combination:

- *Per diem*—wherein the firm is compensated for all the time spent on the project. The firm is reimbursed for travel, subsistence, and other out-of- pocket expenses incurred while away from his or her office. Per diem may also include compensation based on an hourly rate;
- A *retainer*—is used when the services of a firm are not required on a full-time basis. It assures the client of having the services of a certain firm when needed. Usually a retainer is in combination with per diem or hourly rates for the time actually spent in support of the client;
- *Salary Cost Times Multiplier, Plus Expenses*—is compensation for services actually spent on a project, plus an agreed overhead rate, plus reimbursement for direct non-salary expenses. The overhead includes all salary-related costs such as sick leave, vacation, retirement fund, unemployment, and overhead which compensates the engineer for office costs and a margin of profit. The multiplier usually ranges from 2.0 to 3.0. Direct expenses are travel, communications, supplies, and third party contracts;
- *Cost Plus A Fixed Fee*—has the firm reimbursed for the direct costs of all services and supplies including salary costs, overhead, direct non-salary expenses, and a fixed payment to cover contingencies and profit. The fixed payment usually ranges from 4% on small projects to less than 1% on very large projects;
- *Fixed Lump-Sum*—is derived from an estimate of the individual work scope elements times a multiplier, plus a reasonable margin of profit and expenses; and

- *Percentage of Construction Costs*—is based on a prescribed percentage of estimated or actual construction cost. The assumption is made that A&E costs vary in direct proportion to the cost of construction.

Success of a project is dependent upon a complete understanding between representatives of the A&E firm and the client. It should be recognized that some types of architecture, engineering and planning common to airports are unique and should be specifically identified as part of the required services. Care should be taken to assemble a clearly defined working document, which will provide guidance on A&E functions, specifications, types of services required, performance schedules, and methods of compensation. The intent of the consulting contract is to provide for the desired professional services, and completion in every detail, of the described scope of work.

SUMMARY

Airport development in the United States has emerged from the early days of limited federal involvement to the current system in which Federal support remains key to airport survival and growth. The master planning process can be both expensive and time consuming. However, it allows many stakeholders to publicly participate in the future development of an airport. It also serves to introduce some of the complexities associated with a variety of competing interests and issues. One such issue is the environmental impact of airports, which is discussed in detail over the next two chapters.

CHAPTER 6

ENVIRONMENTAL MANAGEMENT

The city will undertake a massive relocation effort, moving 468 tons of dirt by hand, to try to save some tiny endangered shrimp that live at Los Angeles International Airport. The decision ends a six-year debate among the airport agency, U.S. Fish and Wildlife Service and Federal Aviation Administration over what to do with the extensive shrimp habitat. The service had argued that the preserve was necessary because the world's fifth-busiest airport is one of the last refuges for Southern California's rapidly dwindling Riverside fairy shrimp population. But aviation officials contended that protecting the shrimp at LAX was impossible because they require standing water, which attracts birds [that] could be sucked into jet engines, endangering passengers.

Jennifer Oldham, Reporter, Los Angeles Times.[1]

ENVIRONMENTAL AWARENESS

Over the past several decades, airports and their tenants have evolved from being significant generators and repositories of waste, into environmentally aware partners in their communities. In many cases, the catalysts for this evolution were judicial and agency decisions, many of which are well documented in the media. In other cases, airports actively sought environmental expertise and proactively embraced their role as guardians of our environment. As a result, U.S. airports have transitioned from unaware "bystanders" in the

[1]Jennifer Oldham, *City to Move Endangered Shrimp from Airport to Preserve*, Los Angeles Times (Apr. 13, 2005), referring to the sponsor of the Los Angeles World Airport [LAWA].

1960s that were, at best, reactive to environmental concerns, to proactive partners in our communities in the current millennium.

The opening "shrimp tale" above illustrates just one of the many complicated environmental challenges potentially faced by today's airport operators. In this case, the endangered shrimp were first identified a decade ago in the inventory of protected species during the consideration of a proposed airport modernization plan.[2] While officials are wise to expect at least some unforeseen environmental issues with a major expansion effort, few would be prepared for a six-year discourse over the accommodation of a single species' habitat.

Discovering and protecting endangered species can be both an enlightening and frustrating undertaking. At the conclusion of the City of Los Angeles' lengthy environmental process—which, at times, may have seemed as murky as the subject habitat—Deputy Executive Director Jim Richie stated, "We worked long and hard with Fish and Wildlife, and I'm delighted we came to closure on this."[3]

Tiny endangered shrimp are, of course, not the only impediment to the continued operation, expansion and modernization of today's airports. As airport sponsors undertake required environmental studies, they must evaluate and mitigate a myriad of potential impacts to air quality, water quality, coastal resources, wetlands, floodplains, farmlands and twelve other environmental impact categories identified in Federal environmental procedures.[4]

Environmental management is a balancing act. Wildlife and habitat protection must be carefully weighed to assure these measures do not jeopardize the safe operation of aircraft. Socioeconomic impacts and environmental justice issues must be considered prior to initiating any significant development at airports, even if the development would bring much needed economic opportunity to a lower-income community. The benefit of increased air service must be balanced with any additional noise impact on neighboring communities. Thus, the best practices in environmental management are those accomplished in partnership with the communities served and impacted.

A thorough coverage of airport environmental issues would require several chapters, if not an entire book on the subject. However, two must suffice. Thus, this chapter serves to overview the many fac-

---

[2] *Id.*

[3] *Id.*

[4] FAA, *Environmental Impacts: Policies and Procedures*, FAA Order 1050.1E (Jun. 8, 2004), with change 1 incorporated, retrieved from www.faa.gov.

ets involved in environmental management at today's airports, with the exception of the complicated and controversial topic of aviation noise, to which the next chapter is dedicated.

ENVIRONMENTAL POLICY

Protecting the environment is an on-going challenge that began in earnest in the United States in 1969. Environmental management has come to the forefront as a primary function of airport management. Amongst the airport-related environmental issues of the past three decades were storm water runoff, leaking underground storage tanks, air toxins, and noise and land-use compatibility. When it comes to airports, the only issues of compelling social importance that may have surpassed concerns about the environment are concern over aviation security and airport/airspace capacity.

Airports are continuing to evolve, gaining both resources and expertise on environmental issues and management. One researcher believes that airports are far from mature in their capability for excellence in environmental capacity management. The company, Lochard, suggests that there are four generations in environmental capacity management, of which most airports are only at the second generation. Lochard's four generations are as follows:[5]

- *Ignorance*—denial of environmental problems;
- *Measurement*—measure, report, defend and contest;
- *Abatement*—forecast, model, compliance, budgets/ penalties; and
- *Environmental Capacity*—education, cooperative planning, complaint resolution, transparent/independent reporting, information sharing.

The goal, of course, is to transition through the states of being: passive, reactive, and proactive, to the point of finally achieving full collaboration, presumably with the community as well as other essential stakeholders. Through these phases, airports eventually reduce their environmental impact and ultimately increase community tolerance, gaining support for the airport.

---

[5] Lockhard, *4th Generation Aviation Environmental Capacity Management White Paper* (Jan. 2004), retrieved from www.lochard.com/industry/default.asp.

Management of the environment, like safety oversight and economic intervention, is a regulatory process. Government regulations come in three fundamental forms:

- Economic regulation;
- Safety regulation; and
- Social regulation.

Some theorists might argue that administrative regulation is a fourth category. Administrative regulation, however, crosses the boundaries of all categories of regulation and has more to do with policy than form.

Economic regulation involves government intervention to balance the marketplace forces of capital, labor and the consumer.[6] *Safety regulation*, as it relates to air transportation, is about the provision of safe travel. In this instance, the "airway" and its terminal ends, the airports are the infrastructure used by air transportation for the safe transit of aircraft and the movement of cargo and passengers from one point to another. *Social regulation* is about the welfare of society in general. Social welfare, in effect, is designed to protect the human environment. Social regulation shifts regulatory priorities from individual and corporate welfare or from narrow oversight of selected industries to broad control over basic objectives, and from concern with efficient production to promotion of the public (i.e., "social") good.[7]

Administrative regulation is something besides economic, safety or social regulation, and yet it is a part of all three forms. It refers to how laws and regulations are interpreted, and how the "administrative" branch of government enforces them. For example, air transportation policy can be re-molded by administrative objectives that may be different than that expressly stated in the law.

Below are the "keystones" of environmental regulation in the United States, listing in chronological order the central acts of Congress from which emanate legislation directly affecting air transportation. The list is by no means exhaustive, but it does represent salient benchmarks in the genesis of environmental regulation:

---

[6] *See generally* Adam Smith, *An Inquiry Into the Nature and Causes of the Wealth of Nations* (1776).

[7] Larry N. Gerston, Cynthia Fraleigh & Robert Schwab, *The Deregulated Society* (1988), at 32.

- *Federal Water Pollution Control Act* of 1948 (Clean Water Act);
- *Clean Air Act* of 1955;
- *Solid Waste Disposal Act* of 1965;
- *National Environmental Policy Act* of 1969; and
- *Aviation Safety and Noise Abatement Act* of 1979.

However, social regulation began well before 1948 and the Clean Air Act. It has its origins in the social reforms of the Progressive Era from about 1900 to the beginning of World War I. But the hallmark of recent social, or "environmental," regulation is the National Environmental Policy Act of 1969. This act is discussed at length over the next several pages, followed by a more generalized discussion of environmental issues facing today's airport managers.

NATIONAL ENVIRONMENTAL POLICY ACT

The National Environmental Policy Act [NEPA], referred to by its acronym, pronounced "neepa," has become the cornerstone of environmental legislation in the United States. NEPA establishes guidelines for assessing environmental impact and requires an *Environmental Impact Statement* [EIS] whenever an environmental analysis reveals a major federal action would significantly affect the quality of human environment. Individual states may also enact their legislation similar to NEPA. For example, California has a *State Environmental Quality Act.* An *Environmental Impact Statement* in the Federal Act is equivalent to an *Environmental Impact Report* [EIR] in California's State Environmental Quality Act.

Responsible for formulating and recommending national policies to promote improvement of environmental quality in accordance with the Act is the *Council on Environmental Quality* [CEQ] located in the Executive Office of the President. Original guidelines for implementation of the National Environmental Policy Act were prepared by the CEQ in 1973. These rules were principally concerned with the preparation of an Environmental Impact Statement and often resulted in reports which seemingly became their own end product and did little in the way of contributing to decisions which would further national environmental goals. In many cases the environmental review process became an obstacle to progress, without materially aiding in abating environmental concerns. The 1973 guidelines fostered inconsistent agency practices and interpretations of the laws, and resulted in excessive delays in processing environmental reports—with subsequent delays in proposed development.

In response to an executive order from President Jimmy Carter, the CEQ revised its guidelines in 1978, specifically to reduce paperwork and to make the statutorily required environmental analysis more useful. The new procedures were also intended to reduce delays in processing, and to promote better decisions. The most salient principle embodied within the revised guidelines is the use of an early *scoping* process to determine what the important issues are. The guidelines also emphasize real alternatives, reduce the length of environmental impact statements, use plain specific language, and place time limitations in the NEPA process. Early decisions must be made as to whether or not an environmental impact statement is required.

THE NEPA PROCESS

The process of determining environmental impact of a proposed action can be expensive and time-consuming. The environmental studies associated with larger projects may take several years to finish and cost millions of dollars. Figure 6.1, "Environmental Study Process Flow Chart," illustrates the many possible steps of the NEPA process.

Generally the environmental analysis entails two phases: the *Assessment Phase* and the *Declaration Phase*. The actual analysis of the affected environment is conducted in the assessment phase. The declaration phase results in the publication of one, or a combination of four documents, which emanate from the assessment phase:

- An Environmental Assessment [EA];
- A Finding of No Significant Impact [FONSI];
- A Notice of Intent [NOI];
- Environmental Impact Statement [EIS]; and/or
- Record of Decision [ROD].

Figure 6.1—ENVIRONMENTAL STUDY PROCESS FLOW CHART

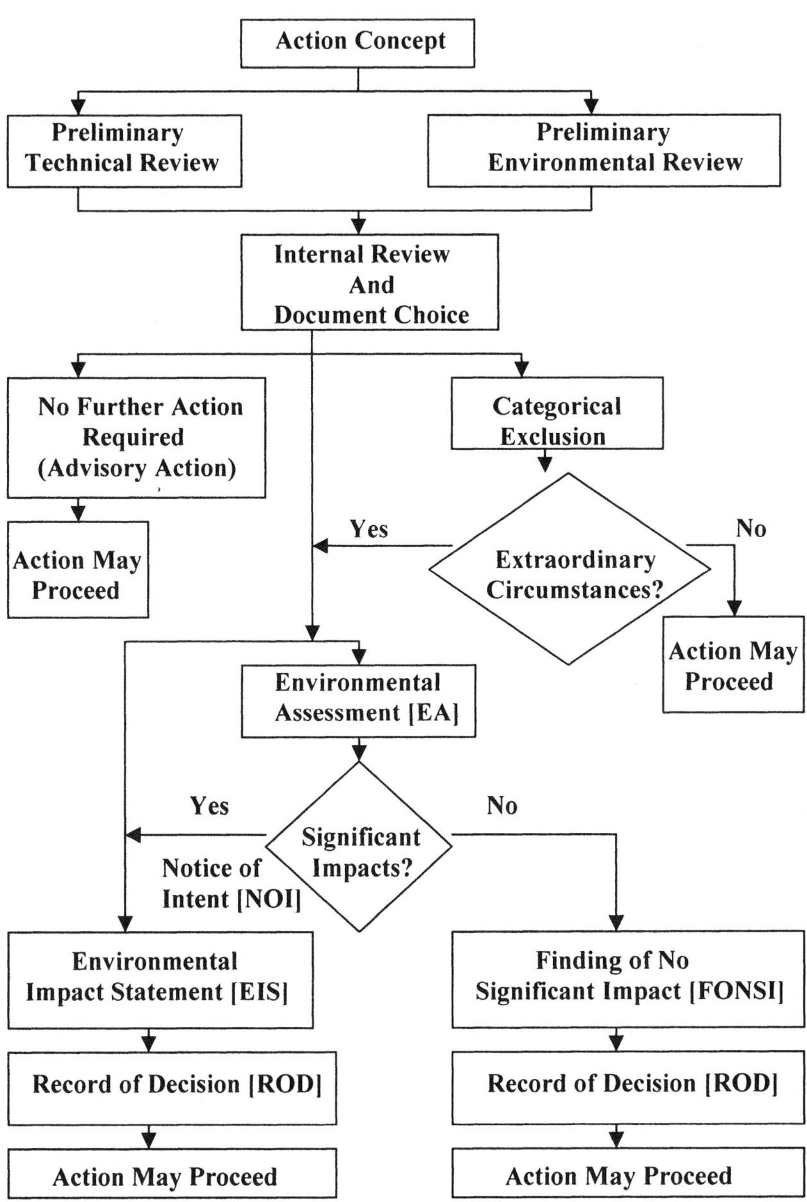

Source: FAA, retrieved from http://www.faa.gov/airports.

An *Environmental Assessment* serves to provide evidence and analysis for determining whether to prepare an EIS or, alternatively, to issue a *Finding of No Significant Impact* [FONSI] (pronounced "fonzee"). The EA assists in an agency's compliance with NEPA, facilitates preparation of an EIS if necessary, and provides a discussion of the need for the proposal. It defines the impacts of the proposal, available alternatives and mitigation strategies, a listing of those persons consulted in the process.

The *Environmental Impact Statement*, on the other hand, is a detailed written statement of the environmental impact of:

- The proposed action;
- Any adverse environmental effects which cannot be avoided should the proposal be implemented;
- The relationship between local short-term uses of the environment and the maintenance and enhancement of long-term productivity; and
- Any irreversible and irretrievable commitments of resources which would be involved in the proposed action should it be implemented.

Conversely, a FONSI, also known as a *Negative Declaration*, presents the reasons why an action will not have a significant effect on the human environment, and why an EIS, therefore, will not be prepared. It includes the environmental assessment or a summary thereof. A *Notice of Intent*, on the other hand, states that an EIS will be prepared and considered. Initially a draft EIS [DEIS] is issued, identifying and addressing the potential environmental effects, along with a *Notice of Availability* [NOA] of the DEIS. The FAA then receives comments, which are taken into consideration in creating the final EIS. After the FONSI or final EIS is issued, a *Record of Decision* is published by the FAA.

Following the national guidelines, individual states have enacted their own legislation similar to NEPA. Reaching out beyond NEPA, and connecting with environmental law predating NEPA are other legislative acts dealing with the aviation industry and its effects upon the environment. Of particular interest are laws regarding conservation of resources, hazardous and solid waste disposal, clean water and air, noise pollution, and wild life management.

AIRPORT PLANNING: THE NEPA COMPONENT

The environment and quality of human life are important! The passage of numerous environmental laws attests to the concern of Congress in this regard. In airport planning and development, environmental feasibility is as important as financial feasibility or engineering feasibility. "Environmental feasibility" means capable of being accomplished from an environmental standpoint. Environmental feasibility has several components, one of which is *political* acceptability. Another is compliance with *regulatory* and *statutory* requirements.

Regulations for implementing the procedural provisions of the National Environmental Policy Act, issued by the President's Council on Environmental Quality, provide for three categories of environmental actions. Every proposed project will eventually be classified into one of these three categories, as listed below:

- Categorical exclusions,
- Actions normally requiring an EA, or
- Actions normally requiring an EIS.

Table 6.1, "Environmental Action Choices," provides general guidelines as to which category a particular project may be categorized. This table lists several environmental actions in each category, so that airports can better estimate the level of environmental analysis typically accompanying such actions.[8]

In general, actions *categorically excluded* are actions that have been found, in normal circumstances, to have no potential for significant environmental impact. Actions normally requiring an EA are actions that have been found by experience to sometimes have significant environmental impacts. Actions having significant impacts will require the preparation of an EIS. The purpose of an EA is to determine whether or not a proposed action will have, or is likely to have, one or more significant impacts.

---

[8] FAA, *National Environmental Policy Act (NEPA) Implementing Instructions for Airport Projects* (formerly, *Airport Environmental Handbook)*, FAA Order 5050-4B (Apr. 2006); and *Environmental Impacts: Policies and Procedures*, FAA Order 1050.1D (Jun. 8, 2004).

Table 6.1—ENVIRONMENTAL ACTION CHOICES

Actions Normally Requiring an Environmental Impact Statement

- First time airport layout plan approval or airport location approval for a commercial service airport located in a standard metropolitan statistical area; and/or
- A new runway capable of handling air carrier aircraft at a commercial service airport in a standard metropolitan statistical area.

Actions Normally Requiring an Environmental Assessment

- Airport location;
- New runway;
- Major runway extension;
- Runway strengthening which would result in a noise increase over noise sensitive areas;
- Construction adversely affecting public roadway;
- Capacity;
- Relocation of residential units;
- Establishment/relocation of an ILS or ALS; and/or
- Development affecting places of historical, architectural, archeological, or cultural significance; land acquisition for conversion of farmland; wetlands, coastal zones, or floodplains; endangered or threatened species.

Categorical Exclusions

- Work on runways, taxiways, aprons, or loading ramps;
- Work on airfield lighting systems;

Table 6.1 (continued)

- Installation of airfield items such as segmented circles, wind indicators, or fencing;
- Construction of passenger handling facilities;
- Construction of entrance and service roadways;
- Grading or erosion control with no off-airport impacts;
- General landscaping;
- Noise compatibility projects;
- Land acquisition and relocation associated with any of the above projects;
- Federal releases of land; and
- Removal of displaced threshold.

Source: FAA, *National Environmental Policy Act (NEPA) Implementing Instructions for Airport Projects* (formerly, *Airport Environmental Handbook)*, FAA Order 5050-4B (Apr. 2006); and *Environmental Impacts: Policies and Procedures*, FAA Order 1050.1D (Jun. 8, 2004).

The purpose of an environmental assessment is to determine if the potential impacts are significant, explore alternatives and mitigation measures, and provide the information to determine whether or not an environmental impact statement is required. The document called an "Environmental Assessment" is simply a record of the preliminary investigations. After reviewing an EA, if the FAA determines that there are no significant impacts or that with appropriate mitigation the impacts could be prevented or minimized to the point that they are not significant the FAA will issue a FONSI. On the other hand, if an EIS is required, it is an FAA responsibility.

The Federal Aviation Administration [FAA] will prepare either a FONSI, or an EIS, but it is often possible to adjust the plans so that significant impacts can be avoided, thus avoiding the necessity to prepare an EIS. Obviously, if there are two development choices available, each of which will meet the need equally well, one with significant impacts and one without, the one without significant impacts can be implemented more readily. Hence, relatively few airport actions require an EIS, but if one is called for, preparation of the EIS in accordance with NEPA is the responsibility of the FAA.

The FAA does not approve a master plan. However, a major product of the master planning effort is the *Airport Layout Plan* [ALP]. A sponsor seeking unconditional approval of a new or revised ALP must, if one is required, submit an EA with the ALP. The FAA will not approve a grant for airport development unless the airport sponsor has a current approved ALP. An ALP is approved unconditionally when all items on the ALP, which are items normally requiring either an EA or an EIS have in fact received environmental approval.

In considering potential impacts, the procedural provisions of NEPA contain specific requirements on the subject of *cumulative* impact. The NEPA provisions also introduce the concept of *tiering* of environmental actions. Although tiering and cumulative impact may, at first glance, appear to be contradictory, they are often mutually supportive terms. Cumulative impact stems from situations where individually minor but collectively significant actions take place over a period of time. The basic idea in the concept of tiering is that decisions should be made when the time is ripe, but need not be made earlier. Even though the environmental documentation and unconditional approval of the ALP may cover only the short term, the environmental documentation, whether it is a categorical exclusion, a FONSI, or an EIS, must consider the cumulative impacts of the short-term development over a longer period.

Environmental analysis can be a complex process. An environmental professional who is experienced with and skilled in the environmental disciplines must undertake the environmental work in connection with airport master planning. Just as the skills of a soil or pavement engineer may be required, there are also requirements for the environmental professional.

PUBLIC INVOLVEMENT

As part of the environmental impact assessment, there are statutory requirements for public participation; there are regulatory requirements for public participation; and, there are often political requirements. Environmental issues cannot be skirted. Especially the aviation community cannot avoid the environment. When confronted by a concern about the environment, the airport manager must meet the issue head-on. Historical litigation has shown that if there is the slightest chance that a proposed action might be controversial on environmental grounds, it is far less trouble to confront the issue in a public information forum than to later resolve the issue in court. Citizen involvement, where appropriate, should be initiated at the earliest practical time and continued throughout the development of the proposed project in order to obtain meaningful input.

Each public participation program should be tailored to the situation. The more complex and far reaching the proposed development, the more complex and far-reaching may be the requirements for public involvement. As a general guideline for public participation programs, the Council on Environmental Quality's regulatory requirements is to,

- make a diligent effort to involve the public in implementing NEPA procedures;
- provide public notice of NEPA related hearings, meetings, and the availability of environmental documentation;
- hold public hearings when appropriate;
- solicit information from the public; and to
- make findings of no significant impact and environmental impact statements and underlying documents available to the public.

For certain projects, even if there appears to be neither public interest nor controversy, an opportunity for a public hearing is required by statute for a:

- New airport;
- New runway; or
- Major runway extension.

In order to meet the requirements of NEPA, the following potential impact categories must each be assessed—identifying both impact and mitigation strategies—and then documented:

- Air quality;
- Coastal resources;
- Compatible land use;
- Construction impacts;
- Department of Transportation Act: Sec. 4(f);

- Farmlands;
- Fish, wildlife, and plants;
- Floodplains;
- Hazardous materials, pollution prevention, and solid waste;
- Historical, architectural, archeological, and cultural resources;
- Light emissions and visual impacts;
- Natural resources, energy supply, and sustainable design;
- Noise;
- Secondary (induced) impacts;
- Socioeconomic impacts, environmental justice, and children's health and safety risks;
- Water quality;
- Wetlands; and
- Wild and scenic rivers.

While this extensive list of potential environmental impacts must be considered prior to the initiation of a federally funded project, this is not the only time the airport must consider its environmental impact. The impact of an airport is a daily consideration. Many larger airports have dedicated environmentalists, teams of environmental experts and access to consultants that help them better manage the airport's environmental programs.

ENVIRONMENTAL IMPACT OF AVIATION

Aircraft *noise* is without question the severest environmental problem currently associated with airports. It can make an airport unpopular no matter how well the airport serves the transportation needs of the community, or how greatly it contributes to the community's economic well-being. Aviation noise extends beyond the boundary of the airport, into areas over which the airport sponsor has no authority. Nevertheless, the airport sponsor is considered responsible for the noise resulting from aircraft operations. Many airports have a dedicated noise officer or a team of individuals dedicated to noise management. Due to the magnitude of the issue, Chapter 7 is completely dedicated to the discussion of aviation noise.

In addition, as listed in the section on NEPA, there are several other significant environmental impacts associated with airports.

Among the most critical are a focus on water, air, leaking underground storage tanks, and hazardous waste.

WATER QUALITY

In the *Water Pollution Control Act* of 1948,[9] Congress recognized the responsibility of states in controlling water pollution. But in addition to recognizing, preserving and protecting the responsibilities of the states, Congress made it a federal policy to support and aid in related technical research and in devising methods for industrial waste treatment to protect the nation's waters.[10]

Provisions of the Clean Water Act were expanded by the *Federal Water Pollution Control Act Amendments* of 1972[11] to restore and maintain the chemical, physical and biological integrity of the nation's waters. The *Environmental Protection Agency* [EPA] was established by President Richard Nixon in 1970, and by 1972, responsibilities for enforcement of the Clean Water Act were transferred to the EPA Administrator. The overall intent of Congress was to develop comprehensive programs for water pollution control, and to develop standards of enforcement, including permits and licenses to permit projects, which might result in pollution discharge. The 1972 amendments were,

- to eliminate discharge of pollutants (by 1985);
- for protection and propagation of fish, shellfish and wildlife;
- to prohibit discharge of toxic pollutants;
- to develop area wide waste treatment management planning processes; and
- to develop technology to eliminate the discharge of pollutants into water.

---

[9] 33 U.S.C. § 1151.

[10] Outlined in the Water Pollution Control Act, otherwise known as the Clean Water Act, were responsibilities to be carried out by the U.S. Surgeon General and by the Federal Works Administrator. Congress established in the Public Health Service a Water Pollution Control Advisory Board to make recommendations relative to technical research and methods of industrial waste treatment.

[11] 33 U.S.C. § 1251.

Additionally, grants were established for scholarship, research and development of new or improved demonstration projects to prevent, reduce and eliminate discharge.

The Water Pollution Control Act of 1948 was amended in 1972 and was again amended by the *Clean Water Act* of 1977. The 1977 act added significantly more funding and expanded the federal wastewater discharge control program. Its overriding purpose was to improve coordination between the Federal government and state and local agencies. State authority was not to be superseded, but federal agencies were to cooperate with state and local counterparts to develop comprehensive solutions to prevent, reduce and eliminate pollution in concert with programs for managing water resources.

A major source of water pollution is storm water run-off, which can remove contaminants from non-point sources. The Clean Water Act is intended to protect rivers and lakes from pollutants washing into these waters due to rainfall and snow melt. Section 402 of the Clean Water Act directs the EPA to establish storm water regulations. In 1990, the EPA issued storm water discharge regulations for municipalities and certain industries, including airports. The regulations make cities and industries responsible not only for storm water flows leaving their properties but for the effluent as well, unless the latter can be measured and sampled as it comes onsite.

Airports, along with municipalities and "other industries," are required to obtain a *National Pollutant Discharge Elimination System* [NPDES] permit for discharge of storm water from areas directly related to manufacturing, processing, or raw materials storage to either surface waters (e.g., lakes, rivers, streams, creeks or ponds) or municipal storm sewers. The NPDES permit is discussed in more detail below.

Water quality impacts may be more of a potential problem, depending upon current water quality and quantity, and the location of proposed development with respect to sources. Just as in certifying that "clean air" standards will be met, if the proposed development involves an airport location, runway location, or a major runway extension, then a certification is required from the governor that there is reasonable assurance the project will be located, designed, constructed and operated in compliance with the applicable "water quality" standards. Impact upon water sources, especially from storm water discharge, will be covered subsequently in more detail.

Routine detailed inventory of *biotic communities* in environmental documents, as was common in the past, is no longer necessary. Consideration of biotic impact now emphasizes *quality*, not quantity, and it is still necessary to be alert to potential impacts of significance on wildlife and waterfowl refuges and on water resources. Other areas requiring consideration are rare and endangered species, alteration of existing habitat, and wetlands. More on this subject is discussed below.

Special consideration has been extended to *floodplains*. If a proposal involves a 100-year floodplain, then some mitigation measures may avoid significant impacts. Consistency of proposed development with approved coastal zone management programs is another requirement.

AIR QUALITY

All airports receiving an allocation from the Aviation Trust Fund for funding of construction must comply with clean air certification. If the proposed development involves an airport location, runway location, or a major runway extension, then a certification is required from the governor of the state wherein the development will take place. The governor must certify that there is reasonable assurance the project will be located, designed, constructed and operated in compliance with the applicable air and water quality standards.[12]

With regards to air quality, *cumulative* impact models must take into account the total expected accumulated emissions from *all* industries in an area being quantified.[13] The airport is one of those industries. However, airports do not produce pollution like factories, but rather, are considered indirect, stationary sources of pollution. And because airports attract other industries, emission analysis often requires going beyond the airport boundary to estimate total impact of an airport *per se*.[14]

---

[12] *See* the *Airport and Airway Development Act* of 1970, as amended, 49 U.S.C.A App. § 2208 (b) (7) (A).

[13] *See* Environmental Protection Agency, *Compilation of Air Pollutant Emissions Factors, Vol. II, Mobile Sources*, AP-42 (4th ed. Sep. 1985).

[14] *See generally* Robert P. Olislagers, *Airports, Airplanes and Air Quality: Issues in Airport Environmental Planning*, a paper presented in fulfillment of requirements for certification as an Accredited Airport Executive [AAE] of the American Association of Airport Executives [AAAE] (Jun. 1992).

Although general aviation airports with less than 180,000 annual operations are not required to establish an air quality analysis,[15] airports with fewer operations have been asked to present such data to environmental agencies. From a planning perspective it is advisable that airports, large and small, include such data in the environmental documentation accompanying an airport master plan. While no airports to date have lost funds as a result of failing to obtain clean air certification, some projects have been *delayed* for failing to obtain certification.[16]

Air pollution is caused primarily by aircraft engine emissions—namely solid particulates, sulfur oxides, carbon monoxide, hydrocarbons and nitrogen oxides. The amounts of each specific emittant are highly predicated upon the size of the aircraft, but also the type of engine used for propulsion; i.e., turbine versus reciprocating. As a rule, jets and other *turbine powered* aircraft emit higher volumes of *solid particulates* and *nitrogen oxides* than do the piston aircraft. Conversely, *piston powered* aircraft discharge more *carbon monoxide* and *hydrocarbons* than do the jets. Aside from aircraft as a point source, other sources of air pollution around airports might be from:

- Airport *construction equipment*;
- Emissions from gasoline operated aircraft *ground service equipment*;
- *Access traffic* entering and leaving the airport;
- Exhaust from *maintenance equipment*;
- *Heating and air conditioning* plants; and from
- The *fuel handling* and storage system.

In the latter, fuel handling and storage, the concern is with vapor emissions. A prevailing environmental issue of the 1990s and into this century is potential leakage from fuel storage facilities. Underground storage systems are discussed below.

---

[15] FAA, *Airport Environmental Handbook*, FAA Order 5050.4A; *see also* Robert P. Olislagers, *Airports, Airplanes and Air Quality: Issues in Airport Environmental Planning*, a paper presented in fulfillment of requirements for certification as an AAE of the AAAE (Jun. 1992).

[16] *See* Robert P. Olislagers, *Airports, Airplanes and Air Quality: Issues in Airport Environmental Planning*, a paper presented in fulfillment of requirements for certification as an AAE of the AAAE (Jun. 1992).

The quality of air Americans breathe was first addressed by Congress in the *Clean Air Act* of 1955,[17] wherein the Federal government recognized State responsibility in controlling air pollution, but provided grants to states and local governments to create "air pollution control districts." In the *Clean Air Amendments Act* of 1970, the Federal government placed special emphasis on research in the effects of air pollutants on public health and welfare. Grants were set up for state and local governments for air quality control and to develop ambient air quality standards and enforcement procedures for regulation of fuels.

Aircraft emissions were added to the statute, and the FAA Administrator was to study and investigate emissions of pollutants from aircraft to,

- determine the extent and effect of such pollutants;
- determine the technological feasibility of controlling these pollutants; and
- prescribe regulations to establish aviation fuel standards.

The Administrator was then to report his or her findings to the EPA, which would follow-up with appropriate regulations.

In 1973, the EPA established production standards to limit emissions of smoke, carbon dioxide, hydrocarbons, and nitrous oxides. As originally drafted, the standards would have applied to all aircraft from the smallest single-engine plane to the largest commercial jet transport. However, in 1977 the EPA relaxed its standards applying to the smaller general aviation fleet and made the standards applicable only to turbine airplanes having engines with at least 12,000 pounds of thrust. The last century closed with limited attention on air quality issues at airports. In fact, the EPA had declared that ambient air quality is only marginally affected by pollution from aviation sources, with an estimated contribution of only 1% of the total air emissions in a community.

AIR TOXICS

The new century ushered in a new focus on airports and air quality, along with a new descriptor for air pollution: *air toxics* (or air

[17] 42 U.S.C. § 1857.

"toxins") and a heightened concern for the negative impact that aviation has on the environment. New research suggested that the aviation industry's total negative impact on air quality might have been poorly measured and substantially underestimated.

Under the *Air Toxics Strategy* (of the Clean Air Act), communities must "provide an integrated strategy for reducing cumulative public health risks in urban areas posed by the aggregated exposures to air toxics from all sources." In addition, NEPA requires that public agencies "analyze and publicly disclose direct and indirect cumulative environmental and social impacts of major federal actions. As such, the airport—taken in total with the "urban soup" of emissions—must be considered in any assessment of air quality.[18]

Airport and aircraft air emissions are a very complex mixture of sources and chemicals that previously had been underestimated. In fact, recent research suggests that there may be as many as 200 compounds associated with aircraft exhaust including: acetone, nickel, chromium and benzene. "Air toxics" as they are termed by the Environmental Protection Agency are broken into six categories:[19]

- *Volatile Organic Compounds* [VOCs], such as benzene, formaldehyde and vinyl chloride;
- *Semi-Volatile Organic Compounds* [SVOCs] such as dioxin and polynuclear aromatic hydrocarbons;
- *Pesticides*;
- *Inorganic compounds* such as hydrogen chloride and hydrazine;
- *Metal compounds*, such as lead, mercury and arsenic; and,
- *Miscellaneous others*, including radio nuclides (e.g. radon), glycol ethers, and fine mineral fibers.

Air toxins can be generated from a number of mobile and stationary sources that originate from activities and equipment at the nations' public airports. These sources include:

- Off-road mobile sources (aircraft , ground support equipment, construction equipment);

[18] Kenneth Mitchell, *Airports and Air Toxins*, available from Author, Air Toxics Assessment and Implementation, EPA, Atlanta, Ga.
[19] *Id.*

- On-road mobile sources (buses, cars, trucks, shuttles);
- Large stationary sources (boilers, generators); and,
- Smaller sources (maintenance, painting/striping, tanks, kitchens, chemical milling, parts cleaning, grounds keeping, electroplating, etc.).

In the Chicago O'Hare Environmental Impact Statement, of primary concern was the existence of *Hazardous Air Pollutants* [HAPs] that were primarily generated from four sources. Motor vehicles contributed more than half of the HAP emissions at 58%, followed by ground service equipment (24%), aircraft (18%) and stationary sources (under 1%). The highest toxicity-weighted HAPs detected in the O'Hare study were emitted from on-road vehicles and ground service equipment (diesel particulate matter, toluene and benzene) and from aircraft (formaldehyde). A large part of the increases in toxins were attributed to airport expansion, with significant discharges coming from construction equipment.[20]

Complex models are used to track the dispersion of air toxics. But generating models is only part of the assessment process. In modeling risk assessment in air toxics, airports should,

- develop the best inventory of HAP emissions from readily available data (both site specific and literature);
- perform air dispersion modeling at specified receptor locations;
- characterize risks and evaluate uncertainties;
- identify major sources and chemicals posing exposures of concern; and
- identify risk mitigation measures for these significant sources and chemicals.[21]

UNNATURAL CLOUD FORMATION

Perhaps one of the most interesting discoveries of the past decade with regard to environmental impact is that aircraft are believed to contribute to the creation of *unnatural clouds*, as their flight creates condensation trails or *contrails*, which are the white lines we see

---

[20] *Id.*
[21] *Id.*

drawn across the skies by aircraft. They are composed largely of water crystals and are considered harmless to humans. However, in 1999, the *Intergovernmental Panel on Climate Change* [IPCC]—comprised of individuals from science and aviation—announced some surprising findings: that contrail formation does affect the cloudiness of the Earth's atmosphere, and therefore may impact atmospheric temperature and climate.[22]

In a publication entitled, "Aircraft Contrails Factsheet,"[23] the EPA echoed the IPCC's conclusions, "Contrail cloudiness might contribute to human-induced climate change. Climate change may have important impacts on public health and environmental protection."[24] As more study is conducted on this subject, recommendations may be forthcoming on making jet exhaust emission standards more stringent or in limiting aircraft operations near sensitive portions of the atmosphere.

SOLID AND HAZARDOUS WASTE

The *Hazardous and Solid Waste Disposal Act Amendments* of 1984 amended the *Solid Waste Disposal Act* of 1965. Like the Clean Water Act of 1948, the 1965 Solid Waste Act was designed to place federal emphasis on improving education and technical research.[25] Another amendment to the Solid Waste Disposal Act was the *Resource Conservation and Recovery Act* [RCRA] of 1976,[26] in which Congress recognized that solid waste represents a potential resource, which could be converted into energy. The intent of RCRA (pronounced "reck-rah") was to promote protection of human health and the environment, while simultaneously conserving valuable material and energy resources through the following:

---

[22] IPCC, *Aviation and the Global Atmosphere* (1999).

[23] EPA, *Aircraft Contrails Factsheet* (Sep. 2000), retrieved from www.faa.gov/regulations_policies/policy_guidance/envir_policy/media/contrails.pdf.

[24] *Id.* at 5.

[25] The Solid Waste Act was to initiate and accelerate a national research and development program for new and improved methods of proper and economic solid waste disposal, including studies directed toward the conservation of natural resources by reducing the amount of waste and by removing and utilizing potential resources in solid wastes. Like the Clean Water Act, the Federal government was to provide technical and financial assistance to state and local governments, and interstate agencies, in planning, development and conduct of solid waste disposal programs.

[26] 42 U.S.C. § 6901.

- Technical assistance;
- Training grants;
- Prohibiting future open dumping;
- Regulatory treatment, storage, transportation and disposal of hazardous wastes;
- Promulgation of guidelines for solid waste collection, transport, separation, recovery and disposal practices and systems;
- Promotion of national research and development programs;
- Promotion of demonstration, construction and application of solid waste management, resource recovery and resource conservation systems which would preserve and enhance quality of air, water and land resources; and
- Establishing cooperative efforts among federal, state and local governments and private enterprise in order to recover valuable materials and energy from solid waste.

In concert with the Clean Water Act, Title VI of the *Hazardous and Solid Waste Disposal Act Amendments* of 1984 (known as the "Leaking Underground Storage Tank Liability and Standards Act") made provisions for control of *Underground Storage Tanks* [USTs] by,

- defining USTs for purposes of this regulation;
- requiring notification to state and local agencies by owners of USTs of their existence;
- promulgation of release, detection, prevention and correction regulations applicable to owners of tanks; and
- establishing new tank performance standards.

In 1988, the EPA issued rules covering the technical requirements for USTs. Under the "Technical Standards and Corrective Action Requirements for Owners and Operators of Underground Storage Tanks,"[27] owners of USTs are required to implement leak detection procedures and to upgrade or replace their tanks. EPA regulations[28] also require that fuel spills or leaks be reported to the EPA and, where there is any possibility of contamination reaching navigable water-

---

[27] 40 CFR Part 280.
[28] 40 CFR Part 302.

ways, the U.S. Coast Guard must be notified as well. Legislation passed in 2005 further fortified RCRA with funding and more stringent underground storage tank standards. The next section discusses underground storage tank issues in depth.

UNDERGROUND STORAGE TANKS

Airport and airline operations require the storage, transport and dispensing of a number of liquids, many of them potentially hazardous. Stored liquids include aircraft fuel, lubricants, deicing fluid, waste oil, and other potentially hazardous products. These products are often used by the airlines, car rental companies, military tenants, fixed based operators, freight/cargo companies, and construction contractors.[29]

Environmental concerns attached to potential leakage from underground storage tanks led to proposals in the mid 1980s for three-pronged legislation intended to prevent slow leak environmental contamination. First, *registration* of all tanks exceeding specified capacities would be required. Beginning in 1986, underground tanks of more than 1,100 gallons had to be registered with appropriate state regulatory agencies.

Second, recommended, but not required, were regular tank *inventory control* programs including periodic environmental audits. Such audits were to be systematic reviews and inspections of environmental records, files, facilities, operations and activities to assess whether the owner was in compliance with all applicable activities.

Third, tank owners were to assume *financial responsibility* for any fuel leak contamination, ostensibly through mandatory insurance coverage for those who could not pay for damages out-of-pocket. Under consideration at that time, and actually created later, was a *superfund* account via the creation of a leaking underground storage trust fund collected through additional taxation on fuels. Owners and operators of tanks would be required to show evidence of financial responsibility in the event of releases from their tanks. However, where financial resources of the owner/operator were not available, such as insolvency or otherwise refusal to cooperate, the EPA could use the fund to pay for corrective action whenever necessary to protect human

---

[29] Minnesota Pollution Control Agency, *MSP International Airport Environmental Fact Sheet* (Mar. 2005), available from Minnesota Pollution Control Agency, St. Paul, Minn. 55155-4194.

health and environment. Current law[30] requires that fuel spills or leaks be reported to the EPA and, where there is any possibility of contamination reaching navigable waterways, the U.S. Coast Guard must also be notified.

Congress in 1984 passed the Leaking Underground Storage Tank Liability and Standards Act, which mandated development of a federal regulatory program for underground tanks, and restricted the type of tanks that could be installed. In the meantime, the Environmental Protection Agency published interim rules stating that the only tanks approved for installation were those designed, constructed and installed to prevent leaks due to corrosion or structural failure, and made of materials compatible with the substances stored. Cathodically protected steel tanks and tanks constructed or clad with non-corrosive materials were permitted if the cathodes would last the lifetime of the tank and if the non-corrosive materials were applied properly. Other than stipulating that tanks were to be installed correctly to prevent leaks, EPA gave little guidance on correct installation procedures.

Under the Environmental Protection Agency's 1988 rules,[31] owners of underground storage tanks are required to implement leak detection procedures and to upgrade or replace their tanks according to a time frame established by the EPA. The rules apply to "underground" storage tanks, which are defined as having 10% or more of their volume below ground. Excluded from the rules are farm and residential tanks that contain less than 1,100 gallons and are not used for commercial purposes; tanks used for storing heating oil for purposes on the premises; tanks that hold less than 110 gallons; and emergency spill and overfill tanks.[32]

It should be understood that a few states (including California and Florida) had already established comprehensive programs covering UST systems prior to the adoption in 1988 of federal guidelines. Moreover, each state has the option to implement the federal rules or develop its own set of guidelines that are at least as stringent as those of the Federal government. In the time that has passed since the federal program was adopted, some state regulations have become more comprehensive than the federal guidelines.

---

[30] 40 C.F.R. 302.

[31] *I.e., The Technical Standards and Corrective Action Requirements for Owners and Operators of Underground Storage Tanks*, 40 C.F.R. 280 (1988).

[32] *Id.*

The Federal Regulation (i.e., 40 CFR Part 280) addresses such areas as the design and installation of new tanks, required leak detection systems, piping, spill and overfill protection as well as record keeping and reporting. The regulation allowed ten years (i.e., until 1998) for the then existing tanks and piping to be protected from corrosion and stated the methods, which had been approved by the EPA. The rule phased in leak detection over a five-year time frame depending upon the age of the tanks.

Other areas included in the rules were corrective action and procedures for tank closures. If a UST system did not have corrosion protection and it remained closed "permanently" (defined as more than twelve months), three requirements had to be met:

- The regulatory authority was to be notified thirty days prior to closure;
- An environmental assessment was to be completed by testing soils and/or groundwater samples to determine if the tank has caused a release which resulted in environmental damage; and
- Depending on local regulatory policies, an underground tank could be either removed or left in place, but in both cases the tank had to be emptied and cleaned by removing all liquids, dangerous vapors and accumulated sludge.

In 1986, Congress also created the Leaking Underground Storage Tank [LUST] Trust Fund and enacted a storage tank tax provision to the "Superfund" program.[33] The Federal UST program receives nearly $70 million per year (of which more than 80% is used for site management and cleanup) and is financed by 0.1 cent per gallon tax on motor fuels. The Fund has two purposes:[34] First, it provides financial support for oversight and enforcement of corrective action taken by a responsible party; and second, it provides money for remediation of sites where the owner/operator is unknown, unwilling or unable to respond (or when emergency action is required).

---

[33] The LUST Trust Fund in 1986 by amending Subtitle I of the RCRA. RCRA initiated the Federal government's *Superfund* program, which was created to finance the remediation of abandoned hazardous waste sites.

[34] EPA, *LUST Trust Fund* (Mar. 2006), retrieved from http://www.epa.gov/OUST/ltffacts.htm.

In addition to other requirements, UST owners must show evidence of "financial responsibility" in the event of releases from their tanks, defined as the ability to finance at least $1 million in cleanup costs per tank release. Financial responsibility can be demonstrated by several means: insurance, self insurance, establishment of an independent trust fund, the use of state funds dedicated for cleanup of leaking tanks, or a combination of these resources. The available option for most operators is insurance, and it should go without saying that most insurance underwriters will require proof that fuel storage systems are not leaking before writing a pollution liability policy to cover them.

The Environmental Protection Agency set minimum construction standards for all USTs installed after 1988. Within a decade all USTs were required to meet the minimum standards. Penalties for owners found in non-compliance can include fines of several thousand dollars per violation. Operators in UST non-compliance may also be shut down.[35]

In August of 2005, the *Energy Policy Act* of 2005, Title XV, Subtitle B (entitled the "Underground Storage Tank Compliance Act of 2005") added amendments to Subtitle I of the Solid Waste Disposal Act.[36] This law will require major changes to existing UST programs.[37] The EPA reports,[38]

> *The UST provisions of the Energy Policy Act focus on preventing releases. Among other things, it expands eligible uses of the Leaking Underground Storage Tank (LUST) Trust Fund, and includes provisions regarding inspections, operator training, delivery prohibition, secondary containment and financial responsibility, and cleanup of releases that contain oxygenated fuel additives.*

---

[35] David Johnson, *In Case You Haven't Started Yet . . . A Primer on 1998 UST Requirements*, Airport Magazine, (Jul./Aug. 1996).

[36] The *Solid Waste Disposal Act* was the original legislation that created the underground storage tank program.

[37] EPA, *New Legislation Requires Changes to the Underground Storage Tank Program* (Sep. 2006), retrieved from http://www.epa.gov/oust/fedlaws/nrg05_01.htm.

[38] *Id.*

While some of the provisions required an August 2006 deadline, others will allow for implementation in subsequent years. The EPA plans to "work closely with tribes, other federal agencies, tank owners and operators, and other stakeholders to bring about the mandated changes affecting underground storage tank facilities."[39]

Unfortunately, the mistakes of the past continue to haunt and cause tension between airports and users. For example, in 2005, the Port of Seattle filed suit against Northwest Airlines for the more than $4 million that the Port paid to clean up jet fuel spilled by Northwest. The Port alleged that Northwest spilled more than 23,000 gallons from its fuel farm in the early 1980s, largely from fuel tanks and pipelines. In addition, the Port claimed that a Northwest underground pipeline ruptured in 1992 causing fuel to pool in the airport's underground baggage system and contaminating a nearby creek. While the Port initiated the clean-up, Northwest claimed that the Port was too ambitious. "The dispute is really over the quantity of soils that should have been removed," said Northwest attorney Randy Steichen. "There's a difference of opinion about what the clean-up standards were and how much had to be hauled away."[40]

Today's larger airports employ environmental monitoring teams and utilize a series of measures to prevent, detect and contain spills, including:[41]

- Construction and installation standards;
- Inspections and visual monitoring;
- Tank floor coatings or secondary containment (to prevent or contain rclcascs;
- Integrity testing or release detection (to test for possible leaks); and
- Overfill protection (to prevent overfill spills).

These well-educated teams—working in concert with airport tenants and users—have the skills to more quickly detect and clean up hazardous spills, thus minimizing environmental damage (preventing

---

[39] *Id.*

[40] Alwyn Scott, *NW Airlines Sued by Port for Fuel Spills*, The Seattle Times (Jul. 2, 2005).

[41] Minnesota Pollution Control Agency, *MSP International Airport Environmental Fact Sheet* (Mar. 2005), available from Minnesota Pollution Control Agency, St. Paul, Minn. 55155-4194, at 2.

fuel from migrating to/through soils and nearby waterways) and extra costs associated with delayed reaction.

STORM WATER DISCHARGE

Primary concerns associated with fuel tank leakage have to do with water contamination. Airport operations entail two kinds of water-related environmental impacts: (1) the effect upon *potable water* intake, and (2) *wastewater discharges*. Water pollution is perhaps the best understood of the environmental concerns, and therefore is the easiest to rectify.

An airport is a point source for wastewater. If the airport chooses to treat its own wastewater, it must establish facilities that meet federal standards in accordance with the Federal Water Pollution Control Act of 1972. If discharges of wastewater are into a municipal treatment or sewer system,[42] the wastewater stream must be pretreated, if necessary, to make it compatible with the treatment system. By the same token, an airport may have its own well water, or may choose to tie into a local water system. If well water is used, it must be inspected and treated, as necessary, to insure potable quality.

The *major* source of water pollution is storm water run-off, which can remove contaminants from non-point sources that are not easily identified. Storm water comes from all areas of the airport, and with it comes any spilled oil, fuel, loose debris, rubber tire deposits and a miscellaneous array of chemicals, paint strippers, cleaning solvents and deicing compounds. The operational necessity of an adequate storm water drainage system as a *physical facility* on the airport was pointed out in Chapter 3. The importance of a proper drainage system is reiterated here as an *environmental* consideration.

The possibility that chemicals may be carried away by water run-off and subsequently cause ecological damage downstream is a deterrent to the use of specific types of weed killers on airports. Weed control is a major operational problem on an airport, but great care

[42] "Sewer systems are often classified according to their use. The two common types of sewer systems include sanitary sewers, which generally convey domestic sewage and industrial waste, and storm sewers, which are designed to convey storm water and other surface waters. Therefore, separate storm sewer systems are only designed to convey storm water." Taken from *Technical Report, LAX Master Plan EIS/EIR*, Ch. 6: Hydrology and Water Quality Technical Report (2001), at 9, retrieved from http://www.laxmasterplan.org/docs/draft_eir_NE/T06_LR.pdf).

must be exercised in the selection and application of chemicals to destroy them. The Clean Water Act is intended to protect rivers and lakes from pollutants washing into these waters due to rainfall and snow melt. Section 402(p) of the Clean Water Act directs the EPA to establish storm water regulations. In 1990, the EPA published storm water discharge regulations for municipalities and certain industries including airports. Simply put, the regulations make airports responsible for storm water flows entering and leaving many sites on the airport. Furthermore, water runoff coming onto airport grounds from a neighboring facility is also the airport's responsibility unless it can be measured and sampled as it arrives onsite.

Airports, along with municipalities and other "industries," are required to obtain a National Pollutant Discharge Elimination System permit for discharge of storm water from areas directly related to manufacturing, processing, or raw materials storage to either surface waters (e.g., lakes, rivers, streams, creeks or ponds) or municipal storm sewers. [43] Also targeted by the rules are airports with aircraft and runway de-icing operations and facilities that use pesticides or herbicides to control weed growth, and facilities using paints or solvents in their operation.

The first phase of the municipal storm water National Pollutant Discharge Elimination System program generally applies to urban areas with a population in excess of 100,000. In addition to regulating other industrial uses, the program requires a NPDES permit for construction activities disturbing at least five acres. Most commercial service airports are included in the Phase I municipal program. In March 2002, the second phase of the NPDES storm water program was activated. This phase automatically regulated all owner/operators of small municipal (separate) storm sewer systems located in urban areas. At that time, the construction activity permit coverage was changed to an acre of disturbed area.[44]

---

[43] "Industrial activity at a transportation facility includes facilities that are either involved in vehicle maintenance (including vehicle rehabilitation, mechanical repairs, painting, fueling, and lubrication), equipment cleaning operations, and airport deicing operations. Since an airport is considered a transportation facility, [airports] and tenants on the airport property that engage in industrial activities are required to be permitted under the industrial NPDES program." Drawn from *Technical Report, LAX Master Plan EIS/EIR*, Ch. 6: Hydrology and Water Quality Technical Report (2001), at 11, retrieved from http://www.laxmasterplan.org/docs/draft_eir_NE/T06_LR.pdf.

[44] *Id.*

The NPDES permitting process continues to evolve. Many state environmental agencies have been empowered to oversee the NPDES permitting and enforcement programs within their states. The NPDES permit holders (airports and their tenants) are required to have plan that assures they,

- eliminate or reduce non-storm water discharges to storm sewer systems and other waters of the nation;
- develop and implement a S*torm Water Pollution Prevention Plan* [SWPPP]; and
- perform monitoring of discharges to the storm water system from their facilities.[45]

The NPDES permits may be obtained either via individual application or group application form. The least preferred method because of cost is to apply for an individual permit requiring submission of sampling data for each storm water *outfall* (point of exit from the storm water system) at each facility. The more preferred method allows industrial facilities, including airports, with similarly expected discharges to join together and submit a group application. The American Association of Airport Executives and its *Airport Research and Development Foundation* [ARDF] submitted a group storm water application on behalf of 605 airports participating in a group application for the NPDES.

A group application requires that at least 10% of the sites participate in run-off sampling.[46] The group permit application contains quantitative and qualitative data based on storm water sampling from outflows of storm water discharge. Some of the items specifically being examined for their presence in the storm water discharge are:

- Oil and grease;
- *Biological Oxygen-Demand* [BOD];
- *Chemical Oxygen-Demand* [COD];
- *Total Suspended Solids* [TSS];
- *Total Kjeldahl Nitrogen* [TKN];

---

[45] *Id.*

[46] Brenda Ostrom, *Predicting Pollutant Loads in Storm Water Runoff From Airports*, an applied project presented in partial fulfillment of the requirements for the degree Master of Technology, Arizona State University (May 1995).

- Nitrate plus nitrite;
- Total phosphorus; and
- The pH of the discharge.

Alternatively, the quantitative testing data parameters may include pollutants limited in an effluent guideline to which the facility is subject, any pollutant listed in the NPDES permit to process wastewater, and/or certain pollutants expected or known to be in the discharge.[47] In addition, the application is to contain the date of the sampling, the rainfall duration and amount, the time of the last 0.1 inch of rain, the maximum flow rate at the point of discharge, the volume of discharge, and the method of flow measurement or estimate.[48]

Control of deicer runoff from airports has become one of the key components of NPDES permits for airports. And airports are coming under increasing pressure not only from the federal government, but from state agencies as well, to prevent pollution from deicing fluid runoff. As a result, many airports are turning to what Karl Bremer calls the "three Rs" for their solutions, to "reduce, recover and recycle" deicing compounds. A number of airports, including Denver International, Salt Lake City International, and Pittsburgh International, have adopted a variety of methods to at least partially recover and recycle glycol.[49]

Deicing compounds have long been identified as a source of pollution when discharged in concentrations too high to allow for gradual breakdown. High concentrations of glycol, for example, can raise the biological oxygen demand of a stream, river or other body of water, choking off the ability of aquatic life forms to survive. As a consequence of the natural decomposition of urea-based deicing compounds, commonly used as a runway deicer, ammonia can be produced in toxic concentrations. The use of urea at airports is declining, but glycol is still commonly used. NPDES permit limits on glycol runoff were first imposed on airports in 1995. There are indications that the EPA may be considering even stricter limits on effluent dis-

---

[47] *See* 40 CFR 122.21 (g) 7 (iii) and (iv).

[48] *See* C. Gemar, *New Storm Water Regulations Impact Industry*, Environmental Progress, (1991), Vol. 10, at 154-157; *see also* Brenda Ostrom, *Predicting Pollutant Loads in Storm Water Runoff From Airports*, an applied project presented in partial fulfillment of the requirements for the degree Master of Technology, Arizona State University (May 1995).

[49] Karl Bremer, *The Three Rs: Reduce, Recover, Recycle*, Airport Magazine (Mar./Apr. 1998), at 42-49.

charges of glycol, and may in the future require airports to account for all ethylene glycol under the federal *Toxic Release Inventory* [TRI].[50]

Currently, to obtain a NPDES permit the EPA requires the applicant to estimate from active sampling both annual and seasonal storm water pollutant loads as well as event mean concentrations for specified pollutants of representative storm events.[51] Several models of varying complexity are available to produce such estimates including:

- The *EPA Simple Method*;
- *Nationwide Regression Equation Model* [NRE];
- The *Program for Predicting Polluting Particle Passage through Pits, Puddles, and Ponds* [P8];
- The *Storm Water Management Model* [SWMM];
- The *Storage, Treatment, Overflow, Runoff Model* [STORM];
- The *Hydrologic Simulation Program, FORTRAN* [HSPF]; and
- The *Quantity-Quality Simulation Model* [QQS].[52]

Except for the EPA Simple Method, all of the aforementioned models were designed to continuously simulate the watershed over extended periods of time.

WILDLIFE PROTECTION AND MANAGEMENT

Another ecological factor having a significant effect upon airport development and operation concerns is wildlife. Not only can airports threaten wildlife, but also wildlife can be a serious threat and costly threat to aviation. "Aircraft collisions with wildlife . . . annually cost the civil aviation industry in the U.S. at least $500 million in direct

---

[50] *Id.*

[51] H.O. Andrews, *Urban Runoff Models Simplify NPDES Process*, Water Environment and Technology, (1993), Vol. 5, at 30-36; *see also* Brenda Ostrom, *Predicting Pollutant Loads in Storm Water Runoff From Airports*, an applied project presented in partial fulfillment of the requirements for the degree Master of Technology, Arizona State University (May 1995).

[52] R. Attanasio & D. Danicic, *Comparing Three Stormwater Pollutant Load Models*, Pollution Engineering, (1993), Vol. 25, at 51-54; *see also* H.O. Andrews, *Urban Runoff Models Simplify NPDES Process*, Water Environment & Technology, (1993), Vol. 5, at 30-36; *see also* S.J. Nix, *Applying Urban Runoff Models*, (1991), Vol. 3, at 47-49.

damage and associated costs, and over 500,000 hours of aircraft down time."[53]

Of principal concern are birds in the vicinity of the air movement area, but other forms of wildlife may be a concern as well. Under NEPA, airports must consider endangered species (both flora and fauna) and potential impacts on biotic communities (wildlife or waterfowl refuges of local, state or national significance). Wildlife found at airports have included deer, elk, dogs, coyotes, snakes, rabbits, crocodiles, birds like gulls, ducks and geese, and many other unwanted visitors. In most cases, proper fencing can keep large animals off the airport, and hunting teams can minimize the need for on-airport control of mammals and reptiles. Birds, on the other hand, are much more difficult to control, and will often require the expertise of professionals experienced in bird control problems.

The safety issue associated with bird strikes has an inverse relationship to the number of engines on a particular aircraft. As the number of engines decreases, the potential for loss of all engines increases in a multiple bird strike (and possible multiple engine damage) situation. The danger is increasing over time as aircraft are being designed with fewer engines. In 1969, 75% of the aircraft had 3 or 4 engines. But by 2008, it is estimated that less than 10% of the world's commercial jet fleet will have 3 or 4 engines. In addition, as aircraft become both faster and quieter, there is less time for wildlife to react. Coupled with the increase in migration of wildlife into urban areas and even airports, the mix of wildlife and airports has become dangerous, and even deadly in some cases.[54]

AGENCIES AND INFORMATION

A great number of federal, state and local agencies are involved in wildlife issues. An interagency memorandum of agreement was finalized in July of 2003, to clarify the roles of several participants that are involved in the protection of aviation from various wildlife hazards. The signatory agencies included: the Federal Aviation Administration, the U.S. Air Force, the U.S. Environmental Protection Agency,

---

[53] Edward Cleary & Richard Dolbeer, *Wildlife Management at Airports: A Manual for Airport Personnel* (2nd ed, Jul. 2005), retrieved from http://wildlife.pr.erau.edu/EnglishManual/2005_FAA_Manual_complete.pdf.
[54] *Id.*

the U.S. Fish and Wildlife Service, and the U.S. Department of Agriculture/Wildlife Services.[55]

A body of information has also been published on the subject, including advisory circulars, portions of federal aviation regulations and regular *CertAlerts (*notices to airport certification personnel). A listing of some of these is included below:[56]

- Advisory Circular 150/5200-32A, *Reporting Wildlife Aircraft Strikes*;
- Advisory Circular 150/5200-33A, *Hazardous Wildlife Attractants on or Near Airports*;
- Advisory Circular 150/5200-43A, *Construction or Establishment of Landfills Near Public Airports*;
- Advisory Circular 150/5200-36, *Qualifications for Wildlife Biologist Conducting Wildlife Hazard Assessment and Training Curriculums for Airport Personnel Involved in Controlling Wildlife Hazards on Airports*;
- CertAlert No. 98-05: *Grasses Attractive to Hazardous Wildlife*;
- CertAlert No. 04-09: *Relationship Between FAA and Wildlife Services*; and
- CertAlert No. 04-16: *Deer Hazard to Aircraft and Deer Fencing.*

While thousands of pages have been written on the topic of airports and wildlife, the discussion of issues, methods and research will likely continue well into the future. Well-attended conferences are held each year on the subject of wildlife management and aviation. An FAA-sponsored website is dedicated to the delivery of this information on Airport Wildlife Hazard Mitigation,[57] and has links to the FAA's National Wildlife Strike Database.[58]

[55] *Id.*

[56] *Id.* Also available from www.faa.gov, in their advisor circular collection.

[57] FAA, Airport Technology Research and Development Branch, *Airport Wildlife Hazard Mitigation Home Page* (updated Jan. 12, 2007), retrieved from http://wildlife-mitigation.tc.faa.gov/public_html/index.html.

[58] FAA, as maintained by Embry-Riddle Aeronautical University [ERAU], *National Wildlife Strike Database Online* (Jan. 2006), retrieved from http://wildlife.pr.erau.edu/public/index1.html.

Clearly, this small section of the environmental management chapter is by no means inclusive. Instead, it is intended to introduce the reader to at least the basics of the very complex and important issues of wildlife protection and management at airports, and in the aviation industry, generally.

FAR PART 139 WILDLIFE GUIDANCE

Under airport certification requirements, public use airports certificated under Title 14 Code of Federal Regulations, Part 139 must ensure that the airport maintains a safe operating environment, including "taking immediate action to alleviate wildlife hazards whenever they are detected." [59] To this end, the Federal Aviation Regulations [FARs][60] (specifically FAR Part 139) provide regulatory guidance for conducting a *Wildlife Hazard Assessment* and creating a *Wildlife Hazard Management Plan,* as deemed necessary by the FAA. This plan is created with guidance from the FAA, as contained in Part 139.337.[61]

The regulation states that each certificate holder (airport) must conduct a wildlife assessment if—on or *near* the airport—an air carrier aircraft experiences multiple wildlife strikes, substantial damage from striking wildlife, engine ingestion of wildlife; or wildlife of a size, or in numbers, capable of causing one of the listed events is observed to have access to any airport flight pattern or aircraft movement area. The FAR further states that the required wildlife hazard assessment required must be conducted by a wildlife damage management biologist who has professional training and/or experience in wildlife hazard management. The wildlife hazard assessment contains several items:

- Actions recommended in the wildlife hazard assessment to reduce wildlife hazards;
- The aeronautical activity at the airport, including the frequency and size of air carrier aircraft;
- The views of the certificate holder;
- The views of the airport users; and

---

[59] *See* Title 14, CFR Part 139.337, retrieved from www.faa.gov.
[60] The regulations under 14 CFR are often referred to as the "Federal Aviation Regulations."
[61] *Id.*

- Any other known factors relating to the wildlife hazard of which the Administrator is aware.

If the (FAA) Administrator determines that a wildlife hazard management plan is needed, the certificate holder must formulate and implement a plan using the wildlife hazard assessment as a basis. The plan must provide measures to alleviate or eliminate wildlife hazards to air carrier operations, be approved by the Administrator prior to implementation, and become integrated in the Airport Certification Manual. A plan must contain several elements which are discussed in FAR 139.337, including (but not limited to):

- Responsible parties and authority, and resources to implement the plan;
- Plans for managing the wildlife population, habitat modification, land use changes, obtaining wildlife permits; and,
- Procedures that identify personnel and responsibilities, provisions for aircraft movement/critical area inspection, wildlife hazardous control measures, communications, plan review, and personnel training.

In all cases, perhaps the most important component of any control program entails focus upon *habitat modifications*. Critters are attracted to habitats that make their lives more comfortable. Disrupted storm drainage systems, for example, may provide an inviting habitat. Standing water may attract mammals and birds alike. Beavers can induce flooding problems on runways and taxiways if allowed to build dams. Wildlife or waterfowl refuges must also be appropriately protected.

Wildlife issues are of significant concern to airport operators. While it is the airport's obligation to assure that wildlife is not needlessly destroyed, wildlife at and around airports must be sufficiently managed to assure that they do not pose a danger to the flying public. Thus, this chapter concludes with a discussion of wildlife control.

WILDLIFE CONTROL STRATEGIES

According to the FAA's wildlife guidance, four basic strategies can be used to control wildlife:[62]

- Aircraft flight schedule modification;
- Habitat modification and exclusion;
- Repellent and harassment techniques; and
- Wildlife removal.

Aircraft flight schedule modification refers to scheduling flights when wildlife activity is not at a peak. While the airport may assist in communicating this activity to users, it is up to the user to make the necessary schedule adjustments, if desired.

In *habitat modification*, the idea is to avoid making potential habitats inviting, or to otherwise eliminate drawing attractions where such conditions have already been created. The intended use of urea, for example, is to control ice on runways and taxiways in winter. Urea may also fertilize the ground where it runs off, thereby promoting grass growth, and subsequently inviting squirrels and other animals to feed and hide in the tall grass. Likewise tall stands of agricultural crops are attractive to rabbits—particularly jack rabbits in the West.

Fortunately, mammals stay on the ground and are thus easier to control than birds. They normally pose less of a hazard, but an aircraft striking a large animal can have catastrophic results. Deer, because of their speed, can appear suddenly. They are quick and unpredictable, and have been known to bound in an effort to clear vehicles such as cars and planes. Unfortunately, elevation of the deer's torso usually increases the hazard because the center of mass is raised to windshield or cockpit levels. Fortunately, mammal strikes accounted for less than 5% of reported aircraft strikes in the United States. But one of those strikes involved an aircraft in flight when a deer was struck with the landing gear. In the U.S., deer and coyotes are the mammals most commonly struck.[63]

---

[62] Edward Cleary & Richard Dolbeer, *Wildlife Management at Airports: A Manual for Airport Personnel* (2nd ed. Jul. 2005), retrieved from http://wildlife.pr.erau.edu/EnglishManual/2005_FAA_Manual_complete.pdf.

[63] FAA, *Wildlife Strikes to Civil Aircraft in the United States 1992-1996*, DOT/FAA/AS/97-3 (1997).

Slower animals present an equal danger. Cattle may be slow to react to an approaching aircraft on the runway. Although reptiles account for less than 1% of animal strikes, alligators are not an uncommon problem at airports in the South. Like cattle, they are slow, and not only are they sometimes large they are also low to the ground. Due to undulations of the runway surface, the pilot of an aircraft on take-off roll may not see the alligator.

Bats can be a problem in the air, but rodent populations of mice, rats, gophers and groundhogs, living in grassy areas on the infields, are not a problem *per se*. But larger birds of prey may look upon such congregations as a food source, will be attracted to the airport, and hence will themselves become hazards to air traffic. Rodents especially attract hawks and owls to airports. Cutting grasses at an optimum height of seven to ten inches can help. The grass should be tall enough to hide small rodents (i.e., food for larger birds) but short enough not to provide shelter for rabbits, pheasants and larger animals.

Airports are, by their very nature, attractive to birds. Airports have open grassy areas, brushlands, wooded areas, and ponding water. Large open areas provide an abundance of seeds, berry-producing plants, grass, insects, grubs and earthworms. Sometimes airports allow cultivation of the land for agricultural production. Farming turns the soil, exposes worms and insects, and provides seeds for birds to feed on. All too often, dumps and landfill areas are in close proximity to the airport and in some cases are located right off the ends of active runways. Dumps particularly attract birds when they are used for the disposal of human refuse. Food occasionally is made available to birds from discarded remnants of meals taken at the airport. Some people intentionally feed birds, which is a practice that should be particularly discouraged at airports.

An estimated 75% of all birds spend their lives within 500 feet of the ground. Consequently, most bird strikes are encountered near the airport in the area of landing and takeoff cycles. Most bird strikes (63%) occur during the daytime. Fifty-five percent occur within 100 feet of the ground, and 88% can be accounted for within 2,000 feet. Fortunately, the preponderance of bird strikes involve the smaller species and cause little damage to aircraft, but on occasion aircraft will collide with larger birds and severe damage ensues. Reportedly, gulls account for more than half of the bird strikes causing severe damage to aircraft—three times as many strikes as waterfowl.

Birds are involved in 97% of reported strikes. In controlling birds or animals it is important to know which species are frequenting the airport since the measures to use will vary with each kind. Gulls, blackbirds, waterfowl, doves, and raptors are the most common bird group involved in aircraft strikes.[64] Because of their size, the biggest bird problem is with gulls. Sparrows, pigeons, and starlings are the most common variety of birds around airports. Sparrows are not a common problem near the flightline, and like pigeons they will stay around buildings. Pigeons, however, will flock to the flightline to feed and can be a real menace. An ongoing trapping program can best control sparrows and pigeons.

Starlings are quite difficult to control. They group together in wandering flocks. Control measures taken against one flock may drive them off, but an entirely new flock may replace them. Scare tactics are usually employed by broadcasting their distress signal, driving at them with a truck and shooting at them with a shotgun.

Crows are a serious threat because of their size, but they are intelligent enough to leave if shot at, especially if a few of their numbers are killed. Unfortunately, killing sometimes becomes necessary with certain species that become immune to less threatening intimidation.

Large bodies of water attract gulls. They will commonly flock together and roost on the runway. Gulls, starlings, robins and crows feed on earthworms on the runway after rains. Gulls also like grasshoppers in grassy areas. Gulls are usually controlled by the same harassment techniques used on starlings (i.e., scare tactics).

The Canadian Wildlife Service and the U.S. Department of Agriculture have both studied the attractiveness of various crops to birds. These studies can be useful to airport managers for guidance as to which types of crops are most acceptable for planting at airports where agricultural activities are allowed. The growing of corn, oats, sunflowers, and milo should absolutely be avoided. The Canadian Wildlife Service recommends that crops not be allowed any closer than 1,200 feet of any runway. The crops recommended are as follows in descending order of preference: hay, alfalfa, flax, soy beans, pasture (although grazing of livestock presents special problems), fall rye, fall wheat, spring wheat, barley, and other grains except corn,

---

[64] *Id.*

oats, sunflowers and milo. Although fall wheat and spring wheat are acceptable, winter wheat should be avoided because it attracts geese.

If the aircraft flight schedule modifications and habitat modification strategies are unsuccessful and/or need to be supplemented, the airport may need to employ a strategy know as, *repellent and harassment techniques.* Bird and animal control can be a frustrating experience. If first attempts are unsuccessful in removing the birds and other critters, the best advice is to call in the experts! A good place to start, whether engaged in a self-control program or seeking the whereabouts and assistance of known professional exterminators is the local state wildlife agency or the U.S. Fish and Wildlife Service. The latter has been a major source of technical assistance. As mentioned earlier, this agency signed an agreement with the FAA to provide assistance upon request to airports having known bird hazards.

A wide range of tactics has been tried to rid airports of animal problems. Each control problem is unique, and listed below are various and sundry solutions that have been tried:

- *Alarms* emit loud, disturbing noises when triggered electronically by switch or electronic eye;
- *Needle strips* placed along roosting edges prevent birds from perching;
- *Distraction devices* such as reflective Mylar ribbons may deter birds from landing in areas of ponding water;
- *Full-height* walls divide hangars and isolate bird problems;
- *Shell crackers and noise bombs* are projectiles fired from a shotgun or flare pistol, respectively, which explode with a loud noise and a flash;
- *Dispersal tapes* emit electronic audio signals that alternately attract gulls to the sounds and then frighten them with unpredictable and loud noises;
- *Bird repellent caulking pastes* are uncomfortably sticky to the bird's feet, and may be used to prevent birds from remaining on treated surfaces;
- *Ultrasonic sound-wave* devices are used particularly in hangars and may repel birds with *Ultra-High Frequency* [UHF] waves of varied pitch, loudness and direction;

- *Nylon netting* has been used to prevent birds from entering hangars and other buildings with beams, rafters, ventilation openings and other recesses;
- *Non-poisonous feed* that, although not fatal, causes stressful symptoms. The distress call emitted may frighten other birds away; and
- *Decoys* or dummies of birds of prey or of serpents have been successfully used to drive away pigeons.

The final tactic associated with wildlife control strategy is *removal.* This is the most extreme measure used to manage wildlife, involving:

- *Traps* and nets may catch birds and/or animals. They can then be transported to new, remote locations; and
- *Poisons, shotguns and other killing devices.* While these are effective, caution must be used when considering extermination. It may be politically sensitive and may also be illegal. It is wise to check with the wildlife service before using such drastic means.

ENDANGERED SPECIES

The *Endangered Species Act* of 1973 [ESA] protects threatened or endangered species and their habitats. The opening chapter quote illustrated the powerful nature of the ESA. One of the busiest U.S. airports was held from expanding due to the presence of a tiny endangered shrimp. In addition, the preservation of a second endangered species' habitat—occupied by the El Segundo Blue Butterfly, and in part overlapped the endangered shrimp's habitat—was also of concern to environmentalists and Los Angeles World Airport officials.[65]

---

[65] Los Angeles International Airport Master Plan Drawing, Technical *Report, LAX Master Plan EIS/EIR*, Ch. 6: Hydrology and Water Quality Technical Report (2001), at 6, retrieved from http://www.laxmasterplan.org/docs/draft_eir_NE/T06_LR.pdf. Los Angeles World Airports [LAWA] is the airport oversight and operations department for Los Angeles, Calif. This department owns and operates Los Angeles International Airport, Ontario International Airport, Palmdale Regional Airport, and Van Nuys Airport. It also runs the FlyAway Bus service. *See* Los Angeles World Airports, *Four Airports, One Vision*, http://www.lawa.org/LAWA.cfm (visited May 11, 2007).

Los Angles is not the only California airport to be affected by endangered species concerns. Endangered snakes at Sacramento cost the airport several millions of dollars. From the late 1980s to 2000, Sacramento filled in several airport wetlands in an attempt to reduce the attraction of the areas to birds, as they were considered a threat to aircraft operations. Unfortunately, the areas being filled in were the habitat for the Giant Garter Snake, a threatened species protected under ESA. As a result, environmentalists sued and the federal government levied penalties on the City of Sacramento. One requirement was an obligation to purchase 300 undeveloped acres in northern Sacramento to be used to create a preserve. Land acquisition and administration costs were estimated to exceed $11 million on completion.[66]

The cost of the preserve's land acquisition will be borne ultimately by the airlines. "It's essentially a cost of doing business," said Sacramento County Airport System assistant director Rob Leonard, who said the added cost will not delay any projects planned by the airport. "It's unfortunate. The airlines are not pleased about that."[67]

Through the decade of the 1970s, many airport development actions were contested on environmental grounds. When Dade County, Florida, proposed an airport in the Florida Everglades as a replacement for Miami International, it was rejected due to serious environmental concerns and resistance. Likewise, when the Los Angeles Airport Authority proposed a replacement airport for Los Angesles International Airport [LAX] in the Antelope Valley in Palmdale, California, a pro-environmental group vehemently opposed the action, thwarting consideration of the site.

Noteworthy of the Antelope Valley and Florida Everglades issues is that in both cases, the proposed developments were to be in locations far removed from the urban settings of metropolitan Miami or Los Angeles. The remote locations were picked at least in part to avoid the significant impact that each proposed airport would have upon the *human* environment. Instead, each proposal met with strong opposition on behalf of the threatened wildlife habitats.

But not only should wildlife receive fair treatment in their habitats, even more paramount, humans, too, are entitled to fair treatment when it comes to airport development. What follows is a discussion

---

[66] Mark Larson, *Airport Pays Millions to Buy Snake Habitat*, Sacramento Business J. (Apr. 25, 2005).

[67] *Id.*

of an important element of the human environment: *environmental justice*.

ENVIRONMENTAL JUSTICE

Environmental Justice [EJ] is defined as, "the fair treatment and meaningful involvement of all people regardless of race, color, national origin, culture, education, or income with respect to the development, implementation, and enforcement of environmental laws, regulations, and policies."[68] Bill Clinton's 1994 Executive Order 12898 requires "Federal Actions to Address Environmental Justice in Minority and Low Income Populations." Additionally, and accompanying Presidential Memorandum and Department of Transportation Order DOT 5610.2, "Environmental Justice," "require the FAA to provide for meaningful public involvement by minority and low-income populations . . . [and] address potential impact . . . that may be disproportionately high and adverse."[69]

From an airport perspective, EJ becomes an issue if low income and/or other underrepresented groups are disproportionately affected by an airport's environmental actions, inactions or procedural processes. The airport environmental disamenity in question might be noise, hazardous waste or a number of other negative externalities generated by the airport and/or its users. EJ also refers to the requirement for protected populations to be fully informed of and involved in the processes associated with major airport decisions, such as receiving invitations to –and meaningful involvement in—public hearings.

One reason it has been difficult to disentangle some key questions regarding environmental justice and airports, is because the "which came first?" question (i.e., the disamenity or the resident) is not always as obvious as it may seem. We've all heard the saying, "If you move next to a dump, don't complain about the flies." But the airport-community relationship is not so simple. Airports regularly experience community encroachment, but in the past, airports have sometimes grown without giving prior notice to the public. It is not always clear how many nearby residents, who moved into homes in the 1970s and 1980s, clearly understood the airport's anticipated rate of

[68] EPA, *Environmental Justice*, retrieved from http://www.epa.gov/compliance/resources/faqs/ej/index.html#faq2.
[69] FAA, *Environmental Impacts: Policies and Procedures*, FAA Order 1050.1E (Jun. 8, 2004), change 1 incorporated, retrieved from www.faa.gov.

growth and potential impact. Noise regulations that prompted the generation of future noise projections were not enacted until the mid-1980s. One scholarly study suggests that both the community and the airport, to some degree, encroached upon one another over the course of several decades, with the residents lacking substantive knowledge of the projected growth and full future impact of the airport.[70]

Thus, even if low income populations appear to be disproportionately affected—for example, by high levels of airport noise or nearby hazardous waste storage—then the question begs, was the purchase an educated or an uneducated one? Essentially, did the person really make a purchase with the understanding that the residence would eventually become unfit for residential living? The opening quote in the next chapter on noise clearly illustrates the sort of misinformation that potential homeowners may encounter, as well as the effort of one airport to help them make a more educated decision.

Clearly, airport decision-makers can and have negatively impacted certain community residents and groups by their decisions. But, historically, while airport decision-makers may have made decisions that impacted lower income or minority residents, they may not have had the awareness provided today. Since the first Federal mandates regarding environmental justice were not instituted until Clinton's 1994 Executive Order, decision-makers before that point were not trained to properly consider environmental justice.[71] Today's public managers are better educated in this area and now have an obligation to consider EJ as an important issue in responsible airport planning, development and environmental management.

OTHER ENVIRONMENTAL IMPACTS

Although this chapter has reviewed several important environmental considerations at today's public airports, many other environmental factors remain virtually uncovered. For example, social im-

---

[70] Robin Sobotta, Heather Campbell & Beverly Owen, *Aviation Noise and Environmental Justice: The Barrio Barrier*, J. of Regional Science (Feb. 2007). This study addresses the timing question in a directly policy-relevant way by examining the growth of a major municipal airport's aircraft operations in relation to the in-migration of noise-impacted residents and, ultimately, studying the airport's implementation of the Federal requirement to provide the community with constructive knowledge of airport noise study results

[71] One reason it has been difficult to disentangle some key questions in the environmental justice literature is because which came first—the disamenity or the minority group—is difficult to observe; *see* F. Liu, *Environmental Justice Analysis: Theories, Methods, and Practice* (2001).

pacts may arise from the disruption of established communities, the necessity for relocation of people, altered transportation patterns, changes in employment, and so forth. And aside from socio-economic impacts, there are other potential impacts upon the man made environment as well. Under various statutes, consideration must be given to the potential impacts of proposals upon public parks, recreation areas, historic sites, and historic and cultural properties, including archeological sites.

Some environmental impacts of an airport could be easily overlooked, but should be considered. If farmland is to be converted to other uses, it must be determined whether any of that land is prime or unique, or of state or local significance, which would be protected under the Farmland Protection Policy Act of 1981. Occasionally, light emissions are an issue when an airport has active nighttime operations (such as air cargo carrier service). For major developments in some areas, energy requirements, which are significant with respect to local supply, may be an issue. Finally, it is common that, because of the surrounding habitat, drainage, water quality, human habitation or other situations particular to the development site, special mitigation measures must be taken during construction.

The FAA's Environmental Program Office assists airports with the implementation of the NEPA and other Federal environmental laws and regulations.[72] Additional guidance on these and other important environmental issues are addressed in the *National Environmental Policy Act (NEPA) Implementing Instructions for Airport Projects* (formerly, the *Airport Environmental Handbook)* and in *Environmental Impacts: Policies and Procedures.*[73]

SUMMARY

Competent environment management is a difficult and expensive undertaking. While there is strong regulatory guidance in many environmental areas, the regulations can be daunting in that they require very specialized expertise and may result in serious airport and personal liability if those who take on this challenge do not pay heed to

[72] FAA's Environmental Program offers valuable information and resource documents retrieved from http://www.faa.gov/airports_airtraffic/airports/environmental/.

[73] FAA Office of Airports, *National Environmental Policy Act (NEPA) Implementing Instructions for Airport Projects*, FAA Order 5050-4B (Apr. 2006) and *Environmental Impacts: Policies and Procedures*, FAA Order 1050.1D (Jun. 8, 2004), retrieved from www.faa.gov.

the guidance. Additionally, smaller airport operators and community feel pinched about some of the environmental requirements that are imposed at times, without funding available at the levels needed to mitigate environmental problems. These often *under* or *un-funded mandates* are a concern to communities that lack the kind of funding needed to address environmental problems that may have been incurred by others, decades prior.

Still, airport operators across the nation are admirably taking on the challenge to be good neighbors and stewards of the environment. The key is to operate today's airports as cleanly and responsibly as possible, so that future airport operators and communities are not left with previous generations' waste and irresponsible behavior.

One additional area that airports are making progress in is the improved management of noise, although many community groups will attest to the fact that the problem is far from being resolved. The next chapter focuses solely on the topic of aviation noise, still considered the severest of all environmental problems facing today's airport operators.

CHAPTER 7

AVIATION NOISE

Be careful with what people tell you. Real estate agents, property developers, neighbors and concerned citizens may not be familiar with aircraft operations . . . So when they tell you that the airport shuts down at night or that the planes usually fly the other way or that it's not that bad or that the noise is getting worse every day or that the flight tracks just got changed or that the property value is going down or anything else, please call the Noise Officer.

Raleigh-Durham International Airport Official Website[1]

THE NOISE SOURCE

Aviation noise is unquestionably the most long-standing and highly controversial environmental issue affecting airports. "Aviation noise," as opposed to "airport noise," is used herein to clarify that the noise source is actually the user (i.e., the aircraft), and not the facility owner (i.e., airport). Indeed, many airport operators can recall a public hearing/forum on noise in which airport personnel were forced to "take the heat" from disenchanted neighbors, while engine manufacturers, aircraft manufacturers and aircraft operators were either absent or seated at the rear of the room. While certainly frustrating (if not impossible) for airport operators to explain decisions made in cockpits—sometimes miles away from the airport—the burden of making airports more compatible by reducing noise impacts and becoming better neighbors falls squarely on the shoulders of airport sponsors.

---

[1] Raleigh Durham Airport, *Tips for Homebuyers* (2006), retrieved from http://www.rduaircraftnoise.com/home/tips.html.

Raleigh-Durham Airport, in its web-based warning to potential new homebuyers (*supra*), is part of a growing movement of airports to be active instead of passive partners in educating homeowners making purchases. Their website continues, "The Noise Officer will discuss flight tracks, current aircraft operations, noise disclosure and future growth at the airport." Other airports are adopting very similar proactive approaches to communicating their message to neighbors and actively embracing them in the decision-making process.

This chapter concludes the review of airport environmental issues with a focus on aviation noise, including a technical discussion of the environmental disamenity, regulatory overview, noise measurement and tracking, noise mitigation strategies, community relations and environmental justice issues.

AIRCRAFT NOISE

Aircraft can pollute the environment in several ways, but the worst pollutant of all is noise. Airplanes emit solid particulate matter, expel noxious gases and toxins, and contribute to global warming due to related unnatural cloud formation; but none of these possibilities has caused the turmoil that noise has. Across the nation aircraft noise has sparked many lawsuits seeking relief from airport related noise.

And yet, aircraft noise is not new; airplanes have always made noise. The original defense against aircraft noise was to remove airports far from population centers so that noise would not be a problem. Using the theory, "If there is no one to hear the noise there is no noise," worked fine in the beginning. But through the years, the tendency of Americans has been to encroach upon airports by building homes and neighborhoods close by, and then sue because airplane noise has supposedly brought the surrounding community to ruin.

Exemplary Dulles International Airport, which was built on 10,000 acres in the Virginia countryside, specifically to remove airplane noise from the populated Washington, D.C. area. Construction began in 1958. Since then the town of Reston developed, nearby Herndon grew rapidly, as did the other close-by communities of Manassas and Sterling Park. Several housing subdivisions were built in and around each of these growing communities. The town of Centreville, which lies directly below a major approach and departure path, was planned by Fairfax County to be a major regional growth center. Within just 25 years land use conflicts became a major problem.

Likewise, when Denver Stapleton was closed in 1995, and replaced with the Denver International Airport, it was anticipated that airport noise complaints would decrease due to the fact that fewer residents lived within the areas that were projected to be at the highest noise levels, relative to Stapleton. However, after the move, Denver airport officials found that noise complaints actually escalated exponentially. Apparently, the community response to an increase of noise above the ambient noise level (which is higher in urban and lower in rural areas) was underestimated. So, while noise models predicted improvements in overall lower noise levels at the new location (since residents were generally farther from the noise at the new location), these models did not predict the (rural) residents' higher level of intolerance for new noise over the prior ambient noise levels.

Clearly, a variable for varying human *perceptions* of acceptable and unacceptable noise in urban or rural settings must be adjusted in future models, if airports want to better predict rural community response to new noise. Both the Dulles and the Denver examples show that computer generated noise models—which will be discussed later in this chapter—are not perfect instruments. Airport sponsors must expect the unexpected when dealing with different people, different environments, and varying perceptions.

The primary concern with noise is that it annoys people by constraining their activities. Some research suggests that it can actually be harmful at higher, sustained levels. It especially interferes with sleep, with normal communications, and with capability to learn. But what is noise? It is not simply sound. More specifically, it is *unwanted* sound, and perception of it will vary greatly from one person to another. For example, individuals show wide variation in their propensity to be wakened or to have their sleep disturbed short of awakening. Older people are generally more susceptible to sleep disturbances than are younger people. The sound of a jet engine may be music to the pilot, but quite the opposite to a concert pianist.

NOISE MEASUREMENT

The unit of measure for sound is the *decibel* [dB]. Each decibel equals a sound pressure level. One dB equals twenty times the logarithmic ratio of the sound pressure in the air to a reference sound pressure (usually 0.0002 dyne per square centimeter). Since this is a logarithmic relation, 2 dB is not twice as great in magnitude as 1 dB, but rather, it is nearly six times as great.

The total amount of sound present is the *overall sound pressure level.* Typically, sound-level meters contain three different response-weighting networks: "A," "B," and "C." The C weighting corresponds to overall sound pressure level. The most commonly used scale is the A weighting since it nearly equates to the human response. The normal human ear does not respond the same to all sound frequencies, but rather, responds to sounds with frequencies between 20 and 15,000 Hertz (the technical unit for cycles per second) and detects frequencies around 1,000 to 2,000 Hertz most efficiently. The *A-weighting* filter discriminates against very high and very low frequencies much as the human ear does. It gives greater weight to frequencies which are heard by human beings and which might be found objectionable by the individual.

Decibels on the A weighted scale are abbreviated dBA. A dBA technically represents only one instant of measurement. However, most references to dBA noise levels for aircraft are an overall yielding of noise for a *single event* such as a takeoff, landing, or flyover. The average person finds that a long-duration noise is more annoying than a shorter-duration noise. Hence, duration of sound is an important factor in measuring noise. The *Sound Exposure Level* [SEL] adds all of the sound energy received during a noise event.

In attempts to more accurately define noise that reflects the annoyance caused by a single aircraft noise event, other standards such as the *Perceived Noise Decibel* [PNdB] and the *Effective Perceived Noise Decibel* [EPNdB] have come into being. The PNdB includes corrective factors beyond the human response weighted A scale. The EPNdB further refines PNdB by accounting for discrete tones in aircraft noise that are sharply annoying such as the whine of a jet engine.

It should be noted that dBA, PNdB and EPNdB all measure *single* noise events. They are not to be confused with ratings given in *cumulative* noise measurement methodologies. Measurement of aircraft noise affecting communities is usually based on aggregates of single aircraft noise events. Worldwide, dozens of noise measurement methodologies have been developed, but within the United States there have been three which have found wide-spread acceptance: *Compos-*

ite Noise Rating [CNR], *Noise Exposure Forecast* [NEF], and *(Yearly) Day-Night Average Sound Level* [DNL or L_{dn} or YDNL].[2]

The oldest system is the CNR, which is based on the PNdB and was specifically designed to correlate aircraft noise with its effect upon humans. Composite Noise Rating is rarely used anymore. Noise Exposure Forecast incorporated several refinements not found in CNR. It uses more detailed information regarding the number of noise events and the type of aircraft involved, and it is based on the EPNdB. Like CNR, its use is no longer a common practice.

Although there is no singularly accepted worldwide methodology, the one that has found the greatest acceptance, and the one most commonly used elsewhere as well as in the United States is DNL or one similar to it. In Europe, for instance, the European Parliament and the Council of the European Union issued a directive relating to the assessment and management of environmental noise known as the *Environmental Noise Directive* [END],[3] which requires that Member States use common noise indicators—L_{den} and L_{night}—to describe environmental noise levels based on Energy Equivalent Noise Level [LEQ]. Like DNL, the LEQ differentiates between daytime and night time activity, with a 10-dBA penalty for night time noise. However, the END does allow Member States to use supplementary noise indicators, such a breaking the 24-hour day into more than two segments.[4]

The day-night average sound level or DNL is the measurement methodology recognized in the United States for use in "Federal Aviation Regulation [FAR] Part 150 studies" to produce Noise Exposure Maps [NEMs] and the footprints or contours of representing noise level that those maps contain. The federally approved model for producing NEMs is the Integrated Noise Model [INM]. Data factored in to the INM include: fleet mix, runway use, wind speed and direction, temperature, takeoff weights, and flight track *bundling*. Bundling refers to the predicted direction and grouping of aircraft paths,

---

[2] According to the FAA Office of Airport Planning and Programming, personal communication (Jan. 2007), all three abbreviations are used interchangeably, with DNL being the most commonly used. L_{dn} is typically used in formulas. YDNL (Yearly Day-Night Average Sound Level) means the 365-day average sound level. While DNL is also supposed to be a yearly average, the FAA reports that, on occasion, DNL will reflect a shorter-term basis, such as when a site is monitored for a period of time that is less than a year.

[3] *The Environmental Noise Directive*, (Jun. 25, 2002), retrieved from http://www.europa.eu.int/eurlex/en/oj/dat2002/1_18920020718en00120025.pdf.

[4] Dave Maundill, *Environmental Noise Mapping*, Building Services & Environmental Engineer (Mar. year unk.)

typically reflecting the merger and separation patterns that are anticipated on departure or arrival."[5]

Figure 7.1, "Airport Noise Contours," illustrates the noise contours generated about the airport. The zones of impact were developed by the U.S. Environmental Protection Agency [EPA] to allow comparison of noise levels from all types of urban sources. In other words, it measures *ambient* noise over a yearly basis. It not only measures aircraft noise but also measures noise created by automobiles, trucks, jackhammers, and so forth—all within the same community setting. Day-Night Average Sound Level uses the simple dBA measurements. It assumes a 10-dBA penalty for nighttime (10:00 p.m.-7:00 a.m.) operations, duration of noise events, and aircraft noise that is above the ambient background level.

A variant to DNL is *Community Noise Equivalent Level* [CNEL], which was developed in California to enforce noise standards enacted by the state legislature. It can be used for predicting community response and for monitoring aircraft operations on the dBA scale. The principal difference between DNL and CNEL is that the latter divides the 24-hour day into three periods rather than two, with operations in the 7:00 p.m. to 10:00 p.m. time frame being assessed a 5-dBA penalty and events from 10:00 p.m. to 7 a.m. incurring a 10-dBA penalty. The philosophy with CNEL is that, as urban noise decreases in the evening (after 7:00 p.m.) the impact of an event is greater and more annoying. After 10:00 p.m. it is assumed to be even more annoying. Both the DNL and the CNEL represent an annual average of the daily energy noise exposure. Much like the California based (CNEL) system Great Britain has developed a variant to the LEQ model, which includes the third 4-hour evening period with a 5-dBA penalty.[6]

The INM generates noise contours or "footprints" that graphically illustrate sound levels around airports. While noise contours can (and should) be validated by ground-based monitors, it is important to point out that the computer-generated contours do not depict *actual* measurements of the noise being emitted by aircraft. Thus, the individual creating the model can, to some degree, alter the result based on the data entered.

---

[5] Hanscom Noise Workgroup presentation, *Aviation Noise Metrics Recommendations* (Feb. 28, 2001), retrieved from http://www.fican.org/pdf/HanscomNoise.pdf.

[6] *See* European Commission Working Group 1, *Executive Summary* (Apr. 1, 1998), retrieved from http://www.xs4all.nl/~rigolett/ENGELS/wg1/execsum.htm.

Figure 7.1—AIRPORT NOISE CONTOURS

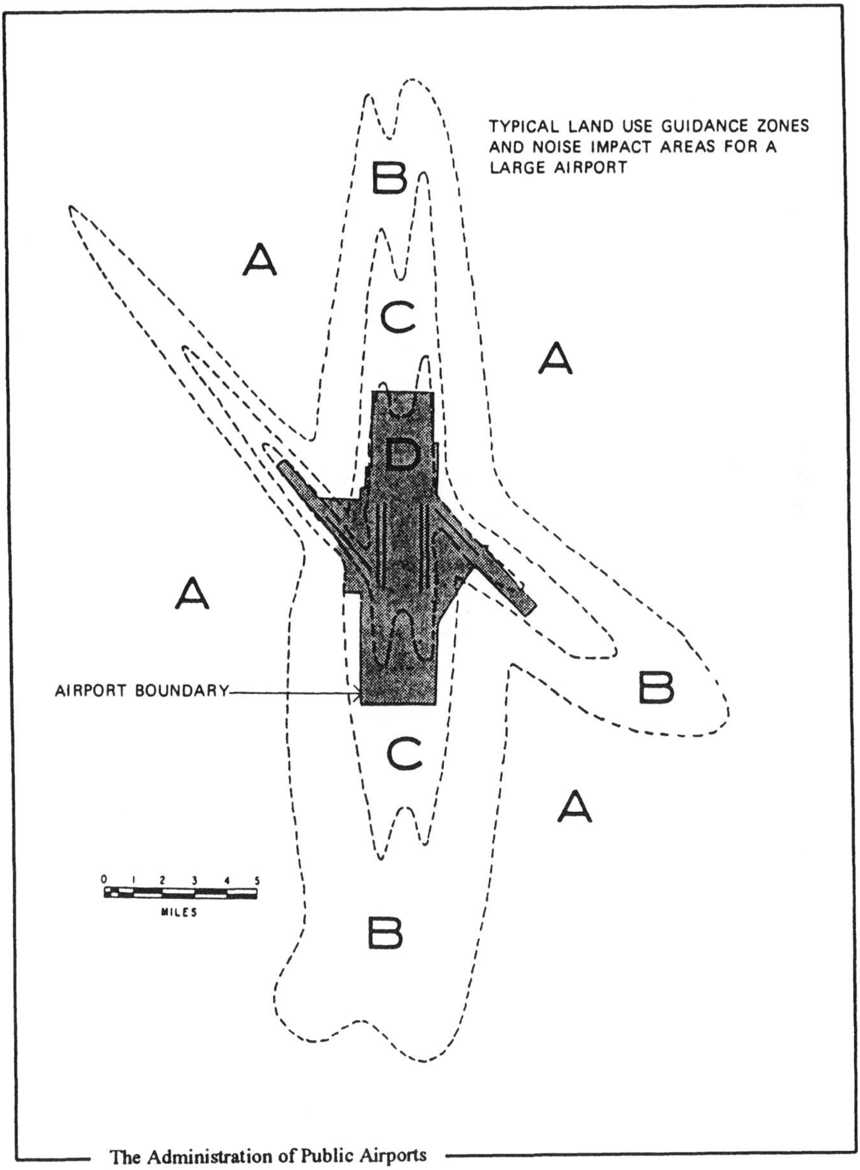
TYPICAL LAND USE GUIDANCE ZONES
AND NOISE IMPACT AREAS FOR A
LARGE AIRPORT
A
B
C
D
A
A
A
B
C
B
A
AIRPORT BOUNDARY
0 1 2 3 4 5
MILES
The Administration of Public Airports

Source: FAA AC 150/5050-6.

"All mathematical models rely on assumptions, and can produce results with some degree of error," reported the Hanscom Noise Workgroup. In the case of the INM, the workgroup reported, "actual measures and model were reported to vary up to 10 dB." [7] While these statements suggest that the INM is not a perfect tool, it is expected that those analysts producing the contours will strive to use accurate data and predictions, and act in an ethical manner in generating the noise contours.

While the Federal Aviation Administration [FAA] reports that the current model and measurement methodology are not scheduled for near-term replacement,[8] many in the noise industry/community actively discuss alternative measurement methodologies for possible use in the INM. Two changes that have been suggested use of the *Time Above* [TA] metric in the INM (to create contours that reflect the length of time noise exceeds a given level) or *Single Event Level Distribution* [SEL/D], which is a histogram distribution of sound exposure level values due to actual (measured) aircraft operations that produce statistical descriptions of aircraft events. Both methodologies reflect an approach that provides "community metrics" (easily understood by the public) and statistical descriptions of single noise events, as opposed to just averages.[9] Recently, flight-tracking software has been extensively used by airport operators to show the actual flights or "events" that occur, thereby helping the community envision the collective impact of several singular events.

COMMUNITY RESPONSE TO NOISE

The effects of noise cover a wide range of human response and varying degrees of annoyance. Noise is vague and difficult to define. Thus, strategies to alleviate airport-related noise are equally difficult to formulate. The historical approach was to define noise in terms of sound pressure, and to equate anticipated human responses to varying levels of sound exposure. Since there is such a wide disparity in individual responses to noise, this approach was not totally satisfactory, and analysts have turned to subjective strategies.

---

[7] *Id.*

[8] Office of Airport Planning and Programming, FAA, personal communication (Jan. 2007).

[9] Hanscom Noise Workgroup presentation, *Aviation Noise Metrics Recommendations* (28 Feb. 2001), retrieved from http://www.fican.org/pdf/HanscomNoise.pdf.

The correlation factors of subjective community response found in the noise measurement methodologies broadly used today were developed for residential communities. Basically, three concentric zones located about the airport delineate the areas of potential noise impact:

- The *primary* impact area is the innermost zone where the greatest noise impact occurs.[10] The primary zone is an area wherein individual reactions would likely include repeated, vigorous complaints. Concerted group action might also be expected;
- The *secondary* zone is the next lesser area of noise impact. Individuals in the secondary zone may complain, and perhaps vigorously.[11] Concerted group action is again possible; and
- The *tertiary* outer zone of noise impact is an area wherein there is moderate exposure to noise, but essentially no complaints would be expected.[12] The noise may, however, interfere occasionally with certain activities of the residents.

Sometimes there is a fourth zone of reference, but it is the unlimited area beyond the boundary of what is considered to be adverse noise exposure.[13] It is an area of minimal-to-no noise impact, wherein there should be absolutely no complaints about aircraft noise.

There is a wide variation in the response to noise amongst individuals. It has been determined by the U.S. Department of Housing and Urban Development [HUD] that, for the range of noise exposure produced by aircraft flyovers, factors other than the physical noise environment influence annoyance judgments. A series of studies by HUD suggested that more than half the measured variation in annoyance response may be due to factors other than noise. Examples of non-acoustic influences are:

- Fear of aircraft crashes;
- Individual susceptibility to noise;
- Proximity to the airport;
- Adaptability to noise;
- Area of residence;

[10] Shown as Zone "D" on Fig. 7.1, "Airport Noise Contours."
[11] Shown as Zone "C" on Fig. 7.1, "Airport Noise Contours."
[12] Shown as Zone "B" on Fig. 7.1, "Airport Noise Contours."
[13] Shown as Zone "A" on Fig. 7.1, "Airport Noise Contours."

- Economic importance of the airport;
- Life-styles;
- Environment attitude;
- Beliefs about the effect of noise on health; and
- Faith in the sincerity of those able to do something about the noise problem.

Confidence in airport administration on the part of the general public can mitigate many of the adverse community responses to noise.

Understanding a community's overall annoyance can be achieved only by taking into account these non-acoustic factors. However, each of the methodologies previously mentioned can provide adequate predictions of average community response. Each can be used as a helpful land use-planning tool, with the understanding that present state-of-the-art methodologies have inherent limitations.

In attempting to improve upon accepted methodologies, airport authorities have tried to correlate the impact of noise upon the community with actual noise complaints. The Environmental Protection Agency warns against such practices. It has been demonstrated that lower-income families suffer more from noise than those in higher income brackets, yet the latter generally register more complaints. Since actual exposure to noise does not necessarily elicit complaints, then numbers of locations of complaints may have little relationship to detrimental noise.

NOISE AND HARM

There is growing evidence that various sorts of environmental pollution cause physical, emotional, psychological, and socioeconomic harm. [14] But many people do not realize that it is not simply a matter of usage or of hyperbole to refer to "noise pollution." Significant evidence indicates that it causes physical and other harm to those overexposed. Research indicates aviation noise can cause a variety of harms, including (but not limited to) communication interference,

[14] Section extracted from Robin Sobotta, Heather Campbell & Beverly Owen, *Aviation Noise and Environmental Justice: The Barrio Barrier*, J. of Regional Science (Feb. 2007). Notably, one researcher in this area, Sanford Fidel (Fidel *et al.*,1995), who has authored studies suggesting no relationship between noise and sleep disturbance, disputes all other studies that suggest noise causes harm—except those pertaining to hypertension (personal communication, Feb. 2000).

sleep disturbance, elevated levels of blood pressure and cholesterol, immune system deficiency, lower birth weight and higher frequency of premature birth, and hearing damage including to unborn babies.[15]

Of particular relevance to minority children, some of these problems may themselves lead to reduced scholastic performance and test scores.[16] In the economic realm, it seems clear that aviation noise can cause significant property devaluation.[17]

NOISE LEGISLATION

The earliest piece of U.S. noise-specific legislation was the 1968 Aircraft Noise Abatement Act, which required the Federal Aviation Administration to consult with the Environmental Protection Agency in the establishment of noise standards for civil aircraft. [18] The 1970 Noise Pollution and Abatement Act then created the Office of Noise Abatement and Control [ONAC] within the EPA. Two years later, the Noise Control Act specifically amended the Federal Aviation Act so that the EPA could become more heavily involved in the regulation of aviation noise. Although the EPA's ONAC did initially attempt to weigh in on some significant aviation noise issues, they were met with extreme resistance from the FAA. In 1981, the ONAC was "temporarily" de-funded and has not been refunded since.

AVIATION SAFETY AND NOISE ABATEMENT ACT

The purpose of the *Aviation Safety and Noise Abatement Act* [ASNA] of 1979 is to provide assistance to airport operators in preparing and carrying out noise compatibility programs, to provide assistance that assures continued safety in aviation, and for other purposes. The Act has the express intent of standardizing noise meas-

---

[15] *See* Walter Holland, *Health Effects of Aircraft Noise* (1997). Unpublished report available from Professor Walter Holland, PO Box 339, Richmond, Surrey, England, TW93RB.

[16] M.S. Haines, Stansfeld, B. Berglund, & R. Job, *Chronic Aircraft Noise Exposure and Child Cognitive Performance and Stress* (1998), in N. Carter & R.F.S. Job (eds.), Proceedings of the 7th International Conference on Noise as a Public Health Problem, 1: 329-334.

[17] Booz, Allen & Hamilton, Inc., *The Effect of Airport Noise on Housing Values: A Summary Report* (Sep. 1994); *see also* M. Espey & H. Lopez, *The Effects of Airport Noise on Residential Property Values*, Growth and Change (2000) Vol. 31, at 408-419; *see also* J. Tomkins, N. Topham, J. Twomey & R. Ward, *Noise Versus Access: The Impact of an Airport in an Urban Property Market*, Urban Studies (1998), Vol. 35, at 243-258.

[18] *Airport Noise Law: Statues and Regulations* (Revised Oct. 20, 2006), retrieved from http://home.netvista.net/hpb/statutes.html.

urement methodologies and land use compatibility programs in the U.S. and for the legal protection of threatened airports.

By no later than one year after passage of ASNA, the Secretary of Transportation (in consultation with the Administrator of the Environmental Protection Agency and other appropriate agencies) was required to,

- establish a single system of measuring noise;
- establish a single system for determining the exposure of individuals to aircraft noise; and
- identify land uses that are normally compatible with various exposures of individuals to noise.

The provisions in ASNA reinforced the fact that, while the federal governmental may provide guidelines for noise measurement, implementation of operational airport noise abatement strategies is the airport's responsibility. In this regard, the Department of Defense [DOD] took an early lead in working toward airport compatibility when in 1973 it set forth DOD policy on achieving compatible use of public and private lands in the vicinity of military airfields. From the military's *Air Installation Compatible Land Use Zones* [AICUZ] program has evolved the Federal government's program for "Noise Control and Compatibility Planning for Airports," (AC 150/5020-1), or what have become commonly known as "FAR Part 150 Studies," of which the two main products are the: (1) *Noise Exposure Map*, and (2) the *Noise Compatibility Program*.

The NEM is prepared using the measurement methodologies (DNL and CNEL) and model (INM) discussed earlier in this chapter. The purpose of an NEM is to depict the airport's present and future noise patterns, and the areas of present and future land use development that are not compatible with those noise patterns. The maps are prepared after consultation with the public, affected local governments, airport users, and the FAA. Utilizing local data and FAR Part 150 land use compatibility guidance, the sponsor determines and labels the non-compatible land uses, including noise sensitive uses such as residential area, schools, hospitals, libraries, rest homes, and auditoriums. After certification as true and correct, the maps and supporting data are submitted to the FAA for review and acceptance.

Upon acceptance of the NEM by the FAA, community members must be given *constructive knowledge* of the proposed noise impacts depicted in the NEM. Constructive knowledge is achieved in two ways: via publication three times in a local newspaper or by directly providing noise-impacted individuals with a copy of the NEM. It is then presumed that persons who subsequently acquire property in noise sensitive areas also have constructive knowledge of the projected airport noise. As such, current and future residents shall not be entitled to recover damages due to airport related noise, so long as the airport's noise levels do not exceed the NEM projections by more than 5 dB over the five-year period projected in the NEM.

Some state and local governments have passed legislation that require potential homeowners be notified of noise impact before completing the purchase of a home, via a *disclosure* document. This serves to "disclose" to prospective buyers that the property they are purchasing is in the vicinity of an airport. Disclosures may be linked with homeowner deeds such that is ceases to be an option to disclose proximity to an airport or the noise associated with aircraft over flight. One tool that is becoming increasingly popular is the establishment of *Airport Influence Areas or Public Airport Disclosure Maps* such as the one presented in Figure 7.2, "Sample Airport Public Disclosure Map."

Airport Influence Area maps are typically produced by the airport sponsor and often registered with a state agency (such as a department of real estate). Influence areas have two main purposes: (1) revealing the potentially noise-impacted areas around airports to current and prospective residents, and (2) providing guidance to planning/zoning commissions as to where airport influence may extend so that compatible land uses can be planned and maintained in those areas. While Part 150 NEMs are only required to project impact over the next five years, influence areas may show areas of projected impact decades into the future. The goal, of course is to reduce or eliminate incremental community encroachment into areas that may be eventually impacted by aviation noise, and reduce the possibility for damage claims.

Figure 7.2—SAMPLE PUBLIC AIRPORT DISCLOSURE MAP

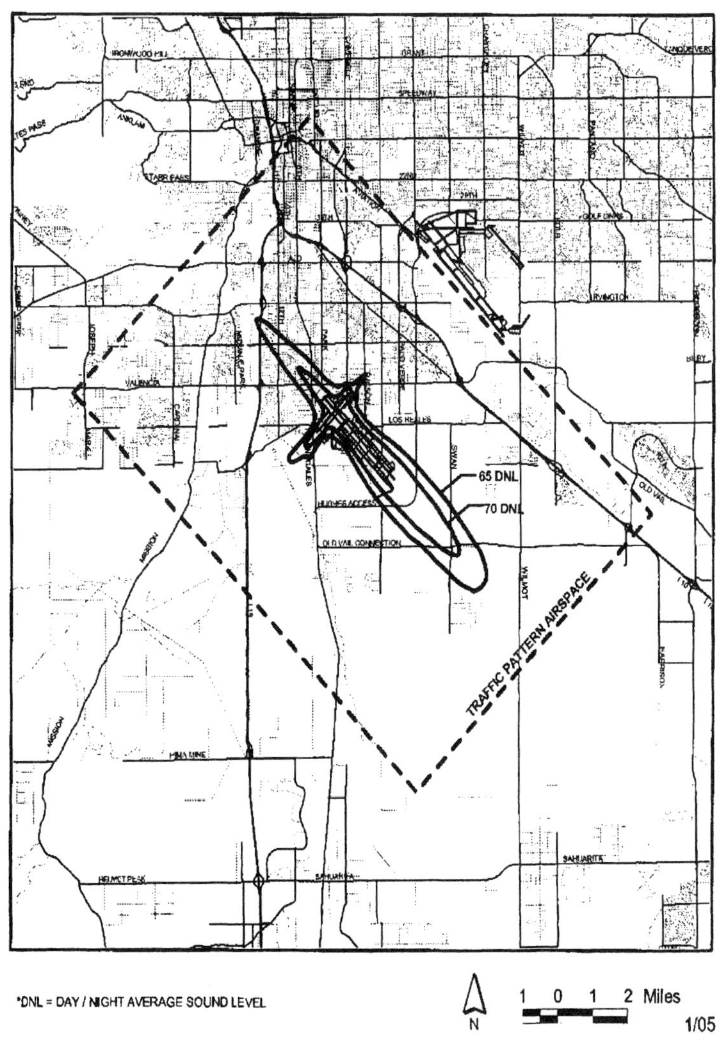

Source: Tucson International Airport, retrieved from http://www.restate.az/ PUBLIC_INFO/Airport_Maps/Territory_in _the Vicinity_of_a_ Public_Airport.html.

The purpose of the other major FAR Part 150-product, the airport's Noise Compatibility Program or NCP, is to formulate possible solutions to the noise problems identified by the noise exposure maps. This is a process in which a number of viable solutions are explored and the most workable of them are selected for full development. Total costs of each alternative are included in the considerations. The entire process is carried out in consultation with the affected local governments, the airport's users, those people impacted by the noise, and with the FAA. The program should include an implementation schedule, should identify who will be responsible for implementing the program, and should identify extent and source of the necessary funds. The total noise compatibility program is then submitted to FAA for approval.

After FAA acceptance of the NEM and publication of the availability of the NCP in the *Federal Register*, the agency has 180 days to complete its review and make a finding. Otherwise, the NEM and NCP are approved by default except for any portion of a program relating to the use of flight procedures for noise control purposes. FAA approval of Part 150 Studies will be given only for those recommendations, which,

- do not compromise safety;
- do not impose an undue burden on interstate or foreign commerce;
- do not discriminate for or against any group or class of users of operators;
- are meaningful and serve to provide real noise abatement;
- comply with federal airport grant agreements, which are funded by the flying public; and
- do not conflict with or invade areas of responsibility vested in the federal government.

No part of the adopted noise map or related information nor any part of the listed compatible land uses can be admitted as evidence, or used for any other purpose, in any suit or action seeking damages or other relief for the noise that results from the operation of an airport. Further, no person acquiring property in an area surrounding an airport and included in the adopted noise map is entitled to recover damages for airport noise after the date of such property acquisition. The only exceptions are where there has been a significant change in aircraft operations; change in airport layout; change in flight patterns; or an increase in nighttime operations.

There is some concern that provisions of this Act which prohibit recovery of damages resulting from aircraft noise may be unenforceable in court. The Fifth Amendment guarantees citizens certain property rights, among which is the right to just compensation for property (rights) taken by a governmental entity. The right of a citizen to recover from *inverse condemnation* (i.e., a "taking" without due process and without compensation) cannot be abrogated by Congress. However, the Act's provisions may prove more beneficial to airport sponsors in tort (civil/negligence) cases where nuisance is the issue rather than property rights or eminent domain.

In a vein similar in philosophy to application of the Noise Exposure Map in FAR Part 150 Studies, when the cities of Burbank, Glendale and Pasadena, California, formed a Joint Powers Authority in order to buy and operate the privately owned Hollywood-Burbank Airport, they obtained funds for the acquisition from the Federal government. In their contractual assurances the cities were required by the FAA to comply with California Governmental Code Section 6546.1 which in part provided that: "In operating the airport, the separate public entity (Joint Powers Authority) shall not permit or authorize any activity in conjunction with the airport which results in an increase in the size of the noise impact area."

In 1975, Lockheed Corporation (the previous airport owner) had applied for variance from state noise standards, and it was because of its inability to work a financially feasible solution to various problems created by aircraft noise, that Lockheed had decided to divest itself of the Burbank Airport. Pursuant to the Airport and Airway Development Act of 1970, the FAA was required to assure that "all possible steps have been taken to minimize (any) adverse effect (upon the environment)." Responsibility to minimize environmental impacts was passed along to the new Joint Powers Authority. Amongst its newly adopted noise abatement rules, air carriers were required to comply with FAR Part 36 and a resolution (Rule 7) which provided in part:

> *Proposed implementation of service by a new carrier, shall be subject to the prior approval of the Commission, which approval shall not*

> *be granted except upon a determination by the Commission that such proposed increase in flight frequencies or such proposed implementation of service by a new carrier will be consistent with the provisions of the existing Grant Agreements between the Authority and the Federal Aviation Administration and any other applicable statutory or contractual restraints governing flight operations at the Airport. . . .*

Hughes Airwest, following adoption of Rule 7, and without Commission approval, increased its weekly flights at Burbank. The airport authority filed suit. The court ruled in favor of the airport, stating that its Rule 7 was reasonable, non-arbitrary and non-capricious.[19] But in a subsequent case, the California Supreme Court held in *Baker et al. v. Burbank-Glendale-Pasadena Authority* that a public airport constitutes a "continuing nuisance."[20] Under this ruling plaintiff could bring successive actions against an airport, effectively providing a perpetual annuity just for living near the airport. Related cases brought against the Authority involved approximately 375 plaintiffs; with each plaintiff subsequent to the initial decision filing new claims against the airport for $100,000 apiece for personal injuries and emotional distress, and $100,000 apiece for property damage—claims totaling approximately $75 million on a potentially recurring basis.

The *Baker* decision was appealed, but *certiorari* was denied (i.e., the Supreme Court would not hear the appeal). In light of decisions in *Baker* and in a companion case, *Blaine et al. v. Burbank-Glendale-Pasadena Airport Authority*, it is interesting to note that the airport not only had a Noise Exposure Map, but also had repeatedly demonstrated its ability to reduce its impact upon the surrounding community by lowering its noise exposure (i.e., reducing the noise contours on the NEM). In the final analysis, the airport was held ultimately responsible for the environmental consequences associated with owning and operating an airport.

---

[19] *See Burbank-Glendale-Pasadena Airport Authority v. Hughes Air Corporation*, Superior Court of the State of California for the County of Los Angeles, Case No. 17926B (Sep. 1980).
[20] *Baker et al. v. Burbank-Glendale-Pasadena Authority*, 39 Cal 3d 862 (1985).

NOISE ABATEMENT

All noise abatement programs are generally aimed at reducing noise at the aircraft and/or airport source. But noise reduction strategies may be grouped into two major categories: (1) *aircraft or engine modifications* wherein the actual sound levels are reduced; and (2) *flight, operational, and land use modifications* which attempt to remove the sound from areas of adverse impact. Airport or engine modifications are discussed in the next few paragraphs while the second category of noise abatement is discussed in an upcoming section entitled, "Operational Procedures."

Through promulgation of FAR Part 36, "Noise Standards: Aircraft Certification,"[21] the FAA has effectively put a lid on aircraft noise escalation by establishing a ceiling on allowable noise produced by jet transport aircraft. FAR Part 36 has been a progressive program, which initially set noise limitations on the manufacture of new aircraft. It has been extended to include the requirement for modification of existing noisy aircraft. Due to the economics of retrofitting an already existing fleet, implementation of FAR Part 36 has been complex and controversial, but it can safely be stated that the trend of excessive aircraft noise is now downward.

Since its issuance in 1969, FAR Part 36 has been amended many times. A 1977 amendment to Part 36 established the noise designations for civil turbojet and transport category airplanes as *Stage 1*, *Stage 2*, or *Stage 3*, as the degree of stringency increased. Those aircraft that could not meet the original 1969 standards were designated as Stage 1 airplanes. Typical airplanes were the Boeing 707 and 720, the Douglas DC-8, and the BAC 1-11. Stage 1 aircraft were phased out in 1985. Stage 2 aircraft included the Boeing 727, 737-100 and 200, 747-100 and some 200's, and the McDonnell Douglas DC-9 and some DC-10s.

AIRPORT NOISE AND CAPACITY ACT OF 1990

The *Airport Noise and Capacity Act* [ANCA] of 1990[22] and the Budget Reconciliation Act of 1990, provided for the development of a

---

[21] 14 CFR 36, *Noise Standards: Aircraft Type and Airworthiness Certification* (1966, as revised in Jul. 2005).

[22] *Airport Noise and Capacity Act* of 1990, 49 USC 47521-47533.

national aviation noise policy, including the phase out of Stage 2 turbojet airplane over 75,000 lbs maximum gross landing weight operations by January 1, 2000. All aircraft over 75,000 lbs are now required to be Stage 3 compliant, with some of the aircraft deemed complaint due to being retrofitted with *hush kits* (which reduce engine noise levels substantially, but not to the level of new Stage 3 aircraft). While hush kits were expected to extend the life of aircraft for a limited number of years, few expected that these exceptions might be used for another decade—but unfortunately they were, causing concern in communities being serviced by "compliant" but noisy hush-kitted aircraft.

The ANCA also prompted creation of a new regulation to prevent communities from imposing unreasonable restrictions on certain users. The result was passage of FAR Part 161: "Notice and Approval of Airport Noise and Access Restrictions,"[23] which requires that any restriction be subjected to an analysis that assures the following statutory conditions or "proofs" have been met, prior to establishment of a noise or access restriction on Stage 3 and certain Stage 2 operations. Under ANCA as enforced through FAR Part 161, any such restrictions require a prior Federal Aviation Administration approval, or the action will be deemed illegal. Conditions that must be met for the FAA to review the proposal are:

- The restriction is reasonable, non-arbitrary, and nondiscriminatory;
- The restriction does not create an undue burden on interstate or foreign commerce;
- The restriction maintains safe and efficient use of the navigable airspace;
- The restriction does not conflict with any existing Federal statute or regulation;
- The applicant has provided adequate opportunity for public comment on the proposed restriction; and
- The proposed restriction does not create an undue burden on the national aviation system.

---

[23] 14 CFR 61, *Notice and Approval of Airport Noise and Access Restrictions* (Sep. 1991, revised Apr. 2001).

Before the passage of FAR Part 161, some restrictions were passed and, as such they were permitted to remain, although some have since rewritten their restrictions in the spirit of the regulation. Interestingly, as of 2007, the FAA Office of Airport Planning and Programming confirmed that no airports have received FAA approval for access restrictions since the passage of FAR Part 161 in 1991.[24] It was explained that this is because no airport could meet all the conditions required to apply, so no applications have ever been submitted. Airports are instead encouraged to work with their users to adopt mutually acceptable restrictions.[25]

Some communities, such as Naples, Florida have resented the nearly impossible hurdles that have been established in the proofs contained in FAR Part 161. The Naples Airport banned Stage 2 jets and, when challenged by the FAA, took the matter to court, incurring more than $3.4 million in legal costs.

Naples was also declined federal funding due to their passage of an unapproved restriction. The FAA's position was that the ban was unjustly discriminatory on the users of a particular type aircraft. The appellate court ruled for the Naples Airport Authority, finding that the ban could continue because the FAA "should have concluded that the Naples community revolves around this particular (quiet) environment, that its economy is based almost entirely on the climate and amenities offered by its outdoor environment, and that its residents and visitors have an expectation of quiet throughout virtually the entire community."[26] After the trial, the FAA continued its refusal to officially approve Naples' ban, but they did release more than $3 million in grants withheld since the ban was implemented.[27]

A NATIONAL NOISE POLICY?

In 1976, the Department of Transportation announced its *Aviation Noise Abatement Policy,* suggesting "a course of action for reducing

---

[24] Reportedly, Jackson Hole Airport was given a special legislative exception that permitted them to ban Stage 2 aircraft operations.

[25] FAA Office of Airport Planning and Programming, FAA, personal communication (Jan. 2007).

[26] *Id.*

[27] John Henderson, *Court Sides with Airport Authority in Jet Ban Dispute*, The Naples Daily News (Jun. 4, 2005).

noise impact."[28] This policy focused on source-noise or reducing noise being emitted from the aircraft and engines, largely through technological innovation. Despite the 1990 Airport Noise and Capacity Act's call for development of a national aviation noise policy, such did not come to fruition for nearly another decade after [ANCA].

On July 14, 2000, the Federal Aviation Administration posted a proposed policy document in the *Federal Register* entitled, "Aviation Noise Abatement Policy 2000." The draft document was presented as "a first step in a process to develop an aviation noise policy,"[29] and would lead to the development of a comprehensive policy statement and guidance document. The draft policy declares itself as summarizes the progress made since the passage of the 1976 Noise Policy,[30]

> *As we stand at the threshold of the 21st century, the achievements realized from the 1976 Policy provide a solid foundation for the future. The successive phase outs of Stage 1 and Stage 2 aircraft are responsible for the larger component of the considerable success in reducing noise levels around the airports. With all civil turbojet aircraft heavier than 75,000 pounds now Stage 3 compliant, the most severe aircraft noise will be limited to within or very near the airport boundaries. The long-term outlook beyond 2000 is for a generally stable situation with respect to noise contours around airports, followed by further reduction as the result of advances in noise abatement technology and the replacement of hush-kitted Stage 3 airplanes by built-as Stage 3 airplanes.*[31]

Six major goals are forwarded in the draft policy, referred to as a "comprehensive update to the 1976 policy," as follows:

---

[28] FAA, *Aviation Noise Abatement Policy 2000*, retrieved from http://www.faa.gov/airports_airtraffic/airports/resources/publications/federal_register_notices/media/environmental_65fr43802.pdf.

[29] *Id.*

[30] *Id.*

[31] *Id.*

- Continue aircraft source-noise reduction;
- Use new technologies to mitigate noise impacts (e.g., Global Positioning System [GPS], automated flight guidance);
- Encourage development of compatible land use in areas of significant noise exposure;
- Design air traffic route and procedures to minimize aviation noise impacts (including areas beyond the airport jurisdiction);
- Provide specific consideration to location with unique noise sensitivities (national parks and refuges; and
- Ensure strong financial support for noise compatibility planning and mitigation projects (using Airport Improvement Program [AIP] noise set-aside, Passenger Facility Charges [PFCs], and exploration of innovative finance and public/private partnerships).[32]

The policy pointed to a decrease in the number of U.S. citizens being exposed to significant levels of noise as evidence of progress since the 1976 policy. However, the policy update also noted that the progress that had been made was being off-set by increasing public expectations for noise reduction.

> *[E]ven as Americans stimulate aviation growth by their increased air travel, they also express an ever-increasing desire for a quieter neighborhood environment. As significant noise around the Nation's airports is dramatically reduced, people will direct more attention to the lower but still annoying noise levels. Unless aircraft noise is addressed with purpose and vigor, it will likely become a potential impediment to the robust airport and airway growth and operation that will be needed as public demand for access to aviation services continues to grow.*[33]

---

[32] FAA, *Proposed Aviation Noise Abatement Policy 2000*, in a presentation delivered to the TRB 8th Annual Meeting (Jan. 7, 2001), retrieved from http://onlinepubs.trb.org/onlinepubs/circulars/EC036/08_Cline.pdf
[33] *Id.*

Clearly, there is a need for a revised noise policy that can provide the "purpose and vigor" suggested in the proposed policy. But, to date, the 2000 draft Aviation Noise Abatement Policy has not emerged from its 2000 "draft" state. The FAA states that this is because most of this proposed policy has already been implemented, and thus, official passage is not necessary.[34] A review of the draft itself suggests, perhaps, another reason why the document may not yet be finalized: an overwhelming concern about legal liability that the federal government may assume if the document were finalized as a "national" noise policy. Interestingly, the word "liability" appears seven times in the document, along with reference to more than 20 legal cases.[35]

The responsibility for determining the permissible noise levels for aircraft using an airport remains with the airport proprietor. This theory originated from a 1946 U.S. Supreme Court case where the United States as operator of a military field was held responsible under the Fifth Amendment to the U.S. Constitution for rendering the owner's property useless as a chicken farm because of low flying airplanes.[36] The precedent was extended to commercial airports in 1962 when it was held that the airport sponsor was the entity that had decided to build an airport at a particular location, and that the sponsor was therefore liable for the taking.[37]

AIR INSTALLATION COMPATIBLE USE ZONES

As mentioned earlier, the Department of Defense preceded the civilian sector by seeking compatible use of public and private lands in the vicinity of military airfields. First, the policy defined mandated restrictions on the uses and heights of natural and manmade objects in the vicinity of air installations. These restrictions provide safety of flight and assure that people and facilities are not concentrated in areas susceptible to aircraft accidents. Second, the policy established desirable restrictions on land use to assure its compatibility with the characteristics, including noise, of air installation operations.

Devised by DOD is the Air Installation Compatible Use Zones or AICUZ program. The objective of AICUZ is to minimize conflicts

---

[34] FAA Office of Airport Planning and Programming, personal communication (Jan. 2007).

[35] *Id.*

[36] *United States v. Causby*, 328 U.S. 256 (1946).

[37] *Griggs v. Allegheny Co.*, 82 S.Ct. 531 (1962).

through reduction of aircraft noise and safety hazards both on and off the air installation, establishment of compatible land use plans for land within the AICUZ footprint, and establishment of a positive plan for coordination with state and local officials, and for maintaining public awareness of the AICUZ program. The AICUZ footprint is made up of land use zones where certain activities can comfortably occur without adverse effects on the health, safety and welfare of area residents, while other activities cannot. The footprint is a composite of *noise exposure* and *accident potential.*

CIVIL AIRPORT COMPATIBILITY PROGRAMS

The Federal government since the late 1940s has recognized the need for adequate land use controls near civil airports. But until more recently there has been no comprehensive approach taken to correct noise impact and land use compatibility problems, other than individual noise abatement programs to solve specific localized problems at select airports. The first comprehensive study undertaken by the FAA at what was then called the *National Aviation Facilities Experimental Center* [NAFEC] near Atlantic City, New Jersey.[38] The project was known as a *Compatible Land Use Zones* [CLUZ] study. It was very similar in scope to the ongoing AICUZ studies then being conducted by the military, but minus the same concerns for potential accident exposure (i.e., the so-called "safety zones").

Following the study at NAFEC, the FAA made plans for a series of pilot programs to be conducted under the auspices of the *Planning Grant Program* [PGP]. Originally, the planning grants were to be called *Airport Noise Control and Environs Compatibility* [ANCEC] studies. The ANCEC plans were to be accomplished by the airport sponsor, individually or in combination with other local and state authorities, airport users, the public, and the FAA, with the goal of reducing as much as possible significant aircraft noise impact to communities adjacent to airports. As stated in the FAA's 1976 *Aviation Noise Abatement Policy*, the objective is to confine aircraft noise exposure levels of 40 NEF (75Ldn) or greater to the area included within the airport boundary, and to the extent possible making land

[38] NAFEC became the FAA Technical Center on May 29, 1980. On May 6, 1996, it was rededicated as the William J. Hughes Technical Center Apr. 11, 1999; retrieved from http://www.tc.faa.gov/genera/history.html.

use activities exposed to levels of 30 NEF (65Ldn) or more compatible with these noise levels. The original program conceived as ANCEC evolved into the *Airport Noise Control and Land Use Compatibility* [ANCLUC] program that was tried in a pilot program at some fifty locations, in most cases with positive acceptance.

In a maze of acronyms like AICUZ, CLUZ, ANCEC, ANCLUC, or some other derivation, the underlying philosophy remains the same. Airport land use compatibility planning includes the planning, implementation and adoption of actions to achieve compatibility between the airport and its environs. It provides guidance in developing procedures and mechanisms that will maximize the compatibility of the airport and the vicinal land uses. The overall goal is to achieve an acceptable balance between the needs and tolerances of both the airport and its neighbors.

Implementation programs contained within airport land use compatibility studies are two-pronged strategies: (1) *operations* modifications, and (2) *land-use* controls. First, they attempt to correct deficiencies in airport design or to realign air traffic and airport operations so that noise may be minimized at the source. Second, actions are taken to correct and realign land uses surrounding the airport so that exposure to unavoidable noise may be reduced. Within these two basic strategies there are a variety of options available to the airport sponsor, state/local governments, and the federal government. All of the options are not available to any one of the agencies alone; hence airport noise compatibility planning takes cooperation of all three levels of control. What follows, although not exhaustive, is a descriptive list of some of the available operational and land-use options.

OPERATIONAL PROCEDURES

Air traffic procedures and aircraft operating modes can be changed in a number of ways to make an airport more compatible with its community, and can be accomplished in such a way that operational efficiency of both the aircraft and the airport are not compromised. The common procedural changes assume the involvement of air carrier and business jet-type aircraft, but turbo-prop and even smaller piston-engine general aviation aircraft should not be discounted as sources of noise annoyance. Noise abatement actions are possible for all types of aircraft.

A reliable correlation has not been shown to exist between sound pressure levels and specific measures of detriment to the underlying community. The degree to which noise is objectionable depends upon characteristics of the sound and population exposure to it. Height of aircraft, time of day, weather conditions, number and types of aircraft, whether people are indoors or outdoors, building construction, and the type of home people live in all affect the responses expressed.

Actual sound exposure to light, single-engine airplanes is far less than that of commercial jet transports, and yet people can be just as annoyed by the smaller aircraft. For instance, the sound made by a single-engine airplane when its power is reduced for landing may be translated into a power failure by the uneducated ear, thus indicating fear that the airplane may crash. Though the *sound* is minimal, it may nevertheless be *noise* to the beholder.

Actual changes employed in specific instances may, of course, vary with the situation. But there are certain basic alternative ways in which operational changes may be implemented. Innovative procedures normally entail the use of one or more of these basic concepts, or in combination. The following paragraphs summarize some of the ways in which operational changes may be implemented.

CHANGES IN AIRCRAFT MIX

To some degree, the natural attrition of older aircraft and subsequent replacement by newer aircraft will automatically bring about a change in aircraft mix. Federal Aviation Regulations (FAR Part 36) aimed at reducing noise at the aircraft source will in time reduce the overall impact of noise at many of the nation's airports, especially the larger ones where jet transports are most common. In some cases, air activity may actually *increase* even while total noise is *decreasing*. This phenomenon can be used, and at least should be taken into consideration, when programming noise abatement strategies.

Intentional changes in aircraft mix can be accomplished by directly prohibiting certain aircraft from operating at the airport. Usually, this type of action is regulatory in nature, but may also be accomplished through development schemes as well. Limitations on runway length or strength may exclude use by unwanted aircraft. Another way might be to construct reliever airports, the use of which would effectively remove certain activities, along with selected aircraft categories, and thus alter the operational mix of aircraft at the primary airport.

ELEVATION OF FLIGHT PATTERNS

There are many situations where normal flight patterns may be elevated, thereby increasing the distance between the noise source, the aircraft, and its underlying impact area. Traffic patterns flown at 800 feet may be just as easily flown at 1,000 or 1,200 feet. This same principle is embodied in the FAA's "keep 'em high" policy where en route traffic is kept as high as possible until it is absolutely necessary to descend for landing.

ELIMINATION OF FLIGHT PATTERNS

Traffic patterns creating critical noise impacts may sometimes be eliminated, or if not eliminated, at least altered to remove them from noise sensitive areas. For instance, a left-hand traffic pattern may be eliminated in favor of using only the traffic pattern on one side of a particular runway. Often by keeping traffic on one side, over flight of developed areas is avoided.

Choice of Navigation Aid [NAVAID] location can also alter a given pattern. Offset approach patterns have been installed at some locations solely for noise abatement purposes. The southerly approach to Washington National Airport is a good example. The flight pattern follows the Potomac River and thereby avoids the city. However, it should be recognized that approaches other than "straight-in" might reduce the margin of safety.

VARIATIONS IN APPROACH/DEPARTURE ANGLE

Changes in glide slope or take-off angles can do two things: increase the angular displacement over noise sensitive areas, and change the aircraft's airspeed. In some instances it is preferable to climb at shallow angles, but at a faster airspeed to over fly close-in areas more quickly. In other situations it may beneficial to climb at high angles and slower airspeeds to avoid land uses which are farther away from the airport. Such a procedure gives the aircraft the opportunity of being as high as possible before over flying a built up area.

Along with choices in angle or airspeed there are attendant variations in power and flap setting. Thrust reductions at the proper time can significantly reduce noise impact. To date, a number of standardized approach and departure profiles have been developed and put into varying degrees of implementation; those developed by the FAA, the Airline Transport Association, Northwest Airlines, and the National Business Aircraft Association are examples.

CHANGES IN RUNWAY UTILIZATION

The use of preferential runways for noise abatement is based upon the same concept that applies to changes in flight routing. It controls the distribution of traffic so that over flight of sensitive areas is minimized. However, wind, weather, and pavement conditions often create limitations on the use of preferential runways for safety reasons, and are considerations that do not necessarily affect proposed changes in flight patterns.

Variations of this basic idea could entail runway modifications such as use of displaced thresholds or runway extensions. Displaced thresholds and/or runway extensions can be used to increase aircraft altitudes over relatively close in community development. However, it should be recognized that it requires a substantial relocation of the take-off or landing spot to bring about any significant change in altitude. Using the standard three-degree glide slope as an example requires a displacement of 1,000 feet in exchange for only fifty-two feet of increased altitude.

CHANGES IN GROUND RUN-UP PROCEDURES

It is not uncommon for the noise of aircraft engine run-ups on the airport surface to carry over to adjacent noise sensitive areas. Corrective actions are to either eliminate or relocate the run-up activity. Another action that can be taken is to install sound attenuation devices. Since most run-up activity is of operational necessity and cannot be readily eliminated, the most viable options are relocation of the aircraft, and/or use of sound suppression equipment. Relocation, of course, is intended to increase distance between the noise source and the receiver, but relocation may consist of simply reorienting the parked aircraft, thus changing the direction of the noise projection.

The greatest proportion of noise emanates from the front end of a turbo-prop airplane and from the rear end of a jet.

Noise suppression equipment may be as sophisticated as *a hush house*, which completely encloses an aircraft. Alternatively, the engine may be removed from the airframe and operationally tested within acoustically treated walls. Or, the "equipment" might be as simple as construction of earth berms and/or natural vegetation. Anything blocking the noise will help. Even buildings and other aircraft can be used as a noise screen.

CURFEWS

Adjustments in the scheduling of operations may reduce noise at times when it is most apt to create public nuisance—at night, for example. These adjustments might also include restrictions in the number of aircraft operations allowed by the airport. There are many possibilities for limiting aircraft operations, including night-time restrictions on all or a particular sector of aircraft operations, scheduling restrictions, restrictions on hourly or daily operations, and so forth.

The major drawback to curfews is their effect upon the total air transportation system and particularly upon air commerce. Restrictions on arrivals will back up into the system and can indirectly restrict departures from other system airports. Nighttime curfews can cause elimination of late scheduled flights from other airports, especially if the flight is from west to east. Not only must the en route flight time be accounted for, but the loss due to time zone change is a consideration as well. In order for a five-hour direct flight from the West Coast to arrive on the East Coast by 10:00 p.m., it must leave by 2:00 o'clock in the afternoon.

Care must be exercised in imposing strict curfews. They may be construed by the courts as being an undue burden on interstate commerce and pre-emptive of exclusive federal regulatory responsibilities over transportation, safety and airspace management; and, therefore, illegal.

AIRCRAFT NOISE LIMITATION

As discussed earlier, Federal Aviation Regulation Part 36 establishes federal limits on aircraft noise emissions. Airports may set limits of acceptable noise as well. The most prominent example of an airport where noise limits have been established is Santa Monica Municipal Airport in California. The City of Santa Monica imposed a series of regulations aimed at reducing noise. A 100-dB maximum as the single-event noise exposure level was one of those regulations. In 1979, the U.S. District Court of Central California upheld the City's right to control noise through the use of their noise-limiting ordinance. Santa Monica subsequently lowered its limit even further.

Of major concern in implementing a similar regulation at any other airport is the difficulty and expense of enforcing it. In California, enforcement is facilitated by Title 21 of the California Administrative Code, which provides noise standards governing the operation of aircraft and airports in the State. Required by the California Standards are clearly identified noise measurement parameters and extremely sophisticated noise monitoring equipment at those airports determined to have a noise problem. Without the umbrella of state legislation a local government may have trouble enforcing this kind of rule. The cost of the necessary equipment may also be prohibitive.

LAND USE CONTROLS

Once the airport's impact upon the community has been established, and the minimized noise impact areas have been defined, a recommended pattern of land use in the vicinity of the airport can be developed. The objective is to ensure land use that is fully compatible according to commonly accepted criteria. Land use/noise compatibility is based upon the disruptive effects of noise on various human activities. Different activities, or uses of the land, have different sensitivities to noise. Uses such as schools, churches, residences, and hospitals are very sensitive to noise. By contrast, manufacturing, industry, and some agricultural uses are relatively insensitive to noise.

To uniformly assess the impact of airport noise upon various land uses, the FAA has compiled a standardized *Land Use Guidance* [LUG] system, which compares in matrix form the levels of noise impact against various land uses. In this case, the noise exposure zones are labeled in ascending order of magnitude, A through D, with A having minimal exposure and D representing the area of most severe exposure. Figure 7.3, "Land Use Guidance," shows each of the four most common noise-estimating methodologies translated into

Land Use Guidance Zones.[39] Also shown are Housing and Urban Development noise assessment guidelines used for site exposure to noise and for screening mortgaging guarantees and other HUD assistance.

Figure 7.4, "Land Use Noise Sensitivity," shows the sensitivity of land uses to varying levels of noise, using the land use categories developed by the Department of Housing and Urban Development and the Federal Highway Administration for their *Standard Land Use Coding Manual* [SLUCM]. The SLUCM has been in use since 1965 as a standard planning reference. But when comparing the various land use categories against the noise sensitivity criteria, the FAA stresses extreme caution. The compatibility of a particular zone with a given level of noise exposure is a suggested achievement goal, not firm criteria. Acceptability of that noise by land users may vary.

Typical airport noise patterns combined with LUG zones were shown earlier in Figure 7.1. Achieving fully compatible land use according to the criteria may not be possible in all cases. When the community has made irreversible commitments and owners and developers make significant investments in land, compromise recommendations may be the best that can be attained. A wide variety of instruments are normally available to local governments and airport sponsors to control the compatibility of surrounding land uses. Generally, they fall into two principal categories: those that involve *ownership* of property rights and provide absolute control, and those that depend upon *administrative and regulatory action* and provide less certain controls. The most generally used controls are zoning, easements, and land purchase.

ACQUISITION IN FEE SIMPLE

Purchase of the land with ownership to all property rights is the most positive form of land use control. It is also the most expensive (at least initially). Acquisition in *fee simple* is appropriate only when there is reasonable doubt that the community has the ability to otherwise adequately control use of the land. The FAA can sometimes aid in the purchase of clear zones, but funds for this purpose are limited. The costs for acquisition must also take into account the removal of the property from the tax roles. But in the long run if the property is resold for compatible uses the net cost can be effectively reduced.

---

[39] The Land Use Guidance Zones (A, B, C, & D) are keyed to Fig. 7.1, Airport Noise Contours."

Figure 7.3—LAND USE GUIDANCE

LAND USE GUIDANCE CHART I: AIRPORT NOISE INTERPOLATION

LAND USE GUIDANCE ZONES (LUG)	NOISE EXPOSURE CLASS	INPUTS: AIRCRAFT NOISE ESTIMATING METHODOLOGIES				HUD NOISE ASSESSMENT GUIDELINES	SUGGESTED NOISE CONTROLS
		L dn DAY-NIGHT AVG. SOUND LEVEL	NEF NOISE EXPOSURE FORECAST	CNR COMPOSITE NOISE RATING	CNEL COMMUNITY NOISE EQUIVALENT LEVEL		
A	MINIMAL EXPOSURE	0 TO 55	0 TO 20	0 TO 90	0 TO 55	"CLEARLY ACCEPTABLE"	NORMALLY REQUIRES NO SPECIAL CONSIDERATIONS
B	MODERATE EXPOSURE	55 TO 65	20 TO 30	90 TO 100	55 TO 65	"NORMALLY ACCEPTABLE"	LAND USE CONTROLS SHOULD BE CONSIDERED
C	SIGNIFICANT EXPOSURE	65 TO 75	30 TO 40	100 TO 115	65 TO 75	"NORMALLY UNACCEPTABLE"	NOISE EASEMENTS, LAND USE, AND OTHER COMPATIBILITY CONTROLS RECOMMENDED
D	SEVERE EXPOSURE	75 & HIGHER	40 & HIGHER	115 & HIGHER	75 & HIGHER	"CLEARLY UNACCEPTABLE"	CONTAINMENT WITHIN AIRPORT BOUNDARY OR USE OF POSITIVE COMPATIBILITY CONTROLS RECOMMENDED

The Administration of Public Airports

Source: FAA AC 150/5050-6.

Figure 7.4—LAND USE NOISE SENSITIVITY

LAND USE GUIDANCE CHART II: LAND USE NOISE SENSITIVITY INTERPOLATION

LAND USE: SLUCM NO.	LAND USE: NAME	LUG ZONE[1]: SUGGESTED	LUG ZONE[1]: STUDY
10	Residential	A-B	
11	Household units		
11.11	Single units—detached	A	
11.12	Single units—semiattached	A	
11.13	Single units—attached row	B	
11.21	Two units—side-by-side	A	
11.22	Two units—one above the other	A	
11.31	Apartments—walk up	B	
11.32	Apartments—elevator	B-C	
12	Group quarters	A-B	
13	Residential hotels	B	
14	Mobile home parks or courts	A	
15	Transient lodgings	C	
19	Other residential	A-C	
20	Manufacturing [2]	C-D	
21	Food and kindred products—manufacturing	C-D	
22	Textile mill products—manufacturing	C-D	
23	Apparel and other finished products made from fabrics, leather, and similar materials—manufacturing	C-D	
24	Lumber and wood products (except furniture)—manufacturing	C-D	
25	Furniture and fixtures—manufacturing	C-D	
26	Paper and allied products—manufacturing	C-D	
27	Printing, publishing, and allied industries	C-D	
28	Chemicals and allied products—manufacturing	C-D	
29	Petroleum refining and related industries [3]	C-D	

LAND USE: SLUCM NO.	LAND USE: NAME	LUG ZONE[1]: SUGGESTED	LUG ZONE[1]: STUDY
30	Manufacturing (continued) [2]		
31	Rubber and miscellaneous plastic products—manufacturing	C-D	
32	Stone, clay, and glass products—manufacturing	C-D	
33	Primary metal industries	D	
34	Fabricated metal products—manufacturing	D	
35	Professional, scientific, and controlling instruments, photographic and optical goods; watches and clocks—manufacturing	B	
39	Miscellaneous manufacturing	C-D	
40	Transportation, communication, and utilities		
41	Railroad, rapid rail transit, and street railway transportation	D	
42	Motor vehicle transportation	D	
43	Aircraft transportation	D	
44	Marine craft transportation	D	
45	Highway and street right-of-way	D	
46	Automobile parking	D	
47	Communication	A-D	
48	Utilities	D	
49	Other transportation, communication, and utilities	A-D	
50	Trade [4]		
51	Wholesale trade	C-D	
52	Retail trade—building materials, hardware, and farm equipment	C	
53	Retail trade—general merchandise	C	
54	Retail trade—food	C	
55	Retail trade—automotive, marine craft, aircraft, and accessories	C	
56	Retail trade—apparel and accessories	C	
57	Retail trade—furniture, home furnishings, and equipment	C	
59	Retail trade—eating and drinking	C-D	
	Other retail trade		

LAND USE: SLUCM NO.	LAND USE: NAME	LUG ZONE[1]: SUGGESTED	LUG ZONE[1]: STUDY
60	Services [4]		
61	Finance, insurance, and real estate services	B	
62	Personal services	B	
63	Business services	B	
64	Repair services	C	
65	Professional services	B-C	
66	Contract construction services	C	
67	Governmental services	B	
68	Educational services	A-B	
69	Miscellaneous services	A-C	
70	Cultural, entertainment, and recreational		
71	Cultural activities and nature exhibitions	A	
72	Public assembly	A	
73	Amusements	C	
74	Recreational activities [5]	B-C	
75	Resorts and group camps	A	
76	Parks	A-C	
79	Other cultural, entertainment, and recreational [5]	A-B	
80	Resource production and extraction		
81	Agriculture	C-D	
82	Agricultural related activities	C-D	
83	Forestry activities and related services	D	
84	Fishing activities and related services	D	
85	Mining activities and related services	D	
89	Other resource production and extraction	C-D	
90	Undeveloped land and water areas		
91	Undeveloped and unused land area (excluding noncommercial forest development)	D	
92	Noncommercial forest development	D	
93	Water areas	A-D	
94	Vacant floor area	A-D	
95	Under construction	A-D	
99	Other undeveloped land and water areas	A-D	

1 REFER TO LAND USE GUIDANCE CHART I, PAGE 12
2 ZONE "C" SUGGESTED MAXIMUM EXCEPT WHERE EXCEEDED BY SELF GENERATED NOISE
3 ZONE "D" FOR NOISE PURPOSES, OBSERVE NORMAL HAZARD PRECAUTIONS
4 IF ACTIVITY IS NOT IN SUBSTANTIAL, AIR-CONDITIONED BUILDING, GO TO NEXT HIGHER ZONE
5 REQUIREMENTS LIKELY TO VARY — INDIVIDUAL APPRAISAL RECOMMENDED.
SLUCM: STANDARD LAND USE CODING MANUAL, SEE PARAGRAPH 21

Source: FAA AC 150/5060-6.

Should the property remain under government control and leased to the private sector, the initial purchase cost will be recovered through time, and the government may assess taxes for the lessee's *possessory interest* in the land.

EASEMENTS

Like fee simple title, an *easement* is a permanent acquisition, but for only part of the property rights. Since it does not involve total transfer of the property, the transaction may oftentimes be far less expensive than a fee simple purchase. There are many types of easements depending upon the select property rights desired. So long as the easement does not significantly reduce the overall value of property, it may be obtained at reasonable cost. The more the easement impairs the usage of the land, the higher the cost will be until at some point it is more cost-effective to purchase the property outright. Easements are classified as either positive or negative. For airport protection purposes, an easement to allow the unobstructed passage of aircraft through the airspace above a parcel of property is an example of a positive easement. Exemplary of a typical negative easement would be one where heights of man-made objects or natural vegetation are restricted from intruding into navigable airspace.

Easements may be obtained by purchase, condemnation, or by dedication. In dedication, the owner may be willing to voluntarily release certain property rights in exchange for some development right such as the right to subdivide.

LAND LEASE

Leasing of land may yield the same positive control as the purchase of property. However, property rights are obtained for a limited period of time only, and not in perpetuity as with title to the land.

ZONING

Certain property rights are always retained by the state such as police power, taxation, eminent domain, and escheat. *Police power* is the inherent power of government to exercise reasonable control over persons and property in the interest of the public's general security, health, safety, morals and welfare. *Zoning* is an exercise of police power. It is the most common and useful land use control. Zoning is advantageous because it can promote compatibility, but at the same time leave land in private ownership and on the tax roles. Unlike outright purchase of land, it is not permanent. Zoning can be readily reversed by legislation. It has some other limitations as well. Zoning is not retroactive, and existing nonconforming uses must be allowed to remain; zoning is limited by jurisdiction, and airport impacts often span more than one governmental jurisdiction, zoning boards may grant variances; and zoning must be applied fairly and be based upon a community plan.

Zoning cannot be used simply because of noise impact. There must be other, more comprehensive reasons for the zoning. The most wide spread use of zoning around airports is for *height and hazard* to protect airspace in the vicinity of the airport from intrusion by high objects.

OTHER CONTROLS

Besides zoning, other controls having either less or special applicability include building codes, health and housing codes, programming of public capital improvements, and cooperation of financial institutions.

- *Comprehensive plans*, while not a direct control, are a basis and policy guide for land use, zoning, transportation, public facilities and capital improvement decisions. The airport land use compatibility plan is a part of the community's comprehensive plan.
- *Subdivision regulations* are usually separated from actual land use controls, but can be a useful tool in controlling urbanization and density in development areas.
- *Building and housing codes* do not control land uses, but do regulate construction standards. Building codes may provide noise reduction through the use of soundproofing materials in building construction.
- *Capital improvement programming* can be one of the more effective ways of controlling undesirable uses. The scheduling of

water and sewer extensions, for example, may determine where future development takes place.

- *Truth in sales and rental ordinances* can be used to discourage development in noise sensitive areas. This is known as the giving of "constructive notice." Such an ordinance may also be used as a defense should legal action be brought against the airport. If people are made aware of the potential exposure prior to taking possession of property, any case against aircraft noise intrusion may be compromised. A truth in sales and rental ordinance simply states that if a property has possible exposure to the influences of airport operations, the owner must divulge that fact to prospective buyers or renters.
- *Voluntary relocation programs* assist residents and local businesses in noise sensitive areas that wish to voluntarily relocate outside the noise impact area. Usually, the associated moving costs are subsidized to make up for loss in property value, transportation expenses, increased costs of new residences, mortgage penalties, realty fees, and so forth. The provisions of the Uniform Relocation Assistance and Real Property Acquisition Policies Act of 1970 are applicable whenever federal programs are involved. Purchase assurance programs may also be associated with relocation programs, in that they guarantee the salability of properties. As any level of government acts, however, it is important that it not solve one problem with another.
- *Mandatory land acquisition programs* use the government's power of eminent domain to relocate homeowners from noise-impacted areas, so the land can be converted to more compatible land use. However, this approach is considered unfair, even hostile, to some residents who may prefer to live with aviation noise as opposed to another disamenity (e.g., crime, poor schools, a long commute, etc.) if forced to relocated to another similarly priced property.[40] Governments must be sensitive to issues of community preference and note that moving people

[40] Sobotta, Campbell & Owen explain, "While it might appear that the airport sponsor is providing the resident with relief from harm, the airport may fail to take into account the tremendous loss of community that can occur when homeowners are forced to move from their chosen—often ethnically connected—communities and then forced to relocate with funds that were issued at levels reflecting the economic devaluation of their property by the disamenity." Robin Sobotta, Heather Campbell & Beverly Owen, *Aviation Noise and Environmental Justice: The Barrio Barrier*, J. of Regional Science (Feb. 2007).

piecemeal out of noise-impacted areas—as has been done in some locales—may cause them even more harm than the original disamenity.[41]

- *Mortgage and construction loans* issued by both private and public lending institutions can influence development if aviation noise criteria are included in their review and approval procedures. The Department of Housing and Urban Development promulgated its noise assessment guidelines,[42] as are shown on Figure 7.2 above. These guidelines are used for screening mortgaging guarantees and other HUD assistance. Veterans Administration and Federal Housing Administration insured loans are subject to review on the basis of HUD's noise assessment guidelines.
- *Insurance limitations* and rate structures have the potential for reducing development in areas exposed to noise, but particularly if exposed to accident potential. Federal Aviation Regulation Part 77 imposes requirements for the public to give notice of any construction activity that may create an aviation safety hazard. If in its airspace review the FAA determines that the object would be an obstruction to air navigation, it is likely that an insurance underwriter would either not insure the structure, or would assign it a higher rate because of its potential risk.

SOUNDPROOFING PROGRAMS

Soundproofing programs are one of the most popular methods of addressing an impacted resident's concerns about noise. For example, the Los Angeles International Airport [LAX] soundproofing program included 9000 residences around two Los Angeles-area airports.[43] Soundproofing involves undertaking acoustical modifications to buildings that are located in high aviation noise impact areas. Examples of modifications include: door and window replacement, and fireplace modifications. Any leaks that might allow noise to penetrate impacted homes are located and corrected. Conveniences like doggie doors are not permitted to remain, unless the homeowner signs an

---

[41] Robin Sobotta, *Communities, Contours and Concerns: Environmental Justice and Aviation Noise*, Unpublished dissertation, Arizona State University, Ariz. (2002).

[42] Depart. of Housing and Urban Development Circular 1390.2 (Jul. 1971).

[43] LAWAs, *Residential Soundproofing News* (fall 2004), retrieved from http://www.lawa.org/docs/SPnewsFa2004.pdf.

agreement stating that they understand noise can enter through such portals.[44]

Home soundproofing can cost between $20-50 thousand per home, depending upon the work required. In exchange for accepting soundproofing of one's home, residents may be required to sign an agreement waiving their right to sue the airport for noise-related damages.[45]

However popular, soundproofing programs are not complete solutions, and sometimes, they appear arbitrary and unfair to residents. Sometimes one house on a block is determined to be within the impacted area, but a neighbor's home is not, yet both sound equally noisy when standing in the front yard. Additionally, while soundproofing programs may improve the interior noise level of the home, exterior levels remain high and harmful. Residents' windows cannot be opened in the summer without subjecting the residents to the previously high noise level. Additionally, playing outside is not a reasonable option for children if the former noise levels persist.[46]

SUMMARY

In its draft National Noise Abatement Policy, the FAA attempted to convey a simple message: "Don't throw out the baby with the bathwater." The document encourages balancing the negative externalities associated with air transportation with the benefits of air transportation. The policy states, "The continued development of aviation growth is a vital element of U.S. transportation, and the aviation industry is, in turn, a powerful generator of economic activity and jobs within communities. Notwithstanding, anticipated technological improvements, aircraft noise will remain and will be a pivotal quality-of life issue."

But, lacking a cohesive national policy, it remains the responsibility of local sponsors to assure that our communities both convenient access to the air transportation and the preservation our precious environmental resources including safe, reasonable levels of noise.

---

[44] *Id.*

[45] LAX Coalition for Economic, Environmental, and Educational Justice, Notice on *Noise Pollution Reduction and Mitigation* (Nov. 24, 2004), retrieved from http://www.environmentaldefense.org/documents/4179_LAX_NoiseOnePager.pdf.

[46] *Id.*

CHAPTER 8

OPERATIONS: SAFETY AND CERTIFICATION

On April 1, 1999, Korean Air flight 36 and Air China 9018, both Boeing 747s, nearly collided at Chicago O'Hare International Airport. Air China had just landed on runway 14R when the tower instructed Korean Air to taxi into position and hold on that runway. After Air China exited runway 14R, the tower instructed them to cross a nearby runway. The tower then cleared Korean Air for takeoff. As the airplane was rolling down the runway, Air China deviated from its assigned taxi route and taxied [back] on to runway 14R. The Korean Air captain saw the 747 taxiing on to the runway but it was too late to stop. Instead, Korean Air 36 lifted off earlier than normal and banked left to avoid striking Air China. The two aircraft, carrying 382 people, missed colliding by about 80 feet.

National Transportation Safety Board Meeting Report[1]

INTRODUCTION

Airports can be dangerous places. As illustrated in the quote above, hundreds of lives could be lost in a moment or two of confusion between the myriad of individuals sharing use of and control over the airfield. As discussed later in this chapter, the prevention of runway

---

[1] NTSB meeting, *Safety Recommendation to the Federal Aviation Administration to Prevent Runway Incursions* (Jun. 12, 2000). Complete public meeting details along with two runway incursion animations (Chicago O'Hare & T.F. Green State Airport near Providence, R.I.), retrieved from http://www.ntsb.gov/Events/2000/incursion/incur_video.htm.

incursions are but one of the major safety initiatives that can be found at airports throughout the country. This is the first of three chapters dealing with the *operational* aspects of airport management; the broad topic of safety is interwoven through each of these chapters.

"Operations," as it is used in this text, has the connotation of "movement." Operations constitute the action side of airport management. Included is the movement of air traffic and surface vehicles; management of access and perimeter roadways, terminal facilities and tenant relationships, automobile parking systems, and airline and general aviation aprons; facilitation of airline passenger circulation, and accommodation of meeters and greeters; implementation of *airport security* and *Aircraft Rescue and Fire Fighting* [ARFF] programs; and monitoring of a sundry list of airfield and terminal activities.

This chapter reviews federal regulatory guidance and popular practices relating to airport safety and certification. Addressed herein are several topics including aviation fuel-handling, aircraft ground handling, issuance of notices to airmen, the operation of ultralights on the airport, air cargo operations, and other topics relating to airfield safety. The focus of the immediate chapter is upon federal *regulatory oversight*, including airport certification, aviation security, and airport rescue and fire fighting.

The next chapter, "Airport and Aviation Security," discusses the reality of airport and airline security, and delves into the dramatic changes experienced by the aviation industry since September 11, 2001, with the onset of the new age of terrorism. Reviewed in that chapter are the evolving regulatory structure, challenges, and technology associated with the new era of airport security.

The final chapter in the series on operations is "Landside, Terminal and Other Operational Activities." That chapter explores the *operational management* of the landside areas (including roadways, ground transportation, and parking facilities), terminal area operation and management (including airport air programs and the emergence of shared use terminal facilities), air cargo operations, and special event coordination.

SAFETY REGULATION

The Federal Aviation Act of 1958 was written in the interest of promoting safety through regulation. It charges the Administrator of the Federal Aviation Administration [FAA] with ultimate responsibility for aviation safety in the United States, within the *special aircraft jurisdiction* of the United States,[2] or where ever the United States has aviation interests. However, safety is everybody's business. A safe flight is the result of the collective effort of many people, not just the aircrew or the government. Safety in flight is the responsibility of design engineers, factory workers, maintenance and line personnel, weather forecasters, air traffic controllers, and many others. In a human chain so long, error is an ever-present possibility.

People cause accidents! More than 80% of all accidents are caused by the unsafe acts of people; that is to say, most accidents are the result of "human error." According to the National Transportation Safety Board [NTSB], few aircraft accidents are attributable to faulty equipment; only 1% is due to airframe failures, 4% to landing gear malfunctions, and 14% to power plant failings. The remainder is attributed to human factors.

The most hazardous portion of aircraft operations is in the airport environment where there are a variety of threats to aviation safety:

- Aircraft are in close proximity to each other, consequently there is a risk of jet, prop, or rotor blast, or even collision;
- Airports store volumes of hazardous materials needed for aircraft servicing such as oxygen, jet fuels and aviation gasoline;
- Aircraft are intentionally exposed to the hazards of low-altitude, low-airspeed, and close proximity with the ground, including actual contact with the ground during landing and take-off; and
- Aircraft must maneuver on the ground, an environment where they are not primarily designed to be. One of the worst disasters in aviation history occurred on the ground at Tenerife where two Boeing 747s collided in dense fog.

An "accident" is defined as an unforeseen or unplanned occurrence. It is an unfortunate event, sometimes unavoidable, but normally resulting from carelessness, unawareness, or just plain ignorance. Although accidents sometimes result from a physical or mechanical condition

---

[2] The "special aircraft jurisdiction" of the U.S. is: (1) any civil aircraft of U.S. registry, (2) aircraft of national defense forces of the U.S., (3) any other aircraft within the U.S., and (4) any aircraft outside the U.S. that has its next scheduled destination or last point of departure in the U.S. *See* Laurence E. Gesell & Paul Stephen Dempsey, *Aviation and the Law* 182 (4th ed. 2005).

that is unsafe, most of the time they are the direct result of someone's wrong action. In the final analysis, most accidents are preventable.

For several reasons, airport management has a direct responsibility for accident prevention. First of all, there are *humanitarian* reasons. But aside from the humanitarian perspective, with which seemingly no one would argue, accident prevention is important because of its cost impact. Hence, airport management has a *fiscal* responsibility. Additionally, there is a *legal* responsibility under tort law. Airport management has an obligation to protect all "invitees" on the airport from negligent harm. And finally, management is *morally* responsible; it holds the power to do something about safety. Management can mandate safe work practices amongst its employees, its tenants and their employees and other airport users.

The key to accident prevention is a *positive attitude* on the part of those capable of doing something about safety. It is an attitude, which accepts the fact that accidents can and will be prevented. Unfortunately, and all too often, it takes a disaster to occur before corrective action is taken. The government, for example, is infamous for its *reaction* rather than its *proaction*. The Federal Aviation Act, which itself is intended to promote air safety, evolved as a reaction to a series of three mid-air collisions involving air carrier aircraft and the obvious need for an improved air traffic control program. The first of these accidents occurred between a Trans World Airlines Constellation and a United Airlines DC-7 which collided over the Grand Canyon in 1956. Subsequent accidents involved a Douglas Aircraft Company DC-7 and an Air Force F-89 near Sunland, California in 1957, and a United Airlines DC-7 colliding with an Air Force F-100 near Las Vegas in 1958.

The Federal Aviation Act of 1958 replaced the Civil Aeronautics Act of 1938 as the basic "Constitution" of aviation law in the United States. It continued the economic regulatory provisions of the Civil Aeronautics Act, but fundamentally it revised the Federal government's air safety program. Specifically, it created the Federal Aviation Agency[3] to provide for the regulation and promotion of civil aviation in such a manner as to foster its development and safety, and to provide for the safe and efficient use of airspace. Aviation safety is the primary role of the Federal Aviation Administration. Theoretically, all of the rules and regulations emanating from the FAA are because of

---

[3] The "Federal Aviation Agency" was later renamed the "Federal Aviation Administration" under the Department of Transportation Act of 1966.

this basic tenet, although promotion of air commerce is a secondary role.

The general powers and duties vested with the Federal Aviation Administrator are:

- *Regulation* of air commerce in such a manner as to best promote its development and safety and fulfill the requirements of national defense;
- *Promotion*, encouragement, and development of civil aeronautics;
- *Control of the use of the navigable airspace* of the United States and the military operations in such airspace in the interest of the safety and efficiency of both;
- Consolidation of *research and development* with respect to air navigation facilities, as well as the installation thereof; and
- Development and operation of a common system of *air traffic control* and navigation for both military and civil aircraft.

Simply stated, the FAA's mission is to ensure the safe and efficient use of the nation's airspace, by military as well as civilian aviation, and to promote civil aeronautics and commercial aviation. The 1958 Federal Aviation Act empowers the Administrator to promote safety in flight by insuring reasonable rules and regulations to regulate and control all "air commerce," defined as,

> *. . . interstate, overseas, or foreign air commerce or the transportation of mail by aircraft or any operation or navigation of aircraft within the limits of any Federal airway or any operation or navigation of aircraft which directly affects, or which may endanger safety in interstate, overseas, or foreign air commerce.*

Effectively, all aviation in the United States is operationally within the purview of the FAA. The existing body of Federal Aviation Regulations [FARs][4] contains rules and regulations and minimum standards governing practices, methods, and procedures concerning:

---

[4] 14 CFR, Ch. I.

- *Definitions*;
- General *rule making* and *enforcement*;
- Design, construction and performance of *aircraft parts*, and appliances;
- *Type certification* and/or approval of aircraft, parts, and appliances;
- *Identification* of aircraft, critical components, replacement parts and nationality;
- *Registration and marking* of aircraft and recording of aircraft title;
- Certification of *airmen*, including medical standards;
- *Airspace* designation and use;
- Certification of *air carriers* and *commercial operators*;
- Certification of *flight schools*;
- Certification of *navigational aids*; and
- Certification of air carrier *airports*.

Further insuring that the FAA is indeed the official federal agency for aviation safety in the United States, Section 304 of the Federal Aviation Act gives the President authority to transfer to the FAA Administrator any functions of government, which relate primarily to selecting, developing, testing, evaluating, establishing, operating and maintaining systems, procedures, facilities, or devices for safe and efficient air navigation and air traffic control. And, Section 308 of the act gives the FAA power to control federal expenditures for the acquisition, establishment, construction, alteration, repair, maintenance, or operation of air navigation facilities on public airports.

The FAA is the official overseer of aviation in the United States, but the primary responsibility for constructing, maintaining, and operating public airports rests with the owner, not the Federal government. Public airport sponsors include municipalities, counties and other public authorities. Unfortunately, this diversity of ownership and responsibility complicates the standardization and balanced development of a national system of airports.

The role of the Federal government with regard to airports is to help identify the needs for airport development, to promote and encourage such development, to provide standards and guides for safe and efficient airport design, construction and operation, and to assure that airports are being operated in accordance with contractual agreements between the airport sponsors and the Federal government. In addition, all of aviation is standardized nationally through regulatory control by the federal government. Local and state governments are therefore prohibited from *preempting* aviation matters, which have been delegated by law to the FAA. In practice, this means that an airport manager has very limited authority in the control of aircraft movement. In the realm of air safety, airport managers are primarily responsible for the airport's compliance with applicable federal rules and regulations. Nevertheless, airport sponsors are directly responsible for all other proprietary aspects of their airport's operation.

NATIONAL TRANSPORTATION SAFETY BOARD

Along with the FAA, the National Transportation Safety Board is also responsible for safety in air transportation. The [NTSB] emanated from the Air Safety Board provisions of the Civil Aeronautics Act of 1938, giving responsibility for accident investigation to the Civil Aeronautics Authority, later to become the *Civil Aeronautics Board* [CAB] under government reorganization in 1940. With the Department of Transportation Act of 1966, the NTSB was created as an agency administratively placed under the purview of the Department of Transportation [DOT]. In 1975, the NTSB became an independent agency of the federal government.

The principal responsibility of the NTSB is accident investigation of all transportation modes and for making final determination as to the *cause* of *all* accidents in transportation. The Board also has responsibility for reviewing on appeal the suspension, revocation, or denial of any certificate or license issued by the DOT Secretary or an administrator such as the FAA Administrator. Additionally, the NTSB conducts special studies pertaining to safety and the prevention of accidents, and makes recommendations that, in its opinion, will tend to prevent accidents and promote transportation safety.

AIR CARRIER AIRPORT CERTIFICATION

The Airport and Airway Development Act of 1970 added to the Federal Aviation Act of 1958 a new Section 612, authorizing the FAA Administrator to issue an *airport operating certificate* to any airport serving (CAB) certificated air carriers, and to establish minimum safety standards for the operation of these airports. The 1970 Act also added to the Federal Aviation Act of 1958 a provision prohibiting any person from operating an air carrier airport without an airport operating certificate, or in violation of the terms of an issued certificate. In addition, action was taken to amend Federal Aviation Regulation Part 121, "Operating Requirements: Domestic, flag, and supplemental operations," to prohibit operations by air carriers into airports that did not hold airport operating certificates.

Federal Aviation Regulation Part 139, "Certification and operations: Land airports serving CAB-certificated air carriers," was established in 1972 to provide for the issuance of airport operating certificates to airports serving those air carriers holding certificates of Public Convenience and Necessity [PC&N] as issued by the Civil Aeronautics Board to those carriers operating "large" aircraft (i.e., over 12,500 pounds maximum certificated takeoff weight) into those airports. Owing to the changing nature and classification of air carriers and "sunset" of the CAB subsequent to adoption of the Airline Deregulation Act of 1978, and in response to pressure from industry and an airport study completed by NTSB to revise FAR Part 139, the so-called "thirty-seat rule" was adopted. The title of FAR Part 139 was changed to "Certification and Operations: Land Airports Serving Certain Air Carriers." Under the thirty-seat rule, the requirement for an airport operating certificate depends on whether the carrier's aircraft have more than thirty seats. Under a 1984 revision, FAR Part 139 was brought into alignment with the thirty-seat rule.

Air carriers were also brought in line with the thirty-seat rule. Companies operating aircraft having a passenger seating configuration (excluding any pilot seat) of more than thirty seats and a maximum payload capacity of more than 7,500 pounds must comply with certification requirements of FAR Part 121. Operators of aircraft having a maximum seating configuration of thirty seats or less and a maximum payload capacity of 7,500 pounds or less are certified under FAR Part 135, "Operating requirements: Commuter and on-demand operations."

As originally written, FAR Part 139 was applicable only to land airports serving *scheduled* air carriers. In 1973, the applicability of FAR Part 139 was broadened to require all airports serving certificated air carriers to hold an air carrier airport-operating certificate. Additional airports not previously included were those serving certificated supplemental air carriers, certificated carriers operating "small" aircraft (i.e., weighing 12,500 pounds or less), certificated air carrier charter operations, and certificated air carriers operating helicopters. Not considered subject to Part 139 were airports at which air carrier training, ferry, check, or test operations were conducted only for reasons of these operations. However, airports used for refueling stops were considered to be rendering services to air carriers and serving CAB-certificated operations. Therefore, they were required to comply with Part 139.

The FAA was having difficulty applying uniformly the safety requirements for air carrier airports to less active airports. In 1974 the FAA amended Part 139 to provide, on an individual basis, the certification and operation of land airports and heliports serving CAB-certificated air carriers conducting only unscheduled operations or operations with small aircraft. These "limited" certificates insured that an airport was properly and adequately equipped to conduct safe operations for the kind of air carrier operation being conducted. However, the FAA usually had lowered standards for compliance with certain Part 139 requirements. Air carrier airports enplaning annually less than .25% of the total number of passengers enplaned at all air carrier airports could petition the FAA for exemption from the aircraft fire fighting and rescue equipment requirements of Part 139 if the regulation requirements were deemed to be unreasonably costly, burdensome, or impractical.

THE NEW PART 139

The latest revision of FAR Part 139, more simply entitled "Certification of Airports," went into effect on June 9, 2004. This revised FAR established certification requirements for airports serving scheduled air carrier operations in aircraft designed for more than 9 but less than 31 passenger seats. Coupled with this change was an amendment of an air carrier operation regulation (14 CFR Part 121) to ensure that air carriers would only operate at airports that were in compliance with the most recent airport certification requirements.[5]

[5] FAA, *Part 139 Certification: Why Was Part 139 Revised?* (2006), retrieved from http://www.faa.gov/airports_airtraffic/airports/airport_safety/part139_cert/?p1=why.

The newest FAR Part 139 changes were undertaken to address perceived deficiencies in a number of areas including:[6]

- A better record keeping system and new personnel training standards to assure Part 139 compliance;
- Improved training of personal for self-inspection, emergency response, and aircraft fueling;
- New training requirements for pedestrians and ground vehicles;
- Clarification of requirements to repair pavement cracks, and maintain safety areas and pavement edge markings;
- New requirements for the airfield sign plan;
- New supplemental wind cone/segmented circle standards;
- Clarification of requirement for determining need for plan and positioning of snow off movement areas; and
- Aircraft Rescue and Fire Fighting revisions relating to new personnel training, a new fire extinguishing agent, revised Hazardous Materials [HAZMAT] response standard; clarification of Index criteria, and extension of ARFF coverage to scheduled operations of small air carrier aircraft.

Under the 2004 update, the regulation now applies to airports with scheduled passenger carrying operations by an air carrier aircraft with more than nine passenger seats and less than 31 seats (referred to as "small" air carrier aircraft). Part 139 also applies to airports with scheduled or unscheduled passenger-carrying operations by an air carrier operating aircraft that are designed to carry at least 31 seats (referred to as "large" air carrier aircraft). While it does not apply to airports operated by the United States (military), it does apply to those portions of a joint-use or shared-use airport that are within the authority of a person serving passenger-carrying operations. There are also special exemptions for Alaskan airports.[7]

One significant change was in the reclassification of airports, and the issuance of new *Airport Operating Certificates*, which are issued under Part 139 for the operation of a Class I, II, III, or IV airport.[8] The certificates are issued, based on a number of factors including average

---

[6] *Id.*
[7] *Id.*
[8] Class I, II and IV airports were previously certificated airports, while Class III airports were newly certificated under the 2004 Part 139 revision.

daily departures, size of aircraft, and whether the passenger air service is scheduled or unscheduled.[9] The certificate holder" is the jurisdictional entity or sponsor that is issued the Airport Operating Certificate. The definitions for each airport classification are as follows:[10]

- *Class I Airport* means an airport certificated to serve scheduled operations of large air carrier aircraft that can also serve unscheduled passenger operations of large air carrier aircraft and/or scheduled operations of small air carrier aircraft.
- *Class II Airport* means an airport certificated to serve scheduled operations of small air carrier aircraft and the unscheduled passenger operations of large air carrier aircraft. A Class II airport cannot serve scheduled large air carrier aircraft.
- *Class III Airport* means an airport certificated to serve scheduled operations of small air carrier aircraft. A Class III airport cannot serve scheduled or unscheduled large air carrier aircraft.
- *Class IV Airport* means an airport certificated to serve unscheduled passenger operations of large air carrier aircraft. A Class IV airport cannot serve scheduled large or small air carrier aircraft.

The terms, conditions, and limitations of an airport operating certificate issued by the FAA are those considered reasonably necessary to assure air transportation safety. The FAA does not certificate general aviation airports, although many states do have licensing procedures for the airports located within their boundaries. State licenses are in addition to FAA requirements and in most cases they include general aviation airports as well as those serving air carriers.

AIRPORT CERTIFICATION MANUAL

To be eligible for an airport operating certificate (other than a heliport, where standard requirements are modified) an applicant must

[9] According to the FAA, "Average Daily Departures" [ADD] means the average number of scheduled departures per day of air carrier aircraft computed on the basis of the busiest 3 consecutive calendar months of the immediately preceding 12 consecutive calendar months. However, if the ADD are expected to increase, then ADD may be determined by planned rather than current activity, as approved by the FAA Administrator.

[10] 14 CFR FAR Part 139, *Certification of Airports* (2004), retrieved from http://www.faa.gov/airports_airtraffic/airports/airport_safety/part139_cert/?p1=regulation.

spell out in an *Airport Certification Manual* [ACM][11] the procedures to be followed in the routine operation of the airport and for response to emergency situations. Additionally, the airport must provide certain equipment and facilities and must insure that the airport's facilities are maintained to specified standards.

The ACM is a working tool in the day-to-day operation of the airport. It provides a means for the airport manager to report to the FAA on the conditions at the airport and the means and procedures to be used to comply with the requirements of Part 139. The ACM is created with guidance provided in Part 139, but ultimately it is the individual operator's manual—with each page stamped and dated as approved by the FAA. It is the FAA enforcement tool for the subject airport.

If an airport chooses to include standards in its ACM that are more demanding than that required in FAR Part 139, then that airport is subjecting itself to a higher level of responsibility if it fails to meet its elevated standards. Thus, most airport operators choose to write an ACM that meets—but does not exceed—the requirements of FAR Part 139.

The FAA employs more than thirty Airport Certification Safety Inspectors to conduct its annual on-site airport certification inspections. In addition, the inspectors are also free to make unannounced inspections. The steps involved in these inspections are presented below:[12]

- *Pre-inspection*—Review of office airport files and airport certification manual.
- *In-briefing with airport management*—Organize inspection time schedule, meet with different airport personnel.
- *Administrative inspection of airport files, paperwork, etc.*—Also includes updating the Airport Master Record (FAA Form 5010) and review of the Airport Certification Manual/Specifications [ACM/ACS], Notices to Airmen [NOTAM]), airfield self-inspection forms, etc.
- *Movement area inspection*—Check the approach slopes of each runway end; inspect movement areas to find out condition of pavement, markings, lighting, signs, abutting shoulders, and safety areas; watch ground vehicle operations; ensure the public is protected against inadvertent entry and jet or propeller blast;

[11] The *Airport Certification Manual* was originally called the "Airport Operations Manual."
[12] This section taken from 14 CFR Part 139, *Certification* of Airports (Feb. 2006), retrieved from http://www.faa.gov/airports_airtraffic/airports/airport_safety/part139_cert/?p1=what.

check for the presence of any wildlife; check the traffic and wind direction indicators.

- *Aircraft rescue and fire fighting inspection*—Conduct a timed-response drill; review aircraft rescue and firefighting personnel training records, including annual live-fire drill and basic emergency medical care training; check equipment and protective clothing for operation, condition, and availability.
- *Fueling facilities inspection*—Inspection of fuel farm and mobile fuelers; check airport files for documentation of quarterly inspections of the fueling facility; review certification from each tenant fueling agent about completion of fire safety training.
- *Night inspection*—Evaluate runway/taxiway and apron lighting and signage, pavement marking, airport beacon, wind cone, lighting, and obstruction lighting. A night inspection is conducted if air carrier operations are (or might be) conducted or if the airport has an instrument approach.
- *Post inspection briefing with airport management*—Discuss findings; issue Letter of Correction noting violations and/or discrepancies if any are found; agree on a reasonable date for correcting any violations, and give safety recommendations.

As stated earlier, each airport is unique. Therefore, airport certification manuals may be presented in a format that best suits the airport's characteristics and operational requirements. At a minimum, the ACM must be current at all times, available for inspection, have portions furnished to involved personnel, and address all required ACM elements. It must be typed and signed by the airport operator. It must also be presented in a format that is easy to prepare, review and revise. Any exemptions that have been granted by the FAA Administrator to the airport must be included in the ACM along with copies of the exemption and any expiration dates.

Based on airport classification, airports must have most of the same basic elements, in order to have it enforceable as Part 139. Typically, these elements are broken out into chapters typically found in each airport's ACM. Table 8.1, "Airport Certification Manual: Sample Table of Contents," is drawn from a model provided by the FAA. In the following pages, these elements are discussed in greater detail.

Table 8.1—AIRPORT CERTIFICATION MANUAL: SAMPLE TABLE OF CONTENTS

Topic	*FAR Part 139 Reference*
General Requirements	
Records	139.301
Personnel	139.303
Paved Areas & Unpaved Areas	139.302 & .307
Safety Areas	139.309
Marking, Signs and Lighting	139.311
Snow and Ice Control	139.313
Aircraft Rescue & Fire Fighting	
Index Determination	139.315
Equipment & Agents	139.317
Operational Requirements	139.319
Hazardous Materials Storage/Handling	139.321
Traffic & Wind Indicators	139.323
Airport Emergency Plan	139.325
Airport Self- Inspection Program	139.327
Pedestrians & Ground Vehicles	139.329
Obstructions/Obstruction Lighting	139.331
Protection of Navaids	139.333
Public Protection	139.335
Wildlife Hazard Management	139.337
Airport Condition Reporting	139.339
Construction Area Marking	139.341
Non-Complying Conditions	139.343

Source: FAA (2006), retrieved from http://www.faa.gov/airports_airtraffic/airports/airport_safety/part139_cert/media/sample_ACM.pdf.

The *Records* and *Personnel* ACM chapters must address record-keeping requirements for airport personnel and Aircraft Rescue and Fire Fighting training, along with records relating to airport fueling agent inspections, self inspection activities, and pedestrian and ground vehicle statistics. Also addressed in the Personnel chapter are key personnel, lines of succession and operational responsibility.

Chapters on *Paved and Unpaved Areas*[13] and *Safety Areas* define and discuss the composition and maintenance of the airfield surfaces. Safety Areas are defined areas comprised of either a runway or taxiway and the surrounding surfaces. These surfaces are for "reducing the risk of damage to aircraft in the event of undershoot, overshoot, or excursion from a runway or the unintentional departure from a taxiway."[14]

The *Airport Marking, Signs and Lighting* chapter in the ACM addresses proper airfield markings, signage and lighting that are found along the taxiways, runways and other areas as noted in airport's official sign plan. Also included are references to the airport beacon(s), approach lighting system(s), obstructions, and maintenance and shielding requirement.

The *Construction and Unserviceable Area Markings* section discusses responsibilities for marking and lighting to prevent aircraft confusion or damage, as well as measures to prevent interruption in utilities and navigational aids. The *Traffic and Wind Indicators* section provides details of the visual indicators available to the flying public.[15]

The ACM chapter on *Obstructions and Obstruction Lighting* discusses the Certificate Holder's requirement to ensure that each object within its authority that is an obstruction is removed, marked and/or lighted. The FAA identifies Advisory Circulars [AC]s as containing "methods and procedures for the lighting of obstructions that are acceptable to the Administrator." Notably (and to the dissatisfaction of some airport operators), this incorporation of an "advisory" document into Part 139, essentially converts the AC to a mandatory document[16].

The *Snow and Ice Control Plan* can be a very large chapter or even equal the size of the rest of the ACM at some heavily snow-impacted

---

[13] Pavements and Soils, along with Snow and Ice Removal are discussed in greater depth in Ch. 11, "Airport Maintenance."

[14] 14 CFR FAR Part 139, *Certification of Airports* (2004), retrieved from http://www.faa.gov/airports_airtraffic/airports/airport_safety/part139_cert/?p1=regulation.

[15] *Id.*

[16] *Id.*

airports. This plan or chapter of the ACM addresses snow and ice-related responsibilities and supervision, equipment, training and procedures, and communications. Priorities in snow removal are covered along with snow positioning and storage, and the issuance of notices/advisories to users.[17]

The ACM chapter on *Protection of Navigational Aids* [NAVAIDS] discusses the airport's requirements to guard against vandalism and theft, as well as the airport's need to prevent interruption of NAVAID visual and electronic signals. In the *Public Protection* Chapter, the airport describes its "safeguards to prevent inadvertent entry to the movement area by unauthorized persons or vehicles," as well as protecting persons and property from aircraft (jet) blast. Fencing is discussed as well.[18]

The final ACM section on *Non-Complying Conditions* confirms that whenever uncorrected, unsafe conditions exist, air carriers will not be permitted to operate in the unsafe areas.

Because of the complexity associated with Aircraft Rescue and Fire Fighting, Hazardous Materials Storage and Handling, the Airport Emergency Plan, the Airport Self Inspection Program, Pedestrians and Ground Vehicles, and Wildlife Hazard Management, these sections are addressed in more depth through the remainder of this chapter.

AIRCRAFT RESCUE AND FIRE FIGHTING REQUIREMENTS

Aircraft rescue and fire fighting equipment and service requirements are determined by a combination of the length of air carrier aircraft (expressed in groups), and the average daily departures of air carrier aircraft.[19] For the purpose of Index determination, air carrier aircraft lengths are grouped as follows:

- *Index A*: aircraft less than 90 feet in length;
- *Index B*: aircraft at least 90 but less than 126 feet in length;

[17] Snow and ice control is discussed in greater depth in Ch. 11, "Airport Maintenance."

[18] *Id. at 17.*

[19] According to FAR Part 139: Except as provided in § 139.319(c), if there are five or more average daily departures of air carrier aircraft in a single Index group serving that airport, the longest aircraft with an average of five or more daily departures determines the Index required for the airport. When there are fewer than five average daily departures of the longest air carrier aircraft serving the airport, the Index required for the airport will be the next lower Index group than the Index group prescribed for the longest aircraft.

- *Index C*: aircraft at least 126 but less than 159 feet in length;
- *Index D*: aircraft at least 159 but less than 200 feet in length; and
- *Index E*: aircraft at least 200 feet long.

The minimum designated Index is Index A. Specified for each index group are the size and capabilities of the vehicle(s) needed. At a minimum, all Indexes require at least one lightweight vehicle providing either 500 pounds of sodium-based dry chemical extinguishing agent or Halon 1211, or clean agent;[20] or 450 pounds of potassium-based dry chemical and water sufficient to produce 100 gallons of *Aqueous Film Forming Foam* [AFFF]. As aircraft progress upward in size each increasing index requires additional equipment.

Minimum equipment for the largest Index (E) include the lightweight vehicle plus two additional self-propelled fire extinguishing vehicles so that the total quantity of water for foam production carried by all three vehicles is at least 6,000 gallons. Each vehicle used to comply with Index B, C, D, or E requirements with a capacity of at least 500 gallons of water for foam production must be equipped with a turret with an appropriate discharge capacity. Each ARFF vehicle required carrying dry chemical, Halon 1211 or clean agent must also meet specific discharge rates. Finally, in addition to the water quantity specified, each AFFF vehicle must carry twice the water needed to generate the appropriate foam-water mix.

A great variety of equipment is used by ARFF units at airports.[21] Larger ARFF vehicles generally have some type of agent-dispensing *turret* mounted on the vehicle or attached to a mechanical arm or *snozzle*. Reportedly, *bumper* or *low-access* turrets are generally the most effective in extinguishing fires. However, to fight an internal aircraft fire, an extendable high-rise turret with a penetrating nozzle can be inserted through the aircraft skin to suppress the fire. Additionally, a *Driver's Enhanced Vision System* [DEVS] with *Forward Looking Infrared* [FLIR] can increase ARFF function and safety.[22]

---

[20] The term, "clean agent" was added to FAR Part 139 in 2004 and is defined in the regulation as, "an electrically non-conducting volatile or gaseous fire-extinguishing agent that does not leave a residue upon evaporation and has been shown to provide extinguishing action equivalent to Halon 1211 under test protocols of FAA Technical Report DOT/FAA/AR-95/87."

[21] FAA guidance on ARFF vehicles is found in AC 150/5220-1C, "Guide Specifications for Water/Foam ARFF Vehicles." *See also*, FAA, *Part 139 Best Practices: ARFF Equipment*, http://www. faa.gov/airports_airtrafic/airports/regional guidance/central/airport_safety/part 139/best_practice/arff/equipment (visited Apr. 27, 2007).

[22] *See* FAA, *Driver's Enhanced Vision System*, AC 150/5210-19 (Dec. 23, 1996).

The requirements for ARFF, or what were once called "Crash, Fire and Rescue" [CFR] equipment have been debated on grounds of insufficient cost/benefit since they were first imposed in 1972. Quoting Russ Hoyt, former Executive Vice President of the American Association of Airport Executives [AAAE] and a long-time opponent of the ARFF requirements mandated by the FAA:

> *As neither the users nor managers of airports could justify the service, few airports provided on-airport CFR prior to federal regulation. With required CFR service at all carrier airports and with no improvement in aircraft occupant survivability, AAAE became insistent that justification for the requirement be provided. This insistence led to the FAA contracting with HH Aerospace for a cost/benefit study. . . . The study was made; its findings fully discussed at a public hearing; comments were invited; and no substantive adverse criticisms were submitted. . . . The study clearly indicates that benefits to aircraft occupants are almost non-existent, particularly at the smaller airports. . . . Although more comprehensive, the study was but one of several that arrived at the same conclusion . . . Therefore, as the saying goes, we rest our case.*

The study referred to above by Mr. Hoyt, commissioned by the FAA and conducted by HH Aerospace Design Company in 1982, gave support to AAAE's and others' claim that the cost of providing required ARFF services at smaller airports far outweighs their value. The study found, during a twelve year period from 1966 to 1978, there was only one life actually saved by ARFF efforts at "smaller airports," defined as having less than 750,000 enplanements annually.

Reportedly, the cost of providing ARFF services at those smaller airports was more than $200 million, which in cost/benefit terms means $200 million per life. As pointed out by Mr. Hoyt, in the macabre business of assigning cost/benefit values to human life, in the FAA's formula for determining the need for air traffic control towers the commonly accepted value of one human life, at that time, was about $500,000. Again quoting Russ Hoyt,

> *I don't want to sound insensitive, but there are 1,500 people killed each year at grade crossings. Now those are entirely preventable deaths. All you have to do is put the road either over or under the tracks. We haven't done it because it is too expensive. We find ourselves in an identical situation in aviation.*

The HH Aerospace Design Company study recommended that ARFF requirements be dropped at airports enplaning fewer than 750,000 passengers annually. In October of 1985, the FAA issued a news release of its proposed revision of FAR Part 139, wherein the FAA would change the requirements for ARFF vehicles at smaller airports. As proposed the FAA would determine on a case-by-case basis the specific vehicle requirements for airports that handle the smallest aircraft. For those smaller airports handling larger aircraft, the proposal called for only one vehicle rather than two.

In 1988, FAR Part 139 was updated to conditionally allow the following reduction in rescue and fire fighting equipment:

> *During air carrier operations with only aircraft shorter than the Index required. . . , the certificate holder may reduce the rescue and fire fighting to a lower level corresponding to the Index group of the longest air carrier aircraft being operated.*

The new Part 139 requires all certificated airports to provide some level of ARFF service, and the FAA has maintained its authority to recognize constraints and reasonableness with regard to ARFF service at airports with small air carrier service. In fact, the revised regulation purportedly allows the FAA to,[23]

> *. . . better exercise its statutory authority to provide appropriate exemptions from some or all*

[23] *Id.* at 11.

> *prescribed ARFF requirements, and establish alternative ARFF compliance measures for airports serving only smaller air carrier aircraft (Class III airports) that may be unable to provide the same level of ARFF services required of airports serving large air carrier operations.*

Thus, on a case-by-case basis, the FAA may consider some limited exemptions from some or all ARFF requirements for airports that have either infrequent or smaller air carrier operations. This exemption allows airports with less than one-quarter of one percent of the total number of annual passenger boardings to request FAA permission to adopt regulatory alternatives for so-called "commuter airports" or those referred to as Class III airports. The goal is to allow alternatives that are least costly, most cost effective or the least burdensome but provide comparable safety at all certificated airports.[24]

The revised Part 139 allows operators of Class III airports to either comply with Index A ARFF requirements or comply with alternate ARFF requirements that provide a comparable level of safety. According to FAR Part 139, these alternate ARFF requirements must,

- be approved by the FAA;
- include provisions for prearranged emergency response services; and
- ensure that emergency responders are familiar with air carrier schedules, airport layout, and airfield communications.[25]

FIGHTING FIRES

Fires associated with flammable product result from ignition of vapors. Vapors from petroleum products mixed with proper amounts of air form explosive mixtures within a limited range called the "explosive range" or "explosive limits." Fuels handled on the airport are in a constant state of flux, passing in and out of the explosive range. The danger of explosion and fire is always present. Aviation fires are the number one safety problem on an airport. Aviation-related fires and explosions are of such critical concern that nearly half of the National

[24] *Id.*
[25] *Id.*

Fire Protection Association's fire codes and standards pertain to aircraft and other aviation-related fire prevention and fire fighting procedures.

The first principle in fighting fires on an airport is to realize that any fire associated with a petroleum product is potentially disastrous! One should not hesitate to call the fire department for professional assistance. Most fires have small beginnings. But this can be deceptive, particularly where petroleum fires are concerned, and may lead to overconfidence and/or reluctance to call for help. Fires can rapidly get out of hand, thus putting firefighters under a severe handicap the later they are summoned. Where airport fires are concerned, there should be no fatal delay in notifying the fire department and seeking professional help.

THE FIRE TRIANGLE

Extinguishing fire entails control of one or more of the three elements of the *fire triangle.* These three elements are *fuel*, *heat* and *air*. Although seldom practicable, wherever possible, the first step is to stop the flow of fuel feeding a fire. This may be done by turning a valve, activating an emergency shut-off switch, or by plugging the leak by any means available. Radiation, conduction, and convection transmit heat, and heat helps the fire spread to other areas. The most effective way to reduce heat and vaporization is with *water* in streams, spray, or a fog. It is nearly impossible to remove all air from a fire, but usually it is possible to dilute the air, smother the fire, or do both where there will no longer be enough oxygen to support combustion. *Dilution* is accomplished with carbon dioxide or water. *Foam* is the best blanketing agent for smothering a petroleum fire.

The Underwriter's Laboratories has grouped fires into three classes, and the National Fire Protection Association has added a fourth class. The four classes of fires are:

- *Class A fires* involve ordinary combustible materials such as wood, brush, grass and rubbish. The effective extinguishing agent for Class A fires is water;
- *Class B fires* occur in flammable liquids such as gasoline, other fuels, solvents, lubricants, paints and similar substances that do

not leave embers. Smothering or cooling is necessary to extinguish Class B fires;

- *Class C fires* are electrical fires involving equipment such as motors, switches and transformers. Smothering is preferred for Class C fires, although the extinguishing agent may not be a conductor of electricity; and
- *Class D* fires are fires in combustible metals such as magnesium, titanium, zirconium, sodium, and potassium. Preferably, a specialized extinguishing agent is used for each type of metal, but time being of the essence, a commonly used dry chemical may have to suffice.

FIREFIGHTING AGENTS

The commonly used agents for aircraft rescue and fire fighting are water, dry chemicals, and/or foam. Water is a generally used element in aircraft rescue and fire fighting, and may be employed as a wetting or cooling agent by applying it as a fog, mist, or stream. It is also used for dilution of foam concentrates in a 3% or 6% solution. Foam is particularly suited for airport-related fire fighting because the water and foam concentrate used for its production can be readily transported and rapidly applied. There are four major types of foam that have been used for aircraft rescue and fire fighting, they are:

- *Protein foam*, which consists primarily of products from a protein hydrolysate (i.e., decomposed protein) plus stabilizing additives and inhibitors;
- *Fluoroprotein foam* which is similar to protein foam but with a synthetic fluorinated surfactant additive (to lower the tension at the surface of the agent);
- *Aqueous Film Forming Foam*, also known as "light water," is the most commonly used foam. It consists of a fluorinated surfactant with a foam stabilizer. The chemical foam produced with AFFF concentrate is suitable for combined use with dry chemicals; and
- *Other synthetic foams*, which generally have as a base hydrocarbon surface active agents.

Dry chemicals are commonly used because of their compatibility with AFFF, and are used wherever a smothering effect is desired. Most dry chemicals contain an ingredient that when exposed to the fire's heat gives off carbon dioxide, thereby producing a smothering effect by excluding available oxygen. Perhaps the most commonly used dry chemical on airports is the brand name *Purple K*, so named because of its color and its basic ingredient potassium (abbreviated as "K" on a table of elements); in this case potassium bicarbonate with silicon additives. Another known brand name is *Super K*, which has as its main ingredient potassium chloride.

In addition to self-propelled fire fighting vehicles, airports have a variety of both portable hand fire extinguishers and wheeled units. Fire extinguishers are available in various sizes and in all types, including pump-tank units. The agent used in the pump-tank type extinguishers is water or an antifreeze solution. Portable fire extinguishers should be inspected frequently for placement in their designated places, for ready accessibility, to insure against having been damaged, and to insure hoses are not clogged. They should be recharged immediately after use and examined at least annually for operability. Pressure extinguishers should be hydrostatically tested every five to twelve years, depending upon the extinguisher. The various portable fire extinguishers other than the pump-tank type are as follows:

- *Soda-acid* extinguishers are the most common water solution types in which gas pressure is used as an expellant. Chemicals used are sodium bicarbonate (baking soda) and sulfuric acid. Soda-acid is used on Class A fires;
- *Antifreeze* solution units are charged with calcium chloride solution. The agent is expelled by gas from carbon dioxide cartridges or produced by chemical reaction. Antifreeze is used on Class A fires;
- *Loaded-stream* extinguishers are charged with alkali metal salt solution and other salts including potassium salts, at least as a portion of the charge. Loaded stream extinguishers are good for Class A or B fires;
- *Foam* extinguishers are usually charged with a water solution of sodium bicarbonate with a foam-stabilizing agent added. Aluminum sulfate solution when mixed with the sodium bicarbonate

produces carbon dioxide gas, and under pressure expels the liquid foam-like bubbles used on Class A and B fires;

- *Vaporizing-Liquid* [VL] (commonly known as "Halon"[26]) comes in either hand-pump units or in stored-pressure extinguishers. The charge is usually bromochloromethane, or in some countries methyl bromide, both of which present a toxic hazard to the operator. The VL extinguishers should be expelled from upwind and should be used only by trained personnel for Class B and C fires. Moreover, Halons were banned by the Montreal Protocol on Substances that Deplete the Ozone Layer;[27]
- *Clean agents* are a newer category.[28] These are electrically non-conducting volatile or gaseous fire extinguishing agents that do not leave a residue upon evaporation and have been shown to provide extinguishing action equivalent to Halon 1211 under test protocols of FAA Technical Report DOT/FAA/AR-95/87.
- *Carbon dioxide* [CO_2] extinguishers are under pressure and when released the CO_2 has a chilling effect on expansion and turns about 30% of the contents into dry ice or snow. It is particularly valuable for dilution of air on Class B fires and as a non-conductor can be used on Class C (electrical) fires; and
- *Dry-chemical* extinguishers have primary agents such as sodium bicarbonate powder, with additives to produce water repellency and free flow. Carbon dioxide, nitrogen, or compressed air expels the agent. Dry chemicals can be used on Class B and C fires.

HAZARDOUS MATERIALS AND FUEL SERVICING

Federal Aviation Regulation Part 139 requires that the airport have procedures for handling and storage of hazardous substances and mate-

---

[26] Halon 1211 and Halon 1301 are trade names for the commercially produced chemical Bromotrifluoromethane.

[27] The Montreal Protocol on Substances that Deplete the Ozone Layer is an international treaty designed to protect the ozone layer by phasing out the production of a number of substances believed to be resopnsible for ozone depletion. The treaty was entered into force on Jan. 1, 1989 and has undergone five revisions since: London 1990, Copenhagen 1992, Vienna 1995, Montreal 1997, and Beijing 1999; *see* Ozone Secretariat, United Nations Environment Program, *The Montreal Protocol on Substances that Deplete the Ozone Layer*, http://ozone.unep.org/pdfs/Montreal-Protocol2000.pdf (visited May 11, 2007).

[28] 14 CFR FAR Part 139, *Certification of Airports* (2004), retrieved from http://www.faa.gov/airports_airtraffic/airports/airport_safety/part139_cert/?p1=regulation.

rials. In 1988, responsibility for fuel servicing was added to the airport's Part 139 responsibility regarding the handling of hazardous materials. This requires the airport to establish fuel handling procedures, safety standards for fire safety, inspection procedures and record keeping, and specialized training.

In a 1984 study of the safety at the nation's airports the National Transportation Board made twenty-one recommendations to the FAA, five dealing with fire fighting and emergencies, and six with *fueling* procedures. The National Transportation Board [NTSB] reported finding "fueling service discrepancies that included leaking fuel trucks, fuel trucks without fire extinguishers, trucks on which the fuel type was not easily identified, fueling being performed without grounding, and fueling being performed without securing the wheels of the truck." To correct these discrepancies the NTSB recommended that fuelers be certified by the FAA, that Federal Aviation Administration be named as fueling inspectors, and that airports be required to include fuel storage and dispensing facilities in their FAR Part 139-required inspections.

The Part 139 rules[29] adopted in 1988 further require each certificate holder to establish and maintain procedures for the protection of persons and property on the airport during the handling and storing of any material regulated by the Hazardous Materials Regulations.[30] This includes, but is not limited to, aviation fuels and lubricants.

Each certificate holder must establish and maintain standards acceptable to the FAA for protection against fire and explosions in storing, dispensing, and otherwise handling fuel, lubricants, and oxygen on the airport. These standards are to cover facilities, procedures, and personnel training. Additionally, the certificate holder is to inspect the physical facilities of each airport tenant-fueling agent at least once every three months.

The fuel handling standards are to address at least the following:

- *Grounding and bonding* of fueling vehicles and aircraft;
- *Public protection*;
- *Control of access* to storage areas;
- *Fire safety* in *fuel farm* and storage areas;
- *Fire safety in mobile fuelers*, fueling pits, and storage areas;

---

[29] 14 CFR §139.321.

[30] 49 CFR § 171.

- *Training* of fueling personnel in fire safety; and
- The airport jurisdiction's *fire code*.

The imposition of regulatory responsibilities for fuel storage and distribution coupled with environmental concerns and the entrepreneurial responsibilities attached to the new public administration paradigm, all beg the question currently being asked by industry observers. "Will the airport of the future . . . become the sole fuel farm owner/operator and fuel distributor"? As changes in the economy continue to impact the airport industry, and environmental regulations challenge traditional ways of doing things, some observers are suggesting that one of the likely outcomes is that airport sponsors will take control of fueling operations on their airports.[31] With the instability of the Fixed Base Operator [FBO] business now being felt at many airports, owning the fuel farm would provide the obvious benefit of ensuring the availability of fuel for local and itinerant users should an FBO go out of business.

Other potential advantages for airports willing to assume control over fueling operations include an ability to prevent a proliferation of requests for self-serving facilities by corporate or other tenants, better revenue control and distribution accountability, and the ability to generate more revenue for the airport.[32]

As Tim Anderson states, ". . . with decreasing access to funds (that) airports have received via traditional means, such as the Airport Improvement Program, and the increasing desire to find alternative sources of revenue to secure the airport's financial future in a changing environment, the control of fueling (offers) obvious potential."[33] David Crowner, manager of the Pullman-Moscow (Washington) Regional Airport, suggests that airports will likely become the sole owners of the fuel farm in order to maintain environmental control.[34] And as Bob Porter, manager of the Arlington (Texas) Municipal Airport, predicts, environmental cautions eventually will force most airports to designate

---

[31] Barbara Cook, *Fueling Your Economic Engine: Is It Time?,* Airport Magazine (May/Jun. 1997), at 12.

[32] Steve Quilty, in Barbara Cook, *Fueling Your Economic Engine: Is It Time?,* Airport Magazine (May/Jun. 1997), at 12.

[33] Tim Anderson, in Barbara Cook, *Fueling Your Economic Engine: Is It Time?,* Airport Magazine (May/Jun. 1997), at 56.

[34] David Crowner, in Barbara Cook, *Fueling Your Economic Engine: Is It Time?,* Airport Magazine (May/Jun. 1997), at 56.

one common area on the premises for all underground and above ground storage tanks in order to localize any potential pollution and reduce mitigation.[35]

The increasing environmental regulations will, in fact, lead to airports becoming owners and operators of the fuel farms. In the view of Fred Anderton, director of Fort Collins-Loveland (Colorado) Airport, ". . . no written contract can sufficiently protect the land owner—the airport—from the liability of a tenant-owned and operated fuel facility. If a tenant elects to mismanage/mishandle a fuel farm, the responsibility will ultimately rest with the airport. The clean-up costs are so great that most fuel vendors facing a clean-up would walk away."[36] Airport sponsors will take control of all responsibilities for refueling operations since the ultimate responsibility for fuel spills and leaking tanks rests with them. Therefore, the airport may as well take over. If the airport sponsor is going to have ultimate responsibility, it will likely want to control as much of the process as possible.[37]

Airport sponsors have a right to be the exclusive purveyor of fuels on their airports,[38] and an airport management team also functioning as the fueling operator can work, ". . . but only if it is run as a business," says David Byers, director of Quadrex Associates, Inc. The cost to deliver fueling services may not allow a significant profit margin.[39] Professor Steve Quilty seconds the opinion. If an airport is to take on the role of sole fuel supplier, "it will require a strong commitment on the part of elected and municipal officials to operate an entrepreneurial business, which many do not have the foresight or willingness to do."[40] Added to the competitive pressures of private enterprise, the government-sponsored business must also consider the public welfare, and higher operational costs, particularly in terms of labor. It is no secret that labor rates usually drop when any function is privatized.

As reported by Bruce Mosley, deputy director of airports for Sacramento County (California) Department of Airports, at the Sacra-

---

[35] Bob Porter, in Barbara Cook, *Fueling Your Economic Engine: Is It Time?,* Airport Magazine (May/Jun. 1997), at 14.
[36] Fred Anderton, in Barbara Cook, *Fueling Your Economic Engine: Is It Time?,* Airport Magazine (May/Jun. 1997), at 15.
[37] *See id.*
[38] *See* Section 308 of the *Federal Aviation Act* of 1958.
[39] David Byers, in Barbara Cook, *Fueling Your Economic Engine: Is It Time?,* Airport Magazine (May/Jun. 1997), at 15.
[40] Steve Quilty, in Barbara Cook, *Fueling Your Economic Engine: Is It Time?,* Airport Magazine (May/Jun. 1997), at 14.

mento airports, airlines have criticized the high cost paid by the county for its fuelers (who are public employees), compared to the costs of the airline (which contracts out the work). The airline was able to pay less than half the county's labor cost, including benefits. But Mosley defends the county's costs by arguing that a low contract wage rate attracts employees with limited communication, reading and math skills. The low wage also generates high turnover as, in many cases, the employee can neither do the work required, which includes computing fuel loads and observing safety practices, nor can the employee live on the low wage received. Thus, in Mosley's observation, public concern over airport safety mitigates against contracting out and/or paying the lower wage for performance of the fueling task on an airport.[41]

In summary, airport sponsors are being held increasingly to higher standards of responsibility and liability for refueling operations. Simultaneously, the investment needed for new fueling technologies plus the expense of environmental requirements is discouraging many FBOs from continuing in the fuel business. As the liability costs for fuel storage and fuel dispensing increase, more and more airports are considering becoming the sole fuel-servicing operator on their airports.[42] But if they are to assume all fueling responsibilities, airport sponsors will have to be firmly committed to the *new public administration* paradigm, which calls for more entrepreneurship in the management of public facilities. This may prove difficult in situations where "the customer service demands of the corporate aircraft user exceed the capacity of entities that are not stimulated by the survival requirements of a for-profit business."[43]

AVIATION FUEL HANDLING

Aviation fuels are categorized as either *Aviation Gasoline* [AVGAS] as *Jet Propulsion* [JP] fuel. Three grades of avgas have been produced for civil use: 80, 100LL (low lead), and 100. These grades replaced 80/87, 91/96, 100/130, and 115/145. Although fuel processors promised the continued availability of 80 octane, leading suppliers have progressively reduced its production. And now, leaded fuels are a

---

[41] Bruce Mosley, *The Best of Both Worlds*, Airport Magazine (Jan./Feb. 1998), at 8-9.

[42] Vic Redding, in Barbara Cook, *Fueling Your Economic Engine: Is It Time?*, Airport Magazine (May/Jun. 1997), at 16.

[43] Bob Showalter, in Barbara Cook, *Fueling Your Economic Engine: Is It Time?*, Airport Magazine (May/Jun. 1997), at 14.

rarity as well. A summary description of aviation fuels, which are, or have been, in common use is shown on Table 8.2, "Aviation Fuels."

Table 8.2—AVIATION FUELS

Fuel Grade	*NATO Code*	*Color*	*Fuel Type*
80/87 (80 Octane)	F12	red	aviation gasoline
91/96	F15	blue*	aviation gasoline
100/130 (100 Octane)*	F18	green	aviation gasoline
115/145	F22	purple	aviation gasoline
Jet A	F30	clear/light straw	kerosene (-37° freezing point)
Jet A-1	F36	clear/light straw	kerosene (-45 °freezing point)
JP-5	F44	clear/light straw	kerosene (high flash point)
JP-8	F34	clear/light straw	kerosene (with antioxidant, anticorrosion, and anti-icing additives)
Jet B	F45	clear/light straw	wide-cut naphtha/ gasoline/kerosene blend
JP-4	F40	clear/light straw	wide-cut naphtha/ gasoline/kerosene blend

* Grade 100LL (low lead) is blue to differentiate it from straight 100 octane.

Since their inception, jet fuel specifications have evolved through a series of alphanumeric designators. The first military specification for jet fuel originated in 1940 and was designated Jet Propulsion 1, or simply JP-1. Through the 1940s jet fuels were improved through series JP-2 and JP-3 with JP-4 introduced in 1951. Today, the most common military fuels are JP-4 and JP-5. JP-6 and JP-7 are classified as special fuels for use in unique flight characteristics only. JP-8 has combat advantages over JP-4, but as yet has not found wide acceptance.

Jet fuels for civilian use have alphabetized designations such as Jet A or Jet B, both of which are characteristically similar to JP-5 and JP-4 respectively. Jet A and JP-5 are kerosene with 20-25% aromatic (benzene ring) bases. Jet B and JP-4 are approximate blends of 65% straight-run gasoline and 35% kerosene, and are commonly referred to as "naphtha" fuels because of their relatively higher volatility when compared to the straight kerosene fuels.

Petroleum products present many hazards, not only to fuel handling personnel but also to safe aircraft operations. Nevertheless, fuels can be handled safely, and aircraft accidents can be minimized if product characteristics are understood and if proper precautionary measures are taken. Even so, all light petroleum fuels are hazardous and proper precautionary measures must be taken *at all times*.

Fuel handling requires both careful handling and strict observance of safety rules to prevent explosions and fires and to prevent inadvertent refueling of aircraft with contaminated fuels. Fuels are "contaminated" when they contain solid foreign matter, free or emulsified water, commingled grades of fuel, or any other material not provided for in the fuel specification.

The common aviation fuel contaminants are water, solids, surfactants, microorganisms, and miscellaneous contaminants, including the intermixing of different grades or types of fuel. Fortunately, the latter problem has been a declining issue. While the NTSB reported twenty-one misfueling accidents from 1980 through 1982, there were only nine from 1983 through 1986. Steve Anderson of Air BP reports that "while misfueling accidents are relatively infrequent today, they still account for a troubling number of serious, reportable accidents each year."[44] Many analysts attribute the reduction to a greater industry awareness of misfueling that spawned an anti-misfueling campaign and, perhaps more importantly, a proliferation of formal aircraft fuel-

[44] Steve Anderson, *Air BP Launches Misfueling Awareness Safety Campaign* (Jun. 12, 2005).

ing and line service *training programs*. Airport oversight of refueling operations mandated by FAR Part 139 since 1988 might also be credited with added refueling safety enhancement.

Next to water, *solid contaminants* are the most likely to be found in aviation fuels. Most common are iron rust, scale, sand, and dirt. However, metal particles, dust, lint from filter material and rags, gasket pieces, rubber, paint, and even sludge produced by bacterial action are included. Microbial growths are common in jet fuels. "Sediment" is the general term applied to solid contaminants. Particles large enough to cause damage are still microscopic in size and are measured on a micron scale. For comparison, one inch equals 25,400 microns. A five-micron particle is considered large enough to cause damage to aircraft and must be filtered out of the fuel.

Filtration of fuels is accomplished with line strainers, micron filters, and water separators. *Line strainers* are screens to remove the coarser materials. They are primarily used to relieve *filter/separators* and to keep large particles out of pumps and meters. "Micron filters" are so called because they remove fine (less than ten microns) particles from fuel. Solid contaminants are retained while fuel passes through the filter. Water is separated from the fuel by its coalescence in the filter and then by falling out of the filter.

The most common of all fuel contaminants is *water*. Aviation fuels absorb moisture from the air as the fuel temperature increases. Water is found in fuels in one of two forms, either suspended or in a solid body of water. There is no practical way of preventing its accumulation. It is drawn from the atmosphere and suspended within the fuel as droplets. The droplets then settle out and coalesce into a pool of water when the temperature of the fuel decreases.

Micro-organic growths of *bacteria* and *fungi* have been found living and growing at the interface between unleaded fuels and the liquid water in tanks. These microbes particularly thrive in turbine fuels. They appear as a soapy, slippery slime and can cause serious corrosion in tanks, or may clog filters, screens and fuel meters. Intermixing (or "commingling") of fuels is the mixing of different types or grades. It can be as serious as any other form of contamination. Mixed grades of avgas reduce the antiknock and volatility of fuels required for reciprocating engines, and can result in engine failure. Leaded gasoline mixed with jet fuel can result in damaging lead deposits in turbine engines. Avgas mixed with jet fuel can cause turbine engines to burn too hot.

To prevent commingling, *separate* fuel systems should handle each type of fuel. Turbine fuels, especially, tend to dislodge rust and scale in the storage tank and pipeline system and require special attention. Likewise, aviation gasoline should not be placed in equipment used for turbine fuels. All fuel-dispensing equipment should be conspicuously marked to indicate the type and grade of fuel (see Table 8.3, "Aviation Fuel Storage Color Coding System").

Table 8.3—AVIATION FUEL STORAGE COLOR CODING SYSTEM

NAMING SYSTEM

- Aviation gasoline grades are printed in white letters and numbers on a red background. Red was chosen for the background as an indication of the special care which must be taken in the handling of the more volatile fuels;
- Jet fuels are painted in white letters on a black background.

BANDING SYSTEM

The color of the single (minimum four-inch) band around the piping or hose is the same color as the dye in the grade of avgas flowing through the line:

- Red for avgas 80;
- Blue for avgas 100LL; and
- Green for avgas 100.

Black bands, each a minimum of four inches wide, are used to identify jet fuel as follows:

- A single black band for Jet A;
- Two black bands for Jet A-1; and
- Three black bands for Jet B.

Source: FAA, *Aircraft Fuel Storage, Handling, and Dispensing On Airports*, AC 150/5230-4 (1982).

Being volatile, fuels emit highly combustible *vapors*. The more rapidly vapors are given off from the fuel, the greater the danger of flash fire due to vapor ignition. This volatility factor varies greatly in the different types of aviation fuel. Gasoline emits vapors the most rapidly of the aviation fuels and is therefore the most volatile. Aviation gasolines have vapor pressures ranging from 5.5 to 7.0 pounds per square inch [p.s.i.]. The least volatile are the kerosene jet fuels, which have vapor pressures in the vicinity of 0.15 p.s.i. The so-called "naphtha" fuels (mixtures of gasoline and kerosene) have a vapor pressure ranging from about 2.0 to 3.0 p.s.i. Generally considered the most hazardous to handle are the naphtha fuels.

Naphtha fuels have a volatility factor in-between kerosene and avgas. In a confined space, naphtha fuel gives off vapor at a rate that will produce a highly flammable mixture. Should a gasoline tank catch fire it will normally burn at a vent, but ignition of a tank of naphtha is very likely to result in combustion and explosion of the air-vapor mixture within the tank.

Kerosene fuels normally *do not* give off sufficient amounts of flammable vapors to be hazardous if they are in closed storage tanks at normal sea level pressures and temperatures. Conversely, while in closed storage tanks, aviation gasoline gives off flammable vapors in such volume that the air-vapor mixture above the liquid surface is *too* vapor-rich to be ignited. However, when released from the storage tank, the air-vapor mixture may rapidly adjust to a highly flammable state.

In either case, if combustion is to occur it requires an igniter source. When two different materials come in contact with each other, *static electricity* is set up by exchange of negative and positive charges across the contact surface. When fuel passes through a pipeline, it builds up a static charge of electricity. Because of lower volatility and higher electrostatic generating tendencies, jet fuels are generally more susceptible to ignition from static electricity than are aviation gasolines. In pumping fuel into a tank, the static build-up can create a spark. The air-vapor mixture in which the spark occurs may likely be within the flammable or explosive range, especially while pumping naphtha-based jet fuels.

In handling aviation fuels the objective is to: minimize the buildup of static charge; avoid flammable air-vapor mixtures; and eliminate as much of the vapor space as possible. Controlling or avoiding flammable air-vapor mixtures and open vapor space is nearly impossible. Therefore, the build-up of electrical-charge in the fuel must be controlled. Following some general rules and procedures can minimize static buildup:

- Avoid pumping contaminated fuels. Water, dirt, or air mixed with the fuel will add to the building of static electricity;
- Do not allow fuel to fall free through the air to the tank bottom;
- Reduce the flow rate where possible. This decreases turbulence and allows more time for the static charge to leak away; and
- Follow standard grounding and bonding procedures as shown on Table 8.4, "Aircraft Grounding and Bonding Procedures."

TABLE 8.4—AIRCRAFT GROUNDING AND BONDING PROCEDURES

FUELING FROM TANKERS

- Connect grounding cable from truck to ground;
- Connect grounding cable from ground to aircraft;
- Bond vehicle to aircraft, either with "Y" or separate bonding cable;
- Bond fuel nozzle to aircraft before opening aircraft filler cap; and
- Disconnect grounding cables in reverse order upon completion.

FUELING FROM HYDRANTS

- Connect grounding cable from dispenser to aircraft;
- For over-the-wing refueling, bond grounding cable from hose nozzle to aircraft before removing aircraft tank cap;
- For under-the-wing fueling discharge electricity by touching nozzle to aircraft prior to connecting; and
- A ground wire is not necessary.

Source: FAA, *Aircraft Ground Handling and Servicing*, AC 00-34 (1972); and *Aircraft Fuel Storage, Handling and Dispensing On Airports*, AC 150/5230-4 (1982).

Adequate control of static discharge requires *grounding rods*. Satisfactory grounding rods may have an acceptable resistance as high as 10,000 ohms, but usually a much lower resistance is readily attainable. Electrodes of pipes or rods 1/2-inch to 3/4-inch in diameter, of galvanized iron, steel or copper-weld steel, driven into the ground, are customarily used as permanently installed ground rods. The usual depth for a grounding rod is six feet below the surface, but may be a minimum of three feet in depth, or may be greater than six feet in order to reach below the permanent ground moisture level. The top of the rod should be flush with the apron, but within a dished-out area to give easy access to the top of the rod, without causing a trip hazard. As an alternative to electrodes driven into the ground, aircraft tie-down bolts may be used if they provide adequate resistance.

Ohms testing of permanently installed electrodes is normally conducted only once at installation and need not be tested periodically unless damaged. Alternative grounding points such as tie-down bolts should be tested annually during the dry season. Usable grounding points should be marked as such by circling each spot with a painted red ring and indicating the date of the last ohms check.

AIRPORT EMERGENCY PLAN

The *Airport Emergency Plan* [AEP] must be an integral part of the ACM.[45] It must insure prompt response to all emergencies and other unusual conditions in order to minimize the possibility and extent of personal injury and property damage on the airport. And it must be sufficiently detailed to provide guidance to all personnel required during disasters and large-scale emergencies. Coordination and other arrangements for mutual assistance from outside agencies are essential.

Under Part 139, the AEP must demonstrate the airport's readiness for a response to each of the following potential emergencies:[46]

- Aircraft incidents and accidents;
- Bomb incidents, including designation of parking areas for the aircraft involved;
- Structural fires;
- Fires at fuel farms or fuel storage areas;

---

[45] Information in this section was drawn largely from FAR Part 139.325.
[46] *Id.*

- Natural disaster;
- Hazardous materials/dangerous goods incidents;
- Sabotage, hijack incidents, and other unlawful interference with operations;
- Failure of power for movement area lighting; and
- Water rescue situations, as appropriate.

An airport's emergency plan must provide, to the extent practicable, for transportation and medical assistance for the maximum number of persons that can be carried on board the largest air carrier aircraft the airport can be reasonably expected to serve. Coordination for medical services is particularly necessary. The combined ambulances of a surrounding group of communities may be insufficient in number to adequately transport all the victims of a major air crash.[47]

The AEP must identify all hospitals, medical facilities, surface vehicles that will be used to transport or house injured or deceased person. Rescue squads, ambulance services, military installations, or government agencies may provide these. In addition, facilities that will be used to house or treat injured or deceased person must be identified along with plans for crowd control and removal of disabled aircraft. Emergency alarm or notification systems and coordination efforts between the airport and air traffic control should be discussed in the AEP along with community and media notification procedures.[48]

Controlling an emergency scene is a difficult task and hard to envision if an airport is relying upon a "tabletop" exercise environment where individuals practice their parts by meeting for a few hours in a room and speaking their part of the response.[49]

> *Dealing with causalities is one of the most challenging parts of an emergency response to prepare for. Event the most detailed tabletop exercise can't give the responders a sense of the conditions and difficulties they will encounter when the real bodies are waiting on the site of an airport emergency, safety officials acknowledge.*

---

[47] *Id.*

[48] *Id.*

[49] Sean Broderick, *Aircraft Rescue and Firefighting: Burn to Learn*, Airport Magazine (Jan./Feb. 2005).

According to William Wilkinson, SFO Manager, Emergency Operations and Planning, when San Francisco International Airport [SFO] held its annual emergency exercise in 2004, several significant lessons were learned:[50]

- Establish positive perimeter control as "ambulatory persons evacuating the aircraft will tend to keep going as far and fast as they can from the crash" and distancing them from needed treatment;
- Confirm that commonly used supplies (such as backboards) are in stock at all times; and
- Ensure that cleared (or "Green") patients don't mix with potentially contaminated (or "Yellow") patients.

Some of most common problems noted at emergency exercises or "disaster drills" center on communications and interagency coordination. Often, drill participants have radios that are not interoperable. Or, radio traffic on the emergency frequency may become so saturated that radios become ineffective. Ambient noise associated with the disaster scene (helicopter and vehicle traffic and other noise) may prevent participants from hearing their radios. Cell phones may be obtained and/or used, but batteries may quickly be discharged.

Multiple *command vans* (representing aviation, fire and police interests) may arrive on scene and each may compete to be the hub for information exchange. Even if an aircraft incident or accident occurs somewhere else in the country, the airport communications center may be overwhelmed with calls about the affected flight or loved ones.

The variety of unexpected observations witnessed at aviation disaster sites in the past give some indication of the range of potential problems one might face during such an emergency. Members of the media may attempt to crawl over the perimeter fence or pretend to be a responder to get better access to the disaster. Individuals may attempt to carry away pieces of the wreckage as souvenirs, without understanding the importance of these objects for passenger identification. Unscrupulous individuals may feign religious or disaster relief organization affiliation to gain access to the site and the "action."

All potentially involved parties must review the plan annually. Class I airports must also hold a full-scale airport emergency plan ex-

---

[50] *Id.*

ercise at least once every three years. The Airport Emergency Plan should be coordinated with both the FAA and the Transportation Security Administration to ensure that the specified emergency procedures are consistent with the airport's approved security plan. Federal Aviation Administration Advisory Circulars contain methods and procedures for the development of an airport emergency plan that are acceptable to the Administrator.[51]

AIRPORT SELF-INSPECTION

Airports are required to conduct self-inspections, and then be held accountable for assuring that Part 139 airfield inspections are conducted by trained personnel, that associated records are kept, that discovered discrepancies are corrected, and that communication occurs rapidly in the event that a problem cannot be immediately correct.[52]

Inspections should be done daily (both in the daylight and nighttime, if air carriers will be operating during those conditions). Also special inspection should be conducted following aircraft emergencies, during construction activities, in adverse meteorological conditions, or when any other unusual conditions that might affect the safe operation of air carrier aircraft.[53]

Self inspectors should be trained in airport familiarization (including airport signs, marking and lighting), the Airport Emergency Plan, the issuance of Notices to Airman, and the airport's procedures for ground vehicles and pedestrians in both the safety and movement areas. Inspection records must be maintained for a year, including any discrepancies found and the corrective action taken. Training records are to be maintained for two years.

PEDESTRIANS AND GROUND VEHICLE OPERATIONS

Numerous accidents and incidents occur every year on airports involving aircraft and ground vehicles.[54] The chapter of the Airport Cer-

[51] *Id. at 47.*

[52] This section is drawn from FAR Part 130.327.

[53] *Id.*

[54] This section is drawn heavily from FAA Office of Airport Safety and Standards, *A Guide to Ground Vehicle Operations on the Airport* (Aug. 1990); and FAA Office of Airport Safety and Standards, *Operating Your Airport Safely: Ideas and Practices* (Mar. 1991).

tification Manual dealing with pedestrians and ground vehicle operations should clearly describe how the airport operator,

- limits access to movement areas and safety areas only to those pedestrians and ground vehicles necessary for airport operations;
- establishes and implements procedures for the safe and orderly access to, and operation in, movement areas and safety areas by pedestrians and ground vehicles, including provisions identifying the consequences of noncompliance with the procedures by an employee, tenant, or contractor; and
- when an air traffic control tower is in operation, how the airport operator ensures that each pedestrian and ground vehicle in movement areas or safety areas is controlled by either two-way radio, is under escort by a someone two-way radio communication., or is controlled by signs, signals, or guards, when it is not operationally practical to have two-way radio communications.

The airport operator must also ensure that each employee, tenant, or contractor is properly trained on airfield procedures and that the training records are maintained for two years. In addition, all accidents or incidents in the movement or safety areas must be maintained for at least a year.

Runway and other movement area incursions are a serious concern at airports. [55] The FAA defines a "runway incursion" as "any occurrence in the airport runway environment involving an aircraft, vehicle, person, or object on the ground that creates a collision hazard or results in a loss of required separation with an aircraft taking off, intending to take off, landing, or intending to land."[56]

The following classifications of runway incursions are recognized by the FAA: [57]

[55]FAA (2006), retrieved from http://www.faa.gov/aso/Runway_Safety/runway_incursions.htm.

[56] FAA Office of Runway Safety (2006), retrieved from http://www.faa.gov/runwaysafety/.

[57] *Id.* at 51. The FAA notes, "All runway incursions are surface incidents, but not all surface incidents are runway incursions. To qualify as a runway incursion, an aircraft that is taking off, intending to take off, landing, or intending to land must encounter both of the following conditions: (1) at least one aircraft, vehicle, pedestrian, or object must be on the runway; and (2) a collision hazard or a loss of separation must occur."

- *Operational Error* [OE]—A failure of the air traffic control system that results in loss of separation;
- *Pilot Deviation* [PD]—The action of a pilot that results in violation of the Federal Aviation Regulations.
- *Vehicle/Pedestrian Deviation* [V/PD]—Any entry or movement on the movement area by a vehicle (including aircraft operated by non-pilots) or pedestrian that has not been authorized by air traffic control.

The FAA identified three major contributory causes of runway incursions including a lack of communication, a lack of airport familiarization, and poor cockpit procedures for maintaining orientation. Problems in each of these areas can be experience by pilots and ground vehicle operators alike.

From the perspective of ground vehicle operators, the first step in preventing incursions and related accidents is to limit access to the air movement area to only vehicles having a real need to be there, and to equip those vehicles with adequate communications equipment. The second step is to train drivers in the use of proper procedures for maintaining orientation and separation. A third step is to conspicuously mark and identify vehicles that will normally have access to the airfield or will be used to escort other vehicles.

Ground vehicles in movement areas should be marked with orange and white-checkered flags and/or with flashing amber beacons or strobe lights. The vehicles should be equipped with good quality radios to ensure reliability. And the radios should have sufficient output power and be equipped with frequency bands as appropriate to communicate with air traffic control, airport fire fighting and rescue services, airport security, and with airport administration.

Pilots, too, can benefit from Runway Incursion awareness. Below are several recommendations:[58]

---

[58] Information was taken from AC 91-73, *Part 91 Pilot and Flight Crew Procedures during Taxi Operations*, and *Part 135 Single-pilot Operations*. According to the FAA these sources provide "guidelines for the development and implementation of standard pilot procedures for conducting safe aircraft operations on the airport surface [and focus] on the activities occurring on the flight deck/cockpit (*e.g.*, planning, communicating, coordinating), as opposed to the actual control of the aircraft (*e.g.*, climbing, descending, maneuvering). Although there are many similarities, taxi operations for single piloted aircraft, as opposed to taxi operations for aircraft that require more than one pilot, present distinct challenges and requirements." This information was taken from *FAA Aviation News* (Nov./Dec. 2003). In addition, runway safety guidance is located at http://www.faa.gov/runwaysafety/cockpit.cfm.

- Read back all runway crossing and/or hold short instructions;
- Review airport layouts as part of preflight planning and before descending to land and while taxiing as needed;
- Know airport signage;
- Review Notices to Airmen information on runway/taxiway closures and construction areas;
- Do not hesitate to request progressive taxi instructions from Air Traffic Control [ATC] when unsure of the taxi route;
- Check for traffic before crossing any Runway Hold Line and before entering a taxiway;
- Turn on aircraft lights and rotating beacon or strobe lights while taxiing;
- When landing, clear the active runway as quickly as possible then wait for taxi instructions before further movement;
- Study and use proper radio phraseology as described in the *Aeronautical Information Manual* in order to respond to and understand ground control instructions; and
- Write down complex taxi instructions at unfamiliar airports.

Standard operating procedures for vehicle operation on the airfield should be developed by airport administration and published in a format available for all employees and contractors to read. Vehicle operators should abide by these rules and regulations. To ensure compliance drivers should be thoroughly familiar with the airport layout. And they should undergo driver training and licensing as appropriate. Aside from the published regulations, there are some basic rules to abide by including conformance to speed limits, being aware of blind/dead spots on the airport, knowing and using accepted terminology, monitoring appropriate frequencies, and ensuring open communications are maintained with the ATC tower.

Air traffic control tower "Light Gun Signals" (Table 8.5) and a proper "Glossary of Terminology" (Table 8.6) are presented on the following two pages. In addition, proper communications at airports generally entail the use of phonetics for aviation as shown in Table 8.7, "Phonetic Alphabet."

Table 8.5—LIGHT GUN SIGNALS

Color and Type of Signal	*Movement of Vehicles, Equip, and Personnel*	*Aircraft on the Ground*	*Aircraft in Flight*
Steady Green	Cleared to cross, proceed or go	Cleared for takeoff	Cleared to land
Flashing Green	Not applicable	Cleared for taxi	Return for landing (to be followed by steady green at proper time)
Steady Red	Stop	Stop	Give way to aircraft; continue circling
Flashing Red	Clear the taxiway/ runway	Taxi clear of runway in use	Airport unsafe; do not land
Flashing White	Return to starting point	Return to starting point on airport	Not applicable on airport
Alternating Red and Green	Exercise extreme caution	Exercise extreme caution	Exercise extreme caution

Source: FAA, *Aeronautical Information Manual* (2005).

Table 8.6—GLOSSARY OF TERMINOLOGY

- ***Acknowledge***—Let me know that you have received my message.
- ***Advise intentions***—Tell me what you plan to do.
- ***Affirmative***—Yes.
- ***Final***—Commonly used to mean that an aircraft is on final approach course or is aligned with a landing area.
- ***Hold***—Stay in place, where you are currently located.
- ***How do you hear me?*** —A question relating to the quality of the transmission or to determine how well the transmission is being received.
- ***Immediately***—Used by ATC when such action compliance is required to avoid an imminent situation.
- **Negative**—No, or permission not granted, or that is not correct.
- ***Out***—The conversation is ended and no response is expected.
- ***Over***—My transmission is ended; I expect a response.
- ***Proceed***—Authorization to begin/continue on authorized routes.
- ***Read Back***—Repeat my message back to me.
- ***Roger***—I have received all of our last transmission. It should not be used to answer a question requiring a yes or a no answer.
- ***Say again***—Used to request a repeat of the last transmission or portion thereof not understood or received.
- ***Speak slower***—Used as a request to reduce speech rate.
- ***Stand by***—Means the person speaking must pause for a few seconds, also means to wait.
- ***That is correct***—The understanding you have is right.
- ***Unable***—Indicate inability to comply with a specific instruction, request, or clearance.
- ***Verify***—Request confirmation of information.
- ***Without delay***—With a sense of urgency, proceed with approved instruction in a rapid manner.
- ***Wilco***—I have received your message, understand it, and will comply.

Source: FAA, *A Guide to Ground Vehicle Operations on the Airport* (Aug. 1990).

Table 8.7—PHONETIC ALPHABET

A	Alpha	N	November	0	Zero
B	Bravo	O	Oscar	1	Wun
C	Charlie	P	Papa	2	Too
D	Delta	Q	Quebec (Kay-bec)	3	Tree
E	Echo	R	Romeo	4	Fow-er
F	Foxtrot	S	Sierra	5	Fife
G	Golf	T	Tango	6	Six
H	Hotel	U	Uniform	7	Sev-en
I	India	V	Victor	8	Ait
J	Juliett	W	Whiskey	9	Nin-er
K	Kilo	X	X-ray		
L	Lima	Y	Yankee		
M	Mike	Z	Zulu		

WILDLIFE HAZARD MANAGEMENT

Airports desiring air carrier services must actively monitor and mitigate wildlife hazards.[59] In fact, entire conferences are held on the issue of wildlife management and a federally funded wildlife tracking website has been established. The Wildlife Hazard Management section of FAR Part 139 continues to evolve, even in the latest revision in 2004. Part 139 requires a Wildlife hazard assessment whenever any of the following occur:[60]

- An air carrier aircraft experiences multiple wildlife strikes;
- An air carrier aircraft experiences substantial damage (such as structural damage) from striking wildlife;
- An air carrier aircraft experiences an engine ingestion of wildlife; or
- Wildlife of a size, or in numbers, capable of causing one of the above events is observed at or near the airport.

A "wildlife damage management biologist" with professional training and/or airport experience (or someone directly supervised by such

[59] This section was drawn largely from FAR Part 139.337.
[60] *Id.*

an expert) must complete this assessment.[61] The wildlife hazard assessment contains analysis of the trigger events; identification of the wildlife and behaviors involved; identification of local habitats that might entice wildlife to/near the airport; a description of the hazard to air carrier ops; and recommended mitigation strategies. The FAA Administrator both approves the assessment and determines (in conjunction with users) whether a wildlife hazard management plan is needed.[62] Wildlife management is discussed in detail in Chapter 6.

A wildlife hazard management plan, if needed, must "provide measures to alleviate or eliminate wildlife hazards to air carrier operations," be approved by the Administrator and becomes part of the Airport Certification Manual. The Plan must identify roles, resources and the prioritization of three important goals: wildlife population management, habitat modification and land use changes. The plan, to be reviewed annually, must also establish how communication will occur between wildlife controllers/observer and air traffic controllers.[63]

AIRPORT CONDITION REPORTING

The management of a public-use civil landing area or airport is responsible for making known (as soon as practical) any condition on or in the vicinity of the airport, existing or anticipated, which would prevent, restrict, or present a hazard to aircraft. Airports certified under FAR Part 139 are subject to certain requirements for dissemination of information concerning conditions on and in the vicinity of their airports that may affect the safe operation of aircraft.

Public notification is normally accomplished by issuing a Notice to Airmen. The same notification coverage should be made when the condition has been corrected or otherwise changed. "Notice to Airmen" refers to information not known sufficiently in advance to publicize by other means concerning the establishment, condition, or change in any component (facility, service, or procedure) of, or hazard in the *National Airspace System* [NAS]. The NOTAM system disseminates information on unanticipated or temporary changes to components of, or hazards in, the NAS until the associated aeronautical charts and related publications have been amended.

---

[61] *Id.*
[62] *Id.*
[63] *Id.*

Airport operators are responsible for providing the appropriate air traffic control facility, normally the associated *Flight Service Station* [FSS] listed in the *Airport Facility Directory*, with a list of employees authorized to furnish NOTAM information. Flight Service specialists are responsible for the classification, accuracy, format, dissemination, and cancellation of NOTAM (D) and NOTAM (L) information. "NOTAM (L)" means dissemination locally by the FSS to the area affected by the aid, service, or hazard being advertised. "NOTAM (D)" means, in addition to local dissemination, transmission will be made beyond the area of responsibility of the FSS. "Airport NOTAM (D) Service Qualification" means that the airport has been designated to receive NOTAM (D) dissemination for certain reportable data elements.

While airport operators are not responsible for determining how a NOTAM is disseminated, they should be aware of the criteria, which the FSS must apply in making that determination. As a general rule, the actual circulation an airport condition report results from the nature of the reported item and the NOTAM service qualification of the airport.

Examples of concerns to be reported via NOTAM are as follows:

- Commissioning or decommissioning of *landing areas* or portions thereof;
- *Airport closure*—total or for only certain categories of aircraft;
- *Conditions* that restrict or preclude the use of any portion of a runway or waterway;
- *Braking action* when poor or nil;
- *Snow, ice, slush, or standing water* conditions;
- Change of *runway identification*;
- *Rubber accumulation* on the runways;
- *Aircraft rescue and fire fighting response* restrictions or non-availability on a certificated airport;
- Commissioning, decommissioning, or outages of certain *approach and runway lighting aids*;
- Commissioning, decommissioning, or outages of certain *electronic navigation aids*; or
- *Special data* information.

There are two principal avenues available to the airport operator for the submission of NOTAM material. The most commonly known (and used) method was referred to above, through the local ATC facility (usually the FSS) by telephone, letter or FAX. Wherever possible, official contractions and abbreviations should be used, and the information should be presented in the following order:

- Identify the affected facility and component;
- Describe the condition of the affected facility, which prompted the NOTAM; and
- Define the effective period of the condition.

If the occasion for a NOTAM is known early enough for regular correspondence to serve as the filing medium, the airport is encouraged to mail the submission to the FAA's *National Flight Data Center*. Whichever routing is followed, airport personnel should keep a log of any NOTAM the airport originates, and should maintain its status. The NOTAM status should be a regular checklist item in the daily routine and airport inspection program.

OTHER AIRFIELD CONSIDERATIONS

While not specifically mentioned in the prior discussion relating to the Airport Certification function, a few remaining items are presented in this chapter. Contract towers, aircraft ground handling and ultralight aircraft are of importance to today's airport operators.

CONTRACT TOWERS

As mentioned earlier in this chapter, the provision of refueling service is moving from the private sector toward the new public administration paradigm, as more and more airports are considering becoming the sole fuel-servicing operator on their airports, air traffic control is a service that is becoming privatized. But as it happened with fuel servicing, air traffic control is an area where some analysts are suggesting airport sponsors might be expected to assume more responsibility, just as it has with refueling activities. This begs the question, "Is air traffic control another service being relegated by the Federal government to the local airport sponsor"? And if so, at who's expense?

In 1982, the Federal government began private contracting for air traffic control services at the lowest activity-level (Level I) *Visual Flight Rule* [VFR] airports. In 1994, the *Federal Aviation Administration Contract Tower* [FTC] program was expanded to include the conversion of FAA Level I VFR towers to contract operators.[64] By early 1998 there were 160 FTC locations. And, for fiscal year 1999, Congress fully funded $47.3 million for the FTC program. Congress also approved a new $6 million cost-sharing provision for contract towers that fall below a 1.0 benefit/cost ratio established by the FAA to authorize contracting out services for ATC tower operation.

Although enhanced safety is touted as a reason for contracting ATC services, the primary objective of the FTC program is to reduce costs to the federal government. The private sector has demonstrated that it can operate a Level I tower for about half what it costs the federal government. The FAA's cost per Level I tower in 1998 was about $508,000 versus approximately $253,000 for contract towers.[65] Enthused by the savings, a number of aviation organizations have endorsed the FTC program.[66] They have all concurred that this is one federal program that enhances safety and services to users while reducing their cost to taxpayers.[67]

As with most privatization initiatives, the greatest savings realized from contract towers are in personnel costs. As a result, not everyone, but especially not organized labor fully endorses the program. One issue being closely watched by the *National Air Traffic Controllers Association* [NATCA] is the wage rate paid to contract tower employees. Likewise, determinations by the Department of Labor require payment of prevailing wages at all federally contracted towers. A second issue of concern to NATCA is organization of contract tower workers. In

---

[64] FAA, *Mission Statement for the Federal Aviation Administration Contract Tower Program* (Mar. 4, 1999), retrieved from http://www.faa.gov/ats/ato/ato310.htm.

[65] U.S. Contract Tower Association, *Annual Report* (1998); The cost at the Charlottesville-Albemarle Airport in the mid-1990s was $325,000 versus the federal cost of about $325,000; at the Central Wisconsin Airport the cost was about 230,000 as opposed to the FAA's $500,000-plus estimate; *see also* Karl Bremer, *FAA's Contract Tower Program: Everybody Wins*, Airport Magazine (May/Jun. 1997).

[66] These groups include the AAAE, the Air Transport Association, Regional Airline Association, National Business Aviation Association [NBAA], National Air Transportation Association, General Aviation Manufacturers Association, and the National Association of State Aviation Officials; *see* U.S. Contract Tower Association, *Annual Report* (1998).

[67] Karl Bremer, *FAA's Contract Tower Program: Everybody Wins*, Airport Magazine (May/Jun. 1997), at 19.

February of 1997, controllers at Central Wisconsin Airport, the first federally controlled tower, voted to join the NATCA.[68]

Most towers in the contract program are simply conversions of existing towers from FAA-operated to private contractor-operated. The National Air Traffic Controllers Association attempted in federal court to force the FAA to take back operation of the air traffic control towers that it once operated. Yet, some airports, such as Central Wisconsin Airport in Mosinee, would not have a tower at all if it were not for the FTC program. In other cases, the tower, such as the one at Salina, Kansas, might have been shut down due to budget cuts.[69] Hence, at least at the margins, the FTC is, indeed, enhancing safety as well as saving money.

Overall, the FTC program is operating at least at the level of comparable federally operated towers. In an audit of the FTC program, the DOT Inspector General [IG] concluded that contract towers provide a quality of service comparable to FAA-operated towers and are staffed by controllers who meet the FAA's training requirements. Contract controllers follow appropriate federal aviation regulations and FAA directives. The FAA certifies the contract controllers just as it does its own. And the majority of the contract controller workforce was trained either by the FAA or by the military. Military controllers are certified by the FAA. Anyone working as a controller must hold an FAA-issued *Control Tower Operator* certificate. Additionally, controllers must hold an FAA-issued *facility rating*, demonstrating competence, qualifications and skills required to control air traffic at the tower to which they are assigned.

Not only are contract towers operated as competently as FAA-operated towers, apparently they are as safe. Looking at 84 airports and at air traffic control incidents occurring between 1992 and 1997, the DOT Inspector General identified 14 incident reports when towers were operated by FAA and only 16 incident reports (i.e., about the same) when contractors operated towers.[70]

One of the appealing aspects of the FTC program is its "flexibility." However, as Patrick McCann, a Washington lobbyist with the Wexler Group representing the U.S. Control Tower Operators, that flexibility could somehow be lessened or jeopardized if the controllers are union-

[68] *Id.* at 2.
[69] *Id.* at 19.
[70] U.S. Contract Tower Association, *Annual Report (*1998).

ized and pay scales are made the same as FAA controllers. Another potential threat to the program could be continued cut backs in the federal budget. Yet, according to McCann, the contract tower program could ultimately grow as a result of FAA budget cuts. "As FAA budgets get squeezed, they'll start staffing Level I towers less and less them selves. Under that scenario the program would surely grow." However, the flaw in McCann's hypothesis assumes the cost of staffing contract towers will continue to be borne by the FAA, and not shifted to airports as a further budget-cutting move. Especially the smaller airport sponsors could find it extremely painful if they had to absorb the $300,000 to $400,000 cost of running an air traffic control tower.[71]

AIRCRAFT GROUND HANDLING

Closely related to air traffic control is the subject of ground handling. This may entail taxiing, towing, parking or aircraft tie-down. Once an airplane leaves the air movement area (the active runways and taxiways) and enters the apron area, it becomes airport management's responsibility to insure that ground-handling operations are conducted safely. Either airport personnel or employees of the airlines and fixed base operators will assist pilots in taxiing and storing their aircraft.

Pilots taxiing aircraft in close quarters or on unfamiliar parking ramps will often require the assistance of ground guides who provide guidance through standardized hand and light signals. When directing an aircraft being taxied, the person giving directions should stay far enough ahead and to the left side of an airplane, or to the right side of a helicopter (i.e., to the pilot's side), so the pilot can clearly see the guide and will have no difficulty in following the guide's hand signals. The ground guide should give clear, positive signals, and should adhere to the standard signals shown on Figure 8.1, "Aircraft Operating Signals," and Figure 8.2, "Helicopter Operating Signals."

During darkness, inclement weather, or other periods of reduced visibility, illuminated or reflective wands should be used. In very congested areas it may be advisable to have additional ground guides to insure wing tip clearance.

---

[71] Karl Bremer, *FAA's Contract Tower Program: Everybody Wins*, Airport Magazine (May/Jun. 1997), at 22-23.

Figure 8.1—AIRCRAFT OPERATING SIGNALS

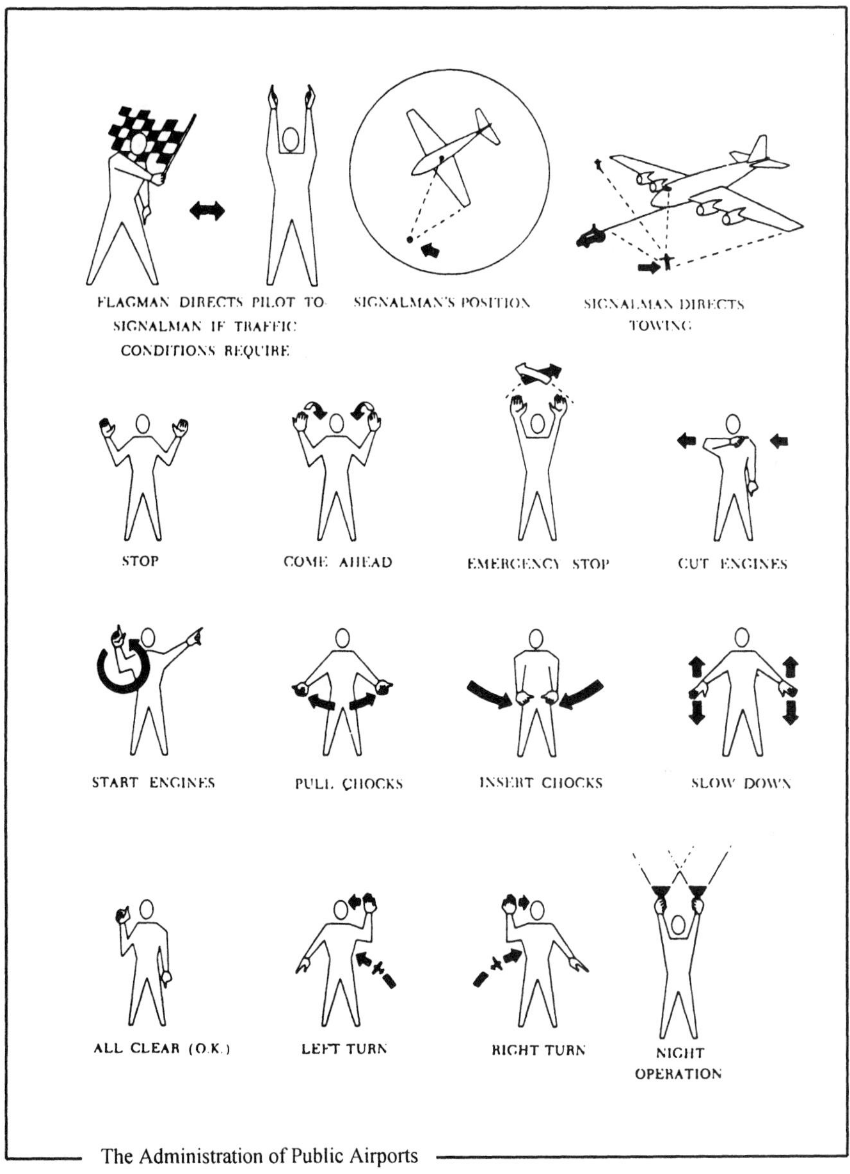

Source: FAA, *Aircraft Ground Handling and Services*, AC 0034.

Figure 8.2—HELICOPTER OPERATING SIGNALS

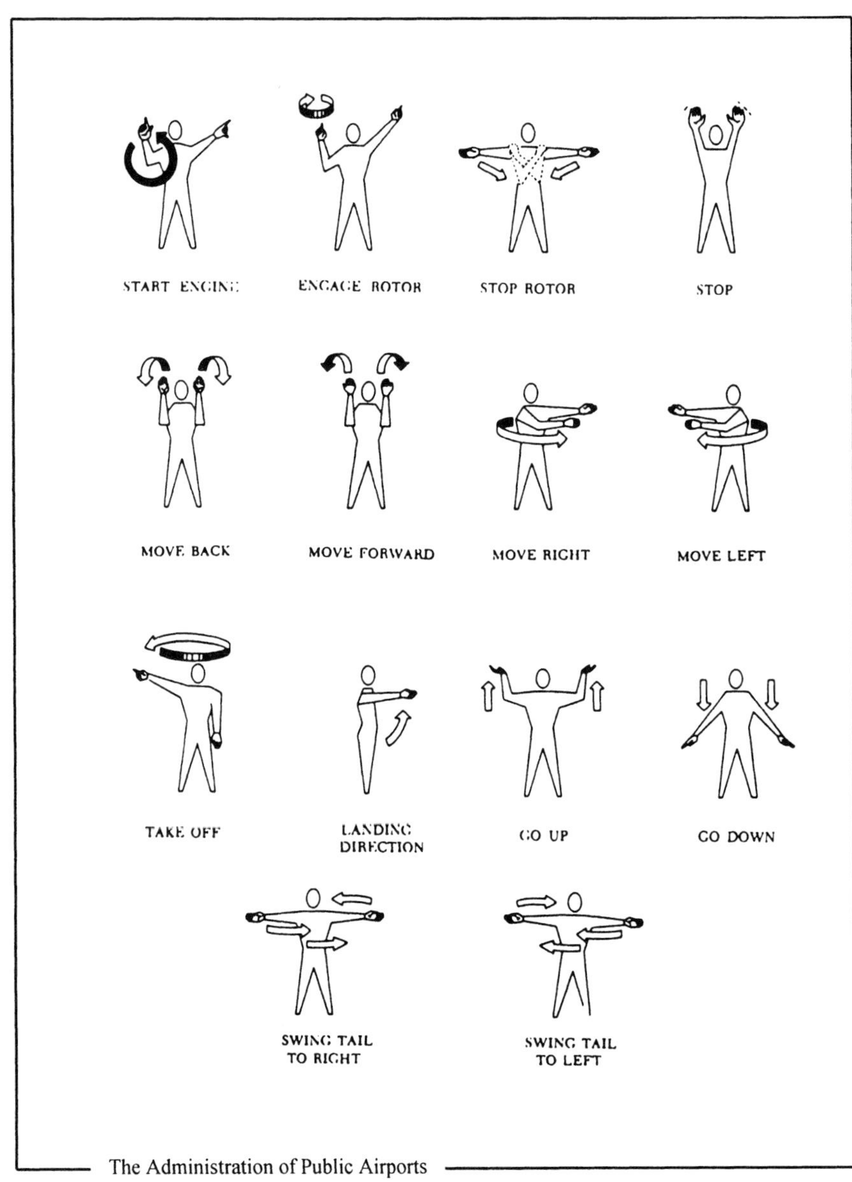

Source: FAA, *Aircraft Ground Handling and Services*, AC 0034.

AIRCRAFT PARKING AND TIE-DOWN

When parking an aircraft it should be chocked fore and aft of its main gear wheels. If it is to remain unattended, or if high winds are expected, the aircraft should be tied down and where possible should have flight control locks installed.

Parking and moving aircraft by hand often necessitates handling the propeller, either to push or pull the airplane, or to reposition the propeller. Before moving or touching the propeller the ignition switches should be checked to insure they are in the "off" position. The airplane, and especially the propeller, is analogous to a gun, which should be "cleared" prior to handling. Certainly, the propeller can be as deadly as a loaded gun. Just as a gun should not be pointed at anyone, one should always stay clear of the propeller blade path, and particular caution should be practiced around warm engines.

Each year numerous aircraft suffer wind damage because they are improperly tied down. Airplanes should be tied down at three points as a minimum. The tie-down ropes should preferably be a synthetic material (polypropylene), one-half inch or larger, and should have at least 3,000 pounds of pull resistance for light, single-engine airplanes; 4,000 pounds for light multi-engine airplanes, and greater pull resistance for larger multi-engine airplanes.

For owners, synthetic materials may be preferred because of their elasticity and non-abrasive qualities. There is less likelihood of damaging the aircraft. Moreover, some aircraft owners may object to the use of chains because they can rust. Nevertheless, some airport managers prefer chains to ropes for ease of handling. If tie-down chains are used, the tensile strength should be increased.

When utilizing ropes, about one inch of play should be allowed, and an anti-slip knot such as a bowline or a square knot should be used. Too much slack allows the aircraft to jerk against the ropes. A rope tied too tightly is easily broken. And it may place inverted stress on the aircraft wing. Only the tie-down rings on the aircraft should be used, never a strut or other part that could be damaged. Ropes should be tied only at ground tie-down rings intended for this purpose, or which are assured can be used safely for tie-down.

ULTRALIGHT VEHICLES

Federal Aviation Regulation Part 103 defines an "ultralight vehicle" as being used or intended for manned operation in the air by a single occupant, intended for sport use, and without a U.S. or foreign airworthiness certificate. If unpowered, it must weigh less than 155 lbs. If powered, it must be less than 254 lbs., carry a maximum of five gallons of fuel, have a maximum speed of 55 knots, and a power-off stall speed of not more than 24 knots. The exception to this rule is the "two place training exemption," which allows a second person on board, so long as one occupant has been deemed qualified to give instruction.[72]

Operationally, ultralight vehicles are handled separately from "other" aircraft. The latter ("aircraft") is defined as a device used for flight. Although ultralight vehicles are indeed intended for use in flight, they do not require FAA registration, an airworthiness certificate, or pilot certification. As a result, they are treated separately and referred to as "vehicles" rather than aircraft.

Development of the modern ultralight vehicle is attributed to John Moody who in 1973 bought a biplane glider. A year-and-a-half later (1975) he rigged a ten-horsepower engine to his glider and using his legs as landing gear became airborne. On a later flight he was observed, and was called by the FAA wanting to know if he was operating an unlicensed airplane. He told them it was a "powered hang glider." It took the FAA six years to make up its mind what to even call the new machines. The controversy over ultralight regulation has never been settled. At airports across the country, attitudes about ultralights have ranged from harmonious integration with normal airport traffic to alienation and a total ban of ultralight operations.

FAA policy with regard to ultralight operations on airports is that,

> *Ultralight vehicle operations are considered an aeronautical activity (FAR Part 103) and, as such, must be normally accommodated on airports, which have been developed with Federal assistance.*[73]

---

[72] Experimental Aircraft Association [EAA], *FAR Part 103 and Ultralight Vehicles: Two Place Training Exemption* (2006), retrieved from http://www.eaa.org/ultralights/far_part103.html.

[73] FAA Administrator, *Airport Compliance Requirements,* FAA Order 5190.6A (Oct. 2, 1989), at 17.

However, this doesn't necessarily mean that they must be operated on conventional runways if ultralight operations can be safely accomplished at a designated ultralight operations area on the airport. An airport operator may make the determination that proposed ultralight operations are unsafe and opt not to allow them to conduct flight operations on the airport.[74] The policy developed relative to ultralight operations at airports is generally applicable to hot air ballooning and parachute drops in the vicinity of an airport. At federally funded airports, the ultimate determination of whether ultralights can safely operate at the airport has been left up to the FAA *Flight Standards District Office* [FSDO] to verify. Non-federally funded airports are not required to accommodate ultralight operations.

The FAA's policy regarding ultralights has been under attack by commercial aviation and by airport operators for years. The American Association of Airport Executives has publicly stated its belief that the FAA should prescribe better training of ultralight pilots for safe operations near airports and that the FAA should encourage the development of separate ultralight parks. The *Air Line Pilots Association* [ALPA] has also supported increased FAA regulation of ultralights.

Ultralights have brought mixed reviews from the general aviation community as well. In some cases, local general aviation operators have ostracized ultralight pilots. At the national level, however, the *Aircraft Owners and Pilots Association* [AOPA] has been a long-time supporter of the ultralight movement, and through its *Flight Safety Foundation* [FSF], it has sponsored a self-regulatory program as an alternative to government regulation.

Ultralights started becoming popular in the mid 1970s, but it was not until 1981 that the FAA proposed rules for governing this segment of aviation. In 1982, FAR Part 103, "Ultralight Vehicles," was promulgated. In essence, FAR Part 103 states that ultralight vehicles are not required to meet airworthiness certification, and ultralight pilots need not meet any aeronautical knowledge, age, or experience requirements nor have airman or medical certificates.

Operational restrictions generally prohibit anyone from operating any ultralight in a manner that creates a hazard. The pilot is to maintain vigilance so as to see and avoid and yield the right-of-way to all aircraft and not operate the ultralight vehicle in a manner that creates a collision hazard. Unless otherwise approved, all ultralight operations

---

[74] *Id.*

are to be conducted in *uncontrolled* airspace during *daylight* hours only.

The philosophy expressed in FAR Part 103 seems to contradict the FAA's regulatory approach. In the words of a past manager of the FAA's General Aviation and Commercial Division, ultralight vehicles are ". . . a large measure of deregulation in a relatively small package." The controversy over ultralights, both internally and externally, led the FAA to defer regulatory action to the private sector via the AOPA and its self-regulatory program. In a letter to the Flight Safety Foundation the FAA stated that based on a review of the ultralight pilot competency and vehicle registration programs submitted by the FSF, it approved the immediate implementation of those programs. The FAA had not yet officially established guidelines of its own for such programs but stated that the FSF had met its (the FAA's) objectives. The approved FSF program was threefold:

- *Pilot competency*, wherein the FAA would recognize, as proof of achievement of a national standard of competency, documents issued under the FSF's ultralight vehicle pilot competency program;
- *Vehicle registration*, wherein the FAA would recognize, on a national basis, registration numbers and vehicle marking requirements issued under the FSF's ultralight vehicle registration program; and
- *Vehicle airworthiness*, wherein the FAA understood that the FSF would submit an ultralight-vehicle airworthiness program in the near future.

By 1984, self-regulating programs calling for airworthiness certification by manufacturers and for vehicle registration and pilot competency by owners and operators were unsuccessful in attracting sufficient participation. The National Transportation Safety Board in early 1985 recommended that the FAA should regulate ultralights, and the pilots who fly them. The NTSB recommended the establishment of minimum requirements for pilots, including a level of knowledge comparable to the general aviation flight rules. The NTSB also recommended FAA registration of all ultralight "aircraft" and that their design and manufacture should be federally regulated as well.

After being criticized by a congressional subcommittee in 1984 for not adopting more stringent ultralight regulations, FAA developed a new ultralight policy in lieu of issuing new rules, which reflected the Congressional as well as NTSB comments. It was anticipated the process of adopting new rules would take at least three years or more to complete. In 1985, AOPA announced it was transferring the Flight Safety Foundation ultralight group to the *U.S. Ultralight Foundation* [USUF], an organization focused on ultralight safety. At the same time, the *U.S. Ultralight Association* [USUA] was formed to promote, protect and represent the industry. Both the USUF and the USUA are located in Frederick, Maryland.

Two decades later, the USUF and USUA continue to represent the ultralight community and bring attention to the needs of the industry. For example, technology has changed considerably, but the weight constraints of the original Part 103 prevent operators from adopting some important safety equipment such as brakes (10 lbs); a self-starter system (36 lbs); improved landing gear system (30 lbs); a gyrocopter pre-rotator system (30 lbs); and a gyrocopter horizontal stabilizer (20 lbs). There is also a push to adjust the weight restrictions to better accommodate those who are physically challenged.[75]

To date, FAR Part 103 remains basically unchanged with the two-place exemption for flight training having been reaffirmed by the FAA in 2004. A series of Advisory Circulars also provide guidance to ultralight operators.[76]

SUMMARY

This chapter reviewed federal regulatory guidance and popular practices relating to airport safety and certification. It touched upon many of the day-to-day operational areas experienced at air carrier airports. The topic of airport operations is a very broad one, encompassing the airside, landside and terminal areas at airports. The next chapter, "Operations: Aviation Security," reviews the extraordinary changes experienced by the industry since entering the age of terrorism in 2001.

---

[75] USUA Staff, *USUA: 20 Years of Service* (Apr. 2005), retrieved from http://www.usua.org/HQNews/Archive/200504.html.

[76] FAA, *Ultralight Vehicle Operations*, AC 103-6; *Ultralight Vehicle*, AC 103-7; *Recommended Airport Traffic Patterns*, AC 90-66A; *Fight Testing Ultralights & Experimental Aircraft*, AC 90-89A; and *Exclusive Rights & Minimum Standards for Aeronautical Activities*, AC 150/5190-5, Change 1.

Landside, terminal and air cargo operations at airports will be explored in Chapter 10.

CHAPTER 9

AIRPORT AND AVIATION SECURITY

Words can't truly capture the events of September 11 and the days that followed, but for commercial aviation, the words "unprecedented," unimaginable" or "surreal" come to mind. The attacks themselves were an indescribable horror, but for airports and airlines, the most unsettling part might have been uncertainty over what was to come.

Avery Vise, Airport Magazine [1]

THE UNIMAGINABLE

Immediately following the tragic events of September 11, 2001, [9/11] airports, airlines and the users could hardly imagine the impact that those events would have on the air transportation industry over the next decade. The impact of 9/11 and subsequent events such as the Heathrow plot of August 2006 have been felt globally and resulted in the expenditure of billions of dollars.[2] For example, in 2007, the Transportation Security Administration [TSA] estimated that in

---

[1] Avery Vise, *Getting the Job Done*, Airport Magazine (Nov./Dec. 2001), at 17.

[2] CNN Staff Reporters, *Police: Plot to Blow Up Aircraft Foiled*, http://www.cnn.com/2006/WORLD/europe/08/10/uk.terror/index.html (Aug. 10, 2006). The 2006 transatlantic aircraft plot was an alleged terrorist plot to detonate liquid explosives carried on board several airliners traveling from the United Kingdom to the United States. The sudden imposition of unprecedented security measures caused chaos and delayed flights for days. *See* Hans Kundnani, *Cost of Airport Upheaval Could Top £300m* (Aug. 22, 2006), The Guardian, UK; *see also* James Sturcke, *US Says 9/11 Suspect Planned Heathrow Attack*, The Guardian, UK, (Sept. 9, 2006).

just three years, their "funding related to aviation security has totaled about $20 billion."[3] The costs associated with increased homeland and aviation security are staggering, and they continue to rise.

Airports, too, have experienced a significant financial strain since 9/11, due to increased labor, technology and infrastructure renovation expenses required to accommodate bigger and heavier security equipment, create TSA personnel break and training rooms, reconfigure passenger queuing and waiting areas, as well as many other changes. Aside from experiencing significant economic instability and a profound level of preparedness vulnerability, airports and their air transportation public and private sector partners witnessed serious erosion in public confidence, convenience and privacy.

This is the second chapter in a series of three that addresses the operational aspects of public airports. The fact that an entire chapter of this book is dedicated to security—when the topic was covered in a few pages in prior editions of this text—is reflective of the massive shift in direction and resources experienced throughout the aviation industry, and in the nation's approach to homeland security. Aviation security is no longer a small component of safety, but rather, is now a seriously considered and fully integrated airport responsibility, as evidenced by increased security personnel, responsibilities and budgetary requirements.

BIRTH OF A NEW NORMAL

Since 9/11, politicians, regulators, airports, aviation industry partners and the traveling public have collectively journeyed toward "a new normal"[4] in the industry, with an aviation security-equilibrium yet to be achieved.[5] American Association of Airport Executives [AAAE] President Charles "Chip" Barclay describes why airports were unprepared in 2001: "We never designed our aviation security systems to withstand a threat from teams of special-operations forces,

---

[3] Government Accountability Office [GAO], GAO-07-448T, Statement of Cathleen A. Berrick, Dir. of Homeland Security and Justice Issues, Testimony before the Subcommittee on Homeland Security, Committee on Appropriations, House of Representatives, *Aviation Security: Progress Made in Systematic Planning to Guide Key Investment Decisions, but More Work Remains*, http://www.gao.gov/new.items/d07448t.pdf (visited Feb. 13, 2007), at. 2.

[4] *Moving toward a New Normal*, Airport Magazine (Nov./Dec. 2001).

[5] This section draws heavily from Robin Sobotta & Laurence Gesell, *Airport and Aviation Security Addendum to The Administration of Public Airports* (4th ed. 1999); and from Laurence E. Gesell & Paul Dempsey, *Air Transportation: Foundations for the 21st Century* (2nd ed. 2005).

comprised of trained suicide pilots, trained for years, with the goals of using the plane as a bomb."[6] The opposition in this clash of ideologies has proven to be both nimble and creative, taking full advantage of the vulnerabilities that arise from social freedoms and robust economic exchange inherent to free-market, democratic societies.

Laurence Gesell and Paul Dempsey explain the difficult nature of the adversary:

> *The first major conflict of the 21st Century came with a new twist: the enemy has no border, no organized army, nor does it have a recognized government. Rather, it hides in the shadows, its uniform is a hooded mask, and like a cancer it has organized cells all over the world from which it carries out its insidious operations. Its dominant motivation is hatred, with the United States as the focus of that loathing. And, it is willing to do anything, including commit suicide, to inflict pain and suffering upon the innocent.*[7]

On September 11, 2001, the "enemy" struck the financial and military centers of America, commandeering fuel-laden jet transports. Nineteen cold blooded killers wearing a martyr's blind boarded four commercial aircraft, hijacked them armed only with box cutters, and then sacrificed their lives by flying two of the planes into the World Trade Center and the third into the Pentagon. Thanks to the quick action and bravery of vigilante passengers aboard the fourth aircraft—likely destined for another economically or politically significant U.S. target—the plane crashed into an open field in the Pennsylvania countryside. Although all aboard perished, luckily there were no injuries

---

[6] Charles Barclay, *Never the Same*, Airport Magazine (Nov./Dec. 2001), at 9.

[7] Although at first glance the movement of radical Islamism has no purpose beyond hatred, one theory suggests that this is but the latest innovation on guerilla warfare; that is to say, engagement in irregular warfare, especially from independent units. The purpose is, as it has always been, to gain power, authority and control—in this case over the Middle East. That once regimes (such as the Royal Saudi Family) are toppled and Western influence is driven from the lands of Islam, what may be described now only as a "criminal conspiracy" will one day coalesce and seek conversion to legitimacy as a recognized governmental authority. *See* Laurence E. Gesell & Paul Stephen Dempsey, *Air Transportation: Foundations for the 21st Century* (2nd ed. 2005).

on the ground. Nevertheless, the few martyrs left aboard the other three aircraft managed to do more damage in less than an hour than did the wave of Japanese airplanes in their attack at Pearl Harbor on December 7, 1941. As reported in *U.S. News & World Report*, "There was fire and smoke everywhere. It was surreal."[8] The attack left 3,212 people dead and reduced the World Trade Center to rubble.[9]

Although the kamikaze-type attack, using fuel-laden wide-body aircraft, shocked many people both in and out of government, it should not have come with such surprise. To have not seen it coming was a "failure of imagination" by U.S. intelligence agencies that made the nation vulnerable to such strikes, reported the National Commission on Terrorist Attacks Upon the United States (hereinafter the 9/11 Commission).[10]

When it comes to blame, the 9/11 Commission laid it equally on two administrations. "Both Presidents Bill Clinton and George Bush . . . told us they got the picture—they understood [Osama] bin Laden was a danger," the commission's report said. "But given the character and pace of their policy efforts, we (the Commission) do not believe they fully understood just how many people al Qaeda might kill, and how soon it might do so." Although it never stated that the attack could have been prevented, the commission report enumerated missed opportunities, especially by the Central Intelligence Agency and Federal Bureau of Investigation.[11]

This was, of course, not the first attempt by a terrorist to hijack an aircraft. In fact, multiple incidences of terrorism involving aircraft have been previously recorded.[12] Nor, to the surprise of many experts, was it the first attempt to hijack an American aircraft for use as a weapon—in and of itself—against a targeted facility. In fact, on at least two prior occasions, aircraft were the selected weapon in unsuccessful crash attempts. One was an attempt by Sam Byck in 1974 to

---

[8] *Id.*

[9] Scot J. Paltrow & Greg Hitt, *Final 9/11 Report Urges and Avoids Blame*, Wall St. J. (Fri., Jul. 23, 2004), at A3.

[10] The National Commission on Terrorist Attacks Upon the U.S. was established in Nov. 2002 to look into almost all aspects of the 9/11 attacks, largely under pressure from families of 9/11 victims who demanded an inquiry. The Bush White House, fearing the possible impact of such a report critical of its handling of the crisis coming out amid the presidential election campaign, blocked the panel's creation for more that a year, until congressional support for an inquiry persuaded the administration to relent. Scot J. Paltrow & Greg Hitt, *Final 9/11 Report Urges and Avoids Blame*, Wall St. J. (Fri., Jul. 23, 2004), at A3.

[11] *Id.*

[12] Kathleen Sweet, *Terrorism and Airport Security* (2002).

kill Richard Nixon by hijacking a Delta DC-9 and crashing it into the White House.[13] The other incident should have given clear warning to intelligence agencies of the distinct possibility of using a large turbo-jet transport as a weapon, even for a suicidal mission.[14] In 1994, Auburn Calloway, a disgruntled pilot employee tried to hijack a DC-10 cargo jet and crash it into the Federal Express headquarters in Memphis.[15] In flight, the distraught employee went after the two pilots with a hammer. During the bloody encounter the captain was able to subdue the assailant long enough to get the aircraft safely on the ground. The notoriety of the event surely should have given federal agencies warning of such possibilities by terrorist groups.

Moreover, official assertions before September 11, 2001, that the U.S. had little reason to suspect that airliners would be used as weapons would appear to be disingenuous. More recent evidence suggests that the federal government had on several earlier occasions taken elaborate, secret measures to protect special events from just such an attack, including the 1966 Atlanta Olympics, and President George W. Bush's inauguration in 2001. In addition, planning for the 2002 Winter Olympics in Utah was underway at the time of the 9/11 attacks, and included such measures. The 9/11 Commission found it curious and wanted to know why the fear of an airborne attack didn't lead to more generalized permanent measures to protect against it.[16]

NATIONAL STRATEGY FOR AVIATION SECURITY

In response to the continuing aviation security concern, the Secretary of Homeland Security was charged by Presidential Directive to create a comprehensive National Strategy for Aviation Security. In March of 2007, the Strategy was released and pronounced, "The security and economic prosperity of the United States depend significantly upon the secure operation of its aviation system and use of the world's airspace by the Nation, its international partners and legiti-

[13] *See* James Clark, *American Assassins: The Darker Side of Politics* (1982).
[14] *See* Robin Sobotta & Laurence E. Gesell, *Airport and Aviation Security Addendum* (2003), to Laurence E. Gesell, The Administration of Public Airports (1999).
[15] The Learning Channel, from the video presentation of *Sky Crimes*, http://www.tlc.discovery.com (visited 1999).
[16] Scot J. Paltrow, *Kamikaze Terrorism Wasn't a New Idea*, Wall St. J. (Thur., Apr. 1, 2004), at A4.

mate commercial interests."[17] The Strategy is designed to align Federal government aviation security programs with those at the state, local and tribal levels to create *layered aviation security.*

The Strategy further states, "Aviation security is best achieved by integrating public and private aviation security global activities into a coordinated effort to detect, deter, prevent and defeat threats to the *Air Domain*, reduce vulnerabilities, and minimize consequences of, and expedite the recovery from attacks that might occur." The air domain is defined as "the global airspace, including domestic, international, and foreign airspace, as well as all manned and unmanned aircraft operating, and people and cargo present in that airspace, and all aviation-related infrastructures.[18] In addition to the Strategy, seven supporting aviation security plans were also released, including:

- Aviation Transportation Security Plan;
- Aviation Operational Threat Response Plan;
- Aviation Transportation System Recovery Plan;
- Air Domain Surveillance and Intelligence Integration Plan;
- International Aviation Threat Reduction Plan;
- Domestic Outreach Plan; and
- International Outreach Plan. [19]

The Strategy discusses a number of items including threats to the air domain, strategic objectives, strategic actions, and roles/responsibilities. It also identifies, threat originators, threat categories, strategic objectives and actions. The three *Threat Originators* identified in the Strategy are *terrorist groups*, *hostile nation-states* and *criminals*. The three *Primary Categories of Threats* are threats to and from aircraft, threats to the aviation transportation system infrastructure, and threats from hostile exploitation of cargo. While terminologies used in the Strategy may be new, the threats have been around for years, as discussed in the next section.[20]

---

[17] Dept. of Homeland Security, *The National Strategy for Aviation Security* (Mar. 26, 2007) at 2, retrieved from www.dhs.gov.

[18] *Id.*

[19] *Id.*

[20] *Id. at* 8-11.

HISTORY OF HIJACKINGS

Like few other commercial activities, an airline embodies the national symbol of the country whose flag it flies.[21] Its existence, and its routes and other commercial activities are a product of national oversight and regulation.[22] For some nations, aviation is a symbol of national aspirations of pride, prestige and global penetration. Moreover, commercial aviation disasters—whether incidental or accidental—are uniquely treated by the media as singular events, commanding the front pages of newspapers, the cover stories of news magazines, and the lead stories of television news broadcasting. For all these reasons, commercial aircraft have been prominent targets of terrorist attacks.[23]

Terrorism has become the nightmare of the modern world. The means by which terrorism manifests itself are as brutal as they are imaginative. They include hijacking aircraft, firing heat-seeking missiles at them, bombing aircraft and airport waiting lounges, gunning down passengers at airports, and more recently, turning aircraft into guided missiles aimed at financial and governmental institutions.

Terrorism is but a symptom of a more pernicious disease. It is the disease of the militarily weak, the politically frustrated, and the religiously fanatic. The Palestinians, the Catholic Irish, the Basques, the Kurds, and a hundred other tribes passionately embrace the natural law imperative of a national homeland. The Islamic Jihad, the Taliban and al Qaeda heed the fundamentalist cry of a supposedly angry God. The Red Army Faction, the Baader-Meinhof Gang and other cells of anarchy aspire to a Marxist utopia. With the prospect of a political solution out of reach, they each suffer from the same malaise that inspires indiscriminate aggression. Anger mixed with desperation can produce a lethal cocktail. Hence, hijacking and other forms of aerial terrorism have developed as a means for the militarily weak to

---

[21] Under "effective ownership and control" requirements, an airline flies the flag of the nation in which it is registered. This contrasts sharply with the "flags of convenience" and "freedom of the seas" principles dominant in international maritime law. Paul Dempsey & Lisa Helling, *Oil Pollution by Ocean Vessels: An Environmental Tragedy: The Legal Regime of Flags of Convenience Multilateral Conventions and Coastal States*, 10 Den. J. Int'l L. & Pol. 37 (1980); Paul Dempsey, *Compliance and Enforcement in International Law: Oil Pollution of the Marine Environment by Ocean Vessels*, 6 N.W. J. Int'l L. & Bus. 459-561 (1984).

[22] Paul Dempsey, Robert Hardaway & William Thoms, *Aviation Law & Regulation* (two volumes 1993).

[23] This section is taken largely from Paul Stephen Dempsey & Laurence E. Gesell, *Air Commerce and the Law* Ch. 15 (2004).

achieve political ends at the expense of the innocent. As Professor McWhinney has observed:

> *The advantages of hijacking . . . as a weapon for achieving major national political objectives by non-military means, have been the unusually small expenditure of money and energy and lives that such action seems to have involved . . . the relative ease with which it has been able to be effected; the enormous international publicity for one's political programme that it has managed to engender; and finally . . . the certain element of perverse sympathy that the hijackings seem to have evoked in many quarters.*[24]

During the infancy of civil aviation, a passenger's principal concerns were the skill of the pilot and the condition of the aircraft. Recent decades have added a third—whether or not a fellow passenger intends to use the occasion to focus the media's attention on a revolutionary cause. The hijacking or destruction of an aircraft is still among the most effective means of capturing a worldwide audience. Professor Paul Wilkinson points out that, "By the end of the 1980s aviation terrorism rivaled technical failure and pilot error as a cause of fatalities in civil aviation."[25]

Hijackings account for the largest percentage of all attacks against civil aviation.[26] Other criminal acts involve: (1) airport attacks;[27] (2) bombings, attempted bombings, and shootings on civil aviation aircraft;[28] (3) commandeering of aircraft;[29] (4) general and charter avia-

---

[24] Edward McWhinney, *Aerial Piracy and International Law* 17 (1971). Prof. McWhinney was then Dir. of McGill University's Institute of Air & Space Law.

[25] Paul Wilkinson, *Terrorism Versus Democracy—The Liberal State Response* (2001).

[26] *U.S. Federal Aviation Administration, Criminal Acts Against Civil Aviation* 3 (2001).

[27] In the 1970s, airports in Tel Aviv and Athens were attacked; in the 1980s, airports in Rome, Munich and Vienna were attacked.

[28] The bombing of Air India flight 182 over the Irish Sea by Sikh separatists, killing all 329 aboard, and the bombing of Pan Am flight 103 over Lockerbie, Scotland, by operatives of the Libyan government, killing all 259 aboard, are notorious examples of explosions that destroyed commercial aircraft. North Korea is also widely believed responsible for a 1987 explosion of a Korean Airlines flight 858 over the Andaman Sea near Burma that killed all 115 passengers and crew aboard. In the late 1970s, surface-to-air missiles brought down Air Rhodesia aircraft. Mistaking it for a military aircraft, in 1988 the U.S.S. Vincennes fired missiles which brought down

tion aircraft incidents;[30] (5) off-airport facility attacks; and (6) shootings at in-flight aircraft.[31]

The motives for aircraft hijacking are diverse. The earliest incidents usually involved political refugees seeking a safe haven. People rebelling against the political environment hijacked aircraft from Cuba to the United States.[32] But many of the Cuban hijackings were not driven by a political purpose; instead, they were the actions of mentally unbalanced individuals seeking an outlet for frustration and repression.[33] During the early 1970s a series of hijackings occurred in which the dominant motive was to obtain money by holding passengers hostage for ransom.[34]

A later series of hijackings was also prompted by political motives but of a different nature than those of the Cold War Era.[35] The hijackings of the late 1970s and the first half of the 1980s were made in an attempt to promote political objectives relating to existing international conflicts.[36] In these decades, politically motivated hijackings

an Iran Air flight 655 A-300 commercial aircraft shortly after taking off from Bandar Abbas, killing all 290 people aboard. Earlier, in 1983, Soviet MIGs also brought down Korean Airlines flight 007, a Boeing 747 that had strayed over its territory, killing all 269 people aboard.

[29] Examples include the 1985 skyjackings of TWA flight 847 and Egypt Air flight 648. R.I.R. Abeyratne, *Legal and Regulatory Issues in International Aviation* 326 (1996).

[30] In 2002, missiles were fired at an Israeli charter aircraft over Nigeria.

[31] These are the categories the FAA has used to report annual criminal incidents since 1986. *Id.*; *see also*, R.I.R. Abeyratne, *The Effects of Unlawful Interference with Civil Aviation on World Peace and Social Order*, 22 Transp. L. J. 449, 455, 461 (1995).

[32] Edward McWhinney, *Aerial Piracy and International Law* 17 (1971).

[33] *Id.* at 17. *See also* D. Hubbard, *The Skyjacker: His Flights of Fantasy* (1971).

[34] Edward McWhinney, *The Illegal Diversion of Aircraft and International Law* 11 (1975). After holding a Northwest Orient Airline Boeing 727 crew hostage, D.B. Cooper parachuted from the jet with $200,000 in ransom money. He was never apprehended. *See* Paul Dempsey, William Thoms & Robert Hardaway, *Aviation Law & Regulation* § 9.04 (1993).

[35] For an analysis of the social and political aspects of hijacking, *see* Abeyratne, *Hijacking & the Tehran Incident: A World in Crisis?*, 10 Air L. 120, 123 (1985). Dr. Abeyratne has identified the various motives of the terrorist: "extracting specific concessions, such as the release of prisoners or payment of ransom; gaining publicity; attracting attention of the international press to the terrorist cause; causing widespread disorder in a society to demoralize and breakdown the existing social order; provoking repression, reprisals, and counter-terrorism; enforcing obedience and cooperation; and punishing the victim of the terrorist attack." R.I.R. Abeyratne, *The Effects of Unlawful Interference with Civil Aviation on World Peace and Social Order*, 22 Transp. L. J. 449, 485 (1995).

[36] *Id.* at 12. *See also* Abeyratne, *Hijacking & the Tehran Incident: A World in Crisis?*, 10 Air L. 120 (1985). In his analysis of the Dec. 1984, hijacking of Kuwait Airways Airbus A-310, Abeyratne states that the "real reason" for the hijacker's terroristic efforts to secure release of persons in Kuwait was actually "to help perpetuate international terrorism." *Id.* at 120.

accounted for more than two-thirds of all hijackings worldwide.[37] This final category of hijackings is the most difficult to control as the militants are willing to undertake tremendous risk for their political cause, and have little fear of imprisonment or death.[38]

The first recorded hijacking was in 1931 when Peruvian revolutionaries commandeered a non-commercial Ford Tri-motor. Although the theory has been subsequently discounted, it was long-suspected that explosion of the Hindenburg Zeppelin at Lakehurst, New Jersey, in 1937 was an act of sabotage.[39] The first actual hijacking of a commercial aircraft was in 1948, when a Cathay Pacific aircraft crashed into the ocean near Macao.

Later, during the first dozen years of modern commercial air travel (1948-1960), there were 29 successful hijackings. In the subsequent six years (1961-1967), there were a total of 16 hijackings. Then, in 1968 alone, there were 30 successful hijackings of aircraft—17 of United States registration.[40] The following year, the number of hijackings was more than double the preceding two decades combined.

One source summarized the events of aerial terrorism during the 20th Century by stating that, "The first wave of hijackings after the Second World War were mostly committed by refugees escaping from communist countries."[41] In the whole history of hijacking since 1947, 61% have been refugee escapes. In the late 1960s there was a veritable explosion of hijacking, including not only hijackings by refugees, but also by United States criminals seeking ransom or a flight to Havana to escape the law.

---

[37] ICAO Doc., LC/Working Draft 744-s(a), *cited in U.S. Doc. A/PV* 1914 A/PV 1914 at 23-25 (1970). Interpol reports that in 1977 35.6% hijackings were made for criminal purposes, and 64.4% were political.

[38] "The average terrorist is a militant who employs tactics aimed at instilling fear in the minds of the international community. His acts are calculated to instill fright and paralyze the infrastructure of a state by totally exhausting the strength of his target." R.I.R. Abeyratne, *The Effects of Unlawful Interference with Civil Aviation on World Peace and Social Order,* 22 Transp. L. J. (1995), at 449, 465. Hijacking "should be viewed as an extortion-oriented act, committed against the international order and world peace which is calculated to take advantage of the most susceptible human quality of the endeavor to protect life at any cost." *Id.* at 479.

[39] Rhee, *Rational and Constitutional Approaches to Airline Safety in the Face of Terrorist Threats,* 49 DePaul L. Rev. (2000), at 847, 849-850. More recent discoveries suggest that ignition of the hydrogen in the Zeppelin was a secondary explosion following ignition of the aircraft's outer skin caused by corona discharges. *See* Richard G. Van Truen, *Oderless, Colorless, Blameless*, Air & Space (Apr./May 1997), at 14-16.

[40] Evans, *Aircraft Hijacking: Its Cause and Cure,* 63 Am. J. Int'l L. (1969), at 695.

[41] Paul Wilkinson, *Weaknesses In Airport Security Must Be Fixed,* The Scotsman (Feb. 8, 2000), at 16.

Then in 1968 came an altogether new type of hijacking when Palestinians used air piracy for the first time as a political weapon to publicize their cause and to force Israel and western governments into releasing Palestinian prisoners from jail. During The following year (1969) there were 82 recorded hijack attempts worldwide, more than twice the total attempts for the whole period 1947-1967.[42]

Prompted by a rash of hijackings worldwide, boarding-gate security searches and screening of passengers and luggage was introduced initially in the United States in 1973. Together with the U.S.-Cuba Hijack Pact, security screening had a significant effect in reducing the number of aircraft hijacking attempts. Airliner hijacking has undergone a welcome overall decline since the peak of 385 incidents in the decade 1967-1976. In the following decade the total had dropped to 300 incidents, and in 1987-1996 this figure was reduced to 212.

But after the Air India bombing in 1985 and the Pan Am bombing over Lockerbie, Scotland in 1988, aviation security concerns switched from simple air piracy to the more ominous prospect of sabotage, bombings, and the threat of terrorism. The volume of hijackings declined, but the level of danger was simultaneously ratcheted up. The TWA hijack to Beirut in 1985 and the 16-day hijack of a Kuwait Airways plane in 1988 showed how sophisticated and ruthless hijackers could still gain publicity for their cause. Moreover, the TWA hijackers were able to use the threat against the U.S. hostages to get 756 prisoners released from jail in Israel and South Lebanon.[43] Nevertheless, after the late 1960s, as the Cuban hijackings decreased in frequency, the total number of aircraft hijackings, regardless of motive, began to decline. In 1968, of the 35 worldwide hijackings, 28 were to Cuba. By 1976, none of the 18 worldwide hijackings went to Cuba.

The worldwide number dropped to five hijackings in 1985, then rose to 39 in 1990. There were 20 hijackings in the year 2000, and 42 incidents of attacks against civil aviation interests worldwide, the largest number since 1994, when 50 were recorded.[44] The number of U.S.-flag aircraft hijacked dropped from a high of 21 in 1980, to one per year from 1988-1991, and zero from 1992-2000. In 2001, there were 21 acts of unlawful interference against commercial aircraft.[45]

---

[42] *Id.*
[43] *Id.*
[44] FAA, *Criminal Acts Against Civil Aviation* 3 (2001).
[45] Of these 21, seven were hijackings (including the four that occurred on 9/11), two were attempted seizures, four were fatality attacks, four were attempted fatalities, two were in-flight

But it was a great mistake to have assumed the hijacking threat had nearly disappeared. With the lull in activity there seemingly came a false sense of security that was abruptly shattered on September 11, 2001, when four U.S. aircraft simultaneously were hijacked in the most lethal act of air piracy in history.[46]

"The nation's vast air, land, and maritime transportation systems are marvels of innovation and productivity, but they are designed to be accessible, and their very function is to concentrate passenger and freight flows in ways that can create many vulnerabilities for terrorists to exploit."[47] The tragic events of September 11, 2001 revealed the profound vulnerability of the U.S. transportation system.

First, *the transportation security umbrella is far more porous than many previously realized.* Although suicide bombers had appeared on the world stage before 9/11, the United States was totally unprepared for the tragic events of that day—though one tried to commandeer an aircraft and ram it into the Eiffel Tower in 1994, there was an Iranian plot to crash a Japanese jet in Israel in 1996, and there was an alleged plan by al Qaeda-linked terrorists to crash an explosives-laden plane from a foreign country into the World Trade Center in 1998.[48] Like France in 1940 shielded behind the anachronistic Maginot Line, America was not prepared to fight the war on terrorism—not for lack of will or determination, but out of complacency. Hijackers to Cuba in the 1960s stimulated the introduction of magnetometers and X-ray machines to detect firearms.[49] The explosion of Pan Am 103 in 1988 brought about a limited introduction of explosion detection technol-

---

attacks, one was an attempted in-flight attack, and one was an attempted act of sabotage. *2001 Annual Civil Aviation Report,* 57 ICAO J. 12, 33 (Nov. 6, 2002).

[46] The tragic events of Sep. 11, 2001 revealed several things. Among them: (1) The transportation security umbrella is far more porous that we realized; (2) The U.S. is unduly reliant on a single mode for intercity passenger transportation, an addiction desirable from neither a national security nor national economy perspective; (3) Multimodal intercity transportation passenger alternatives are poor or nonexistent; and (4) Intermodal connectivity is poor or nonexistent in many parts of the U.S.

[47] Trans. Research Board, *Deterrence, Protection and Preparation: The New Transportation Security Imperative 1*, TRB Special Report (2002), at 270, "Designed and organized for the efficient, convenient, and expeditious movement of large volumes of people and goods, transportation systems must have a high degree of user access." *Id.* at 12.

[48] *See* Scot J. Paltrow, *Kamikaze Terrorism Wasn't a New Idea*, Wall St. J. (Thur., Apr. 1, 2004), at A4. *See also* Federal Research Division Report (1999); *Congressional Joint Inquiry on Intelligence Relating to Sep. 11* (Jul. 2003); *see also* Daniel Benjamin & Steven Simon, *The Age of Sacred Terror* (Oct. 2002).

[49] *See* Paul Dempsey, William Thoms & Robert Hardaway, *Aviation Law & Regulation* §§ 9.37, 9.38 (1993).

ogy. But terrorists armed with box cutters, hijacking commercial aircraft and converting them into guided missiles, were wholly off the radar screen.[50]

Second, *the United States is unduly reliant on a single mode of transportation (i.e., commercial aviation) for intercity passenger transportation—an addiction desirable from neither a national security nor national economy perspective.* For the three days the U.S. Federal Aviation Administration grounded commercial aviation, most stranded passengers had no means of reaching distant destinations. Amtrak is a skeletal system that serves only a limited number of city-pairs. Most of the U.S. intercity passenger transportation system lacks redundancy. Multimodal intercity transportation passenger alternatives are poor or nonexistent.[51]

Third, *transportation is an essential component of the infrastructure that supports the U.S. economy.* The United States is a service economy in a broader global economy that relies on the ability to move its brainpower to business destinations around the world. Transportation accounts for between 15-20% of Gross National Product [GNP], but it is the one-fifth of the economy that makes the other four-fifths possible.[52] Transportation links remote buyers and sellers, allowing economies to thrive under the law of comparative advantage. When the commercial aviation industry was shut down for three days, and as passengers began to curtail travel in the psychological wake of the horror of 9/11, the U.S. economy took a significant hit. As a consequence, the United States suffered undue economic harm.

Finally, *intermodal connectivity is poor or nonexistent in many parts of the United States.* Unlike Europe, the overwhelming numbers of U.S. airports have no access to the intercity or intracity rail system, and the few that do, have relatively poor connections.[53]

---

[50] From what is known of how the hijackers of those four aircraft did, in entering U.S. airports in Boston, New York and Washington, with box cutters, they broke no laws. It is therefore clear, that airport and aircraft security was asleep.

[51] *See Presentations from the Intermodal Founding Fathers of North American Conference,* 28 Transp. L. J. 373-562 (2001); *Symposium on Intermodal Transportation,* 27 Transp. L. J. 295-496 (2000).

[52] *See* Paul Dempsey & Laurence Gesell, *Airline Management: Strategies for the 21st Century* (1997).

[53] *See Presentations from the Intermodal Founding Fathers of North American Conference,* 28 Transp. L. J. 373-562 (2001); *Symposium on Intermodal Transportation,* 27 Transp. L. J. 295-496 (2000).

LAW AND POLICY

Both safety and security are highly regulated in air transportation; yet, they are opposite sides of the coin. Both are focused on protecting the traveling public and property from damage. But safety is concerned with *unintentional* injury, while security is about *intentional* harm. This dichotomy is analogous to the difference in tort law between negligence, and intentional torts (such as assault and battery).

International and domestic law have worked in a complimentary fashion to arrest aircraft hijacking, piracy, terrorism, and other forms of unlawful interference with commercial aviation as has United States' legislation addressing international and domestic problems related to aircraft hijacking and other forms of aerial terrorism. To better understand the historical response to aerial terrorism, a chronological understanding of the evolution of law and policy in aviation is essential, as the development of aviation policy has long been a reactive, rather than a proactive, process.[54] Presented below is an overview of international as well as domestic law and policy dealing with the threat of terrorism.

MULTILATERAL CONVENTIONS, RESOLUTIONS, AND DECLARATIONS

International law aimed at subduing threats and attacks on aviation and airport security is based upon several multilateral conventions drafted under the auspices of the U.N. International Civil Aviation Organization [ICAO],[55] including:

- *The Tokyo Convention of 1963*—the Convention on Offenses and Certain Other Acts Committed on Board Aircraft[56] requires

---

[54] For example, establishment of the Federal Aviation Agency in 1958 followed three tragic crashes the preceding year, one that took the life of a U.S. Senator. Paul Dempsey & Laurence Gesell, *Air Transportation: Foundations for the 21st Century* 229-231 (1997).

[55] ICAO is composed of some 188 Contracting States and thereby encompasses virtually the entire civil aviation community. The basic aims and objectives of the ICAO are to ensure safe and orderly growth of international civil aviation throughout the world and to promote safety of flight in international air navigation. For discussion of the role of the ICAO, *see* Kotaite, *Security of International Civil Aviation-Role of ICAO,* 7 Annals Air & Space L. (1982), at 95.

[56] *Convention on Offenses and Certain Other Acts Committed On Board Aircraft*, a.k.a., The Tokyo Convention (Sep. 14, 1963), 20 U.S.T. 2941, T.I.A.S. No. 6768, 704 U.N.T.S. 219, reprinted in 58 Am. J. Int'l L. 566 (1959) All subsequent citations are to the materials reprinted.

that a hijacked aircraft be restored to the aircraft commander and passengers be permitted to continue their journey;

- *The Hague Convention of 1970*—the Convention for the Suppression of Unlawful Seizure of Aircraft[57] declares hijacking to be an international "offense" and requires that the State to which an aircraft is hijacked to extradite or exert jurisdiction over the hijacker and prosecute him, imposing "severe penalties" if he is found guilty;
- *The Montreal Convention of 1971*—the Convention for the Suppression of Unlawful Acts Against the Safety of Civil Aviation expands the definition "offense" to include unlawful acts against aircraft or air navigation facilities, and the communication of false information, and requires prosecution thereof;
- *Annex 17*—in 1974, ICAO adopted Annex 17 to the Chicago Convention on Civil Aviation of 1944[58]; beyond incorporating several of the requirements of the Tokyo, Hague and Montreal Conventions, the Annex requires that member States establish a governmental institution to regulate security and a national civil aviation security program that prevents weapons, explosives or other dangerous devices aboard aircraft, the checking and screening of aircraft, passengers, baggage, cargo and mail, and requires that security personnel be subjected to background checks, qualification requirements, and be adequately trained;
- *The Montreal Protocol of 1988*—the Protocol for the Suppression of Unlawful Acts of Violence at Airports Serving International Civil Aviation, Supplementary to the Convention for the Suppression of Unlawful Acts Against the Safety of Civil Aviation added airport security to the international regime; and,
- *The Montreal Convention of 1991*—the Convention on the Marking of Plastic Explosives for the Purpose of Detection[59] prevented the manufacture, possession and movement of unmarked explosives.

---

[57] Convention for the Suppression of Unlawful Seizure of Aircraft, a.k.a. The Hague Convention (Dec. 16, 1970), 22 U.S.T. 1641, T.I.A.S. No. 7192, reprinted in 10 I.L.M. 133 (1971).

[58] Convention on International Civil Aviation (Dec. 7, 1944), 61 Stat. 1180, T.I.A.S. No. 1591, 15 U.N.T.S. 295. *See* Dempsey, *The Role* of *the International Civil Aviation Organization on Deregulation, Discrimination, and Dispute Resolution,* 52 J. Air L. & Com. 529 (1987).

[59] Convention for the Suppression of Unlawful Acts Against the Safety of Civil Aviation, a.k.a. The Montreal Convention (Sep. 23, 1971), 24 U.S.T. 564, T.I.A.S. No. 7570, reprinted in 10 I.L.M. 115.

In order to have domestic legal standing for these conventions and protocols, the U.S. must pass reflective, enabling legislation. Professor Murray Henner explains, "To a great extent, enabling domestic legislation in the United States has been ratified so that the provisions of various international conventions now have actionable or *implementable* legal effect. For example, the Aircraft Sabotage Act of 1984 implements the Montreal Convention of 1971 and the Antihijacking Act of 1974 implements the Hague Convention of 1970. The United States has also passed other relevant domestic legislation including but not limited to the Foreign Airport Security Act of 1985. . . ."[60]

Several air security agreements have emerged entirely outside ICAO auspices, including, the European Convention on the Suppression of Terrorism (The European Convention),[61] and the Bonn Declaration on Hijacking (The Bonn Declaration).[62] The European Convention of 1977 provided that hijacking would not be deemed a political offense for purposes of extradition. The Bonn Declaration of 1978, an agreement of G-7 leaders, provided that all flights would be ceased immediately to or from any nation which refused to prosecute or extradite a hijacker, or return the hijacked aircraft.

Though constituting an important portion of the legal arsenal to curb acts of violence against civil aviation, the Conventions are limited in their application to contracting States.[63] Of the 188 ICAO member States, a number failed to ratify the Conventions, particularly the plastics explosive convention.[64] Nonetheless, ICAO members are

---

[60] Murray Henner, *A Call for a New International Protocol Relating to Aviation Security in Light of Recent Technological and Global Developments Subsequent to 9/11*, Int'l J. of Technology, Knowledge and Society (2005/2006), Vol. 1, at 2-3, retrieved from http://ijt.cgpublisher.com/product/pub.42/prod.109/m.1?.

[61] *European Convention on the Suppression of Terrorism*, opened for signature, Jan. 27, 1977, reprinted in 15 I.L.M. 1272 (1976).

[62] *Joint Statement on International Terrorism*, Pub. Papers 1308 (Jul. 17, 1978), reprinted in 17 I.L.M. 1285 (1978). The seven economic powers that participated in the drafting of the Bonn Declaration were Canada, France, W. Germany, Italy, Japan, the United Kingdom and the United States.

[63] *The Convention for the Suppression of Unlawful Seizure of Aircraft*, Dec. 16, 1970, 22 U.S.T. 1643, 860 U.N.T.S. 105, entered into force Oct. 14, 1971, with 140 ratifications in 1994. *The Convention for the Suppression of Unlawful Acts Against the Safety of Civil Aviation*, Sep. 23, 1971, 24 U.S.T. 567, 974 U.N.T.S. 177, entered into force on Jan. 26, 1973, with 150 ratifications..

[64] Nicholas Matte, *Treatise On Air-Aeronautical Law* 372 (1981). As of 1981, 106 States had ratified the Tokyo Convention, and 109 had ratified the Montreal Convention. As of 2002, 173 States had ratified the Tokyo Convention, 175 had ratified Hague, and 176 had ratified Montreal. Of ICAO's 188 member States, 15 States had not ratified the Tokyo Convention of 1963, 13 had not ratified the Hague Convention of 1970, 12 had not ratified the Montreal Convention

obliged to abide with Annex 17 to the Chicago Convention, which incorporated several of the Conventions' requirements. The acceptance of the Conventions by a broad spectrum of the economic powers may lead to the development of customary international law[65] on the subject, in which case the provisions could be enforced against both signatories and non-signatories.

UNILATERAL RESPONSES TO AERIAL TERRORISM: UNITED STATES LEGISLATION

This section addresses the ways in which the United States government has attempted to combat aerial terrorism. As the world's largest aviation market, the U.S. exerts enormous influence on international aviation, for airlines and flights from airports that do not meet its security requirements are prohibited access to the United States. Hence, U.S. law and regulation has an impact disproportional even to the large global market share of U.S.-flag airlines and U.S. passengers, for the impact of isolation can be economically painful.

Protecting the public against terrorist acts is a tremendously important task. But governmental institutions that provide security must not be blind to the impact their processes, procedures, and costs have on industry profitability, passenger convenience, personal privacy, and individual liberty. It is the careful balancing of these conflicting objectives that is the formidable task of enlightened government.

The first hijacking of a U.S. commercial aircraft occurred in 1961.[66] Congress promptly responded by declaring hijacking and certain related activities federal crimes.[67] After defining the crime in that

---

of 1971, and 108 had not ratified the Convention on the Marking of Plastic Explosives for the Purpose of Detection of 1991. *Status of Certain International Law Instruments,* 57 ICAO J. 35 (No. 6, 2002).

[65] An international customary law rule is common usage or State practice felt to be legally obligatory by those who follow it. Sasella, *The International Civil Aviation Organization: Its Contribution to International Law*. 8 Melb. U. L. Rev. 41 (1971).

[66] *United States v. Davis,* 482 F.2nd 893, 897-898 (9th Cir. 1973).

[67] On Sep. 5, 1961, the U.S. Congress amended § 902 of the Federal Aviation Act of 1958 to impose criminal penalties upon persons convicted of hijacking. Pub. L. No. 87-197, § 1, 75 Stat. 466. *See* Paul Dempsey, William Thoms & Robert Hardaway, *Aviation Law & Regulation* § 9.21 (1993). The 1961 Act has been scattered throughout Title 49.

Prior to 1961, hijacking an aircraft in the U.S. was usually held to be kidnapping or obstruction of commerce. *See Bearden v. United States,* 304 F.2d 532, 534-535 (5th Cir. 1962), *vacated on other grounds,* 372 U.S., 252 (1963), *obstructing commerce affd,* 320 F.2d 99, 104 (5th Cir. 1963), *cert. denied,* 376 U.S. 922 (1964). However, the Federal Aviation Act of 1958, Pub. L. No. 85-726, had authorized the FAA to issue such rules and regulations as necessary to provide

year, the United States discovered that the solution to this new type of terrorism was not to be realized by the imposition of penalties.[68] The problem was, and is, far more complex than traditional crimes. It follows then that unconventional measures may be necessary to rid the skies of would-be pirates. The solution to this complex problem can only be realized by drafting legislation that improves airport security, destroys hijackers' incentives, and imposes sanctions not just on the hijacker himself, but on his support system and on any country willing to grant him a sanctuary.

In the ensuing decades, the United States created a body of law designed to combat terrorism both domestically and abroad. Some of this legislation is intended to fulfill the nation's obligation as a party to the relevant international conventions or treaties, described above.[69] Still other laws have been enacted in response to the problem in United States domestic air travel caused by hijackings to Cuba.[70] Others still, were adopted to deal with particular catastrophes—Pan Am 103's explosion over Lockerbie, Scotland, Trans World Airlines [TWA] flight 800's explosion over Long Island, New York, and the World Trade Center/Pentagon attacks on September 11, 2001. Most of the statutes in force today can be divided into two broad categories: those designed to deter air piracy and those designed to punish the perpetrator, although newer pieces of legislation served to create a new agency and to promote private sector involvement in the improvement of aviation security. Succinctly summarized, the principal objectives of each these laws follows:

- *The Antihijacking Act of 1974* implemented the Hague Convention of 1970; it imposed penalties for carrying weapons or explosives aboard aircraft, and a penalty of 20 years imprisonment or death if a passenger is killed during a hijacking; it au-

---

for national security and safety in air transportation. It also prohibited the transportation of explosives or other dangerous articles in violation of FAA rules.

[68] During the decade following the 1961 hijacking legislation, more than 120 attempts were made to hijack U.S. aircraft.

[69] *See e.g.*, The Antihijacking Act of 1974, Pub. L. No. 93-366, § 101, 88 Stat. 409-410, 413 (1974) implements the Convention for the Suppression of Unlawful Acts Against the Safety of Civil Aviation (The Hague Convention), 24 U.S.T. 564, T.I.A.S. No. 7570.

[70] As early as 1971, the FAA began to promulgate rules designed to increase security in and around the nation's airports, especially those airports located near large Cuban immigrant populations. For details about then current regulations, *see* 14 C.F.R. Part 107 (1986).

thorized the President to suspend the landing rights of any nation that harbors hijackers.

- *The Air Transportation Security Act of 1974* authorized the screening of passengers and baggage for weapons.
- *The Aircraft Sabotage Act of 1984* implemented the Montreal Convention of 1971; it imposed penalties of up to $100,000 or 20 years imprisonment, or both, for hijacking, damage, destruction or disabling an aircraft or air navigation facility.
- *The International Security and Development Act of 1985* authorized expenditures for enhancing security at foreign airports.
- *The Foreign Security Airport Act of 1985* required the U.S. Department of Transportation Secretary to assess security at foreign airports, and notify the public or suspend service if a foreign airport fails to correct a security breach; it also required that foreign airlines serving the United States adopt and implement security procedures prescribed by the U.S. government.
- *The Aviation Security Improvement Act of 1990* mandated background checks for airline and airport employees, and imposed additional training, educational and employment standards upon them; it also required deployment of bomb-detection technology for baggage.
- *The Federal Aviation Administration Reauthorization Act of 1996* required passenger profiling, explosive detection technology, procedures for passenger/bag matching, and certification for screening companies.
- *The Omnibus Consolidated Appropriations Act of 1997* authorized the purchase of advanced screening equipment for baggage.
- *The Aviation Security Improvement Act of 2000* required fingerprinting and background checks of airport and airline security personnel at Category X airports.[71]
- *The Aviation and Transportation Security Act of 2001* federalized the airport screening function, establishing the new Transportation Security Administration under the Department of Transportation to regulate security in all modes of transportation; it also enhanced baggage screening procedures, and im-

[71] 49 U.S.C. § 44903 (2002).

posed more stringent personnel qualifications on security employees.

- *The Homeland Security Act of 2002* consolidated 22 agencies, including the TSA, into a new cabinet-level Department of Homeland Security. The agency was given jurisdiction, *inter alia,* over transportation security, customs, immigration and agricultural inspections.
- *The Support Anti-Terrorism by Fostering Effective Technologies Act of* 2002 [SAFETY] "allows sellers of anti-terror technologies [to] have the ability to immunize themselves from liability arising out of a terrorist event," thus encouraging innovation and introduction of cutting edge technologies. To achieve protection, an interested company must register their device with the Department of Homeland Security [DHS] as a *Qualified Anti-Terrorism Technology* [QATT].
- *The Intelligence Reform and Terrorism Prevention Act of 2004*, most notably, created the position of Director of National Intelligence. It also called for the development of "comprehensive technical and operational system requirements and performance standards for the use of biometric identifier technology in airport access control systems (including airport perimeter access control systems) to ensure that the biometric identifier systems are effective, reliable, and secure."[72]

In addition, several fiscal year federal spending bills have been passed over the last decade, and are instrumental is assuring that need appropriations are available for the security and safety initiatives suggested in the above laws.[73]

AVIATION SECURITY BEFORE 9/11

Before 9/11 and the subsequent reorganization of security agencies and regulations in the United States, the provisions of FAR Part 107,

[72] TSA, *Guidance Package: Biometrics for Airport Access Control*, (Sep. 30, 2005), retrieved from http://www.tsa.gov/assets/pdf/biometrics_guidance.pdf.

[73] An example of this can be found in a Fiscal Year 2006 Dept. of Homeland Security spending bill, P.L. 109-90, which helped to both fund DHS and Aviation security initiatives, as well as serving to protect airports wishing to use private screeners.

"Airport Security," and FAR Part 108, "Airplane Operator Security," formed the fundamental regulatory structure for the security of persons and property against acts of *criminal violence* and *aircraft piracy*.[74] Part 107 provided for the control of access to air operations areas by unauthorized persons and ground vehicles. Further, no person was allowed entry to a "sterile" area without submitting to the screening of his or her person and property in accordance with the procedures being applied by the airport to control access to that area.

Part 108 was designed to prevent or deter the carriage aboard airplanes of any explosive, incendiary, or a deadly or dangerous weapon on or about each individual's person or accessible property, and the carriage of any explosive or incendiary in checked baggage. Under Part 108, airlines were to: prohibit unauthorized access to their airplanes; ensure that baggage carried aboard their aircraft was checked in by an identified agent; prohibit unauthorized access to cargo and checked baggage; and conduct security inspections of their airplanes.

A third regulation, FAR Part 109, "Indirect Air Carrier Security," provided additional protection against criminal activity. This part prescribed aviation security rules governing each air carrier (including air freight forwarders and cooperative shipping associations) engaged indirectly in air transportation of property. Each indirect air carrier was required to have a security program designed to prevent or deter the unauthorized introduction of explosives or incendiary devices into any package cargo intended for carriage by air.

These federal aviation regulations were designed to ensure the security of airports serving scheduled air carriers required to have screening programs. In other words, *air carriers* have had the responsibility of preventing and deterring carriage of weapons and explosives aboard their aircraft by potential hijackers. Conversely, *airports* serving the applicable carriers have been responsible for preventing and deterring unauthorized access to the air operations area, and for providing law enforcement support at passenger screening stations.

Since their inception in 1972, FAA security regulations were designed to meet hijacking and other criminal threats, as they were then perceived. Between 1972 and 200l, while there were some exceptions, a "typical" hijacker was expected to be a male who was working alone, would chose a metal-based weapon, and would be both

[74] This section is drawn heavily from Laurence E. Gesell, *The Administration of Public Airports* Ch. 12 (4th ed. 1999).

intimidated and detected by the security technology of that era—largely the magnetometer (metal detector) and the x-ray machines. The act would be triggered for one of three primary reasons: depression or mental illness, greed, or the perceived need for transport due to political issues. Regardless, a hijacker in that era was expected to be interested in survival and relatively unsophisticated in their planning efforts. Because of the historical decline in aircraft hijackings around the world, it was assumed that procedures had been adequate to protect the traveling public. Even though there were occasional exceptions to the typical hijacker profile, the guard as a nation and an industry was allowed to degrade to an unacceptable level. But as stated above, the tragic events of September 11, 2001 revealed the profound vulnerability of the U.S. transportation system.

For the most part these operations involved large transport type airplanes, generally conducted by air carriers with Certificates of Public Convenience and Necessity [PC&N] (originally issued by the Civil Aeronautics Board [CAB] and later by the Department of Transportation). Operating rules for these carriers were set out in Federal Aviation Regulation Part 121, and for this reason, FAA security regulations were initially placed in that part. After passage of the Airline Deregulation Act of 1978 and the CAB's liberalized policies and broad authority granted to commuters to conduct scheduled operations with large aircraft, numerous commuter air carriers held authority to conduct operations similar to those that were previously conducted only by holders of CAB Certificates of PC&N. These airplanes were operated over routes formerly served by CAB certificate holders, and the operations were conducted without being subject to full FAA security requirements.

To ensure consistent application of FAA's security rules and to achieve the necessary level of security, Federal Aviation Regulation Part 108, "Airplane and Airport Operator Security" evolved, which based security requirements upon airplane complexity instead of CAB authorizations. Note the original Part 108 carried a different title than a later version. In the later version, Part 108 applied to "airplane operators," but not to airports. The airports' responsibilities were then totally contained within Part 107. Basically, the requirements of Part 108, as pertains to aircraft size, remained the same.

THE CHANGING THREAT

Over the years, the perceived threat to airports and the aviation industry has changed, and it has become broader and less predictable. Before 1960, security problems at airports were confined to conventional crimes: vandalism, theft, assault and battery, trespassing, and so forth. But since the late 1960s airports have become the target of international crimes such as terrorism, air piracy, sabotage, and overt acts of aggression. As noted above, between 1963 and 1971, The International Civil Aviation Organization [ICAO] convened several times for the purpose of drafting measures to counteract terrorism: the Tokyo Convention of 1963, Hague Convention of 1970, and the Montreal Convention of 1971. ICAO adopted a set of standards and recommended procedures in 1974 for the security of civil aviation.[75]

In 1969, the FAA established a Task Force on Deterrence of Air Piracy. And in 1971, the FAA issued a Notice of Proposed Rule Making [NPRM] for landmark revisions to airport and airline security measures. Emanating from that NPRM was FAR Part 107, "Airport Security." The current aviation security architecture (as described above) was designed around the threat observed 30 years ago. Unfortunately, the would-be airplane hijacker of 20 or 30 years ago has become a more diversified outlaw.[76] International terrorism has become much more sophisticated and has greatly intensified, suggesting that it is time to redesign the security systems architecture.[77] The system has been upgraded since 9/11, but it is still designed around the threat of 30 years ago. As the 9/11 Commission reported in 2004, the Transportation Security Administration is focused on fighting "the last war." "The current efforts do not yet reflect a forward-looking strategic plan systematically analyzing assets, risks, costs and benefits."[78]

The most recent threats of terrorist activities have been against infrastructure, transportation, water and power utilities, financial institutions, and political conventions. Aviation *per se* is but a small part

---

[75] The document, *Standards and Recommended Practices—Security—Safeguarding Civil Aviation Against Acts of Unlawful Interference*, was published as Annex 17 to the original Chicago Convention of 1944; *see* Atef Ghobrial & Ken Fleming, *A Model for Developing an Airport Security Plan*, J. of Avn./Aerospace Ed., Vol. 4, No. 2 (winter 1994), at 27.

[76] Barbara Cook, *High-Tech Security: The Future is Now*, Airport Magazine (Jan./Feb. 1997), at 34.

[77] *See* Laurence E. Gesell, *The Administration of Public Airports* 602-612 (4th ed. 1999).

[78] Scott McCartney, *From X-rays to Cargo, Security Gaps Remain*, Wall St. J. (Wed., Jul. 28, 2004), at D2.

of the big picture. In fact, threats against civil aviation have a very low incidence rate of only .003% of all terrorist attacks.[79] The airport itself is looking more like the target than are the aircraft using it. And some attacks worldwide have involved unconventional weapons such as the gas attack against innocent civilians in the Tokyo subway. Now bombings have become part of the shock strategy of transnational special interest groups and radical extremists. The attacks on the World Trade Center in New York and the Pentagon in Washington, D.C. are prime examples. The FBI has become concerned with the size of devices now being used in terrorist attacks. While the number of individual attacks has decreased, the devastation of the attacks that are staged is greater.[80] Thus the character of the threat has changed since the first airport security regulations were implemented in the 1970s. It has moved from the days of a lone individual boarding an airplane with an explosive capable of bringing down an aircraft, to the reality of large-scale bombs and the possibility of mass devastation within airport terminals, if not cities.

AVIATION SECURITY CHANGES AFTER 9/11

Subsequent to the attacks of September 11, 2001, reporters for *U.S. News & World Report* reported "The terrorists flew on devil's wings in a horrifying moment, singular in history.[81] They changed the course of a presidency, a nation, and, quite likely, the world." There was a strong suspicion that Osama bin Laden had choreographed the plan of terror and devastation that fundamentally changed the basic calculus for life for not only Americans but for millions around the world. But shortly following the attacks no one knew for sure who it was who had attacked the United States. Nevertheless, President George W. Bush immediately declared war. He just couldn't name the enemy.[82]

---

[79] Cathal Flynn, in Barbara Cook, *High-Tech Security: The Future is Now*, Airport Magazine (Jan./Feb. 1997), at 16.

[80] John O'Neill, in Barbara Cook, *High-Tech Security: The Future is Now*, Airport Magazine (Jan./Feb. 1997), at 16.

[81] This section draws heavily from Robin Sobotta & Laurence E. Gesell, *Airport and Aviation Security Addendum* (2003), to Laurence E. Gesell, The Administration of Public Airports (4th ed. 1999).

[82] Edward T. Pound, David E. Kaplan, Douglas Pasternak, Chitra Ragavan, Linda Robinson, Angie Cannon, Richard J. Newman, Mark Mazzetti, Bruce B. Auster, Kevin Whitlaw, Gloria

President Bush's formal response to the tragedy, "Security the Homeland, Strengthening the Nation," addresses two reasons why terrorism is—and will continue to be—a serious issue of concern for Americans: First, the characteristics of American society that its citizens cherish—freedom, openness, great cities and towering skyscrapers, and modern transportation systems—make the country vulnerable to terrorism of catastrophic proportions. America's vulnerability to terrorism will persist long after justice is brought to those responsible for the events of September 11. Second, the technological ability to launch destructive attacks against civilian populations and critical infrastructure spreads to more and more organizations and individuals with each passing year.[83] Another reason is that the very machine (the airplane) that helps to bring us all together by reducing both time and space, has made us all more vulnerable.[84]

Clearly, America's treasured personal freedoms coupled with its economic and political philosophies make the threat to the U.S. transportation system "a permanent condition," as bluntly noted by Mr. Bush in his address. In response, Congress and the Bush administration took many administrative and regulatory steps to address the changing threat against the United States and the world community. These resulted in the passage of legislation and associated regulations that created a new cabinet-level office, new security regulations, and strengthened security procedures.

ORGANIZATIONAL CHANGES: FAA, TSA and DHS

With the November 2001 passage of the Aviation and Transportation Security Act, several organizational and regulatory changes were prompted that, ultimately, have affected the aviation industry. The ATSA created the Transportation Security Administration and prompted several changes, including a mandate for 100% screening of all checked bags by air travelers and the requirement that all U.S. airport screening personnel be federally employed (with the exception of few select test programs for privatization). In addition, the ATSA mandated the fortification of commercial aircraft cockpit doors, addi-

---

Borger, Michael Tackett, Rochelle Sharpe, Ricardo Castillo, & Juli Hilliard, *Under Siege*, U.S. News & World Report (Sep. 24, 2001), at 10.

[83] George Bush, *Securing the Homeland Strengthening the Nation*, http://www.whitehouse.gov (visited 2003).

[84] *See* Editors, *The Security Puzzle*, Av. Wk. & Space Tech. (Aug. 23/30, 2004), at 56.

tional federal air marshal presence on commercial aircraft, and hijack training for flight crews.

On March 1, 2003, the newly formed Department of Homeland Security became responsible for oversight of the TSA.[85] "DHS is responsible for protecting the movement of international trade across U.S. borders, maximizing the security of the international supply chain, and for engaging foreign governments and trading partners in programs designed to identify and eliminate security threats before these arrive at U.S ports and borders."[86] Two weeks prior to its takeover by DHS, the TSA—which had already been granted the responsibility for security in all other modes of transportation—assumed all civil aviation security functions previously held by the Federal Aviation Administration [FAA]. In a *Federal Register* notice, TSA also announced the intended federalization of all airport security screeners and assumed responsibility "for the day-to-day security screening operations for passenger air transportation and intrastate air transportation under U.S.C. 44901 and 44935 . . . [including] hiring, training, testing, and deploying or arranging for Federal security screeners."

While the Department of Homeland Security has been credited with many successes since 9/11, some still feel that serious vulnerabilities in U.S. security remain. Former Inspector General of the Department of Homeland Security Clark Kent Ervin explains,

> *It is an exaggeration to say that America is as vulnerable to a terrorist attack as it was on [9/11] but it is not much of an exaggeration. There is still a big gap between how much more secure we can be and how secure we really are. As long as the 'vulnerability gap' remains as wide as it is today, America remains an open target.*[87]

The quick creation of DHS in response to a terrorist act, in a quixotic way, may have actually "worked against the imperative of securing the homeland."[88] On this, Ervin writes,

---

[85] DHS, *Travel and Transportation*, http://www.dhs.gov (visited 2003).

[86] *Id.*

[87] Clark Kent Ervin, *Open Target: Where America is Vulnerable to Attack* (2006), at xii.

[88] *Id.* at 21.

> *People have come to believe that the fact that we have not been attacked again, and the fact that [DHS] was created in response to the first attack, proved that the department has succeeded in securing the homeland. Of course, given the manifold security gaps that remain, the department has really done no such thing. Rather than having created a department to secure the homeland, we have attempted to secure the homeland simply by the act of creating a department.*[89]

There is some speculation that U.S. citizens and their government may be experiencing a false sense of security associated with the creation of the lumbering DHS organization. Ervin compares today's DHS officials—who claim significant progress in fortifying national security since 9/11, citing the lack of a terrorist act since that date—with French officials in the 1930s and 1940s who believed that the Maginot Line would protect them from a German invasion.[90] Unfortunately, "when put to the test, [the Maginot Line] proved to be no match for Hitler's bloodthirsty legions"[91] who traveled over some forested, largely unprotected terrain along non-traditional routes to invade France. Ervin concludes that the DHS and the nation may, likewise, be "put to the test"[92] by clever and persistent terrorists, if DHS does not recognize its "Maginot mentality,"[93]

> *People chosen to lead the department may be under the comforting illusion that its very existence is our sure defense against terrorism, but the terrorists know better. In claiming that the homeland is more secure than it really is, and in attributing that security largely to an ill*

---

[89] *Id.*

[90] The Maginot Line was a supposedly impregnable barrier (comprised of a wall and fortresses) built by the French between 1929-1940 as a superior barrier against an attack from Germany, Robert Wilde, *The Maginot Line* (2001), retrieved from http://europeanhistory.about.com/library/weekly/aa072001c.htm.

[91] Clark Kent Ervin, *Open Target: Where America is Vulnerable to Attack* (2006), at 21.

[92] *Id.*

[93] Robert Wilde, *The Maginot Line* (2001), retrieved from http://europeanhistory.about.com/library/weekly/aa072001c.htm.

conceived, hastily constructed, and poorly performing government bureaucracy, we are only deceiving ourselves.[94]

Aside from the pure size and funding of the DHS bureaucracy, societal belief in the value of physical barriers and technology (versus human ingenuity and deception) may also serve to create a false sense of security. Again, potential similarities can be found when compared to the Maginot Line scenario, about which Ian Ousby writes,

Time treats few things more cruelly than the futuristic fantasies of past generations, particularly when they are actually realized in concrete and steel. Hindsight makes it abundantly clear that the Maginot Line was a foolish misdirection of energy when it was conceived, a dangerous distraction of time and money when it was built, and a pitiful irrelevance when the German invasion did come in 1940.[95]

The federal government claims it is well aware of its deficiencies in the area of homeland security. In fact, in 2007, the Government Accountability Office [GAO] issued a report on the need for DHS to continue making improvements in support of better securing the U.S. air transportation system. In her testimony before the House of Representatives Homeland Security Committee, Homeland Security and Justice Issues Director Cathleen A. Berrick stated,

DHS and TSA have undertaken numerous initiatives to strengthen the security of the nations aviation system . . . however, much work remains. Meeting the congressional mandates to screen airline passengers and checked baggage alone was a tremendous challenge. [More recently], TSA has turned its attention

[94] Clark Kent Ervin, *Open Target: Where America is Vulnerable to Attack* (2006), at 21.

[95] Ian Ousby, *Occupation: The Ordeal of France* (1997), at 14, as cited in Robert Wilde, The Maginot Line (2001), retrieved from http://europeanhistory.about.com/library/weekly/aa072001c.htm.

> *to, among other things, strengthening passenger prescreening; more effectively allocating, deploying, and managing the TSO [Technical Standing Order] workforce; strengthening screening procedures; developing and deploying more effective and efficient screening technologies; and improving domestic air cargo security.*[96]

Indeed, the TSA's first few years were challenging and they failed to meet some stated goals of their initial two-year (post 9/11) plan for major aviation security activities. TSA's response to some deadlines was not timely or were met with questionable means (such as the 100% Explosive Detection Systems [EDS] checked bag deadline which was ultimately "achieved" a year late and, in some cases, by means other than EDS, such as trace detection, bag matching, dogs, and compliance waivers. Critics were concerned whether the Bush Administration was more concerned about pleasing politicians (to satisfy political agendas and the public demand for improved customer service), than with achieving true security improvements.

Airline executives—reluctant to appear critical of the TSA—say that problems have cropped up for a variety of reasons, not all of them the agency's fault. For example, in the rush to install baggage-screening systems by the earlier-mentioned deadline, the TSA resorted to screening many bags by having technicians wipe them with pads, and then analyze the pads for signs of explosives. The job could be automated by using scanning machines instead, but installing those giant machines, and the conveyor belts needed to make effective use of them, has lagged, partly for budgetary reasons and partly due to shortages in equipment availability. From the onset, airports have been asking for—and denied—the right to move ahead on putting security solutions into effect. Until only recently, they were under funded and/or met with resistance until the regulatory agency could identify funding and/or the 'appropriate' solutions."[97]

---

[96] Cathleen A. Berrick, Dir. of Homeland Security and Justice Issues, before the Subcommittee on Homeland Security, Committee on Appropriations, House of Representatives, *Aviation Security: Progress Made in Systematic Planning to Guide Key Investment Decisions, but More Work Remains,* GAO-07-448T, http://www.gao.gov/new.items/d07448t.pdf (visited Feb. 13, 2007).
[97] David Plavin, *Rushed Airport Security*, N.Y. Times (Nov. 23, 2002), at A26.

In subsequent years, the TSA has encountered additional challenges at airports. In its collaborations involving state and local governmental agencies (e.g., airport sponsors) and in interface with users (e.g., passengers and tenants), both Congress and governmental agencies have had to continually balance seemingly opposing goals in a new-age aviation security continuum, with the opposing ends being optimal states of *aviation security/safety & intelligence gathering* and *passenger privacy & convenience,* as illustrated below:

Privacy & Convenience ⟵⟶ **Security & Intelligence**

"Optimal" *security and intelligence* on the far right encourages the highest levels of passenger and property security and safety. It is a state where the transportation security officials and their partners have access to highly accurate watch lists, generated from intense intelligence gathering activities, and unfettered access to personal records (supported by information-collection tools and agency information-sharing networks such as allowed within the USA Patriot Act[98] or the proposed Computer-Assisted Passenger Prescreening System [CAPPS]).[99] The right side also favors the most intense screening measures and technology including biometric-based tools (which might be more physically revealing or invasive). The right side presumes screeners have ample time to *thoroughly* process all travelers.

---

[98] *Uniting and Strengthening America by Providing Appropriate Tools Required to Intercept and Obstruct Terrorism Act of 2001* (P.L. 107-56), a.k.a. the USA PATRIOT Act or simply the *Patriot Act* (Oct. 26, 2001).

[99] See the description of CAPPS below. The Uniting and Strengthening America by Providing Appropriate Tools Required to Intercept and Obstruct Terrorism Act of 2001 (Public Law 107-56), known as the USA PATRIOT Act or simply the *Patriot Act*, was formed in response to the terrorist attacks against the U.S., and dramatically expanded the authority of American law enforcement for the stated purpose of fighting terrorism in the U.S. and abroad. It has also been used to detect and prosecute other alleged potential crimes, such as providing false information on terrorism. Federal courts have ruled that some provisions are unconstitutional infringements on civil liberties. In March of 2007, the DOJ released an internal audit that found that the FBI had engagged in "improper and illegal uses" of their national security letter authorities in obtaining information from private citizens and institutions, which were termed "serious misuses," but "did not involve criminal misconduct." Office of the Inspector General, U.S. Dept. of Juststic, *A Review of the Federal Bureau of Investigation's National Security Letters* (Mar. 2007), at xxviii, http://www.usdoj.gov/oig/special/s0703b/final.pdf (visited May 11, 2007).

At the opposite end of the spectrum to the far left, "optimal" *privacy and convenience* includes factors such as passenger processing speed (over accuracy), comfort (short waits and baggage assistance), courtesy (including special treatment such as shorter lines for first class passengers, etc), access (such as having friends/family permitted beyond the checkpoints), and personal privacy issues (such as physical privacy and the protection of personal information). Privacy issues are discussed in more depth in a later section entitled, "Security Procedures: Needed Protection or Invasion of Privacy."

As time passes subsequent to whatever is the most recent terrorist incident, policy makers, regulators and others are pressured to move toward the left side of the continuum. Periodically, though, a new incident creates an adjustment back to the right compelling procedural changes. For example, there was the "Heathrow Plot" of August 2006, in which several U.S.-bound flights were targeted for attack by suicide bombers hiding liquid explosives in carry-on luggage. Rules relating to the carriage of liquids were changed, with some passenger inconvenience and delays. However, the inconvenience was fairly well tolerated due to a belief that the threat was credible and because the public saw a valid need to impose new restrictions.

SECURITY GUIDELINES FOR AIRPORT PLANNING

As a result of the changing threat, designers of security systems must make some hard decisions on just "how much they can do." The cost of security has gone up. The U.S. now spends $5.3 billion a year on transportation security and 90% of that goes to aviation.[100] Countermeasures against mass attack and the use of unconventional weapons are expensive. The nation must be vigilant not to over-spend, as it did in response to concerns regarding the year 2000 panic. The United States alone spent approximately $122 billion to fix the Y2k problem, yet not a single computer nor a single power grid came crashing down anywhere on the planet on New Year's day 2000.[101]

The 9/11 Commission concluded that while commercial aviation remains a possible target, "terrorists may turn their attention to other modes." Ships, trains and mass transit are far more vulnerable than

---

[100] Scott McCartney, *From X-rays to Cargo, Security Gaps Remain*, Wall St. J. (Wed., Jul. 28, 2004), at D2.

[101] *See* Patricia Sullivan, *Computer Pioneer*, Washington Post (Jun. 25, 2004), at B6.

airplanes these days."[102] As John O'Neill emphasizes, "Terrorists can attack anything, anywhere and anytime, and we cannot protect everything all the time."[103] One of the strongest strategies—as in homeowner protection—may well be encouraging would be terrorists to attack another, more convenient facility. O'Neill points out that, "By themselves, physical changes in a potential target don't eliminate terrorism. . . . They deflect it to a less well-protected target."[104]

Atef Ghobrial and Ken Fleming suggest that airport security plans must now be much more comprehensive than those associated with older aviation security requirements. In order to protect passengers, staff, airlines, aircraft, and property, airports are going to have to develop, implement, and maintain a complete and comprehensive security program for the airport system.[105]

The security system architecture will vary considerably for each airport situation due to terminal design, utilization, and other local factors.[106] Unfortunately, says Nicholas Bodouva, transportation facilities architects have not been included in the dialogue about security systems design. Thus far, the discussions of enhanced security have been confined largely to procedures and equipment, not the (terminal) building itself. Questions about terminal design requirements represent challenges not only to building design creativity but also to client/architect collaboration; a task complicated further by needing to ensure that security procedures remain "secret," while at the same time creating an atmosphere that says "safe."[107]

There are three basic components to security architecture design:

- Procedures mandated by government;
- Equipment, especially baggage and passenger screening machinery at strategic checkpoints; and
- The building itself, the planning of which can only be greatly affected by the first two.[108]

---

[102] *Id.*

[103] John O'Neill, in Barbara Cook, *High-Tech Security: The Future is Now*, Airport Magazine (Jan./Feb. 1997), at 16.

[104] *Id.*

[105] *See* Atef Ghobrial & Ken Fleming, *A Model for Developing an Airport Security Plan,* J. of Aviation/Aerospace Ed., Vol. 4, No. 2 (winter 1994), at 27.

[106] Committee on Commercial Aviation Security, *Detection of Explosives for Commercial Aviation Security*, NMAB-471 (1993).

[107] William Nicholas Bodouva, *Security by Design*, Airport Magazine (Jan./Feb. 1997), at 35.

[108] *Id.*

Bodouva asks, "As a building type, are airports destined to become the 1990s equivalent of overseas embassies, with their beefed-up structural systems and other terrorism-resistant features?" And, indeed, Bodouva has valid concerns. Entrances to terminal buildings may very well have to accommodate new screening procedures and equipment. For example, in response to the relentless terrorist acts of the Liberation Tigers of Tamil Eelam, the Sri Lankan government redesigned the entrance to its airport terminal at Colombo; there the parking lot adjacent to the terminal was eliminated and curbside access and baggage screening was moved to an area behind a blast wall packed with sloping soil.[109]

As more advanced screening devices for carry-on baggage are mandated, the area required for the security checkpoint may increase as much as 40%. Additionally, the screening of baggage away from public areas will require the allocation of substantial floor space within the terminal or in baggage make-up areas.

As Bodouva states, "It is important to recognize that architects are being asked to plan for technology that has not been fully developed."[110] Moreover, if one assumes that terminals may well be designed and built without due consideration of new improved technologies in passenger and baggage screening, the lack or inadequacy of available floor space may compromise security systems.

In response to airports' request for guidelines that might enable them to better plan, design and construct airport facilities to incorporate current and future security requirements, the TSA created a planning document entitled, "Recommended Security Guidelines for Airport Planning, Design and Construction." This comprehensive document was released in June of 2006 and contains several important sections, relating to security planning including recommended guidelines for the following major areas of interest:[111]

- *Airport Layout and Boundaries* (security areas, other vulnerable areas, chemical and biological agents, boundaries and access points, etc.);

---

[109] Paul Dempsey, *Airport Planning and Development* 349 (2000).

[110] *Id.*

[111] TSA, *Recommended Security Guidelines for Airport Planning, Design and Construction* (Jun. 2006), retrieved from www.tsa.gov/assets/pdf/airport_security_design_guidelines.pdf.

- *Airside* (aircraft movement, parking, roads, vulnerable areas, cargo areas, etc.);
- *Landside* (natural barriers; landside roads, parking, and facilities, entry control points, interior and exterior spaces, systems and equipment, emergency response, etc.);
- *Terminal* (security architecture, terminal area users and infrastructure, sterile areas, public areas, non-public areas common use areas , terminal vulnerable areas, chemical and biological threats, etc.);
- *Security Screening* (passenger security screening checkpoints, baggage screening, cargo screening, etc.);
- *Access Control and Alarm Monitoring Systems*;
- *Video Surveillance, Detection and Distribution* (Closed-Circuit Television [CCTV], operational/technical issues, system design, infrastructure);
- *Power, Communications and Cabling* (power, infrastructure, airport network security, telecom, radio frequency, data transport, etc.); and
- *International Aviation Security* (foreign security requirements and U.S. Federal Inspection Services [FIS] and homeland security requirements).

These recommended airport planning security guidelines contain several planning tools (appendices) for airport planners and security officials. These include a suggested airport vulnerability assessment process, an airport security space planning tool, information on airport blast protection, and several planning checklists (for each of the major areas of interest that were bulleted above).[112]

Much has changed since 9/11. New agencies have been created, replacing the security responsibilities of the FAA. The body of aviation security regulations ceased being called "Federal Aviation Regulations" and are now reorganized and re-titled as "Transportation Security Regulations" (see Table 9.1, "Air Transportation Security Regulations Changes"). And, private screeners have been replaced by an administrative structure and a cadre of career federal security screening personnel. These developments, along with other changes in the security protocol, are discussed over the next several pages.

---

[112] *Id.*

Table 9.1—AIR TRANSPORTATION SECURITY REGULATION CHANGES

Regulatory Subject	*New TSRs (49 CFR):*	*Largely Taken from old FARs (14 CFR):*
Passenger Civil Aviation Security Service Fees	Part 1510	Part 129.3
Protection of Sensitive Security Information	Part 1520	Part 191
Civil Aviation Security (on-board security and other issues)	Part 1540	Portions of 107, 108 and 91
Airport Security	Part 1542	Portions of 107, 108 and 91
Aircraft Operator Security: Air Carriers and Commercial Operators	Part 1544	Part 108
Foreign Air Carrier Security	Part 1546	Part 129
Indirect Air Carrier Security	Part 1548	Part 109
Aircraft Operator Security under General Operating and Flight Rules	Part 1550	SFAR 91

Source: Federal Register (Feb. 22, 2002), Vol. 67, No. 36, at 7939-8384.

REGULATORY CHANGES

The airport security architecture and protocol remains fundamentally the same as before, albeit significantly beefed-up, [113] but concomitant with the organizational changes made at the federal level were several regulatory changes as shown in Table 9.1. As stated above, the *Federal Aviation Regulations* [FARs] that previously formed the regulatory backbone of aviation security were replaced by *Transportation Security Regulations* [TSRs]. Although many of the changes are essentially a renumbering/relocation of FARs to TSRs there are a number of changes in the regulations of note, and that are discussed below. Irrespective of implemented changes, much cynicism remains regarding the effectiveness of those changes and/or the TSA's responsiveness (or lack thereof) to needed change.

For example, a *New York Times* editorial warned that "airport operators and airlines should be concentrating on how to meet the requirements, not how to dodge them."[114] David Z. Plavin, President of the Airports Council International-North America said that, "No airports 'balked' at the baggage-screening deadline with which Congress encumbered the Transportation Security Administration. From the onset, airports have been asking for—and denied—the right to move ahead on putting security solutions into effect. Until only recently, they were often met with hostility, then ignored, then informed that they would be told of the 'appropriate' solutions."[115]

SECURITY CHECKPOINT PROTOCOL

Airport security screening systems have varied principally only in where the screening takes place and have conformed to compliance with evolving legal precedence that remains fundamentally unaltered since 9/11.[116] At each screening point, appropriate signs advise the individual of the screening requirement and that the exercise of the individual's option to refuse to undergo the required screening process would result in denial of passage beyond the screening point. Additionally, wherever an X-ray baggage inspection system is used, appropriate signs must advise the individual of the X-ray inspection sys-

---

[113] 49 CFR 1542 describes the airport security under the TSA.
[114] Editorial, *Airport Security*, N.Y. Times (Sep. 20, 2002).
[115] Leo Plavin, *Rushed Airport Security*, N.Y. Times (Nov. 23, 2002), at A26.
[116] *See* Laurence E. Gesell, *Aviation and the Law* Ch. 6 (3rd ed. 1998).

tem. The initial screening process is conducted using either a *walk-through metal detector* (or magnetometer) or a *hand-held metal detector*. If the person being screened does not alarm the detector, the person is cleared to proceed beyond the screening point. If the metal detector alarms, the person must be reprocessed to determine the cause of the alarm.

In reprocessing, the person causing the alarm divests his or her person of metal and is then reintroduced through the metal detector. If the walk-through metal detector continues to alarm during reprocessing, the person must undergo additional screening. The hand-held metal detector is then used to determine and isolate the area of the alarm. Once the area has been isolated, the cause of the alarm should be determined, with the passenger's assistance, through a consent frisk either by observation, physical inspection of outer garments, or by having the passenger present the contents of a pocket for inspection. Under no circumstances is the passenger allowed beyond the screening point unless screening personnel are first assured that the passenger is not carrying any dangerous objects.[117]

Property processing is conducted by using an X-ray device and/or by physical inspection of the item. If no weapon, explosive or incendiary device is discovered the carry-on article may be permitted beyond the screening point. Metal detectors are normally not used to screen carry-on articles. If during the screening process, a weapon, explosive, incendiary device, or other contraband is discovered; the law enforcement officer takes custody of the item and initiates appropriate law enforcement action.

The airport operator must provide Law Enforcement Officers [LEOs] in the number and in a manner adequate to support the airport security program and each air carrier passenger screening system. Airport police are full-fledged peace officers. They are uniformed, carry a badge, armed and authorized to use a firearm, and have authority to arrest (with or without a warrant) for felony crimes.

Canines [K-9s] are an important component of airport security programs. The nation's canine program was launched in 1972 when a bomb-sniffing dog named Brandy found an explosive device on a Trans World Airlines [TWA] jet at John F. Kennedy Airport that was

---

[117] It is of note that several of the 9/11 hijackers set off metal detectors at Washington's Dulles Airport. But surveillance camera tapes show that the screeners waved hand-held metal detectors around but never resolved what had set off the metal detectors. *See* Scott McCartney, *From X-rays to Cargo, Security Gaps Remain*, Wall St. J. (Wed., Jul. 28, 2004), at D2.

bound for Los Angeles. Brandy reportedly found the device just 12 minutes before it was due to detonate.[118] Many U.S. airports now have dogs trained to sniff and search baggage, aircraft and terminals for explosives.

The FAA first employed bomb-detection dogs in 1972 with the object of trying ". . . to have them located so that no airplane would ever be more than 30 minutes from an airport with dog teams." By 1986, there were between 60 and 70 dogs at airports across the country. Since then, at least four agencies looking into airport security system deficiencies—the National Research Council's Committee on Commercial Aviation Security in 1988, and the Government Accounting Office in 1994, the White House Commission on Aviation Safety and Security in 1996, and the National Commission on Terrorist Attacks Upon the United States in 2004—have called for the increased utilization of dogs. Following the attacks of 9/11 the federal government's Explosives Detection Canine Team Program has rapidly expanded to include more than 425 teams at 75 airports and 13 mass transit systems.[119]

Historically, LEO presence requirements varied—initially from a requirement to be stationed at the screening point, to a later "flexible response" model where the LEO could be summoned as needed within a specified period of time, depending upon the airport's passenger activity level. Much discretion was given to the FAA Administrator to determine the acceptability of each airport sponsor's law enforcement support system.[120] After 9/11, however, if the TSA provides law enforcement presence, airport police are then required to back up the TSA as needed.[121]

---

[118] *TSA's Fine K-9s*, Airport Report Magazine (Jan./Feb. 2003), at 9, 11.

[119] Senate Resolution 104 (Mar. 9, 2007).

[120] Subsequent to the TSA assuming responsibility for airport security, it has "looked at what is before it to be controlled," and has "rubricized" airport categories to its own liking. The TSA has been silent on what criteria it uses to categorize the airports. But generally they are categorized as Category I, II, III, etc., with the most prominent Category I airports being classified as Category X. With prior LEO response programs under Part 108, the response time varied depending upon the size of the airport. At Category I airports (screening over two million people annually) the response time could not exceed five minutes, and at selected Category IA airports could not exceed one minute. At Category II airports (screening 500,000 to two million) the response time was 10 minutes. At Category III (less than 500,000 to two million) the response time was 15 minutes. And, for Category IV airports (serving air carriers with less than sixty seats) the response time could be as much as 20 minutes.

[121] When TSR 1542 was created, the following was noted in the Federal Register, (Fri., Feb. 22, 2002), Vol. 67, No. 36, Rules and Regulations:

Security risks associated with airline *employees* became an issue with the crash of a Pacific Southwest Airlines [PSA] commuter jet near Paso Robles, California, in December of 1987. The crash occurred after a former PSA employee, flying as a passenger, opened fire with a gun during the flight. The procedures to guard against air piracy that had been in place for nearly 20 years had served their purpose well, but in the PSA crash, they failed. Moreover, with the introduction of "plastic" explosive materials, they were no longer as effective against the threat of concealed explosives. Emanating out of the PSA crash, the FAA in 1988 amended airport security regulations to better control airport access including that attempted by airline and airport employees. However, even today, there exist some loopholes by which airport employees may access a sterile concourse from the ramp without having been screened.

Although 49 CFR 1542, "Airport Security" was largely based on the old FAR Part 107 (also called "Airport Security"), the new regulation contains many changes. TSR 1542 requires the designation of an Airport Security Coordinator to work closely with the TSA to create and implement the Airport Security Program [ASP] (referred to as a "complete program"). The plan must contain several elements:

- The name, means of contact, duties, and training requirements of the *Airport Security Coordinator* [ASC];
- A *description of the secured areas*, including a diagram with dimensions detailing boundaries and features; access control measures; measures used to perform the access control functions; Procedures to control movement within the secured area

---

The airport operator must provide law enforcement personnel to support its security program and to support each system for screening persons and accessible property required under Parts 1544 or 1546. This screening includes the inspection of individuals and property, as well as other security measures such as those that take place at the ticket counter, such as Computer Assisted Passenger Prescreening System. TSA will be assuming responsibility for law enforcement presence for the inspection of individuals and property as necessary. When TSA assumes this duty at the airport, the airport will no longer need to perform this function on a routine basis. However, the airport operator will continue to provide a law enforcement presence and capability that is adequate to ensure the safety of passengers in accordance with 49 U.S.C. 44903(c), including covering screening before TSA law enforcement assumes this duty. Airport law enforcement will also be expected to back up TSA law enforcement officers at screening locations should the need arise. TSA will work closely with law enforcement agencies at each airport to ensure that all agencies cooperate in providing for the safe and secure operation of the airport.

and ID media requirement; and a description of the notification signs;

- A *description of the Airport Operations Area* [AOA], including a map detailing boundaries and pertinent features; each activity or entity on, or adjacent to, an AOA that affects security; measures used to perform the access control functions; and measures to control movement within the AOA, including identification media as appropriate; and description of notification signs;
- A *description of the Security Identification Display Area* [SIDA], including a map detailing boundaries and pertinent features; each activity or entity on, or adjacent to, a SIDA;
- A *description of the sterile areas,*[122] including a diagram with dimensions detailing boundaries and pertinent features; access controls to be used when the passenger-screening checkpoint is non-operational and the entity responsible for that access control; and measures used to control access;
- Procedures regarding fingerprint-based *criminal history records checks*;
- Personnel *identification* systems;
- *Escort* procedures;
- *Challenge* procedures;
- *Training* programs;
- *Law enforcement* support;
- Record keeping systems;
- Procedures and facilities used to support *TSA inspections* as required in TSR 1544 and 1546;
- Contingency plan;
- Procedures for the *distribution, storage, and disposal* of security programs, and other sensitive or classified information;
- Procedures for posting of *public advisories*;
- *Incident management* procedures;
- *Alternate security procedures* to be use in natural disasters, and other emergency or unusual conditions;
- *Exclusive area agreements*; and
- Airport *tenant security* programs.

[122] *I.e.*, the areas where passengers and baggage have been screened for security purposes.

AN EXPLOSIVE EVOLUTION

In response to the tragic loss of Pan Am 103 in 1988, Presidential Executive Order 12686 established the President's Commission on Aviation Security and Terrorism. The Aviation Security Improvement Act of 1990 was enacted, in large part, to implement the recommendations of the President's Commission on Aviation Security and Terrorism. The 1990 act amended the Federal Aviation Act of 1958 by adding a new sub-section, "Employment Standards," directing the FAA Administrator to prescribe minimum standards for hiring and continued employment of air carrier and airport security personnel.

Subsequent to the bombing of Pan Am 103, FAR Part 107 was amended many times in piecemeal fashion and in response to individual aviation disasters. Then in response to the crash of TWA Flight 800 in 1996, the President's Commission alone made 57 recommendations for improving aviation safety. Between passage of the Aviation Security Improvement Act in 1990 and 1999 both FAR Parts 107 and 108 had been in rewrite effectively for more than eight years. The final rewrite of those federal aviation regulations came just before the attacks in 2001. But much attention was being focused on requirements for security screening companies and personnel. The *Threat Image Projection* [TIP] system was proposed for installation on existing baggage X-ray machines and designed to measure the performance of screeners by randomly placing realistic images of threatening objects onto the screen. The TIP system is one component of an overall computer-based *Screener Proficiency Evaluation and Reporting System* [SPEARS]. SPEARS will be used to select, train, evaluate and monitor X-ray-screening employees.[123]

The Pan Am 103 incident highlighted not only the difficulty of detecting modern plastic explosives but also the growing capability of terrorist groups. The FAA effort to find a technical counter-terrorism solution accelerated in the aftermath of Flight 103. FAA broadened its research in programs such as:

- Working with aircraft manufacturers to develop techniques to *harden an aircraft* against the effects of a midair explosion;

[123] *See* Karl Bremer, *The Security Blues—Will Part 107 Rewrite Ever Surface?* Airport Magazine (Mar./Apr. 1999), at 28-29.

- A major new initiative in the *human factors* of using technologies for screening;
- Additional work in identifying suspects through the application of *profiles and questioning*; and
- Special programs for *Thermal Neutron Analysis* [TNA] enhancement, the process of nuclear resonance absorption and vapor detection device.

When baggage is introduced to the TNA machine, neutron radiation activates elements in the bags, which then briefly emit gamma radiation measured by deflectors. The unique signature of gamma radiation can identify hidden objects. The FAA installed several TNA units at airports around the world, and although reportedly pleased with the results, remained officially undecided about proceeding with the TNA program. Ultimately, critics contended that TNA was not cost-effective and had a high rate of false alarms, particularly when testing woolen articles. Wool contains high concentrations of nitrogen, and can be misidentified as explosives. In one test of the TNA, the machine processed 500 to 1,000 bags per day. When required to detect 2.5 pounds or more of explosives, the unit had a false alarm rate of about 5%. When set to detect less than one pound of explosives the rate went up to 20%.

Passage of the Aviation Security Improvement Act of 1990 temporarily blocked any further procurement of TNA devices pending more research. The act directed the FAA to "accelerate and expand the research, development, and the implementation of technologies and procedures to counteract terrorist acts against civil aviation. The FAA requested that the Committee on Commercial Aviation Security be extended to provide advice regarding the implementation of the Aviation Security Improvement Act of 1990. The FAA asked for help in two key areas: *systems analysis and architecture* for explosive detection systems that could inspect passenger baggage and the development of *test protocols and performance criteria* for such systems.

In evaluating the "enemy" capabilities, against which counterterrorist measure must be designed, terrorists have literally dozens of choices of explosives, as shown in Table 9.2, "Chemicals and Other Demolitions Paraphernalia (Used in Truck Bomb Attacks Against U.S. Government Facilities)."

Table 9.2—CHEMICALS AND OTHER DEMOLITIONS PARAPHERNALIA (USED IN TRUCK BOMB ATTACKS AGAINST U.S. GOVERNMENT FACILITIES)

Substance	***Amount*** *(where available)*
Urea Crystals	1,000 lbs. (47% purity)
Nitric Acid	105 Gals.
Sulphuric Acid	60 Gals. (93% purity)
Ammonium Nitrate (fertilizer)	108 bags (50 lbs. each)
Nitro-Glycerine	
Potassium Nitrate	
Methenamine	
Hydrogen	4 Bottles (4 feet long)
Sodium Azide	
Magnesium Azide	
Aniline Reagent	
Ethanol	
Battery Acid	18 liters
Liquid Nitromethane (racing fuel)	3 drums (50 gals. each)
Tovex blasting gelatine	
Shock Tube	
Anhydrous Hydrazine (boiler cleaner)	

Source: DHS Information Bulletin, *Potential Indicators of Threats Involving Vehicle Borne Improvised Explosive Devices* [VBIEDs], www.mipt.org/pdf/dhsbulletinvbied.pdf (visited Apr. 27, 2007).

However, the explosive of choice seems to be the high energetic "plastic" explosives that are widely available. Using plastic explosives, small, powerful bombs can be inexpensively constructed. These *nitrogen-based* (nitramine) explosives have three qualities that make them attractive to the terrorist:

- They have *high-energy yields* per unit weight;
- They have *small critical diameters* (i.e., the small diameter that can sustain detonation); and
- They require *little or no confinement* (i.e., heavy metal walls).

As a result, the focus in research and design of explosive detection devices is to search primarily for systems that can detect plastic explosives. Nevertheless, there are other types of explosives and devices that also pose significant threats.

There are basically three general types of mechanical security detection techniques recognized by the FAA: (1) *enhanced X-ray* machines; (2) *vapor detection* systems; and (3) *particle detection* equipment such as TNA. A fourth and far less sophisticated detection system uses *dogs* to sniff out and detect explosives. Enhanced X-ray differentiates between organic and inorganic materials to aid in identifying explosives in luggage. Unlike X-ray machines, vapor detectors key on minute traces of explosive compounds captured in air samples. Table 9.3 "Explosive Detection Devices" [EDD] lists a variety of devices that had been explored as of the mid-1990s.

In the past decade, the TSA has explored other interesting approaches including Nuclear Quadrupole Resonance, X-Ray Diffraction, Multi-view X-ray, and Neutron and Gamma Ray. In addition, combined technologies have been considered such as Nuclear Quadrupole Resonance in conjunction with CT technology.[124] Also, Explosive Trace Detection [ETD] used in conjunction with X-ray imaging for object identification.[125]

---

[124] At airports, the machines can scan several hundred bags an hour using Computerized Tomography [CT], formerly known as Computed Axial Tomography (CAT or CT scans), which uses medical imaging technology to generate a three-dimensional image to "compare the density of objects inside luggage to the density of known explosives." *See* Beth Kassab, *Screening Machines to Take Backstage Role: The Large Machines will be Moved to Free Up Space in OIA's Ticketing Area*, The Orlando (FL) Sentinel (Mar. 20, 2006).

[125] Robin C. "Chuck" Burke, *Technology Briefing*, TSA, (date unknown).

Table 9.3—EXPLOSIVE DETECTION DEVICES

EDD Technique	*Principle of Operation*	*Characteristic Detected*
Thermal Neutron Activation [TNA]	Low energy neutrons captured by nitrogen atoms, resulting de-excitation produces characteristic gamma rays.	Nitrogen content
Elastic Neutron Scattering	Monoenergetic neutron source used to scan objects; elastically back-scattered neutrons are detected.	Carbon, nitrogen, oxygen content calculated from neutron energy loss
Pulsed Fast Neutron Activation [PFNA]	Fast pulses of neutron beams used to excite characteristic gamma rays.	Provides carbon, nitrogen, and oxygen compositional information
Photon Activation	A powerful electron linear accelerator produces brems-stahlung X-rays, which in turn produce a radioactive isotope of nitrogen when encountering nitrogen atoms. The resultant nitrogen isotope has a 10 minute half life, and decays by emitting a positron.	Nitrogen content
Nuclear Resonant Absorption [NRA]	Proton beam bombards a target to produce high energy gamma rays which preferentially excite nitrogen atoms.	Nitrogen content
Fast Neutron Associated Particle [FNAP]	High energy neutrons produced from a deuteriumtritium reaction are ejected in known directions relative to an ejected associated alpha particles. These fast neu-trons activate nuclei by inelastic scattering which results in emis sion of characteristic gamma rays. Correlation of the direction of the gamma rays with the alpha parti-cles yields directionality.	Relative amounts of carbon, nitrogen, and oxygen

Table 9.3 (continued)

EDD Technique	*Principle of Operation*	*Characteristic Detected*
Duel Energy X-ray	Alternating X-ray beams of high and low energy levels produce two different images due to differences between the photoelectric and Compton attenuation coefficiencies of the different elements. By comparing the images, the areas with light elements can be identified.	Average atomic number, density, and shape
Backscatter Analysis X-ray	Compares normal X-ray transmission image with a Compton backscatter image. By comparing the images, the areas with light elements can be identified.	Average atomic number, density, and shape
Extremely Low-Dose X-ray	Same as backscatter analysis X-ray but at a lower X-ray intensity level.	Average atomic number, density, and shape
Coherent X-ray Scattering	X-ray diffraction.	Crystal structure
Dual Energy X-ray Computed Tomography [CT]	A CT image is a map of the X-ray attenuation coefficient in each voxel. Attenuation depends on density and composition. Differences between photoelectric and Compton attenuation coefficients at two different energy levels are used to solve for density and composition.	Shape, atomic number, and density
Vapor/Particle Detection Devices	Devices employ a variety of methods, including: gas chromatography; chemical luminescence; and/or mass spectrometry.	Volatility, molecular weight, and electron affinity

Source: Committee on Commercial Aviation Security, *Detection of Explosives for Commercial Aviation Security*, NMAB-471 (1993).

Not withstanding other technological advances in security technology, K-9 units remain one of the most effective tools for combating crime and terrorism. For reasons that are not altogether understood, dogs are able to sense the volatility and possibly other characteristics of explosives. But more advanced, scientifically reliable technology is needed.

The terrorist bombing of Pan Am Flight 103, which killed 270 people, clearly demonstrated the need for new technology to detect explosives. The Aviation Security Improvement Act set a goal for the FAA to have new explosive detection equipment in place by November 1993. Questioning whether the goal had been met, members of Congress asked the Government Accounting Office to examine the FAA's progress in developing new security technology and to specify actions the FAA could take to improve its security research program. In May of 1994, the GAO reported the FAA had made little progress toward meeting the goal for deploying new explosive detection systems. Although several devices had shown promise, technical problems had slowed development and approval of the devices. Similarly, the FAA's efforts to enhance aircraft survivability following an internal explosion (by hardening baggage containers) were promising but were also several years from completion. Finally, the FAA lacked a strategy to guide its and the airlines' efforts to implement explosive detection equipment, nor had the FAA resolved such issues as cost, weight, and durability of hardened baggage containers.[126]

Unfortunately, within two years of the GAO report there was an explosion aboard Trans World Airlines Flight 800 just after takeoff. The explosion of TWA Flight 800 off Long Island on July 17, 1996 killed 230 people. No one knew for sure what caused the explosion. It could have been a mechanical malfunction, or there was a theory that because one of the fuel tanks was partially empty, vapors in the tank may have exploded. But the possibility of a bomb having been placed aboard the aircraft or even a missile fired from the coast of Long Island Sound as the aircraft was climbing out was also suspected. Fearing sabotage, the White House Commission on Aviation Safety and Security was formed, chaired by Vice President Al Gore, to investigate what might be done to enhance aviation safety and security.

---

[126] GAO, *Aviation Security: Development of New Security Technology Has Not Met Expectations*, GAO/RCED-94-142 (May 19, 1994).

On September 5, 1996, the Gore Commission announced its proposals to fight terrorism. Basically, the recommendations were a reiteration of what had already been presented:

- To install state-of-the-art *bomb-detecting equipment* in airports;
- To fund *research and development* necessary to make the technology more effective and readily available;
- Increase the number of *bomb-sniffing dog teams*;
- A mandatory *match between passengers and their luggage*; and
- Better screening of passengers through computerized *profiles*.

The report highlights the fact that much of its work was based on addressing the public's *emotional needs*. And, Robert Hahn laments, "The sad truth is that the threat of airline terrorism cannot be eliminated unless air travel is banned. . . ."[127] But as Al Gore resolved,

> *We may never see an end to terrorism, but we are sure going to do our level best to combat it and reduce to an absolute minimum level humanly possible the risk to American citizens traveling on airlines.*[128]

In 1996 President Clinton signed into law the Federal Aviation Administration Reauthorization Act, which included some wide-ranging security measures recommended by Al Gore's aviation security commission. It authorized the installation of new bomb-detection scanners to examine both carry-on and checked baggage at major airports, funding for new FBI agents to be assigned to airport security, increased inspection of mail on board flights, and increased use of bomb-sniffing dogs.[129]

Shortly after 9/11, President Bush signed the Aviation and Transportation Security Act, which directed the federal government to assume the screening of all commercial airline passengers for weapons, explosives and other hazardous/dangerous items. Since that date, the

---

[127] *See* Karen Walker and Dave Knibb, *Blood, Sweat and Gore*, Airline Business (Apr. 1997).

[128] U.S. News Story Page, *Gore Announces Proposals to Fight Air Terrorism*, http://www.cnn.com/US/9609/05/airport.security/index.html (visited Feb. 18, 1999).

[129] U.S. News Story Page, *Clinton Signs Airport Security Measures Into Law*, http://www.cnn.com/US/9610/09/faa/index.html (visited Feb. 18, 1999).

TSA federalized screening at more than 440 commercial service airports. According to the TSA, about 45% of federal screening hours are spent screening bags, while 55% is spent screening passengers.[130]

NEW EXPLOSIVE DETECTION TECHNOLOGY

There has been a variety of solutions to security concerns that have been implemented at airports in the United States and around the Globe in hopes of reducing security risks. These include changes in personnel selection, training, and retention practices; an increased use of canine security applications; new or increased perimeter and facility surveillance methods; and an increased incorporation of new technologies. While many question the obvious (how would these actions have prevented the events of September 11, 2001?) others question the practicality or inconvenience to which they've been subjected since the 100% checked bag rule went into affect.

Unfortunately, the federal government's security initiatives have been beset with negative externalities such as passenger delays, explosive detection inaccuracies, and related slow processing speeds, and the challenges (as well as the infrastructure accommodation costs) associated with the mandated installation of these very large, heavy pieces of equipment.

Perhaps the most visible of these security technology "solutions" are the explosive detection systems that travelers have seen introduced into airport lobbies, as required by the 100% checked bag screening initiative. The Aviation and Transportation Security Act (as amended by the Homeland Security Act) ultimately required that by December 31, 2003, all checked baggage being loaded onto commercial aircraft be 100% screened for explosives.[131] The TSA uses two types of devices to detect explosives in checked bags: *Explosive Trace Detection* or ETD and *Explosive Detection Systems* or EDS. Table 9.4, "EDS and ETD Machines Deployed," shows the number of EDS and EDT machines deployed at U.S. airports in 2004 by airport security category. Both of the types of devices the TSA uses to screen checked baggage for explosives (EDS and ETD) have limitations that

---

[130] Subcommittee on Aviation, *Airline Passenger Baggage Screening: Technology and Airport Deployment Update* (Jun. 29, 2006), at 1.

[131] Homeland Security Act (PL 107-296).

create operational efficiency and require additional backup screening methods.

Table 9.4—EDS AND ETD MACHINES DEPLOYED

Category	*Airports*	*EDS Units*	*ETD Units*
X	21	679	2833
I	61	467	2401
II	50	71	695
III	124	9	744
IV	190	2	473

Source: GAO analysis of data presented in Airport Magazine (May/Jun. 2005), at 58.

The ETD machines are roughly the same size as a common laser printer and cost only a few thousand dollars. They can detect minute traces of explosive residue, which may have been transferred to baggage surfaces through direct contact. ETD machines have extremely high detection rates and very low false-positive rates. But, unfortunately, the process for collecting trace samples is slow, labor intensive, and highly susceptible to human error. They work best as a primary means of explosive detection at low-throughput airports. Nevertheless, to meet the baggage-screening deadline, TSA deployed ETD machines extensively.[132] As of mid-2006, more than 7,400 EDT machines were deployed.

Conversely, EDS machines can be as large as a minivan, weigh up to 17,000 pounds and cost over $1 million each, with an equal amount of money needed for fortifying floors and building expansion for housing this technology. In addition, older models are labor intensive. Newer models are less labor labor-intensive, and can be highly automated and networked to scan bags by the hundreds each hour. They use computer tomography or other advanced methods to scan objects and compare density to the density of known explosives. The problem is that these machines have high incidence of both false-positive and false-negative alarms. Many common objects have densities similar to

[132] Subcommittee on Aviation, *Airline Passenger Baggage Screening: Technology and Airport Deployment Update* (Jun. 29, 2006), at 2.

commercial and military grade explosives; thus a high number of false-positive indications can result. And since they require the presence of a sufficiently large mass of explosive to function properly, there is a high likelihood of a false-negative alarm if small amounts of explosive are present. One of the biggest problems is the size of the EDS machines. Most terminals require significant modification prior to installation.[133]

The first EDS was certified in 1999, and currently three EDS manufacturers have received official TSA certification: (1) L-3 Communications, (2) GE Security and (3) Reveal Imaging Technology. By June of 2006, more than 1,700 EDS had been purchased by the TSA for use at airports.[134]

The aviation community has put pressure on the TSA to move the EDS machines out of terminal lobbies (free-standing EDS) and to integrate them into the airport's automated baggage systems (in-line EDS). In-line EDS have higher explosive detection capability, on-screen alarm resolution, better false-positive rates, less staffing, lower maintenance, and less out-of-service time. In-line systems are categorized as follows:[135]

- High speed fully integrated in-line systems;
- Medium speed fully integrated systems;
- Mini in-line system; and
- Micro in-line system (in testing).

The first two in-line options, while fast, require rather extensive terminal modifications such as reinforced flooring and electrical upgrades, and thus only 23 airports had converted to full in-line systems as of mid-2006. Unfortunately, installation of an in-line EDS would require extensive terminal and baggage conveyor system modification at most airports.[136] Funding for these systems contin-

---

[133] *Id.*

[134] *Id.*

[135] *Id.*

[136] Necessary modifications include reinforced flooring, Information Technology [IT] networking, electrical upgrades, new conveyor systems, and sundry other new facilities. Airport officials have estimated the total cost for integration of EDS nationwide to be around $5 billion. As of Jul. 2004, eight airports had converted to full in-line operations, with an additional ninth airport in the process. An additional eight airports had signed letters of intent with the TSA, and 12 more had approved plans and were awaiting federal funding approval. *Id.*

ues to be a problem, as the TSA cites a lack of available funds. Some airports have used the Airport Improvement Program, their own revenue, or Passenger Facility Charges to fund inline EDS.[137] While the fully integrated EDS in-line systems are both large and expensive, in the long run their processing efficiency and reduced labor costs will allow the expense to be recouped in 1-5 years.[138]

Many airports are seeking an alternative to the larger and expensive in-line systems. One option growing in favor at airports is one called "In-line Lite." This creative approach eliminates the need for complex construction by utilizing vertical space and open pockets of baggage room space to create the Baggage Handling System [BHS] component of in-line system.[139] In addition, to the In-line Lite option, TSA also continues to explore *Next Generation EDS Technology* via its Phoenix Project (lowering false alarms, increasing throughput, and improving detection) and its Manhattan 2 project.[140]

In addition to EDS and ETD, the TSA is also testing newer technologies such as Human and Document Trace Detection units. Current walk-through explosives detection *Trace Portals* have been constructed by Smiths Detection and GE Corporation. Trace portals work by sending puffs of air onto a person and then checking the ambient air for traces of explosives. Explosive trace detection document scanners can detect explosives on paperwork.[141]

Introduction of federal TSA employees as screeners, installation of baggage screening equipment, and other modifications to the way passengers are screened have had a strong visual impact. One important change in airport security is the changing of the industry's perception of how to conduct a thorough risk assessment and, generally, the receptivity for application of new solutions to a variety of security-related concerns. "Effective risk management means moving from the concept of controlling crises to embracing the idea of mak-

---

[137] U.S. House of Representatives, Subcommittee on Aviation, hearing on *In-Line Explosive Detection Systems: Financing and Development* (Jul. 14, 2004) and Subcommittee on Aviation, *Airline Passenger Baggage Screening: Technology and Airport Deployment Update* (Jun. 29, 2006), at 1-7.

[138] *Id.* at 3.

[139] Rodger L. Dickey, *Inline Lite—Inline Right?* Airport Magazine (May/Jun. 2005), at 50-53.

[140] Subcommittee on Aviation, *Airline Passenger Baggage Screening: Technology and Airport Deployment Update* (Jun. 29, 2006), at 5.

[141] Robin C. "Chuck" Burke, *Technology Briefing*, TSA (date unknown).

ing decisions proactively to forestall problems before they happen."[142] This more proactive approach includes consideration of both physical and financial risks.

Indeed, economic (including revenue considerations) and liability concerns have been elevated to an unprecedented status in risk planning. "Risk assessment entails estimating the magnitude of the identified risks in order to prioritize them on the basis of their potential ramifications. According to the level of risk, a notification plan is prepared to alert key decision-makers."[143]

ECONOMIC STATE OF THE AVIATION INDUSTRY

"Aviation is key to our nation's economic health," said Delta Air Lines Chairman and CEO Leo F. Mullin, as he cited the industry's provision of 1 million jobs, $17.7 million in taxes, support for the $700 billion tourism and travel industry, and carriage of 620 million passengers and 22 billion tons of cargo, annually.[144] Unfortunately, the economic and societal impacts of the attacks were profound and threaten the continued provision of these economic benefits.

According to the Air Transportation Association, the 2001 industry losses for just the nine major airlines totaled $7.4 billion. Wall Street analysts estimate the air carriers' losses to be approximately $14 billion for the two years proceeding March 2003.[145] Then, from 2003 to 2007, several bankruptcies, restructurings and mergers occurred. In his January 2007 testimony to the Committee on Commerce, Science and Transportation Assistant DOT Secretary Andrew Steinberg discussed the status of the airline industry,

> *The U.S. airline industry remains in the midst of an historic restructuring. Over the last five years, U.S. network airlines have reduced their annualized mainline costs excluding fuel by more than 25%, or nearly $20 billion. While some of the cost savings were the product of*

[142] Gerald Fitzgerald, *Risk Assessment in a New Environment*, Airport Magazine (May/Jun. 2003), at 38.
[143] *Id.*
[144] Leo Mullin, Testimony before the Subcommittee on Aviation: House Committee on Transportation and Infrastructure, http://www.house.gov (visited (2003).
[145] Air Transport Assn., *State of the Airline Industry One Year After 9/11* (Sep. 24, 2002).

> *identifying greater operational efficiencies, most of the savings were generated by renegotiation of existing contractual arrangements with creditors, aircraft lessors, suppliers and airline employees and achieved either through the bankruptcy process itself or under threat of bankruptcy. 22 percent of industry capacity is still operated in bankruptcy—down from a high of 46 percent in 2005 but still substantial by any measure. The result is that several carriers that were on the precipice of liquidation just five years ago now have much lower cost structures that should allow them to return to profitability over the short term.* [146]

Steinberg attributed this major industry restructuring to a "confluence of intense competition, structural conditions in the industry, and a series of exogenous events that temporarily depressed air travel demand or increased costs (e.g., the September 11th terrorist attacks, the war on terror, greater security burdens, Severe Acute Respiratory Syndrome [SARS], and much higher fuel prices)." During this time, the airlines successfully focused on six major areas of cost reduction: labor, fuel, IT/reservations/customer service, (travel agent) commissions, fleet/maintenance (retiring older aircraft), and pensions. Steinberg reported, "In 2006, the industry recorded its first annual profit since 2000, estimated to be $2 billion on revenues of nearly $123 billion."[147] However, in 2007, there was concern about the long-term airline industry outlook which Steinberg reported as "more uncertain." The problems that contribute to this uncertainly include:

- Many networked carriers are still highly leveraged;
- Fuel and labor costs—which constitute some of the largest expenses incurred by the industry—are expected to increase;
- Some international markets still constrain competition (e.g., United Kingdom, China, Japan, Latin America);

---

[146] Andrew Steinberg, DOT Assistant Secretary for Avn. & Intl. Affairs, Testimony before the Committee on Commerce, *Science and Transportation*, retrieved from http://testimony.ost.dot.gov/test/steinberg1.htm (Jan. 24, 2007).

[147] *Id.*

- The cost of capital to U.S. carriers has increased due to cross-border investment restrictions;
- Airlines delayed investments in fleet renewal and other new techniques, which is bound to reduce their competitiveness in the long run; and
- Carrier bankruptcy tends to result in the bankrupt carriers (with renegotiated contracts) having a competitive advantage over those airlines that did not seek such protection.

Airlines are "particularly susceptible to this phenomenon because the business is highly responsive to economic cycles." As Steinberg explains:

> *Just as most network airlines are now expected to turn an operating profit, most lost substantial sums in the last several years; when one carrier finds itself in trouble, typically most others do. Consequently, when one firm falls behind on its aircraft lease payments, its lessors may lack the economic leverage to reclaim assets (because they cannot redeploy them profitably elsewhere)—and thus don't. This is compounded by the ability of airlines operating in Chapter 11 to win significant savings on their leases and postpone reconfirmation of leases, allowing bankrupt airline managers to 'time' the bottom of the market and gain a capital cost advantage over their competitors.* [148]

Airports, too, have had parallel losses since 9/11, in part associated with the air carriers experiencing financial difficulties. Steinberg noted, "Airports that are reliant on large airline tenants face a similar bargaining dynamic in difficult financial times for the industry and must also make concessions that keep failing companies afloat."[149] While in 2006, it was reported that airports

---

[148] *Id.*
[149] *Id.*

"have performed admirably overall, increasing credit ratings, generating adequate revenues, and convincing financial markets to lend monies for expansion,"[150] airports still face challenges.

After 9/11, airports were financially affected on at least three levels: airline financial troubles, increased security-related costs, and decreased concession revenues. For example, new TSA security requirements resulted in increased costs for security personnel, technology acquisition, and infrastructure remodeling. Also, many airports experienced an immediate loss (due to the grounding of aircraft) and thereafter due to loss in post-checkpoint concession revenues, as meters-and-greeters were prohibited from going beyond the checkpoints. Finally, some airports were prohibited from allowing proximal parking (i.e., within 300 feet of terminals) for several months, due to TSA concerns about car bombs, or Large Vehicle-Bourne Improvised Explosive Devices [LVBIEDs], thus greatly reducing parking revenues.

Studies have shown that the largest amount of explosives able to be loaded into an automobile (from a compact to a full sized sedan) is between 500 to 1,000 pounds. Because the heavy load would likely depress the vehicle onto its springs, it would send a signal that it might be an LVBIED. A rental moving truck could carry as much as 10,000-20,000 pounds of explosives and still look like it is empty, but the truck itself might draw attention. Still, it is most likely that a minivan, van or small truck would be used as the LVBIED.[151] Although the TSA did modify the 300-foot rule in 2002 (linking the separation of parked vehicles from terminals to the DHS's threat bulletin system), it is generally perceived that the lack of advance knowledge of threat-level changes makes this modification of little value.

After 9/11, it was feared that already ailing air carriers might go bankrupt, unless federal financial stabilization was provided. Airlines were suffering, economically, from reduced demand (due to a slowing economy) and rising labor costs.[152] Just 11 days after the attacks, the Air Transportation Safety and System Stabilization Act of 2002 (the Stabilization Act) was signed by President Bush to provide airline loan guarantees of up to $10 billion as well as direct

---

[150] *Airport Financial Trends: A Preliminary Look at 2000-2005 Data*, Airport Magazine (Jun./Jul. 2006), at 25.

[151] Kevin Miles, FBI, Los Angeles, *Possible Indicators of the Presence of a Large Vehicle Bourne Improvised Explosive Device (LVBIED)*, http://www,google.com (visited Jul. 30, 2004).

[152] House of Representatives Financial Subcommittee on Aviation, *Hearing on Financial Condition of the Airline Industry* (Sep. 22, 2001).

compensation for losses, where appropriate.[153] The House Committee on Transportation and Infrastructure's Subcommittee on Aviation, in its Hearing on the Financial Condition of the Airline Industry, reported that, as of September 2002, the Stabilization Act directly compensated passenger and cargo air carriers more than $4.5 billion in direct compensation.[154]

Unfortunately, the air transportation industry remains in economic peril. "The dark aftermath of September 11th only served to throw the proverbial gasoline on the fire," stated American Airlines president and CEO Donald Carty. In his congressional testimony, "[We moved] aggressively to reduce costs . . . [but] the cumulative effect of new government taxes, fees, mandates, and restrictions has added billions of dollars in costs to the airlines—costs that Washington simply cannot continue to expect us to pay and at the same time assume we will survive." Carty continued, "Just to survive day-to-day, airlines have had to take on massive debt, and as a result, our balance sheets and credit ratings are deteriorating rapidly. In fact, the average U.S. carrier is now 90% leveraged."[155]

Carty continued, "As for the security challenges we as a nation face, I believe that security is better than it's ever been, and getting better. The bottom-line is, however, that providing for the security of our nation's citizens and fighting the wars on terrorism are national security issues and fundamentally governmental functions. As such, if the U.S. government determines what specific regime needs to be in place to secure our nation's airways, it should pay for it."[156] While Congress was responsive to initial pleas for assistance (passing the Emergency Wartime Supplemental Appropriations Act of 2003, which offered $2.3 billion to U.S. airlines for the expense and lost revenue associated with aviation security), Congress was ultimately less responsive in subsequent requests for assistance.

The United States is not alone in its concern about the economic impact of a terrorist incident. At a March 2007 Asia-Pacific Economic Cooperation Transportation Ministers' Meeting, Australia's Deputy Prime Minister and Minister for Transport and Regional

---

[153] P.L. 107-42.

[154] House of Representatives Financial Subcommittee on Aviation, *Hearing on Financial Condition of the Airline Industry* (Sep. 22, 2001).

[155] Donald Carty, Testimony before the House Committee on Transportation and Infrastructure, Subcommittee on Aviation (Sep. 24, 2003).

[156] *Id.*

Services Mark Vaile estimated that the economic impact of a terrorist attack on a large passenger aircraft in Australia to be $30 billion.[157] Key in economic survival is to recognize the economic vulnerabilities associated with a closely networked transportation system and to build "the capacity of all economies to create an environment for the secure and efficient movement of passengers and freight across the region." Vaile explains,

> *The networked nature of the region's transport system means that attacks in one economy can have far reaching ramifications for other economies, so improving preventative security in the transport sector is an important challenge for all economies in the region. Cooperation, collaboration and capacity building offer significant opportunities for all economies to enhance their transport security frameworks. For example, developing comprehensive transport security strategies that focus on the international intermodal movement of cargo door-to-door, and in particular focusing on the high-risk transfer points is an important economic priority for the economy.* [158]

At an October 2005 international security conference, airport executives openly shared issues, and potential solutions for unresolved aviation security problems. One common problem shared by airports across the globe is concern about security costs. In Dublin, Airport Director Robert Hilliard focused on the need "to balance the cost of security with the required security regiment, and predicted dire consequences if this warning is ignored." Speaking on behalf of the European Commission's Energy and Transport Unit, Aviation Security and Maritime Director Eckerd Seibohm echoed Hilliard's concerns about security costs, particularly those associated with the European Civil Aviation Conference and European Union security requirements.[159]

---

[157] Mark Vaile, as quoted in Jim Ensom, *Call for Tighter Airline Security*, South Africa—GlobalContinuity.com (Mar. 26, 2007).
[158] *Id.*
[159] Jeff Price & Sean Broderick, *International Issues,* Airport Magazine (Sep./Oct. 2005), at 80.

In addition, European airport and aviation officials share a common concern that, if passengers suffer much more inconvenience due to intensified airport security, they may switch to trains and other modes of transportation that are available. Hilliard concluded, "We need to balance security needs versus getting passengers through."[160] Finally, intelligence and information sharing is as much a concern abroad as it is for U.S. airports. Seibohm commented, "Intelligence agencies are protecting information that airports need."[161]

SECURITY PROCEDURES: NEEDED PROTECTION OR INVASION OF PRIVACY

As mentioned earlier in this chapter, while some analysts discuss the need to continue making meaningful improvements in air transportation security, others feel the pendulum has swung too far in the opposite direction, particularly in the area of privacy concerns. American Civil Liberties Union [ACLU] legislative counselor Katie Corrigan suggested a "three-prong analysis" before Congress implements additional security measures. First, any new security proposals must be genuinely effective rather than creating a false sense of security. Second, security measures should be implemented in a non-discriminatory manner. Individuals should not be subjected to intrusive searches or questioning based on their perceived or actual race, ethnic origin, or religion, or based on proxies for such characterizations. Finally, if a security measure is determined to be genuinely effective, the government should work to ensure that its implementation minimizes its costs to fundamental freedoms including the right to due process, privacy and equality.[162]

Of particular concern to the ACLU and others concerned about the strong potential for discrimination—particularly that based on gender, race or religion—is the possibility of compromised privacy when an airline collects and analyzes personal data in an effort to predetermine those who may be at higher risk of committing acts of air piracy. Using an FAA grant, Northwest Airlines developed the first profiling system, referred to as *Computer-Assisted Passenger Prescreening System* [CAPPS]. By analyzing more than 40 pieces of

---

160 *Id.* at 79.
161 *Id.* at 80.
162 Katie Corrigan, Testimony before the House Committee on Transportation and Infrastructure, Subcommittee on Aviation (Feb. 27, 2003).

secret information collected by the airlines, the computer selects a number of individuals (referred to as "selectees"), as well as some randomly selected travelers, all of whom are subjected to heighten security procedures.[163] Currently, more advanced versions of CAPPS are being tested in the U.S., although for all intents and purposes CAPPS II is officially "dead." The government's controversial plan to screen passengers before they board the plane was officially terminated—but the TSA promised it would return in a new form with a new name. Homeland Security spokeswoman admitted that "The name CAPPS II may be dead, but the process of creating an automated passenger pre-screening system to replace (the current) CAPPS will continue."[164]

CAPPS II was a limited, automated prescreening system authorized by Congress in the wake of 9/11. The intent was to modernize the prescreening process by authenticating travelers' identities and performing risk assessments to detect individuals who may pose a terrorist-related threat or who have outstanding federal or state warrants for crimes of violence. The TSA considers CAPPS II (or a derivative) to be a critical element in its "system of systems" approach to security including: thorough screening of baggage and passengers by highly trained federal employees, more impregnable aircraft through fortified cockpit doors and use of reinforced baggage containers, thousands of Federal Air Marshals aboard record numbers of flights, and armed and deputized Federal Flight Deck Officers.[165]

Under CAPPS II, airlines asked passengers for expanded amounts of reservation information, including full name, date of birth, home address, and home-telephone number. With this expanded information, the system would quickly (i.e., within five seconds or so) verify the identity of the passenger and conduct a risk assessment utilizing commercially available data and current intelligence information. The risk assessment would result in a recommended screening level, categorized as: (1) *no risk*, (2) *unknown or elevated risk*, or (3) *high risk*.

Once the system had computed a traveler's risk score it would send an encoded message to be printed on the boarding pass indicat-

---

[163] *Id.*

[164] Ryan Singel, *Life After Death for CAPPS?*, Wired News, http://www.wired.com (visited Sep. 13, 2004).

[165] U.S. Department of Homeland Security, *CAPPS II at a Glance*, a TSA Fact Sheet (Feb. 20, 2004).

ing the appropriate level of screening by screeners at security checkpoints.[166] On the positive side, this would work well for the *majority* of travelers—as most utilitarian proposals do. However, for the minority, including people misidentified by say having the same name as a suspected terrorist it would deny them free access to travel. Thus, there is the potential of violating the basic rights of some people.

ACLU's Corrigan claims, "Profiling is an ineffective security measure . . . not rooted in specific facts or evidence that an individual is a terrorist. Instead, [it] has been used pursuant to a cost-benefit analysis that certain security devices are too expensive to be used on each and every passenger."[167] Because the ACLU feels it is likely that terrorists will quickly learn the profile parameters, they would thus employ others who do not fit the profile to carry their bombs or hijack aircraft. Further, the ACLU is very concerned that privacy rights and illegal searches will result from "super profiles" that are reportedly being developed by the DOT, which is "funding private research on artificial intelligence techniques that would rate the risk of each passenger that boards a plane."[168]

Undaunted, the TSA announced in September 2004 that it would test a new pre-screening system for airline passengers known as *Secure Flight,* which the TSA said will result in a more accurate, less intrusive screening process. Secure Flight is intended to replace the controversial CAPPS II program and allow the TSA to take over responsibility for checking airline passengers' names against watch lists—a function that under CAPPS was handled by the airlines.[169]

Not unsurprising, the same groups that protested against CAPPS II asserted that the new program was little more than "a clone of the old one." The ACLU acknowledges that the job of government security officials is daunting, and they endorse the goal of keeping terrorists off airplanes. But they fear that a "capricious and unpredictable security bureaucracy" will trample on individual rights.[170]

In another "pre-screening program" the TSA is currently testing and deploying the *Registered Traveler* [RT] Program, which offers

---

[166] *Id.*

[167] Katie Corrigan, Testimony before the House Committee on Transportation and Infrastructure, Subcommittee on Aviation (Feb. 27, 2003).

[168] *Id.*

[169] AAAE, *TSA Unveils New Screening System*, Airport Report (Sep. 1, 2004), at 1.

[170] David Hughes, *'Secure Flight' Draws Fire*, Av. Wk. & Space Tech. (Nov. 1, 2004), at 54.

airport security screening benefits such as shorter lines, to passengers agreeing to provide personal information and undergo biometric identity checks (e.g., fingerprints or iris scans) in advance.[171] The TSA has published a copy of its RT business model on the American Association of Airport Executive's [AAAE] website.[172] The model "provides a concept baseline for discussions with airports and service providers interested in RT" and "details on issues such as screening benefits and payment to fees to TSA for its role in RT." [173]

AAAE provides another essential service to the airport community: the *Transportation Security Clearinghouse* [TSC], created in December of 2001 to more quickly process aviation employee fingerprints after 9/11. The TSC serves to expedite fingerprint processing and name-based checks via required federal channels, allows for centralized billing, permits the authorized viewing (airports/airlines) of investigation results, assists the industry in the purchasing of biometric equipment, and facilitates access to training.[174]

Today, the TSC has facilitated more than a million biographical background checks for members of the aviation community.[175] Minneapolis-St.Paul Airport alone has processed more than 20,000 prints through the clearing house.[176] The TSC has been very successful in reducing wait times and costs to the industry. Amazingly, since 2001, the TSC has reduced fingerprint processing time from 52 days to four hours! The AAAE's TSC "has advanced far beyond its initial mandate to process Criminal History Record Checks [CHRC] for the airport community and is poised to offer the resources needed to bring identify management and biometrics solutions to future federal government security challenges."[177]

---

[171] Audrey Warren, *Frequent Flyers Line Up to Bypass Extra Searches*, Wall St. J. (Wed., Jul. 21, 2004), at D9.
[172] The Registered Traveler business model can be access on line at http://www.aaae.org/govberment/150_Transportation _Security_Policy/.
[173] AAAE Staff Report, *TSC Volume Reaches New Milestone,* Airport Magazine (Apr./May 2006), at 21.
[174] AAAE Staff Report, *Inside TSC,* Airport Magazine (May/Jun. 2005), at 25.
[175] AAAE Staff Report, *TSC Volume Reaches New Milestone*, Airport Magazine (Apr./May 2006), at 20.
[176] *Id.* at 23.
[177] *Id.* at 21.

BIOMETRICS

As mentioned earlier in this chapter, the *Intelligence Reform and Terrorism Prevention Act of 2004* called for the development of "comprehensive technical and operational system requirements and performance standards for the use of biometric identifier technology in airport access control systems (including airport perimeter access control systems) to ensure that the biometric identifier systems are effective, reliable, and secure."[178] Biometrics are physiological or behavioral characteristics that can be measured to identify an individual's identity.[179] Biometrics are quickly becoming an important tool for use by airports and security agencies alike.

In its position paper, *The Application of Biometrics at Airports*, Airport Council International [ACI] states it "recognizes the benefit of using biometrics to confirm personnel identify for border control, airport passenger processing and airport access control, to improve airport security, efficiency and facilitation." A biometric sample (face, fingerprint and iris are the three specified in the ICAO standard) is "captured and compared against data on database, a Machine Readable Travel Document [MRTD] or on a smart card.[180]

OTHER SECURITY CHANGES: APPROACH, POLICY AND PERSONNEL

The impact on the aviation industry—and, in particular the airport industry—is only the beginning of a larger initiative to address the technological capabilities of those who wish to attack the "American Way of Life." These include changes in the cockpit and in the general perception of the "appropriate way" to handle hijackers or terrorists. Citizens once warned to act submissive are being raised to the status of heroes for their acts to thwart violence on board aircraft.

Likewise, there has been an about-face in federal policy on flight crew response to terrorists and/or hijackers on board aircraft. In keeping with this change was a push and subsequent approval for permitting qualified airline pilots to carry weapons on-board aircraft. "Un-

---

[178] TSA. *Guidance Package: Biometrics for Airport Access Control*, (Sep. 30, 2005), retrieved from http://www.tsa.gov/assets/pdf/biometrics_guidance.pdf.

[179] ACI, *The Application of Biometrics at Airports,* Position Paper (Nov. 2005), retrieved from http://www.airports.org.

[180] *Id.*

der Title XIV of the Homeland Security Act of 2002,[181] the Arming Pilots Against Terrorist Act established a program to deputize qualified volunteer commercial passenger airline pilots to serve as Federal Flight Deck Officers [FFDO], to defend the cockpit of an aircraft against acts of criminal violence or air piracy."[182]

While the FFDO program has already graduated and deployed a number of candidates, some concerns remain. For example, some perceive that the required psychological testing is "excessive and designed to fail a large number of candidates." In addition, the FFDOs are deputized for five years, so long as they re-qualify every six months. Some feel this amount of recurrent training is excessive. However, requalifying with firearms every six months is not unusual for law enforcement officers. There is a concern about the fact that neither the TSA nor the State Department has engaged in discussions with foreign nations for recognition and acceptance of FFDOs internationally.[183]

In addition to passenger and crew changes, the TSA initially reinvigorated the Federal Air Marshal [FAM] program with increased personnel hires, modernized training facilities, increases in the number of flight segments, and an increased budget. More recently, though, there have been budget reductions in this area. To make up for FAM shortages—particularly during heightened threat level conditions—the TSA has engaged in the cross training of some Customs agents as FAMs.

Federalizing more than 40,000 security screeners into TSA employment signaled the federal government's overt assumption of the aviation security role at the nation's 400 plus commercial service airports. While some laud this as a necessary move to elevate security, others question whether the TSA's additional focus on customer service might compromise their original mission of deterring the carriage of weapons aboard aircraft and acts of air piracy.[184]

---

[181] P.L. 107-296.

[182] House of Representatives, Subcommittee on Aviation, *Hearing on the Status of the Flight Deck Officer Program* (May 8, 2003).

[183] *Id.*

[184] Blake Morrison, *Feds Take Over Airport Screening: Better-trained Force Doesn't Shed Skeptics*, USAToday (sometime in 2002), at A1.

SCREENING PARTNERSHIP PROGRAM

Contained within the Aviation and Transportation Security Act of 2001 was the initiation of a two-year pilot program, during which five airports would be permitted to utilize private screeners, which would still be paid for and overseen by the TSA. The goal of this option was to allow for the option of larger-scale re-privatization of the checkpoint screening function under the *Screening Partnership Program* [SPP] otherwise referred to as an "opt-out" of the federalized screening program. Despite the fact that all airports have since been invited to apply for privatization of their screening, only one additional airport has taken advantage of this option.[185]

There are a number reasons that have been given by airports as to why they have not pursued the SPP offer, of which the most commonly cited is liability. The General Accountability Office stated that the most pressing issue was "whether and to what extent private screening contractors and airports would be liable in the event that threat objects or weapons were not detected . . . leading to a terrorist incident," a GAO study reported, [186] although subsequent legislation has largely addressed this concern. According to Sioux Falls Airport Director Mike Marnach, "the real problem is there's no financial incentive at the moment to make the switch back to private screeners. The savings we obtain all go back to the federal government."[187]

Another concern relates to the possible ramifications of airports releasing the TSA from its duties and replacing them with privatized help. Janine Punt with Covenant Security states, "There's a sense in the airport community that the TSA will eventually pass the cost of the screeners down to the airports."[188] One unanticipated function airports were forced to absorb in 2006 was the monitoring of the screening checkpoint exit lanes. Airports claim this responsibility was a non-budgeted expense, and thus unfair. While the TSA granted a 90-day extension to airports assuming the responsibility, the function was ultimately turned over to airports.[189]

---

[185] GAO Report, as discussed in John Croft, *Airports Shun Private Screening*, Airport Magazine, (Jun./Jul. 2006) at 39; *see also* AAAE, *Airport Officials Testify on Screening*, Airport Report (Apr. 1, 2006), at 1.

[186] *Id.*

[187] *Id. at* 41.

[188] *Id.*

[189] AAAE, *TSA to Extend Exit Monitoring Deadline*, Airport Report (Jan. 15, 2006), at 1.

One of the newer technologies that may be helpful to passengers and screeners alike is SmartCheck, currently being tested. A "SmartCheck scan" is a voluntary option to the traditional "pat down" search and is intended for passengers undergoing secondary screening, although it has been controversial due to the fact that the image generated is quite revealing. SmartCheck uses backscatter X-ray to create an outline depicting contraband and threats, but reportedly does not reveal facial or other sensitive features. In addition, the SmartCheck system cannot store, transmit, export or print the images it generates for screeners.[190]

GENERAL AVIATION AIRPORTS

Amidst the heavy emphasis on security at U.S. air carrier airports, the impact on general aviation airports has been a mere afterthought. Guidance for GA airport operators has been lacking despite envisioned concerns about terrorists using crop-dusting aircraft for chemical/biological attacks against communities, livestock or agricultural areas as well as other criminal uses (or abuses) of larger general aviation aircraft. A Corporate jet loaded down with explosives and/or biological agents could be just as effective as a commercial airliner if it were crashed into a sports stadium or arena full of spectators. Yet, access to a GA aircraft is loosely guarded relative to its commercial counterpart. More often than not the flight crew, with time on their hands while they wait for passengers to return, can be found napping in the back of the plane.

What could be an easier target than someone asleep in an open aircraft that is re-fueled and ready to go? In response to this and other concerns, the TSA created, "Security Guidelines for General Aviation Airports" in May of 2004, which is "intended to provide GA airport owners, operators and users with guidelines and recommendations that address aviation security concepts, technology and enhancements."[191] However, the "guidance" is advisory in nature and therefore not mandatory. Included in the *Security Guidelines* is the "Airport Characteristics Measurement Tool," which provides a point-based assessment scale for suggested airport security en-

---

[190] AAAE, *Screening System Tested in Phoenix*, Airport Report (Mar. 1, 2007), at 3.
[191] TSA, *Security Guidelines for General Aviation Airports*, TSA Information Publication A-001 (May 2004).

hancements.[192] Public use airports and heliports incur higher points than private use airports and heliports, and both are ranked in identified categories of location, based aircraft, runway length and type, and operations. The greater the total points, the more enhancements suggested, ranging from community watch programs to intrusion detections systems and closed-circuit television.

The Aircraft Owners and Pilots Association [AOPA] is also quite proactive on the issue of GA security. It has developed the AOPA *Airport Watch* initiative, enlisting the help of 650,000 general aviation pilots to watch for and report suspicious activities at U.S. airports. AOPA has created a video and a brochure, as well as having established a toll-free hotline to receive security-related calls.[193]

NEWER THREATS: SURFACE-TO-AIR MISSILES, LVBIEDs, AND BIOTERRORISM

While the protectors of the air transportation system struggle with finding solutions to extant security problems, terrorists continually threaten to introduce new hazards. These more diabolical threats, such as shoulder-fired missiles and chemical or biological terrorist attacks will require specialized training and technology solutions, which, unfortunately, have yet to be perfected.[194]

The downing of TWA Flight 800 in 1996—although eventually attributed to a mechanical malfunction—was initially considered to be the possible result of a surface-to-air missile.[195] Several more recent incidents involving the use of *Man-Portable Air-Defense Systems* [MANPADS] against commercial aircraft have prompted additional concern. Confirmed incidents involving the use of MANPADS include an al Qaeda attempt to down an Israeli aircraft in Kenya, two similar incidents in Bagdad, and one in Mombasa. In response, the FBI conducted inspections at 80 U.S. commercial service airports and confirmed the vulnerability of carriers to a missile attack.[196] However, due to the million-dollar-plus price tag associated with equipping a

---

[192] *Id., see* Appendices A and B of the guidance document for more information.

[193] AOPA, *Airport Watch*, retrieved from http://www.aopa.org/airportwatch/.

[194] Phillip Shenon, *A Nation at War: Domestic Security: Missile Threat is Bringing Stricter Rules for Airports*, N.Y. Times (Mar. 30, 2003), at B11.

[195] *See* Laurence E. Gesell, *The Administration of Public Airports* (4th ed. 1999).

[196] Phillip Shenon, *A Nation at War: Domestic Security: Missile Threat is Bringing Stricter Rules for Airports*, N.Y. Times (Mar. 30, 2003), at B11.

passenger aircraft with missile detection/deflection capability, reliance is being placed on increased intelligence reconnaissance and surveillance near airports. Actions vary by airport. For example, the *New York Times* reported that San Francisco International Airport increased road patrols and Coast Guard surveillance while Boston Logan officials have provided "local clam diggers with mobile phones to allow them to call in if they see suspicious activity."[197] To secure George Bush Intercontinental Airport, Houston enlists volunteer riders on horseback to patrol nearby woodlands.[198]

In the meantime, higher tech solutions are being sought. In November 2006, DHS selected three companies to receive more than $7 million in funding, "to support efforts to counter the potential threat posed to commercial aircraft by shoulder-fired, anti-aircraft missiles." In announcement of the award, DHS stated that Raytheon Company, Northrop Grumman Space Technology and L-3 Communications AVISYS Corporation are to use the funds to "evaluate and demonstrate emerging counter-MANPADS technology solutions that show the most promise in defeating this threat."[199] In addition, DHS will "test whether drones flying at 65,000 feet about the nation's busiest airports could be used to protect planes from being shot down by terrorist using shoulder-fired missiles."[200] The drones will be equipped with missile warning systems and linked to anti-missile lasers on the aircraft or on the ground. Equally of concern are Large Vehicle Borne Improvised Explosive Devices. An LVBIED is essentially a truck or car bomb that can be detonated strategically to inflict damage, injury and death. The best defense against this type of threat is for airport operators to first understand the impact that such a blast can have on a structure and those occupying a structure. Airport operators should then take action to minimize the congregation of people in vulnerable areas, better separate vehicles from areas of concern and generally fortify airport structures to better withstand a potential blast.

The most densely populated areas at airports are within commercial aircraft, followed by the terminals with their passenger queues, common areas, sidewalk queuing areas (e.g., curbside check-in), and

---

[197] *Id.*

[198] Amy Schatz, *To Secure Airport, Houston Enlists Volunteer Riders*, Wall St. J. (Thur., Sep. 16, 2004), at A1.

[199] AAAE, *DHS Awards Anti-MANPADS Contracts*, Airport Report, (Nov. 1, 2006), at 2. Man-Portable Air-Defense Systems, or MANPADS, are shoulder-launched surface-to-air missiles.

[200] Mimi Hall, *Drones Could Defend Airports*, USA Today (Mar. 23-25, 2007), at 1A-2A.

curbside bus/ground transportation waiting areas.[201] Figure 9.1, "Vehicle Explosives Capacity, Blast Range and Evacuation Distance," shows how the size of a vehicle can affect the vehicle's load, and ultimately the lethal air blast range. Figures 9.2, "Blast Impact on Structures," and 9.3, "Vehicle Bomb Explosion Hazard by Weapon Yield and Stand-off" illustrate the structural impact of blast from a vehicle bomb explosion, as a function of weapon yield and stand-off.

Equally horrifying is the targeting of an airport for a biohazard attack with the purpose of infecting a few isolated travelers in the short term, but populations globally in the longer term. Air transportation has already been identified as a favored target for terrorists as it represents both the economic power and freedom that adversaries of the U.S. wish to compromise. First responders (police, fire fighters, medical assistance, etc.) are fairly well prepared for chemical or radiological attack, but they have very limited capability for response to the more silent attack posed by a bioterrorism strike.[202] Despite the myriad of improvements in homeland security undertaken since 9/11, many observers feel that chemical or biological terrorism has not been taken as seriously as other terrorist threats.

In 2005, 95% of communities surveyed about their concerns believe there will be another terrorist attack in the U.S. within four to five years, with 13% specifically concerned about biological threats. Unfortunately, nearly a third of those surveyed rated their local preparation as "poor."[203] Department of Homeland Security funding to state agencies has been both helpful and controversial, due particularly to the distribution methods employed.

---

[201] Brian Chow, Clifford Grammich, & Terry Schell, *Designing Airports for Security—An analysis of Proposed Changes at LAX*, Issue Paper- Public Safety and Justice (2003), retrieved from http://www.rand.org/publications/IP/IP251/IP251.pdf_.

[202] A. Avary, A. Bowles, M. Denoff, A. Oberg, R. Sobotta, & R.J. Wielebski, *Biodefense Concerns, Technology and Potential Applications: A Global Review and a Focus on Clark County, Nevada* (May 2003). *See also* A. Carl, R. Sobotta, K. Sommer, P. Vana, & M. Voss, *Biodefense Concerns, Technology and Potential Applications: A Global Review with a Focus on First Responders and Phoenix, Arizona* (May 2003). *See also* K. Freibott, A. Oberg, R. Sobotta, & J. Yamada, *Biodefense Concerns, Technology and Potential Applications: A Global Review and a Focus on Health Care Facilities* (May 2003); all papers available from Embry-Riddle Aeronautical University, Prescott, Ariz.

[203] McGraw-Hill Co. conducted this survey of 1200 officials at a 2004 conference in Washington, D.C.

Figure 9.1—VEHICLE EXPLOSIVES CAPACITY, BLAST RANGE AND EVACUATION DISTANCE

ATF	VEHICLE DESCRIPTION	MAXIMUM EXPLOSIVES CAPACITY	LETHAL AIR BLAST RANGE	MINIMUM EVACUATION DISTANCE	FALLING GLASS HAZARD
	COMPACT SEDAN	500 Pounds 227 Kilos *(In Trunk)*	100 Feet 30 Meters	1,500 Feet 457 Meters	1,250 Feet 381 Meters
	FULL SIZE SEDAN	1,000 Pounds 455 Kilos *(In Trunk)*	125 Feet 38 Meters	1,750 Feet 534 Meters	1,750 Feet 534 Meters
	PASSENGER VAN OR CARGO VAN	4,000 Pounds 1,818 Kilos	200 Feet 61 Meters	2,750 Feet 838 Meters	2,750 Feet 838 Meters
	SMALL BOX VAN *(14 FT BOX)*	10,000 Pounds 4,545 Kilos	300 Feet 91 Meters	3,750 Feet 1,143 Meters	3,750 Feet 1,143 Meters
	BOX VAN OR WATER/FUEL TRUCK	30,000 Pounds 13,636 Kilos	450 Feet 137 Meters	6,500 Feet 1,982 Meters	6,500 Feet 1,982 Meters
	SEMI-TRAILER	60,000 Pounds 27,273 Kilos	600 Feet 183 Meters	7,000 Feet 2,134 Meters	7,000 Feet 2,134 Meters

Source: Department of the Treasury, Bureau of Alcohol, Tobacco and Firearms [ATF], *Vehicle Bomb Explosion Hazard and Evacuation Distance Tables* (May 2004), retrieved from http://www.atf.gov/pub/fire-explo_pub/i54001_old.htm.

First responders report that existing, relatively inexpensive bio-detection equipment is limited and typically requires 12-24 hours to produce secondary (laboratory) confirmation. The existing airborne bio-hazard detection technology is beset with disadvantages. It is expensive, large, typically requires high concentrations of pathogens in order to detect them (yielding false negatives at lower, still infectious levels), and it is highly sensitive to environmental conditions (yielding false positives in dusty, high vibration or multiple pathogen conditions). In addition, existing airborne detection methods are limited generally to a small library of "bad bugs," allowing opportunity for creative terrorists to use other pathogens.[204]

---

[204] *Id.*

Figure 9.2—BLAST IMPACT ON STRUCTURES

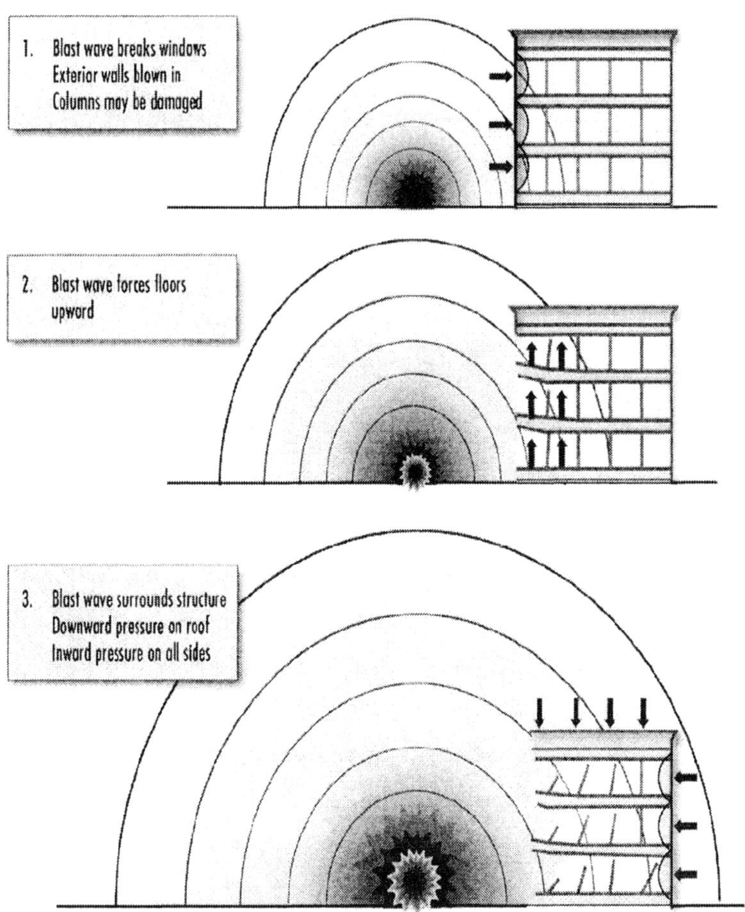

Source: Federal Emergency Management Agency [FEMA], *Explosive Blast* (Apr. 2004), retrieved from http://www.fema.gov/pdf/fima/426_ch4.pdf.

Figure 9.3—VEHICLE BOMB EXPLOSION HAZARD BY WEAPON YIELD AND STAND-OFF

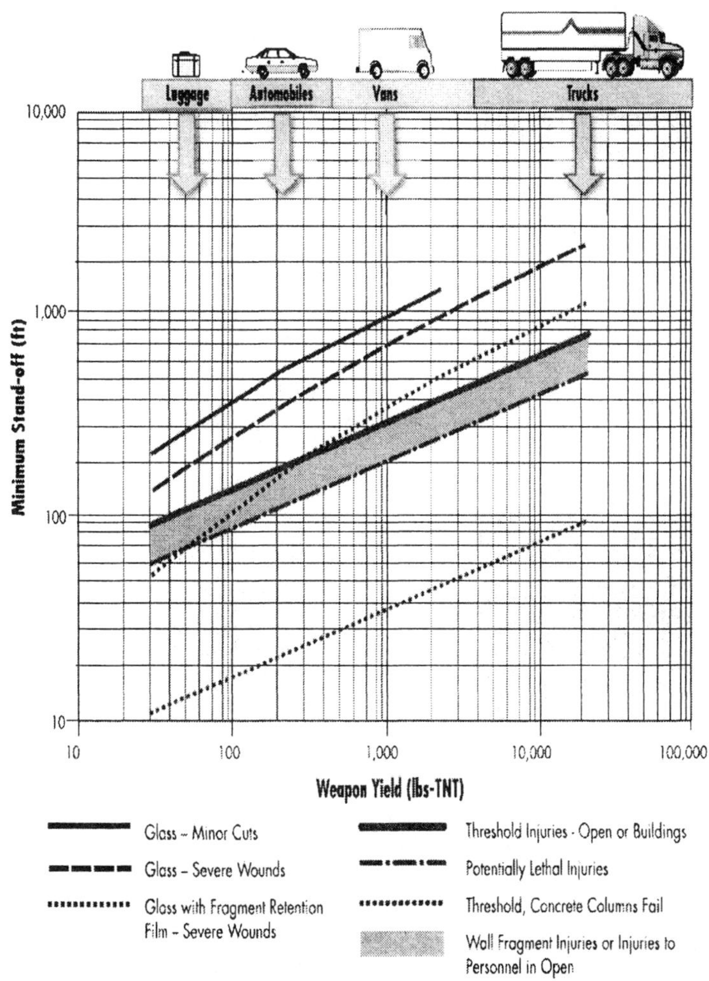

Source: FEMA, *Explosive Blast* (Apr. 2004), retrieved from http://www.fema.gov/pdf/fima/426_ch4.pdf.

SECURITY CHANGES—PROGRESS OR POMP?

This chapter sheds light on the changes that have occurred in the aviation industry since the 9/11 attacks. Although some progress has been achieved—organizationally and procedurally—those who seek to terrorize the Free World can still find creative ways to achieve their ends. In addition to reviewing the delicate balance that exists between the continued viability of the aviation industry and the need to maintain a strong security position, this section examines whether substantive progress has been made.

While Donald Carty testified that he perceived aviation security is improving, others have questioned whether the so-called improvements are truly meaningful or merely superficial.[205] Indeed, many of the regulations remain the same, having only been renumbered and renamed. As Scott McCartney indicates,

> *Security screeners are still hunting sharp objects. But sharp objects aren't likely to enable a terrorist to commandeer a plane today because of hardened cockpit doors and far more vigilant passengers and crews. Meanwhile, we aren't doing enough to screen for bombs. While we scan checked luggage for plastic explosives, we don't scan carry-on-luggage. While we X-ray shoes for bombs, we don't check people. Odds are the next bomber wouldn't be a shoe bomber but a belly bomber.*[206]

Is America any safer now than prior to the attacks? The 9/11 Commission reported, "America is safer, but far from safe." There are still gaps. The Council on Foreign Relations observed, "Following September 11, the government instituted an unprecedented number of new security measures that officials say make it safer to fly, and airline travel remains statistically far less risky than driving. But despite the new, more rigorous safeguards—many of them

---

[205] Donald Carty, Testimony before the House Committee on Transportation and Infrastructure, Subcommittee on Aviation (Sep. 24, 2003).

[206] Scott McCartney, *From X-rays to Cargo, Security Gaps Remain*, Wall St. J. (Wed., Jul. 28, 2004), at D2.

mandated by the ATSA—officials say they cannot offer a blanket guarantee of safety. Nevertheless, both federal officials and consumer advocacy groups are encouraging the public not to be afraid to fly. But experts say there are simply too many airports and commercial flights in the United States to ensure that determined terrorists willing to die will not find a way to use an aircraft in a future attack."[207] "In the end, perfection in security isn't possible—unless the airplane never leaves the ground."[208] According to the Emergency Response and Research Institute:

> *Although security was boosted, there are still holes that could allow future attackers to slip through. These include inadequately trained security staff and governmental reticence to commit extra resources such as the intelligence agencies to conduct profiling of all passengers. Taking a more active approach to stopping hijackers in the air and at the gate is a great step, but there is less risk if these perpetrators can be stopped before they even load their luggage.*[209]

In this regard, The Government Accounting Office[210] conducted 1,164 tests at 127 airports from September 2002 to February 2004 by trying to sneak weapons past screeners. What the federal investigators found is that airport screeners often fail to spot weapons—whether they are federal employees or private-security screeners.[211]

Additionally, critics of the TSA and Congress also cite continuing deficiencies in air cargo screening as well as the pressing need to "address other priorities, including intelligence capability and

---

[207] Council on Foreign Relations, *Terrorism: Questions and Answers* (2003).

[208] *See* Scott McCartney, *From X-rays to Cargo, Security Gaps Remain*, Wall St. J. (Wed., Jul. 28, 2004), at D2.

[209] Emergency Response and Research Institute (2003).

[210] Effective Jul. 7, 2004, the GAO's legal name became the Government Accountability Office, *GAO Human Capital Reform Act* of 2004, P.L. 108-271.

[211] Amy Schatz, *Federal, Private Airport Screeners Do Poorly in Tests*, Wall St. J. (Fri., Apr. 23, 2004), at A4.

security of ports, railroads, and trucking."[212] Air cargo activities are an example of one airport activity that was not initially addressed, but later came to the forefront after more pressing security issues had been prioritized. In fact, the needed for improved air cargo security measures is an issue that has moved up as a priority to members Congress in the past couple of years.

A 2005 GAO report explains that air cargo operations are an airport's responsibility,"[213]

> *. . . to the extent that air cargo operations areas overlap with areas of the airport designated as security identification display areas (SIDA), pursuant to 49 C.F.R. part 1542. Individuals working in a SIDA must have an airport-approved photo identification that is displayed at all times above the waist on the individual's outermost garments. To obtain a SIDA identification badge, a person must successfully undergo a fingerprint-based criminal history records check and successfully complete security training. In addition, SIDA access requirements must include procedures for challenging all persons not displaying appropriate SIDA photo identification.*

New rules are just one weapon in the war against terrorism. In order for these rules to be effective, they must be clearly written, evenly enforced, and reasonably financed. "One of the worst things you can do is to write a rule with 17 interpretations" stated Cargo Airline Association President Steve Alterman. There could be impacts on the [air cargo industry] depending on how the TSA interprets some of the words."[214] Community officials are concerned as well that, while security rules can help in achieving national standardization, they may also trigger a negative economic externality. These rules may be *unfunded mandates,* which unreasonably force

---

[212] *Peering Into Billions of Bags*, N.Y. Times (Dec. 31, 2003), at A18. *See also* Scott McCartney, *From X-rays to Cargo, Security Gaps Remain*, Wall St. J. (Wed., Jul. 28, 2004), at D2.

[213] GAO, *Aviation Security: Federal Action Needed to Strengthen Domestic Air Cargo Security*, GAO-06-76 (Oct. 17, 2005).

[214] John Croft, *Boxed In*, Airport Magazine (Jan./Feb. 2005), at 38.

local communities to finance federal security initiatives, relative to a community's financial resources or perceived threat level.

SUMMARY

Clearly, airport sponsors and users have yet to achieve the "new normal" referenced early in this chapter. With each new threat that is revealed—both in the U.S. and abroad—airport and community vulnerabilities are revealed, and corresponding changes initiated. While some claim that the government should be more proactive, others complain that the current cost of increased aviation security is already a burden to airports and their users. Many in the industry feel that we may never be completely secure at our airports or in our communities—that it is not a matter of *if* there will be another terrorist attack on the United States but *when*.

Despite the plethora of new technologies and procedures, the key to proactive aviation may be in refraining from using all the tools at once. Instead, there is value in randomized use of a fairly extensive collection of security options. In a 2006 presentation on the nation's aviation security system, TSA Administrator Kip Hawley said that "unpredictability must continue to be a part of aviation security so terrorists will not know the specific measures they will face at any given time." On any given day, an airport may bring in K-9 teams, introduce additional or randomized screening, or employ behavior pattern recognition techniques. Hawley also discussed a "layered approach" to security where trade-offs are based on relative risk.[215]

In the final analysis, all actors and aspects of airport and aviation security including the air transportation industry, intelligence officials, technology providers—as well as the rules and the regulators—must coordinate efforts. The ultimate mission of protecting the public must be achieved without imposing undue burdens on passenger convenience and privacy, or on delicate airport and aviation industry finances. Airports have found that these goals can be difficult to achieve, and may be conflicting, in some cases. Irrespective, the threat remains and the bar continues to elevate. As this book was going to print in the summer of 2007, the vulnerability of the airport infrastructure was again revealed in the foiled attempt to blow up fuel tanks at New York's John F. Kennedy Airport.

---

[215] AAAE, *TSA's Hawley Addresses Airport Officials*, Airport Report (Apr. 1, 2006), at 1-2.

CHAPTER 10

LANDSIDE, TERMINAL AND OTHER OPERATIONAL ACTIVITIES

SFO's new International Terminal was designed from the ground up to take maximum advantage of [technology]—and to speed the passenger's journey from planeside to curbside. All of the terminal's equipment—everything from computer terminals to baggage belts—is designated "common use" [so] it can be assigned to any flight of any airline at the terminal. What really sets this terminal apart is what you can't see—a network of intelligent software modules called the SmartAirport Operations Center that continually monitors the status of gates, baggage belts, check-in counters and other resources. Operations personnel—not software programmers—input the rules by which the SmartAirport Operations Center makes decisions.

Excepts from News Release, Ascent Technology[1]

INTRODUCTION

This is the third of three chapters focusing on airport operations. While the first two chapters address the pressing issues of airfield safety/certification and aviation security, the operation of today's airports encompasses many complex areas of paramount interest to airports and their users. As users demand greater convenience and efficiency, airport operators must employ increasingly unique strategies, including impressive technological advancements like those men-

[1] Ascent Technology, *SFO's New International Terminal Soars Proving Where True Beauty Lies: In the Software*, http://www.ascent.com/case-sfo.html (visited Jan. 30, 2007), at 1.

tioned in the opening quote, for the management of operational activities.

In addition, environmental and legal pressures require airport operators to likewise employ higher standards of responsibility and liability in all operational areas of the airport. As such, airport managers must assume oversight of *many landside, terminal* and *airside* activities that were once the exclusive responsibility of airport tenants. Due to the heavy focus on airside safety and certification issues in Chapter 8, this chapter will initially focus on the two remaining operational centers of activity: landside and terminal operations, and then close with additional areas of operational concern that were not previously addressed.

Airside, landside and terminal areas are by no means independent of one another. In fact, the management (or lack thereof) over one of these areas can have a significant impact over activities occurring in the other areas. For example, consider the case of an airfield pavement construction project where a landside haul route is needed to carry soil or gravel away from the site. If haul vehicles are not properly cleaned after the loading process, a debris trail can run for miles, exposing the public to personal property damage or a safety concern, and the airport to related liability.

Because there are some areas of airport operations and activities that can affect landside, terminal *and/or* airside areas in a variety of sometimes overlapping ways, this chapter discusses these types of operational activities separately. Airport construction and air cargo operations are two such activities that fall into this category, and thus are addressed in separate sections in this chapter.

At smaller airports, individuals serving in operational roles may move from airside to the curbs and into the terminals to resolve or monitor a variety of situations. At larger areas, specialized positions may be dedicated to one or more of the three areas, or even have a very-focused job description that only works on one or two major tasks within one of the three areas. For example, in addition to the more generalized landside, airside and terminal areas of focus, specialized staff may be appointed to monitor air cargo activities, ground transportation activities or parking at the airport.

This chapter concludes the coverage of airport operational activities; however, new business approaches and associated revenue generating activities are covered in greater detail in Chapters 12, "Airport

Finance and Economics," and 13, "The Airport Marketplace: Revenues and Rates."

LANDSIDE

While landside or so-called "curbside" activities are generally considered the less glamorous counterpart to airside activities, they are nevertheless an enormously critical aspect of airport operations. Often, the first exposure to the airport is from the curb, and the impression can be lasting. It can also affect future travelers in their decision to use a particular airport over other available options within a reasonable distance of their home.

For those entering the airport as arriving passengers, the first impression may be gleaned from inside the terminal: the airports restrooms, its restaurants, the ability to easily make connections, the airport's paging system, or its terminal services (custodial or information) personnel. Airport terminal areas are discussed below.

Anyone who has traveled to a major airport has likely stepped outside the terminal building onto a curb in order to secure some form of ground transportation, whether a taxi, mass transportation, or a shuttle to a car rental facility. For some travelers, a personal vehicle is waiting in an airport or tenant-operated parking structure. Family, friends or business associates waiting on the curb may also be involved in the pick up travelers, and develop an impression of the airport, based on the ease of access, roadway signs, the curbside management practices and personnel, the waiting lines exiting the parking garage, or a variety of other landside factors.

Anyone who has arrived in a new city needing to find a taxi or shuttle can confirm the importance of a well-planned and monitored ground transportation program. Yet, despite the obvious need for balanced landside and airside facilities, airport managers often find themselves with inadequate landside facilities. The traveling public, then, must make the best of what they have.

GROUND TRANSPORTATION

In part, landside problems can be a labor or management issue. It can also be related to the airport's *design*. Many simple and curvilinear terminals that were later expeditiously converted to satellite or pier terminals—to increase airside aircraft parking space—have insufficient landside or curbside space. Accommodation of curbside demands was a second thought, if considered at all.

In addition to curb space issues, the airport industry has limited numbers of individuals with specific expertise in *management* of landside activities. Only in the past decade have ground transportation issues become a nationally recognized area of expertise. Compounding the issue of managing curbside activities in a confined space is the national move toward deregulation of ground transportation in many states. Although this has served to promote competition amongst ground transportation operators, ground transportation deregulation has its difficult "side-effects." Among these are keeping up cleanliness and safety in vehicles that have been released from the regulatory constraints that previously had addressed these important issues.

Travel and tourism industry professionals believe that a visitor's first impression of a community may be established within the airport terminal or in the first few feet outside the terminal doors. Some passengers find the securing of some type of commercial or courtesy transportation (e.g., rental car, a taxi, shared ride commercial vehicle or courtesy shuttle) to be a routine experience, while others consider it to be a stressful venture. Regardless, commercial Ground Transportation [GT] and courtesy shuttle services provide important short-haul transportation to a variety of destinations including other terminals, hotels, businesses, rental car agencies and parking structures.

A bad experience with a ground transportation operator can not only sour a trip, but it can establish a negative reputation for the airport sponsor that fails to correct the obvious landside problems encountered by the traveling public. This "bad" reputation for an airport with landside problems can last for years, even though the service or facilities are improved. Indeed, some airports have been identified as places of concern, based solely upon the reputation of their ground transportation operators. Commensurately, some privately published tourism guides have observed to contain public warnings about airports where ground transportation was considered to be poorly managed and where travelers may be considered potential "victims" of under or unregulated and unscrupulous GT operators.

The approach to managing commercial GT operators varies from airport to airport and may incorporate a number of management tools including: state and local laws, a competitive bid process, contracts, vehicle and driver permitting, vehicle inspections, background investigations, driver training classes, procedural requirements. Airports and their local or regional enforcement authority may employ specialized enforcement personnel to enforce rules and procedures, as well as conduct "sting" or other covert enforcement operations. Sometimes local "grandfathered" GT operations of a specialized nature may be permitted at one airport and prohibited at another.

At larger airports, a single large contract operator or several smaller operators may be selected and permitted to provide commercial ground transportation services. Decisions on which operator(s) are selected may be based on vehicle size and year, safety issues, operator business experience, driver experience and/or other relevant factors. There is a significant workload associated with the permitting and inspection of hundreds of vehicles and operators. The permitting and inspection processes may be conducted by a state, regional or airport entity. The fee structure for patrons may be based on zones, distances traveled from departure point, and waiting times. It may also include an adjustment for peak traffic periods, the number of passengers and the number of stops (in shared ride situations).

A key determinate of the approach to be used in managing ground transportation activities may also be established via the legal challenges that airport operators will inevitably face in trying new approaches. New approaches, while providing increased safety and value to travelers and communities, should be expected to generate some legal resistance. Over the past 20-30 years, airports have found some comfort in sharing with one another the management approaches that have withstood key legal challenges.

When enforcement is required so too is due process. Airport officials must be prepared to provide due process (such as an appeal process or judicial review procedure) for those accused of breaking the rules. Airports likewise have an obligation to monitor the airport curbs and roadways, and provide enforcement against *scooping* or unauthorized pick-up of fare-paying customers at specific locations at the airport or in the community, depending upon the local jurisdictions' laws and rules. Since the airport is a lucrative place for ground transportation operators to work, it is not uncommon to find unauthorized operators who may risk large fines or other enforcement mechanisms to secure a fare-paying customer, who may be victimized by a non authorized operator's unsavory business practices or non-inspected vehicle.

RENTAL CAR OPERATIONS AND MANAGEMENT

While vehicle rental operations include landside and terminal elements, the greatest impact is felt on the landside, with particular emphasis on rental vehicle cueing/storage/return and transport of passengers to and from remote vehicle facilities.

As Chapter 13 discusses in more detail, rental car operations can be an important source of revenue for commercial service airports. They also enable smaller airports to provide a necessary convenience for passengers. However, such revenue streams and passenger conveniences are not without their impact at the airport including parking facility and curb congestion, as well as the safety impact associated with a high-traffic interface between vehicles and people.

Airports have taken a variety of approaches to managing car rental operations at airports, ranging from smaller airports—where a Fixed Based Operator [FBO] might have a number to call for a rental car to be delivered on demand, to the busiest commercial service airports that may provide multiple shuttles or light rail transport to a consolidated car rental storage and processing facility on or near the airport.

Some airports provide vehicle storage for rental vehicles near the terminal buildings, a feature that some passengers prefer. Other passengers prefer riding a rental car shuttle to a less congested, off-airport location where the vehicle is collected. On-airport access to rental car vehicles serves to increase roadway traffic and sometimes increase safety concerns. This is all too often due to the driving behavior of some rental car transport personnel or "jockeys" who are paid to drive vehicles from an off-airport storage location to an on-airport pick-up location convenient to customers. Airports have found the car rental operator's need for quick service for passengers must be balanced with enforcement and education to assure that all of its many drivers operate in a safe and courteous manner. Measures must also be in place to address complaints associated with these employees, potential accidents, customer claims/disputes, and abandoned vehicles (occasionally left by passengers who don't want to be late for their flights).

As a note of caution, however, the airport must avoid assuming any additional liability that might be associated with any earnest attempt to manage car rental operations from a safety perspective. In one case, and although no major vehicle-pedestrian accidents had occurred, Phoenix Sky Harbor International Airport [PHX] proactively added speed bumps to the rental car storage/pick-up area of a parking garage in an effort to respond to complaints about the so-called rental car "jockeys" driving at excessive rates of speed in the parking structure. Unfortunately, and even though they were clearly marked, several incidents resulted from elderly people tripping over the newly added speed bumps and incurring significant facial, head and other injuries. Inasmuch as it could not be affirmatively determined that the speed bumps did in fact prevent accidents from occurring between speeding rental vehicles and passengers, and as a result of the trip/fall incidents, the airport ultimately decided to remove the speed bumps. As a matter of liability, even if such an accident (between a speeding vehicle and a pedestrian) might eventually occur, such an incident would more likely be the primary responsibility of the rental car agency, as opposed to the airport sponsor who had been the primary recipient of claims for injury/damages associated with the elderly trip/fall accidents.

While on the subject of rental car agencies, one topic that continues to be of concern to these operators and to passengers alike is that of the so-called pass-through "recovery fees." At certain airport locations where the auto rental agency is an on-airport concessionaire, the agency is required to collect *mandatory* airport related charges from its customers and to remit them to the airport; these may be referred to as "Customer Facility Charges," "Airport Facility Charges," or "Transportation Facility Charges." At other locations, the car rental agency may have elected to impose *non-mandatory* related charges to recover or recoup all or a portion of its expenses related to a type of overhead. At certain airport locations where the car rental agency is an on-airport concessionaire, it may have elected to impose a charge, often referred to as a "Concession Fee Recoupment" or "Concession Fee Recovery," to recover all or a portion of the concession fees which it is obligated to pay to the airport. Further, many airports impose a fee on revenue from off-airport rental car transactions (typically when the customer exits the airport using the off-airport company's shuttle bus) at locations where rental agency is an off-airport concessionaire. In such cases the agency may elect to impose a charge to recover all or a portion of this fee from customers. The fee, which varies by airport, usually appears separately in the charges section of the rental agreement as an "Airport Fee," or the like. Hence, the customer is made aware of the charge and often attributes the extra charge to the airport and not to the rental agency.[2]

While some of these concession fees are linked to specific community projects, many rental car operators find them burdensome and unfair, particularly when they appear to have no connection to the airport or the traveler (such as a stadium fee). Airport Facility Charges may include a construction or other fee for a *consolidated* car rental facility. They may also be a customer fee for common rental car ground transportation systems, to cover the cost of the vehicle (bus) as well as its operation and maintenance costs. When an airport or a community imposes such fees, they should consider the potential for resistance from the car rental industry and travelers who may resent such fees, if deemed unfair or unrelated to a vehicle rental.[3]

In contrast, the customer fee method of financing consolidated facilities may also yield an important benefit in terms of competition. This approach reportedly "allows smaller renal car companies the opportunity to come on airport without a huge capital requirement, allowing them to compete on the same level (on the expense side) as the larger companies."[4] It also allows the focus to be on customer service as opposed to impressive infrastructure.

Aside from the issue of fees, car rental companies are also concerned about space, including the availability of space in the terminal as well as land in close proximity (say within 10 miles) of the airport. They are also concerned about the financing of the improvement in these spaces. Car rental agencies normally wish to be involved in the design of the consolidated facilities. As of 2000, more than 20 commercial service airports had established a consolidated car rental facility or were actively planning for the creation of one. In this regard, car rental agencies expect that facilities will be planned and operated

---

[2] *See* National Car Rental, *National Rental Policies*, http://www.alamo.com (visited Mar. 31, 2007).

[3] Barbara Cook, *Airports and the Car Rental Industry*, Part 2, Airport Magazine (Jan./Feb. 2000), at 18.

[4] James Brenda & John F. Brown, Co., as cited in *Airports and the Car Rental Industry*, Part 2, Airport Magazine (Jan./Feb. 2000), at 22.

in a manner that assures their business goals of being more cost efficient than current approaches, more operationally efficient, and being more customer friendly.[5]

VEHICLE ACCESS AND TRAFFIC CONTROL

Vehicular access, traffic control and parking are important concerns at today's airports. Vehicle demands and the approaches to meeting these demands vary greatly from airport to airport. It is important to note that airport planning and design choices have a substantial impact on operational priorities. Some airport roadway systems are designed as closed loop or a "dead end" to discourage through traffic, while others offer an "expressway" of sorts to commuting traffic wishing to use the airport roads in order to avoid stoplights or city street congestion. Likewise, airports have many approaches to traffic control on the curb. Some have strict enforcement procedures while others are more lax. Approaches to vehicle parking are equally diverse. Some airports offer free or reduced parking as an incentive for passengers to use the airport. They may commingle parking for air travelers, ground transportation cueing, meeters-and-greeters, rental cars, and airport employees. Others establish tiered rates for various lengths of passenger stay and separate parking structures though distance and/or with electronic equipment.

Control of traffic accessing the airport and terminal curbs is increasingly considered as an important issue for both the airport and the traveling public. With original development funds prioritizing airside construction, the landside infrastructure deteriorated or became congested. Airport management responded to this problem by heightening the presence of operations personnel on access roads and by implementing curb management programs. *Curb management* and *enforcement* are controversial topics. No one wants a speeding or parking ticket. Some airport visitors feel they should have the "right" to access the airport—a public facility—without paying a charge (such as that incurred in using a parking facility). As such, they exercise this "right" on the curb and have been known to challenge to curb enforcement personnel to preserve this "right."

Obviously, if everyone were to park on the curb, rather than in the parking structures, there would be no room for the plethora of vehi-

---

[5] *Id.*

cles that would overwhelm the terminal curb. And, if everyone were to be allowed to speed to avoid missing a flight, the roadways would be unsafe. Hence, enforcement of laws for roadway and curb management have become a major source of work for landside personnel (or police representatives, depending upon the jurisdictional control of the roadways and curbs), and a potential source for customer complaints as well. Although citations are never desirous to the receiver, roadway and curb management personnel must have tools for use in enforcing the laws. Handled diplomatically, though, roadway and curb management efforts can be viewed as reasonable and effective measures that need to be taken to maintain public safety.

INTERMODAL INTERFACES

A variety of intermodal interfaces can be found at airports, ranging from co-located bus stations, to trains, to light rail lines that now may be, in part, funded by airport *Passenger Facility Charges* [PFCs][6]. Multimodal transportation options may be designed for on airport (between terminals, or from the curb to a parking structure), to access specific facilities near the airport (consolidated car rental facilities or parking structures) or to provide community-wide transportation access. Airport intermodal interfaces are very common in Europe, but have been gaining in popularity in the United States over the past decade or two, with increase planning and funding mechanisms coming to light. Intermodalism provides new incentives for passengers to use new transportation modes as part of their larger travel experience.

Following the physical costs of construction, operation and maintenance, another major cost associated with these systems may be that of additional vulnerabilities and the need for additional layers of security. Encouragement of intermodalism essentially pushes out the airport boundary, making the accompanying intermodal interfaces and multimodal vehicles of greater interest to terrorists who previously may have been focused on aircraft or the airport itself. As aircraft operators and airports "harden" themselves—and then consider moving airport "entry" points further and further from the airport center—large groups of queuing passengers (at intermodal interface points) may become the terror targets. At one point, Los Angeles World Airports [LAWA] discussed the potential closure of [LAX]'s inner loop

[6] PFCs are discussed in greater detail in Ch. 12.

roadway system and the replacement of that system with an off-airport (remote check-in) site. Passenger would leave their vehicles in a massive remote lot, and then use light rail to access the terminals. While it was initially believed that this could reduce security concerns associated with Large Vehicle-Borne Improvised Explosive Devices [LVBIEDs] along the curbs, for both financial reasons, and the security reasons discussed above, the plan was eventually shelved.

PARKING

Although parking, as a *concession*, is discussed elsewhere, it is important to view parking from an *operational* perspective in this chapter. Failure to appropriately plan for necessary parking or staffing for parking facilities can result in passenger inconvenience or missed flights. If parking is in a remote location, shuttle service will need to be provided. Although there is a trend at larger airports to remote-park facility employees, this can result in substantial employee dissatisfaction and dissension. Likewise, passengers can be adversely affected by lack of planning for peak events such as holidays. Airport staff should review prior years' parking statistics and current estimated enplanements (often available from the airlines) to determine the capacity required for holidays and other peak periods.

An important part of managing the parking function is the tracking of vehicles for use in revenue control. There are several approaches to the revenue collection process at airports. Patrons may pay a flat fee or use an access card upon entry to a lot, and be permitted to stay for a fixed period or indefinitely, depending upon the posted or agree-upon terms and conditions. If the cost of parking is to be calculated based upon a per hour or per day basis, the airport may employ more complex means to track vehicle use and revenue. Parking lot use and revenue tracking relies upon the accurate recording of entry/exit data and associated charges; it also requires specific information about users in order to allow further crosschecking for loss prevention.

Common technology at many parking facilities allow for the recording of a date and time stamp. The complex component of parking lot tracking and auditing is the linking of entry/exit information with a particular users. User/vehicle confirmation can be done with an access card or an *Automatic Vehicle Identification Tag* [AVIT], but this is not practical for non-regular users of a parking facility. If a magnetic strip ticket (with entry time/day only recorded) is the principle document produced, airports may seek to further identify the user/vehicle for loss prevention purposes.[7]

A simple (but labor intensive) way to identify specific users/vehicles is for parking employees to walk the lots on a nightly basis and record license plate information from the vehicles. Another method involves the use of *License-Plate Recognition* [LPR] hardware (camera image capture) and with *Optical Character Recognition* [OCR] software to record specific information into a data base. All information is uploaded to the facility management system computer and then used to cross check charges as the patron exits. Thereafter, local business rules are used to address situations where the information collected is found to be incongruent.[8]

An on-going challenge for the airport operator is to allow quick and convenient access (but potentially more costly) parking options for short-term users (those needing parking for less than a day, and often just a few hours), while allowing lower cost (but somewhat less convenient) solutions for long-term parking customers. Many airports are supportive of private lots located in close proximity to the airports, and offering shuttle service to/from the lot at the airport curbs. Other airports have flat-rate lots that they open in undeveloped airport areas as "overflow" lots for use during peak periods such as holidays.

Two solutions for short-term parking needs are worthy of note in this section. The first involves *metered* or *short-term parking spots* (highly enforced areas within parking structures) that allow short-term patrons close, but limited duration access for terminal access and passenger interface. The need for these non-traditional short-term loading areas—as an alternative to curbside waiting—became a necessity with increased security concerns since September 11, 2001.

The other solution is perhaps one of the simplest and most convenient of parking options for parties meeting arriving passengers. It is the *cell phone lot* or *arriving passenger queuing lot*. These lots may be found a bit further from the airport terminal, but are conveniently equipped with flight information displays and may be used at low or no cost on a short term basis. As the name suggests, individuals can remain in their vehicle at these lots until they establish cell-phone

---

[7] Joseph F. Wenzel, *Parking Revenue Control: What Is; What May Be*, Airport Magazine (Jul./Aug. 2005), at 16.

[8] *Id.*

contact with their arriving passenger, at which point they proceed to the proper curb and affect an immediate pickup. In extreme cold or heat, though, this solution may be considered a less desirable option.

Without a doubt, airport parking concepts and revenue generating strategies will continue to evolve along with emerging technologies. Other innovative parking technologies are discussed in the upcoming Airport Marketplace chapter.

TERMINAL AREAS

Fixed terminal design is a thing of the past. The newest designs are planned with the need for airports to evolve and respond quickly to changes in air transportation and the airport marketplace.

> *In the not so distant future, passengers will go from drop-off into terminal buildings largely devoid of the fortress-like ticket counters and their long lines. With perhaps a quick stop at a kiosk for an e-ticket boarding pass and baggage check, they'll breeze through security and enjoy the pleasures of a huge concourse area that is more like a shopping mall than a place to board an aircraft . . . Security concerns combined with 21st century technology.*[9]

As the opening quote to this chapter suggested, airport terminal design must now encompass state of the art technology, which is managed by Operations personnel rather than software programmers. High-tech Operations Centers, like that being used in San Francisco's new international terminal, reportedly enable "SFO to derive maximum utility from every asset with less waiting by passengers. That flexibility, combined with the intelligence of the SmartAirport Operations Center, gives the International Terminal a functional edge that rivals its aesthetic appearance."[10]

Four of the most dynamic areas within terminals are those dedicated to: ticketing/check-in, baggage processing, security check-

[9] Ascent Technology, *SFO's New International Terminal Soars Proving Where True Beauty Lies: In the Software*, http://www.ascent.com/case-sfo.html (visited Jan. 30, 2007), at 1.
[10] *Id.*

points, and gate areas. The previous chapter discussed changes at the checkpoints. The next section focuses on baggage processing improvements, while later sections discuss the development of shared facilities in the other terminal areas.

BAGGAGE PROCESSING

The August 2006 international security event, triggering the liquids ban in carry-on luggage, is an example of one incident that highlighted a need for increased airport flexibility in its baggage processing. Clearly, as the air transportation industry expands, increased amounts of luggage will be carried by passengers, processed through the increasingly complex airport environment, and stored in aircraft. For the airport operator, this translates into a need to facilitate potentially longer lines at checkpoints, the need for innovations in the baggage handling process and the need for increased space for associated processing equipment.

Over the past decade, many airports have approved the installation of automated baggage systems for common use by several tenants, or for use by a specific tenant. While there have been sometimes numerous reports of inoperative systems, and/or lost or damaged luggage associated with these automated systems (such as that widely reported at Denver International Airport shortly after the new airport opened in 1995), they have been considered a key to reducing labor costs, increasing efficiency and increasing accountability for passenger property.

With the more recent mandates to install in-line *Explosive Detection Systems* [EDS] for checked baggage screening even more accountability is required. Howard, Needles, Tammen and Bergendoff [HNTB] Deputy Planning Manager Scott Hyde explains,

> *Since 9/11, EDS has been the generator of changes in baggage tracking systems, because you can no longer have conveyor systems that move bags from point A to point B . . . With EDS, you have to plan for a system that feeds baggage into a central location for explosives screening,*

and continue to track it if it is pulled out for future explosives' residue inspection.[11]

The perfect combination for increased accountability is highly reliable hardware, coupled with the latest in sorting and tracking software. Manufacturer and integrator Glidepath recently installed an advanced software-driven baggage tracking system at Adelaide Airport in Australia as well as at Boise Airport in the U.S. Glidepath's proprietary software, GlideSort, is specifically designed for repetitive transactions in the "sorting, screening and reconciliation of outbound baggage in a cost-effective way," according to Business Director John Gude. "GlideSort has been designed to electronically track and provide graphic information on baggage—from check-in through sorting and reconciliation. It provides the TSA with a graphics-based, statistical representation of the bag's security status.[12]

To meet the need for increased efficiency on the world's increasingly larger airports, faster systems and higher levels of reliability are necessary. "New airport facilities are larger and the baggage must travel longer distances between the terminal and gates," explains Portec (Conveyor Systems) Manager Michael Anderson.[13] In fact, whereas older systems were moving baggage at a rate of 800 feet per minute, newer systems are being designed to operate at the rate of 2,000 feet per minute, with significant improvements at the "bottleneck" points of the system.[14]

Using a *Radio Frequency Identification Systems* [RFID]-based approach as introduced in the last chapter, a coupling of several hardware and software systems can provide both benefits and problems. Technology-based systems have already been shown to enhance airport security and decrease incidences of lost or misdirected luggage.[15] But, in very complex environments using multiple systems the RFID component is the key to assuring that multiple manufacturers' equipment effectively interact with others' equipment. In 2006, Las Vegas McCarran became a world-leader in RFID use of the International Air Transport Association [IATA] standard 920 Hertz [Hz] passive Ultra-

---

[11] Paul Seidernman & David J. Spanovich, *Expediting the Baggage Handling Process*, Airport Magazine (Oct./Nov. 2006), at 30.

[12] *Id. at 31.*

[13] *Id. at 30.*

[14] *Id. at 31.*

[15] *Id. at 32.*

High Frequency [UHF] RFID-embedded luggage tags. At Hong Kong International Airport, a test RFID program was initiated in 2004, but not completed until 2007.

It is projected that RFID-based baggage systems can reduce lost baggage by nearly 40 percent over traditional methods of tracking luggage. Still, due to cost, bar coding, and not RFID remains the current standard in the industry.[16] Bar coding costs about 6 cents per unit, while RFID is currently triple the cost, per unit. As an alternative to a per-bag approach to RFID use, some airports have used RFID to identify baggage trays, allowing the RFID chip to remain in the system while the baggage or cargo in the tray changes.

Baggage systems are also beginning to evolve in response to another trend—one of common-use or shared-use equipment and facilities at airports. "Passengers will check baggage at one central location rather than at individual airline ticket counters, and the bags will then go though EDS screening as part of the sorting process."[17] While some airports are on the cutting edge of new processing technology, others prefer to wait until the technology matures. Still other airports cite concerns with the projected costs and coordination required for automated, in-line baggage systems, particularly when multiple carriers must share these systems. Oakland International Airport's Aviation Director Steve Grossman noted that installation of an in-line baggage handling and EDS at every airport could cost collectively more than $3.4 billion.[18]

Reportedly, common-use baggage processing equipment will serve to maximize use of EDS, while increasing baggage throughput rates. Shared equipment and facilities are discussed at length in the next section.

---

[16] *Id.*
[17] *Id.* at 31.
[18] *Id.* at 33.

COMMON-USE FACILITIES

As introduced in the opening quote for this chapter, the concept of common-use facilities at airports is fast becoming one of the most significant and influential trends. The general concept is hardly a new one, using runways as an example. One can hardly imagine the airport attempting to establish a dedicated runway for each and every airline. Due to the lack of capacity in a growing transportation system airport managers are being challenged to use creative approaches.

Clearly, though, the common-use concept is not limited to the baggage system sharing noted in the previous section, and it is certainly not limited to U.S. airports. In fact, common-use equipment and facilities are much more common oversees than domestically, with air carriers often claiming "common-use" as the desired standard, due to reduced labor, capital and maintenance costs. Lufthansa reportedly told the New York/New Jersey Port Authority that the airline prefers common-use as a standard, only bringing in their proprietary processing systems when no common-use options are presented.

Common Use Terminal Equipment [CUTE] is an older term that includes the sharing of the traditional airline check-in desk. But like the technology, the terminology is also changing. The "next generation" of common use will be defined by two principle terms: *Common Use Passenger Processing Systems* [CUPPS] and *Common Use Self-Service* [CUSS]. The former (CUPPS) encompasses all "agent-facing devices" that are designed for common use such as ticket counters and baggage processing systems. The latter (CUSS) refers to a device that faces the passenger and is described as, "a shared kiosk offering convenient passenger check-in whilst allowing multiple airlines to maintain branding and functionality."[19]

The use of CUSS equipment and systems is generally considered a win-win scenario for airports, customers and airlines. The International Air Transportation Association reports that customers benefit from easier and faster passage through the airport, faster check-in and the opportunity for remote check-in (car parks, train stations, car rental return facilities). Airlines benefit from economy-of-scale benefits, the reduction of airport counter requirements, and the improvement of staff productivity. In fact, the International Air Transport As-

[19] IATA, *2007 CUSS Fact Sheet*, http://www.iata.org/NR/rdonlyres/132A888C-A991-4539-BE9B-7F95FEF7C58C/0/CUSSStatusforAirportsDecember06.pdf.

sociation reports an average per check-in saving to the airlines of $2.50 and an anticipated $1 billion annual savings to the industry when the market penetration of CUSS reaches 40%. Some airlines, though, have reportedly expressed concerns about common-use reducing their ability to protect their "market share" at a given airport, which for some can be better accomplished with exclusive-use facilities.[20]

IATA believes that airports will also benefit from common-use in the form of improved capacity utilization (limiting the need for new infrastructure) and in managing the concourse "real-estate" and airline/passenger flow processes. Some smaller airports are not as interested in common-use. These airports believe that *exclusive-use* facilities and agreements better obligate future airline service, and also serve to satisfy covenants associated with the acquisition and retirement of revenue bonds.[21]

The move toward common-use is one that can assist airports to potentially move further along the continuum (of potentially privatized options) toward increased airport privatization.[22] However, some may dispute this claim. Admittedly, while the development of a shared-use space approach may in fact *reduce* private entity (i.e., a single airline) control over exclusive spaces, it can be likewise argued that a shared-use system can also increase the likelihood of choice and open competition that privatization is meant to encourage. Las Vegas currently claims that it is the only airport in the country to be completely common-use, and it boasts a rich blend of air service options.

At John F. Kennedy Airport [JFK] in New York, Terminal 4 is an example of the link between common-use and successful privatization. JFK's Terminal 4 claims the distinction of being "the only privatized terminal in the U.S.," in great part the airport attributes its success to the terminal's initial design and operation as 100% common-use. The so-called "terminal of last resort" at JFK, is a low-start-up-cost option for seasonal, international and charter commercial traffic. In addition to common-use spaces and systems, the terminal's operator, JFK International Air Terminal, LLC, offers airlines a choice of four ground-handling agents for customer use.[23]

---

[20] *Id.*
[21] *Id.*
[22] Privatization is discussed in greater detail in Ch. 15.
[23] Alan Maca, President, JFK International Air Terminal, LLC (personal communication Feb. 2007).

To make common-use more "user friendly," airline lease or use agreements may include a *Preferential Use Clause* which assures a particular tenant first use of the premises over other users, so long as the active use of the area can be confirmed. *Remain Over Night* [RON] or the overnight parking of aircraft may be excluded as an "active use" of the premises and thus, might require an air carrier to relocate the aircraft for another carrier's use. [24]

Effective common-use involves several partners including a *platform provider* to provide the physical technology or hardware (usually the airport or a designated vendor), an *application provider* (which is usually a software developer and an airline or vendor function), and an *operational service provider* (which may be a vendor and/or airport employees) to service the equipment. Depending upon the source of an outage of service the operational service provider or an airline may be held responsible for CUSS outages.

IATA has taken the lead on establishing the standards for these systems. A comprehensive CUSS standard currently exists prompting CUSS-compliance kiosks to be in use at more than 100 major airports.[25] More than twenty European airports are CUSS-compliant, with a handful compliant in the U.S., the Americas, North Asia and Africa. But it is clearly a trend of the future. One of the most dynamic areas in airports today is the development and implementation of the common-use concept at check-in counters, baggage systems and in passenger check-in. However, the concept is expected to gain wide acceptance in other traditionally exclusive areas. Common-use is expanding to hold rooms and gates, loading bridges, aprons, preconditioned air and power sharing, the so-called "European model for ground handling" (privatized services provided to the user at the time of use), and even shared telephone systems where technology options exist.[26]

It is rather ironic that, while an entire chapter of this text heralds the emergence of airports as the new "marketplace" of the future—

---

[24] Alan Maca, President, JFK International Air Terminal, LLC., Personal Interview (Feb. 2007), E-mail contact: amaca@jfkiat.com. *See also* Greater Orlando International Airport, *Common Use Facilities Operating Procedures* (Oct. 1, 2004), http://www.orlandoairports.net/goaa/avleasing/common_use_facilities.pdf.

[25] Greater Orlando International Airport, *Common Use Facilities Operating Procedures* (Oct. 1, 2004), http://www.orlandoairports.net/goaa/avleasing/common_use_facilities.pdf, with data current as of 2007. It is estimated that, by the end of 2008, the number of CUSS-compliant airports will increase to more than 140.

[26] *Id.*

with branding being a key to strong revenue generation strategy—that "plain vanilla" common-use facilities and systems are being simultaneously introduced. While it might appear that airports are encouraging airline partners to abandon traditional branding efforts that were associated with exclusive-use space, this assumption would be incorrect. Newer signage technology is expected to eventually address this issue, as airport operators and technology managers seek ways to effectively enable robust branding for the users in these shared spaces.

Fortunately, gone are the days of using a roll of Mylar that is hand cranked up to display the logo of a current user. One key technology that will make common-use areas more passenger-and-tenant friendly is digital *dynamic signage* that will allow tenants to fully brand the space, during the time in which a particular user is occupying and paying for it. With the use of the newest in dynamic sign systems—which may eventually encompass entire walls in the gate or ticketing areas—spaces can be quickly converted between users, allowing users to display magnificent colors, logos and information. Terminal signage is discussed in greater detail below.

WAY FINDING AND TERMINAL SIGNAGE

An emerging area of interest in terminal development is that of *way finding*, or making public spaces easier to negotiate by improved signage, intuitive architecture and planning for mistake recovery; that is to say, finding the right way after having gone astray. New forms of signage are transforming sometimes confusing terminals into spaces that a stranger can comfortably negotiate. Gene Fuller explains the use of signage as a necessary "language" at airports:

> *Airport language is a spectacle, an interface for social relations between human and machines. Signage intensives social relations— reconfiguring territories of geophysical/ architectural space into territories of recognition that speak to a productive power of language that is fundamentally non-representational. . . . The traveler navigates through a highly textually mediate space where the signs not only enact semioticised territories, but also directly inter-*

> *vene into the material machinic process of traveling.* [27]

Directions are just one function of today's terminal signs. *Airport Magazine* Editor Clifton Stroud states, "Aesthetics, emergency communications and advertising revenue all play a part in implementing new signage."[28] The delivery of convenient and timely flight information can allow the passenger to remain longer in revenue-generating airport areas. For example, increasingly more airports are including large and comprehensive *Flight Information and Display Systems* [FIDS] in terminal (and retail area) redesign projects.

Factors to consider in signage include placement, character size and color (including hue, saturation and brightness). Approximately eight percent of males are color blind (with difficultly distinguishing between green and red), while a smaller percentage of men have difficulty distinguishing between yellow and blue.[29]

Newer dynamic technologies include *Plasma*, *Liquid Crystal Displays* [LCD] and *Light Emitting Diode* [LED] technologies. Airports must balance costs with function, and currently, the choice for most airports is LED. Trans-Lux Vice President Gene Coyne states that LED is the most practical choice for airports, because "The life expectancy of an LED sign is about 100,000 hours or about 7.5 years if the sign is on 24/7. Plasma has a much shorter life expectancy and certain images will eventually burn onto the screen. . . ."[30]

AIRPORT ART PROGRAMS

Several airports in the U.S. have significant art collections and some even employ full-time curators. Three well-respected airport art programs and/or collections can be found at Phoenix Sky Harbor International Airport [PHX], Dallas/Fort Worth International Airport [DFW] and Philadelphia International Airport [PHL]. When DFW opened its new International Terminal D, its Skylink stations hosed a

---

[27] Gene Fuller, *The Arrow—Directional Semiotics: Wayfinding in Transit*, as cited in Clifton Stroud, Signage in the Digital Age, Airport Magazine (Oct./Nov. 2006) at 22. "Semiotics" and "machinic architecture" deal with automobility, way finding and media designed to move the traveler from point to point.

[28] Clifton Stroud, *Signage in the Digital Age*, Airport Magazine (Oct./Nov. 2006), at 22.

[29] *Id.* at 22-23.

[30] Gene Coyne, as quoted in Clifton Stroud, *Signage in the Digital Age*, Airport Magazine (Oct./Nov. 2006), at 23.

multi-million dollar art display. Phoenix has both fixed and rotating art exhibits, as well as some high-quality public viewing areas, and in 2005 was seeking accreditation by the American Association of Museums. Philadelphia has 13 public art exhibition sites within its seven terminals.[31]

One of the catalysts for this movement was federal, state and/or local rules/efforts that permit a portion of airport capital improvement funds to be expended on pubic art. For example, in early 2000, Seattle-Tacoma International Airport [SEA-TAC] invested one percent of its $4.1 billion Capital Improvement Program in publicly visible or accessible projects for art."[32] The airport also has an Art Oversight Committee to oversee purchases.

At some airports, art has also become a revenue generating activity. Albany Art and Culture Program Director Sharon Bates oversees such a program at the Albany (New York) International Airport [ALB] exhibit and retail outlet. The terminal features a 2,500 square foot gallery and the Departure retail outlet, which "offers merchandise that reflects the theme or concept of the exhibit."[33]

WI-FI

The above section on airport art programs illustrates one trend at airports—blending pleasure with the business of air travel. If properly designed, airport terminal spaces can be productive spaces, especially if the traveler has access to a few electronic necessities. Two of those items are *Wireless-Fidelity* [Wi-Fi] *hotspots* (wireless internet access points) in the terminal and easy access to electrical outlets, to enable charging and use of a traveler's computer or cell phone.

When airports provide insufficient electrical outlet access, customers become creative, running recharging cords from seats to nearby plugs, sometimes sitting on the floors next to an outlet, sometimes causing fellow passenger inconvenience if not a trip hazard. The fix for the lack of electrical outlets is considered more of a future design consideration, with a few vendors having proposed some innovative approaches to "selling" electrical power at airports.

---

[31] Barbara Cook & Betsy Woods, *Beyond the Exhibition*, Airport Magazine (Sep./Oct. 2005), at 58.
[32] *Id.*
[33] *Id.*

The Wireless-Fidelity or Wi-Fi issue is perhaps one of the most dynamic technology issues to affect today's airports. A Boston-based researcher, the Yankee Group estimates the number of U.S. Wi-Fi "hot spots" at 72,480 in 2007.[34] *USA Today* reports the number of worldwide airport locations with Wi-Fi hotspots exceeded 1,650 in 2007, of which more than 500 of those locations are at U.S. airports.[35] Wi-Fi has wiggled onto airports in a variety of ways, sometimes through a private vendor or through an airline. For example, by 2005 JetBlue had established Wi-Fi networks at five major airports (Long Beach, JFK, Oakland, Fort Lauderdale and Orlando).[36]

Airports are not always in sync with their tenants on the approach to providing Wi-Fi services at airports. For example, from 2000-2005, Continental Airlines was offering complementary Wi-Fi to its frequent fliers at twenty President Club lounges across the nation. That same year, the Massachusetts Port Authority [MASSPORT]—charging $7.95 per day for public Wi-Fi access at Boston Logan International Airport—insisted that Continental turn off the antenna that provided the complementary service, citing public safety and management reasons.[37] Later that year, Continental filed a complaint with the Federal Communications Commission [FCC], asking them to overturn the airport's order.

While Boston Logan officials conceded that "dedicated public safety networks and *Wireless Local Area Networks* [WLANs] generally don't share the same frequency," they stated that "public safety agencies want to use Wi-Fi, and that a proliferation of Wi-Fi antennas in the airport could cause signal interference." Christine Gill, a partner with McDermott, Will and Emery, LLP, the Washington law firm representing the Massachusetts Port Authority explained, "We have tried to make it clear in the filings that this is not the backbone for the public safety network in the airport. They have their own proprietary networks that would not be subject to interference, but they want to make use of the Wi-Fi network, too."[38]

Airline officials and their supporters claimed the issue was more about money than safety, citing the airport's annual revenues of

---

[34] Bloomberg, *Boston Wi-Fi Spat Born in Airport Lounge May Set U.S. Rules* (Feb. 20, 2006).
[35] USA Today, *Hotspot Finder: Wi-Fi Locations*, http://usatoday.jiwire.com/hotspots-hot-spot-airport-directory-browse-by-country.htm (Mar. 2007).
[36] John Croft, *Wanted: Wireless*, Airport Magazine (Sep./Oct. 2005), at 67-69.
[37] Carmen Nobel, *Airport Seeks Ban on Free Airline Wi-Fi*, PC Magazine (Jan. 9, 2006).
[38] *Id.*

$200,000 from its Wi-Fi provider. Logan officials, however, maintained its safety position, contending that there should be only one centrally managed public network and that the Boston airport officials should be the logical operators of such a network. "They actively manage the Wi-Fi network, they encrypt it, they offer control over it, and they can shut down the network in an emergency if they need to," Gill said. "It's a management function more than anything else." [39]

In late 2006, though, the FCC disagreed, and issued a decision in favor of Continental Airlines. In this latest of major rulings that have been birthed at U.S. airports, the FCC explained their decision,

> *Today's declaratory ruling reaffirms the Commission's dedication to promoting the widespread deployment of unlicensed Wi-Fi devices. It clarifies that American consumers and businesses are free to install Wi-Fi antennas under our OTARD rules—meaning without seeking approval from their landlords—just as they are free to install antennas for video programming and other fixed wireless applications.*[40]
>
> *Today's decision ensures that the Wi-Fi bands remain free and open to travelers, who can make productive use of their time while waiting to catch their next flight in an airport. They will be able to choose from among multiple providers, including members-only airport lounges as well as coffee shops or businesses that may choose to attract customers by offering Wi-Fi service at lower prices than the airport authority offers.*

While, in the above decision, the FCC clearly sought to encourage competition, the Wi-Fi industry is not without its dark side. As such, there may be future claims of too much freedom from a victimized passenger who may feel an airport has not done enough to protect passengers from potential Wi-Fi-based attacks that may occur on airport property. Preston Gralla presents one such concern, where passengers could fall victim to "free" Wi-Fi scams:

---

[39] *Id.*

[40] Over the Air Reception Device [OTARD] (i.e. Antennas and dishes).

You could end up being the target of a "man in the middle" attack, in which a hacker is able to steal the information you send over the Internet, including usernames and passwords. And you could also have your files and identity stolen, end up with a spyware-infested PC and have your PC turned into a spam-spewing zombie. The attack could even leave your laptop open to hackers every time you turn it on, allowing anyone to connect to it without your knowledge.[41]

Gralla further explains how this occurs:

You go to an airport or other hot spot and fire up your PC, hoping to find a free hot spot. You see one that calls itself "Free Wi-Fi" or a similar name. You connect. Bingo—you've been had! The problem is that it's not really a hot spot. Instead, it's an ad hoc, peer-to-peer network, possibly set up as a trap by someone with a laptop nearby. You can use the Internet, because the attacker has set up his PC to let you browse the Internet via his connection. But because you're using his connection, all your traffic goes through his PC, so he can see everything you do online, including all the usernames and passwords you enter for financial and other Web sites.

In addition, because you've directly connected to the attack PC on a peer-to-peer basis, if you've set up your PC to allow file sharing, the attacker can have complete run of your PC, stealing files and data and planting malware on it. You can't actually see any of this happening, so you'd be none the wiser. The hacker steals what he wants to or plants malware, such as

[41] Preston Gralla, *Don't Fall Victim to the 'Free Wi-Fi' Scam: Those Wireless Connections Could be a Trap*, Computer World (Jan. 19, 2007).

> *zombie software, then leaves, and you have no way of tracking him down.*[42]

Wireless "ad hoc" hazards and attacks may actually be quite common. In fact, Gralla states that Authentium, Inc. (a security company) "has found dozens of ad hoc networks in Atlanta's airport, New York's LaGuardia, the West Palm Beach, Florida, airport and Chicago's O'Hare. Internet users have reported finding them at LAX airport in Los Angeles."[43] Arguably, a recognizable, airport-controlled Wi-Fi system may assist in the prevention of travelers from falling prey to sort of attack.

Control over Wi-Fi access also means control over any advertising messages that might be broadcast to the users. Other issues associated with Wi-Fi service are those of inadequate bandwidth and the work/costs associated with setting up new service. Jeff Heiser, senior software engineer with *Live TV* noted regional differences in installation complexity and costs, associated with the JetBlue Wi-Fi initiative. Heiser reported that some of the [western] airports were more difficult collaborators. "While airlines in some cases can negotiate with an airport for space to set up access points for private Wi-Fi Systems, other airports are not willing or able to make such concessions. Airports that have concession agreements with a single wireless provider can be tough nuts to crack; while those with a so-called 'neutral host' . . . can be easier." The inclusion of third parties in the process may result in the imposition of fees (to the airline or customer) for the passage of data through their networks.[44]

Free airport wireless access is often cited as a selling point of smaller airports and their community-promoting partners. In Chattanooga, Tennessee, Airnet partnered with the airport to provide Wi-Fi service at the airport. "We are thrilled to be able to offer this service to our airport for its travelers frequenting our city as well as the airport staff," says Keith Campbell, Airnet's Chief Operations Officer. "With a visitor's first impression to Chattanooga through our airport, what better way to assist the wonderful job [the airport and/or man-

---

[42] *Id.* Personal Computer [PC].

[43] *Id.*

[44] John Craft, *Wanted: Wireless; Airlines Target Private Wi-Fi for Data Dumps*, Airport Magazine (Sep./Oct. 2005), at 68-69.

ager is] doing for us and show our travelers what Chattanooga has to offer." [45]

AIRPORT COMMUNICATIONS CENTER

A critical element at busier commercial service airports is the airport's communication center, which may be co-located with the airport's operations center or simply linked to it via electronic means. While communications centers are being addressed in this section (on passenger terminals) these centers may actually be physically housed in a variety of airport locations ranging from maintenance buildings to fueling facilities. Communications functions may be centralized or they may be fragmented to various locations with specific tasking to perform communications in support of the police and/or fire personnel, in support of operations and maintenance personnel or in the performance of other functions including paging, monitoring of airport doors, gates, and checkpoints, etc.

Calls into or out of the communications center involve safety or security issues, the proper handling of which may result in life or death decisions. The telephone and radio lines into and out of the center may be continually recorded. Usually, though, these nerve centers serve a support function in enabling communications between various units on the airports, with tenants and with the community.

Increasingly, the issue of communications interoperability is of importance to police, fire and airport personnel. During an emergency or other serious event, it is important for those working the incident to have the opportunity to communicate with each other. In making equipment acquisitions, airport operators would be wise in planning and purchasing systems that assure interoperability between users.

AIRPORT CONSTRUCTION

Airport construction can be both exciting and treacherous. [46] From an operational perspective, an airport construction project prompts many safety and security concerns. Construction activity normally involves the presence and movement of personnel, equipment, and

---

[45] *Free Wireless to be Available at Chattanooga Airport*, The Chattanoogan (Jan. 25, 2007).

[46] This section draws heavily from FAA, *Operational Safety on Airports During Construction*, AC 150/5370-2E (Jan. 17, 2003); *see also* FAA Office of Aviation Safety and Standards, *Operating Your Airport Safely: Ideas and Practices* (Mar. 1991).

materials on or adjacent to the aircraft movement areas and within active terminal buildings. Construction projects involve several phases, including the *Pre-design, Design, Preconstruction, Construction* and *Inspection* phases. [47]

Airport construction activities typically involve two or more stakeholders, each with important responsibilities: the airport operator, the construction contractor (and their subcontractors/vendors), and various tenants (particularly if planning/construction activities are on leased property). Other important stakeholders include police and fire personnel who may have to access the construction areas during emergencies, or the traditional communications chains that notify airport users of unusual activities or hazards (e.g., such pilots, via the Flight Service Station as will be discussed later in this section).[48]

The first step in all cases is for the airport operator to either develop internally or otherwise approve construction safety plans. Details for developing a construction safety plan can be found in the FAA's Advisory Circular on *Operational Safety on Airports during Construction*.[49] Safety and security concerns with regard to construction projects can be best viewed from the three perspectives that have been continually presented throughout the airport operations chapters, from the *airside*, *landside*, and *terminal* area perspectives.

AIRSIDE CONSTRUCTION ISSUES

Obviously, not all construction projects on airports affect the airside portion of the operations equation. Those that do, though, prompt both serious safety concerns for maneuvering and parked aircraft, as well as people on board, and those who service aircraft. There are many important operational safety issues that should be discussed prior to the start of a construction project. To assure safety during construction, it is essential that a number of safety considerations be addressed during the design and pre-construction phases and included in the safety plan checklist which has several elements: [50]

---

[47] FAA, *Operational Safety on Airports During Construction*, AC 150/5370-2E (Jan. 17, 2003), at 1.

[48] *Id.* at *1-2.*

[49] *Id.*

[50] *Id.* at 3-4.

- Scope of work;
- Runway and taxiway lighting;
- Procedures for protecting runway and taxiway safety areas, obstacle-free zones and object free areas; [51]
- Navigation Aids [NAVAIDS], areas and operations affected by the construction;
- Methods of separating vehicle and pedestrian construction traffic from airport movement areas;
- Procedures and equipment (such as barricades) to delineate a closed construction area from airport operational areas;
- Limitations on construction;
- Required compliance of contractor personnel with safety and security measures; [52]
- Locations of stockpiled construction materials, construction site parking and access/haul roads;
- Radio communications;
- Vehicle identification;
- Trenches and excavation, and cover requirements;
- Procedures for notifying Aircraft Rescue and Fire Fighting [ARFF] personnel if water lines or hydrants must be deactivated or emergency access roads rerouted or blocked;
- Emergency notification procedures for medical and police response;
- Use of temporary visual aids;
- Wildlife management;
- Foreign Object Debris [FOD] control provisions;
- Hazardous Materials [HAZMAT] management;
- Issuance of Notices to Airmen [NOTAMs];
- Inspection requirements;
- Procedures for locating and protecting existing underground utilities, cables, wires, pipelines, and other underground utilities;
- Procedures for contacting responsible points of contract for all involved parties, including off-duty contact information, and

[51] As further outlined in FAA, AC 150/5300-13, *Airport Design*, and includes limitation on equipment height and stockpiled material.
[52] Including, but not limited to 49 CFR 1542 relating to transportation security regulations, and 14 CFR 139 relating to airport certification and airfield safety.

contact information for individuals responsible for navigational aids, in the event that the construction project creates a temporary outage of a NAVAID;

- Vehicle operator training;
- Penalty provisions for noncompliance with airport rules, regulations or the safety plan; and,
- Any special conditions that affect the operation of the airport and require a portion of the safety plan to be triggered (such as low visibility or snow-removal operations).

Some important occasions to review and discuss the operational impact of construction projects are during the plans review phase and during the construction project pre-bid and/or pre-construction meeting. It is at these phases of a construction project that many major airside safety concerns might be mitigated. A sampling of discussion items might include those that follow.

Airport familiarization should include airport rules and layout briefings (often obtained through structured airfield safety classes held by airport management), aircraft right-of-way issues, airfield access and escorts, vehicle haul routes, and *safety area incursion* issues (i.e., problems with unauthorized entrance onto the runways and/or taxiways). Unfamiliar construction workers and equipment/ aircraft right-of-way issues need to be covered including the need for airfield escorts, vehicle haul routes, and movement and safety area incursions. If a construction haul route involves aircraft operating areas, haul route traffic and debris (falling from trucks) should be addressed. Regular inspections, spillage prevention and clean-up options should be discussed.

Obstructions to air navigation need to be addressed. Upon application for a building permit, the construction company should complete and submit a *Notice of Construction* for review by the FAA and disseminated for comment to many other potentially affected entities.[53] This notification to the FAA addresses the final height of the structure to be constructed relative to the imaginary surfaces and safety areas at airports that are protected through a weave of federal aviation regulations,[54] advisory circulars and related provisions in the airport's approved Airport Certification Manual.

---

[53] FAA Form 7460-1, *Notice of Construction or Alteration.*

[54] *E.g.*, FAR Part 77, *Objects Affecting Navigable Airspace.*

However, the construction notification normally does not include dimensions of construction equipment (such as cranes) that are required on site. All barricades, temporary markers, or other objects that have to be used in the safety area need to be as low as feasible, of low mass, and easily collapsible if impacted by aircraft. If they are not attached to the surface, they need to be weighted down or anchored. If they are affixed to the surface, they need to be "frangible" (i.e., easily broken) near the ground. Construction equipment, vehicles, personnel, and materials should not penetrate obstacle free zones or safety areas. Unavoidable obstructions and activities may require issuance of a NOTAM, marking, lighting, relocated or displaced thresholds, or runway/taxiway closure. Obstructions, hazards, and closed portions of airport operations areas must be adequately marked. Airport hazards such as open manholes, excavations, stock-piled materials, and all objects that penetrate the primary or transitional surfaces must be adequately lighted.

Equipment, debris and materials often found at airport construction sites pose a variety of hazards to aircraft and people. As much as possible, debris, holes, open trenches, and ponded water on pavement surfaces need to be eliminated. FOD or *foreign objects* such as nails, stockpiles, and other loose debris may be ingested into aircraft engines, block critical aircraft intakes, or severely damage aircraft tires, brakes, control surfaces or landing gear. Or it may be blasted about, causing substantial injury or even death to individuals working within and around construction sites.

Jet and propeller blast, aircraft wing tip clearance and barricade visibility are all special issues with regard to airports and aircraft traffic. Because of the constant existence of blast, the barricades must be durable and heavy. Visibility must be maintained so that barricading and/or cones can be clearly seen at night, at high aircraft speeds and from the perspective of a variety of pilot vantage points ranging from five- to fifty-feet cockpit heights.

Contractors should be briefed on the airport's requirement to notify pilots of potential safety hazards through the NOTAM process. Several common examples of items requiring notices should be discussed such as changes to landing/taxiway areas, lighting aids, navigational aids, and changes in airport conditions. Construction activities can often result in hazardous conditions. The NOTAM system disseminates information on unanticipated information, including construction activities, or temporary changes to components of, or hazards that are not otherwise published on associated charts and related publications.

The potential for electrical outages affecting lighting and NAVAIDs is a major concern that should be addressed if the contractor is doing any major electrical work or digging in areas where electrical lines may be affected. If outages are planned, appropriate movement area closures or alternate lighting plans should be discussed. Procedures and contact numbers of FAA Airway Facilities personnel should also be listed so that they can be notified of unanticipated utility outage or a cable cut occurring that impacts FAA navigational aids.

Coordination, especially with air traffic control representatives and affected tenants, is critical. Not only is coordination required in the Airport Certification Manual, it is simply "good business" to keep all affected parties in the loop. Revised vehicular control procedures or additional equipment and the movement of personnel in the airport operations area need to be coordinated. There needs to be effective coordination of construction activities during winter with the airport snow removal plan. Any planned disruptions of the tower line-of-sight need to be coordinated with Air Traffic Control [ATC].

Liability issues may fall under the jurisdiction of the airport manager's office, operations, engineering or business office. Adherence to proper *insurance* requirements (often differing in various locations on the airport) is an important issue to cover during the pre-design/pre-construction phase. Additionally, there should be a chain of notification and authority to change safety-oriented aspects of the construction plan, with designation of responsible representatives of all involved parties and their availability. Finally, the construction site should be inspected daily, if not more often, for hazards. Additionally, construction inspectors trained in airport safety should be used to monitor construction activities.

LANDSIDE AND TERMINAL CONSTRUCTION ISSUES

The plans review phase, as well as the construction project pre-bid and/or pre-construction meetings, also provide an opportune environment for discussion of landside and terminal area construction issues. A list of discussion items might include those that follow.

Both *traffic laws* and *local traffic demands* must be discussed when the construction project involves roadways and/or terminal curbs. If a traffic manual is available from the airport sponsor, it should be given to the contractor. If none is available, ample discussion of rules, potential project impacts, and airport sponsor expectations should occur before the start of the project.

Roadway signs and pavement markings should be discussed so that appropriate measures can be taken to assure that pavement markings and signs properly alert drivers to potential hazards or changes in roadway conditions. *Traffic control* and lane closures or changes should be discussed prior to implementation. The repercussions of a poorly planned lane restriction may be a missed flight or the cause of a traffic accident. Traffic control should also be discussed and coordinated such that appropriate personnel are on hand to direct traffic (when such cannot be controlled through marking and signage). *Sidewalk closures or restrictions* need to be adequately marked and as convenient to pedestrians as possible. If pedestrians do not have sidewalk access, they may resort to walking in the street where they can become a road hazard. Proper planning and detours keep pedestrians from acting in an unsafe manner.

If *haul routes* involve airport roads, issues such as vehicle parking (curbside), haul route roadway congestion, and debris (falling from trucks) should be addressed. Regular inspections, spillage prevention and clean-up options should be discussed. The potential for interference or outages of utilities involving electrical lines, gas lines, telephone lines, alarm and computer feeds, etc., should be an item of discussion as applicable.

Construction can create *attractive nuisances* and *unforeseen hazards.* Because individuals of all ages and capacities frequent airports, construction projects must be scrutinized for a variety of users. The unexpected as well as the expected must be anticipated. Individuals, who may be physically or mentally challenged, disoriented in a new place, or simply curious must be taken into consideration. A child may swing on temporary poles, pick up a forgotten tool, or attempt to drink the contents of an open bottle. Also to be considered is what might occur if a person tried to sit on a pile of construction materials or what would happen if a physically challenged person had to maneuver around construction debris with a wheel chair. Dust, smoke, noxious solvents and glues should all be considered items to avoid in enclosed terminal spaces. All these scenarios and more, if unchecked, could lead to unnecessary injuries and airport liability. One of the best ways to help keep a construction site safe is for airport personnel to conduct *frequent inspections*, viewing the site from the perspective of a passenger. As the next section reveals, special events must also be monitored as they present "special" challenges.

SPECIAL EVENTS

Airports by their very nature become focal points for special events and activities. A number of airports have regular yearly events that tax the airport facilities and its staff. In addition, due to the popularity of air travel, celebrities, politicians, sports figures and other Very Important Persons [VIPs] frequent airports. As a result, special events and accommodations have become a way of life for those in operational capacities at airports.

VIP ARRIVALS AND DEPARTURES

Prominent government officials and candidates, religious leaders, celebrities and sports figures are among those that may draw crowds of people to the airport. Some local residents may come to the airport to honor visiting dignitaries, while others may come in protest. With such a variety of individuals arriving at the airport, some basic considerations include parking accommodations, physical space in the arrival/departure area as well as general security and safety concerns.

MOVIE PRODUCTIONS OR COMMERCIAL PHOTOGRAPHY

At times, airports may play host to movie crews or still photography "shoots." These types of activities may be limited in scope by local laws or airport rules. Often, airport escorts are required for visitors to have access to sensitive or secured areas. Insurance requirements must be met and necessary permit(s) must be obtained prior to the commencement of the activity. Planning should be undertaken to minimize the effect of the production on the traveling public and airport tenants.

It is important to note that movie productions often involve "creative" individuals who may not readily accept (or may be too preoccupied to remember) the strict safety or security limits that must be imposed in the airport environment. For example, during one "film shoot" at a major commercial service airport, after being given detailed airfield security, safety and escort instructions, a film director was then being escorted toward an approved airside location for filming, with the escort vehicle leading the director in a separate car. Unexpectedly, the director suddenly turned his vehicle toward the runway. The airfield escort quickly responded by driving her vehicle in the path of the director's vehicle causing him to abruptly stop. While the escort's maneuver prevented the director from reaching the runway, it was nevertheless a distressing moment. When asked his rationale for leaving the escort's lead, the director responded that the "light (toward the runway) was incredible" so he spontaneously decided to "check out the location."

Similar problems have been reported at airports with regard to production company use of electrical power (overloading circuits in the terminal), blinding pilots (with excessive lights toward ramp or movement areas) and propping open security doors in secured areas. While film crews may be proficient at their craft, it should be presumed that they need a watchful eye and firm guidance in areas that could compromise airport safety or security. It is also helpful to have a permitting process (and a film office) for production activities and oversight. This process may require the payment of fees and obtaining permits; a discussion of insurance/liability issues; the scheduling of escort and other necessary personnel (electrical, mechanical, operational); rules/regulations; tenant and user communications; and the repercussions associated with lack of compliance.

MAJOR COMMUNITY EVENTS OR INCIDENTS

Local events or incidents often draw both anticipated and unforeseen visitors to the community. The associated glut of visitors can heavily affect the local airport. Whether it is a major sporting event, a natural disaster, a hot media story or some other event, the primary airport (and even reliever airports) must quickly adapt to the needs of the traveling public. The key to handling the demands of a special event lies in active communication and coordination with airport users, community leaders, government officials, airport tenants and the myriad of service industries that accommodate the traveling public.

If an event requires the lighting of a fire, such as that used to signal the beginning of a disaster drill, the communication center and members of the media should be notified so that community members do not mistake the smoke for an aircraft incident or accident.

AIR CARGO OPERATIONS

"Air cargo" is a generic term, which applies fundamentally to anything that goes into the hold of an aircraft, with the exception of baggage.[55] The latter (baggage) is associated with the carriage of passengers and is included as part of the individual passenger's airfare. Air Cargo is in three forms: *air freight*, *mail*, and several types of expedited small-package service captured under the rubric of *air express*.

Air cargo operations differ significantly from air passenger operations. The process of moving freight is much more complex than passenger traffic. It involves packaging, extensive and complex documentation, arranging for insurance, pick-up and/or collection from the shipper, preparing dangerous and hazardous goods documentation, customs clearance at origination and destination, and final delivery. This complexity has encouraged the growth of specialty firms—the *freight forwarders*—that perform some or all of these tasks on behalf of the shipper.[56]

An air freight forwarder or consolidator is an *indirect* air carrier. It assembles and consolidates property for shipment by air; is responsible for the transportation of property from its point of receipt to its destination; and utilizes, for the whole or part of the actual transport of the goods, the services of a *direct* air carrier.[57] The air freight forwarder provides an interface between the shipper and the airline. In short, it is a third party, which arranges for the shipment of air cargo. Since deregulation, air freight forwarders have become as central to the retailing of the airline's freight service as travel agents are to the

---

[55] This section is drawn heavily from Paul Stephen Dempsey & Laurence E. Gesell, *Air Transportation: Foundations for the 21st Century* (1997).

[56] Rigas Doganis, *Flying off Course: The Economics of International Airlines* 327 (2nd ed. 1991). *See also* William E. O'Connor, *An Introduction to Airline Economics* 129-130 (2nd ed. 1982). In Europe the "forwarder" is known as a "consolidator," which may be a more accurate term, since the essence of a forwarder's function is to *consolidate* many shipments into one large shipment and then to offer the consolidated shipment to the airlines.

[57] *See* the Civil Aeronautics Board [CAB] Glossary in Robert M. Kane, *Air Transportation* (12th ed. 1996).

retailing of airline passenger business, though their role may be eroding.[58]

The introduction of wide-body aircraft, ancillary developments such as containerization, electronic transmission of documents, and automated ground handling of shipments have revolutionized the air cargo industry, which in turn has had an impact on airport operations and infrastructure. For the infrastructure to be effective, it requires an airport environment conducive to cargo operations. There must be minimum delay to the movement of cargo through terminals, cargo must be protected from damage and theft, there must be the ability to load and unload aircraft swiftly, and costs must be contained. Most of all, air cargo terminals need an abundance of space. The tendency of the industry to dispatch cargo at the end of the day for delivery at the destination the following morning creates a concentration of trucks around the terminals during pick-up and delivery times.[59]

Operations at cargo terminals are *labor intensive*, despite extensive use of complex sorting and conveying apparatus. It takes labor to receive the shipments; to process paperwork; to compute and collect charges; to weigh, sort and allocate each piece of cargo to its proper flight; and to provide proper security.[60] There must be adequate space to accommodate a sizable work force. In addition, air cargo traffic behaves very differently than passenger handling. Air carrier terminals are designed around typical peak hour operations. Following the peaks in passenger traffic, terminal congestion typically subsides, but not so with cargo. In the cargo terminal, freight may have to be stored in transit, temporarily awaiting dispatch.

On the input side of cargo flow through the terminal, over a very short period of time (i.e., the typical peak hour) the aircraft payload arrives in a "batch." The batch is then sorted. Cargo that is inbound and not transferred directly is checked in, stored, processed, and stored again prior to delivery in relatively small shipments (i.e., up to container size).

---

[58] Assuming the airline's rates for pick-up and delivery are included, the rates offered by the freight forwarder for door-to-door service are usually lower than the rates shippers would pay if they dealt directly with the airlines. The freight forwarder makes up the difference, plus a profit, by *consolidating* shipments and obtaining a quantity or volume discount from the airline for the larger shipment.

[59] *Id.* at 125.

[60] *Id.* at 126.

The export operation is the reverse process. Small packages or shipments are received, processed, stored, and assembled into the payload for a particular flight. The aircraft is then loaded as expeditiously as possible. However, loading/unloading times can vary considerably depending on factors such as:

- The type of cargo and whether it is *unitized* or in small shipments;
- The *type of shipper*—for example, terminal operations are simplified when freight forwarders rather than private shippers are involved;
- *Domestic versus international* cargo, where domestic shipments require less documentation;
- The level of *transfer between terminals*, where so called "across the apron" transfer to another terminal may require special handling;
- If *surface shipments* are involved, where inter-modal processing, transfer and reloading must be accomplished;
- *Interlining* which may likely require less processing than other import cargo; and
- Whether *all-freight operations* are involved. Dramatic peaks of cargo flow and severe overloading of the cargo apron characterize all-freight operations. Conversely, the use of passenger aircraft implies that cargo will be remotely loaded at the passenger terminal apron.[61]

Add to the turmoil of the terminal operation the activities of air freight forwarders. In many cases, on-airport facilities are provided not only for the airline, but also for freight forwarders. Many airlines welcome freight forwarders for providing intermediary service between the airline and the shipper. As indicated above, freight forwarders can expedite the flow of cargo through the terminal. By taking care of many of the shipping procedures, the freight forwarder allows the airline to concentrate on the provision of air transport.[62] Irrespective, the separate operation of the freight forwarder occupies

---

[61] Norman Ashford, H.P. Martin Stanton & Clifton A. Moore, *Airport Operations* 275-278 (1991).
[62] *Id.* at 271-272.

limited space in what already may be overcrowded conditions in the terminal.

In short, air cargo terminals require a lot of space to accommodate aircraft, cargo storage and processing, and an environment conducive to a large work force. Such space is at a premium at major international airports. Added to the space requirements, local community concerns about noise and congestion, as well as air traffic and/or landside capacity constraints are significant factors, which may limit air cargo terminal operations. This has led some observers to conclude there ought to be a separate airport altogether, devoted exclusively to freighters. Suggested is that such a "cargo-port" could be built in the hinterland, far out from the city, where space would be more abundant and land would be cheaper. Noise problems would be reduced, congestion at regular airports would be reduced, and passenger service would indirectly benefit. In addition, cargo would move unhindered by the congestion at the passenger airports.[63]

The problem with the above vision, however, is that it ignores the fact that most air cargo moves in the *bellies* of passenger aircraft, especially in the U.S. Such a concept may work well for an all-cargo service provider, though it too needs inter-modal access to highways linking urban centers to the airport. But, even there, many of the integrated carriers use the cargo capacity of passenger airlines to complement their services. In the final analysis, although they are separate and distinct segments of the air transportation industry, the carriage of passengers and the transport of air cargo are an *integrated* function. Each must be accommodated at major airports, and ways must be found to enhance the environment for air cargo operations at predominantly passenger-handling airports. Accordingly, airport operators must advocate and attempt to provide a market-oriented airport policy and encourage the growth and facilitation of international cargo.[64]

Recognizing potential constraints to accomplishing an environment conducive to air cargo operations, airport managers have identi-

---

[63] William E. O'Connor, *An Introduction To Airline Economics* 127 (2nd ed. 1982). The concept identified here as a "cargo-port" resembles the "wayport" created by James Sheppard, except that instead of a passenger terminal it would be a remotely located airport for all-cargo operations. In its basic form, Sheppard's wayport would be an airport built at a remote site and would provide a place where airlines could inter-connect passengers. There would be no local traffic. There would be neither enplanements nor deplanements, only passengers making connections.

[64] Douglas V. Leister, Stuart E. Robinson, Erwin von den Steinen & Ingrid M. Kollist, *An Analysis of The United States International Air Cargo Market 1975-1986* 54 (1988).

fied the major issues confronting them today. With the assistance of the *Airport Operators Council International* [AOCI],[65] a survey was taken of the top ten U.S. international air cargo airports about their approach to air cargo operations.[66] Information provided by the top ten airports addressed five principle issues affecting international air cargo operations: curfew restrictions, slot availability, cargo facilitation, transit operations, and sort centers.[67]

- *Curfew restrictions*—Many airports allow full 24-hour operations, while some airports have limited flexibility due to noise concerns. Included in many noise abatement strategies is a requirement for air carriers to convert to "Stage 3 aircraft" that meet the noise levels prescribed in 14 CFR Part 36.
- *Slot availability*—For the most part, U.S. airports are not subject to landing or take-off slot restrictions. At some airports, however, the Federal Aviation Administration's "high density rules" apply. These airports are limited to the hourly number of allocated operations (takeoffs and landings) that may be reserved for the specific classes of users of those airports.
- *Cargo facilitation*—U.S. airports offer a variety of cargo-handling arrangements subject to policies that differ primarily because of different management philosophies. The major impediment to flexible cargo facilitation is lack of space, which is a growing problem among the larger air carrier airports.
- *Transit operations*—There may not be sufficient facilities and services available at some airports to allow all carriers to service their own transient needs. Most airports, however, allow airlines to handle other airlines. In some cases (Anchorage and Honolulu, for example), newer, longer-range non-stop equipment has permitted traditional stopover points to be overflown, particularly by passenger aircraft. This could free up facilities for more cargo operations.
- *Sort centers*—The air cargo "sort center" concept for connecting air freight movements is the all-cargo counterpart to the

[65] This organization is now the Airports Council International [ACI].

[66] The airports included: New York's J.F. Kennedy, Miami, Los Angeles, San Francisco, Chicago O'Hare, Boston Logan, Atlanta Hartsfield, Honolulu, Houston Intercontinental, and Newark.

[67] Douglas V. Leister, Stuart E. Robinson, Erwin von den Steinen & Ingrid M. Kollist, *An Analysis of The United States International Air Cargo Market 1975-1986* 54-60 (1988).

> "hub-and-spoke" system introduced by passenger carriers. The sort center attempts to optimize efficiency through simultaneous aggregation and disaggregation of freight from widely dispersed origins and destinations. Typically, large fleets of planes and trucks stand by for post-sort loading to accomplish delivery to ultimate destinations.

As mentioned earlier, air cargo activities, such as package sorting and aircraft loading are often conducted during evening hours. This nighttime activity can generate lighting and nighttime noise impacts that may be considered an irritation to local communities. In addition, vehicle operations to and from the air cargo area may cause increased evening traffic as well as additional air and noise pollution from idling or moving vehicles. Thus, airport operators should take special care, when able, to consider proper location of the cargo operation, such that they are located as far from residential areas as reasonably possible.

SUMMARY

Operations personnel at airports range from the "jack of all trades" person who may perform generalized security, safety and ground transportation oversight, to those at airports having departments or divisions with hundreds of workers, each with specialized duties and areas of responsibility. While this chapter and the last two chapters provide a wealth of information on several operational areas of great concern to today's airports, they fall well short of encompassing all the operational challenges encountered by public airport managers and their staff. To cover all of the operational aspects would go beyond the scope of one volume. Clearly, though, rapid technology changes will continue to dramatically change the way airports are managed. In addition, major global events challenge airport operators to continually review their management and operational practices.

Equally diverse and challenging are maintenance operations at today's public airports. The topic of maintenance, with specific emphasis on grounds keeping, snow removal and airfield pavements, is the focus of the next chapter.

CHAPTER 11

AIRPORT MAINTENANCE

We do everything we can to provide the best surface possible.
It's up to the carrier to decide if they can use it.

John Swedyk, Operations Manager,
Cleveland Hopkins Airport[1]

INTRODUCTION

A well-conceived, properly applied maintenance program is essential to the operation of any airport, and it must entail continuous implementation to be effective. The program must be carried out with sufficient consistence and competence that a high level of trust is generated by those who must use the airport and airfield during the most challenging of meteorological conditions, from blistering heat to a winter blizzard.

Proper maintenance of the airport is important for a variety of reasons including:

- Preservation of capital investment;
- Assurance of a safe operating environment;
- Compliance with sponsor assurances attached to federal funding grant agreements; and
- Compliance with appropriate Federal Aviation Regulations [FAR]s.

---

[1] As cited in Clif Stroud, *Getting Ready for a Tough Winter*, Airport Magazine (Aug./Sep. 2006), at 77.

There is a strong link between airfield maintenance and safety, particularly that required in order to maintain certification for a commercial airport. FAR Part 139 "Certification of Airports" requires the airport have specific procedures in place for snow removal and storage, as well as the maintenance of paved and unpaved areas, safety areas, marking and lighting systems, traffic and wind direction indicators, and prevention of power failure to Navigation Aids [NAVAIDs]. In fact, when FAR Part 139 was substantially revised in February of 2004, a number of maintenance-related requirements were clarified, including:[2]

- Repairing pavement cracks;
- Marking pavement edges;
- Runway and taxiway identification system plan;
- Controlling and removing snow and ice;
- Notifying air carriers of field conditions; and
- Documenting airfield self-inspections and airport condition reports.

Further, where federal funds have been used to develop airport facilities, airport agreements generally impose on the airport sponsor a continuing obligation to preserve and maintain airport facilities in a safe and serviceable condition. These contractual agreements require the sponsor to carry out a continuing program of preventative maintenance and minor repair activities which will ensure that the airport facilities are at all times maintained in the way they were designed to be used.[3]

This chapter discusses the importance of properly maintaining airport grounds and the airfield pavement areas. While a variety of important maintenance functions are referenced, this chapter focuses on the extensive and sometimes specialized airport maintenance areas of *grounds-keeping*; *snow* and *ice control*; and *pavement construction, maintenance* and *repair*.

---

[2] 14 CFR FAR Part 139, *Certification of Airports* (2004), retrieved from athttp://www.faa.gov/airports_airtraffic/airports/airport_safety/part139_cert/media/part139_final_rule.pdf.

[3] FAA, *Airport Compliance Requirements*, FAA Order 5190.6A (Oct. 2, 1989).

MAINTENANCE PROGRAM

"Maintenance" is the work of keeping the airport in proper condition. It is the process of preserving the airport in a state of good repair. Depending upon the airport's state of disrepair, maintenance assumes one of two general forms. If performed before difficulties have developed, it is *preventive maintenance*. If, on the other hand, serious failure has already occurred, and repairs are required, it is *corrective maintenance*. Where preventive maintenance leaves off and where corrective maintenance begins is often a matter of individual perception. In some cases, however, the difference between preventive and corrective actions is more clearly defined. For example, the Federal government will not provide financial assistance for routine maintenance such as a runway slurry coat application. On the other hand, reconstruction of the runway with an asphalt overlay may be federally fundable if the overlay is intended for other than maintenance repair; to increase the load bearing capacity of the pavement, or to increase runway surface friction, for example.

Although not federally fundable, the value of preventive maintenance can be demonstrated, and if properly applied can affect significant savings in unnecessary or deferred construction expense. Minor defects rapidly become major ones, and can result in costly repairs. In general, preventive maintenance can substantially reduce the need for extensive repairs or replacement.

Maintenance expenses are a major item. Reportedly, the cost of airport facilities maintenance averages 38% of the typical operating budget. Yet, despite the economics, facilities and equipment must be maintained to insure safe and efficient operation. Airports certified for air carrier operations under FAR Part 139 must be inspected daily, the results must be logged, and corrective action must be timely to insure the airport is operationally safe.

During the inspection, emphasis is placed on:

- *Weather hazards* such as snow, ice or slush on the operational areas;
- *Obstacles* in the primary, transition, and approach surfaces;
- *Public protection* including fencing and gate security;
- *Pavement surface hazards* such as erosion, displacement or debris;

- *Construction hazards* including holes, ditches, and obstacles such as improperly parked vehicles; and
- *Bird hazards* and any other maintenance deficiencies.

As a practical matter, managers of general aviation airports should also perform similar operational inspections in conjunction with routine maintenance inspections.

To reduce maintenance costs, the time, effort, and cost of airport maintenance can be greatly minimized through proper planning, design and construction of facilities. Buildings such as passenger terminals, which are subject to heavy traffic, should be pre-designed to withstand abuse. Maintenance through proper construction can result in long-term savings and prolonged facility life. For instance, floors of brick or cement tile do not require special care, while the maintenance of marble terrazzo is more complicated. Exposed brick or stone walls require minor maintenance, but wooden, plastered, and painted walls take very special care. Carpet selection can also be critical. The life of a carpet is short and maintenance can be very costly. Restrooms must be meticulously clean. If designed to withstand high-pressure washers and quick evacuation of excess water, they are much easier to keep clean. Even the cleaning and maintenance of the areas outside of buildings can be reduced if adequate planning and design of landscaping is done before installation. Low-maintenance shrubs and ground covers, automatic irrigation systems, and adequately placed trash receptacles may preclude hours of maintenance performance.

MAINTENANCE AREAS OF SPECIALIZATION

At smaller airports, one or more general maintenance workers may accomplish a variety of maintenance tasks or functions. A maintenance worker who operates a sweeper on the taxiway may also be expected to unstop a toilet or repair the seal on a hangar door. At larger airports, the division of labor may be more specialized. A maintenance division or department may include hundreds of employees with a variety of specialized areas including, but not limited to the following:

- *Airfield maintenance* (runways, taxiways, infields, safety areas, etc.);
- *Building maintenance* (physical or structural repairs);
- *Mechanical maintenance* (doors and conveyors, baggage systems, security/ticketing systems, etc.);
- *Communications or equipment maintenance* (telecommunications, radio equipment, common use equipment, etc.);
- *Grounds maintenance* (ground cover/landscaping, trees, etc.);
- *Custodial or janitorial* maintenance (generally cleanliness of floors, bathrooms, trash removal, etc.);
- *Electrical maintenance* (airfield, terminal, and roadway lighting; lighted signs, etc.);
- *Street maintenance* (sweeping and roadways, signage install/repair, etc.);
- *Fleet maintenance* (vehicle engine and body routine maintenance and repairs);
- *Information technology* (computer systems acquisition and maintenance); and
- *Specialty areas* (sign-making and installation, airfield/roadway marking, NAVAIDs, etc).

Sometimes, airport employees are based at the airport, while others may be employees of the airport's sponsor—charged to respond to the airport when specific maintenance services are required. Airports may also have established contracts for the provision of certain necessary maintenance functions. In these cases, the specific maintenance services are either provided routinely (such as nightly terminal janitorial services or quarterly runway rubber removal services) or in an on-call or emergency basis (such as significant pavement repairs).

With established facilities, the key to reducing maintenance expense is through periodic inspection and early detection. *Preventive maintenance* entails a programmed approach of inspection and follow-up corrective action. *Routine maintenance* should be scheduled whenever appropriate and in anticipation of future problems. A maintenance plan should be established enabling advanced cost-benefit consideration in all areas, and especially to the major cost items such as pavement repair. Routine preventive maintenance will lengthen utility life and thereby reduce replacement cost. A periodic condition survey is strongly recommended to detect the need for maintenance or rehabilitation, especially to reveal early symptoms of pavement distress.

In addition to routine daily airport inspections, there should also be periodic, comprehensive inspections conducted by qualified individuals; preferably by a team of inspectors. Maintenance planning requires a team effort with input from designers, project managers, users and maintenance personnel. Routine maintenance inspections should also be a team effort, headed by an airport management representative and accompanied by a maintenance supervisor. Moreover, all that use or work at the airport should conduct comprehensive self-inspection programs and should communicate deficiencies to someone in a position to implement corrective action referred to as *corrective or emergency maintenance*, depending upon the severity of the problem.

Maintenance is environmentally important as well, especially in the area of energy conservation. Maintenance of existing mechanical and electrical systems can be essential to energy efficiency. Routine preventive maintenance has been estimated to save as much as 10% of an airport's annual utility budget. Additionally, preventive maintenance will extend equipment life and reduce replacement costs.

Airport maintenance takes on the many facets normally associated with the operation of any large institution. It includes custodial and janitorial services, power plant maintenance, repair and maintenance of vehicles, and so forth. With few exceptions, the procedures employed in airport building maintenance need to match the same standards used at other, non-airport structures subject to high volumes of pedestrian traffic. For example, salt is used extensively on airports in the Snow Belt. Yet, salt is an archenemy of terrazzo flooring; it enters the terminal building on the boots and shoes of passengers and visitors, and can gradually disintegrate tile flooring. Terrazzo floors, therefore, must be sealed periodically with a liquid chemical sealant, and then cleaned and maintained with an alkaline cleaning solution, although the newest forms of Terrazzo require less maintenance than that of prior decades. Aside from salt damage, all floors need to be cleaned of dirt, oil and grime to minimize unnatural wear.

As stated, maintenance of an airport terminal building is much like that of any large building subjected to high volumes of pedestrian traffic. Not to slight the importance of proper building maintenance, but the thrust of this chapter addresses facilities unique to airports; in particular the airfield. Airport maintenance entails upkeep of extensive areas of open turf and expansive paved areas, which support specific (airport) operational needs. Owing to extensive runway, taxiway and apron lighting systems, airports may also be unique in having extremely high utility costs.

Each of the fore-mentioned areas of maintenance specialization can be very important to airports, and thus, several chapters could be dedicated to the subject of maintenance at airports. The focus of this chapter is in three major areas: *grounds-keeping*, *snow and ice removal*, and a more lengthy discussion on *pavement construction, maintenance and repair*. These areas were selected because of the specialized nature of the airfield and the extraordinary demands placed on that environment by arriving and departing aircraft weighing hundreds of thousands of pounds that can generate jet blast exceeding 100 miles per hour.

GROUNDS MAINTENANCE

Grass and weeds are a nemesis, yet an inherent part of a healthy airfield. Mowing grass serves a variety of purposes, and grass is an important part of maintaining an airport. It enhances the aesthetics. It controls bird and animal hazards by eliminating inviting habitats. It allows pilots and air traffic controllers an unobstructed view of paved areas, lights and signs. And it minimizes the danger of potential brush fires.

Mowing is perhaps the most intense outdoor maintenance operation at the airport. It is a chore, and an expensive one at that, but the resulting healthy grass is important to soil conservation and for protection against erosion. Healthy ground cover is needed, especially on sloping terrain subject to erosion by rainfall runoff. Turf coverage inhibits rapid and destructive water runoff. Roots hold the turf together, and prevent erosion of the topsoil. Airfield turf is a functional surface, which controls wind and water erosion, reduces dust, and stabilizes the runway overruns, shoulders, and other areas used by regular or emergency traffic.

Proper grounds-keeping also aids in drainage management, the operational and environmental importance of which was emphasized earlier in this text. Erosion of the surface by water runoff may cause obstruction of drainage ditches by weeds, brush, and other accumulation of debris. Dense sod helps to stabilize open ditches and prevent debris accumulation. The airfield drainage system should be checked in the spring to insure storm sewer inlets are not blocked and to clean away all silt, foliage and debris from the grates. There should be no ponding of water or erosion around inlets. Broken structures and deteriorated pipes should be repaired. And, open ditches should be cleaned of debris, overgrowth and obstructions. The turf at pavement edges should also be checked and noted for areas of damming and channeling of flow parallel to the pavement. Federal Aviation Regulation Part 139 allows for no greater than a three-inch lip where the turf abuts the pavement.

Turf maintenance is a lot of labor-intensive work, but it need not be a problem so long as there is a management program designed to give intelligent and timely attention to soil needs. Grounds-keeping practices normally fall into one of five categories: fertilizing, watering, mowing, cultivating, and control (of disease, insects, and weeds).

Fertilizing supplements the natural food supplies of the soil, and balances the plant growth requirements. Nitrogen, phosphorous, potash, and lime are the elements around which most fertilizing programs are planned. The key element for turf grass is nitrogen; one or more annual applications are normally required for satisfactory growth.

Where there is an annual rainfall of less than thirty inches, lime, phosphorous and potash are likely to be deficient. Rainfall in many locales precludes the need to water. If supplemental *watering* is necessary, an irrigation engineer or a manufacturer of irrigation equipment should be consulted. Additionally, a local horticulturist ought to be consulted to determine exact fertilizer needs. There are inherent differences in nutritional requirements of different grasses, and organic, compost-type fertilizers may be advisable.

There are wide regional variations in soil and climate affecting plant growth. Most airfield turf is in sandy soil, with no irrigation, and in an environment non-conducive to regular mowing, fertilizing or other turf maintenance practices. Nevertheless, turf specialists agree that combining organic fertilizers with the right grass types and proper reseeding and mowing programs can aid in providing both healthy and attractive airport groundcovers.

Mowing serves a threefold purpose in promoting healthy grass growth:

- It aids in controlling weeds and helps to promote density of the cover;
- Grass is normally maintained at a height of cut that promotes deep rooting, thus minimizing erosion; and
- It reduces the potential for grass fires associated with accumulations of dry dormant growth.

Mowing height and frequency of cut are the key elements to successful mowing, and are a function of the type of grass and its rate of growth. A rule of thumb is to cut grass so as not to remove more than one-third to one-half of the leaf surface at any one cutting.

A thin, weedy ground cover, lacking perennial species of grasses should be renovated. *Cultivation* and fertilizers may renew the area, but weed removal and reseeding may be needed as well to restore the cover to good health. Fall is the best time to cultivate and apply fertilizers. Seeding is best done in the spring.

Weeds are usually not a serious problem, and in fact, they may be of some benefit. Along with other more desirable growths, weeds prevent dust and stabilize the soil against erosion. They are also helpful in establishing a good stand of grass. However, weeds should be controlled from spreading and taking over grassy areas. Weeds are classified as annuals, biennials, or perennials, depending upon their individual root lives of one, two, or more years. Mowing just as the blossoms begin to open will kill most annuals and a few of the perennials.

Chemicals are useful on small areas for killing individual plants, groups of plants, or for discouraging growth adjacent to runways, taxiways, aprons, and around edge lighting systems. Weed-killing chemicals can be obtained for varying periods of potency. Some are designed for a one-time kill, while others are designed to sterilize the soil for a period of years. Needless to say, scrutiny must be given to the selection and application of de-weeding chemicals. Generally, the most acceptable weed control procedures adopt the use of chemicals in combination with mowing. Burning over weeded areas should be avoided. It destroys organic matter, lowers soil fertility, and may intensify soil erosion.

Although there are many costs for items such as fuel, supplies and equipment, labor is usually the principal expense involved in grounds maintenance as well as snow and ice removal (where necessary). Airport mowing programs, like snow removal programs, tend to be unique to each airport situation, and managers use varying techniques to control costs. One cost-saving tool used is plant growth retardant. But weed killers that destroy all plant life may also encourage soil erosion. Therefore, to stabilize barren soil, soil penetrants and/or sealants may be applied.

Retardants allow growth but inhibit cell division. When the complete costs of mowing are totaled, including insurance, replacement of cutting blades and depreciation of mowing equipment, at some airports and for some operations, plant growth retardants may be more economical than mowing. Plant retardants, however, may present environmental concerns.

Another way to reduce grounds maintenance cost is to find new uses for land that would otherwise grow grass. On the infields this could be *farming*, for example. Allowing a farmer to work the soil has a two-fold economic benefit. First, the farmer maintains the land and thus reduces direct grounds-keeping costs to the airport. Second, farming can produce revenues. The farmer may pay rents on the land either directly or by sharing in the sale of crops. It goes without saying that for safety compliance it may be necessary to properly train farmers in airfield procedures before allowing them onto the air movement area.

Where there are no alternatives to mowing, some managers have found that they can cut labor and operations costs by using different types of mowers and tractors. The paramount consideration is usually to get the turf mowed quickly and as economically as possible. For airport mowing, there are four basic types of tractor-powered mowers in general use. These basic types of mowing machines are designed to cut in one of two ways, by either *shearing* or by *impact* action. The four types of mowers are as follows:

- *Reel* mowers have horizontally mounted blades, which rotate against a cutting bar to shear the grass. Basically they are like the household push-mower. They are poor in cutting high or wet grass, but excellent in maintaining tiff or golf course type greens.
- The *cutter bar* is also a shearing type mower. Most cutter bar installations are side-mounted wings with a scissors action clipping mechanism, incorporating many moving parts. Conse-

quently, maintenance of this equipment is high. Another disadvantage is slow cutting speed. Advantages are an easily adjusted cutting height and the ability to reach hard-to-get-at places.

- *Rotary* mowers have a long (impact) cutting blade, which rotates at high tip speeds in a horizontal plane. They are rugged machines that require little maintenance and lend themselves to a variety of airport tasks. The rotary mower can be used effectively in rough weeds, in light brush, and over relatively rough terrain. A major disadvantage is safety, because objects picked up by the blade tend to be hurled outward with great velocity. Another disadvantage is a tendency to collect wet grass, which blocks the discharge chute.
- The *flail* (or "vertical rotary") mower gets its name from the fact that it "flails" the grass. It consists basically of a horizontal shaft designed to rotate at moderately high speeds, and attached thereto are a number of free-swinging cutter blades referred to as "flails." These blades rotate in a vertical plane about the horizontal shaft, and centrifugal force holds them straight out where they impact the grass during operation. They can be used in areas ranging from small to vast, smooth or rough, clean or trashy, level or steeply banked. Vegetation may range from fine, closely cropped lawns to tough, thick, high grass or weeds and brush. Maintenance of this mower entails a frequent exchange of cutter blades. But, the vertical, as opposed to horizontal, cutting action makes the flail mower much safer than the rotary mower.

SNOW AND ICE CONTROL

Keeping an airport clear and operational during snowstorms is more of an art than a science. Yet the problem and its solution are so critical for airports in the northern latitudes that symposiums are held annually addressing the subject, and various awards are given for outstanding performance in removing ice and snow. The nature of such awards, if not for valor at least represents a reward for unrelenting tenacity and good old fashion hard work. Many have stated that the way to beat snow is with advance preparation, keeping the equipment in top shape, getting the most accurate weather forecasts, and having the crews out early. But, it takes more than cunning, equipment, and weather forecasts. It takes a tireless, hard-working crew continuously removing snow until it stops falling. As one airport manager once put it, "When the snow comes, you go out and move it until it stops—there's no other way."[4]

WEATHER SCIENCE AND TECHNOLOGY

Ultimately, snow removal involves planning, with a key to planning being an understanding of weather science and the use of modern technology tools. Weather must be tracked accurately in order for an airport to properly deploy its equipment, materials and qualified human resources. Busier snow-impacted airport facilities have designated centers of operation, equipped with the latest in weather-related technology. They work in conjunction with their tenants to share information and communication and to coordinate plans of action during the snow season.

Chicago's O'Hare International Airport for example has the ability to track weather with its "Command Central." The "snow desk" houses a variety of weather forecasting equipment and a team of experts responsible for coordinating snow removal activities and communicating with all concerned parties on the field. The airport stands ready to mobilize some 100 pieces of snow removal equipment and more than 200 personnel in order to keep its runways, taxiways, roadways and gates operable.

New developments in technology have given airports and users important tools to better ensure aviation safety and efficiency in adverse weather conditions. Some of the latest weather technology improvements include:[5]

- An improved national radar network (158 sites) established by the Federal government over the past two decades;
- Availability of that Aviation Digital Data Service [ADDS] with free on-line aviation weather information[6] with new experimental capabilities being tested in 2007-08;[7]

---

[4] Anonymous.

[5] Bruce Carmichael, *Improving Aviation Through Weather Science*, Airport Magazine (Dec./Jan. 2007).

[6] National Weather Service, available at http://adds.aviationweather.gov.

[7] National Center for Atmospheric Research, retrieved from http://weather.aero.

- Availability of the Weather Support to Deicing Decision Making [WSDDM], pronounced "wisdom," which is a real-time ground de-icing weather information system;
- Incorporation of Next Generation Weather Radar [WSR-88D] with color-coded images; and
- Incorporation of Aviation Routine Weather Report [METAR] surface weather reports from Automated Surface Observation System [ASOS] stations.

Airport and aircraft operators appreciate the benefits obtained from use of these advanced systems, and have teamed with governmental agencies, researchers and technology developers to further the testing and advancement of new generation weather technology devices. WSDDM, for example, has been demonstrated at several airports including Chicago O'Hare International and New York LaGuardia International airports, and has been well received, in part, due to its simplicity. *Airport Magazine* contributor Bruce Carmichael elaborates:

> *WSDDM's graphic displays, run on personal computer workstations, are strategically located at airline station control, dispatch and deicing facilities, airline and city snow desks, and FAA air traffic manager positions. The system requires little meteorological knowledge, minimal training to operate, and enables decision makers to obtain valuable information in seconds, allowing them to anticipate both the onset and termination of snow at the airport and surrounding regions.*[8]

The WSDDM system is currently being used to support weather operations at Denver and Minneapolis-St. Paul International airports where,

> . . . *snowfall and weather information is used by ground personnel conducting aircraft deic-*

[8] Bruce Carmichael, *Improving Aviation Through Weather Science*, Airport Magazine (Dec./Jan. 2007).

> *ing operations, airline station control managers cording flights, airport managers coordinating runway plowing activities, and air traffic controllers involved in gate-hold program planning.*[9]

An additional application of WSDDM, referred to as Check-Time, "gives pilots specific information about how long they can wait for take-off following deicing operations."[10]

The monitoring of aviation and airport weather conditions is a collaborative effort that involves multiple stakeholders from national laboratories[11] and federal agencies.[12] This collaboration is supported and facilitated by the Next Generation Air Transportation System [NGATS] Joint Planning and Development Office. The WSDDM system has been determined to be eligible for Federal funding via the Airport Improvement Program.

SNOW REMOVAL PLAN

As with other grounds-keeping, snow removal should have a pre-established program. As mentioned in Chapter 8, Federal Aviation Regulation Part 139 (Section 313) requires a snow plan in the Airport Certification Manual.[13] The snow plan needs include instructions and procedures for,

- prompt removal or control, as completely as practical, of snow, ice, and slush on each movement area;
- positioning snow off the movement area surfaces so all air carrier aircraft propellers, engine pods, rotors, and wing tips will clear any snowdrift and snow bank as the aircraft's landing gear traverses any portion of the movement area;

---

[9] *Id.*

[10] *Id.*

[11] Including the National Center for Atmospheric Research, National Oceanic and Atmospheric Administration and the MIT Lincoln Laboratories.

[12] Dept. of Commerce, Dept. of Defense, National Aeronautics and Space Admin.

[13] 14 CFR FAR Part 139, *Certification of Airports* (2004), retrieved from http://www.faa.gov/airports_airtraffic/airports/airport_safety/part139_cert/media/part139_final_rule.pdf.

- selection and application of authorized materials for snow and ice control to ensure that they adhere to snow and ice sufficiently to minimize engine ingestion;
- timely commencement of snow and ice control operations; and
- prompt notification of all air carriers using the airport when any portion of the movement area normally available to them is less than satisfactorily cleared for safe operation by their aircraft.

When the Federal Aviation Administration [FAA] announced the Part 139 update in 2004, it used an example to explain why smaller airports would be required to improve their snow and ice control programs,

> *On March 17, 1993, a BAC–BA-Jetstream 3101 aircraft was making a night instrument approach to Raleigh County Memorial Airport in Beckley, WV. Because the runway was not properly plowed, and berms of snow concealed the runway lights at ground level, the captain lost control after touchdown, and the airplane sustained substantial damage. This rule [requires smaller] airports to develop tailored snow and ice control plans . . . Although many of these classes of airports already have procedures for snow and ice removal, this rule will formalize consistent plans across all airports with scheduled air carrier services. The FAA concludes that this low-cost requirement to standardize responses to snow and ice conditions at certificated airports will significantly help prevent the kind of accident discussed above.*[14]

In addition to the direction found in FAR Part 139, airports must also follow the guidance provided in several FAA Advisory Circulars [AC]s pertaining to winter operations that "reveal methods and procedures for snow and ice control equipment, materials, and removal

[14] *Id.*

that are acceptable to the Administrator" and those that might qualify for Airport Improvement Program [AIP] funding. For example, FAA Advisory Circular 150/5200-30A *Airport Winter Safety and Operations* instructs airports on several facets of snow and ice control, including field reporting and the intricacies of friction measurement. This document guides airports,

> *. . . in the development of an acceptable airport snow and ice control program and to provide guidance on appropriate field condition reporting procedures[which] can enhance aircraft safety when provided to pilots during winter operations. For this reason, many airports use runway friction measurement equipment to provide an indication of the existing friction on runways contaminated by snow or ice during aircraft operations and during snow removal operations.*[15]

The FAA warns that there are some conditions during which friction testing may yield erroneous readings, "For example, friction testing should not be made on loose snow over 1 inch (2.5cm) or slush over 1/8 inch (3mm) deep."[16] Procedures and performance specifications for Continuous Friction Measurement Equipment [CFME] are found in FAA AC 150/5320-12C, *Measurement, Construction and Maintenance of Skid Resistant Airport Pavement Surfaces.*

Each airport must design its own program according to its specific needs and the availability of snow removal equipment. Not only are snow removal plans unique to site-specific airports, but according to Larry Hedrick, former manager of both the Buffalo International Airport and the Niagara Falls International Airport, "It's like fighting a war—each battle is different, and different strategies are needed for each encounter." In response to the needed flexibility, two snow plans are recommended—one plan that confirms that the airport will comply with 139 snow removal requirements, and another detailed

[15] FAA, *Runway Friction Surveys During Winter Operations*, retrieved from http://www.airtech.tc.faa.gov/safety/friction.asp (Nov. 2004).
[16] *Id.*

enough to provide specific guidelines, yet flexible enough to accommodate various snowstorm conditions.

The more detailed plan must impart an awareness and understanding of what is expected. It should outline the standards, which are to be adhered to by those conducting the snow removal operation. In general, the plan should include:

- A statement as to the *purpose* of the plan;
- A listing of *responsible personnel* and agencies with appropriate notification procedures;
- A *method of notifying airport users* on a frequent and continuing basis of the existing conditions, including communications and NOTAM responsibilities;
- A listing of available snow removal *equipment* and equipment obtainable in emergencies;
- A *prioritization of service* for each runway and taxiway;
- *Starting times/indicators* for snow removal operations;
- Air traffic control and other *safety considerations*; and
- *Inspection procedures* and standards expected.

The person responsible for the snow removal activities should coordinate with the FAA Flight Service Station or with the National Weather Service to obtain the: (1) anticipated time of snowfall beginning; (2) estimated duration of snowfall; (3) expected depth of snow; and (4) prevailing wind direction and temperature expected during and after snowfall.

SNOW REMOVAL METHODS AND EQUPIMENT

To carry out snow removal procedures, there are two basic methods of removing snow and ice: *mechanical* and *chemical*. Hot water and electric heating systems have been investigated, but from a cost-benefit analysis, mechanical and chemical methods continue to be the most acceptable means of removing snow and ice from paved surfaces. Most snow removal is accomplished mechanically, but may be augmented with chemicals to prevent or remove ice accumulations. The three mechanical tools used are the plow blade, snow blower, and brush. The most effective program results from the combined use of all three. The only differences between an *airport plow* and a standard highway plow are perhaps the reversible capability of the blade direction, and a modified blade which provides greater casting distance, the need for which will be shown later. Blades are available in steel, steel with carbide steel cutting edges, rubber, and polyurethane. The choice depends on desired characteristics. Steel works effectively on dry, packed snow, but not so well on slush. Rubber and polyurethane edges last longer and are not as apt as steel blades to damage the runway surface or in-pavement centerline lights. Rubber and polyurethane also make less noise and causes less vibration, thus contributing to greater operator comfort. Rubber works well on slush, but not as well as steel does on dry, packed snow.

The blade is primarily used to stack the snow, whereas the *blower*, or "rotary snow plow," is the principal tool for removal of snow. Blowers come in single and two-stage configurations. The single-stage blower works faster, but the two-stage blower removes hard-packed snow banks more easily.

The *brush*, which is a standard multi-purpose brush, can be used year-round. For snow removal, it is used to clean up the residue left by the plow and/or blower, to clear surfaces of light snow, or to remove sand previously spread for improved runway traction. Brushes are available with either steel or synthetic bristles. Steel bristles generally perform better, but nylon or polypropylene bristles are more effective on wet snow and slush. Bristle types can be mixed if so chosen. Some managers, however, shy away from the use of steel bristles because broken-off steel bristles can become a greater Foreign Object Damage [FOD] hazard than plastic bristles.

With snow removal techniques, the intention is to eliminate the need for repeated passes and extensive cleanup of isolated snow accumulations, and also to avoid burying the runway or taxiway lights and the subsequent work of uncovering them. For the most *efficient* removal of snow, initial passes are made at the runway edge, moving the snow towards the centerline and away from the lights. Passes are then made down the centerline, moving the snow toward the windrows made by the initial passes and short of runway edge. Two windrows are created on either side of the runway centerline; both of which are on the hard surface, clear of the edge lights and in good position for removal by the blower.

The most *expeditious* way to remove snow is to plow from the centerline outward in both directions to avoid having to move large accumulations of snow. Passes are made with sufficient speed to cast the snow a sufficient distance to scatter and not create areas of greater accumulation. If there are strong crosswinds it may not be possible to plow in both directions without a blowback of snow that has been cast into the wind. Advantage should be taken of strong wind by plowing from the upwind to the leeward side of the runway. In this situation an initial pass on the runway edge will serve to protect the lighting.

Snow removal is an emergency condition! As such, decisions must be made to determine what kind and how much equipment is adequate. A major concern of all airport managers is the most efficient use of available resources. The question of snow equipment can be a dilemma, since like fire equipment typically only limited funds are committed towards the purchase of equipment that has only limited use.

The basic snow removal technique described above can be used at smaller airports and with minimum equipment. For efficient snow removal operations at airports served exclusively by propeller-driven aircraft weighing less than 12,500 pounds, the FAA recommends one or more high-speed snow blowers, supported by at least one snowplow. However, for budgetary reasons, some small airports may have to make do with less equipment. At a minimum, it has been suggested that a small airport could get along with just two units: a *dump truck* with a tailgate spreader and a front-mounted reversible plow; and a medium-sized *tractor* with a rear-mounted blower and a front-mounted hydraulic drive broom.

Larger airports will normally require more equipment and more involved techniques. At airports served by turbojet aircraft or scheduled air carriers, the FAA recommends, at a minimum, one or more high-speed snow blowers, supported by a minimum of two snow plows per snow blower, one truck-mounted hopper-spreader and/or one liquid spraying rig, and a front-end loader. However, typically, major air carrier airports will have additional equipment.

The size and duration of storms, the customary number of storms occurring during any given season, and the prevailing visibility conditions during storms determine the equipment and snow-removal programming of a given airport. Take for instance the example of Chicago's O'Hare cited above. At one count, O'Hare had 13 deicers, 10 brooms, 33 plows, 18 blowers and 23 spreaders. But Chicago is subjected to *very* harsh winters. Compare this with Atlanta's Hartsfield

International Airport where cost-effective combat is much different against Southern winters. The climate in Northern Georgia is not harsh enough to warrant a sophisticated and expensive snow and ice removal program. Nevertheless, operations at Atlanta have been significantly impaired by snow and ice conditions.

In formulating its program, Atlanta copied Metropolitan Nashville Airport's liquid de-icing operation. Using modified agricultural equipment, it purchased three 1,500-gallon tanks with forty-foot spray booms to mount on twelve-foot flatbed trucks; two 500-gallon, pickup mounted tanks with ten-foot booms; one 9,000-gallon mobile tanker; and four replacement plows for dump trucks. Along with runway de-icing fluid, in the early 1980s, that was the sum total snow and ice removal equipment used by the then second busiest airport in the United States!

At larger airports, the decision to buy more equipment is predicated upon the funds available, the frequency and amount of snowfall, and the urgency by which the operational areas must be cleared. Air carrier airports with frequent operations and high volumes of traffic will require highly efficient snow removal programs. The savings generated through continued operations may well offset the cost of snow equipment.

Some airports have even participated in the design of their equipment, such as Minneapolis–St. Paul International Airport's [MSP] involvement in the development of Oshkosh's "H-Series" snow blower. MSP Field Maintenance Planning Manager Lee Spangrud explained, "We've had long standing relations with [Oshkosh] and they're very open to us making suggestions on their equipment." Some of the suggestions relate to the inclusion of new technology while others are simpler, such as a larger windshield and the inclusion of cup-holders.[17]

More recently, airports have found value in the purchase of smaller, so-called "utility vehicles" that have a one-person cab and a powerful diesel engine. These units are purchased with a variety of attachments (e.g., snow blower, angle plows, rear spreaders, V-plows, power angle sweepers, front and boom-mounted flail mowers, etc.) making them useful in all seasons. While these utility vehicles are not considered the first line of defense in a snow storm, they are ideal

---

[17] Clif Stroud, *Getting Ready for a Tough Winter*, Airport Magazine (Aug./Sep. 2006), at 53.

for accessing tight areas such as those around airfield signs and lights.[18]

Multifunction units are indeed gaining in popularity. In 2006, Cleveland Hopkins International Airport [CLE] purchased six Oshkosh multi-function, high-speed, tow-behind units to add to its impressive fleet. "Our conga line would have plow, brooms and blowers—three different kinds of equipment manned by three different drivers. This multifunction unit allows us to combine all those into one," stated Fred Szabo, CLE Commissioner. Due to the high speed of these units, the average clearance time of a runway dropped from 40 to 25 minutes.[19]

If multiple pieces of equipment are available, the airport manager must decide how best to use them as a team. Two general techniques may be employed, phased clearance and high-speed team plowing. *Phased* clearance uses a team of plows operating in a train, starting from the centerline and staggered towards the runway edge. A solo plow works the runway edges to clear a zone adjacent to the runway lights. The second phase brings in the snow blowers to clear the runway of the windrows created by the plows. Blowers work at a slower speed than the plows.

To overcome this handicap, and to increase the clearance process, it requires a heavier outlay on equipment and acquisition of enough blowers to keep up with the plows. Short clearing times can be achieved through *high speed* plowing. High speed team plowing assumes the runway is not cleared until snow has been thrown over the runway lighting. To achieve the shortest possible clearing time, the blowers must work concurrently with the plows; snow blower capacity must match plowing capacity; and the equipment works in pairs, with one plow and one blower forming a unit.

Two related issues that the airport snow control teams need to manage are the management of drifting snow, and the storage and removal of snow. Snow fences and snow trenches can help in the battle against drifting snow. Snow fences should be carefully placed away from runway safety areas and in a manner that does not penetrate any critical surfaces. Specific areas are generally preserved for the storage of snow, but at times the operator must seek a way to dis-

---

[18] John Croft & Sean Broderick, *Big Jobs for Small Tools*, Airport Magazine (Feb./Mar. 2006), at 38.

[19] Clif Stroud, *Getting Ready for a Tough Winter*, Airport Magazine (Aug./Sep. 2006), at 54.

pose of the snow when the storage space is expended. One piece of snow removal equipment gaining in popularity at airports is the portable snow melting unit. These units do not require special permits and, reportedly, can melt up to 60 cubic yards of snow per hour.[20]

ICE CONTROL AND REMOVAL

Snow clearance is performed principally by mechanical means. In contrast, *ice* removal can be done *chemically, thermally or mechanically*. Thermal systems are those that are contained within the pavement itself. Mechanical methods for controlling ice include scraping and cutting with a variety of specialized blades or serrated cutting edges, attached to plow moldboards. On softer ice, a squeegee can be used. Mechanical methods can be both slow and destructive to pavements. The majority of the ice control undertaken at airports is accomplished by chemical means.[21]

Ice control procedures are categorized as *anti-icing* (preventing a bond from forming) or *deicing* (ice removal after formation). The broader term that is used to encompass both is *airfield deicing agents*. The FAA elaborates, "Anti-icing, which is recommended over deicing, is accomplished by concentrating either thermal or chemical energy at the pavement surface. Because of the high costs of installing pavement heating systems and the large amounts of energy [needed to operate them, using] approved airside chemicals is generally more economical." The FAA notes that, "the most difficult task in winter maintenance occurs when snow or ice bond to the pavement. Thus the primary effort should be directed at bond prevention" or anti-icing.[22]

The greatest probability of ice formation occurs during periods when there are freezing temperatures and snow accumulation is of insufficient depth (generally less than one-half inch) to warrant removal. Unlike new fallen snow, compacted snow and ice cannot be completely removed by mechanical means. The porosity of the pavement allows entry of water below the surface, hence forming a bond when it freezes. The adhesive strength of ice to pavement can be as high as the tensile strength of the ice itself, and attempts at removing

---

[20] Sean Broderick, *Beware the Dragon*, Airport Magazine (Feb./Mar. 2006), at 43.
[21] FAA, *Airport Winter Safety and Operations*, AC 150/5200-30A (Oct. 1991), at 25-26.
[22] *Id.* at 26.

ice by mechanical means alone can result in damage to the pavement surface.

Unless procedures are established to promptly remove accumulations of snow, the formation of ice may occur. Ice can also form from the snow residue left after removal by plow and blower. Brooms are used to brush away the residue. Chemicals are then laid down to act as an anti-bonding agent. If ice has already formed, however, heated sand can be spread on the ice or snow-pack to create friction. Or, as some airports have employed, *flame-throwing weed burners* can be used to melt the ice, followed by brushing and application of chemical agents.

Qualities of anti-icing or de-icing agents must meet three requirements to be effective. First, they must be chemically neutral after the thawing process so that they are not destructive to aircraft or the runway. Second, the thawing process must take place rapidly. And third, the thawing effect must persist for a reasonable length of time. Available airport runway chemicals are comparatively expensive, and are not as effective as highway chemicals. But highway chemicals should not be used on airports because of their highly corrosive properties. In fact, some airports prohibit chloride salts or other corrosive chemicals on aircraft areas. Although not recommended, pelletized agricultural fertilizers have been commonly used because of their lower cost.

AIRFIELD DEICING AGENTS

Airfield deicing agents are produced generally in two categories: *solids* and *liquids*. Liquid deicers are sometimes used with solid deicers as a pre-wetting agent to help solid particles adhere to the pavement during high winds. Common airport de-icing agents that have been used include glycol based fluids and potassium acetate base fluids. In addition, solids such as urea may be used.

Urea is a soluble, crystalline solid found in urine or made synthetically. Sometimes, urea is combined with heated sand to prompt both melting and friction. Urea is available in both solid and liquid form. The most common form is agricultural grade urea in pill form. Urea is effective down to approximately minus seven degrees Centigrade. And, although more expensive than sand, urea is relatively inexpensive.[23] Because historically urea has been the pavement deicer of

[23] In 1996 dollars, about $300 per ton; *see id.*

choice, it is against the performance and cost of urea that alternative deicers are compared.

One solid that may be used to increase friction is sand. Dry sand is the cheapest agent to use, although most aircraft operators decry its use, especially if used on the runways. High aircraft speeds and wind currents expose aircraft surfaces to sand abrasion and predispose engines to ingestion of blowing sand. Nevertheless, most airports are still using heated sand because of its effectiveness and relatively low cost. Stringent specifications as to the size of aggregate and amount of fines allowed in sand used in airport operations have been established by the FAA. As determined in FAA tests, jet engines can safely ingest sand particles if they have been applied properly and are within the prescribed specifications.

However, it has been found that the problem with sand is the "fines," and not the average grain of sand. Fines will adhere to certain engine components instead of passing through, subsequently creating a buildup and blockage. Secondly, fines will hold moisture once the temperature drops below freezing. This moist sand turns into hard, stone-like clumps that can cause engine damage if ingested. An alternative to sand is urea. But urea can cost twice as much as heated sand and can only be applied effectively before ice has formed. Moreover, urea presents environmental concerns of such significance that an active search is underway to find an adequate replacement.

Once ice has accumulated it requires substantial amounts of urea (or an alternative) to melt the ice, whereas an application of sand may provide instantaneous improvement in friction quality. However, when ice has formed and no preventive measures have been taken, urea pellets are often mixed with sand prior to application.

As an alternative, *sodium acetate* is available in solid form. And it may be used in conjunction with a liquid deicer (such as ethylene or propylene glycol or potassium acetate) as a pre-wetting agent. Sodium acetate reacts with ice faster than urea, and it takes only about two-thirds as much sodium acetate as urea to achieve similar results. The greatest disadvantage for using sodium acetate is its cost, which is four to five times higher than urea.[24]

Another choice is *sodium formate.* It is a granular-based material that has several advantages as a deicer. It is more effective at low

[24] Dean Mericas & Bryan Wagoner, *Runway Deicers: A Varied Menu*, Airport Magazine (Jul./Aug. 1996), at 12.

temperature than urea. And it requires only about half of the volume to achieve the same results. Additionally, sodium formate-base granular pavement deicer has significantly lower Biological Oxygen-Demand [BOD] than any other alternative deicing material. It can be used in conjunction with liquid deicers, and an additional advantage is its shape. It is an irregularly shaped crystal that resists being blown around in the wind. Its disadvantage is cost, but it is only marginally more expensive to use than urea. The cost per volume of product is nearly three times more expensive than urea, but because it goes twice as far the net cost is only about 1.5 times that of using urea.

Calcium Magnesium Acetate [CMA] is a solid deicer commonly used on highways and bridges where concrete spalling and bridge corrosion are of concern. It has also been approved by the FAA for use on airport pavements. However, CMA has not found wide acceptance for airport use because of two factors. It is available only in pill form, which is easily blown around in the wind. And it is slower acting than other approved deicers. Thus, CMA has limited advantages for airfield deicing.[25] Closely related to CMA is *Magnesium Calcium Acetate* [MCA].

Potassium acetate is produced by several chemical companies as a liquid-form runway deicer. It has a number of significant advantages over both the glycol-based deicers and urea. It melts snow and ice faster and at lower temperatures. Its biggest advantage environmentally is that it does not produce ammonia when it decomposes. However, it has only a marginally lower environmental impact than either urea or propylene glycol. But it is lower, and that is a distinct advantage as environmental concerns mount (as will be discussed further below). As for cost, it is about the same as for propylene glycol.[26]

Ethylene glycol (or alternatively propylene glycol) is the key component in most anti-icing fluids. It has been widely used in combination with urea for airfield pavement deicing and also for pre-wetting solid compounds. The primary advantage of glycol is its effectiveness at low temperatures and its ability to melt through existing snow and ice.[27] But, unfortunately, ethylene glycol is classified as a hazardous substance under U.S. law. A key question for airlines and airports concerning glycol-based deicing and anti-icing fluids is what to do

[25] *Id.* at 13.
[26] *Id.* at 14.
[27] *Id.* at 13.

with the fluids once they have been used. Hence, as with urea there is an on-going search for either replacement compounds or for ways to contain the residual impact of using such compounds.[28]

ENVIRONMENTAL CONSIDERATIONS

Selection of deicing/anti-icing compounds for a given airport have historically been a function of local weather conditions and available resources including equipment, personnel and funds. Now, environmental factors must be included into the selection process, with the most likely concerns being BOD and ammonia concentrations. The selection process is compounded by the fact that the same deicing compounds used at one airport may not be acceptable at another airport. Each airport is unique, and the configuration of airfield drainage collection and conveyance systems is a critical factor. Taking a variety of factors into consideration, airport managers must decide on an appropriate mix of deicing/anti-icing compounds.[29] Dean Mericas and Bryan Wagoner suggest that there are some common issues that must be considered including:

- *Relative contributions* of pavement deicers *to the total pollutant load* in storm water runoff;
- *Reductions in total pollutant load* in storm water runoff that may be achieved through use of alternative deicers;
- *Performance requirements* in terms of snow, ice and operating temperatures; materials storage and handling requirements and capabilities; and
- Last but not least, *cost*.[30]

Containment and subsequent treatment of contaminated runoff from *aircraft deicing* is a possibility because aircraft deicing can be confined to a small, isolated area. Containment of *airfield deicing* compounds is another matter. Pavement deicers are applied over a very large area and widely distributed. And even if pavement deicers could be captured and stored on-site, treatment would be technologi-

---

[28] Staff, *Recycling Offers Disposal Solution*, Avn. Wk. & Space Tech. (Sep. 11, 1993); *see also* Staff, *Search Underway for Efficient Fluids*, Avn. Wk. & Space Tech. (Sep. 11, 1993).
[29] *See* Dean Mericas & Bryan Wagoner, *Runway Deicers: A Varied Menu*, Airport Magazine (Jul./Aug. 1996), at 14-15.
[30] *Id.* at 46.

cally and economically infeasible. Thus, as a study conducted by Transport Canada in 1990 concluded, it is impractical to mitigate the impact of urea use and alternative pavement deicing materials should be sought.[31]

Although glycol-based chemicals have been used for many years, contamination of water sources from deicer runoff has forced many airports to either abandon their use or develop elaborate recovery facilities with which to control their disposal. Urea, used in high concentrations, has become an environmental concern. It can cause *eutrophication* (accelerated aging) of lakes and waterways. Calcium magnesium acetate, and related magnesium calcium acetate are touted as viable alternatives to glycol-based runway deicers, as well as urea. These more recently developed products are applied in the same manner as urea.

The principal environmental concern with deicing fluids is related to the oxygen consumed during decomposition of these chemicals. Oxygen consumption occurs when bacteria decompose organic materials and use oxygen in the process. The depletion of oxygen can have a negative impact on aquatic life. The potential for oxygen consumption is expressed as Biological Oxygen Demand exerted over some time frame, typically five days (i.e., BOD_5). Biological oxygen demand may be further differentiated depending upon whether it is *Carbonaceous Biological Oxygen Demand* [CBOD] or *Nitrogenous Biological Oxygen Demand* [NBOD]. The environment concern with urea is related to the ammonia released when urea breaks down. The ammonia contributes to NBOD. In addition, ammonia is potentially toxic to aquatic life.[32]

Environmentally friendly, alternatives are continually being sought by airport operators and the FAA. One innovation in the testing process is the use of *Freezing Point Depressant* [FPD] chemicals to pavement prior to a winter storm. In the anti-icing process, FPDs serve to prevent or weaken bonds between ice and pavement surface, without the environmental impacts associated with other chemicals.[33]

Additionally, a pavement texturing process is currently being evaluated to determine if these textures can "retain anti-icing characteristics in advance of a winter storm event and throughout the dura-

---

[31] *Id.*

[32] *Id.* at 11.

[33] FAA Airport Technology R & D Branch, *Alternative Methods to De-Icing Runways*, retrieved from http://www.airtech.tc.faa.gov/safety/deice.asp (Nov. 2004).

tion of multiple storm events without reapplication of chemical agents."[34] Over the past few years, the FAA has also experimented with *textured aggregate coating systems*, referred to as "Anti-Icing Smart Pavement Overlays." Testing continues as the agency attempts to "determine the ability of the treated surfaces to retain anti-icing properties over a series of winter storm events and the durability of these surfaces under controlled traffic and snow removal operations."[35]

While this section of the chapter highlighted the technology, materials, plans and procedures that airports use to respond to the challenges of winter options, the snow and ice control systems at airports are not perfect. The December 2005 Southwest Airlines accident in Chicago, for example, prompted important questions about winter operations safety at airports and the need for a greater margin of safety. The incident prompted new guidance for airports (still in the draft/evolving stage, as this book goes to press), as discussed below:

> *The . . . accident at Chicago's Midway Airport, where a Southwest 737 landed in bad weather, overshot the runway and ended up in the street on top of a car, has prompted the FAA to issue an Operational Specification/Management Specification that will add an additional 15 percent safety margin for landing minimums above the Landing Distance Available [LDA].*[36]

While the FAA's proposal has met with resistance from airport operators who feel that the suggested margin is too large (and thus burdensome to obtain and maintain), the airport community clearly would be even more distressed to see a repeat of the accident. The thousands of workers and "snow bosses" (senior snow plow operators) that comprise the snow and ice control community at U.S. airports, have a very high level of pride in their long-term success in achieving both efficiency and safety objectives.

---

[34] *Id.*
[35] *Id.*
[35] *Id.*
[35] *Id.*
[36] Cilf Stroud, *Getting Ready for a Tough Winter*, Airport Magazine (Aug./Sep. 2006), at 56.

In summary, airport managers who must contend with severe winter weather say the trick to successful snow removal is maintaining close coordination with the weather bureau and staying ahead of the snowstorm. Staying ahead of the snowstorm takes the right equipment and *available* personnel. Snow removal, like mowing, is labor intensive and costly. Labor costs for snow removal are particularly staggering when personnel must be kept on the payroll year-round. One strategy used to reduce associated labor costs is to employ farm workers who are otherwise unemployed in the winter, and who already know how to operate similar equipment such as plows.

PAVEMENTS

Along with the familiar air traffic control tower, runways and taxiways are among the most distinguishing features of an airport. But, while these structures seem relatively simple—involving construction, use and maintenance of a relatively flat piece of pavement—the design and preservation of these surfaces requires a significant commitment of both human and economic resources.

Many of these important air transportation landing and taxiing surfaces have been constructed with federal, state and local funds, following lengthy planning processes. However, despite the best planning efforts of all involved parties, some paved airfield areas at airports are currently underutilized while others are overtaxed, relative to forecast activity and loads. The FAA discusses this and the resulting impacts:

> *Many pavements were not designed for servicing today's aircraft, which impose loads much greater than those initially considered. Also, the frequency of takeoffs and landings at many airports has increased considerably. Both factors result in accelerated deterioration of the pavement structure. To assure safe operations, airports must make special efforts to upgrade and maintain pavement serviceability.*

While airport sponsors generally understand that, without these surfaces, airports would be useless, the expense and value of maintaining airport pavements may be scrutinized, particularly at smaller airports facing annual budgeting challenges. These fiscal challenges and the fore-mentioned changes in surface use have resulted in an increased need for proactive guidance and management—in the form of formal pavement maintenance programs—often mandated by the Federal government.

There are many issues to be considered when discussing pavements at airports. In the following pages, pavement types, design issues, maintenance programs, common deficiencies, repairs and coatings, and pavement markings are all presented and discussed.

PAVEMENT TYPES

Airport pavements are designed with firm, stable, smooth, all-weather surfaces, which can support loads imposed by the critical aircraft using the airport. There are two principal types of pavement surfaces, *flexible* and *rigid*, each supported by base and/or sub-base "courses," or layers of select underlying materials. Other surface courses include overlays and sealing mixes such as fog seals, slurry coats and chip seals, which will be discussed later in this chapter.

Flexible pavements consist of a bituminous wearing surface placed on a base course, and when required by sub-grade conditions, a sub-base, as illustrated in Figure 11.1, "Typical Flexible Pavement Structure." The entire flexible pavement structure is ultimately supported by the sub-grade. The bituminous surface or wearing course must prevent the penetration of surface water to the base course. It must provide a smooth, well-bonded surface free from loose particles, which might endanger aircraft or persons. It must resist the shearing stresses occasioned by aircraft loads. And it must furnish a texture of non-skid qualities, yet not cause undue wear on tires.

The *base course* is the structural component of the flexible pavement. It has the major function of distributing the imposed wheel load pressures to the pavement foundation, the sub-base and/or sub-grade, as shown in Figure 11.2, "Distribution of Load Stress in Flexible Pavement."

Figure 11.1—TYPICAL FLEXIBLE PAVEMENT STRUCTURE

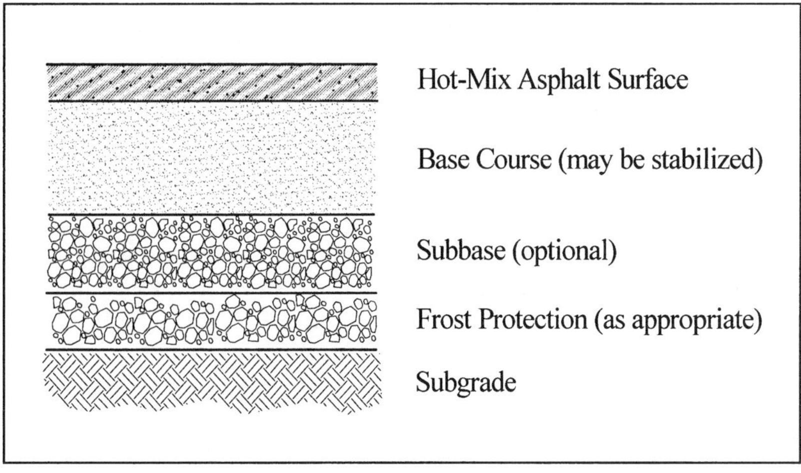

Figure 11.2—DISTRIBUTION OF LOAD STRESS IN FLEXIBLE PAVEMENT

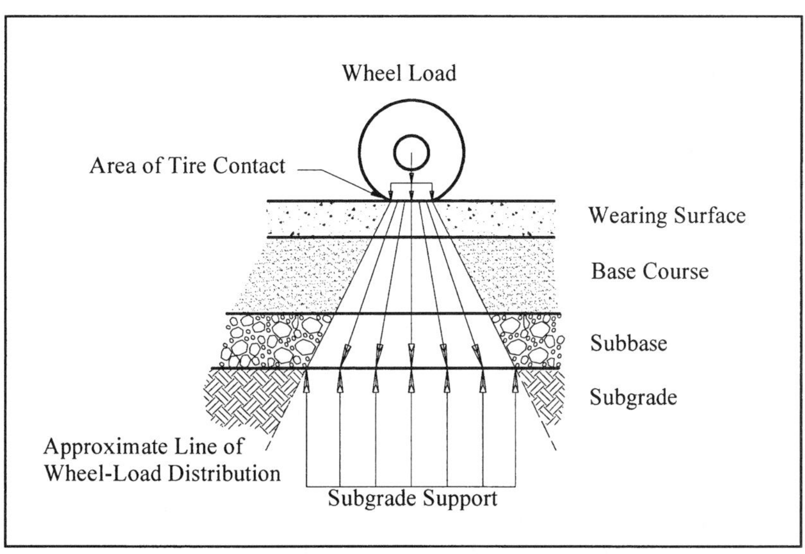

Source for Figures 11.1 & 11.2: FAA, *Guidelines and Procedures for Maintenance of Airport Pavements*, AC 150/5380-6A, (Jul. 14, 2003).

The base course must be of such quality and thickness as to prevent failure in the sub-grade. It must withstand the stresses produced in the base itself. It must resist vertical pressures that tend to produce consolidation and result in distortion of the surface course. And the base course must resist volume changes caused by fluctuations in its moisture content. Base courses consist of a variety of treated and untreated materials. Untreated materials consist of crushed or uncrushed aggregates. Treated bases include additives such as cement, bitumen, lime, fly ash, or a combination of stabilizers mixed with the crushed or uncrushed aggregates.

A *sub-base* is included in areas where the frost action is predicted to be severe, or where the sub-grade soil is considered to be inferior. The function of the sub-base is similar to that of the base course. However, since it is farther removed from the surface and is subjected to lower loading intensities, the quality of the materials used is not as strict as for the base course. Sub-base courses are made up of stabilized or un-stabilized granular material, or a stabilized soil.

The sub-grade *soil* is also of concern, but the sub-grade soils are subjected to lower stresses than the surface, base, and sub-base courses, and sub-grade stresses decrease with depth. Nevertheless, the sub-grade soil is compacted to specification prior to placement of sub-base, base, and surface materials on it. In areas where freezing temperatures occur (with frost-susceptible soil and a high ground water table) a frost protection layer may be included between the sub-base and sub-grade. The impact of ice crystals (frost) on pavements is illustrated in Figure 11.3, "Formation of Ice Crystals in Frost-Susceptible Soil."

Rigid pavements at airports are composed of Portland Cement Concrete [PCC] usually placed upon a granular or treated sub-base course,[37] resting on a compacted sub-grade. As with flexible pavements, a frost protection layer may be included between the sub-base and sub-grade if needed. Figure 11.4, "Typical Rigid Pavement Structure," illustrates a typical rigid pavement structure.

The concrete surface must provide an acceptable non-skid surface. It must also prevent the infiltration of surface water and provide structural support to a moving or static (non-moving) aircraft, transferring the wheel load as shown in Figure 11.5, "Transfer of Wheel Load to Foundation in Rigid Pavement Structure."

---

[37] Under certain conditions a sub-base is not required.

Figure 11.3—FORMATION OF ICE CRYSTALS IN FROST-SUSCEPTIBLE SOIL

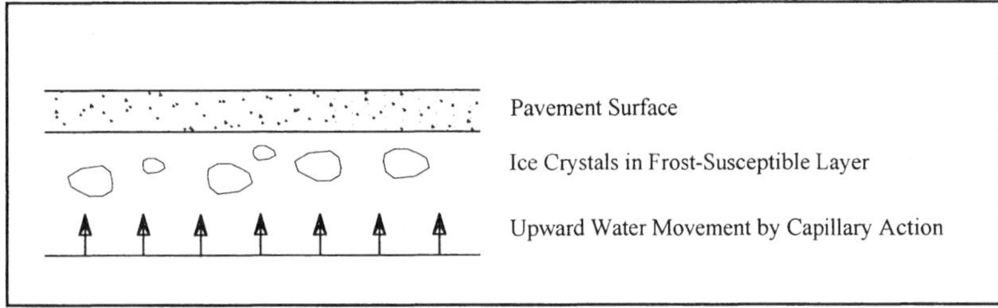

Figure 11.4—TYPICAL RIGID PAVEMENT STRUCTURE

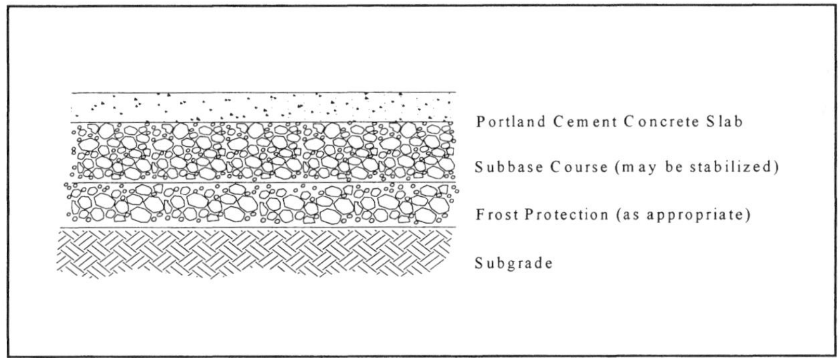

Figure 11.5—TRANSFER OF WHEEL LOAD TO FOUNDATION IN RIGID PAVEMENT STRUCTURE

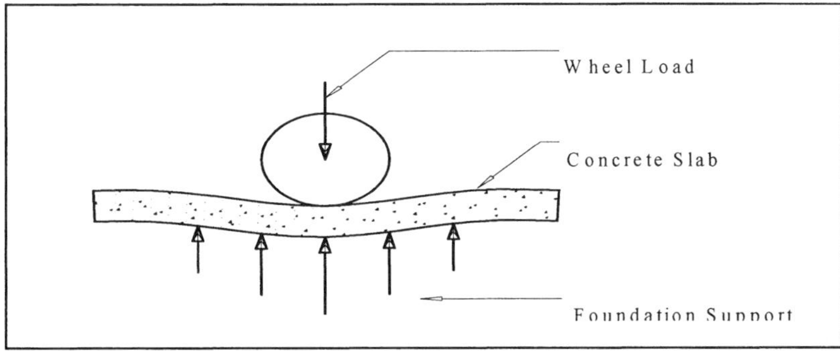

Source for figures 11.3 to 11.5: FAA, *Guidelines and Procedures for Maintenance of Airport* Pavements, AC 150/5380-6A, (Jul. 14, 2003).

The purpose of the sub-base underlying rigid pavement is to provide uniform, stable support for the pavement slabs. A minimum thickness of four inches of sub-base is normally required under rigid pavements. As with flexible pavements, the sub-grade materials underlying a rigid pavement are also compacted to provide adequate stability and uniform support. However, the compaction requirements for rigid pavements are not as stringent as for flexible pavement due to the relatively lower sub-grade stress.

Variations in temperature and moisture content can cause volume changes and slab warping and produce stresses of significant magnitude in rigid pavement. In order to reduce the detrimental effects of these stresses and to minimize random cracking, the pavement is divided into sections by joints.

Pavement *joints* are categorized according to the function a joint is to perform. The categories are expansion, contraction, and construction joints, as presented below:

- *Expansion joints* provide for pavement expansion, isolate intersecting pavements, and isolate structures from the pavement;
- *Contraction joints* provide controlled cracking when the pavement contracts due to curing shrinkage, decreasing moisture content, or temperature drop; and
- *Construction joints* are used when two abutting slabs are poured at different times, and there must be a joint placed between them.

For a variety of reasons, airport pavement *overlays* may be required on either rigid or flexible surfaces. Overloading may have damaged a pavement. Similarly, a pavement in good condition may require strengthening in order for it to serve heavier aircraft than those for which it was originally designed. Or, a pavement may require an overlay simply because it has been worn by time, service and the elements.

As with pavement surfaces in general, airport pavement overlays are of two types, Portland cement concrete or bituminous concrete. Overlays of either bituminous or concrete pavement are constructed on top of an existing pavement. A "sandwich pavement" is an overlay pavement containing a granular separation course.

PAVEMENT DESIGN

Pavement design is based upon the *critical aircraft* using or expected to use the airport. From forecasts of aircraft activity, the "design" aircraft is selected on the basis of the one requiring the greatest pavement thickness. And, it may not be the heaviest aircraft. Airport pavement design takes into consideration aircraft load, landing gear type and geometry, and traffic volume.

Aside from required runway length, the most important operational design consideration for both rigid and flexible pavements is *aircraft loading*. The maximum landing weight is usually only about three-fourths of the maximum take-off weight. Therefore, the maximum gross takeoff weight of the critical aircraft is accepted as the typical aircraft load in calculating the pavement thickness required.

The landing gear type and configuration dictate how the aircraft weight is distributed to the pavement and determine pavement response to aircraft loading. In 1958, the FAA adopted a policy of limiting maximum federal participation in airport pavements to a pavement section designed to serve a 350,000-pound aircraft with a DC-8-50 series landing gear configuration. In addition, the intent of the policy was to insure future aircraft would be equipped with landing gear that would not stress pavements more than the referenced 350,000-pound aircraft.

Aircraft manufacturers have accepted and followed the 1958 policy and have designed aircraft landing gear to conform to the policy even though over the years, aircraft gross weights have substantially exceeded 350,000 pounds. This has been accomplished by increasing the number and spacing of landing gear wheels.

The three landing gear configurations are single-gear, dual-gear, and dual tandem-gear. Wide-body aircraft, beginning with the B-747, the DC-10, and the L-1011, represent a radical departure from the geometry assumed for dual-tandem geared aircraft. Due to the large differences in gross weights and gear geometry, separate design curves have been prepared for wide-body aircraft.

Another operational factor considered important in pavement design is the *traffic volume*. Information on aircraft operations is available from the airport master plan, and from a variety of sources including FAA terminal area forecasts, airport activity statistics, and air traffic activity reports. With regard to air traffic counts, an aircraft *operation* is either a takeoff or a landing. For the purpose of pavement design, the number of departures is used, and forecasts of annual departures by aircraft type are needed.

The determination of *pavement thickness* is a complex engineering task of interacting variables, wide variations in climate, and anticipated aircraft loading. Pavement design is as much an engineering art as it is a science. There are no strict mathematical solutions for determining pavement thickness, although the FAA has prepared design curves for that purpose. Pavement design is a professional determination based on theoretical analysis of load distribution through pavements and soils, and analysis of experimental pavement data, as well as performance of pavements under actual service conditions. The FAA has developed data, which have generally proven satisfactory. Nevertheless, local pavement design must be accomplished by a professional civil engineer.

Pavement design is segregated into two categories: design of pavements to service *light aircraft*, and pavements designed for *heavy aircraft*. Pavements for light aircraft are defined as landing facilities normally intended to accommodate aircraft weighing less than 12,500 pounds (i.e., "utility aircraft"), but not exceeding a gross weight of 30,000 pounds. Pavements designed to serve aircraft of 30,000 pounds gross weight or more are based on more critical evaluation. Although pavement design is a complex determination, at a minimum, the following pavement thickness is required for the various pavements serving light aircraft:

- *Flexible pavements* require a two-inch minimum surface course;
- *Rigid pavements* require five-inch surfaces for aircraft weighing 12,500 pounds, and six-inch surfaces for aircraft between 12,500 and 30,000 pounds; and
- *Bituminous overlays* should be a minimum of two inches thick.

PAVEMENT MAINTENANCE

Airports that have received federal funds for airfield pavements are required to perform preventative maintenance on the surfaces designated for those funds. If any future project calls for replacement or reconstruction of the pavement, the airport sponsor must provide proof to the FAA that they have designed and implemented an effective pavement maintenance management program.[38] The sponsor is required to continually assess the airport pavement conditions and the management program.[39] On this issue, the FAA states,

> *The requirement to establish a pavement maintenance management program applies to any pavement at the airport which has been constructed, reconstructed, or repaired, with federal assistance. All grants involving pavement rehabilitation or reconstruction contain a grant assurance that addresses the pavement maintenance obligation.*[40]

The FAA is not the only agency interested in seeing that an airport is serious about preserving its expensive pavement assets. State transportation agencies also recognize the importance of proactive airport maintenance programs. For example, in Wisconsin, a copy of the airport pavement maintenance program must be submitted to the state agency if an airport wishes to be considered for specialized airport maintenance funding.[41]

In the interest of promoting the best development of an efficient and effective pavement maintenance program, airport operators should have an understanding of the life cycles of pavements and the available guidance to airports on establishing their pavement maintenance programs.

---

[38] Special Airport Improvement Program grant conditions now require many airports to develop and maintain an effective airport pavement maintenance management program. *Guidelines and Procedures for Maintenance of Airport Pavements*, AC 150/5380-6A.

[39] P.L. 103-305, Sec. 107 amends 49 U.S.C. § 47105, and in the assurances signed by the airport sponsor receiving federal funds.

[40] FAA Airports Central Region, *Airport Obligations: Pavement Maintenance*, retrieved from http://www.faa.gov/airports_airtraffic/airports/regional_guidance/central/airport_obligations/pavement_maintenance (Feb. 9, 2006).

[41] Wisconsin Bureau of Aeronautics, *Wisconsin Airport Maintenance Programs* (Undated brochure), retrieved from http://www.dot.wisconsin.gov/library/publications/topic/air/airportmaint.pdf.

PAVEMENT LIFE CYCLE

Pavements have a somewhat predictable useful life expectancy, with the initial years being rather stable, followed by an accelerated drop in pavement condition over time. The deterioration is attributable to several factors, as the FAA explains,

> *Traffic loads in excess of those forecast during pavement design can shorten pavement life considerably. Normal distresses in the pavement structure result from surface weathering, fatigue effects, and differential movement in the underlying sub-base over a period of years. In addition, faulty construction techniques, substandard materials, or poor workmanship can accelerate the pavement deterioration process. Consequently, airport pavements require continual routine maintenance, rehabilitation, and upgrading.*

Figure 11.6, "Typical Pavement Life Cycle Curve," illustrates pavement deterioration throughout its life cycle.

Figure 11.6—TYPICAL PAVEMENT LIFE CYCLE CURVE

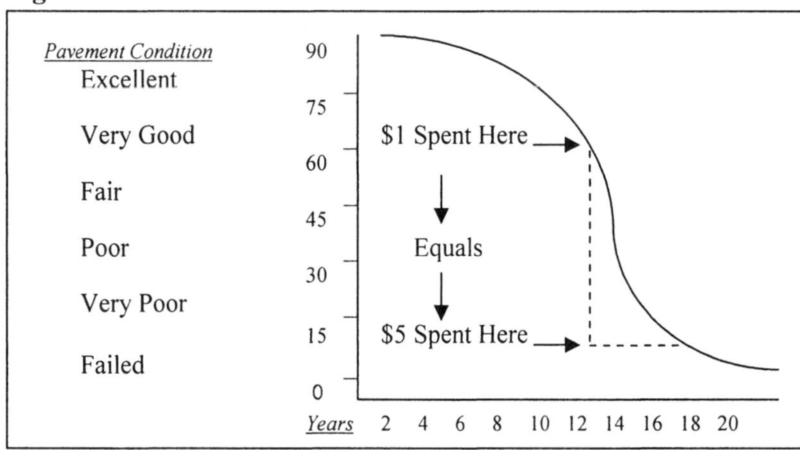

Source: FAA. *Airport Obligations: Pavement Maintenance*, http://www.faa.gov/airports_ airtraffic/airports/regional_guidance/central/airport_ obligations/pavement_maintenance (visited Feb. 2006).

The above figure also depicts the importance of considering the value of early investment in preventative maintenance. Clearly, it is more economical to invest in pavements when the pavement can still be rejuvenated, as opposed to attempting to revive pavement later, when it can be far (even by order of magnitude) more costly and may require reconstruction.

PAVEMENT MAINTENANCE PROGRAM

The estimated design life of bituminous pavement is about twenty years. With an initial seal coat it may easily go for five years without any maintenance. The pavement deteriorates only slightly the first few years. But as runway pavement deterioration progresses, the cost of restoring it increases dramatically with time, until at some point, the pavement reaches an unserviceable level and must be reconstructed. The key to cost/benefit maintenance is to determine that point in time when maintenance should be undertaken.

Under the supervision of professional airport engineers and airfield maintenance personnel most large air carrier airport runways receive programmed maintenance. Unfortunately, this has not happened at smaller commercial and general aviation airports. In fact, many have been allowed to deteriorate until expensive rehabilitation became necessary to save the runway. There is an underlying politico-economic reason for this having happened.

In 1982 the General Accounting Office [GAO] investigated this happening and conducted a report as part of a follow-up to the Airport Development Aid Program [ADAP]. As a condition for receiving funds from this program airport sponsors agreed to properly maintain their airport facilities, including the runways. What the GAO found is that especially local governments were allowing runways at small airports to deteriorate faster than was necessary. In effect, they were "deferring" maintenance for lack of operational funds.

Note, that while the Federal airport program funds airport *development,* it does not authorize the funding of airport *maintenance* projects. Therefore, if maintenance is to be performed it must be done using local funds only. Yet, small commercial and general aviation airports are barely able to meet their operational budgets. The 1982 GAO report validated that many small airport operators simply lack the resources necessary to maintain the runways. Consequently, they had allowed their runways to deteriorate until they were in such serious condition that they required rebuilding. Although reconstruction was hundreds of thousands of dollars more expensive than the cost of preventive maintenance, the local 10% share (for reconstruction under federal programs) was less expensive for the airport sponsor. The Federal government picked up the remaining bulk of the cost from the aviation user trust fund.

The GAO report concluded that unnecessary deterioration of pavement was needlessly costing millions of dollars per year.[42] The report identified three main factors contributing to the problem: (1) the lack of local funds, (2) many small airport managers have limited experience with pavement maintenance, and (3) the FAA was neither monitoring the situation nor taking corrective action. The report made three recommendations. The GAO recommended the FAA strictly enforce the grant assurances. It urged the FAA to work more closely with airport owners to develop meaningful airport maintenance programs. And the GAO suggested an advisory circular be printed giving general guidelines for maintenance of airport pavements.

In 1982, the FAA revised its advisory circular with guidelines and procedures for maintaining airport pavements.[43] In 1988, the FAA published an advisory circular presenting the concept of a "Pavement Management System."[44] In 1994, Congress amended the United States Code with regard to airport sponsor's grant assurances.[45] For all federal projects approved after January 1, 1995, to replace or reconstruct airport pavement, the airport sponsor must assure or certify that it has implemented an effective airport *Pavement Maintenance-Management Program* [PMMP]. The PMMP is expected to include at a minimum a pavement history, an inspection schedule, record keeping, an information retrieval system, and it must employ the use of FAA advisory circulars on "guidelines and procedures for maintenance of airport procedures" and a "pavement management system."[46]

Most airports today have a structured PMMP that addresses both preventative measures and the need for repairs. The FAA states that

[42] GAO, *Runways at Small Airports are Deteriorating Because of Deferred Maintenance: Action Needed by FAA and the Congress* (1982).
[43] FAA, *Guidelines and Procedures for Maintenance of Airport Pavements*, AC 150/5380-6 (Dec. 1982).
[44] FAA, *Pavement Management System*, AC 150/5380-7 (Sep. 28, 1988).
[45] P.L. 103-305, Sec. 107 amends 49 U.S.C. § 47105, *Sponsor's Grant Assurance No. 11.*
[46] *I.e.*, AC 150/5380-6 and AC 150/5380-7.

an effective PMMP should also, "address key elements that will permit tracking of pavement maintenance activities [and] must be provided with sufficient resources and commitment if it is to succeed." A sample pavement maintenance program can be found on the FAA's website that can be used in conjunction with FAA advisory circular guidance on pavements.[47]

A PMMP should assure the provision of safe and functional pavements for the activity anticipated, at the lowest possible cost. The FAA states, "The major objective in the design and construction of these pavements is to provide adequate load-carrying capacity and good ride quality necessary for the safe operation of aircraft under all weather conditions."[48] As with all substantial investments, airport operators hope to achieve the greatest possible return on their investment.

The FAA suggests the following elements be contained within a pavement maintenance management program:

- *Pavement Inventory* including the location of all runways, taxiways, and aprons; type of pavement; dimensions, construction year (or most recent rehabilitation); and identification of surfaces constructed with federal financial assistance.
- *Inspection Schedule* including detailed (annual)[49] and "drive-by" inspections (monthly).
- *Record Keeping* of the detailed inspections for five years, including types of distress, their locations, and remedial action, scheduled or performed, must be documented. For drive-by inspections, the date of inspection and any maintenance performed must be recorded.
- *Information Retrieval Method* to assure that records will be readily available when requested by the FAA, and be retained on file for five years.
- *Program Funding* to support the PMMP should be included.[50]

[47] FAA, *Guidelines and Procedures for Maintenance of Airport Pavements*, AC 150/5380-6A (Jul. 14, 2003), retrieved from the FAA's pavement maintenance website at http://www.faa.gov/airports_airtraffic/airports/regional_guidance/central/airport_obligations/pavement_maintenance, (Feb. 9, 2006).

[48] *Id.*

[49] At airports where an ASTM D5340 PCI survey has been conducted and recorded, the frequency of inspection may be extended to three years.

[50] *Id.*

The reference document for the PPMP is to be Advisory Circular 150/5380-6, "Guidelines and Procedures for Maintenance of Airport Pavements," for maintaining airport pavements and establishing an effective maintenance program. This advisory circular discusses various types of pavement distress and provides recommended corrective actions that should be undertaken during preventive and remedial maintenance. Additionally, the FAA recommends adherence to the American Society for Testing and Material Standards [ASTM] D 5340, "Standard Test Method for Airport Pavement Condition Index Surveys," when conducting preventive maintenance inspections. This standard uses the visual distress identification and rating system known as the *Pavement Condition Index* [PCI].

Developed by the U.S. Army Corp of Engineers Construction Engineering Research Lab, the *PCI method* to determining pavement distress serves to create a *PCI Value*[51] for airfield pavements through a visual survey of asphalt surfaces or jointed Portland cement concrete pavements. The PCI is a numerical rating of pavement condition, ranging from 0 to 100, with 0 being the worst possible condition and 100 being the best.[52] PCI Value is determined as follows:

- Divide pavement section into sample units and select sample units for inspection;
- Identify and record pavement distress in sample units;
- Compute PCI of sample units based on distress within sample unit; and,
- Compute PCI of section.

Pavement Condition Index distresses on *asphalt* surfaced pavements and Portland cement *concrete* pavements are presented in Figure 11.7, "PCI Distress Types for Airfield Pavements." The type, level of severity, and quantity of pavement distress within each sample unit is recorded through visual inspection. Sixteen types of distresses are identified on asphalt surfaced pavements, while fifteen are identified on PCC pavements.[53]

---

[51] City of Belmont, Calif., *Pavement Condition Index (PCI) Method*, retrieved from www.belmont.gov/SubContent.asp?CatId=240000622.

[52] This method has been adopted by the FAA to determine pavement condition, AC 150/5380-6, *Guidelines and Procedures for Maintenance of Airport Pavements.*

[53] City of Belmont, Calif., *Pavement Condition Index (PCI) Method*, retrieved from www.belmont.gov/SubContent.asp?CatId=240000622.

Figure 11.7—PCI DISTRESS TYPES FOR AIRFIELD PAVEMENTS

Distress Types on Asphalt Pavements	***Distress Types on PCC Pavements***
Alligator Cracking	Blow-up
Bleeding	Corner Break
Block Cracking	Longitudinal, Transverse, Diagonal Cracks
Corrugation	Durability (D) Cracking
Depression	Joint Seal Damage
Jet Blast Erosion	Patching –Small
Joint Reflection Cracking	Patching Large and Utility Cuts
Longitudinal and Transverse Cracking	Pop outs
Oil Spillage	Pumping
Patching and Utility Cut Patching	Scaling, Map Cracking and Crazing
Polished Aggregate	Settlement or Faulting
Raveling and Weathering	Shattered Slab/Intersecting Cracks
Rutting	Shrinkage Cracks
Shoving	Joint Spalling
Slippage Cracking	Corner Spalling
Swell	

Source: FAA, *Guidelines and Procedures for Maintenance of Airport Pavements*, AC 150/5380-6A (Jul. 14, 2003).

PAVEMENT DISTRESS AND REPAIR

Deceivingly, one of the least durable types of construction is pavement. Pavements deteriorate and fail. Bituminous pavements are destroyed by the elements. Not only are pavements exposed to sun and water damage, but bituminous surfaces are subject to volatilization of the asphalt mix as well. And, like asphalt, concrete pavements need occasional maintenance too. Despite the fact that the PCI Index identifies many specific types of distresses, the various types generally fall into four broad categories:

- Cracking;
- Distortion;
- Disintegration; and
- Loss of skid resistance.

Compounding the problems of normal distress, pavements fail because of faulty construction, inadequate bearing capacity, and differential movement in the underlying sub-base. Many existing runways were built years ago and were not designed for today's aircraft, greater loads, and increased frequency of operations. General aviation runways, that for years required little maintenance, suddenly fail when exposed to dynamic increases in operations by new, heavier air carrier activity. It is little wonder that there is a perpetual demand for the maintenance and rehabilitation of pavements.

Preventive Maintenance [PM] will substantially reduce the need for extensive repairs. The ultimate solution is to correct minor deficiencies before they get expensive, or at least to patch distressed areas to prolong pavement life and put off more costly solutions. Necessary repairs are a function of the type and magnitude of failure. PM consists of cold and hot bituminous patches, crack and joint sealing, cement mortar patches, fog and slurry seals, and cleaning, sweeping and other mechanical treatments of surface irregularities.

Normal *aircraft utilization* of a bituminous runway can also be considered as a type of routine maintenance. It has been accepted for many years that lack of traffic is an important factor that affects the rate of deterioration in flexible pavements. Active traffic is necessary for flexible pavement life. Without traffic the pavement shrinks from oxidation and a void condition develops. The void relieves itself by cracking at the surface. Oftentimes, a vibratory roller is used to relieve the stresses causing reflective or shrinkage cracking.

An *overlay* is pavement that is constructed on top of a runway when the existing surface can no longer be maintained satisfactorily at a serviceable level, or when it may require strengthening to serve heavier aircraft than those for which the pavement was originally designed. Pavement overlays are of Portland cement concrete, bituminous concrete, or a combination of both. A bituminous overlay may be placed on rigid pavement; or vice versa, a concrete overlay may be placed on a flexible surface

Maintenance of rigid pavements generally consists of sealing joints, repair of cracks, and replacement of broken areas, spalling, deep surface scaling, or other deep depressions. Instead of a bituminous patch in deep holes, a cement mortar mix may be preferable. The choice of repair methods is dependent upon the pavement type and deficiency observed. Chapters 5 and 6 of Advisory Circular 150/5360-6A provide a detailed listing of equipment (e.g., saws, jackhammers, pavement grinders, vibratory plate compactors, heating kettles, sandblasting equipment, etc.) and repair methods involving pavement removal/replacement, patching, seals and other measures. Table 11.1, "Pavement Conditions" shows a variety of common pavement problems associated with flexible as well as rigid pavements.

Joints are intentionally installed in concrete pavements to control cracking and provide for natural movement of the pavement. Materials used to seal joints deteriorate and work out of the joint. The joints must be re-sealed to prevent water drainage into the sub-base. Joint sealing is not a seasonal maintenance procedure, but rather, should be done whenever the old joint sealant has deteriorated to the point that it no longer prevents the entry of foreign materials. Joints, as well as distress cracks, should be re-sealed only when they are wide open or working open. Sealing materials will not penetrate tight cracks.

Routine maintenance of runways should collect FOD materials and should include sweeping and removal of rocks, gravel and other foreign objects. The airport should either own for itself, or otherwise have access to pavement sweeping equipment that it can use. A rotating brush can be used on runways and taxiways where debris can be swept onto the adjoining turf. However, on aprons and large expanses of pavement it requires a sweeper with a vacuum to pick up the debris and a hopper to retain it.

Table 11.1—PAVEMENT CONDITIONS

Bituminous Pavements
• *Cracks*—vertical cleavage such as block cracks; joint reflection cracks; slippage cracks; and longitudinal (parallel to centerline) and transverse cracks (across centerline). • *Alligator (fatigue) cracking*—interconnecting cracks forming a series of small polygons, which resemble an alligator's skin. • *Spalling*—breaking away of pavement along cracks, joints, or edges. • *Depressions and Rutting*—the formation of longitudinal depressions under traffic in the wheel paths. • *Waves*—transverse undulations at regular intervals, two feet apart. • *Corrugation, Shoving and Swelling*—transverse undulations at regular intervals. Shoving results in bulging of the pavement surface. • *Depressions or Potholes*—bowl-shaped holes or "birdbath" areas of varying sizes in low areas and resulting from localized disintegration. • *Raveling*—progressive disintegration from the surface downward, or edges inward, by the dislodgment of aggregate particles. • *Pumping*—ejection of water from the sub-base through cracks, joints, or edges when the pavement is subjected to passing heavy loads. • *Patching*—corrections made to pavement defects such as filling in holes, utility cut patching, seal coating, tarring of cracks, etc. • *Loss of Skid Resistance* from *Bleeding* and *Fuel Spillage* which softens asphalt—a film of bituminous material on the pavement surface.

Table 11.1 (continued)

Portland Cement Concrete Pavements
• *Cracking*—vertical cleavage. Several types noted in the PCI list include corner breaks; intersecting cracks; shrinkage cracks; durability cracks; and longitudinal, transverse and diagonal cracks. • *Shattered slab*—where intersecting cracks break up the slab into four or more pieces. • *Raveling*—progressive disintegration from the surface downward, or edges inward, by the dislodgment of aggregate particles. • *Pop outs*—crater-like depressions caused by the forcing off of part of the pavement surface by expansion of underlying coarse aggregate. • *Map Cracking, Crazing or Scaling*—peeling away of the surface. • *Disintegration and Spalling*—breaking or chipping of the pavement at joints, cracks, or corners, resulting in fragments with feather edges. • *Blow-up*—localized buckling or shattering, usually at a transverse crack or joint, and caused by excessive longitudinal pressure. • *Pumping or blowing*—ejection of mixtures of water, clay and/or silt along cracks and along pavement edges, caused by downward slab movement and the passing of heavy loads. • *Settlement or Faulting*—differential vertical displacement. • *Patching*—correction of pavement defects with bituminous or quick set solutions, sometimes forming uneven surfaces. • *Loss of Skid Resistance*—due to build-up of contaminants.

Source: W.R. Lovering, *Asphalt Pavement Maintenance* (1970), with updates from ASTM Standard D 5340 (2007); and FAA, *Guidelines and Procedures for Maintenance of Airport Pavements*, AC 150/5380-6A (Jul. 14, 2003).

Runways should also be cleaned periodically to remove surface deposits of rubber. A build up of tire rubber on the runway can result in a loss of runway friction. Rubber deposits or old pavement markings may be removed with high-pressure water, with chemicals (solvent cleaning), high velocity impact abrasives (e.g., sandblasting), or by mechanical grinding. Sometimes, mechanical grinders may also remove pavement roughness.[54]

Rubber deposits, rainwater accumulation, worn or polished pavement, or snow and ice are all conditions that precipitate a loss in runway friction. All are potentially hazardous conditions. Where runway friction loss is a common problem, airport management will likely use a *decelerometer* to test the runway during periods of questionable surface friction. The "decelerometer" is a device used to measure and record the coefficient of friction between various road or runway surfaces and a measuring wheel.

SEALANTS AND FILLERS

Sealants and fillers are used in all joints to prevent water from getting through to the sub-base. Water under the pavement undermines and erodes the soil. To correct for voids under Portland cement and to stabilize the base and restore the original grade, an asphalt underlayment may be pumped beneath the slabs. Environmentally heated, the softened bituminous underlayment may attempt to escape through expansion joints in the concrete. Silicone joint sealant may be used with two-fold purpose: to prevent water from penetrating the surface downward, and to prevent seepage of asphalt from the bottom up.

The environment is the worst enemy of bituminous pavements, especially when the pavement is subjected to extremes like freeze/thaw or wet/dry combinations. The most harmful environmental factor is *oxidation*, which ages the asphalt and makes it brittle. Placement of a seal coat over the pavement minimizes oxidation. For this purpose, there are five basic types of seal coats:

- *Fog seal* (or sprayed bituminous surface treatment) is a light application of asphalt emulsion mixed with water. It may be used to prevent circulation of air through the mix, or may be

[54] FAA, *Guidelines and Procedures for Maintenance of Airport Pavements*, AC 150/5380-6A, (Jul. 14, 2003).

used to moisten a pavement surface dried out from weathering. A fog seal works reasonably well at slowing down the oxidation process;

- A *slurry coat* (or sand-bituminous mixture) is a mixture of emulsified asphalt and sand aggregates. It is a heavy-duty protective coating, which fills cracks and provides a thin overlay. The basic material of coal tar pitch emulsion has been used for more than seventy-five years for this purpose;
- *Coal tar seal* emulsions, or emulsions with silicones or rubber in them, can be used as an effective seal against fuels and other solvents. They are used wherever fuel spillage is anticipated. They keep the fuel from eroding the pavement;
- *Chip seal* is an emulsion containing small "pea" (i.e., pea-size) gravel. Sometimes rubber is used to retain the aggregates. Discretion and employment of an engineer experienced with chip seals are imperative on airport applications. The loose aggregate from a chip seal can damage propellers or jet engines if ingested; and
- *Plant mix seal*, or what is commonly referred to as a "popcorn" friction course, is an open, graded surface using large aggregate. Like chip seals, it is common practice to add rubber to the mix for aggregate retention. The purpose of the friction course is to allow water to flow between the large aggregate and thus prevent hydroplaning.

SPECIAL TREATMENTS

The following paragraphs describe non-standard procedures, or those considered "special" treatments for unusual conditions. Some of these procedures or products, because of their recent innovation, are still associated with their inventor or manufacturer. They may be considered state-of-the-art in pavement renovation.

ROLL-ON PAVEMENT REPAIRS

Thought to be effective against reflective cracking is a roll-on surface covering consisting of a non-woven polypropylene fabric, which combines with asphalt to form an impermeable stress-relieving membrane. Bad cracks are filled with hot asphalt mix. A tack coat is spread on the pavement over which the fabric membrane is laid. A one and one-half to three-inch asphalt leveling course is then placed on top of the fabric.

REJUVENATING AGENTS

A cold-water emulsion of petroleum resins and oils is used in conjunction with a heater-scarifier process for overlaying existent asphalt concrete pavements. The old surface is heater-scarified and then treated with the rejuvenating agent to revitalize and re-plasticize the old asphalt mix. An asphalt overlay is subsequently applied to provide a flexible, long lasting surface. The process provides economic savings by enabling a thinner lift of new asphalt in combination with re-processing of the old asphalt surface. The rejuvenating agent provides a positive initial bond and avoids delaminating problems.

RUBBERIZED COAL TAR SEALERS

Jet fuel and other solvents spilled on unprotected bituminous pavement breaks-down the asphalt binders, resulting in chuckholes and loose surfaces. A surface treatment of a rubberized coal tar emulsion will seal the pavement and make it resistant to penetration from water, gasoline, oil, deicing chemicals and petroleum products.

FRICTION TREATMENTS

Wet and flooded runways result in a loss of tire braking and traction for landing aircraft, particularly due to hydroplaning where the aircraft tire footprint is lifted off the runway surface. Other causes of traction loss are normal pavement wear, pavement abnormalities, and rubber deposit build-up. The most effective surface friction treatment is to cut grooves in the pavement, either laterally or longitudinally. The grooves allow water to dissipate and preclude dynamic hydroplaning. Runway grooving is most effective in Portland cement, but may be cut in asphalt pavement as well, although the flexibility of asphalt allows the grooves eventually to be pressed together. A more effective friction treatment for bituminous pavement is to apply a friction course of aggregates mixed with a coal tar pitch emulsion (i.e., a "popcorn" friction surface).

NON-DESTRUCTIVE TESTING

An accurate and complete evaluation of existing pavement is a key factor in determining maintenance requirements. Qualitative analysis of runway composition is categorized as either *destructive* or *non-destructive*. The former includes expensive and time consuming tests including the taking of pavement core samples, borings, test pits, etc. Destructive testing is, as the name implies, a process entailing at least partial destruction of the runway integument.

Conversely, non-destructive tests do not disrupt the pavement. An effective and cost-saving example of non-destructive testing techniques is *vibratory* (or dynamic) testing. This test measures the amount the pavement responds (or deflects) under a known vibratory load. It measures the strength of the composite pavement system. Vibratory testing is particularly effective on flexible pavements, but rigid pavements may also be examined with this technique to test for density, voids, pumping, load transfer, and reseating.

QUICKSET PATCHING

Tying up a runway for sufficiently long periods to conduct repairs presents extremely difficult operational problems. Cold asphalt patches can be applied quickly and economically, but repairs of this type are only temporary. Permanent repairs normally entail hot asphalt mixes for flexible pavements and poured concrete sections in the case of rigid pavement repairs.

Alternatively, there are quick-set patching products available for the maintenance of concrete and asphalt runways. In some cases, permanent repairs can be made with these quickset materials. Asphalt-based patching products especially designed for repairs can be used on either asphalt or concrete to affect a permanent repair. Or, epoxy concrete can be applied specifically to Portland cement. Epoxy concrete, containing resins and binders, is mixed at the job site with sand, gravel, or stone. Properly mixed, it will set in less than six hours, thus allowing overnight repairs and cause minimum traffic disruption.

Another type of quickset material for use on rigid pavements is *magnesium phosphate* concrete, which contains neither Portland cement, gypsum, nor epoxies. It needs no additives except water, but aggregates can be added to increase the yield of the patching materials.

STEEL FIBROUS CONCRETE

The minimum thickness for poured concrete is normally about six inches. However, for increased load bearing capacity, design criteria may specify a foot or more in thickness. The use of steel fibrous concrete can significantly reduce the normal thickness requirement of the concrete pavement. It may also reduce the number of joints needed. Steel fibrous concrete is strengthened by the addition to the concrete mix of inch-long *steel slivers* for increased flexural strength.

PLASTIC FIBROUS CONCRETE

The plastic fibrous concrete technique uses *polypropylene fibers* added to bituminous pavement to give it added strength. The fiber creates a harder, yet more flexible surface that will better resist reflective cracking due to freeze/thaw, and rutting from traffic loading, especially during hot weather.

SOIL-CEMENT

Soil-cement is a recycling technique involving the use of a motorized grader and traveling mixer to pulverize the old asphalt mat and blend it with underlying granular and soil materials. The combined material is then mixed with Portland cement and processed to form a new cement-stabilized base material.

PLASTIC WEBS

Plastic webs may be used as an alternative to the gravel-based airport pavement base. A plastic, *honeycombed containment grid* is laid down in place of the traditional base material. The honeycombs are filled with sand. The confined sand then has the strength to receive the surface overlay.

CONCRETE PAVERS

Concrete "pavers" or interlocking blocks are hand-sized, interlocking concrete blocks usually about four-inches wide by eight-inches long and three-inches thick. The blocks are bedded in sand, and the small, sand-filled joints transfer loads to adjacent units by shear force. When assembled the interlocking blocks form a paved surface.

Protecting the surface is important, but what may be overlooked is the importance of the soil underneath the pavement. The next section discusses the soils that are critical to pavement health.

SOILS

The *soil* (or sub-grade) forms the foundation for pavement. The first six inches to one foot of sub-grade is compacted to help improve its load-bearing ability. It is the soil, and not the pavement, that actually carries the loads imposed by aircraft using the airport's paved surfaced area. The pavement serves to *distribute* the imposed load over the ground.

The importance of identification and evaluation of the soil cannot be overemphasized. Soil conditions are an important factor affecting runway construction. Soil conditions include the elevation of the water table, the presence of water bearing strata, and field properties such as structure, identification, plasticity, moisture content, and density.

To determine the physical properties of soils and to provide an estimate of their behavior under various conditions, soils are tested for such characteristics as particle size, plastic limit, liquid limit, plasticity index, and moisture density. Supplemental tests may look at shrinkage factors, permeability, organic materials, or bearing ratio. The strength of materials intended for use in flexible pavement structures, for example, is measured by the *California Bearing Ratio* [CBR] test.

The CBR test is basically a penetration test conducted at a uniform rate of strain. The force required to produce a given penetration in the material under test is compared to the force required to produce the same penetration in standard crushed limestone. The result is expressed as a ratio of the two forces. Thus, a material with a CBR value of "15" means the material in question offers 15% of the resistance to penetration that standard crushed stone offers.

For many years the FAA used its own method of soil classification. But, In 1978, the FAA changed from its own system to the *Unified Soil Classification System* (ASTM D-2487) developed by the American Society for Testing Material [ASTM], based on the results of a research study which compared three methods of soil classification. The research study concluded the Unified System is superior in detecting properties of soils that affect airport pavement performance. Since many past records contain references to the older (FAA) method, an overview of both the FAA and Unified Systems of soil classification are presented in this chapter.

Under the old FAA system, soils were classified into thirteen groups according to soil analysis. Soil classification required three basic tests: mechanical analysis, liquid limit, and plastic limit. *Mechanical analysis* determines quantitatively the distribution of particle sizes. The *liquid limit* of soil is the water content point at which the soil passes from a plastic to a liquid state. The *plasticity index* indicates the range of moisture content over which a soil remains in a plastic state before it changes into a liquid.

In the Unified Soil Classification System, soils are classified into 15 groups or types ranging from well-graded gravel and gravel-sand mixtures with little or no fines, to peat, muck and other highly organic soils (See Table 11.2, "Unified Soil Groups." The types of soil are then organized into three major divisions. The initial division is based on the separation of course and fine-grained soils and highly organic soils (See Table 11.3, "Unified Soil Classification System"). Course-grained soils are further subdivided into gravels and sands. Gravels and sands are then classed according to whether or not fine material is present. Fine-grained soils are subdivided into two groups on the basis of liquid limit or the amount of moisture the soil can hold. A separate division of highly organic soils is established for materials not generally suitable for construction purposes.

In the design of pavement, *stabilization* of the sub-grade is considered when there are certain conditions such as poor drainage, adverse surface drainage, frost or the need for a stable working platform. Soil stabilization is the procedure whereby the properties of a soil are improved to the extent it will meet the requirements for pavement bases and sub-bases.

Table 11.2—UNIFIED SOIL GROUPS

Soil Group—Description
GW—Well-graded gravel and gravel-sand mixtures, little or no fines.
GP—Poorly graded gravel and gravel-sand mixtures, little or no fines.
GM—Silty gravel, gravel-sand-silt mixtures.
GC—Clayey gravel, gravel-sand-clay mixtures.
SW—Well-graded sands and gravelly sands, little or no fines.
SP—Poorly graded sands and gravelly sands, little or no fines.
SM—Silty sands, sand-silt mixtures.
SC—Clayey sands, sand-clay mixtures.
ML—Inorganic silts, very fine sands, rock flour, silty or clayey fine sands.
CL—Inorganic clays of low to medium plasticity, gravelly clays, silty clays, lean clays.
OL—Organic silts and organic silty clays of low plasticity.
MH—Inorganic silts, micaceous or diatomaceous fine sands or silts, plastic silts.
CH—Inorganic clays or high plasticity, fat clays.
OH—Organic clays of medium to high plasticity.
PT—Peat, muck and other highly organic soils.

Source: FAA, *Airport Pavement Design and Evaluation*, AC150/5320-6D (Jul. 1995).

Table 11.3—UNIFIED SOIL CLASSIFICATION SYSTEM

Major Divisions	*Unified Soil Group Symbols**
Course-grained Soils (more than 50% retained on No. 200 sieve)	
• Gravel 50% or more of coarse fraction retained on No. 4 sieve	
Clean Gravel	GW GP
Gravel with Fines	GM GC
• Sands less than 50% of coarse fraction retained on No. 4 sieve	
Clean Sands	SW SP
Sands with Fines	SM SC
Fine-grained Soils (50% or less retained on No. 200 sieve)	
• Silts and Clays Liquid Limit 50% or less	ML CL OL
• Silts and Clays Liquid Limit Greater than 50%	MH CH OH
Highly Organic Soils	PT

* See Table 11.2, "Unified Soil Groups."

Source: FAA, *Airport Pavement Design and Evaluation*, AC 150/5320-6D (Jul. 1995).

The design of pavements in areas subject to frost action or in areas of permafrost is a complex problem requiring detailed study. The detrimental effects of frost action may be manifested in frost heave or in loss of foundation support through frost melting.

Soil is considered to have poor drainage if it cannot be drained because of its composition, or because of site conditions; i.e., because the soil has an affinity for moisture, or water flows into the area. Clays and silts are examples of impervious soils, which, because of their affinity for moisture are unstable. Soil that has good drainage remains well drained and stable under all conditions.

MARKINGS

Runway and taxiway markings are essential for the safe and efficient use of airports, and their effectiveness is dependent upon proper maintenance to maintain an acceptable level of conspicuity. As discussed in Chapter 3, runways are marked in accordance with operational usage; i.e., visual, non-precision instrument, or precision instrument. The color of markings used on runways is *white*, while that used on taxiways or for marking deceptive, closed, or hazardous areas is *yellow*. On light-colored runway pavements, outlining them with a black border at least six inches in width can increase the contrast of the markings

Advisory Circular 150/5340-1J, "Standards for Airport Markings" (April 2005) contains the latest standards for airport marking. In 2008, enhanced taxiway markings (comprised of a solid yellow centerline bordered by a dashed line on both sides, all outlined in black) will become the standards at airports enplaning 1.5 million or more passengers annually. In some locations the use of striated markings, consisting of painted stripes four inches to six inches wide, with equal width of unpainted area, has been effective in reducing frost heave of the pavement. This method also increases the coefficient of friction over the marking area. However, since this method results in reduced marking conspicuity, frequent maintenance is required to provide an acceptable marking system.

There are two basic types of paints used on airports: acrylic or *water-based* paints, and *oil-based* paints. On new overlays or new pavement it is recommended that acrylic paint be used because oil-based paints tend to soak in. Oil-based paints are recommended for older pavement. Oil-based paints are easier to work with. They spray better, look better and last 50% longer. However, recent trends are towards more generalized use of acrylics, primarily because of ecological reasons. Petroleum based solvents evaporate from oil-based paints. Whether water- or oil-based, reflective beads may be added to runway and taxiway paints to make the markings even more conspicuous.

SUMMARY

This chapter on maintenance focused on three areas of interest for most airport operators: grounds-keeping, snow and ice control, and pavements. Maintaining public airports is a task that is growing in both complexity and costs, arising from labor, materials, equipment, and infrastructure demands. The next two chapters delve more deeply into the cost- or fiscal-side of airports, with a review of airport finance, economics and the airport as a robust marketplace.

CHAPTER 12

AIRPORT FINANCE AND ECONOMICS

The difference between airports and commercial entitles such as airlines . . . can be summed up this way, 'Airport operators as public entitles make money to provide service. Airlines provide service to make money. There is a huge difference between the two.'

James Wilding, President and CEO,
Metropolitan Washington Airports Authority[1]

INTRODUCTION

Airport finance and related economic issues are critical areas of knowledge for effective airport management. Airport operators must balance their budgets, understand complex financial issues, obtain capital improvement funding, and promote the economic benefit of the airport facilities to their communities. A discussion of finance is not complete, though, without a discussion of *control*; those who "hold the purse strings" wield power over financial aid recipients.

The opening quote above reflects the dramatic fiscal and political changes being foist upon those who are in charge of assuring that the busiest of airports are being operated with economic efficiency—akin to running a business, yet so different. While airport operators recognize the need to operate their airports in innovative ways, some feel a

---

[1] James Wilding as quoted by Sean Broderick in *Wilding: Need for Airport-Government Policy Framework*, Airport Magazine, (Jan./Feb. 2003), at 18.

level of frustration in having to constantly remind others that airports are, in fact, not a business nor an arm of the Federal government, but instead exist for the purpose of local governance and the provision of important community services.

James Wilding, President and Chief Executive Officer [CEO] of the Metropolitan Washington Airports Authority, perceives that airports may now be the subject of too much regulation and federal government oversight, and states that this may be due to a "lack of common understanding about how airports are run and the balancing act airport executives face."[2] He states,

> *Everyone understands the airlines, aircraft manufacturers and most of the tenants that occupy an airport are for-profit businesses, and that's how they're run and regulated. But airports combine enormous commercial and governmental dimensions, making them impossible to pigeon-hole as either for-profit or for private.*[3]

Even members of the federal government—who should be well aware of the public sector constraints—can be considered part of the problem. Wilding continues,[4]

> *The perplexing and increasingly troubling aspect of the airport-federal relationship comes from the federal government's unwillingness to value from the public nature of airport operators and from its apparent view of itself as an economic regulator of airports. Remarkably these federal tendencies have not evolved from any clear federal policy framework of statute or regulation. . . . When public policy considerations needed to be weighed, the federal government was quick to overlook or ignore the nature of airport operators as local public entities and*

---

[2] *Id.*
[3] *Id.*
[4] *Id.*

> *to proceed as if the airports operators were private, commercial entitles.*

Wilding is not alone in his concerns about where airports should appropriately be positioned along a continuum between public and private sector opportunities/expectations and associated levels of regulatory oversight.

While some note that "airports are monopolies and therefore, need close governmental regulation"[5] to better assure competition, Wilding resists the insertion of the federal government into local matters and calls for a "framework that should help the Federal government "restrain itself when attempting to over involve itself in airport matters that are vested to local public bodies—the airport operators."[6] He concludes, "This is the time for airport operators and the local government officials whose communities they serve to focus on restoring the freedom airports need to operate as both public transportation entities and successful businesses."[7]

Airports throughout the nation and around the globe are struggling with similar challenges between the "old way" of running airports—minimum risk and minimum potential for revenues—and the new way of operating airports that require vision and creativity, more traditional business skills, and a fair tolerance for risk, in exchange for the increased potential for greater efficiencies and revenue generation. They are also struggling for the continued right to maintain localized financial and administrative control over their significant air transportation assets, while significant financial resources remain controlled largely by federal officials.

This chapter explores the complex public finance and budgeting roles of airport operators. The next chapter continues with a related discussion about emerging business-like trends at airports and the *new airport marketplace*.

AIRPORT FINANCE

Finance is about where and how to obtain fiscal resources, but it also has to do with fiscal decision-making. For instance, if one must

[5] Sean Broderick, *Wilding: Need for Airport-Government Policy Framework*, Airport Magazine (Jan./Feb. 2003) at 18.
[6] *Id.* at 4.
[7] *Id.*

choose between adding a new terminal or extending the existing terminal, the process by which one chooses is also called finance. "Finance," as presented herein, has two general meanings: (1) the management of money, and/or (2) the provision of capital. That is to say, it may be the on-going, day-to-day management of income and expenses, or it may refer to the arrangement of financing to pay for capital improvements. Both perspectives as related to airport finance are addressed in this chapter.

Finance has the connotation of managing funds—especially large sums of money—particularly in corporations and in government. Private sector, or *corporate finance*, is associated with marketplace allocation of resources directed largely by competition and consumer choice. The three phases typically addressed in corporate finance are planning (including budgeting), raising capital and investing capital.

Public finance, on the other hand, traditionally focuses on the provision of goods and services through expenditure programs (or "budgets"), and the financing of those programs through collection of revenues. Revenues are primarily collected in the form of taxes, but with proprietary activities such as airports, revenues may also be derived through the assessment of fees on particular users. *User fees* are those fees associated with the cost of providing services, as calculated through comprehensive cost accounting practices and implemented via rates and charges programs. In order to provide public sector goods and services, it is necessary to purchase products, mostly from the private sector. Government expenditures, through the budgetary process, serve as the counterpart of cost outlays for business firms.

THE BUDGET

The business of finance involves the circulation of money. It deals with credit, investments, and other monetary provisions. It is the acquisition and use of money. As pointed out in the introduction, in the public sector, nearly synonymous with finance is budgeting. As commonly understood, a "budget" is the forecast by a government of its expenditures and revenues for a specific period of time, usually for one *fiscal* year. Budgeting has also found widespread adoption in the private sector, in corporations as well as individual and family budgets. But governmental budgeting is not solely a matter of finance in the narrow sense as it might be with a family or with a small business.

The public budget, particularly at the national level, is a reflection of fiscal policy.

Like all government budgets, the "airport budget" is a plan of estimated expenditures during a given period of time, including the proposed method of financing those expenses. To the student of public administration, the term "budget" brings forth a variety of abstract if not esoteric notions, but in this text the subject, hopefully, is more straight-forward. It is relatively easy to say what a budget is. It is much more difficult to develop and explain sophisticated theories about budgeting. The intent here is merely to define budgeting, and to show its application to the administration of public airports.

Resources are limited, and government agencies compete with each other for limited public funds. Although some administrators might cynically state that budgeting, reduced to its simplest political terms, means getting approval for as much money and resources as possible; more optimistically, it is a planning and management tool. By another definition, a "budget" is a financial program for future operations. It is a *plan* that represents the effects of varying levels of activity upon costs and revenues. It is a projected operating statement of profit or loss; or more ideally, in the public sector it ought to be a "balanced budget." The strategy normally taken by a public entity in the operation and management of a community airport assumes the role of serving the *public convenience and necessity*. In other words, it involves notions of public welfare, and does not have profit as an express motive. That is, it has not had profit as an express motive until recently. To the airport manager, the "budget" is a tool for limiting and controlling spending. It determines how much or how little the airport manager may spend, and hence, sets outside limits of potential accomplishment within a specified time period.

HISTORY OF BUDGETING

Budgeting originated in Europe, but remained comparatively simple until the advent of World War I. The word "budget" is derived from Old French *bougette*, meaning "little bag." When the British Chancellor of the Exchequer makes the annual financial statement, he is said to "open" the budget or receptacle of documents and accounts. As in Europe, budgeting in the United States evolved with the significant increases in governmental spending that accompanied the war effort. However, the impetus for public budgeting in America began during the Progressive Era, well before WWI began.[8]

The budgeting system of the Federal government rests on the Budget and Accounting Act of 1921. But adoption of the 1921 act was preceded by more that than three decades of civil agitation for budgetary reform at all levels of government. Influenced by the same reform pressures that brought about the Budgeting and Accounting Act, state and municipal governments tended to adopt budgetary practices similar to those of the federal government.[9]

In the movement to reform budgetary practices, it is often argued that the business community was the origin and model of improved public financial practices in the United States. But in reality government officials working in concert with academics invented, imported from other governments, and modified public budgeting in the U.S. Although the business community encouraged the government to adopt more efficient financial management techniques, public officials generally resisted copying business practices, which at the time were not very good, at times even corrupt.[10]

The city manager form of government is one example of a reform recommendation promoted by businessmen and adopted by government. Budget reformers often advocated the adoption of business techniques. And although government officials generally resisted in doing so, the impression has lingered that business practices were superior to those in the public sector. Budget reformers like Henry Bruere, Frederick Cleveland, W.F. Willoughby and Charles G. Dawes fostered this impression.

Henry Bruere was one of the directors of the New York Bureau of Municipal Research. It was an independent analytical and critical organization established to study fiscal issues and reform recommendations to government. Bruere attributed some of the budget innovations adopted by government to recommendations made by railroad financier E. H. Harriman and others associated with the New York Bureau of Municipal Research. But it was wealthy backers, including Harriman, who sponsored the New York Bureau of Municipal Research.[11] Suspicions abound about the possible ulterior motives surrounding

[8] *See* Encyclopaedia Britannica, *Budget, Governmental* 364 (1969).
[9] *Id.*
[10] Irene S. Rubin, *Who Invented Budgeting in the United States?*, Public Administration Review, Vol. 53, No. 5 (Sep./Oct. 1993), at 438.
[11] *See id.*

backers of the "research bureaus" that sprang up about the same time that the government was beginning to economically regulate industry. Concerns about the efficiency of government management by these wealthy financiers seemingly had more to do with how the government might regulate their affairs than it did with government efficiency.

One of the major stimuli for the improvement of accounting and reporting in railroads was the creation of the Interstate Commerce Commission [ICC] in 1887. Once the ICC set up accounting systems and imposed them on private sector organizations, the government was pressured to adopt analogous measures for itself. As Frederick Cleveland argued, if the government was to impose major accounting changes on business, it had better impose similar changes on itself. Cleveland was the director of President Taft's Economy and Efficiency Commission, but he had been a director of the New York Bureau of Municipal Research.[12]

W.F. Willoughby was another member of Taft's Economy and Efficiency Commission. Like Cleveland, Willoughby also argued that if government was going to economically regulate business, it had first to put its own house in order.[13] After the commission was dissolved, Willoughby became director of the Institute for Government Research, another research bureau investigating government fiscal reform. The Brookings Institution traces its beginnings to 1916 with the founding of the Institute for Government Research. Like its predecessor, the Brookings Institution functions as an independent analyst and critic, committed to publishing its findings for the information of the general public. Brookings is financed largely by endowment and by the support of philanthropic foundations, corporations, and private individuals.[14]

Charles Dawes was another businessman who in 1921 was trying to set up business practices in government. He was the first director of the Bureau of the Budget. His major focus was to press for the import of business accounting and especially *balance sheets* to government. He argued that business used balance sheets and accruals of assets and liabilities, so too should government. Arguing strongly that government ought to operate like business he said that,

---

[12] *See id.*
[13] *See id.*
[14] The Brookings Institution, *About Brookings*, retrieved from http://www.brook.edu/about/aboutbi.htm (Jan. 30, 1999).

> *Every habit, every custom, personal or administrative . . . which militated against the recognition in government business of those principles of business organization incident to successful private administration, we have fought from the beginning. . . .*[15]

There is still an impression held by many that government ought to operate like business, and that private is almost always better than public management.[16] Supporters of this position point to *command economies* (government-driven, such as that attempted in the former Soviet Union) as historically unsuccessful, and subsequently replaced by *market economies*. As evidence, innovations like zero-base budgeting, benchmarking, and total quality management were invented for business and then touted for the public sector.

Some of the contemporary business management concepts and strategies, which have evolved over the years, and which seem to replace one another as newer innovations come into vogue are presented below. These various management strategies are designed to enhance financial management and facilitate the accomplishment of organizational objectives. These are some of the more popular techniques that have been tried:

- *Management by Objectives* [MBO] is a performance and results-oriented technique. The manager knows what the objectives are, measures performance and results, and makes the necessary changes to achieve the desired results.
- *Management by exception* is a technique used to assist managers in identifying when and where attention is needed. Concentration is given to critical issues and the trivial matters are deferred or diverted.
- *Participative management* is the process of involving people in decisions that affect them. It emphasizes the notion of letting subordinates share in the organizational goal-setting and decision-making process.

---

[15] Charles G. Dawes, *The First Year of the Budget of the United States*, 229 (1923).

[16] Robert Poole of the Reason Foundation, for example, states there "is a very clear belief that private managers freed of government shackles generally do a better job of managing the business and providing higher service levels"; *see* Robert W. Poole Jr., *Airport Privatization: What the Record Shows*, Reason Foundation, Policy Study No. 124 (Aug. 1990).

- *Planning-Programming-Budgeting-Systems* [PPBS] is a process formulated in the 1960s by the U.S. Defense Department. This system's approach shifts the emphasis from accounting to economics of cost-benefit. It assumes resources are scarce and choices and costs are everywhere involved; that input/output calculations can be determined even in the absence of a profit factor. All objectives must be defined as precisely as possible through planning (the process of determining objectives); programming (translating objectives into time-phased requirements); and budgeting (transferring required resources into spending requests).
- *Organizational effectiveness* is an on-going interactive process which views organizations as systems and attempts to develop normative strategies for change, predicated upon hard data. It is goal oriented, rational, and based on experience. It follows a four-step circular process of data collection and diagnosis, action planning, implementation of change, and evaluation and feedback.
- *Zero-based budgeting* is an attempt to begin the budgetary process afresh. In its ideal form zero-based budgeting is impractical and therefore practically impossible to achieve, but it is commonly used in modified forms. Annual re-evaluation and justification of all programs and expenditures is the essence of this management process. It allows for complete rethinking and redirecting of programs, rather than dependence upon the last budget for determination of future expenditures. Zero-base budgeting focuses the budget process into a comprehensive analysis of objectives and needs, combining planning and budgeting into a single process.
- *Total Quality Management* [TQM] is a system for managing a company or organizations in which the workers are organized by teams to create a shared vision of how to continuously improve their processes. Progress is measured against five identified causes of problems: (1) *material* (metal, paper, information, and so forth, used in the production process); (2) *machines* (tools used to change the materials of production); (3) *methods* (what is done to change the process of production); (4) workforce (the knowledge, skills, motivation, cooperation, etc. of those employed in the process); and (5) environment (the

physical conditions, political atmosphere or company culture).[17]

- *Benchmarking* is an attempt to compare one organization against another to see how it measures up in such areas as management training, scheduling and delivery, workforce and productivity, quality methods and results, and energy and environment. Benchmarking is "the search for best practices that will lead to superior performance." It is a process for measuring one company's methods, processes, procedures, products, and service performance against those of companies that "consistently distinguish themselves in that same category of performance." And, once measurements have been made, benchmarking is a tool for setting appropriate, measurable objectives for improvement.[18]

Admittedly, some of the above techniques have been effective in improving management in the public sector. But the argument that business financial practices were better during the budgetary reform period of the Progressive Era (from about the 1890s to World War I) are way overstated. There are at least three evidences that the role of earlier business techniques as a model have been exaggerated:

- First, the quality of financial management in the private sector in the late 1890s and early 1900s was generally poor;
- Second, much of the development of the government budgeting reform agenda came from the experience of government practitioners and academics, not the private sector; and
- Third, the development of budget reform proposals by government officials preceded the recommendations of the early "research bureaus."

As Irene Rubin argues,

> *The role of business techniques as a model has been greatly exaggerated. The history of early*

[17] Transformation, *Total Quality Management*, retrieved from http://www.transfmn.com/tqm1.html (May 26, 1998).
[18] Alberta Research Council, *Performance Benchmarking*, http://www.chatsubo.com/cchrei/changing/vol3-1/performance.html.

> *public budgeting in the United States suggests that the public should have more confidence in the public sector's capacity for experimentation, evaluation, and reform.*[19]

It is important to remember this today, because the supposed superiority of private over public sector management is again being touted as an argument for privatization of the public sector, and used as a reason for contracting out and for reducing the scope of government services.

THE BUDGETARY PROCESS

In the evolution of budgetary concepts in the United States, there are three basic types that have resulted:

- The first form is the *line item budget*, which classifies expenditures according to types of purchases; i.e., accounting for each item of supplies, equipment, and personal services. Under this system, estimates for the coming year's budget are usually based on quantities of supplies used in the preceding year;
- The second type is the *program budget*, which deals in gestalts (or wholes) instead of details. In essence, the program budget states what facilities, personnel or equipment are needed, in what location, at what cost, and in what time span; and
- The third category is the *performance budget*. Under this procedure, services are broken down into work loads or units of performance, thus creating units of measurement to be used in calculating the labor and material inputs required to achieve the objectives of a given program.

There is no pat answer as to how long a budget period should last. Normally, a budget is for one fiscal year, but for planning purposes it is good practice to plan ahead for at least five years. The budgetary process is ongoing and has individual, yet overlapping phases. The new budget is often in preparation before the ink has had a chance to

---

[19] Irene S. Rubin, *Who Invented Budgeting in the United States?*, Public Administration Review, Vol. 53, No. 5 (Sep./Oct. 1993), at 439.

dry on the currently adopted budget. The budget cycle has four principal phases:

- The initial phase is *preparation* by an executive agency (e.g., the airport director, county administrator, or city manager.
- The budget is then submitted to the legislative body (the airport commission, county board of supervisors, or city council) for *approval* in the second phase.
- *Execution*, or expenditure, is the third phase, taking place throughout the fiscal period.
- The final phase is an *audit* by the government's auditor ensuring honesty in dispensing public funds, and as a deterrent against needless waste.

REVENUES

In providing facilities and services for the convenience of aircraft, travelers and the storage and handling of mail and cargo, airports incur expenses, but at the same time they create offsetting revenues. The airport's revenues originate from three principal source categories: (1) *aeronautical operating revenue* such as landing fees, terminal and international arrival area rental, apron charges/tie-downs, FBO revenue: contract or sponsor-operated, cargo and hangar rental, and aviation fuel tax and fuel sales; (2) *non-aeronautical operating revenue* including land and non-terminal facilities, Terminal sources (food and beverage, retail and other), rental cars, and parking; and (3) *non-operating revenue* including interest income, grant receipts and passenger facility charges.[20]

Over the past couple of decades, airport revenue generating activities have gone through an exciting evolution. As a result, a significant portion of the next chapter is dedicated to revenue-generating innovations and other relevant business activities/strategies. The next chapter looks at the airport as a marketplace and addresses in greater detail the revenue sources identified above.

---

[20] FAA, *Operating and Financial Summary Form 5100-127*, as an appendix to AC 150/5100-19. (Apr. 2001), retrieved from http://forms.faa.gov/forms/faa5100-127.pdf.

EXPENSES

In analyzing and comparing airport revenues and expenses, it is seemingly much easier to identify potential revenues in advance than it is to anticipate the expense side of the profit/loss equation. The determination of airport-projected expenses is complicated by the public and governmental nature of the airport. Barring explosive growth, revenues associated with airport operations are more clearly foreseeable because of established rental agreements and set rates. Expenses, on the other hand, are not so rational, and may not be borne in the same fashion by all airport operators.

The nature of the airport's expenses depends upon a number of factors such as the location of the airport within its governmental and administrative hierarchy, and its financial structure. As will be pointed out in the succeeding chapter, hidden expenses are often buried in the budgets of supporting governmental departments. The engineering department may perform maintenance; the local fire department and local law enforcement agencies may provide police and fire protection; staff services such as accounting, legal services, and planning assistance may come from pooled resources. The budgets of these respective governmental subdivisions may have budgetary allowances for support of the airport, which may be paid out of the general fund account.

In some cases cross-departmental charges may be made against the airport, but may not include the total costs of providing the services. For instance, labor costs may be attributed to airport support. But the costs for tools, equipment and their maintenance may be borne entirely by the supporting department. Average man-hour costs may be used rather than costs based upon actual per-person wages. And, overhead costs such as sick leave, vacation, retirement or insurance may not be cost applied.

Certainly, public trust demands that the total costs for governmental operations must be accounted for, but *balancing* of the budget may very likely not occur until the overall (general fund) budget (i.e., "the bottom line") is tallied. In order to truly ascertain what it costs to operate an airport, the airport's accounting system must exist in a nearly autonomous state; that is to say, in an *enterprise account*, as it would likely be for an airport special district, or as it would exist if it were purchased by private enterprise.

Airport costs are typically divided into the two major categories of either *operating* or *non-operating* expenses. Operating expenses are the daily, "out-of-pocket," expenses incurred in the operation of the airport. Operating expenses usually exclude depreciation, debt service, and capital improvements, which are the principal non-operating expenses. Other non-operating expenses consist of interest payments, contributions to government, and other miscellaneous costs.

Operating costs generally consist of what are called the "Operations and Maintenance" [O&M] expenses. The operations costs include the general and administrative expenses along with the costs of providing specific services related to day-to-day airport operations. Maintenance costs are related to maintaining and repairing airport facilities. The O&M expenses may or may not include all of the personnel costs involved in the operation of the airport. Typical O&M expenses are:

- Maintenance of grounds, facilities and equipment;
- Salaries, wages, and overhead budgets;
- Costs for outside professional services;
- Tools and equipment; office, clothing, and personal supplies;
- Administrative costs for transportation, travel, professional memberships, and entertainment;
- Utilities;
- Insurance; and
- Communications and household expenses.

Debt service repayment is the most prominent of the non-operating expenses. Debt service refers to money required to pay the interest on outstanding debt, which is usually incurred through bonding for capital improvements. It may also include the principal, or face amount of the bond. Although considered poor accounting practice, debt repayment of the principal is sometimes treated as expense. The justification for doing so is that the payments may be approximately equal to depreciation. Since the motive for charging interest is profit, then interest is clearly a legitimate expense entry. At any rate, the necessary funds to cover debt service obligations, including the principal, are cash outlays. They therefore represent a non-operating expense to the airport.

"Depreciation" is the lowering in value of a commodity due to the passage of time and use. The loss in value is an expense to the owner. The costs of depreciation are calculated for buildings, structures, and equipment, predicated upon their anticipated service lives. Methods of depreciation may vary with accounting practices, but items normally considered depreciable are structures such as buildings, hangars, navigational and lighting aids, equipment, and so forth. Items not considered depreciable are land, earthwork, demolition costs and projects that will not require replacement. Pavement construction costs may or may not be considered depreciable since their upkeep is normally inclusive in O & M expenses.

COST EFFECTIVENESS

Analyses of airport revenues and expenses indicate a number of factors that result in unusually high or low revenue and expense relationships. Among these are:

- *Maximized utilization of existing facilities*—Airport facilities being used at or near capacity have higher revenue to expense relationships;
- *Rates set at project operating levels*—Fees and costs that are set high in anticipation of expected operating expenses and debt service enable the airport to more adequately cope with financial management. Fees and charges should be designed to provide a source of revenue for airport development (a reserve account or sinking fund should be established);
- *Airport in the long haul route system and/or a terminal end*—Concession revenues increase with route stage lengths and whether or not trips begin or end at the airport. For example, auto rental and auto parking revenues are low at predominately connecting airport terminals;
- *Location as a servicing facility*—The airport's location can make it a major service and refueling stop, thus increasing fuel flowage rates and other revenues;
- *Proper capital improvement planning*—failure to anticipate future facility funds can result in substantial capital investment that cannot be easily amortized;

- *High maintenance costs*—Large land holdings that are kept fallow, or paved areas in excess of needs, result in needless expense. Maximized use of the land, and abandonment of useless pavement, can improve the revenue/expense balance;
- *Security and Airport Rescue and Fire Fighting* [ARFF] *requirements*—The costs for rescue and fire fighting capability, and for police services, must be closely monitored to provide adequate protection, but at the same time kept within the bounds of necessity. Personnel costs for these services are among the highest on the airport and are a primary cause of deficit spending at smaller air carrier airports;
- *Intra-airport transportation*—At expanding airports the costs of providing passenger ground transportation from terminal-to-terminal, or to remote satellite parking lots is a major financial consideration;
- *Hub-and-spoke*—There is a significant potential for generating increased airport revenues associated with the cost efficiencies airlines achieve through hub-and-spoke networks. Airports that form the hubs are in a position to extract a portion of the cost savings in exchange for providing the hub facility; and
- *Investment in non-aviation property*—Land uses (particularly industrial) not related to airport operations can provide an expanded revenue base.

A sample end-of-the-year financial operating statement for a large commercial service is presented in Figure 12.1, "Typical Airport Operating Statement." The *operating statement* is an end-of-year accounting of the airport's annual budget. Included in the operating statement are operating revenues and expenses, non-operating revenues and expenses, and a reporting of the airport's net assets. A typical budgeting and accounting system will sub-divide the major line items into sub-items.

If the operating statement could have been accurately foreseen at the beginning of the year it would be the projected budget for that year. While forecasts are never completely accurate, the end-of-year statement should reasonably match the beginning-of-year airport budget.

Figure 12.1—TYPICAL AIRPORT OPERATING STATEMENT

OPERATING (REVENUES/EXPENSES) AND OPERATING LOSS (INCOME)		
	Current Year (*$000*)	*Previous Year*
Operating Revenues		
Aviation Revenue		
Landing Fees	$ 147,990	$ 149,176
Building Revenues	133,635	133,176
Other Aviation Revenues	60,336	66,108
Concession Revenue	228,230	200,789
Airport Sales and Services	2,575	2,655
Miscellaneous	1,467	3,676
Total Operating Revenue	574,233	545,567
Operating Expenses		
Salaries and Benefits	237,588	211,373
Contractual Services	156,576	142,736
Administrative Expenses	4,057	3,412
Materials and Supplies	45,967	43,127
Utilities	29,023	24,173
Total Operating Expenses[21]	499,057	459,647
Operating Income Before Depreciation [22]	75,176	85,920
Depreciation & Amortization	(76,189)	(75,973)
Operating (Loss) Income	(1,013)	9,947

[21] This figure is the total operating expenses before depreciation and amortization.
[22] This figure is the total operating income before depreciation and amortization.

Figure 12.1 (continued)

NON-OPERATING (REVENUES/EXPENSES) AND CHANGE IN NET ASSETS		
	Current Year ($000)	*Previous Year* [23]
Non-Operating Revenues (Expenses)		
Passenger Facility Charges	$ 122,283	$ 116,013
Interest Income	33,106	33,775
Change in Fair Value of Investments	(3,376)	(18,229)
Interest Expense	(23,847)	(25,965)
Bond Expense	(361)	(387)
Gain on Sale of Securities	3,867	988
Other Non-Operating Expenses	(29)	(2,159)
Other Non-Operating Revenues	6,425	949
Total Non-Operating Revenue, Net	138,065	104,985
Operating Loss/Income [24]	(1,013)	9,947
Income Before Capital Grants	137,052	114,932
Capital Grant Contributions	1,798	7,593
Change in Net Assets	138,850	122,525

NET ASSETS		
	Current Year ($000)	*Previous Year* [25]
Net Assets, Beginning of Year	$ 2,322,160	$ 2,199,635
Changes in Net Assets	138,850	122,525
Net Assets, End of Year	2,461,010	2,322,160

Source: City of Los Angeles Department of Airports, *Statements of Revenues, Expenses and Changes* in Net Assets (for the years ending Jun. 30, 2005 and 2004).

[23] Imported from prior page calculations of operating loss or income.
[24] This figure is the total operating expenses before depreciation and amortization.
[25] Imported from prior page calculations of operating loss or income.

CAPITAL BUDGETING

Budgets usually combine two or more sub-budgeting processes. The operating budget with its revenues versus expenses will also have non-operating revenues and expenses. Included in the non-operating expenses will be provisions for the repayment of bonds and other capital debt, of which capital budgeting may be an entire process in and of itself.

In budgeting there needs to be a differentiation made between *capital budget* and *capital budgeting.* The capital "budget" involves planned expenditures in fixed assets. Capital "budgeting" is the whole process of evaluating projects (airport improvements) to be included in the capital budget. In the private sector, this is usually determined by Net Present Value [NPV], Internal Rate of Return [IRR], and profitability index or payback period. In the public sector, other factors such as level of service issues, community requirements, grant-driven parameters, or political motivations may affect the capital budgeting process.[26]

Capital budgeting is usually associated with development in accordance with the master planning process. Schedules and cost estimates of improvements proposed in the master plan are developed on the basis of *short-range* (five years), *intermediate* (ten years), and *long-range* (twenty years) forecasts of aeronautical demand. The establishment of the airport master plan's economic feasibility (i.e., the balance between annual cost of capital investment and airport revenues) is vital to securing financing for proposed plan improvements.

The implementation schedule and cost estimates evolve from technical and financial considerations. *Technical considerations* include determination of time needed to acquire land, develop engineering or architectural designs and complete construction. The *financial considerations* relate to the availability and timing of capital financing. Federal and state aid may be limited; existing indebtedness could delay early debt incurrence; or the financial market may not be suitable for debt financing.

Hence, the capital budget incorporates a financial feasibility study and economic analysis. It is a traditional cost-benefit analysis that measures the airport operator's ability to cover potential costs for

---

[26] Per conversation with Javad Gorjidooz, Professor of Finance at Embry-Riddle Aeronautical University, Prescott Campus, Ariz. (Feb. 28, 2007).

capital improvements. The costs for various alternative development concepts, including projected expenses for operations, maintenance, and administration, are weighed against potential revenues. Typical revenue producing centers, as discussed in more depth in the next chapter, include: the landing area, aircraft aprons and parking areas, airline terminal buildings, automobile parking lots, cargo buildings, aviation refueling systems, hangars, commercial facilities, and other revenue producing areas such as open land, which could be used for farming or other commercial activities.

Traditionally there have been five resources that are used separately or in combination to finance airport development:[27]

- *Airport Cash Flow (rates and charges, concession revenue, rentals, fees, etc.)*—Airport revenues include receipts from airline rates and charges such as landing fees and rentals, and revenue from airport concessions. Airport revenues are used to pay O&M expenses, to finance "pay as you go" capital projects, and are pledged to pay bondholders both principal and interest. At most commercial service airports, the financial and operational relationship between an airport and the airlines it serves is defined in legally binding agreements that specify how the risks and responsibilities of airport operations are to be shared between the two parties. Commonly referred to as "airport use agreements," these contracts generally specify the methods for calculating the rates airlines must pay for use of airport facilities and services, as well as identify the airlines' rights and privileges, which in some cases include the right to approve or disapprove any major proposed airport capital development projects (which the airlines are required to finance). Airport rates and charges programs, and the associated use fees are discussed in the next chapter.
- *Debt Financing, such as Revenue and General Obligation Bonds*—In the 1950s and early 1960s, General Obligation [GO] bonds were more widely used than revenue bonds for airport development. GO bonds are backed by the taxing authority of the issuer. Since the 1960's, airport revenue bonds

[27] This subsection was drawn largely from: National Civil Aviation Review Commission, *Airport Development Needs and Financing Options*, (Jun. 1997), retrieved from http://www.library.unt.edu/gpo/NCARC/airports/Default.htm.

have been the major financing mechanism for capital improvements at large, medium, and some small hub airports. These financial instruments pledge the airport's revenue streams to repay bondholders. Debt financing is discussed at length later in this chapter.

- *Airport Improvement Program* [AIP]—Since the agency's inception in 1958, the FAA has managed federal grants for airport planning and capital improvement projects. Until 1970, these grants were appropriated from the general fund; in that year, the Airport and Airway Trust Fund and the resulting grant program entitled the Airport Development Aid Program [ADAP] and Planning Grant Program [PGP] were established by Congress. Revenues for the trust fund are derived from passenger ticket taxes and other excise taxes. The Airport and Airway Improvement Act of 1982 combined the planning and funding mechanism into one program called the Airport Improvement Program or AIP.
- *Passenger Facility Charges* [PFCs]—In 1990, Congress removed the statutory prohibition on airports charging a per passenger enplanement fee. Funds from PFCs were intended to finance airport capital improvements, with emphasis placed on capacity, security and noise/environmental mitigation projects. PFCs are discussed later in this chapter.
- *State and Local Grants*—Aviation aid from state governments is considerable. State-imposed fuel taxes, aircraft registration fees are examples of revenue sources for state aviation programs. Sometimes state and local governments fund airports from their general fund or a special fund (support by tax and user revenues, respectively).

As mentioned in earlier chapters, the National Plan of Integrated Airport Systems [NPIAS] identifies the airports of significance to national air transportation for a period of approximately ten years. The Airport Capital Improvement Plan [ACIP] [28] is a document that is designed to provide the NPIAS funding details and is contained in a Federal Aviation Administration [FAA] on-line database referred to as NPIAS-ACIP. The ACIP "provides additional details including the anticipated sources of funds for specific NPIAS development ex-

---

[28] FAA, *Airport Capital Improvement Plan,* FAA Order 5100.39A. (Aug. 22, 2000).

pected to be undertaken within the next three to five years, and consider likely to be funded by the AIP.

Individual airport financial plans parallel and support the airport's master plan implementation schedule. These will vary according to the type and activity level of the airport and its ability to generate revenue. Low activity commercial service airports historically have operated without operating revenue surplus. Conversely, commercial service airports with high activity usually generate sufficient revenue to support revenue bond financing for capital improvements.

In the private sector, the capital budgeting process involves selection of new investment proposals, which will best add to the wealth of the firm. The financial operations of a modern airport are comparable with those of complex and highly diversified business enterprises. And, although historically there has been no overt profit-taking motive in governmental activities, there are concerns about capacity and service levels. As shown in Figure 12.1 (above), the debt service (in this case listed as "interest expense") for a large airport can mount into the millions of dollars. Capital investment must be just as carefully programmed here as it is in the corporate sector.

TIME VALUE OF MONEY

Forecasting is but one of the tools to be used in the mathematics of finance.[29] Although forecasting was discussed previously as a function of the master planning process, it is equally important and interrelated with all business financial decisions. Forecasting is a preliminary step in financial planning. All business and public administration decisions require forecasting to some degree. The attempt in forecasting, like other rational economic actions, is to reduce uncertainty about the future. Forecasts can be used as indicators of whether or not budgetary plans and financial decisions are consistent with the future and with the goals and objectives of the airport.

In financial planning it is helpful to have an understanding of the present versus future value of money, or what is referred to as the "time value use of money,"[30] and how to use the appropriate mathematical tools to calculate the time value of money.

---

[29] The authors appreciate the significant contributions to this section made by Javad Gorjidooz, Ph.D., Professor of Finance, Embry-Riddle Aeronautical University, Prescott, Ariz.

[30] Sometimes referred to as "opportunity cost," "economic cost," and/or "opportunity use of money."

The mechanics of finance are *compounding* and *discounting.* When the future value of a cash flow is calculated, the cash flow is being *compounded.* When the present value of a cash flow is calculated, the cash flow is being *discounted.* If one borrows money from a bank, the bank wants to be paid back something for the *use* of the money it lends. The amount charged by the bank is the *compound interest.* The bank uses compound interest to charge the borrower for the "use" of the money.

The principle of interest can be readily appreciated since most people are exposed daily to the notion of credit. What is not so easy to understand is the *opportunity use* of money. Basically, it is a function of whether money is more valuable now or later. If a choice had to be made between accepting a dollar now or taking it later, most people would choose to have the dollar now. This is because the dollar will earn a return, or can be invested in such a way that it will increase in value over time with the interest it can earn.

To demonstrate, suppose an airport manager would spend $200 per year over the next five years in maintenance of a ramp sweeper. If the manager were to buy a new one it would cost $500 for the sweeper, but only $40 per year in maintenance. Which option should the manager choose? It is not as simple as adding and comparing the totals for each alternative. In the first year alone, there is a difference of $300, which if tied up in equipment, cannot be used for any other purpose. The use of that $300 is worth something. It is worth its compound value. The decision needing to be made is whether the money could best be spent on the sweeper, saved, or alternatively invested.

Another way of observing compound value with which most people are familiar is to look at inflation. Suppose an airport manager is anticipating the need for a new ramp vehicle, which now costs $5,000. Also, assume that the current inflation rate is a high 15%. If inflation remains at 15%, the same vehicle will cost $5,750 next year. If the airport manager has $5,000 now, it is probably advisable to buy the vehicle, before the price goes up. Should the money be retained in a bank paying say 5%, it would be worth only $5,250 a year later. If the money were saved in a bank for a year rather than invested in the vehicle, the airport would lose $500 in opportunity use of money value. Thus, in this case saving the money until the vehicle is actually needed would be a poor investment decision.

In making decisions between alternative investment proposals, one must be able to evaluate the merits of each project. Discounting and compounding are the basis by which each investment can be put on an equal scale. Varying projects have different cash outlays and different revenue lives. By reducing each project through discounting to its present value, the earnings project can be evaluated in terms of its worth today. Table 12.1, "Time Flow Equations," shows various equations to use in solving present value and future value of a single amount or a stream of equal payments. Tables 12.2 through 12.5 present pre-calculated values of compounding and discounting of a single amount and an annuity of $1 at varying rates from 1% to 20% annual interest for periods of up to 20 years.

Table 12.1—TIME FLOW EQUATIONS

To Find	*Given*	*Use Table*	*Formula*
F	P	12.2	$F = P\,(1+r)^{n}$ $F = P\,(FVIF\ r, n)$
P	F	12.3	$P = \frac{F}{(1+r)^{n}}$ $P = F\,(PVIF\ r, n)$
F	D	12.4	$F = D\,\frac{[(1+r)^{n} - 1]}{r}$ $F = D\,(FVIFA\ r, n)$
D	F	12.4	$D = F\,\frac{r}{[(1+r)^{n} - 1]}$ $D = \frac{F}{(FVIFA\ r, n)}$

Table 12.1 (continued)

To Find	*Given*	*Use Table*	*Formula*
P	D	12.5	$P = D \dfrac{[1-(1+r)^{-n}]}{r}$ $P = D\,(PVIFA\ r, n)$
D	P	12.5	$D = P \dfrac{r}{[1-(1+r)^{-n}]}$ $D = \dfrac{P}{(PVIFA\ r, n)}$
Present value of a perpetual annuity where payments continue forever is calculated as follows:			
P	D and r	N/A	$P = \dfrac{D}{r}$

Where:

P = Present value or worth
F = Future value or worth
r = Interest rate
n = Number of time periods (years)
D = Uniform series of payments, benefits or receipts taking place at year end
(FVIF r, n)* = Future value interest factor at the rate of r for period of n
(PVIF r, n)* = Present value interest factor at the rate of r for period of n
(FVIFA r, n)* = Future value interest factor of annuity at the rate of r for period of n
(PVIF r, n)* = Present value interest factor of annuity at the rate of r for period of n

* Interest factors are pre-calculated in Tables 12.2 through 12.5

Table 12.2—FUTURE VALUE OF $1 AT THE END OF n PERIODS

n	1%	2%	3%	4%	5%	6%	7%	8%	9%	10%	11%	12%	13%	14%	15%	16%	17%	18%	19%	20%
1	1.010	1.020	1.030	1.041	1.051	1.062	1.072	1.083	1.094	1.105	1.116	1.127	1.138	1.149	1.161	1.173	1.184	1.196	1.208	1.220
2	1.020	1.040	1.061	1.082	1.104	1.126	1.149	1.172	1.195	1.219	1.243	1.268	1.294	1.319	1.346	1.373	1.400	1.428	1.457	1.486
3	1.030	1.061	1.093	1.126	1.159	1.194	1.230	1.267	1.305	1.344	1.384	1.426	1.469	1.513	1.558	1.605	1.653	1.702	1.753	1.806
4	1.040	1.082	1.125	1.170	1.217	1.265	1.316	1.369	1.423	1.480	1.539	1.601	1.665	1.732	1.801	1.873	1.948	2.026	2.107	2.191
5	1.050	1.102	1.158	1.216	1.276	1.340	1.407	1.477	1.551	1.629	1.710	1.796	1.886	1.980	2.079	2.183	2.292	2.407	2.527	2.653
6	1.060	1.124	1.191	1.262	1.338	1.419	1.504	1.594	1.689	1.791	1.898	2.012	2.133	2.261	2.397	2.540	2.693	2.854	3.026	3.207
7	1.070	1.145	1.225	1.311	1.403	1.501	1.606	1.718	1.838	1.967	2.105	2.252	2.410	2.579	2.759	2.952	3.159	3.380	3.616	3.870
8	1.080	1.166	1.260	1.360	1.469	1.587	1.714	1.851	1.999	2.159	2.332	2.518	2.720	2.937	3.172	3.426	3.700	3.996	4.316	4.661
9	1.090	1.188	1.295	1.412	1.539	1.677	1.828	1.993	2.172	2.367	2.580	2.813	3.066	3.342	3.642	3.970	4.328	4.717	5.142	5.604
10	1.100	1.210	1.331	1.464	1.611	1.772	1.949	2.144	2.358	2.594	2.853	3.138	3.452	3.797	4.177	4.595	5.054	5.560	6.116	6.727
11	1.110	1.232	1.368	1.518	1.685	1.870	2.076	2.305	2.558	2.839	3.152	3.498	3.883	4.310	4.785	5.311	5.895	6.543	7.263	8.062
12	1.120	1.254	1.405	1.574	1.762	1.974	2.211	2.476	2.773	3.106	3.479	3.896	4.363	4.887	5.474	6.130	6.866	7.690	8.613	9.646
13	1.130	1.277	1.443	1.630	1.842	2.082	2.353	2.658	3.004	3.395	3.836	4.334	4.898	5.535	6.254	7.067	7.986	9.024	10.197	11.523
14	1.140	1.300	1.482	1.689	1.925	2.195	2.502	2.853	3.252	3.707	4.226	4.818	5.492	6.261	7.138	8.137	9.276	10.575	12.055	13.743
15	1.150	1.322	1.521	1.749	2.011	2.313	2.660	3.059	3.518	4.046	4.652	5.350	6.153	7.076	8.137	9.358	10.761	12.375	14.232	16.366
16	1.160	1.346	1.561	1.811	2.100	2.436	2.826	3.278	3.803	4.411	5.117	5.936	6.886	7.987	9.265	10.748	12.468	14.462	16.776	19.461
17	1.170	1.369	1.602	1.874	2.192	2.565	3.001	3.511	4.108	4.807	5.624	6.580	7.699	9.007	10.539	12.330	14.426	16.879	19.748	23.105
18	1.180	1.392	1.643	1.939	2.288	2.700	3.185	3.759	4.435	5.234	6.176	7.288	8.599	10.147	11.974	14.129	16.672	19.673	23.214	27.393
19	1.190	1.416	1.685	2.005	2.386	2.840	3.379	4.021	4.785	5.695	6.777	8.064	9.596	11.420	13.589	16.171	19.244	22.900	27.251	32.429
20	1.200	1.440	1.728	2.074	2.488	2.986	3.583	4.300	5.160	6.192	7.430	8.916	10.699	12.839	15.407	18.488	22.186	26.623	31.948	38.337

Table 12.3—PRESENT VALUE OF $1, RECEIVED IN n PERIODS

n	1%	2%	3%	4%	5%	6%	7%	8%	9%	10%	11%	12%	13%	14%	15%	16%	17%	18%	19%	20%
1	0.990	0.980	0.971	0.961	0.951	0.942	0.933	0.923	0.914	0.905	0.896	0.887	0.879	0.870	0.861	0.853	0.844	0.836	0.828	0.820
2	0.980	0.961	0.942	0.924	0.906	0.888	0.871	0.853	0.837	0.820	0.804	0.789	0.773	0.758	0.743	0.728	0.714	0.700	0.686	0.673
3	0.971	0.943	0.915	0.888	0.863	0.837	0.813	0.789	0.766	0.744	0.722	0.701	0.681	0.661	0.642	0.623	0.605	0.587	0.570	0.554
4	0.962	0.925	0.889	0.855	0.822	0.790	0.760	0.731	0.703	0.676	0.650	0.625	0.601	0.577	0.555	0.534	0.513	0.494	0.475	0.456
5	0.952	0.907	0.864	0.823	0.784	0.746	0.711	0.677	0.645	0.614	0.585	0.557	0.530	0.505	0.481	0.458	0.436	0.416	0.396	0.377
6	0.943	0.890	0.840	0.792	0.747	0.705	0.665	0.627	0.592	0.558	0.527	0.497	0.469	0.442	0.417	0.394	0.371	0.350	0.331	0.312
7	0.935	0.873	0.816	0.763	0.713	0.666	0.623	0.582	0.544	0.508	0.475	0.444	0.415	0.388	0.362	0.339	0.317	0.296	0.277	0.258
8	0.926	0.857	0.794	0.735	0.681	0.630	0.583	0.540	0.500	0.463	0.429	0.397	0.368	0.340	0.315	0.292	0.270	0.250	0.232	0.215
9	0.917	0.842	0.772	0.708	0.650	0.596	0.547	0.502	0.460	0.422	0.388	0.356	0.326	0.299	0.275	0.252	0.231	0.212	0.194	0.178
10	0.909	0.826	0.751	0.683	0.621	0.564	0.513	0.467	0.424	0.386	0.350	0.319	0.290	0.263	0.239	0.218	0.198	0.180	0.164	0.149
11	0.901	0.812	0.731	0.659	0.593	0.535	0.482	0.434	0.391	0.352	0.317	0.286	0.258	0.232	0.209	0.188	0.170	0.153	0.138	0.124
12	0.893	0.797	0.712	0.636	0.567	0.507	0.452	0.404	0.361	0.322	0.287	0.257	0.229	0.205	0.183	0.163	0.146	0.130	0.116	0.104
13	0.885	0.783	0.693	0.613	0.543	0.480	0.425	0.376	0.333	0.295	0.261	0.231	0.204	0.181	0.160	0.141	0.125	0.111	0.098	0.087
14	0.877	0.769	0.675	0.592	0.519	0.456	0.400	0.351	0.308	0.270	0.237	0.208	0.182	0.160	0.140	0.123	0.108	0.095	0.083	0.073
15	0.870	0.756	0.658	0.572	0.497	0.432	0.376	0.327	0.284	0.247	0.215	0.187	0.163	0.141	0.123	0.107	0.093	0.081	0.070	0.061
16	0.862	0.743	0.641	0.551	0.476	0.410	0.354	0.305	0.263	0.227	0.195	0.168	0.145	0.125	0.108	0.093	0.080	0.069	0.060	0.051
17	0.855	0.731	0.624	0.534	0.456	0.390	0.333	0.285	0.243	0.208	0.178	0.152	0.130	0.111	0.095	0.081	0.069	0.059	0.051	0.043
18	0.847	0.718	0.609	0.516	0.437	0.370	0.314	0.266	0.225	0.191	0.162	0.137	0.116	0.099	0.084	0.071	0.060	0.051	0.043	0.037
19	0.840	0.706	0.593	0.499	0.419	0.352	0.296	0.249	0.209	0.176	0.148	0.124	0.104	0.088	0.074	0.062	0.052	0.044	0.037	0.031
20	0.833	0.694	0.579	0.482	0.402	0.335	0.279	0.233	0.194	0.162	0.135	0.112	0.093	0.078	0.065	0.054	0.045	0.038	0.031	0.026

Table 12.4—FUTURE VALUE OF $1 ANNUITY FOR n PERIODS

n	1%	2%	3%	4%	5%	6%	7%	8%	9%	10%	11%	12%	13%	14%	15%	16%	17%	18%	19%	20%
1	1.0	2.010	3.030	4.060	5.101	6.152	7.214	8.286	9.368	10.462	11.567	12.682	13.809	14.947	16.097	17.258	18.430	19.614	20.811	22.019
2	1.0	2.020	3.060	4.122	5.204	6.308	7.434	8.583	9.755	10.950	12.169	13.412	14.680	15.974	17.293	18.639	20.012	21.412	22.840	24.297
3	1.0	2.030	3.091	4.184	5.309	6.468	7.662	8.892	10.159	11.464	12.808	14.192	15.618	17.086	18.599	20.157	21.761	23.414	25.117	26.870
4	1.0	2.040	3.122	4.246	5.416	6.633	7.898	9.214	10.583	12.006	13.486	15.026	16.627	18.292	20.023	21.824	23.697	25.645	27.671	29.778
5	1.0	2.050	3.152	4.310	5.526	6.802	8.142	9.549	11.027	12.578	14.207	15.917	17.713	19.598	21.578	23.657	25.840	28.132	30.539	33.066
6	1.0	2.060	3.184	4.375	5.637	6.975	8.394	9.897	11.491	13.181	14.972	16.870	18.882	21.015	23.276	25.672	28.213	30.905	33.760	36.785
7	1.0	2.070	3.215	4.440	5.751	7.153	8.654	10.260	11.978	13.816	15.784	17.888	20.141	22.550	25.129	27.888	30.840	33.999	37.379	40.995
8	1.0	2.080	3.246	4.506	5.867	7.336	8.923	10.637	12.488	14.487	16.645	18.977	21.495	24.215	27.152	30.324	33.750	37.450	41.446	45.762
9	1.0	2.090	3.278	4.573	5.985	7.523	9.200	11.028	13.021	15.193	17.560	20.141	22.953	26.019	29.361	33.003	36.973	41.301	46.018	51.159
10	1.0	2.100	3.310	1.641	6.105	7.716	9.487	11.436	13.579	15.937	18.531	21.384	24.523	27.975	31.772	35.949	40.544	45.599	51.158	57.274
11	1.0	2.110	3.342	4.710	6.228	7.913	9.783	11.859	14.164	16.722	19.561	22.713	26.211	30.095	34.405	39.190	44.500	50.396	56.939	64.202
12	1.0	2.120	3.374	4.779	6.353	8.115	10.089	12.300	14.776	17.549	20.655	24.133	28.029	32.392	37.280	42.753	48.883	55.749	63.439	72.052
13	1.0	2.130	3.407	4.850	6.480	8.323	10.405	12.757	15.416	18.420	21.814	25.650	29.984	34.882	40.417	46.671	53.738	61.724	70.748	80.496
14	1.0	2.140	3.440	4.921	6.610	8.535	10.730	13.233	16.085	19.337	23.044	27.271	32.088	37.581	43.842	50.980	59.117	68.393	78.968	91.024
15	1.0	2.150	3.472	4.993	6.742	8.754	11.067	13.727	16.786	20.304	24.349	29.001	34.352	40.504	47.580	55.717	65.075	75.836	88.211	102.443
16	1.0	2.160	3.506	5.066	6.877	8.977	11.414	14.240	17.518	21.321	25.733	30.850	36.786	43.672	51.659	60.925	71.673	84.140	98.603	115.379
17	1.0	2.170	3.539	5.141	7.014	9.207	11.772	14.773	18.285	22.393	37.200	32.824	39.404	47.102	56.109	66.648	78.978	93.404	110.283	130.031
18	1.0	2.180	3.572	5.215	7.154	9.442	12.141	15.327	19.086	23.521	28.755	34.931	42.218	50.818	60.964	72.938	87.067	103.739	123.412	146.626
19	1.0	2.190	3.606	5.291	7.297	9.683	12.523	15.902	19.923	24.709	30.403	37.180	45.244	54.841	66.260	79.850	96.021	115.265	138.165	165.417
20	1.0	2.200	3.640	5.368	7.442	9.930	12.916	16.499	20.799	25.959	32.150	39.580	48.496	59.196	72.035	87.442	105.930	128.116	154.739	186.687

Table 12.5—PRESENT VALUE OF $1 ANNUITY FOR n PERIODS

n	1%	2%	3%	4%	5%	6%	7%	8%	9%	10%	11%	12%	13%	14%	15%	16%	17%	18%	19%	20%
1	0.990	1.970	2.941	3.902	4.853	5.795	6.728	7.652	8.566	9.471	10.368	11.255	12.134	13.004	13.865	14.718	15.562	16.398	17.226	18.046
2	0.980	1.942	2.884	3.808	4.713	5.601	6.472	7.326	8.162	8.983	9.787	10.575	11.348	12.106	12.849	13.578	14.292	14.992	15.679	16.352
3	0.971	1.913	2.829	3.717	4.580	5.417	6.230	7.020	7.786	8.530	9.253	9.954	10.635	11.296	11.938	12.561	13.166	13.754	14.324	14.878
4	0.962	1.886	2.775	3.630	4.452	5.242	6.002	6.733	7.435	8.111	8.760	9.385	9.986	10.563	11.118	11.652	12.166	12.659	13.134	13.590
5	0.952	1.859	2.723	3.546	4.329	5.076	5.786	6.463	7.108	7.722	8.306	8.863	9.394	9.899	10.380	10.838	11.274	11.690	12.085	12.462
6	0.943	1.833	2.673	3.465	4.212	4.917	5.582	6.210	6.802	7.360	7.887	8.384	8.853	9.295	9.712	10.106	10.477	10.828	11.158	11.470
7	0.935	1.808	2.624	3.387	4.100	4.767	5.389	5.971	6.515	7.024	7.499	7.943	8.358	8.746	9.108	9.447	9.763	10.059	10.336	10.594
8	0.926	1.783	2.577	3.312	3.993	4.623	5.206	5.747	6.247	6.710	7.139	7.536	7.904	8.244	8.560	8.851	9.122	9.372	9.604	9.818
9	0.917	1.759	2.531	3.240	3.890	4.486	5.033	5.535	5.995	6.418	6.805	7.161	7.487	7.786	8.061	8.313	8.544	8.756	8.950	9.129
10	0.909	1.736	2.487	3.170	3.791	4.355	4.868	5.335	5.759	6.145	6.495	6.814	7.103	7.367	7.606	7.824	8.022	8.201	8.365	8.514
11	0.901	1.713	2.444	3.102	3.696	4.231	4.712	5.146	5.537	5.889	6.207	6.492	6.750	6.982	7.191	7.379	7.549	7.702	7.839	7.963
12	0.893	1.690	2.402	3.037	3.605	4.111	4.564	4.968	5.328	5.650	5.938	6.194	6.424	6.628	6.811	6.974	7.120	7.250	7.366	7.469
13	0.885	1.668	2.361	2.974	3.517	3.998	4.423	4.799	5.132	5.426	5.687	5.918	6.122	6.303	6.462	6.604	6.729	6.840	6.938	7.025
14	0.877	1.647	2.322	2.914	3.433	3.889	4.288	4.639	4.946	5.216	5.453	5.660	5.842	6.002	6.142	6.265	6.373	6.467	6.550	6.623
15	0.870	1.626	2.283	2.855	3.352	3.784	4.160	4.487	4.772	5.019	5.234	5.421	5.583	5.724	5.847	5.954	6.047	6.128	6.198	6.259
16	0.862	1.605	2.246	2.798	3.274	3.685	4.039	4.344	4.607	4.833	5.029	5.197	5.342	5.468	5.575	5.669	5.749	5.818	5.877	5.929
17	0.855	1.585	2.210	2.743	3.199	3.589	3.922	4.207	4.451	4.659	4.836	4.988	5.118	5.229	5.324	5.405	5.474	5.534	5.585	5.628
18	0.847	1.566	2.174	2.690	3.127	3.498	3.812	4.078	4.303	4.494	4.656	4.793	4.910	5.008	5.092	5.162	5.222	5.273	5.316	5.353
19	0.840	1.547	2.140	2.639	3.058	3.410	3.706	3.954	4.163	4.339	4.487	4.611	4.715	4.802	4.876	4.938	4.990	5.033	5.070	5.101
20	0.833	1.528	2.106	2.589	2.991	3.326	3.605	3.837	4.031	4.192	4.327	4.439	4.533	4.611	4.675	4.730	4.775	4.812	4.843	4.870

Using Tables 12.1 through 12.5, the following are examples of how to solve time value of money problems. Assume interest at 4% compounded annually in all of the problems.

TIME FLOW EXAMPLE A

\$100 at the end of each year for thirteen years will repay a present debt of how much?

$$P = D \frac{[1 - (1+r)^{-n}]}{r}$$

$$P = 100 \frac{[1 - 0.6006]}{.04}$$

$$P = 100 \frac{[0.3994]}{.04}$$

$$P = 100 \ (9.985)$$

$$P = \$998.5$$

Using Table 12.5,

P = D (PVIFA 4%, 13)

P = \$100 (9.986)

P = \$998.6

Note: Answers to problems solved using the tables may differ slightly, due to rounding of the pre-calculated interest factors.

TIME FLOW EXAMPLE B

A payment of how much now is acceptable in place of a payment of $1,500 eighteen years hence?

$$P = \frac{F}{(1+r)^n}$$

$$P = \frac{1500}{2.028}$$

$P = \$740.45$

Using Table 12.3,

P = F (PVIF 4%, 18)

P = $1,500 (0.494)

P = $741

Note: Answers to problems solved using the tables may differ slightly, due to rounding of the pre-calculated interest factors.

TIME FLOW EXAMPLE C

A present investment of $10,000 will secure a perpetual income of how much per year?

$$P = \frac{D}{r}$$

D = P (r) = $10,000 (.04) = $400

TIME FLOW EXAMPLE D.1

An annual end-of-year investment of how much is required to provide \$22,000 at the end of twenty years?

$$D = F \frac{r}{[(1+r)^n - 1]}$$

$$D = 22{,}000 \frac{.04}{[2.191 - 1]}$$

$$D = 22{,}000 \frac{.04}{1.191}$$

$$D = 22{,}000\ (.03358)$$

$$D = \$738.76$$

Using Table 12.4,

D = F / (FVIFA 4%, 20)

P = \$22,000/ (29.778)

P = \$738.80

Note: Answers to problems solved using the tables may differ slightly, due to rounding of the pre-calculated interest factors.

TIME FLOW EXAMPLE D.2

In the event a period of time greater than that listed in the interest tables is desired, the interest rate 4% may be derived by compounding n years $(1+ r)^{n}$ using the appropriate combination of years. Using the same situation as above, but substituting thirty years for twenty years, the solution looks like this:

$$D = F \frac{[\quad r \quad]}{[(1+r)^{n} - 1]}$$

$$D = 22{,}000 \frac{[\quad .04 \quad]}{[(1.04)^{20}\,(1.04)^{10} - 1]}$$

$$D = 22{,}000 \frac{[\quad .04 \quad]}{[(2.19)\,(1.480) - 1]}$$

$$D = 22{,}000 \frac{[\ .04\ ]}{[3.243 - 1]}$$

$$D = 22{,}000 \frac{[\ .04\ ]}{[2.243]}$$

$$D = 22{,}000\ [.01783]$$

$$D = \$392.26$$

TIME FLOW EXAMPLE E.1

The future worth of $5,000 twenty years hence is how much?

$F = P(1+r)^n$

$F = 5{,}000\ (2.191)$

$F = \$10{,}955$

Using Table 12.2,

F = P (FVIF 4%, 20)

F = $5,000 (2.191)

F = $10,955

Note: Answers to problems solved using the tables may differ slightly, due to rounding of the pre-calculated interest factors.

TIME FLOW EXAMPLE E.2

As in Example E.1, suppose the period is longer than 20 years, which is the maximum shown on the table? If the period were 37 years, the solution would be:

$F = P(1+r)^n$

$F = 5{,}000\ (1.04)^{17}\ (1.04)^{20}$

$F = 5{,}000\ (1.948)\ (2.191)$

$F = 5{,}000\ (4.268)$

$F = \$21{,}340$

Using Table 12.2,

F = P (FVIF 4%, 20) (FVIF 4%, 17)

F = $5,000 (2.191) (1.948)

F = $21,340

Note: Answers to problems solved using the tables may differ slightly, due to rounding of the pre-calculated interest factors.

ACCOUNTING

Accounting is not just bookkeeping; it is the *reporting* function of the continuing budget cycle. Keeping books amounts to a detailed recording of information. “Accounting,” on the other hand, is the total process of collecting, analyzing, and interpreting data. Accounting produces data necessary for analysis. The results help management make decisions and formulate policy.

Accounting systems are tailored to the needs of the airport and will vary from airport to airport, not only as a function of airport size, but also according to the nature of the supporting government’s accounting system. The accounting system for a small municipal airport will most likely be inadequate for larger airports.

Airports in the U.S. are normally financed internally in one of three ways, two of which usually apply to county and municipal airports, and the third is almost exclusively applicable to authorities and special districts. County and municipal airports are either set up as a separate airport fund, or are included as a line item within the *general fund account*. Financial support is drawn from the general fund budget. A special district (or authority) normally has its own separate accounting system.

To fully account for all revenues and expenses, and to adequately report profitability, a separate airport accounting system may be necessary. However when airports are small it is oftentimes less than cost-effective to establish a separate airport account. Moreover, unless airport revenues can fully cover expenses, it may be politically advantageous to keep the airport budget within the general fund, from which the airport must be subsidized. Local authorities would prefer not having to report deficit spending on what many people may consider as a facility operated for a special interest group. As a result, smaller, non-profitable airports are usually part of the general fund; as are many other services provided by a county or municipality such as parks, beaches and other recreational and service activities.

In general fund accounts, there still is an attempt to accurately portray the true cost of the airport's operation, but many of the actual costs get buried in the budgets of supporting departments, and therefore show up as an expense for those departments rather than an airport expense. Services such as accounting, secretarial help, maintenance, and administration (particularly from upper management such as the city manager or county administrator) are often not included in the airport's operating budget, because general fund operations may or may not cost-apply their services to each other. Incidental items like office supplies and photocopy services may also be obtained at no applied cost to the airport. The airport may be insured under the local government's blanket coverage, and thus will not have to account for payment of the premium other than perhaps for an aviation rider to cover exposure for aviation-related risks beyond the normal coverage limits. Countless expenses can get lost in the shuffle, making it nearly impossible to measure the true economic efficiency of the airport's operation.

As noted above, there may be political reasons for retaining the airport within the general fund account. As indicated previously, most airports operate at a net loss. Assuming the airport's operating budget is a sub-account of the city or county general fund, if airport expenses are kept within the operating budget, then airport expenses not included in the operating budget will be absorbed by the general fund. Thus, expenses over and above the airport's operating budget are not readily apparent. Expenses (representing a net loss) which are "out of sight" are "out of mind," and, therefore, are subject to less scrutiny by the public. Not only are the net losses hidden, but it has not been uncommon for an airport manager to claim a "profit" for having an operating budget surplus at the end of the year, even though the actual fiscal costs may have well exceeded the revenues when the capital (or non-operating) costs were included.

The general fund is used to account for the general, overall operations of the local government. Short of establishing a special district, and aside from the general fund, one of several types of accounts may be established by local governments to segregate activities for cost purposes:

- *Special revenue funds* collected from special revenue sources and set apart for special purposes;
- *Debt service funds* (or "sinking fund") for repayment of principal and interest on long-term debts;
- *Capital project funds* for development and construction programs;
- *Trust and agency funds* for accounts held in trust for others, donations for example;
- *Special assessment funds* to account for particular improvements or services such as street improvements or water and sewer for select beneficiaries;
- *Intra-governmental service funds* for transactions within the government such as general stores, garage, or central duplicating; and
- *Enterprise funds* (or accounts) for businesslike operations.

The separate accounting system most applicable to airports is the *enterprise fund.* The characteristics of a public service "enterprise" are such that services are rendered primarily to the general public. Charges made are intended to recover the cost of providing the service. And the services rendered are those that have been identified with the public service enterprise expenditure function (i.e., airport and other aviation-related services).

No matter which type of accounting system used, and although not always practical to achieve, an important principle for which the airport manager should strive is *cost accounting.* Cost accounting, which is discussed in more detail in the next chapter, is the allocation of costs to the major associated cost areas. Cost accounting (or "cost allocation") identifies revenues that can be used to offset the costs of the principal expense areas. The major areas are basically four:

- The landing area(s);
- The terminal(s);
- Hangar area(s); and
- Other non-aviation-related areas (e.g. industrial sites and business centers).

In allocating costs, it is important to apply costs and revenues not only by major area, but by user as well. Nothing will get an airport manager into more trouble with the airport community than to intentionally assess charges to one area in order to pay for costs in another, particularly if the users are general aviation versus air carrier. The two are often like "oil and water," and great care must be exercised in deriving revenues from the general aviation sector to be used to cover air carrier related expenses. The same is true for air carrier revenues applied to general aviation. The principles and application of cost allocation are discussed in more detail in the next chapter.

DEBT FINANCING

Key public airports are a part of the National Plan of Integrated Airport Systems, and as such are eligible for federal and state aid, the aggregate of which can amount to over 90% funding through the use of other than local tax monies. There are programs airports can undertake that would be otherwise impossible without outside help. However, federal and state grants do not necessarily follow a rational pattern of need. Certain items are eligible for aid while others are not. At best, the airport sponsor must provide a minimum of 10% of the capital improvement cost. At worst, paying for the project may be entirely the responsibility of the airport.

Traditionally, airport financing has been accomplished through the use of municipal bonds, which are interest-bearing certificates of public indebtedness. [31] The four most common types of municipal bonds are *general obligation bonds, revenue bonds, commercial paper* and *private activity bonds*[32]. When a public entity needs to borrow money, it may do so from an investment house willing to purchase its bond offer. The bond is the written promise of the governmental agency to pay a specified sum of money, at specified dates in the future, together with periodic interest at a specific rate.

---

[31] Information about bonds throughout this section were largely extracted from two sources: Standard & Poor's, *Learning Library—Municipal Bonds*, retrieved from www.axaonline.com/rs/axa/print/5062_print.html (Oct. 2005) and the National Federation of Municipal Analysts, *Recommended Best Practices in Disclosure for Airport Debt*; retrieved from www.nfma.org/disclosure/rbp_airport.pdf (May 2004).

[32] Standard & Poor's, *Learning Library—Municipal Bonds*, retrieved from www.axaonline.com/rs/axa/print/5062_print.html (Oct. 2005), at 1.

Municipal bonds differ from corporate (private sector) bonds in a number of ways. First, the interest paid on municipal issues is usually exempt from federal taxes and sometimes state and local taxes as well, hence they are often referred to as "tax-exempt" bonds. The second difference is in how municipal bonds are retired, relative to corporate bonds. "Corporate bonds are usually issued with 'term' maturities, but many municipal bonds are issued with 'serial' maturities (or several maturity dates). A portion of the principal matures with each maturity date until the entire principal has been paid off."[33]

In addition, longer-term "municipals," as they are called, may have a *call provision* allowing the issuer to retire the bond early (on the call date), especially if the prevailing interest rate is below the bond's *coupon* (original redemption) date. Usually corporate bonds are issued in $1,000 amounts on the over-the-counter-market and at the exchanges. Municipals are generally issued in $5,000 amounts and are only available in the over-the-counter market.[34]

Of great importance to airports and investors alike is whether the bond is issued as a *private purpose* (or private activity) bond. "If the municipal bond is a 'private purchase' bond, the income is taxable unless specifically exempted," making them less desirable.[35] Since more than 80% of the bonds that have been issued for airport capital projects are categorized as private-activity bonds, airports would like to see reform in this area. ACI-NA explains,

> *While airports are owned and operated by state and local governments and serve a vital public purpose [most of their bonds are] "private activity" bonds [and] interest on the bonds is subject to the Alternative Minimum Tax, which raises the cost of borrowing. [The] private activity [classification] ignores the public benefits . . . Reform would also allow airports to "refund" or refinance their bonds, taking advantage of lower interest rates.*[36]

---

[33] *Id.*

[34] *Id.*

[35] *Id.*

[36] Airport Council International-North America, *ACI-NA Announces Principles for FAA Reauthorization*, retrieved from http://www.aci-na.org/asp/pressdetail.asp?art=1491 (Feb. 5, 2007).

Interest rates for state and local government agencies' bonds are customarily very low when compared to other commercial loans. Because bonds and other municipal securities are exempt from federal income taxation, they are inviting to investors as a tax shelter. The investor may realize lower per annum return of marginally 2% to 4% from the bond, and the money saved by not paying taxes on it may be substantially above the amount returned from alternative investments.

General Obligation, or GO bonds are municipal bonds that are secured by the general taxing power of the local government. This means that if necessary general taxes could be raised to meet the bond obligation. General obligation bonds are known as "full faith and credit" bonds, because there is an absolute requirement upon the issuer to stand behind them. Although not necessarily so, general obligation bonds are usually payable from *ad valorem* (according to value) property taxes and other general revenue. They are further guaranteed indirectly by the limitations placed upon total general obligation indebtedness, which a local government may have outstanding. Almost universally the debt cannot exceed a given percentage—for example, 5% or 10%—of the valuation of taxable property. Because of their extremely low risk, general obligation bonds are normally marketable at lower interest rates than are revenue bonds.[37]

Larger airports, however, tend not to rely upon general obligation financing. Local governments typically reserve such bonds for other public programs, where the users cannot be identified, and for activities that cannot generate sufficient revenues to cover the costs of capital indebtedness. Additionally, since obligation bonding places pressures on the local government's debt limit and on its credit rating, qualified airports generally use revenue bonding. Revenue bond obligations are backed by the revenues earned by the public (airport) enterprise. Revenue bonds have limited liability and do not constitute a general obligation backed by the government's taxing power. Where GO bonds require voter approval, revenue bonds do not.

The least expensive way to finance a public improvement is through GO bonds, but for several reasons—chief among them what many are calling unrealistic debt ceilings—communities are forced to look for other ways of financing; particularly for special use activities like airports. Where the project to be financed does not benefit all

[37] National Federation of Municipal Analysts, *Recommended Best Practices in Disclosure for Airport Debt*; retrieved from www.nfma.org/disclosure/rbp_airport.pdf (May 2004).

citizens equally, the revenue bond is particularly attractive because it has an underlying "user pays" philosophy. However, revenue bonding is not available to all airports that would seek it. The issuer of the bond must be able to demonstrate the enterprise's ability to generate sufficient funds to pay back the loan. Thus, an airport's financial strength, and its ability to be self-sustaining, is best measured through its success in attracting *private investment capital.*

Three forms of revenue bonds applicable to airports are *General Airport Revenue Bonds* [GARBs], *passenger facility charge* supported bonds, and *special facility revenue bonds*. The revenue stream for each form differs. GARBs are backed by the airport's entire revenue stream, while PFC-supported bonds rely on anticipated revenues from FAA-approved PFCs. Special facility revenue bonds are "tax exempt bonds secured solely by the financing payments of a corporate borrower, most typically an airline..."[38]and are considered a "hybrid area of airport finance that incorporates elements of project finance and corporate debt analysis." Those who assess credit risk and quality of a municipal debt issue require full disclosure of both financial and operating information at the subject airport.[39]

To finance a project designed to generate income used to pay interest and retire principal, entails analysis of earnings, past or future, compared with bond performance requirements, which oftentimes are too stringent for smaller airports to meet. Revenue bonding has been used for many years to finance development at large, medium, and some small-hub airports able to demonstrate an adequate earnings record, stable air service, and the potential for sustained future growth necessary to secure user-charge type loans.

Most small hubs, non-hubs and the preponderance of general aviation airports usually do not have the substantial earnings history sought by the investment houses. Added to the smaller airports' dilemma are the results of deregulation and reduced or eliminated service by the major air carriers. Assurance of stability in air service is another factor that investors and rating agencies look for in considering the merits of a bond offering. During the regulatory years, when airlines and airports were "wedded" to each other by the Civil Aeronautics Board [CAB], airport executives were counseled to obtain *residual* agreements or modified *compensatory* agreements, since

---

[38] *Id.*
[39] *Id.*

such provisions made the lender's' jobs easier.[40] But while this may have been the case for many years, the market (i.e., investors and rating agencies) has come to understand that the *inherent demand* for air traffic is the real driving force behind an airport's credit.[41]

Given their disadvantaged situation smaller airports have improved their bonding potential through a variety of alternative arrangements:

- One alternative might be *bond insurance*. By insuring the principal and interest payment, the airport's rating may be improved and thereby made more attractive to investors.
- Another alternative is the *self-liquidating general obligation bond*. It may be advantageous for certain airport users to repay the bond indebtedness through increased airport rates earmarked for debt-service repayment since bonds may be secured at lower interest rates than other financing arrangements. By demonstrating how the bonds can be repaid, voters may be convinced to support a general bond campaign. Additionally, the self-liquidating debt may be excluded from the net community debt due to the bond's self-sustaining nature.
- The *combined revenue/obligation bond* (or "double-barrel bond") is another alternative. These bonds are secured by a pledge of back-up tax revenues to meet principal and interest requirements in case airport revenues are insufficient.
- *Sponsoring governments cooperative agreements* are yet another alternative. In order to provide additional bonding security nearby governments may agree to deposit money into a reserve fund. Thus, in an emergency, where the airport is unable to cover the debt payment, monies may be used from the reserve fund for that purpose. The cooperative governments would then replenish the reserve fund.
- Another alternative is the *gross revenue pledge with back-up taxing authority*. In situations where small airports (or their supporting local governments) have the legal capability to obtain tax support for airport operations, the bondholders may be given the first claim against airport revenues. If necessary *ad*

---

[40] *See* George Doughty, *Everyone's Problem*, Airport Magazine (Nov./Dec. 1996).

[41] Michael Lexton, Manageing Director, Lehman Brothers, *Airport Financing*, a letter to the editor, Airport Magazine (May/Jun. 1997), at 34-35.

valorem taxes may be levied to pay for operations and maintenance expenses.

- A *limited revenue pledge bond* is an arrangement similar to a self-liquidating general obligation bond in that the bonding is secured against revenues pledged by one or more airport tenant operator. For example, where concessionaires will operate a terminal building, the terminal could be constructed and financed through revenue bonding, and secured by contractual revenue guarantees. There are similarities between this and the special facility bond discussed earlier, although limited revenue pledge has a GO bond backing.
- *Swap agreements* (or "swaptions") may be tied to current and future bond issues. While they may subject the airport to risk, these agreements may also save the airport millions of dollars, and are considered an innovative way to manage debt.[42] For example, Las Vegas McCarran has more than twenty swap agreements tied to current bond issues.

All of the financing ramifications listed above still represent one or a combination of the two basic types of municipal (general obligation and revenue) bonds available, but each demonstrates how the marketability of a small airport bond issue might be improved. Largely the bond rating assigned to the debtor determines the marketability of a bond. A bond rating is a judgment of the investment quality of a long-term obligation and is based upon a likelihood the debtor will be able to repay the loan. Bond ratings are simple, easy to understand classifications of credit risks, based on four primary factors: economy, debt, finances, and administration/management strategies.[43]

There are three principal bond-rating agencies: *Moody's Investors Service*, *Standard and Poor's Corporation* and *Fitch Ratings*. Each company assigns a letter grade to bonds to reflect in its judgment the investment quality of the bonds. The long-term obligation issuer credit rating scales for these entitles are shown in Table 12.6, "Bond Rating Scales."

---

[42] A rate swap agreement gives the buyer the right to pay (receive) a fixed rate on a given date and receive (pay) a floating rate index. For an up front premium, it is designed to give the holder the benefit of an agreed upon strike rate (the level at which the agreement is entered) if the market rates are higher.

[43] Moody's Investors Service, Inc, *Moody's Rating Symbols and Definitions*, (Aug. 2003), retrieved from www.moodysaia.com.

Table 12.6—BOND RATING SCALES

Moody's Investors Service

Rating	*Description*
Aaa	Best Quality/Smallest Risk
Aa*	High Quality
A	Upper Medium Grade
Baa	Medium Grade
Ba	Speculative Elements
B	Lack Desirable Investment Characteristics
Caa	Poor Standing
Ca	Highly Speculative
C	Extremely Poor

Standard and Poor's Corporation

Rating	*Description*
AAA	"Extremely Strong" - Highest Rating
AA*	"Very Strong" - High Rating
A	"Strong" - Low High Rating
BBB	"Adequate"
BB	Speculative, but "Less Vulnerable" than B
B	Speculative, but "More Vulnerable" than BB
CCC	Very Highly Speculative and "Currently Vulnerable"
CC	Outright Speculation and "Highly Vulnerable"
Regulatory Supervision Due to Financial Condition	
SD or D	Selective Default or Default – Has Failed to Pay

Fitch

Rating	*Description*
AAA	Highest Credit Quality
AA*	Very High Credit Quality
A	High Credit Quality
BBB	Good Credit Quality
BB	Speculative
B	Highly Speculative
CCC, CC, D	High Default Risk
DDD, DD, D	Default

* Note: Sub-AAA Bonds may be listed as 1, 2 or 3 (Moody's) or as + or – (S&P and Fitch). Sources: Moody's Investors Service, Inc, *Moody's Rating Symbols and Definitions*, (Aug. 2003), retrieved from www.moodysaia.com; Standard & Poor's, *S&P Long-Term Issuer Credit Rating Definitions* (May 2002), retrieved from www2.standardandpoors.com; and *Fitch-Definitions of Bond Ratings*, retrieved from www.treasurer.ca.gov/ratings/fitch.asp (Jan 2007).

Additionally, there are specific rating scales issued by each of the bond-rating agencies for medium term note rankings, short-term note rankings, and sector specific ratings (such as U.S. municipal and tax-exempt rating).

The National Federation of Municipal Analysts has identified recommended information disclosures, including: financial, management and governance, the local economic base, airport demand, legal analysis, airline use and lease agreements and capital planning and facilities design. The following information is reflective of that required in a *financial information disclosure* so that the credit characteristics of an airport bond issue can be determined:

- *Income Cash Flow Statement* (Current Airline and non-airline revenues, operating and non-operating revenues, intergovernmental revenue, federal and state grants, rates and charges, Operating and Maintenance expenses, annual capital expenditures and debt service coverage.)
- *Balance Sheet Information* (detailed presentation of all short and long-term debt, schedule of gross and remaining principal and interest payments, commercial paper program summary, lines of credit, other indebtedness, and cash/liquid assets and fund/reserve details.
- *Financial Forecasts* (forecasted debt service, O&M expenses, airline and non-airline revenues, PFC collections and interest income, and application of PFC revenues).
- *Supplementary Information* (previous versus current cost projections, and a discussion of variances, another analysis of debt service and revenue forecasts).[44]

The marketing procedure for bonds is almost always to sell the entire issue of bonds in a block to one dealer or to a syndicate of dealers. Brokerage of municipal bonds is almost non-existent, and each dealer will purchase, price, and sell the bonds on his or her own account. The normal chronological order of the bond process is to,

- *determine the need* for capital improvement, and identify the estimated project cost;

[44] National Federation of Municipal Analysts, *Recommended Best Practices in Disclosure for Airport Debt*, retrieved from www.nfma.org/disclosure/rbp_airport.pdf (May 2004), at 2.

- *determine the government's authority to issue bonds*, and examine any restrictions on additional financing;
- *investigate possibilities of assistance* from the federal, state or nearby local government levels;
- *analyze the legal and financial feasibility* by examining existing debt, historical and prospective financial operations, and whether or not the requirements for bonds can be met through an earnings test;
- *prepare a prospectus* which presents comprehensive information about the bonds and advertises them for sale; and finally
- *sell the bonds* at public sale.

FINANCE AFTER DEREGULATION

The Airline Deregulation Act of 1978 significantly altered the economic regulatory system, which had controlled the airline industry for nearly forty years. The Airline Deregulation Act,

- reduced economic regulation;
- terminated oversight by the Civil Aeronautics Board;
- guaranteed *Essential Air Service* [EAS] to small communities;
- provided EAS subsidies where necessary;
- allowed the airlines freedom of market entry and exit;
- reduced authority over domestic routes;
- terminated authority over domestic routes and fares; and
- shifted anti-trust law responsibility (in-part) to the airlines.

Deregulation of the airline industry radically changed the market climate not only of the airlines but also of the airports they serve. In the post deregulation era, the *airport-as-a-market* brought on a new, and yet old, phenomenon called "hubbing." It was an "old" phenomenon, in that airlines have been "hubbing and spoking" out of centralized airports for years. Yet it was also "new," because of the contemporary trend to create new hubs for economic development. Airlines hub generally for three reasons: (1) to capture connecting traffic, (2) to generate economies of scale, and (3) to create greater frequency of service.

It should be noted that both the airports and the airlines benefit from hubbing and spoking. Airports too are in a tough competitive fight for business and for the opportunity to be one of the hubs. In the new strategy airlines realign their routing systems by eliminating marginal point-to-point routes and concentrating on connecting hubs at one or more airports. Connecting passengers thereby stay on the same carrier rather than interline, thus concentrating business for the hubbing airline.

Airports strive to become hubs because they benefit from larger markets than their own, and thus generate increased revenue, which can be used for facility development, and also to provide economic development for the local community. Development of hub airports by the air carriers caused trends in enplanements to shift. And it fostered rethinking of capital planning. Airports can financially benefit from becoming hubs, but there are potential vulnerabilities.

The airlines take on more responsibility for enplanement trends, and the financial health of a particular carrier can play a key role in the viability of a connecting hub airport. Sometimes an airport can become dependent upon a single airline. If that one airline were to fail, the community could be left with high debt service and underutilized facilities. A brighter outlook, however, assumes that if the airport-as-a-market can attract more passengers as a hub, it can also attract replacement airline service should the original carrier fail. Hence, the airport retains its ability to repay its debts.

One outcome of airline deregulation has been concentration of the major carriers into the lucrative, high-density markets, and reliance upon third-level carriers to backfill unsatisfied demand in the smaller, less lucrative rural markets. The result for airports has been to strengthen the financial positions of most large and medium-sized airports, while increasing difficulties in financing the development of smaller facilities. Following the advent of deregulation, airports along with the airlines faced uncertainties of a newly created *laissez-faire* marketplace. In the new, unregulated environment, large and medium-sized airports, as a market, were able to increase their ability to generate income as a result of increased service from the major carriers. However, smaller airports have not fared as well.

As one of the goals of airline deregulation, the government was to maintain a "comprehensive and convenient system of continuous scheduled service to small communities."[45] Instead, the promise of greater "frequency" of service brought with it disruptions in service

---

[45] *See* the *Airline Deregulation Act* of 1978.

and higher costs. On average, air carrier service to small communities has been neither "continuous" nor "convenient." Moreover, revenue bases shrink as airports decrease in size. Smaller airports have difficulty generating sufficient revenues to cover even their operating costs, let alone locating financing for new development. The disruptions in service after deregulation made it that much more difficult for smaller airports to finance new development. They are not only unable to attract money from the bond market, but many have been looking for innovative ways to fund their operations budgets. Look, for example, at Daytona Beach, Florida.

In the mid-1980s, officials at the Daytona Beach Airport proposed an auction of its $2.5 million in Airport Improvement Program entitlement funds which were designated for airside projects. The plan called for selling its allocated AIP funds to another AIP eligible airport at a discounted rate. In exchange, it was hoped that the non-AIP money used to purchase the "restricted" funds could then be used at Daytona Beach's discretion for operations and for non-AIP eligible terminal construction. When the FAA disallowed the sale of AIP funds, airport authorities proposed a swap whereby another airport would provide non-AIP funded terminal construction at Daytona Beach, which would in turn provide AIP funded airside improvements at the other airport. The FAA responded by ruling that *any* transfer of AIP entitlements would be disallowed.

Financing developments at smaller airports has not improved since deregulation in 1978. Larger airports, nevertheless, remain in a strong, if not stronger position to borrow money. In its report to Congress in 1984, the Congressional Budget Office [CBO] investigated key financial ratios in evaluating the economic vitality of the nation's largest airports. Four indicators often used by investment counselors to judge the value of a municipal enterprise include the following:

- The *operating ratio* is derived by dividing operating and maintenance expenses by operating revenue. This ratio measures the share of revenues absorbed by operating and maintenance costs. A relatively low operating ratio indicates financial strength by signifying that only a small share of revenue is required to satisfy operating requirements. A high ratio (close to one) indicates that relatively little additional revenue is available for capital spending.

- The *net takedown ratio* is calculated as total revenue minus operating and maintenance expenses, divided by gross revenues. The net takedown is similar to the operating ratio, but also includes non-operating revenues (such as interest income). It is a slightly broader measure of the share of airport revenues remaining after payment of operating expenses.
- The *debt-to-asset ratio* is calculated as gross debt minus bond principal reserves, divided by net fixed assets plus working capital. An enterprise's debt-to-asset ratio measures the fraction of total assets provided by creditors. Creditors prefer low debt ratios because each dollar of debt is secured by more dollars of assets. This can be important if assets have to be sold to pay off bondholders.
- The *debt service safety margin* is defined as gross revenues less operating and maintenance expenses and annual debt service, divided by gross revenues. This ratio measures both the percentages of revenues available to service an airport's new debt, and the financial cushion in the event of an airport's achieving unexpectedly low revenues.

The first two ratios (operating ratio and net takedown ratio) measure the availability of revenues beyond those needed to pay regular operating expenses. The last two indicators (debt-to-asset ratio and debt service safety margin) measure an airport's ability to support existing and new borrowing for capital investment.

Purchasers of airport revenue bonds look for assurances that an airport can generate net revenue (that is, gross revenues net of operating and maintenance costs and debt service requirements) sufficient to pay interest over the term of the bonds and to repay the principal. When compared to other financially self-sufficient municipal enterprises, such as electric utilities, water supply systems, and sewage treatment authorities, airports appear to carry high levels of debt relative to the value of their assets. Nevertheless, net airport revenues appear comparatively strong, due in part to a strong history of airport solvency and responsibility, in which there is no record of an airport defaulting on its debt in more than fifty years.[46]

---

[46] Moody's Investor Service 2000 as cited in Richard de Neufville & Amedo Odoni, *Airport Systems: Planning, Design and Management* 246 (2003).

Though major airports serving the preponderance of national enplanements have shown increasing ability to finance development, they have not been able to keep up with demand. Overall, the capacity of the nation's airport system has been outstripped by expanding demand. The Federal government must accept much of the blame for allowing the system to be overwhelmed by what were predictable increases in air travel. The Administration and some members of Congress are seemingly at fault for having maintained an Aviation Trust Fund surplus rather than spending it on air transportation improvements. The problem has now grown beyond the ability of the existing Trust Fund mechanism.

By 1990, a dramatic change in the approach to financing capital improvements was being actively pursued by airport operators. At that time, at least twenty large commercial airports were accommodating operations in excess of the airport's design capacity, with the demand at as many as forty-seven airports expected to exceed capacity by the end of the century. To rectify deficiencies in the National Plan of Integrated Airport Systems, the Airport Operators Council International and the American Association of Airport Executives jointly determined that more than $75 billion would have been needed through the year 2000 to finance the *identified* capital projects to meet the then forecast demand. Because airport development funds substantially exceeded the projected Trust Fund revenues and airports could not finance the necessary massive expansion, Congress adopted the Passenger Facility Charge, or PFC as an additional funding mechanism in 1990, which nearly two decades later, has proved to be of great benefit to airport operators.

PASSENGER FACILITY CHARGES

The PFC (a.k.a. "passenger facility fee") is a surtax added to the air passenger's fare, which is collected by the airlines and then conferred to the airport for use in future development. These PFC funds must be used only at the airport where they are collected, on projects "that enhance safety, security, or capacity; reduce noise; or increase air carrier competition."[47] The evolution of the PFC program has a history that has spanned nearly four decades, and has been the subject

[47] FAA, *Passenger Facility Charges*, retrieved from www.faa.gov/airports_airtraffic/airports/pfc/ (Feb. 2007).

of much debate in the industry and in Congress. Despite the fact that PFCs have resulted in a significant improvement over the prior AIP-dominated approach to capital funding at airports, many concerns remain.

HISTORICAL OVERVIEW

Although prohibited for many years, the so called "head tax" is now accepted as a reasonable fee in the recovery of airport costs.[48] Until 1990, locally imposed per passenger charges were illegal in the United States, except for a brief period in 1972-1973, following a Supreme Court ruling that had legalized it.[49] In response to the court decision legalizing "head taxes," certain airport sponsors rushed to impose related charges, with some collecting the taxes for off-airport, non-aviation related uses.

The Supreme Court ruling allowing the collection of per passenger taxes, with no restrictions placed on where the moneys might be applied, was in direct conflict with Federal policy related to expenditures from the Aviation Trust Fund. Moreover, federal agencies were strongly opposed to allowing airports to impose their own charges upon passengers who were already contributing to the Aviation Trust Fund by way of taxes collected by the airlines. To more fully understand the policy conflict, it should be realized that airport sponsors that receive Aviation Trust Fund assistance, must give assurances to the federal government that all moneys generated at the airport will be returned to the airport, and will not be used for any other (i.e., non-airport) government activity.

The airlines, too, reacted to the court decision with understandable opposition for fear that excessive taxes might drive consumer demand down. Hence, those opposing the imposition of local head taxes (i.e., federal agencies, the airlines, and consumer advocacy groups) successfully exhorted Congress subsequently into outlawing locally imposed charges.

In 1973, Richard Nixon signed into law the Anti-Head Tax Act, which prohibited the collection of taxes (by local authorities) based

---

[48] *See* Robert A. Bunnell, *Passenger Facility Charges: Are We Finally Ready?*, Airport (Jan./Feb. 1990).

[49] *See Evansville-Vanderburgh Airport Authority District. v. Delta Airlines*, 405 U.S. 707, 92 S.Ct. 1349, 31 L. Ed. 2d 620 (1972); *see also Northeast Airlines, et al. v. New Hampshire Aeronautics Commission, et al.*, N.H. Supreme Court (Feb. 24, 1972).

upon individual passenger enplanements. However, following passage of the Act, President Nixon stated that he would have ". . . favored a moratorium rather than a prohibition on the taxes. . . .," so the issue could be studied more closely. Therefore, he directed the Secretary of Transportation to conduct a study of the prohibition. In 1974, the FAA completed its study and found that, while funds were needed for airport development, ". . . head taxes may or may not be the most effective way to increase financing." The issue was left open-ended, and consequently, the battle over head taxes continued, with local airports seeking alternative ways to finance airport development.

By 1988, airport proprietors collectively (principally through the Airport Operators Council International, and the American Association of Airport Executives) declared that it was time once again to raise the issue of local funding. But, on this go-around, the head tax issue was combined with the overriding, critical and national issue of declining airport capacity and increasing delays being experienced in the air traffic and airspace system. The argument used by airport sponsors was that a local funding mechanism was necessary to enhance capacity.

Former Secretary of Transportation Samuel Skinner, who sought more local participation in funding the transportation system through user fees, reinforced the airport owners' position. Additionally, one of the central components of Mr. Skinner's national transportation policy for airport financing was a passenger facility charge. Sufficient congressional support was obtained, and by a vote of 405 to 15, the Aviation Safety and Capacity Expansion Act, which included PFCs, was passed in 1990. The Aviation Safety and Capacity Expansion Act is part of Title IX of the Omnibus Budget Reconciliation Act of 1990. Section 9110 of the Budget Reconciliation Act, entitled "Passenger Facility Charges," allowed an airport, approved by the Secretary of Transportation, to impose $1.00, $2.00, or $3.00 fee per enplaning passenger to help finance airport projects.

In 2000, the PFC ceiling was raised to $4.50 to adjust for inflation that had occurred since 1990. As of 2007, more than 70% of airports collecting PFCs were authorized at the maximum rate of $4.50.[50] PFCs may only be collected for the first two enplaning PFC-

[50] ACI–NA, *ACI-NA Announces Principles for FAA Reauthorization* (Feb. 5, 2007), retrieved from http://www.aci-na.org/asp/pressdetail.asp?art=1491.

authorized airports on a traveler's outbound flight, along with the last two enplaning PFC-authorized airports on the return flight.[51]

The fees collected: (1) may not exceed amounts necessary to finance specified projects; and (2) must be used on an eligible airport-related project (those enhance safety, security, or capacity; reduce noise; or increase air carrier competition). In other words, the fees collected specifically *cannot* be applied to non-airport programs, although in 2004, the FAA did announce the potential for PFC funding eligibility for certain ground access transportation programs (e.g., heavy or light railroads).[52]

Air carriers are required to collect the locally imposed fee as part of their ticketing of passengers. The airlines then transfer the funds to the airport sponsor. From the year 2005 forward, airlines are permitted to keep 11 cents of each PFC collected and remitted, as compensation for the costs associated with PFC collection.[53] In addition, air carriers have the opportunity to invest the PFCs—from the time they are collected until they are remitted on the last day of the month *following* the month in which they are collected.[54]

Although now legitimized, Passenger Facility Charges have not been imposed without challenge.[55] And, while PFCs have provided

---

[51] FAA, Passenger Facility Charge Branch, *Draft Passenger Facility Charge Audit Guide for Air Carriers*, retrieved from www.faa.gov/airports_airtraffic/airports/pfc/audit_guides/media/air_carriers_audit.doc (Jul. 2002).

[52] FAA, *Notice of Policy Regarding the Eligibility of Airport Ground Access Transportation Projects for Funding Under the PFC Program*, Federal Register Vol. 69, No. 27. (Feb. 10, 2004); also information on PFC eligible projects retrieved from www.faa.gov.

[53] FAA, *Revision to Passenger Facility Charge Rule for Compensation to Air Carriers*, Federal Register, Vol. 69, No. 53. (Mar. 18, 2004), retrieved from http://www.faa.gov/airports_airtraffic/airports/resources/ publications/federal_register_notices/media/pfc_69fr18Mr0415.pdf.

[54] *Id.* at 48.

[55] *See Northwest Airlines v. Federal Aviation Administration*, CCH 24 AVI 17,901 (1994), where the question was raised whether an airport authority must provide air carriers with written notice of individual projects being considered for funding through imposition of Passenger Facility Charges. The Airport Authority requested permission to impose a $3.00 PFC on all passengers enplaned at Memphis International Airport. The application identified four primary projects to be financed with PFC revenue. In addition, the application identified a backup project, should any one of the primary projects not be approved. Memphis failed to mention this alternative "noise compatibility project" when it consulted with Northwest and other airlines prior to submitting its PFC application. Fundamentally, the court deferred to the FAA's reasonable interpretation of the PFC statute. However, because the FAA had violated the consultation provisions of the statute with respect to the airport authority's proposed alternative project, the court concluded that Memphis could not expend its PFC funds to finance the alternative "noise compatibility project."

some needed relief, airports and their professional associations claim the current combination of Airport Improvement Program and PFC funds still remain insufficient to meet the future needs of a steadily growing, but aging system of airports.

In 2007, the Airport Council International-North America board of directors issued six Reauthorization Principles which suggest that Congress "provide airports with the necessary tools to fund projects benefiting their local community and help continue to meet growing airline and passenger demands." These reauthorization principles include:

- Increase the PFC rate ceiling and give airport flexibility in rate setting;
- Streamline FAA's management of the PFC program;
- Increase and strengthen the AIP;
- Improve the Airport and Airway Trust Fund to foster financial stability;
- Treat airport bonds as tax-exempt public purpose bonds; and
- Allow airports more financial flexibility.[56]

In their support of these principles, the ACI-NA explained that there are some significant opportunities for improvement both in the amount of funds that could be collected and in the way that the PFC and Airport Improvement Program administration could be improved.

First, ACI-NA notes that the PFC funding ceiling should be increased to $7.50 to counteract anticipated inflation through the year 2011. They explain that, while many airports have committed to multi-year construction programs, they were not able to project the incredible cost inflation in construction costs that many have experienced since 2000. Without congressional authorization for an increase in the rate ceiling, airports will either need to scale back or delay some construction plans.[57]

Airports also are requesting improved management processes in both the PFC program and in the FAA Grant Assurance Program. ACI-NA suggested that FAA's PFC application and approval process

---

[56] *Id.* at 27. *Also note*, these principles were issued to "guide the industry's lobbying efforts on the Federal Aviation Reauthorization process," as the authorizing legislation was due to expire in Sep. 2007.

[57] *Id.*

be replaced with an "impose, report and review" that would allow continued revenue accumulation to continued to occur, despite any FAA delays in processing requests for PFC use. They also stated that the Assurance process should be streamlined and simplified "to eliminate obsolete and redundant provisions, focus on unauthorized diversion of aviation revenues and employer airports to sustain themselves as non-profit entities."[58]

With regard to Airport Improvement Program funding, ACI-NA would like Congress to "strengthen points of order and budget processes" to make it "difficult for appropriators to fund AIP below the authorized amounts." They would also like to see Congress include a "guaranteed General Fund Contribution" to assure a "stable and predictable funding stream" for the AIP that is not currently available.[59]

While this section focused on the support of the nation's airports, these facilities should be duly recognized for the many contributions that they provide to their communities, both tangible and intangible. The next section reviews these economic and other benefits of airports to the communities they serve.

ECONOMIC IMPORTANCE OF AIRPORTS

Airports play a significant role in generating and sustaining local, state and national economies. There are distinct economic advantages for a community that has viable air transportation facilities. Although these economic advantages are difficult to quantify, they are nevertheless important to the community's economic health and vitality.

Recognized is that air transportation is of paramount importance to the nation's economy. The airlines carry the bulk of the world's air commerce. Air carriers have shrunk all distances in terms of time and convenience and have given rise to significant increases in the numbers of people now traveling by air. Since the late 1950s and the advent of the commercial jet transport, there has been a marked shift in traffic volume from surface to air transportation. Commercial air transportation is of major importance, socially, politically and economically.[60] And, airports are the terminal ends of the commercial air transportation system. Although not as visible to the general public as

---

[58] *Id.*

[59] *Id.*

[60] *See* Robert Kane, *Air Transportation* (12th ed. 1996).

the airlines, general aviation is of significance as well. The airlines serve only about 600 of the nation's airports. General aviation extends the air transportation system to the remaining 19,000 plus landing sites in the United States.

Since the late 1960s, there have been a number of studies looking at the economics of airports and their importance to the communities they serve. The general consensus of studies by the FAA, by the General Aviation Manufacturers Association, the Aircraft Owners and Pilots Association, and other organizations has concluded that:

- Airports are part of the *community development* program. Most airports, because of their impact on local economies, have had active community planning programs, aggressively supported by community leaders and civic organizations. The airport is an important element in the development of a balanced community.
- Airport development is a *catalyst for business* and industrial growth. In most or all of the airports studied, the broad census measures of "value added by manufacture," "volume of retail trade," "volume of wholesale trade" and "volume of service business," among others, registered increases in rates of growth following construction of a new airport or the modernization of existing facilities. Some of the reasons why commercial activity is enhanced by available air transportation resources are because sales representatives can visit widely scattered customers. Service personnel and replacement parts can be ferried in and out to assist local businesses and industries. And business professionals can attend meetings in cities hundreds or thousands of miles away without driving or being away from their businesses for prolonged periods of time. The pace of business activity in many cases would be severely restrained without ready access to air transportation. Some businesses would be handicapped to the point of being non-competitive within their respective industries.
- Airports *attract new industry*. Community leaders and heads of new industries have stated that the availability of air transportation was a strong factor in decisions to locate in their respective communities. New industries not only provide more employment and improve the community's economy, but also

serve to increase property tax revenues for county and local governments.

- Airports are a factor in *retaining existing industry*. Not only have airports helped to retain existing industry, air transportation has become increasingly more important to local industry representatives by helping them retain and improve their competitive positions in local, national, and international markets.
- Airports provide *access to the global air transportation network*. With an airport, a community is tied into the more than 19,000 airfields in the conterminous United States and, broadly speaking, to all of the airports in the world. Virtually every major town in the U.S. is directly accessible from the local airport. Conversely, every major town in the U.S. has direct access to the local airport. Users include not only businesses and industry, but the general public as well.
- Airports are a *nucleus for industry*. Airports are commonly found in the center of commercial and industrial development. Sound land use planning dictates industrial land-use in and around airports for compatibility. For many airports such development has occurred without the benefit of a formal land use plan. Rather, the presence of an airport seems to possess certain magnetism for industry. Some industries locate at or near airports because they have a direct need for access to air transport facilities. Others may have an indirect need for being near an airport such as: (1) convenience for traveling employees, associates and clients; (2) convenience for shipping or receiving products or materials by air; and/or (3) convenient proximity to an associated business located at the airport. Sometimes firms locate at airports for no apparent reason, but are simply attracted to the airport's "mystique" and glamour. In some cases it is advantageous for certain (especially) general aviation airports to devote surplus airport property to industrial use, and to in turn use the industrially related revenues to support airport operations. Thus, the availability of commercial space can attract a broad spectrum of businesses to the airport.
- Airports are a *boon to the local economy*. Money directly spent at the airport generates further spending in the community.

This phenomenon is known to economists as the "multiplier" or "spin-off" effect or impact.

ECONOMIC ACTIVITY MEASURES

The four general types of impact are on-airport direct impacts (would not occur if airports did not exist), off airport direct impacts (visitor spending), airport dependent impacts (would suffer if airport did not exist) and the spin-off (multiplier) effects.[61]

An increase in the aggregate income of a community arises from each increment of new spending. The *economic multiplier* is a chain reaction, which starts with the first person receiving new money in a hypothetically closed economic system. That person then has money with which to buy goods from the next person in the chain, and so on. Each time the original dollar spent changes hands, the stimulating effect upon the economy is diminished until finally it is spent for goods outside the system. The multiplier effect is usually about 2.0 to 3.0. So for each new dollar spent, it is worth roughly $2 to $3 to the local economy.

Airports also generate "new" money in several ways: through airport related jobs, consumer spending by the air traveler, and revenues collected from airport users. Even the monies derived from the federal share of airport development projects bring new prosperity to the local economy.

Still, it has been difficult at best to quantify the economic benefits of an airport to those who might question the value of airports. The absolute value of airports has been elusive. No one yet has been able to adequately demonstrate what an airport is actually worth to the community it serves other than through the abstract theory of the multiplier effect, the reality of which is difficult for many people to grasp. Yet, in the absence of being able to profit from their airports—an opportunity long denied by federal grant assurances—the economic multiplier is the only way a public airport sponsor has of realizing the economic benefits of owning and operating an airport. More importantly, it has been difficult to show that an airport is worth subsidizing if for no other reason than because of its economic benefit to the

---

[61] Virginia Airport System, *Commonwealth of Virginia Economic Impact Study,* retrieved from http://www.doav.virginia.gov/Downloads/Studies/2004%20VEI/VEI%202004%20Chapter%20Two.pdf (2001).

community. In many cases elected officials insist an airport must "pay its way" through direct user-support, and it can be difficult to persuade them otherwise when there are no positive data to the contrary.

Because it is difficult for many people to fully comprehend the abstractness of the multiplier effect, its demonstration is told in the story of the airport manager at the Dunsmuir Airport in Northern California, who doused each dollar that passed through the airport with a cheap, but distinctive perfume. Every time one of those dollars passed through the cash registers of local stores, merchants were physically reminded by their senses of where the dollar originated. Nevertheless, this example of the multiplier effect, although graphic, is not very scientific. In order to demonstrate to the community the value of its airport, many airport sponsors have conducted *economic impact studies* of their airports upon the local community so that they could then demonstrate by statistical inference the direct and indirect values received from the airport's operation. The authors of economic impact studies review impact by measuring a variety of factors, including:[62]

- *Dollar impact* of the airport on the local economy, wherein the measure is "value added," meaning the sum of all expenditures by the suppliers and users of aviation services on payrolls (wages, salaries, employee benefits), rent, utilities, materials, supplies, services, and taxes paid in the area;
- *Suppliers* of aviation services who are those firms and agencies directly involved in the movement of passengers and air cargo. These suppliers include airlines, commuter air services, airport businesses (such as auto rental agencies, airport shops, security services), travel agencies, air cargo agencies, ground transportation (taxi, bus and limousine operators), fixed base operators, and government agencies (such as the Federal Aviation Administration and the airport authority);
- *Users* of aviation services who include those firms and agencies using aviation services to move supplies, products, and employees. A portion of the total value added by user firms is attributed to aviation, based on air transportation as a portion of total U.S. inputs;

---

[62] Some information in this section drawn from FAA, *Estimating* the *Regional Economic Significance of Airports,* retrieved from http://www.faa.gov/airports_airtraffic/ airports/aip/bc_analysis/media/ economic_significance_1992.pdf (Sep. 1992).

- *Air travel and tourism* impacts, which include the expenditures at the airport and within the community by visitors arriving by air. These visitors impact the economy through expenditures for local transportation, lodging, restaurants, entertainment, and retail purchases;
- *Economic impact of general aviation*, which is measured as the imputed value of air miles flown for business or recreational purposes by general aviation aircraft based at the airport(s) in the economic study area;
- *Primary (or direct) impact*, which is the initial expenditures made and jobs created by suppliers and users of aviation services;
- *Induced impact*, which results from multiplier effects as primary spending by suppliers and users of aviation services circulates through the local economy; and the
- *Total economic impact*, which is the sum of primary and induced impacts, measuring the jobs, payrolls, and total expenditures contributed to the area.

Typically, a variety of surveys are used to collect relevant data. Survey efforts may include the following:

- Airport Manager Survey;
- Airport Tenant Survey;
- Airport Dependent Business Survey;
- Corporate Based Aircraft Ownership Survey;
- Air Carrier Visitor Survey; and
- General Aviation Visitor Survey.[63]

A variety of entities may generate economic impact studies including airport sponsors, regional or state entities (department/division of transportation), federal agencies and organizations. Terms commonly used in economic impact studies include *measured effects* and *calculated effects*. Measured effects are those that capture employment, expenditures, and cargo and passenger numbers of interest. Calcu-

---

[63] Virginia Airport System, *Commonwealth of Virginia Economic Impact Study* (2001), retrieved from http://www.doav.virginia.gov/Downloads/Studies/2004%20VEI/VEI%202004%20 Chapter%20Two.pdf.

lated effects include tourism numbers, business generation and sales figures which are generally derived from formulas relating to business activities in the city or region of interest.

More recently, airport economic impact studies have been increasing in sophistication with advanced models and new approaches to determining the multiplier effects. More than 500 public and private sector agencies have employed the most popular economic impact-planning model, *Impact Analysis for Planning* [IMPLAN], which incorporates countywide data with industry-wide detail.[64] In addition, specialized IMPLAN-based state or county multipliers are used to calculate the "recycling of dollars" and to best "quantify the effect of continued reinvestment of output."[65]

Economic impact or benefit studies should be considered a valuable public relations tool.[66] They demonstrate the positive aspects of the airport and emphasize the sometimes hidden economic importance. These studies may also help to overcome adverse publicity perhaps generated from noise or other unwanted side effects of airport operation, or potentially to keep the airport property from being converted to non-aviation use.

Economic impact studies can look at an individual airport or all the activities in a state or region. The results of a 1999 study of the aviation-related jobs, activities and facilities in Arizona revealed a

---

[64] According to the Commonwealth of Virginia, IMPLAN is highly effective because it uses, "U.S. Commerce Department data (including National Income and Product Accounts) on inter-industry technology relationships (also known as input-output structural matrices), countywide employment and income data from the Bureau of Economic Analysis [BEA] and Bureau of Labor Statistics, and its own industry and county-specific estimates of local purchasing rates (regional purchase coefficients). It is enhanced over most other input-output models in that it also includes coverage of public sector activity and consumer activity (reflected in its social accounting matrix). The industry detail is at the level of 528 industries, and is based on categories of the BEA, which correspond to 3 and 4-digit groups in the Standard Industrial Classification system." FAA, *Notice of Policy Regarding the Eligibility of Airport Ground Access Transportation Projects for Funding Under the PFC Program*, Federal Register Vol. 69, No. 27. (Feb. 10, 2004); also information on PFC eligible projects retrieved from www.faa.gov.

[64] FAA, *Revision to Passenger Facility Charge Rule for Compensation to Air Carriers*, Federal Register, Vol. 69, No. 53. (Mar. 18, 2004), retrieved from http://www.faa.gov/airports_airtraffic/airports/resources/ publications/federal_register_notices/media/pfc_69fr18Mr0415.pdf.

[65] *Id.* at 47, at 2-18.

[66] It is notable that some feel that the term "economic impact" is not an appropriate descriptor as a true "impact" study should include both economic benefits and the direct and indirect economic costs associated with the continued operation and maintenance of the facility. Most economic impact studies do not include all costs associated with the airport in question. As an alternative, some suggest the use of the term "economic benefit studies" although this term has not gain wide acceptance.

$26 billion dollar benefit to the state of Arizona.[67] In the Phoenix Airport system (as in many other commercial service airports across the country), the airport's impact study noted that airport revenue generation or aviation user fees paid for every airport item from terminal buildings to employee salaries to pencils. No taxes were collected from the general public at large. In short, an important message was generated that the City's airports pay their own way, while simultaneously generating millions of dollars of economic activity for the local communities.

SUMMARY

The dominant approach to public finance (and hence to the budgetary process) is perhaps best reflected by Richard Musgrave's conceptualization of the proper role of the public sector.[68] He perceives the public sector as having three functions to perform in assisting the economy to achieve its goals:

- Equitable *distribution* of income;
- *Stabilization* of economic conditions; and
- *Efficient* allocation of resources.

The latter criterion, *efficiency*, is measured by whether or not social benefits exceed the social costs incurred in producing the benefits. In the private sector efficiency is easier to measure since the analyst can use positive tools to measure prices and costs of production. In the public sector, more normative measurements must be relied upon to measure social benefits. Nevertheless, the nature of the efficiency objective is clear. It is to allocate resources such that the difference between social benefits and social costs is maximized. With the *distribution* criterion, however, there is widespread disagreement on what is most preferred. Irrespective of the varied opinions regarding distributive goals, in order to achieve the third criterion of *stability* in the airport case, the allocation of resources must, of necessity, lead to the continued operation of the airport and the provision of airport services.

---

[67] Lee McPheters & Robin Sobotta for the Arizona Dept. of Aeronautics, *State of Arizona Aviation Economic Impact Study* (1999).
[68] Richard Musgrave, *The Theory of Public Finance* (date unknown).

Economist Jonathan Gruber offers a slightly differing but equally interesting view of this issue. Gruber suggests that when presuming that competitive market equilibrium is the most efficient outcome for society, there are just two reasons why governments may wish to intervene in market economies: in response to *market failures* or for *redistribution*.[69] While Musgrave addressed (re)distribution, Gruber suggests that market failure is the only other valid reason for government to intervene in market economies. Market failure occurs when "a competitive outcome fails to maximize total social efficiency." When individuals are seeking only to meet their individual or corporate needs, the total social value may not be recognized or maximized. In the case of airports, it is likely that many, particularly smaller airports would cease to exist if government were not permitted to intervene. While some will always question the importance of airports (and the need to support those facilities), a community's seriously underserved transportation needs would inevitably be viewed as a market failure.

In the final analysis, the purpose of the budgetary procedure is to integrate efficiency, distribution, and stability such that the airport sponsor might continue to provide maximized airport services to the public at the lowest possible cost. The basic principles of rational budgeting are four:

- To evaluate expenditures and the means of financing the expenditures simultaneously;
- To weight the expenditures on the basis of net social benefits;
- To minimize the total weighted social costs of the revenue system; and
- To achieve aggregate stability.

Accomplishment of these four budgeting principles is the ideal, but in practice, budgetary processes seem to fall short of fulfilling these requirements for several reasons. For example, taxes and other revenues are usually considered separately from expenditures. Moreover, in the ideal budgetary process there is no ranking of objectives, yet legislators appear to establish political priorities among the economic objectives. When distribution becomes important, programs

[69] Jonathan Gruber, *Public Finance and Public Policy* (2nd ed. 2007), at 9.

are adopted which may conflict with efficiency. When stability is of concern, legislators may use expenditure variations as a stabilizing tool and without consideration of its effect upon economic welfare. And finally, sometimes government programs (financed by taxes and revenues) produce social costs greater than the amounts collected and the benefits to be derived from them.

In a perfect marketplace economy, social net benefits would be maximized, and there would be no need for government intervention. But because of imperfect competition and other externalities, private markets are not perfect. The resulting distribution failures in imperfect marketplace economies imply that public activity (i.e., government intervention and/or proprietary activity such as airport operation) is necessary in order to attain the desired pattern of resource distribution within society. Ideally, then, government expenditure and revenue policies should be designed to move the economy closer to the goals of a more perfect economy. However, the presumption of market failure does not imply society is necessarily better off with government intervention. It cannot be assumed that government will succeed where the private sector has failed. If the government activity cannot move the economy closer to the goals of efficiency, equity and stability, then perhaps the activity should remain in (or be returned to) the private sector, where even though imperfect, it may be less imperfect than the government alternative.

The onus of insuring that airports operate efficiently in the public sector is on airport management, and the competence of the airport manager can be measured best by the net social benefits produced at the airport for which the manager is responsible. The public is demanding that airport administrators be held fully responsible for managing society's airport facilities efficiently. The advent of new forms of public entrepreneurship and the evolution of the airport marketplace are tools available for public administrators, and will be discussed at length in the next chapter. If public administrators cannot live up to the challenges presented by the new form of public administration and the evolving airport marketplace, then indeed a strong argument exists for the further exploration of privatization.

CHAPTER 13

THE AIRPORT MARKETPLACE: REVENUES AND RATES

Today's airline passengers want an in-airport experience that includes "grab and go" food selections, yet they also demand upscale, sit-down restaurants. High-end retail shops are edging out conventional souvenir shops. And, travelers want personal services that go beyond the traditional shoe-shine stand and ATM.

Barbara Cook, Deputy Editor, Airport Magazine[1]

THE EMERGING MARKETPLACE

In the 21st century, airports have emerged as remarkable marketplaces of the future, with their operators impressively managing millions in important revenue-generating activities. Gone are the mundane, unbranded retail and Food & Beverage [F&B] shops of yesteryear, run by a single Master Concessionaire. Today's airports feature upscale retail concepts, name brand presence, and a phenomenal range in consumer choice and convenience. They employ street-level pricing practices and new approaches in the management of their lucrative concessions. Proper use of new tools and terms translate into an increase in the economic benefit of airports to the communities they serve. These tools also empower airport operators in fairly as-

[1] Barbara Cook, *Upscale Retail and F&B Outlets Dominate New Airport Concessions*, Airport Magazine (Aug./Sep. 2006), at 24.

sessing rates in charges to aviation users, while maximizing revenue generation from non-aviation revenue sources.

This is the second of two chapters on the subject of finance and business practices. The preceding chapter, "Finance and Economics" introduced the concepts of basic airport finance, including budgeting and capital budgeting streams. This chapter delves more deeply into approaches that airports have used to transform their public-sector facilities into robust retail marketplaces supportive of traditional and innovative revenue generating activities. The chapter concludes with a review of economic, financial and other business practices employed in the daily operation of airports, such as the rates and charges programs, cost accounting, pricing, and leasing.

21st CENTURY AIRPORT MARKETS

Airports are one of the latest organizations to discover the value and necessity of a well-designed and implemented marketing effort. Since the advent of airline deregulation, marketing has been an exciting, evolutionary process for airport sponsors. Airport operators have become willing partners in learning the best application for available marketing functions—to the extent permissible for public sector entities that must also honor their commitment to providing competent and ethical governance, in the context of receiving governmental funding.

Like traditional businesses, airports desire to grow at the expense of their competitors. But as competitive pressures have increased for both airports and airlines, and as more airports have begun to market themselves aggressively, it is becoming necessary to develop more sophisticated techniques to maintain a competitive edge. The pressures forcing airports to compete include the freedom accorded airlines under deregulation to select airports they will serve, and consolidation of remaining airlines into select hub-and-spoke operations, and privatization in the public sector. Unfortunately, this competition has forced airports to see the airlines, rather than passengers, as their primary customers. The rule of airport marketing has traditionally been, "keep the airlines happy and everything else follows."[2]

But, as the industry transitions from simple landlords collecting rent to a more entrepreneurial model in the development of complex

[2] Mike Howarth, *Good Relations*, Airline Business (Jun. 1996), at 68.

marketplaces, the old airline-dominated model is becoming antiquated. While air transportation is the primary reason airports exist, airport operators now recognize that the average traveler has a variety of needs, other than a cup of coffee, a hot dog and a newspaper. Today's traveler is coming to the airport much earlier, creating longer loiter time in the airport terminal. They also have a need to be productive in the course of busy lives. Accomplishing something—whether business or leisure in nature—is a desired goal of air travelers today.

In addition to communications, the media, citizen participation, favorable employee relations, *marketing* is also a tool of public relations. The American Marketing Association once defined "marketing" as, "the performance of business activities that direct the flow of goods and services from producer to consumer or user." It is traditionally viewed as the entrepreneurial function of "finding customers." Marketing consists also of "those activities necessary and incidental to bring about exchange relationships." In this latter sense, the airport is the marketplace where the exchange of air transportation services and goods takes place. Nevertheless, airports *per se* have not been market producers. Traditionally, they have merely provided a place where the (airline) producer could transact business. In effect, until airports were required like other business to market their product, airport sponsors have been little more than "property companies."[3]

However, following deregulation of the airline industry in 1978, many airports were thrust into new roles of "marketing" their facilities and communities, in order to compete with other airports to attract both airline service and air travelers. Airlines, for example, have stated a need to develop "some kind of partnership" with the communities and airports they serve especially where a potential hub is involved. And, at large airports where hubs have been in operation for years, airport management must still come to realize the value of marketing. Even the largest airports need to promote themselves to ensure communities understand the economic benefits they provide. Thus, it may be said that marketing, too, is a form of public relations.

In an authoritarian or otherwise government-controlled economy, goods and services are allocated by government edict. Conversely, in a free or mixed economy, the *market system* serves as the mechanism for the distribution of resources. Before deregulation the Federal gov-

---

[3] *Id.*

ernment, through the Civil Aeronautics Board, determined by issuance of *Certificates of Public Convenience and Necessity* [PC&N] what was in the best interest of the traveling public. Certificates of PC&N are still required under Section 401 of the Federal Aviation Act. However, with deregulation of the airlines, the public's "need" is determined by the marketplace. In order to receive their "401" certification airlines need only to demonstrate that they are "fit, willing and able" to serve the market.

The Airline Deregulation Act of 1978 gave the airlines the freedom to experiment in the marketplace, to seek out potentially lucrative markets, and to abandon community-served transportation where it was not profitable. Airports, then, find themselves in a position of having to attract the airlines and to demonstrate that the area they serve is, or could be, a worthwhile market. Airports are marketing to the traveling public, but more importantly, are focusing marketing efforts toward the airlines.

THE MARKETING MIX

Analysis of the market, or "marketing," is defined by the American Marketing Association as "the performance of business activities that direct the flow of goods and services from producer to customer or user." Individual markets can also be described in marketing terms. Marketing is the process of conducting marketing research, determining an appropriate product or mix of products, accurately pricing the product, promoting the product through advertising and selling, and establishing a system of efficient distribution. Marketing's four basic components, referred to as the four "Ps" of the *marketing mix* are:

- Price;
- Product;
- Place (a.k.a. Distribution); and
- Promotion.[4]

---

[4] Marketing is generally summed up in marketing texts as the classical four "Ps" of marketing: *price*, *product*, *place*, and *promotion*, although some sources include *marketing research* as a fifth critical element. Joel Evans and Barry Berman, *Marketing, 9e: Marketing in the 21st Century* (2007), retrieved from Atomicdogpublications.com.

The marketing mix is typically set upon a solid foundation of *marketing research* that enables decision makers to bring the most appropriate selection of goods and services to a desired *target audience.* Marketing research is the gathering, reduction, and analysis of market data. This could range from simple inquiry to complex statistical manipulation. The first step taken by the T.F. Green Airport in Warwick, Rhode Island, for example, required little more than an investment of time and some stamps. They started writing to all the air carriers, asking for additional service and lower airfares. Target audiences are composed of final customers (individuals who buy for home, family or personal use) or organizational customers (such as governmental organizations or corporations that buy for resale, for use in their operation, or in the production of other goods).[5]

A marketing strategy combines the marketing mix in such a way as to produce desired, measurable results. Each of the four components of the marketing mix should be manipulated and implemented in preplanned ways to achieve an entity's marketing objectives. The *price* is what the customer must pay for goods and services, and is influenced by the customer's perceived value of those goods and services. The *product* determination and mix provides the customer with a system of preferences, and encompasses packaging and the branding of the product or service.

Place or distribution involves consumer access to goods or services, and all the logistics associated with the tracking, transfer and storage of goods and services. The distribution component assures that the desired good or service is readily available to consumers when and where wanted. *Promotion* informs, persuades or reminds people about goods, services, image, ideas, community involvement or impact on society.[6] Promotion furthers the growth and establishment of the business. Sometimes, however, a service effectively sells itself. The promotional mix is comprised of advertising, public relations; direct marketing (a.k.a. personal selling) and sales promotion (usually including sponsorships).

The marketing mix must satisfy the needs or wants of a target group. In the case of airports, there may be multiple target audiences and specific marketing plans/objectives associated with each, such as the:

---

[5] *Id.*

[6] *Id.*

- *General Public*—to promote positive community relations and support for airport presence and development;
- *Traveling Public*—to increase use of the airport and it's tenant's goods and services;
- *Policy Makers*—to increase political and legislative support;
- *Airlines*—to encourage new or improved (more frequent or larger aircraft) domestic or international service, and to increase competition resulting in lower fares; and
- *Concessionaires*—to increase goods/services and F&B variety and quality, and to promote revenue-generation.

Marketing an airport and its variety of goods and services can be an expensive and challenging task, in light of the choice that people have in a highly mobile society.

> *Passengers with a choice of airports may drive substantial distances to gain a cheaper fare. And passenger and cargo airlines may be reluctant to institute or expand service without solid assurances that the service will be profitable. Faced with these economic realities, airport managers are employing a variety of marketing tools to build recognition, demand and air service at their facilities.*[7]

In the following pages, tools that the airport manager can use—the four elements of the marketing mix—are discussed and supplemented by examples of innovative strategies used by airports throughout the country.

PRICE

Pricing is theoretically the single, most important instrument of competition in a market economy. Airport rates and charges, as discussed in an earlier chapter, is the typical method of determining airport pricing for airport users. While a well-run rates and charges programs provides a strong framework for financial solvency, it may not

---

[7] Barbara Cook, *Making Their Pitches*, Airport Magazine, (Apr./May 2006) at 26.

always yield the type of service choices that are needed and/or wanted in a community. To entice new service into a community, ingenuity is often employed, but must be done in a way that is equitable to existing tenants.

Airports, in order to attract air carriers, may offer discounted rents on counter space, gates and support buildings. However, an airline chief executive officer once stated, "low airport rental alone will not attract a carrier." There must be a market to serve. If a market has indeed been demonstrated, airport rental rates may well be accepted by the carrier as merely the cost of doing business. But, if rates are perceived to be unreasonable, air carriers will nevertheless contest them.

In one case study, the City of Yakima, Washington, told its major carrier, (at that time) Republic Airlines, it would have to accept higher airport user fees or leave. The airport was operating at a deficit and the City established a policy that local taxpayers would receive a fair return from their airport investment. Included in negotiations with the City were Republic Airlines, Cascade Airways, Horizon Airlines and Air Olympia. Agreement was reached with Cascade, Horizon and Air Olympia.

Republic denounced the City for what they called its unreasonable position. They said they would rather leave the airport than stay where they were not wanted. City officials questioned whether Republic might have already decided to leave Yakima and had encountered convenient justification for its decision. Republic officials denied any ulterior motives, but based on the 50,000 annual enplanements at Yakima it could be questioned whether Republic's DC-9s were the airplane for the market after deregulation.

Republic pulled out, but subsequently passenger enplanements, frequency of flights, and airport revenues went up. Cascade Airways introduced forty-eight-passenger twin turbo-prop aircraft. Horizon was already using aircraft of comparable size. Daily flights increased to eighteen compared with eight by Republic. The community lost jet service, but it was replaced by higher frequency.

Maybe Yakima was lucky, and perhaps in other circumstances discounted costs to the carrier may be more effective. In 1986, the Alabama State legislature voted to exempt carriers with hubs in that state from virtually all taxes on aircraft and equipment—including the State's 1.3 cents per gallon fuel tax—as an incentive. Some states and local communities have since taken some extraordinary pricing steps to either attract or retain air service.

Over the past decade, innovative financial incentives have been offered by airports seeking the introduction or expansion of commercial air service. For example, Southwest Florida International Airport has a program that provides reduced rates to qualified airlines during their inaugural year of service. The airport director reports success in the program, "Because it gives airlines the opportunity to test new service with reduced financial risk."[8]

Little Rock National Airport's *Air Service Development Program* offers reduced gate rental charges and landing fees for six months, along with support for advertising the new service. A participating carrier must either sign an operating agreement for one year, or repay the amount invested in that carrier (waived fees, marketing, etc.). Little Rock's Airport Manager Phillip Launius explains the payback requirement, "We view (the program) as a two-way street rather than a give-away-the store program."[9]

The issue of airport pricing is also discussed later in this chapter, as part of a larger discussion on the issue of airport rates and charges.

AIRPORT PRODUCTS AND SERVICES

Product determination and mix provide the customer with a system of preferences. In Yakima the capacity of one major carrier was exchanged for frequency of service and selection offered by three smaller carriers. In Alabama, a hub is defined as an airline operation of fifteen or more daily departures to five or more destinations for at least six days a week, during six or more months a year.

In the post-deregulatory era, the key to *air carrier* survival has seemingly been the adoption of a strong hub position and to use local traffic to support high-frequency hub operations. Airlines have also survived and gotten stronger through market concentration. The key to *airport* survival has been through attraction of new carriers and retention of the old ones. A marketing strategy must illuminate the importance of the various "products" that the airport has to offer to its target markets. Each product found at an airport is comprised of a

---

[8] Robert Ball, A.A.E. as quoted by Barbara Cook, *Making Their Pitches*, Airport Magazine (Apr./May 2006), at 41.

[9] Phillip Launius, as quoted by Barbara Cook, *Making Their Pitches*, Airport Magazine (Apr./May 2006), at 41.

bundle of attributes which collectively, create the user's impression of the facility as a whole.

Typical products found in the airport environment include the airport/terminal (general image, cleanliness, comfort, convenience, etc.) and the air carrier service (convenience, frequency, destinations, pricing, image, reliability, equipment, frequent flyer programs). Also, concessions (selection/brands, pricing, speed of service), parking (proximity, prices, transport to terminal) and other service-providers such as Fixed Base Operator [FBO] and cargo carriers (services, hours of operation, prices, reliability) are the products of the airport.

In some cases, the airport "product" can be effectively expanded and promoted as an extension of the local community, with its more desirable services and attributes. In Lansing, Michigan, for instance, the airport joined with a coalition of 140 local corporations to "raise the community's profile in efforts to attract additional air service," stated Executive Director Robert Selig. The creation of the coalition prompted the creation of much more appealing bundle of attributes than those traditionally associated with the airport. Coupled with an advertising campaign and a new "full service website with airline, hotel and car-rental booking engine," the airport recorded an 18.5 percent increase in passenger boardings" after its transformation.[10]

PLACE AND DISTRIBUTION

Distribution is the bringing together of the consumer with the good or service. It also involves all the logistics associated with the marriage of the two, including the physical movement, storage and tracking of goods or services from the producer to the customer. The Allentown-Bethlehem-Easton Airport [A-B-E] in Pennsylvania developed a two-prong marketing effort that ties the distribution and promotion elements together. First, the airport tried to convince travelers to use A-B-E instead of New York or Philadelphia airports. Consumers were educated that by using A-B-E, they already had access to national air transportation and did not have to travel to larger, more congested airports. And second, it tried to convince airlines to offer enough flights, at attractive fares, to make the desired flights available and convenient for prospective passengers.

---

[10] *Id.* at 38.

In the example of airports, distribution would also include ease and clarity of access to and through the airport complex, to service(s) offered, and could include ease of transition from the roadway to the curbs, parking facilities, and terminal areas prior to reaching the gates. When a community has limited or no access to the national air transportation system, improving distribution would generally involve a concerted effort to improve the *access* to air service. It could also mean providing convenient ground transportation to transport travelers to a neighboring airport—but few airport operators would likely consider that to be a desirable approach.

PROMOTION

Promotion has its own mix of elements, which collectively can be of great value to airport operators. The *promotional mix* (not to be confused with the marketing mix, mentioned earlier) includes advertising, public relations (including publicity), personal selling and sales promotion. *Advertising* is "paid, non-personal communication regarding goods, services, organizations people, places and ideas that is transmitted through various media."[11] Advertising can easily become the most expensive element of an airport's promotional plan.

The second element of the promotional mix, *Public Relations* is defined in the field of marketing as "any communication to foster a favorable image."[12] Because of the critical importance of public relations for airports, it will be covered in greater depth in Chapter 14.

Personal selling (sometimes referred to as direct marketing when no intermediary agent is used) is the third element.[13] Personal selling involves "oral communications with one or more prospective buyers [or prospective users] by paid representatives for the purpose of making sales." At airports, this varies depending on the "product" that is being "sold". The airport manager can be a compelling marketer for the airport. Airlines, airport employees, concessionaries and many other can individually or collectively encourage use of the airport and purchase of goods and services.

The fourth element, *sales promotion* is defined as "paid marketing communications activities (other than advertising, publicity, or per-

---

[11] Joel Evans & Barry Berman, *Marketing, 9e: Marketing in the 21st Century (2007)*, retrieved from Atomicdogpublications.com.

[12] *Id.*

[13] *Id.*

sonnel selling) that intend to stimulate customer purchases or dealer effectiveness."[14] Notably, some marketing resource manuals or videos include event or activity *sponsorship* as a method of sales promotion; other sources separate out sponsorship as a fifth promotional element.[15]

The elements of the promotional mix as defined above are clearly oriented toward for-profit organizations. Still, modified for today's airport operators, these elements suggest a valuable assortment of tools for promoting airports to their clients—particularly air travelers and airport tenants, both of whom have many choices.

Advertising is an important component of the promotional mix at airports. A-B-E built its program around the slogan "Going somewhere? Fly A-B-E." The slogan was placed on coffee mugs, baggage tags and other items distributed by the airport. Similarly, The T.F. Green State Airport had a program of low-cost marketing ideas to remind area residents to use *their* airport. They thought it would be a great idea to put on the desk of every travel agent in the state one of those pads of notepaper that looks like a cube, and put "Go Green" on the side. They followed up with green promotional luggage tags. They also decided on a "Go Green" billboard on Interstate 95 and ads in Rhode Island newspapers.

Milwaukee's General Mitchell Field [MKE] invested $165,000 in its "Avoid the Chicago ORDeal! Fly MKE" campaign, during which prospective flyers were encouraged to register on the airport's website (AvoidTheChicagoORDeal.com), during which travelers could compare air fares and parking fees in a calculator operated by Orbitz.com.[16]

Promotions have been extended to prospective air cargo tenants as well as evidenced by the campaign undertaken by Ohio's Rickenbacker International Airport. The airport,

> *. . . developed a marketing campaign that contrasts Rickenbacker with traditional cargo gateways. Phase one of the campaign consisted of three mailings using a non-*

[14] *Id.*

[15] For more discussion on this, *see* the 1999 video, *Marketing*, Produced by the Standard Deviants Academic Team of John McCarty (American University) & Barbara Rosenthal (Miami-Dade Community College), ISBN: 1421356902.

[16] Barbara Cook, in *Making their Pitches*, Airport Magazine (Apr./May 2006), at 37.

> *aviation theme that went to 300 industry decision-makers. One mailing stated that congestion at traditional gateways means a carrier needs luck to land on time, while at Rickenbacker, delays aren't a problem. The mailing included luck charms. . . .*

Likewise, in 2005, The Metropolitan Washington Airports Authority [MWAA] also launched a cargo advertising program for Dulles International Airport. The campaign was "intended to develop a brand identity for Dulles, raise awareness of the airport's low operating costs, its central location on the east coast and the network of interstate highways that connect to the airport." The target audiences included airlines, freight forwarders, and other third-parties (e.g., FBOs).[17]

REVENUE SOURCES

Airports are more than just a place to land or take off; they are an economic entity. They provide facilities and services for the convenience of aircraft operation, travelers and the storage and handling of mail and cargo. In providing these services airports incur expenses, but at the same time they create offsetting revenues. The airport's operational revenues originate from three principal source categories:

- Aeronautical operating revenue;
- Non-aeronautical operating revenue; and
- Non-operating revenue.[18]

Aeronautical operating revenues are comprised of revenues derived from a variety of aviation-related sources including:[19]

- Landing fees;
- Terminal and international arrival area rental;
- Apron charges/tie-downs;

---

[17] *Id.*

[18] FAA, *Operating and Financial Summary*, Form 5100-127, as an appendix to AC 150/5100-19. (Apr. 2001), retrieved from http://forms.faa.gov/forms/faa5100-127.pdf.

[19] *Id.*

- FBO revenue: contract or sponsor-operated;
- Cargo and hangar rental; and
- Aviation fuel tax and fuel sales.[20]

Non-aeronautical operating revenues includes revenues derived from a variety of non-aviation-related sources such as:

- Land and non-terminal facilities;
- Terminal sources (food and beverage, retail and other);
- Rental Cars; and
- Parking.[21]

In the following pages, select aeronautical and non-aeronautical sources will be discussed in detail. *Non-operating revenue,* which include interest income, grant receipts and passenger facility charges were detailed in the prior chapter on "Airport Finance and Economics."[22]

AERONAUTICAL REVENUES

Landing area and terminal revenues generate the greatest share of aeronautical revenues at airports. Fees associated with cargo operations can also be substantial at some airports.

LANDING FEES

Most airports serving air carriers charge some form of landing fee for air carrier operations, and there are a number of ways in which landing fees may be determined. At many commercial service airports, the fees that are associated with operation and maintenance, (and sometimes the construction or reconstruction) of the landing areas are tallied using complex *cost accounting* methods detailed later in this chapter.

Usually the fees are then assessed to the users on the basis of certificated Maximum Gross Weight [MGW] on landing, but other meth-

[20] FAA, *Operating and Financial Summary*, Form 5100-127, as an appendix to AC 150/5100-19. (Apr. 2001), retrieved from http://forms.faa.gov/forms/faa5100-127.pdf.
[21] *Id.*
[22] *Id.*

ods of calculating charges may be made according to aircraft category and/or by flat fee, collected for each landing or aggregated by accounting period such as monthly or annually. It is not an uncommon practice for smaller airports to use fuel flowage charges in lieu of landing fees. Some charge both.

As the volume of enplanements increases, the more likely it becomes that the airport will use the gross landing weight method; and the preponderance of airports using the landing weight method will charge so many cents per each thousand pounds of (certified) MGW landing weight. In some cases a combination of schedules is used, with the larger airplanes being assessed by gross weight and the smaller airplanes charged a flat fee.

Landing fees for general aviation are not particularly common other than for commercial operations. As a revenue source the administrative costs associated with collecting landing fees from general aviation are usually beyond cost benefit. It generally requires the airport to post a "follow me" truck to "chase" each landing aircraft for the purpose of exacting the fee, or to have some alternative (and potentially elaborate) mechanism by which to collect the fee. One reported system uses a computerized billing procedure. The owner of the registration ("N") number[23] on the aircraft observed landing is sent an invoice using the national aircraft registration address.

Some of the larger and busier air carrier airports have begun charging landing fees for general aviation aircraft, but in most cases the General Aviation [GA] landing fees have been levied as a deterrent (to their operations) rather than for true revenue collection purposes. Because of air traffic saturation these airports may be attempting to prompt general aviation to use reliever airports by assessing what are often excessive and seemingly unreasonable charges to GA.

TERMINAL REVENUES

Terminal revenue refers to those revenues generated from tenants that are actively engaging in aeronautical activities. These spaces include ticket counters, baggage claim areas, passenger holding rooms, airline or air cargo offices, airline terminal-based maintenance areas, and international arrival areas. It does not apply to activities like the

[23] An "N" number refers to first letter being an "N" in the numbers issued to U.S.-registered aircraft. In other countries, the first letter is different.

concessions that could be conducted at a non-airport location (albeit, not as lucratively), which will be discussed later.

Charges to airlines or other aeronautical users are established by the airport sponsor or its oversight authority using a variety of methods. These charges may reflect past practice, may be calculated as a function of the cost of operating and maintaining the space, or may be adjusted to reflect development costs incurred by the tenant.

The long-term conveyance of real estate for a specified rent constitutes a "lease." *Leaseholds* are distinguished from *concessions* (discussed later in this chapter) in that the users pay a flat rental fee rather than a percentage of the gross sales or profits. The method of charging for rent most commonly used is a certain rate per square foot of space; usually on an annual basis, but rental rates may be calculated monthly or otherwise. Sometimes terminal fees are established not as leases, but as short-term (such as 30-day) use agreements.

The duration of leases or agreements may be a function of the airport's approach to financial management. This is discussed later in this chapter.

APRONS, HANGARS, CARGO AND FBO REVENUES

Apron or ramp fees include charges for aircraft servicing, aircraft parking fees and other related activities. In addition, there are usually fees for hangar storage. Charges for the use of certain facilities at the interface between the aircraft parking apron and the terminal building complex might be considered an apron or ramp fee. Oftentimes, the air carriers will have exclusive use of passenger loading ramps, gates, and boarding areas, and they will have these areas included in their leasehold agreements. But where there are insufficient airport facilities for each carrier's sole use, the carriers may be forced to share. Charges in the form of ramp fees may be allocated according to each airline's prorated use of the apron areas.

These charges may be collected directly by the airport operator, or alternatively, the ramp may be partially or totally operated as a concession, with the airport receiving a cut of the revenues. If a concessionaire provides the service of parking or storing aircraft for the airport, the concession normally collects the fees and pays a percentage of the collection to the airport proprietor.

Aircraft parking is categorized as either *transient* or *permanent* storage. Charges for transient parking are normally collected on a daily basis, with rates varying according to aircraft size and category. Permanent storage fees are usually collected monthly.

Ancillary ramp services such as providing auxiliary power units for engine starts, towing, and other aircraft servicing are generally provided by fixed base operators, or by the airlines. However, the airport may, on occasion, provide special services such as security, and it will make appropriate charges for these supplementary services.

Hangars are another source of ramp-related revenue. However, almost without exception airports rarely have enough hangars to satisfy the demand for them. Oftentimes there is only limited room available for new hangar development, the cost of constructing hangars is high and the return on investment is usually very low. Hence, hangar development has evolved into a variety of ownership options. Some hangars may be owned by the airport and rented directly to users. In some cases hangars are built and owned by the users who pay only for rental of the bare land upon which the hanger sits.

In some cases fixed base operators build hangars on rented land and then rent directly to the hangar user. In other cases, the airport may own the hangar(s), and rent to an FBO who in turn will sub-let the hangars. Hence, there are a variety of ways by which airports derive hangar-related revenues.

It should be recognized that in many cases an operator might be both a lessee in one instance and a concessionaire in another. For example, an FBO may lease facilities for its business (maintenance and flight) operation while at the same time paying (fuel flowage) concession fees for dispensing fuels. The airline may lease its office and hangar facilities, but may also pay concession (or landing) fees in connection with the number of landings it performs.

FUEL AND LAND REVENUES

Fuel and oil flowage fees are a system by which the airport charges a fixed fee (usually a few cents) for every gallon of aviation gasoline, jet fuel, or engine lubricating oil delivered for use at the airport. This practice started when airport proprietors initially got out of the fuel dispensing business. As the refueling operations were transferred to fixed base operators the airports still wanted to receive some portion of the revenues derived from gasoline sales. Thus, the airport applied a surcharge for each gallon sold.

Since the airlines normally refueled their own airplanes, it was primarily general aviation pilots who bought their fuels from purveyors on the airports, and it was they who generally paid the fuel flowage surcharge. As a result, fuel flowage became a general aviation related charge. Though traditionally viewed as a general aviation user fee, the practice has crossed over to the air carrier sector. Fuel flowage fees sometimes substitute for landing fees, particularly at smaller, predominantly general aviation airports. Although fuel flowage did not begin as a user charge, but rather was a concession fee, through time and practice it has become an indirect airfield use fee.

Where there is land in excess of the airport's operational needs, leasehold agreements may be entered into to provide an expanded revenue base in support of the fiscal operation of the airport. The most compatible use of airport land other than for aviation operations is in either agricultural or industrial/commercial uses. These non-aeronautical uses are the subject of the next section.

NON-AERONAUTICAL REVENUES

Food and beverage, retail, parking, and rental car operators are all considered non-aviation related activities. Thus, they form a secondary market whose business livelihood is dependent upon the primary market of air commerce. They provide ancillary services to users of the primary market and as such may be subjected to market-based rates for use, as opposed to rates based on space Operations and Maintenance [O& M] costs.

TERMINAL CONCESSIONS

With enlarged and enhanced facilities, as well as generally longer dwell times (associated with heightened security since 9/11), there is increasing demand for concessions at airports. The most common concessions found at airport terminals are food and beverage or F&B services and retail merchandisers. Airport services are a growing sector in the non-revenue-generating category. Airports may host full service restaurants, cocktail lounges, hotels, banks, beauty salons, barbershops, shoe shine stands and a vast variety of retailers including those catering to golfers and specialty beverage connoisseurs (e.g., PGA Shop and Starbucks). According to Sue and O.B. Schooley:

> *There are many components to a great concessions program; no two programs are exactly the same. Like the paints an oil painter chooses to cover a blank canvas, the mix of concessions is critical to a concessions program development.*[24]

Available floor space and imagination is the only real limitation on the number and variety of concessions that could conceivably locate in the terminal. There are concessions that may not be essential to the traveling public, but which nevertheless may be a convenience and therefore in the public's interest to allow them in the terminal area. Examples are duty free shops, gift shops, boutiques, stationers, and vendors of flowers, candy, or fruit, and even auto service stations. Amusement centers, television viewing areas and sleeping booths are also examples of convenience type concessions.

Airports must be partners with their tenants in the planning of retail areas, in order to achieve maximum revenues. Passenger behavior and analysis techniques suggest five steps that could be taken in the planning of airport concession areas:

- Understand the customer;
- Determine what they will buy;
- Create a shopping environment;
- Motivate shopping behavior; and
- Make it easy to buy.[25]

Concession activities at airport terminals constitute one of the principal sources of airport revenue, and depending upon airport size can amount to well over 50% of the airport's gross income. Concession revenues are associated predominantly with air carrier airports,

---

[24] Sue & O.B. Schooley, *Concession: Beyond "The Numbers"*, Airport Magazine (Sep./Oct. 2005), at 61.

[25] The source for these steps is Stephen Freibrun, Principal Associate, The Center for Airport Management, *Converting Your Vision into a Plan*, ERAU/ACI-NA Concession Seminar, Las Vegas, Nev. (Nov. 12, 2004).

but they may be a major source of revenue at larger general aviation airports as well. As a rule, the amount of revenues generated collectively by the concession operators correlates directly with either the enplanements volume at air carrier airports, or the number of aircraft operations at general aviation airports.

Pricing guidelines for concessions are rather complex, but are usually based upon a minimum rental payment and a percentage of the concessionaire's gross income. In theory, the value of the concession rents is tied to the opportunity of serving the primary market that is provided by the airport sponsor. A percentage of the gross income is therefore thought to reflect the economic value of the concessionaire's location advantage at the airport. In other words, airport traffic is the market generator. For owning and operating the airport, the proprietor is entitled to receive a (income) share of the business that it brings to the concessionaire. The value of that service graduates with an expanding market of airport users (reflected by an increase in passenger enplanements and/or aircraft operations).

TERMINAL MALLS AND MARKETPLACES

Airport terminal concessions have infamous reputations for offering over-priced, yet poor quality products. However, the 1990s ushered in a renaissance in airport food service and retail sales. The current trend is to upgrade the terminal marketplace in terms of both higher quality and lower price, and to make it more competitive with off-airport shopping centers. The airport terminal also serves as the 21st century gateway to the communities the airport serves. As Stephen Freibrun states:

> *The success of an airport's concession program is measured by a number of economic and intrinsic factors [such as] the positive experience that a traveler has as the airport, resulting in the traveler's desire to return to the community; the businesses that want to relocate to the area because of its transportation facilities; and the amount of pride a commu-*

> *nity has for its airport because of its superb customer service and excellent facilities.*[26]

Airport sponsors are attempting to improve upon services by adopting an economic philosophy of going after volume rather than margin. Seemingly they are finding it more lucrative to lower space rents and to take a lower percentage of the gross receipts in order to encourage more business volume. Moreover, one of the roles of the airport is in keeping airport customers satisfied. Airports are for people, and anyone who walks into the airport terminal is a potential customer. In the United States there are over two billion such potential customers every year. There are roughly 600 million annual enplanements, which in turn become another 600 million deplanements at another airport. These passengers are matched by an equal (or greater) number of meeters-and-greeters at either end. Added to this is the number of airline and airport employees who go to work every day at the airport.

The combined 2.5 billion potential customers make up a huge market sector! And, as surveys have shown, airport customers are typically more affluent than are customers at local city malls. As a result, these travelers—comprised of more and more women and other diverse groups—have become the targets of new marketing and merchandising strategies aimed at the customers who desire both a convenient and a comprehensive retail shopping experience. Additionally, the number and variety of retail services are increasing at airports. As reported by *Airport* Magazine:

> *Services are beginning to get a lot of attention than five or six years ago, as well as product lines that cater to the female traveler as she becomes more a part of the mainstream. Airports are looking for manicures and massages. You will start to see a large line of health/beauty stores, primarily for the female traveler.*[27]

---

[26] *Id.*

[27] Delaware North Companies Travel Hospitality Services, *National v. Retail Brands*, Airport Magazine (Aug./Sep. 2006), at 27.

Airport terminals may never attract shoppers to the extent downtown shopping malls do, but airline passengers as well as airport meeters-and-greeters are potential customers who often find themselves with leisure time to spend at the airport. The current marketing trend is an attempt to capture discretionary dollars from airport visitors by encouraging them to eat and/or shop at airport terminal malls.

Most travelers seemingly consume airport "junk food" as a last resort, but studies have shown that more than 60% of passengers regularly buy food and/or beverages each time they are at the airport. Many spend their time reading, and nearly 40% of business travelers, and 30% of leisure travelers buy something to read at the airport. Retail stores are the least frequented establishments. Less than 15% of the airport customers shop at airport retail stores, citing high prices and low quality as the reasons.

Nevertheless, airport shopping centers have in some cases become distinctive marketplaces. Moreover, airports are developing shopping malls with food courts that are anchored by nationally known franchisers like Burger King, McDonalds, and Pizza Hut, and interspersed with restaurants and other purveyors with local themes. Surveys have shown that travelers say they prefer "brand-named" food places where quality is consistent. Conversely, when it comes to retail goods, travelers say they prefer goods indigenous to the area rather than generic items.

Although some airports deal directly with each concessionaire, many concession management approaches or models exist. These models and examples of airports (using three-letter designators) where they are being used are listed below:

- Prime (ATL)
- Multiple or Direct Leasing (SFO, DEN)
- Master (OAK)
- Developer (PIT, PHL).[28]

A *prime* is a concessionaire who operates several concessions in a single category, with some subcontracts to Disadvantaged Business Enterprises (DBEs). There may be a few primes, but only one master, as discussed below. In a *multiple or direct leasing* model, the "airport

[28] Leigh Fisher Associates, *Concession Management Approaches*, Airport Magazine (Aug./Sep. 2006), at 29.

awards multiple concession agreements to a number of concessionaires, each with one or more units."[29] Individual concession operators may be referred to as "independents." A *master* concessionaire "operates all or a substantial majority of the airport's concessions, subcontracting some units to DBEs."[30] While heavily used in the prior century, this approach has become rare. Finally, a *developer* "subcontracts all concession spaces to others and manages the program on behalf of the airport."[31]

The choice of one of the listed concession management models relies upon a number of factors including the type of passenger traffic (origin/destination or transfer), the size of the airport, the nature of existing agreements, etc. Smaller airports may not have sufficient revenue generation capabilities to insure the success of multiple independents (associated with a direct leasing model). Thus, they may opt for another model such as that selected by the Louisville Regional Airport Authority, who's Property Manager Lew Bleiweis explains,

> *We looked at our enplanements, the distribution of those enplanements throughout the terminal building and other influencing factors and determined it would be best to pursue a prime concessionaire for each of the two categories of concessions. . . . [E]ven though our enplanements are good, they are weighted to one side more than the other. With this in mind, we felt a stand-alone operator could not be successful and needed the whole operation to carrying the slower concourse.* [32]

Vendors are encouraged contractually or by other means to maintain prices competitive with off-airport stores. This practice has come to be known in some circles as "street pricing" (a.k.a. "street-level pricing"). Some contracts, for example, prohibit concessionaires from pricing products higher than what they charge at other local (but off-airport) locations.

---

[29] *Id.*
[30] *Id.*
[31] *Id.*
[32] Barbara Cook, *Retail's Reach*, Airport Magazine (Sep./Oct. 2004), at 51-52.

Since the late 1980s, airports have been implementing strategies to dispel negative perceptions about airport concessions and to increase airport revenue. Of more than 20 airports surveyed in one 1995 street-pricing study, most airports reported having a formal street level pricing policy in their retail tenant leases, with the remainder reporting such a policy under development. Those formal policies ranged from "not a penny above" street prices to a "defined acceptable mark up limit" (e.g., 5% to 15%).

The approach to street or street-level pricing today remains inconsistent. At a popular airport retail conference held in San Francisco in 2005, airport officials described their approach to street-level pricing in a variety of ways, such as: prices found in a similar controlled setting (such as a mall or other planned shopping centers with development costs), prices on the street plus a percentage mark-up (10% or 20%), or the best of several price samplings from a variety of pre-designed off-airport locations. Sometimes prices are simply adjusted in collaboration between airport and tenant, with the goal of making prices more reasonable to the traveling public.

Some facilities feel they need active enforcement of their street pricing policies. Market forces may serve to bring prices closer to street level, but tenants should be expecting at least some random monitoring. Los Angeles International Airport, believes that they have such a variety of concessions at the airport that the "competition seems to maintain prices at very close to street level." Nevertheless, they believe that monitoring of prices is crucial to ensure reasonable prices.[33] Philadelphia International Airport has a set of guidelines for assuring compliance with its street-pricing policy, as follows:

- Merchants are required by lease to adhere to street pricing;
- Merchants are required to submit retail pricing reports quarterly;
- Developer provides digital template for required information;
- Developer enforces policy with comprehensive reviews and active oversight (secret shopper program);
- Pricing discrepancies result in penalties, which may include monetary fines; and

---

[33] Staff, *Prices In U.S. Airports Compete Head-On With Street Retail*, World Airport Retail News (Nov. 5, 1995), at 1-10.

- Multiple offences can lead to merchant default or termination.[34]

The newest passenger retail services and for-pay amenities include business services, financial services and personal services such as health clubs and massages. In addition, the presence of national brand products also helps to stabilize pricing at lower levels or makes pricing appear to be more in line with the perceived value of the goods or services. For instance, a McDonalds or Burger King restaurant charging the same prices as at their other establishments can serve as a control on pricing by other (independent) food service vendors with whom they are in competition at the airport.

A *brand* is a set of distinguishing characteristics that differentiates one company, entity, product or service from another.[35] "When a customer encounters these characteristics, branding creates in that consumer the thoughts and emotions associated with the product or service."[36] A barrage of branding efforts can be found at airports, including that pertaining to the community, the airport, the retail environment, individual stores and individual product or services. Airports are best served in considering all the branding efforts that may be underway and devising strategies for mutual benefit.

An example of superior branding and retail coordination can be found at Seattle-Tacoma International Airport [SEA-TAC] with their "central terminal" complex that features the Pacific Marketplace. Retail shops and food and beverage concessions were selected using a model that promoted the airport's desire to highlight the geographic and cultural highlights of the region. A robust marketing campaign serves to generate interest in the specialized concessionaires, while equally supporting the airport's larger branding efforts. If revenue generation is an indicator of success, SEA-TAC has been wildly successful. In 2007, one F&B operator is anticipating revenues in excess of $10 million and one retail store reported a single sale in excess of $22,000 in 2006![37]

---

[34] James Tyrell, *Philadelphia International Airport Case Studies*, ERAU/ACI-NA Concession Seminar Presentation, Las Vegas, Nev. (Nov. 11, 2004).

[35] Jeff Van Hoosear & Jason Evans, *Brands in the Boardroom: Key Branding Issues for Senior Executives*, Intellectual Assets Management Magazine, retrieved from www.iam-magazine.com, as referenced in Pursuing Strong Brand, of Knobbe Martens Olson & Bear, LLP, at 5.

[36] *Id.*

[37] Public statement made by SEA-TAC personnel (and validated with the subject retail concessionaire), ERAU/ACI-NA Airport Retail Concession Conference, Seattle, Wash. (Nov. 2006).

One emerging issue in the area of branding is the quest for the proper balance between *national brands* versus *local brands*. While hurried passengers may want the familiarly of a national brand, The Paradies Shops counter that, "Local brands play a very important part of the concessions program, because the airport traveler typically wants to purchase something indigenous to the area and take home the experience."[38] Still, the days of rows of airport souvenir shops are fast coming to an end.

In the transition airports must be mindful of the hidden costs associated with airport concessions. These "back of the house" issues such as problems with lack of storage space, ramp access issues, off-site warehousing, environmental/health issues, transportation issues, and security concerns can present operating and pricing constraints to concessionaires, and at times to the airport as well. The "liquids restrictions" imposed by the Transportation Security Administration [TSA] in 2006, for example, created challenges for concessionaires and airports alike. However, it should also be noted that the restriction presented opportunities as well for concessionaires by creating increased sales beyond the security checkpoints.

Irrespective, by keeping costs and prices low, and by offering brand name goods, the hopeful expectation is that airport consumers might be better served, more revenue might be generated to support airport operations, and the airport terminal market might no longer be perceived as a place of overly priced goods and service.

RENTAL CARS AND PARKING REVENUES

Two significant sources of non-aeronautical revenue are rental car operators and parking activities, with the revenues surpassing the retail and F&B numbers at times. For example, while Las Vegas McCarran Internal Airport's estimated annual retail *and* F&B annual revenues to exceed $158 million in 2005, their rental car revenue estimates for the year were $218 million.[39]

Since 50% or more of the air passengers arrive at the airport by car, automobile parking is a very important revenue-producing activity. Parking operations can be owned and operated by airports, by

---

[38] Barbara Cooke, *Upscale Retail: National vs. Local Brands*, Airport Magazine (Aug./Sep. 2006), at 27.

[39] PowerPoint Slide Presentation, *McCarran International Airport Concessions Tour*, (Nov. 10, 2005).

private vendors, public-owned and contractually operated, or via another public/private partnership model. Just as airports have seen dramatic changes in their retail and F&B areas, they have also experienced transformations in their parking programs, including new technology and new services. Valet parking, for example, is increasing in popularity at commercial service airports. Some airports are considering allowing more comprehensive vehicle services such as car washes and maintenance.

Technology has benefited airports in their management of parking operations. In 2005, Orlando became the first airport in Florida to automate its parking payment system, for use by vehicles equipped with toll-road transponder devices. Not only will this system decrease delays for users, but it is anticipated to eventually reduce the number of staffed exit lanes required at parking facilities.[40]

To enhance the parking experience, airports are also installing new devices to guide users and track their garage use. When a vehicle enters a parking facility at Boston Logan International Airport, a camera records the license number and time of arrival into its database. Thereafter, passengers are guided by a series of illuminated signs to vacant spaces.[41] The technology saves labor costs, increases passenger satisfaction, and eliminates problems associated with lost tickets.

OTHER REVENUES

The most common non-aviation revenues come from leases for ground space, office and warehousing buildings. Agricultural leases can be granted where other uses are unlikely, such as the open infield areas between the runways, taxiways, and other operational areas. Although the return on the land is minimal, agricultural use has a dual economic advantage for the airport. First, there is the direct revenue received for use of the land. And second, the farmer's attention to the land eliminates the need to seed, fertilize or mow weeds. Thus, the airport sponsor can realize substantial savings in grounds maintenance expenses.

Other important sources of non-aviation revenues at airports include: advertising, ground transportation and gaming (slot machines).

---

[40] J. Jackson, *Orlando Airport Automates Parking Payment System for Vehicles with E-Pass*, Knight-Rider Tribune Business News (Feb. 23, 2005).

[41] B. Mohl, *Forget Where You Parked Your Car? Logan is Spending Millions to Track Available Spaces and Help Travelers Navigate its Busy Garages*, Boston Globe (Mar. 13, 2005).

For the year 2005, Las Vegas McCarran estimated revenues of $11.4 million in advertising, $32 million in ground transportation, and 56.5 million in gaming revenues.

Airports have had mixed approaches pertaining to the possible revenues associated with Wireless-Fidelity [Wi-Fi] Internet access and battery charging locations and stations. The Dallas Morning News reports,

> *Keeping electronic gadgetry juiced up is a growing frustration for business travelers, who are carrying more devices and waiting longer in airports, in part because of added security. Replenishing computer and cell phone batteries between flights often entails sitting on the airport floor. Some travelers inadvertently create tripwires as their power cords stretch between power outlets and their seats. For Dallas/Fort Worth International Airport, that frustration may prove to be an opportunity.*[42]

Graduate students are examining whether adding certain amenities (e.g., power outlets) at Dallas/Fort Worth International Airport [DFW] would attract more connecting passengers. "Connecting passengers are crucial for DFW, accounting for about two-thirds of the airport's 60 million passengers each year," states reporter Suzanne Marta. The goal is to create a strategy that "makes the most of the airport's investments and sales opportunities."[43]

NON-OPERATING REVENUES

Just as there are hidden economic advantages attached to agricultural land-use grants on the airport, there may also be other sources of revenues that are not readily apparent, or which are not applicable to all airports in general. These may be considered *non-operating* revenues.

---

[42] Suzanne Marta, *D/FW to Survey Passengers on Recharging Needs*, The Dallas Morning News (Fri., Jan. 12, 2007).
[43] *Id.*

As pointed out later in this chapter, few airports are economically self-sustaining. Most require some form of subsidy. The level and manner in which an airport receives outside subsidies may represent an obscure revenue source. For example, personal property taxes collected for aircraft ownership and *possessory interest* taxes for use of government owned lands both represent revenue derived from airport users. Personal property taxes are collected on chattel (i.e., non-real estate) properties, which may be considered luxuries. Boats, campers, and airplanes are typical properties for which *ad valorem* taxes are collected. Privately owned real property is also taxed, but government-owned property is not taxable. However, when private parties take *possession* of public property through leasehold or some other agreement, then the property is once again subject to taxation. Such a tax is commonly referred to as a "possessory interest" tax.

Although possessory interest and personal property taxes are usually collected by the State and devoted to non-aviation uses such as schools and other community needs, they nevertheless represent a revenue source to the community, which is produced by the airport. It may be considered an equitable exchange for the community to return monies or to subsidize the airport by an amount equal to the personal property and possessory interest taxes associated with the airport, where it can be demonstrated that such funds are necessary for continued airport operation.

Providing utilities such as water or electricity may derive another form of revenue. Some airports receive considerable income through the purchase of utility services at wholesale rates and re-sale of those services to airport tenants at retail prices. In this way, the airport can find itself the operator of a mini-utility company. For example, the airport may receive its water from the municipal source and will pay for that water based on the records of a master meter. The water may then be distributed to the various tenants through individual lease site meters, with individual charges assessed to each user. The airport will pay the city for water received on the airport, and will in turn apply a handling charge to the bill passed on to the tenant.

Another form of revenue may be income derived from the sale of *surplus property*. A strategy used by some airport authorities has been to develop, or to otherwise sell for development, that property not needed for airport operations, then to use the sale receipts for airport specific development and operation.

An example of airport land sold for development occurred in Santa Maria, California. The Santa Maria Airport District received approximately 3,000 acres of land along with its airfield from the Federal government following World War II. In support of airport expansion through the decade of the 1970s, the Airport District set aside some 250 acres for industrial park development. The park site was subdivided, with subsequent sale of most of the parcels. The monies received from the land sale were then used for revenue-producing development on the airport. As a result, the District was able to systematically develop its airport according to a master plan, and was able to retain ownership of the entire airport operational area along with buildings and facilities. All of this would not have been possible had the airport depended upon its own revenue tax base or for help from the local municipality. The remaining unsold industrial parcels could then be leased to further expand the airport's revenue base.

Still another source of income may be from *investments*. Funds accumulated in excess of current budgetary needs may be invested in the money market; into certificates of deposit, time deposits, U.S. Treasury securities, and other governmental investments authorized by law. Interest earned can compound the value of cash on hand, and may represent additional income to the airport through the *opportunity- or time-use of money*.

Any funds an airport may receive over and above its normal operating revenue, and which it can use to overcome its financial deficit constitute supplemental revenue. Subsidies and grants-in-aid, including federal airport grants, are in this category of income.

FOREIGN TRADE ZONE/ DUTY FREE OUTLET

A Foreign Trade Zone [FTZ] or Duty Free Outlet [DFO] is a restricted access site in or near a Customs Port of Entry. These *Duty Free* areas are the U.S. version of a "customs free zone." They are remnants of the "free ports" of early trade history where relatively independent maritime cities made special efforts to create an environment wherein trade would flourish.[44] As nation states emerged and subsequently imposed customs laws within their borders, they did not

---

[44] Today, the city-state of Singapore is perhaps the nearest approximation to the historic free port.

completely eliminate free trade areas, but rather, compressed the free port's size to a "zone" of free trade within the city.[45]

In the United States, a Free Trade Zone is a designated site that is licensed and overseen by the Foreign Trade Zones Board in Washington, D.C., and supervised by the U.S. Customs Service of the Department of the Treasury. Within the Foreign Trade Zones special customs procedures may be applied pursuant to the Foreign Trade Zones Act of 1934.[46] The Federal Trade Zones Act is administered through two sets of regulations: the Foreign Trade Zone Regulations (15 CFR Part 400) and the Customs Zone Regulations (19 CFR Part 146).[47]

Foreign Trade Zones have been in existence since the Act was passed in 1934, and every U.S Customs Port of Entry is entitled by law to an FTZ. The *special purpose FTZ*—or "subzone"—is a type of FTZ approved for use by a single company, usually an industrial plant, authorized to operate outside the geographic boundaries of a *general purpose FTZ*. A Foreign Trade Zone is another tool to get companies to locate in a given area. Airports with FTZ status can benefit from the value those potential investors and cargo customers return to the airport.[48]

For customs entry purposes, FTZ procedures allow domestic activity such as storing, displaying, assembling, processing and manufacturing of foreign items to take place as if it were procedurally conducted outside the U.S. Customs territory. The procedures are designed to help improve the international competitiveness of firms engaged in domestic economic activity. The objective is to counterbalance customs advantages available to overseas producers who export their products to the United States and other markets in competition with products made in the U.S. The FTZs tend to be known for their services to firms *importing* products and components for eventual sale in the United States, but the greatest benefits accrue to companies that

---

[45] Kenneth A. Cutshaw, *Foreign Trade Zones: Good For Business*, Airport Magazine (Sep./Oct. 1997), at 37; *see also* Dept. of the Treasury U.S. Customs Service, *Foreign Trade Zones: U.S. Customs Procedures and Requirements*, (1979); *see also* John J. Da Ponte, Jr., Executive Secretary Foreign Trade Zones Board, *Updated Rules for Foreign Trade Zones Reflect Big Increase in Zone Activity*, Business America (Nov. 4, 1991), at 9; *see also* Editorial, *Zoned for Business*, Airport Magazine (Nov./Dec. 1991), at 50.

[46] 19 U.S.C. 81a-81-u, *Foreign Trade Zones.*

[47] U.S. Customs and Border Protection, *About Foreign-Trade Zones & Contact Info*, available at http://www.cbp.gov (visited Mar. 2, 2007).

[48] *Id.*

re-export items, because they are the ones accorded the optimal zone benefit of duty-free treatment.[49]

The significant advantage for re-exporters is the *inverted tariff*. The business can elect to pay duties on either the component material used in the production of the final product or for the finished product, depending on which duty is lower. For products manufactured within the FTZ there can be significant savings by not having to pay duties on what becomes waste, scrap, defective, damaged or obsolete during the manufacturing process. Another advantage can be in eliminating tariffs on exports from the FTZ. Customs duties are paid only when the imported items are transferred into the customs territory of the United States, not when they enter the FTZ. Thus, a business can inventory or manufacture a product duty free within an FTZ. A primary objective of the FTZ program, and one that overrides the collection of customs duties, is the creation of jobs in the United States and to stimulate the use of U.S. made goods and products in the United States and abroad.[50]

Since 1970 there has been an explosive growth in Foreign Trade Zones. In 1970, there were nine approved general-purpose FTZs. By 1997, there were over 225. In 1970, there were seven special-purpose FTZs. By the end of 1997, more than 250 subzones had been approved, bringing the total to nearly 500 FTZs.

Foreign Trade Zones are now common at airports around the United States. Airports that host international airlines are using the FTZ more frequently to save money by locating their fuel farms within them. The FTZ program allows domestic refineries to compete on equal footing with international refineries and airports can benefit in the interim. Entities given authority to operate a Foreign Trade Zone usually opt to contract with private firms to operate the facilities and provide services to FTZ users. Successful airports are recognizing and capitalizing on the changing nature of the world economy and aviation's role as an economic center. They are tying together various modes of transportation with industrial needs. Moreover, there is a large potential for generating non-aviation revenues such as industrial parks and other commercial initiatives. A Foreign Trade Zone could be one of those initiatives.[51]

---

[49] *Id.*
[50] *Id.*
[51] *Id.*

While some FTZ/DFO commercial developments at airports are generally considered beneficial, such projects are not without their critics. In 2007, a major international carrier suggested that fares could rise if airports focus too much on commercial developments unrelated to aviation. It was perceived that certain retail projects on airport land could lead airport operators to assess airlines with higher fees to improve their return on capital. Qantas' Government and International Relations Manager, David Hawes, said some commercial developments might negatively affect aeronautical development and hinder "aviation and tourism activity over the longer term."[52]

He referred to Sydney airport's proposal to develop a Duty Free Outlet and bulky goods depot, notwithstanding the inability projected under its (master plan) to provide enough parking spaces for aircraft due to the limited development footprint. Hawes concluded, "While airport operators had the right to pursue non-aviation business, the primary purpose of airports had to be maintained."

DISADVANTAGED BUSINESS ENTERPRISE

Because of a "national legacy of discrimination against women and people of color" legislation and regulatory guidance has evolved over several decades to provide opportunities for the socially and economically disadvantaged.[53] Airports receiving Airport Improvement Program funds[54] must submit a Disadvantaged Business Enterprise or DBE program and three participation goals[55] including one each for:

- Federally funded projects (Part 26);
- Concessions other than car rentals (Part 23); and
- Car rentals.

The federal DBE program originally began as a Minority/Women-Owned Business Enterprise [MBE/WBE] Program in 1980. Cur-

[52] John Masanauskas, *Qantas Warns on Airport Shopping*, Australia-The Melbourne Herald Sun (Thurs., Feb. 1, 2007).
[53] This section taken largely from the following source: ACI–NA, Business Diversity Subcommittee, *An Orientation on Airport DBE Programs.*
[54] Airports receiving FAA grants for airport planning or development and who will award prime contracts exceeding $250,000 in FAA funds must have a DBE program.
[55] There are a couple of exceptions to this that only affect small airports.

rently, the DBE Program is authorized by the Transportation Equity Act for the 21st Century [TEA-21]. Following two legal challenges which rose to the level of the Supreme Court, a requirement was established that a disparity study be conducted prior to creating local DBE programs. In addition, the Supreme Court ruled that race-conscious affirmative action programs must begin to meet a strict scrutiny standard of review.[56]

Several aspects of the DBE program proved to be key in its survival including:

- Goal setting process based on the number of ready willing and able DBEs in local markets;
- Race Neutral measures to achieve DBE goals (i.e., measures intended to help all small businesses, not just DBEs); and
- Personnel net worth standard ($750,000) which is a limit on the personal assets of a DBE certification applicant, not including the applicant's primary residence or the interest in the business being considered for DBE certification.[57]

To be eligible as a DBE or an Airport Concession Disadvantaged Business Enterprise
[ACDBE], a business must be for-profit, considered a "small business," and the controlling member(s) of the business (51%) must be socially and economically disadvantaged.

Socially disadvantaged pertains to an individual that has been subject to race or ethnic prejudice or cultural bias stemming from beyond the individual's control. Although certain groups are automatically considered socially disadvantaged due to ethnicity or gender, others may qualify by providing a preponderance of evidence that they were raised with a similar cultural bias.

As a result of the Supreme Court ruling in *Richmond v. Croson*,[58] meeting the socially disadvantaged component alone is not enough.

[56] *See City of Richmond v. J.A. Croson* 87-998 (1989); *see also Adarand Constructor, Inc. v. Pena*, 515 US 200 (1995).

[57] ACI–NA, Business Diversity Subcommittee, *An Orientation on Airport DBE Programs*.

[58] *City of Richmond v. J.A. Croson Co.*, 488 U.S. 469, 490 (1989). *Croson* involved a minority set-aside program in the awarding of municipal contracts. Richmond, Va., with a black population of just over 50% had set a 30% goal in the awarding of city construction contracts, based on its findings that local, state, and national patterns of discrimination had resulted in all but complete lack of access for minority-owned businesses. Because appellant city failed to

The candidate must also show they are *financially disadvantaged* (as noted in the personal net work standard).

The measurement of success in a DBE program is whether the goals established were indeed accomplished. Goals are typically established by using FAA's recommended methodology, and should be a reflection of the diversity of companies available in the airport's region. Some airports have exceeded their DBE expectations, and have experienced success. In the development of its Model Concession Program, seven of ten concessions selected were DBEs.[59]

AIRPORT RATES AND CHARGES

Establishment and collection of user charges and the terms of leases involves the underlying philosophy of airport management, adopted policy regarding rates and charges, and the very concept of governmental function. The answer to the question of what the airport ought to charge for its services depends upon where the airport lies within the scale of governmental functions.

APPROACHES TO FINANCIAL MANAGEMENT

The financial and operational relationship between the airport and its tenants is defined in legally binding agreements specifying how the risks and responsibilities of airport operation are to be shared between the two parties. Although these agreements are most commonly referred to as "leases," they are more than a common lease. The agreement is a combination of a lease upon real estate (as is commonly understood) and an *operating* agreement between the involved parties. The contracts, more appropriately termed "airport use agreements," establish the terms and conditions governing the (private) tenant's use of the (public) airport property. Although financial management practices differ greatly among public airports, most are typically based on one of three very different approaches with important implications for airport pricing and investment practices:

---

identify the need for remedial action in the awarding of its public construction contracts, its treatment of its citizens on a racial basis violated the Equal Protection Clause.

[59] SEA Managing Dir. Mark Reis, *Concessions of the Future*, ERAU/ACI-NA Airport Concession Conference: Top-Line Strategies for Bottom Line Results, Seattle, Wash. (Nov. 1, 2006).

- One method is the *residual cost*, or "single cash register" approach.[60] Once the airport's costs are determined, revenues (excluding airline fees) are subtracted from these costs to determine what additional revenue is needed if the airport is to cover its costs. Excluded (airline) fees are then set so that they bring in the remaining deficit. This approach seeks to balance *total* airport costs with total revenue.
- The second method is the *cost of service*, or "multiple cost center" approach. The airport is divided into cost centers, and the fees and charges for each revenue-producing cost center are set so that the revenue from the cost center covers the cost allocated to it. To the accountant this is known as "cost allocation."
- The third method is the *public subsidy* approach. The local government airport sponsor offsets the difference between revenue and expenses by subsidizing the airport operation.

The "cost of service" and "public subsidy" financial management strategies may be grouped into one, the *compensatory approach.* In the compensatory approach, the airport sponsor assumes the major financial risk of running the airport and charges tenants and users fair equitable rates set so as (and wherever possible) to recover the actual costs of the facilities and services that they use. While most airports select either the compensation or the residual cost approach, at least one major airport (Las Vegas McCarran International Airport) utilizes them in combination: residual for the airfield and compensatory for the terminal.

Historically, lease agreements have not provided airports with the flexibility needed in deregulation. Many of the essential air service airports found themselves locked into exclusive airline agreements that had been entered into long before deregulation. *Traditional* airline leases (i.e. "residual cost"), or what many call "Chicago" or "O'Hare" contracts, are long-term (twenty to thirty year) agreements, under which signatory airlines effectively have a say in "managing" the airport along with the airport operator. Distinguishing features of the traditional lease are:

[60] This is sometimes referred to as the "single till" approach.

- *Majority-in-interest* provisions wherein significant capital projects, and sometimes the airport budget, must be approved by *signatory* airlines;
- *Residual cost* methods of determining what the airlines are to pay the airport sponsor. Usually the airlines pay the difference up to a specified amount between revenues from all other sources and the airport's total expenses. The result is for the airport to at best break even. More often, however, there is a deficit the taxpayers must make up; and
- *Exclusive rights* of the individual airlines to their terminals, ticket counters, passenger lounges, gates, concourses, office space, cargo and other air carrier areas.

The "traditional" leases have become a standard in the industry because of adopted financing mechanisms, with over half of the medium and large air carrier airports engaged to some degree in the residual cost approach. For fifty years the Civil Aeronautics Board [CAB] managed airline routes, wherein the Federal government guaranteed the profitability of the airlines *de facto* through subsidies. Thus, the airlines, backed up by the airports as markets, were a good bond risk. Since most airport capital improvements are financed through the sale of revenue bonds, long-term leases with the airlines were needed to secure financing. In exchange for their signatures on the leases, and a commitment to provide air service, the airlines demanded a say in how airport monies were to be spent. Hence, contracts evolved which granted airlines the right to vote on airport projects, and gave them a part to play in the overall management of the airport. However, at these airports there still may be some non-signatory airlines that have different terms and conditions.

Since deregulation, the "airport-as-a-market" has become more dominant than the existence of service by any one airline. The Federal government no longer guarantees the longevity of a given airline serving an airport. Yet, capital development is a long-term proposition. The question now is whether or not any airlines will be serving the market twenty to thirty years down the road once construction and/or expansion of facilities has been completed. Assurance that *some* airline will serve the market must be derived from the inherent demand generated by the airport and must come from granting newcomers access and allowing for the effects of free market economics.

The test of the airport-as-a-market cannot be settled when any one airline has exclusive rights, which may bar the entry of another. If the incumbent airline decides to discontinue service, the airport may likely suffer an interim loss of air transportation.

The quality of the airport-as-a-market is relative. If another airline believes it to be a good market it will enter to fill the void, but financing may likely be secured and guaranteed only by the promise of continuous air carrier service. In turn, continuous service can only be guaranteed if those airlines wishing to serve the airport are given the opportunity to do so. A real dilemma arises when the airport sponsor lacks the power, flexibility, or ability to provide additional facilities to new airlines.

Airport landlord/tenant relationships vary widely. The extreme opposite from the traditional or "Chicago" lease is one in which tenant airlines get no vote at all on rates, charges, or capital projects. They do not have (long-term) exclusive rights to airport facilities, but rather, have short-term agreements, and use gates, concourses, ramps and other facilities, which are amenable to sharing on a demand basis. Examples of airports setting air carrier rental rates by ordinance and without air carrier approval are Sky Harbor International Airport in Phoenix and McCarran International Airport in Las Vegas. Although deregulation has not caused radical changes in financial management of airports there have been signs of shift in management policy and practice toward the "compensatory approach."

Airports having the latitude to establish rates as they deem necessary are fortunate, but at some point a decision had to be made by the airport sponsor to provide certain facilities at its own expense in order to retain rights over the use of facilities by more than one carrier. An airline company cannot be expected to pay for facilities a future carrier may demand; they can only be expected to pay for their own needs. If a baggage conveyor system, for example, may potentially serve more than one carrier, an existent airline cannot reasonably be expected to pay the total costs associated with the conveyor. The airport sponsor must be willing to subsidize the tenant airlines for the unused portion of the system.

In the case of Phoenix, Arizona, city leaders had the good fortune and/or insight to recognize that Sky Harbor Airport would grow and, in the long run, it would be unnecessary to subsidize the airlines. Other situations where growth is not so evident may require the community to subsidize the air transportation system if they are to retain or lure air carrier service.

Where the tenant develops capital improvements without governmental assistance, it is often necessary that the tenant obtain long-term rights to property in order to secure favorable bank financing. Granting of long-term agreements and the subsequent loss of flexibility is the price to be paid if the airport sponsor is forced or chooses to relegate the financing of capital improvements to the private sector.

ECONOMIC PHILOSOPHY

Before establishing a price for a service (or a commodity), one must first determine what it costs to produce the service, and second, what the service might be worth to a potential customer. Similarly, such an analysis ought to take place in the provision of public goods. Or, in the instant situation, one might ask, "For what is the airport charging?" The answer to this question depends upon where the airport lies within the scale of governmental functions. Citizens pay taxes in exchange for services, which will promote the most benefits to the most people. Is an airport one of those services? If so, it should be supported by general tax revenues the way public parks or fire and police departments are. If, on the other hand, the airport serves only an elite minority, then they should be the ones who bear the entire costs of the government owning and operating the airport.

Proponents of the former philosophy point out the economic benefit to the community, which the airport brings. Some of these benefits were listed in the previous chapter. Airport advocates believe these benefits serve the common welfare of the community, far outweighing the deficit costs of maintaining the airport. Opponents, on the other hand, argue that airports are for the privileged few, and governmental support of an airport constitutes a subsidy of special interests. Their opinion is moderated to some extent where air carriers and the notion of public transportation is interjected, but they still maintain the users should bear the costs for airport operation; user charges being defined as a payment over and above the user's obligations for the general government support. They argue that the individual beneficiaries can be identified and appropriate portions of the costs can be allocated to individuals on the basis of use. Under these conditions—

so the argument goes—the airport should operate as a commercial venture, and thereby pay its way.

It may be safely assumed that airports lie somewhere in-between the two foregoing positions. By statistical inference, airports are essential to modern transportation, and therefore are indeed necessary for a community's well being. If an airport is essential to the welfare of the community, then it follows that there is an inherent obligation on the part of government to provide this service. That is, of course, if it cannot otherwise be provided by private enterprise. Herein lies the answer to ameliorating the two opposing arguments for and against public support of airports. Private enterprise, user charges, and the government, collectively support the operation of air transportation facilities. The *degree* to which the public sector must participate in subsidizing the airport is the political issue. As pointed out in Chapter 12, all but a select few airports are, from a practical standpoint, incapable of self-support. Most airports rely on some form of subsidy.

The establishment and collection of user charges and rent from negotiated leases is not a simple matter. It involves the underlying philosophy of airport management, the adopted policy regarding rates and charges, and the very concept of governmental function. The functions of government can be classified into three general areas:

- *Protective services* are the basic idea of organized government, entailing protection of life and property;
- *Redistributive activities* provide services or additional income to those who would not otherwise enjoy them if not provided by the government; and
- *Proprietary services*, which under other circumstances would be performed by private, profit-making organizations.

Airports fall primarily within the realm of proprietary services. If airports could have been viably developed and sustained within the private sector, they would have been. But private airports are rapidly disappearing. During the 1950s, half of the U.S. public-use airports were privately owned. This is no longer true. Now, few public-use airports are privately owned. The reasons for the closing of privately owned airports have been varied and complex, but the most common problem cited is financial, particularly due to high property taxes. Other problems cited are the high costs of capital improvements and maintenance, lack of land for expansion, overwhelming environmental issues, land use controls, and personal plans of the owner, often involving retirement and sale of the airport. Small airports have been plums for land developers. According to many former airport owners, high real estate taxes and pressure from developers put (or enticed) them out of business. Many airports could hardly survive. Unreasonably high improvement and operating costs induced many private owners to allow their airports to deteriorate and to use them only as a temporary means of paying taxes while land values increased. These airports became stepping-stones to more profitable residential and commercial land uses.

The low profit margins of particularly smaller airports make them unattractive as long-term business ventures. Private enterprise has not until recently been interested in airports *per se*. But it has been interested in investing in airlines and in select services at airports offering a greater margin for profit. Historically, the actual business of running airports has been a function economically relegated to the governmental sector. Owing to the general public demand for airports, the government has had to step in and provide such services. Thus, airports are a joint venture between private enterprise and government.

Airports are monopolistic in character, which may be another good reason for having the government operate them. One analogy would be to liken airports to public streets, parks and so forth. More appropriately, they are akin to *public utilities* such as municipal water, power or gas systems. The system users can be readily identified, and they can be expected to pay reasonable costs for the services they receive. The free-public-use concept is valid only where the individual beneficiaries cannot be so readily identified. A pure public utility is one which:

- *Is subject to regulatory control* in its geographic area of operation;
- *Rates are charged* to the public; and
- *A* percentage of return on investment *(profit) is allowed.*

Aside from the fact that true public utilities are privately owned, a public airport generally meets the three basic criteria, although the usual philosophy is neither to make a profit nor to lose money in the operation. Profit—meaning personal advantage or gain—by the government is normally viewed as an impingement upon the rights of free enterprise, since government represents unfair competition in a *laissez-faire* economy. Airport pricing schemes are customarily designed with the objective of breaking even, or at least of reducing losses to a minimum.[61] Revenue maximization is normally important in fulfilling the objective, but within the realm of "reasonableness" in assessed charges by a public agency.

Air transportation is a service industry. The airport's product is the provision of a place for the service transaction to occur. In making charges for airport facilities, the intent is to recover all or part of the cost of constructing, maintaining and operating the airport. Great care must be made to insure that all costs for long-term operation are accounted for. All too often in the past, airport sponsors have underpriced airport services in order to encourage aviation growth on the airport and in the community. The result was to lock inequitable financial agreements into perpetuity. As costs began to escalate, these airports were unable to increase revenues accordingly.

The most important element underlying pricing strategy, in probably any field of endeavor is to maintain flexibility. Airports likewise must have the right to adequately charge for services. And they must be able to recover costs for both long and short-term agreements. If pricing flexibility is restricted, the end results are detrimental not only to the airport sponsor, but to the user as well, since airport services are bound to be curtailed.

Airport charges can be categorized in two ways, as either *short-term* or *long-term.* Short-term arrangements are the most flexible and are generally based upon *direct user fees*. They are normally established in some form of rate structure or rental agreement. Direct user fees comprise those charges most directly associated with use of the public areas of the airfield such as landing fees, aircraft storage, transient tie-down fees, and fuel flowage. *Long-term agreements* are leases (rather than rental) of land, terminal floor space, and other buildings.

Pricing flexibility and property manageability became particularly critical following passage of the Airline Deregulation Act of 1978,

---

[61] FAA policy requires airports to maintain a fee and rental structure that "makes the airport as financially sustainable as possible." This long-standing policy was reiterated in 1999 in the FAA's policy on airport revenue diversion; *see Policy and Procedures Concerning the Use of Airport Revenue*, Federal Register (Tues., Feb. 16, 1999); *see also* Karl Bremer & Holly Arthur, *The Revenue Quagmire*, Airport Magazine (May/Jun. 1999).

and the inherent necessity to provide "free access" to airlines wanting to move into new markets. Free access was a cornerstone of airline deregulatory policy. If deregulation was to work, passenger gates, ticket counter areas, and aircraft apron space would have to be made available to all potential entrants.

Against threats of discontinued federal funding and potential litigation, the Department of Transportation and the Federal Aviation Administration were demanding airport operators negotiate leases incorporating the airport's authority to provide for additional airlines' needs. Airports needed the flexibility to take, if necessary, from airline tenants the facilities needed by new entrants. At the same time, environmental issues were pressing the need for airport sponsors to reduce the liability for noise-related impact on nearby residents. Noise abatement is viewed by the airport sponsor as a proprietor's responsibility, but also as a "right." The FAA on the other hand considers itself solely responsible for determining efficient and safe use of the airspace, including capacity of airport runways and taxiways open to the public. The programs of airport proprietors and the FAA's sovereignty in airspace are, and have been, in conflict. The FAA thus found it necessary to develop federal policy in response to use restrictions (including rules imposed for environmental reasons) which were enacted by airport authorities and were producing inconsistent or undesired results from a national perspective of maximizing air traffic system capacity and minimizing delay.

In January of 1986 the FAA published its *Notice of Proposed Rule Making* (NPRM), and later that same year published final access rules. In its stated policy, the FAA objective was to "ensure sufficient airport capacity to meet the demands of the American public for air transportation services . . . (and) to clearly define the roles of the FAA and airport proprietors. . . ." The FAA stated that the *provision* of airport capacity is a local responsibility of airport operators and communities, but that airport facilities developed with Federal funds should be operated to capacity levels consistent with airside capacity, except as limited by appropriate noise compatibility programs. The FAA reserved for itself the right to determine efficient and safe runway and taxiway operating levels, and to impose operational limits and allocation procedures in such situations.

The procedures adopted by the FAA incorporated the issuance of, and the buying and selling of airline arrival and departure slots. The

FAA rule permitted air carrier and commuter operator air traffic slots (i.e., air traffic control reservations) at capacity-constrained hub airports. The slots could be transferred for any reason. The rule also adopted certain procedures for the allocation and use of slots including a "use-it-or-loose-it" provision.

The FAA initially withdrew 5% of the slots then in use by air carriers and commuters (by lottery), and redistributed these slots (by lottery) to other air carrier and commuter operators. Thereafter, if an airline did not actively use its slot, it was subject to being withdrawn, even if the carrier had purchased the slot from another airline. Lotteries were to be held periodically to reassign available slots.

Although the airlines and the airports lined up on opposite sides, most in the industry voiced opposition to the buy/sell rule in favor of some other plan. The airlines were primarily in opposition to reassignment of slots. Airport sponsors were concerned with proprietary rights to the slots, believing the public and the airports had made as much of an investment in airport facilities as the airlines that stood to benefit from the buy/sell rule.

PRICING

The advent of California's "Proposition 13" movement in the mid-1970s, and the notion of decreased taxes and less government developing nationally, there has been an attendant shift from general fund tax support to the "user pays" philosophy. Airport users have always been expected to pay their fair share of transportation costs. However, the notion of fairness has been given broader meaning. With reduced general service tax bases, airport sponsors are increasingly motivated to transfer more and more of the economic burden of operating the airport upon its users.

Since, hypothetically, airports are not supposed to make a profit, the rates charged for providing specific services have been established to recover only the costs of providing those services. It is herein that the definition of *user pays* has taken on new meaning. True user pays philosophy demands that *all* costs of providing facilities be fully recovered. This includes administrative costs, operations and maintenance costs, capital recovery, and depreciation.

Heretofore, rate structures have in most cases been established, not so much as a function of the airport's need to recover costs, but more in accordance with the rates and charges of other nearby airports. This parity approach to rate setting has in most cases kept user charges artificially low, disallowing recovery of the necessary funds to pay for the services rendered, let alone the needs for future capital investment.

Bringing the rates in line with actual fiscal requirements is a difficult and politically sensitive task requiring extensive public relations and marketing efforts. Airport users are loath to consider as part of their obligation the full economic responsibility of the airport, including the recapture of land costs, initial development costs incurred by the airport sponsor, economic life and long-term amortization of facility improvements predicated upon future values of money. They are quick to point out the lower charges (serving their advantage) for similar services at nearby airports. They are inclined to reduce the costs of providing services down to their simplest terms, amortized over a given period of time, at no interest, and not including sundry hidden costs associated with administering the services. Unfortunately, this is the same approach taken over the years by airport management, although unknowingly, resulting in many cases with a disadvantaged rate structure for the airport sponsor.

It can be very difficult to recover from a disadvantaged price structure. As the attempt is made to increase rates, no matter how justified, the backlash from airport users can be intolerable. Nobody likes to pay more, whether the increased charge is just or not. It can be extremely difficult to explain the reasons for increased prices to an irrational group of people looking out for their self-interest and concerned only with what *they* must pay, and not with the overall financial obligations the sponsor may have in operating an airport.

Fortunately, if the rates are reasonably set they will stand the test of time. The public is never agreeable to paying for something previously received for nothing. But with time and education they will learn to accept the increased charges. The shock of paying increased charges eventually subsides, and the once-considered high charges become the status quo. For precedence, one can look at the history of parking meters. People were once enraged by the installation of parking meters on public streets. The righteous indignation suffered at the time has long since been forgotten. Reasonable increases in airport fees are analogous to the parking meter situation and tend to run the same course in terms of public acceptance.

But what constitutes a "reasonable charge"? In light of the fact that few airports are capable of fully paying their way, it is necessary for the airport to maximize its revenues, but never at the price of injustice to its tenants and users. Each tenant must have the opportunity to generate sufficient revenues to recover costs and to make an expected profit. Yet it cannot be at the public's expense without some counter-balancing public welfare benefits. And, if the tenant is unable to generate sufficient revenues to pay the going rent, the laws of economics hypothesize that he or she will seek alternative opportunities elsewhere.

COST ALLOCATION

Accepted airport accounting principles advocate the *allocation of costs* to specific user areas, particularly with regard to aeronautical activity and users. The underlying philosophy suggests that investment be allocated according to relative economy and fitness. From the standpoint of economic rationale, it is believed that user charges determine the appropriate amounts of investment. This economic principal calls for making user charges as direct as possible in an attempt to relate cost to demand. It makes those responsible for certain costs and getting the benefit of the facilities pay in proportion to their use and the costs, which they cause. The more direct the charges the more ideal is the cost allocation process.

However, it is broadly accepted that true cost allocation may not be attainable while at the same time providing well-rounded aviation services to the general public. The process required to engage in allocation of costs involves several steps.[62] The airport sponsor must,

- establish a policy on cost allocation and communicate this to users;
- divide the airport into functional areas or *cost centers* such as landing areas, ramps and hangars, terminal buildings, and other leased areas;
- track and record operations, maintenance and other relevant costs (labor, equipment, materials, etc.) in a process referred to as *cost accounting*;

[62] Some information from this section is drawn from Amedeo R. Odoni in a PowerPoint presentation, *Airport User Charges and Financing*, (Nov. 7, 2002).

- create *revenue centers* to be referenced in the cost recovery process, referred to as *cost allocation*;
- calculate user charges from per-unit costs associated with each revenue centers, referred to as *pricing;* and
- adjust the rates and charges program to reflect necessary changes in payments, and communicate to/with users.

In cost allocation the expenses attributable to each area are established and charges are made to recover each area's costs. It is a violation of the cost allocation principle to cross credit revenue from one area to another since this tends to break down the connection between cost and demand. An example would be to take general aviation parking revenues to pay some of the costs for operating the air carrier terminal; i.e. costs for facilities not necessarily used by the one paying the charges.

Cost allocation is limited to the precept that price should be related to cost, but *price discrimination* (or the relative advantages and disadvantages of value-of-service pricing) inherently enter into airport rate setting schemes. It seems hypocritical for airport management to advocate cost allocation while at times applying funds from high revenue-generating centers to pay for non-related activities. Nevertheless, the nature of providing balanced airport services seemingly makes it necessary.

Obviously, the profit margins of all airport tenants are not alike, and often the non-aviation related activities generate more income than do those engaged directly in air commerce and air transportation. For example, a fixed base operator offering training and service as its main product has a much lower potential for profit than does a concession such as a restaurant and cocktail lounge. As a result, it is not uncommon for concessions to contribute a proportionately larger share of revenue to the airport than many of the directly related aviation activities. Although such price discrimination may at times be taking place, it does not necessarily mean airport management is not trying to allocate costs to the best of its ability under the circumstances. For instance, the concession revenues may be used for reinvestment within the terminal area. If necessary, though, the concession revenues might also be used in indirect support of other airport functions. Nothing more classically demonstrates this issue than the debate between automobile rental companies and the airport sponsor over not only what the rental agencies are charged but how the revenues are applied to the airport's cost structure.

When the automobile rental industry first began tapping the airport market back in the 1960s, someone arbitrarily picked a formula of 10% of gross proceeds as the cost of doing business at the airport. The formula has become an industry standard. And at some airports, the rental agencies also pay square footage charges for the terminal space they use. The price charged the auto rental agencies far exceeds the direct costs incurred by the airport for accommodating them. In effect, the automobile rental companies are subsidizing operation of the airport. Indirectly, they are thereby subsidizing the airlines.

The rental companies, of course, argue that airports should not use revenues derived from their operations to pay for airline-related facilities. If the airports are going to cross-allocate automobile rental revenues they ought to be used for landside, not airside development. After all, they contend, their on-airport space requirements are not being met. And the automobile rental industry is a significant part of the ground transportation system, not air transportation.[63]

In recent years, some of the larger automobile rental car activities have been able to negotiate their percentage-based obligation as low as 8%. And, some shift in allocation of automobile rental agency revenues is occurring with the expiration of long-term residual airline agreements at many airports. Nevertheless, the 10% formula remains the standard. The problem on the airport side is that there are dwindling resources for capital improvements, so airports are being pushed in the other direction economically to continue cross-allocating revenues and applying them wherever they are needed.[64] Moreover, there are two arguments supporting the notion of non-aviation related activities helping to financially support the directly related aviation operations; which just incidentally, remains the airport's primary reason for being.

The *joint-product* argument, as applied to an airport, states air commerce is the primary activity, which produces the market for secondary activities such as concessions. In this concept, the profits of the secondary market are deducted from the costs of producing the primary product. Still, some economists oppose the use of the

---

[63] Danna K. Henderson, *Airports and Rental Car Companies*, Airport Magazine (Jan./Feb. 1997), at 24-25.
[64] *Id.*

joint-product concept, arguing that joint-product applies when a secondary product (say hides) is produced as the result of the production of a primary product (say meat). Since a concession is not a byproduct of airline production, the joint-product analogy is inappropriate. More appropriately, the concept of "derived demand" may be applicable.

Derived demand is also known as the "shopping-center" argument.[65] The price in derived demand is based not so much on economic theory as it is upon bargaining power. In this theory, the primary tenant can bargain a lower rent because it generates the market for other lessees. The analogy is that airlines, fixed base operators, and other aviation activities are the primary tenants who are entitled to lower rental rates because of their pulling power. Therefore, non-aviation related activities are expected to pay higher rents.

Here too, as in the joint-product analogy, there are some weaknesses. In the real market, the airlines and the FBO's are not in as strong of a bargaining position as a major storeowner would be in dealing with the owner of a shopping center. Normally, there is only one airport and if the air service is to operate in the community it must bargain with the sole airport proprietor. The fact that, in so many communities, the airlines are given credit for concession revenues results from acceptance on the part of the airport sponsor of either the principle of joint-product and/or derived demand.

Although acceptance of the principles of joint-product and derived demand is apparently hypocritical, there still exists the underlying principle of cost allocation as a desirable goal. But there is always the overriding necessity for the airport to meet its bottom-line commitments, even if cross-crediting revenues become necessary. Such practice may be repugnant to the certified accountant, but it should be recognized the airport is not always a perfect economic market, especially when public subsidies are required for its continued operation. What would happen to the airport if reinvestment were made into non-aviation activities because of their profit-making abilities, while at the same time the aviation activities were neglected because of their minimal money making qualities? There could very well be no airport at all.

---

[65] In marketing, derived demand occurs when organizational customers make purchases based on the anticipated demand of final customers. It is not used in this context here.

The cost allocation purest would say, "Raise the rents to meet the costs," but it is not that simple. Rate changing has an impact upon the airport users. Additional costs incurred by the commercial air carriers are not readily passed through to passengers. Even after passage of the Deregulation Act of 1978, air carrier rates remain subject to economic forces. And where the airline industry has always been competitive, it is even more so with the advent of regulatory reform.

Airlines have few alternatives in recovering additional airport-related costs. They can reduce other costs such as the quality of in-flight services, or they can elect to reduce frequency of service. Deterioration in the level of service can be more economically detrimental to the airport than offset increases in airport charges may warrant.

Yet airport-related costs constitute a minimal percentage of airline expenses and, combined with the regulatory controls associated with air carrier operations and the competitive nature of the industry, are insensitive to cost increases at individual airports. Conversely fixed base operators are much more sensitive to increases in airport charges than are the commercial airlines. The price of airport services is a greater portion of the FBO's total cost of operation. In passing the costs along there are two groups of FBO customers: those using aviation for business reasons, and those who use it for pleasure and recreation (or training). The businessperson may be able to accept the increased charges as the cost of doing business, but increased charges can result in lost customers who fly for pleasure, or who are taking flight training.

In many ways the concessionaire's ability to pass along increased charges is more limited than that of either the airline or the fixed base operator. This is particularly true where the concessionaire deals in extremely price sensitive products such as boxed candy, souvenirs, or gifts. If the price for a product is significantly more expensive at the airport than elsewhere, the customer is more apt to wait and buy it later. Where commodities are relatively insensitive to price such as tobacco, non-prescription medicines, and food products, it is much easier to pass increased prices along. But does the airport sponsor increase charges to one group of concessionaires and not to another? Price discrimination within a special activity group may be totally unacceptable.

A final point with regard to allocation of costs is the question of federal aid and other governmental subsidies. The argument for subsidy recovery through cost allocation is that if not recovered from the airport users, all aid will be passed on to airport tenants and users, without benefit to the airport operator. The counter-argument states that that is what subsidies are supposed to do! The user has already paid for federal Airport Improvement Program [AIP] support by directly or indirectly contributing user fees to the trust fund. If federal aid funds were recovered in the form of user charges, they would constitute a double charge and would amount to private capital grants to the airport sponsor.

The airport sponsor's ability to generate additional revenues through rate increases has its limitations. Pricing flexibility is essential for the airport sponsor, but cost control is just as important to the airport tenants. The two must be firmly balanced in airport lease negotiations and rate structure. In pricing the airport's services, there are three areas of special consideration to be discussed in the next three sections: establishment of *equitable rate structures*, *appraisal of airport land values*, and *lease negotiation techniques*.

RATE STRUCTURES

Much is written on the subject of pricing airport services, and while the economic philosophies fostered by these writers may be prudent and reasonable, rate setting is a subjective assessment of what charges should be made for services at a given airport. One need only thumb through the pages of published industry surveys to find that there are no established standards for airport rates and charges. Nevertheless, there are systematic ways to arrive at equitable prices, and as evidenced by the myriad of rate schedules in use, the established charges are not at all arbitrary. In fact, many of the schedules are quite complex and are indicative of a great deal of independent thought and/or politics in their formulation.

In pointing out the inequities of airport pricing economists in the past have repeatedly stated that in most cases the established fees were based upon the charges of neighboring airports. No consideration was given to whether or not the fees were reasonable and, more importantly, whether or not the costs of providing the services were adequately recovered. Although there is some merit to the accusation, it should be remembered that market values are established by *comparison*. As the owners of surrounding airports make surveys of fees charged at neighboring airports, a rate structure evolves. This structure may bear little relation to the actual costs of providing services, but as shown by the variety of rate schedules in existence, airport sponsors have not simply duplicated the rates charged by others. More likely they have used the charges made by others as guidelines in formulating rate schedules applicable to their own management situations. Such an approach has merit, although the adequacy of recovering costs may still be in question.

In conducting surveys of the charges made by other airports, ideally the selected airports should be as comparable as possible. It is difficult at best to find one airport that can be identically compared to another. However, airports with similar characteristics can be readily located. The most equitable measure can be found in comparable operational situations and in similar economic settings. By operational similarity the comparisons to be used should be based on like volumes of air traffic, based aircraft, whether the airport is air carrier or general aviation, and whether or not there are industrial land leases with associated broad revenue bases. Additionally, the airports selected for comparison should be situated in areas with socio-economic and demographic similarities. As with any statistical analysis, the more data available the better. Data from several selected groups should be compiled as equitable comparisons. Examples of desirable groupings could be national or regional comparisons, socio-economically comparable counties or cities, or similar airports immediately proximate to the airport in question.

From analyses of the prices charged by other similar airports, the limits of a fair market value may be derived. This prevailing market value can then be used as a baseline from which to determine proposed rates. It is not suggested this derived value be immediately adopted, but rather it is recommended as a point of departure from which to evaluate its efficiency in recovering the costs of providing services and facilities.

In the argument between an airport being a public facility funded with general tax revenues, or being a commercial enterprise, it was stated that airports generally fall somewhere in between. It follows then that airports are quasi-commercial entities, attempting to relate cost to demand, but normally not expecting to profit. The users are nevertheless expected to pay (only) for the services they receive, as opposed to payment for all airport services provided to the community at large.

Ideally, users should pay only for the services they receive. Out of context, it is readily possible to determine the direct costs for providing specific services such as aircraft tie-downs, hangars, and so forth, but total cost determination is a complex matter. The applicable rates should reflect the cost of providing the facility, capital recovery, return on the land, administration and maintenance, depreciation, and all costs directly or indirectly associated with the facility both long and short-term. This is the true user-pays philosophy, but it is not complete. Yet to be established is the value of using the entire facility including common use areas. The distribution of costs for miscellaneous areas is not so easily accounted for, and it is here where sound judgment comes into play.

All aircraft do not have the same requirements for airfield facilities, principally because of varying weight and performance characteristics. Heavier airplanes require thicker pavement to withstand increased loads. High performance and larger airplanes require longer runways. Should the lighter aircraft operators be expected to pay for portions of the runway they don't need? Is the Visual Flight Rule [VFR] pilot supposed to pay for sophisticated navigational aids not used by that pilot? In establishing rates, the costs must be distributed according to an increasing scale proportional to the demands placed upon the facilities. Larger airplanes must be expected to pay for more than just the additional area they require on the parking ramp.

Judgmentally, the costs for overall use of the airfield are added to the basic costs of providing specific facilities. At this point the ratemaking analyst has two numbers in hand: the prevailing market value, and the short-term costs of providing airfield facilities. Accountability for long-term considerations must now be established.

Marginal cost for capital improvement of airfield facilities rises in a step-wise function, since airfield capacity is not a continuous variable. In the short run, airfield facilities are fixed, and the volume of traffic is sustained at something less than capacity. As long as the traffic increases at a rate less than capacity, the average operations and maintenance costs decline and the marginal costs approximate zero. When traffic exceeds capacity, additional facilities must be built to accommodate the increased traffic volume. The economic efficiency of the airfield is altered by the sudden increase in capacity. Debt service for capital improvements increases and so does the cost of operation and maintenance of the expanded area. Who pays for the sudden economic burden? These projected capital improvement costs must be anticipated and incorporated into earlier pricing schemes, even though the need for additional facilities is only a forecast of future requirements.

Once the long-term costs of providing user services have been incorporated into a potential fee schedule they may be aggregated with other potential sources of revenue and compared against the projected bottom-line expense requirements for operating the airport. If there is still a shortage, it must be made up by increasing user fees, through outside subsidies, or by cross-crediting revenues; then a finalized rate schedule can be established. If the prevailing rate structure at other airports is higher than the derived rate structure to recover actual costs, then rates may be equitably established at or near the prevailing market value. On the other hand, if the derived rates are already at or above the prevailing market, serious consideration must be given to the two latter choices of seeking outside subsidies or violating the principle of cost allocation by cross-crediting revenues.

Once rates are established, arrangements should be made for an annual review, with provisions made for uniformly increasing (or decreasing) the rates. In anticipation of the opposition expected from airport users, which almost always attends a rate increase, it is advisable to devise a method of setting airport rates and charges that will preclude future confrontations between airport management and airport users. Those users who are expected to pay any increased charges should be anticipating the change rather than shocked by it.

A method used by some airport authorities is to adjust the rates upwards or downwards annually in relation to an economic indicator such as the adjusted *consumer price index*. This seems to be one of the most rational, defendable ways of bringing about an automatic change in the rate structure. However, there is an inherent danger in following a *national* indicator, which may not reflect *local* economic fluctuations. At capacity-constrained airports revenues may increase more rapidly than expenses. Where capacity exceeds demand the expense may increase more rapidly than revenue. This disproportionate shift may not occur at the same rate as the consumer price index.

REAL ESTATE APPRAISAL

Airport sponsors are periodically reminded by the FAA that they have a legal obligation to be self-sustaining. Part of achieving that goal is to properly appraise the value of properties under the airport's control. A "real estate appraisal" is an estimated evaluation of property. But what is meant by "value"? People perceive the meaning of value in different ways:

- *Condemnation value* is the cost of restoring an owner to a position had before property is taken;
- *Insurance value* is the cost of replacement;
- *Inheritance-tax value* of property is a matter of court determination; and
- *Fair market value* is determined between a willing seller and a willing buyer.

It is the latter, fair market value, which generates the most common concept of value. It is the one generally used by the courts. A more specific definition of "fair market value" is that, which,

> *. . . the land will bring if exposed for sale in the open market, with a reasonable time allowed to find a purchaser buying with knowledge of all the uses and purposes to which it is best adapted and for which it is capable of being used.*

The value of airport property may have an even different meaning. As airport proprietors, governments are engaged in quasi-commercial activities wherein profit is not expected. Additionally, it may be recalled there is a cost-demand relationship where the airport sponsor may be attempting only to recover the cost of providing facilities and services. There is a distinct contrast between "value" and "cost." The former refers to economic advantage resulting from ownership. The latter term has to do with the sacrifice involved in acquiring the property.

The difference between the cost of land and its value represents an economic rent, or surplus. And "surplus" is another term for "profit."

In appraising airport property there can be a wide disparity between the cost of the land and its fair market value. The appraisal must first answer the question of who is to receive the benefit of the economic rent. Ultimately the rents should accrue to the benefit of the public who is *using* air transportation.

Some experts might argue that when the lessor is a public body and the lessee a private business regulated in the public interest, there is no justification for the establishment of leasehold prices that will divert economic rents generated by the lessee to the lessor. However, the notion that airports are not to profit is self-imposed. There is no mandate to that effect, only politics. The airport proprietor adheres to this principal as a matter of policy and depending upon the airport's need to recapture economic rents accruing to the land. Seemingly, the U.S. Department of Transportation's Office of Inspector General is of the opinion that airports in general need to be more efficient in striving to at least break even, if not to generate a profit.

Airport sponsors were reminded by the FAA again in 1994 that they have a legal obligation to be self-sustaining. Cited by the DOT Inspector General were a variety of violations commonly found at airports, including:

- Leases below fair market value;
- Leases below market to governmental agencies;
- Failure to market vacant land;
- Failure to include reasonable escalation or re-negotiation clauses; and
- Aeronautical land leases below fair market rental value.[66]

All of these failures point out the need for adequate appraisals.

Whether or not the airport sponsor elects to participate in the collection of economic rents, it should nevertheless retain the option. If economic rent from one area of the airport is needed in another area, and it will help support the overall operation of the airport, such transfers are often made in the public's welfare interest. The airport proprietor may legitimately disperse airport funds as necessary to support the agency's overall responsibilities. Thus, leases usually provide for

---

[66] Bruce D. Greenberg, *Real Estate Appraisals: Getting Your Money$ Worth*, Airport Magazine (Sep./Oct. 1997), at 48.

a periodic revaluation so the lessor can collect a portion of the increasing economic rent value of the property.

Whether preparing appraisals, airport rental studies, acquisition assignments, or easement valuations, ideally the appraiser uses comparable data to draw a value conclusion. Comparable sales and/or comparable rentals must have a strong degree of similarity. All too often, appraisers inexperienced with airport properties, when valuing *inside-the-fence* holdings, acquire their comparable sales or rentals in the general vicinity of the airport being valued, but not necessarily on the airport itself. And, they solely use this *outside-the-fence* local data for comparison, which is inappropriate. Properties being valued inside the fence have the benefit of airport amenities, unlike properties outside-the-fence.[67] Additionally, airport properties are tied to an aviation sub-economy different from the outside. Land uses on airports have two distinct functions and each implies a different valuation procedure. There is land used to produce airfield, terminal, hangar and other aviation services. There is also land in excess of aviation needs, which may be devoted to other business and commercial uses.

By contractual agreement between the airport sponsor and the Federal government, economic rents are to be returned, in one way or another, to the air transportation public. Should the airport sponsor elect not to participate in the economic rents of the aviation-related properties, the surplus will be channeled to the public through the lessee. Land utilized by commercial and industrial tenants who provide no airport services at all is a different matter. These non-aviation-related lands should be valued by the usual appraisal methods while taking into account the amenities of property on the airport. Rental profits can then be returned to the traveling public through the airport sponsor. Such funds can be used to reduce the bottom-line airport expenses, thereby allowing for reduced rates to the airport users. This is another way in which cross-crediting revenues can be a benefit to the airport, and can be done within the realm of accepted fiscal principals.

Sound property appraisal theory and practice recognizes three approaches to the determination of value. The courts have leaned toward the notion that a thorough appraisal will entail working through all three approaches:

---

[67] *Id.* at 49.

- Cost;
- Market comparison; and
- Capitalization of income.

The *cost* approach to value is comprised of two types of cost: *replacement* and *reproduction*. The cost method states that the value of an existing property is limited by the cost of either replacing or reproducing it, less an allowance for depreciation. Depreciation is the margin of difference between the new and the old. Reproduction involves reproducing a replica building with today's costs. Usually it is more appropriate on airports to use replacement costs, new.

The *market comparison* approach, also known as "the comparable sales method," is most commonly used if only one method is being employed. It entails comparison of like properties, one of which was recently sold. It is an effective approach, but sometimes nearly comparable properties are unavailable. Two parcels of airport property may look alike, but one may have land use restrictions that the other does not or, perhaps, there have been no recent sales of like parcels.

The *capitalization of income* method is also known as "the income method." Capitalization involves the determination of an income stream through the technique of discounting; i.e., accounting for the opportunity use of money and compounding its value through time. When capitalizing the value of vacant land, the technique usually employed is the *land residual* method, which implies that the relevant use of the land is its "highest and best use." This is the best economic use to which the land can be placed in light of any restrictions placed on the land such as aviation-use only, zoning regulations, availability of utilities, and so on. Consider, for example, a parcel used solely for aviation related business; it would be grossly unfair to compare its value to parcels zoned "industrial."

The technique most directly applicable to the market is the one that will render the most acceptable value, but it is best to apply all three appraisal techniques whenever practicable. If each method is applied in a non-biased manner, it is unlikely all three derived values will be the same. But the results may be compared and can aid in the final determination of value. Whichever method is used, the appraisal process follows a relatively standard format. It is an orderly procedure involving the following elements:

- *Identification of the property*—wherein property is identified by address and legal description; the kind of property it is; the nature of the interest being appraised such as fee simple, easement, lease, etc.; the purpose for the appraisal; and the date of the estimate;
- *Preliminary survey*—which is the first phase of field work and involves a physical inspection of the property and surrounding area;
- *Planning the appraisal*—entails formation of a judgment regarding the most profitable use of the property. The valuation of real estate should be based upon the most profitable (or highest and best) use to which the property can be put; i.e., its highest and best use;
- *Acquisition of data*—should include recent comparable sales, listings, and other evidence of market value; and
- *Analyses of the data*—wherein one or a combination of the three valuation techniques should be used; i.e., the market, cost, or the income methods.

LEASEHOLD AGREEMENTS

A "lease" is a contract between the property owner (the lessor) and another party (the lessee), the terms of which provide the lessee with legal possession of the property for an agreed duration of time, for a specified rent, and under specified performance obligations.

There are two types of ownership in a lease agreement, the lessor's and the lessee's. The lessor's interest is simply the right to collect the rent and to repossess the property at the end of the agreement, or sooner if the contract is otherwise terminated. The lessee's interest is the economic rent, which is the difference between the value of the property and the contract rent (cost), although the lessor, as part of the primary rent, might also share in the economic rents. The lessee's interest also includes the present value of improvements and the value of any improvements left for the lessor at the end of the lease term. There are basically four types of leasehold agreements:

- The conditions of the *straight lease* remain constant throughout its term;

- The *graduated lease*, also known as a "step-up lease," provides for changes in rent at stated intervals;
- In the *revaluation lease* there are provisions to periodically (usually every five or ten years) re-valuate the property and to charge rents at the then current rental value; and
- The *percentage lease* calls for rents equivalent to a stated percentage of the business sales. There may also be a guaranteed minimum rent attached to the agreement.

Fiscal management varies amongst airports and there is no standard lease or contract philosophy that can be applied to all situations. Lease policies and contractual procedures vary with the different types, sizes, and categories of airports. Generally, however, there will be standardized leases established at individual airports to deal with routine contractual agreements. The very routine negotiations are sometimes in the form of a use permit, granting the tenant certain rights and privileges in exchange for recurring use of airport services. The *use permit* is a type of user's fee, but in written contractual format. Standardized agreements for use of the airfield, terminal buildings, and hangars may be uniform as to rates, privileges and duration.

The notion of a lease normally infers a negotiable agreement based upon individual circumstances and having a sense of permanency. Leases are usually long-term and often involve the investment or exchange of large sums of money. Negotiated agreements are the usual manner in which airlines, fixed base operators, and concessionaires secure airport real estate and building floor space.

SUMMARY

Airports continue to walk a fine line between maximizing revenues and respecting the limits associated with a public sector model, where the bottom line may not always be conveyed in numbers but rather in the purveyance of effective governance. Effective and efficient delivery of necessary services is an increasingly exciting and complex role for airports as they evolve into dynamic marketplaces.

Historically, getting on the aircraft was the "main experience" for a traveler, but the landscape is changing. As airlines continue to reduce services on board the aircraft, airports and their tenants must be prepare to take on increasing levels of service. Customers have indicated a willingness to pay more for quality and availability of needed goods and services. In response, concessionaires are planning efforts to "up-market" by taking the leadership in becoming the "main experience" in the airport environment.[68] "People want the function of a food court, without the look of a food court."

As the lines blue between tenants and their services (airlines versus airport food for carry-on to the aircraft) airports would do well to cross traditional boundaries to meet the needs of tenants and passengers alike. For example, Newark Airport officials reportedly invited JetBlue officials into the selection process for the F&B concessionaires in JetBlue's assigned concourse. As a result the airline and concessionaire both benefited from a coordinated strategy that maximized passenger satisfaction, accommodated "JetBlue Experience" branding considerations (e.g., enabling sushi selections for their passengers), and enabling the concessionaire to meet revenue generation requirements.[69]

Travelers are now facing longer dwell times largely due to security. During this time, they are seeking ways to either maximize their business productivity or decrease their stress level. The concept of the "third place" as coined by Starbucks, acknowledges that aside from work and home, people need another place where they can have their needs met. Airports must also cater to the changes in global demographics. The customer is evolving into a traveler with more sophisticated needs including that for healthier food and a desire to experience regional tastes and culture. Airports must continue to evolve accordingly.

---

[68] Future industry projections provided by Elie Maalouf, Pres./CEO, HMS Host Corp., *Concessions of the Future*, presented at the Top-Line Strategies for Bottom Line Results session of the ERAU/ACI-NA Airport Concession Conference in Seattle, Wash. (Nov. 1, 2006).

[69] Comments made by panel members, *Concessions of the Future*, ERAU/ACI-NA Airport Concession Conference: Top-Line Strategies for Bottom Line Results, Seattle, Wash. (Nov. 1, 2006).

CHAPTER 14

PUBLIC RELATIONS, SOCIAL AND ETHICAL RESPONSIBILITIES

When people go on vacation, they don't want to put their values on vacation. People look for expenditures that support their values.

James Soares, Director of Social Responsibility,
Salt Lake Brewing Company[1]

PUBLIC RELATIONSHIP

The relationship an airport manager has with the public is predicated upon public perception, which may be either favorable or unfavorable. The airport's important stewardship role and its proactive use of public relations—good and bad—are inescapable facts of life in airport management. If the airport is considered to be more of a burden than a benefit, and little is done to promote the airport's good will, its critics will instead promote its negative aspects. And, nothing is more important to public administrators than the public's opinion about their honesty, truthfulness and personal integrity.

Likewise, positive public opinion of the airport—including the airport sponsor and the many businesses operating through or at airports—relies on a foundation of ethical conduct and the use of re-

[1] *Green and Organic Business Solutions for Airport Concessions: Good for Community and Your Bottom Line*, ERAU/ACI-NA Airport Concession Conference: Top-Line Strategies for Bottom Line Results, Seattle, Wash. (Nov. 1-3, 2006).

sponsible, socially aware governance, operational and business practices. As the opening quote suggests, an increasing number of travelers appreciate (if not demand) the use of such practices at their airports. Airports and their concessionaires both benefit from the increased revenues that travelers spend at establishments that reflect and support their values. Over the past two to three decades, airports and their tenants have progressed in their understanding and encouragement of public engagement, education and empowerment.

PUBLIC RELATIONS: AN EDUCATIONAL PROCESS

Considered by many airport managers to be the most important aspect of their jobs is *public relations*. The complexities of the times make it necessary for diversified groups to seek ways of working together, if not in total harmony, then at least in peaceful coexistence. Public relations is the art of developing reciprocal goodwill and understanding. Moreover, it is an educational process, not merely to transfer knowledge to the public, but to understand the public position as well. In other words, it is an educational give-and-take process.

Public relations has no generally accepted meaning, but does connote a notion of *accommodation*. The term "relation" is a quality determined only by comparing two or more things. The relationship an airport manager has with the public is predicated upon how the public perceives the manager. That perception may be either good or bad. Yet public relations has come to mean only the former, positive aspect. The intent of public relations is to create an attitude of acceptance. The role of the public relations manager is to counsel and communicate with the public in such a way as to promote the goodwill and understanding referred to earlier. Public relations—good and bad—is an inescapable fact of life for airport management. If nothing is done to promote the airport's good will, its critics may instead promote its negative aspects.

In a 1946 study, conducted by the Opinion Research Corporation for a group of industrial clients on the subject of "How to Get Along in the Plant Community," it was determined that "living right" is not enough. Companies that actually paid the highest wages, provided the steadiest employment, and had the most pleasant working conditions were not necessarily thought of as the best employers. They received high ratings only when they made it a point to inform employees and their communities of their comparative benefits. In airport management, it cannot be assumed the public knows that the airport is an asset to the community; the public must be shown!

Since the airport is an important transportation hub, and therefore vital to the community's well being, the public should be made to understand the role the airport plays in the community. According to the Airport Council International–North America [ACI-NA], the goals of an airport public relations program are to,

- establish the airport in the minds of the general public and special public as a facility dedicated to *serving the public* interest;
- communicate to these publics those actions and policies of the airport authority with the goal of establishing and building *good will* among those served by the aviation facilities;
- *maintain a liaison* with residents of the area served by the aviation facilities through authorized news media representatives;
- assist community, civic, and special interest groups in obtaining information that will create a better *knowledge and understanding* of the operation and objectives of the airport authority;
- establish a *good working relationship* with airport tenants and federal, state and local agencies with interests corollary to those of the airport authority;
- *answer general and environmental complaints* on an individual basis, initiating action to investigate complaint particulars, where appropriate;
- establish and maintain programs designed to *enhance and improve employee morale*; and
- *handle special requests* of the public and news media and coordinate activities designed to meet those requests; i.e., tours, staff appearances at civic and community functions, feature stories, etc.

THE PUBLIC

In the section above, definition was given for the latter part of the term "public relations." The first half of the term (i.e., public) needs some explanation as well. Who is the "public"? The semantics of the word infers populace, or the people as a whole. Certainly, an airport's public relations representative cannot be expected to satisfy *all* of the people. The public's attitudes toward the airport are not formed or changed overnight, and these long-time developing attitudes often become polarized into separate and distinct camps. Oftentimes, people are either airport supporters or they are not. The National Business Aircraft Association [NBAA] has stated, there are ". . . only two reasons why an airport should have trouble with the community: either the airplane does not serve a useful purpose to the majority of the people . . . or the majority of the people do not understand the useful purposes the airplane serves."

It follows then, that the art of airport public relations is a strategy game to win over the *majority* of the population in support of the airport. This stratagem can be approached in one of two ways, either active or passive. A *passive* public relations plan is one of on-going good will. For a particular cause—usually a controversy over the airport—an *active* program may be undertaken to counteract the adverse publicity being generated by specified groups.

Segments of the public must be identified who will be receptive to public relations programs—programs which are oriented toward those groups who hopefully can be swayed or encouraged (as applicable) in their opinions. It is important, however, not to overlook elements at the extreme ends who normally would not be considered impressionable; i.e., groups in vehement opposition to the airport, or, at the opposite end of the spectrum, the airport users. Some people may never be enthusiastic supporters of the airport, but when educated they may more adequately understand airports and aviation, and be more agreeable to working out differences. Frustration causes anger, and people rarely get angry at what they understand.

A classic example of the progress that may be made through working directly with an adversarial group occurred in the late 1970s with the Westchester County Airport near White Plains, New York. Westchester is a very busy airport located within an area of exclusive home development on the fringes of New York City. The airport serves scheduled air carriers, but is predominantly used by corporate aviation and large numbers of business jets. These jets were the source of noise impact upon a community that had significant political influence with which to fight back. In opposition to the airport and its noise was the Northwest Greenwich Association, composed of local homeowners and their association president, Joan Caldwell.

The answer to working out the perceived differences between the operators of Westchester County Airport and those of the Northwest Greenwich Association was found in a decision-making process involving broad *citizen participation*, and which, in particular, included Joan Caldwell's involvement. In Ms. Caldwell's words, the actions taken to work out differences between her group and the airport operator could be termed "negotiations." But so successful was the "Westchester Experiment" that Ms. Caldwell was later invited to address a National Business Aircraft Association conference on airport noise abatement. In fact, she took the place of counsel for Westchester County (her adversary) who was unable to attend the conference. A sound public relations program transformed an extremely hostile group, headed by a dedicated political activist, into a cooperative forum capable of arriving at a peaceful solution to their differences.

At the other end of the scale from the strong adversarial groups are the clearly pro-aviation people, the airport users themselves. Although general aviation can no longer be associated with the wealthy alone, the nature of aircraft ownership and operation does pre-suppose an element of financial success. Individually, these operators possess significant political influence. Where air carrier airports are concerned, the body of air travelers represents another reservoir of political influence.

In addition to better *communications* and *education*, raw *political clout* should not be overlooked as a tool to benefit the airport. Airports are important to the community's economy, and there should be little reluctance to employ those people most concerned about that economy and the community's well being. Many of the community's influential people frequent the airport and would be willing to help the airport if asked. Public relations is a *campaign*, not a *skirmish*! Use of political clout is fair play. The power of influential leaders or in combination with organizations is tremendous. The political system in the United States is designed to reflect popular will through representative rule. It is therefore not uncommon to have government controlled by organized minorities.

A salient point to remember is that airport problem solving necessarily must include support of *non-aviation* people. And, the greatest attention must be spent with the *uncommitted* public. The firm supporters and the irrevocable opponents are readily recognizable, and neither is likely to change position. Too much effort with either may be wasted. Time spent with the *internal* public may turn into "preaching to the choir." Too much time with an adversarial group may be as non-productive as "talking to the wall." The *external* publics must be reached if the public relations program is to be successful.

Major public segments must be identified, and priorities given to the group(s) which can be educated most productively. Some public relations programs canvas two or more groupings, while other programs are designed to solve problems peculiar to a specific group. The major groups that collectively comprise "the public" are:

- Airport users;
- Potential airport users;
- The community at large;
- Lawmakers (the FAA, state and local governments, etc.); and
- The aviation industry.

PUBLIC ACCEPTANCE

Although begun as simple *publicity*, the field of public relations now attempts to do more than just *propagandize*. It encompasses many functions, concepts, and techniques, which are designed to win the good will of others. Since the term, "public relations," has no generally accepted definition, but rather infers certain notions of manipulating the minds of others and of influencing their decisions, people are wary of those who try to do so. The problem is further compounded by a general distrust in governmental agencies, of which the airport authority or sponsor is one. Unfortunately, an inherent characteristic of administrative institutions is a preoccupation with secrecy. Uncovered secrecy and/or the management of news only fuels the prevailing distrust in government. This leads not only to distrust in government, but also to interagency distrust amongst the various segments and levels of government.

An underlying philosophy that ought to be representative of the role of public relations in government is couched in statements by such noted revolutionaries as Thomas Jefferson and Patrick Henry, and embodied within the spirit and letter of the law of the Freedom of Information Act of 1966. Thomas Jefferson said it is "a matter of the highest importance to furnish the citizens with full and correct information." Patrick Henry stated government must be prevented from "governing with the veil of secrecy the common routine of business, for the liberties of the people never were, or never will be, secure when transactions of their rulers may be concealed from them." However, Mr. Henry did admit that *some* secrecy is necessary.

Congress during its 1962 Freedom of Information hearings was reminded that there must be a workable balance between "the citizen's right to know and his right to keep private what he has confided to his government." In signing the Freedom of Information Act into law on July 4, 1966, President Lyndon Johnson suggested that citizens were entitled freely to,

> *. . . information that the security of the Nation permits . . . (but) No one should be able to pull curtains of secrecy around decisions which can be revealed without injury to the public interest.*

The function or role of a governmental agency in public relations is to,

- *advertise* by conducting a reporting program that describes the government and tells the public what it is doing. There exists a public's right to know, and an obligation upon the government to tell them;
- conduct *sales* through reporting and persuasion. The public must know why certain administrative measures are being taken if they are to support them;
- promote *learning* by establishing a channel for two way communications, and by listening to what the public wants, needs, and likes; and
- foster *image-building* to build public confidence.

Representing the Northwest Greenwich Association in her address to the NBAA, Joan Caldwell emphasized that, from the residents' point of view, the Westchester Experiment was then working and working well, because of three principal elements:

- *Trust* in the motives of those wishing to sit down and talk with her association;
- *Respect* for the sincerity of the airport manager and users towards solving their differences; and
- *Confidence* in not only the sincerity to do something, but the ability to do it.

The aftermath of the 1960s and the Freedom of Information Act left a climate of "full disclosure" and of an "open society." Communicating the views of the airport operator to the public is complex and competitive. Achieving receptiveness is not a simple matter. The community is composed of many groups, and public interests are the result of varied and diverse personal prejudices, experiences, and values. To reach the public, communications must be honest and straightforward. A public relations program should never be a cover-up. A skeptical audience will quickly see through the cosmetics. Public relations is a function of *personality*, and a deceitful person cannot readily gain nor retain the public's confidence.

Along with the public's general distrust of government, there is also the notion of *consumerism*, which can erect an additional barrier to effective communications. Normally associated with the manufacturer or seller of goods and services, so widespread is the idea of consumerism that, like a public utility, it affects the operation of an airport as well. Both the airport authority and its tenants (the airlines, fixed base operators and concessionaires) provide products and services to the community. For the general public, it is difficult to determine who is responsible for providing which services. The public often is not aware of who airport management is or what it does. The airport may be blamed for poor services provided by its air carriers. Conversely, the airlines may get credit for facility improvements on the airport accomplished by airport management.

Poor consumerism is the result of a breakdown (given or implied) of contractual relations between the consumer (the buyer) and the provider (the manufacturer or seller). When it happens, consumers coalesce in their complaints and unite to demand either change on the part of the manufacturer, or protection from government. The airport authority may find itself in a public relations campaign to overcome adverse publicity generated by one or more of its tenants.

With a potential wall of negativism between the airport and its community, how does airport management go about winning public support? There are no clear-cut guidelines, since each situation will vary. But there are some basic principles, which can be considered; principles that apply to the public relations practitioner, and principles that lead to influencing behavior. From the aspect of the receiving public, consider the following:

- Most people are looking for changes in their environment;
- They may wish to make changes, but do not know how;
- Since nobody's life is in complete harmony, people are often predisposed in two or more directions;
- People have many personal interests and cannot keep track of them all;
- People's attitudes are latent and though a predisposition exists, action does not result unless it is triggered;
- People constantly want new information and must necessarily develop new attitudes to match; and
- When radical changes occur in their personal environments, people faced with new conditions and deeply rooted behavior patterns are often unable to satisfy basic needs.

In short, individually the public does not necessarily represent a unified front, but more likely is *seeking guidance and direction from leaders*. This provides an opportunity for airport management to provide leadership in matters concerning airport operations and their impact upon the community. To provide guidance to a searching audience, primary elements leading to conviction and motivation are as follows:

- Information must be *acceptable*. It is necessary that a public relations program be timely, and include statements the audience is pre-set to accept;
- The program must be *compatible* with the audience. They must be able to relate to its message;
- The message must be presented with intensity. It must have *prominence* if it is to capture attention;

- Communication must have *visibility*. Exposure in television, in the newspaper, and through other mass media has the greatest power to sway public opinion;
- Exposure leads to another principle, *pervasiveness*. The public must be surrounded by the mood of the idea, and to become absorbed in its message;
- The message should be presented repeatedly and in several ways. A variety of impressions results in *diffusion*; and
- Communications must be *persuasive*. The deliverer must be personally involved with the message, and must be able to move others to believe it.

PUBLIC RELATIONS TOOLS

The essence of public relations is *communications*, focused upon target individuals and/or groups. There can be little question about the value of using radio, television, the newspapers, and more recently the internet in reaching the masses, and in providing the pervasive atmosphere necessary. But there is a whole checklist of mechanisms besides the mass media, which can prove useful in reaching out to the public. Some are common knowledge, while others are not. Some can be used to reinforce statements given through other media, and thus give variety to the way the message is presented. Perhaps it is desirable to narrow the field, and to direct attention toward smaller groups of people or to a specific individual. Dictated by individual situations, there are innumerable ways to interact with the public. After all, the art of public relations is really a matter of *common sense*.

For example, the communication of *airport economic benefits* is of great value in airport public relations. Almost everyone can relate to money, and it is of particular concern to the public how airport funds are generated and how they are spent. Not only is the public made up of taxpayers, but communities include company stockholders, investors and potential investors, investment banking firms, institutional investors, commercial banks, security analysts, local, state and national leaders, business and industry; all of whose primary interest is financial. The economic health of the airport directly or indirectly affects the community, and the airport's economic well being is dependent upon the economic and social health of the community. Financial news press releases may be well received.

Another area, which for years was neglected as a focal point for public relations effort is *employee relations*. Good employee morale is important to both the airport and the community, especially if the airport is large and employs many workers. Often, the first person a traveler meets or speaks with is an airport employee; thus, employees are a decisive factor in achieving public relations objectives. Management's plans and programs are more likely to succeed when employees understand and accept them. Employees have a lot at stake personally in what becomes of the airport. An informational channel should be established through newsletters and other periodic publications and bulletin board announcements. Further, employees and airport volunteers who regularly interface with the public should receive specialized training to enable these community "ambassadors" to properly welcome and assist travelers and other airport visitors. A uniformed worker often is considered to be an important resource, authoritative on the airport, its services and the local community. While workers typically have primary employment tasks associated with their position, non-emergency workers should, at the very least, be approachable and sufficiently knowledgeable to direct airport visitors or travelers to locations where information is available.

Airport managers are themselves principal public relations tools. They should be identifiable to the public, and they should maintain high standards of appearance. They should be cordial to airport visitors, and most of all should be good sales representatives. Good sales people know their products, therefore, the airport manager must be astute and must continually circulate on the airport, attend applicable conventions and seminars, communicate with others in the airport and aviation industry, and generally keep abreast of significant upcoming developments. The airport manager must have the answers when called upon to respond. He or she must keep in touch with groups and agencies concerned about aviation, including elected officials, the chamber of commerce, tourist and convention bureaus, commerce departments, and planning and zoning agencies; and to let these groups know where the airport stands on the issues.

Visitor programs and airport *special events* are a good medium of communication. Examples may be tours, exhibits, an open house, a flight show, groundbreaking ceremonies, dedication of new facilities, and inauguration of new services. Visitors should be made welcome, and courtesy must always be extended, especially when complaints are being registered. Prompt and efficient handling of complaints may be one of the most important factors in a public relations program.

Citizen participation in the public planning and decision-making processes can be yet another channel for public relations. Involvement with airport programs is one of the best ways for the public to become educated. "Citizen participation" can be defined as a representative cross section of affected citizens interacting with governmental officials in the planning, development, and/or operational process. The traditional means of involving the public has been through public hearings where the public becomes informed, is able to influence decisions, and where citizens can receive adequate response from government. Although public hearings have not proven to be the most adequate forums for continuing evaluation and discussion of alternatives and issues, they do give the general public an opportunity to express their opinions. Where greater public involvement is desired in the decision-making process, a citizen's group is usually formed to represent the public at large.

There are generally two categories of citizen participation programs, each applicable to the level of citizen involvement. There is a *minimal* level for simple and non-controversial programs, and a *comprehensive* level for more complex and/or controversial programs. The minimal level entails a public information program and public informational meetings, whereas the comprehensive level involves creation of an organized citizen's planning group, workshops, and includes a more formal series of public hearings.

A planning process that does not include an adequate public participation program may meet with strong citizen reaction and ultimate disapproval. The Federal Aviation Administration's *Airport Master Plans* advisory circular prioritizes the creation of a *public involvement program* as the first element or step of the master planning process. Likewise, at the completion of the master planning process, a variety of public-oriented deliverables are required including the following: [2]

- Technical Report—containing the results of the analysis;
- Summary Report—containing "pertinent facts, conclusions, and recommendations for public review";
- Airport Layout Plan Drawing Set;

[2] FAA, *Airport Master Plans*, AC 150/5070-6B (Jul. 29, 2005).

- Web Page; and
- Public Information Kit.

MEDIA INVOLVEMENT

One prominent communications firm describes their public relations efforts as "value creation through free media or earned media."[3] Without a doubt, the development of good relations with the media and the effective utilization of media opportunities can be an invaluable part of an airport's public relations program.

There are generally two types of media which can be used in support of the airport public relations efforts: *popular media* such as electronic (radio, television, internet) and print (newspaper and magazine) communications; and *project media* such as newsletters, flyers, posters, meeting notices, airport web sites, and so forth. As involvement increases and significant numbers of citizens become active in an airport's public involvement or participation program, the program will become more newsworthy, and will generate the interests of reporters. Effective use of the news media is important not only to projects that require public participation, but more generally, in support of the airport's public relations program and daily community outreach efforts.

Involvement of the news media in airport public relations programs is a two-way street of mutual benefits. A good public relations program must have effective news coverage, and the media depends upon having a source of news to report to its subscribers. It is important that a good relationship be established with local editors and reporters. An airport manager does not have to be a professional publicist to let the media know what is happening at the airport. He or she does need to have a story to report though. In working with publicity media there are some guidelines that should be followed, and there should be a sound understanding of who the media is and what it represents. Mismanagement of the media can be disastrous!

In a free and democratic society—such as in the United States with its constitutional guarantees of a free press—the communications media are closer to having absolute sovereignty than any other element in society. This is especially the case for those media with

---

[3] Advantage Communications, Inc., *The Role of Public Relations*, http:// advantageci.com/Services/PublicRelationsEventPlanning/TheRoleofPublicRelations/tabid/61/Default, (visited about Jan. 2007).

little or no direct competition such as local newspapers and television stations; i.e., the ones with which airport management is most likely to come in contact. Because there is a certain degree of sovereignty in the press, and because there is so much power in the press, two-way communications between airport management and the media is not an equal pattern. Editorial judgment decides what it will use, when it will use it, and in what form. The sovereignty of the media must be recognized and accepted. The consolation is that responsible media have a policy of being accurate and fair.

Good journalism requires that reporting not be editorialized by the source. Sometimes errors are made, but they must be ignored unless they are gross mistakes. To avoid erroneous coverage the trick is to know the reporters, and be available when the news breaks. Unfavorable news often results because no knowledgeable or informed people are available when the story is written. Reporters work to close deadlines and they may not have time to run down all of the sources.

Working with the media usually takes on one of three forms:

- Airport management may *respond to the requests* of the communications media;
- Management *may arrange for media coverage* and dissemination of information on routine or otherwise anticipated events; or
- Management may use its initiative to *stimulate the media* into carrying airport-related news and viewpoint.

Some general guidelines for accommodating the news media include the following:

- Get to know the local news people and learn what they consider news;
- Channel the news through one knowledgeable staff person, or through a pre-designated substitute in case of absence;
- Help the media obtain accurate, complete, and timely news. One should not guess or give off-the-cuff answers which could possibly be wrong;
- Be candid, available, and willing to talk with reporters. Do not be evasive;

- Be objective and admit the obvious (e.g., "a plane just landed 'gear up' on the runway" or "a female passenger was transported by ambulance to the hospital"), but refrain from making statements unless you *know* the facts to be accurate (e.g. "the pilot probably forgot to put the gear down" or "I don't think that she will survive").
- If you don't know the answer to a press question, state that you do not have the information, but will look into the matter and provide information when able. Then keep your word;
- Be fair with all reporters. However, one should respect a reporter's right to an "exclusive" story, and never tip off a rival;
- Be prompt in reporting stories, especially unfavorable news. It is better for a reporter to hear the news directly than to chance third party renditions which may have an even more unfavorable slant;
- Avoid stretching or distorting the facts, or otherwise seeking publicity for the sake of publicity;
- Ignore insignificant reporting errors, but if necessary bring them to the attention of the reporter who covered the story, not the reporter's superiors;
- Establish an open or designated gate policy at the airport for reporters, especially during emergencies, which will assure access (escorted, if necessary) to restricted areas. If you designate a room for press to use during an emergency that does not have view of the emergency scene, don't be surprised if it is not well utilized. At times, multiple reporters may arrive at multiple locations and request escort and/or access. One should establish procedures to be used during emergencies that will aid reporters in obtaining their stories and photos, without interfering with emergency services. Expect that if not reasonably accommodated, members of the media may take extreme measures to self-accommodate and gain access; and lastly,
- Remember that there is no such thing as "off the record." If information is divulged, one should expect that it might be reported.

The role of a public relations program is to *listen*, to *counsel*, and to *communicate*. At times, the public must be educated or informed about something that is basically wrong. Public relations entails inviting and listening to any comments or concerns expressed by members of the media, users or the general public, diplomatically correcting that which is wrong, and professionally communicating that which is right.

In summary, it is apropos to quote from a speech, presented by an expert in the field, Charles Spence, then Vice President for Public Relations for the Aircraft Owners and Pilots Association [AOPA]:

> *Air transportation is essential today, and air transportation cannot exist without favorable public opinion. When the airport is criticized, we must resist the temptation to become paranoid. Our entire social structure is and will continue to be under intense scrutiny. Those elements of it, which are worth saving, will be saved. But the court of first and last resort is public opinion. And public opinion can be directed to support airports. . . . The challenge faced by all of us in aviation is to help the public understand that airports are for people who DON'T fly.*

SOCIAL RESPONSIBILITY

As nation's airports have grown in size and impact, surrounding communities have, too, become more aware of both the benefits and costs of these facilities. Prior chapters have examined airport economic and air transportation benefits, as well as the substantial environmental impacts associated with the nation's collection of air transportation facilities. While the earlier chapter discussions of environmental disamenities clearly illustrate the importance of implementing effective mitigation strategies, this section centers on an important change that is occurring in airport *stewardship* with regard to the community. Airports are increasingly evolving from earlier years as rudimentary, reactionary entities (i.e., those employing piecemeal environmental or social strategies, sometimes reluctantly) into willing, proactive, socially responsible partners acting in concert with the needs and expectations of their communities.

Social responsibility is the proactive and comprehensive consideration of "the consequences of a person's or firm's (or agency's) acts as they might affect the interests of others."[4] In the case of airports, this involves full consideration of the societal impacts associated with both the current level of activity, as well as those associated with any projected decreases or increases. Social responsibility requires airport operators to be accountable to society in policy and practice, with regard to access, employment, environment, finance, safety, security, and other issues of importance to the community. While airport operators realize they cannot please everyone, airports are increasingly employing more and more proactive and innovative measures to ensure operation in a socially responsible manner.

For several years, the private sector has recognized the value of selecting environmentally friendly business practices that also serve to increase profitability. So-called "green" business practices feature win-win strategies, in which the business institutes green (environmentally friendly) practices, while reaping green (financial incentives) as a result of the practice. For example, modern hotels proudly notify their guests with in-room signage of the fact that towels and sheets may not be washed daily, as part of a hotel industry-wide ecologically responsible initiative. Granted, while the practice clearly reduces water and energy uses, it also serves the additional benefit of reducing the hotel's utility, labor, and detergent costs.

While, over time, airports have adopted some recycling programs, energy reduction initiatives and other environmentally friendly measures such as waste oil collection sites to help reduce their *ecological footprint* in the community, they historically lacked the financial (profit) incentives that drive many successful green business practices. While, historically, some environmentally friendly measures did indeed reduce airport expenses (such as utility costs), the driving force was more toward environmental compliance rather than financial gain.

More recently, though, as airport managers are compelled to operate more transparently (e.g., when operating as an enterprise fund or account), they are increasingly seeing the financial value of innovative green business strategies. In addition, as the opening quote to this chapter suggested, airport concessionaires like the Salt Lake Brewing

---

[4] Peter D. Bennett (ed.), American Marketing Association, *Dictionary of Marketing Terms* 267 (2nd ed., 1995).

Company are tailoring food and beverage offerings to a new generation of travelers that seek out services employing green business strategies. Some of the practices used by the Salt Lake Brewing Company include:

- Use of waterless urinals that reduce water usage and save the company about 33% of annual water costs;
- Donation of a nickel per *Chasing Tail Ale* bottle caps to selected animal/human therapy and animal protection causes; and
- Use of reclaimed items in the construction and decorating of their business, such as old street cobblestones for wall décor and old wine barrels that were used to construct a wall.[5]

James Soares, Director of Social Responsibility for the Salt Lake Brewing Company, notes that for the last point, innovation and patience are important. He says, "The key is in changing the way you go about acquiring materials."[6] This goal of being socially and, particularly, environmentally responsible—when carried out over decades and even centuries—becomes a larger goal of achieving *sustainability*. Sustainability is "meeting the needs of the present without compromising the ability of future generations to meet their own needs."[7]

Environmental groups have pushed for the reduction of emissions and the ecological footprint left by both airplanes and airports. In response, airports have devised innovative plans that go beyond simple compliance. For example, Boston Logan Airport was the first U.S. airport to receive Leadership in Energy and Environmental Design [LEED] certification for sustainable or *green design*, construction and operation.[8] LEED sustainability principles focus on five areas: site development, water savings, materials selection, indoor air quality, and energy efficiency.[9]

---

[5] James Soares, *Green and Organic Business Solutions for Airport Concessions: Good for Community and Your Bottom Line*, ERAU/ACI-NA Airport Concession Conference: Top-Line Strategies for Bottom Line Results, Seattle, Wash. (Nov. 1-3, 2006).

[6] *Id.*

[7] American Friends Service Committee, *Glossary of International Trade Terms*, retrieved from www.afsc.org/trade-matters/learn-about/glossary.htm (Feb., 2007).

[8] Helen Walters, *Airport Design Takes Off: Amid Terrorism, Increased Traffic, Green Concerns, Facilities Face New Needs*, Business Week, (Feb. 2, 2007).

[9] US Green Building Council, (2007), retrieved from http://www.usgbc.org/DisplayPage.aspx?CategoryID=19.

Sustainability is not a new issue in transportation, but despite years of discussion and debate, full integration of sustainable concepts into all phases of transportation planning has not yet been achieved. In the preface of the 2005 Integrating Sustainability into Transportation Planning Conference Proceedings, the tenuous balance between the benefits and impacts of the transportation system is evident:

> *The concept of sustainability has a powerful grip on people. Few could disagree that attainment of a sustainable transportation system is desirable; however, many challenges lie along the path to achieving such a system. The nation's transportation system has enhanced quality of life through increased access to health care, education, employment, recreation, and a wide range of consumer goods. These benefits have not been achieved without costs. The negative impacts of the transportation system include congestion; fatalities and injuries; noise, air, and water pollution; greenhouse gas emissions; diminishing energy resources; and biological and ecosystem damage. The challenge of a sustainable transportation system lies in minimizing these costs while offering strong transportation benefits.*[10]

Particularly in the last decade, airport sponsors and their tenants have become much more creative and collaborative in achieving a more comprehensive approach to social responsibility. Seattle-Tacoma International Airport is recognized as an impressive example of social and environmental responsibility through proactive, comprehensive use of a wide variety of innovative strategies including:

---

[10] Transportation Research Board [TRB], *Integrating Sustainability into Transportation Planning—Preface,* Conference Proceedings 37, (Conference held Jul. 11-13, 2004, proceedings published in 2005), retrieved from http://onlinepubs.trb.org/onlinepubs/conf/CP37.pdf.

- A "lattes to landscaping" program, in which beverage concessionaires cooperate in recycling (to compost) more than 120 tons of coffee grounds annually;
- A comprehensive waste recycling program which saves $120,000 annually in solid waste costs and prompts the annual recycling of more than 90 tons of scrap metal;
- Annual collection and reuse of 12,000 gallons of concession cooking oil/grease as bio-diesel fuel (with concessionaires each personally paying $2000 per grease transporter and the vendor hauling away the grease at no charge to the airport or its tenants);weekly collection of more than 500 pounds of food to be donated to local food banks;
- Airport purchase and use of *green power* (from Bonneville Power Administration); and
- Collection of foreign newspapers from international airlines, and donating them to local foreign language schools. [11]

There are usually both benefits and costs to social responsibility.[12] Some benefits include worker and public health, cleaner air and water, more efficient use of resources, economic growth, improved business/agency image, public education, improved safety/security, and/or a better standard of living for the community members. Costs might include an unequal distribution of benefits, fiscal costs, traveler or user inconvenience/delays, loss of privacy, and loss of resources allocated to prevention. Achieving a reasonable balance between benefits and costs can be both difficult and rewarding. Ethical responsibilities and related challenges faced by public administrators are discussed throughout the remainder of this chapter.

ETHICAL RESPONSIBILITIES

As stated above, the relationship an airport manager has with the public is predicated upon how the public perceives that manager. The public must perceive the manager as being a person of honesty and

---

[11] Doug Holbrook, Manager, Utilities and Business Management, Port of Seattle, *Green and Organic Business Solutions for Airport Concessions: Good for Community and Your Bottom Line*, ERAU/ACI-NA Airport Concession Conference: Top-Line Strategies for Bottom Line Results, Seattle, Wash. (Nov. 1-3, 2006).

[12] Joel R. Evans & Barry Berman. *Marketing, 9e.: Marketing in the 21st Century* (2007).

integrity. Additionally, people prefer to do business with others they like and trust. And one's perception of another will be guided by the other person's ethical conduct. The communication of and adherence to *ethical standards* is thereby another component of public relations.

In the study of ethics, theorists have developed unique frameworks with which to understand ethics.[13] But fundamentally, ethics is the study of human behavior as it relates to right and wrong conduct.[14] "Ethics" refers to personal character, or what it takes to be a good person. The word "ethics" is derived from the Greek *ta ethica*, meaning the nature of the virtuous life, or the right way to live.[15] Ethics is the science that deals with conduct, in so far as it is considered as right or wrong, good or bad.[16] It is a matter of "duty." Ethics in ancient times signified moral philosophy (*philosophia moralis*), which was also called the *doctrine of duties*.[17]

---

[13]Some of these *epistomologies* include: *Deontology* (*deontos*, Greek)—which is the study of rights and duty or obligations, with the belief that a person knows the difference between right and wrong; the moral rightness or wrongness of an act is to be defined in terms of its production of goodness or badness; *Descriptive Ethics*—describe how some people, members of cultures, or societies address moral issues; *Ethical Egoism*—approves of behavior motivated merely by an individual's desire for personal gain; it views behavior motivated by self-interest as ethical, and it looks at personal greed as collective altruism; *Metaethics*—is the analyzing of moral language; good and bad (or evil), right and wrong, propriety and impropriety, duties and rights, obligations and claims, or justice and injustice; *Natural Law Theories*—hold that moral principles or laws reflect the nature or rational order of things; that is to say, they exist in nature irrespective of human intervention; *Normative Ethics*—are an inquiry into the norms or principles of justifiable behavior and the values they embody; *i.e.*, into what kinds of acts are right or permissible; *Right-based Theories*—take the basic concept of morality to be rights, freedoms and claims; assumed is an entitlement to act or have others act in a certain way; if one has a right to do something, then someone else has a correlative duty to act in a certain way; *Social Contract Theories*—take morality to consist of a set of rules establishing how members of society ought to treat each other—by hypothetical contract, which consists of giving up personal freedoms to a sovereign power in exchange for a set of rights, duties, and government protection; *Teleology* (*teleios*, Greek)—looks at the end consequences of a person's conduct; each class or kind of thing has an end (or *telos*) that will be good to the extent that it fulfills the natural functions of its kind; *Utilitarian Theories*—are based on the utility of what is useful is good; the moral worth of actions or rules is judged solely in terms of goodness or badness and the greatest utility (or happiness); that is to say, whatever promotes happiness is utility and therefore good; and *Virtue Theories*—where the study is of the moral character of the individual, rather than rightness or wrongness of actions; *see* David Theo Goldberg, *Ethical Theory and Social Issues* (2nd ed. 1995); *see also* Jacques P. Thiroux, *Ethics: Theory and Practice* (1977); *see also* William H. Shaw & Vincent Barry, *Moral Issues in Business* (5th ed. 1992).

[14] Herbert M. Bohlman & Mary Jane Dundas, *The Legal, Ethical and International Environment of Business* 34 (2nd ed. 1993).

[15] David Theo Goldberg, *Ethical Theory and Social Issues* (2nd ed. 1995).

[16] John Dewey & James H. Tufts, *Ethics* (revised ed. 1908/1932).

[17] Immanuel Kant, *Fundamental Principles of the Metaphysic of Morals* Introduction (1785).

"Ethics," or "moral philosophy," is used herein as philosophers have traditionally used the terms, as words arising from the study of what is *good* or *right*. It is the study of what people *ought* to pursue; i.e., what is good or what are right actions. However, "morality" and "ethics" do not have the same exact meaning. Even though they are often used synonymously, there is a distinction. The terms have different origins and cultural connotations. "Ethics" stems from the Greek *ethos*, whereas "moral" is from the Latin (i.e., Roman) *mores*. In the contemporary sense, "We might refer to someone's 'personal ethics' or character while 'morality' is often used in discussions about social conventions and custom."[18] Where the focus of ethics is on the individual, *morality* refers to the social rules that govern or limit one's conduct. Morality is about doing what is good or right according to the rules. The Latin *mores* denotes *rectus*, meaning "straight" or "according to rule"; that is to say, correct social behavior. "Good" is connected with the German *gut*, with the same root in Greek, meaning "valuable for some end." Since ethics can be thought of as the study and science of morals,[19] in the contemporary sense, to be ethical is indeed nearly synonymous with being moral.

In business or politics, ethics has to do with proper decision-making. "Business ethics" seeks to understand business practice, institutions, and actions in light of human values.[20] In Pastin's conception, the ethics of a person or firm is simply, "the most fundamental ground rules by which the person or firm acts." "Good ethics," he says, is a matter of making "right decisions."[21] To aid associates in making "right decisions" agencies often create bureaucratic rules referred to as "codes of conduct." For example, the United States Military Code of Conduct is the moral guide for the behavior of U.S. military members who are evading or captured by hostile forces. Likewise, civilian agencies may have a code outlining the responsibilities of or best practice for the individual or organization, such as a set of principles of good corporate behavior adopted by a business. The code of conduct for the American Association of Airport Executives [AAAE] is presented below on Table 14.1, "AAAE Code of Ethics."

---

[18] David Theo Goldberg, *Ethical Theory and Social Issues* 3 (2nd ed. 1995).
[19] Herbert M. Bohlman & Mary Jane Dundas, *The Legal, Ethical and International Environment of Business* 16, 29 (2nd ed. 1993).
[20] T. Donaldson & P.H. Werhane (eds.), *Ethical Issues in Business* 2 (1983).
[21] Mark Pastin, *The Hard Problems of Management: Gaining the Ethical Edge* xii, 24 (1986).

Table 14.1—AAAE CODE OF ETHICS

As a professional Airport Executive in the performance of my duties and responsibilities, I pledge to:

1. Be dedicated to the safe, efficient, and economic operation of airports and the national air transportation system and believe that professional management is the method to achieve this objective.

2. Be dedicated to the highest ideals of honor and integrity in all public and personal relationships in order to earn and retain the respect and confidence of public officials, employees, and the general public.

3. Refrain from participation in the election of the members of the employing governmental body and from all partisan political activities that would compromise the performance of a professional executive.

4. Resist any encroachment on professional responsibility and duties, believing that the executive should be free to carry out official policies without interference and handle each problem without discrimination on the basis of principle and justice.

5. Neither seek nor accept any favor or gift from persons or firms under which circumstances could be reasonably inferred that the favor would influence or compromise the executive or governing body.

6. Submit policy proposals to the employing governmental body and officials, provide them with facts and advice on matters of policy as a basis for making decisions and establishing airport goals, implement and execute policies adopted by the governing officials.

7. Recognize that elected and/or appointed officials are responsible for the establishment of airport policies and that policy execution is the responsibility of the airport executive.

Table 14.1 (continued)

8. Keep the community informed on airport affairs; encourage communication between the users, citizens, and all public officials; emphasize friendly and courteous service to the public, and constantly seek to improve the quality and public image of the airport executives.
9. Handle all personnel matters on the basis of merit in order that fairness and impartiality govern the executive's decision pertaining to appointments, salary adjustments, promotions, and discipline.
10. Strive to continually improve professional competence and ability through education and research, and to encourage the professional development of associates and subordinates.
11. Conduct myself in my public and personal life in a matter in accordance with the rules of civil and criminal law.

Source: AAAE Code *of Ethics*, (May 2005), retrieved from http://www.aaae.org/members/100_About_AAAE/175_Code_of_Ethics/.

Presented below are a set of recommended guidelines excerpted from the *Code of Ethics and Guidelines* of the American Society for Public Administration [ASPA], whose motto is "advancing excellence in public service."

- The public administrator must demonstrate the highest standards of personal integrity, truthfulness, honesty and fortitude in all public activities in order to inspire confidence and trust in public institutions. Perceptions of others are critical to the reputation of an individual or a public agency. Nothing is more important to public administrators than the public's opinion about their honesty, truthfulness and personal integrity. It may even overshadow competence as the premier value sought by citizens in their public officials.
- The public administrator should serve in such a way as to not realize undue personal gain from the performance of official duties. The only gains the administrator should seek from pub-

lic employment are salaries, authorized fringe benefits, respect, and recognition for work.

- Public employees should not undertake any task in conflict, or viewed as in conflict, with job responsibilities, but rather should avoid any interest or activity in conflict with the conduct of official duties. This general statement addresses a fundamental principle that public employees are trustees for *all* the people.
- The public administrator should support, implement, and promote merit employment and programs of affirmative action. These efforts should assure equal employment opportunity through the administrator's recruitment, selection, and advancement of qualified persons from all elements of society. The administrator should oppose any discrimination because of race, color, religion, sex, national origin, political affiliation, physical handicaps, age, or marital status, in all aspects of policymaking.
- The administrator should eliminate all forms of illegal discrimination, fraud, and mismanagement of public funds, and should support colleagues if they are in difficulty because of responsible efforts to correct such discrimination, fraud, mismanagement or abuse. Furthermore, all associates and subordinates should be informed that no illegalities in office will be tolerated. In support of this concept, all public servants should support authorized investigative agencies and the concept of auditors reporting to committees independent of management.
- Answers to questions on public policy should be complete, understandable, and true. The administrator should serve the public with respect, concern, courtesy, and responsiveness, recognizing that service to the public is beyond service to oneself.
- Administrators should strive for personal professional excellence and encourage the professional development of associates and those seeking to enter the field of public administration. Staff members should be encouraged to participate in professional activities and associations. They should also be reminded of the importance of doing a good job and of their responsibility to improve the public service.
- The administrator should accept as a personal duty the responsibility to keep informed about present and emerging issues and

to administer the public's business with professional competence, fairness, impartiality, efficiency, and effectiveness.

- Citizens expect government to be compassionate, well organized, and operating within the law. Administrators should approach organization and operational duties with a positive attitude and should constructively support open communication, creativity, dedication, and compassion.
- Much information in public offices is privileged for reasons of security or because of laws and ordinances. There should be respect for and protection of privileged information to which administrators have access in the course of official duties.
- In conformance with agency guidelines, the administrator should exercise whatever discretionary authority the administrator has under the law to promote the public interest. For example, there are occasions when a law is unenforceable or has become obsolete. In such cases the administrator should recommend that the law be modernized. If an obsolete law remains in effect, the administrator should determine if the law is or is not to be enforced.
- Finally, the administrator should be familiar with constitutional government, and should respect, support, study, and when necessary, work to improve federal and state constitutions and other laws which define the relationships among public agencies, employees, clients, and all citizens. As a *citizen*, the administrator should work for legislation in the public interest.

The last item above is the fundamental basis for ethics in the public sector. Defending and supporting state and federal constitutions is the first and foremost responsibility of all public administrators. It follows that the ethical practices of public administrators ought to conform to the ethical foundations of constitutional law. A discourse on constitutional law has been handled elsewhere and is beyond the scope of this text.[22] But what can be appropriately addressed here are the theoretical constructs that together form the ethical foundation found in the *United States Constitution*, which is exemplary of modern constitutions. It is a document that can be described as a written rather than merely a hypothetical social contract. And where the U.S.

---

[22] *See e.g.*, Laurence E. Gesell & Paul Stephen Dempsey, *Aviation and the Law* (4th ed. 2005).

Constitution is an expressed contract, the *Declaration of Independence* was a declared breach of a prior but relied upon natural social contract, the violation of which compelled the American colonists to forge a new contract, and to put the contract in writing.

LAW AND ETHICS

Roscoe Pound argued that society's ethics, its moral ideas, give us the law.[23] Jean Jacques Rousseau stated,

> *What makes the constitution of a State really solid and lasting is the due observance of what is proper, so that the natural relations are always in agreement with the laws on every point, and law only serves, so to speak, to assure, accompany and rectify them.*[24]

Thus, stated as an axiom, "law follows morality."[25] Ethics and morality, then, precede the law and can include acts that are wrong in and of themselves (*malum in se*), because they are not right; as well as acts which society believes ought to be prohibited by government (*malum prohibitum*), because they are not good. Speeding, for example, is against the law. Yet, there is nothing inherently immoral about speed. But when it might endanger others, it becomes wrong. Likewise, there is nothing illegal about greed. But when the avarice of capitalism reaches beyond reasonable bounds it becomes immoral, and may result in what is referred to as "white collar crime." Ivan Boesky and Michael Milken, for example, were not burglars, robbers, or common thieves, yet both went to prison for causing harm by what amounted to the same thing.[26] Stock manipulation is *malum prohibi-*

---

[23] Roscoe Pound (1870-1964) was an American jurist, educator, and a leader in the reform of court administration in the U.S..

[24] Jean Jacques Rousseau, *Du Compac Social, The Social Contract or Principles of Political Right* Book II (1762).

[25] This section draws heavily from Laurence E. Gesell, *Aviation and the Law* (3rd ed. 1998).

[26] In 1987, Ivan Boesky, a Wall Street speculator in corporate takeovers, plead guilty in federal court to a felony charge of stock manipulation. In 1990, Michael R. Milken, a junk bond financier at Drexel, Burnham & Lambert, plead guilty to six felonies, including conspiracy, securities fraud, mail fraud, and filing false tax forms. William H. Shaw & Vincent Barry, *Moral Issues in Business* (5th ed. 1992).

tum, while theft is *malum in se*. In either case, there is an immoral gain at someone else's expense.

Laws *malum prohibitum* are created by legislatures and, therefore, are subject to change. Conversely, acts *malum in se* are of eternal nature. In the latter case, one is motivated to do what is morally right out of either concern for others or just because it is right. Included in what is meant by morality are conventional norms against lying, cheating, stealing, or otherwise harming other people. Acts *malum in se*, and the prohibition against harming other human beings, are a social convention that is fundamental to religious doctrines.

Most religions provide believers with an eternal or spiritual perspective. Additionally, they provide certain moral guidelines, values and commitments to adhere to as acceptable standards in this life. Much of law throughout the world is grounded in religious tenets, with Western law having its roots in the Judeo-Christian tradition. Its morality is likewise grounded in the *utilitarian* and *social contractarian* philosophies, each of which takes its inspiration from religious, although not necessarily Judeo-Christian, doctrine.

One example of a religious tradition that runs parallel to the philosophies of utility and contract is the *Golden Rule*, which is to say, "Treat others the way you would have them treat you." The Golden Rule, or some derivation of it, seems to be a convention shared by the entire global population. Similar edicts can be found in all of the major world religions:[27]

- Good people proceed while considering that which is best for others is best for them selves (Hinduism).[28]
- Thou shalt love thy neighbor as thyself (Judaism).[29]
- Therefore all things whatsoever you would that men should do unto you, do ye even so unto them (Christianity).[30]
- Hurt not others with that which pains your self (Buddhism).[31]
- What you do not want done to yourself, do not to others (Confucianism).[32]

---

[27] William H. Shaw & Vincent Barry, *Moral Issues in Business* 9-10 (5th ed. 1992).
[28] *Hitopadesa*.
[29] *Leviticus* 19:18.
[30] *Matthew* 7:12.
[31] *Udanavarga* 5:18.
[32] *Analects* 15:23.

- No one of you is a believer until he loves for his brother what he loves for himself (Islam).[33]
- Treat the earth and all that dwell thereon with respect (Native American).[34]

THEORETICAL CONSTRUCTS

In the Golden Rule, one can find the seeds of both social utility and the social contract. Utilitarianism and the social contract are philosophical constructs that came out of the Era of Enlightenment, to be borrowed in the writing of the Declaration of Independence and the United States Constitution, and operationalized as fundamental principles in the basic law of the land. The social contract takes morality to consist of a set of rules establishing how members of society ought to treat each other—by hypothetical contract, which consists of giving up personal freedoms to a sovereign power in exchange for a set of rights, duties, and government protection. The utilitarian theory is based on the "utility" of what is useful is good. The moral worth of actions or rules is judged solely in terms of goodness or badness and the greatest utility (or happiness); that is to say, whatever promotes happiness is utility and therefore good. One can trace the historical development of each of the utilitarian and contractarian philosophies through a genealogy of its prophets.

SOCIAL UTILITY

Study of both the utilitarian as well as social contractarian perspectives begins best with Thomas More (1477-1535). More railed in his work, *Utopia*, at the idolization of money and at the idea that kings and merchants might consider them selves richer for having a well-filled exchequer[35] even though the citizens were destitute.[36] In criticizing the state, and its policies that effectively made it impossible for commoners to be other than paupers and thieves, More was

---

[33] *Traditions.*
[34] Anonymous, but most likely from the 19th Century, found on a poster by Paul H. Morgan (1994).
[35] The term *exchequer* refers to an individual or agency that collects and manages revenues or items of value for the government. Additionally, the term describes a table, room or location where a government's valuables are collected and/or stored. Here, the authors refer to the latter.
[36] C.N. Starcke, *Laws of Social Evolution and Social Ideas* 9, 12-13 (1926).

making (individual) human welfare the ultimate standard. Human welfare (or happiness) is the ultimate standard of right and wrong in utilitarianism. By his emphasis upon the consumer, More was placing the individual before the state—a fundamental precept in the social contract.

Thomas More described his perfect commune in *Utopia*; a social organization built on the interests of the consumer. In the moral philosophy of the eighteenth century this view found its philosophical formula in the *doctrine of utility* and its principle: The greatest possible happiness of the greatest possible number. The "formula" for the principle of utility builds on the will of God. Based on the formula for utility, how one is to know the will of God is explained by Starcke:

> *The essence of God being love, only that which inspires benevolence towards one's fellowmen can be acknowledged as the will of God and, in this way, the welfare of humanity becomes the criterion of the Divine Law.*[37]

In this intricate train of thought, the criterion of virtue is the will of God. If society takes the place of the will of God, it can only mean that universal welfare should be the leading principle of moral conduct.[38]

After the American War of Independence, and especially after the advent of the Industrial Revolution, English society had been subjected to a number of changed trade conditions. The demand for removal of obstacles to free trade gave advantage to the thoughts of two contemporary writers of the late 18th century, Adam Smith and Jeremy Bentham.

Like Thomas More, Adam Smith also railed against the British Mercantile System. In 1759, he wrote his *Theory of Moral Sentiment*, which emphasized mutual sympathy and happiness as the decisive factor in social life. His seminal work, *An Inquiry into the Nature and Causes of the Wealth of Nations* (1776), was published in the same year as the American Declaration of Independence. His latter work was timely in the transformation from a feudal society to capitalism

---

[37] C.N. Starcke, *Laws of Social Evolution and Social Ideas* 16-17 (1926).

[38] *Id.* at 16.

and free trade. American capitalism was the ideal of that transformation.

Democratic capitalism is personified by Adam Smith. His philosophical views epitomize the ideology of individualism and the free market that underscores capitalism in America and the Western World. In *Wealth of Nations*, Adam Smith describes an economy where the market forces of capital, labor and the marketplace (or consumer) are perfectly balanced and kept in balance by the "invisible hand" of competition. In his "perfectly" competitive system, the value of work resolves itself in fair wages for the worker, at the same time provides reasonable profits for the capitalist, and the consumer pays a "natural" (i.e., not inflated) price for commodities.

Adam Smith best expressed the ideal of American capitalism in stating that, "By pursuing his own interest he (the individual) frequently promotes that of society more effectually than when he really intends to promote it." The invisible hand is more than an apology for capitalism; it is the first discovery of a general sociological principle, that the collective result of individual behavior is not the same as the individual behavior. In this sense, personal greed can translate into collective altruism.[39]

By focusing on the (individual) consumer, he does not measure *The Wealth of Nations* by their passive riches, but by their active social processes, wherein the favorable condition of production lies in the consumer's interest and in a free and competitive market. Smith's argument was that the division of labor and the specialization of production, the greatest possible market freedom, and the fewest possible artificial barriers to trade, are the conditions most favorable to the creation of wealth. Conversely, favoring the rich at the cost of the poor was a direct hindrance to the formation of wealth.[40] Adam Smith conceptualizes a vision of perfect liberty, where an individual would be left "perfectly free to pursue his own interest his own way."[41]

Adam Smith (1723-1790) was a contemporary of Jeremy Bentham (1748-1832), and there was a close relationship between the two men.[42] Whereas Smith (an economist) had intended to prove that social welfare depends on harmony in the economic domain (where

[39] *See* James Inverarity, Pat Lauderdale & Barry Feld, *Law and Society: Sociological Perspectives on Criminal Law* 96 (1983).
[40] *See* C.N. Starcke, *Laws of Social Evolution and Social Ideas* 9-10 (1926).
[41] Adam Smith, *An Inquiry Into the Nature and Causes of the Wealth of Nations* (1776).
[42] C.N. Starcke, *Laws of Social Evolution and Social Ideas* 19 (1926).

everybody could freely seek his own happiness), Bentham (a social engineer) was trying to prove that happiness depends on construction of the right social organization. He argued that the welfare of all depends on the welfare of each, and that social organization should aim at the construction of such harmony.[43] Like Thomas More, what burned deepest in Bentham's soul was anger at the indifference of the state toward the victims of its (mercantilist) policy—the poor.

Although David Hume (1711-1776) and others had used the term "utility" in their moral writings, it was Jeremy Bentham who first formulated an explicitly utilitarian moral theory. Bentham's concept of social utility is a form of *hedonism*, and a belief that right conduct is determined by the balance of pleasure over pain that a given act can produce.[44]

An Introduction to the Principles of Morals and Legislation (1789) is probably Bentham's best known work. In it, he describes his doctrine of utility—that the aim of society ought to be the achievement of the greatest happiness for the greatest number. It was Bentham's belief that pain and pleasure could be measured quantitatively. If utility could be measured in quantitative terms, then it followed that ethical and social decision making might be reduced to a quasi-mathematical science. Bentham called his science *hedonistic* or *felicific* calculus.

It was Jeremy Bentham who first formulated the theory of social utility, but it was seemingly his student, John Stuart Mill (1806-1873), who coined the term "utilitarianism." Mill was one of the Philosophical Radicals, or Benthamites, who pursued various social and political reforms along the utilitarian lines laid down by Jeremy Bentham. However, in his most famous work, *Utilitarianism* (1863), Mill revised Bentham's version of utility. Where Bentham had suggested that all pleasures were of equal value, Mill differentiated the various pleasures, and argued for the superiority of the "higher pleasures of the mind."

Mill also gives some indication of an affinity for the social contract theory in his book, *On Liberty* (1859). In it, he suggests that only

---

[43] *Id.* at 18.

[44] There are two fundamental types of utilitarianism. In *Act Utilitarianism* there is one, and only one, moral obligation, the maximization of happiness, for which every action is to be judged according to how well it maximizes happiness. In *Rule Utilitarianism* utilitarian standards should be applied not to individual actions but to moral codes as a whole, suggesting that societies should adopt rules that maximize happiness. William H. Shaw & Vincent Barry, *Moral Issues in Business* 78 (5th ed. 1992).

the principle of self-protection alone can justify either the state's tampering with the liberty of the individual or any personal interference with another's freedom. In his theory of justice, Mill determined that justice involves the violation of the rights of the individual. And, if the individual has a right to something, then he has a valid claim on society to protect him in the possession of that thing (*à là* the social contract). What Mill's "utilitarianism" identifies as "rights" are certain moral rules, the observance of which is of utmost importance in the maximization of happiness. The utilitarian theory of justice ties the question of economic distribution to the promotion of social well being, or happiness.[45]

Mill defended his brand of utilitarianism by conceiving the principle as Bentham had: happiness alone is desirable as an end, and it consists in pleasure and freedom from pain.[46] Mill defined utilitarianism as,

> . . . *[t]he creed which accepts as the foundation of morals, Utility, or the Greatest Happiness Principle, holds that actions are right in proportion as they tend to promote happiness, wrong as they tend to produce the reverse of happiness. By happiness is intended pleasure, and the absence of pain; by unhappiness, pain, and the privation of pleasure.*[47]

Utilitarianism has popular appeal, because it is easy, says John Rawls.[48] Its appeal has been a function of its simplicity, egalitarianism, and comprehensiveness. According to Goldberg, it,

> . . . *holds the promise of a single, simple and general quantitative calculus for ethics, government, economics, and the law . . . utilitarianism has continued to offer a method for determining efficient rules for law, politics, and economic distributions.*[49]

---

[45] William H. Shaw & Vincent Barry, *Moral Issues in Business* 108-109 (5th ed. 1992).
[46] David Theo Goldberg, *Ethical Theory and Social Issues* 126 (2nd ed. 1995).
[47] John Stuart Mill, *Utilitarianism* Ch. II (1863).
[48] John Rawls, *A Theory of Justice* (1971).
[49] David Theo Goldberg, *Ethical Theory and Social Issues* 128-129 (2nd ed. 1995).

However, contemporary utilitarians no longer interpret "utility" simply as pleasure versus pain, but rather, refer to preferences, interests, benefits, welfare or other technical references to distribution.[50] Utility interpreted this way is more in line with the philosophy of Henry Sidgwick (1838-1900). Sidgwick was an English philosopher best known for his ethical studies. His most prominent work was *Methods of Ethics* (1874). Although critical of the older utilitarians such as Jeremy Bentham and John Stuart Mill, Sidgwick formulated a utilitarian position that actions are right or wrong on the basis of their conformity with the *general welfare.* Sidgwick supported utilitarianism because he said it best described the morality of ordinary common sense.

THE COMPACT OF LAW

The rules of the game of law are conceived as granting the people rights and liberties, while at the same time subjecting them to duties and responsibilities.[51] Likewise, the *social contract* theory holds that a state is originally created through a voluntary agreement entered into by hypothetical individuals living in a natural state of anarchy.

Although John Locke is generally thought of as the exponent of the social contract, the concept may be at least as old as the Romans. One can also find the theory in the writings of St. Thomas Aquinas.[52] In an argument suggesting that trust implies a contract, trust is the *mandatum* of Roman law, meaning a form of consensual contract. Whereas the Roman *mandatum* might imply something about the social contract, in the writings of St. Thomas Aquinas, the theory blossoms fully.

In the Thomist system, the teachings of the Bible, the doctrines of Roman law, and the principles of Aristotle's *Politics* are brought together. The Bible, for instance, teaches that law emanates from God. But it also teaches that David made a covenant with his people. In the theory of Roman law, by *Lex Regia*, power conferred upon the emperor must proceed from the people. Finally, Aristotle seemed to favor a monarchy of the one best man. However, he also endorsed the right of the masses not only to elect the magistrate but also to call him

[50] *Id.* at 129.
[51] Readers Digest, *You and the Law* (Henry V. Poor, advisory ed. 1971).
[52] Sir Ernest Barker, *Introduction, Social Contract: Essays by Locke, Hume, and Rousseau* viii-x, xiii (1947).

to account. St. Thomas balances the three concepts of authority (the Bible, Roman law and Aristotle's politics) in the ideas of *principium*, *modus*, and *exercitium*.

As Sir Ernest Barker explains,

> *. . . [T]he principium, or essential substance of authority is ordained of God, . . . but its modus, or constitutional form (be it monarchy, aristocracy, democracy, or a mixed form), is determined by the people, . . . and its exercitum, or actual enjoyment is conferred—and as it is conferred may also be withdrawn—by the people.*[53]

Thus, in *De Regimine Principum*, St. Thomas states that government is instituted by the community, and may be revoked or limited by the community if the government is tyrannical. This was the general view through the Middle Ages. Feudalism, for example, was a system of contract, under which each man could say to his lord,

> *I will be to you faithful and true . . . on condition that you keep me as I am willing to deserve, and all that fulfil (sic) that our agreement was, when I to you submitted and chose your will.*[54]

From the Middle Ages, the enlightened philosophers eventually picked up the concept of the social contract.

Whereas Thomas Hobbes (1588-1679) used the concept of the social contract to justify the absolute *power of the state*,[55] with John Locke the social contract theory challenged the divine right of kings as the basis for a state's legitimacy. In doing so, it laid the foundation for theories of constitutional government. Locke related law and government to the social contract, but did so from the perspective of *individual rights*, as did Jean Jacques Rousseau later. It was the political theory of Locke, which had a profound effect on England. It pene-

---

[53] *Id.* at ix.

[54] From a Wessex document "Of Oaths" (circa A.D. 920), in Sir Ernest Barker, *Introduction*, Social Contract: Essays by Locke, Hume, and Rousseau ix (1947).

[55] Thomas Hobbes, *Leviathan* (1651).

trated into France, and passed through Rousseau into the French Revolution. It was carried into the American colonies, and passed through Samuel Adams and Thomas Jefferson into the American Declaration of Independence.[56]

To Locke and to Rousseau goes much of the credit for the principles and underlying philosophy of not only the Declaration of Independence, but also of the United States Constitution. Both theorists are recognized for their conceptualizations of the social contract. Legal scholars in interpreting the Constitution often consult the writings of both Locke and Rousseau. Moreover, the U.S. Constitution may be viewed as if it were a type of (written) social contract.

Basing his argument on the social contract, Thomas Hobbes, a 17th century English philosopher, justified absolute government as the sole means of protecting society from the selfish nature of its individual members. His argument is presented in his most famous work, *Leviathan; or the Matter, Form, and Power of a Commonwealth, Ecclesiastical and Civil* (1651).

In *Leviathan*, Hobbes argues that the natural "condition of man" is constant "warre (sic) of every one against every one else." In making his argument, he uses the terms "warre" and "nature" interchangeably. The "right of nature," he says,

> *. . . is the liberty each man hath to use his own power as he will himself for the preservation of his own nature; that is to say, of his own life; and consequently, of doing anything which, in his own judgment and reason, he shall conceive to be the aptest means thereunto.*[57]

So long as this natural right of every man to every thing exists, there can be no security for anyone. Seeking protection and self-preservation in the "war of all-against-all," civil society arises only by convention. From self-interest, people make peace and obtain security as a consequence of their delegation of total power to the state—which, in a state having absolute power, is a *monarchy*. "Death,"

---

[56] Sir Ernest Barker, *Introduction*, Social Contract: Essays by Locke, Hume, and Rousseau xvi (1947).

[57] Thomas Hobbes, *Leviathan*, Ch. XIV (1651).

Hobbes says, is the worst of evils, and "The passions that incline men to peace are . . . fear of death. . . ."

Hobbes posits some fundamental laws of nature, the first of which, he argues, is to seek peace. The second law is derived from the first:

> *. . . that a man be willing, when others are so too, as far as for peace and defence (sic) of himself he shall think it necessary, to lay down this right to all things; and be contented with so much liberty against himself.*[58]

This mutual transferring of right is execution of the (social) contract, or what Hobbes calls the "mutual contract."[59] It need not require the swearing of an oath, "[f]or a covenant, if lawful, binds in the sight of God, without the oath, as much as with it." One makes the covenant by conforming to the "laws of nature," which are "immutable and eternal." Once the contract has been made, in Hobbes' perspective, the subject is obligated irreversibly to obey its laws (which are the laws of nature), and of the commonwealth (e.g., the people of a state).

By *civil laws*, Hobbes understood to mean laws that men were bound to observe because they are members of a commonwealth. "Civil law is to every subject those rules which the Commonwealth hath commanded him. . . ."[60] Hobbes' mutual (or social) contract thereby grants absolute power to the sovereign. He concluded that rebellion against the state breaks society's basic contract and is punishable by whatever penalty the monarch may exact in order to protect all subjects from a return to the original state of nature.

John Locke (1632-1704) opposed Hobbes' view that people in the natural state are "nasty, brutish, and short." Instead, the natural state of man is one of happiness and tolerance. Men "are born free and rational." He also did not agree that individuals surrender their rights in exchange for an absolute sovereign who would be the source of all morality and law. Rather, the social contract preserves *preexistent* natural rights of the individual to life, liberty, property, and the pursuit of happiness.

---

[58] Thomas Hobbes, *Leviathan* (1651); Hobbes equates this law to the golden rule of the gospel: "Whatsoever you require that others should do to you, that do ye to them."

[59] *Id.* at Ch. XV.

[60] Thomas Hobbes, *Leviathan* Ch. XXVI (1651).

Locke suggested there are two "foundations" (or human laws versus the law of God and the law of nature) that bear up societies. One is the natural inclination whereby all people desire sociable life and fellowship. The other an order (a social compact) expressly or secretly agreed upon. The latter is that which is called the law of a commonwealth.

Men being by nature free, equal, and independent, cannot be put out of their state of happiness and subjected to the political power of another without giving their own consent. Such consent is freely given "by agreeing with other men, to join and unite into a community for their comfortable, safe and peaceable living . . ." and ". . . a greater security against any that are not of it."[61] And, by consenting with others in a *social compact* to make one body politic under one government, each person puts himself "under an obligation to every one of that society to submit to the determination of the *majority*."

However, the agreement is not irreversible as it is in the case of Thomas Hobbes' contract. Locke was an advocate of civil and religious liberties. He denied the divine right of kings, arguing that government is based on the *consent of the people*. Locke set forth the view that the state exists to preserve the natural rights of its citizens. But when a government fails in that task, its citizens have the right—even the duty—to withdraw their support, and at times to rebel.

In agreement with Locke on the matter, Jean Jacques Rousseau (1712-1778) stated,

> *. . . there is in the State no fundamental law that cannot be revoked, not excluding the social compact itself; for if all citizens assembled of one accord to break the compact, it is impossible to doubt that it would be very legitimately broken.*[62]

However, Rousseau did not agree with Locke on the issue of the will of the majority. Rather, Rousseau maintained that the state was created to preserve freedom of the individual. The state is a unity and as such expresses the general will for the common good of securing

---

[61] John Locke, *Concerning Civil Government* Ch. VIII (1690).

[62] Jean Jacques Rousseau, *Du Compac Social, The Social Contract or Principles of Political Right* Book IV (1762).

freedom, equality, and justice, regardless of the will of the majority. The majority may, in fact, wish for something contrary to the common good.

Another point of departure for Rousseau is in construction of the social contract. Locke, and others, had assumed the social contract to be an historical event. To Rousseau, the social contract was a *theoretical construct*, not a reality. In *The Social Contract*, he opens his dissertation by saying,

> *Man is born free; and everywhere he is in chains. One thinks him self the master of others, and still remains a greater slave than they.*[63]

He goes on to say that,

> . . . *since no man has a natural authority over his fellow, and force creates no right, we must conclude that conventions form the basis of all legitimate authority among men.*[64]

And in response to Hobbes, he states that,

> . . . *it is an empty and contradictory convention that sets up, on the one side, absolute authority, and, on the other, unlimited obedience. It is not clear that we can be under no obligation to a person from whom we have the right to exact everything.*[65]

The "problem," he says,

> . . . *is to find a form of association which will defend and protect with the whole common force the person and goods of each associate, and in which each, while uniting himself with*

---

[63] Jean Jacques Rousseau, *Du Compac Social, The Social Contract or Principles of Political Right* Book I § 1 (1762).
[64] *Id.* at Book I § 4.
[65] *Id.*

> *all, may still obey himself alone, and remain as free as before.*[66]

This, he says, . . . "is the fundamental problem of which the Social Contract provides the solution."[67] And finally,

> *. . . each man, in giving himself to all, gives himself to nobody; and as there is no associate over whom he does not acquire the same right as he yields others over himself, he gains an equivalent for everything he loses, and an increase of force for the preservation of what he has.*[68]

Within the social contract, as envisioned by Rousseau, there is found,

- an hypothetical association of individuals;
- who are willing to subordinate their freedoms to a government;
- that derives its authority from the people; and
- will use its sovereignty to defend and protect the person and goods of each of its associates.

Individual sovereignty is given up to the state in order to achieve freedom, equality, and justice. Jean Jacques Rousseau proclaimed that, "By social compact we have given the body politic existence and life; we have now by legislation to give it movement and will."[69] But when a state fails to act in a morally acceptable way, it ceases to exert genuine authority over the individual, who is then free to rebel.

A contemporary of Jean Jacques Rousseau's was Immanuel Kant (1724-1804), who formulated his own concept of the *original contract* theory.[70] To Kant there was a contractual basis for the just society that began from an original, or *a priori*, state of nature. "In all social contracts . . . " Kant said, " . . . we find a union of many individu-

---

[66] Jean Jacques Rousseau, *Du Compac Social, The Social Contract or Principles of Political Right* Book I § 6 (1762).
[67] *Id.*
[68] *Id.*
[69] *Id.*
[70] *See* Immanuel Kant, *The Fundamental Principles of the Metaphysic of Morals* (1785).

als for some common end which they all share." In the Kantian perspective, the social contract envisions an objective, hypothetical third person, in an "original position," who contracts for conditions as yet unforeseen. Assumed is the contracting person will not agree to conditions which might turn out to be adverse to that person's best interests, but rather, chooses to optimize the conditions wherein he or she might later be situated.

APPLIED ETHICS

Out of the Era of Enlightenment came the ethical foundations for the evolution of modern law (and creation of the United States Constitution). Utilitarians proclaim that universal welfare (or happiness) should be the leading principle in the conduct of life. The divine right of kings is thus supplanted as society takes the place of the will of God, which thereby describes what is called "natural law." As Calvi and Coleman explain, Thomas Jefferson incorporated the concept of natural law into the Declaration of Independence when he invoked the notion that persons are endowed by their Creator with certain "inalienable rights." He also invoked the theory of the social contract, *à là* Locke and Rousseau,[71] when he emphatically stated that governments are instituted among men to protect those natural rights and that when a sovereign abuses the power granted to it by its subjects, it is the right of the people to alter and abolish it.

The Declaration of Independence and its underlying philosophy, grounded in Locke and Rousseau, put a new twist on the relationship between the people and their government, by proclaiming that government derived its power from the consent of the governed, not by some accident of royal birth. Implicit in the concept of government by consent is the idea of majority rule.[72] American democracy is, by definition, utilitarian, because it attempts to provide the greatest happiness to the greatest number. It is, at the same time, grounded in the theory of the social contract, placing the individual before society and above the state. However, such a view about the generalized application of utilitarian and contractarian theories is not without its critics.

---

[71] Jean Jacques Rousseau, *Du Compac Social, The Social Contract or Principles of Political Right* Book (1762).

[72] *See* James V. Calvi & Susan Coleman, *American Law and Legal Systems* 56 (3rd ed. 1997).

David A.J. Richards, for example, demands that adherence to social utility, or to the social contract, ignores history by obfuscating "the interpretation of historical meaning of the American constitutional system." He argues that to properly understand the U.S. Constitution, one must "take seriously the multiple layers of interpretive history" the founders used in constructing the Constitution. In short, interpreting the U.S. Constitution is no easy task that can be reduced to simple conventions like utilitarianism and the social contract.[73]

However, the elusiveness of sorting out the "layers of interpretive history," that Richards finds necessary to understand constitutional construction, makes the ease of using conventional theories, such as utilitarianism and the social contract, appealing and instructive in understanding constitutional law (and its ethical foundations). Hence, both the utilitarian and contractarian perspectives are instrumental in helping one to come to grips with the morality and substance of constitutional law.

Reduced to the simplest terms, ethical decision making within the utilitarian concept of justice would suggest that such decisions should be made to satisfy as large of a majority of one's constituents as possible. That is to say, to make as many people as "happy" by the decision as possible. In the belief that social welfare should depend only on the welfare levels of individual citizens, at the very least the policymaker's choice criterion should respond positively to an increase in the welfare of individual citizens. Ideally, the policy of choice should make certain individuals better off while at the same time making no one worse off.[74]

Where the policymaker must choose between the status quo and a policy change that will make some individuals better off and others worse off, the choice criterion is to maximize the utility of society as a whole by improving the lot of the least privileged, and in this way provide the most pleasure to the most people.[75] Sometimes, however, in order to minimize the pain and suffering of the majority, a minority must of necessity have imposed upon them even greater pain and suffering. These are times when the policymaker is caught in a dilemma between acts of omission and commission—where one can never do nothing.[76] Herein lies the inherent weakness of utilitarianism.

---

[73] David A.J. Richards, *Foundations of American Constitutionalism* 11-17 (1989).

[74] Edith Stokey & Richard Zeckhauser, *A Primer for Policy Analysis* 270-273 (1978).

[75] John Rawls, *A Theory of Justice* (1971).

[76] Garrett Hardin, *The Tragedy of the Commons*, Science Vol. 162 (1968), at 1243-1248.

By providing the most pleasure to the most people, the most quantifiable justice is satisfied. But there still remains a tolerance for unhappiness, and even injustice, in a minority of the population. It is this residual injustice which renders the utilitarian model in and of itself unacceptable.

Embodied in the contractarian theory are notions of *individual* rights. Within the Declaration of Independence, there is an appeal to natural law wherein it is stated that all men are, along with life itself, endowed (by their creator) with certain "unalienable" rights, and that among these are *liberty* and the pursuit of *happiness*. Justice in the American liberal democratic tradition prioritizes human rights and may be characterized as a form of "modern individualism," redefined by Lowi as "conservatism,"[77] which asserts an inalienable right to self-govern,[78] but grants autonomy only within certain limitations.

The underpinnings of this individualism are conservative ideals of liberty, equality, community, and justice: *Liberty*, because one of the deeply held values in American life is that of freedom, freedom to be left alone, and to pursue happiness and success as it is individually perceived.[79] *Equality*, incorporating not only a right to equal participation,[80] but also political equality and a republican form of government where it is incumbent upon citizens to participate.[81] *Community*, because of the Jeffersonian injunction to love your country more than self,[82] the admonition of Christ to "love thy neighbor as thyself,"[83] or as Adam Smith said, ". . . it is a great precept of nature to love ourselves only as we love our neighbor, or what comes to the same thing, as our neighbor is capable of loving us."[84]

From the individual perspective, all people are interrelated and integrated economically, technically, and functionally with the community around them. Hence, people join together for mutual benefit, and they survive as human beings more through cooperation than by

---

[77] Theodore Lowi, *The End of Liberalism* 4 (2nd ed. 1979).

[78] Robert Bellah, Richard Madsen, William Sullivan, Ann Swindler & Steven Tipton, *Habits of the Heart* 142 (1971).

[79] *Id.* at 23.

[80] John Rawls, *A Theory of Justice* 22 (1971).

[81] Robert Bellah, Richard Madsen, William Sullivan, Ann Swindler & Steven Tipton, *Habits of the Heart* 30 (1971).

[82] *Id.* at 31.

[83] *Matthew* 22:39.

[84] Adam Smith, *The Theory of Moral Sentiments* (1759).

competition.[85] And finally, *justice*, in the sense that equal opportunities are guaranteed by fair laws and political procedures that are applied in the same way to everyone.[86] Justice is where regular and impartial administration of public rules are applied. Justice is where each person has an equal chance to pursue his or her own individual interests. Justice also strikes a balance in the tensions between liberty, equality and community. Although liberty has the highest priority,[87] liberty must of necessity be constrained in the service of equality and community in order to promote at least minimum levels of acceptable social justice.

These conservative ideals of liberty, equality, community, and justice are embodied in the framework of the social contract. These are the ideals which members of society have a right to expect. Conversely, it is an obligation upon government to grant to its citizens such rights. Having given up certain personal freedoms to the government in exchange for these rights, the government accepts the duty to protect its citizens with these rights.

If moral philosophy can be defined as "sympathy,"[88] or as "empathy," then notions of *caring* and *cooperation*, being synonymously related terms, have much to do with promoting justice; and more importantly, in minimizing injustice. Public administrators, in accepting their positions of authority, and as personal representatives of the government, have an obligation to protect the individual rights of citizens. In effect, they are obliged to treat all citizens equally in the way they would like to be treated themselves given similar circumstances (i.e., to apply the golden rule). If they do not, then citizens have every right to demand their removal from office.

Social contract theorists attempt to work out the liberties of the individual rationally. However, the contractarian places that rationality into the hands of some hypothetical third person, a condition that makes it far too easy to manipulate choices and to generate convenient conclusions.[89] For example, it may be presumptuous to assume the public administrator, however objective that person might be, can truly act like the hypothetical third person in making rational deci-

[85] Petr Kropotkin, *Mutual Aid* (1910).
[86] Robert Bellah, Richard Madsen, William Sullivan, Ann Swindler & Steven Tipton, *Habits of the Heart* 25 (1971).
[87] John Rawls, *A Theory of Justice* 243-251 (1971).
[88] Adam Smith, *The Theory of Moral Sentiments* (1759).
[89] Bruce A. Ackerman, *Social Justice in the Liberal State* 337 (1980).

sions for another individual. No public administrator is immune to outside political influences in their decision making. Conversely, the utilitarian perspective fails to take individualism (and liberty) seriously enough.[90]

Recognizing the inherent injustices in not only the classical utilitarian, but the intuitionist conceptions of justice as well, John Rawl's guiding aim was to work out a theory of justice that would be a more viable alternative to those doctrines, which he says "have long dominated our philosophical tradition." His initial response was to strike a compromise between utility and the social contract.[91] But his ultimate answer[92] was to return to the contractarian concept, to raise it to a higher level of abstraction, and to describe "justice as fairness" in the Kantian perspective—fairness in this case meaning a balance of competing claims.

Human rights are the outcome of Kant's "original contract."[93] In Rawls' perspective, "The force of justice as fairness would appear to arise from two things: the requirement that all inequalities be justified to the least advantaged, and the priority of liberty." Hence, supporting Rawls' "original position" are his two basic *principles of justice*, which are:

- *The Liberty Principle*—Each person is to have an equal right to the most extensive basic liberty compatible with a similar liberty for others; and
- *The Difference Principle*—Social and economic inequalities are to be arranged so that they are both (a) reasonably expected to be to everyone's advantage, and (b) attached to positions and offices open to all.[94]

---

[90] *Id.* at 342.

[91] *See* John Rawls, *Outline of a Decision Procedure for Ethics*, The Philosophical Review (1951), at 60; *see also* John Rawls, *Justice as Fairness*, The Philosophical Review (1958), at 67; *see also* John Rawls, *The Sense of Justice*, The Philosophical Review (1963), at 72.

[92] John Rawls, *A Theory of Justice* (1971).

[93] *See* Immanuel Kant, *Kant's Political Writings* (Hans Reiss, ed. & H.B. Nisbet, trans. 1970) in James Sterba, Justice: Alternative Political Perspectives (1980).

[94] John Rawls, *A Theory of Justice* 250 (1971).

SUMMARY

A revolution prompted the Declaration of Independence and ultimately led to writing the United States Constitution with its grounding in theories of social utility and the social contract. As Donald Menzel points out, "We are living through revolutionary times and we only partly recognize that reality."[95] He states that "[e]thical passages into 21st Century public management may be smooth and safe or they may be rough and dangerous." And there are plenty of reasons why they might be the latter and not the former. It is going to be difficult for public administrators in the future to protect individual liberties as described above. Menzel identifies five powerful forces of change encompassed in the current "revolution" and mitigating against personal freedoms.

The first force is *computerization*, which is transforming every facet of life. Alvin Toffler spoke of a future when change would be so rapid that people would no longer be able to adapt, and society would grind to a halt, causing a sociological and psychological "shock wave."[96] The force of computerization, although not slowing things down to the conditions described by Toffler, is indeed becoming a challenge to many in society, including a challenge of their ethical standards. Personal privacy, for example, is under attack. It takes only minutes to obtain a credit check or a criminal investigation background check. For that matter, a complete history can be obtained from the Internet on almost anyone with a social security number and a credit card account.

The second force is the *information explosion*. This force is inextricably linked to computerization, but it has more to do with the *volume* of information than with personal privacy. There is so much information available that people are having difficulty digesting it. There is a glut of information that frustrates those who are trying to select from it that which might be personally meaningful. As Menzel explains, ". . . it is overwhelming us, perhaps dumbing us down"! And what are the ethical challenges? To what extent does freedom of information extend? Is there such a thing as too much information in

---

[95] This section draws heavily from Donald C. Menzel, *Ethical Passages Into 21st Century Public Administration*, PA Times, Vol. 21, No. 7 (Jul. 1998), at 6.

[96] Alvin Toffler, *Shock Wave* (1970).

a democracy? Most importantly, who is it that might presume to have the authority to withhold information?

The third force sweeping the globe is *privatization.* It is revolutionizing the way governments are structured and operated and is discussed at length in the next chapter. Entrepreneurship in the public sector is a complete reversal of roles, making the government overseer a competitor. To what extent might the government ethically and fairly compete with private enterprise? What and where are the conflicts of interest?

The fourth force is *globalization* and is linked to the "fifth wave" of infrastructure discussed in Chapter 16. Air transportation made the world smaller. But as Menzel explains, communications including the Internet, e-mail and direct TV are shrinking the world at "warp speed." The ethical challenges lie in negotiations between peoples with cultural differences. The ethical standards guiding the negotiators may lie at opposite ends of the spectrum. What may be considered customary business practice in one part of the world may be considered unethical, even illegal bribery in another part of the world.

Ironically, the fifth force is *democratization.* The freedoms afforded under democracy render the world from a security standpoint unsafe. This presents challenges in making the world safe while still maintaining democratic ideals and freedoms. Moreover, if leaders and people of emerging democracies are not up to the ethical challenges, some observers would contend that allowing them to govern themselves might be dangerous.

These revolutionary forces, computerization, the information explosion, privatization, globalization and democratization, will challenge the ethics of individual public administrators. But as Woodrow Wilson, the father of modern public administration, noted, an ethical administrator is one who accepts responsibility and is competent. Moral responsibility begins with the individual.

CHAPTER 15

PRIVATIZATION AND PUBLIC ENTREPRENEURSHIP

The City of Los Angeles never has received five cents return on the work and investment that it has made. It is interesting to note that under our law and regulation, Hertz can make a profit, United Airlines and American Airlines can make a profit, the restaurant operator can make a profit, everyone can make a profit from the public investment except the people who actually own it. They are not allowed to take money from the airport in to the general treasury of the City. The money must remain on the airport.

Clifton Moore, former Director of Airports,
City of Los Angeles [1]

THE MOTIVATION TO PRIVATIZE

Many of the world's airports are currently experiencing major congestion problems. In response, there has been a significant worldwide trend to privatize government services and facilities since the middle of the 1980s.[2] Proponents claim that privatization would inject much needed capital into the aviation infrastructure. Conversely, opponents argue that local governments—the sponsors of most public airports in the United States—favor privatization only because they see it as a means of diverting airport generated funds into other mu-

---

[1] Reason Foundation, *Airport Privatization: Can It Work?,* A Transcript of a Reason Foundation Seminar (Mar. 20, 1990), at 15-16.
[2] Richard de Neuville, *Airport Privatization Issues for the United States*, Massachusetts Institute of Technology (unpublished draft, 1999).

nicipal purposes, which would thereby result in higher costs for airlines and passengers.[3]

Regardless of how the goal might be achieved, unless something is done to add air traffic system capacity, air transportation may reach gridlock early in this, the 21st Century.[4] The problem is serious, yet governments are in a dilemma as to how to go about improving the system effectively, both in terms of management and development of physical facilities.

There has long been a debate regarding the scope of government involvement revolving around two conflicting issues: *efficiency* and *equity*.[5] While the United States traditionally has favored private ownership and control of economic enterprises, recognized is that some functions are so affected with the "public interest" that government involvement is a prerequisite. Airports are a classic example of a *public* enterprise that may be distinguished from a *private* enterprise because of the role they play in serving the public interest. Public enterprises typically operate as government-approved monopolies supplying an indispensable service to society.[6] However, this does not preclude privatization to varying extents. Energy companies, for example, are often privately owned and operated as public utilities. Airports, too, have historically involved some form of privatized activity.

The problem with expanding airports to meet the growing demands of society is not so much about management or management style as it is about finance and how to pay for the improvements. But with local and national budgets stretched and basic services such as education under-funded, many governments simply don't have the money to improve airports.[7] Consequently, many airport sponsors both in the United States and throughout the world are looking at private investment as a way to ease the financial strain. Some analysts even go so far as to see privatization as the panacea for addressing the

---

[3] Government Accounting Office [GAO], *Airport Privatization: Issues Related to the Sale or Lease of U.S. Commercial Airports* (Nov. 7, 1996).

[4] The International Air Transport Association states that by 2010, fifty of the world's major airports, many of them in the U.S., will be operating beyond their capacity. *See* Kyle Pope, *Airport Privatization Begins to Take Off, Led by Britain's BAA*, Wall St. J. (Sep. 24, 1996), at A1.

[5] Lawrence J. Truitt & Michael Esler, *Airport Privatization: Full Divestiture and its Alternatives*, Policy Studies J., Vol. 24, No.1 (1996), at 100.

[6] *See id.*; *see also* J.P. Garfield & W.F. Lovejoy, *Public Utility Economics* (1964).

[7] Kyle Pope, *Airport Privatization Begins to Take Off, Led by Britain's BAA*, Wall St. J. (Sep. 24, 1996), at A1.

daunting demands for future air transportation infrastructure development.

As Robert Poole of the Reason Foundation argues, the motivations driving the current interest in privatization of U.S. airports include:

- General constraints in public budgets;
- Capacity bottlenecks on the ground and in the air;
- Changes in airport markets, such as commercialization and globalization;
- Escalating airport infrastructure operations and maintenance expenses;
- Interest in airports as catalysts for regional economic development; and generally,
- A growing need for airports to do more with less.

Charles Sander, Vice President of Airport Operations for Unisys Global Transportation refers to privatization as the "Enterprise Approach," and suggests that it:

- Increases operating efficiencies;
- Increases airport revenues;
- Improves airport amenities;
- Creates potential new revenue streams for local, state and international governments; and it
- Reduces risks to airport-related project development.[8]

Advocates for airport privatization such as Robert Poole of the Reason Foundation or Charles Sander at Unisys can present a strong case for private investment into airports from the corporate vantage point and with regard to profit-making. However, from the perspective of other stakeholders—the airlines, passengers and other airport users, perhaps even from the airport sponsors themselves—the proponents' argument for privatization weakens. Airports serve a purpose beyond venture capitalism and management efficiency.

---

[8] *See* Charles Sander, *Airport Privatization: Trends and Opportunities,* Part I, http://www.unisys.com (visited Sep. 21, 2006). Sander does not define "enterprise," but assumed is that he means "private enterprise." However, it should be recognized that governments, too, may operate an enterprise, or enterprise account, as one of its proprietary functions. Hence, the issue is more of private vs.public management of the enterprise.

As Richard de Neuville argues,

> *Because there always will be a public interest in the operation of major commercial airports, that are both vital assets to the community and potential monopolies, it is generally impractical to transform airports into wholly private businesses. Most privatization projects involve substantial regulation of the private investors, detailing the design of their services, the prices they may charge, and their openness to users.*[9]

Moreover, by de Neuville's accounting U.S airports are already among the most privatized in the world, leaving little scope for privatization in the United States compared to elsewhere. Conversely, overseas, privatization has taken on momentum, particularly in the privatization of airports that were previously owned and operated by principally national governments and city states. The movement began following deregulation (or liberalization) of the airlines in the 1980s. By 1996 at least fifty countries other than the United States had expressed interest in some form of private sector participation at commercial airports.[10] Then in 1998 alone, as many as fifty-seven airports in fifteen countries turned to some form of privatization for a variety of reasons—lack of capital, infrastructure development, cost savings and efficiency, to name a few. By 2006 more than twenty countries had consummated the sale or lease of airport facilities in whole or in part.[11] Virtually all of the above activity occurred outside the United States.[12] But, as previously stated, U.S. airports are already amongst the most privatized in the world, depending on how one defines privatization. Although all commercial airports in the United

---

[9] Richard de Neuville, *Airport Privatization Issues for the United States*, Massachusetts Institute of Technology (unpublished draft, 1999).

[10] *See* GAO, Airport *Privatization: Issues Related to the Sale or Lease of U.S. Commercial Airports* (Nov. 7, 1996).

[11] Argentina, Australia, Austria, Bahamas, Bolivia, Cambodia, Canada, Chile, Colombia, Denmark, Dominican Republic, Germany, Hungary Italy, Japan, Malaysia, Mexico, New Zealand, Singapore, South Africa, Switzerland & the United Kingdom. *See* Charles Sander, *Airport Privatization: Trends and Opportunities,* Part I, http://www.unisys.com (visited Sep. 21, 2006).

[12] Holly Arthur, *Airport Privatization: A Reality Check*, Airport Magazine (Sep./Oct. 1998).

States are publicly owned, the private sector plays a significant role in their operations and financing.[13]

Nevertheless, in the United States, for a time, expanded, even *de novo* privatization of governmental services, or the use of the private sector to attain public goals, took center stage in federal, state, and local government attempts to reform service delivery and lower cost.[14] But the general movement to privatize governmental services in the United States may have peaked out. In a 1995 survey of city officials, Dilger, Moffett and Struyk conclude there may be a slowdown in the dramatic growth of privatization.[15] Irrespective, the number of privatized services in America's largest cities suggests the privatization movement has made a significant impact, and that privatization is now firmly entrenched.[16]

According to a 1997 survey of privatization activity in state governments conducted by the Council of State Governments, privatization is a tool that states have been trying in order to save money and hopefully to provide better services. Many governors, legislative leaders, and state agencies view privatization as a practical, cost-saving initiative. Amongst state agencies, transportation departments privatized the most programs and services, followed by administration and general services, corrections, and social services.[17]

Although it may now be widely accepted as a viable, alternative service delivery option, privatization, meaning outright sale or lease, is an altogether different matter than outsourcing for limited service provision. As Richard Leone, former chairman of the Port Authority of New York and New Jersey, states, privatization "just doesn't make sense for big airports in communities like New York and New Jersey." Selling major airports to private operators could leave strategic public assets loaded with debt, deteriorating from lack of investment

---

[13] GAO, Airport *Privatization: Issues Related to the Sale or Lease of U.S. Commercial Airports* (Nov. 7, 1996).

[14] Bruce A. Wallin, *The Need for a Privatization Process: Lessons for Development and Implementation*, Public Administration Rev., Vol. 57, No. 1 (1997), at 11.

[15] Privatization here meaning outsourcing of certain services such as vehicle towing, solid waste collection, building security, street repair, ambulance service, printing services, street lighting/signals, drug/alcohol treatment centers, employment and training, and legal services.

[16] Robert Jay Dilger, Randolph R. Moffett & Linda Struyk, *Privatization of Municipal Services in America's Largest Cities*, Public Administration Rev., Vol. 57, No. 1 (Jan./Feb. 1997), at 21-25.

[17] Keon S. Chi & Cindy Jasper, *Private Practices: A Review of Privatization in State Government*, Council of State Governments (Mar. 1998).

and unable to support the communities they serve.[18] But that does not mean that sponsors of larger airports have not attempted to sell their airports as a means of reducing costs, increasing revenues, or outright as a way to divert airport generated funds into local coffers.[19]

Airlines, in particular, are wary of privatization. As Mosley suggests, the airlines and other airport tenants want "the best of both worlds." They want efficiently run airports, but simultaneously enjoy the benefits of government subsidized operations.[20] Yet, even the airlines acknowledge that something must be done. All around the world airports are in trouble. Terminals are congested, passengers are frustrated and airlines are starting to panic about the increasing gridlock. In 1996 the number of passengers was forecast to more than quadruple by the first decade of the 21st Century.[21] The events of September 11, 2001 intervened, the passenger count subsided, and concerns about airport congestion were temporarily put aside. But now the numbers are back up and exceeding the pre-9/11 volumes. And, airports have failed miserably to keep pace with the projected growth. As more airports move into the private sector, airlines are hoping for better service and investment but are worrying about higher prices—ironically, in an environment they helped to create.

The effects of airline deregulation fueled the drive for airport privatization. Deregulation led to widespread adoption of the hub-and-spoke strategy by the major carriers. The establishment of strategic airport hubs generated problems of severe congestion at many of the world's largest commercial airports, especially during peak travel periods.[22] Managers of airports large and small have found it necessary to competitively market their airports in order to either take advantage of the "hubbing" phenomenon, or in some cases to even be a part of the air transportation network at all. For larger airports, traditional leases became particularly problematic with the advent of deregulation. Many new entrant airlines have been either restricted, or otherwise unable to obtain access to airports they wanted to serve. In

---

[18] *See* Staff, *Privatization Could Leave Major Airports in Debt, Port Authority Chairman Warns*, Avn. Wk. & Space Tech. (May 25, 1992).

[19] *See* GAO, Airport *Privatization: Issues Related to the Sale or Lease of U.S. Commercial Airports* (Nov. 7, 1996).

[20] Bruce H. Mosley, *The Best of Both Worlds*, Airport Magazine (Jan./Feb. 1998), at 8.

[21] Kyle Pope, *Airport Privatization Begins to Take Off, Led by Britain's BAA*, Wall St. J. (Sep. 24, 1996), at A1.

[22] Lawrence J. Truitt and Michael Esler, *Airport Privatization: Full Divestiture and its Alternatives*, Policy Studies J., Vol. 24, No.1 (1996), at 101.

most cases gates are limited, and the few existing gates in service are controlled by incumbent airlines. The granting of air traffic slots to certain airlines by the Federal government has had a similar effect in excluding service, especially to smaller carriers.[23]

At the same time that airlines were consolidating operations at strategic hub airports, well-organized citizen groups attempted to block expansion of airports in the areas where they live. In addition to the airlines consolidating their operations and the evolution of anti-airport development groups, declining public investment in airports has exacerbated these problems.[24] As a result, airport privatization is gathering pace even though there has been remarkably little discussion in the literature of how the privatization process should be structured; that is to say, how should the rules for privatization be written.[25]

Look, for instance, at the privatization of the Indianapolis International Airport [IND]. Michael Boggs suggests that the Indianapolis privatization was motivated more by politics "based on the mayor's agenda. . . ." than by economic efficiency—even though the contract between IND and its private contractor, BAA Indianapolis, LLC, has at its core an "efficiency guarantee." The contractor's compensation is based on either increasing non-airline revenues and/or decreasing operating costs.[26]

The issue of privatization remains a contentious one, which is fraught with uncertainty. Airport privatization is not without its critics. Airlines oppose it over concern that private operators will raise fees. In Argentina, for example, airlines through the International Air Transport Association [IATA] have sought a revision of the terms of the long-term concession awarded to the Aeropuertos Argentinas 2000 [AA2000] consortium to operate thirty-three of the country's airports including Ezeiza, Aeroparque and Cordoba. IATA is concerned that airlines will be faced with escalating airport charges to cover the $171 million annual concession fee AA2000 agreed to pay

---

[23] There has long been widespread support in Congress to improve competition within the airline industry, insure the provision of airline service to small and medium hub communities, and grant priority to smaller carriers in obtaining slots at major hubs. *See* Karen walker, *Bill Favors Small Cities, Airline Business* (Aug. 1998), at 11.

[24] Lawrence J. Truitt & Michael Esler, *Airport Privatization: Full Divestiture and its Alternatives*, Policy Studies J., Vol. 24, No.1 (1996), at 101.

[25] Bruce A. Wallin, *The Need for a Privatization Process: Lessons for Development and Implementation*, Public Administration Rev., Vol. 57, No. 1 (1997), at 11.

[26] Michael Boggs, The *Politics of Privatization*, Airport Magazine (Sep./Oct. 1998), at 33.

the Argentine government and a compulsory $1.3 billion capital investment program.[27]

Not only are the airlines concerned about the prospects of airport privatization, the general aviation industry opposes privatization not only because it could result in higher fees, but also because it might be denied the use of commercial airports. Labor also is generally opposed because of the threat of job elimination and/or decreased benefits.[28] For example, in the privatization of Rhode Island's six-airport system under the State Department of Transportation in 1993, thirty-three employees responsible for maintenance and operations were reduced to only seven, including the general manager, at the five general aviation airports.[29]

Cost cutting inevitably begins with reducing the work force, and revenue enhancement generally means an increase in rates and charges. In effect, privatization may not be the panacea that some advocates have perceived it to be. Nevertheless, if privatization could be combined with the development of a new wave of air transportation infrastructure, perhaps a public/private partnership might alleviate the future reality of a capacity-locked system.

The air traffic and airspace system, including airports, is an integrated system, and experience has shown facilities controlled exclusively by private companies tend to be proprietary, and inflexible to system requirements for change. A real dilemma arises when the airport sponsor lacks the power or ability to provide additional facilities to airlines wishing to enter the market at the sponsor's airport. Although deregulation has not caused radical changes in financial management of airports, there have been signs of shift in management policy and practice toward the *compensatory approach*, as discussed in Chapter 13. With the compensatory approach, sponsors can have more direct control over available airport facilities. Additionally, with the concentration of airlines into hub-and-spoke networks, larger airports have become viable business enterprises with a propensity for profit. The possibility of profit has spawned a movement toward airport self-sufficiency at a minimum, but ostensibly toward total privatization of airports at the extreme.

---

[27] Tom Gill, *Argentinian Airport Fray*, Airline Business (Sep. 1998), at 22.

[28] Lawrence J. Truitt & Michael Esler, *Airport Privatization: Full Divestiture and its Alternatives*, Policy Studies J., Vol. 24, No.1 (1996), at 101.

[29] John F. Infanger, *An Airport Corporation*, Airport Business (May 1997), at 15.

PROFITABILITY

By definition, "profit" equals revenues minus expenses. As in the corporate world, assessment of the potential profitability of airports can best be measured by the relationship between revenues and expenses. The economics of all airports involve the same basic relationship between each one's revenues and expenses. The underlying principle for all airports certainly is to maximize revenue and minimize expense, but certain types of airports have a propensity to make more money than do others.

Additionally, and although the economic basics are relatively the same amongst airports, there is a difference in revenue and expense distribution which reflects differing types of air passenger transportation and other commercial activity. As the proportion of air carrier movements goes up, so does the percentage share of revenue from air carrier-related concessions such as auto rental agencies, restaurants, and auto parking. As this percentage of air carrier-related revenue goes up so does the ability of the airport to actually pay its way, ultimately reaching true economic self-sufficiency.

At strictly general aviation airports, those with industrial land uses have a distinct advantage over those that do not. As with concessions at air carrier airports, the more industrial activity a general aviation airport can generate the better are its chances of operating in the black.

There are at least three studies from which to derive the potential profitability of airports. In the first one in 1974, the Federal Aviation Administration [FAA] published a financial and statistical survey of representative airports in the United States. The study shows how airport operating revenues and expenses vary by airport size, operations, and location. Data were collected from ninety-two air carrier and eighty-four general aviation airports and were compiled in a format that conveniently permits analytical comparison of airports in a *relatively* consistent and uniform manner.

However, accountability for operating and non-operating expenses may vary from one airport to another, and the elusiveness of some critical expense items makes the determination of airport profitability extremely difficult to predict and compare. In analyzing data collected by the FAA in 1974, care had to be taken in compiling the results, which are subsequently presented in this chapter. At the smaller airports, the reporting of non-operating expenses is often sketchy and unreliable. Moreover, the scatter plots of the data are widely dispersed, indicative of a low correlation between the variables being measured (in this case the non-operating expenses), and an indication that the data may not be consistent. As a result, non-operating expenses are excluded from the data in Figure 15.1, "Small and Non-Hub Airports Operating Profit Margin," and Figure 15.2, "Commercial and Industrial GA Airports Operating Profit Margin."

Figures 15.1 and 15.2 reflect the statistics of small non-hub and General Aviation [GA] airports predominantly found in general fund accounting systems wherein the airport sponsor's intent is to break even with operating budgets while accounting for capital improvement expenses in separate accounts within the general fund accounting system. What this means is that small air carrier airports and certain general aviation airports are generally capable of meeting operating expenses, but must be subsidized in their capital improvement programs. Less active general aviation airports and those devoted exclusively to training and service for the general aviation community cannot even meet their operating expenses, let alone expect to generate profit. A flat trend line in Figure 15.3, "Service and Training GA Airports Operating Profit Margin," that never rises above the break-even point, demonstrates the non-profitability of service and training airports; i.e., airports that have aviation related land uses only.

At the large and medium hub airports the reporting of revenue and expense line items more completely reflect all of the operating and non-operating data. The larger airports usually have distinct and inclusive accounting systems and they are less likely than the smaller airports to have any dependence upon intergovernmental assistance or to have expense items hidden within the general fund accounting system. Figure 15.4, "Large and Medium Hub Airports Net Profit Margin," shows the point at which air carrier airports may be expected to generate net profits after all expenses (including non-operating expenses) have been paid.

Figure 15.1—SMALL AND NON-HUB AIRPORTS OPERATING PROFIT MARGIN

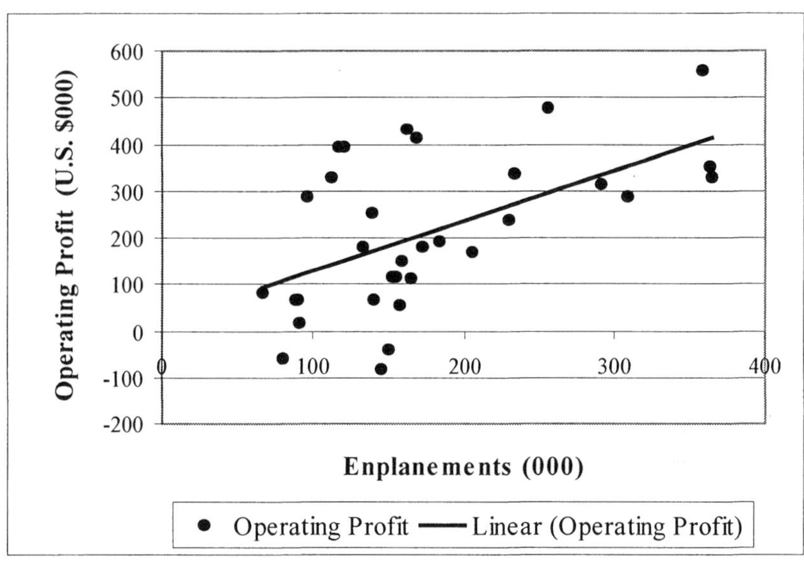

Figure 15.2—COMMERCIAL AND INDUSTRIAL GA AIRPORTS OPERATING PROFIT MARGIN

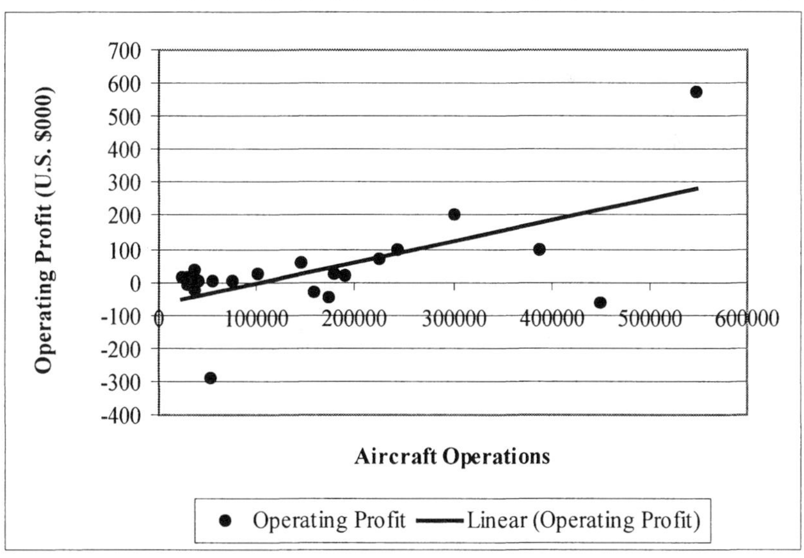

Figure 15.3—SERVICE AND TRAINING GA AIRPORTS OPERATING PROFIT MARGIN

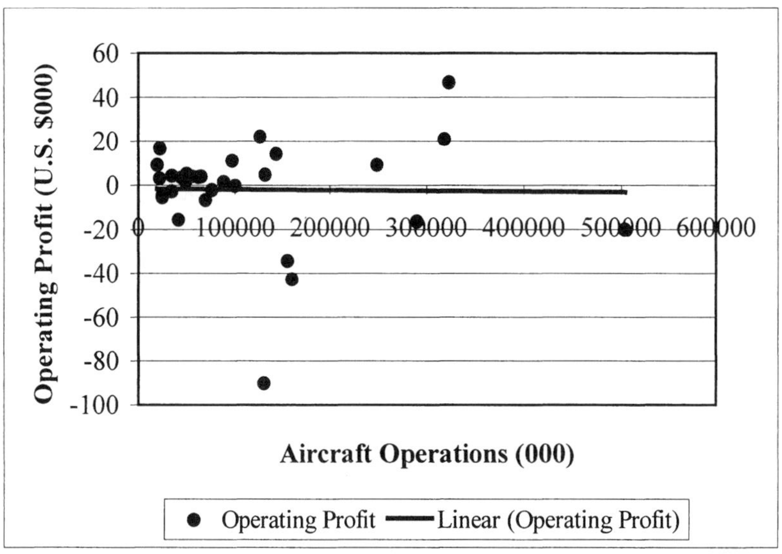

Figure 15.4—LARGE AND MEDIUM HUB AIRPORTS NET PROFIT MARGIN

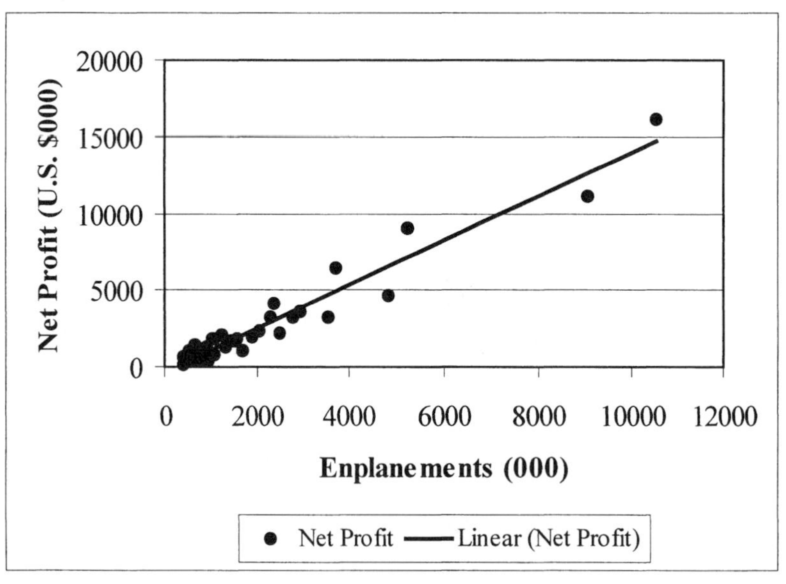

DATA ANALYSES

The Federal Airport Act of 1946 contained provisions for standardized accounting by all airports receiving federal grant funds. "Standardized," however, means acceptable to standard accounting practice, and does not have the same connotation as standardized within the meaning of say the *Uniform System of Accounts and Reports* [USAR] required of the airlines. Since accounting systems may not be exactly alike, comparing one accounting system against another can be a comparison of the proverbial "apples and oranges." The attempt in analyzing the airports in the FAA study was to organize them as nearly as possible into groups with similar characteristics.

Since there is no standard accounting system adopted for all airports, each may have its own definition for revenue and expense items. In the FAA study, operating revenues were defined to exclude contributions by local governments or appropriations of tax funds. Operating expenses excluded depreciation, debt service, and capital improvement costs. Non-operating expenses consisted of interest, contributions to government, and other miscellaneous expenses. They did not include capital improvement costs or repayment of loan principal.

Airports were grouped into air carrier and general aviation classifications. *Air carrier* airports were those having scheduled service by domestic trunk, local service, or large intrastate carriers (i.e., definitions used prior to airline deregulation). Each air carrier airport was further sub-categorized into *large*, *medium*, *small*, or *non-hub*.[30] *General aviation* airports included those with commuter air carrier service. General aviation airports were divided into two sub-categories: c*ommercial/industrial* airports and s*ervice/ training* airports.

Analyses of all airport categories showed that, as a group, the *only* airports having true economic independence were the *large hub* airports. Although air carrier airports larger than non-hub showed operating profits, only the large hubs earned sufficient revenues to fully meet operating and non-operating expenses, and still have the ability to finance large capital improvements. Large hub airports have a high

[30] When the 1974 FAA survey of revenues and expenses at representative airports in the U.S. was analyzed for presentation in the first edition of this text (1979) there were 3,250,00 enplanements in the U.S. Therefore, a large hub airport enplaned 3,250,000 passengers or more; a medium hub enplaned between 800,000 to 3,249,999 passengers; a small hub beween 150,001 and 799,999 passengers; and a non-hub airport enplaned 150,000 passengers or less.

proportion of air carrier operations with broad concession and commercial/industrial revenue bases. All other airports had a decreasing ability to operate without some form of subsidy, albeit federal grants for capital improvement. As airports decreased in size their marginal propensity to pay for non-operating and capital investment expenses diminished, until finally in the non-hub category some airports were no longer able to cover all of the operating expenses.

Figure 15.5, "Non-Hub Airports Operating Profit Margin," plots the regression of non-hub operating revenue and expense data. With approximately 10,000 annual enplanements, an air carrier airport may be expected to cover its operating expenses, but only marginally. As shown on Figure 15.5, operating revenue proportionally increases very gradually with increased enplanements, thus indicating the requirement for large subsidies for capital improvement and other non-operating expenses.

In contrast, Figure 15.6, "Large Hub Airports Net Profit Margin," shows the availability of tens of millions of dollars for capital investment at large hub airports, even after the non-operating expenses have been rectified.

At general aviation airports, where purely aviation service and training takes place, there is little likelihood of the airport sustaining its own operation. As shown in Figure 15.3 above, service and training airports are not expected to break even in operating expenses until attaining well over 600,000 annual operations. As a practical matter, this means that this type of airport may never be able to pay its way. The expected break-even point does not occur until some time after it has reached saturation of the air traffic and airspace system.

Representing the upper limit in Figure 15.3 is the Tamiami Airport in Miami, Florida. Tamiami is part of the Dade County Airport system and receives much of its financial support from revenues generated at Miami International, which is a large hub airport. Fortunately, this kind of symbiotic, or system-supporting relationship, provides for the maintenance of many of the nation's general aviation airports. The Richard L. Jones (Tulsa Riverside) Airport near Tulsa, Oklahoma, is another example, which derives support from a larger air carrier airport, in this case from Tulsa International Airport. Likewise, Phoenix Sky Harbor Airport subsidizes Deer Valley and Goodyear Airports in Arizona. And, there are many other such examples throughout the U.S.

Figure 15.5—NON-HUB AIRPORTS OPERATING PROFIT MARGIN

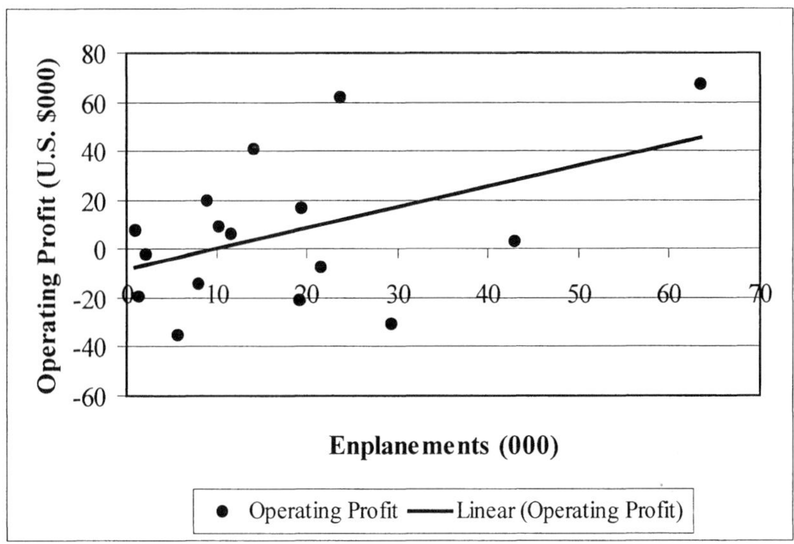

Figure 15.6—LARGE HUB AIRPORTS NET OPERATING PROFIT MARGIN

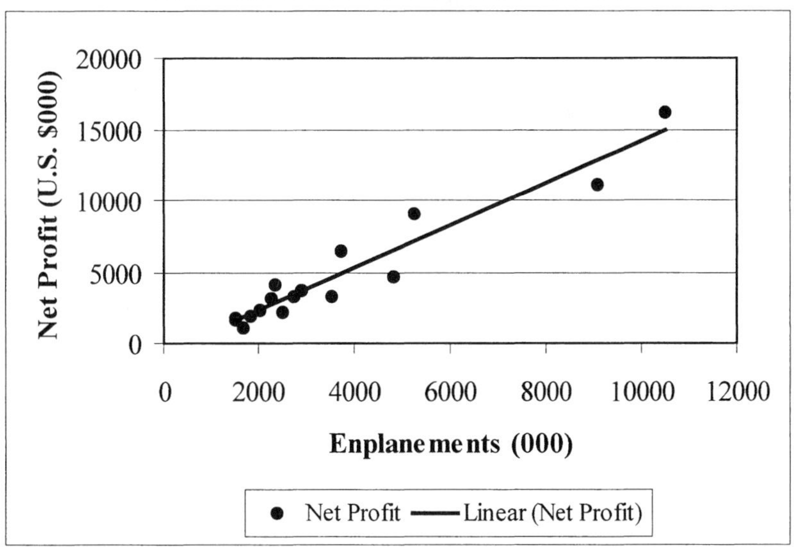

At airports where there is non-aviation related industrial activity, the revenue base is significantly expanded. Where the service/training type of airport does not break even until approximately 600,000 annual operations, as shown in Figure 15.2 above, the commercial/ industrial airport starts making an operating profit at around 100,000 operations, after which the profit margin significantly increases.

The salient point brought out by Figures 15.1 through 15.6 is an underlying principle of "the highest and best use of the land." Land that is devoted exclusively to aviation use yields very low return. It appears that the key to airport profitability, whether the facility is an air carrier or general aviation airport, lies in either increasing aviation user costs or relying more upon non-aviation related revenue sources. The marginal funds needed to run airports, by-and-large, currently come from non-aviation related industrial and commercial rents and concessions. Nevertheless, to strive for the ideal of economic independence, the aviation-related rate structure should be maximized to the extent possible, while staying within the bounds of *fair* market equity for the airport services provided. For airports receiving federal grant assistance it is required. Federal airport grant programs stipulate that the,

> *. . . rental structure for the facilities and services being provided the airport users . . . will make the airport as self-sustaining as possible under the circumstances existing at that particular airport, taking into account such factors as the volume of traffic and economy of collection, except that no part of the Federal share of an airport development project for which a grant is made . . . shall be included in the rate base in establishing fees, rates, and charges for users of that airport. . . .*

The FAA study, completed over three decades ago, using data even older, is based upon 1971 dollars. Due to the passage of time and ensuing inflation, the validity of the study's results would suggest that they might be somewhat dated. Unfortunately, there has been no other comparable study completed since then, from which to draw more current, if not more valid conclusions. However, there is at least one study that was completed in 1984 by the Congressional Budget Office, which although not exactly like the 1974 FAA study, its results seemingly re-validate the analytical relationships of the 1974 data shown herein. There is also an *Airline Business* survey of thirty-six airport "companies" and their reported profits for 1996, which, when combined with other available data, can be analyzed for comparison and validation.[31]

Although the monetary variable of the 1974 FAA study is in 1971 dollars, and would have to be inflated to current dollars to provide more reliable results, the break-even points for given airport categories seem to retain the same relationships in terms of passenger enplanements and aircraft operations. A current rule of thumb for private sector airport investors is that they should not consider buying an airport enplaning fewer than *one million passengers*, and it is only when the *five million* mark is reached that the investment is considered attractive.[32] The analyses presented below seem to support the reported rule of thumb.

CONGRESSIONAL BUDGET OFFICE STUDY

Another study, which appears to validate analyses of the 1974 study presented above, is a *Congressional Budget Office* [CBO] study. In 1984, the CBO released the results of its very comprehensive analyses of air carrier airport economics. However, the CBO study, although comprehensive for its intended purpose, was very dissimilar to the one conducted by the FAA in 1974. Where the FAA compared the finances of all public airport categories, the CBO study focused upon the (sixty) larger and busier air carrier airports only. Nevertheless, the CBO study did allude to the approximate breakeven point for certain airports. The intent of the study was to determine if Congress should continue or adjust the Federal government's role in financing civilian airports. In short, the study was to determine whether or not the largest, self-sufficient airports might be "de-federalized" (i.e., removed from the federal airport subsidy program).

Federal financial assistance has played a critical role in building America's system of airports. Nearly 40% of that assistance has gone

---

[31] *See* Richard Whitaker, *Runway Successes*, Airline Business (Dec. 1997), at 47-49.

[32] *See* Tom Gill, *Stampede to Market*, Airline Business (Apr. 1998), at 50.

to the nation's seventy-one large and medium-sized commercial airports. These same seventy-one facilities serve almost 90% of all commercial passengers. In recent years, many of these major airports have demonstrated an ability to finance their capital spending needs through a combination of retained earnings and conventional financing in the municipal bond market. This apparent capacity of many airports to obtain adequate financing in the private sector not only raises the issue of the federal role in airport finance, but it also indicates positive cash flow and economic self- sufficiency. In essence, it makes the same analytical assumptions about medium and large air carrier airports that were deduced from the 1974 FAA report.

As a result of their strong financial status, most large and medium-sized airports have relatively easy access to non-federal capital through the municipal bond markets. Pointed out by the CBO, "Though the bulk of these funds was raised by large and medium-sized airports, even some smaller airports achieved a measure of success in the bond market."

For purposes of studying, describing and analyzing their financial management policies, the CBO categorized airports into groups according to passenger enplanements (or "boardings"). In their groupings:

- *Large Airports* handled 1% or more of all yearly passenger boardings in the United States. Twenty-four airports fell into this category, with boardings of at least 3,091,521 travelers in 1982;
- *Medium-Sized Airports* handled between 0.25% and 1% of all passenger boardings. Forty-seven airports fell into this category, with at least 772,880 and no more than 3,091,521 boardings in 1982;
- *Small Airports* had scheduled service but handled no more than 0.25% of all passenger boardings and no fewer than 2,500 boardings. This category included 489 airports; and
- *General Aviation Airports* were those that served aircraft owned by private individuals or firms, and that were used predominantly for business and recreational flying. *Reliever Airports* were, and are general aviation airports, which offer potential to "relieve" traffic congestion at nearby commercial airports.

The CBO defined large and medium-sized airports "as those handling more than 772,880 boardings, and it determined the large and medium-sized airports were financially self-sufficient, and "some smaller airports" were marginally self-sufficient. It follows then that the breakeven point would be anticipated at somewhere in the neighborhood of that 772,880 enplanements figure for medium sized airports; or, very close to the one million passenger mark as identified for large hub airports in the analysis of the 1974 FAA data above.

By interpolation of data represented in Figure 15.4, "Large and Medium Hub Airports Net Profit Margin," the breakeven point coincides with the assumption that true self-sufficiency will occur at just under one million enplanements. Thus, the more current (1984) data and conclusions compiled by the Congressional Business Office seem to give credence to the results of regression analyses of the earlier, but much more comprehensive data, collected by the FAA in its 1974 report.

AIRLINE BUSINESS SURVEY

Analyses of even more recent information gathered in 1996 further validates both the 1984 CBO study and analyses of medium and large hub airports in the 1974 FAA survey. In 1996, *Airline Business* magazine surveyed thirty-six airport management companies and airport authorities, supplemented with data obtained from Airports Council International [ACI], to ascertain the profitability of air carrier airports.[33] What the staff at *Airline Business* found was that the thirty-six reporting airports made a collective net profit of over $2.4 billion (U.S.). "Net profit" meant "after tax and extraordinary items." Not surprisingly, British Airports Authority [BAA] was the largest and most profitable. Nevertheless, public airport authorities for airport systems in Los Angeles and New York demonstrated the potential for equally impressive profit generation. Although in the case of public airports receiving federal grant assistance, the marginal income above the break-even point is officially not called "profit."

By comparing the results of profitability (or revenues above required levels, if you will) compiled by *Airline Business* with passen-

[33] Richard Whitaker (ed.), *Runway Successes*, Airline Business (Dec. 1997), at 47-50.

ger enplaning data obtained from ACI,[34] the data reveal the approximate breakeven point for large air carrier airports. As shown in Figure 15.7, "International Airports Net Profit Margin," the break-even point for world class airports on average is about five million enplaning passengers.

Figure 15.7—INTERNATIONAL AIRPORTS NET PROFIT MARGIN

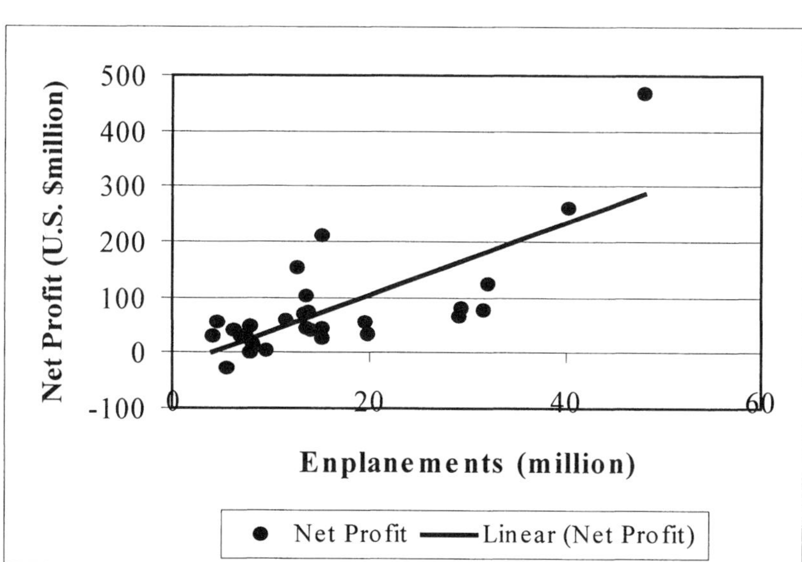

For large U.S. airports only, the break-even point is on the high side at about six to seven million enplanements, as shown in Figure 15.8, "U.S. Airports Net Profit Margin." For non-U.S. airports the break-even point is on the lower side at approximately two to three million enplanements, as shown on Figure 15.9, "Non-U.S. Airports Net Profit Margin."

[34] Airports Council International, *The Worlds Airports in 1997 (Preliminary)*, http://www.airports.org/pax97.html (May 18, 1998).

Figure 15.8—U.S. AIRPORTS NET PROFIT MARGIN

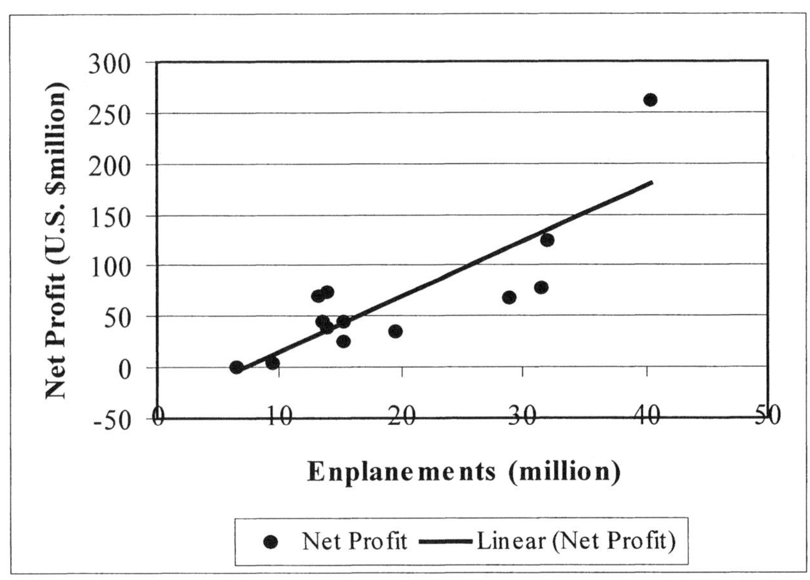

Figure 15.9—NON-U.S. AIRPORTS NET PROFIT MARGIN

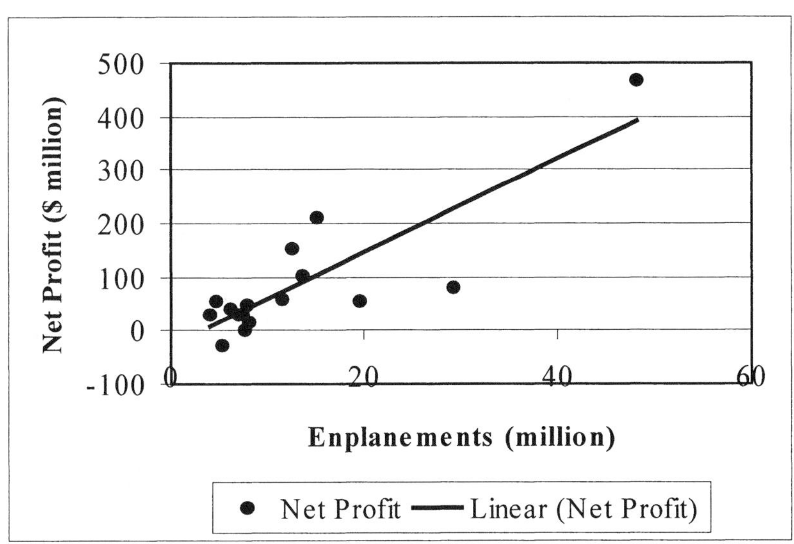

IMPLICATIONS FOR PRIVATIZATION

The Congressional Budget Office study alluded to an approximate financial breakeven point where these larger airports (those with approximately three quarters of a million enplaning passengers or more) are seemingly able to finance their own operations and capital requirements without needing outside subsidization. The intent of the CBO study was to determine if Congress should continue or adjust the federal government's role in financing civil airports, and whether or not the largest, self-sufficient airports might be "de-federalized." In part, the current Passenger Facility Charge [PFC] program, which allows airports to collect a per-passenger enplanement tax in lieu of receiving all or a portion of their entitlements to federal aviation trust fund monies, emanated from the results of the CBO study.

Although certain airports may be self-sufficient, it should nevertheless be recognized these airports did not achieve their current positive economic positions without some form of government subsidy. Federal financial assistance, along with substantial long-term investment by state and local government airport sponsors, has played a critical role in building the nation's and the world's system of airports. Of the airports in the U.S. National Plan of Integrated Airport Systems [NPIAS], fewer than 10% are privately owned. The reason is economics! Although there are profitable cost centers on airports, the costs of overall airport operation are greater than the revenues produced. Because of the economics, ownership and operation of public airports has been historically relegated primarily to state and local governments, but subsidized by the Federal government.

Of the federal assistance provided to public-use airports, nearly 40% has gone to the Nation's approximately seventy large and medium-hub commercial airports which serve about 90% of all commercial passengers. Many of these same commercial airports have empirically demonstrated an ability to finance their capital spending needs through a combination of retained earnings and conventional financing in the municipal bond market. This apparent capacity of certain airports to obtain adequate financing in the private sector not only raises the issue of the federal role in airport finance, but also demonstrates positive cash flow, economic self sufficiency, and most importantly, indicates a propensity for select airports to generate profits.

In an effort to determine the fiscal viability of certain public airports, the Congressional Budget Office studied the economics of the largest U.S. air carrier airports.[35] The intent of the 1984 study was to determine whether Congress should continue or adjust the Federal government's role in financing civilian airports. In short, the study was aimed at determining whether the largest airports might be totally self-sufficient, with no need for outside financial assistance. Most importantly, the CBO wanted to know if the major air carrier airports might be "de-federalized." In other words, could they be removed from the federal airport subsidy program? In the final analysis the CBO determined there were seventy-one airports, serving some 90% of all commercial passengers, which were capable of being self-sufficient. The CBO determined these airports were generally able to operate without federal assistance, and were capable of funding capital improvements through alternative financing mechanisms.

When it was looking at which airports might be de-federalized, the Congressional Budget Office determined that both large and medium hub airports had "demonstrated an ability to finance their capital spending needs through a combination of retained earnings and conventional financing in the municipal bond market."[36] Although there is a diminishing ability below the large hub category, the CBO determined that not only were the large hub airports fully capable of financing their capital needs, but that medium airports might also be able to meet their capital requirements through some form of municipal bonding.

As discussed in Chapter 12, there are generally two types of municipal bonds, and most airport financing is accomplished through the use of either *general obligation bonds* or *revenue bonds*, or some derivation of the two. Larger airports tend to rely upon revenue bonds, which are backed by revenues earned by the airport.[37] Revenue bonds have limited liability and are not backed by the taxing power of the local government. In order to qualify for revenue bonding, the airport must demonstrate, with margin to spare, the public enterprise's ability to generate sufficient funds to pay back the loan. Not all medium-hub airports are able to meet the loan market's income-to-debt ratio requirements. Instead they must rely on general obligation bonds

---

[35] CBO, *Financing U.S. Airports in the 1980s* (1984).

[36] *Id.*

[37] Paul Dempsey, Andrew Goetz & Joseph Szyliowicz, *Denver International Airport: Lessons Learned* 183-225 (1997).

that are secured by the airport sponsor's taxing power. This means that, if necessary, general taxes could be raised to meet the bond obligation. A totally privatized airport would not have access to general obligation bond funds. But even for government-owned facilities the problem with general obligation bonding is that there are legal limitations placed upon total general obligation indebtedness that the local government may incur. The airport may not have high enough priority within the government's varied public service and welfare concerns to qualify for general obligation bonds. As a result, some medium and smaller sized airports may not be able to finance all of their capital needs absent some form of subsidy from the outside.

In the final analysis, the CBO suggested the seventy-one identified airports were potentially capable of being de-federalized. But that does not necessarily mean privatized. Local governments would still remain involved. Since fiscal viability of some of the medium hubs is in question, in reality there are probably fewer than seventy-one (of the more than 3,000) airports in the National Plan of Integrated Airports that are capable of economic independence under government sponsorship, let alone privatized. When the CBO did its study there were twenty-four large hub airports and forty-seven medium hubs. Hence, the number of airports fully capable of being economically independent at that time was probably closer to twenty-four than to seventy-one.

In part, the current Passenger Facility Charge program (discussed in Chapter 12, which allows airports to collect a per-passenger enplanement tax in lieu of receiving all or a portion of their entitlements to Aviation Trust Fund moneys, emanated from the results of the CBO study.[38] The Aviation Safety and Capacity Expansion Act of 1990 authorizes the collection of a PFC which allows an airport to impose a fee per enplaning passenger (at that specific airport) to help finance "airport-related projects." The PFC program is an attempt to eliminate outside (particularly federal) subsidy and to impose stricter cost allocation upon the users of the system. The Act requires air carriers to collect the locally imposed fee as part of their ticketing of passengers. The airlines then transfer the funds to the airport sponsor.

Airlines generally opposed the imposition of Passenger Facility Charges for fear that excessive taxes might drive consumer demand down. Consumer advocacy groups likewise opposed the PFC because

---

[38] *Id.* at 281-283.

in the final analysis this cost allocative principle would shift the burden of indirect (airport-related) travel costs to the consumer, thereby driving the direct cost of travel up. Nevertheless, the PFC became a reality in 1990 and the system moved a step closer to becoming defederalized.[39]

The supposed de-federalization of certain airports has suggested to some deregulation advocates that these same airports be "deregulated" as well. Airline deregulation led to radical changes not only for the airlines, but also for the airports they serve. Critics of the governmental process would argue that airports ought to be privatized to make them more economically efficient.

Privatization, like deregulation, has its roots in the free market economics of Adam Smith.[40] One of the anticipated benefits of privatization is that it might increase revenues and/or decrease costs.[41] Another underlying theme of privatization is grounded in a belief that management by private enterprise, motivated by profit, is somehow always more efficient than government management. And, there are some studies that support the position that the private sector is more economically efficient than the public sector.[42]Robert Poole of the Reason Foundation, for example, states there "is a very clear belief that private managers freed of government shackles generally do a better job of managing the business and providing higher service levels."[43]

What is meant by airport privatization in the contemporary ("deregulatory") sense entails the government relinquishing control over

---

[39] In 1998 an attempt was quashed at raising the upper limit of the PFC charge to $4.

[40] The reference here is to the treatise on free market economics by Adam Smith, *An Inquiry Into the Nature and Causes of the Wealth of Nations* (1776/1937). *See* Robert C. Moe, *Exploring the Limits of Privatization*, Public Administration (Nov./Dec. 1987).

[41] The Airport Research and Development Foundation [ARDF] of the AAAE, *An Airport Executive's Guide To Privatization* (1992).

[42] These include David F. Linowes, Professor of Political Economy & Public Policy, University of Illinois, testimony before the House Committee on the Budget (Mar. 1, 1995); Fuat Andic, *Privatization Theory and Policy*, United Nations Industrial Development Organization (Apr. 1, 1193; John Hilke, *Cost Savings from Privatization: A Compilation of Study Findings*, Reason Foundation (Mar. 1993); José A. Gómez-Ibáñez & John R. Meyer, *Going Private: The International Experience with Transport Privatization*, Brookings Institution (Nov. 16, 1993). *See* GAO, Airport *Privatization: Issues Related to the Sale or Lease of U.S. Commercial Airports* (Nov. 7, 1996).

[43] Robert W. Poole Jr., *Airport Privatization: What the Record Shows*, Reason Foundation, Policy Study No. 124 (Aug. 1990); *see also* Laurence E. Gesell & Sehyun Oh, *Entrepreneurship: and Airports in the Public Sector*, a paper presented at the 35th Airport Management Short Course of the Southwest Chapter of AAAE (Jan. 18, 1995).

management of the airport to the private sector, either through a management contract, lease, or by outright sale.[44] In transferring an airport, either by management or by lease or sale to the private sector, at issue is the public interest in the airport and its services, and profit taking from a service center traditionally viewed as a non-profit governmental function. Underlying the advocacy of privatization is a notion suggesting greater efficiency naturally results when there is a profit motive. According to Spencer Dickerson of the American Association of Airport Executives [AAAE],

> *As the airport would be driven by profit, allocation of resources would be more efficient, and business judgment, instead of political considerations, would be used to conduct operations.*[45]

Likewise, Robert Poole argues public enterprises (could) produce steady streams of revenues, and private owners (would) have strong incentives to run them efficiently.[46] Poole, in fact, questions why airports need operate at all "essentially as break-even public services," when instead they could be "robust, cash-generating businesses."[47] Both Poole and Dickerson appear to overlook the natural monopoly characteristics of airports. Land and environmental constraints severely inhibit the ability of new airports to be built to discipline the ability of the unregulated monopolist to extract monopoly rents from tenant airlines and their passengers. Hence, government oversight, perhaps to the point of business constraint would still be required in the public interest. Moreover, is it really the profit incentive that is necessary to improve airport efficiency or might some form of increased accountability on the part of public managers be sufficient to meet public service goals?

But if profit were indeed a concurrent requirement of privatization, where would the money come from to pay for the privatization of public airports? "Obviously from the airlines and their customers," declares Robert Aaronson, past president of the Air Transport Asso-

---

[44] Laurence E. Gesell, *Airport Privatization* (Part I): The Rush to Deregulate, a paper presented at the 34th Airport Management Short Course of the Southwest Chapter of AAAE (Jan. 6, 1994).
[45] Spencer Dickerson, *To Privatize Or Not To Privatize*, Airport Magazine (May/Jun. 1990).
[46] Robert W. Poole, *Invest in Infrastructure—Privatize*, Wall St. J. (May 5, 1992).
[47] Robert W. Poole, *Viewpoints*, Los Angeles Times (Mar. 25, 1992).

ciation [ATA].[48] If profit must exist in order to have efficiency, and if Poole is right in his view that airports ought to be run strictly as profit ventures, then the question might be, "Profit at who's expense and/or to who's benefit?" Privatization could be "fixing" something the traveling public really doesn't want fixed, especially if profit is to be at the public's expense.

The expectation of privatization is that the increased efficiency will overcome the siphoning of profits. However, if private enterprise turned out to be less efficient than anticipated, airport users would likely question the necessity for profit if it came out of their pockets without countervailing benefits to the consumer.[49] Proponents of privatization are quick to point out that at airports, which have been privatized, business increased after it became privatized. Thus, they submit this as proof positive that airport privatization is more efficient. However, there may be a failure in their cause and effect argument. Business may have increased not as result of privatization but of a natural growth in demand. Hence, there may be a correlation but not a basis for a finding of cause.

The General Accountability Office reports:

> *Private airport owners or lessees can generate profits and a return on their investment in two ways—by increasing efficiency and by charging users higher prices. However, whether private firms would operate airports more efficiently than public owners (and pass on some of the cost savings to users) is uncertain and would likely vary among airports. According to airport management firms, some airports are not good privatization candidates because opportunities to increase revenue or cut costs are limited.*[50]

In effect, and in certain cases, public management may be as efficient as private management

---

[48] Robert A. Bunnell, *Is Your Airport A Pot Of Gold*, Airport Magazine (May/Jun. 1992).

[49] *Id.*

[50] GAO, Airport *Privatization: Issues Related to the Sale or Lease of U.S. Commercial Airports* (Nov. 7, 1996).

INFRASTRUCTURE CAPACITY

The International Civil Aviation Organization [ICAO] special committee on Future Air Navigation Systems [FANS] was tasked with planning for global implementation of a future air navigation system to accommodate the projected growth and diversity of civil aviation well into the 21st Century.[51] As part of the National Airspace System Plan updates, the United States has also been measuring the demand/capacity of its air traffic and airspace system. The bottleneck in the system has been the congestion experienced not only in the airspace network but also, at the terminal ends, the airports.

Congestion results from the inability of the infrastructure at the terminal ends (specifically the runways, but also taxiways, gates, passenger handling facilities and access roads) to accept traffic from the en route system. As Robert Horonjeff argued many years ago, the key to relieving congestion is in acquiring more "landside" (airport) capacity.[52] Thus, the solution to the long-standing controversy over airport congestion, as pointed out by Horonjeff, would seem simple—build more runways! Implementation of that solution, however, is not so simple. There are a lot of barriers to developing new airports, not the least of which is money. It will take a lot of money, and where is that money going to come from, if not from the private sector if governments are strapped for money or carrying excessive burdens of debt? Privatization may well be a partial answer to the dilemma. As airline executive Stephen Wolf suggests, needed is a partnership of private and public sector leaders to bring about long-term economic growth and to develop a national agenda by targeting the public infrastructure and other areas of economic importance.[53]

Presented in the next chapter are at least three evolving developments, all of which provide some promise of hope in solving the government fiscal dilemma with regard to air transportation infrastructure development and in providing additional system capacity. One of these solutions is evolving naturally. The other two solutions, however, require vision and true entrepreneurial spirit, but at the same time need to be closely monitored by government to protect the public interest. In these two solutions of hopeful expectation lies a greater

---

[51] ICAO, *International Aviation in the 21st Century*, Aviation Safety J. (winter 1992).

[52] Stated in a presentation to a meeting of the Radio Technical Commission for Aeronautics (about 1974).

[53] Stephen Wolf, *A Word form United Airlines, Vis a Vis* (Jul. 1992).

reliance upon the private sector. The first development is the hope of attracting private investment. The other expectation is for an innovative advancement of the airport infrastructure.

GOVERNMENT PRIVATIZATION

The movement toward more reliance upon the private sector (i.e., "privatization") was not only a wave of the 1980s and 1990s but into the 21st century as well. All governmental service areas are currently undergoing scrutiny for potential private intervention. As Robert Poole points out, ". . . governments around the world are privatizing virtually every kind of public works infrastructure," including airports.[54]

Privatization is not new, but it has found renewed interest, and was particularly popular with the Reagan and George H.W. Bush administrations. Specifically, President Bush by executive order sponsored a privatization initiative in 1992 to remove some of the barriers to the privatization of municipally and state-owned infrastructure assets. Airport privatization, in particular, was central to that initiative.[55]

The Clinton administration, on the other hand, was looking more at public/private partnerships than at strictly privatization of governmental functions.[56] For an idea of what such a partnership might look like at the state level, look at the Rhode Island State airport privatization initiative. In an effort to revitalize a sagging airport system, Rhode Island officials turned to privatization, in partnership with a commercial aviation operator. In 1992, the Rhode Island Airport Corporation [RIAC] was formed as a quasi-private organization by the state's economic development authority to oversee the State Department of Transportation's system of one air carrier airport and five general aviation airports. The RIAC focuses on management of the

---

[54] Robert W. Poole, Jr., *Invest in Infrastructure—Privatize*, Wall St. J. (Tue., May 5, 1992).

[55] Seemingly consumed by the War on Terrorism, as of 2007, President George W. Bush had not signed any legislation to promote development of U.S. aviation infrastructure. In 2001 the Air Transportation Safety System Stabilization Act was passed to provide a perceived need the Nation's commercial airline system in the aftermath of the Sep. 11, 2001 terrorist attacks. In 2003 the administration sent to Congress Aviation Investment and Reform Act for the 21st Century (AIR-21) reauthorization in the form of the Centennial of Flight Aviation Authorization Act (Flight-100) to provide for investment in safety, research, air traffic control modernization, airport infrastructure improvements and environmental initiatives. As of May 2007 it had not been acted upon.

[56] Al Gore, *Report of the National Performance Review: Creating a Government that Works Better and Costs Less* (1993).

T.F. Green State Airport, while it contracts with Hawthorne Aviation, a sixty-year veteran of the general aviation industry, to manage and develop its five general aviation airports.[57] Other examples of private management contracts for the operation of publicly owned airports in the United States include both commercial and general aviation airports:

- Addison Airport, Texas;
- Albany County Airport, New York;
- Atlantic City International Airport, New Jersey;
- Burbank-Glendale-Pasadena Airport, California;
- Danielson Airport, Connecticut;
- Fort Worth Alliance Airport, Texas;
- Indianapolis International Airport, Indiana;
- Los Angeles County Airports (Brackett Field, Compton Airport, El Monte Airport, Fox Field, Whitman Airport), California;
- Morristown Municipal Airport, New Jersey;
- Republic Airport, New York;
- Rickenbacker International Airport, Ohio;
- Rochester International Airport, Minnesota;
- Stewart International Airport, New York;
- Teterboro Airport, New Jersey;
- Westchester County Airport, New York; and
- Windham Airport, Connecticut.

In addition, several government sponsors have tried to sell or lease their airports whole or in part, including:

- Atlantic City International, New Jersey;
- Baltimore-Washington International Airport, Maryland;
- Greater Peoria Regional Airport, Illinois;
- Indianapolis International Airport, Indiana;
- John Wayne/Orange County Airport, California;
- Kennedy International Airport, New York;
- LaGuardia Airport, New York;

[57] John F. Infanger, *An Airport Corporation*, Airport Business (May 1997), at 14.

- Logan International Airport, Massachusetts;
- Los Angeles International Airport, California; and
- Stewart International Airport, New York.

LAISSEZ-FAIRE ROOTS

Privatization, like deregulation, has its intellectual roots in the free market or *laissez-faire* economic theory of Adam Smith.[58] In the United States, wherever society has had a need for goods and services, which could be produced profitably, the provision of such services has been left to the private sector. As George Bush senior stated in 1992, "Private enterprise and competitively driven improvements are the foundation of our Nation's economy and economic growth." Public infrastructure development in the United States has traditionally involved private enterprise. The public and private sectors, and the prosperity of each, are "inextricably linked."[59] Hence, private investment in America's infrastructure is not innovative, nor is the privatization of airports a novel idea. In fact, most airports in the United States began as privately owned operations.[60] Furthermore, most landing sites in the U.S. today are still privately owned. But while the number of privately owned airfields continues to increases, those open to the public have diminished, leaving mostly publicly-owned facilities to serve the needs of the air transportation industry.

The reason principal airports in the U.S. are in public ownership is economics. Although there are profitable cost centers on airports, the expenses associated with the overall operation of most airports have been greater than the revenues produced. Because of the economics, ownership and operation of public-use airports have been historically relegated primarily to state and local governments. Nevertheless, there is currently a propensity for the largest airports to make a profit. And coupled with a general disappointment in government performance there is a renewed interest in airports by the private sector.

---

[58] Ronald C. Moe, *Exploring the Limits of Privatization*, Public Administrative Review (Nov./Dec. 1987) at 453.

[59] *Id.*

[60] James Ott, *Bush Order Opens Door for Airport Privatization*, Avn. Wk. & Space Tech. (May 11, 1992) at 24.

The public sector is also finding an interest in airport privatization, and government entities have turned to the private sector in an effort to increase revenues and/or reduce costs.[61] To overcome the apparent shortage of public funds, governments are looking to expand their tax bases, promote development of new facilities in the "traditional manner" (i.e., through private capital investment), and there is growing public support for direct user charges[62]

In general, any form of private intervention may be referred to as "privatization," which ". . . encompasses a broad range of arrangements under which activities once engaged in by government are to varying degrees turned over to private hands."[63] The counterpart to privatization in the private sector is "outsourcing." The latter (outsourcing) became part of the business lexicon during the 1980s and generally refers to the delegation of non-core operations from internal production to an external entity specializing in the management of that operation. Grover Starling suggests that "privatization," defined in technical terms, involves a continuum (as shown in Figure 15.10, "Privatization Continuum"), with the public sector (government) on the far left and the private sector (the marketplace) on the far right, with a variety of intermediary or mixed forms in between:

Figure 15.10—PRIVATIZATION CONTINUUM

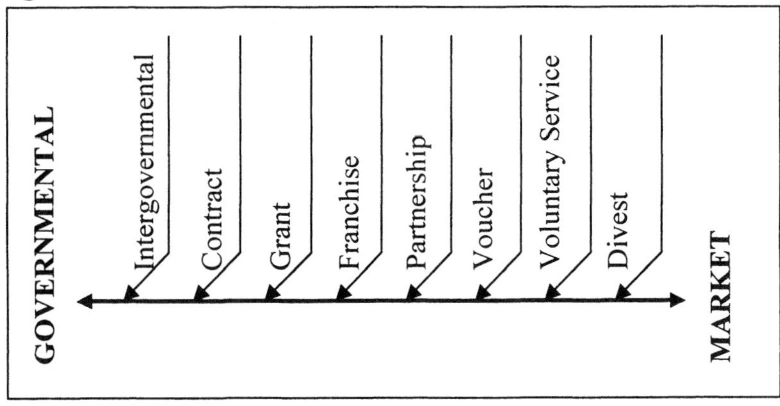

Source: Grover Starling, *Managing the Public Sector* (6th ed. 2002).

---

[61] ADRF of AAAE, *An Airport Executive's Guide to Privatization* 17 (1992).

[62] *Id.* at 12.

[63] Harold J. Sullivan, *Privatization of Public Services: A Growing Threat to Constitutional Rights*, Public Administration Rev. (Nov./Dec. 1987).

Of the several meanings of privatization, the most common forms in the airport sector consist of:

- The *contracting* out by government to private firms of operations, maintenance or management of a service previously or traditionally provided by government employees;
- The *private development* of new facilities of a type that has been traditionally provided by the government, accompanied by government oversight; and
- The *sale or lease* of existing government-owned enterprises to a private firm, usually with restrictions and obligations as to how the enterprise will run.[64]

AIRPORT DEREGULATION

What is meant by airport privatization in the more contemporary ("deregulatory") sense entails the government relinquishing control over management of the airport to the private sector, either through a management contract or by lease or outright sale. In 1992, President George H.W. Bush issued Executive Order 12803 defining privatization as, ". . . the disposition or transfer of an infrastructure asset, such as by sale or by long-term lease, from a state or local government to a private party." In transferring an airport, (by management, lease or sale) to the private sector, at issue is the public interest in the airport and its services, and profit-taking from a service center traditionally viewed as a non-profit governmental function.

And where would the money come from to pay for the privatization of public airports? The most likely source, of course, is from the end users, the customers. Hence, there is conservative resistance to the idea of privatization from both users and providers of air transportation services, and much criticism of its merits.

Still, advocates of privatization seem to tout it as a general cure-all for the problems facing society. As Robert Poole, of the Reason Foundation, contends, ". . . America's bridges, waterworks and airports won't work properly until they are in private hands."[65] But

[64] ADRF of AAAE, *An Airport Executive's Guide to Privatization* 17 (1992) at 12; *see also* Robert W. Poole, Jr., *Airport Privatization: What the Record Shows*, Reason Foundation, Policy Study No. 124 (Aug. 1990) at 3; *see also* Timothy Chandler & Peter Feuille, *Municipal Unions and Privatization*, Public Administration Rev. (Jan./Feb. 1991) at 15.
[65] Robert W. Poole, Jr., *Invest in Infrastructure—Privatize*, Wall St. J. (Tues., May 5, 1992).

Poole goes too far! Efficiently operated public enterprises do exist. And there are plenty of examples of misdirected privatization to make one skeptical of its merits under all circumstances. Look at the Pentagon, for instance, where cost overruns are infamous! "If government by private contract really were the answer to all our ills, Pentagon spending would be a model of efficiency."[66]

To the critics of airline deregulation, its outcome is another example that might lead one to question the merits of privatization. And yet, the Heritage Foundation, the Reason Foundation, and Unisys all strongly advocate the deregulation of airports as well. William Laffer of the Heritage Foundation states that the air system's problems are the result of "unfinished deregulation." The real problem (with air traffic congestion) . . ." he says, ". . . lies with the failure to deregulate the other components of America's air transportation network—the airports and the air traffic control system."[67] In a like vein, Robert Poole suggests, "Congress freed up the airlines to compete and grow, but left the essential infrastructure—the airports and Air Traffic Control [ATC] system—in their static, bureaucratic pre-deregulation condition. The result is a growing set of problems, most notably delays, congestion, and questions about safety levels."[68] Charles Sander says there is an "opportunity to reinvent the airport . . . that given the success of privatization efforts in the United Kingdom, Europe and Indianapolis, the benefits of airport privatization can no longer be ignored in the United States." However, Sander does admit that "airport privatization does not mean divestiture by the government. . . ."[69]

Airport deregulation infers that the government ought to extract itself from the management of airports, and to relinquish that responsibility to the private sector. But before all "rush to deregulate" and further "dismantle America,"[70] consider first that the success of airline deregulation is still a matter of debate. When measured by the explicit goals and promises of the Airline Deregulation Act of 1978,

---

[66] Robert Kuttner, *Privatization is Not a Cure-All*, Wall St. J. (Thurs., Apr. 30, 1992).

[67] Tom Belden, *Privatization of Airports Gaining Favor*, Phoenix Gazette (Thurs., Mar. 28, 1991).

[68] Robert W. Poole, Jr., *Privatizing Airports*, Reason Foundation, Policy Study No. 119 (Jan. 1990).

[69] Charles Sander, *Airport Privatization: Trends and Opportunities, Parts II and III*, http://www.unisys.com (visited Sep. 21, 2006).

[70] *See* S. J. Tolchin & M. Tolchin, *Dismantling America: The Rush to Deregulate* (1983).

airline deregulatory policy has certainly failed on every point.[71] At the dawn of the 21st century the airline industry is in a tailspin.

A popular theme since the 1970s has been reduction in the size of government. And, "[t]he notion of less government is becoming more popular with taxpayers who are skeptical about government's ability to do business efficiently."[72] Reduced government was the underlying idea spawning airline deregulation, and some proponents would still advocate privatization if for no other reason than to "eliminate government." However, a position advocating less government at any cost is extreme, and ignores why governments exist at all. As Ronald Moe suggests, "[s]upporters of the privatization movement view their role as advocacy of a cause and thus feel little need to consider the possible limitations to their arguments."[73] Less government at any cost also ignores the existence of a primary difference between public and private management.

As Moe and Gilmour argue, "[t]he theoretical foundation" of public administration "is in public law." It is "founded on the body of the Constitution and the Bill of Rights and articulated by a truly enormous body of statutory, regulatory, and case law to ensure continuance of a republican form of government and to protect the rights and freedoms of citizens at the hands of an all-powerful state." "The distinguishing characteristic of governmental management is that the actions of governmental officials must have their basis in public law."[74]

While the so-called "new public administration" encourages public managers to become entrepreneurial and to exert leadership, public managers have, heretofore, been excluded by law from the political arena. However instrumental or enlightened the new approach may

---

[71] *See* Paul Stephen Dempsey & Laurence E. Gesell, *Air Transportation: Foundations for the 21st Century* (1997); *see also* Melvin A. Brenner, *Airline Deregulation—A Case Study in Public Policy Failure* (1988); *see also* Paul Stephen Dempsey, *Deregulation Has Spawned Abuses in Air Transport*, Av. Wk. & Space Tech. (Nov. 21, 1988); *see also* Paul Stephen Dempsey, *The Deregulation Mess, Air and Space* (Sep. 1989); *see also* Paul Stephen Dempsey, *Flying Blind: The Failure of Airline Deregulation* (1990); *see also* Laurence E. Gesell, *Airline Re-Regulation* (1990); *see also* Laurence E. Gesell & Martin T. Farris, *Airline Deregulation: An Evaluation of Goals and Objectives*, 21 Trans. Law J. (1992).

[72] Wendy Quinones, *Contract Management Helps Airports Get Down to Business*, Airport Services Management (May 1986).

[73] Ronald C. Moe, *Exploring the Limits of Privatization*, Public Administration Rev. (Nov./Dec. 1987) at 458.

[74] Ronald C. Moe & Robert S. Gilmour, *Rediscovering Principles of Public Administration: The Neglected Foundation of Public Law*, Public Administration Rev., Vol. 55, No. 2 (1995), at 135-146.

appear, the model of the market-oriented public manager is inherently problematic for democratic governance. Because entrepreneurship in the government sector implies that public managers might be motivated by self-interest and act opportunistically stands in stark contrast to the traditional ideal of the "ethical agents who administer the public's business with the common good in mind."[75] Although the ideal may not be realized in modern governance, any perceived threat to the ideal might be cause for some alarm.

As with the *institutional imperative*, which motivates public bureaucrats to advance the self-interest of their agencies and themselves above the public's interests,[76] the inherently self-interested, risk-taking, and rule-breaking orientations of public entrepreneurs might well fuel the anxieties of many who feel that the bureaucracy is already too powerful. Such anxiety provides ammunition for those who believe that what is needed are more, not fewer, constraints to keep public entrepreneurs accountable.[77] Until more is known about how to ensure accountability, skeptics of the new public administration, like Terry, reject the new model.[78] Moe, on the other hand, advocates "the legal paradigm" of entrepreneurial government, wherein ". . . a conceptually sound enabling statute, supplemented by comprehensive, yet flexible, general management laws is a necessary basis for effective agency management."[79]

At a minimum, any government contemplating privatization will have to take certain precautions not only to protect the public interest, but to facilitate the privatization initiative.[80] Based on privatization experiences in certain state and local governments,[81] the U.S. General Accountability Office has identified six lessons for federal officials

---

[75] Linda Kaboolian, *The New Public Management: Challenging the Boundaries of the Management vs. Administration Debate*, Public Administration Rev., Vol. 58, No. 3, (May/Jun. 1998), at 190.

[76] *See* Ch. 7.

[77] *See* Larry D. Terry, *Administrative Leadership, Neo-Managerialism, and the Public Management Movement*, Public Administration Rev., Vol. 58, No. 3 (May/Jun. 1998), at 198.

[78] *See generally* Larry D. Terry, *Administrative Leadership, Neo-Managerialism, and the Public Management Movement*, Public Administration Rev., Vol. 58, No. 3 (May/Jun. 1998).

[79] Ronald C. Moe, *Lets Rediscover Government, Not Reinvent It*, Government Executive, Vol. 25 (Jun. 1993), at 47.

[80] The British government was aware of the dangers when it passed the 1986 Airports Act, imposing some tight controls on new airport companies operating privatized airports in the British Isles; *see* Rigas Doganis, *The Airport Business* 30 (1992).

[81] In Georgia, Indiana, Massachusetts, Michigan, New York, and Virginia.

(and ostensibly for any government level) contemplating privatization projects:

- Privatization can be best implemented when there is a *committed political leader* to champion it;
- Governments need to establish organizational and analytical *structure for privatization projects*;
- Governments need to have *enabling legislation* to encourage privatization activities;
- *Reliable and accurate cost data* on government activities are needed to assess the overall performance of activities targeted for privatization;
- Governments need to develop *strategies to help their employees make the transition* to a private-sector environment; and
- Governments need to *monitor and evaluate performance* of private sector providers to ensure that the government's expectations are protected.[82]

PUBLIC VERSUS PRIVATE MANAGEMENT

Another underlying theme of the "privatization movement" is grounded in the belief that management by private enterprise is somehow always more efficient than government management. Poole, for example states, there ". . . is a very clear belief that private managers freed of government shackles generally do a better job of managing the business and providing higher service levels." Poole's generalization, however, is conjecture. Corporate bureaucracies can be every bit as inefficient as government bureaucracies. And it is interesting how analysts, both for and against privatization, can use the same example to support one over the other. Take, for example, the "Chicago Flood" of April 1992, resulting when an underground tunnel collapsed.

Poole argues it ". . . was not the failure of a concrete structure that was at fault . . . it was the failure of a political structure. . . ."[83] As Chicago Mayor Richard Daley said when told that city workers had known about the tunnel problem for several days before it collapsed,

---

[82] GAO, *Privatization: Lessons Learned by State and Local Governments*, GAO/GGD-97 (Mar. 1997).

[83] Robert W. Poole, Jr., *Invest in Infrastructure—Privatize*, Wall St. J. (Tues., May 5, 1992).

"Let's privatize the (expletive deleted) place."[84] Poole suggests it was ". . . political pressure that led to the phenomenon of 'deferred maintenance'—the politician's term for allowing public facilities to crumble."

Poole's arguments would suggest that all management within government is inefficient, and the answer to such inefficiency, in all cases, is privatization. However, using that same "Chicago" incident, Kuttner points out that, "part of the blame lies with Mayor Richard M. Daley's downsizing of government."[85] Six months before the tunnel collapsed, "Mayor Daley eliminated the Department of Public Works as a cost-saving measure. Some of its functions were transferred to other agencies; other functions were contracted out (i.e.; privatized). At the same time of the flood it was no longer clear which agency, public or private, was responsible for tunnel maintenance."

Similar case studies can be used to argue the pros and cons of airport privatization. As stated above, privatization of airports is not a novel idea, nor is the notion of private investment in the airport infrastructure a recent inspiration. As Bunnell points out, "The presence of private money at the world's airports is not new. For a very long time, funding has come from airport tenants—primarily the airlines—to finance capital improvements in line with airport/tenant leases."[86] At airports where tenants have invested in capital improvements on airports without government assistance, it has been necessary for those same tenants to obtain long-term rights to property in order for them to secure favorable bank financing. By relying heavily upon private investment many communities were able to develop their airports where they would not have had sufficient capital otherwise. Traditional airport leases have for decades granted long-term (typically from twenty to forty years) agreements to airlines, fixed base operators, and other airport tenants, in order to promote private investment in the airport infrastructure.

It should be noted, however, that in most cases the granting of long-term, exclusive rights to public (airport) property has resulted in a subsequent loss in management flexibility. "Residual cost" or what some people refer to as "Chicago" or "O'Hare" contracts became the traditional form of lease agreement. In residual cost contracts, the

---

[84] *Id.*

[85] Robert Kuttner, *Privatization is Not a Cure-All*, Wall St. J. (Thurs., Apr. 30, 1992).

[86] Robert A. Bunnell, *Is Your Airport a Pot of Gold?*, Airport Magazine (May/Jun. 1992).

tenants (usually the airlines) pay the difference up to a specified amount between revenues from all other sources and the airport's total expenses. In many cases the result has been for the airport to at best break even. More often, a deficit resulted, which local taxpayers had to make up. Development of the airport at private expense usually produced economic generation for the community, and therefore provided a public benefit, but the tradeoff was a loss of management control, which later acted against the public interest.

Traditional leases became particularly problematic with the advent of airline deregulation. Many newcomers to the airline industry were either restricted, or unable to obtain access to airports they wished to serve. In most cases gates were limited and the few existing gates were controlled by incumbent airlines. The granting of air traffic slots to certain airlines by the Federal government had a similar effect in excluding service, especially to smaller carriers. The air traffic and airspace system, including airports, is an integrated system, and experience has shown facilities controlled exclusively by private companies tend to be proprietary, and inflexible to system requirements for change.

Another problem that came with deregulation was airline failures resulting in bankruptcy and the tying up of limited airport facility resources pending the outcome of the bankruptcy proceedings. Bankruptcy law has since been corrected to allow the immediate return of airport facilities to airport sponsor control, but bankruptcy still remains as an issue of consideration if not an impediment to airport privatization. A privatized airport could go bankrupt, and it is unclear to what extent the airport's activities might be disrupted as a result. The local community, for example, might have to buy back the airport to ensure its continued operation as an airport. As the Government Accountability Office explains,

> *Certain Bankruptcy Code provisions may, in effect, hinder or prevent a local or state government from canceling a lease or management contract to protect other creditors, even if the lease or contract contains a default clause. Furthermore, the local or state government's ability to substitute a new operator may be restricted even if the bankrupt opera-*

> *tor's performance deteriorates. Moreover, certain Bankruptcy Code provisions authorize the trustee, subject to court approval, to reject certain agreements, which could include a lease or management contract.*[87]

Historically, the net outcome of the private/public partnership investments in airport development has been a mixture of advantages and disadvantages. Airport infrastructures were developed where, were it not for private investment, they may not have been developed. But barriers to competition were set up as well, with, in some cases, an associated net loss in economic efficiency and needed flexibility.

From a public interest perspective, airports developed and managed primarily by government sponsors have seemingly been more efficient, and more flexible. Irrespective, private investment has always had a role in the development of U.S. infrastructures. Hence, there are few examples of airports in the United States developed exclusively with public funds. Perhaps the foremost example of such an airport developed largely through public funding is the Phoenix Sky Harbor Airport in Arizona. As a result, Phoenix officials are apparently better positioned to manage and control their airport facilities than are most other airport sponsors of similarly sized airports.

In the decade between 1980 and 1990, Phoenix Sky Harbor was able to rapidly expand to meet a tripling demand in enplanements, while at the same time controlling its costs. However, the airport became face-to-face with the catastrophic possibility that its then primary carrier, America West, might have gone out of business when it filed for Chapter 11 (bankruptcy) protection in the early 1990s. Had America West failed to recover from Chapter 11, Phoenix Sky Harbor nonetheless still would have been able to effectively shift utilization of its terminal assets, and thereby control costs until the air transport market in Phoenix once again stabilized.[88]

It would appear that Phoenix has been a model of government efficiency, standing in the face of those who would argue that private is hands-down better than public management. Even so, Robert Poole tried to promote the sale of Phoenix Sky Harbor in 1990, arguing that

[87] GAO, Airport *Privatization: Issues Related to the Sale or Lease of U.S. Commercial Airports* (Nov. 7, 1996).

[88] Phoenix was able to negotiate 30-day agreements instead of leases for terminal space, thereby providing even greater control over airport assets in the event of bankruptcy.

it would give a one-time windfall of about $544 million, put the property back on the tax roles, and provide funding for major capital investments at the airport. In response, Neilson "Dutch" Berthoff, then Phoenix Aviation Director, confidently rejected the notion of private enterprise being able to run Sky Harbor better than the City. He pointed out that it was unlikely for Phoenix to yield control of a facility that is crucial to economic development and pumps billions of dollars annually into the local economy.[89]

In response to zealous advocacy for airport privatization, Robert Kuttner suggests that, "privatization is not a cure-all."[90] "There is no permanent formula for what should be public and what should be private." Privatization may not be a panacea, but neither should it be hastily dismissed. As Poole might counterpoint, it may still be ". . . attractive as a way of generating increased investment in airport capacity and addressing the problem of concentrated hubs."[91] And, as the American Association of Airport Executives points out in its sponsored project report on airport privatization,

> *Application of privatization to publicly owned, air carrier airports is neither a panacea nor an empty concept for addressing current-day airport problems. It is a tool to be considered and used when it fits a problem that requires fixing.*[92]

Privatization may be an opportunity for fixing a management problem, but it is not a panacea. It is but one alternative to management and "requires fixing" is the operative term. Yet, what may be "required" is a subjective determination. The concept of privatization is subjective as well. But at a minimum, privatization implies that there is an underlying profit motive. That is to say, "privatization" is nearly synonymous with "profitization." It is the prospect of profit that attracts investors. But as Kuttner submits, ". . . the incursion of a

---

[89] Ken Western, *Phoenix Urged to Sell Sky Harbor Airport*, The Arizona Republic (Feb. 8, 1990) at E-1.

[90] Robert Kuttner, *Privatization is Not a Cure-All*, Wall St. J. (Thurs., Apr. 30, 1992).

[91] Robert W. Poole, Jr., *Privatizing Airports*, Reason Foundation, Policy Study No. 119 (Jan. 1990) at 3.

[92] ADRF of AAAE, *An Airport Executive's Guide to Privatization* 17 (1992).

profit-motivated vendor into public spaces sometimes overwhelms the public purpose of the endeavor."

THE PROFIT MOTIVE

A prevailing consensus suggests that greater efficiency naturally results when there is a profit motive. According to Dickerson, "[a]s the airport would be driven by profit, allocation of resources would be more efficient, and business judgment, instead of political considerations, would be used to conduct operations."[93] Likewise, Robert Poole argues that public enterprises (could) produce steady streams of revenues, and "private owners (would) have strong incentives to run them efficiently";[94] effectively, as ". . . robust, cash-generating businesses."[95]

If profit must exist in order to have efficiency, and if Poole is right in his view that airports ought to be run strictly as profit ventures, then again the question might be, "profit at who's expense and/or to who's benefit?" Privatization could be "fixing" something the public doesn't want fixed, especially if the profit is at public expense. Airport users would certainly question the necessity for profit if it came out of their pockets.[96] Moreover, what is meant by "airport profitability" and how important is it really?

Whether an airport "profits" or not is relative to its micro and macro-economic perspectives; "micro-economic" here meaning the airport-as-a-market, and "macro-economic" defined herein as the community or region served by a given airport. Most airports at the micro-economic level do not make a profit, nor are they intended to. As a rule, governments, including airport sponsors, are not supposed to show a profit. Airports, specifically, are not supposed to make a profit, per the assurances made by airport sponsors to the Federal government in exchange for airport development grants. The Federal government requires that all proceeds be reinvested in the airport. In most cases, airports cannot profit anyway, at least not "reasonably." With the possible exception of a few medium and large hub airports, most airports are publicly subsidized.

---

[93] Spencer Dickerson, *To Privatize or Not To Privatize*, Airport Magazine (May/Jun. 1990).
[94] Robert W. Poole, Jr., *Invest in Infrastructure—Privatize*, Wall St. J. (Tues., May 5, 1992).
[95] Robert W. Poole, Jr., *Viewpoints*, The Los Angeles Times (Mar. 25, 1990) at D3.
[96] Robert A. Bunnell, *Is Your Airport a Pot of Gold?*, Airport Magazine (May/Jun. 1992) at 17.

What must be kept in perspective is that airports are not an end unto themselves. Airports are there to serve their communities, not the other way around. An airport's value may not lie in whether it makes a profit as an enterprise, but rather, if it economically benefits the community as a whole. In other words, does the community "profit?"

Since the late 1960s, there have been numerous studies looking at the economics of airports and their importance to the communities they serve. The general consensus of studies by the FAA, the General Aviation Manufacturers Association [GAMA], the Aircraft Owners and Pilots Association [AOPA], and other organizations, concludes there are distinct economic advantages for communities having airports in terms of attracting and retaining industries, and creating new jobs. Airports are significant economic multipliers, irrespective of their profitability. In most cases the added cost of operating an airport is far offset by the economic benefits derived by the community.

As previously discussed, in 1984 the Congressional Budget Office released its results of a comprehensive analysis of the economics of the largest and busiest air carrier airports in the United States. The study alluded to an approximate financial breakeven point where these larger airports (those with approximately three quarters of a million enplaning passengers or more per year) are seemingly capable of financing their own operations and capital requirements without the need for subsidy from the outside.[97] Of the more than 3,000 airports in the NPIAS, only about sixty or seventy airports might meet the criteria and be capable of profiting as a business. More realistically, perhaps only about two dozen airports as stated before.

Again, the intent of the 1984 CBO study was to determine if Congress should continue or adjust the Federal government's role in financing civil airports; in short, whether or not the largest, self-sufficient airports might be "defederalized." Because certain airports are demonstrating the potential for profitability, not only has the question of de-federalization come up, but the notion of privatizing those airports has gained popularity as well.

[97] Most private sector investors would not consider buying an airport with fewer than one million enplaning passengers, and it is only when the five million mark is reached that the investment is considered to be attractive. Tom Gill, *Stampede to Market*, Airline Business (Apr. 1998).

Although certain airports may be self sufficient, it should nevertheless be recognized that these airports did not achieve their current positive economic positions without some form of government subsidy. Federal financial assistance, along with substantial long-term investment by state and local government airport sponsors, has played a critical role in building the nation's system of airports. Private investment has also played a role, but because of the net cost of airport operation, ownership and operation of public airports has been historically relegated primarily to state and local governments, but subsidized heavily by the federal government.

Of the federal assistance provided to public-use airports, nearly 40% has gone to the nation's seventy or so large and medium-hub commercial airports, which serve almost 90% of all commercial passengers. Ironically, these are the same commercial airports identified in the CBO study as having demonstrated an ability to finance their capital spending needs through a combination of retained earnings and conventional financing in the municipal bond market. Irrespective of the heavy federal subsidization, this apparent capacity of certain airports to obtain adequate financing in the private sector not only raises the issue of the federal role in airport finance, but also demonstrates positive cash flow, economic self-sufficiency, and most importantly, indicates a propensity for select airports to make a profit. Hence, coupled with the current fiscal crises in government, the potential profitability in airport operation is attracting private enterprise.

The profitability of the largest airports, however, is seemingly not a problem that "requires fixing." The problem, if there is one, lies in the non-profitability of the other 3,000 plus airports in the NPIAS. And, whether private enterprise can fix the "problem" by making many of these airports profitable is highly doubtful, when historically it was the private sector that relegated the problem to the public sector in the first place—because the private sector was unable to make airports profitable.

PUBLIC GOODS

The prospect of privatizing currently operating facilities raises serious questions. Are the proponents of privatization groping for an answer to a socio-economic dilemma, or is it the avarice of capitalism? There is concern, for example, that privatization might transfer the proceeds of what are now profitable cost centers to private interests, to make them even more profitable, but with no apparent public benefit. As Kuttner suggests, ". . . a dogmatic approach may actually cost taxpayers more money."[98]

In the absence of profitability, the provision of airport services was left to the government and thereby became defined as "public goods." In one definition, public goods have two critical properties: one is it is not *feasible* to ration their use (i.e., to exclude any individual); and second, it is not *desirable* to ration their use.[99] These two factors have an impact upon economic efficiency in the public sector.

Productive efficiency, in fact, may not be one of government's strong suits, if for no other reason, because *public interest* is at the heart of government service provision. "Public agencies characteristically are structured to guarantee due process and administrative fairness, to ensure all considerations get proper weight and that no citizen's rights are violated"[100] If access to a public-use airport is a "public good," then "[w]ho is best able to safeguard that public good—the public sector or free enterprise"?[101] Certainly, the public sector is best suited to the protection of civil rights, but it still does not discount the possibility of private management on behalf of the government sponsor of say an airport.

GLOBAL PRIVATIZATION

Management (of particularly smaller public airports) by a private firm (usually a fixed base operator) ". . . is nothing new."[102] Additionally, many activities, or concessions, have been, and are operated by companies as private ventures on airports, or as privately managed activities on behalf of the airport sponsor. Parking lots are commonly operated and managed by contractors, with a share in the proceeds going to the airport. In Canada a private consortium built, owns and is

---

[98] Robert Kuttner, *Privatization is Not a Cure-All*, Wall St. J. (Thurs., April 30, 1992).

[99] Joseph E. Stiglitz, *Economics of the Public Sector* (1986).

[100] Spencer Dickerson, *To Privatize or Not To Privatize*, Airport Magazine (May/Jun. 1990) at 132.

[101] *Id.*

[102] Wendy Quinones, *Contract Management Helps Airports Get Down to Business*, Airport Services Management (May 1986) at 40-45.

operating Terminal 3 at Pearson International Airport in Toronto.[103] At Atlanta's Hartsfield International Airport, some cargo facilities are privately owned.[104] Also, numerous airport facilities, including terminals at Kennedy, O'Hare, and Cincinnati,[105] were privately paid for and developed, as were hangar facilities at hundreds of airports across the United States.

In some cases even large airports have been sold, leased, or managed under contract. However, most of the privatized activity by outright sale has taken place outside the United States. Since the early 1980s (and the advent of airline deregulation in the United States), airports in most places other than the U.S. have been in the process of being transformed from central or local branches of government into dynamic and commercially oriented enterprises capable of generating substantial profits. The change has come about as close ties between governments and airports have been *liberalized*.[106] Simultaneously, airport managers have been given greater freedom to operate commercially in order to produce profits or to otherwise reduce deficits.[107]

For many years a number of airports operated as private companies, although such airports, while being private in a legal sense, did not have the commercial freedom which a truly privately owned company would have. Moreover, in many cases, the company shareholders have been one or more central or local government departments or other government organizations. For example, most of the larger German airports were government-owned companies.[108] Milan has had private minority shareholders, but its majority shareholders have been central and state holding companies.

---

[103] ADRF of AAAE, *An Airport Executive's Guide to Privatization* 23 (1992); *see also* Paul McKnight, *The Evolution of Devolution: Privatization, Canadian Style*, Airport Magazine (May/Jun. 1990) at 108-131.

[104] TADRF of AAAE, *An Airport Executive's Guide To Privatization* (1992), at 20.

[105] GAO, *Airport Privatization: Issues Related to the Sale of U.S. Commercial Airports*, testimony Report No. T-RCED-96-82.

[106] Liberalization is a term used in some other countries as a counterpart to deregulation. In the U.S. But, it has a slightly different meaning. Deregulation connotes extraction of the government from the regulatory process. Liberalization connotes a more liberal approach by government while it is still engaged in economic intervention. Hence, privatization likewise takes on a slightly different meaning outside the U.S. The British Airports Authority, for example, is a private company, but highly regulated by the central government of Great Britain. In the final analysis, the U.S. government has not extracted itself totally from economic intervention, nor have other countries totally privatized their airlines and airports.

[107] Rigas Doganis, *The Airport Business* xii, 1 (1992).

[108] *Id.* at 26, 28.

The first actual airport privatization, where a government authority transferred airport title to the private sector, was the British government's sale of British Airports Authority.[109] In 1987, the British government authorized the sale of British Airports Authority by offering public shares of the Authority, which operates London's Heathrow, Gatwick, and Stansted airports, and four airports in Scotland.[110]

A number of other governments are pursuing airport privatization as well, including Denmark, Greece and New Zealand.[111] The Turks, Poles, Czechoslovakians, Malaysians, and Australians are working on it too.[112] The Greek government received proposals for a consortium at the new Athens International Airport. Consultants studied the potential for privatizing Changi Airport in Singapore. The Council of Ministers in Spain announced that airports would be permitted to operate with functional autonomy and private capital.[113]

Collectively, there is much worldwide interest in airport privatization in its various forms, from complete privatization by transfer of title, to partial privatized involvement. In Copenhagen, for example, the Airports Authority was formed to allow for bank financing, but the government still owns 75% of the authority. Table 15.1, "Foreign Countries with Airport Privatization," lists fifty countries that had some form of private sector participation at the beginning of 1997.

Now more than ever government sponsors are in the mood to sell their airports. With a growing shortage of airport capacity, coupled with steep government deficits, hundreds of airports around the world, from Mexico to Argentina to Russia, are going on the block.[114] What follows are some examples by world region.

---

[109] Robert W. Poole, Jr., *Privatizing Airports*, Reason Foundation, Policy Study No. 119 (1990), at 7.

[110] Robert W. Poole Jr., *Airport Privatization: What the Record Shows*, Reason Foundation, Policy Study No. 124 (Aug. 1990), at 4.

[111] *Id.*

[112] Joan Feldman, *Is Airport Privatization a Good Idea?*, Air Transport World (1989), at 26.

[113] AAAE & ARDF, *An Airport Executive's Guide To Privatization* (1992), at 24.

[114] Kyle Pope, *Airport Privatization Begins to Take Off, Led by Britain's BAA*, Wall St. J. (Sep. 24, 1996), at A1.

Table 15.1—FOREIGN COUNTRIES WITH AIRPORT PRIVATIZATION

Albania	China	Indonesia	Qatar
Algeria	Colombia	Italy	Russia
Argentina	Costa Rica	Jamaica	Singapore
Australia	Denmark	Japan	Slovakia
Austria	Dominican Republic	Macau	Switzerland
Bahamas	Ecuador	Malaysia	Thailand
Bolivia	Egypt	Mexico	Trinidad and Tobago
Brazil	Germany	Myanmar	Turkey
Bulgaria	Greece	New Zealand	United Kingdom
Cambodia	Hong Kong	Pakistan	Uruguay
Cameroon	Hungary	Panama	Venezuela
Canada	India	Peru	Vietnam
Chile		Philippines	

Source: GAO, Airport *Privatization: Issues Related to the Sale or Lease of U.S. Commercial Airports* (Nov. 7, 1996).

LATIN AMERICA

Most Latin American airports typically are described as "cramped," "old" and "substandard." They have been compared to airport terminals in the United States thirty and even forty years ago.[115] "Virtually every country in Latin America is privatizing its airports," says airport consultant Robert Aaronson. The countries considering private airport management form a list as diverse as the region, which is not limited to the bigger or more politically stable nations. Panama and Haiti, for example, are looking to attract foreign investors. Cuba might even be an airport privatization project, especially if U.S. policies with the island were to change, says airport consultant Mauricio Gutierrez.[116] The Bolivian airport system was sold to U.S.-based Airport Group International [AGI].[117] Airports in Uruguay, Peru and Chile are also being privatized. The Uruguayan gov-

[115] Beth Kanter, *Latin American Airports: An Investor's Paradise*, Airport Magazine (May/Jun. 1998), at 61.
[116] *Id.* at 60.
[117] Tom Gill, *Stampede to Market*, Airline Business (Apr. 1998).

ernment is requiring investors to Build, Operate, and Transfer [BOT] a new terminal and extend two runways at the Montevideo airport.[118] Costa Rica's Juan Santamaria Airport at San Jose is also being privatized through management, operation and expansion. Like other Latin American airports, the need for private management at the Juan Santamaria Airport stems from overcrowding, increased traffic and the absence of public money for improvement.[119]

Certainly the larger countries like Brazil and Argentina are looking to private investors to help finance airport expansion. In early 1998, Argentina formally announced that the Aeropuertos Argentina 2000 consortium (led by Milan-based Societa Esercizi Aeroportuali [SEA]) would manage thirty-three of the country's biggest airports for the next thirty years. Ezeiza International Airport and the regional Aeroparque, both in Buenos Aires, were chosen as the first two (of the thirty-three) Argentine airports to be sold to the private consortium.[120]

More so than the airports in Argentina, aviation analysts say that Brazil's airports would be highly attractive investments because they would not require as much development work as other country's airports in the region. Infraero, the Brazilian government's airports authority, has already been working with private companies, which it contracts on a project-by-project basis. However, as of this writing, Brazil had not announced any intentions to fully privatize any of its airports through sale. Nevertheless, pressure from Brazil's rapidly expanding airlines could encourage more extensive privatization.[121]

Not all privatizations in Latin America have capital investment commitments written into the contracts. The Mexican government, for example, believes regulation will ensure the necessary investments. Moreover, the government believes many of its airports need minimal investment, and if they do require investment, construction costs are low. But this is not true for Mexico City where expansion for a needed fifth runway is not possible. A new airport will need to

---

[118] *Id.* at 51; *see also* GAO, Airport *Privatization: Issues Related to the Sale or Lease of U.S. Commercial Airports* (Nov. 7, 1996). Under a BOT contract, a private entity finances, builds or modernizes, and operates a facility and obtains revenue from its operation. After a certain period, ownership of the facility transfers to the government.

[119] Beth Kanter, *Latin American Airports: An Investor's Paradise*, Airport Magazine (May/Jun. 1998), at 62.

[120] *Id.* at 61; *see also* Brian Homewood, *Latin Airport Sales Closer*, Airline Business (Dec. 1997), at 18; *see also* Tom Gill, *Stampede to Market*, Airline Business (Apr. 1998), at 50.

[121] Brian Homewood, *Latin Airport Sales Closer*, Airline Business (Dec. 1997), at 18.

be built in either Texoco or Hidalgo State, which is estimated to cost up to $5 billion (U.S.).

EUROPE

With most privatizations, government sponsors and investors have wanted to move cautiously to see if privatization would work. Following the BAA experiment in England, many airports in Europe began selling shares on the common market, while governments retained regulatory control and full ownership. The Vienna International Airport was a good example of early privatization, where the government retained control while soliciting private investors. By 1993, 27% of the airport's shares were in the hands of private investors, with the rest being divided among the republic, province and city. At the same time, the Copenhagen Airport in Kastrup, Denmark, was in the process of being privatized. In 1990, the airport organization changed status from being a government agency to a state-owned public limited company. This change allowed the minister of transport to sell up to 49% of the shares in the company.[122]

As in other parts of the world, in Europe privatization is also gathering pace. The Portuguese government intends to sell its airport authority, ANA. It also plans to contract for a new airport in Lisbon that will be developed and operated privately. Russia too, is bringing in private money. In the spring of 1998, Aéroports de Paris [ADP] signed a contract for a twenty-five year concession to build and operate a third, international terminal at St. Petersburg.[123]

In 1997, BAA, the former British Airports Authority, bought a 70% stake in Naples/Capodichino, Italy's third largest airport.[124] Heretofore, airports in Italy have been subject to multiple owners and operators. For instance, in Rome, Leonardo da Vinci Airport at Fiumicino has been subject to private law, the state owns the land on which the airport is built, but the airport company has many owners. Management of the airport has been provided by Alitalia Airlines (Italy's national airline), which owns 49% of the airport shares. The rest of the ownership has been divided between the state holding company (Istituto per la Ricostruzione Industriale [IRI]), Italstat, and Rome's

---

[122] Lucinda D. Wold, *International Perspectives on Airport Privatization*, an honor thesis at Arizona State University (fall 1993), at 10-11.
[123] Tom Gill, *Stampede to Market*, Airline Business (Apr. 1998), at 50-51.
[124] *Id.*

Chamber of Commerce. The airport in Milan has been owned and operated in basically the same way.[125] The Italian government plans to move the entire system into the private sector.[126]

The German government is selling six major airports, including three in Berlin, and one each in Frankfurt, Hamburg and Köln-Bonn. The situation in Berlin is unique. The airport in former West Berlin was under control of the Berlin Airport Company, which was a state-owned limited liability company. Subsequent to the reunification of Germany, the three Berlin airports came under the Berlin-Brandengurg Airport Holding Company (Berlin Brandenburg Flughafen [BBF]), owned jointly by the federal government, the city of Berlin, and the state of Brandenburg.[127] In 1997, the BBF approved privatization of the company. As part of its privatization, the BBF planned for the closure of two of Berlin's three airports (Tegel and Tempelhof) and to concentrate on Schönefeld. The latter was to be known as the Berlin Brandenburg International Airport, and to be the first European airport development to depend almost entirely on private funds.[128]

Other privatization initiatives in Germany include the Dusseldorf and Munich airports. In 1997, Dusseldorf Airport, Germany's third largest, entered into negotiations for a 50% stake in the airport.[129] And, in 1998, Flughafen München and Lufthansa signed an agreement to finance and operate Munich Airport's Terminal 2, which was completed in 2003.[130]

ASIA AND THE PACIFIC RIM

In Japan, there have been discussions about privatization of both Narita Airport and the airport at Osaka. Although there are no current plans to privatize Narita, Osaka is being seriously considered. The

---

[125] Lucinda D. Wold, *International Perspectives on Airport Privatization*, an honor thesis at Arizona State University (fall 1993), at 11-12.

[126] Tom Gill, *Stampede to Market*, Airline Business (Apr. 1998), at 50-51.

[127] Lucinda D. Wold, *International Perspectives on Airport Privatization*, an honor thesis at Arizona State University (fall 1993), at 11.

[128] Michael A. Taverna, *Berlin Oks Airport Privatization, New International Facility*, Avn. Wk. & Sp. Tech. (Oct. 6, 1997); *see also* Tom Gill, *Stampede to Market*, Airline Business (Apr. 1998), at 50-51.

[129] Michael A. Taverna, *Berlin Oks Airport Privatization, New International Facility*, Avn. Wk. & Space Tech. (Oct. 6, 1997)

[130] Staff, *Digest*, Airline Business (Jul. 1998), at 77.

New Tokyo International Airport Authority sees no reason to privatize the Narita Airport since it is "successful" under the existing (governmental) management. Nevertheless, the authority receives subsidies for operation of the airport.[131]

Airports in Singapore and Taiwan have considered privatization, but because of security reasons it will likely be limited in both places. The Civil Aviation Authority [CAA] of Singapore, which is an organization under the Ministry of Communication, runs the Changi Airport. In 1989, the Singapore government hired consultants to examine the feasibility of privatizing the airport.[132] The CAA has three functions: regulating, licensing, and Air Traffic Control. The CAA decided that it would privatize only if the organization could do so as a complete entity. The responsibility for ATC operations is shared by the Singapore Air Force. Because of national security issues, and the shared responsibility with the Air Force, the CAA as a whole cannot be privatized. Nevertheless, the CAA contracts many of its operations to private companies for services such as baggage handling and concessions.[133]

Similarly, Chiang Kai-Shek Airport is operated by Taiwan's Civil Aeronautics Administration [CAA], within the Ministry of Transportation and Communications. The CAA, which also operates Taiwan's domestic airport, Sungshan, has considered privatizing Chiang Kai-Shek, but will not consider privatizing Sungshan because it is under control of the China Air Force. A study to privatize Chiang Kai-Shek as a whole was presented to the minister of transportation and communications. He determined that the airport could be only partly privatized. Hence, the lounge and check-in areas of the passenger terminal and also the cargo terminal were planned for privatization.[134]

One of the world's most ambitious airport privatization programs is taking place in Australia. Fifty-five year leases were granted for three of Australia's airports. The selected bidders, requiring that major ownership be Australian, took over their airports July 1, 1997, at a cost of $3.337 billion (Australian). In addition, they were required to

---

[131] Lucinda D. Wold, *International Perspectives on Airport Privatization*, an honor thesis at Arizona State University (fall 1993), at 8.

[132] Rigas Doganis, *The Airport Business* (1992); *see also* Lucinda D. Wold, *International Perspectives on Airport Privatization*, an honor thesis at Arizona State University (fall 1993), at 8.

[133] Lucinda D. Wold, *International Perspectives on Airport Privatization*, an honor thesis at Arizona State University (fall 1993), at 9.

[134] *Id.*

spend more than $500 million (Australian), collectively, over the following decade to improve core airport facilities. Brisbane, the nation's fastest growing airport, went to Brisbane Airport Corporation Limited for. Australia's second busiest airport, Melbourne, was leased to Australia Pacific Airports Corporation for $1.307 billion (Australian). Perth Airport, on Australia's West Coast, was awarded to Airstralia Development Group for $643 million (Australian).

The remaining nineteen airports, including Sydney, continued to be nationally owned and operated by the Federal Airports Corporation [FAC], which was established in 1988 as a self-supporting business enterprise. However, subsequent to making leasing arrangements for Brisbane, Melbourne and Perth, the government then asked for expressions of interest on leases for the next fifteen airports.[135] Although Sydney was expected to be the main attraction of Australia's airport privatization program, noise became a political issue prompting location of a new airport. The FAC pledged not to sell the Sydney lease until the noise problem had been alleviated and a decision made on a second airport.[136]

AFRICA AND THE INDIAN SUB-CONTINENT

In late 1997, the government announced its intentions to sell 49% of the Airports Company South Africa [ACSA]. Of the 49%, 20% would go to a strategic equity partner, 10% would be offered to local investors, 9% was earmarked for the company's employees and 10% for the National Empowerment Fund for historically disadvantaged persons. The strategic partner selected would have the option of later acquiring an additional 10%.[137]

In the 1996/1997 financial year, ACSA showed a net profit of $33.1 million (U.S.). At least twenty-nine private airport operators from Europe, North America and Asia expressed an interest in the privatization of South Africa's nine state-owned airports, including three gateway airports in Johannesburg, Cape Town and Durbin as

---

[135] At Adelaide, Alice Springs, Archerfield, Canberra, Coolangatta, Darwin, Essendon, Hobart, Jandakot, Launceton, Moorabbin, Mount Isa, Parafield, Tennant Creek, & Townsville, *see* Adele C. Schwartz, *Australia: On Top of Privatization Down Under*, Airport Magazine (Sep./Oct. 1997), at 42.

[136] Adele C. Schwartz, *Australia: On Top of Privatization Down Under*, Airport Magazine (Sep./Oct. 1997), at 41-42.

[137] Roger Makings, *South Africa to Sell Airports*, Airline Business (Dec. 1997), at 20.

well as others in Kimberly, Port Elizabeth, Gearge, East London, Bloemfontein and Upington. Required in the solicitation was that the strategic partner be an internationally recognized airport operator. Additionally, the strategic partner was expected to assist ACSA to develop its operational expertise and non-aeronautical businesses and to enhance ACSA's profitability and value.[138]

UNITED STATES PRIVATIZATION

In the United States, no commercial airport has (as of 2007) been sold outright to private enterprise. For that matter, there may not be an example of a *complete* privatization anywhere, not even the supposed privatization of the British Airports Authority. Critics argue the BAA transfer does a "disservice to the privatization argument. . . ." British Airports Authority, they contend, was developed and controlled as an instrument of the national government. And, despite its "refinancing," it is one of the least privatized airports to the extent "privatization" denotes lack of government involvement in the contemporary "deregulatory" sense.[139]

Thus far, all but one attempt to sell or lease a commercial airport in the United States has been abandoned after encountering various legal obstacles. In 1986, Atlantic City, New Jersey, leased its terminal at Atlantic City International Airport and its general aviation airport to a private management firm. The lease required minimum payments of $400,000 annually to the city. Seemingly the lease was an anomaly, because FAA officials cannot fully explain why Atlantic City was allowed to divert revenue in 1986, when the agency opposed similar lease proposals by Albany County, New York, in 1989, Los Angeles in 1992, and Orange County, California in 1995.[140]

The first serious attempt after Atlantic City to transfer an already established public airport to private hands occurred in 1989 when Albany County, New York, attempted to sell, or alternatively to lease, its airport to the highest bidder.[141] Albany County considered a plan

---

[138] *Id.*

[139] ADRF of AAAE, *An Airport Executive's Guide To Privatization* (1992), at 23.

[140] GAO, *Airport Privatization: Issues Related to the Sale of U.S. Commercial Airports*, Testimony Report Number T-RCED-96-82.

[141] *See* Robert A. Bunnell, *Is Your Airport A Pot Of Gold?*, Airport Magazine (May/Jun. 1992), at 37-41.

to turn over the County Airport to Lockheed Air Terminal [LAT][142] and its partner British-American, through a long-term lease or outright sale in exchange for the promise of a new $100 million terminal along with a hotel and related developments. The Federal Aviation Administration declined to approve either proposal. The snag in the deal reportedly was the *assurance* requirement of the federal government that airport revenues would be spent for capital projects or for operating costs of the airport.[143] It appeared as if Lockheed wanted to "siphon" profits from the airport, although the company said it ". . . only expected to be paid fees for its services, as it is at almost two dozen other airports."[144]

Additionally, the Federal government said it was not satisfied ". . . that Lockheed could fulfill all of the responsibilities of a public airport owner, many of which are governmental in nature; or that Albany County (intended) to maintain the full and complete oversight of an airport sponsor."[145] In 1991, Albany County and Lockheed agreed to a management contract giving Lockheed day-to-day control but left the County with ultimate responsibility for the airport.[146]

In 1992, the City of Los Angeles looked into the possibility of selling or leasing Los Angeles International Airport, but dropped the idea when it was confronted by threat of suit by the FAA. In 1995, Orange County, California, likewise sought to sell John Wayne Airport as a way to obtain revenue for its general fund after the County filed for bankruptcy in December 1994. The County abandoned its privatization effort after concluding that any sale or lease proceeds could not be retained for its general fund.[147]

Short of sale or lease of public airports, there has long been a reliance on the private sector for reducing costs and improving services. Some municipalities have gone so far as to contract out management of their entire airport to the private sector. Historically, at smaller air-

---

[142] A division of the aerospace company of the same name.

[143] James Ott, *FAA Rejects Two Proposals to Privatize Albany Airport*, Av. Wk. & Space Tech. (1989), at 44.

[144] Robert A. Bunnell, *Is Your Airport A Pot Of Gold?*, Airport Magazine (May/Jun. 1992), at 20.

[145] James Ott, *FAA Rejects Two Proposals to Privatize Albany Airport*, Av. Wk. & Space Tech. (1989), at 44; *see also* Seth Payne & E. Schine, *Buyers Are Starting to the Airports*, Business Week (Oct. 2, 1989), at 38.

[146] *See* Robert A. Bunnell, *Is Your Airport A Pot Of Gold?*, Airport Magazine (May/Jun. 1992), at 20.

[147] GAO, *Airport Privatization: Issues Related to the Sale of U.S. Commercial Airports*, testimony Report Number T-RCED-96-82.

ports, this may have entailed a lease to a local Fixed Base Operator [FBO]. And while airport management contracts have tended to be with smaller airports, in September 1995, the Indianapolis Airport Authority signed a ten-year contract with a private firm, BAA Indianapolis, LLC, to manage its system of airports.[148]

Although there have been no sales of public airports in the United States, private "management" of larger, air carrier and general aviation airports such as at Albany County has become common. The largest such airport currently operated by a private firm in the United States is the Burbank-Glendale-Pasadena Airport in California, which has been under contract since 1978 to Lockheed Air Terminal.[149] The Burbank airport, however, is a unique privatization. It began as a *private* airport, owned and operated by the Lockheed Corporation. Although the field was profitable according to Viggo Butler, then president of Lockheed Air Terminal [LAT],[150] it was transferred to public ownership because in 1975 Lockheed was unable to work out a financially feasible solution to various environmental problems resulting from aircraft noise.[151] The airport was sold to an authority representing the three cities, and Lockheed resumed management under a governmental umbrella.

By 1990, Lockheed was in operation at twenty-two airports or terminals in the U.S. and internationally.[152] Including the Burbank-Glendale-Pasadena Airport, among the larger U.S. airports currently managed by the successor to LAT, Airport Group International, are Rickenbacker Airport in Columbus, Ohio, Republic Airport on Long Island, Stewart International Airport north of New York City, and of course, Albany County.

Another important contract operator was Pan Am World Services, formerly part of Pan American World Airways. Pan Am World Services became a subsidiary of Johnson Controls, Inc., which operated Westchester County Airport in White Plains, New York, Atlantic City International, Bader Field, and Teterboro Airport, all in New Jer-

---

[148] *Id.*

[149] Lockheed Air Terminal is now Airport Group International.

[150] Tim W. Ferguson, *Landing a Profit by De-Socializing an Industry*, Wall St. J. (Mar. 13, 1990), at A17.

[151] *See City of Burbank v. Lockheed Air Terminal*, 411 U.S. 624 (1973); *see also* Laurence E. Gesell, *Aviation and the Law* 595-596 (3rd ed. 1998).

[152] Robert W. Poole, Jr., *Privatizing Airports*, Reason Foundation, Policy Study No. 119 (Jan. 1990), at 5.

sey.[153] It also operated the Grand Canyon Airport for a while, but eventually management of the airport reverted back to the State of Arizona.

Currently, JFK International Air Terminal, LLC, claims that its agreement to build and operate Terminal 4 at Kennedy Airport (for common use and with a choice of four ground handling companies) is the "only privatized terminal in the U.S."[154] However, aside from the common-use aspect, the agreement is materially no different than JetBlue's agreement for the old Trans World Airlines Flight Center building (Terminal 5) at the same airport; or for that matter, British Airport Authority's management at Indianapolis. JetBlue will operate the remodeled Terminal 5 under a 34-year lease, after which it will revert back to the airport.[155] In none of these cases is it truly a fully privatized initiative; meaning privatized ownership.

Gary Rice, airport services director for Airport Group International suggests that perhaps it is time to take a closer look at privatization. In his estimation, ". . . we are now facing the 'mother' of all regulatory changes, privatization," and he asks, "Are we so afraid of change that we throw up road blocks to the rewards of privatization"? In support of airport privatization, Rice argues,

> *Economic theory forecasts that goods and services produced in the most efficient manner creates the strongest total economic system. Airports being managed inefficiently are a drain on the economy.*[156]

But Truitt and Esler warn, ". . . to the extent that privatization increases efficiency, completely privatizing airports would not result in as great an increase in efficiency as many proponents might hope." Moreover, ". . . to the extent that private managers could run airports more efficiently than their public counterparts, the gains in efficiency would not be without costs."[157]

---

[153] *Id.*

[154] Alan Maca, President of JFK International Air Terminal, LLC, personal communication (Feb. 2007).

[155] AAAE, *New JetBlue Terminal Set for JFK*, Airport Report (Aug. 15, 2004).

[156] Gary Rice, *Airport Privatization: A Closer Look*, Airport Magazine (Mar./Apr. 1997), at 34-35.

[157] Lawrence J. Truitt & Michael Esler, *Airport Privatization: Full Divestiture and its Alternatives*, Policy Studies J., Vol. 24, No.1 (1996), at 109.

To test the potential efficiency of airport privatization Congress passed the *Federal Aviation Administration Authorization Act* of 1996, establishing an airport privatization pilot program in the United States.[158] The 1996 Reauthorization Act authorizes the Secretary of Transportation (and through delegation, the FAA Administrator) to exempt a sponsor of a public use airport that has received federal assistance, from certain federal requirements in connection with the privatization of the airport by sale or lease to a private party.[159]

Specifically, the Administrator may exempt the sponsor from all or part of the requirements to use airport revenues for airport-related purposes, to pay back a portion of federal grants upon the sale of the airport, and to return airport property deeded by the Federal government upon transfer of the airport. The Administrator is also authorized to exempt the private purchaser or lessee from the requirement to use all airport revenues for airport related purposes, to the extent necessary to permit the purchaser or lessee to earn compensation from the operation of the airport.

Participation in the privatization project is limited to five airports, each characterized by a different level of privatization. In all cases, the lease agreement must ensure:

- The airport will continue to be available for public use on reasonable terms and conditions without unjust discrimination;
- The operation of the airport will not be interrupted if the private operator experiences bankruptcy or other financial difficulty;
- The private operator will "maintain, improve, and modernize" airport facilities through capital investments, and submit a plan for these actions;
- Airport fees imposed on air carriers will not increase faster than inflation unless a higher amount is approved by at least 65% of the air carriers using the airport;
- Fees imposed on general aviation operators will not exceed the percentage increase in fees imposed on air carriers;
- Safety and security will be maintained "at the highest possible levels";

[158] Public Law No. 104-264 (Oct. 9, 1996), Sec. 149, which adds a new Section 47134 to Title 49 U.S.C.

[159] *See* Sec. 149 of the *Federal Aviation Administration Authorization Act* of 1966.

- Adverse effects of noise from operations at the airport will be mitigated to the same extent as at a public airport;
- Adverse effects on the environment from airport operations will be mitigated to the same extent as at a public airport;
- Collective bargaining agreements cover airport employees on the date of the sale or lease; and
- The FAA Administrator must find that the transfer will not result in unfair and deceptive trade practices or unfair methods of competition.[160]

In addition, an operator of an airport receiving air carrier service by aircraft having more than thirty passenger seats must hold an (FAR Part 139) operating certificate. Such certificates are non-transferable. Therefore, a new operator must obtain a new certificate.

As of this writing, the pilot program comprises Stewart International Airport in Newbergh, New York, and Brown Field, a general aviation airport in San Diego, California. Under the FAA Reauthorization Act, which outlines the FAA's *Pilot Program on Private Ownership of Airports*, one of the five airports must be a general aviation facility, and not more than one may be a large hub. The Empire State Development Corporation, acting on behalf of the Stewart Airport, selected United Kingdom-based National Express to be a long-term lessor of the facility. It was likely that San Diego would also consider a long-term lease arrangement.[161] In other words, neither the Stewart Airport nor Brown Field "privatizations" were destined to be "total privatizations"; that is to say, outright sales. The only remaining applicant for one of the pilot slots is New Orleans Lakefront Airport. Damaged by Hurricane Katrina, its application was put on hold.[162]

PRIVATIZATION PROS AND CONS

The major contractors identified above, as well as some lessor operators, are seemingly at the forefront of an emerging industry. Poole gives three reasons why the interest in airport privatization is grow-

---

[160] *Id.*

[161] Holly Arthur, *Airport Privatization: A Reality Check*, Airport Magazine (Sep./Oct. 1998), at 28-30.

[162] Reason Foundation, *Annual Privatization Report* (2006).

ing.[163] The first reason given is there is not enough infrastructure capacity to meet air transportation demands. The hope of privatization is that it might attract more net investment, and the attraction of capital will generate more revenue, and thereby help finance expansion of the nation's airport capacity.

Second, since the advent of airline deregulation, there has been decreasing airline competition at certain hub airports. Managers of privately operated airports, it is argued, might be better negotiators in dealing with airlines as tenants, and through private investment might be able to expand airport capacity and attract more airline competition.

And third, airports represent a sizeable capital investment for which local airport sponsors are not allowed (by federal grant assurances) to earn any kind of a return. Privatization is one means of generating profits, which could be used to do other useful things in the community.

The first two reasons given for privatization expansion are under girded by a clear belief that private managers freed of government constraints generally do a better job of managing business. Proponents argue privatization would lead to efficiencies and increased capacity; the underlying premise, again, being a widely held perception that business management by the private sector is superior to management found in the public sector. They argue privatization leads to lower operating costs, more productivity, and therefore greater efficiency. But, the supposed "efficiencies" to be derived from privatization are not altogether clear.

Opponents to privatization, for instance, contend it would increase costs to users and would restrict access to general aviation. The argument for public provision of "public goods" is that it is more efficient to have them publicly provided. Joseph Stiglitz submits,

> *. . . there are two sources of inefficiencies that may arise from the private provision of public goods. First, when there is no marginal cost to an additional individual using a good, then, . . . it should not be rationed. But if it is to be privately provided by a firm, the firm must*

[163] Reason Foundation, *Airport Privatization: Can It Work?*, A transcript of a Reason Foundation Seminar (Mar. 20, 1990).

> *charge for its use; and any charge for its use will discourage individuals from using it. Thus when public goods are privately provided, an underutilization of these goods will result.*[164]

In short, discrimination will ensue, the cost per unit of production will go up, and the efficiency, therefore, will go down. Economic efficiency assumes prices are close to the marginal unit cost of production. And, if a profit margin must be built into the cost of production, price, it would seem, must increase, and therefore, may not be at its most "efficient" level.

From a financial perspective, and in certain situations, it may be advisable to privatize, but seemingly only at the margins. And to make the generalization that private management is superior to public management is not altogether valid. One must still ask, if management of airports could be better served in the private sector then in the past why was the responsibility relinquished to the government? Tim Ferguson responds to the question by suggesting that "Washington's aid guidelines stifle business-like practices in countless ways and are one of the primary reasons why U.S. airports fell into public hands and have remained there."[165] There is little evidence, however, to support Ferguson's contention. Aside from the large and medium hubs, the economic reality is that most (smaller) airports are not profitable, and are, therefore, unattractive as long-term ventures, other than to management companies who assume only limited risk, yet are nevertheless assured of a profit.[166] The GAO reports that in most cases, private managers are compensated on a fixed fee basis, sometimes including a performance incentive payment.[167]

---

[164] Joseph Stiglitz, *Economics of the Public Sector* (1986).

[165] Tim W. Ferguson, *Landing a Profit by De-Socializing an Industry*, Wall St. J. (Mar. 13, 1990), at A17.

[166] For example, in exchange for managing the five general aviation airports belonging to the Rhode Island State DOT, the management company receives: costs, including those for staff, reimbursable based on an approved budget; $65,000 per year management fee; and a 30 % incentive fee of actual operational bottom line improvement over the base year 1996 actual operation bottom line. Presumably a decreased deficit (albeit still a deficit) is treated as an improvement in the bottom line. *See* John F. Infanger, *An Airport Corporation*, Airport Business (May 1997), at 14-15.

[167] GAO, Airport *Privatization: Issues Related to the Sale or Lease of U.S. Commercial Airports* (Nov. 7, 1996).

FINANCIAL ENTREPRENEURSHIP

Privatization of even the largest airports may be advantageous to arbitrageurs at this time only because the public sector has already paid the sacrifice of long-term investment in airports, the cost of which might now be discounted to the private sector's advantage. There is some doubt that airports would be sold at their actual value. A potential privatization target airport can be valued only by its future potential income, not the true cost of development, which in most cases far exceeds the revenue-stream value.

There is a distinct difference between "value" and "cost." The former refers to *economic advantage* resulting from ownership. The latter has to do with the *sacrifice* involved in acquiring the property. In an attempt to "break even," governments are notorious for being concerned only with the current year's budget, and charging only for the direct costs of providing services.[168] The difference between the cost of land and its value represents an economic rent, or surplus, and "surplus" is another term for "profit," which, as already stated, airport sponsors in the U.S. are not supposed to collect. In the liquidation of airport property, for political expediency airport sponsors may be satisfied with collecting only part of their sunken costs, while transferring the excess value to the private sector at little or no cost in order for the latter to profit in the long-term investment.

In the determination of value, real property appraisal theory recognizes three approaches:

- *Cost*;
- *Market comparison*; and
- *Capitalization of income*.

Sound appraisal practice normally incorporates all three methods of appraisal. Yet, in the sale of airports, market comparisons would be rare, and capitalization of income would likely entail deep discounting of the airport value in order to produce a viable income stream and allow for reasonable profits. The result would be to shift greater reliance upon the replacement cost method, further suggesting air-

[168] The lack of concern for economic efficiency on the part of government agents, of course, is one argument for privatization.

ports would be transferred at cost, if not reduced cost, but certainly not at value.

The private sector wants discounted value and also seems interested in buying only those airports that have already achieved profitable operational levels; i.e., an airport with an infrastructure that is in place, and ". . . which is a mature industry."[169] For example, major hubs like Los Angeles International Airport and Phoenix Sky Harbor Airport have either been urged to sell, or are otherwise self-motivated in selling.[170] Some other airports involved in privatization initiatives include Boston Logan, T.F. Green in Rhode Island, and Baltimore-Washington International.[171]

By-and-large, the airports at Los Angeles and Phoenix are financially self-sustaining public enterprises, and "[a]irport authorities that are currently operated in a business-like manner with minimal political interference, high productivity, lean staffing and aggressive use of competitive bidding may have little to gain from privatization."[172] Look at Los Angeles, for example. According to a study ordered by the airport commission, Los Angeles International Airport would make twice as much money for the City of Los Angeles if it remains in city hands instead of being sold.[173] In most cases, if airport sponsors were allowed to divert airport generated revenues into other (non-airport related) municipal uses, they would not be interested in selling their airports.

Although private enterprise may be interested in acquiring "mature" airports, "small and medium-sized airports are considered by experts to have greater potential for privatization than larger, more complex facilities" —because they are the ones that "need fixing."[174] The smaller airports typically operate at a deficit, and their sponsors are the governments most apt to be looking for fiscal relief through privatization. If an airport cannot reasonably be made profitable (os-

---

[169] Reason Foundation, *Airport Privatization: Can It Work?*, A Transcript of a Reason Foundation Seminar (Mar. 20, 1990), at 8.

[170] *Id.* at 15; *see also* Ken Western, *Phoenix Urged to Sell Sky Harbor*, Arizona Republic (Feb. 8, 1990), at E1.

[171] Robert A. Bunnell, *Is Your Airport A Pot Of Gold?*, Airport Magazine (May/Jun. 1992), at 17.

[172] *Id.* at 101.

[173] Michael A. Dornheim, *Study Shows Private LAX Ownership Would Give Lowest Payback to City*, Avn. Wk. & Space Tech. (Jun. 8, 1992), at 36.

[174] James Ott, *Bush Order Opens Door for Airport Privatization*, Avn. Wk. & Space Tech. (May 11, 1992) at 24.

tensibly at the user's expense), then little interest will be expressed by private enterprise in buying these non-profitable airports. Modern capitalism seemingly holds more interest in those situations where it can be "rationally" protected against potential losses.[175] Hence, "[a] more probable scenario is for title and supervisory control to remain in the hands of governments, with long-term management contracts for private companies."[176]

With non-profitable airports, the private sector may be interested only in "skimming the cream" where profits may be taken, and leaving for the public sector the responsibility of maintaining the cost centers which have negative bottom lines. Rather than selling and allowing marginal profits (if any) to be siphoned off by finance entrepreneurs, wouldn't it be more "efficient" to allow public sector managers to cross allocate and use excess proceeds from profitable cost centers to offset the costs of the negative cost centers? That is to say, cross allocation.

A typical contract for privatization of a non-profitable airport entails "operational" management, wherein the contractor attempts to negotiate a guaranteed margin of profit, but leaving with the airport sponsor the responsibility for non-profitable capital improvements, sovereignty issues (*infra*), and for airport liability. Within such a scenario, although called a *contractor*, in reality the contract manager is not much different than an *employee*. Under the laws of negligence, the contract "employee" is usually considered the responsibility of the employer whether employed directly or not.[177] This could leave the government sponsor saddled with not only the financial responsibility

---

[175] *See* Max Weber, *The Theory of Social and Economic Organization* (A.M. Henderson & T. Parsons trans. 1947). In Max Weber's perspective on capitalism (and the modern institutional order), the free market economy is dependent upon rational-legal authority, not only internal to the organization in its "bureaucracy," but also externally, upon the "rationality of economic action." As Anthony Giddens interprets Weber, "Modern rational capitalism has need, not only for the technical means of production, but of a calculable legal system and administration in terms of formal rules." Anthony Giddens, *Introduction* (1976), in Max Weber, The Protestant Ethic and the Spirit of Capitalism (T. Parsons trans. 1976). By "rational," Weber was referring to marketplace efficiency; the most rational means of orienting economic activity. As Inverarity, Lauderdale & Feld explain, rationality does not mean "reasonable" in the colloquial sense, but rather, is used in the technical sense to mean rules and procedures. James M. Inverarity, Pat Lauderdale & Barry C. Feld, *Law and Society: Sociological Perspectives on Criminal Law* (1983); *see also* Ch. 7.

[176] James Ott, *Bush Order Opens Door for Airport Privatization*, Avn. Wk. & Space Tech. (May 11, 1992) at 24.

[177] *See Emelwon, Inc. & Kaiel Thompson McAlister v. United States,* CCH 10 AVI 17,718 (1968).

for the airport's deficit, but with legal liability as well, while the private sector manager profits with minimal risk.

RETURN ON INVESTMENT

The third reason cited by Poole (*supra*) in support of privatization perhaps has the greatest merit. Local airport sponsors have begun to look at airports as one of their largest capital investments, from which they are not earning any kind of direct return. As Clifton Moore, then director of airports for the City of Los Angeles, complained, everyone else on the airport is allowed to make a profit except the airport owner.[178] What Mr. Moore is referring to are conditions (or "assurances") which are attached to federal airport grants requiring all monies generated on the airport to be invested back into the airport. A medium or large hub airport represents an investment of millions of dollars, if not billions when one considers the nature of long-term investment and the opportunity use of money. Yet, airport sponsors are unable to realize a direct financial return on this investment other than economic multiplier effect. Additionally, the huge investment is tied up in high value property that is kept exempt from property taxation, typically the local government's largest single source of revenue for the general fund.

As Robert Poole notes in his suggestion that the City of Phoenix should sell its airport, selling Sky Harbor and other public airports would permit them to keep most of the revenues they generate, rather than sending the money to Washington to be distributed across the country. To demonstrate, Sky Harbor generated about $42 million per year in ticket taxes in 1990, but got back only $7 million in annual federal airport development grants. Additionally, Phoenix could have collected an estimated $9.5 million in annual property taxes if the airport had been in private hands.[179]

On the surface, demands that revenues derived from airport operations remain on the airport might seem reasonable, particularly for airports operating at a deficit. In such cases, all funds ought to be returned to the airport for its operation and improvement. But what about those medium and especially large hubs that now find them-

---

[178] *See* the quote by Mr. Moore under the heading for this chapter.

[179] Ken Western, *Phoenix Urged to Sell Sky Harbor Airport*, Arizona Republic (Feb. 8, 1990) at E-1.

selves with large propensities to profit? Assuming federal subsidies were terminated, there are no valid reasons why sponsors of potentially profitable airports shouldn't be able to use the profits of their investments to pay for any and all public social programs and welfare concerns for which they are responsible. As Clifton Moore says, why can't the airport sponsor "profit" like all other ventures on the airport? What valid reason can be given other than an unfounded fear that the airport might suffer if revenues are diverted?

One argument against removal of proceeds from the airport is that airports might be drained of their assets. Other countering arguments, philosophically, may have something to do with sound cost allocation and the notion that governments ought not to make a profit. Also in question, however, is whether excess revenues really constitute a profit if they are cross allocated for *re-investment* in the provision of other community services. However, airport sponsors already cross allocate within airport cost centers. Cross allocation of airport proceeds, or "cross subsidization," is a standard practice worldwide.[180] True cost allocation on airports is seemingly not achievable if simultaneously the airport sponsor is attempting to provide well-rounded aviation services to the public. It has therefore become standard practice on airports to transfer funds from profitable centers to help pay for less profitable activities; i.e., to "cross allocate" funds.

Cross allocation is a mechanism for *redistribution*, and redistribution of wealth is but one of the traditional functions of government. And, assuming it is acceptable to cross allocate amongst airport activities, the justification for doing so within a given activity could be extended to allow airport sponsors to divert funds (ie., cross allocate) from airport to non-airport cost-centers. Allowing airport sponsors to cross allocate amongst all of its various government responsibilities and activities would aid local communities in paying for non-airport-related public expenses.

Still, skeptics seem to fear that by taking excess proceeds from the airport and spending them on other-than-airport programs and other social needs might detract from the importance of the airport and in the degree of support given it by its sponsor. Such an attitude, seemingly fostered by the Federal government, may be overly paternalistic. Certainly the integrity of the nation's air transportation system must be protected. But in the final analysis the local airport sponsor is the

---

[180] Tom Gill, *Argentinian Airport Fray*, Airline Business (Sep. 1998), at 22.

one responsible for its airport, as well as the welfare of its community, not the Federal government. Assuming the airport is producing a profit, why would any reasonable airport sponsor deliberately choose to kill the proverbial "golden goose"? Economic rationality would suggest that just the opposite would be the case. It would be more likely that the sponsor would be motivated to hire a sound business manager to run the airport. Sound fiscal practice requires sufficient reinvestment to perpetuate any viable business. Diversion of funds to the detriment of the (airport) business would be tantamount to fiscal irresponsibility. Moreover, the Federal government has the means and authority necessary to inspect the airport for safety compliance and to demand that the airport be maintained properly.

Not only is an airport part of the National Plan of Integrated Airport Systems, its ultimate purpose is to serve its (local) community. The airport could serve its community even better by providing for more than just its air transportation needs. By allowing proceeds from the airport to pay for other community needs, the airport's economic importance would be magnified, thereby providing even more popular support for the airport. Airport sponsors would have an added incentive to invest in their airports.

Certainly, there would be the opportunity for some errant (if not irresponsible) politician(s) to misuse airport revenues. But an airport sponsor would be far more inclined to lend its support to an airport providing direct and tangible financial returns than to one offering only the indirect benefits of economic multiplier effects. Moreover, irrespective of the current federal prohibition against revenue diversion, there already exists the opportunity to neglect, if not otherwise abuse the airport financially. The airport sponsor need only withhold funding support. The net result is the same as any supposed revenue diversion. This is especially true where the airport is a subsidized operation.

Rather than privatizing certain airports, and turning the potential profits over to private enterprise, it might serve the public interest better for the government sponsor to maximize profits, and to use those profits which are over and above the needs of the airport to invest in other social programs? One resistance to doing so may be that it is not only a form of profitization, but the profits are paid for at the expense of the airport user—the same argument employed by users against privatization. However, in the majority of cases, it is the other way around. Airports are usually subsidized by the general public but to the airport user's benefit. In those few instances where airports have the propensity to profit, they ought to be allowed to do so, particularly if those "profits" would be applied to programs in the greater interest of the community.

One reason airport sponsors are turning to privatization is because of stifling federal policy. By barring sponsors from using their excess airport revenues for other than airport purposes, local governments are finding privatization appealing because it offers at least one way to realize direct financial benefits from their airport investments. Unfortunately, it may not be the most economically efficient nor socially productive way to provide airport services. Nevertheless, if airport sponsors are to be barred from taking proceeds off their airports, then maybe it is time to consider privatization of at least that segment of the national airport system which is capable of being profitable to the private sector, particularly if it is the only way available for government sponsors to realize direct financial benefits from their investments. Federal policy requiring re-investment of all funds back into the airport needs to be reviewed in light of the only other alternative available to airport sponsors for them to profit from their airport investments—that of selling the airport to private interests at discounted value.

THE SOVEREIGNTY ISSUE

If airports were to be privatized, government sponsors would still be saddled with the responsibility for their airport operations. There are other concerns besides economics. Legal concerns, for example, may override economic considerations. Although advocates of privatization see limitless opportunities, most public administrators are generally aware that limits do exist. Consequently, there has been a manifest resistance by public officials to the privatization challenge.

Organized public sector resistance was perhaps nowhere more apparent than in the FAA's rejection of Albany County's attempt to privatize its airport. The FAA gave indications it would look unfavorably toward (perhaps any) privatization attempts. Even so, such staunch resistance was tempered by President George H.W. Bush's directive to federal agencies for them to "assist state and local governments in their efforts to advance the objectives. . . ." of his executive order on infrastructure privatization. Still, such efforts by the administration to privatize may only be supported "to the extent permitted by law"[181] Acknowledged is that there are limitations, if not legal barriers, to total privatization of public assets.

The U.S. Constitution, statutory law, and the political culture all tend to promote and reinforce the separate and distinct basis for the public sector from that which is private. At issue is *sovereignty* and whether or not the privatized activity is an instrumentality of the (sovereign) government. At times privatization might result in the relegation of sovereign powers, and, if not illegal, may at a minimum be contrary to serving the public interest.

As Ronald Moe points out, "The debate over the definition of sovereignty is hoary with age. . . .,"[182] But he suggests certain attributes fundamentally inhering to a sovereign:

- It possesses the legitimate right to use coercion to enforce its will (and force subjects to conform to its laws);
- Only a sovereign may legitimately go to war with another sovereign;
- Sovereigns are infallible (e.g., "the king can do no wrong");
- A sovereign is indivisible and cannot assign its attributes to a private party and remain sovereign;
- A sovereign may disavow debts but cannot go bankrupt. The right to declare bankruptcy is a personal or private right not inhering to a sovereign; and
- The sovereign has the right to take private property (i.e., "eminent domain") to promote public purpose.

All of the attributes listed above inhere to the Federal government, most to the states, and some to local governments as representatives of the State. Since the majority of airports are operated by local governments, sovereignty may be an issue. In considerations of privatization, the first question should be, "Does the performance of the function necessarily invoke the powers properly reserved to the sover-

[181] George Bush, Executive Order 12803, *Infrastructure Privatization*, Federal Register, Vol. 57, No. 86 (Mon., May 4, 1992).
[182] Ronald C. Moe, *Exploring the Limits of Privatization*, Public Administration Review (Nov./Dec. 1987).

eign?" Or, "Is the function largely private in character, requiring none of the coercive powers of the sovereign?"

Management of public airports does, at times, require the use of coercive (police) powers. Therefore, at a minimum, it would seem that some form of government oversight is necessary even in those instances where privatization occurs through outright sale. As submitted by E. Tazewell Ellett, former FAA general counsel and attorney in the attempt by Albany County to privatize its airport,

> *Public entities should not get out of airports totally . . . where we are headed is a public entity continuing to hold title to an airport, but leasing out the operation to a company. . . . The public entity continues to control and conduct the supervision the FAA requires, but the private entity with the long-term lease can go to the bank and borrow money based on the lease, build and develop an airport.*[183]

SUMMARY

"Total privatization," defined as the sale of an airport to a private enterprise, is perhaps an economically appropriate consideration in the United States only with the (seventy or so) large and medium hub airports, which are already profitable. Seemingly, those select airports might be able to function in the public's interest just as any other public utility operated in the United States. Nevertheless, there is stiff opposition to privatizing the largest airports. As Richard Leone, former chair of the board of directors for the Port Authority of New York and New Jersey, argues, "[s]elling major airports to private operators could leave strategic public assets loaded with debt, deteriorating from lack of investment and unable to support the communities they serve"[184]

Leone lists three reasons why public airports should remain public.[185] First, "anybody who wanted to buy the airports would have to

[183] James Ott, *Bush Order Opens Door for Airport Privatization*, Avn. Wk. & Space Tech. (May 11, 1992) at 24.
[184] Staff, *Privatization Could Leave Major Airports in Debt, Port Authority Chairman Warns*, Avn. Wk. & Space Tech. (May 25, 1992), at 34.
[185] *Id.*

borrow heavily," and the 1980s demonstrated the dangers of such leveraged buyouts. Second (assuming airports were sold for their true "value") the required debt service payments would make it difficult for a private operator to invest in airport maintenance and improvements. And third, a private operator could not manage the variety of legal, community and intra-governmental problems that arise in airport management.[186] At a minimum, some powers would have to remain with the government. This is precisely why the Lockheed Corporation in the late 1970s found it necessary to transfer its (privately-owned) Burbank airport to the public sector.

With the remaining (approximately 3,000) airports in the national system of airports, some degree of *partial* privatization might be appropriate, but only where it can be adequately demonstrated that improved efficiencies would, in fact, be achieved. Profiting from a public asset by a private enterprise, if it is at the public's expense does not and cannot represent economic efficiency. If prices must be increased, and public goods must be rationed solely for the sake of making a profit for a private operator, it clearly would not serve the public interest, and it would be far better for the airport to remain totally within the public sector. But if it can be truly demonstrated that privatization of an airport would generate more revenue and thereby help finance expansion of infrastructure capacity, improve upon day-to-day management, and allow local airport sponsors to capitalize on their investments, then, indeed, it would be a strong argument for privatization.

Perhaps the greatest opportunity for privatization is associated with the concept developed by John Kasarda that he calls the "aerotropolis") (pl. "aerotropoli"),[187] which is a new type of urban form comprised of aviation-intensive businesses and related enterprises extending about 15 miles outward from major airports. It is similar in form and function to a traditional metropolis, which contains a Central Business District [CBD] at its core, surrounded by clusters of aviation-related enterprises and commuter-linked suburbs.[188] The airport at the center of the aerotropolis is surrounded by tens of thousands of acres of light industrial space, office space, upscale

---

[186] *Id.*

[187] *See* John D. Kasarda, *Aerotropolis: Airport-Driven Urban Development*, Urban Land Institute on the Future: Cities in the 21st Century (2000); see also John D. Kasarda, *From Airport City to Aerotropolis*, Airport World (Aug.-Sep 2001), Vol. 6, No. 4, at 42-45.

[188] *Aerotropolis*, http://en.wikipedia.org (visited Jun. 2, 2007).

retail mix, business-class hotel accommodations, restaurants, entertainment, recreation, golf courses, and single and multiple-family housing.[189] Aerotropoli typically attract industries related to time-sensitive manufacturing, e-commerce fulfillment, telecommunications and logistics; hotels, retail outlets, entertainment complexes and exhibition centers; and offices for business people who travel frequently by air or engage in global commerce. Clusters of business parks, logistics parks, industrial parks, distribution centers, information technology complexes and wholesale merchandise marts would locate around the airports and along the transportation corridors radiating from them.

Currently, aerotropoli can be found in varying stages of development surrounding major airports worldwide, particularly in Asia, where newer airports are being built on large tracts of open land. Among the most notable aerotropoli, existing or under development, are those associated with the following airports:

- Beijing Capital International Airport (China);
- Dallas-Fort Worth International Airport (Texas);
- Detroit Metropolitan Wayne County Airport (Michigan);
- Dubai World Central International Airport (United Arab Emirates);
- Hong Kong International Airport (China);
- Incheon International Airport (Korea);
- Kuala Lumpur International Airport (Malaysia);
- Los Angeles-Ontario International Airports (California);
- Memphis International Airport (Tennessee);
- Schiphol Airport (The Netherlands);
- Singapore Changi Airport (Singapore); and
- Suyamabhumi International Airport (Bangkok).[190]

Kasarda suggests that "airports will shape business location and urban development in the 21st century as much as highways did in the 20th century, railroads in the 19th and seaports in the 18th" Aerotropoli and other forms of future airport infrastructure are the subject of the next chapter.

---

[189] Devany K. Donigan, *The Aerotropolis*, an unpublished student paper, Eastern Michigan University (Fall 2002).

[190] *Aerotropolis*, http://en.wikipedia.org (visited Jun. 2, 2007).

CHAPTER 16

FIFTH WAVE INFRASTRUCTURE

A Collector-Distributor is the technical name;
Wayport is the romantic name.

James E. Sheppard,
Inventor of the Wayport Concept[1]

LEGITIMATE ENTREPRENEURSHIP

Privatization, at least defined as "total," may not be part of the "wave" of the future. What seems more likely is that there will be a continuation, albeit enhanced, of the traditional partnership between the public and private sectors in the development of the airport infrastructure such as the emerging aerotropolis concept. Suggested in the previous chapter were three reasons for the current interest in privatization (i.e., to attract capital investment, improve management, and generate profits). Suggested here is a fourth reason supporting privatization not previously mentioned. A partnership between government and private enterprise might provide legitimate entrepreneurial opportunities for profitization, while at the same time increasing system capacity and generating an economic multiplier for the community, thereby allowing both the public and private sectors to benefit.

By "legitimate" entrepreneurship, what is meant has no reference to the positive, lawful aspect of the term. Rather, the reference here is to the moral perspective; that is to say, to what is reasonable, justifi-

[1] Nat M. Turnbull, Jr. & James E. Sheppard, *Airports and Real Estate Development: New Trends and Approaches*, presented by The Industrial Development Research Council, Inc. (1990).

able and acceptable to society. Inferred by "legitimate" is the fundamental meaning of "entrepreneurship"; that is to say, the "taking of risks for the sake of profit." Moreover, referred to are the legitimate profits of production, and not the "financial entrepreneurship" and arbitrage that characterized the decade of the 1980s.

One recent example of a private/public partnership in airport development is the Alliance Airport north of Fort Worth. Although not necessarily suggesting the Alliance project as a model for future development, it is an example of the fourth reason for privatization, and of legitimate entrepreneurship and private airport investment. *Build, Operate and Transfer* [BOT] projects are another example, such as the Terminal 3 project at Pearson International Airport in Toronto. But the Alliance experience entailed development of an entirely new airport.

Alliance Airport was created in 1989 as a quasi-private project. It was developed in a public/private partnership between the Perot Group, the City of Fort Worth, and the Federal Aviation Administration [FAA]. Needed was a facility to *relieve* congestion at the Dallas-Fort Worth Airport. Of the airport's 3,400 acres of land, the Perot Group dedicated 418 acres to the City for operational runway/taxiway use. The remaining property remained privately owned for use as an industrial airpark.

Now anyone familiar with airport economics will recognize that airside related land-use is non-profitable, while lands devoted to industrial use are the most profitable on general aviation airports. The Perot Group retained property that would generate even more profit than non-airport related industrial land uses (because of the land's association with, and proximity to the airport). Nevertheless, it should be noted that the Perot Group, in the spirit of "entrepreneurship," donated land for the airport as an *investment*, and was relying upon the overall success of the land development project surrounding the Alliance Airport. Additionally, government officials *requested* the donation from the Perot group because of the need for a reliever airport.[2]

Since the Perot Group retained properties traditionally used to generate revenues for re-investment back into the airport, the City of Fort Worth may have been left with a public deficit in its operation and maintenance of the airport. But the deficit, if one is generated, is

---

[2] Ross Perot, Jr., on Peter Jennings, *Who is Ross Perot?*, The American Broadcasting Corp. (1992).

likely to be less than had the City developed an airport without the ancillary urban and commercial development found around Alliance. As H. Ross Perot, Jr. explains, "Alliance is more than an airport it is an industrial, commercial and residential center."[3] Because the airport was developed as part of a greater economic center, the airport-related rents have a propensity to be higher than had the City developed an airport on its own.

The airport-as-a-business may be non-profitable, and the (public) airport sponsor may be left with a direct liability. However, the costs of airport operation may be more than offset by the economic benefits derived by the community. A significant multiplier effect results from the creation of jobs and spending in the community. Additionally, the real property tax base will be substantially increased, including the taxes derived from the industrial airport property left in private ownership with the Perot Group. The bottom line is that the costs of the airport may be insignificant when compared to the economic impact and fiscal return to the community. In other words, the community may still "profit" even though the airport per se may not.

One lesson of the Alliance project is that the greatest opportunities for private investment, and "legitimate entrepreneurship," may lie not in back filling public managers with private managers (within an already existing infrastructure), but in investment in altogether new facilities. There is the opportunity to invest in projects like Alliance, and in the next generation or *wave* of airport infrastructure development. Robert Poole suggests *wayports* might ". . . provide an ideal opportunity to test the idea of airports as for-profit enterprises."[4] He refers to wayports as ". . . free-standing hubs; i.e., airports based in remote (and therefore low-cost) areas." Others, like Clifton Moore, suggest that what is needed are *superhubs*, capable of a full range of services.[5] Still others point to the unused capacity of airports currently not included in the hub-and-spoke network. Sam Hoerter suggests the advent of the regional jets offers the promise of more effectively, and efficiently serving many of these underutilized airports.[6] But there are other developments within the structure of the airline industry that

---

[3] *Id.*

[4] Robert W. Poole, Jr., *Privatizing Airports*, Reason Foundation, Policy Study No. 119 (Jan. 1990).

[5] *See* Reason Foundation, *Airport Privatization: Can It Work?*, a transcript of a Reason Foundation Seminar (Mar. 20, 1990).

[6] Sam Hoerter, *A Break With Tradition*, Airport Magazine (Jul./Aug. 1998), at 6.

add to Mr. Hoerter's argument. The changing environment within the airline industry is discussed in this chapter, along with a look at the potential for change in the way airports are structured.

SUPERHUBS AND WAYPORTS

In response to ever-increasing traffic constraints at certain U.S. airports, one suggestion offered by James Sheppard as a solution to the capacity problem was the development of a (hypothetical) category of airports he calls "wayports."[7] Although none have yet been built (at least under the rubric of a wayport) a wayport (by whatever name) would be an airport built at a remote site, which would provide a place where airlines could inter-connect passengers. There would be no local traffic. In fact, there would be neither enplanements nor deplanements, only passengers making connections. A wayport, in effect, would be a hub-and-spoke activity, remotely located to remove congestion from urban areas and high-density terminals. Theoretically, airlines could perform connections without experiencing the flight delays and congestion associated with large and medium hubs.

Assumed by proponents of wayports is that airlines need airports in addition to existing facilities where they might connect flights and passengers with minimum congestion and delay. It is further assumed that airlines are willing to develop hub-and-spoke activities at other than market generating centers. But herein is where the argument for wayports becomes weak, because it lacks either an understanding of how airports have been financed, or to otherwise suggests how the such airports might be financed.

Without enplanement and/or deplanement activity, there would be few of the revenue generating centers normally associated with large commercial airports (e.g., parking lots and automobile rentals) that have been the mainstream of revenue generation outside of government subsidies. The cost for operating such airports would have to be paid for by the airlines, to be ultimately borne by the traveling public, or otherwise to be heavily underwritten by government. This brings the dilemma full-circle. Government lacks the available funding either for new airport development or for expanded airport operations and maintenance. And because the airlines themselves would have to

---

[7] James E. Sheppard, *Wayports: A Concept Whose Time Has Come*, Airport Services Management (May 1989).

pay for the infrastructure, without the prospect of reasonable return on their investments they have been opposed to the concept. In response to political pressures, successive (Reagan, Bush, and Clinton) administrations opposed the wayport concept, as have federal agencies such as the Department of Transportation [DOT] and the FAA. Therefore, to date, no wayports (by name) have been developed, and few (if any) professionals within the airport or the airline industries have supported the wayport concept. In 1990, a yearlong DOT-FAA study found that wayports would be impractical, and the concept has seemingly become a moot issue.

The outlook for new capacity in the existing system is bleak because of restrictions imposed by noise and environmental issues, lack of physical space, and most importantly, because of insufficient funds. The outlook for development of any major new airports in *metropolitan* areas is dismal, as evidenced by the fact that only one major airport in America (Denver) has been built since Dallas/Fort Worth was completed in 1974. And even if billions of dollars were available for this purpose, public opposition could indefinitely doom or delay new urban airports. The synopsis of Mr. Sheppard's argument is that new airports are needed, but where or how will they be built?[8] Suggested in this chapter, is that a derivation of the wayport idea, coupled with private investment, is at least one answer—if not the most viable solution—to provide additional air transportation infrastructure capacity.

Within the framework of the wayport concept, low-cost rural land would be utilized, and for the foreseeable future there could be almost unlimited long-range airport and airspace capacity, since airport configurations could be optimized with inexpensive land that otherwise would have only limited use. The problem, says Clifton Moore, retired general manager of Los Angeles Airports Department, is that the wayport would need an extensive surface infrastructure to make it work. He foresees high-speed rail lines, and accessibility to automobiles—and linkage to connecting airports.[9]

What Mr. Moore is suggesting is a variant to the wayport concept. Wayports, in their most basic form, would have no enplaning or deplaning passengers. What Moore is describing is a "superhub," served

---

[8] James E. Sheppard, *Wayports: A Concept Whose Time Has Come*, Airport Services Management (May 1989).

[9] *See* Reason Foundation, *Airport Privatization: Can It Work?*, a transcript of a Reason Foundation Seminar (Mar. 20, 1990).

from populated areas directly by high-speed rail, bus, tilt-rotor, helicopter and/or commuter aircraft. A true wayport, on the other hand, would have no need for elaborate access systems. The underpinning of what is suggested supposes superhubs, and not wayports, are the more likely wave of the future. Los Angeles, for example, intends to go ahead with its plans for an airport at Palmdale, north of the City. Likewise, the State of Arizona has been conducting a seemingly perpetual investigation into the possibility of a regional airport centrally located between Phoenix and Tucson.[10] Both the Palmdale and Central Arizona projects, if (or when) they come to fruition will likely develop into superhubs.

Narrowly defined, a wayport, at least in its initial phase of development, would be an airport built at a remote site that would provide a place where airlines could inter-connect passengers and cargo. Initially there might not be any local traffic; that is to say, there may be neither enplanements nor deplacements. There would only be passengers making connections. Nevertheless, the wayport concept does not preclude Origin and Destination [O&D] traffic in its ultimate development. Moreover, it need not be remotely located. In effect, wayports might be to passenger traffic, what sorting centers are to air cargo operators.[11]

In response to ever increasing traffic constraints at certain U.S. airports, the (hypothetical) category of airports known as wayports was offered as a solution. As described by its inventor (James Sheppard), a wayport could act as a "collector/distributor" or "expediter."[12] Traffic at wayports would bypass aviation's choke points, much the way the interstate highways bypass congested city streets.[13]

---

[10] Casa Grande, Ariz., surfaced from three separate studies as the most likely location.

[11] Fully integrated cargo sorting centers came into existence subsequent to cargo deregulation in 1977. Prior to that time, smaller versions existed in Los Angeles, New York, Minneapolis, and the one created at Memphis by Federal Express (now FedEx). Seaboard World Airlines sorted international freight in New York. Northwest Airlines sorted freight at its hub in Minneapolis, and Flying Tigers sorted international freight at Los Angeles. By 1987 there were a number of full-blown sort centers throughout the United States: Airborne Express at Wilmington, Ohio; Burlington Air Express at Fort Wayne, Indiana; Consolidated Freightways at Indianapolis; Emery Worldwide at Dayton, Ohio; Federal Express at Memphis, Tennessee and sub-hubs; Flying Tiger Line at Columbus, Ohio; and United Parcel Service at Louisville, Kentucky and sub-hubs. There are sort centers around the world as well, particularly in Europe. Examples are Lufthansa'a Cologne and Frankfurt centers, and Sabena's center in Brussels, as well as FedEx's center at the former Clark Air Force Base at Subic Bay, Philippines; *see* Paul Stephen Dempsey & Laurence E. Gesell, *Air Transportation: Foundations for the 21st Century*, Ch. 7 (1997).

[12] James E. Sheppard, *The Wayports Concept*, an unpublished paper (spring 1989).

[13] Brian O'Donnell, *A New Course for the Future*, Tampa Tribune (Feb. 9, 1992), at 1.

The term, "wayport," is a meaningful derivation of "waypoint," the latter term being used by air traffic control and generally meaning a geographic fix that is off-set from the normal, published routes. Air traffic bypasses the published routes via waypoint fixes.[14] The wayport concept has been but one attempt at describing the future airport system, or improvement upon what otherwise has been referred to as the *fifth wave of economic infrastructure* development.

THE FIFTH WAVE

America's first great cities were the ports, where merchant ships from around the world brought goods.[15] These seaports were the *first wave* of economically related infrastructure development. Major rivers and canals linked cities to form the *second wave* of economic development. Railroad development prompted the *third wave*. The interstate highway system became the *fourth wave*, by shifting the mass movement of people and goods to cars and trucks. World-class international airports are the *fifth wave*, and although Samuel Skinner, former Secretary of Transportation in the George H.W. Bush administration, did not support the *wayport* concept *per se* (see *infra)*, he declared that in the 21st century, economic growth will indeed be dependent upon an adequate system of airports.[16] Full development of the fifth wave of infrastructure, whatever the airports might be called, must ultimately unlock the impending gridlock, in order to provide for the unimpeded transport of passengers and the globalization of economic transactions.

Full development of the fifth wave of economic infrastructure is yet to be adequately described. But it will have to be a system of international jetports that will spell relief for the existing system of origin/destination airports, and will link global commerce and transportation. One attempt at describing what the advanced fifth wave might look like was the wayport system. Although the term "wayport" was seemingly appropriate, the wayport concept proved highly controversial, in part because of confusing terminology, in part because of lack

---

[14] *See* FAA, *Air Traffic Control*, AC 7110.65G (Mar. 5, 1992), at 2-53, and G75.

[15] *See* John D. Kasarda, *A Global Air Cargo-Industrial Complex for the State of North Carolina* (1990); *see also* Donald D. Meyers, *Flying High: Arizona Could Become Major Transportation Hub*, Phoenix Gazette (Sep. 28, 1991), at A13.

[16] *See* Donald D. Meyers, *Flying High: Arizona Could Become Major Transportation Hub*, Phoenix Gazette (Sep. 28, 1991), at A13.

of common definition of how such an airport would operate, in part because of conservative resistance to a new concept, but mostly because the airlines opposed it. Consequently, it was not a concept embraced by the Reagan or Bush administrations.[17] Nevertheless, former Secretary of Transportation Skinner described the wayport concept ". . . as an industrial concept like Alliance."[18]

The new generation of international jet ports have been variously called "gateways," "superhubs," "global airports," "transfer hub airports," as well as "wayports," but the latter term has seemingly gained the most worldwide appeal to connote an altogether new system of airports. For purposes of describing the future system of airports, in this book the fifth wave of airport infrastructure development will be referred to simply by as "advanced fifth wave" airports. The advanced fifth wave is a global concept of airports, which would not only relieve airspace capacity constraints, but would support a new generation of supersonic/hypersonic aircraft and super-large transports.[19] The advanced fifth wave system could also relieve congestion and improve quality of life in the metropolitan areas—and do it at a fraction of the cost of improved navigation aids, added runways, or expanded hub airports.

Although seemingly put on hold by countervailing politics and an alternative airport site made available by the closing of Williams Air Force Base,[20] the Arizona Partnership for Air Transportation [APAT] suggested development of a fifth wave type of airport centrally located in Arizona. In its promotion of a new international jetport, APAT "chose" to call its proposal a "regional international airport"[21] Inclusion of the term "regional," however, was very misleading, if not overused. Unfortunately, the terminology APAT was using was too

---

[17] Transportation Research Board [TRB] Committee, *Airport System Capacity*, TRC Special Report 226 (1990).

[18] Staff, *FAA Panel Finds Little Near-Term Benefit in Wayports Concept*, Aviation Daily (Mar. 23, 1990).

[19] Boeing plans to build two larger, longer-range versions of the 747, which would be able to fly 8,500 nautical miles and carry 500 passengers in three-class seating (about 20% more than the 757-400). Boeing is also developing a stretch version of its 777, which will seat 550 people in single-class seating, and fly 5,700 nautical miles, which could replace many older 747s, which are less efficient to operate and maintain. Airbus Industrie also foresees a requirement for aircraft larger than the current 747 series. It forecasts a need for over 800 aircraft of 600 seats or more within the next 20 years; Paul Stephen Dempsey & Laurence E. Gesell, *Air Transportation: Foundations for the 21st Century* 86 (1997).

[20] Now called Williams Gateway Airport.

[21] *See* Donald D. Meyers, *Flying High: Arizona Could Become Major Transportation Hub*, Phoenix Gazette (Sep. 28, 1991), at A13.

reflective of an already existing system of airports wherein "regional" has come to mean a greater metropolitan region or a Standard Metropolitan Statistical Area [SMSA]. For example, Atlanta's Hartsfield International Airport, as well as airports in Orlando, Dallas-Fort Worth, Denver and Phoenix, can all be described as "regional international airports."[22] Yet, what APAT was really trying to create could more accurately be described as a futuristic concept, "the fifth wave" as it were, of economic infrastructure development.

Unfortunately, the national debate on wayports has concentrated on *location* rather than *function*. Nevertheless, future fifth wave airports, including wayports or whatever they may be called, should "function" so as to:

- Offer massive, low cost, long range, additional capacity to entire regions or multi-state areas;
- Off-load excess connecting operations from the growing number of congested airports (where use of such airports would be induced and there would be no forced segregation of origin and destination and transfer activities);
- Meet the operating needs of future operations of larger (1,000 seat), faster (supersonic, hypersonic), and potentially noisier aircraft;
- Meet the full operating needs of industry (with twenty-four hour operations, mail, small package and cargo handling, training flights, maintenance bases, and so forth);
- Provide site layout and fully zoned buffer areas for unlimited capacity expansion as, and when, needed;
- Be built in areas unconstrained by airspace, physical or environmental limitations;
- Provide for long-haul intercontinental operational capabilities;
- Strategically positioned in the national airspace and hub-and-spoke system to be attractive to primary users; and
- Developed with the latest state-of-the-art technology and design.

---

[22] *See id.*

Such new airports might be strategically located in the "metro-edge," just outside the metropolitan area served by one or more congested airports. They might be located at appropriate surplus military airfields near an emerging metropolitan area with sufficient near-by land where a large airport site might be located; other under-used airports (if thirty to forty-year long-range expansion can be provided at low cost); as well as in rural underdeveloped sites.[23]

Additionally, an advanced fifth wave airport could be a hub-and-spoke activity, remotely located to relieve high-density urban area terminals by removing connecting traffic. At major hubs like Dallas-Fort Worth, connecting traffic can account for up to 65% of total traffic.[24] Theoretically, airlines could perform connections without experiencing the flight delays and congestion associated with many of the existing large and medium hubs. Initially having small amounts of O&D traffic, if the new generation airports were, by design, wayports, they would need only minimal conventional airport facilities to start with. Because of these initial savings, fifth wave concept airports could be started for as little as one-third of the cost of a new conventional, metropolitan airport.[25]

Low-cost rural land would be utilized, and the fifth wave of infrastructure development would have almost unlimited long-range airport and airspace capacity since the configuration could be optimized with inexpensive land. Fifth wave airports could be staged at each location on an as-needed basis to meet evolving growth, but the acquisition of their land requirements from the outset would assure needed future airport capacity, and facilities sufficiently large to handle all new generations of aircraft.[26] Included would be 15,000 feet runways and one to two million pound pavement strengths to accommodate the next generation of larger and faster cargo and passenger aircraft.[27]

---

[23] Correspondence with James E. Sheppard (Jun. 25, 1992); *see also* Donald J. Reilly, *Challenge 2010: Planning for the U.S. Airport Capacity Needs of the Year 2010 and Beyond* (Feb. 4, 1992).

[24] Jacqueline Gallacher, *Wayports: A Way Out, Airline?*, Airline Business (Jul. 1989), at 38.

[25] James E. Sheppard, *The Wayports Concept*, an unpublished paper (spring 1989), at 3; *see also* Jacqueline Gallacher, *Wayports: A Way Out, Airline?*, Airline Business (Jul. 1989), at 38.

[26] *See* Donald J. Reilly, *Challenge 2010: Planning for the U.S. Airport Capacity Needs of the Year 2010 and Beyond* (Feb. 4, 1992), at 10.

[27] James E. Sheppard, *The Wayports Concept*, an unpublished paper (spring 1989), at 2; *see also* Donald J. Reilly, *Challenge 2010: Planning for the U.S. Airport Capacity Needs of the Year 2010 and Beyond* (Feb. 4, 1992), at 17.

As warranted by demand, eventually a ground infrastructure and other conventional facilities would have to be added to accommodate increases in O&D traffic and to develop the rudimentary airport to its full capacity. The facility could be built/expanded on an *as-needed* modular basis.[28] Envisioned in the infrastructure development would be tilt-rotor (or other vertical/short takeoff) aircraft, high-speed rail lines including magnetic levitation ("mag-lev") trains, and highway networks connecting the metropolitan areas and other hub airports with the new generation airport. With a high-speed infrastructure feeding the fifth wave airport, O&D traffic would not necessarily begin or end at the airport itself, but rather could originate/terminate at the terminal ends of the surface infrastructure, in the metropolitan centers or at hub airports.

To date, no airports strictly defined as wayports have been developed. The FAA in the past has "snubbed" the notion of wayports "with studied indifference."[29] Reportedly, there was no interest within the George H.W. Bush administration in funding a massive airport expansion program, nor any willingness to take on the political responsibility for determining the locations for a system of wayports.[30] Hence, the wayport concept was not well received either by the FAA or by the public. The FAA has allegedly refused to fund any projects called "wayports," and reportedly, the Arizona Partnership for Air Transportation (*supra*) "chose" to call its project a "regional international airport" because the Bush administration (acting through the FAA) would not fund it if APAT had called it a wayport proposal.

It is unfortunate, but the FAA's actions undoubtedly contributed to the confusion over wayport concept terminology. Additionally, the agency's lack of direction in formulating a policy around fifth wave infrastructure development has become a hindrance to progress in alleviating the constrained capacity problem confronting the air transportation industry. Not only did the Administration stonewall the

---

[28] Donald J. Reilly, *Challenge 2010: Planning for the U.S. Airport Capacity Needs of the Year 2010 and Beyond* (Feb. 4, 1992), at 17.

[29] Zack Binkley & James E. Castro, *Snubbing Wayports Flies in the Face of Sense*, Herald-Dispatch (Jul. 25, 1991), at A8.

[30] Ironically, the Federal Government did sponsor development of the Mid-America Airport near Lambert Field in Saint Louis, but across the river in Illinois. Mid-America was completed at a cost of more than $330 Million. Yet, two years later the brand new airport sat idle, unable to attract any airline service; *see* CNN Headline News (May 28, 1999). As 2007 the airport was served by only one airline, Allegiant Air; *see MidAmerica Home: St. Louis Airport,* http://www.flymidamerica.com/ (visited May 11, 2007).

wayport concept, but other reports indicate key congressmen may have been "sitting" on the wayport idea to protect the interests of local constituencies. At any rate, in 1990, a yearlong DOT-FAA study found that wayports would be impractical, and the concept seemingly became a moot issue within the agency.

The FAA study, however, was fundamentally flawed because it limited its evaluation of wayports to "near-term" (five to ten-year) benefits. Additionally, the FAA panel reportedly had no organizational meetings to review the "wayport concept," which was to be the primary focus of their study![31] It should be noted that wayports have always been advocated as a "long-term" concept, and a subsequent 1992 report (see *infra*),[32] which was contracted by the FAA, provided the FAA with the long-term industry recommendations.[33]

Irrespective of attempts to squelch the wayport idea per se, fifth wave concept airports are still very much alive, and have generally found worldwide acceptance. As Sheppard explains, one of aviation's worst fears is that it will indefinitely face artificial constraints caused by gridlock and delay, and the [wayport] concept presents one of the few viable alternatives to solving the impending problem.[34] This was reinforced in a 1992 report submitted to Leon Griggs, then FAA assistant administrator for airports.[35]

Congress, in its Airport and Airway Safety and Capacity Expansion Act of 1987, mandated that the Secretary of Transportation develop ". . . an overall airport system plan through the year 2010, which will assure the long-term availability of adequate airport system capacity." The final report was prepared by Donald Reilly, former president of the Airport Operators Council International [AOCI], with participation by representatives of airlines, airports, labor and general aviation. The Report concluded that, other than building new

[31] Staff, *FAA Airport Capacity Panel Fails to Hold Promised Meetings*, Aviation Daily (Dec. 5, 1989), at 419; *see also* Staff, *FAA Panel Finds Little Near-Term Benefit in Wayports Concept*, Aviation Daily (Mar. 23, 1990), at 573.

[32] *See also* Donald J. Reilly, *Challenge 2010: Planning for the U.S. Airport Capacity Needs of the Year 2010 and Beyond* (Feb. 4, 1992).

[33] Correspondence with James E. Sheppard (Jun. 25, 1992).

[34] James E. Sheppard, *Wayports: A Concept Whose Time Has Come*, Airport Services Management (May 1989); *see also* Donald R. Cress, *The Issue of Wayports*, a paper presented to the Aeronautics & Space Engineering Board, Commission on Engineering & Technical Systems, National Research Council (Oct. 18-19, 1990), at 1.

[35] *See* Donald J. Reilly, *Challenge 2010: Planning for the U.S. Airport Capacity Needs of the Year 2010 and Beyond* (Feb. 4, 1992); *see also* Staff, *Report to FAA Recommends Wayports as Best Way to Meet Long-Term Needs*, Aviation Daily (Feb. 20, 1992).

airports in metropolitan areas, no other approach ". . . appears capable of fully handling the 200% to, perhaps, 300% increase in air travel demand that could develop by the year 2010 or soon thereafter," than the wayport concept.[36]

The synopsis of Jim Sheppard's argument is that new airports are needed, but where or how will they be built?[37] Suggested by Mr. Sheppard in his wayport concept, and reinforced by arguments made in this chapter for the development of fifth wave airports, coupled with private investment, is at least one answer—if not the most viable solution—to provide additional air transportation infrastructure capacity for an evolving air transport system.

EVOLVING AIRLINE INDUSTRY STRUCTURE

In the first decade of the New Millennium, the air transportation industry was struggling to recover from the worst economic crisis in its entire history, the trauma of which was brought on by a series of setbacks that began with airline deregulation, followed by a rash of consumer complaints and safety concerns, constrained airport capacity resulting in inordinate traffic delays, economic recessions and spikes in oil prices, two wars in the Middle East, and topped off by acts of terrorism around the world and a system now constrained by heightened alert and enhanced security procedures. In the process several traditional hub-and-spoke airlines have been brought to the very brink of extinction. In the meantime, a new low cost modeled emerged to challenge the old. Yet the new, low-cost point-to-point model is only a partial answer. But whether the Majors "can shift focus fast enough to survive" remains a serious question.[38] What this means for airports is reflected in the old adage, "As aerospace goes, so go the airlines." Or likewise, "As the airlines go, so goes the airports."[39]

Anthony Velocci suggests that we should "Say goodbye to the U.S. airline industry as we know it. A dramatic transformation is un-

---

[36] Donald J. Reilly, *Challenge 2010: Planning for the U.S. Airport Capacity Needs of the Year 2010 and Beyond* (Feb. 4, 1992), at 16-17.

[37] James E. Sheppard, *Wayports: A Concept Whose Time Has Come*, Airport Services Management (May 1989).

[38] Anthony Velocci, Jr., *Can Majors Shift Focus Fast Enough to Survive?*, Av. Wk. & Space Tech. (Nov. 18, 2002), at 52.

[39] This section draws heavily from Laurence E. Gesell & Paul Stephen Dempsey, *Air Transportation: Foundations for the 21st Century* 454-476 (2005).

derway, although it still may be imperceptible to most of the flying public."[40] And as Edmund S. Greenslet, head of ESG Aviation Services, submits, "The domestic airline landscape is changing before our eyes, and the consequences for the traditional airlines are only beginning to be felt."[41] In effect, what is emerging is an air transportation system comprised of six principal market niches:

- Long haul hub-and-spoke carriers;
- Short haul point-to-point carriers;
- All cargo carriers;
- Regional carriers;
- Air charter networks; and a
- Small Aircraft Transportation System [SATS].[42]

Accepting that the new and evolving air transport structure will be comprised of the above groupings, reasonable domestic market share assumptions for each of the passenger enplanement segments could conceivably be as follows: long haul hub-and-spoke carriers 45%; short haul point-to-point carriers 25%; regional carriers 20%; with air charter networks and SATS sharing the remaining 10%.[43]

Rather than concluding that some new form of airport development is likewise inevitable, might there not be some way to more efficiently use already existing, yet underutilized infrastructure assets? To this end, Sam Hoerter provides some insight by suggesting that the introduction of regional jets represents such a "break with tradition."[44] In fact, operators of the regional jets have already brought about a reconfiguration of the air transportation route system. The Low Cost Carriers [LCCs] are also contributing to change.

There is no "silver bullet" for the airlines' dilemma, nor is it clear what direction the airline industry is taking. However, there are some indications as to what form it may take. As Robert Crandall suggests, "New low cost carriers have already figured out how to make the business efficient and profitable. Now all they need is a little more

---

[40] *Id.*
[41] *Id.*
[42] *See* Laurence E. Gesell & Paul Stephen Dempsey, *Air Transportation: Foundations for the 21st Century* 454-476 (1997).
[43] *Id.*
[44] Sam Hoerter, *A Break With Tradition*, Airport Magazine (Jul./Aug. 1998).

competition."[45] What follows is a description of the evolving airline industry.

FULL SERVICE CARRIERS

As the "airline crisis" slowly ebbs around the world, the profile of a revamped industry is in some ways taking shape along familiar lines.[46] In other respects it may look nothing like the past. Keith Johnson suggests that "[major] airlines are fretting about budget rivals and security fears. But the biggest threat to improving profits may be their own addiction to flooding the market with flights and bigger planes packed with more seats"[47]—a process known in the industry as "capacity dumping." With prospects for increased demand, Asian, European and U.S. carriers all introduced routes, increased frequency of service and added more seats in their schedules. Most full-service carriers increased capacity on long-haul international routes, which is the market the low cost carriers are least likely to penetrate. The so-called Southwest model is not the one that best fits what Robert Crandall describes as the "long-haul niche." Although critics contend that the large hub-and-spoke system is flawed, Crandall maintains it is here to stay,[48] as did Leo Mullin, former Chief Executive Officer [CEO] of Delta.[49] It is the only viable model for the full service carriers. Even so, Crandall concedes that hubs will become less important. And now that the overriding factor in airline choice is pricing, not connection time or frequency, Crandall predicts "Legacy carriers will inevitably wish to allocate more aircraft to point-to-point flying."[50] This shift away from the hub-and-spoke airports to direct flights has been described as "fragmentation" of the industry.

However, "when people say the (hub-and-spoke) model is broken, they're moving their jaw without putting their brain in gear," states Crandall. There are 5,500 to 6,000 city pairs in the U.S., of which no more that 500 will support non-stop service. By his reckoning that's less than 10% of the domestic market. But Crandall is speaking more

---

[45] Robert Crandall, *Out of a Tailspin: A Recipe for Airline Rescue*, Wall St. J. (Tues., Dec. 10, 2002).
[46] *See* James Ott, *Change, Or Else!*, Av. Wk. & Space Tech. (Jul. 21, 2003), at 55.
[47] Keith Johnson, *Flying in the Face of Doubt*, Wall St. J. (Thurs., Mar. 11, 2004), at B2.
[48] Robert Crandall, *Out of a Tailspin: A Recipe for Airline Rescue*, Wall St. J. (Tues., Dec. 10, 2002).
[49] Leo Mullin, Speaking to the Aero Club of Washington, D.C. (Jun. 19, 2003).
[50] Frances Fiorino, *Man with a Plan*, Av. Wk. & Space Tech. (Sep. 27, 2004), at 45.

from the perspective of the full service airline manager than that of the low cost or regional carrier. It depends upon the size and efficiency of the aircraft being utilized versus the market demand. Crandall's point of reference is the market that can generate at least 100 passengers a day. For a carrier operating large jet aircraft (meaning 100 seats or more) such as the full service carriers, then the relative market for direct service is restricted to the size of the aircraft.

Leo Mullin suggests that of the 30,000 city-pair markets where air service is currently available, only 5% have adequate traffic to support non-stop, point-to-point flights. The other 95%, he says can only be served through the hub-and-spoke system, with its ability to gather and consolidate traffic.[51] Like Crandall, Mullin is speaking of another paradigm. His assessment of the point-to-point potential is incorrect if one considers smaller, more efficient aircraft to fit the market.

Nevertheless, consensus has suggested that the direct, low fare niche market consists of about 20% of the supposedly hub-and-spoke market. Yet, the low fare carriers have captured roughly 30% of the market to date and they continue to push the envelope out. But the low fare carriers are seemingly up against the outer limits of their niche. If this is indeed the case, which has not necessarily been empirically demonstrated, then 60% to 70% of the market ostensibly will have to be maintained by the full service carriers, and via the hub-and-spoke model.

Crandall is "skeptical that the industry will ever be competitive as long as there are so many carriers selling what has evolved into a commodity product, of which there is an excess for the sake of customer convenience."[52] Conventional wisdom is suggesting that failing airlines should be allowed to fail. And in the process, the industry should consolidate naturally until airline capacity reaches actual demand.[53] Given that the airlines can control their appetites for expanded market share and can bring excess capacity under control, it is assumed that if costs can be brought in line with the LCCs, the full service carriers could become profitable. Perhaps the majors would be well advised to stay within their long haul, hub-and-spoke niche. But their compulsion to produce excess capacity would appear to be insatiable. The Majors seem determined to hold on to the lion's share of

---

[51] Leo Mullin, Speaking to the Aero Club of Washington, D.C. (Jun. 19, 2003).

[52] Robert Crandall, *Crandall's Rx for Airlines*, Av. Wk. & Space Tech. (Nov. 18, 2002), at 54.

[53] *See* Editorial, *Courageous Steps Required to Reform Airlines*, Av. Wk. & Space Tech. (Nov. 18, 2002), at 82.

the market, at the expense of becoming everything to everybody. Look for example at the restructuring of United Airlines domestically and Qantas Airlines internationally. In the process of restructuring these two airlines one gets a glimpse at a future airline industry, which is segmented into the variety of niches identified above.

AIRLINES WITHIN AIRLINES

United has looked at three separate "segments" or "niches" to provide a "family of products" to meet customers' different and "relevant" needs.[54] The first tier is the traditional full-service hub-and-spoke system. The second tier "airline within an airline" is Ted, which is a direct, low-cost carrier to compete head-to-head with other low cost Southwest type competitors. The third tier system is United Express and its affiliates, to compete with other Regional carriers and to feed United's hub-and-spoke system. Ironically, United tried the airline-within-an-airline concept in the early 1990s, then jettisoned it as unprofitable, brand diluting, and distracting; as did Continental and US Airways. It is unclear why Ted will succeed where other such experiments have failed, but United is committed.

Qantas is even more diversified. Under CEO Geoff Dixon, Australia's largest and the world's second oldest airline dating back to 1920 has undergone a fundamental transformation from an integrated airline into five segmented carriers.[55] Qantas International and Domestic is the core operation and includes Qantas Freight. QantasLink is comprised of four separate regional airlines: Airlink, Eastern Australia Airlines, Sunstate Airlines and Impulse Airlines. Australian Airlines is a full-service, international leisure (or charter) carrier that commenced operation in 2002. Another carrier-within-a-carrier is Jetstar, which is a domestic low cost carrier, largely modeled after Southwest Airlines in the U.S. but operating Airbus A320 equipment rather than Boeing 737 airplanes. As an added amenity, the A320s are equipped with all leather seats. Jetstar began operations in May of 2004.[56]

According to Geoff Dixon, Qantas wants "to be one of the airlines that takes part in *consolidation* [of the industry]."[57] What Dixon is

---

[54] *See* Susan Carey, *UAL Strategy Chief Outlines Plans*, Wall St. J. (Fri., Dec. 13, 2002).
[55] Jens Flottau, *New Horizons*, Av. Wk. & Space Tech. (Jul. 12, 2004), at 42.
[56] *See* Qantas, *Subsidiary Companies*, http://www.qantas.com.au (visited Jul. 21, 2004).
[57] Jens Flottau, *New Horizons*, Av. Wk. & Space Tech. (Jul. 12, 2004), at 42 (emphasis supplied).

calling a "consolidated" industry is another way of describing what a new "restructured" airline industry might look like. But there is another dimension to the new and evolving air transport system, particularly in the U.S. but internationally as well, which must be included to round out the vision. *Airports* form the terminal ends of the air transport system. Passengers begin and end their journeys at airports.

In the United States, most trips begin at one of the airports in the National Plan of Integrated Airport Systems [NPIAS]. Around the globe, international passengers board aircraft at a comparable national airport within their own countries. Airports, like the air transportation system in general, are important to everyone, and not just to the direct consumers of aviation services. Airports are the gateways to commerce and to the modern transportation world.

In the U.S. alone there were 19,847 total U.S. airports in 2006. Of the 19,000 plus facilities, 5,261 were open to the public. Of the airports open to the public, 3,431 are included in the 2007-2011 NPIAS and considered significant to national air transportation. And of the NPIAS airports, 517 are "commercial service airports," defined as "public airports receiving scheduled passenger service and having 2,500 or more enplaned passengers per year."[58]

Since the advent of airline deregulation in 1978, the "airport-as-a-market" has become more dominant than the existence of service by any one airline. Deregulation radically changed the market climate of the airlines, and the air transport industry, including airports. Rather than having government dictate where air transport markets might best be served, greater reliance was placed upon a more natural evolution of the economic marketplace.

The airlines responded to the economic freedom by attempting to rationalize the marketplace to their own advantage. Deregulation led the carriers to want two things—market dominance and lower cost of operation.[59] A phenomenon associated with airline deregulation has been the creation of new tools of competition. After price competition, the principal instrument of competition coming out of deregulation has been the hub-and-spoke concept.[60] Thornton called it the primary "weapon of war" in the unleashed competition following de-

---

[58] FAA, *National Plan of Integrated Airport Systems 2007-2011*, report to Congress (Sep. 29, 2006).

[59] Karen Walker, *Bespoke Fortunes*, Airline Business (Jan. 1997), at 35.

[60] *See id.* at 451-457.

regulation.[61] Some call them "fortress hubs," where a single airline controls the lion's share of gates, takeoff and landing slots, and passengers, and smothers new entrants with additional frequency, capacity, and acres of discounted seats.[62]

THE HUB-AND-SPOKE SYSTEM

The hub-and-spoke system has been an economic strategy designed to capture a greater share of the market. Using the hub-and-spoke system, the airline can put far more cities into its system and it can effectively capture passengers by making it difficult and expensive for them not to use the hub airline's services.[63] But airline hubs are bottleneck connections travelers must transit when they fly to their destinations.

"Hubbing," as it has been called, results from airlines offering large numbers of connecting flights to other cities from a few "hub" airports. It came about because the airlines found the hub allowed them to take advantage of network and scale economies, while offering frequent service to a geometrically increasing array of city-pair markets.[64] Plugging networks together in regional, national and global code-sharing alliances is yet another way to expand the array of origin/destination city-pairs available on any given hypothetical airline.

Hubbing is a corporate strategy where large airlines dominate traffic at many airports by forming hub-and-spoke networks. A carrier uses spoke flights, flown by its own planes or those of smaller regional lines that major airlines control through purchase or agreement, to generate passenger flow for flights to and from its hub operations. The introduction of regional jets is now enlarging the "catchment" area around strategic hubs to 500 nautical miles. The network creates sizable economies that inhibit entry into hub markets by competitors. The captive origin-and-destination passenger provides a stable base on which carriers may load fixed costs, while consumers complain of "monopoly pricing at fortress hubs."

---

[61] R.L Thornton, *Airlines and Agents: Conflict and the Public Welfare*, J. of Air Law & Commerce (1986), at 52.

[62] *See* Paul Dempsey, *Predatory Pricing & Monopolization in the Airline Industry: A Case Study of Minneapolis/St. Paul*, Trans. L. J. (2002), at 29; Paul Dempsey, *Predation, Competition & Antitrust Law: Turbulence in the Airline Industry*, J. of Air Law & Commerce (2002), at 67.

[63] Barbara Byer, in Karen Walker, *Bespoke Fortunes*, Airline Business (Jan. 1997), at 35.

[64] Adib Kanafani & Atef Ghobrial, *Airline Hubbing—Some Implications for Airport Economics*, an unpublished seminar paper (1984).

The "hub-and-spoke" should not be confused with the DOT categorization of the airport hub system based on demographics. But in a study of 43 airports falling under the FAA's "large-hub" classification, the U.S. Government Accounting Office found fares to be generally "much higher" in 1995 at the 10 airports that are either affected by operational constraints or where one airline accounts for the vast majority of enplanements. High fares at fortress hubs have been well reported, but the solutions are less well documented. The indisputable fact remains that the hub-and-spoke concept is now so deeply established that any fundamental change would be extremely controversial and difficult to bring about.[65]

The airlines argue that the hub-and-spoke system offers convenience and access to city-pairs that otherwise might not be viable markets.[66] This, they say, translates into convenience for the customer and higher yields to the airline.[67]

Before deregulation, while Atlanta (for Delta) and Pittsburgh (for Allegheny, now US Airways), were moderately concentrated, no airline dominated more than 45% of the capacity or market share of any major airport in the United States (as measured by gates, passengers, or takeoffs and landings). Subsequent to deregulation, airlines began consolidating their operations around hub-and-spoke networks. These networks soon accounted for 70% of the flights offered by domestic airlines.[68] Capacity concerns were exacerbated as the infrastructure of gates and landing slots at the major airports became consumed by the dominant carriers, leaving little room for significant new entry.[69]

Strategically located hubs allow carriers to blanket the nation (even the globe) with ubiquitous service. For example, United established hubs at Chicago, Denver, San Francisco, and Washington, D.C.

---

[65] Karen Walker, *Bespoke Fortunes*, Airline Business (Jan. 1997), at 32.

[66] *Id.*

[67] "Yield" means the air transport revenue per unit of traffic carried in air transportation. It may be calculated and presented several ways (*e.g.*, passenger revenue per passenger mile, per aircraft mile, per passenger ton mile and per passenger. *See* Paul Stephen Dempsey & Laurence E. Gesell, *Air Transportation, Foundations for the 21st Century* 566 (1997).

[68] *American-Sponsored Study Blasts Criticism of Hubs*, Aviation Daily (Jul. 31, 1990), at 197.

[69] 88% of the gates at the 66 largest U.S. airports are leased to airlines, and 85% of the leases are for exclusive use; *Intelligence*, Aviation Daily (Aug. 20, 1990), at 323. Some upstarts have focused on the remaining, smaller airports. In the early 1980s, America West focused on Phoenix and Las Vegas. In the 1990s, WesternPacific began operations at Colorado Springs, and American Trans Air focused operations on Indianapolis. Several major carriers (*i.e.*, TWA, Braniff and Eastern) unsuccessfully attempted to establish a hub at Kansas City. In the 1990s, upstart Vanguard Airlines also focused operations at Kansas City; *see* Aviation Daily (Jan. 30, 1996), at 150. Many of these experiments failed because of inadequate local O&D traffic base.

(Dulles). American Airlines developed hubs at Chicago, Dallas/Ft. Worth, Miami, San Juan, San Jose, Nashville, and Raleigh/Durham, and assumed the St. Louis hub when it absorbed Trans World Airlines [TWA]. Delta built hubs at Atlanta, Dallas/Ft. Worth, Salt Lake City, and Cincinnati. Northwest has hubs at Detroit, Minneapolis/St. Paul and Memphis.

By the late1990s, legacy airlines controlled more than half the enplanements at more than half of 50 largest airports in the United States.[70] However, as the hub-and-spoke phenomenon takes on less importance in the age of pricing over frequency and/or connection, an increasingly larger share of total enplanements is being given up to low-cost and regional point-to-point carriers that increasingly are bypassing the hubs and disseminating traffic to other non-hub airports.

To counter the loss, and stay competitive the majors are themselves starting to provide more direct flights, and in smaller aircraft. United and Delta turned to airlines-within-airlines with Ted and Song respectively. American, on the other hand, has reduced flights and now spreads its schedules out rather than bunching them closely together at hubs. Moreover, American has managed to cut its costs and increase its aircraft utilization to bring it more in line with Southwest and other low cost carriers. In addition American in some cases has customized its aircraft (such as the MD-80) to fit the market better. By more closely adapting to the LCC model American, alone amongst the legacy carriers, was able to claw its way back to profitability in the second quarter of 2004.[71]

The trend is global and dynamic. Economic recession in the 1980s prompted airlines to wind down many smaller, less efficient hubs (American Airlines jettisoned Nashville, Raleigh/Durham, San Jose and St. Louis, Delta at Dallas for example). The economics of the early 21st century are forcing further restructuring. Downsizing a hub is a painful process. Every spoke eliminated deprives other spokes of traffic feed, causing the synergies of the hub to unravel.[72] Nevertheless, airline management must be sufficiently agile to withdraw from markets which are producing unsatisfactorily, and re-deploy resources

---

[70] *See generally* Paul Stephen Dempsey & Laurence E. Gesell, *Airline Management: Strategies for the 21st Century* 200-215 (1997).

[71] Scott McCartney, *Hit Hard by Low-Cost Airlines, AMR Tries Behaving Like One*, Wall St. J. (Jun. 7, 2004), at A1.

[72] James Hirsch, *Big Airlines Scale Back Hub-Airport System To Curb Rising Costs*, Wall St. J., (Jan. 12, 1993), at A1, A6.

to more lucrative markets. Brian Harris, vice president at Wall Street's Lehman Brothers, concludes the industry remains "over-hubbed" and would be more (economically) efficient if there were fewer, larger-sized hubs. Hub economics work better (i.e., are more profitable) where there are larger (and fewer) hubs in big cities.[73]

Hubbing is advantageous (to airline operators) because it allows enhanced marketing opportunities via geometric proliferation of city-pair markets that can be served. The number of passengers enjoys a corresponding exponential growth, while labor staffing increases at a much more moderate rate.[74] Figure 16.1, "Hub-and-Spoke vs. Linear Route Model," shows the advantages of the hub-and-spoke system over linear routes by increasing the city pairs served (in this particular model) from 6 to 36 through the hub city, "H."[75]

To work, a hub must have a large number of flights ("banks," as they are called) from a large number of origins converging at an airport in close time proximity, so that passengers can readily transfer to flights departing to an equally large number of destinations. This requires a large number of gates and ground personnel. Nevertheless, significant network economies may be achieved via hubbing.

While good for the airlines and the airports that serve them, both origin/destination and many connecting passengers pay a yield premium for the frequent service hubbing allows. At the concentrated "fortress hub," consumption of airport infrastructure often translates into higher yields. The most attractive airports from a financial standpoint are congested hubs near large business communities. The more congested the airport, the scarcer the air transportation resource becomes. And, scarce resources lead to higher prices.[76] Yields at concentrated airports are more than 20% higher per mile for passengers who begin or end their trips there than at un-concentrated airports.[77]

---

[73] *See* Karen Walker, *U.S. Hubs Need to be Consolidated*, Airline Business (Feb. 1998), at 74.

[74] Dan Reed, *American Eagle* 157 (1992).

[75] Paul Stephen Dempsey & Laurence E. Gesell, *Airline Management: Strategies for the 21st Century* 206-208 (1997).

[76] Alexander ter Kuile, *Hub Fever*, Airline Business (Dec. 1997), at 67.

[77] General Accounting Office [GAO], *Airline Competition: Higher Fares and Reduced Competition at Concentrated Airports* (1990).

Figure 16.1—HUB-AND-SPOKE vs. LINEAR ROUTE MODEL (Hypothetical Route Structure to Serve Nine Cities)

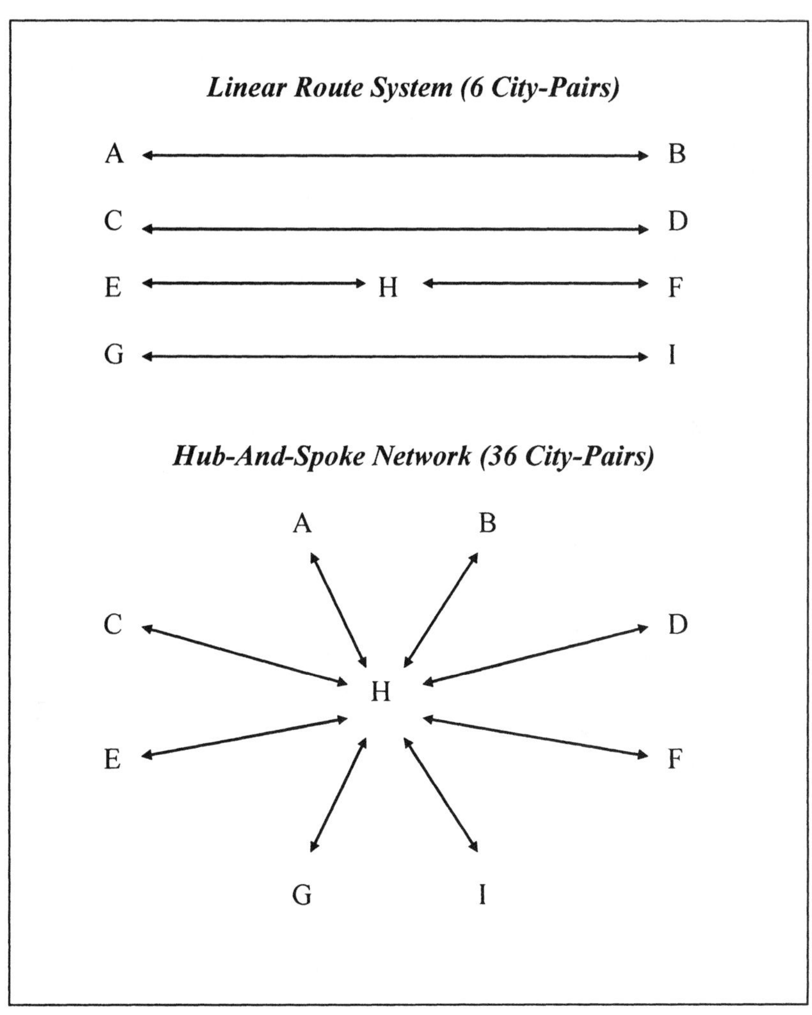

Source: Laurence E. Gesell & Paul Stephen Dempsey, *Airline Management: Strategies for the 21st Century* 207 (1997).

Airlines with more gates, takeoff and landing slots (at capacity constrained airports), and/or code sharing agreements charge significantly higher prices than those without.[78] In fact, flights at airports where *majority-in-interest clauses*[79] reduce expansion opportunities result in 3% higher fares; flights at slot controlled airports result in 7% higher fares; and carriers with code-sharing arrangements charge 8% higher fares.[80] An airline, which doubles the number of its gates, enjoys a 3.5% increase in fares.[81]

Hubbing also results in a yield premium for certain connecting markets, particularly for city-pairs less than 1,500 miles in distance, and for smaller cities without multiple hub connections. Some hub carriers have learned to focus on this high-yield connecting traffic, and avoid the local O&D price wars with low cost airlines.[82]

International carriers also employ their gateways as venues for *sixth freedom* [83] connecting traffic. For example, royal Dutch Airlines puts enough capacity on the North Atlantic to transport the entire population of the Netherlands to the United States in a single summer. Most of the traffic is funneled through its hub at Amsterdam Shiphol, from or to points beyond.

Nevertheless, hubbing sacrifices equipment and labor utilization and consumes more fuel than a linear route system in markets sufficiently dense to support nonstop service. Clearly also, the United States is over hubbed by duplicative parallel route networks connecting virtually every conceivable city-pair market. To trim costs and reduce capacity, carriers in the 1990s began downsizing or closing

---

[78] In 1985, before the DOT decreed these public resources could be bought and sold at market, the 8 largest airlines controlled only 70% of the slots. The success of consolidation and the hub-and-spoke strategy reached a peak in 1988 when the eight largest U.S. airlines controlled 96% of the landing and takeoff slots at the four slot-constrained airports (i.e., Chicago O'Hare, Washington National, and New York's Kennedy and LaGuardia). GAO, *Airline Competition: Industry Operating and Marketing Practices Limit Market Entry* 4 (1990).

[79] *I.e.*, documents allowing airline control over some key airport decisions.

[80] Paul Dempsey, Robert Hardaway & William Thoms, *Aviation Law & Regulation* § 5.05 (1993). GAO, Testimony of Kenneth Mead before the Aviation Subcommittee of the U.S. Senate Commerce Committee 6 (Apr. 5, 1990).

[81] *Id.* at 6.

[82] Maurice Myers, Address before the Salomon Brothers Transportation Conference, New York, N.Y. (Nov. 17, 1994).

[83] *Sixth freedom* is the right to carry traffic between two foreign countries via its own country of registry. Sixth freedom can also be viewed as a combination of third and fourth freedoms secured by the country of registry from two different countries. *Third freedom* is the right to carry traffic from its country of registry to another country. *Fourth freedom* is the right to carry traffic from another country to its own country of registry.

selected hubs. The net effect of giving up the smaller hub operations was to become entrenched in the remaining larger hubs. The major airlines are now relying more than ever on their "fortress hubs."

By the mid-1990s, U.S. domestic commercial aviation had divided itself into two dominant types of service providers: (1) the *ubiquitous network hub carriers* (e.g., United, American, Delta, Northwest) emphasizing connecting traffic; and (2) the *short-haul nonstop point-to-point carriers* (e.g., Southwest) focusing on O&D traffic.[84] Internationally as well, new long-haul point-to-point carriers have emerged (e.g., Virgin Atlantic) to compete along side the established international network carriers (e.g., British Airways).

Hub-and-spoke networks significantly altered the air transportation route structure. The major airlines overloaded large-hub airports, while leaving many airports that did not integrate into their hub systems without regular airline service.[85] Nearly 70% of all domestic passengers are enplaned at the 31 large-hub primary airports. Large and medium hubs combined enplane almost 90% of the domestic enplanements.[86] Large airports are left with air traffic and airspace capacity constraints, while smaller airports go looking for air carrier service.[87] But the trend of consolidating into few large hub airports is currently being reversed, starting with the introduction of regional jets. The downside is that those same airports that were capacity constrained before by hub-and-spoke operations are now constrained even further by increased numbers of smaller aircraft.

[84] Southwest type operations embrace a point-to-point linear route system, which allows more productive equipment and labor utilization, and more efficient fuel consumption than does a hubbed operation. Southwest avoids congested airports, focusing instead on secondary airports in many markets, thereby allowing a quick turn around time (15 minutes is the goal).

[85] *See generally* Melvin A. Brenner, James O. Leet & Elihu Schott, *Airline Deregulation* (1985).

[86] FAA, Report to Congress; *National Plan of Integrated Airport Systems 2001-2005*, (Aug. 28, 2002).

[87] The FAA considers an airport congested when average delay per aircraft is in excess of five minutes. In 2000 there were 18 airports that accounted for most of the severe air traffic delays in the U.S.: New York LaGuardia, Newark Int'l., Philadelphia Int'l., Atlanta Harstfield, Boston Logan, New York John F. Kennedy, Detroit Metropolitan, Chicago O'Hare, Dallas-Ft. Worth, Washington Dulles, Minneapolis-St. Paul, St. Louis Int'l., Los Angeles Int'l., San Francisco Int'l., Phoenix Sky Harbor, Miami Int'l., Houston George Bush, and Cincinnati-No. Kentucky Int'l. FAA, Report to Congress; *National Plan of Integrated Airport Systems 2001-2005*, (Aug. 28, 2002).

REGIONAL JETS

The evolving system is further segmenting the marketplace into niche markets and at the same time is looking to recapture airport capacity lost as the Majors concentrated on development of the hub-and-spoke system. The introduction of regional jets opened the prospect of serving the "real needs" of many forgotten travelers who move between cities that generate fewer than 100 passengers a day each way. Sam Hoerter points out that "Traditional jetliners from previous generations were vastly oversized for the markets and, consequently, airline operators were forced to devise specific operating strategies to match these large aircraft to smaller markets."[88] Hence, there developed the notion that few markets could be served efficiently (via the hub-and-spoke strategy). The airplane came first, and passenger behavior was then molded to fit the product. Hoerter predicted that the Regional Jet [RJ] represented "such a break with past tradition that the future [held] the potential to be very different from the past."[89] And, indeed it has. The potential for direct, point-to-point service is greater. And, the number of viable city-pairs has been expanded for the hub-and-spoke operators. The prospect of the former could relieve airport congestion, but with the latter the potential for gridlock is only compounded.

FRACTIONAL OWNERSHIP

Congestion, delays and other passenger inconveniences associated with the airline crisis have sent many business travelers looking for alternatives. Where able, corporations are turning to ownership and operation of their own aircraft. Because business aircraft have access to more than just the 546 scheduled air carrier airports, not only can executives travel when and where they want and spend less time doing it, there are other business advantages as well. The introduction of corporate jets into the air transport system also translates into more privatization opportunities in the development of private terminal facilities to service the business traveler.

A study by Arthur Anderson consultants indicates total shareholder returns for large-capitalization companies that operate aircraft

---

[88] Sam Hoerter, *A Break with Tradition*, Airport Magazine (Jul./Aug. 1998), at 6.
[89] *Id.*

exceeds the returns generated by non-operators by 141%. For small capitalization companies, it is 92%. Among the Standard and Poor's [S&P] 500 companies sales growth is nearly double that of non-operators.[90] As a result, sales of business aircraft set a blistering pace between 2000 and 2002.

New options emerged in the form of fractional ownership that allows corporate travelers—fed up with hassles of commercial flights—to hop into the private-jet market.[91] By 2003 sales began to taper off but the potential for the fractional business market remains undeveloped.[92] Between 1998 and 2002 the fleet of fractionally owned aircraft grew by 182%.[93] Honeywell Aerospace is upbeat about the future. By 2012, Honeywell expects the fractional ownership fleet to comprise 10% of the active business aircraft worldwide, up from about 6% in 2003. Fractional ownership is also taking root in Europe. Executive Jet Aviation's NetJets Europe began service in 1997.[94]

In addition to fractional ownership the business climate is upbeat for air taxi charters in corporate-type jet aircraft as well. However, there has existed an unfair market advantage in favor of the fractional operators. Comparing fractional ownership programs to air taxi operations is much like time-share condominium ownership versus the rental of hotel suites. The former is exclusive while the latter is available to the public in common. Fractional ownership operations are similar to fly-for-hire air taxis but not subject to the same rules. Air taxis operate under Federal Aviation Regulation [FAR] Part 135, "Operating Requirements: Commuter and On-Demand Operations." Fractionals may operate under the less stringent requirements of FAR Part 91, "General Operating and Flight Rules."[95] The FAA considers

---

[90] *See* Anthony Velocci, Jr., *Booming Bizjet Market Tied to Practical Benefits*, Av. Wk. & Space Tech. (Oct. 16, 2000).

[91] Susan Carey, *Fare Wars Hit the Jet Set: Sharing a Plane for Less*, Wall St. J. (Oct. 23, 2002), at D1.

[92] Anthony Velocci, Jr., *Where Biz Aviation is Going*, Av. Wk. & Space Tech. (Oct. 6, 2003), at 36-37.

[93] Anthony Velocci, Jr., *Bizjet Fractional Ownership Remains Relatively Strong*, Av. Wk. & Space Tech. (Sep. 9, 2002), at 61.

[94] Edward H. Phillips, *Fractional Ownership Taking Root in Europe*, Av. Wk. & Space Tech. (Jul. 24, 2000), at 194.

[95] To make the operations more compatible and to bring fractional ownership more under control by the FAA, in 2000 the Administration chartered the Fractional Ownership Aviation Rulemaking Committee [FOARC]. The committee was comprised of 27 officials representing fractional ownership program managers and owners, on-demand charter operators, aircraft manufacturers, corporate flight departments, traditional aircraft management companies, aircraft financing and insurance companies, and industry trade associations to make recommendations

most FAR Part 91 operations as "non-commercial," while FAR Part 135 operations are "commercial" and therefore more restrictive.[96]

Warren Buffet, chairman of Executive Jet parent company Berkshire Hathaway, projected the fractional market could reach 20,000 owners domestically.[97] NetJets, the industry leader, is a unit of Berkshire Hathaway. So dynamic has been the growth industry that it has caused certain airlines to test the waters, although two pulled out of the market—at least for the time being. For example, American Airlines' parent company AMR bailed out in 1997 after deciding to stick through the crisis to its core airline operation.[98]

When AMR dropped the initiative, former AMR CEO Robert Crandall and Donald Burr, founder of now-defunct low-fare airline People Express, picked up the gauntlet by founding the Burr/Crandall Air Taxi Company to provide private, on-demand, point-to-point air transportation. Reportedly the company has ordered 75 Adam Aircraft A700 AdamJet twin-engine airplanes.[99] Burr and Crandall named their "next-generation air taxi operation," Pogo, saying, "We wanted to find a name that would suggest both 'unconventional' and 'approachable,' one that conveys the idea of quickly "hopping" from one place to another." Donald Burr will be the CEO of Pogo.[100]

United Airlines' holding company, UAL, placed a huge $1.25 billion order for 35 business jets from General Dynamics Corporation's Gulfstream Aerospace to launch its Avolar subsidiary. UAL probably miscalculated how much money would be required to make the operation viable and subsequently cancelled the order. Besides financial-related considerations, timing also became a factor and UAL

---

for regulatory oversight of the growing corporate-type air transport sector. Recommendations from FOARC resulted in a Notice of Proposed Rulemaking [NPRM] for modifications to both FAR Part 91, Subpart K and to FAR Part 135 that will become effective Feb. 17, 2005. Under the revised rules the fractionals will be subject to slightly more restrictive rules while the rules governing the air taxis will be slightly less restrictive. *See* John Croft, *Fractional Ruling Promises Air Taxi Bonus*, Av. Wk. & Space Tech. (Aug. 6, 2001), at 62.

[96] Barbara Cook, *The Factions of Fractional Ownership*, Airport Magazine (Jul./Aug. 2000), at 40-42.

[97] *Id.*

[98] Susan Carey, *Fare Wars Hit the Jet Set: Sharing a Plane for Less*, Wall St. J. (Oct. 23, 2002) at D1.

[99] The A700 first flew in Jul. 2003 and by May 2004 had accumulated more than 150 hours of flight testing toward FAA certification, which is tentatively scheduled for the first quarter of 2005. *See* Av. Wk. & Space Tech. (May 31, 2004), at 23.

[100] SpeedNews, *Pogo and You're There*, email@speednews.com (Fri., Jul. 16, 2004).

closed its fledgling fractional operation in March 2002, subsequent to the terrorist attacks.[101]

Delta Air Lines also entered the air taxi/fractional ownership arena with its Delta AirElite, but did so by either purchasing or otherwise forming working relationships with already existing companies. Delta Air Lines entered the business aviation market in January 2000 when it acquired Comair Jet Express, a charter operator, from its Comair Holdings parent. The name was changed to Delta AirElite in October 2001. An exclusive partnership was later formed with Bombardier Flexjet to provide fractional ownership. Rather than partial ownership in specific aircraft Delta AirElite offers blocks of flight time for purchase. Fractional ownership can be had by buying as little as 25 hours of guaranteed flight time. Hence, Delta AirElite offers both charter services and fractional ownership under its operational plan.[102]

Delta's continued operation of Delta AirElite solidifies the air charter and fractional ownership operations as new segments of the air transportation industry. Moreover, Aviation Data Service president John Zimmerman says, "Don't misread United's decision to pull the plug on [its] operation. . . . While the fractional-ownership market has cooled . . . we expect steady growth to continue for the foreseeable future."[103] United may be back as may some other airlines, to join a host of independent fractional ownership providers including: MaverickJets, Flight Options, FlightTime, TravelAir, eBizJets, and Flight Options.

From the network of operating business jets, a spin-off product has emerged whereby excess seats can be sold to the general public. By listing available seats along with origin and destination information and times of departure, the seats can then be brokered to customers wanting to acquire the seats. Reportedly, these excess seats on charter business jets have a selling price comparable or just slightly higher than first class accommodations on regular commercial airlines.

As reported by Anthony Velocci, Jr., "UAL's decision to integrate business jets into its worldwide fleet—and the likelihood other major

---

[101] Anthony L. Velocci, Jr.. *UAL Places Huge Order for Gulfstream Bizjets*, Av. Wk. & Space tech. (Jun. 18, 2001), at 94; *see also* Anthony L. Velocci, Jr., *Avolar Failure Belies Strength of Fractionals*, Av. Wk. & Space Tech. (Apr. 1, 2002), at 36; *see also* Susan Carey, *Fare Wars Hit the Jet Set: Sharing a Plane for Less*, Wall St. J. (Oct. 23, 2002) at D1.

[102] *See* Delta AirElite *Home Page*, http://www.airelite.com (visited Jul. 22, 2004).

[103] John Zimmerman *quoted in* Anthony L. Velocci, Jr., *Avolar Failure Belies Strength of Fractionals*, Av. Wk. & Space Tech. (Apr. 1, 2002), at 36.

carriers will follow—is a testament to the perceived market for fractional ownership of business aircraft."[104]

SMALL AIRCRAFT TRANSPORTATION SYSTEM

According to Robert Crandall, there are 5,500 to 6,000 city pairs created from a base of 546 commercial airports in the NPIAS. With access to as many as 5,314 airports that are open to the public the total origin and destination airports for the fractional ownership/charter jet industry can be expanded exponentially. If aircraft had access to all of the 19,000 plus landing facilities in the United States the city-pairs could be nearly infinite. To this end, the Small Aircraft Transportation System, or SATS, developed by the National Aeronautics and Space Administration [NASA], in partnership with DOT/FAA and state and local aviation and airport authorities, holds the potential to revolutionize the way Americans travel by air and to make nearly all of the 19,000 landing facilities accessible, both public and private.

The NASA-led SATS initiative is focused on development of advanced technologies in flight. The SATS initiative proposes a new generation of advanced small (jet) aircraft to provide air transportation services to primarily general aviation airports and to all remote areas. Four operating capabilities will be developed to enable safe and affordable access to virtually any runway in the nation in most weather conditions. These advanced operating capabilities will rely on on-board computing, advanced flight controls, highway-in-the-sky heads-up visual displays, and automated air traffic separation and sequencing.[105]

SATS grew out of a recognized need for a small aircraft transportation system to relieve safety and congestion problems not only in the air, but on America's highways as well. Highways and roadways, particularly in urban areas, are often plagued with delays and accidents. Likewise, the nation's 30 largest airports are nearing gridlock, resulting in frequent delays and flight cancellations. With 3,431 air-

---

[104] Anthony L. Velocci, Jr., *UAL Places Huge Order for Gulfstream Bizjets*, Av. Wk. & Space Tech. (Jun. 18, 2001), at 94.

[105] NASA Langley Research Center, *Small Aircraft Transportation System (SATS)* Home Page, http://sats.larc.nasa.gov. (visited Jul. 22, 2004); *see also* Scott E. Tarry & Brent D. Bowen, *Optimizing Airspace System Capacity Through a Small Aircraft Transportation System: An Analysis of Economic and Operational Considerations*, J. of Air Trans. Worldwide (2001), Vol. 6, No. 1.

ports included in the 2007-2011 NPIAS, more than 5,261 airports open to the public, and over 19,000 total landing sites, a small aircraft transportation system that is both a safe and affordable alternative would provide almost limitless air traffic and airport capacity to the current air transportation system.[106]

The Proof of Concept research and development phase will demonstrate the SATS operational capability in four major areas:

- Higher volume operations in non-radar airspace and at non-towered airports;
- Lower landing minimums at minimally equipped landing facilities;
- Increased single-pilot crew safety and mission reliability; and
- En route procedures and systems for integrated fleet operations.

Pieces of the SATS and several SATS concept aircraft already exist and the Proof of Concept research and development phase ends in 2005. It is anticipated that SATS will continue development through the following decade, during which time it is hoped that regulations, airspace procedures, and industry products will be developed to accommodate SATS traffic. The full deployment phase could occur as early as 2015, and SATS could be fully operational by 2020.[107]

A FRESH LOOK AT HELICOPTER AIR TRANSPORTATION

It has been more than 30 years since the end of the scheduled helicopter transport era. Much has changed in the technology, economics and environmental impact of helicopters. It is time to once again look at the viability of helicopters as a mode of transport in the urban environment and perhaps to revisit the concept of using helicopters for personal mobility rather than as scheduled carriers.[108]

---

[106] FAA, *National Plan of Integrated Airports [NPEAS]*, 2007-2011.

[107] NASA Langley Research Center, *Small Aircraft Transportation System (SATS)* Home Page, http://sats.larc.nasa.gov. (visited Jul. 22, 2004); *see also* Scott E. Tarry & Brent D. Bowen, *Optimizing Airspace System Capacity Through a Small Aircraft Transportation System: An Analysis of Economic and Operational Considerations*, J. of Air Trans. Worldwide (2001), Vol. 6, No. 1.

[108] Laurence E. Gesell, *The Evolution of Helicopter Air Transportation*, an unpublished paper prepared for the Urban Mobility and Helicopter Seminar scheduled in Tempe, Ariz.(Oct. 28, 1999) but cancelled.

From the business-jet charter scenario presented above, the ongoing SATS research and development program, the example of on-demand limousine/bus service found in many cities, and the Emergency Medical Services [EMS] helicopter service model in operation across the country, there emerges a vision for an on-demand helicopter transportation system operating (hypothetically) within the greater metropolitan area. The system would operate much like on-demand airport bus (or limousine) services currently serving major hub airports to/from the outlying areas. Unlike helicopter systems in the past, which operated on programmed routes with scheduled times of arrival/departure, the system envisioned would operate on-demand with random routings to heliports/helipads scattered throughout the metropolitan area. Such a system is currently in operation in Sao Paulo, Brazil, where gridlock on the ground has motivated the development of rooftop heliports on perhaps one in three skyscrapers throughout the urban environment. Today, commuters by the hundreds crisscross the city in helicopter air taxis.[109]

Thus, in the scenario of personalized mobility, helicopter transportation would come "full circle" from notions of operating a helicopter out of one's garage, to the provision of scheduled air carrier service on off-airway routes, to on-demand air limousine service. Although not yet becoming the individual mobility envisioned in owning and operating one's personal helicopter, more personalized mobility to and from more conveniently located destinations would move the process a step beyond the inconvenience of waiting and moving in mass by scheduled air carrier service. Transportation is about time and place utility—of providing the right service at the right time and at the right place. Departure and arrival locations within the scenario of personalized helicopter air transport would be in greater proximity to the passenger's desires, and at more convenient times—not unlike SATS but on a smaller geographic scale.

Hence, what is envisioned is more like the individual "mobility" foreseen with the advent of the practical helicopter, as opposed to the "mass transit" services offered by scheduled air carriers operating on fixed routes. Such a scenario brings helicopter transportation full-circle, reflecting a recognized evolutionary pattern as shown in Figure 16.2, "Evolution of Helicopter Air Transportation."

---

[109] *See* Discover Atlas, *Brazil Revealed* (2006).

Figure 16.2—EVOLUTION OF HELICOPTER AIR TRANSPORTATION

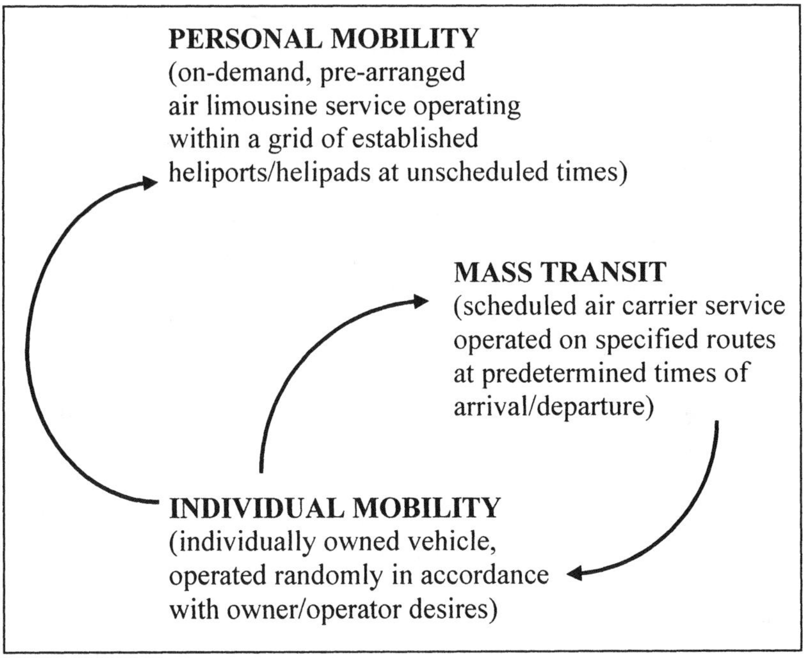

PERSONAL MOBILITY
(on-demand, pre-arranged air limousine service operating within a grid of established heliports/helipads at unscheduled times)

MASS TRANSIT
(scheduled air carrier service operated on specified routes at predetermined times of arrival/departure)

INDIVIDUAL MOBILITY
(individually owned vehicle, operated randomly in accordance with owner/operator desires)

Source: Laurence E. Gesell & Paul Stephen Dempsey: *Air Transportation: Foundations for the 21st Century* 472 (2005).

SUMMARY

Clearly there is an identified need for private intervention in the development of terminal facilities and an *overlay* of several global jetports. This new type of airport is yet to be effectively defined although the term most commonly used to refer to the new-generation airports worldwide has been "wayport"; a word etiologically rooted in the air traffic and airspace system, and perhaps the best term (functionally) describing the future generation of airports. But owing to any resistance to using the term to describe future generation airports, "advanced fifth wave" is used generically in this book to mean any one of several alternative terms referring to fifth wave economic infrastructure development. Irrespective of terminology, the underpinning of what is suggested is that wayports, superhubs, global airports, regional international airports, or whatever one might call the advanced fifth wave of air transportation infrastructure development, are the most viable alternative available in solving the evolving gridlock dilemma. And, in the development of these new airports, there not only is an opportunity for entrepreneurship there is a *need* for private investment in a public/private partnership.

An initial system of four to six fifth-wave airports in the United States of the proper size and capacity could meet America's long-range needs. Fifth wave airports could also be located in South America, Europe, the Pacific Rim, and Africa.[110] In Europe, for example, ATC-Lease Management, a financial service organization has promoted what it has called the "European Gateway Airport," which differs in location although not in function from the wayport concept. The principle is the same, except that *existing* airports would be redesigned to incorporate operation of Mach-5 aerospace passenger planes and one thousand-ton freighters.[111] Shannon, Ireland, would be the first candidate for a fifth wave airport in Europe. Second choices would be Porto, Portugal, and Prestwick, Scotland.[112] A fifth wave airport located on the western borders of the former Soviet Union would also provide a convenient European location, meeting all of the necessary requirements of a future generation airport, while providing a major boost to the depressed economy in that area.[113]

Another site in Western Siberia emerged as a selected fifth wave airport location. The industrial city of Omsk signed an agreement with the Central-Midwest International Airport group to work together toward building cargo hubs in Omsk and in the hills near Pond River, Kentucky.[114] The Omsk group envisioned a mid-America site for a distribution center for not only the U.S. but for Central and South America as well. It might be noted that the Transportation Research Board [TRB] also recommended a site in the Kentucky-

[110] James E. Sheppard, *The Wayports Concept*, an unpublished paper (spring 1989), at 2.
[111] Kurt Pischl, in a letter to Karen Mogan, legislative assistant to Rep. J. Roy Rowland (Apr. 19, 1989).
[112] *Id.*
[113] J.R. Wilson, *Wayport Solution to Saturation*, Janes Airport Review (about 1989 or 1990).
[114] Keith Lawrence, *Russians the Toast of Muhlenberg*, Owensboro Messenger Inquirer (Jun. 6, 1992).

Indiana region as one of three sites forming the "backbone" of the fifth wave system in the United States.[115]

Locations that have considered a fifth wave concept airport in the U.S. include: Alabama, Arizona, Arkansas, California, Colorado, Florida, Georgia, Kentucky, Mississippi, Nebraska, New York, North Carolina, North Dakota, Oklahoma, Virginia, West Virginia, and Washington.[116] The wayport concept may not be dead after all. The Arkansas and Florida proposals are of particular note in terms of privatization. In Arkansas a public/private partnership was formed to create a major cargo distribution center and industrial airport designed to serve mid-America. The airport project was begun by Sam Walton, and has had federal funding support combined with private backing by the Walmart store chain, Tyson Foods, and J.B. Hunt.[117] The proposed airport has been described as "an industrial concept like (Fort Worth) Alliance." It has also been called a "wayport."[118]

One of the most ambitious private efforts in the U.S. to build an inter-modal transportation center, including a wayport, is located in Martin County, Florida, about 105 miles from Orlando and Miami. Aeroplex—A Florida Wayport proposes development entirely with private funds and is a plan to build one of the world's first fully private commercial international airports.[119] Planned on a 22,559-acre site are two parallel runways, each runway 15,000 feet long, an industrial park and a commercial center including a free trade zone. In addition, there is a lake resort and hotel complex with golf course, surrounded by a 10,000 acre citrus tree zone, which includes the beforementioned lake for irrigation and storm water runoff. The "aeroplex" is to have a toll road connecting it with Interstate 95 and the Florida Turnpike, and a planned tie into a rail line that runs between Miami and Palm Beach. Aeroplex is programmed from the outset to serve origin and destination traffic, as well as transfer traffic.

Before leaving the Aeroplex project, it is of note that in October 1993, the FAA granted a favorable airspace determination for Aero-

---

[115] Ben Wolfe, *Central-Midwest International Airport*, a report of the Central City Economic Development Corp. (Apr. 1992); *see also* TRC Committee, *Airport System Capacity*, Special Report No. 226 of the Transportation Research Board (1990).

[116] Staff, *FAA Examined Other Alternatives to Expanding DFW Airport*, Aviation Daily (Jan. 24, 1992), at 148.

[117] Tyson Foods is a poultry processing firm; J.B. Hunt owns a large freight trucking company.

[118] Staff, *Arkansas Project Boosts Concept*, Aviation Daily (Dec. 4, 1990).

[119] Staff, *FAA Acts to Save Plan for Fully Private Commercial Airport*, Aviation Daily (Dec. 1, 1993).

plex. Yet, Aeroplex is defined by its developers as a "wayport." Maybe this finding by the FAA (under the Clinton administration) signaled a change, if only temporary, in federal policy towards wayports. Reportedly, one of the first things asked for by Secretary of Transportation Frederico Peña, was information about wayports. Apparently consumed by the war on terrorism, the George W. Bush administration has been relatively silent with regard to the air transportation industry, other than promotion of terrorism relief legislation.

Although not yet a reality, wayports and other fifth wave airports developed largely through private investment are beginning to happen—if not actually, then at least in vision. But it takes time to develop new airports. Unless the process can be expedited through privatized involvement in a partnership between the public and private sectors (as it was for the Alliance Airport), and adoption in full by the Federal government of the fifth wave concept, it would take, at a minimum, fifteen to twenty years to see the reality of any new air transport airports. In the meantime, the existing infrastructure will continue to be taxed beyond its capabilities. Democratic governments are infamous for being *reactive* rather than *proactive*. Like the development of adequate superhighways in large metropolitan areas, advanced fifth wave airports most likely will not be developed until it appears almost too late. But eventually, the reality of gridlock and its toll in time, money and frustration will call for government (re)action.

Without private investment, fifth wave airports may not come on line at all. But irrespective, development of the advanced fifth wave of infrastructure will inevitably require federal, state and local government involvement as well. When the government does react, it ought to be in a public/private partnership, using the Alliance project as its model. That is to say, the government might build the basic facilities to support the safe movement of aircraft (runways, taxiways, navigation aids, and so forth). Although revenues may be generated from landing fees and aircraft parking structures, because safety is an overriding concern, the air and ground movement areas may not be *profit* centers. And subsidy funding for the basic infrastructure ought to come from the Aviation Trust Fund, passenger facility charges, and/or some other form of user tax, while relying on the private sector, including the airlines, to invest in revenue generating profit centers (e.g., terminals, parking lots, concessions, etc.).

CHAPTER 17

AIRPORT LIABILITY

It is ancient doctrine that at common law ownership of the land extended to the periphery of the universe—Cujus est solum ejus usque ad coelum. But that doctrine has no place in the modern world. The air is a public highway. . . . Yet, it is obvious that if a landowner is to have full enjoyment of the land, he must have exclusive control of the immediate reaches of the enveloping atmosphere.

William O. Douglas, U.S. Supreme Court Associate Justice.[1]

PROPRIETARY NATURE OF AIRPORTS

As explained in the opening chapters of this book, the preponderance of airports included in the National Plan of Integrated Airport Systems [NPIAS] are—as airports are in most of the world—publicly owned and operated. That is to say, the ownership and operation of airports that are open and available to the traveling public are, by default, a governmental responsibility. And, as there are public versus private airports, the legal status of each varies as well. Privately owned airports are clearly proprietary—and one of the functions of government is also proprietorship. But the legal status of a government is not the same as it is in private enterprise. The functions of publicly owned airports may or may not be considered proprietary depending upon the circumstances. For example, police functions (i.e., "protection of health, welfare, safety and morals of society") are government responsibilities not related to proprietorship. In addition,

[1] Mr. Justice Douglas delivering the opinion of the Court in *United States v. Causby*, 328 U.S.256 (1946).

the courts have held that the acquisition, improvement, maintenance, and operation of a governmentally owned and operated airport, for use by the general public, and for the general benefit of the public, are within the scope of governmental services.[2]

However, along with its rights with regard to owning airports, government sponsors also have responsibilities for the consequences of operating those airports just as other proprietors might have. Airport-related law cases associated with the *proprietary* function of government-owned and -operated airports, begin with the landmark *United States v. Causby* case in 1946.[3] With respect to the environment, the responsibility for determining the permissible noise levels for aircraft using an airport remains with the airport proprietor. This precept originated from the *Causby* case, where the United States, as operator of a military field, was held responsible under the Fifth Amendment to the U.S. Constitution for rendering the Causby's property useless as a chicken farm because of low flying airplanes. The precedent set in the Causby case was extended to commercial airports in 1962, in *Griggs v. Allegheny Co.*, when it was held that the County, as the airport sponsor, was the entity that had decided to build an air-

[2] In *American Airlines, et al. v. Louisville and Jefferson County Air Board*, CCH 6 AVI 17,587 (1959), the question was whether an airport is within the normal scope of governmental services. The U.S. District Court declared in a memorandum that the arbitration provisions of certain airport leases were invalid and unenforceable. The trial court found that "the Air Board was without authority to contract to delegate to arbitrators its public and discretionary duty to fix rentals for the use of the facilities of the airport." On appeal, the court stated that the attack, upon the validity of its covenant to submit the renewal rentals and fees to arbitration, rested upon a ground that goes to the very formation of the contract to arbitrate in the first place; in particular, the authority of the Air Board as a public body to make such a covenant. The case was remanded to the District Court.

[3] In *United States v. Causby*, 328 U.S. 256 (1946), the Causbys owned a chicken farm underlying the approach path to a (leased) military airfield. The Causbys claimed that noise and glaring lights at night, of military planes landing or leaving the airport, interfered with the normal use of their property as a chicken farm and with the night's rest of their family. As a result, they had to give up their chicken business. As many as six to ten chickens were killed in one day when they became frightened and flew into walls. A total of 150 chickens were lost in this way. The Causbys submitted a claim to the federal government for the loss of their property. The claim ultimately reached the U.S. Supreme Court for a ruling. The Supreme Court agreed with the lower U.S. Court of Claims that there had been a diminution of value in the property, and that the frequent and low-level flights (outside of the minimum prescribed altitudes) were the direct and immediate cause. The court's opinion seems to indicate mere flight over land does not constitute a taking, but rather must be attended by something else such as noise and glare. The court found that flights over private land are not a taking unless flown so low and so frequently as to be a direct and immediate interference with enjoyment and use of the land.

port at a particular location, and that the County was therefore liable for the *taking* of property in *inverse condemnation*.[4]

Public airport sponsors have authority to acquire property for airport use through purchase, lease or through exercise of their power in *eminent domain*. In 2005 the U.S. Supreme Court in a narrowly divided (5-4) decision ruled that eminent domain could be used even to transfer land from one private owner to another private party to further economic development. In other words, the Court held that the general benefits a community enjoyed from economic growth—creation of new jobs, increased taxes and other revenues, revitalization of a depressed or blighted urban area, and so forth—qualifies as a public use so long as the receiving private entity serves as the legally authorized agent of the government.[5]

Airport sponsors, however, are not simply owners of property engaged in private enterprise, they are governmental authorities as well. In the furtherance of social utility, one of the functions of government is the *redistribution of wealth* for the good of the majority. Some economists[6] have argued that rate setting and cost recovery schemes should attempt to be *allocative* (i.e., to associate revenues with their cost-generating centers). But recognized is that airports are not perfect markets. In fact, empirically demonstrated is that few airports are capable of economic independence. Most airports cannot balance

---

[4] *See Griggs v. Allegheny Co.*, 82 S.Ct. 531 (1962). The Griggs owned a family residence at the end of the northeast runway at the Greater Pittsburgh Airport. Due to sloping terrain up to the residence, regular flights over the house made it impossible for people to converse or talk on the telephone. The residents were unable to sleep, the windows would often rattle and at times plaster fell from the walls and ceilings. The house was rendered unusable as a family residence. It was determined that there was a taking, but the party responsible for the unauthorized taking—the Federal government, the aircraft owners, or the airport proprietor—was in question. The U.S. Supreme Court found that it was the airport sponsor that was liable. It was the promoter, owner, and lessor of the airport. It was the airport proprietor who took the air easement in the constitutional sense. The airport proprietor decided where the airport would be built, what runways it would need, their direction and length, and what land and navigation easements would be needed; *Condemnation* is the act of judicially converting private property to public use under *eminent domain*. Property is taken without consent of the owner, but with just compensation. *Inverse condemnation* occurs when a public entity takes or damages property without going through the legal procedure of condemnation, and does so without compensation to the owner.

[5] *Kelo v. City of New London*, 545 U.S. 469 (2005); *see also* U.S. Supreme Court Media, *The OYEZ Project*, http://www.oyez.org/cases/2000-2009/2004/2004_04_108/ (visited May 11, 2007).

[6] Milton Friedman, for example, and also Alfred Kahn, the former Civil Aeronautics Board [CAB] Director and so called "father of airline deregulation"; *see* Laurence E. Gesell, *Aviation and the Law* 10-11 (3rd ed. 1998).

revenues with expenses, and therefore, cannot effectively allocate costs. Although cost allocation is held as a desirable goal of airport management, true cost allocation is not attainable while at the same time providing well-rounded aviation services to the traveling public (i.e., the consumer).

Although it may be philosophically difficult to accept the practice of cross allocating resources from one cost center to another, a subjective if not qualitative defense has shown income redistribution to be justifiable where it is necessary to satisfy social utility. Nevertheless, redistribution of wealth means "taking" from one to give to another.[7] In serving the interests of the majority, a minority may be disadvantaged. Hence, as John Rawls points out, utilitarianism "does not take seriously the distinction of persons."[8]

The result of all of this in actual application is that the government becomes a legitimized *Robin Hood.* Those who can afford it pay more and those who can least afford it pay less.[9] One tenant may be paying what are considered exorbitant rents, while a neighbor tenant may be paying very low rent, or might even be subsidized! Take for example the airport-related costs to an automobile rental agency. Their rental contract normally calls for about 10% of their gross income to be paid to the airport for rental space and for the privilege of doing business on the airport. The net rent amounts to thousands of dollars per square foot of occupied terminal floor space where commercial exchange actually takes place with customers. Compare this with rental of say only ten to twenty dollars per square foot of floor space by the airlines. This disparity has not gone unnoticed by the automobile rental companies, nor has it gone unchallenged.[10]

---

[7] Reference here is to the possible violation of the Fifth Amendment to the U.S. Constitution, and the "taking" of property without due process under the Fourteenth Amendment.

[8] John Rawls, *A Theory of Justice* (1971).

[9] In *Kelo v. City of New London*, 545 U.S. 469 (2005), the U.S. Supreme Court held that the City of New London's taking of private property to sell for private development qualified as a public purpose/use, as the City had followed an economic development plan, despite the fact that the land would not be used by the public. Here, the government played a reverse Robin Hood role, taking from the poor (homeowners) and giving to the rich (developers). *See* U.S. Supreme Court Media, *The OYEZ Project,* http://www.oyez.org/cases/2000-2009/2004/2004_04_108/ (visited May 11, 2007).

[10] In *Alamo Rent-a-car v. Sarasota-Manatee Airport Authority*, CCH 20 AVI 18,175 (1987), Alamo challenged whether an airport may impose charges upon non-airport tenants who regularly use the airport for commercial purposes. This case is one of a series of actions brought by *off-airport* automobile rental agencies in an attempt to avoid paying airport charges related to commercial automobile rental operations on certain airports, including the defendant in this case, the Sarasota-Manatee Airport Authority; *see also Airline Car Rental, Inc v. Shreveport*

Another example is the rate paid for parking automobiles versus the rate charged for temporary storage of an airplane. The fees, say five to ten dollars, charged for overnight parking of an aircraft may only marginally pay the costs of parking apron development, construction and maintenance. Conversely, one can pay as much or more to park a car for just two or three hours at some airports.

Automobile parking revenues and rents collected from auto rental agencies are major sources of income for an air carrier airport. Revenues from these two sources constitute the lion's share of surplus funds available to the airport sponsor which can be used to make up for deficits in other, particularly aviation-related land-use areas.

In cross allocating funds from one cost center to another, airports seemingly violate certain principles of distributive justice, and yet government in order to support the airport and to provide a facility for all who come legitimizes it. The practice is seemingly justified by the canon of *social utility*,[11] but irrespective of the social advantages, the one paying the greater share of the burden may feel his or her individual rights are being violated, and the potential for a lawsuit is generated no matter how just the government's intentions.

Along with proprietary and redistributive powers airports may exercise their *police powers* to regulate the operation of their airports. Promulgation of aviation related rules and regulations designed to protect the public safety, health and welfare have been upheld by the courts as a valid exercise of police power,[12] so long as the local regu-

---

Airport Authority, CCH 21 AVI 17,201 (1987). The U.S. Court of Appeals reversed a district court ruling on equal protection challenge by Alamo. But because the district court did not reach several of Alamo's alternative grounds for relief, the appellate court remanded for consideration of those contentions. For example, the district court did not reach Alamo's claims that the user fee: constituted an unreasonable burden on interstate commerce; denied it due process of law in violation of the Fourteenth Amendment and the Florida Constitution; and/or was enacted in violation of Florida's statutes; *see also Airline Car Rental, Inc. v. Shreveport Airport Authority*, CCH 21 AVI 17,201 (1987). There the question was whether an off-airport automobile rental company may conduct business on an airport without an agreement with the airport. Airline claimed the Airport Authority was requiring them to pay for the privilege of conducting business on the airport in violation of the Commerce Clause and in violation of state and federal Equal Protection Clauses. The U.S. District Court granted summary judgment in favor of the Airport Authority, finding that the resolution was passed under lawful authority and it did not place an impermissible burden on interstate commerce.

[11] The Canon of Social Utility is justice, which advances the common good, or public interest, over the interests of the individual. *See* Nicholas Rescher, *Distributive Justice* (1966).

[12] In *R E. Stagg v. Municipal Court of Santa Monica, et al.*, 2 Cal App 3d 318 (1969), the question was whether aviation related rules and regulations designed to protect the public safety, health and welfare are a valid exercise of police power. The superior court determined the City of Santa Monica had no authority to pass an aviation-related ordinance, because the State had

lations are reasonable and do not conflict with existing state or federal regulations.[13] Local governments may regulate their airports, so long as they do not regulate those aspects of aircraft operation which have been *pre-empted* by the Federal government,[14] nor pass regulations which unduly burden interstate commerce.[15]

In short, airports have obligations that are at times in opposition. On the one hand they represent government authority, with police

---

reserved for itself the power to regulate all aspects of the air transportation field not reserved by the Federal government. The appellate court disagreed. The City owned the airport and a charter city has plenary (full) powers with respect to municipal affairs not expressly forbidden to it by the state. The operation of a municipally owned airport had been expressly committed by state statute to the local agency. The Government Code of California provided that a municipality may acquire property for *use* as an airport. The appellate court concluded that the city ordinance in question might also be upheld as a valid exercise of the municipality's police power. The California Constitution empowered cities and counties to make and enforce "such local, police, sanitary, and other regulations as are not in conflict with general laws."

[13] In *American Airlines, et al. v. Town of Hempstead, et al.*, 348 F 2d 369 (1968), the question was whether local aviation rules and regulations may conflict with existing state or federal regulations. The primarily residential Town of Hempstead, New York passed a local noise ordinance forbidding anyone from operating a mechanism or device (including airplanes) which created excessive noise within the town. The U.S. District Court found that the ordinance was an unconstitutional burden on interstate commerce; the area in which the ordinance operated had been preempted by federal legislation and regulation; and, the ordinance was in direct conflict with valid applicable federal regulation. The district court ruling was affirmed on appeal.

[14] *In Burbank v. Lockheed Air Terminal, Inc*, 411 U.S. 624 (1973), the issue was over whether a local government could impose a curfew on jet operations at a privately owned airport. The City of Burbank had passed an ordinance prohibiting jet operations at the Hollywood-Burbank Airport between the hours of 11 p.m. and 7 a.m. The critical issue in this case was an argument that the ordinance was invalid because Congress by its enactment of the Federal Aviation Act of 1958, and the Noise Control Act of 1972, had preempted state and local control over aircraft noise. The Federal Aviation Act provides in part, "The United States of America is declared to possess and exercise complete and exclusive national sovereignty in the airspace of the United States. . . ." There is no express provision of preemption in the Noise Control Act, but the court concluded that the scheme of federal regulation of aircraft noise is so pervasive that there is preemption. The FAA in conjunction with the Environmental Protection Agency [EPA] has full control over aircraft noise, preempting state and local oversight. Thus, state and local governments remain unable to use their police powers to control aircraft noise by regulating the flight of aircraft. The U.S. Supreme Court, in the majority, held the Burbank ordinance invalid.

[15] In *Santa Monica Airport Association v. City of Santa Monica*, 481 F. Supp. 927 (1979), the question was whether an airport proprietor can restrict aircraft operations for noise abatement; and specifically, whether it can impose a ban on jet operations. In a move aimed at reducing aircraft noise, the City of Santa Monica imposed a series of ordinances restricting aircraft operations, including a total ban on jet aircraft either landing or taking off at the Santa Monica Municipal Airport. Each of the ordinances was challenged under the U.S. Constitution—on *preemptive* grounds, on *equal protection* grounds, and as an impermissible *burden on interstate commerce*. As to all of the ordinances in question, except the jet ban, the court found them to be an *indirect* burden on interstate commerce. The ordinance banning jets presented different legal questions. It was held unconstitutional on two alternative grounds; first, because it violated the Equal Protection Clause; and second, it imposed an impermissible burden on interstate commerce.

powers and the duty to protect the general public. On the other hand, they are proprietary entities, responsible for their own actions, just as other private individuals, with a duty to avoid depriving individuals of their civil rights under common law. Specifically at issue in the management of public airports are the First, Fourth, and Fifth Amendments of the U.S. Constitution. All public administrators are obligated (usually by oath) to preserve and defend state and federal constitutions and to uphold the law.

COMMON LAW

The U.S. common law system may be separated into civil law and criminal law. *Criminal law* is statutory. It is positive, written law found in rules, regulations and penal codes. A "crime" is an act, or an omission, which has been defined and made punishable by law. Criminal violations are acts against *society*. Criminal law may be described by its severity and the penalties assigned to commission of an illegal act, as follows:

- A *felony* is a crime so serious that it may be punishable by death or by imprisonment in a state or federal penitentiary. It is a crime referred to by the Constitution as "capital" or "infamous."
- *Misdemeanors* are serious, but of less severity than felonies. They, accordingly, have associated with their commission less severe penalties. They are, however, still considered crime in its truest sense.
- A *violation*, or in some states what may also be known as an *infraction* of the law, is an offense, but is one normally considered as something less than crime. It usually carries with it a comparatively weak penalty—a fine for a traffic ticket for instance.

Where criminal law is a violation against society, *civil* law involves injury to an *individual*. Although civil law has a broader meaning, it is sometimes referred to by one of its forms, "tort" law, although the law of torts gives reference to acts of *negligence*. Contract law, for example, is also a form of civil law, but does not include negligence. Torts are generally undefined and, therefore, common, widespread and varied. Torts involve the violation of an individual's right to freedom from bodily injury, property damage, injury to personal reputation, and/or a taking of one's rights without just cause.

To constitute a tort, it must be clearly established that actual damage and/or injury did in fact occur. An act, even though malicious, which causes no damage is insufficient cause for legal action. Furthermore, an accused must be directly or indirectly responsible for the damages caused either intentionally or by way of that person's negligence. *Intent* is an essential element of a tort. In other words, unavoidable accidents are not a tort.

If the damages were unintentional, but nevertheless caused through accidental interference, then the person at fault may have been *negligent*. Negligence is said to exist when:

- There is an *obligation to protect* others against unreasonable risks;
- There has been a *failure to conform* to a reasonable standard;
- The conduct of the person supposedly at fault is so closely related to the incident as to have caused it—to have been the *proximate cause*; and
- *Actual damages* did result.

The key element in negligence is the connection between the act and the injury resulting from it. "Proximate cause" is the direct and immediate cause to which an injury or loss can be attributed. It is the cause that without which the injury would not have happened. Again, unavoidable accidents are not negligence.

The U. S. common law system is thus made up of both civil and criminal elements. Table 17.1, "Common Law System," illustrates this bifurcation of the law, and subcategorizes civil law into its various forms around which attorneys tend to specialize.

Civil and criminal law are both described above as distinct and separate ways by which laws may be perpetrated. It is possible, however, for a person to be simultaneously guilty of trespassing the bounds of both civil and criminal law. For example, a person breaking the law may at the same time be harming someone through negligence.

Table 17.1—COMMON LAW SYSTEM

BRANCHES:	***Criminal***	***Civil***
AREAS:	Felony Misdemeanor Infraction	Contract Property (real) Probate Intellectual Property Corporate Family Creditor's rights Tort Administrative
PROOF:	Beyond reasonable doubt	Preponderance (weight)
PARTIES:	Public grievance	Private dispute
CONSEQUENCES:	Liberty at issue	Money/ Damages at issue
PURPOSE:	Maintain order	Resolve disputes

PROTECTION AGAINST WRONGS

Enumerated in the Constitution are the basic rights of United States citizens. In this section, those rights are looked at in the context of the available defenses against being wronged. Outlined below are the common causes for litigation when there has been some form of interference with personal rights.

- *Freedom of movement*—A person has the right to unrestricted freedom of movement. If a person has been illegally restrained, that person may file charges for *false arrest* or for *false imprisonment.*
- *Misuse of legal process*—On occasion public officials abuse their powers of office and willfully use them against individuals. A person has the right to be free from deliberate misuse of the law and the courts. Such violations give rise to charges of *malicious prosecution.*
- *Interference with person*—Individuals have the right to be free from bodily injury, and not to be threatened. Charges of assault and battery may result—*assault* if there have been threats, and *battery* if there has been actual injury to their physical person.
- *Peace of mind*—People have the right to freedom from unnecessary mental suffering. Malicious acts, which cause mental strain are called *emotional anguish.*
- *Privacy*—People have the right to non-interference with individual privacy. A person has the right to be left alone and to have their personal privacy protected.
- *Interference with reputation*—The individual is expected to have freedom from unwarranted (and untruthful) attacks on his or her character. *Defamation of character* if written or printed is *libel*; if maliciously uttered it is *slander.*
- *Property rights*—A person has the right to unrestricted enjoyment and use of both real and personal property. If that right has been violated, the person has been deprived of *quiet enjoyment.* If there has been undue annoyance, inconvenience, discomfort or injury, which has caused the loss of quiet enjoyment, then there is *nuisance.* If there has been unpermitted access onto land or into a building, then *trespass* has been committed. A person also has the right to unrestricted, uninter-

rupted enjoyment of personal property. If there has been interference with the right to personal property, the person doing it is said to be "converting" the property to his or her own (but unauthorized) use.

- *Contracts and business relationships* are also forms of property. If there has been an interference with contractual relationships, then there may have been *breach of contract*, or perhaps *breach of warranty*. Other interferences with contractual relationships might involve *fraud*, *deceit* and *misrepresentation*. A person has the right to freedom from cheating and trickery.

AIRPORT SECURITY

All types of street crimes occur on airports just as they do elsewhere, but the area of criminal law where airports are most liable is in the enforcement of airport security provisions. The strongest defense against lawsuit is to conform to established airport security screening procedures. The system has been tested by trial and error and the currently established procedures, including those adopted following the events of September 11, 2001, are the result of court precedence. Where airport sponsors as well as the Transportation Security Administration [TSA] carefully conform to the rulings established in prior court proceedings the exposure level is significantly reduced. Emanating from court decisions in this area, the following airport screening procedures have evolved.

At each screening point, appropriate signs advise the individual of the screening requirements and that the exercise of the individual's option to refuse to undergo screening would result in denial of passage beyond the screening point. Additionally, wherever an X-ray baggage inspection system is used, appropriate signs must advise the individual of the X-ray inspection system.

Prior to spring of 2006, proceeding past signage was not construed as a *voluntary* consent to being searched.[16] In other words, the pas-

[16] *United States v. Gerald Kroll*, 481 F 2d 884 (1973) addressed the issue of unwarranted search and seizure. Metal hinges on the defendant's brief case activated the magnetometer at the screening point, whereupon a U.S. Marshal directed the defendant to open the file section. The marshal felt Kroll's actions were *suspicious* and, therefore, asked the defendant to empty the contents of an envelope found in the brief case. It contained an amphetamine and a partly consumed marijuana cigarette. The defendant claimed the search was illegal and asked that the evidence be suppressed. The government claimed the search was reasonable and pointed out that warnings were posted at the airport advising passengers they were subject to being

senger still had the right to refuse further screening and to leave the airport even after having passed through the magnetometer. All of that seems to have been changed by a Ninth Circuit ruling. Now, passengers may not back out of the checkpoint screening process once they are partway though it.[17] Although technically the rule applies only within the Ninth Circuit Court district,[18] pragmatically it has been adopted by the TSA and is therefore the standard now used everywhere within the jurisdiction of the United States.

The initial screening process is conducted using either a walk-through metal detector or a hand-held metal detector. If the person being screened does not alarm the detector, the person is cleared to proceed beyond the screening point (unless otherwise "selected" for secondary screening by the TSA or an authorized agent). If the metal detector sounds an alarm or the search is considered "inconclusive," and the person insists on entering the sterile area, the person must be reprocessed (i.e., submitted to a secondary search) to determine the cause of the alarm.[19] In reprocessing, the person causing the

---

searched, and that passengers thereby consented to being searched. After an evidentiary hearing, the district court granted the defendant's pretrial motion to suppress; holding that while it was reasonable to inspect the defendant's attaché case, it was not reasonable to inspect the contents of the envelope. The U.S. District Court allowed suppression of the evidence and the U.S. Court of Appeals affirmed the determination.

[17] *See United States v. Aukai*, 04-10226 (9th Cir., Mar. 17, 2006). Daniel Kuuloloha Aukai arrived at the Honolulu Int'l. Airport for a flight to Kona, Hawaii. At the time he had no official identification on his person. He nevertheless voluntarily passed through the magnetometer and did not set it off. However, because he had not presented identification he was flagged for a secondary screening. Aukai protested that the procedures would make him late for his flight, and at one point he attempted to leave the area designated for secondary screening. Eventually, a glass pipe and methamphetamines were found on his person. Later, he plead guilty to charges that he knowingly possessed and intended to distribute 50 grams or more of methamphetamine, but with the right to appeal a motion to suppress the evidence found at the screening. His claim was that, while initially consenting to the screening, he later revoked that consent by electing not to fly rather than undergo the secondary screening. The trial court ruled against Aukai and he appealed. A three-judge panel of the U.S. Court of Appeals for the 9th Circuit ruled that travelers cannot prevent the secondary search. In the court's opinion, "Allowing a passenger in Aukai's position to revoke his consent prior to the secondary screening would . . . encourage airline terrorism by providing a secure exit where detection was threatened." *See also Airport Can Offer Screenings That Travelers Can't Refuse*, Air Safety Wk (Apr. 10, 2006).

[18] *I.e.*, those states included in the 9th Circuit: Alaska, Arizona, California, Hawaii, Idaho, Montana, Nevada, Oregon, and Washington

[19] *United States v. Cecil Epperson*, 454 F 2d 767 (1972) looked at the issue of what *constitutes a legitimate search and seizure*. As the defendant Epperson passed through a magnetometer, the instrument disclosed an unusually high reading. Epperson produced several metal objects, but the device still gave a positive reading. Thereupon, the marshal searched the jacket Epperson was carrying and found a loaded .22 caliber pistol. Epperson was convicted of attempting to board an aircraft while carrying a concealed dangerous weapon. The decision of the Magistrates Court was sustained by the U.S. District Court, and Epperson appealed. He claimed the pistol

alarm divests his or her person of metal and is then reintroduced through the metal detector. If the walk-through metal detector continues to alarm during reprocessing, the person must undergo additional screening. The hand-held metal detector is then used to determine and isolate the area of the alarm. Once the area has been isolated, the cause of the alarm should be determined, with the passenger's assistance, through a consent *frisk* either by observation, physical inspection of outer garments, or by having the passenger present pocket contents for inspection. Under no circumstances is the passenger allowed beyond the screening point unless screening personnel are first assured that the passenger is not carrying any dangerous objects. Failure to clear the metal detector a second time justifies the more intrusive search of a pat down or frisk.[20] Property processing is conducted by using an X-ray device and/or by physical inspection of the item. If no weapon, explosive or incendiary device is discovered the carry-on article may be permitted beyond the screening point. Metal detectors are normally not used to screen carry-on articles. If during the screen-

---

and ammunition should not have been introduced into evidence because they were the products of an illegal search. He argued that the use of the magnetometer was a "search," in violation of the Fourth Amendment. The appellate court agreed that the use of the magnetometer in these circumstances was a "search" within the meaning of the Fourth Amendment. But the Constitution does not forbid searches and seizures. It forbids only those that are *unreasonable*. The search for the sole purpose of discovering weapons and preventing air piracy fully justified the minimal invasion of personal privacy resulting from the use of a magnetometer. The U.S. Court of Appeals affirmed the conviction of the lower courts.

[20] In *United States v. Ramon Albarado*, 495 F 2d 799 (1974), the precedent was set for requiring the person being screened to pass through the metal detector a second time before conducting a pat down search. Defendant Albarado placed his carry-on luggage on the table, and it was searched. He then passed through the magnetometer and activated it. A U.S. Customs Officer motioned for Albarado to open his coat. The officer then patted him down and felt a bulge in his inside jacket pocket. It was a package wrapped in aluminum foil, containing counterfeit $20 bills. Albarado was convicted in the U.S. District Court for possession of counterfeit currency and he appealed. In determining the reasonableness of a search, the need for the search must be balanced against the invasion of privacy involved. While the magnetometer may not be the most efficient means to conduct a search, balanced against this is the absolutely minimal invasion of privacy involved. There is no detention at all. There is no "probing into an individual's private life and thoughts. . . ." Passing through a magnetometer has none of the indignities involved in fingerprinting, paring of a person's fingernails, or a frisk. The use of the device does not excessively annoy, frighten or humiliate those who pass through it. A frisk, on the other hand, is considered a *gross* invasion of one's privacy. Rather than conduct an immediate pat down search, the court ruled that it would be easier and more effective merely to ask the passenger to remove all metal items and return through the magnetometer (a second time). This procedure is clearly preferred over the immediate frisk because, while still a search, it entails far less invasion of the privacy or dignity of a person than to have a stranger poke and pat one's body in various places. Thus, the appellate court found the frisk to have been unlawful and reversed and remanded with directions that a motion to suppress the evidence be granted.

ing process, a weapon, explosive, incendiary device, or other contraband is discovered the Law Enforcement Officer [LEO] takes custody of the item and initiates appropriate law enforcement action.

In the airport screening process there is an undertone of *passive* crime prevention; that is to say, it is an "administrative" search, with the specific purpose of keeping weapons and explosives off airplanes and preventing hijackings, rather than looking for evidence as part of a criminal investigation. The law enforcement officer is present to prevent acts of violence aboard aircraft. The LEO is not there for ordinary crime prevention, but rather, is there to observe the public in general, and the passengers or others being screened in particular, and to be on the alert for acts or potential acts of criminal violence. The LEO's presence is intended to deter individuals from engaging in violations of the law and to give confidence to screening personnel who often find themselves the targets of ill-will by those opposed to the screening process.

If not conducted within the guidelines of the law, the screening process may be deemed "unreasonable," and therefore an illegal search.[21] The Fourth Amendment of the U. S. Constitution protects people against illegal search and seizure,

> *The right of the people to be secure in their persons, houses, papers, and effects, against unreasonable searches and seizures, shall not be violated, and no warrants shall issue, but*

[21] *United States v. Henry Bell*, 464 F 2d 667 (1972) *questioned* what justifies a pat down search. When defendant Bell passed through the magnetometer, the device was activated. A deputy marshal requested that Bell pass through the magnetometer a second time. Bell complied and again the device registered. Bell consented to being "patted down." The marshal then proceeded to pat down Bell from chest to hips and in the process felt hard objects in his raincoat pockets. When opened the objects were seen to contain glassine envelopes containing heroin. Bell argued he was the victim of an unlawful search and seizure, to which the court did not agree. The marshal's request that he submit to a pat down search did constitute a "stop and frisk," but did not offend any Fourth Amendment rights of the defendant. A contention that the use of the magnetometer constituted an unreasonable search was, in the court's opinion, baseless. The bodily pat down of Bell by the marshal was a frisk fully within the *Terry* test. In *Terry v. Ohio*, 392 U.S. 1 (1968), the Supreme Court rejected the concept that the police officer, conducting a stop and frisk, must have probable cause for making an arrest. There was no arrest here until after the contraband had been discovered. The Supreme Court in *Terry* required something less for the frisk but still required that the police officer have a reasonable belief some criminal activity might take place and a reasonable belief the suspect may have a weapon which would present a danger to himself or others. Such were the circumstances in this case. The U.S. Court of Appeals affirmed the district court conviction.

> *upon probable cause, supported by oath or affirmation, and particularly describing the place to be searched, and the persons or things to be seized.*[22]

The courts have determined Fourth Amendment protection is not confined to the home. It extends to *wherever* the person may be—at the airport for instance. And, it is assumed every person may have secrets pertaining to his or her family, business or social relations. It is further assumed a person's secrets may be no one else's business but one's own. If a person's personal affairs are disgraceful, they are nevertheless to be of no concern to others, and are not to be exposed without justifiable occasion. Irrespective, one should be aware of the screening process before entering the airport and should avoid carrying items that may be sensitive, whether it be sex paraphernalia, pornography, drugs, drug equipment, or anything else that one chooses to keep secret, let alone weapons and explosives.

The justification for a search is supported by "probable cause." Search and seizure is not allowed unless the facts and circumstances would warrant a person of *reasonable* caution (certainty) to believe seizable property *will* be found on a particular person or in a particular place. It follows that arrest should not take place unless the officer's information at the moment of arrest would warrant a person of reasonable caution (certainty) to believe the suspect had committed or

---

[22] In *United States v. Frank Lopez*, 328 F. SUPP. 1077 (1970), the court ruled that the use of a metal detector is a reasonable search allowable under the Fourth Amendment. No warrant was obtained for a search of the defendant nor, as a practical matter, could one have been expected. The court determined that the anti-hijacking system depends upon being able to swiftly sift out potential hijackers for closer scrutiny while permitting all passengers including selectees (like the defendant) to board unless weapons are discovered. The government argued that continuing the boarding process after reading the posted and clearly observable signs that stated "PASSENGERS AND BAGGAGE SUBJECT TO SEARCH" amounted to implied consent to searches such as occurred in this case. But, the court found there was no evidence of express consent. Still it concluded that contraband seized as a result of a properly circumscribed investigatory frisk predicated on information generated by a well administrated federal anti-hijacking system is admissible in evidence. Such a seizure comports with established Fourth Amendment principles, and were it not for the special circumstances surrounding airport searches, the court would not have hesitated to deny this motion to suppress. While evidence discovered during a frisk pursuant to this anti-hijacking procedure would normally have been admissible, the special circumstances to the instant case required suppression because security personnel had identified the defendant as a "selectee" using modified criteria not authorized by proper FAA authority. Since without this evidence the government had no case, the indictment was dismissed.

was committing an offense. Conditions under which a legal search and seizure may be authorized are as follows:

- Upon a *warrant* (court order) based on probable cause;
- Incident to *lawful arrest* based on probable cause;
- A *stop and frisk* ("pat down") search for dangerous weapons;[23]
- A search of *mobile premises*;
- *Emergency administrative searches* such as health and safety inspections; and/or
- Upon *consent*.

The situation of a passenger simply boarding an aircraft cannot in any way be construed to meet the above criteria for search and seizure. Nevertheless, in light of the serious threat posed by air piracy suspicious behavior may be sufficient cause for a pat down search.[24]

---

[23] In *Terry v. Ohio*, 392 U.S. 1 (1968) the U.S. Supreme Court determined that one search which may be conducted under conditions not requiring probable cause, is the *stop and frisk*, or "pat down" search. From the *Terry* case, the courts decided that an officer may, on *less* than probable cause, stop and frisk a suspect for weapons if the officer believes that criminal activity may occur, or that the person with whom the officer is dealing may be armed and dangerous.

[24] In *United States v. Bobby L. Lindsey*, 451 F.2d 701 (1971), the question being asked is whether a suspect may be frisked based upon observations of suspicious appearance and behavior. The defendant Lindsey had not yet passed through the security screening point, but was patted down on the basis of his suspicious behavior and presentation of false identification. The pat down search produced two aluminum-wrapped packages containing heroin. Lindsey was tried and convicted in U.S. District Court and appealed. His contention was that the heroin was inadmissible evidence because it was obtained by an unlawful search and seizure. The U.S. Court of Appeals, in applying *Terry* to the case at hand, believed the arresting officer's reactions to the unusual behavior of the defendant were justified. In the context of a possible airplane hijacking with the enormous consequences which may flow therefrom, and in view of the limited time in which the officer had to act, the level of suspicion required for a *Terry* investigative stop and protective search should be lowered. Therefore, despite the fact that it may be said the level of suspicion present in the instant case was lower than in *Terry*, it was sufficiently high to justify the marshal's actions; *United States v. Abraham Piña Moreno*, 475 F 2d 44 (1973) also looked at what constitutes a reasonable suspicion of a suspect's behavior. Abraham Piña Moreno was observed deplaning at San Antonio International Airport. He appeared to be looking for someone and was unusually wary of the airport security guards. He was visibly nervous, a condition which became more pronounced when he realized he was under surveillance. Shortly thereafter he left the airport by taxi but returned two hours later, going first to a ticket counter. Obviously very nervous, he switched from one line to another, several times before going to another airline counter where he finally bought a ticket. After purchasing the ticket he went into a restroom. He seemed to be protecting or covering something, and there was a prominent bulge on the left side of Moreno's coat. This aroused an officer's suspicion that Moreno might be carrying some kind of weapon or explosive device. When the officer questioned Moreno, he was given an account that the officer knew from his observations to be untrue. When Moreno "started to turn" the officer thought Moreno was going to attempt to "run out of the restroom." A pat down search was conducted, which yielded three cellophane wrapped packages containing

FOURTH AMENDMENT ENFORCEMENT

It is the latter two conditions stated above (emergency administrative searches and consent) upon which airport searches are predicated. As stated above, prior to spring 2006 and the court's ruling in *Aukai*, if the passenger initially refused to be searched after only one alarm, and there were no other conditions leading one to reasonably suspect a crime had or was occurring, the person was allowed to freely depart. But now, and in light of heightened concerns about aviation security, once the traveler has started the screening process, authorities may subject the person to secondary screening, including a pat down. Irrespective, a hastily exercised search of the person, even if weapons or contraband are found, could result in non-admissible evidence. The courts have held that evidence obtained illegally cannot be used in court.

In 1914, the U.S. Supreme Court determined that evidence illegally obtained couldn't be used in *Federal* prosecution for any purpose.[25] In 1949, the U.S. Supreme Court in *Wolf v. Colorado* held that *State* courts were not constitutionally required to exclude illegally obtained evidence.[26] In 1961, however, the Supreme Court reversed itself by overruling *Wolf* and decided the Fourth Amendment *requires* the state courts to exclude evidence obtained by unlawful search and seizures.[27] One search, which may be conducted under conditions not requiring probable cause, is the *stop and frisk*, or "pat down" search. This allowable exception was established in *Terry v. Ohio*.[28]

From the *Terry* case the courts decided an officer may, on *less* than probable cause, stop and frisk a suspect for weapons if the officer believes criminal activity may occur or the suspect may be armed and dangerous. The *Terry* precedent permits a law enforcement officer to stop and frisk a suspect based only on the officer's reasonable *suspicion* that a suspect *probably* has or will commit a crime. But

---

heroin. Moreno filed a motion to suppress as evidence the heroin seized in the airport search. In denying the motion, the district court recognized "the strong need for reasonable searches and seizures in furtherance of the public interest against air piracy." Moreno was convicted in the U.S. District Court for unlawful possession of heroin in an attempt to distribute, and he appealed. The U.S. Court of Appeals upheld the lower court's finding in view of defendant's unusual nervousness and apprehensive behavior.

[25] *Weeks v. United States*, 232 U.S. 383 (1914).

[26] *Wolf v. Colorado*, 331 U.S. 25 (1949).

[27] *Mapp v. Ohio*, 367 U.S. 643 (1961).

[28] *Terry v. Ohio*, 392 U.S. 1 (1968).

suspicion means something more than a mere hunch, guesswork, gut feeling or intuition. It must be supported with *facts*, which the officer may later point to for the court, to justify his or her suspicion. Otherwise, the suspicion will not be considered by the courts to have been made by a reasonable person under similar circumstances.

A stop and frisk must be limited to a pat down search of a suspect for *weapons* that would be dangerous either to the officer or to others. Additionally, the crime, which is suspected, must be connected with a weapon. For example, a suspected drunk would not likely be armed. Conversely, a potential hijacker would be expected to be armed and dangerous.

In applying the *Terry* case to passenger screening situations, a pat down search in a typical passenger-screening situation is to be used only as a *last* resort. The passenger having failed to pass through a metal detector the first time, is then required to divest himself or herself of metal on his or her person and resubmit to the metal detection screening device. The screening personnel may alternatively use a portable (hand held) detection device to determine the source location of the cause for alarm. Of importance is the fact a passenger alarming a metal detection device indicates only that the passenger has on his or her person metal for which no one has accounted. It does not provide reasonable grounds for suspicion that crime has, or is about to take place.

When a passenger has unexplained metal on his or her person, which cannot be cleared by the screening personnel, the passenger is requested to consent to a pat down search by the law enforcement officer. If the passenger declines the frisk and chooses instead to depart, the person ordinarily may do so. In Daniel Aukai's case, he was subjected to a secondary search as a matter of procedure because he lacked personal identification. If on the other hand the passenger demands on entering, or even attempts to enter the "sterile" area (meaning the area wherein all persons have been screened or otherwise cleared), or to board an aircraft, a pat down search is authorized. If a weapon or explosive device is found on that person, or in the carry-on items, there is "probable cause" for arrest.

When a person consents to a frisk, the pat down search is limited to detection of weapons or explosives. If contraband is discovered, rather than weapons or explosives, it is admissible as evidence in court only so long as it was found where a reasonable person might have searched for weapons or explosives.

CRIMINAL CASE LAW

A person's right to privacy must be protected, and yet the TSA, for the health, safety and welfare of the travelling public, requires that all passengers undergo metal detection device screening and search of carry-on items. In the potential clash between individual rights and public safety, there were twenty cases in the decade between 1971 and 1981 that reached the U.S. Court of Appeals for decision. None of them reached the Supreme Court.

Out of that body of twenty litigated actions, sixteen cases involved contraband such as drugs and counterfeit money. Four cases involved weapons. From these twenty cases, as well as those tried previously and since, have emanated certain established precedents:

- The Federal courts have ruled that in a constitutional sense, screening by means of a metal detection device is a search within the scope of the Fourth Amendment. That is to say, it *is* a search, but one which is authorized within certain limits;[29]
- The Federal courts have rejected the theory that persons being screened consented to search on the basis a waiver of constitutional right to fly on an air carrier is a form of duress or subtle coercion;[30] and
- The Federal courts have held that passenger screening searches fall within the *emergency administrative search doctrine* exception and are constitutionally valid on the basis that all persons desiring to fly on air carrier aircraft are required to undergo screening. In other words, the requirement is not discriminatory. Furthermore, the serious threat of air piracy *is* an emergency situation.[31]

In summary, there is a discretionary fine line between lawful and unlawful screening of air passengers. It is extremely important for

[29] *See United States v. Cecil Epperson*, 454 F 2d 767 (1972).

[30] *See United States v. Gerald Kroll*, 481 F 2d 884 (1973).

[31] *See United States v. Bobby L. Lindsey*, 451 F 2d 701(1971); *see also United States v. Abraham Piña Moreno*, 475 F 2d 44 (1973).

TSA as well as airport personnel and law enforcement officers to adhere strictly to the established procedures.

FIRST CLAIMS

The primary concern of airport security liability is in enforcement of the Fourth Amendment. But also of concern in airport liability is protection of First Amendment (or "first claims") rights. The first claims are freedom of *speech*, of the *press*, of *religion*, and of *peaceable assembly.*

On the one hand, the airport has a responsibility to *enforce* First Amendment violations. Illegal communication, for example, would include oral or written materials, which are restricted by police power. A person is not free to overthrow civil order, for instance. The limits of freedom of speech and of writing must be considered in context with other clauses in the Constitution. Communications may not be indirect, or otherwise injurious to the public morals, private reputation or safety. A person may not, for example, give false information such as falsely reporting a bomb during airport screening.[32]

The airport also has an obligation to *protect* First Amendment rights. But how to balance the rights of individuals against the rights of society is not always easily discernible. For instance, religious or political activists have a right to practice free speech, particularly in a public place such as the airport. Conversely, many passengers may find the activists' practices a nuisance. In the public interest, the airport sponsor may regulate solicitation on the airport premises in a manner that is reasonable or necessary.[33] However, because most airports are public property, ordinances attempting to control the exercise of First Amendment rights must be limited and must legitimately

[32] In *United States v. Marvin R. Feldman*, CCH 10 AVI 18,351 (1969) the defendant falsely reported a bomb. Marvin R. Feldman was charged with violating the United States Code, which makes it illegal to impart or convey false information. While seated at a lunch counter at Dulles International Airport, another person seated next to him asked what was ticking. Mr. Feldman replied to the query with, "it could be a bomb." After searching Feldman's suitcase a wind-up Westclox alarm clock was discovered. He was arrested for reporting false information. Feldman attacked the constitutionality of the statute for depriving him of his First, Fifth and Sixth Amendment rights. And because he claimed the statute violated due process of law. The U.S. District Court found the statute, (18 U.S.C.A., § 35a) to be clearly constitutional and denied the defendant's motion for dismissal. It has never been deemed an abridgment of freedom of speech or press to make a course of conduct illegal merely because the conduct was in part initiated, evidenced or carried out by means of language, either spoken, written or printed.

[33] *See State v. Daquino*, 361 U.S. 944 (1960).

serve the public interest.[34] The courts have overruled ordinances broadly disallowing First Amendment activities in airport terminals.

In *Jamison v. St. Louis*, the evidence indicated the airport director's unvarying practice was to deny all requests for permission to protest or solicit except those accompanied by a court order.[35] Jesse Jamison believed he was discriminatorily discharged from his employment by an airline because of his mental illness. And he was denied permission by the airport director to peacefully protest his discharge by standing silently in an unsecured spot on the terminal concourse with a sign stating the "airline discriminates against the handicapped." The U.S. Court of Appeals found the airport director's procedure for determining who could exercise First Amendment rights at the airport defective, because it gave the airport director *complete* and *unguided* discretion to rule on the exercise of First Amendment rights.

In another case the distribution of literature by a religious group was held to be protected speech and the central terminal area of a major international airport was held to be a "public forum."[36] The airport board had adopted a resolution banning *all* First Amendment activity. Alan Howard Snyder, a minister of the Gospel for Jews for Jesus was threatened with arrest if he did not stop distributing literature on a pedestrian walkway in the Central Terminal Area. The U.S. appellate court ruled the airport board's desire to limit the uses of the airport complex to airport-related purposes did not justify the "total" denial of free speech exercise within the terminal. In another similar case, the courts would not enjoin the airport sponsor from enforcing its regulations with respect to the exercise of First Amendment rights in *non-public* areas of the airport.[37]

In a case dealing with the media's First Amendment rights, an airport's total ban on the placement of news racks inside its airline passenger terminal was challenged.[38] In a non-jury trial, the U.S. District Court found that the First Amendment protects distribution of newspapers via the use of news racks. It also determined that, for purposes of disseminating news, an airport is a *public forum*. Finally, the district court concluded that the airport violated the newspaper compa-

[34] See *International Society for Krishna Consciousness v. Englehardt*, 425 F Supp 176 (1976).
[35] *Jamison v. City of St. Louis*, 828 F 2d 1280 (1987).
[36] *Jews for Jesus, et al., v. the City of Los Angeles*, CCH 19 AVI 18,401 (1986).
[37] *International Society for Krishna Consciousness v. Lee*, CCH AVI 17,270 (1992).
[38] *Multimedia Publishing Company of South Carolina v. Greenville-Spartanburg Airport District*, CCH 24 AVI 17,474 (1993).

nies' First Amendment rights. Accordingly, it enjoined the airport to permit the newspaper companies to place news racks in eight locations inside the terminal building. The airport appealed.

The U.S. Court of Appeals determined the constitutionality of the airport's news rack ban; first by deciding whether the distribution of newspapers through news racks located on that property was entitled to First Amendment scrutiny. If it were entitled, two further questions would be raised: (1) what type of forum for First Amendment purposes was this public property?, and (2) could the challenged ban survive the constitutional scrutiny appropriate to the regulation of expression in that type of forum?

The appellate court determined that the airport's ban on newspaper vending machines violated the First Amendment of the United States Constitution, because it was not reasonably necessary to preserve the airport for its intended purpose of facilitating air travel and commercial activity. Although the airport terminal is *not* a public forum the government's power to regulate expressive activity on public property is still limited. In this case, the ban against news racks placed a substantial burden on the newspaper companies' expressive conduct within the terminal, since the alternative for distributing newspapers—the airport gift shop and vending machines in a parking garage—was insufficient to provide easy access, unlimited availability, and visibility. The newspaper machines did not create major aesthetic problems. There was no evidence that the airport's concession revenue would be reduced by the presence of the machines. And the machines were inanimate objects that would create only a minimal amount of congestion. Concerns that a bomb might be placed in a newspaper machine were unfounded because the airport had never experienced a bomb threat, and, in fact, newspaper machines had never been used in any U.S. airport for the placement of a bomb.

Although during pendency of this appeal, it was established in *International Krishna. v. Lee* that airline terminals of the sort at issue in this case, are not public forums, this court concluded that the *total* ban here challenged was nevertheless unconstitutional.[39] The appellate court therefore affirmed the district court's decision, declaring that the ban violated the First Amendment and had to be lifted.

---

[39] *Society for Krishna Consciousness, Inc. v. Lee*, 112 S.Ct. 2701 (1992).

ENTRUSTMENT TO OTHERS

Another area of fundamental rights directly affected by airport operations is tied to the Fifth Amendment, which states in part,

> *[n]o person shall be . . . deprived of life, liberty, or property, without due process of law; nor shall private property be taken for public use, without just compensation.*

A *bailment* occurs when personal property is handed over to another for a specific purpose, under either an express or implied agreement. And, when the contract is completed or the purpose for which the property was delivered is fulfilled, it is understood the property will be returned to its original owner. Bailment occurs not only for commercial purposes such as repair, cleaning, storage, and so forth, but lending property to a friend or neighbor creates a bailment as well.

An aircraft delivered to a mechanic for repair creates a bailment. Allowing a friend to use an aircraft is also a bailment. Delivery of an aircraft to an airport sponsor or to a Fixed Base Operator [FBO] for storage may likewise create a bailment. The one (the owner) who delivers the aircraft to the mechanic is the *bailor*. The one (e.g., the mechanic) to whom the property is delivered is the *bailee*.

In a bailment the bailee has certain responsibilities. The bailee must reimburse the bailor for any loses or damages to the bailor's property while in the bailee's care.[40] It must be returned in its original condition. Unless agreed upon the bailee may not use the property for his or her own benefit.

---

[40] In *Burton Quam v. Nelson Ryan Flight Service,* 144 N.W. 2d 551 (1966) the plaintiff, Burton Quam, was assigned a parking place for his single engine airplane on the defendant FBO's premises. One of the tie-down ropes broke during a severe storm, resulting in damage to the plane. The jury found that there had been breach of duty on the part of the FBO, because it failed to provide equipment, which was safe for its *intended use*. On appeal, the Supreme Court of Minnesota ruled that one who furnishes equipment for compensation for a business use by another, under circumstances where the person retains the *exclusive* right to maintain the equipment, and it is foreseeable that damage might result from defects to it, owes a duty to use reasonable care to provide equipment which is safe for its intended use and free from defects of which the person has knowledge, or which could have been discovered by use of reasonable care.

The bailor must also assume certain responsibilities. If the bailor fails to retrieve the property within a reasonable period of time, the bailee may have the right to dispose of the property to satisfy the lien against it. If the bailee has taken reasonable precautions to protect the property, and yet the property is still damaged for reasons beyond his or her control, the bailor may be responsible for the property.[41] Should the bailor deliver the property to the bailee in faulty and dangerous condition, and not notify the bailee of the condition, the bailor may be responsible for damages or injury. Implied in the above situations are certain general rules covering the bailor's (owner's) rights in bailment:

- The bailee does not own the property and possession reverts to the owner;
- The bailee may not dispose of the property (unless the bailor fails to fulfill the terms of the agreement);
- The bailee must be warned of hidden (dangerous) defects;
- The bailee must take reasonable care of the property;
- The bailee may be liable for loss or damage caused by the bailee's negligence;
- The bailee is generally not liable for loss or damage beyond the bailee's control;
- The bailee must return the exact property received; and
- The bailee may not use the property without permission and if the bailee does, the bailee is almost always liable for loss or damage. The wrongful use or wrongful taking of personal property is known as "conversion."

---

[41] In *John Clemson v. Butler Aviation-Friendship, Inc.*, 296 A. 2d 419 (1972), John Clemson entrusted his airplane to Butler Aviation for repairs. While in Butler's care, a Butler employee found a man sprawled across the front seats, the victim of suicide. There was extensive damage done to the plane. The instrument panel had been smashed and apparently pieces of glass had been used in the suicide attempt. Clemson brought suit against Butler for damage to the airplane "while in the care and custody of Butler for repairs," and for the three day delay in making the repairs. Butler sued Clemson for the cost of the repairs. The Baltimore County Circuit Court entered judgment in each suit in favor of Butler. The Court of Appeals of Maryland affirmed that the bailee, Butler, *had* exercised ordinary care and diligence in safeguarding the airplane, and could not be held accountable for the activities of the suicide victim. No evidence was presented to indicate that Butler should have anticipated damage would take place.

BANKRUPTCY

Bankruptcy is a state of being declared judicially "insolvent." That is to say, the fair value of the property owned by an individual (or business), or the flow of income, is insufficient to cover the person's debts. The property of one declared bankrupt is subject to seizure and distribution amongst creditors. Bankruptcy proceedings may be voluntary or involuntary. The *debtor* files a *voluntary* bankruptcy, whereas the *creditors* file an *involuntary* bankruptcy.

Bankruptcies are categorized according to the chapter under which they are filed. The references are to procedures outlined by Chapter in the National Bankruptcy Act (Title II U.S.C.). The following is an overview of the contents (by chapter) of National Bankruptcy Act:

- *Chapter 7* is liquidation. It is a complete termination of the business, and according to the Act is intended to ". . . close up the estate as expeditiously as possible. . . .";
- *Chapter 9* contains the procedures by which the debts of a municipality may be adjusted. It may be recalled that in the mid-1970s New York City was threatened by bankruptcy, and should it have been necessary the city would have done so under this chapter;
- *Chapter 11* is a reorganization, which leaves the "debtor in possession." Under this chapter a plan is formulated to make the company solvent while it remains in operation; and
- *Chapter 13* is an adjustment of the debts of an individual with a regular income. It is much like Chapter 11, but for the individual. In other words, a plan is formulated which may result in achieving solvency.

BANKRUPTCY PROCEDURE

The bankruptcy process involving property rentals on airports begins when a petition is filed with the bankruptcy court. The process then proceeds as follows:

- The filing of the petition automatically stays (i.e., restrains) creditors from collecting on claims, enforcing liens, or evicting tenants;

- The stay continues until the bankruptcy proceedings are ended;
- The debtor remains in possession of rental premises;
- The debtor has sixty days to resume, reject, or assign the lease;
- The debtor may assume the lease only by curing *all* defaults (i.e., not just rent alone, but other conditions of the lease as well); and
- Pre-bankruptcy defaults must be cured before the lease may be assigned.

In a bankruptcy proceeding, a trustee (or receiver) is appointed by a *federal* court. The trustee takes over while the debtor is insolvent or unable to pay debts. The trustee's role is to:

- Take charge of the estate;
- Investigate irregularities such as *fraudulent transfer* or *preferential transfer*;
- Assure creditors are treated fairly;
- Receive claims;
- Liquidate property; and
- Distribute available funds.

Irregularities such as fraudulent and/or preferential transfer are not uncommon where bankruptcy is involved. These irregularities result from attempts by debtors to retain assets at the expense of creditors. *Fraudulent transfer* is the transfer of money or property to "defraud" creditors. A common example of fraudulent transfer might be the transfer of company funds to relatives just prior to filing for bankruptcy.

Preferential transfer occurs when certain, preferred creditors are paid in full while leaving others partially or totally unpaid. It is an unfair distribution of limited assets. This could be a likelihood especially where a supplier is controlled by the same company as the insolvent company.

Also common in bankruptcy proceedings are high levels of suspicion amongst creditors who feel an automatic (whether real or imaginary) sense of being cheated when they become aware they may not receive what is due them because of bankruptcy proceedings. It is the responsibility of the trustee to protect the interests of creditors and to discern whether potential allegations of wrongdoing have any foundation and to investigate those suspect irregularities.

Swift Aire Lines v. Crocker Bank is one case example of an airline in bankruptcy. Braniff's bankruptcy is another. More specifically, *Swift* is a good example of a trustee attempting to fulfill his responsibilities to assure all creditors were treated fairly, and to rectify any irregularities. Additionally, this case is an example of the impact upon the airport of an airline in bankruptcy. Terminal facilities and lease holdings were tied up in bankruptcy proceedings for months, causing disruption in air service to the community.[42]

The effects of bankruptcy on creditors and others are varied. Creditors may sell aircraft and other assets to liquidate debts and to realize at least partial recovery. But at a minimum, the estate will likely be tied up in the bankruptcy proceedings for months, and sometimes years, while claims are filed and the liquidation process takes place. Moreover, certain creditors have priority and will be paid before other general creditors. Taxes and administrative fees of the trustee (the appointed bankruptcy attorney) for instance are paid before other creditors.

In aviation bankruptcies there are at least two recognized ways for creditors to avoid having their property rights tied up in bankruptcy proceedings. First, Chapter 11 of the Bankruptcy Act provides that where there is a *purchase-money equipment security interest* (i.e., the right to demand and receive property), the creditor may have the right to take possession of *aircraft* per the terms of a lease or conditional sales contract. Such a right connected with aircraft ownership cannot be affected by a court ruling to enjoin such a taking.

---

[42] The allegations in *Swift* were twofold: (1) that Crocker Bank failed to live up it its obligation to honor an irrevocable letter of credit to Swift Aire for $775,000 based on a technicality; and (2) that Justin Colin, the principal stockholder in Swift, intentionally bankrupt the airline in a Chapter 7 filing in order to avoid personal responsibility for the $775,000 letter of credit. The trial court concluded that Crocker's refusal to honor the letter of credit was an attempt to "elevate form over substance." It was also pointed out in the lower court proceedings that, "[t]he (Swift) Board of Directors, being controlled by Colin, might have been reluctant to draw on the letter of credit." The trial court upheld the trustee's complaint against the bank for wrongful refusal to honor the letter of credit. On appeal, however, the appellate court reversed the lower court's ruling sustaining Crocker's defense that there had not been "strict compliance" with the terms of the letter of credit agreement. Furthermore, by filing Chapter 7 bankruptcy Swift (controlled by Colin) made it impossible for anyone to draw against the letter of credit. The appellate court also found no irregularity in the latter action. *Swift Aire Lines, David Farmer as Trustee v. Crocker National Bank and Justin Colin*, 30 B.R. 490 (1983).

Another priority creditor may be the landlord in real property leasehold or rental agreements. The landlord is entitled to rents that are owed and on-going while the property is tied up in bankruptcy. In the case of an airport as the landlord, however, this creditor priority right may be of limited benefit. Airports are established as a public service to fulfill the transportation needs of the community. Rental monies are not the primary objective. In fact, rental agreements with airlines, air carriers, and other fixed base operations are often below cost in order to attract their services. Thus, with limited airport land or building assets tied up in bankruptcy, to the exclusion of other air carriers, it may offer little consolation for the airport to receive the rental monies in the interim while public air transportation needs are not served. Quoting Paul B. Gaines, then Director of Aviation for Houston, Texas, in the reorganization petitions of Braniff International and Continental Airlines,

> *During each of these painful proceedings, airport proprietors lost control over the use of aircraft gates and terminal space, and in some cases, these facilities sat idle when the bankrupt airline closed or reduced its operations. . . This situation was compounded when other airlines were anxious to serve or expand their existing service, and the proprietor was precluded by law from making use of these scarce facilities.*

In other related cases the Chapter 11 carrier was able to lease out its protected gates at a profit while paying the airport proprietor the below breakeven cost of the original lease. Even though large air carrier airports have other available terminal and airfield assets, and may be served by multiple carriers, the loss of any space at all at already over-crowded airports can be noticeably detrimental to airport operations. Imagine, then, the effect of bankruptcy on smaller airports where the loss of space used by even one carrier is proportionally magnified. Or take the example of San Luis Obispo, California, where Swift Aire Lines was its sole carrier when it filed for bankruptcy under Chapter 7. Limited terminal space and an extensive leasehold were tied up for nearly two years, ultimately at the expense of more than 100,000 passengers in each of those years.

Fortunately, subsequent amendments to the Bankruptcy Act require an air carrier to relinquish unused terminal space within a much shorter time period. According to Paul Gaines, "The change in federal law will help assure that scarce airport gates and terminal space are made available to airlines willing and able to provide needed air service." Along with changes in the bankruptcy code, there are certain measures that airport operators can take to minimize the impact of tenant insolvency. Some of these measures are:

- *Shorter lease terms*—leases ending by term expiration during the bankruptcy proceedings cease to be property of the estate;
- *Additional guarantees*—debts not collectable from the bankrupt debtor may be collected from a guarantor;
- *Insecurity clauses*—by requiring regular financial statements, the landlord is able to terminate a lease prior to bankruptcy based upon the financial insecurity of the tenant;
- *Additional events of default*—provide for termination or modification of the lease if the landlord is given reason to believe compliance with the lease might be impaired;
- *Notice and cure provisions*—shorten or eliminate the length of time a tenant is given to cure a non-payment or other default;
- *Consensual landlord's liens*—include a lease provision granting the landlord a consensual lien (or reversion to the landlord) in case of bankruptcy;
- *Security assurances*—require tenants to provide security assurances (such as a bond) that will survive the duration of bankruptcy proceedings;
- *Use provisions*—include lease provisions restricting the use of the property for which it is being leased; and
- *Require performance*—give immediate notice to a defaulting tenant.

The above suggestions provide assurances against bankruptcy proceedings. However, the threat of bankruptcy, at least by the airlines, has seemingly been replaced in the near-term by concerns of non-competition. Following the advent of airline deregulation in 1978, air carrier solvency became an issue of growing concern. Associated with a string of airline company bankruptcies was an adverse public image of airline companies that along with the actual insolvency of airlines affected the industry as a whole. This period of high bankruptcy rate was followed by a period of consolidation amongst major carriers, coupled with a movement toward alignment of regional carriers under the umbrellas and colors of the larger, dominant airlines. Consolidation seemed to be the answer to industry-wide insolvency. But then the market began to fragment and reorganize into the so-called "legacy" carriers, Low Cost Carriers [LCCs], and regional carriers, followed by bankruptcy of the largest including United, Delta, Northwest and US Airways. Hence, concerns about bankruptcy of the airline industry have continued.

LIENS

A "lien" is a cloud on a title. By definition it is a legal claim on property as security (or interest) for a debt or charge, under which the property may be seized and sold to satisfy the debt. A lien can be in effect without actual possession of the property in question.

Liens come in various forms, and lien holders are included in what are termed "favored creditors"; that is, lienors (or lien holders) usually come ahead of others for what is owed them. A seller, for example, may transfer title under a conditional bill of sale. As a "condition" of the sale, payment must be made in full before title is fully transferred. The seller is said to hold a *chattel* mortgage, a "chattel" being personal property rather than real property. The seller retains the right of repossession for non-payment. Other examples of liens are: lawyer's, mechanic's, storage, innkeeper's, garageman's, dry cleaner's, and law violator's liens.

Southern Jersey Airways v. National Bank of Secaucus is an example of a case involving bailment, a mechanic's lien, favored creditor status, and a conditional sales agreement. Also demonstrated is the importance of expeditiously registering any title changes in aircraft with the FAA. In *Secaucus* the owner of an aircraft handed it over to Southern Jersey Airways for repair.[43] Subsequently, the owner defaulted on his conditional sales agreement with the National Bank of Secaucus, and the latter appointed a bailiff to take possession of the airplane. The bailiff purported to take possession, and posted a notice

---

[43] *Southern Jersey Airways, Inc. v. National Bank of Secaucus*, CCH 11 AVI 17,463 (1970).

of public sale. The bailiff sold the plane at public sale, and the bank purchased it as the highest bidder. However, throughout the entire process, the aircraft was physically in the hands of Southern Jersey Airways. They refused to surrender possession, relying upon their statutory mechanic's lien.

The Bank of Secaucus recorded its security agreement with the FAA. Southern Jersey Airways did not record its mechanic's lien until after the bank purported to seize and sell the aircraft (to itself) after default on the loan by the owner. The bank brought suit against Southern Jersey Airways for possession of the aircraft.

Under the Federal Aviation Act of 1958, the FAA maintains a system of both *registrations* of aircraft ownership, and for recordation of *conveyances* of aircraft and of other security instruments. Recognizing the priority of recorded security interest in the federal system of aircraft registration, and owing to the fact the bank recorded its interests prior to Jersey Airways filing of its mechanic's lien, the Atlantic County Court entered a judgment in favor of the bank.

In the appeal by Southern Jersey Airways, the New Jersey Superior Court, Appellate Division, did not place in question the priority of the federal recordation system. At issue, rather, was whether or not a mechanic's lien constitutes a recordable security interest. New Jersey law[44] granted a possessory lien for sums due for the storage, maintenance, keeping or repair of aircraft, and further stated, "The lien shall be superior to all other liens. . . ."[45] The Uniform Commercial Code, adopted in New Jersey, reads, "When a person in the ordinary course of his business furnishes services or materials with respect to *goods subject to a security interest*, a lien upon goods in the possession of such person given by statute or rule of law for such materials or services *takes priority over a perfected security interest* unless the lien is statutory and the statute expressly provides otherwise."[46]

The appellate court was convinced that Congress, in passing the 1958 Federal Aviation Act, did not intend necessarily to displace and pre-empt all state law bearing upon priorities of lien and title interests in aircraft. Rather, it was the intent of Congress to substitute, for the multiplicity of state registration or recording systems, a single pre-

---

[44] N.J.S.A. 2A: 44-1.
[45] N.J.S.A. 2A: 44-2.
[46] N.J.S.A. 12A: 9-310.

emptive federal system. Most decisions involving the Federal Aviation Act have carefully delineated federal recording provisions as preemptive and exclusive only in respect of place, requirements of recording, and the effect of failing to record a federally *recordable conveyance or instrument.* It is erroneous to assume that Congress has preempted the entire field of conveyancing of interests in aircraft.

The statutory description of recordable rights makes it doubtful that Congress contemplated recordation of a mechanic's lien. A "conveyance" is defined in 49 U.S.C.A., as "a bill of sale, contract of conditional sale, mortgage, assignment of mortgage, or other instrument affecting title to or interest in, property." It is evident that the 1958 Act contemplates a *written* instrument. Even if a lien were a recordable instrument, in the instant case, recording of the mechanic's lien would have afforded no constructive notice to the bank which had taken its interest previously. Additionally, a search of the record by the bank before its investment would not have discovered a mechanic's lien, even if it had been recorded.

The court concluded that,

- failure to record the lien did not invalidate it;
- federal recording of the bank's interest did not afford it priority over Southern Jersey Airway's recording (federal recordation is not a matter of a race to see who can record first); and
- the relative priorities in this case had to be determined according to state law, giving priority to a mechanic's lien.

Thus, the judgment was reversed and remanded. A mechanic's lien does not constitute a security interest that should be recorded.

Another type of lien is an *innkeeper's lien.* If a person stays in a motel but fails to pay the bill, the "innkeeper" may retain the person's luggage as a lien. Likewise, ordinances have been written by local governments authorizing impound of aircraft for non-payment of tie-down or storage fees. If an aircraft is left for repair and the bill for the repairs is not met, the mechanic may refuse to surrender the vehicle until the bill is paid. This is a "mechanic's" or "garageman's" lien. A lien may be placed against property for non-payment of legal fees. This is called an "attorney's" lien.

Property may be confiscated and secured against civil penalties for violations of Federal Aviation Regulations [FAR]s. Confiscation may occur in association with other federal violations as well; customs, drug enforcement, and postal violations are examples. Many aircraft have been seized for the illegal carriage of drugs, and some of these aircraft have not only been confiscated but have been added to the fleets of customs and drug enforcement agencies for use in law enforcement.

Most property is ostensibly subject to lien action. Exceptions, unless a consensual agreement has been reached, are real property, life insurance, clothing, and books and tools used for business.

FIXED BASE OPERATORS

The term "fixed base operator" is derived from the fact that the operator's service provision is geographically "fixed" at a given airport, as opposed to an airline, which has multiple stations throughout its system. Fixed base operations, often referred to in the acronym "FBO," are private enterprises offering air taxi services, flight training instruction, aircraft maintenance and repair, aircraft refueling service, aircraft storage and parking, and other ground support services to the general aviation community.

Because the majority of public airports are owned and operated by state and local governments, FBOs operating on those airports become tenants of a government (proprietor) landlord. Airports are similar to public utilities. They are monopolistic in character, and airport tenants (including FBOs) have little or no choice in shopping around for airport facilities from which to operate. Airport tenants are not only subjugated to their landlord, but the landlord in this case is a governmental bureaucracy with far reaching authority through its police powers. And the landlord, in this case, may be insulated from responsibility for its actions through certain immunities from prosecution.

Airport tenants are disadvantaged negotiators. They may find it difficult to negotiate for what they consider to be reasonable rental terms or to receive equitable and non-discriminatory treatment. Hence, rental agreements, and the right to conduct business, are primary issues with many FBOs.

Another prominent area of legal concern for the FBO is bailment. Fixed base operators are primarily in the business of renting their property and/or servicing the property of others. In either case, bailment usually occurs for which the FBO has legal responsibility. The primary FBO concerns, then, seem to focus on the one hand with rents, fees and charges imposed by the (airport) landlord. On the other hand there is the issue of fair and equitable treatment along with entrustment of the personal property of others. In the context of airport operations, the latter issue is of concern when the airport sponsor assumes responsibility for fixed base operations.

Airport charges can be categorized in two ways, as either *short-term* or *long-term*. Short-term arrangements are the most flexible and are generally based upon direct user fees. They are normally established in some form of rate structure or rental agreement. Direct user fees comprise those charges most directly associated with use of the public areas of the airfield such as landing fees, aircraft storage, transient tie-down fees and fuel flowage. Long-term agreements are leases (rather than rental) of land, terminal floor space, and other buildings.

Where the tenant is to develop capital improvements without governmental assistance, it is often necessary that the tenant obtain long-term rights to property in order to secure favorable bank financing. The granting of long-term proprietary rights to public land for private use brings up the issue of *possessory interest* taxes. When real estate is transferred to the public sector, it is removed from the property tax roles and is no longer a source of revenue for the government. Conversely, if it is transferred to the private sector, it is again taxable. If, however, title to property is retained by the government but turned over through rental or long-term lease to the private sector for private commercial purposes, this conversion of the land may again subject it to taxation.[47] Thus, the tenant may be responsible for possessory taxes over and above the leasehold agreement.

---

[47] For example, *see Reading Municipal Airport Authority v. Schuylkill Valley School District*, CCH 12 AVI 17,307 (1972). In *Reading* there was a question of whether hangars, leased by an airport to an FBO, were subject to taxation. The airport authority borrowed money to purchase two buildings containing 16 T-hangars. It leased the T-hangar buildings to a fixed base operator. The FBO in turn leased the sixteen T-hangars to owners of private aircraft based at the airport. The issue in this case was whether the two buildings were entitled to exemption from local property taxation. The county tax assessor, as well as the Pennsylvania Court of Common Pleas, determined the buildings were not tax exempt. Where buildings are provided to a *private* business entity with no restriction as to use or charges for use, and available for rental by that private business organization to persons of its unfettered choosing, there is not a public use. The hangars, therefore, were not entitled to the public subsidy of tax exemption. The airport authority appealed, but the Commonwealth Court of Pennsylvania affirmed the lower court's ruling.

As airports are not supposed to make a profit, or at least are to turn any profits back into the airport, the rates charged for providing specific services generally are established to recover only the costs of providing those services. Bringing the rates in line with actual fiscal requirements is a difficult and politically sensitive task. The airport's view of what constitutes a reasonable charge may be very different from that of its tenants. As few airports are capable of fully paying their way, it is necessary for the airport to maximize its revenues, but not at the price of injustice to its tenants and users. Each tenant must be able to generate sufficient revenues to recover its costs and must be able to make a reasonably expected profit. If a tenant in private business is unable to generate sufficient revenues, the laws of economics hypothesize that the tenant will seek alternative opportunities elsewhere. But in a monopoly there are no choices, the airport tenant must, voluntarily where possible but involuntarily if necessary, obtain equitable lease arrangements. That sometimes means taking the airport sponsor to court.

Rents and fees are perhaps the most common ground for disagreement between tenants and the airport sponsor, but this is by no means the only area where differences arise. Another prominent area is in *discrimination*, or its opposite *exclusive rights*; i.e. antitrust. Fixed base operators, especially when there is only one on an airport, often serve a dual role both as entrepreneurs and as managers of the airport for the airport sponsor. When FBOs develop a close working relationship with the airport sponsor (or at least closer than others), there is a tendency for them to receive preferential treatment over existing or potential competition.

Section 308 of the Federal Aviation Act, however, specifically prohibits exclusive rights by stating, "There shall be no exclusive right for the use of any landing area or air navigation facility upon which Federal funds have been expended." Even though Section 308 prohibits exclusivity, the FAA for many years supported a policy of protectionism for airport-based operators, at times sanctioning the airport sponsor's decision to have only one fixed base operator on its airport.

In the philosophical dichotomy between providing an atmosphere conducive to open competition, while at the same time protecting certain businesses, airport managers find themselves squarely between competing interests and a lawsuit erupts over charges of antitrust violation.

ANTITRUST IMMUNITY

In 1984 Congress granted to local governments, including airport authorities, *antitrust immunity*. By definition a "trust" as used herein is a combination of business firms by agreement, and which reduces, or is intended to reduce, competition. Thus, "anti-trust" means against monopolistic agreements.

Congress in 1890 passed the Sherman Act, which was intended to discourage the concentration of smaller businesses into monopolies. It declared illegal "every contract, combination in the form of trust, or otherwise, or conspiracy in restraint of trade among the several states." It prescribed punishment by fine or imprisonment or both for "every person who shall monopolize, or attempt to monopolize, or combine or conspire . . . to monopolize any part of the trade or commerce among the several states." Under the provisions of this act, decisions handed down in 1911 by the Supreme Court ordered the dissolution of the targeted Standard Oil Company and the American Tobacco Company. It was an act to protect trade and commerce against unlawful restraints and monopolies.

The Clayton Act of 1914 was enacted in response to labor concerns over right to organize and became a supplement to existing laws against unlawful restraints and monopolies and for other purposes. This law was intended to remove ambiguities in the Sherman Act by making certain specific practices illegal. Price discrimination among buyers was forbidden, along with exclusive selling and tying contracts, if their effect was to lessen competition. The Clayton Act also clearly stated there was no provision in antitrust laws to forbid the formation of labor unions.

The antitrust laws are codified in Title 15 of the United States Code. As adopted into Section 408 of the Aviation Act of 1958 (as amended by the Airline Deregulation Act of 1978) antitrust activity is unlawful, *except as approved by the government*. If the activities of a local government (hence an airport) are authorized by the State, the local government's competitive activities are protected by the "state action" exemption to the federal antitrust laws.[48] The Airline Deregu-

[48] See *Parker v. Brown*, 317 U.S. 341 (1943).

lation Act of 1978 discontinued antitrust immunity (in part) for the airlines. Subsequent to the 1978 Act, and through the edict of governmental deregulatory policy, the courts and the U.S. Justice Department began to concentrate their efforts on enforcing antitrust violations. Supreme Court decisions in 1978 and 1982 virtually stripped local governments of any antitrust immunity assumed shared with the states. Hundreds of antitrust suits against airports were subsequently filed. On the horns of a dilemma, airport operators needed to restrict the number of concessionaires such as restaurants, parking lot companies, taxi operators, and others, in order to maintain services at levels the airport facilities were capable of handling.

In response to "public convenience and necessity," Congress in 1984 passed a law[49] to limit liability of local governments including airport authorities, to injunctive relief only. The law removed the threat of potential liability for treble (monetary) damages for antitrust violations. A plaintiff could hope to stop the government from its antitrust actions, but was barred from seeking monetary compensation for damages.

Historically, the courts have been reluctant to grant injunctions against public airports since such action could threaten the availability to the public of scheduled air transportation services.[50] Although not related directly to aviation, but in fact dealing with monopoly over sewage treatment in the area of city services, the U.S. Supreme Court, in a 1985 Wisconsin municipal antitrust case, broadened the exemption from antitrust prosecution for local governments including air-

---

[49] H.R. 6027.

[50] *See Loma Portal Civil Club v. American Airlines, Inc.*, 394 P 2d 548 (1964). In *Loma Portal*, plaintiffs resided in the Loma Portal area of San Diego, just west of Lindbergh Field. The plaintiffs sought from the court an injunction against the defendant airlines, to *prohibit* operation of their jet aircraft "at low altitudes in close proximity to such residences in such manner and at such times as to interfere unreasonably with the normal use and enjoyment by plaintiffs of their homes." There were no claims for damages. This was important because it characterized the case only as an action to *enjoin* a claimed nuisance, and not to recover any damages for injury. It is well established that public policy denies an injunction and permits only the recovery of damages where private property has been put to a public use by a public service corporation and the public interest has intervened. The Supreme Court of California held that a request in superior court for an injunction to prohibit a nuisance was properly denied, as a matter of law. Under the facts of this case, (i.e., the operation of aircraft with federal airworthiness certificates in federally-certificated, scheduled passenger service, in conformity with federal safety regulations, in a manner not creating imminent danger, and in furtherance of the public interest in safe, regular air transportation of goods and passengers) an injunction is not available. However, the court noted that nothing in their findings was intended to be a determination of the rights of landowners to seek *damages*.

ports. The Supreme Court held that anti-competitive conduct by a municipality is protected by the state action exemption to the federal antitrust laws where it is authorized by the state, even though the state does not "compel" or actively supervise the anti-competitive conduct.[51]

TORT LIABILITY

In dealing with a State or with the Federal government on tort issues, a private citizen must contend with the doctrine of *sovereign immunity* when bringing suit against the government. Such is not necessarily the case with local governments including airport sponsors. In the exercise of governmental functions the airport sponsor may benefit from extension of the state's sovereign immunity. On the other hand, the courts in some instances have held that the local government in its operation of an airport was acting in a purely proprietary capacity. In certain aspects of airport operation the local government possesses all the necessary powers to operate an airport—that is, to obtain or sell property, to regulate the airport, and to charge fees for its use. As proprietors, airports may charge fees to recoup the costs of operation, so long as the fees are reasonable.[52] Airports may also assess charges as a (governmental) regulatory function such as the imposition of fees in an attempt to divert traffic to another airport.[53] But where proprietary regulations have been unreasonable or

---

[51] See *Town of Hallie et al. v. City of Eau Claire*, 85 L Ed 2d 24, (1985).

[52] *The issue in American v. Massachusetts Port Authority*, 560 F 2d 1036 (1977) was whether an airport may charge for the utility of facilities not used. The MASSPORT increased its landing fees to offset the cost of three construction projects, all of which were deemed by the airlines to be of little or no use to them. Plaintiffs, eighteen airlines, sought a declaratory judgment that the action of MASSPORT was an unconstitutional burden on interstate commerce. The U.S. District Court dismissed the complaint, and granted summary judgment for MASSPORT. The court relied upon language in *Evansville-Vanderburgh v. Delta Airlines*, 405 U.S. 707, 92 S.Ct. 1349, 31 L. Ed. 2d 620 (1972), wherein that court determined that a tax may not be "excessive in comparison with the government benefit conferred." The overwhelming thrust of the language was toward a comparison of the tax with costs incurred in connection with construction of facilities. The appellate court in this case stated it could not see how a federal system, recognizing state sovereignty, could work on a basis of customer judgments of benefits received. If taxes, such as landing fees, were to be subject to attack from each user, depending upon the particular *utility*, their imposition could be a matter of endless and shifting controversy.

[53] In *Aircraft Owners and Pilots Association v. Port Authority of New York and New Jersey*, 305 F Supp 93 (1969), there was a question of whether an airport may impose a fee in an attempt to divert traffic to another airport. The Port Authority, for the professed purpose of relieving congestion and achieving maximum efficient operation of its three major airports, and with the professed intention of influencing general aviation operators to transfer their operations else-

discriminatory, or especially where they have conflicted with state or federal regulatory schemes, they have been held invalid.

In an attempt to divert, or to otherwise discourage general aviation, including commuter carriers, from using Logan International Airport, the Massachusetts Port Authority [MASSPORT] proposed implementation of its Program for Airport Capacity Efficiency [PACE] which would have dramatically increased landing fees. Three lawsuits, combined in a class action to challenge PACE, were brought by the National Business Aircraft Association, the Aircraft Owners and Pilots Association, and by the New England Legal Foundation with the Regional Airline Association. In an initial finding, a federal district court judge ruled that the MASSPORT plan for fee increases was legal. He determined the fees were reasonable, were not discriminating, and did not preempt any power intended by Congress to rest with federal authorities. Still, he questioned why the general aviation fee increase was so dramatic—between 250 to 300%!

Taking an opposing position, and subsequent to the ruling in the district court, an Administrative Law Judge [ALJ] for the Department of Transportation [DOT] rendered his preliminary decision in the DOT's investigation of the MASSPORT fees. The ALJ ruled that the PACE proposal violated grant assurances pursuant to Section 511 of the Airport and Airway Improvement Act of 1982, because the fees were not "fair and reasonable." It was "discriminatory" under Section 511. It violated the *Anti-Head Tax Act*,[54] because it was not "reasonable." It "invaded" the authority of the DOT in violation of section

---

where during peak traffic periods, adopted a minimum charge for takeoff during defined peak operating periods. Claiming discrimination, plaintiffs sued to enjoin any further enforcement of the regulation. The FAA intervened by acknowledging the fee and that it was intended to provide traffic relief and not to correct a safety problem. The FAA itself had imposed an increased minimum charge for landing at Washington National Airport, put into effect to relieve congestion. In deciding the discrimination issue, the U.S. District Court said there was no basis for denying the FAA and airport owners the power to differentiate among kinds of flights. All persons have equal rights of access to the navigable air space, but one aircraft approach may represent the right of over 150 passengers to have access to the navigable airways and landing areas. The next plane may represent the right of one or of two persons to have access to the airways and landing areas. To treat them alike in allocating scarce landing and take-off time and space is to ignore, and not to recognize the basic right of equal access to airways and landing areas. Considerations of safety and of efficient utilization of the air space are both valid grounds upon which to establish preferential assignments of landing and take-off times, and are perfectly compatible with the interest of every person in the protection of his or her freedom of access to navigable airways and related landing areas. The district court granted the defendant's motion for summary judgment, and the action was dismissed.

[54] 49 U.S.C. §1513.

307 of the Federal Aviation Act of 1958. It was contrary to the prohibitions set forth in Section 105 of the Federal Aviation Act. It was preempted by federal law and thus unlawful. And the fee structure violated the Commerce Clause of the U.S. Constitution and was therefore unlawful.

The class action suit was finally settled in 1991, following a court decision in 1988, which ultimately found the higher fees to be unlawful. Under the settlement, those who paid excess fees were refunded the difference, plus one year's interest, minus fees and expenses. The settlement cost MASSPORT an estimated $2.68 million, plus interest.

Public airports have, more or less, been granted antitrust immunity, and in some instances immunity for their actions as governmental agencies. Nevertheless, airport sponsors still have tort liability. Their liability for injuries resulting from negligent operation depends to an extent upon whether in the specific instance the airport operation is a *proprietary* or a *governmental* function. Most tort actions are the result of hazardous conditions that contribute to accident and personal injury or property loss. Liability for injury often results from lack of supervision or failure to exercise the due care of a reasonable person (i.e., to be "negligent").

In most instances airport sponsors may be held liable for negligence in failing to maintain the airport in a safe condition, failure to protect airport users and visitors (i.e., "business invitees") from reasonably foreseeable dangers, or failure to discharge the duty of a bailee in caring for property.[55] In tort liability a "guest" assumes much of the liability of the host. But a "business invitee" is offered a higher degree of care than are non-commercial guests. The business

---

[55] *See Slapin v. Los Angeles International Airport*, 65 Cal App 3d 484 (1976). In *Slapin* it was held that the airport was liable as a proprietor for reasonably foreseeable dangers. Plaintiff Herman Slapin was assaulted and severely injured by unknown persons while in a parking lot at Los Angeles International Airport. The allegation was that for some time prior to the assault, the defendant airport knew the parking lot was dangerous and unsafe unless properly supervised, maintained, patrolled and protected. Nevertheless, the airport "carelessly, negligently, and improperly owned, operated, managed, maintained, supervised, controlled, lighted and secured said parking area in such a fashion and manner so as to maintain a dangerous condition of property." The Superior Court of Los Angeles County sustained the city's *demurrer* to the complaint, that to the extent the plaintiffs' complaint sought recovery for failure of the city to provide sufficient patrolling or police protection at the parking lot, it failed to state a cause of action. A public entity is specifically *immunized* from liability for such failure by Government Code. Plaintiffs appealed, contending this immunity should not apply to a situation where the governmental entity is engaged in a *proprietary* function; *i.e.*, operating a parking lot for paying patrons. The California Court of Appeal agreed by holding that plaintiffs were entitled to attempt to prove their negligence cause and the case was remanded.

operator owes an invitee ordinary care and warnings of known hazards. Airport management, as a proprietor, has a legal duty to react to, and prevent, any conditions or actions, which in themselves create a dangerous or hazardous situation. The courts have held that airports must be kept safe for invitees and other users.[56]

TORT IMMUNITY

Most courts have not regarded state laws as granting governmental immunity in the operation of public airports. Rather, airports are generally viewed as proprietary in nature, and the government sponsors held liable for torts accordingly, except where states have *expressly* granted tort immunity for local government operation of an airport.[57] In most instances the local government's liability for torts arising from airport operation is the same as that of a private person. The general rule is that municipalities are immune from suit in the exercise of their governmental functions, but are not immune for their proprietary or businesslike activities.

For example, associated with its government police powers, an airport is responsible for preventing unauthorized access to air opera-

---

[56] In *Brown v. Sioux City, Iowa*, 49 NW 2d 853 (1951), C.A. Brown sued the city of Sioux City, Iowa, alleging in his petition that he rented certain property located at the municipal airport, for the purpose of maintaining and establishing colonies of bees thereon, and that the city was negligent in spraying the airport property with chlordane, such that his bees were sprayed. The bees picked up the poisonous substance and carried it back to the bee colonies, with the result that his bees died, his honey was permeated with the poisonous substance and rendered unfit, and the hives also were rendered unfit for further use. His petition alleged that the city operated the Sioux City Airport in its proprietary capacity. At the conclusion of the evidence, the trial court submitted to the jury the questions of defendant's negligence, plaintiff's freedom from contributory negligence, and whether the defendant was acting in a *governmental* or *proprietary* capacity. After a verdict for the plaintiff for $1,500, the trial court sustained the defendant's motion for judgment notwithstanding the verdict, on the ground "that the operation of the air base was a governmental function. The plaintiff appealed. In its review, the Iowa Supreme Court concluded that it is the established rule in most jurisdictions, that a municipality, in the exercise of its *purely governmental function*, is not liable for negligence. But this rule of governmental immunity is to be strictly construed. In renting for revenue, the city was functioning in its *proprietary* capacity. The city cannot accept and exercise the special privilege of leasing its property to tenants without assuming the responsibilities and liabilities flowing from that relationship.

[57] The question of airport immunity from tort liability was addressed in *Joseph H. Scotti v. City of Birmingham* 337 SO. 2d 350 (1976). Scotti sued the City of Birmingham, Alabama, after sustaining injuries in a fall allegedly caused by a wet slippery mat at an entrance doorway of the Birmingham Municipal Airport. The defendant, City of Birmingham, filed a motion for summary judgment, contending it was *immune* by state law from liability for its negligence at the airport. The motion was granted and the action dismissed. Scotti appealed from the judgment of dismissal. The Alabama Supreme Court affirmed the circuit court judgment in favor of the city, finding it immune from suit for negligence.

tions areas and for providing law enforcement officers. The exercise of state police powers may afford certain immunities for the airport. However, in protecting the public against security risk, airport authorities must respect the civil rights of the traveling public. Moreover, airports are responsible for protecting the well being of "invitees" (i.e., passengers and other airport customers) just as any other private enterprise.

ENVIRONMENTAL ISSUES

Environmental issues cannot be skirted, especially not by the aviation community. When confronted by a concern about the environment, the airport sponsor must meet the issue head-on. Historical litigation has shown that if there is the slightest chance a proposed action might be controversial on environmental grounds, it is far less trouble to prepare an Environmental Impact Statement [EIS] than to resolve the issue in court. If in doubt as to whether or not an EIS is necessary, it is normally considered more expedient to go ahead and prepare an EIS rather than to chance its necessity later. For example, in the case of Atlanta Hartsfield Airport, the performance of an EIS was required retroactively after the National Environmental Policy Act [NEPA] of 1969 was enacted.[58] The absence of an EIS has proven to be the weakest defense an airport proprietor can have.

Aircraft can pollute the environment in several ways, but the worst pollutant of all is noise. Airplanes emit solid particulates, expel noxious gases, and theoretically can affect the ozone layer; but none of these possibilities has caused as much turmoil as has noise. Aside from aircraft as a point source, other sources of air pollution around airports may be from airport construction equipment and emissions from the following: gasoline operated aircraft ground service equip-

---

[58] In *City of Atlanta v. United States of America, et al.*, CCH 16 AVI 18,453 (1982), the City of Atlanta submitted an Airport Layout Plan [ALP] to the FAA, which provided for a considerable upgrading of the facilities at Hartsfield International Airport. The FAA approved the Plan on June 12, 1968 (*i.e.*, before the NEPA became law on January 1, 1970). The question before the U.S. District Court was the applicability of the provisions of NEPA to these actions. The FAA contended that NEPA required it to prepare at least an Environmental Assessment [EA] before taking any action. The city disagreed and brought this action for a declaratory judgment that NEPA was inapplicable. The issue before the court was not the retroactive application of NEPA to federal actions taken before July 1, 1970; rather it was the application of NEPA to federal actions occurring after NEPA became effective in a project undertaken before NEPA's effective date. Defendant FAA's motion for summary judgment was granted. Plaintiff City of Atlanta's motion for summary judgment was denied.

ment, access traffic entering and leaving the airport, exhaust from maintenance equipment, heating and air conditioning plants, and from the fuel handling and storage system. Airport operations can also adversely impact water sources. Water pollution is perhaps the best understood of the environmental concerns, and therefore is the easiest to rectify. The major source of water pollution is storm water run-off, which can remove contaminants from pavement surfaces. Another ecological factor that can have a significant effect upon airport development and operation is wildlife. Of principal concern are birds in the vicinity of the air movement area, but other forms of wildlife may be a problem too.[59]

AIRCRAFT NOISE

Aircraft noise is without question the severest environmental problem associated with an airport. It can make an airport unpopular no matter how well the airport serves the transportation needs of the community, or how greatly it contributes to the community's economic well being. Across the nation aircraft noise has sparked lawsuits seeking relief from airport-related noise.[60] Public opposition to airport noise has become increasingly vocal and sophisticated. In many instances, court actions are initiated to restrict or close airports.

The primary concern with noise is that it annoys people to the point where it constrains an individual's activities. It especially inter-

[59] In *Safeco Insurance Company of America v. City of Watertown, South Dakota, and Safeco Insurance Company of America v. United States of America,* CCH 16 AVI 18,201 (1981), plaintiff, as subrogee of its insured, brought these actions, (consolidated for trial) to recover for property damage to a twinjet aircraft, which crashed on take-off from the Watertown Municipal Airport. The plaintiff brought action against the City of Watertown as operator of the Airport, and sued the U.S. under the Federal Tort Claims Act [FTCA]. Almost immediately after takeoff the plane encountered a flock of Franklin gulls. Some of the gulls were ingested into the airplane's engines. All power was lost, and the aircraft crashed. To make out a cause of action under the FTCA, the plaintiff had to overcome the authority of a number of cases, the essence of which stated that the mere provision for government safety inspections, or the ability to stop an activity for failure to comply with safety standards, does not impose liability on the government for failure to do so. Thus, the complaint against the United States for negligent failure to discover and correct the bird problem had to be dismissed. However, this court had no hesitation in finding that the operator of a public airport has a duty independent of federal statutes and regulations to the pilots using the airport to use reasonable care to keep the airport free from hazards—or at least to use reasonable care to warn of hazards not known to the pilots. The district court found that the Watertown Airport, under the circumstances, owed the pilots a duty to warn them of the possible presence of gulls; that defendant City of Watertown breached this duty by failing to so warn; and that the failure to warn was the proximate cause of the crash.

[60] For more discussion related to aviation noise *see* Ch. 7.

feres with sleep and with communications. Noise is more than sound—it is *unwanted* sound. It is a *nuisance*. To demonstrate the noise liability issue surrounding airports, the case of the Burbank-Glendale-Pasadena Airport is instrumental. In 1975, Lockheed (the original owner of the Burbank-Glendale-Pasadena Airport) had applied for variance from state noise standards, and it was because of its inability to work a financially feasible solution to various problems created by aircraft noise, that Lockheed had decided to divest itself of the Burbank Airport. Pursuant to the Airport and Airway Development Act of 1970, the FAA was required to assure that "all possible steps have been taken to minimize (any) adverse effect (upon the environment)." Thus, that responsibility was passed along to the new Joint Powers Authority amongst its newly adopted noise abatement rules, air carriers were required to comply with FAR Part 36 and a resolution (Rule 7) which provided in part:

> *. . . proposed implementation of service by a new carrier, shall be subject to the prior approval of the Commission, which approval shall not be granted except upon a determination by the Commission that such proposed increase in flight frequencies or such proposed implementation of service by a new carrier will be consistent with the provisions of the existing Grant Agreements between the Authority and the Federal Aviation Administration and any other applicable statutory or contractual restraints governing flight operations at the Airport. . . .*

Hughes Airwest, following adoption of Rule 7, and without Commission approval, increased its weekly schedule of flights at Burbank. The airport authority filed suit. The court ruled in favor of the airport, stating that its Rule 7 was a reasonable, non-arbitrary and non-capricious regulation.[61] In *Baker v. Burbank-Glendale-Pasadena Airport*, the California Supreme Court in 1984 held that a public airport

[61] *The Burbank-Glendale-Pasadena Airport Authority v. Hughes Air Corporation*, Superior Court of the State of California for the County of Los Angeles, Case No. 17926B (1980).

constitutes a "continuing" nuisance.[62] Under this ruling a plaintiff could bring successive actions against an airport, effectively providing that person with a perpetual annuity just for living near the airport. In light of decisions in *Baker* and in a companion case, *Blaine et al. v. Burbank-Glendale-Pasadena Airport*, it is interesting to note that the airport had not only produced a Noise Exposure Map [NEM], but it had repeatedly demonstrated its ability to *reduce* the airport's impact upon the surrounding community by lowering its noise exposure (i.e.: reducing the noise contours on the NEM).

LAND USE CONTROLS

Once the airport's impact upon the community has been established through production of a NEM, and the minimized noise impact areas have been defined, a recommended pattern of land use in the vicinity of the airport can be developed. The objective is to ensure land use that is fully compatible according to commonly accepted criteria. Yet, achieving fully compatible land use according to the criteria may not be possible in all cases. When the community has made irreversible commitments and owners and developers make significant investments in land, compromise recommendations may be the best that can be attained. A wide variety of instruments are normally available to local governments and airport sponsors to control the compatibility of surrounding land uses. Generally, they fall into two principal categories: those that involve *ownership* of property rights and provide absolute control, and those that depend upon *administrative and regulatory action* and provide less certain controls. The most generally used controls are zoning, easements, and land purchase.

ACQUISITION IN FEE SIMPLE

Purchase of the land with ownership to all property rights is the most positive form of land use control. It is also the most expensive (at least initially). Acquisition in *fee simple* is appropriate only when there is reasonable doubt that the community has the ability to otherwise adequately control use of the land. The FAA can sometimes aid in the purchase of clear zones, but funds for this purpose are limited. The costs for acquisition must also take into account the removal of

---

[62] *Kenneth L. Baker et al. v. Burbank-Glendale-Pasadena Authority*, 197 Cal. Rptr. 357 (1984).

the property from the tax roles. But in the long run if the property is resold for compatible uses the net cost can be effectively reduced. Should the property remain under government control and leased to the private sector, the initial purchase cost will be recovered through time, and the government may assess taxes for the lessee's *possessory interest* in the land.

EASEMENTS

Like fee simple title, an *easement* is a permanent acquisition, but for only part of the property rights. Since it does not involve total transfer of the property, the transaction may oftentimes be far less expensive than a fee simple purchase. There are many types of easements depending upon the select property rights desired. So long as the easement does not significantly reduce the overall value of property, it may be obtained at reasonable cost. The more the easement impairs the usage of the land, the higher the cost will be until at some point it is more cost-effective to purchase the property outright.

Easements are classified as either *positive* or *negative*. For airport protection purposes, an easement to allow the unobstructed passage of aircraft through the airspace above a parcel of property is an example of a positive easement. Exemplary of a typical negative easement would be one where heights of man-made objects or natural vegetation are restricted from intruding into navigable airspace.

Easements may be obtained by *purchase*, *condemnation*, or by *dedication*. In dedication, the owner may be willing to voluntarily release certain property rights in exchange for some development right such as the right to subdivide.

LAND LEASE

Leasing of land may yield the same positive control as the purchase of property. However, property rights are obtained for a limited period of time only, and not in perpetuity as with title to the land.

ZONING

Certain property rights are always retained by the state such as police power, taxation, eminent domain, and escheat. *Police power* is the inherent power of government to exercise reasonable control over persons and property in the interest of the public's general security, health, safety, morals and welfare. *Zoning* is an exercise of police power. It is the most common and useful land use control. Zoning is advantageous because it can promote compatibility, but at the same time leave land in private ownership and on the tax roles. Unlike outright purchase of land, it is not permanent. Zoning can be readily reversed by legislation. It has some other limitations as well. Zoning is not retroactive, and existing nonconforming uses must be allowed to remain; zoning is limited by jurisdiction, and airport impacts often span more than one governmental jurisdiction, zoning boards may grant variances; and zoning must be applied fairly and be based upon a community plan.

Zoning cannot be used simply because of noise impact. There must be other, more comprehensive reasons for zoning. The most wide spread use of zoning around airports is for *height and hazard* to protect airspace in the airport vicinity from intrusion by high objects.

OTHER CONTROLS

Besides zoning, other controls having either less or special applicability include building codes, health and housing codes, programming of public capital improvements, and cooperation of financial institutions.

- *Comprehensive plans*, while not a direct control, are a basis and policy guide for land use, zoning, transportation, public facilities and capital improvement decisions. The airport land use compatibility plan is a part of the community's comprehensive plan.
- *Subdivision regulations* are usually separated from actual land use controls, but can be a useful tool in controlling urbanization and density in development areas.
- *Building and housing codes* do not control land uses, but do regulate construction standards. Building codes may provide noise reduction through the use of soundproofing materials in building construction.
- *Capital improvement programming* can be one of the more effective ways of controlling undesirable uses. The scheduling of

water and sewer extensions, for example, may determine where future development takes place.

- *Truth in sales and rental ordinances* can be used to discourage development in noise sensitive areas. This is known as the giving of "constructive notice." Such an ordinance may also be used as a defense should legal action be brought against the airport. If people are made aware of the potential exposure prior to taking possession of property, any case against aircraft noise intrusion may be compromised. A truth in sales and rental ordinance simply states that if a property has possible exposure to the influences of airport operations, the owner must divulge that fact to prospective buyers or renters.
- *Voluntary relocation programs* assist residents and local businesses in noise sensitive areas that wish to voluntarily relocate outside the noise impact area. Usually, the associated moving costs are subsidized to make up for loss in property value, transportation expenses, increased costs of new residences, mortgage penalties, realty fees, and so forth. The provisions of the *Uniform Relocation Assistance and Real Property Acquisition Policies Act* of 1970 are applicable whenever federal programs are involved. Purchase assurance programs may also be associated with relocation programs, in that they guarantee the salability of properties.
- *Mortgage and construction loans* issued by both private and public lending institutions can influence development if aviation noise criteria are included in their review and approval procedures. The Department of Housing and Urban Development [HUD] promulgated its noise assessment guidelines[63] for screening mortgaging guarantees and other HUD assistance. Veterans Administration and Federal Housing Administration insured loans are subject to review on the basis of HUD's noise assessment guidelines.
- *Insurance limitations* and rate structures have the potential for reducing development in areas exposed to noise, but particularly if exposed to accident potential. Federal Aviation Regulation Part 77 imposes requirements for the public to give notice of any construction which may create an aviation safety hazard.

[63] HUD, Circular 1390.2 (Jul.1971).

If in its airspace review the FAA determines that the object would be an obstruction to air navigation, it is likely that an insurance underwriter would either not insure the structure, or would assign it a higher rate because of its potential risk.

AVIATION SAFETY AND NOISE ABATEMENT ACT

Implementation of operational airport noise abatement strategies is the airport's responsibility. In this regard, the Department of Defense [DOD] took an early lead in working toward airport compatibility when in 1973 it set forth DOD policy on achieving compatible use of public and private lands in the vicinity of military airfields. From the military's *Air Installation Compatible Land Use Zones* [AICUZ] program has evolved the Federal government's program for "Noise Control And Compatibility Planning For Airports," (AC 150/5020-1), or what have become commonly known as "FAR Part 150 Studies."

The purpose of the *Aviation Safety and Noise Abatement Act* of 1979 is to provide assistance to airport operators in preparing and carrying out noise compatibility programs, to provide assistance that assures continued safety in aviation, and for other purposes. The Act is a decisive one and has the express intent of standardizing noise measurement methodologies and land use compatibility programs in the U.S. and for the legal protection of threatened airports.

By no later than one year after passage of the Noise Abatement Act the Secretary of Transportation (in consultation with the Administrator of the Environmental Protection Agency and other appropriate agencies) was to:

- Establish a single system of measuring noise;
- Establish a single system for determining the exposure of individuals to aircraft noise; and
- Identify land uses which are normally compatible with various exposures of individuals to noise.

A product of an FAR Part 150 Study is the Noise Exposure Map. The purpose of the NEM is to depict the airport's present and future noise patterns, and the areas of present and future land use development which are not compatible with those noise patterns. The maps are prepared after consultation with the public, affected local governments, airport users, and the FAA. Utilizing local data and FAR Part 150 land use compatibility guidance, the sponsor determines and labels the non-compatible land uses, including noise sensitive uses such as residential area, schools, hospitals, libraries, rest homes, and auditoriums. After certification is true and correct, the maps and supporting data are submitted to the FAA for review and acceptance. Upon acceptance of the NEM by FAA, and publication by the sponsor to give reasonable notice, persons who subsequently acquire property in noise sensitive areas shall be presumed to have *constructive knowledge* of the existence of the NEM. And they shall not be entitled to recover damages due to airport related noise.

The purpose of the other major FAR Part 150 product, the airport's *Noise Compatibility Program* [NCP], is to formulate possible solutions to the noise problems identified by the noise exposure maps. This is a process in which a number of viable solutions are explored and the most workable of them are selected for full development. Total costs of each alternative are included in the considerations. The entire process is carried out in consultation with the affected local governments, the airport's users, those people impacted by the noise, and with the FAA. The program should include an implementation schedule, should identify who will be responsible for implementing the program, and should identify extent and source of the necessary funds. The total noise compatibility program is then submitted to FAA for approval.

After FAA acceptance of the NEM and publication of the availability of the NCP in the *Federal Register*, the agency has 180 days to complete its review and make a finding. Otherwise, the NEM and NCP are approved by default except for any portion of a program relating to the use of flight procedures for noise control purposes. FAA approval of Part 150 Studies will be given only for those recommendations, which:

- Do not compromise safety;
- Do not impose an undue burden on interstate or foreign commerce;
- Do not discriminate for or against any group or class of users of operators;
- Are meaningful and serve to provide real noise abatement;

- Comply with federal airport grant agreements, which are funded by the flying public; and
- Do not conflict with or invade areas of responsibility vested in the federal government.

No part of the adopted noise map or related information, or any part of the listed compatible land uses can be admitted as evidence, or used for any other purpose, in any suit or action seeking damages or other relief for the noise that results from the operation of an airport. Further, no person acquiring property in an area surrounding an airport and included in the adopted noise map is entitled to recover damages for airport noise after the date of such property acquisition. The only exceptions are where there has been a significant change in aircraft operations; change in airport layout; change in flight patterns; or an increase in nighttime operations. There is some concern that the provisions of this Act which prohibit recovery of damages resulting from aircraft noise may be unenforceable in court. The Fifth Amendment to the U.S. Constitution guarantees its citizens certain property rights, among which is the right to just compensation for property (rights) taken by a governmental entity. The right of a citizen to recover from *inverse condemnation* (i.e., a "taking" without due process and without compensation) cannot be abrogated by Congress. However, the Act's provisions may prove more beneficial to airport sponsors in tort (civil/negligence) cases where nuisance is the issue rather than property rights or eminent domain.

In a vein similar in philosophy to application of the Noise Exposure Map in FAR Part 150 Studies, when the cities of Burbank, Glendale and Pasadena, California, formed a Joint Powers Authority in order to buy and operate the privately owned Hollywood-Burbank Airport, they obtained funds for the acquisition from the Federal government. In their contractual assurances the cities were required by the FAA to comply with California Governmental Code Section 6546.1 which in part provided that: "In operating the airport, the separate public entity (Joint Powers Authority) shall not permit or authorize any activity in conjunction with the airport which results in an increase in the size of the noise impact area."

In 1975, the Lockheed Corporation (the previous airport owner) had applied for variance from state noise standards, and it was because of its inability to work a financially feasible solution to various problems created by aircraft noise, Lockheed had decided to divest itself of the Burbank Airport. Pursuant to the Airport and Airway Development Act of 1970, the FAA was required to assure that "all possible steps have been taken to minimize (any) adverse effect (upon the environment)." The responsibility to minimize environmental impacts was passed along to the new Joint Powers Authority. Amongst its newly adopted noise abatement rules, air carriers were required to comply with FAR Part 36 and a resolution (Rule 7) which provided in part:

> *Proposed implementation of service by a new carrier, shall be subject to the prior approval of the Commission, which approval shall not be granted except upon a determination by the Commission that such proposed increase in flight frequencies or such proposed implementation of service by a new carrier will be consistent with the provisions of the existing Grant Agreements between the Authority and the Federal Aviation Administration and any other applicable statutory or contractual restraints governing flight operations at the Airport. . . .*

Hughes Airwest, following adoption of Rule 7, and without Commission approval, increased its weekly schedule of flights at Burbank. The airport authority filed suit. The court ruled in favor of the airport, stating that its Rule 7 was a reasonable, non-arbitrary and non-capricious regulation.[64] But in a subsequent case, the California Supreme Court held in *Baker et al. v. Burbank-Glendale-Pasadena Authority* that a public airport constitutes a "continuing nuisance."[65] Under this ruling a plaintiff could bring successive actions against an airport, effectively providing that particular person with a perpetual annuity just for living near the airport. Related cases brought against the Burbank-Glendale-Pasadena Airport involved approximately 375 plaintiffs; with each plaintiff subsequent to the initial decision filing

---

[64] *See The Burbank-Glendale-Pasadena Airport Authority v. Hughes Air Corporation*, Superior Court of the State of California for the County of Los Angeles, Case No. 17926B (Sep. 1980).

[65] *Baker et al. v. Burbank-Glendale-Pasadena Authority*, 39 Cal 3d 862 (1985).

new claims against the airport for $100,000 apiece for personal injuries and emotional distress, and $100,000 apiece for property damage—claims totaling approximately $75 million on a potentially recurring basis.

The *Baker* decision was appealed to the U.S. Supreme Court for its consideration, but *certiorari* was denied (i.e., the Supreme Court would not hear the appeal). In light of decisions in *Baker* and in a companion case, *Blaine et al. v. Burbank-Glendale-Pasadena Airport Authority*, it is interesting to note that the airport not only had a Noise Exposure Map, but had repeatedly demonstrated its ability to reduce its impact upon the surrounding community by lowering its noise exposure (i.e., reducing the noise contours on the NEM). In the final analysis, the airport was held ultimately responsible for the environmental consequences associated with owning and operating an airport.

SUMMARY

The most notable areas for litigation involving airports are airport land use control, property rights, and cases emanating from airports as a nuisance, especially due to airport-related noise and other environmental concerns. Litigants have experimented with three principal causes in recovering damages:

- By claiming *nuisance*;
- Charging *trespass*; and/or
- By *inverse condemnation.*

The most successful method has been the latter, under which damages are represented by an unconstitutional taking of property without just compensation.[66]

---

[66] In *Greater Westchester Homeowners v. City of Los Aangeles*, 603 P2d 1329, 160 Cal. Rptr. 733 (1979), plaintiffs, as homeowners near the two north runways at Los Angeles International Airport, sued the City in inverse condemnation for property damage, and on a nuisance theory, for personal injuries caused from aircraft generated noise, smoke and vibrations. In defense, the City argued that the nuisance claim was inappropriate for two reasons. First, because the noise emanated from aircraft in flight where the Federal government exercises exclusive dominion. The airport operator was, therefore, federally preempted. Second, operation of aircraft is sanctioned by law and, therefore, the resulting aircraft noise emissions cannot constitute a nuisance.

However, Federal preemption *per se* is not a valid defense. And, it is recognized that a property owner has a constitutionally founded remedy of inverse condemnation for property

Land use regulatory controls are pursuant to police power—the power to protect the public health, safety, and welfare.[67] Whereas the government may regulate the use of property, if regulation goes too far it becomes a "taking." The Fifth Amendment to the United States Constitution states in part, ". . . nor shall private property be taken for public use, without just compensation." State constitutions contain similar language.

Whenever the state "takes" private property for public use the owner must be justly compensated. In contrast, when there is only regulation of the uses of private property (police powers), compensation does not have to be paid. Whether or not compensation is due, and how much, and whether or not there has been an invalid exercise of police power under the due process clause, are normally at the root of most land use cases.

One recent ruling coming out of Nevada that centers on the "uncompensated taking" issue has airports across the U.S. concerned that other state courts may find the ruling persuasive. In *McCarran v. Sisolak* the Nevada Supreme Court determined in 2006 that the district court properly concluded that a county height restriction ordinance effected a "per se" taking of the airspace above private land that is located within the departure critical area of an airport approach zone.[68] Appellate Clark County operates McCarran International Airport and had adopted height restriction ordinances limiting the development of respondent Steve Sisolak's airspace. The district court concluded the height restriction ordinances effectuated a *per se* taking, and a jury awarded Sisolak compensatory damages of $6.5 million. Thereafter, the district court awarded Sisolak attorney fees, cost and prejudgment interest, bringing the total award to more than $16.6 million.[69] Because the height restriction ordinances authorize airplanes to make a permanent, physical invasion of the homeowner's airspace, the Nevada Supreme Court concluded that a regulatory *per*

---

damage or loss caused by noise. The court also found significant the City's involvement in the creation and maintenance of the nuisance in question was continuous. It was the City that decided to build and then expand the airport in the vicinity of a residential area. The court held that the claims for personal injuries were founded upon nuisance that had not been federally preempted.

[67] *See Harrell's Candy Kitchen v. Sarasota-Manatee Airport Authority*, 111 SO 2d 439 (1959).

[68] *McCarran International Airport v. Sisolak,* 122 Nev. Adv. Op. No. 58 (Jul. 13, 2006).

[69] *See* Andrews Publications Litigation Reporter, *High Court Upholds $16.6 million Award to Nevada Landowner*, http://news.findlaw.com (visited Apr. 19, 2007).

se taking occurred, requiring an award of just compensation and, accordingly, affirmed the district court's judgment.

Airport-related noise as a problem is associated with people living in close proximity to airports. When citizens are subjected to noise in their habitats they rebel and seek compensation for what they consider to be an intrusion on their peace and quiet. Although the Federal government would seem to be the only entity clearly possessing sufficient authority to control airport noise, the liability for injury suffered by those living near airports has been clearly placed by the courts with the airport proprietor. Saddled by the courts with the responsibility for noise nuisance, yet lacking the authority to do something about it short of federal preemption, airports have become increasingly more frustrated. With two cases ruled in favor of airport proprietors in 1985, airport sponsors were subsequently granted more authority to manage their noise control problems.

In one case the Port Authority of New York and New Jersey issued a rule prohibiting aircraft non-compliant with FAR Part 36 from using Kennedy Airport.[70] Arrow Air, an airline flying Douglas DC-8's from New York to Puerto Rico and other U.S. points, after receiving a federal exemption from Part 36 filed suit in U.S. District Court for a temporary restraining order against enforcement of the local rule. The district court judge ruled in favor of the Port Authority on all three of Arrow's major arguments: (1) that the carrier's exemption from FAR Part 36 should federally pre-empt locally adopted rules; (2) that the Port Authority's rule placed undue burden on interstate commerce; and (3) that the Port Authority acted discriminately and arbitrarily in refusing to exempt Arrow from its rule.

According to the court, airport proprietors now have significant leeway in formulating policies different from federal policies, provided they do not conflict. The airport's authority had been broadened subsequent to the Aviation Safety and Noise Abatement Act. In the court opinion,

> *Congress has authorized airport proprietors to enact reasonable, non-discriminatory noise regulations. . . . The Port Authority's final rule fully meets these criteria, and any effect on*

---

[70] *Arrow Air, Inc. v. The Port Authority of New York and New Jersey*, (1985).

> *commerce is both incidental and authorized by Congress.*

In the month following the New York trial, Ecuatoriana Airline challenged a similar Los Angeles International Airport noise rule. Ecuatoriana wanted to service Los Angeles with a Boeing 707. The U.S. District Court denied Ecuatoriana's request for injunction against the Los Angeles Airport. Here again, the airline argued that federal law preempted the local rules. The court rejected the preemption argument, and also, arguments that the rules violated treaty agreements and due process.

Even though the FAA had granted exemptions to the airlines, the federal courts in New York and Los Angeles ruled that since the airport is ultimately responsible for local noise suits, the airport must be given the authority to remedy any noise unacceptable to the community. Moreover, the courts ruled that because the Federal government has chosen not to accept responsibility for noise suits, and Congress (in the Aviation Safety and Noise Abatement Act of 1979) authorized airport proprietors to enact reasonable, non-discriminatory regulations, "local noise rules adopted by airports and meeting these criteria shall be upheld."

APPENDIX A

FORECASTING

For more detailed planning activities, a variety of tools may be used to examine and forecast airport demand and capacity. In the following pages, two such tools are provided: bivariate regression analysis used in trend-line forecasting and long range methods for determining airport demand/capacity.

REGRESSION ANALYSIS

A first step in analyzing relationships between two variables is to plot the data on a *scatter diagram* (or *scatter plot*). Each dot on the scatter plot represents the intersecting relationship between the dependent and independent variables. Data are plotted on two axes with the horizontal x axis being the independent variable and the vertical y axis being the dependent variable. The two variables are related to, or *correlated* with, each other. The closer the dots cluster around a central *regression line*, the higher the correlation. Conversely, the more the dots are scattered, in buckshot fashion, the less they are correlated. Correlation is described as "positive" when high values of one variable are associated with high values of the other variable, in which case the dots have an upward direction to the right, as shown:

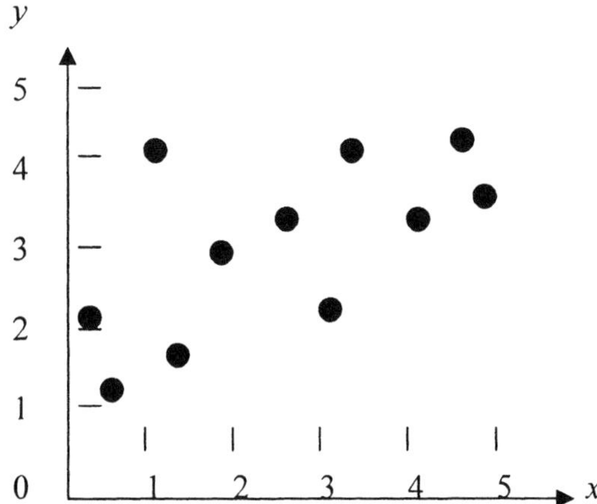

When high values of one variable occur with low values of the other, the variables are inversely or "negatively" correlated, and the direction of the dots is to the right and down. If the plotted points on a scatter diagram generally follow a straight line, there is a *linear* relationship between the two variables. If a curved line gives the best fit, the correlation is *curvilinear*, or *nonlinear*.

The scatter diagram is a graphic means of presenting the relationship between two variables, and may be used mechanically to produce a simple forecast. One method that can be used is to visually estimate *a line of best fit* or *regression line* (or the line that most closely follows the plotted points as plotted below:

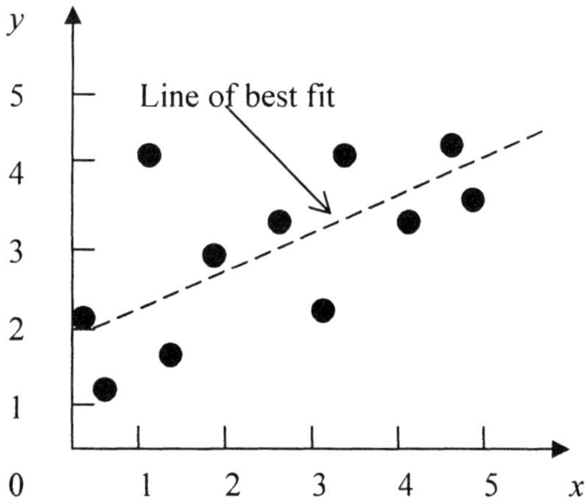

Such forecasts may be produced manually through the use of either a French curve or a straight edge. *Mechanical* extrapolation of the regression line then results in a forecast of expected relationships between the two variables. This is a rapid method that may suffice for rough estimates or very short-term forecasts, but most business decisions regarding finance and capital investment require more specific, *mathematical* calculations.

A generalized approach to estimating both linear and nonlinear relationships is "least squares analysis." Least squares analysis is based on a mathematical method of positioning the line to minimize the sum of the squares of the distances from each point to the line. In the example shown below, the line would be selected by the least squares method such that $(Y_1)^2 + (Y_2)^2 + (Y_3)^2 + (Y_4)^2$ would be the minimum possible value. Hence, it gets its name—least squares. In the least squares method, the line of best fit is positioned by determining the equation for the regression line:

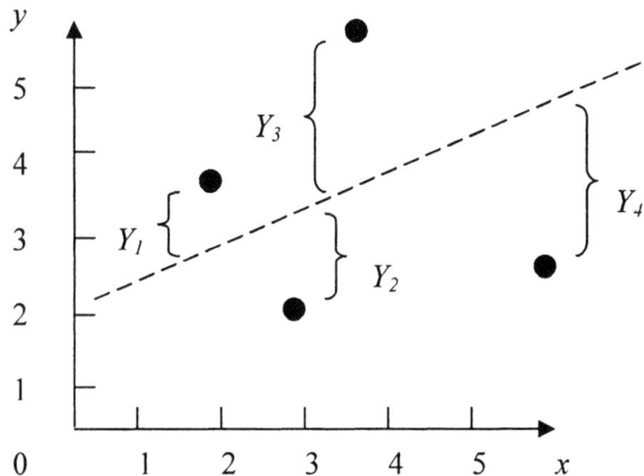

Least squares estimation of the dependent variable regressed against only one independent variable is *bivariate regression*. If the dependent variable is regressed against time, the bivariate regression is referred to as a *trend line analysis*. The regression expresses the average relationship between the dependent and independent variables as a line or mathematical equation. It is defined as "the amount by which the conditional expectation of one of two correlated variables is closer to the mean of its set than are given values of the second to the mean." The dependent variable is designated *y*, and the independent variable(s) is/are designated *x*. The dependent variable is then expressed as some function of the independent variable(s).

The formula for the bivariate regression is:

$$Yc = a + bx$$

Where, *Yc* is the computed or expected value of *y* (i.e., the value on the line for a given value of *x* and the relationship described by the line). The constant *a* is the value of *Yc* at the *y* axis when $x = 0$ (i.e., it is the location where the line intersects the vertical, *y* axis). The term *b* is the increase in *Yc* for each unit increase in *x*. The value of *b* is therefore the slope of the line, and the slope of b is termed the "regression coefficient."

The linear least squares method enables the analyst to take a group of data points and mathematically compute a and b for the straight line that best fits these points. In order to compute the values of the slope and y intercept for a regression line, the data must be arranged in a prescribed manner. But first, interim equations must be solved for a, b, the mean values of x and y, and the total number of data points (n) in the sample population (see Table A.1, "Statistical Symbols" for an explanation of the statistical symbols used in regression analyses). For example, in the following sample of x and y variables there are 6 x and 6 y:

x	y
1	2
2	4
3	6
4	8
5	10
6	12

In the equations, x is the independent variable and y is the dependent variable.

The arithmetic mean (average) of all the values of the independent variables is represented by $\bar{x}$ calculated:

$$\bar{x} = \frac{\Sigma x}{n}$$

The arithmetic mean (average) of all the values of the dependent variables are represented by $\bar{y}$ calculated:

$$\bar{y} = \frac{\Sigma y}{n}$$

Table A.1—STATISTICAL SYMBOLS [1]

Symbol	Description
$Yc = a + bx$	Form used to describe the average relationship between the two variables and to carry out the regression analysis process
a	The dependent variable whose value is estimated in the regression analysis
b	The slope of the line, or the amount by which the computed value of y changes with each unit change in x
x	The independent variable from which the regression estimates are made
$\bar{x}$	Arithmetic mean of a sample of x values
$\bar{x} = \frac{\Sigma x}{n}$	Form used to describe the arithmetic mean of x values.
Σ	Sum of
Σx	Sum of x values
n	Number of observations in a sample
$\bar{y} = \frac{\Sigma y}{n}$	Form used to describe the arithmetic mean of y values
$b = \frac{\Sigma xy - n\bar{x}\bar{y}}{\Sigma x^2 - n(\bar{x})^2}$	Equation used to determine the value of b

[1] The symbols represent numerical values. For example, the symbol Σ means to sum what is indicated; *i.e.*, Σx means to add all the x values together; Σx^2 means to add all the x^2 values together; and $\Sigma x y$ means to add all the $x y$ product values together.

Table A.1 (continued)

$a = \bar{y} - b\bar{x}$	Equation used to determine the value of *a*
$r^2 = \dfrac{\Sigma (y - Yc)^2}{\Sigma (y - \bar{y})^2}$	The measure used to determine the sample coefficient of determination
$\Sigma (y - Yc)^2$	The sum of the vertical deviations of *y* values from the regression line
$\Sigma (y - \bar{y})^2$	The sum of the squared vertical deviations from the horizontal line
r	Correlation coefficient between *x* and *y*
r^2	Coefficient of determination; a measure of the amount of correlation between *y* and *x*, explained in terms of the relative variation of the *y* values around the regression line and the corresponding variation (sum of squared deviations) around the mean of the *y* variable
Logarithm	The exponent that indicates the power to which a number is raised to produce a given number
Common log	A logarithm whose base is 10
Natural log	A logarithm with *e* (approximately 2.71828) as a base

The equation for computing the slope, *b*, is:

$$b = \frac{\Sigma\, x\, y - n\, \bar{x}\, \bar{y}}{\Sigma\, x^2 - n\, (\bar{x})^2}$$

Having determined the slope *b*, the intersection point, *a*, on the *y* axis, or the computed value of *y* when $x = 0$, can be computed as:

$$a = \bar{y} - b\, \bar{x}$$

The computational formulas presented above enable the analyst to calculate the slope, *b*, and *y* intercept, *a*, which exactly define the positioning of the best fitting line. Knowing the equation for the regression line, the analyst can use it to estimate values of the dependent variable *y*, based on knowing the corresponding value of the independent variable *x*. There are generally two ways to use the equation to get the results. The first way is *graphically*, and the second is *algebraically.* In the graphic method, and knowing the equation, the analyst plots the regression line and then reads values from the graph as in the visual method presented above using the scatter diagram. Only now the line is much more accurate. To plot a straight line given its equation $Yc = a + bx$, *Step one* is to draw a set of coordinate axes as follows:

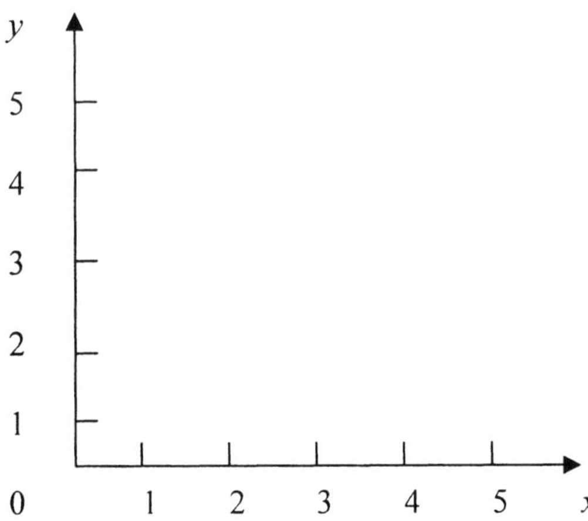

Step two is to place a point on the y axis at the value of the y intercept of the equation (the value of a). This is the value of y when $x = 0$. For example, to plot the line representing the equation $Yc = 2 + \frac{1}{2} x$, place a point on the vertical axis at 2.

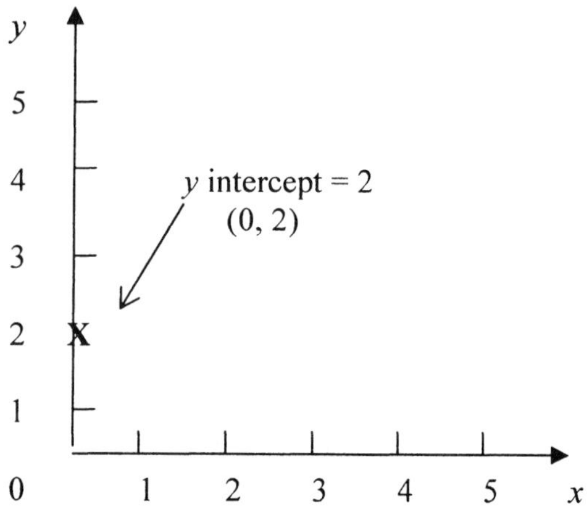

Step three is to pick any other value of x, say 2, solve the equation for y, and plot that point. It should be remember that a data point (x, y) is plotted right and up (just as in map reading).

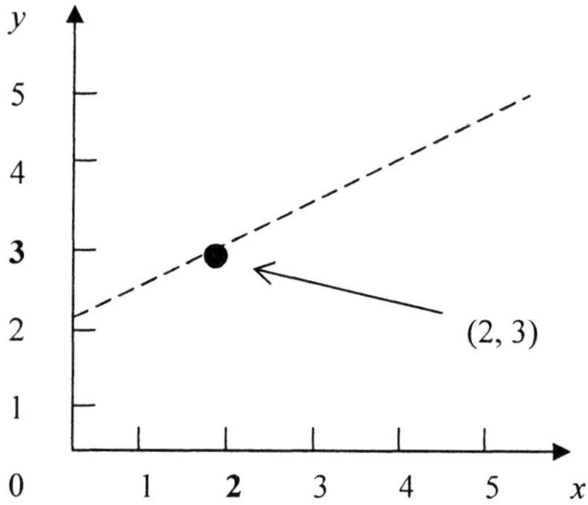

Once the line has been plotted, the values of the dependent variable can be determined for corresponding values of the independent variable in the same manner as the visual method. The analyst enters on the *x* axis at the given *x* value, traces up vertically to the line and then horizontally to the *y* axis, and reads the dependent variable's value. For example, after plotting the equation $Yc = 2 + \frac{1}{2}x$, the analyst solves for $x = 5$, by entering the *x* axis at 5, goes vertically to the line, then horizontally to the y axis and interpolates the answer, $Yc \approx 4.6$.

The algebraic method enables a more mathematically *precise* answer to be determined. Once the equation of the best fitting regression line has been determined by the least squares method, the analyst merely substitutes the value of *x* and then solves the equation for *y*:

$$Yc = 2 + \tfrac{1}{2}x$$
$$Yc = 2 + (\tfrac{1}{2} \times 5)$$
$$Yc = 2 + 2.5$$
$$Yc = 4.5$$

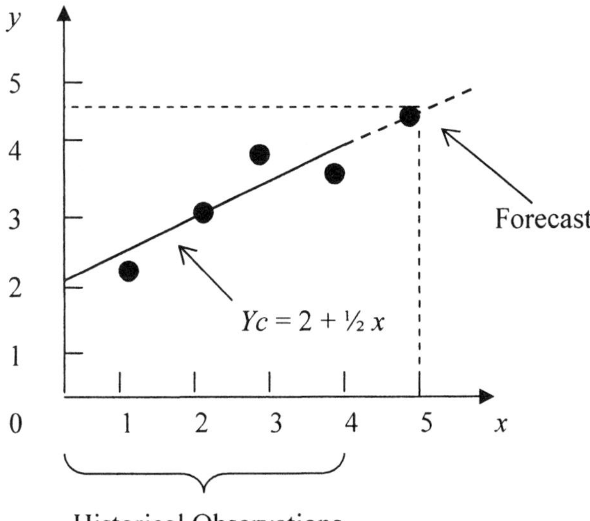

Note that in the case above, data points 1 through 4 are the historical observations upon which the regression is formed. Since observation 5 is beyond the historical data, it is a *projected forecast.*

What follows are two examples of algebraically calculating trend line forecasts. The first example uses least squares to determine the line of best fit in a *linear* regression. The subsequent example demonstrates *non-linear* forecasting using logarithmic functions.[2]

- Regression Example A—At the hypothetical Lazy 8 Airport there were 23 based aircraft in 1980; 50 in 1990; and 111 in the year 2000. The regression will project the number of based aircraft that would be expected in the year 2010. Note that 2010 is observation number 4; year 2020 would be observation number 5, etc. The observations can be for any period of time in weeks, months, years, and so on, but each observation must be a measure of the same thing. In other words, time periods may not be mixed with one observation representing one year and another observation representing a decade. In this example, the observations are all in decades. It would not be appropriate to use interim years such as 2001 or 2013, unless all observations were on an annual basis.

Year	x	y	xy	x^2
1980	1	23	23	1
1990	2	50	100	4
2000	3	111	333	9
	6	184	456	14
2010	4			

$$\bar{x} = \frac{\Sigma x}{n} = \frac{6}{3} = 2$$

$$\bar{y} = \frac{\Sigma y}{n} = \frac{184}{3} = 61.3$$

[2] The example uses common logarithms, however, whether common or natural logarithm is used is not significantly material.

$$b = \frac{\Sigma xy - n\,\bar{x}\,\bar{y}}{\Sigma x^2 - n\,(\bar{x})^2} = \frac{456 - (3)(2)(61.3)}{14 - (3)(2)^2} = \frac{88.2}{2} = 44.1$$

$$a = \bar{y} - b\,\bar{x} = 61.3 - (44.1)(2) = 61.3 - 88.2 = -26.9$$

$$Yc = a + bx = 26.9 + (44.1)(4) = 150 \text{ (based aircraft in 2010)}$$

In the Regression Example A above, the trend line is straight, or linear as shown in Figure A.1, "Linear Regression Lazy 8 Airport."

**Figure A.1—LINEAR REGRESSION
LAZY 8 AIRPORT**

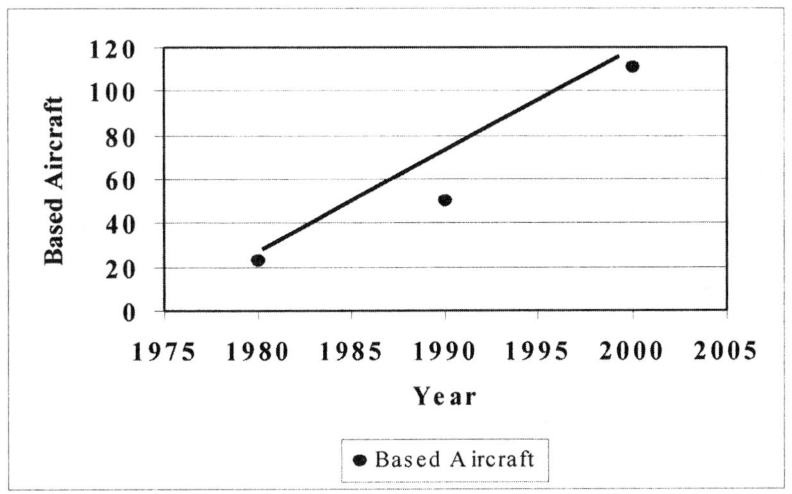

When observing the scatter plot if the trend line is seemingly non-linear—in other words, if it seems to curve—it is best to solve the regression logarithmically. Regression Example B demonstrates the use of common log in the analysis (see Figure A.2, "Logarithmic Regression—Lazy 8 Airport"). The logarithmic value of a number can be obtained from a logarithmic table (see Table A.2, "Common Logarithms"), or can be obtained using a calculator with logarithmic function.

**Figure A.2—LOGARITHMIC REGRESSION—
LAZY 8 AIRPORT**

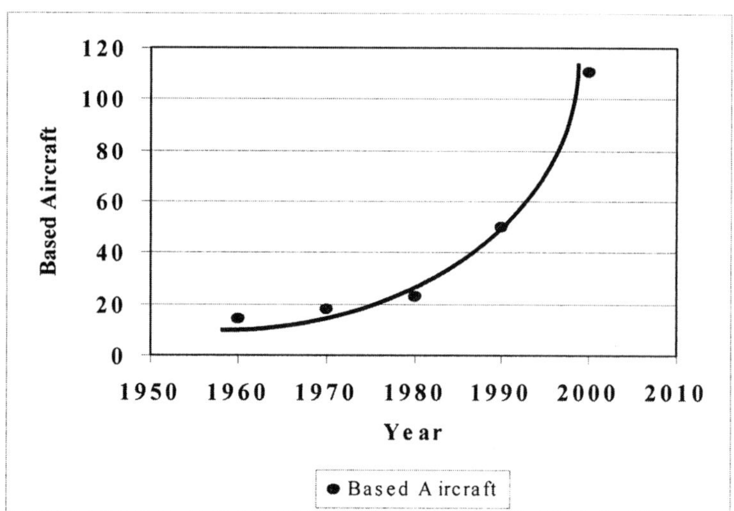

From the equation that follows (in "Regression Example B" below), it can be seen that the common logarithmic value of 14 is 1.1461. For two-digit numbers, the logarithmic equivalent begins with a 1 followed by a decimal point and the appropriate value from Table A.3. Three-digit numbers begin with 2, then a decimal point and the appropriate value from the table. For example, the number 111 translates into 2.0453. The vertical numbers on the left-hand column of Table A.2 are two-digit numbers. The third digit of a three-digit number is taken from the horizontal column at the top of Table A.2. To translate the number 111 into log, find 11 in the left hand column; find the third digit number at the top of the table where the horizontal and vertical columns meet find the value 0453; place a 2 and a decimal point in front of 0453; i.e., 2.0453. Table A.2 can be used to convert any two or three digit number into common log.

Table A.2—COMMON LOGARITHMS

	0	1	2	3	4	5	6	7	8	9		0	1	2	3	4	5	6	7	8	9
10	0000	0043	0086	0128	0170	0212	0253	0294	0334	0374	55	7404	7412	7419	7427	7435	7443	7451	7459	7466	7474
11	0414	0453	0492	0531	0569	0607	0645	0682	0719	0735	56	7482	7490	7497	7505	7513	7520	7528	7536	7543	7551
12	0792	0828	0864	0899	0934	0969	1004	1038	1072	1106	57	7559	7566	7574	7582	7589	7597	7604	7612	7619	7627
13	1139	1173	1206	1239	1271	1303	1335	1367	1399	1430	58	7634	7642	7649	7657	7664	7672	7679	7686	7694	7701
14	1461	1492	1523	1553	1584	1614	1644	1673	1703	1732	59	7709	7716	7723	7731	7738	7745	7752	7760	7767	7774
15	1761	1790	1818	1847	1875	1903	1931	1959	1987	2014	60	7782	7789	7796	7803	7810	7818	7825	7832	7839	7846
16	2041	2068	2095	2122	2148	2175	2201	2227	2253	2279	61	7853	7860	7868	7875	7882	7889	7896	7903	7910	7917
17	2304	2330	2335	2380	2405	2430	2456	2480	2504	2529	62	7924	7931	7938	7945	7952	7959	7966	7973	7980	7987
18	2553	2577	2601	2625	2648	2672	2695	2718	2742	2765	63	7993	8000	8007	8014	8021	8028	8035	8041	8048	8055
19	2788	2810	2833	2856	2878	2900	2923	2945	2976	2989	64	8062	8069	8075	8082	8089	8096	8102	8109	8116	8122
20	3010	3032	3054	3075	3096	3118	3139	3160	3181	3201	65	8129	8136	8142	8149	8156	8162	8169	8176	8182	8189
21	3222	3243	3263	3284	3304	3324	3345	3365	3385	3404	66	8195	8202	8209	8215	8222	8228	8235	8241	8248	8254
22	3424	3444	3464	3483	3502	3522	3541	3560	3579	3598	67	8261	8267	8274	8280	8287	8293	8299	8306	8312	8319
23	3617	3636	3655	3674	3692	3711	3729	3747	3766	3784	68	8325	8331	8338	8344	8351	8357	8363	8370	8376	8382
24	3802	3820	3838	3856	3874	3892	3909	3927	3945	3962	69	8388	8395	8401	8407	8414	8420	8426	8432	8439	8445
25	3979	3997	4041	4031	4048	4065	4982	4099	4116	4133	70	8451	8457	8463	8470	8476	8482	8488	8494	8500	8506
26	4150	4166	4183	4200	4216	4232	4249	4265	4281	4298	71	8513	8519	8525	8531	8537	8543	8549	8555	8561	8567
27	4314	4330	4336	4362	4378	4282	4409	4425	4440	4456	72	8573	8579	8585	8591	8597	8603	8609	8615	8621	8627
28	4472	4487	4502	4518	4533	4548	4564	4579	4594	4609	73	8633	8639	8645	8651	8657	8663	8669	8675	8681	8686
29	4624	4639	4654	4669	4683	4698	4713	4728	4742	4757	74	8692	8698	8704	8710	8716	8722	8727	8733	8739	8745
30	4771	4786	4800	4814	4829	4843	4857	4871	4886	4900	75	8751	8756	8762	8768	8774	8779	8785	8791	8797	8802
31	4914	4928	4942	4955	4969	4983	4997	5011	5024	5038	76	8808	8814	8820	8825	8831	8837	8842	8848	8854	8859
32	5051	5065	5079	5092	5105	5119	5132	5145	5159	5172	77	8865	8871	8876	8882	8887	8893	8899	8904	8910	8915
33	5185	5198	5211	5224	5237	5250	5263	5276	5289	5302	78	8921	8927	8932	8938	8943	8949	8954	8960	8965	8971
34	5315	5328	5340	5363	5366	5378	5291	5403	5416	5428	79	8976	8982	8987	8993	8998	9004	9009	9015	9020	9025
35	5441	5453	5465	5478	5490	5502	5514	5527	5539	5551	80	9031	9036	9042	9047	9053	9058	9063	9069	9074	9079
36	5563	5575	5587	5599	5611	5623	5635	5647	5658	5670	81	9085	9090	9096	9101	9106	9112	9117	9122	9128	9133
37	5682	5694	5705	5717	5729	5740	5752	5763	5775	5786	82	9138	9143	9149	9154	9159	9165	9170	9175	9180	9186
38	5798	5809	5821	5832	5843	5855	5866	5877	5888	5889	83	9191	9196	9201	9206	9212	9217	9222	9227	9232	9238
39	5911	5922	5933	5944	5955	5966	5977	5988	5999	6010	84	9243	9248	9253	9258	9263	9269	9274	9279	9284	9289
40	6021	6031	6042	6053	6064	6075	6085	6096	6107	6117	85	9294	9299	9304	9309	9315	9320	9325	9330	9335	9340
41	6128	6138	6149	6160	6170	6180	6191	6201	6212	6222	86	9345	9350	9355	9360	9365	9370	9375	9380	9385	9390
42	6232	6243	6253	6263	6274	6284	6294	6304	6314	6325	87	9395	9400	9405	9410	9415	9420	9425	9430	9435	9440
43	6335	6345	6355	6365	6375	6385	6395	6405	6415	6425	88	9445	9450	9455	9460	9465	9469	9474	9479	9484	9489
44	6435	6444	6454	6464	6474	6484	6493	6503	6513	6522	89	9494	9499	9504	9509	9513	9518	9523	9528	9533	9538
45	6532	6542	6551	6561	6571	6580	6590	6599	6609	6618	90	9542	9547	9552	9557	9562	9566	9571	9576	9581	9586
46	6628	6637	6646	6656	6665	6675	6684	6693	6702	6712	91	9590	9595	9600	9605	9609	9614	9619	9624	9628	9633
47	6721	6730	6739	6749	6758	6767	6776	6785	6794	6803	92	9638	9643	9647	9652	9657	9661	9666	9671	9675	9680
48	6812	6821	6830	6839	6848	6857	6866	6875	6884	6893	93	9685	9689	9694	9699	9703	9708	9713	9717	9722	9727
49	6902	6911	6920	6928	6937	6946	6955	6964	6972	6981	94	9731	9736	9741	9745	9750	9754	9759	9763	9768	9773
50	6990	6998	7007	7016	7024	7033	7042	7050	7059	7067	95	9777	9782	9786	9791	9795	9800	9805	9809	9814	9818
51	7076	7084	7093	7101	7110	7118	7126	7135	7143	7152	96	9823	9827	9832	9836	9841	9845	9850	9854	9869	9863
52	7160	7168	7177	7185	7193	9868	9872	9877	9881	9886	97	9868	9872	9877	9881	9886	9890	9894	9899	9903	9908
53	7243	7251	7259	7267	7275	7284	7292	7300	7308	7316	98	9912	9917	9921	9926	9930	9934	9939	9943	9948	9952
54	7324	7332	7340	7348	7356	7364	7372	7380	7388	7396	99	9956	9961	9965	9969	9974	9978	9983	9987	9991	9996

- Regression Example B—For the Lazy 8 Airport used in Example A, there are more data available than was previously presented. But when plotting the data for years prior to 1980, it is found that the earlier historical trend line is curved, or non-linear. Thus, rather than uniform progression, there is logarithmic progression. Using common log, the regression analysis is accomplished as shown below.

Year	x	y	y(common log)	xy	x^2
1960	1	14	1.1461	1.1416	1
1970	2	18	1.2553	2.5106	4
1980	3	23	1.3617	4.0851	9
1990	4	50	1.6990	6.7960	16
2000	5	111	2.0453	10.2265	25
	15	216	7.5074	24.7643	55

2010	6
2020	7
2030	8 (etc.)

$$\bar{x} = \frac{\Sigma x}{n} = \frac{15}{5} = 3$$

$$\bar{y} = \frac{\Sigma y}{n} = \frac{7.5074}{5} = 1.5015$$

$$b = \frac{\Sigma xy - n\,\bar{x}\,\bar{y}}{\Sigma x^2 - n\,(\bar{x})^2} = \frac{24.763 - (5)(3)(1.5015)}{55 - (5)(3)^2}$$

$$= \frac{24.763 - 22.5225}{55 - 45}$$

$$= \frac{2.2418}{10} = .2242$$

$$a = \bar{y} - b\ \bar{x} = 1.5014 - (.2242)\,(3) = 1.5015 - .6725$$

$$= .829$$

$$Yc = a + bx = .829 + (.2242)\,(6) = .829 + 1.3452$$

= 2.172 (which is a logarithmic value; the antilog is required to convert back to a final number)

= 149 (based aircraft in the year 2010)

In observing the plotted data for the Lazy 8 Airport, the growth prior to 1980 was relatively slow compared to the more dynamic increase in based aircraft after 1980. The analyst may be aware of reasons not reflected in the data why more owners chose to base their airplanes at the airport after 1980, which makes the data prior to that time questionable. Or perhaps there is some other explanation for the sudden influx in based aircraft after 1980 that makes the data prior to that time questionable. Judgmentally, the analyst may decide that data prior to 1980 are no longer applicable and therefore may be disregarded. Given sufficient justification, it is acceptable to take such action. In other words, forecasting is "an art not a science."

This example demonstrates the permissiveness of using only the applicable data. It also allows the choice of using the linear regression analysis performed in Regression Example A versus the logarithmic analysis used in Regression Example B. However, one should keep in mind that the examples shown herein are for instructive purposes. More realistically, airport forecasting entails more sophisticated statistical modeling using multiple variables.

Multivariate regression enables the forecaster to measure the joint effect of any number (n) of independent variables upon a dependent variable. The *multiple regression* equation describes the average relationship between these variables, and this relationship is used to predict or control the dependent variable. By measuring the simultaneous influence of several factors, the forecaster has a more powerful and realistic tool of analysis than in considering only one independent variable. The multivariate analysis may be accomplished manually, but the use of computer programs greatly facilitates the calculations.

Multiple regression analysis represents the simultaneous influence of a set of independent variables, which could include those listed above as "factors affecting demand forecasting," or others, upon the dependent variable. The equation can be written:

$$Yc = a + b_1x_1 + b_2x_2 + b_3x_3 + \ldots b_nx_n$$

Where, Yc is the computed or estimated value of the dependent variable y and $x_1, x_2, x_3, \ldots x_n$ are the independent variables. The term a is the value of Yc when all the x's are zero. The terms $b_1, b_2, b_3 \ldots b_n$ are the net regression coefficients. Each measures the change in Y per unit of change in that particular independent variable, assuming all other variables are held constant.

The confidence placed in regression analyses is demonstrated in three terms: r^2, the *F-statistic*, and the *t-statistic*. The *coefficient of determination* is r^2 (or R^2 in the multivariate case). It is a statistic that expresses the amount of variation in the dependent variable explained or accounted for by the independent variable(s) in a regression equation. It compares explained variation to total variation, and can range from 0.00, with no variation at all, to 1.00, where all variation is explained (i.e., perfect explanation). For example, an r^2 of .40 infers that the independent variable(s) provides 40% of the correlative explanation for the dependent variable. The higher (or closer to 1.0) the coefficient of determination is, the higher the correlation (if not "causal" relationship) there is between the variables.

Once calculated, the regression should be tested for its reliability. The test is to find r^2, which is a measure of the amount of correlation between y and x, explained in terms of the relative variation of the y values around the regression line and the corresponding variation around the mean of the y variable (the sum of squares deviation). The coefficient of determination can be interpreted as the percentage of the variation of y values that can be attributed to the variation in the x values; i.e., how strongly y's variation is associated with x's variation. For example, $r^2 = .81$ would mean that 81% of the variation in the y variables could be explained by the x variable, and the remaining 19% is either unexplained or is the result of some other variable. A perfect correlation between x and y is 1.0, thus, a high r^2 value, of say .95, would mean that the data points producing the high coefficient of determination would be very nearly in a straight line, as follows:

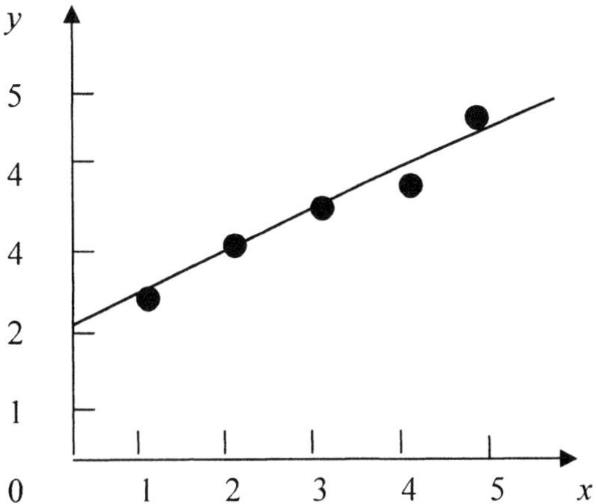

Conversely, if the data points are randomly scattered across the graph in a broad pattern, as shown below, so that no straight line could adequately represent them, then r^2 would approach 0.

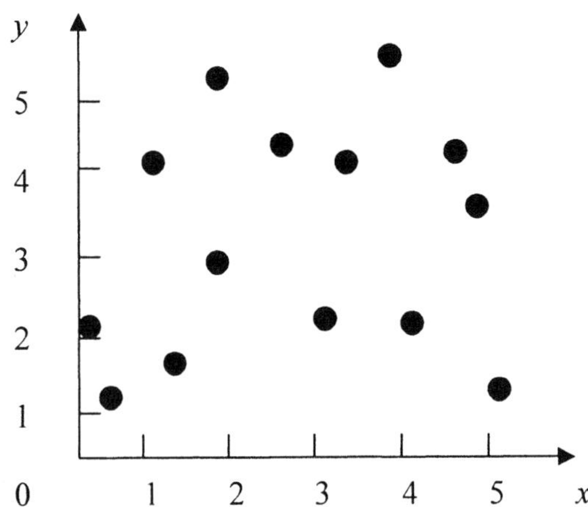

The coefficient of determination is expressed,

$$r^2 = 1 - \frac{\Sigma (y - Yc)^2}{\Sigma (y - \bar{y})^2}$$

Regression Examples D and E demonstrate the coefficient of determination for the regression analyses performed in Regression Examples A and B respectively.

- Regression Example D—Before finding the coefficient of determination, the regression ($Yc = a + bx$) must be solved for each observation.

$Yc = a + bx$

Year	$Yc = -26.9 + (44.1)(x)$
1980	$Yc = -26.9 + (44.1)(1) = 17.2$
1990	$Yc = -26.9 + (44.1)(2) = 61.3$
2000	$Yc = -26.9 + (44.1)(3) = 105.4$

$\Sigma (y - Yc)^2$

Year	y		Yc		$y - Yc$		$(y - Yc)^2$
1980	23	–	17.2	=	5.8	=	33.64
1990	50	–	61.3	=	–11.3	=	127.69
2000	111	–	105.4	=	5.6	=	31.36
					.1		192.69

$\Sigma (y - \bar{y})^2$

Year	y		$\bar{y}$		$y - \bar{y}$		$(y - \bar{y})^2$
1980	23	–	61.3	=	–38.3	=	1466.89
1990	50	–	61.3	=	11.3	=	127.69
2000	111	–	61.3	=	49.7	=	2470.09
					.1		4064.67

$$r^2 = 1 - \frac{\Sigma (y - Yc)^2}{\Sigma (y - \bar{y})^2} = \frac{192.69}{4064.67}$$

$$= 1 - .0474 = .9526$$

- Regression Example E—In solving the coefficient of determination for Regression Example B, which was logarithmic, the same process is employed, as in Example A, however it must be accomplished logarithmically.

$Yc = a + bx$

Year	$Yc = .829 + (.2242)(x)$
1960	$Yc = .829 + (.2242)(1) = 1.0532$
1970	$Yc = .829 + (.2242)(2) = 1.2774$
1980	$Yc = .829 + (.2242)(3) = 1.5016$
1990	$Yc = .829 + (.2242)(4) = 1.7258$
2000	$Yc = .829 + (.2242)(5) = 1.9500$

$\Sigma (y - Yc)^2$

Year	Yc		y		$y - Yc$		$(y - Yc)^2$
1960	1.0532	–	1.1461	=	–.0929	=	.0086
1970	1.2774	–	1.2553	=	.0221	=	.0005
1980	1.5016	–	1.3617	=	.1399	=	.0196
1990	1.7258	–	1.6990	=	.0268	=	.0007
2000	1.9500	–	2.0453	=	–.0953	=	.0091
					.0006		.0385

$\Sigma (y - \bar{y})^2$

Year	y		$\bar{y}$		$y - \bar{y}$		$(y - \bar{y})^2$
1960	1.1461	–	1.5015	=	–.3554	=	.1263
1970	1.2553	–	1.5015	=	–.2462	=	.0606
1980	1.3617	–	1.5015	=	–.1398	=	.0196
1990	1.6990	–	1.5015	=	.1975	=	.0390
2000	2.0453	–	1.5015	=	.5438	=	.2957
					.0001		.5411

$$r^2 = \frac{\Sigma(y - Yc)^2}{\Sigma(y - \bar{y})^2} = \frac{.0385}{.5411}$$

$$= 1 - .0712 = .9288$$

The *F-statistic* (or *F-ratio*) is a test statistic formed by the ratio of two mean-square estimates of the population error variance. It compares explained variation to unexplained variation, and is used to test the hypothesis that the dependent variable in a regression equation is statistically unrelated to any of the independent variables. Desired is a large "*F*" or a high ratio of explained to unexplained variance. A value of zero means that the independent variable(s) provide no explanation of the variation in the dependent variable. For example, suppose that a reported *F*-statistic was 7.011. It is compared with the appropriate entry in a statistics table of *F*-values to determine whether it is significant at various confidence levels. Unless otherwise stipulated, the *statistical significance* confidence level is conventionally set at 95%. If the reported *F*-value is greater than the listed entry in the table (for the appropriate degrees of freedom), it is accepted as statistically significant.

The *t-statistic* is a test of significance for continuous variables where the population variance is unknown and assumed is that the sample has been drawn from a normally distributed population. It is similar to the *F*-statistic, and in multivariate regression is used to test whether an individual independent variable's regression coefficient (b) is significantly different from some hypothesized regression coefficient (b^*). As with the *F*-statistic, the calculated *t*-statistic is compared with a listed entry in a statistics table of *t*-values to determine its significance (usually 95%). For example, if the reported *t*-statistic was say 2.65, and the listed entry was 2.00 for the 95% confidence level, the statistical significance would be acceptable.

DEMAND/CAPACITY ANALYSES

Using a hypothetical Chandelle Airport as a test case, demonstrated below is an example of how airport capacity would be calculated with the aid of Chapter 2 of AC 150/5060-5, "Capacity and Delay Calculations for Long Range Planning." Demonstration of the long-range method is for instructive purposes, and it should be kept in mind that the "long-range" method is the simplified procedure. Normally, the capacity calculations for individual airports follow a much more detailed and complex procedure.

The long-range procedure is a two-step process. *Step one* is to determine the gross calculations in order to determine *Annual Service Volume* [ASV] and average delay per aircraft in minutes. *Step two* is to make *adjustments* by modifying the "airfield useable time." To accomplish the analysis a worksheet is provided.[3]

AC 150/5060-5 Worksheet

Aircraft Mix				Mix Index %	Configuration		Capacity Ops/Hour (000)		ASV	Annual Demand	Annual Demand / ASV	Average Delay per Aircraft (minutes)		Minutes of Annual Delay (000)	
%A	%B	%C	%D	(C+3D)	No.	Sketch	VFR	IFR	(000)	(000)		Low	High	Low	High
1	2	3	4	5	6	7	8	9	10	11	12	13	14	15	16

Determine the percentage of aircraft classes C and D using or expected to use the airport. The current demand at the Chandelle Airport is as follows:

Operations per year	
Single-engine piston	121,440
Multi-engine piston	20,240
Turboprop	6,256
Military	8,600
Corporate Jet	2,944
Rotorcraft	3,680
Air carrier (large)	251,635
Air carrier (heavy)	34,314
Total	449,109

[3] FAA, *Airport Capacity and Delay*, AC 150/5060-5, Figure A5-1, Appendix 5 (Sep. 23, 1983).

The mix is determined from a table of given aircraft mixes:

AC 150/5060-5 Aircraft Mix Table

Aircraft Class	Maximum Certificated Takeoff Weight (lbs.)	Number of Engines	Wake Turbulence Classification
A	12,500	Single	
B	or less	Multi	Small (S)
C	12,500 – 300,000	Multi	Large (L)
D	over 300,000	Multi	Heavy (H)

- From the current demand, determine the *mix index*; i.e., the percentage of C + 3D aircraft:

$$\%(C + 3D) = \frac{C + 3D}{\text{Total Demand}} = \frac{251{,}635 + (3 \text{ x } 3431\%}{449{,}109}$$

$$= \frac{354{,}577}{449{,}109} = .79 = 79\%$$

- Of the nineteen typical runway layouts given in AC 150/5060-5 (Figure 2-1, "Capacity and ASV for Long Range Planning"), identify the runway configuration that most closely resembles the Chandelle Airport runway configuration—assume that at the Chandelle Airport there are three parallel runways. Two of the runways are 3,500 feet apart, and are sufficiently distant from one another to allow at least limited simultaneous IFR operations. The third runway is 700 feet from its nearest counterpart, a sufficient distance to allow simultaneous VFR operations. Accordingly, from Figure 2-1, runway configuration number 7 is selected as the closest approximation of the runway configuration at the Chandelle Airport.

AC 150/5060-5 Figure 2-1

Runway-use Configuration	Mix Index % (C+3D)	Hourly Capacity Ops/Hour VFR	IFR	Annual Service Volume Ops/Year
700' to 2499'	0 to 20	295	119	625,000
	21 to 50	219	114	475,000
3500' +	51 to 80	184	111	455,000
	81 to 120	161	117	510,000
	121 to 180	146	120	645,000

- Obtain the hourly capacity from Figure 2-1: IFR = 111; VFR = 184.
- Obtain the annual service volume from Figure 2-1: 455,000.
- Calculate the aircraft delay from AC 150/5060-5 (Figure 2-2, "Average Aircraft Delay for Long Range Planning"). First, calculate the ratio of annual demand to annual service volume:
-

$$\frac{\text{Annual demand}}{\text{Annual service volume}} = \frac{449{,}109}{455{,}000} = .99$$

Enter the graph in Figure 2-2 at the ratio of annual demand to annual service volume. Go up vertically until intersecting the upper boundary line then go left horizontally to intersect the annual delay scale. The upper portion of the band (or high average delay per aircraft) applies to airports where air carrier operations are dominant. The full width of the band applies to airports where general aviation operations are dominant, with the lowest band representing the low average delay per aircraft. Total annual aircraft delay is calculated by multiplying the average delay by the annual demand:

4 x 449,109 = 1,796,436

AC 150/5060-5 Figure 2-2

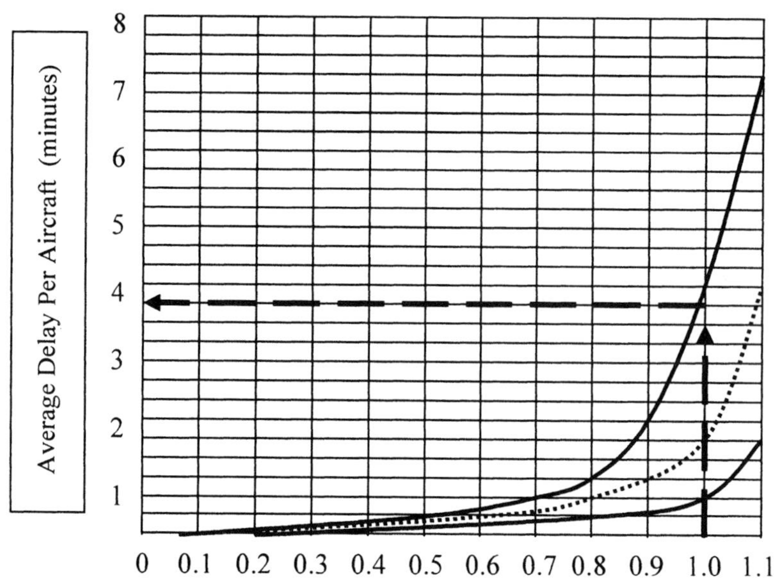

The completed worksheet for the capacity and delay calculations for the Chandelle Airport should look as follows:

AC 150/5060-5 Worksheet Completed

Aircraft Mix				Mix Index %	Configuration		Capacity Ops/Hour (000)		ASV	Annual Demand	Annual Demand / ASV	Average Delay per Aircraft (minutes)		Minutes of Annual Delay (000)	
%A	%B	%C	%D	(C+3D)	No.	Sketch	VFR	IFR	(000)	(000)		Low	High	Low	High
1	2	3	4	5	6	7	8	9	10	11	12	13	14	15	16
28	8	56	8	79	7		184	111	455	449	.99	1	4	499	1,796

It should be noted that in the example using the Chandelle Airport, the ratio of annual demand to annual service volume is nearly 1:1, resulting in an average delay of four minutes per aircraft; i.e., traditionally understood to be the acceptable delay factor for air carrier airports. Additionally, and as noted above, airport facilities should be planned and developed when demand reaches or is forecast to reach 60% of capacity. In this case demand has nearly reached the available capacity, assuming there are no mitigating factors in the capacity calculations.

APPENDIX B

TOPICAL INDEX

APPENDIX C

NAME INDEX

APPENDIX D

ACRONYMS

9/11	September 11, 2001
A&E	Architecture and Engineering
AA2000	Aeropuertos Argentinas 2000
AAAE	American Association of Airport Executives
AAE	Accredited Airport Executive
AARF	Airport Rescue and Fire Fighting
A-B-E	Allentown-Bethlehem-Easton Airport
AC	Advisory Circular
ACDBE	Airport Concession Disadvantaged Business Enterprise
ACE	Aviation Capacity Enhancement Plan
ACI	Airport Council International
ACI-NA	Airport Council International–North America
ACIP	Airport Capital Improvement Plan
ACLU	American Civil Liberties Union
ACM	Airport Certification Manual
ACS	Airport Certification Specifications
ACSA	Airports Company South Africa
ADA	American with Disabilities Act
ADAP	Airport Development Aid Program
ADCUS	Advise Customs
ADD	Average Daily Departures
ADDS	Aviation Digital Data Service
ADOT	Arizona Department of Transportation
ADP	Aéroports de Paris
ADSM	Airfield Delay Simulation Model
AEP	Airport Emergency Plan
AFFF	Aqueous Film Forming Foam
AGI	Airport Group International
AIA	American Institute of Architects
AICUZ	Air Installation Compatible Land Use Zones
AIL	Airborne Instruments Laboratory
AIM	Aeronautical Information Manual
AIP	Airport Improvement Program
Air-21	Aviation Investment and Reform Act for 21st Century
ALB	Albany (New York) International Airport
ALJ	Administrative Law Judge
ALP	Airport Layout Plan
ALPA	Air Line Pilots Association
ALS	Approach Light System
AMA	Air Movement Area
AMPAP	Airport Management Professional Accreditation Programme
ANA	All Nippon Airlines
ANCA	Airport Noise and Capacity Act
ANCEC	Airport Noise Control and Environs Compatibility
ANCLUC	Airport Noise Control and Land Use Compatibility

Acronyms

AOA	Airport Operations Area
AOCI	Airport Operators Council International
AOPA	Aircraft Owners and Pilots Association
APA	American Planning Association
APAT	Arizona Partnership for Air Transportation
ARC	Airport Reference Code
ARDF	Airport Research and Development Foundation
ARFF	Aircraft Rescue and Fire Fighting
ARIMA	Autoregressive Integrated Moving Average
ARSA	Airport Radar Service Area
ARTCC	Air Route Traffic Control Centers
ARTS II	Automated Radar Terminal System II
ARTS IIA	Automated Radar Terminal System IIA
ARTS IIE	Automated Radar Terminal System IIE
ARTS III	Automated Radar Terminal System III
ARTS IIIA	Automated Radar Terminal System IIIA
ARTS IIIE	Automated Radar Terminal System IIIE
ARTS	Automated Radar Terminal System
ASC	Airport Security Coordinator
ASCE	American Society of Civil Engineers
ASDE	Airport Surface Detection Equipment
ASNA	Aviation Safety and Noise Abatement Act
ASOS	Automated Surface Observation System
ASP	Airport Security Program
ASPA	American Society for Public Administration
ASPM	Aviation System Performance Metric System
ASR	Airport Surveillance Radar
ASTM	American Society for Testing and Material Standards
ASV	Annual Service Volume
ATA	Air Transport Association
ATC	Air Traffic Control
ATCO	Air Taxi/Commercial Operator
ATCRBS	Air Traffic Control Radar Beacon System
ATCT	Airport Traffic Control Tower
ATCTF	Air Traffic Control Terminal Facilities
ATF	Alcohol, Tobacco and Firearms
ATL	Atlanta Hartsfield International Airport
ATM	Automated Teller machine
ATO	Air Traffic Organization
ATSA	Aviation and Transportation Security Act of 2001
AVGAS	Aviation Gasoline
AVIT	Automatic Vehicle Identification Tag
AWOS	Automated Weather Observation System
AWOS I	Automated Weather Observation System I
AWOS II	Automated Weather Observation System II
AWOS III	Automated Weather Observation System III
BAA	British Airports Authority
BBF	Berlin Brandenburg Flughafen
BEA	Bureau of Economic Analysis
BHS	Baggage Handling System
BOAC	British Overseas Airways Company
BOD	Biological Oxygen-Demand
BOT	Build, Operate, and Transfer

BPV	Present Value of VFR tower Benefits
BRITE	Bright Radar Indicator Tower Equipment
BTS	Bureau of Transportation Statistics
CA	Conflict Alert
CAA	Civil Aeronautics Administration
CAA	Civil Aeronautics Authority
CAA	Council on Aviation Accreditation
CAB	Civil Aeronautics Board
CAC	Commuter and Small Certificated Air Carrier
CAD/CAM	Computer-Aided Design and Computer Aided Manufacturing
CAPPS	Computer-Assisted Passenger Prescreening System
CAPPS II	Computer-Assisted Passenger Prescreening System II
CBD	Central Business District
CBO	Congressional Budget Office
CBOD	Carbonaceous Biological Oxygen Demand
CBR	California Bearing Ratio
CCTV	Closed-Circuit Television
CEO	Chief Executive Officer
CEQ	Council on Environmental Quality
CFME	Continuous Friction Measurement Equipment
CFO	Chief Financial Officer
CFR	Code of Federal Regulations
CFR	Crash, Fire and Rescue
CHRC	Criminal History Record Checks
CIP	Capital Improvement Plan
CLE	Cleveland Hopkins International Airport
CLUZ	Compatible Land Use Zones
CM	Certified Member
CMA	Calcium Magnesium Acetate
CNEL	Community Noise Equivalent Level
CNR	Composite Noise Rating
CO_2	Carbon dioxide
COD	Chemical Oxygen-Demand
CPV	Present Value of VFR tower Costs
CRJ	Canadair Regional Jet
CRS	Computer Reservation System
CT	Computed Tomography
CUPPS	Common Use Passenger Processing Systems
CUSS	Common Use Self-Service
CUTE	Common Use Terminal Equipment
dB	Decibel
dBA	Decibels on the A weighted
DBE	Disadvantaged Business Enterprise
DEN	Denver International Airport
DEIS	Draft Environmental Impact Statement
DEVS	Drivers Enhanced Vision System
DF	Direction Finder
DFO	Duty Free Outlet
DFW	Dallas/Fort Worth International Airport
DH	Decision Height
DHS	Department of Homeland Security
DME	Distance Measuring Equipment

DNL	Day-Night Average Sound Level
DOD	Department of Defense
DOJ	Department of Justice
DOT	Department of Transportation
EA	Environmental Assessment
EAA	Experimental Aircraft Association
EAS	Essential Air Service
EDD	Explosive Detection Device
EDS	Explosive Detection Systems
EEC	European Economic Community
EIR	Environmental Impact Report
EIS	Environmental Impact Statement
EJ	Environmental Justice
EMS	Emergency Medical Services
END	Environmental Noise Directive
EPA	Environmental Protection Agency
EPNdB	Effective Perceived Noise Decibel
ERAU	Embry-Riddle Aeronautical University
ESA	Endangered Species Act
ETD	Explosive Trace Detection
EU	European Union
F&B	Food and Beverage
FAA	Federal Aviation Agency/Administration
FAAP	Federal Aid to Airports Program
FAC	Federal Airports Corporation
FAF	Final Approach Fix
FAM	Federal Air Marshal
FANS	Future Air Navigation Systems
FAR	Federal Aviation Regulation
FBI	Federal Bureau of Investigations
FBO	Fixed Base Operator
FCC	Federal Communications Commission
FEMA	Federal Emergency Management Administration
FFC	Foreign Flag Carrier
FFDO	Federal Flight Deck Officer
FIDS	Flight Information and Display Systems
FIS	Federal Inspection Services
FLIR	Forward Looking Infrared
FNAP	Fast Neutron Associated Particle
FOARC	Fractional Ownership Aviation Rulemaking Committee
FOD	Foreign Object Damage/Debris
FONSI	Finding of No Significant Impact
FORTRAN	IBM Mathematical Formula Translating System
four Ps	Price, Product, Place and Promotion
FPD	Freezing Point Depressant
FSDO	Flight Standards District Office
FSF	Flight Safety Foundation
FSS	Flight Service Station
FTC	Federal Aviation Administration Contract Tower
FTCA	Federal Tort Claims Act
FTZ	Foreign Trade Zone

NDB	Non-Directional Beacon
NEF	Noise Exposure Forecast
NEM	Noise Exposure Map
NEPA	National Environmental Policy Act
NEXRAD	Next Generation Weather Radar
NGATS	Next Generation Air Transportation System
NGWR	Next Generation Weather Radar
NIMBY	Not In My Back Yard
NLA	New Large Aircraft
NOA	Notice of Availability
NOTAM	Notice to Airman
NPA	New Public Administration
NPDES	National Pollutant Discharge Elimination System
NPIAS	National Plan of Integrated Airport Systems
NPRM	Notice of Proposed Rule Making
NPV	Net Present Value
NRA	Nuclear Resonant Absorption
NRE	Nationwide Regression Equation Model
NTSB	National Transportation Safety Board
NWS	National Weather Service
O&D	Origin and Destination
O&M	Operations and Maintenance
OAK	Oakland International Airport
OCR	Optical Character Recognition
ODALS	Omni-Directional Approach Light Systems
OE	Operational Error
OI	Operational Improvements
OMB	Office of Management and Budget
ONAC	Office of Noise Abatement and Control
OPSNET	Operational Network
ORD	Chicago O'Hare Airport
OTARD	Over The Air Reception Devices
p.s.i.	per square inch
P8	Program for Predicting Polluting Particle Passage through Pits, Puddles & Ponds
PACE	Program for Airport Capacity Efficiency
PANCAP	Practical Annual Capacity
PAPI	Precision Approach Path Indicators
PAR	Precision Approach Radar
PC	Personal Computer
PC&N	Public Convenience and Necessity
PCC	Portland Cement Concrete
PCF	Passenger Facility Charge
PCI	Pavement Condition Index
PD	Pilot Deviation
PFC	Passenger Facility Charge
PFNA	Pulsed Fast Neutron Activation
PGA	Professional Golfers' Association
PGP	Planning Grant Program
PHL	Philadelphia International Airport
PHOCAP	Practical Hourly Capacity
PHX	Phoenix Sky Harbor International Airport

PIO	Public Information Officer
PIT	Pittsburgh International Airport
PM	Preventive Maintenance
PMMP	Pavement Maintenance-Management Program
PMT	Passenger-Miles of Travel
PNdB	Perceived Noise Decibel
POSDCORB	Planning, Organizing, Staffing, Directing, Coordinating, Reporting & Budgeting
PPBS	Planning-Programming-Budgeting-Systems
PPS	Precise Positioning Service
PSA	Pacific Southwest Airlines
PVASI	Pulsating Visual Approach Slope Indicator

QATT	Qualified Anti-Terrorism Technology
QQS	Quantity-Quality Simulation Model

RCLS	Runway Centerline Light Systems
RCRA	Resource Conservation and Recovery Act
RDSM	Runway Delay Simulation Model
REIL	Runway End Identification Light
RFID	Radio Frequency Identification Systems
RFP	Request for Proposals
RIAC	Rhode Island Airport Corporation
RJ	Regional Jet
RNAV	Area Navigation
ROD	Record of Decision
RON	Remain Over Night
ROT	Runway Occupancy Time
RPM	Revenue Passenger Miles
RPZ	Runway Protection Zone
RT	Registered Traveler
RTCA	Radio Technical Commission for Aeronautics
RVR	Runway Visual Range

S&P	Standard and Poor's
SAFETY	Support Anti-Terrorism by Fostering Effective Technologies Act of 2002
SARS	Severe Acute Respiratory Syndrome
SATS	Small Aircraft Transportation System
SDF	Simplified Direction Facility
SEA	Societa Esercizi Aeroportuali
SEA-TAC	Seattle-Tacoma International Airport
SEL	Sound Exposure Level
SEL/D	Single Event Level Distribution
SFL	Sequenced Flashing Lights
SFO	San Francisco International Airport
SIDA	Security Identification Display Area
SIMMOD	Simulation Model
SLUCM	Standard Land Use Coding Manual
SMSA	Standard Metropolitan Statistical Area
SPEARS	Screener Proficiency Evaluation and Reporting System
SPP	Screening Partnership Program
SPS	Standard Positioning Service
SPSS	Statistical Package for the Social Sciences
STARS	Standardized Terminal Automation Replacement System

STOL	Short Take Off and Landing
STORM	Storage, Treatment, Overflow, Runoff Model
SVOC	Semi-Volatile Organic Compound
SWMM	Storm Water Management Model
SWPPP	Storm Water Pollution Prevention Plan
TA	Time Above
TACAN	Tactical Air Navigation
TDD	Telecommunications Devices for the Deaf
TDWR	Terminal Doppler Weather Radar
TDZL	Touchdown Zone Lights
TEA-21	Transportation Equity Act for the 21st Century
TERPS	Terminal Instrument Procedures
TIP	Threat Image Projection
TKN	Total Kjeldahl Nitrogen
TNA	Thermal Neutron Analysis
TPHP	Typical Peak Hour Passengers
TQM	Total Quality Management
TRACAB	Terminal Radar Approach Control in the Tower Cab
TRACAN	Tactical Air Navigation
TRACON	Terminal Radar Approach Control
TRB	Transportation Research Board
TRI	Toxic Release Inventory
TRSA	Terminal Radar Service Area
TSA	Transportation Security Administration
TSC	Transportation Security Clearinghouse
TSO	Technical Standard Orders
TSR	Transportation Security Regulation
TSS	Total Suspended Solids
TWA	Trans World Airlines
U.S.	United States
UAL	United Airlines
UAS	Uninhabited or Unmanned Aircraft Systems
UHF	Ultra-High Frequency
USAR	Uniform System of Accounts and Reports
UST	Underground Storage Tank
USUA	United States Ultralight Association
USUF	United States Ultralight Foundation
V/PD	Vehicle/Pedestrian Deviation
VA	Veterans Administration
VASI	Visual Approach Slope Indicator
VBIED	Vehicle Borne Improvised Explosive Device
VFR	Visual Flight Rule
VIP	Very Important Person
VL	Vaporizing-Liquid
VOC	Volatile Organic Compound
VOR	Very High Frequency Omni-Directional Range
WBE	Women-Owned Business Enterprise
Wi-Fi	Wireless-Fidelity
WLAN	Wireless Local Area Network
WSDDM	Weather Support to Deicing Decision Making

WSR-88D	Weather Radar
Y2K	New Year's Day 2000
YDNL	Yearly Day-Night Average Sound Level

APPENDIX E

ABOUT THE AUTHORS

LAURENCE E. GESELL

Laurence Gesell is Professor of Science, Technology and Society in the School of Applied Arts and Sciences at the Polytechnic Campus of Arizona State University and Professor of Transportation in the Interdisciplinary Studies in Transportation Systems in the Graduate College on the ASU Main Campus. Previous faculty appointments have included Adjunct Professor for Embry-Riddle Aeronautical University (1986-1989); Lecturer in the College of Business at California Polytechnic State University in San Luis Obispo (1983-1984); and Instructor in the Department of Aviation at Northern Virginia Community College (1976-1979).

Prior to ASU, Laurence Gesell was the Airports Manager for the County of San Luis Obispo, California (1979-1984). He is an Accredited Airport Executive [A.A.E.] with the American Association of Airport Executives and Certified Airport Executive [C.A.E.] with the Southwest Chapter of the American Association of Airport Executives. From 1973-1979, he was an aviation consultant and airport planning project manager with Howard, Needles, Tammen and Bergendoff, a leading design firm of architects, engineers and planners. Dr. Gesell is a commercially rated pilot, retired Lieutenant Colonel, Master Army Aviator, and veteran of the Vietnam conflict, where he was awarded the Distinguished Flying Cross, 39 Air Medals (including one for valor), Bronze Star with oak leaf cluster, and the Army Commendation Medal.

Laurence Gesell holds the following degrees: B.A. (in Public Administration), Upper Iowa University (1976); M.P.A., University of San Francisco (1982); and Ph.D. (in Justice Studies), Arizona State University (1990). He has authored 19 books, numerous professional papers, journal articles and final consultant reports. His principal areas of teaching and research interest are air transportation systems management and planning, public policy and regulation, as well as justice, law and society and the ethical foundations of law. He is a 2008 inductee into the Arizona Aviation Hall of Fame.

ROBIN R. SOBOTTA

Robin Sobotta is Chair of the Department of Business and Associate Director of the Global Security and Intelligence Studies Program at Embry-Riddle Aeronautical University-Prescott. Prior to ERAU she was a Transportation Research/Faculty Associate at Arizona State University (1997-1999) and was instrumental in producing the *Arizona Aviation Economic Impact Study*. Dr. Sobotta has been principal investigator and/or researcher in several funded projects including those focusing on Unmanned Aviation Vehicle/Systems, Multimodal Transportation and Bioterrorism Defense, and Explosive/Biohazard Detection Systems. Concurrent with her academic service, she was Project Manager and Technical Consultant to NASA-Dryden Flight Research Center (2005-2006) where she conducted research relating to unmanned systems as well as border-security related activities, and offered business analysis on emerging marketing opportunities.

Dr. Sobotta was an Airport Duty Manager at Phoenix Sky Harbor International Airport (1984-1997) where she also served as Public Information Officer Manager at Sky Harbor and Assistant to the Manager at Deer Valley Municipal Airport. During the 1980s, she held internships at Sky Harbor, Oceano and San Luis Obispo County airports, as well as Muskegon County International Airport. She is an Accredited Airport Executive [A.A.E.] and Advisor for the ERAU-Prescott Student Chapter of the American Association of Airport Executives. She served on the Governor's Commission for Non-Traditional Employment for Women (1993-1999), received the City Manager's Award for Excellence in Public Service (1986) and has received numerous awards for teaching and faculty excellence.

Robin Sobotta holds a B.S. degree (Political Science and Public Relations/Advertising) from Grand Valley State University; an M.B.A. (Aviation) from ERAU; and a Ph.D. (Public Administration) from Arizona State University. She has authored numerous professional, papers, articles and consulting reports. Her principal areas of teaching and research are airport administration, planning, operations and marketing; airport and aviation security; and border security and intelligence.

GA	General Aviation
GAMA	General Aviation Manufacturers Association
GAO	General Accounting/Accountability Office
GARB	General Airport Revenue Bond
GCA	Ground Controlled Approach
GIS	Global Information Systems
GNP	Gross National Product
GO	General Obligation
GPS	Global Positioning System
GT	Ground Transportation
HAI	Helicopter Association International
HAP	Hazardous Air Pollutant
HAZMAT	Hazardous Material
HIRL	High Intensity Runway Lights
HNTB	Howard, Needles, Tammen and Bergendoff
HSPF	Hydrologic Simulation Program, FORTRAN
HUD	Department of Housing and Urban Development
Hz	Hertz
ID	Identification
IAP	International Airport Professional
IATA	International Air Transport Association
ICAO	International Civil Aviation Organization
ICC	Interstate Commerce Commission
IFR	Instrument Flight Rule
IG	Inspector General
ILS	Instrument Landing System
IMPLAN	Impact Analysis for Planning
IND	Indianapolis International Airport
INM	Integrated Noise Model
IPCC	Intergovernmental Panel on Climate Change
IRI	Istituto per la Ricostruzione Industriale
IRR	Internal Rate of Return
IT	Information Technology
ITWS	Integrated Terminal Weather System
JAL	Japan Airlines
JFK	John F. Kennedy Airport
JP	Jet Propulsion
JPDO	Joint Planning and Development Office
K-9	Canine
KLM	Royal Dutch Airlines
LAN	Local Area Network
LAT	Lockheed Air Terminal
LAWA	Los Angeles World Airports
LAX	Los Angeles International Airport
LCC	Low Cost Carrier
LCD	Liquid Crystal Displays
LCRAC	Large Certificated Route Air Carrier
LDA	Landing Distance Available
LDA	Localizer Directional Aid

Lden	Day Sound Level
LDIN	Lead In Lights
Ldn	Day-Night Average Sound Level
LED	Light Emitting Diode
LEED	Leadership in Energy and Environmental Design
LEO	Law Enforcement Officer
LEQ	Energy Equivalent Noise Level
Leq	Equivalent Sound Level
LIRL	Low Intensity Runway Lights
LLC	Limited Liability Company
LLP	Limited Liability Partnership
Lnight	Night Sound Level
LOC	Localizer
LORAN	Long Range Navigation
LORAN-C	Long Range Navigation C
LPR	License-Plate Recognition
LRR	Long-Range Radar
LUG	Land Use Guidance
LUST	Leaking Underground Storage Tank
LVBIED	Large Vehicle-Borne Improvised Explosive Device
M&S	Metering and Spacing
MALSR	Medium Intensity Approach Lighting System with Runway Alignment Indicators
MANPADS	Man-Portable Air-Defense Systems
MAP	Missed Approach Point
MASSPORT	Massachusetts Port Authority
MBA	Master of Business Administration
MBE	Minority Business Enterprise
MBO	Management by Objective
MCA	Magnesium Calcium Acetate
METAR	Aviation Routine Weather Report
MGW	Maximum Gross Weight
MIRL	Medium Intensity Runway Lights
MKE	Milwaukee's General Mitchell Field
MLS	Microwave Landing System
MPA	Master of Public Administration
MRTD	Machine Readable Travel Document
MSAW	Minimum Safe Altitude Warning
MSP	Minneapolis–St. Paul International Airport
MWAA	Metropolitan Washington Airports Authority
N (number)	U.S. aircraft registration beginning with letter N
NAFEC	National Aviation Facilities Experimental Center
NAP	National Airport Plan
NAS	National Airspace System
NASA	National Aeronautics and Space Administration
NASP	National Airport System Plan
NATCA	National Air Traffic Controllers Association
NAVAID	Navigation Aid
NBAA	National Business Aircraft Association
NBOD	Nitrogenous Biological Oxygen Demand
NCP	Noise Compatibility Program